The Cambridge Handbook of Heritage Languages and Linguistics

Heritage languages are minority languages learned in a bilingual environment. These include immigrant languages, aboriginal or indigenous languages, and historical minority languages. In the last two decades, heritage languages have become central to many areas of linguistic research, from bilingual language acquisition, education, and language policies to theoretical linguistics. Bringing together contributions from a team of internationally renowned experts, this handbook provides a state-of-the-art overview of this emerging area of study from a number of different perspectives, ranging from theoretical linguistics to language education and pedagogy. Presenting comprehensive data on heritage languages from around the world, it covers issues ranging from individual aspects of heritage language knowledge to broader societal, educational, and policy concerns in local, global, and international contexts. Surveying the most current issues and trends in this exciting field, it is essential reading for graduate students and researchers, as well as language practitioners and other language professionals.

SILVINA MONTRUL is Professor of Linguistics in the Department of Spanish and Portuguese and in the Department of Linguistics at the University of Illinois at Urbana-Champaign. Her recent publications include *Heritage Language Acquisition* (2016) and *El bilingüismo en el mundo hispanohablante* [Bilingualism in the Spanish-speaking world] (2013).

MARIA POLINSKY is Professor of Linguistics at the University of Maryland, College Park, and director of the National Heritage Language Research Center at UCLA. Recent publications include *Deconstructing Ergativity* (2016) and *Heritage Languages and Their Speakers* (2018).

Genuinely broad in scope, each handbook in this series provides a complete state-of-the-field overview of a major sub-discipline within language study and research. Grouped into broad thematic areas, the chapters in each volume encompass the most important issues and topics within each subject, offering a coherent picture of the latest theories and findings. Together, the volumes will build into an integrated overview of the discipline in its entirety.

Published titles

The Cambridge Handbook of Phonology, edited by Paul de Lacy

The Cambridge Handbook of Linguistic Code-switching, edited by Barbara E. Bullock and Almeida Jacqueline Toribio

The Cambridge Handbook of Child Language, Second Edition, edited by Edith L. Bavin and Letitia Naigles

The Cambridge Handbook of Endangered Languages, edited by Peter K. Austin and Julia Sallabank

The Cambridge Handbook of Sociolinguistics, edited by Rajend Mesthrie

The Cambridge Handbook of Pragmatics, edited by Keith Allan and Kasia M. Jaszczolt

The Cambridge Handbook of Language Policy, edited by Bernard Spolsky

The Cambridge Handbook of Second Language Acquisition, edited by Julia Herschensohn and Martha Young-Scholten

The Cambridge Handbook of Biolinguistics, edited by Cedric Boeckx and Kleanthes K. Grohmann

The Cambridge Handbook of Generative Syntax, edited by Marcel den Dikken

The Cambridge Handbook of Communication Disorders, edited by Louise Cummings

The Cambridge Handbook of Stylistics, edited by Peter Stockwell and Sara Whiteley

The Cambridge Handbook of Linguistic Anthropology, edited by N.J. Enfield, Paul Kockelman and Jack Sidnell

The Cambridge Handbook of English Corpus Linguistics, edited by Douglas Biber and Randi Reppen

The Cambridge Handbook of Bilingual Processing, edited by John W. Schwieter

The Cambridge Handbook of Learner Corpus Research, edited by Sylviane Granger, Gaëtanelle Gilquin and Fanny Meunier

The Cambridge Handbook of Linguistic Multicompetence, edited by Li Wei and Vivian Cook

The Cambridge Handbook of English Historical Linguistics, edited by Merja Kytö and Päivi Pahta

The Cambridge Handbook of Formal Semantics, edited by Maria Aloni and Paul Dekker

The Cambridge Handbook of Morphology, edited by Andrew Hippisley and Greg Stump

The Cambridge Handbook of Historical Syntax, edited by Adam Ledgeway and Ian Roberts

The Cambridge Handbook of Linguistic Typology, edited by Alexandra Y. Aikhenvald and R. M. W. Dixon

The Cambridge Handbook of Areal Linguistics, edited by Raymond Hickey

The Cambridge Handbook of Cognitive Linguistics, edited by Barbara Dancygier

The Cambridge Handbook of Japanese Linguistics, edited by Yoko Hasegawa

The Cambridge Handbook of Spanish Linguistics, edited by Kimberly L. Geeslin

The Cambridge Handbook of Heritage Languages and Linguistics

Edited by

Silvina Montrul
University of Illinois, Urbana-Champaign

Maria Polinsky
University of Maryland

CAMBRIDGE
UNIVERSITY PRESS

University Printing House, Cambridge CB2 8BS, United Kingdom

One Liberty Plaza, 20th Floor, New York, NY 10006, USA

477 Williamstown Road, Port Melbourne, VIC 3207, Australia

314–321, 3rd Floor, Plot 3, Splendor Forum, Jasola District Centre, New Delhi – 110025, India

103 Penang Road, #05–06/07, Visioncrest Commercial, Singapore 238467

Cambridge University Press is part of the University of Cambridge.

It furthers the University's mission by disseminating knowledge in the pursuit of education, learning, and research at the highest international levels of excellence.

www.cambridge.org
Information on this title: www.cambridge.org/9781108487269
DOI: 10.1017/9781108766340

© Cambridge University Press 2021

First published 2021

Printed in the United Kingdom by TJ Books Limited, Padstow Cornwall

A catalogue record for this publication is available from the British Library.

Library of Congress Cataloging-in-Publication Data
Names: Montrul, Silvina, editor. | Polinsky, Maria, editor.
Title: The Cambridge handbook of heritage languages and linguistics / edited by Silvina Montrul, Maria Polinsky.
Description: Cambridge ; New York : Cambridge University Press, 2021. | Series: Cambridge handbooks in language and linguistics | Includes bibliographical references and index.
Identifiers: LCCN 2020042868 (print) | LCCN 2020042869 (ebook) | ISBN 9781108487269 (hardback) | ISBN 9781108719995 (paperback) | ISBN 9781108766340 (epub)
Subjects: LCSH: Bilingualism. | Multilingualism. | Heritage language speakers. | Linguistic minorities. | Linguistic minorities—Education.
Classification: LCC P115 .C38 2021 (print) | LCC P115 (ebook) | DDC 306.44/6—dc23
LC record available at https://lccn.loc.gov/2020042868
LC ebook record available at https://lccn.loc.gov/2020042869

ISBN 978-1-108-48726-9 Hardback

In memory of Olga Kagan and Janne Bondi Johannessen: Outstanding scholars and tireless advocates for heritage languages, linguistics, and education whose work will continue to inspire so many.

Contents

Figures and Tables

Figures

Tables

Contributors

Abdulkafi Albirini Utah State University
Sharon Armon-Lotem Bar-Ilan University
Netta Avineri Middlebury Institute of International Studies
Fatih Bayram UiT The Arctic University of Norway
Sara Beaudrie Arizona State University
Elabbas Benmamoun Duke University
Shereen Bhalla Hindu American Foundation
Melissa A. Bowles University of Illinois at Urbana-Champaign
Bernhard Brehmer University of Konstanz
Maria M. Carreira California State University, Long Beach
Charles B. Chang Boston University
Huay Chen-Wu University of California, Santa Barbara
Maria Cecilia Colombi University of California, Davis
Grazia Di Pisa University of Konstanz
Irina Dubinina Brandeis University
Cristina Flores University of Minho
Kleanthes K. Grohmann University of Cyprus
Paola Guerrero-Rodríguez University of Florida
Agnes Weiyun He Stony Brook University
Andrew D. Hoffman Pennsylvania State University
Tania Ionin University of Illinois at Urbana-Champaign
Jill Jegerski University of Illinois at Urbana-Champaign
Susan Joffe Bar-Ilan University and
Oranim Academic College of Education
Janne Bondi Johannessen University of Oslo
Hyun-Sook Kang University of Illinois at Urbana-Champaign
Chae-Eun Kim University of Hawai'i
Kendall King University of Minnesota

Olesya Kisselev University of Texas at San Antonio

Kimi Kondo-Brown University of Hawai'i at Mānoa

Tanja Kupisch University of Konstanz and
UiT The Arctic University of Norway

Oksana Laleko State University of New York at New Paltz

Jin Sook Lee University of California, Santa Barbara

John M. Lipski The Pennsylvania State University

Na Liu Chabot College

Terje Lohndal NTNU – Norwegian University of Science and Technology and
UiT The Arctic University of Norway

Andrew Lynch University of Miami

Natalia Meir Bar-Ilan University

Silvina Montrul University of Illinois at Urbana-Champaign

Naomi Nagy University of Toronto

William O'Grady University of Hawai'i

Adriana Ojeda University of Florida

Diego Pascual y Cabo University of Florida

Natalia Pavlou University of Cyprus

Maria Polinsky University of Maryland

Kim Potowski University of Illinois, Chicago

Michael T. Putnam The Pennsylvania State University

Itxaso Rodríguez-Ordóñez California State University, Long Beach

Jason Rothman UiT The Arctic University of Norway and Universidad
Antonio de Nebrija

Lorena Sainzmaza-Lecanda Independent scholar

Joseph Salmons University of Wisconsin – Madison

Lara Schwarz Technical University of Dortmund

Maria Schwedhelm University of Minnesota

Corinne A. Seals Victoria University of Wellington

Irina A. Sekerina College of Staten Island and The Graduate Center,
City University of New York

Ronald Shabtaev Bar-Ilan University

Roumyana Slabakova University of Southampton and
NTNU – Norwegian University of Science and Technology

Neal Snape Gunma Prefectural Women's University

Kate Stemper University of Minnesota

Julio Torres University of California, Irvine

Linda Tsung The University of Sydney, Australia

Joel Walters Bar-Ilan University and
Talpiot Academic College of Education

Terrence G. Wiley Arizona State University

James Hye Suk Yoon University of Illinois at Urbana-Champaign

Lubei Zhang Southwest Jiaotong University, China

Acknowledgments

We are pleased and proud to present this volume, which gathers the inspiration, foresight, dedication, and work of many colleagues. We are grateful to Helen Barton at Cambridge University Press for inviting us to work on this title and to Isabel Collins for guiding us through the production process to bring forth this new collection in the Cambridge Handbook series. We are also deeply grateful to all the authors who contributed state-of-the-art overviews on heritage languages and who then took it upon themselves to review other chapters in this volume.

The spirit of this volume, and our vision of it, grew from the annual Heritage Language Institutes at the National Heritage Language Resource Center at the University of California, Los Angeles (UCLA), which started in 2007 and whose main goal has been to bring together scholars from diverse disciplines to discuss the state of heritage languages, heritage language linguistics, and heritage language education from a global perspective. While different communities of heritage languages and heritage language groups present their own unique characteristics, at the heart of the annual institutes has been the purpose of studying heritage languages on a global scale and focusing on commonalities among heritage languages and cultures.

We dedicate this handbook to the memory of two colleagues who have been at the forefront of this effort and whose vision is represented here: Olga Kagan and Janne Bondi Johannessen.

Introduction

Heritage Languages, Heritage Speakers, Heritage Linguistics

Silvina Montrul and Maria Polinsky

Heritage languages are minority languages learned in a bilingual or multi-lingual environment.[1] They include languages in diaspora spoken by immigrants and their children, aboriginal or indigenous languages whose role has been diminished by colonizing languages, and historical minority languages that coexist with other standard languages in diverse territories. All these examples indicate that in any given context a heritage language instantiates one of the languages in a bilingual society; thus, heritage languages fall under the rubric of bilingualism. Bilingualism is not a new phenomenon, socially, demographically, or linguistically, but attention to heritage languages has been relatively new in bilingualism research, with first mentions of heritage speakers in English research studies dating back to the 1990s (Cummins 1991).

Throughout this handbook, we will follow this definition of heritage language and heritage speakers:

> A language qualifies as a heritage language if it is a language spoken at home or otherwise readily available to young children, and crucially this language is not a dominant language of the larger (national) society. [...] [A]n individual qualifies as a heritage speaker if and only if he or she has some command of the heritage language acquired naturalistically [...]. (Rothman 2009: 156)

Two comments related to this definition are in order. First, the concept of heritage is extremely broad. In principle, it can include connections to one's family history, ethnic affiliation, attribution or appropriation, and cultural links. The understanding of cultural and ethnic heritage may include

---

[1] While we recognize the difference between bilingualism and multilingualism, in the discussion here we use the term "bilingualism" as a shorthand for the sake of brevity.

reference to a language that was at some point spoken by a particular group, and return to that heritage often involves the revival of a language associated with that group or the revival of traditional songs or narratives in that language. Such language revival is typical of heritage groups broadly understood (compare Fishman 2001 and discussion in Polinsky and Kagan 2007). As long as revival efforts involve adult learners of the language associated with a given group, they do not qualify as heritage speakers in the narrow sense, the sense used in this handbook: bilingual speakers who were exposed to the minority language from birth or very early childhood. Thus, while the concept of heritage is wide-ranging, the concept of heritage language is quite specific and well-defined.

Second, research on heritage languages has prompted extensive discussion of the nature of native speakerhood (see Kupisch and Rothman 2018). Are heritage speakers native speakers or should they be treated as a special group? And if yes, what kind of group? Empirical research on heritage speakers often shows they are different from monolingual baseline but even more different from second-language learners. As bilingual speakers become more and more recognized in linguistic research, the need to identify heritage speakers as a special group within native speakers is also becoming more apparent. On the educational side, this kind of recognition is important as it allows us to validate heritage speakers' and heritage learners' special needs as language users and removes the stigma of "not speaking right" often associated with these speakers. On the linguistic side of things, the idea that heritage speakers are native speakers springs from the recognition of a heritage language as a coherent linguistic system, with its consistent rules and operations. Differences between a heritage language and a monolingual baseline should thus be accounted for in the same way we account for differences between dialects within a single language.

Heritage language speakers typically grow up in situations of subtractive bilingualism, and by young adulthood they have variable degrees of knowledge and command of their heritage language. They are the second generation of immigrants born in the new society, children of immigrants, and young children who immigrate before puberty (immigrant children). Children of immigrants tend to be simultaneous bilinguals growing up, exposed to the heritage, home language, and the majority language early on. Immigrant children had a period of monolingualism in their homeland and bring knowledge of their native language on immigration, although the degree of acquisition of their native language depends on their age at immigration and whether they received schooling. For example, a four-year old may not have gone to school, but an eight- or nine-year-old most likely did. The linguistic knowledge of an eight- or nine-year-old is more advanced than that of a four-year old, at least in vocabulary, semantics, and pragmatics. In indigenous or aboriginal populations, migration is from rural areas to big cities, but the processes and outcomes of language contact and change at different ages are very similar to the international situation of immigrants and their children. In cases of historical minority languages, their official or non-official status within their territories determines the level of availability of the language beyond the home sphere and their ultimate survival across generations. For example, competence in Basque varies greatly in Spain where Basque has co-official status with Spanish in its territory, compared to competence in the Basque spoken in France, where the language does not have any status and is not protected (Rodríguez-Ordóñez 2016).

What drew both of us to study heritage languages and heritage speakers we encountered in our own classrooms and in the community were their complex characteristics. When speakers of standard and non-standard national languages migrate and gradually begin to use their language less as they start their life in a new language, their original language shows distinguishing and distinguishable concomitant changes in structure (phonology, morphology, syntax, semantics, and pragmatics). The amount and degree of changes, the focus of many of the studies in this field, vary by grammatical area, by the age of the speaker, by the age of immigration or extensive exposure to the majority language, by the size of the speech community, by the vitality of the language beyond the home, by access to schooling, by attitudes, and by issues related to identity, among other factors.

There are at least two broad groups of heritage speakers that have attracted the attention of researchers: those in the "wild" and those in the "classroom" (Polinsky and Kagan 2007). Many heritage speakers come to the university language classroom because they are aware that their language is different. They lack vocabulary and expressions beyond the home context. Many cannot read and write, or they have a sense that their grammar needs development. These are the so-called **heritage language learners**, those who are trying to regain what they feel they have lost if they did not acquire it in a formal classroom environment. Understanding the linguistic needs of heritage language learners, how they differ from those of typical adult second language learners, and how to address them, has been at the forefront of the research agenda around heritage language education and the work of the National Heritage Language Resource Center led by the late Olga Kagan. **Heritage language speakers** are those in the wild, naturalistic learners and users who are not seeking to learn their heritage language in the classroom.

Heritage languages are precious linguistic, cultural, and personal resources for individuals and for society, but, due to their minority status, many are vulnerable to loss, gradual or imminent. Preserving heritage languages and transmitting them to future generations is not only of paramount importance for the individuals, families, and communities that speak them, but for scientific research as well. Research has shown that bilingual children with high proficiency in two languages who continue to use the languages along the lifespan enjoy cognitive, cultural, and economic benefits of bilingualism if the home language is maintained. Academically, heritage languages have a great deal to teach us about different languages, cognition, society and culture, language acquisition and bilingualism, linguistic models of human language, and education and language policies. Critical questions we are addressing here are: First, why are heritage languages vulnerable to loss at the cognitive and societal level? Second, how can we prevent language loss? Third, how can we regain a language we have lost? How can we support language maintenance and growth? These questions can be answered from the macro-level by looking at the broader sociolinguistic and sociopolitical factors that drive language status, language attitudes, language identity, and ultimately language use, and from the more micro-level of specific language features, language processing, acquisition, and cognition within individuals.

It is well known that heritage speakers form a very heterogeneous group when we consider the age of acquisition of the majority language, their degree of daily use of the heritage language during the lifespan, and access to the heritage language beyond the home during their lifetime, among other factors. But in the last two decades, our interest has been to map and characterize the universality of heritage languages; that is, when we look at different heritage languages in the same sociopolitical environment or in other environments, what do they have in common? In Montrul (2008, 2016) and Polinsky (2018), among many other sources, we have written about how different heritage languages show structural similarities. Recurrent similarities across different heritage languages can reveal the universality of the underlying cognitive and linguistic processes that shape these grammars (Polinsky 2018). What we know so far is that some aspects of heritage speakers' grammars (aspects of phonology and syntax) converge with, and do not differ significantly from, the grammars of fluent speakers of the language (in the homeland or in the diaspora); whereas other aspects of their grammar (morphology, long-distance dependencies, syntax-discourse interface) diverge or differ from the grammars of fluent speakers of the language, leading to what appear to be nonnative or nontarget effects. Nonnative effects arise for many reasons: insufficient input and use of the heritage language during a formative time in language development, differences in the input due to structural changes present in the input providers (intergenerational transmission), effects of the dominant language, and insufficient proficiency to deploy fast and efficient language processing of the heritage language, among others. Today, we believe that despite these differences, heritage speakers do not have random grammars; their language follows principles of universal language design, such as propensity for one-to-one mappings, preference for acoustically salient, perceptual material, morphological and syntactic restructuring, and preference for default settings. Yet there are also differences between heritage languages spoken in different sociolinguistic and sociopolitical contexts that remain to be understood, as well as the role of the majority language in effecting many of the changes seen in heritage language speakers.

As we have already mentioned, the study of heritage languages is not new, but it used to be the concern of sociolinguists, anthropological linguistics, and folklore studies. Not being standard languages, heritage languages were pretty much at the fringe of scientific language research. Much has changed in the last two decades, as heritage languages and their speakers have now become a central focus of different areas of linguistic research, from bilingual language acquisition, education and language policies, to theoretical linguistics. Much of the growth in the field has been propelled by growing recognition that the majority of the world population is bilingual and multilingual, yet our theories of language have been strictly concerned with describing the linguistic competence and language use of standard, idealized native speakers. Although monolingualism and standard languages are well represented in theoretical fields of linguistics in general, there has been an increasing tendency to include heritage languages and their speakers as critical data sources for theoretical linguistics, psycholinguistics, and sociolinguistics. A good example of this recent development is the demonstration that Children of Adult Deaf Adults (CODAs), or heritage speakers of American Sign Language, engage in code-blending, a unique linguistic phenomenon afforded to bimodal bilinguals, akin to code-switching in spoken languages bilingualism. Code-blending is different from code-switching, which is also used by bimodal bilinguals, and is produced with varying amounts of overlap between signed components and spoken components (Lillo-Martin et al. 2016: 739). These unique data from heritage speakers of American Sign Language led Lillo-Martin et al. (2016) to propose a language synthesis model that adds a signed dimension to the phonology component of vocabulary insertion. In this way, models of language strictly conceived on the basis of monolingual data can accommodate bilingualism and different manifestations of language (spoken, signed). Another more urgent contributing force to moving heritage languages from the periphery to the center has been the quest for solutions to applied concerns, such as teaching heritage languages in the classroom at the college level and in elementary and high schools. As a result, heritage language teaching and education has also become a central topic in Applied Linguistics more generally.

Along with the theoretical and empirical expansion of the field, we are also seeing rapid expansion of the study of heritage language outside the USA. Although immigrant languages in the United States have been the driving force behind the "new" field since the 1990s, the last ten years have seen exponential growth in the study of heritage languages in Europe and other parts of the world. This is apparent from the widespread acceptance of the term "heritage language" and its use in research work in different languages (compare Spanish *lengua de herencia*, French *la langue d'héritage*, German *Herkunftssrpache*), a practice virtually unknown in Europe ten years ago. What has changed is the scientific focus on individuals (cognitive, psycholinguistic, experimental linguistic approaches) and how these relate to society (sociolinguistics, education, language policies), along with the realization that understanding heritage languages and their speakers calls for collaboration and interaction between different areas of linguistics that have been traditionally isolated from each other.

The volume we present here, *The Cambridge Handbook of Heritage Languages and Linguistics*, aims to provide a state-of-the-art comprehensive view of this emerging area of linguistics from different perspectives: theoretical linguistics, experimental approaches to heritage languages, sociolinguistics, language education, and language policy. *The Handbook* focuses on issues ranging from individual aspects of heritage language knowledge, acquisition, loss, and maintenance to broader societal, educational, and policy concerns covering global and international contexts. One of the overarching goals of the *Handbook* is to bring theoretical and applied approaches to heritage language under the same cover in a manner that would allow them to inform each other and pave the way to new research across different subfields. In keeping with this overarching goal, we have brought together a series of chapters that describe heritage languages in different parts of the world, address theoretical and educational aspects of heritage language research, and discuss social aspects of heritage language use.

Part I: Heritage Languages around the World

This part provides sociolinguistic overviews and demographic descriptions of heritage language communities in different parts of the world, covering a wide range of geographical areas, such as immigrant languages in the United States and Europe, minority languages in Europe and Asia, and Indigenous languages in Latin America, Canada, and Australia. The purpose of this part is to showcase the range of variation of heritage languages and heritage language communities, underscoring the fact that heritage speakers are not a homogeneous group, and that even the same language can have a different destiny as a heritage language in different parts of the world. The chapters illustrate how heritage languages differ with respect to whether their speakers are literate, functionally literate, or illiterate, depending on the writing system, multilingualism in the homeland, place of a given language in the educational system, and other characteristics.

Heritage languages also differ with respect to the patterns of immigration or length of presence in a given territory, the size of the relevant language community, its sociolinguistic vitality, and the cultural and ideological commitment to a given language. All these characteristics determine to a large extent the ranges of proficiency observed in heritage speakers of different groups.

In an ideal world, it would be desirable to have a chapter on heritage languages in each country, but that goal is still unattainable, and the absence of chapters discussing heritage languages in a particular country or part of the world is a clear indication of areas where future work is needed.

Part II: Research Approaches to Heritage Languages

Language is both a grammatical system that develops in the minds of individual speakers and a social construct that allows individual speakers to communicate, form groups on the basis of their communication and use of language, and at the same time, define their own linguistic identities through sociolinguistic and communicative practices. In recent years, heritage languages have increasingly been recognized as a unique source of insight into knowledge of language, and their data have contributed a great deal to the development of linguistic subfields and theory construction. The chapters in this second part of the volume address different approaches to the study of heritage languages, from corpus research to generative linguistics. From an empirical perspective, heritage speakers and heritage languages raise many important questions for research, and this part of the volume also includes chapters outlining the range of research designs and methodologies that have been applied to this population to date and that are related to different approaches and methodologies.

Part III: Grammatical Aspects of Heritage Languages

This part focuses on structural aspects of heritage languages and their relevance for theoretical linguistics. The chapters in this part of the handbook discuss phonetics and phonology, semantics, pragmatics, and morphosyntax of heritage languages. Theoretically-grounded studies of heritage language systems show that heritage language grammars are systematic in many respects. Some elements of these systems are comparable to what is found in the baseline, whereas others can, and must be, accounted for by restructuring of the original system.

The majority of chapters in this part of the handbook rely equally on production and comprehension data from heritage languages, which allows the authors to produce important results, separating issues of online processing that can be grouped under the rubric of the "mapping problem," along with fundamental changes in the underlying representations in heritage grammars, ones that make these grammars different from the grammar of the baseline language. Another recurrent theme in the chapters of this part of the handbook has to do with differences between baseline speakers (L1s), heritage speakers, and proficiency-matched L2 speakers. A common pattern observed across different linguistic domains is that heritage speakers are different from L1s, while together, L1s and heritage speakers are more similar to each other, to the exclusion of L2 speakers. This recurrent result is important in the way it underscores the affinity between baseline speakers and heritage speakers, especially in comprehension, and a significant advantage that heritage language speakers hold over L2 speakers, even more advanced ones.

Part IV: Heritage Language Education

An increasing trend in many postsecondary foreign language classes worldwide is the presence of heritage language learners. The education of heritage language speakers as adults at the university level has been the driving force behind heritage language education, especially in North America, Europe, and Australia. At the same time, there is a natural relationship between the extent to which heritage languages are taught in elementary and high schools around the world, the availability of bilingual education and community schools to help heritage language children develop, maintain, and use their heritage language to communicate with family members, or to eventually be able to use it in professional contexts. Moreover, the availability of different educational models to promote heritage language education is inextricably linked to attitudes and ideologies about the heritage languages, the political status of the heritage language in the territory or community, and language policies at a national or regional level. The chapters in this part present and discuss different types of educational models promoting heritage language development, as well as language policies that determine the availability of heritage language education in different parts of the world.

In discussing the chapters of Part I, we have already mentioned a great number of blank spots in the description of heritage language. Blank spots are also present in other areas of heritage language analysis, and in that respect, the chapters of this handbook reflect both the state of the field and areas awaiting further inquiry and investigation.

References

Cummins, J. 1991. Heritage Languages. *Canadian Modern Language Review* 47 (4), 635–641.

Fishman, J. 2001. 300-plus Years of Heritage Language Education in the United States. In J. K. Ranard and S. McGinnis (eds.), *Heritage Languages in America: Preserving a National Resource*. Washington, DC: Delta Systems; and McHenry, IL: Center for Applied Linguistics, 81–98.

Kupisch, T. and J. Rothman. 2018. Terminology Matters! Why Difference Is Not Incompleteness and How Early Child Bilinguals Are Heritage Speakers. *International Journal of Bilingualism* 22(5), 564–582.

Lillo-Martin, D., R. Müller de Quadros, and D. Chen Pichler. 2016. The Development of Bimodal Bilingualism: Implications for Linguistic Theory. *Linguistic Approaches to Bilingualism* 6(6), 719–755.

Montrul, S. 2008. *Incomplete Acquisition in Bilingualism: Reexamining the Age Factor*. Amsterdam: John Benjamins.

Montrul, S. 2016. *The Acquisition of Heritage Languages*. Cambridge: Cambridge University Press.

Polinsky, M. 2018. *Heritage Languages and Their Speakers*. Cambridge: Cambridge University Press.

Polinsky, M. and O. Kagan. 2007. Heritage Languages: In the "Wild" and in the Classroom. *Language and Linguistics Compass* 1, 368–395.

Rodríguez-Ordóñez, I. 2016. *Differential Object Marking in Basque: Grammaticalization, Attitudes and Ideological Representations*. Unpublished PhD dissertation, University of Illinois at Urbana-Champaign.

Rothman, J. 2009. Understanding the Nature and Outcomes of Early Bilingualism: Romance Languages as Heritage Languages. *International Journal of Bilingualism* 13(2), 155–163.

Takanishi, R. and S. Le Menestrel (eds.) 2017. Promoting the Educational Success of Children and Youth Learning English. *National Academy of Sciences, Engineering & Medicine 2017*. Washington, DC: The National Academy Press.

Part I

Heritage Languages around the World

1

Slavic Heritage Languages around the Globe

Bernhard Brehmer

1.1 Historical and Social Context

The history of Slavic people has always been shaped by migration and relocation processes. As a result, Slavic-speaking minority communities nowadays form a considerable part of minority communities around the world (see for an overview Sussex 1982, 1984, 1993; Moser and Polinsky 2013; Hill 2014). These Slavic minority communities differ considerably with regard to the time of their establishment in the respective host countries, the geopolitical circumstances and motivations that led to the emigration of Slavs from their countries of origin. In general, three different types of Slavic heritage communities can be distinguished:

1. Communities whose members did not emigrate themselves, but where the political boundaries have been shifted due to wars and other geopolitical cataclysms. These speakers often experienced a rather abrupt change of the political and social status of their mother tongue by turning overnight into speakers of minority languages. For instance, Russian turned into a minority language in most of the successor states after the disintegration of the Soviet Union in 1991. Depending on the status of Russian and the sociolinguistic situation in the respective countries (see Pavlenko 2008a, 2008b for an overview), the conditions for the acquisition of Russian and identity formation in the generation that was born after the dissolution of the Soviet Union differ greatly (Laitin 1998). This has obvious consequences for the maintenance of Russian by heritage speakers in these states. Other Slavic heritage communities emerged due to an earlier reshifting of boundaries in Europe. Thus, Polish minority communities exist in many Eastern European countries where speakers of Polish have been living for centuries (e.g., as part of the Polish-Lithuanian Commonwealth) but

were turned into an autochthonous minority after the post–World War II border changes. The sociolinguistic and linguistic situation in these Polish language islands and autochthonous communities in the Czech Republic (Teschen Silesia, Zaolzie), Slovakia (Spisz, Orawa), Lithuania, Belarus, and Ukraine have been the object of extensive research by (mostly) Polish linguists in recent decades (see Rieger 2001 for an overview).

2.   Diaspora communities that emerged due to the deportation of Slavs from their homelands. In the period between the two world wars or during/after World War II, Poles, Russians, Ukrainians, and Belarusians were deported as forced laborers to Germany, and Polish settlers were displaced by Soviet authorities from Poland mainly to Kazakhstan and Siberia. Most of them repatriated to their countries of origin when the political circumstances changed, but some of them moved to other countries (esp. Canada and the United States) or stayed in their new homeland, giving rise to new generations of Slavic heritage speakers. More recently, the civil wars surrounding the collapse of Yugoslavia in the 1990s brought about the evacuation and expulsion of people from Croatia, Bosnia-Herzegovina, and Serbia-Montenegro. Some of them gained political asylum or were accepted as war refugees in Western European countries, and others joined relatives who were already living in Western Europe or overseas (for Australia see Hlavac 2003: 14).

3.   Heritage communities that emerged following a (more or less) voluntary and active emigration of Slavs from their homeland due to (i) religious, (ii) political, or (iii) economic reasons, or a mixture of motivations.

Religious reasons have been the driving force for the emigration of the Russian Old Believers, i.e., splinter groups from the Russian Orthodox Church such as the *molokane* or *doukhobortsy*, who were persecuted by the official state and church authorities and therefore fled from tsarist Russia to various destinations, including Canada (Schaarschmidt 2000), Poland (Zielińska 2017), or Bulgaria and Romania (Steinke 1990), in the eighteenth century. They formed groups within themselves, which gave them the feeling of a strong connection to their homeland, and tried to keep isolated from the host communities in fear of losing their own religious and cultural identity, which had obvious consequences for language transmission to the next generation. Similarly, Catholic Bulgarians (the so-called Paulicanians) left Northern Bulgaria when it became part of the Ottoman Empire. First they fled to Siebenbürgen, but later settled in the Banat region (Star Bišnov and Vinga), which was then under Austrian rule. These chain migrations were also typical for the groups of Russian Old Believers (Steinke 2013). A more recent example is the emigration of Jews from the former

Soviet Union that started in the 1970s as a consequence of political liberalization. People of Jewish descent were allowed to leave the Soviet Union for Israel, although many of them actually ended up in the United States (Zemskaja 2000: 771). Jewish emigration also played an important role after the fall of the Iron Curtain, when Jews from the states of the former Soviet Union were granted the right and possibility to replenish Jewish communities in Israel, Germany, the United States and other countries (see Isurin 2011).

Political emigration has been another central push factor that spawned a considerable number of Slavic-speaking communities mainly in Western Europe and the Americas. One typical example is the emigration of highly educated aristocrats and representatives of the so-called Old Intelligentsia, which was evoked by the Bolshevist revolution in 1917 and the subsequent civil war in Russia. They formed numerous groups in various European capitals, such as Berlin, Paris, Prague, and Belgrade, and were very dedicated to staying true to their Russian roots in order to be able to return to Russia if the political situation changed. When this did not happen, many of them resettled in other countries, especially the United States (see Zemskaja 2000: 770f.). Similar waves of politically motivated or even forced emigration resulted from failed upheavals in different countries of the Soviet bloc, e.g., in 1956 (Poland), 1967–71 (Czechoslovakia, Poland, Croatia), and 1980/81 (Poland) (see Kamusella 2013: 209).

Economic considerations have motivated emigration from the Slavic homeland mainly since the middle of the nineteenth century. With regard to the United States, Hill (2014: 2117) states that:

> [s]ome 1.5 million Slavs, including 83,698 Czechs, 320,047 Slovaks, 738,012 Poles, 102,036 Ruthenians and Ukrainians and 53,454 Russians, besides an undisclosed number of South Slavs, arrived between 1899 and 1908, boosting very small Slavonic enclaves into large ethnic communities, with the rising industrial centres such as Chicago, Detroit, Pittsburgh, Cleveland, Buffalo and New York still the strongest bastions of the Slavonic element in the USA.

The majority escaped economic depressions in the Slavic homelands and opted for a better life overseas. Better economic conditions abroad also figured as an important pull factor for many inhabitants of Yugoslavia in the 1960s and 1970s to leave their homes: At that time, some countries, such as Germany or Australia, signed bilateral treaties with Yugoslavia and opened their labor market for "guest workers" from Yugoslavia. This was expected to be a temporary immigration. Many Croats, Serbs, and Slovenes, however, who initially had planned to return to Yugoslavia and had, therefore, transmitted their Slavic home language to their children who had already been born abroad, later decided not to return to their homelands, because their standard of living in the host country was markedly better in comparison to that which they could expect back in Yugoslavia (see Stölting-Richert 1988 for Western Europe and Hlavac 2003 for Australia). Massive economic problems that accompanied the transformation process in Eastern European countries after the demise of communism in the late 1980s and early 1990s evoked new waves of temporary or permanent emigration from these countries. For some countries in Western Europe, North America, Australia, and New Zealand, this led to a replenishment of already established Slavic communities, which helped to decelerate the trend of language shift to the majority language and to prevent these communities from ageing (Stoffel 2000). Last, but not least, the accession of several Slavic countries to the European Union (Czech Republic, Slovakia, Slovenia, and Poland in 2004, Bulgaria in 2007, and Croatia in 2013) facilitated the emigration of people from these countries (among them also highly skilled workers) to other EU member states. For instance, an estimated 2.5 to 3 million Polish citizens left Poland in the first decade of the 2000s for other European Economic Area countries, mainly Britain, Ireland, and Sweden (see Kamusella 2013).

This brief sketch of the different social and historical contexts of the establishment of Slavic diaspora communities worldwide indicates that there can be no unified account with regard to the sociolinguistic situation and structural characteristics of Slavic heritage languages. The heritage communities differ substantially with regard to their time of establishment and their linguistic and cultural proximity to the surrounding community; their legal, social, and sociopolitical status; their degree of integration into the host country; their establishment of supplementary schools and cultural organizations; and their predominant attitudes toward maintenance of the Slavic heritage language, to mention only a few of the relevant linguistic and sociolinguistic factors that shape their ethnolinguistic vitality (see Section 1.3 for further details).

This chapter will mostly focus on Slavic heritage languages spoken in Western Europe, Israel, North and South America, Australia, and New Zealand, i.e., in countries where the majority language is not Slavic. It is these Slavic communities on which most research has been conducted by adopting a heritage linguistics approach in the narrow sense (see Section 1.2). This does not mean, however, that one could not integrate the findings of the rich literature on autochthonous Slavic minorities, e.g., the Sorbs in Germany, Carinthian Slovenes in Austria, or Polish minority communities in the Czech Republic, Lithuania, Belarus, or Ukraine, into this overview, as the acquisitional scenario for the current speakers of these minority languages is essentially the same as for "typical" heritage speakers of Slavic languages in other parts of the world.

1.2   Research on Slavic Heritage Languages

A striking feature of linguistic research on Slavic heritage languages is the rather unequal distribution of scholarly attention with regard to individual languages. This is certainly connected to the differing numbers of speakers of individual Slavic languages in general and in countries outside their homelands. Thus, it comes as no surprise that most research is focused on Russian, Polish, Ukrainian, and Croatian as heritage languages. Russian heritage speakers have been the object of a multitude of studies, both regarding sociolinguistic issues and structural aspects. Besides studies dealing with Russian as a heritage language in individual countries (see, among others, for Russian in Argentina: Urban 2004; Finland: Viimaranta et al. 2018; France: Golubeva-Monatkina 1995; Germany: Isurin and Riehl 2017; Israel: Kopeliovich 2011; United States: Polinsky 2000, 2006; Dubinina and Polinsky 2013), many studies are also devoted to a comparison of Russian as a heritage language in different countries (e.g., Zemskaja 2001; Ždanova 2009a; Kagan et al. 2019; Minkov et al. 2019; Nikunlassi and Protassova 2019). Similar overviews are available for Polish (Dubisz 1997; Sękowska 2010) and Croatian (Hlavac and Stolac 2021).

Other Slavic heritage languages have been studied mostly with regard to individual countries in which they form larger cultural or linguistic enclaves, e.g., Bulgarian in Canada (Slavkov 2015), Croatian and Serbian in Australia (Hlavac 2003), Germany (Stölting 1980), New Zealand (Stoffel 1981), Sweden (Ďurovič 1983), and the United States (Albin and Alexander 1972; Jutronić-Tihomirović 1985); Czech in Australia (Cigler 1983), Austria (Balhar et al. 1999), and the United States (Kučera 1990); Macedonian in Australia (Hill 1989; Hlavac 2016); Slovak in the United States (McCabe 2016); Slovene in Germany (Štumberger 2007) and the United States (Šabec 1993); and Ukrainian in Canada (Žluktenko 1990; Hudyma 2011) and the United States (Odarčenko 1990). Not all studies focus exclusively on heritage speakers; some of them also consider representatives of the first generation of immigrants, thus allowing insights into qualitative aspects of input in the Slavic L1 that the heritage speakers are exposed to. Systematic comparisons of Slavic heritage speakers with first-generation immigrants (Polinsky 2000; Nagy and Kochetov 2013; Brehmer and Mehlhorn 2015; Hlavac 2016), however, are still scarce.

1.3   Language Maintenance and Shift

Sussex (1993: 1030) states that "émigré Slavonic communities have striven long to maintain their languages and cultures in the diaspora. Some communities have been remarkably successful over a number of generations, like the Poles in Panna Maria, Texas." There are, however, considerable differences concerning the success of Slavic heritage language maintenance in the individual communities. In his review of previous research on language shift in Slavic diaspora communities in the New World, Hill (2014: 2123) stresses that "different nationalities demonstrate a different preparedness to maintain L1: while Croats (other than Dalmatians), Ukrainians and Poles seem fiercely defensive of L1, Macedonians, Serbs and even Russians appear to accept the change to L2 as inevitable and even desirable." Language attitudes alone, however, are not a sufficient predictor for language maintenance: Stoffel (2000: 821) concludes that "[f]or Croatians and Poles, language appears to be more central to their ethnicity than for Serbs. However, this is not necessarily reflected in their L[anguage] M[aintenance]: the Serbian and Russian Orthodox communities with their close connection of language, culture and religion have maintained language better."[1] Nevertheless, he interprets findings of previous research on various Slavic L1 communities in North America and Australia as showing analogous patterns of language preservation or shift (Stoffel 2000: 816ff.):

Before World War II, Slavic home languages were preserved and passed on to the next generation especially in bigger cities and towns where Slavic-speaking immigrants formed the local majority population in some districts, e.g., in the northeastern United States (see Polish-dominated neighborhoods in Milwaukee, Chicago, and Buffalo) or in block settlements in the prairie provinces of Canada (Manitoba, Saskatchewan, and Alberta) (Henzl 1981: 313f.; Magocsi 2013: 16). After World War II, these Slavic communities began to disappear gradually due to changing demographic patterns in urban centers. Geographical distance and the isolation imposed by the Iron Curtain cut these communities off from their home countries after World War II. This accelerated the shift to the majority languages between the first and second postwar generations. As a consequence, the loss of Slavic L1 and lack of transmission to the next generation characterized Slavic-speaking communities of the New World by the 1970s. In scarce communities, sociolinguistic circumstances fostered the retention of the Slavic home language (see Stoffel 2000: 817). These favorable factors included compact settlements, low mobility, cohesive social units (e.g., churches, social, or cultural organizations [clubs, societies]), community schools to support transmission of the Slavic L1, and local media in that language (Magocsi 2013: 14ff.; Hill 2014: 2123f.). Communities of Russian

[1] Differences between individual Slavic-speaking communities are also reported in Achterberg (2005) for Germany as the host country. However, the differences regarding self-perceived ethnolinguistic vitality are rather small, with the Russian-, Bosnian/Croatian/Serbian-, and Polish-speaking groups scoring higher on the index than the other Slavic-speaking communities (see Achterberg 2005: 234ff.).

Old Believers in Canada, Alaska, Oregon (Sussex 1993: 1004; Schaarschmidt 2000), and some European countries like Bulgaria or Romania (Steinke 1990) formed isolated and inwardly directed enclaves, which helped them to preserve their own language (mostly archaic dialects with some innovative features) and culture. Their religious otherness,[2] strong internal solidarity, and fear of losing their identity fostered isolation, which prevented linguistic assimilation until the second half of the twentieth century (Steinke 2013).

The political and social changes following the demise of communism in the countries of the former Warsaw Pact and the breakup of Yugoslavia in the 1980–1990s fundamentally changed the *external setting* for heritage language maintenance in Slavic diaspora communities worldwide (see Stoffel 2000: 818ff.):

1. Politically unimpeded migration and economic problems during the transformation process triggered massive waves of emigration from Central, Southeastern, and Eastern European countries. This influx of new vintages of Slavic-speaking migrants led to a significant numerical replenishment of diasporic Slavic communities.[3]

2. The new waves of speakers enriched the linguistic environment of the heritage speakers, e.g., by introducing recent linguistic developments that occurred in the standard or substandard varieties of the Slavic languages spoken in the homeland, but never made their way into the varieties spoken by many older migrants.

3. The more open policies and travel regulations promoted revitalization of heritage languages, e.g., by paying long- or short-term visits to the homeland, which motivated individuals to maintain, improve, or relearn their home language. Furthermore, institutions in the home countries provide support for the cultural and linguistic revitalization of diaspora communities. This support is now mostly free of political bias, in contrast to communist times. Many universities in the Slavic metropolises organize summer schools that sometimes explicitly address heritage speakers living abroad.

4. Even if heritage speakers lacked the financial means to visit their countries of origin, the establishment of the Internet and other new communication technologies offered ways to stay in contact with friends and relatives in their countries of origin. Modern communication technologies such as social networking websites, Skype, satellite

---

[2] The role of religion as a strong unifying force in Slavic communities and as an important functional domain, where the heritage language preserves its dominant function and is used on a regular basis, is highlighted in many publications on language maintenance in Slavic communities (see Hill 2014: 2124 for an overview).

[3] Remennick (2003) describes cases where the growing presence of Russian after 1989 and the subsequent rising of the sociolinguistic status of speakers of Russian in Israel motivated Jews who emigrated from the Soviet Union to Israel in the 1970s to return to the use of Russian in family settings after many years of oblivion.

TV, and radio programs, as well as easy access to periodicals and information websites in the home language, allow heritage speakers to participate in the mainstream of everyday life in the countries of origin (see also Kamusella 2013: 219f.).

5. The ongoing globalization and economic development of the countries of the former Eastern bloc foster new ways of economic and cultural cooperation between East and West. This has a potential impact on the market value of knowing a Slavic language in the business world. There seems to be a growing propensity in host countries for viewing heritage speakers as a resource in the national and international market spheres, drawing on their linguistic as well as cultural expertise (see Remennick 2003; Laleko 2013).

6. Globalization also supports the emergence of highly mobile societies. Members of Slavic-speaking communities abroad now have the possibility to engage in temporary remigration or permanent transmigration, i.e., they maintain a binational lifestyle, which obviously enhances the need for language maintenance.

Parallel to these changes, many countries in general experienced a growing linguistic diversity in their population. In order to adapt to these developments, some of them changed their language policies regarding linguistic minorities. According to Stoffel (2000: 822), the "so-called language ethnic revival has increased the prestige of most migrant languages" in North America and Australia since the 1980s, which resulted in the "formulation of a favourable migration policy and the creation of a multicultural setting." Larger Slavic communities, e.g., the Russian-speaking community in Australia, the Croatian minority in New Zealand, and the Ukrainian community in Canada, benefited from these new policies that placed more emphasis on integration than on straightforward assimilation of minorities.[4] In the European context, the 1992 European Charter for Regional and Minority Languages was designed by the Council of Europe in order to protect and promote autochthonous regional and minority languages in Europe (see Grin 2003). While national implementations of the Charter still show weaknesses, many Slavic minorities have gained more language rights and benefited from the establishment of social and cultural organizations as well as ethnic schools (see contributions in Lebsanft and Wingender 2012). However, some successor states of the former Soviet Union (e.g., Latvia, Lithuania, and Estonia) refused to ratify the Charter because of their hesitation to grant rights to the Russian-speaking minority. Whereas the

---

[4] In Israel massive immigration of Russian-speaking Jews in the 1990s coincided with "a general decline in Hebrew monolingual nation-building ideology, as well as a national identity crisis of 'post-Zionist' Israeli society. This massive immigration wave was one of the major factors that propelled Israeli society towards multilingualism; challenged the 'melting pot' policy towards ethnic minority groups, as well as the dominance of Hebrew as the realization of monolingual ideology." (Kopeliovich 2011: 108).

sociolinguistic situation of many "old" Slavic diaspora communities in Eastern Europe considerably improved after the political turnover, "new" Russian minority communities face local language policies that disfavored the development of Russian by subsequent generations (Wingender 2012).

The overall favorable changes in the sociolinguistic conditions after the dissolution of the Soviet bloc, however, did not always hamper the tendency to language shift. In her report on the vitality of the Russian-speaking community in the United States, Laleko (2013) observes a steady decline in the use of Russian, even among recent arrivals. Her findings corroborate previous statements that Russian – like many other heritage languages in the United States – obviously does not survive beyond the second generation. One factor that negatively impacts heritage language vitality is that the Russian communities in the United States tend to be rather small and speakers of Russian therefore do not live in clearly defined ethnic or linguistic neighborhoods. This limits the possibility of using Russian outside the home or to gain access to community schools (Laleko 2013: 89). Zemskaja (2001) observes that among members of the so-called fourth emigration wave, which started in the middle of the 1980s and was mainly driven by the economic crisis in post-Soviet Russia, there is on average less motivation and desire for a continued use of Russian and for developing the skills necessary for its maintenance and transmission to subsequent generations. They often opted for permanent immigration, which made quick integration into the host society and, therefore, rapid adoption of the majority language top priority (see also Laleko 2013: 97f.). Migration policies that enable fast naturalization of immigrants, e.g., by automatically granting citizenship for generations born in host countries, further contributed to a certain loss of ethnic and linguistic identity among second-generation immigrants and boosted tendencies to abandon the heritage language (Stoffel 2000: 818). The fact that most newly arriving immigrants from Central and Eastern Europe nowadays are characterized by prior knowledge of English facilitates their integration in Anglophone countries and possibly also contributes to the tendency not to mingle with older residents of the same communities in the host countries. On the other hand, prior knowledge of the language of the host country is generally deemed a prerequisite for keeping the two codes apart, which itself promotes maintenance of the home language (Stoffel 2000: 823).

In contrast to the situation in the United States as sketched by Laleko (2013), Slavic heritage languages seem to remain quite vital in other parts of the world. Speakers of a Slavic minority language in countries where they form a sizable group in comparison to the local population exhibit a strong tendency to retain their languages. This applies to some Polish-speaking communities in Western Europe, especially in Anglophone countries (Kamusella 2013), or the Russian-speaking community in Israel (e.g.,

Remennick 2003; Kolčinskaja and Najdič 2009; Isurin 2011; Yelenevskaya 2015). In the latter case, Russian-speaking Jews represent the largest minority community, comprising 30–40 percent of the local population in some districts (Kolčinskaja and Najdič 2009: 103). See Chapter 4 for more details on the status of Russian in Israel.

The prospects for heritage language maintenance in Slavic-speaking communities abroad depend primarily on individual financial resources and on personal preferences and attitudes regarding the emotional and practical value attached to heritage language maintenance. Due to their geographical proximity to the countries of origin, Slavic communities in Europe and Israel may have better prospects for keeping their heritage languages vital compared to Slavic communities overseas.

1.4   Slavic Heritage Languages between Standard and Dialect

Not only have the sociolinguistic conditions for heritage language maintenance changed but also the varieties that heritage speakers are exposed to in families have undergone significant shifts. Stoffel (2000: 809) distinguishes between three stages, depending on the time when the first generation of immigrants arrived in the New World: (i) pre–World War II Slavic settlers were mostly speakers of dialects that they brought with them from their homeland and, consequently, transmitted to the next generation(s)[5]; (ii) post–World War II generations (settlers who arrived between 1945 and 1980 and their offspring) commonly used both dialects and the standard varieties; (iii) post–1989 immigrants and their offspring mostly speak standard-based varieties.

Until the massive replenishment of Slavic diaspora communities in the 1980–1990s, there were indeed some close-knit Slavic communities in the New World who shared a common local or regional background and therefore preserved their original dialects to an even higher degree than speakers of the same dialects in the homeland (see Filipović 1998; Stoffel 1994). Today, due to the establishment of community schools; the influx of media both from the country of origin (which can be accessed via the Internet) and the host country; and new waves of immigrants who bring with them standard-based idioms, dialectal input seems to play a minor role for heritage language acquisition. Possible exceptions can be found in

---

[5] Some groups used the standard varieties of the time when they left their homeland, e.g., highly educated representatives of the first wave of Russian immigrants to Europe and North America after the Bolshevik revolution in 1917. Yet, the majority of Slavic emigrants at that time were peasants or unskilled workers with no command of the standard variety.

autochthonous Slavic minority communities in Central and Eastern Europe (e.g., the Polish minority communities and linguistic enclaves in Ukraine [Rieger et al. 2002], Lithuania [Mędelska 1993], or Slovakia [Rieger 2001]) but also in some communities of Russian Old Believers. Thus, colloquial Doukhobor Russian in Canada has in general a Southern Russian dialectal base but incorporated a lot of borrowings from Canadian English as well as Ukrainian. Ukrainian influence was prominent during the temporary settlement of Doukhobors in the province of Saskatchewan, where they had intense contact with neighboring settlers from Galicia (including cases of intermarriage). This influence stopped after the Doukhobors resettled to British Columbia, where no Ukrainian settlers were present (Schaarschmidt 2000). Old Believers in Romania and Bulgaria also continued to use their own local Russian dialects and not the standard variety of Russian, which was established only after the Old Believers left tsarist Russia. But even afterward, they refused to adopt the standard variety of Russian due to a deeply rooted mistrust of the Russian (and later Soviet) state as representative of the antichrist that led to a rejection of everything that was printed in Russia. Only after 1945, when Russian became an obligatory foreign language in Bulgarian and Romanian schools, did the influence of the Russian standard language increase (Steinke 2000: 760). This pressure from the standard language boosted insecurity for those generations who were already born in the host country concerning which of the varieties they should follow, i.e., the dialectal variety spoken in the family or the Russian standard language that they learned at school (Sussex 1993: 1009).

The presence of speakers of various dialectal backgrounds in the minority community was another factor that contributed to dialect levelling and a shift to the standard variety (see Albijanić 1982: 19). In some cases, heritage languages mix different dialects, which leads to a combination of dialect features that cannot be found in any given dialect of the homeland: According to Dubinina and Polinsky (2013: 167), heritage Russian in the United States exhibits a mixture of features from various dialectal variants of Russian, with traits from Southern Russian dialects occurring also in the speech of families who come from other territorial backgrounds. This mixing of features is not restricted to elements stemming from various dialects of the Slavic L1. Apart from dialects[6] and the pervasive influence of the surrounding majority language, Slavic heritage languages can also show properties that can be traced back to other languages. Stoffel (1982) reports that the speech of Croatians (Dalmatians) in New Zealand exhibits influence

---

[6] This also includes influences from other varieties of the respective Slavic languages, e.g., in the case of Czech heritage speakers, the distinction between so-called written Czech (*spisovná čeština*) and common Czech (*obecná čeština*) (Henzl 1982; Kučera 1990). On dialect mixing in Serbo-Croatian variants spoken by heritage speakers in Sweden, see Ďurovič (1987).

not only from New Zealand English but also from Maori. Other triglossic situations include Russian heritage speakers in Western Europe or North America from families where other languages of the former Soviet Union besides Russian are spoken (Visson 1985); heritage speakers of Sorbian who grew up in bilingual Sorbian-German families in Australia or the United States (Stoffel 2000: 810); or speakers of so-called Aegean Macedonian in Germany, who display features from their original Macedonian dialect, Greek, and German (Hill 2014: 2120).

Whether Slavic heritage languages can be considered clear-cut regional varieties of the respective standard languages spoken in the home countries is up for debate. Sussex (1993: 1010) states that "the better established émigré Slavonic languages can, in certain functional respects, be almost as stable as dialects, at least over the time span of the first generation." Polish linguists tend to classify Polish variants spoken abroad generally as viable regional varieties of Polish labelled "Polonia dialects" (*dialekty polonijne*); these include varieties spoken by subsequent generations born in the host countries (see Sękowska 2010: 37ff.). Walczak (2001: 571f.) stresses that the mechanisms that shape the lexical systems of these local varieties are essentially the same as those that can be observed in the history of Polish. He admits, however, that the impact of the surrounding majority languages on the phonetic and grammatical system of these Polonia varieties cannot compare to developments of Polish varieties spoken in the homeland. Other claims concerning the stability of forms used in diaspora communities concern the lexical level as well. Thus, Ždanova (2009b: 92) treats lexical features like *rabarbar* "rhubarb" (instead of Standard Russian *reven'*) or *aronija* "black chokeberry" (instead of *černoplodnaja rjabina*) found in Latvian heritage speakers of Russian as regional features comparable to regional lexical variants in the homeland. Other researchers underscore the decidedly unstable nature of Slavic heritage language varieties. Hill (2014: 2119) concludes that "Slavonic languages in alloglossic environments typically display (…) weak norms, redolent of Bickerton's (1975) variation within a creole community, with acrolects, mesolects and basilects."[7] In some extreme cases, heritage varieties have developed a distinct literary norm, which was sometimes even taught at community schools (see Steinke 2013: 30f. on Banat Bulgarian). In Slavic linguistics, these local varieties are known under the label "Slavic (literary) microlanguages" (Duličenko 1981).

Slavic heritage languages have not always been exclusively the recipient languages with regard to language change. Heritage Ukrainian in Canada

---

[7] For the sake of brevity, I will use labels like "American Polish", "Australian Macedonian", "Latvian Russian" etc. to refer to Slavic heritage languages in Section 1.5. This does not mean that I consider these distinct contact varieties of the respective homeland languages.

and the United States is an interesting case of influence of a heritage language on the standard spoken in the homeland; after Ukrainian became the sole official state language (*deržavna mova*) in independent Ukraine, representatives of the North American Ukrainian diaspora played an active role in setting the norms of modern Standard Ukrainian. The North American Ukrainian diaspora refused to implement Soviet models for the development of Ukrainian during the Cold War period, and the "pure" Ukrainian standards used by North American heritage speakers of Ukrainian were treated as important reference points during the reform of the Ukrainian language and orthography after 1991 (see Taranenko 2013).

1.5   Structural Properties of Slavic Heritage Languages

The structure of Slavic heritage languages is shaped by the same processes as reported for other heritage languages: (a) transfer from the surrounding majority language(s); (b) preservation of archaic and/or dialectal features; (c) divergence from the standard language, be it due to insufficient input, qualitative shift in the varieties that heritage speakers are exposed to, or internal processes of restructuring that sometimes show parallels to processes that drive the development of the language in the homeland. This section offers an overview of noncanonical features which can be found in different Slavic heritage languages, primarily with a focus on properties that emerge in production.

1.5.1   Phonetics and Phonology

Sussex (1993: 1014f.) mentions as a general feature that heritage speakers often have trouble distinguishing phonologically contrasting pairs in the Slavic heritage language. For example, the distinction between palatalized and non-palatalized consonants is abandoned by merging the palatalized consonants with the non-palatalized series, which leads to a loss of palatals and an increase in homophones. This tendency can be observed in Swedish Croatian, American Czech, or Australian and American Polish, where Polish *proszę* 'please' and *prosię* 'piglet' are both realized as ['prɔʃɛ], i.e., the distinction between /ʃ/ and /ɕ/ is lost (Hill 2014: 2129). Walczak (2001: 571) also notes the loss of affricates in French Polish, which are replaced by simple fricatives. The elimination of single phonemes most often affects those that are missing in the majority language or phonetically difficult to produce, e.g., Czech /r̝/, which is replaced by [ɹ], [ʒ], [dʒ] or [ʃ] in American Czech (Henzl 1982), or the Ukrainian fricative glottal /ɦ/, which is usually substituted by [h] in Canadian Ukrainian (Hudyma 2011: 185).

Frequent phonetic changes on the segmental level include the aspiration of initial voiceless stops (see for American Russian: Polinsky 2000: 796; German Russian: Brehmer and Kurbangulova 2017; American Polish: Sussex 1976); the replacement of velarized Slavic [ł] by a lighter, less velar [l] (Sussex 1993: 1013), or the substitution of trilled [r] by a flapped [ɹ] (for French Russian: Zemskaja 2000: 776; German Russian: Besters-Dilger 2013: 196; German Slovene: Štumberger 2007: 96; Australian Polish: Sussex 1976). Dental stops frequently become postdental/alveolar (Hudyma 2011: 185 on Canadian Ukrainian; Sussex 1976 on Australian Polish). Simplification of consonantal clusters has been noted for American Czech; for example, *nedlik* instead of *knedlík* 'dumpling' (Henzl 1981: 311). For Slavic heritage languages spoken in Anglophone countries, Sussex (1993: 1014) reports a progressive loss of assimilation of voice and place/manner of articulation in consonant clusters as well as the removal of word-final devoicing of voiced obstruents under the influence of English. The latter tendency, however, could not be found in American Russian (Polinsky 2000: 796).

As for the vowels, Polinsky (2000: 796) reports that speakers of American Russian "consistently shift all of their vowels backwards and lower them," e.g., [i] becomes [ɨ], front unrounded [e] becomes central unrounded [ə], and low front [a] sounds like either the central unrounded [ɐ] or the low back unrounded [ɑ]. Other frequently mentioned phenomena include the diph-thongization of stressed vowels and reduction of unstressed vowels (for Australian Polish: Sussex 1976; Canadian Ukrainian: Hudyma 2011: 185).

Most of these and other changes are generally accounted for by the influence of the surrounding majority languages, which affects sounds that are nearly identical in both languages and only slightly differ in their articulatory settings. For some speakers of heritage Russian, Zemskaja (2000: 776) notes the retention of old pronunciation norms that have now been almost lost in homeland Russian, e.g., the assimilative softening of consonants in words like *ži[zʲnʲ]* 'life'. Preservation of dialectal features is reported for smaller and relatively closed Slavic heritage communities, e.g., the Polish community in Panna Maria (Texas) whose speakers still show the so-called Masurian pronunciation (*mazurzenie*), i.e., the merger of Polish retroflex fricatives and affricates /ʂ, ʐ, t͡ʂ, d͡ʐ/ into the alveolar series /s, z, t͡s, d͡z/ (Rappaport 1990).

Research on intonational patterns in Slavic heritage languages is still scarce: Andrews (1993) observed some types of intonational interference from American English in the realization of declarative sentences and yes/no-questions by heritage speakers of Russian in the United States. Sussex (1993: 1014) adds some evidence on the influence of English patterns of stress and vowel-quality reduction in unstressed syllables on fixed-stress Slavic heritage languages like Polish or Czech and on the fixation of word stress in American Russian for words that show mobile stress patterns in homeland Russian (e.g., pronunciations like **rukú* instead of *rúku* 'hand$_{Acc.Sg.fem.}$' in analogy to the nominative *ruká*).

1.5.2 Morphology and Morphosyntax

Several studies describe a major restructuring of the *case system* in Slavic heritage speakers that significantly affects the grammatical structure of the heritage languages, as Slavic languages (apart from Bulgarian and Macedonian) are generally characterized by a highly inflectional system of noun morphology. Sussex (1993: 1017) provides an overview of studies on different Slavic heritage languages in the United States (Croatian, Czech, Polish, Russian, Slovak, Slovene), which all attest a heavy reduction of case morphology. Thus, American heritage speakers of Russian basically use just one unmarked case form (nominative) for all functions except that of the indirect object that is rendered by the accusative (instead of the dative in Standard Russian) (see Polinsky 2006, 2008a): *rasskazyvaj *Lenu$_{Acc}$ *moja$_{Nom}$ *skazka$_{Nom}$* instead of *rasskazyvaj moju$_{Acc}$ skazku$_{Acc}$ Lene$_{Dat}$* 'tell Lena my fairy tale' (Polinsky 2000: 796). All other oblique case forms are replaced by the unmarked case (nominative), which is also used after prepositions, see *s *moi$_{Nom}$ *druz'ja$_{Nom}$* (target: *s moimi$_{Instr}$ druz'jami$_{Instr}$* 'with my friends'), where the expected instrumental case after the preposition *s* 'with' is substituted by the nominative. In the European context, we find comparable evidence: Ďurovič (1983: 24) summarizes his findings on case marking by heritage speakers of Croatian/Serbian in Sweden by formulating an implicational hierarchy of case loss in the investigated children: nominative/accusative < genitive < locative < instrumental < dative < vocative. Thus, children who consistently mark the locative case still retain the genitive and the nominative/accusative, but not vice versa. Again, the system obviously gravitates toward a two-case system (nominative and accusative), with prepositions developing into core markers of the functions of the oblique case forms.[8] Analyzing heritage Polish in Sweden, Laskowski (2014) observes that the nominative shows a clear tendency to function as the unmarked case. The nominative frequently occurs in place of different dependent cases, with the accusative and genitive being better retained than the instrumental and, particularly, the locative and dative cases (Laskowski 2014: 199). The fact that these instances of a more or less systematic restructuring of the case systems were attested mostly in settings where the majority languages exhibit poor noun morphology (English, Swedish) was mostly accounted for by seeing cross-linguistic influence as an important driving force for the reduction of case forms.

---

[8] For a similar tendency in New Zealand Croatian see Stoffel (2000: 813f.). Here, the "casus generalis" that substitutes dependent case forms can have a nominative or accusative desinence.

However, research on case morphology of different Slavic heritage languages in Canada could not confirm a general tendency of a levelling of case forms in an English-dominant surrounding (Łyskawa and Nagy 2019, see also Preston and Turner 1984). There is also less evidence of systematic case levelling in Slavic heritage languages spoken in Germany (Anstatt 2011, 2013; Besters-Dilger 2013; Štumberger 2007), although in many instances, nominative replaces forms of dependent cases in less-proficient heritage speakers (see, e.g., for German Slovene: Štumberger 2007: 97f.). Following Sussex (1993: 1018) we can conclude that "[t]he issue of how much case loss is found in émigré Slavonic, and how it is to be modelled, remain open questions." Recent research suggests that case maintenance in Slavic heritage languages is sensitive to the onset of acquisition of the majority language and to the amount of exposure to the heritage language at home (see Schwartz and Minkov 2014; Gagarina and Klassert 2018).

Generally speaking, there is a tendency in Slavic heritage languages for dependent-case forms to be replaced by prepositional phrases. The prepositions are either followed by nouns in the unmarked case (see American Slovak: okolo *krk$_{Nom}$ instead of okolo krku$_{Gen}$ 'around the neck', Sussex 1993: 1018), or by dependent-case forms, where the preposition explicitly marks the semantic content of the case (see French Polish teściowa *od Janka$_{Gen}$ 'mother-in-law of Janek' instead of a bare genitive: teściowa Janka$_{Gen}$, Walczak 2001: 571).

The morphological distinction between animate and inanimate masculine nouns is systematically weakened; the special accusative form of animate masculine nouns in the direct object position is replaced by the nominative; see German Russian oni uvidjat *medved'$_{Nom}$ 'they will see the bear' (instead of medvedja$_{Acc}$); for German Polish see Anstatt (2013). In a similar manner, the genitive of negation, i.e., the normative use of the genitive form of the internal argument of negated verbs, is often replaced by the accusative, which leads to the use of the accusative as the default case for marking direct objects; see German Polish nie$_{neg}$ rozbiłbym *szybę$_{Acc}$ instead of szyby$_{Gen}$ 'I wouldn't break the window' (see Polinsky 2000: 796 for American Russian; Preston and Turner 1984 for American Polish).

Similar to the reduction of the case system, heritage speakers of Russian in the United States also show a substantial restructuring of the *gender system* (see Polinsky 2008a): The three-way gender system of homeland Russian with masculine, feminine and neuter gender is reduced to a binary masculine–feminine contrast. Intermediate and low-proficient heritage speakers treat all nouns ending in a consonant as masculine, and those ending in a vowel as feminine. The neuter gets lost mainly because of two factors: (i) it is by far the most infrequent gender in Russian and one needs sufficient input to acquire it; (ii) due to the qualitative reduction of Russian vowels in unstressed syllables nouns ending in unstressed /o/ (which are by default neuter) and nouns ending in /a/ (typically feminine nouns) both end in an /a/-like vowel, thus leading heritage speakers to consider these to be feminine. Although more proficient heritage speakers retain the three-way gender system better, they still rely almost exclusively on morphonological cues, i.e., the ending of the noun, to determine its gender rather than on the declensional class which provides more reliable morphological gender assignment cues. Such American Russian speakers treat as neuter only nouns ending in stressed /o/, whereas neuter nouns ending in unstressed /o/ are assigned to the class of feminines. While no such consistent restructuring of the gender system has been reported for other Slavic heritage languages, errors in gender agreement are mentioned as frequent deviations from the homeland baseline. This applies to violations of gender agreement rules on noun-modifying adjectives, like in New Zealand Croatian *svakin$_{Masc}$ subota$_{Fem}$ 'every Saturday' (Stoffel 2000: 813f.), numerals, like Swedish Polish *dwa$_{Masc}$ korony$_{Fem}$ 'two crowns' (Laskowski 2014: 98) or past tense verbs, as in Swedish Polish krew$_{Fem}$ *leciało$_{Neut}$ 'blood was running' (Laskowski 2014: 98). For heritage Polish, additional problems occur in distinguishing between masculine-personal (virile) and non-personal (non-virile) gender forms in the plural, with the latter gender covering all nouns that belong to the masculine-inanimate, feminine, and neuter gender in the singular, but encompassing also masculine animate nouns that do not denote persons (animals, etc.). Some Polish heritage speakers completely lose the distinction between virile/non-virile and show inconsistent agreement patterns, e.g., my *strzelałyśmy$_{Non-Pers}$ i później poszliśmy$_{Masc-Pers}$ do domu 'we were shooting and then we went home' (Laskowski 2014: 100), or overgeneralize one of the two gender forms in the plural. For German Polish, we found that the virile form often became generalized on verbs (e.g., Sylwia i moja mama *mieli$_{Masc-Pers}$ urodziny 'Sylwia and my mom had birthday'), whereas numerals tended to show non-virile agreement. Adjectives showed no clear preference for one or the other form (see also Laskowski 2014: 99ff. for Swedish Polish). Typically, heritage speakers have fewer problems assigning gender to nouns with transparent lexical, morphological, or phonological gender cues. Nouns with unclear gender cues (like feminines ending in consonants) or epicene nouns pose problems for heritage speakers (see Schwartz et al. 2014 and Laleko 2018 for heritage Russian; Brehmer and Rothweiler 2012 for heritage Polish).

Number agreement between subject and verb seems rather infrequently affected in Slavic heritage speakers. However, Štumberger (2007: 101f.) observes an almost consequent loss of the dual in Slovenian heritage speakers in Germany that is replaced by the respective plural forms, e.g., in te dva *imajo$_{Pl}$ dve *hčerke$_{Pl}$ (target: in te dva imata$_{Du}$ dve hčerki$_{Du}$) 'and these two have two daughters'. Laskowski (2014: 101f.) mentions violations in subject–verb agreement in syntactic constructions with predicative complements introduced by the deictic element *to* 'this', where the auxiliary verb *być* 'to be' sometimes occurs in the singular despite a plural predicative complement, e.g., *to* *jest$_{Sg}$ *kwiaty*$_{Pl}$ instead of *to sq*$_{Pl}$ *kwiaty*$_{Pl}$ 'these are flowers'.

Gagarina and Klassert (2018) found that verbal inflection in young heritage speakers of Russian in Germany is much more robust than case inflection. They account for this observation by claiming that "case on nouns in Russian is one of the least transparent morphological categories; it is characterized by high syncretism and multiplicity of manifestations and thus it is more challenging for language acquisition as compared to the iconic and transparent tense-person verb inflection" (Gagarina and Klassert 2018: 11). However, studies on West and South Slavic heritage languages revealed weakened verbal inflection "even to the extent of erasing the distinction between singular and plural in the Serbo-Croat spoken in Sweden" and the emergence of paradigms "where the [personal] pronouns are now the only means of marking the person–number distinction" (Sussex 1993: 1018). A similar reduction of verbal person–number paradigms that leads to frequent subject–verb agreement errors has been found in American Russian (Polinsky 2000: 798). Levelling of stem alternations that regularly occur in Slavic verb inflection is another widespread phenomenon in Slavic heritage languages: Heritage speakers tend to normalize different conjugational patterns by avoiding morphonological alternations that differentiate between the infinitive and present tense stems, see heritage Russian *iskat'*, *iskaju (target: *išču*) 'to search, I search', *remontirovat'*, *remontirovaju (target: *remontiruju*) 'to repair, I repair' (Zemskaja 2000: 779) or American Czech *plakat, on* *plaká (target: *pláče*) 'to cry, he cries' (Henzl 1981: 311). Stoffel (2000: 814) mentions an example in New Zealand Croatian where the infinitive stem is adapted to the present tense forms: *peret (target: *prati*), *peren, pereš* 'to wash, I wash, you wash'.

Tense-aspect systems of Slavic languages represent another vulnerable domain for heritage speakers. Several studies report on the loss of distinction between perfective and imperfective aspect in Slavic heritage languages (see Hill 2014: 2128). Laskowski (2014: 110) observes the "neutralisation of the functional opposition between the present forms of imperfective verbs and non-past forms of perfective verbs" among child heritage speakers of Polish in Sweden. Thus, they frequently use non-past forms of perfective verbs that serve to express future completed events in Standard Polish as a narrative present tense, see *Dziewczynka siedzi*$_{Ipf.Pres}$ *na wymalowanym ławce i* *przyjdzie$_{Pf.non-Past}$ (target: *przychodzi*$_{Ipf.Pres}$) *inna dziewczynka i się* *siądzie$_{Pf.non-Past}$ (target: *siada*$_{Ipf.Pres}$) *na ławce.* 'A girl sits on a painted bench, and then comes another girl and sits down on the bench'. As illustrated by this example, the imperfective form is typically used to describe a background situation (a static state in this case, or a situation that develops in time), while the perfective form in the non-past tense retains a perfective meaning, i.e., denotes a state resulting from the action described by a preceding verb (Laskowski 2014: 112). However, the use of non-past perfective verbs in the habitual function of the present tense was also found in Laskowski's data (Laskowski 2014: 113). Synthetic perfective future tense forms are almost entirely lost and replaced by analytic imperfective future in low-proficient heritage speakers of Australian Russian, possibly under transfer from English where analytic forms express future events (Sussex 1993: 1019). For American Russian, there is conflicting evidence regarding the preservation of aspectual distinctions: Studies on low-proficient speakers of American Russian revealed a tendency toward lexicalization of aspectual markers (Pereltsvaig 2005, 2008; Polinsky 2006, 2008b): Some verbs are used exclusively in the imperfective aspect; others are restricted to the perfective form. Which of the two aspects gets lexicalized depends on the lexical properties of the verbal roots, with inherently telic verbs occurring in the perfective form (like *vstretit'* 'to meet'), and verbs denoting unlimited processes or states (like *verit'* 'to believe' or *sidet'* 'to sit') lexicalized in the imperfective. Laleko (2011: 15f.) provides a typology of deviations from the baseline: She distinguishes between instances where heritage speakers use (i) forms with the opposite aspectual value from the one that would have been used in homeland Russian; (ii) forms with the same aspectual value, but with deviant morphological marking, e.g., missing, superfluous, or wrong prefixes or suffixes; (iii) periphrastic constructions to convey aspectual meanings. Bar-Shalom and Zaretsky (2008), on the other hand, found almost no overt aspectual errors in production of high-proficient speakers of American Russian.

Speakers of American Russian also seem to have lost the conditional in their heritage language, replacing it with simple past tense forms that morphologically build on the same *l*-participle in Russian, but without the conditional marker *by* (Polinsky 2000: 798). For adult Polish heritage speakers in Germany, Błaszczyk (2018) found that they either omitted the conditional marker altogether or tended to overmark the conditional by using the marker *by* twice. Furthermore, they preferred a fixed position of the clitic marker *by* that occurred either before the *l*-participle or in the Wackernagel position.

1.5.3　Syntax

Syntactic innovations in Slavic heritage speakers can be traced back to different sources: Several noncanonical constructions are obviously linked to the reduction of the inflectional system that limits the means of marking grammatical relations (see Section 1.5.2): Reduction in verbal inflection is sometimes compensated for by an *overextension of personal pronouns* to mark the subject in prototypical or partial null subject languages, cf. reports on the use of overt subject pronouns even in cases of co-ordination of clauses in German Croatian/Serbian (Stölting 1980), American Croatian (Jutronić-Tihomirović 1985), German Slovene (Štumberger 2007), Australian Polish (Sussex 1976) or American Russian (Dubinina and Polinsky 2013). Loss of word-order flexibility is another development linked to the levelling of case distinctions. Compare the tendency to strict SVO order in low-proficient speakers of New Zealand Croatian who retain only the nominative: *Ja dajen profesor knjiga* 'I give the professor a book' (Stoffel 2000: 814). This tendency is obviously reinforced by the corresponding fixed SVO order in English. Influence of dominant word order patterns of the majority languages can be found in other cases as well: Preposed possessives in heritage Polish replicate patterns of word order inversion in English (*mojej*$_{Gen}$ *siostry*$_{Gen}$ *tata*$_{Nom}$ 'my sister's father', Sussex 1993: 1020) or Swedish (*babci*$_{Gen}$ *siostra*$_{Nom}$ 'grandma's sister', Laskowski 2014: 118). V2 word order patterns of the majority language can also impact on the placement of constituents in Slavic heritage languages, see the tendency to postpone the subject after the verb due to Swedish V2 in Swedish Polish: *W domu mam *ja 27 książki* 'At home have I 27 books' (Laskowski 2014: 118).[9]

Further types of transfer from the majority language include the use of relative clauses with uninflected *co* (comparable to the English relative 'that') as the general relative pronoun (replacing inflected relative pronouns like *który* 'who, which') in Swedish Polish; *co* here replicates the Swedish uninflected relative *som*, see *książka, co ja pożyczyłem* instead of *książka, którą*$_{Acc}$ *ja pożyczyłem* 'the book that I have borrowed' (Laskowski 2014: 120f.). Constructions of this type resemble comparable uses of uninflected *co* in informal Polish, but lack the obligatory enclitic exponent of the dependent case determined by the head of the relative structure: *książka, co ją*$_{Acc}$ *pożyczyłem* (Laskowski 2014: 121). For different heritage varieties of Polish, the overextension of demonstrative pronouns like *ten* 'this' and numerals like *jeden* 'one' have been observed that function to mark (in)definiteness, similar to definite and indefinite articles, which are mostly present in the majority languages of these communities (e.g., for Swedish Polish Laskowski 2014: 106ff.).

Syntactical innovations include simplification, e.g., (i) loss of double negation in Swedish Polish (Laskowski 2014: 119); (ii) loss of fixed rules for the placement of enclitic elements, especially in South Slavic heritage languages, see German Serbian *smo se lepo igrali* instead of *lepo smo se igrali* 'we have played nicely' (Hill 2014: 2127f.); (iii) infrequent use of participles and gerunds that are replaced by relative clauses or conjoined clauses

---

[9] We did not find German V2 effects in the word order in German Russian declarative clauses (Brehmer and Usanova 2015).

(Sussex 1993: 1019); (iv) reduction of reflexives that are replaced by their non-reflexive counterparts, and (v) substitution of reflexive and possessive-reflexive pronouns with simple personal and possessive pronouns, see Swedish Polish *dostałem* *mój (target: *swój*) *pokój* 'I got my [own] room' (Laskowski 2014: 108).

1.5.4   Lexicon and Semantics

Research on language contact has established that the lexicon is most susceptible to influence from other languages, and Slavic heritage languages are no exception to this rule. Consequently, lexical borrowings from the majority languages represent a universal trait of Slavic heritage languages around the globe (see Sussex 1993: 1021–1030 or Hill 2014: 2125–2127 for an overview). As this presumably does not differentiate Slavic heritage languages from other heritage languages, I will focus only on some changes found in Slavic.

Code-switching between the majority and the heritage language is a frequent phenomenon, especially among more proficient heritage speakers (see, among many others, Schmitt 2000). The code-switching between English and Croatian by heritage speakers of Croatian in Australia indicates that Croatian mostly remains the matrix language, but that varies across individual heritage speakers (Hlavac 2003). Based on Muysken's typology (Muysken 2000), we observed a clear preference of Russian heritage speakers in Germany for the insertion of single German constituents into Russian as the matrix language, whereas alternations occurred only infrequently (Brehmer 2018).

Direct lexical transfers from the majority language affect both those cultural references of the host country that lack an equivalent or short designation in the heritage language (e.g., names of measures, currencies, weights, social institutions) and lexical replacements due to (temporary) lexical-access problems or due to the special role of the referent in the host community. Examples of the former type are American Russian *grinkart* 'greencard' or *kèš* 'cash', and the latter type is represented by *bedrum* 'bedroom', *èkspiriens* 'experience' or *drajvat'* 'to drive' (Zemskaja 2000: 777). More proficient heritage speakers tend to adapt the transfers to the phonological and grammatical patterns of the heritage language, see American Slovene *strajk* 'strike' (besides *štrajk* as an established borrowing from English in homeland Slovene) or *devaluirati* 'to devaluate' (Sussex 1993: 1024). Phonological and morphological integration of such borrowings can vary. In Australian Croatian, "some English phonemes like /ə/, /ð/, /w/ or /ə/ are never replaced in otherwise phonologically-integrated transfers," because comparable phonemes are absent from Croatian (Hlavac 2003: 331). Morphological integration raises the question of gender assignment, which is not always straightforward. Thus, the English *book* would be expected to be masculine in Slavic, because it ends in a hard consonant. However, it becomes the feminine *buka* in American Czech, American Ukrainian, and Pennsylvanian Croatian, possibly because of the feminine gender of the Slavic word it replaces (Czech *kniha*/ Ukrainian *knyha*/ Croatian *knjiga* 'book') (Sussex 1993: 1025). Sometimes morphological transfer leads to functional doubling: Italian diminutive nouns are integrated into Italian Russian with the addition of the Russian diminutive suffix {/očk/}: *ty moja stellinočka* "you are my little starlet' (from Italian *stellina* 'little star' < *stella* 'star') (Goletiani 2009: 131f.).

Loan translations are another common trait in Slavic heritage languages, see American Slovene *mehke pijače* 'soft drinks' (Sussex 1993: 1027), American Polish *suche wino* 'dry wine' (Walczak 2001: 570), or American Croatian *zatvoriti odgovor* 'to conclude an answer' (Jutronić-Tihomirović 1985: 68). There is a strong tendency to generalize the collocations of semantically light verbs in the majority language, see extensions of phrasal combinations with verbs meaning 'to do', 'to take', or 'to have' and different nouns in Slavic heritage varieties: American Russian *delat' den'gi* 'to do (= make) money', French Russian *imet' restoran* 'to have a restaurant', Australian Polish *brać autobus* 'to take a bus' etc. (Sussex 1993: 1027f.; Stoffel 2000: 815).

Semantic extensions of single Slavic words, due to a broader semantics of their equivalents in the majority language, are common; see the additional meaning 'telephone call' of American Russian *telefon* ('telephone', Zemskaja 2000: 777), 'latest' of French Polish *ostatni* ('last', following French *dernier*, Walczak 2001: 570), 'to vote' in German Russian *vybrat'* ('to choose', motivated by ambiguous German *wählen*, Besters-Dilger 2013: 196), or 'yeah' of the Australian Croatian discourse marker *da* ('yes', Hlavac 2003: 333).

Apart from these primarily contact-driven changes, there are also cases of internal restructuring and/or reduction within the lexicon: Sussex (1993: 1021) reports on a simplification of the system of prepositions in American Slovak. Here, the distinction between the prepositions *od* and *z*, which both have the meaning 'from' and govern the genitive in homeland Slovak, but differ with regard to their semantic combinability,[10] is abandoned. *Od* becomes the only preposition meaning 'from' in American Slovak, whereas *z* replaces the phonetically close preposition *s* 'with' and also takes over the government of the instrumental case from *s*. However, *od* is often also confused with *o* 'about' and in these instances followed by the prepositive case. Similar tendencies have been noted in American Croatian, where the preposition *na* tends to replace all other prepositions, see **na* (target: *u*)

---

[10] *Od* is used only with nouns denoting persons, and *z* is used elsewhere.

Kaliforniji 'in California', *na* (target: *pri*) *ruki* 'at hand', *na* (target: *po*) *noči* 'at night' (Jutronić-Tihomirović 1985: 56). This kind of conflation of functions can also be found in unprefixed verbs of motion: Whereas the baseline distinguishes between unidirectional motion verbs (e.g., Russian *idti* 'to go') and verbs that convey a multidirectional or repetitive motion (e.g., Russian *xodit'* 'to go'), heritage speakers often abandon this distinction, see heritage Polish *dzieci *szły* [target: *chodziły*] *do szkoły* 'the children went to school' (Walczak 2001: 571, see also Pfandl 1997 for German Russian).

1.5.5 Pragmatics and Register Variation

One of the common pragmatic characteristics of heritage speakers is their limited knowledge of formal registers in the heritage language. They normally use the heritage language only orally in contact with family members, which leads to a lack of knowledge of elements that are characteristic for written or more formal registers. Consequently, the mixture of different styles, especially the use of colloquial or substandard expressions in more formal speech situations requiring higher registers, is frequently mentioned in research on Slavic heritage speakers (see, among others, Zemskaja 2001, Polinsky and Kagan 2007, or Ždanova 2009b on heritage Russian). Speakers of Doukhobor Russian seem to have suffered from a loss of variability in expressive means (e.g., diminutives) to be used in informal settings, which limits the possibilities to adequately express different degrees of intimacy and age/status relations between the interlocutors (Vanek and Darnell 1971). The limitation of the spectrum of social interactions to family or informal encounters has obvious consequences for the acquisition of verbal markers of social distance. Thus, heritage speakers often lack polite (distant) pronouns of address or apply and interpret them inappropriately (see, e.g., Wolski-Moskoff 2018 for American Polish or Vanek and Darnell 1971 for Doukhobor Russian). This does not mean that heritage speakers in general are not capable of expressing their communicative intentions outside the family circle in a socially acceptable manner; see Chapter 27 with examples from American Russian.

1.5.6 Writing and Spelling

Many heritage speakers lack literacy skills in their Slavic L1. The acquisition of writing and reading skills is additionally impeded by the fact that the East and South-East Slavic languages (Russian, Belarusian, Ukrainian, Bulgarian, Macedonian, and Serbian) use the Cyrillic script, which means that in many instances heritage speakers would have to master two different script systems, one for the majority and the other for the heritage language. Mastering the Cyrillic script is often viewed as a sign of loyalty toward the heritage culture (Brehmer 2015a), and biscriptual writing skills can be exploited for several purposes, including switching of the script system as a contextualization cue for signaling additional information (Brehmer 2015b). There are, however, many instances where heritage speakers who have acquired (limited) productive writing skills in Cyrillic transfer graphemes from the majority language alphabet (Usanova 2019).

Spelling rules represent another problematic domain for heritage speakers. Due to their limited experience in reading and writing texts in the heritage language, heritage speakers often apply phonetic spellings, which increases the number of spelling errors in Slavic languages with a high amount of historical (e.g., Polish) or morphological spellings (e.g., Russian). Spelling is also affected by transfers from the majority language, e.g., when texts of Russian heritage speakers in Germany reflect the German principle to use capitalization in rendering nouns, or when diacritics in New Zealand Croatian are replaced by digraphical spellings (Stoffel 2000: 813).

1.6   Conclusions

Heritage speakers of Slavic languages constitute a large proportion of heritage speaker communities worldwide. Some Slavic heritage communities like the Croatians in New Zealand or the Ukrainians in Canada can look back at 150 years of life in diaspora and, therefore, have a "generally recognized privileged status" in these countries (Stoffel 2000: 807). Slavic heritage communities in the Western world that emerged as a result of large-scale migration waves are often similar to other migrant communities. On the other hand, Slavic heritage communities that emerged as a result of changing borders in postwar periods or the demise of large multiethnic states like Yugoslavia and the Soviet Union represent a different case, one that was only marginally discussed here. In both cases, however, "[s]urvival in linguistic minorities under foreign domination is a skill which the Slavs have practised over long periods. They learnt many mechanisms to overcome linguistic repression" (Sussex 1993: 1006). This included a strong feeling of loyalty toward the home language and culture as well as the establishment of institutions (churches, clubs, community schools, etc.) that supported language and culture maintenance. Nevertheless, intergenerational language shift to the majority languages was a widespread phenomenon before the political turnover in Central and Eastern Europe at the end of the 1980s. New waves of emigration, as well as the improvement of the sociolinguistic situation of many autochthonous Slavic heritage communities in the countries of the former Eastern bloc, resulted in the fact that "the major Slav migrant languages have been given a renewed lease of life and will continue into the 21st century" (Stoffel 2000: 825). It remains to be seen, though, whether the large share of Slavic-speaking communities outside the traditional range of the Slavic-speaking world (Americas, Israel, Western Europe), current migration patterns, and the new mobility in a globalized world will indeed suffice to make Slavic heritage languages "a permanent fixture in the host societies and cultures for the generations to come" (Kamusella 2013: 216). Recent research on heritage speakers of Russian in the United States suggests that the preservation of family ties remains the core motivation for language maintenance (Laleko 2013: 99).

On the linguistic level, Slavic heritage languages reveal striking parallels regarding the restructuring, partial reduction, and simplification of phonology, grammar, and the lexicon. While the majority language without doubt exerts a pervasive impact on the respective Slavic heritage grammar and lexicon, parallel developments in the same heritage language spoken in different countries hint at more universal principles of language change being at play in reshaping heritage grammars. As some heritage languages have received more attention than others, more systematic comparative research is needed to shed additional light on these language-independent developments. Future research should also take into account autochthonous Slavic heritage communities and hitherto largely neglected Slavic languages like Belarusian, Bulgarian, or Slovak.

References

Achterberg, Jörn. 2005. *Zur Vitalität slavischer Idiome in Deutschland: Eine empirische Studie zum Sprachverhalten slavophoner Immigranten*. Munich: Sagner.

Albijanić, Aleksandar. 1982. San Pedro Revisited: Language Maintenance in the San Pedro Yugoslav Community. In Roland Sussex (ed.), *The Slavic Languages in Emigre Communities*. Carbondale, IL: Linguistic Research, 11–22.

Albin, Alexander and Ronelle Alexander. 1972. *The Speech of Yugoslav Immigrants in San Pedro, California*. The Hague: Martinus Nijhof.

Andrews, David R. 1993. American Intonational Interference in Émigré Russian. A Comparative Analysis of Elicited Speech Samples. *Slavic and East European Journal* 37(2), 162–177.

Anstatt, Tanja. 2011. Sprachattrition: Abbau der Erstsprache bei russisch-deutschen Jugendlichen. *Wiener Slawistischer Almanach* 67, 7–31.

Anstatt, Tanja. 2013. Polnisch als Herkunftssprache: Sprachspezifische grammatische Kategorien bei bilingualen Jugendlichen. In Sebastian Kempgen, Monika Wingender, Norbert Franz, and Miranda Jakiša (eds.), *Deutsche Beiträge zum 15. Internationalen Slavistenkongress Minsk 2013*. Munich: Sagner, 25–35.

Balhar, Jan, Stanislava Kloferová, and Jarmila Vojtová. 1999. *U nás ve Vídni. Vídeňští češi vzpomínají.* Brno: Masaryk University.

Bar-Shalom, Eva and Elena Zaretsky. 2008. Selective Attrition in Russian-English Bilingual Children: Preservation of Grammatical Aspect. *International Journal of Bilingualism* 12(4), 281–302.

Besters-Dilger, Juliane. 2013. Russian in Germany: Intermediate Results on L1 Attrition. In Michael Moser and Maria Polinsky (eds.), *Slavic Languages in Migration.* Vienna: LIT, 189–204.

Bickerton, Derek. 1975. *Dynamics of a Creole System.* Cambridge: Cambridge University Press.

Błaszczyk, Izabela. 2018. *Wenn man die polnische Sprache erbt...Beschreibung und empirische Analyse zum Irrealis-Marker by im Polnischen und seiner Verwendung bei Herkunftssprechern mit Deutsch als dominanter Sprache.* PhD dissertation, University of Regensburg. (Retrieved from epub.uni-regensburg.de, last accessed May 26, 2020).

Brehmer, Bernhard. 2015a. The Cyrillic Script as a Boundary Marker between "Insiders" and "Outsiders": Metalinguistic Discourse about Script Choices in Slavic-German Bilingual Computer-Mediated Communication. In Konstanze Jungbluth, Peter Rosenberg, and Dagna Zinkhahn-Rhobodes (eds.), *Linguistic Constructions of Ethnic Borders.* Frankfurt: Peter Lang, 55–80.

Brehmer, Bernhard. 2015b. Script-Switching und Digraphie im Netz: Schriftpräferenzen und Schriftkontakt in der bilingualen slavisch-deutschen Internet-Kommunikation. In Vittorio Tomelleri and Sebastian Kempgen (eds.), *Slavic Alphabets in Contact.* Bamberg: Bamberg University Press, 59–93.

Brehmer, Bernhard. 2018. Typen von Sprachmischungen in zweisprachigen russisch-deutschen Familien: ein intergenerationeller Vergleich. In Sebastian Kempgen (ed.), *Deutsche Beiträge zum 16. Internationalen Slavistenkongress in Belgrad 2018.* Wiesbaden: Harrassowitz, 69–79.

Brehmer, Bernhard and Tatjana Kurbangulova. 2017. Lost in Transmission? Family Language Input and Its Role for the Development of Russian as a Heritage Language in Germany. In Ludmila Isurin and Claudia Maria Riehl (eds.), *Integration, Identity and Language Maintenance in Young Immigrants. Russian Germans or German Russians.* Amsterdam: Benjamins, 225–268.

Brehmer, Bernhard and Grit Mehlhorn. 2015. Russisch als Herkunftssprache in Deutschland: Ein holistischer Ansatz zur Erforschung des Potenzials von Herkunftssprachen. *Zeitschrift für Fremdsprachenforschung* 26(1), 83–121.

Brehmer, Bernhard and Monika Rothweiler. 2012. The Acquisition of Gender Agreement Marking in Polish: A Study of Bilingual Polish-German Children. In Kurt Braunmüller and Christoph Gabriel (eds.), *Multilingual Individuals and Multilingual Societies.* Amsterdam: Benjamins, 81–100.

Brehmer, Bernhard and Irina Usanova. 2015. Let's Fix It? Contact-Induced Changes in Word Order Patterns of Russian Heritage Speakers in

Germany. In Hagen Peukert (ed.), *Transfer Effects in Multilingual Language Development*. Amsterdam: Benjamins, 159–186.

Cigler, Michael. 1983. *The Czechs in Australia*. Melbourne: AE Press.

Dubinina, Irina and Maria Polinsky. 2013. Russian in the USA. In Michael Moser and Maria Polinsky (eds.), *Slavic Languages in Migration*. Vienna: LIT, 161–187.

Dubisz, Stanisław (ed.) 1997. *Język polski poza granicami kraju*. Opole: University of Opole.

Duličenko, Aleksandr D. 1981. *Slavianskije literaturnye mikrojazyki: Voprosy formirovanija i razvitija*. Tallinn: Valgus.

Ďurovič, Ľubomír (ed.) 1983. *Lingua in Diaspora: Studies in the Language of the Second Generation of Yugoslav Immigrant Children in Sweden*. Lund: Lund University.

Ďurovič, Ľubomír. 1987. The Development of Grammar Systems in Diaspora Children's Language. *Slavica Lundensia* 11, 51–85.

Filipović, Rudolf. 1998. Sjedinjene Američke Države. In Mijo Lončarić (ed.), *Hrvatski jezik*. Opole: University of Opole, 287–294.

Gagarina, Natalia and Annegret Klassert. 2018. Input Dominance and Development of Home Language in Russian-German Bilinguals. *Frontiers in Communication-Language Sciences* 3, 40.

Goletiani, Liana. 2009. Processy zaimstvovanija v reči russkojazyčnyx ėmigrantov v Italii. In Vladislava Ždanova (ed.), *Russkij jazyk v uslovijax kul'turnoj i jazykovoj polifonii: sbornik statej*. Munich: Sagner, 129–138.

Golubeva-Monatkina, Natalija I. 1995. Leksičeskie osobennosti russkoj reči potomkov russkogo zarubež'ja vo Francii. *Rusistika segodnja* 1, 70–92.

Grin, François. 2003. *Language Policy Evaluation and the European Charter for Regional or Minority Languages*. Basingstoke: Palgrave Macmillan.

Henzl, Vera M. 1981. Slavic Languages in the New Environment. In Charles Ferguson and Shirley Brice Heath (eds.), *Language in the USA*. Cambridge: Cambridge University Press, 293–321.

Henzl, Vera M. 1982. American Czech: A Comparative Study of Linguistic Modifications in Immigrant and Young Children Speech. In Roland Sussex (ed.), *The Slavic Languages in Emigre Communities*. Carbondale, IL: Linguistic Research, 33–46.

Hill, Peter. 1989. *The Macedonians in Australia*. Perth: Hesperian Press.

Hill, Peter. 2014. The Slavonic Languages in Emigre Communities. In Karl Gutschmidt, Sebastian Kempgen, Tilman Berger, and Peter Kosta (eds.), *Die slavischen Sprachen. The Slavic Languages. An International Handbook of Their Structure, Their History and Their Investigation*. Vol. 2. Berlin and Boston: de Gruyter, 2116–2135.

Hlavac, Jim. 2003. *Second-Generation Speech: Lexicon, Code-Switching and Morpho-Syntax of Croatian-English Bilinguals*. Frankfurt: Peter Lang.

Hlavac, Jim. 2016. *Three Generations, Two Countries of Origin, One Speech Community: Australian-Macedonians and Their Language(s)*. Leipzig: Biblion Media.

Hlavac, Jim and Diana Stolac. 2021. *Diaspora Language Contact: The Speech of Croatian Speakers Abroad*. Berlin and New York: de Gruyter.

Hudyma, Khrystyna. 2011. Ukrainian Language in Canada: From Prosperity to Extinction? *Working Papers of the Linguistics Circle of the University of Victoria* 21, 181–189.

Isurin, Ludmila. 2011. *Russian Diaspora: Culture, Identity, and Language Change*. Berlin and Boston: de Gruyter.

Isurin, Ludmila and Claudia Maria Riehl (eds.) 2017. *Integration, Identity and Language Maintenance in Young Immigrants: Russian Germans or German Russians*. Amsterdam: Benjamins.

Jutronić-Tihomirović, Dunja. 1985. *Hrvatskij jezik u SAD*. Split: Logos.

Kagan, Olga, Miriam Minkov, Ekaterina Protassova, and Mila Schwartz. 2019. Osobennosti russkogo jazyka u mnogojazyčnyx podrostkov v Germanii, Izraile, SŠA i Finljandii. In Julija Men'šikova and Ekaterina Protassova (eds.), *Mnogojazyčie i obrazovanie*. Berlin: Retorika, 49–60.

Kamusella, Tomasz. 2013. Migration or Immigration? Ireland's New and Unexpected Polish-language Community. In Michael Moser and Maria Polinsky (eds.), *Slavic Languages in Migration*. Vienna: LIT, 205–231.

Kolčinskaja, Evgenija and Larisa Najdič. 2009. Čerty lingvističeskogo portreta russkix tinejdžerov v Izraile. In Vladislava Ždanova (ed.), *Russkij jazyk v uslovijax kul'turnoj i jazykovoj polifonii: sbornik statej*. Munich: Sagner, 103–117.

Kopeliovich, Shulamit. 2011. How Long is 'the Russian Street' in Israel? Prospects of Maintaining the Russian Language. *Israel Affairs* 17(1), 108–124.

Kučera, Karel. 1990. *Český jazyk v USA*. Prague: Univerzita Karlova.

Laitin, David D. 1998. *Identity in Formation: The Russian-speaking Populations in the Near Abroad*. Ithaca, NY: Cornell University Press.

Laleko, Oksana. 2011. Restructuring of Verbal Aspect in Heritage Russian: beyond Lexicalization. *International Journal of Language Studies* 5(3), 13–26.

Laleko, Oksana. 2013. Assessing Heritage Language Vitality: Russian in the United States. *Heritage Language Journal* 10(3), 382–395.

Laleko, Oksana. 2018. What Is Difficult about Grammatical Gender? Evidence from Heritage Russian. *Journal of Language Contact* 11, 233–267.

Laskowski, Roman. 2014. *Language Maintenance – Language Attrition: The Case of Polish Children in Sweden*. Frankfurt: Peter Lang.

Lebsanft, Franz and Monika Wingender (eds.) 2012. *Die Sprachpolitik des Europarates: Die "Europäische Charta der Regional- oder Minderheitensprachen" aus linguistischer und juristischer Sicht*. Berlin and Boston: de Gruyter.

Łyskawa, Paulina and Naomi Nagy. 2019. Case Marking Variation in Heritage Slavic Languages in Toronto: Not So Different. *Language Learning* 70(1), 122–156.

Magocsi, Paul Robert. 2013. Slavic Immigrant Cultures in North America: The Language Factor. In Michael Moser and Maria Polinsky (eds.), *Slavic Languages in Migration*. Vienna: LIT, 11–21.

McCabe, Marta. 2016. Czech and Slovak as Heritage Languages in the Southeastern United States: The Potential of Transnationalism for Language Maintenance. *International Journal of the Sociology of Language* 238(2), 169–191.

Mędelska, Jolanta. 1993. *Język polski na Litwie w dziewiątym dziesięcioleciu XX wieku*. Bydgoszcz: Wyd. Uczelniane WSP.

Minkov, Miriam, Olga E. Kagan, Ekaterina Protassova, and Mila Schwartz. 2019. Towards a Better Understanding of a Continuum of Heritage Language Proficiency: The Case of Adolescent Russian Heritage Speakers. *Heritage Language Journal* 16(2), 211–237.

Moser, Michael and Maria Polinsky (eds.) 2013. *Slavic Languages in Migration*. Vienna: LIT.

Muysken, Pieter. 2000. *Bilingual Speech: A Typology of Code-Mixing*. Cambridge: Cambridge University Press.

Nagy, Naomi and Alexei Kochetov. 2013. VOT across the Generations: A Cross-Linguistic Study of Contact-Induced Change. In Peter Siemund, Ingrid Gogolin, Monika Schulz, and Julia Davydova (eds.), *Multilingualism and Language Contact in Urban Areas: Acquisition – Development – Teaching – Communication*. Amsterdam: Benjamins, 19–38.

Nikunlassi, Ahti and Ekaterina Protassova (eds.) 2019. *Russian Language in the Multilingual World*. Helsinki: University of Helsinki.

Odarčenko, Petro V. 1990. *Ukrajins'ka mova v Ameryci*. Toronto: Novi Dni.

Pavlenko, Aneta. 2008a. Multilingualism in Post-Soviet Countries: Language Revival, Language Removal, and Sociolinguistic Theory. *International Journal of Bilingual Education and Bilingualism* 11, 275–314.

Pavlenko, Aneta. 2008b. Russian in Post-Soviet Countries. *Russian Linguistics* 32, 59–80.

Pereltsvaig, Asya. 2005. Aspect Lost, Aspect Regained: Restructuring of Aspectual Marking in American Russian. In Paula Kempchinsky and Roumyana Slabakova (eds.), *Aspectual Inquiries*. Dordrecht: Springer, 369–395.

Pereltsvaig, Asya. 2008. Aspect in Russian as Grammatical Rather Than Lexical Notion: Evidence from Heritage Russian. *Russian Linguistics* 32, 27–42.

Pfandl, Heinrich 1997. Abweichungen im Gebrauch der Verben der Fortbewegung bei in Österreich lebenden Sprecher(inne)n mit russischer Erstsprache und frühem Ausreisealter. *Mitteilungen für die Lehrer slawischer Fremdsprachen* 73(6), 13–27.

Polinsky, Maria. 2000. The Russian Language in the USA. In Lew Zybatow (ed.), *Sprachwandel in der Slavia: Die slavischen Sprachen an der Schwelle zum*

21. Jahrhundert. Ein internationales Handbuch. Vol. 2. Frankfurt: Peter Lang, 787–803.

Polinsky, Maria. 2006. Incomplete Acquisition: American Russian. *Journal of Slavic Linguistics* 14, 191–262.

Polinsky, Maria. 2008a. Gender under Incomplete Acquisition: Heritage Speakers' Knowledge of Noun Categorization. *Heritage Language Journal* 6(1), 40–71.

Polinsky, Maria. 2008b. Without Aspect. In Greville G. Corbett and Michael Noonan (eds.), *Case and Grammatical Relations.* Amsterdam: Benjamins, 263–282.

Polinsky, Maria and Olga Kagan. 2007. Heritage Languages: In the 'Wild' and in the Classroom. *Language & Linguistics Compass* 1, 368–395.

Preston, Dennis R. and Michael Turner. 1984. The Polish of Western New York: Case. *Melbourne Slavonic Studies* 18, 135–154.

Rappaport, Gilbert. 1990. Sytuacja językowa Amerykanów polskiego pochodzenia w Teksasie. In Władysław Miodunka (ed.), *Język polski w świecie.* Krakow: PAN, 159–178.

Remennick, Larissa. 2003. From Russian to Hebrew via *HebRush*: Intergenerational Patterns of Language Use among Former Soviet Immigrants in Israel. *Journal of Multilingual and Multicultural Development* 24(5), 431–453.

Rieger, Janusz. 2001. Język polski na Wschodzie. In Jerzy Bartmiński (ed.), *Współczesny język polski.* Lublin: Wyd. UMS, 575–590.

Rieger, Janusz, Iwona Cechosz-Felczyk, and Ewa Dzięgiel 2002. *Język polski na Ukrainie w końcu XX wieku.* Warsaw: Semper.

Šabec, Nada. 1993. Language Maintenance among Slovene Immigrants in the USA. *Slovene Studies* 15(1–2), 151–168.

Schaarschmidt, Gunter. 2000. Doukhobor Russian in Canada: Present Trends and Prospects for Survival. In Lew Zybatow (ed.), *Sprachwandel in der Slavia: Die slavischen Sprachen an der Schwelle zum 21. Jahrhundert. Ein internationales Handbuch.* Vol. 2. Frankfurt: Peter Lang, 831–841.

Schmitt, Elena. 2000. Overt and Covert Codeswitching in Immigrant Children from Russia. *International Journal of Bilingualism* 4(1), 9–28.

Schwartz, Mila and Miriam Minkov. 2014. Russian Case System Acquisition among Russian-Hebrew Speaking Children. *Journal of Slavic Linguistics* 22, 51–92.

Schwartz, Mila, Miriam Minkov, Elena Dieser, Ekaterina Protassova, Victor Moin, and Maria Polinsky. 2014. Acquisition of Russian gender Agreement by Monolingual and Bilingual Children. *International Journal of Bilingualism* 19(6), 726–752.

Sękowska, Elżbieta. 2010. *Język emigracji polskiej w świecie: Bilans i perspektywy badawcze.* Kraków: Wyd. Uniwersytetu Jagiellońskiego.

Slavkov, Nikolay. 2015. Language Attrition and Reactivation in the Context of Bilingual First Language Acquisition. *International Journal of Bilingual Education and Bilingualism* 18(6), 715–734.

Steinke, Klaus. 1990. *Die russischen Sprachinseln in Bulgarien*. Heidelberg: Winter.

Steinke, Klaus. 2000. Russisch in der Diaspora. In Lew Zybatow (ed.), *Sprachwandel in der Slavia: Die slavischen Sprachen an der Schwelle zum 21. Jahrhundert. Ein internationales Handbuch*. Vol. 2. Frankfurt: Peter Lang, 753–766.

Steinke, Klaus. 2013. *Sprache und Konfession in der Migration (am Beispiel der Altgläubigen im Osmanischen Reich und der Banater Bulgaren)*. In Michael Moser and Maria Polinsky (eds.), *Slavic Languages in Migration*. Vienna: LIT, 23–37.

Stoffel, Hans-Peter. 1981. Observations on the Serbo-Croatian Language in New Zealand. *New Zealand Slavonic Journal* 8, 53–64.

Stoffel, Hans-Peter. 1982. Language Maintenance and Language Shift of the Serbo-Croatian Language in a New Zealand Dalmatian Community. In Roland Sussex (ed.), *The Slavic Languages in Emigre Communities*. Carbondale, IL: Linguistic Research, 121–140.

Stoffel, Hans-Peter. 1994. Dialect and Standard Language in a Migrant Situation: The Case of New Zealand Croatian. *New Zealand Slavonic Journal* 21, 153–170.

Stoffel, Hans-Peter. 2000. Slav Migrant Languages in the "New World". In Lew Zybatow (ed.), *Sprachwandel in der Slavia: Die slavischen Sprachen an der Schwelle zum 21. Jahrhundert. Ein internationales Handbuch*. Vol. 2. Frankfurt: Peter Lang, 805–830.

Stölting, Wilfried. 1980. *Die Zweisprachigkeit jugoslawischer Schüler in der Bundesrepublik Deutschland*. Berlin: Osteuropa-Institut FU Berlin.

Stölting-Richert, Wilfried. 1988. Linguistic, Sociological and Pedagogical Aspects of Serbo-Croatian in West-European Diaspora. *Slavica Lundensia* 12, 11–21.

Štumberger, Saška. 2007. *Slovenščina pri Slovencih v Nemčiji*. Ljubljana: Znanstvenoraziskovalni inštitut Filozofske fakultete.

Sussex, Roland. 1976. Preliminaries to a Linguistic Analysis of Australian Polish. In Roland Sussex (ed.), *Proceedings of the Polish Colloquium*. Melbourne: University of Melbourne, 63–76.

Sussex, Roland (ed.) 1982. *The Slavic Languages in Emigre Communities*. Carbondale, IL: Linguistic Research.

Sussex, Roland (ed.) 1984. The Maintenance of the Slavonic Languages Abroad. *Melbourne Slavonic Studies* 18 (Special Issue).

Sussex, Roland. 1993. Slavonic Languages in Emigration. In Bernard Comrie and Greville G. Corbett (eds.), *The Slavonic Languages*. London: Routledge, 999–1036.

Taranenko, Oleksandr. 2013. Movna prysutnist' ukrajins'koji zaxidnoji diaspory v sučasnij Ukrajini. In Michael Moser and Maria Polinsky (eds.), *Slavic Languages in Migration*. Vienna: LIT, 125–160.

Urban, Angela. 2004. *Russisch-spanischer Sprachkontakt in Argentinien. Die russische Emigration nach Argentinien und deren sprachliche Folgeerscheinungen dargestellt am Beispiel der russischen Sprachgemeinschaften in Buenos Aires und Oberá, Misiones.* Vienna: Praesens.

Usanova, Irina. 2019. *Biscriptuality: Writing Skills among German-Russian Adolescents.* Amsterdam: Benjamins.

Vanek, Anthony L. and Regna Darnell. 1971. Canadian Doukhobor Russian in Grand Forks, B.C.: Some Social Aspects. In Regna Darnell (ed.), *Linguistic Diversity in Canadian Society.* Edmonton and Champaign: Linguistic Research, 267–290.

Viimaranta, Hannes O., Ekaterina Protassova, and Arto Mustajoki. 2018. Russian-Speakers in Finland: The Ambiguities of a Growing Minority. *Revue d'Etudes Comparatives Est-Ouest* 49(4), 8–40.

Visson, Lynn. 1985. Russian in America: Notes on the Russian Spoken by Émigrés. *Russian Language Journal* 145/146, 185–191.

Walczak, Bogdan. 2001. Język polski na Zachodzie. In Jerzy Bartmiński (ed.), *Współczesny język polski.* Lublin: Wyd. UMS, 563–574.

Wingender, Monika 2012. Russisch als neue Minderheitensprache im östlichen Europa. Die "Europäische Charta der Regional- oder Minderheitensprachen" und die Diskussion um das Russische in Nachfolgestaaten der UdSSR. In Franz Lebsanft and Monika Wingender (eds.), *Die Sprachpolitik des Europarates: Die "Europäische Charta der Regional- oder Minderheitensprachen" aus linguistischer und juristischer Sicht.* Berlin and Boston: de Gruyter, 165–189.

Wolski-Moskoff, Izolda. 2018. Knowledge of Forms of Address in Polish Heritage Speakers. *Heritage Language Journal* 15(1), 116–144.

Yelenevskaya, Maria. 2015. An Immigrant Language in a Multilingual State: Status and Group Competition (Russian in Israel). *Russian Journal of Communication* 7(2), 193–207.

Ždanova, Vladislava (ed.) 2009a. *Russkij jazyk v uslovijax kul'turnoj i jazykovoj polifonii: sbornik statej.* Munich: Sagner.

Ždanova, Vladislava. 2009b. K probleme lingvističeskogo statusa russkogo jazyka diaspory. In Vladislava Ždanova (ed.), *Russkij jazyk v uslovijax kul'- turnoj i jazykovoj polifonii: sbornik statej.* Munich: Sagner, 89–101.

Zemskaja, Elena A. 2000. O jazyke russkogo zarubež'ja. In Lew Zybatow (ed.), *Sprachwandel in der Slavia: Die slavischen Sprachen an der Schwelle zum 21. Jahrhundert. Ein internationales Handbuch.* Vol. 2. Frankfurt: Peter Lang, 767–785.

Zemskaja, Elena A. (ed.) 2001. *Jazyk russkogo zarubež'ja: obščie processy i rečevye portrety.* Moscow and Vienna: Jazyki slavjanskoj kul'tury.

Zielińska, Anna. 2017. *The Multilingualism of the Old Believers Living in Poland.* Warsaw: Institute of Slavic Studies.

Žluktenko, Jurij O. 1990. *Ukrajins'ka mova na linhvistiyčnij karti Kanady.* Kiev: Naukova Dumka.

2

Heritage Languages in Europe

Tanja Kupisch

2.1 Introduction

It is widely agreed that a heritage language (HL) is a minority language acquired in a regional or national environment where it represents neither an official language nor the language of the majority of the population, i.e., the societal language. Therefore, the distinction between *majority* and *minority* language is crucial in the context of HL research, though it is not straightforward in countries with several official languages, whose use depends on the region (e.g., Belgium, Switzerland, and Spain). Generally, a HL is described as being acquired as a first language in a naturalistic setting, either as the only first language or as one of two or more first languages, through one or several family members. Definitions and descriptions of heritage speakers (HSs) vary, however (see Benmamoun et al. 2013; Fishman 2001; Flores et al. 2017; Kupisch and Rothman 2018; Montrul 2008, 2016; Rothman 2009; Putnam et al. 2018; Polinsky 2018; Polinsky and Scontras 2020), as do the extra-linguistic circumstances under which HLs are acquired, and the latter often lead to differences from monolingual speakers. Some definitions refer to the degree of mastery of the languages, implying that bilinguals are not HSs if they are highly proficient. Herein, I make no such a priori assumptions about mastery.

Currently, there seems to be no consensus concerning the types of minorities whose languages count as HLs. Within the context of political philosophy, Kymlicka (1995) distinguishes three types of ethnic (minority) groups based on three sources of multiculturalism: (i) national minorities, (ii) indigenous peoples, and (iii) immigrant groups. For example, in Sweden, the Finnish are a national minority, the Sámi represent an indigenous minority, and there are various migrant minorities, e.g., Iranian, Syrian, and Lebanese. Indigenous minorities differ from migrant minorities in being original settlers of a given region in contrast to groups that have occupied, settled, or colonized the area later. In the US context, somewhat similarly, Fishman (2001) distinguishes between (i) indigenous HLs spoken by autochthonous minorities, (ii) colonial HLs, such as Dutch or Swedish, and (iii) HLs of recent migrants. It is open to debate whether the following types of speakers should be subsumed under the label of HSs: speakers of national minorities, e.g., Danish in Germany; dialect speakers, e.g., Venetan in Italy; *neo* or *new speakers*, e.g., late learners of Basque with Basque ancestry who have had no exposure to Basque during childhood. The linguistic research on HSs has mostly been concerned with migrant minorities, and this is also the focus of this chapter.

In order to understand the situation of HSs in Europe, it is important to keep in mind the different types of minorities and what distinguishes them. In what follows, it will be evident that migrant minority languages are less protected than other types of minority languages, although they are higher in number, both with regard to the diversity of languages and the number of speakers (see Extra 2001). Turkish and Arabic, for example, are spoken by millions of people in Europe.

2.2   Linguistic Diversity in Europe

With more than 700 million inhabitants on a surface of ~10 million square kilometers, and currently 45 countries (including transcontinental Russia and Turkey), Europe is densely populated and represents a relatively urbanized area of the earth. Most of the official national languages in Europe are Indo-European and part of the Germanic, Romance, or Slavic language families (with ~200 million speakers per family). Other Indo-European families with far fewer speakers are Albanian, Hellenic (Greek), and Baltic (Latvian, Lithuanian). Non–Indo-European families include Uralic (Finnish, Estonian, Hungarian), Turkic, and Semitic (Maltese). Besides national languages, some statistics mention about sixty regional and minority languages and numerous indigenous languages (e.g., Special Eurobarometer 2012: 2), but the number of sixty is probably a crude underestimation. The inclusion of minority languages, recognized or not, would extend the variety to include many more Indo-European and some non–Indo-European languages (e.g., Romanes, Welsh, and Basque). The Charter of Regional or Minority Languages (Council of Europe 1992) lists eighty-three regional or minority languages, but since almost half of the states have not ratified the charter, the actual number is probably much higher.

At first blush, this scenario seems to be inessential, given the existence of individual countries elsewhere in the world, such as India or Papua New Guinea, which have 700–900 languages. However, as Gogolin (2002) points out, the picture changes drastically once migrants and their languages are taken into account. In an ordinary primary school with 200 children in Hamburg, Germany, for instance, she found that only 50 percent of the children had a monolingual background, while the other 50 percent came from fifteen different countries and spoke twenty different languages. A survey by Fürstenau et al. (2003) reported 90 different languages spoken by primary school children in Hamburg.

From a language policy and planning perspective, the Council of Europe has committed to the protection of multilingualism. The European Charter for Regional or Minority Languages (Council of Europe 1992) ensures that regional or minority languages are recognized as part of Europe's cultural heritage. Their protection and promotion is seen as essential to fostering democracy, cultural diversity, education, and economy. However, the Charter only applies to regional and minority languages, defined as "languages traditionally used within a given territory of a state by nationals of that state who form a group numerically smaller than the rest of the state's population" (Council of Europe 1992: Article 1). It does not apply to the languages of migrants or to dialects. The 2008 European Union (EU)[1] Strategy for multilingualism (i) seeks to develop multilingualism further, (ii) encourages EU citizens to learn and speak more languages, and (iii) ensures that citizens have access to EU legislation, procedures, and information in their own languages. The EU pursues the long-term objective that every citizen should have practical skills in at least two languages beyond his/her mother tongue. In 2012 the EU commissioned a survey with the objective of understanding citizens' language use, experiences, perceptions, and attitudes toward multilingualism (Special Eurobarometer 2012: 386). Proportional to the EU population, the most widely spoken native languages are German (16 percent), Italian (13 percent), English (13 percent), and French (12 percent), and the most widely spoken foreign languages are English (38 percent), French (12 percent), German (11 percent), Spanish (7 percent), and Russian (5 percent). Most Europeans speak the official language of their country of residence as their native language, but 54 percent of all Europeans can hold a conversation in at least one additional language; a quarter can speak at least two more languages. Most Europeans (67 percent) consider English as the most useful language, while agreeing to 81 percent that all languages spoken within the EU should be treated equally. Moreover, although 69 percent think that Europeans should be able to speak a common language, they do not believe that any one language should have priority over others.

---

[1] Only twenty-seven European states are members of the EU. Most of the information provided in the following reflects primarily the EU because comparable information for the other states is less readily available.

Despite this generally positive attitude toward multilingualism, as reflected by EU policies, the Eurobarometer did not explicitly address questions about the use and attitudes toward minority, indigenous, and immigrant languages. Within the German context, for example, Gärtig et al. (2010) carried out a survey on language prestige, reporting attitudes toward minority languages. It turned out that Germans welcome the protection of autochthonous minorities, but among the minority languages in Germany (Danish, Sorbian, Frisian, Low German, and Romani) only Danish receives large support, having a higher prestige and being the national language of the neighboring country Denmark. Furthermore, Germans embrace multilingualism, thinking that English, French, and Spanish should be taught as subjects in schools. They like French-, Italian-, English-, or Spanish-sounding foreign accents. However, they do not necessarily like Russian, Turkish, or Polish-sounding accents, and a third of the respondents mentioned comprehension difficulties in conversations with migrants (244–247) and were against giving them the opportunity to use their native languages exclusively in some contexts (236). Although this observation is based on a single country, it suggests that when (some) Europeans think and speak about protecting multilingualism, they may not primarily have immigrant minority speakers in mind.

Immigrant minority languages in Europe differ greatly from one another in terms of prestige, number of speakers, distance to the home country, and where they are spoken. Some originate in nation states elsewhere in Europe as a result of migration from South to North for economical and/or political reasons. This primarily concerns migration from Greece, Italy, Portugal, and Spain. However, most immigrant minority language speakers come from outside of Europe. The largest number of foreign citizens in Europe live in France, Germany, Spain, and the United Kingdom, and the largest variety of nationalities can be found in Germany and the United Kingdom, with ~70 nationalities according to the Ethnologue (Eberhard et al. 2019). Citizenship and language background varies depending on the country. For example, migrants of Turkish origin predominate in Germany and in the Netherlands, migrants from the former colonies in Portugal and Spain, from Albania in Greece, from the Maghreb in France, from the former Soviet Union in Estonia, Latvia, and Lithuania, from the former Yugoslavia in Sweden, Indian languages in the United Kingdom, and Congolese in Belgium.

The remainder of this chapter summarizes research on HSs in Europe. The major sections are devoted to research on early childhood (2.3), primary school/ adolescent years (2.4), and adulthood (2.5), respectively, which have so far largely been treated as independent areas of research. The thematic organization of subsections therefore also varies. I make reference to (morpho-)syntax, phonology, and vocabulary, but given the large scope of this chapter and limited space, the list of studies is not exhaustive. The goal is to uncover common themes and outcomes in each research area as well as missing links.[2]

2.3 Early Development of Heritage Speakers

2.3.1 Separation, Mixing, Dominance

In the first half of the twentieth century, bilingualism was still thought to be subtractive for normal development. Not only was it associated with a delay in vocabulary, disadvantages in writing skills, and repeating rhythms, but even with "mental confusion" (e.g., Saer 1923: 23). Indeed, Saer's (1923) study originated in Europe, based on Welsh-English bilinguals in Wales. The idea that bilingualism conferred disadvantages for learning and general cognitive development continued to prevail for at least fifty more years, until systematic evidence for the contrary began to accumulate. During the second half of the twentieth century, more and more case studies on bilingual development were conducted, using audio-recordings of natural-istic data and observing the linguistic development in children's two lan-guages separately. These studies mostly included HSs, although none of the below mentioned studies used that label.

Volterra and Taeschner (1978) raised the important question of what phases child bilinguals pass through during their early development and which strategies they pursue. Based on data from two German-Italian girls in Italy, i.e., HSs of German, they proposed that bilingual children initially have a fused lexicon with words from their two languages (Stage I), then separate lexicons but fused grammars (Stage II), before finally separating lexicon and grammar (Stage III, ~2;6–3 years). Though much criticized, the study paved the way for subsequent research on bilingual development, confirming Volterra and Taeschner's view or advancing the opposing view that bilingual children separate their language systems from early on. Redlinger and Park (1980) investigated mixing patterns in four bilingual children around the age of 2 years, arguing in favor of a fused lexicon, which is gradually separated as mixing decreases. Their participants grew up in Germany with Spanish, French, or English as their HLs. Lanza (1997, 2001) provided data from Siri, who grew up in Norway with English as her HL. Contrary to Redlinger and Park, Lanza interpreted mixing as indicative of language dominance rather than a fused language system. In her study, data from both languages were considered and systematically divided by

---

[2] For lack of space, I have excluded findings on the societal language, although considering both HL and societal language will ultimately be essential for a more comprehensive understanding of HL acquisition (see, however, fn. 4, 6, and 7 for examples).

context. In the English context, mixing was more frequent and included both functional and lexical elements, while in the Norwegian context mixing was less frequent and restricted to lexical elements. A claim related to the idea of a fused lexicon was that language mixing is due to vocabulary gaps. According to Clark's (1987) Principle of Contrast, any difference in form marks a difference in meaning. In a bilingual setting, this would imply that cross-linguistic synonyms (i.e., translation equivalents) are avoided or used with reference to difference concepts. Quay (1995) investigated an English-Spanish child in the United Kingdom, using daily diary records and weekly video recordings in both language contexts to study the child's lexicon and, especially, the existence of translation equivalents. At 1;11, 50 percent of the child's vocabulary were English words (150 items), 35 percent were Spanish words (105 items), and 13 percent were ambiguous between English and Spanish (375). Thus, fewer words were unique to the HL Spanish compared to English, indicating that vocabulary developed more slowly in the HL. Crucially, between 0;11 and 1;10, the proportion of words with equivalents increased along with vocabulary in general. At 1;10, there were fifty-four equivalent pairs, contradicting the claim that bilingual children code-switch because they do not have the means to make a choice.

Some studies investigated the development of general proficiency (language dominance) in the two languages of simultaneous bilingual children. While the HL literature often states that the societal language becomes dominant over time – implying that the HL is initially the dominant or only language– research on simultaneous bilinguals has shown that this is not the only possible scenario. Kupisch (2007) provided longitudinal data from four bilingual children in Germany (ages 1;6–3 years), all with Italian mothers and German fathers, comparing their two languages in terms of Mean Length of Utterance (MLU), verb and noun types, absolute number of utterances, and upper bound (the longest utterance) based on 30–45 minute recordings. Two of the children were relatively balanced: one was dominant in German, whereas one child was dominant in the HL. The study shows that even if parents use the *one parent-one language* strategy at home and there is additional exposure to the societal language outside the home, there can be various trajectories for the early development of the HL.

Another research focus toward the end of the twentieth century was the question of whether bilingual children develop their two syntactic systems independently. Crucially, studies that addressed this question selected phenomena that differed between the bilinguals' two languages, and often included language data from both the societal language and the HL (even though the label "HL" was not used). For instance, Meisel (1989) investigated the acquisition of word order in two German-French children growing up in Germany, showing that the children pursued language-specific paths in German and French that resembled those of monolinguals in the respective languages. Further evidence for language separation in the area of morphology and syntax has been provided in De Houwer's (1990) case study of Kate, who grew up in Belgium with English as her HL (see also De Houwer (2008) for an overview of relevant studies).

2.3.2 Cross-linguistic Influence: Accelerated and Decelerated Development

By the turn of the last century the idea that bilingual children develop two separate language systems was generally accepted. However, this does not exclude potential interaction between the two languages that may lead to accelerated or decelerated development. But under what conditions does cross-linguistic influence (CLI) obtain? Most of the studies pursuing this question included longitudinal data and comparisons to age-matched monolingual children. Müller and Hulk (2001) studied Dutch-French, German-French, and German-Italian children in the Netherlands and Germany (aged 1;10–4), focusing on object drop in the Romance languages, i.e., the children's HL. The bilinguals omitted clitic object pronouns for longer periods of time than monolingual children matched by age and MLU. However, there was no difference in the qualitative type of omissions, and the children stopped omitting object pronouns once they had acquired constructions relevant to the left sentence periphery,[3] just like monolingual children. The study promoted the idea that bilingual and monolingual children pursue the same acquisition paths, although there may be differences in speed of acquisition.

Slight delays have also been observed in the acquisition of grammatical gender. Kupisch, Müller, and Cantone (2002) studied gender marking in three Italian and French HSs in Germany. The children produced a few more instances of target-deviant gender marking than age-matched monolinguals, especially in French, where gender assignment is less transparent than in Italian. Similarly, the acquisition of gender in Spanish as a HL may be delayed when acquired along with Dutch, which has a very opaque gender system (Hulk and van der Linden 2010). Brehmer and Rothweiler (2012) found delays in the acquisition of neuter gender in Polish HSs in Germany, but since neuter gender is also protracted in monolingual Polish, the delay may have been due to insufficient exposure to Polish rather than simultaneous exposure to German. There are also cases where heritage bilinguals acquire gender on a par with monolinguals, although a delay

---

[3] The left periphery links syntax to discourse and it is relevant to object omissions in topic drop languages, such as Dutch and German. The authors argued that the extended phase of object omissions may be due to indirect CLI from the Germanic languages.

could have been expected. For example, Hulk and van der Linden (2010) found no delay for children (aged 4 years) acquiring French in the Netherlands, and Kuchenbrandt (2005) found no delay in children (aged 1;7–2;3) acquiring Spanish in Germany. A comparison of these studies shows that delays cannot be attributed to bilingualism per se, but depend on the language combination, the transparency of gender assignment systems, and language-external factors.

Examples of deceleration were also found in phonological development. Lleó (2002) has shown that Spanish children in Germany were temporarily delayed compared to monolinguals in their production of words with unfooted syllables, i.e., prosodic structures that are comparatively marked. However, the delay was already overcome by the end of the children's second year. Delays may be caused by temporary periods of transfer, i.e., children incorporate a property from language A into language B and this property is not normally part of language B. For example, Lleó and Rakow (2005, 2006) and Lleó (2018) studied Spanish children in Germany in their production of spirants and assimilation of nasal codas – two phonological processes that exist in Spanish but not in German. When the data collection stopped (age 5), the children had not acquired the two phenomena, producing voiced stops instead of continuants as a result of transfer from German. Cross-sectional data from 7-year-old's still showed a lot of individual variation, suggesting that not all individuals might eventually have acquired coda assimilation and spirantization. Another example of transfer can be found in Kehoe et al.'s (2004) study of Voice Onset Time (VOT) in four German-Spanish bilinguals growing up in Germany. One of the children, Niels, produced long lag VOT in Spanish, arguably due to transfer from German, which has long lag VOT.

Mayr and Siddika (2018) studied the production of stop sounds in Sylheti heritage children (ages 3;7–5;0) in the United Kingdom. The children grew up in Wales, which has a large concentration of Bangladeshi HSs. Sylheti is an Indo-Aryan language spoken in Bangladesh. It has voiced breathy and non-breathy stops / $g^ɦ$ $b^ɦ$; b ḍ ̪d g / and the voiceless stops / t̪ ʈ k /. Unlike English, which distinguishes short lag VOT (voiced stops) and long lag VOT (voiceless stops), Sylheti distinguishes prevoicing (voiced) vs. short lag (voiceless). The children were accurate in their Sylheti production of /$g^ɦ$/ and /$b^ɦ$/ with breathiness, but their Sylheti stops were mostly produced with short lag and rarely with prevoicing (18 percent). The absence of prevoicing could be a developmental pattern, since prevoicing is generally acquired late. However, age-matched third-generation children did not produce prevoicing at all, suggesting that prevoicing is particularly susceptible to change over generations.

As pointed out earlier for grammatical gender, bilinguals are not always delayed in acquiring the phonological properties of the HL. For example,

Kehoe (2002) studied vowel length in Spanish heritage children in Germany, including data from both languages (ages 1;11–2;6). The phonemic inventory of Spanish includes only five vowels, while German has a larger inventory with short and long vowels. While the children's acquisition of vowel length in German was delayed, they acquired Spanish vowels akin to monolingual Spanish children.

Sometimes CLI results in acceleration, i.e., bilingual children acquire certain linguistic properties faster than monolinguals. Kaltsa et al. (2019) have shown that Greek children in Germany are relatively fast in acquiring Greek gender. Within phonology-oriented research, Lleó, Kuchenbrandt, Kehoe, and Trujillo (2003) examined the acquisition of codas in Spanish heritage children in Germany. Codas are abundant in German, while their occurrence in Spanish is restricted. The children in this study ceased to drop Spanish codas at earlier ages than age-matched monolingual children, arguably due to their experience with codas in German. Kehoe (2018) studied the acquisition of /r/ in the same children. The /r/-sound is (typically) a uvular approximant [ʁ] in German, while Spanish makes a phonemic distinction between the alveolar tap [ɾ] and the trill [r]. Although phonetic and phonological complexities challenge the acquisition of the /r/-sound, the children acquired German /r/ akin to monolinguals (except in articulatorily complex clusters), and they outperformed monolinguals in Spanish, i.e., their HL.[4]

2.3.3 Summary

Studies on early bilingual development have received scarce attention in the HL literature, possibly because bilingual children have not always been labeled as HSs. However, the early years are essential for naturalistic language learning, and findings as to which properties are affected by CLI (or not) might help understand acquisition outcomes at later ages. Research on child bilinguals has provided crucial insights: Bilingual children have separate lexicons and grammars for each language from early on; compared to monolinguals their vocabularies are typically smaller in each language but larger overall; the development of individual phenomena is determined by intra- and extra-linguistic factors jointly. For instance, CLI does not occur across the board, and language dominance matters but can be overridden by intra-linguistic factors, such as markedness or complexity. Since most longitudinal studies stop around age 5 or earlier, they leave open whether

---

[4] HL acquisition can also lead to accelerated development in the societal language, as shown for article use in German with HL Italian (see Kupisch 2007) and grammatical gender in Dutch with HL French, Spanish, or Greek (Hulk and van der Linden 2010; Egger et al. 2018) but our discussion here is restricted to the HL.

properties that are affected by CLI early on will eventually be acquired in a way similar to the (monolingual) baseline.

2.4 HSs during Primary School and Adolescence

2.4.1 Delays and Cross-linguistic Influence

Delays are perhaps most apparent in the domain of vocabulary. For example, Montanari et al. (2018) have investigated the vocabulary knowledge of 126 German-Russian children aged 6–11 in Germany. Results show that while the proportion of cognates and vocabulary items exclusive to the societal language increases in number, the number of items exclusive to the HL decreases, indicating that vocabulary development in the HL Russian slows down substantially over the course of primary school attendance. Klassert et al. (2014) studied the vocabulary of sixty German-Russian children (4–7 years old) in Germany, focusing on verbs and nouns in a picture-naming task. Especially when naming nouns, the 5 and 6 year olds showed an advantage in German over Russian. In German, the bilinguals were generally outperformed by monolinguals, but comparable to only one-year younger monolinguals despite having had less exposure. In Russian, their HL, bilinguals could name fewer nouns than monolinguals at all age groups, and this difference remained even in comparison with one-year younger monolinguals. The study points to delays in both languages, but the children catch up fast in the societal language, and they learn more within less time, even if they appear to be delayed in terms of age.

Unlike in vocabulary acquisition, delays in the acquisition of syntax (and its interfaces) are typically linked to CLI. Woods (2015) studied German-English bilinguals in the United Kingdom (ages 4;9–8;8) with regard to the dative alternation in both languages.[5] The author reports unidirectional CLI into German (the HL), where language-specific restrictions of the dative alternation were delayed. Similarly, Serratrice et al. (2009) investigated 6–10 year old Italian HSs in the United Kingdom in their use of articles in generic plural subjects. In these types of sentences Italian requires an article, while English requires bare nominals, as illustrated by (1).

(1)   It.   Le /(*Ø)   fragole   sono   rosse. (generic)
              DEFART.PL   strawberries   COP.3PL   red
              "Strawberries are red."

In an acceptability judgment task, the bilinguals accepted significantly more ungrammatical bare nouns compared to monolingual Italian children and adults, suggesting that the HSs of Italian were more affected by their

---

[5] Woods did not refer to her participants as HSs given minimal dominance and high fluency, but they fall under the common descriptions of HSs.

dominant English input. Like Serratrice et al. (2009), Kupisch and Pierantozzi (2010) studied articles in subject DPs in HSs of Italian in Germany (ages 6–10), but using a Truth Value Judgment Task to tap into the interpretation of articles. The Italian definite plural article is ambiguous between a specific and a generic reading, while the German equivalent has a specific reading (the generic reading is expressed via bare nouns, like in English). Thus, Italian *Le fragole sono rosse* (see 1b) can refer to strawberries in general but also to specific ones. By contrast, the German translation equivalent, illustrated in (2), can only have a specific interpretation.

(2)   Ge.   **Die**   Erdbeeren   sind   rot. (specific)
            DEFART.PL strawberries COP.3PL red
            "The strawberries are red."

Therefore, under the influence of German, Italian HSs might be more inclined to interpret Italian plural subject DPs as specific. The bilingual children in this study gave more generic responses in Italian than they did in a corresponding German task, suggesting that they were sensitive to the semantics of the definite article in Italian. However, they did so less often than monolingual children from Italy. The study suggests that children acquire the properties of the HL but CLI is likely to occur if there are partially overlapping structures in the two target languages.

2.4.2   Stretching the Limits

Most studies on HSs at school age show that the children acquire the specific properties of their HL. While they often differ from monolinguals due to CLI, they tend to stay within the limits of what is acceptable in the HL, as the following studies show:

Brehmer and Usanova (2015) investigated CLI in verb placement in Russian, based on the written texts of twenty German-Russian bilingual adolescents (around 15 years) in Germany. The children were attending secondary school (Gymnasium) and were either born in Germany or had moved there at the age of 6 years or earlier. They spoke Russian at home. German is a V2 language with some flexibility in word order, but the verb must stay in the second position. Russian word order is entirely determined by information structure, which means that the verb can occupy any position (V1, V2, V3, V4 etc.); verb-initial structures are frequent in narratives. CLI from German could thus lead to less flexible word order in Russian at the expense of pragmatically motivated verb placement. Contrary to such expectations, the results for main clauses showed no narrowing down of word order options. Instead, the HSs showed even more variation in their word order patterns than expected. However, they produced fewer V1-structures, possibly due to the overuse of subject pronouns in sentence-initial positions (as a result of CLI from German). This study indicates that, under the influence of the societal majority languages, HSs nevertheless exploit the variation inherent to the HL system, with some consequences for pragmatic felicitousness.

Anstatt (2008) studied aspect and tense in narratives told by Russian-German bilinguals aged 3–9 years, comparing them to monolingual children and adults. The narratives of the monolingual Russian children and adults were predominantly anchored in the Perfective past, and those of monolingual German children and adults predominantly in the present. Present tense can also be used in Russian but it is marginal here; the same is true for the perfective past in German. The heritage children used Perfective in German and Present in Russian to a greater extent than monolinguals. In other words, they were influenced by their respective other language, but they nevertheless produced structures that are acceptable (albeit marginal) in the target systems. The author interpreted her findings in terms of bilingual bootstrapping: Children aim at the successful narration of a story and they exploit their resources in both languages.

Santos and Flores (2016) studied adverb placement and VP-ellipsis, two constructions related to verb movement, in European Portuguese HSs in Germany. VP-ellipsis is a process whereby a verb phrase can be omitted if it is identical with a previously uttered VP, normally in a coordinated structure, as in (3a or b).

(3)   a.   Teresa had offered flowers to her mother and Anna had _ too.
       b.   Today the father won't bring the car to the garage but the mother will.

Twenty heritage children (9–11 years) were compared to monolingual and L2 controls. The heritage children patterned with monolinguals in terms of adverb placement and VP-ellipsis, but with L2 controls in preferring pronoun substitution over ellipsis. For instance, in a case like (3b), they would add *bring it there* at the end of the subordinate clause, which would be required in the equivalent German structure). The children's preference is arguably due to CLI from German. Importantly, pronoun substitution is a possible option in European Portuguese, albeit one that is dispreferred by monolinguals.

Several authors have observed the tendency in the Turkish spoken in Germany to overuse subject pronouns. Turkish is a pro-drop language, while German requires overt pronouns. For example, Pfaff (1991) studied narratives in four 8–9 year old children growing up in Berlin, finding that the most German-dominant child overused overt pronouns in Turkish. As Pfaff (1991: 124) notes, there are two possible not mutually exclusive interpretations for this: Transfer of the non–pro-drop setting from German, or a communicative strategy that provides greater redundancy when the communicative systems in the HL have become frail. In other words, the overuse of overt elements need not be a direct influence from

German, but it could be a strategy to express reference morphologically in cases where the children lack other linguistic means (see also Section 2.5.1).

Finally, in some cases, CLI may lead to new distinctions in the HL. One example from phonology is Queen's (2001, 2006) study of intonation patterns in Turkish heritage children (aged 10–12) in Germany. The bilinguals used the same two distinct rising contours in German and Turkish. One resembled the rising L*H% pattern that is characteristic for German, and the other resembled the rising L*HH% pattern that is characteristic for Turkish. These intonational contours are used as strategies for cuing specific narrative functions, the former marking continuation and the latter discourse coherence, which are also found in monolinguals. However, the bilinguals used them more frequently and in different pragmatic contexts as the monolinguals, indicating interaction between the languages to the extent of blending.[6]

2.4.3 Summary

Until recently, primary school children and adolescents counted as understudied populations. In the meantime, a fair number of studies have been carried out. Some of them seem to point to delays in the HL but, as the previous examples have shown, it is hard to distinguish CLI from delay. In many studies, children employed structural options that are possible in their HL, but they overused them compared to the baseline.

2.5 Adult Bilingual HSs

Research on adult HSs has generally focused on acquisition outcomes compared to monolinguals and, not surprisingly, found differences. Several studies have gone beyond highlighting differences, asking *how* heritage grammars differ. Roughly, the scenarios fall into three categories: (i) HSs are more inclined to use a construction that is shared by their two languages at the expense of a structure that is unique to one language (see also Section 2.4.1, example 2). In this scenario, properties of the societal majority language and CLI play a crucial role. (ii) HSs develop a new property, which is marginally or not at all related to the societal language, and this property is also in the process of evolving in related varieties but more slowly due to norming or standardization. Here, HSs may anticipate or mirror language change. (iii) Heritage grammars are like monolingual grammars or even more conservative.

---

[6] At this age too, HL exposure can positively affect the development of the societal language. Tamburelli et al. (2015) showed that Polish–English bilingual children in the United Kingdom (ages 7;01–8;11) outperformed monolinguals in their production of English-like nonwords beginning with complex clusters. The effect is arguably due to CLI from Polish, which allows a greater range of consonant clusters than English.

2.5.1 Contact-Induced Change and CLI

Moro (2015) investigated HSs of Ambon Malay in the Netherlands, focusing on tense and aspect markers. Ambon Malay is an Austronesian language spoken by Moluccans on the Ambon Island in Indonesia. The language lacks a grammaticalized tense system, but it optionally expresses aspect (progressive, perfective, and iterative). Dutch, the contact language, marks the past/non-past distinction as well as finiteness. Based on spoken data from video-descriptions, the authors analyze the frequency and distribution of aspect markers. Results show that the progressive marker *ada* has undergone a change in frequency. It is still used as a progressive marker but it is also overextended as a marker of present tense (and possibly finiteness), i.e., distinctions not expressed in the original language or in Ambon Malay speakers from Indonesia. Markers of perfective and iterative aspect are used less by the HSs than by a control group from Ambon.

Aalberse, Zou, and Andringa (2017) studied definiteness marking in Mandarin Chinese HSs in the Netherlands. In Dutch, definite articles express definiteness; demonstratives can be used in this function too, but they have a more specialized meaning. Mandarin Chinese has no articles. Instead, word order and verb type determine whether a noun is interpreted as definite, indefinite, or generic. Demonstratives, often together with classifiers, can be used to encode definiteness, but definiteness marking is not their primary function, like in Dutch. Generally speaking then, Dutch and Mandarin Chinese both encode definiteness, but they differ in the way it is realized. Since both languages can mark definiteness via demonstratives, the authors expected increased use of these elements in heritage Mandarin Chinese as a sign of functional extension. Based on video retelling data, the authors compared first-generation Mandarin Chinese speakers (born in China or Malaysia), second-generation HSs (born in the Netherlands or moved there before age 7), and a control group from China. As expected, with already mentioned (definite) referents, the control group from China used demonstratives less frequently (14 percent) than first-generation (24 percent) and second-generation speakers (36 percent) in the Netherlands. Similarly, Doğruöz and Backus (2009) observed that Turkish HSs in the Netherlands tended to use subject pronouns in contexts where monolingual Turkish speakers would drop them (see also Section 2.4.2). Importantly, the baseline language allows reference marking by means of subject pronouns, but their use is restricted to particular pragmatic contexts, while the use of subject pronouns in Dutch is unrestricted. Thus, the contact language might play a role in promoting the observed changes in the heritage grammars.

Finally, an area in which CLI from the societal language is hard to disregard is the global pronunciation of HSs. Kupisch et al. (2014b) have investigated the perceived accents of four groups of HSs (Italian HSs in

Germany, French HSs in Germany, and German HSs in Italy and France). Indeed, most speakers in these studies were deemed foreign when speaking their HL and the perceived accent source was the societal language. This was also confirmed in studies with Turkish HSs (Kupisch et al. 2020) and Italian HSs (Lloyd-Smith et al. 2020).[7]

2.5.2 Emergent and New Distinctions Already Present in the Baseline

Differences between HSs and monolinguals may also be mirrored by incipient changes in the target grammar or varieties thereof, compromising the idea that all divergence between heritage grammars and the baseline varieties they are compared to is due to CLI alone.

Rinke, Flores, and Barbosa (2017) found that HSs of Portuguese in Germany omitted clitic object pronouns more than first-generation speakers and controls from Portugal. However, omission of clitic object pronouns has also been observed in Brazilian Portuguese, where it has spread diachronically along a referential hierarchy with omissions being more likely in less referential (e.g., inanimate) contexts than in more referential (e.g., animate) contexts. Closer analysis of Rinke et al.'s data revealed that, indeed, the HSs dropped pronouns especially when the denoted referent was inanimate, but sometimes also when the denoted referent was animate. The authors proposed that the HSs extended contexts of clitic object omissions to more referential contexts. The parallelism in heritage Portuguese and Brazilian Portuguese indicates that HLs evolve in the same way as natural languages and sometimes independently of the properties of the contact language.[8] Similarly, in Rinke and Flores' (2017) study of clitic object pronouns in European Portuguese HSs in Germany, the HSs performed differently from monolinguals, but the type of omissions were reminiscent of properties of spoken varieties of Portuguese. Thus, the context of HL acquisition might promote linguistic changes that are already inherent to the baseline variety.

Doğruöz und Backus (2009) and Backus et al. (2011) have reported innovation in indefinite article use in Turkish HSs in the Netherlands. While in the Turkish spoken in Turkey, the numeral *bir* "one" has taken

---

[7] For accents, there can also be CLI into the societal language. Kupisch et al. (2020) found that German-Turkish speakers are sometimes perceived as foreign-sounding when speaking German. Mayr and Siddika (2018) found that Sylheti HSs in the United Kingdom produced voiced stops in English with a voicing lead (40 percent), arguably due to CLI from Sylheti, which has voicing lead. Note, however, that both studies have offered explanations alternative to CLI.

[8] German, the societal language in this study, allows topic drop but not object drop.

over some article functions, over some article functions, it does not have the same expansion as articles in fully grammaticalized article systems, where indefinite articles denote specific or nonspecific referents (compare 4a vs. 4b).

(4)   a. Mary has **a dog** (and she loves it)   (specific)
       b. Mary wants **a dog** (but she hasn't decided which one). (nonspecific)

Similarly, Backus et al. (2011) report that HSs in the Netherlands used bir in many contexts where speakers from Turkey would not use it, probably (also) due to contact with Dutch – a language in which indefinite articles can denote both specific and nonspecific referents.

   In the lexical domain too, there are examples of innovation. Turkish heritage children in Germany (Pfaff 2000) and Turkish HSs in the Netherlands (Doğruöz and Backus 2009) show a tendency to increasingly use lexical collocations with the light verb *yapmek* "do" in a range of functions that are different from those used in Turkish in Turkey. For instance, in the noun–verb collocations [N-yap] as in *Fransızca yap-in* "do French," *yap* is used instead of a more specific lexical verb such as *oku-* "read", as in *Fransızca oku-* "read/study French," the variant used in Turkish as spoken in Turkey. In Turkish in Turkey, two types of similar noun–verb collocations co-occur, [N-yap] and [N-et] (both roughly translating into "do"), but the latter is the unmarked one, and the distribution of the two depends on sociolinguistic factors, such as generation and social pressure from peers. Treffers-Daller et al. (2016) investigated the use of *-yap* and *-et* among HSs of Turkish in Germany, comparing them to those found among Turkish monolinguals. The HSs used significantly fewer [N-et] and more [N-yap] than the monolingual controls.

2.5.3 Maintenance and Overcorrection

In a series of experiments with a small group of HSs of French in Germany, Kupisch et al. (2014a) have shown that when there is abundant contact with the HL, notably when the HL constitutes the language of instruction at school, the HL may develop exactly like the baseline variety. One phenomenon they considered was the position of adjectives, which can be pre- or postnominal in French, depending on the intended meaning and phonological properties of the adjective. The HSs placed adjectives correctly before or after the noun, although adjectives in German are prenominal and one could have expected overuse of this position due to CLI. Another study focused on articles in generic subject nominals, which require an article in French but not in German (compare 5a vs. 5b).

(5) Fr. **Les**   tournesols   sont   jaunes. (generic)
          DEFART.PL   sunflowers   COP.3PL   yellow
     Ge. Sonnenblumen   sind   gelb.
          sunflowers   COP.3PL   yellow
          "Sunflowers are yellow."

Again, the HSs were successful in providing articles in obligatory contexts (see also Barton 2016). The third property tested was gender marking. Here, the HSs were successful in marking the agreement relation between determiner and adjective, although they occasionally failed to assign the correct gender, especially when there were no cues or contradicting cues for gender assignment. The same speakers were investigated in their use of functional and lexical prepositions in spontaneous speech. Prepositions are particularly challenging due to their hybrid nature between lexical and functional elements, and errors may be expected in particular with nonfunctional elements because of their lower token frequencies. The corpus contained more than 2,000 instances of prepositions, but target deviant uses were below 2 percent.

Although HSs' global pronunciation is subject to CLI from the societal language (see Section 2.5.1), not all individual phonological properties, segmental or supra-segmental, are affected. Lein et al. (2016) investigated the production of the voiceless velar stop /k/ in HSs of French. The stop /k/ is produced with short lag VOT in French but with long lag VOT in German. Thus, bilingual exposure might lead to realizations of French /k/ within the long lag range. Although the speakers in this study were perceived to be accented, Lein et al. found no differences in the speakers' production of /k/ compared to speakers from France. Similarly, Einfeldt et al. (2019) studied the production of geminate consonants, comparing HSs of Italian with German-Italian bilinguals from Italy and monolinguals. In Italian, the distinction between short and long (geminate) consonants is phonemic, while German has only short consonants. Therefore, CLI from German could lead to smaller durational contrasts between the HSs' singletons and geminates. Contrary to expectations, and although the speakers were perceived to be accented, their short and long consonants differed more in length than those of the controls from Italy. When regional background was taken into account, it became evident that the origin of the HSs' parents played a role: Speakers whose parents came from Northern Italy showed the smallest contrast between long and short consonants and this was mirrored in the controls from Italy, thus indicating that the HSs maintained some of the dialect features of their parents' speech. As for why gemination was generally maintained, the authors argued that relevance in the target system, i.e., whether or not a contrast is phonemic, may work against CLI from the dominant language. Moreover, the study underlines that dialectal variation can sometimes explain deviance from monolinguals.

A small number of studies have revealed a tendency for HSs to regularize the system toward some default, norm, or contrast to the societal language. The aforementioned example of gemination is a case in point. An example from syntax is Kupisch's (2014) study of adjective placement in HSs of Italian in Germany. Italian adjectives can precede or follow the noun, depending on the adjective class and the intended meaning, but the post-nominal position is more frequent. The HSs in this study overaccepted postnominal nouns, although German allows only prenominal adjectives. Thus, they used the default position in Italian, although it exhibits a contrast to German. Similarly, in a study of definiteness effects, Kupisch et al. (2017) have shown that HSs of Turkish in Germany generally behaved on par with speakers from Turkey but in some cases they changed accept-able sentences into more formal variants thereof, thus being more conser-vative than the controls from Turkey.

2.5.4 Summary

The given examples show that research on HSs has gone beyond pointing out differences between monolinguals and HSs, which undoubtedly exist (though not across the board), just as they exist among monolingual speakers from different regions. The various scenarios suggest that HSs may anticipate language change, especially if the contact language pro-motes such changes, but also that HSs may resist language change and overstress properties unique to the HL, thus showing increased language awareness or even more conservative behavior compared to monolinguals. As observed in Sections 2.4.2, 2.5.2, and 2.5.3, adult HSs often stay within the limits of what is possible in the baseline or related varieties.

2.6   Conclusions

This chapter has provided examples of studies of HSs in Europe, pointing out that not all relevant work was originally labelled in terms of HL research. Studies range across preschool and primary school children, adolescents as well as adults. The questions of interest in each of these areas have differed, but CLI is a common denominator. I conclude with three observations. First, there are hardly any comparisons across generations, neither longitudinal nor cross-sectional, although similar properties have been identified as vul-nerable. Interestingly, studies on child bilinguals have often pointed to bidirectional CLI, while instances of CLI into the societal language become less frequent with age. Phonology seems to be the area where CLI into the majority language is most likely (see footnote 7). Future research could focus on comparisons across ages, not only to discuss the plausibility of divergent outcomes or attrition but also to identify the ages when HLs need most support to be maintained. Second, in terms of languages, the Romance and Slavic families as well as Turkish are well represented. Research on Germanic languages is scarce, because speakers of Germanic languages typically constitute small minorities in Europe. Moreover, minorities speaking non–Indo-European languages, even if large, as in the case of Arabic, are underrepresented. Finally, research drawing analogies with other situations of language contact and change, including, e.g., dialectology, are highly desirable if we want to take the important step beyond observing differences between mono- and bilinguals and toward explaining why certain differences obtain.

References

Aalberse, S., Y. Zou, and S. Andringa. 2017. Extended Use of Demonstrative Pronouns in Two Generations of Mandarin Chinese Speakers in the Netherlands: Evidence of Convergence? In E. Blom, L. Cornips, and J. Schaeffer (eds.), *Crosslinguistic Influence in Bilingualism: In Honor of Aafke Hulk*. Amsterdam: John Benjamins, 25–48.

Anstatt, T. 2008. Aspects and Tense in Storytelling by Russian, German and Bilingual Children. *Russian Linguistics* 32, 1–26.

Backus, A., A. Doğruöz, and B. Heine. 2011. Salient Stages in Contact-Induced Grammatical Change: Evidence from Synchronic vs. Diachronic Contact Situations. *Language Sciences* 33(5), 738–752.

Barton, D. 2016. Generische Nominalphrasen bei deutsch-französischer Zweisprachigkeit: Zur Verwendung des Definitartikels bei erwachsenen Herkunftssprechern. PhD Dissertation, University of Hamburg.

Benmamoun, E., S. Montrul, and M. Polinsky. 2013. Heritage Languages and Their Speakers: Opportunities and Challenges for Linguistics. *Theoretical Linguistics* 39(3–4), 129–181.

Brehmer, B., and M. Rothweiler. 2012. The Acquisition of Gender Agreement Marking in Polish: A Study of Bilinual Polish-German-Speaking Children. In K. Braunmueller and C. Gabriel (eds.), *Multilingual Individuals and Multilingual Societies*. Amsterdam: John Benjamins, 81–100.

Brehmer, B., and I. Usanova. 2015. Let's Fix It? Cross-Linguistic Influence in Word Order Patterns of Russian Heritage Speakers in Germany. In H. Peukert (ed.), *Transfer Effects in Multilingual Language Development*. Amsterdam: Benjamins, 161–190.

Clark, E. V. 1987. The Principle of Contrast: A Constraint on Language Acquisition. *Mechanisms of Language Acquisition* 1, 33.

Council of Europe. 1992. The European Charter for Regional or Minority Languages. Retrieved from www.coe.int/en/web/european-charter-regional-or-minority-languages/text-of-the-charter.

De Houwer, A. 1990. *The Acquisition of Two Languages from Birth*. Cambridge: Cambridge University Press.

De Houwer, A. 2008. How Different Are Monolingual and Bilingual Acquisition? *Ilha do Desterro* 43, 127–148.

Doğruöz, A. S., and A. Backus. 2009. Innovative Constructions in Dutch Turkish: An Assessment of Ongoing Contact-Induced Change. *Bilingualism: Language and Cognition* 12(1), 41–63.

Eberhard, D. M., G. F. Simons, and C. D. Fennig. 2019. *Ethnologue: Languages of the World*.

Egger, E., A. Hulk, and I. Tsimpli. 2018. Crosslinguistic Influence in the Discovery of Gender: The Case of Greek-Dutch Bilingual Children. *Bilingualism: Language and Cognition* 21(4), 694–709.

Einfeldt, M., J. van de Weijer, and T. Kupisch. 2019. The Production of Geminates in Italian-Dominant Bilinguals and Heritage Speakers of Italian. *Language, Interaction, and Acquisition* 10(2), 177–203.

Europäische Komission 2012. Die europäischen Bürger und ihre Sprachen. Report. Special Eurobarometer 386. Retrieved from https://ec.europa.eu/commfrontoffice/publicopinion/archives/ebs/ebs_386_de.pdf

Extra, G. 2001. The Immigrant Minority Languages of Europe. In B. Kortmann and J. van der Auwera (eds.), *The Languages and Linguistics of Europe: A Comprehensive Guide*. Berlin/Boston: De Gruyter Mouton, 467–481.

Fishman, J. A. 2001. 300-Plus Years of Heritage Language Education in the United States. In J. K. Payton, D. A. Ranard, and S. McGinnis (eds.), *Heritage Languages in America. Preserving a National Resource. Language in Education: Theory and Practice*. McHenry, IL: Delta Systems Inc., 81–97.

Flores, C., T. Kupisch, and E. Rinke. 2017. Linguistic Foundations of Heritage Language Development from the Perspective of Romance Languages in Germany. In P. Trifonas and T. Aravossitas (eds.), *Handbook of Research and Practice in Heritage Language Education*. Champaign, IL: Springer, 1–18. https://doi.org/10.1007/978-3-319-38893-9_12-1

Fürstenau, S., I. Gogolin, and K. Yagmur. 2003. *Mehrsprachigkeit in Hamburg: Ergebnisse einer Sprachenerhebung an den Grundschulen in Hamburg*. Münster/New York: Waxmann.

Gärtig, A. K., A. Plewnia, and A. Rothe. 2010. *Wie Menschen in Deutschland über Sprache denken: Ergebnisse einer bundesweiten Repräsentativerhebung zu aktuellen Spracheinstellungen*. Arbeitspapiere und Materialien zur deutschen Sprache 40. Mannheim: Institut für Deutsche Sprache.

Gogolin, I. 2002. *Linguistic Diversity and New Minorities in Europe. Guide for the Development of Language Education Policies in Europe: From Linguistic Diversity to Plurilingual Education*. Reference Study, Strasbourg: Council of Europe.

Hulk, A. and E. Van der Linden. 2010. How Vulnerable Is Gender? In P. Guijarro-Fuentes and L. Domínguez (eds.), *New Directions in Language*

Acquisition: Romance Languages in the Generative Perspective. Newcastle-upon-Tyne: Cambridge Scholars, 107–132.

Kaltsa, M., I. M. Tsimpli, and F. Argyri. 2019. The Development of Gender Assignment and Agreement in English-Greek and German-Greek Bilingual Children. *Linguistic Approaches to Bilingualism* 9(2), 253–288.

Kehoe, M. 2002. Developing Vowel Systems as a Window to Bilingual Phonology. *International Journal of Bilingualism* 6, 315–334.

Kehoe, M. 2018. The Development of Rhotics: A Comparison of Monolingual and Bilingual Children. *Bilingualism: Language and Cognition* 21(4), 710–731.

Kehoe, M. M., C. Lleó, and M. Rakow. 2004. Voice Onset Time in Bilingual German-Spanish Children. *Bilingualism: Language and Cognition* 7(1), 71–88.

Klassert, A., N. Gagarina, and C. Kauschke. 2014. Object and Action Naming in Russian-and German-Speaking Monolingual and Bilingual Children. *Bilingualism: Language and Cognition* 17(1), 73–88.

Kuchenbrandt, I. 2005. Gender Acquisition in Bilingual Spanish. In J. Cohen, K. T. McAlister, K. Rolstad, and J. MacSwan (eds.), *Proceedings of the 4th International Symposium on Bilingualism (ISB4)*. Somerville: Cascadilla Press, 1252–1263.

Kupisch, T. 2007. Determiners in Bilingual German-Italian Children: What They Tell Us about the Relation between Language Influence and Language Dominance. *Bilingualism: Language and Cognition* 10(1), 57–78.

Kupisch, T. 2014. Adjective Placement in Simultaneous Bilinguals (German-Italian) and the Concept of Cross-Linguistic Overcorrection. *Bilingualism: Language and Cognition* 17(1), 222–233.

Kupisch, T. and C. Pierantozzi. 2010. Interpreting Definite Plural Subjects: A Comparison of German and Italian Monolingual and Bilingual Children. In K. Franich, M. Iserman, and L. Keil (eds.), *Proceedings of the 34th Annual Boston University Conference on Language Development*. Somerville, MA: Cascadilla Press, 245–254.

Kupisch, T., and J. Rothman. 2016. Terminology Matters! Why Difference Is Not Incompleteness and How Early Child Bilinguals Are Heritage Speakers. *International Journal of Bilingualism* 22(5), 564–582. https://doi.org/10.1177/1367006916654355

Kupisch, T., A. Lloyd-Smith, and I. Stangen. 2020. Perceived Global Accent in Turkish Heritage Speakers in Germany: The Impact of Exposure and Use for Early Bilinguals. In F. Bayram and D. Tat (eds.), *Studies in Turkish as a Heritage Language*. Amsterdam: John Benjamins, 207–228.

Kupisch, T., N. Müller, and K. F. Cantone. 2002. Gender in Monolingual and Bilingual First Language Acquisition: Comparing Italian and French. *Lingue e Linguaggio* 1, 107–150.

Kupisch, T., A. Belikova, Ö. Özçelik, I. Stangen, and L. White. 2017. Restrictions on Definiteness in the Grammars of German-Turkish Heritage Speakers. *Linguistic Approaches to Bilingualism* 7(1), 1–32.

Kupisch, T., D. Barton, T. Lein, J. Schröder, I. Stangen, and A. Stöhr. 2014a. Acquisition Outcomes across Domain in Adult Heritage Speakers of French. *Journal of French Language Studies* 24(3), 347–376.

Kupisch, T., D. Barton, K. Hailer, T. Lein, I. Stangen, and J. Van de Weijer. 2014b. Foreign Accent in Adult Simultaneous Bilinguals? *Heritage Language Journal* 11(2), 123–150.

Kymlicka, W. 1995. *Multicultural Citizenship: A Liberal Theory of Minority Rights.* Oxford: Clarendon Press.

Lanza, E. 1997. Language Contact in Bilingual Two-Year-Olds and Code-Switching: Language Encounters of a Different Kind? *International Journal of Bilingualism* 1(2), 135–162.

Lanza, E. 2001. Language Mixing and Language Dominance in Bilingual First Language Acquisition. In E. V. Clark (ed.), *The Proceedings of the Twenty-Fourth Annual Child Language Research Forum.* Stanford, CA: Center for the Study of Language (CSLI), 197–280.

Lein, T., T. Kupisch, and J. Van de Weijer. 2016. Voice Onset Time and Global Foreign Accent in German-French Simultaneous Bilinguals during Adulthood. *International Journal of Bilingualism* 20(6), 132–149.

Lleó, C. 2002. The Role of Markedness in the Acquisition of Complex Prosodic Structures by German-Spanish Bilinguals. *International Journal of Bilingualism* 6(3), 291–313.

Lleó, C. 2018. Aspects of the Phonology of Spanish as a Heritage Language. *Bilingualism: Language and Cognition* 21(4), 732–747.

Lleó, C., and M. Rakow. 2005. Markedness Effects in Voiced Stop Spirantization in Bilingual German-Spanish Children. In J. Cohen, K. T. McAlister, K. Rolstad, and J. MacSwan (eds.), *Proceedings of the 4th International Symposium on Bilingualism (ISB4).* Somerville, MA: Cascadilla Press, 1353–1371.

Lleó, C., and M. Rakow. 2006. Nasalassimilation und Prosodische Hierarchie im monolingualen und bilingualen Erwerb des Spanischen und des Deutschen. In C. El Mogharbel, and K. Himstedt (eds.), *Phonetik und Nordistik. Festschrift für Magnús Pétursson zum 65. Geburtstag.* Frankfurt am Main: Hector, 95–117.

Lleó, C., I. Kuchenbrandt, M. Kehoe, and C. Trujillo. 2003. Syllable Final Consonants in Spanish and German Monolingual and Bilingual Acquisition. In N. Müller (ed.), *(Non)Vulnerable Domains in Bilingualism.* Amsterdam: John Benjamins, 191–220.

Lloyd-Smith, A., M. Einfeldt, and T. Kupisch. 2020. Italian-German Bilinguals: The Effects of Heritage Language Use on Accent in Early-Acquired Languages. *International Journal of Bilingualism* 24(2), 289–304. https://doi.org/10.1177/1367006919826867

Mayr, R., and A. Siddika. 2018. Inter-Generational Transmission in a Minority Language Setting: Stop Consonant Production by Bangladeshi

Heritage Children and Adults. *International Journal of Bilingualism* 22(3), 255–284.

Meisel, J. 1989. Early Differentiation of Languages in Bilingual Children. In K. Hyltenstam and L. Obler (eds.), *Bilingualism across the Lifespan: Aspects of Acquisition, Maturity and Loss*. Cambridge: Cambridge University Press, 13–40.

Montanari, E. G., R. Abel, B. Graßer, and L. Tschudinovski. 2018. Do Bilinguals Create Two Different Sets of Vocabulary for Two Domains? *Linguistic Approaches to Bilingualism* 8(4), 502–522.

Montrul, S. A. 2008. *Incomplete Acquisition in Bilingualism: Re-examining the Age Factor*. Amsterdam: John Benjamins.

Montrul, S. A. 2016. *The Acquisition of Heritage Languages*. Cambridge: Cambridge University Press.

Moro, F. 2015. Aspectual Distinctions in Dutch-Ambon Malay Bilingual Heritage Speakers, *International Journal of Bilingualism* 31(1), 78–92.

Müller, N., and A. Hulk. 2001. Crosslinguistic Influence in Bilingual Language Acquisition: Italian and French as Recipient Languages. *Bilingualism: Language and Cognition* 4, 1–21.

Pfaff, C. W. 1991. Turkish in Contact with German: Language Maintenance and Loss among Immigrant Children in Berlin (West). *Journal of the Sociology of Language* 90, 98–129.

Pfaff, C. W. 2000. Development and Use of *et-* and *yap-* by Turkish/German Bilingual Children. In A. Göksel and C. Kerslake (eds.), *Studies on Turkish and Turkic languages*. Wiesbaden: Otto Harrassowitz, 365–373.

Polinsky, M. 2018. *Heritage Languages and Their Speakers*. Cambridge: Cambridge University Press.

Polinsky, M., and G. Scontras. 2020. Understanding Heritage Languages. *Bilingualism: Language and Cognition* 23(1), 4–20. https://doi.org/10.1017/S1366728919000245. .

Putnam, M., T. Kupisch, and D. P. Cabo. 2018. Different Situations, Similar Outcomes: Heritage Grammars across the Lifespan. In S. Aalberse, A. Backus, and P. Muysken (eds.), *Studies in Bilingualism 54*. Amsterdam: John Benjamins, 251–279.

Quay, S. 1995. The Bilingual Lexicon: Implications for Studies of Language Choice. *Journal of Child Language* 22(2), 369–387.

Queen, R. 2001. Bilingual Intonation Patterns. Evidence of Language Change from Turkish-German Bilingual Children. *Language in Society* 30 (1), 55–80.

Queen, R. 2006. Phrase-Final Intonation in Narratives Told by Turkish-German Bilinguals. *International Journal of Bilingualism* 10(2), 153–178.

Redlinger, W. E., and T. Z. Park. 1980. Language Mixing in Young Bilinguals. *Journal of Child Language* 7(2), 337–352.

Rinke, E., and C. Flores. 2014. Morphosyntactic Knowledge of Clitics by Portuguese Heritage Bilinguals. *Bilingualism: Language and Cognition* 17(4), 681–699.

Rinke, E., C. Flores, and P. Barbosa. 2017. Null Objects in the Spontaneous Speech of Monolingual and Bilingual Speakers of European Portuguese. *Probus* 30(1), 93–119.

Rothman, J. 2009. Understanding the Nature and Outcomes of Early Bilingualism: Romance Languages as Heritage Languages. *International Journal of Bilingualism* 13(2), 155–163.

Saer, D. J. 1923. The Effect of Bilingualism on Intelligence. *British Journal of Psychology: General Section* 14, 25–38.

Santos, A. L., and C. Flores. 2016. Comparing Heritage Speakers and Late L2-Learners of European Portuguese: Verb Movement, VP Ellipsis and Adverb Placement. *Linguistic Approaches to Bilingualism* 6(3), 308–340.

Serratrice, L., A. Sorace, F. Filiaci, and M. Baldo. 2009. Bilingual Children's Sensitivity to Specificity and Genericity: Evidence from Metalinguistic Awareness. *Bilingualism: Language and Cognition* 12(2), 239–257.

Tamburelli, M., E. Sanoudaki, G. Jones, and M. Sowinska. 2015. Acceleration in the Bilingual Acquisition of Phonological Structure: Evidence from Polish–English Bilingual Children. *Bilingualism: Language and Cognition* 18(4), 713–725.

Treffers-Daller, J., M. Daller, R. Furman, and J. Rothman. 2016. Ultimate Attainment in the Use of Collocations among Heritage Speakers of Turkish in Germany and Turkish–German Returnees. *Bilingualism: Language and Cognition* 19(3), 504–519.

Volterra, V. and T. Taeschner. 1978. The Acquisition and Development of Language by Bilingual Children. *Journal of Child Language* 5(2), 311–326.

Woods, R. 2015. The Acquisition of Dative Alternation by German-English Bilingual and English Monolingual Children. *Linguistic Approaches to Bilingualism* 5(2), 252–284.

3

Heritage Languages in Southeastern Europe

Natalia Pavlou and Kleanthes K. Grohmann

3.1 Introduction

The study of heritage speakers lies at the forefront of language development in contexts of contact across linguistic borders, as throughout southeastern Europe. Geographically, this area consists of the wider Balkan peninsula, including the Hellenic Republic of Greece with its many islands, and extends to neighboring locations, in particular Turkey and, the focus of the present chapter, Cyprus. The interaction between speakers led toward extensive use of the dominant language in many situations as evident from the borrowing of many linguistic features and contact-induced language change. The Balkan area has been considered a *Sprachbund* or "linguistic area" where the interactions between speakers have led to the diffusion of a number of shared linguistic characteristics through various processes of contact-induced changes, some of which have resulted in favor of the use of the dominant language (see Friedman and Joseph 2014 and pertinent references cited).

While use of a dominant language is part of any definition of "heritage language," other instances offer a more complete picture of the dominant minority language pair, such as large-scale speaker communities of Russian, Bulgarian, and Romanian in Cyprus. However, the dominance of one language over another also characterizes minority languages, as can be observed for the Cypriot Maronite Arabic community, which demonstrates the moribund status of a heritage language (Sanna) as an immediate result of using the dominant language (Cypriot Greek). With each of these cases contributing to the profile of "heritage" languages, this chapter will discuss heritage languages in southeastern Europe, with particular emphasis on Cyprus, and explore some of the social, historical, and linguistic issues.

The appearance of all these different contexts that may qualify as heritage languages raises a basic question: What exactly are the factors that define the term "heritage" – and are these factors common across all different linguistic situations and complexities? Factors such as *linguistic hegemony* and *co-overt prestige* can possibly explain the emergence of a dominant language and the status of the different languages examined here as heritage or not. Moreover, the extent to which these particular factors are also applicable in other contexts can be identified as well. What then sets heritage languages apart from these contexts? The identification and labeling of these varieties as heritage languages relies on the more careful examination of the grammar of each one of these, identifying phenomena showing *transfer* or *divergent attainment* (Polinsky 2018). In the first, grammar exhibits an interplay between the learner's first (heritage) language and second (dominant) language. Concerning divergent attainment, new emerging phenomena in grammar that constitute innovations not found elsewhere appear in the heritage language.

In this chapter, we present different linguistic contexts in southeastern Europe, with an emphasis on language varieties spoken in Cyprus. A particularly interesting aspect about this island is that it involves complex sociolinguistic conditions, such as target-like L1 "low" variety interrupted in its acquisition path by the "high" variety taught in the school environment, while at the same time providing the opportunity to examine the interaction of minority languages spoken with their corresponding dominant language(s). In Section 3.2, a historical overview relates language contact to contexts where dominant languages are created and established. Section 3.3 discusses the socio-psychological factors that may describe such situations, while Section 3.4 examines linguistic features that may appear in a heritage speaker's grammar. Most importantly, the discussion there aims to supply the essential background of candidate heritage language contexts in southeastern Europe and to examine the conditions that define them as such. Section 3.5 briefly concludes.

3.2   Historical Overview and Demographics

The social and historical conditions that led to the development of the present status applied to different linguistic communities are a crucial aspect for an understanding of what triggers the creation and existence of varieties in different contexts characterized by the use of a dominant and a home language, similarly to a definition of heritage language. In this section, we provide an overview of different linguistic contexts in the Balkans and the eastern Mediterranean that share the characteristic of the existence of a dominant language as a result of different historical, economic, and social circumstances.

The Balkans are a linguistic area identified through vast multilingual contact between languages that changed to share common structural and lexical characteristics even if they are genealogically unrelated or only distantly related (Friedman and Joseph 2014). Languages that form the Balkan *Sprachbund* ("Balkan languages") are often listed as "Albanian, Modern Greek, Balkan Romance (Romanian, Aromanian, and Meglenoromanian), and Balkan Slavic (Bulgarian, Macedonian, and the southernmost dialects of the former Serbo-Croatian)" (Friedmann 2017: 1) and are associated with several different Indo-European branches (Albanian, Hellenic, Romance, and Slavic). But they also include Slovene in the north and Turkish in the east, at least two major dialects of Albanian, Geg (North) and Tosk (South), plus a host of other varieties and dialects as well as minority language, such as Romani (Indo-Aryan).

In the times of the Ottoman Empire, division of the region was not based on geographical or ethnic units, but rather on the division of the population into religious groups. The founding of nation states started happening during the nineteenth century, decreasing the immediate need for linguistic convergence in the whole Balkan area but still allowing the existence of ethnic groups within the different nations. Before the formation of nation states, ethnic groups were associated with languages, religions, and socio-economic status, yet less with territories, with Slavs being mostly farmers and many Albanians as well as Aromanians transhumant shepherds. Based on this, economic exchange relations forced cross-linguistic communication (Lindstedt 2000). During this time, cross-linguistic contacts were also asymmetrical: Since the thirteenth century, Greek had been regarded as the most prestigious with Romani at the opposite end of the scale. Speakers of Macedonian, Bulgarian, Albanian, and Aromanian learned Greek and used these languages, creating a multilingual profile. This would then trigger a context where Greek was one of the languages that would gain the status of prestigious or socially dominant language in order to satisfy needs for communication and contact, possibly forcing some of the speakers' first languages, such as the ones mentioned previously, into heritage language status.

Greek did not only dominate the linguistic context in the Balkan region but also moved east to different locations, including the island of Cyprus. With regard to Cyprus, the official languages are Greek and Turkish, which stand for the official languages of Greece and Turkey, respectively. The majority of the population is made up of native speakers of Cypriot Greek (CG), the local variety of which has been further divided into town speech and village Cypriot or village speech (Newton 1972). Town speech, also known as urban Cypriot or local Cypriot *koiné* (Karyolemou and Pavlou

2001), is a variety mostly based on the speech of educated speakers. Village speech, on the other hand, is a term used to describe a host of geographic-ally based linguistic varieties (Newton 1972). Village and town Cypriot form a continuum with village Cypriot as the basilect and town Cypriot as the acrolect (Karyolemou and Pavlou 2001). Standard Modern Greek (SMG) is perceived as the prestigious language that dominates any contexts charac-terized by formal register. An intermediate variety between CG and SMG, Cypriot Standard Greek (Arvaniti 2010) has been argued to be the result of divergence and lack of knowledge of the differences between these two varieties by Greek Cypriot speakers. In some formal registers, code-mixing and code-switching show aspects of leveling and koinezation and a shift from a regional dialect continuum to a register continuum (Tsiplakou et al. 2006). In these cases, the regional dialect leveling leads to a reduction of the differences between dialects and a gradual homogenization of the vernacular speech of a region appears (Kerswill 2013).

It follows that such a context, following a simple definition of a heritage language, also allows the use of a dominant language and a variety that is the first language of the speakers – but in a completely different setting than the one typically described.

Not every context in which different languages appear to have some function in that particular society can be subsumed under a "heritage" status. English has a distinctive status among Greek Cypriots following its extended prestige and use in court until 1989 (Karoulla-Vrikki 2001) and the British Forces Cyprus at Sovereign Base Areas in different parts of the island following the establishment of the Republic of Cyprus in 1960. English is taught very early on in the school curriculum – exposure typic-ally starts at pre-school age and continues throughout elementary and high-school education as well as private classes preparing pupils for general certificates in the language. What sets this situation apart from other heritage contexts is perhaps the learning of English as a second language, which is not the socially dominant language but rather a language used for professional purposes (possibly a situation comparable to the purpose of learning Spanish in the United States for professional development or "US Spanish") and which furthermore shows extensive use of borrowed words (Terkourafi 2011); it is possibly better classified as its own (emerging) variety (viz. "Cyprus English"; Buschfeld 2013). It only has an expected heritage language status for British people living in Cyprus, estimated at 24,000 people according to the 2011 census (plus many more if, e.g., UK-born Cypriots are also included). In these cases, English would be the first language of these speakers, who have acquired either CG or SMG (or even Turkish) as the dominant languages while residing in Cyprus.

With this set of languages as the most recognizable ones when it comes to languages of Cyprus, there are other less known languages spoken on the island. Based on the European Charter for Regional or Minority languages, the Republic of Cyprus recognized Armenian and Cypriot Maronite Arabic as minority languages. There are also Roma that date back to the arrival of "Atsiggani" after 1571 (Pelekani 2018), who are speakers of Kurbetcha, identified as a creole of the above-mentioned Romani and Cypriot Turkish, which will not be discussed further in this chapter.

Armenians first began to acquire a distinctive ethnic identity in the 1890s when the first waves of refugees from Asia Minor began to arrive on the island following the Hamidian massacre (1894–1896), the Adana massacre (1909), and the main Armenian Genocide (1915–1920), which was followed by "the 1921–1923 massacres and deportations" (Hadjilyra 2009: 14). Armenians that survived the killings totaled, according to reports, 9,000 refugees from Constantinople, Smyrna, and Cilicia, out of which 1,300 remained on the island. With the passing of time, the social and linguistic gaps between the locals ("deghatsi") and the refugees ("kaghtaganner") disappeared, as can be witnessed by 1,077 Armenians choosing to officially be part of the Greek Cypriot community in the 1960 referendum. It is calculated that up to 3,500 Armenians lived in Cyprus, with a census of as early as 1881 reporting Armenian as the mother tongue for this population. Table 3.1, built on Hadjilyra (2009: 21), summarizes the number of speakers declaring Armenian as their mother tongue based on different censuses between 1881 and 1956. (The 1960 census did not ask for mother tongue information, but there were 3,628 registered Armenian residents in Cyprus.)

Armenians in Cyprus speak the Western variety of Armenian; speakers of Eastern Armenian reside elsewhere. The earliest Armenian school facility reported in Cyprus was in 1927, while all three, Armenian, Greek, and English, are languages of instruction in certain schools in Cyprus even today. Armenian is also used on radio shows and since 2002 it has been recognized as a minority language of Cyprus. Within this context, Armenian could also be classified as a heritage language for the speakers

Table 3.1 *Native Armenian speakers in Cyprus (1881–1956)*

Census	Armenian native speakers
1881	168
1891	216
1901	505
1911	551
1921	1,162
1931	3,317
1946	3,678
1956	4,549

and younger generation that still learn and speak it in their early years, with the more dominant languages being used at a later stage and in more formal contexts. Armenian seems to be different from other minority languages that have not been preserved or promoted for use and teaching, raising the question whether all instances of minority languages can be classified as heritage languages for the speakers who speak them (especially since these speakers' fluency levels fluctuate widely).

Another minority language in Cyprus, Cypriot Maronite Arabic or Sanna, is classified as a severely endangered understudied Arabic variety in the *UNESCO Atlas of the World's Languages in Danger*, spoken primarily in the village of Kormakitis in northwestern Cyprus. It is estimated to have one terminal speaker by 2074 (Karyolemou 2010). Sanna speakers in north Cyprus and their linguistic competence are perceived and described as being closest to the actual place of origin in addition to any effects of language contact with Greek (more specifically, CG) or Turkish. This speech community is reported to consist of approximately 100 competent speakers of a variety of Arabic that is unique to Cyprus (Borg 1985) and which remains to this day understudied – yet the speakers are fully competent in both Sanna and CG. Sanna is spoken on a daily basis by the residents of the village, while CG is found extensively in contexts of code-switching or conversing with (non-Maronite) Greek Cypriots visiting the community.

With very little known about relevant historical or archival work, Maronites share the common belief that they moved to Cyprus at the beginning of the seventh century, possibly after moving from Syria to Attalia. Subsequent immigrations led to population growth to 80,000 people across sixty villages (Karyolemou 2010). An estimated number of 6,000 people who identify as Maronites are dispersed all over Cyprus and are part of a large community with their own churches and cemeteries. Historically, the process of Maronite assimilation into mainstream Greek Cypriot culture and language was set in motion by the historical facts of 1974 when they were uprooted from their ethnically homogeneous villages and forced to resettle in towns in the part of the island controlled by the Republic of Cyprus. There are some villages considered to have been the biggest settlements of Maronite Arabs throughout the years: Kormakitis, Karpasia, Asomatos, and Agia Marina Skillouras. Yet Sanna is reported to have been preserved only in Kormakitis (today's place of stay for most speakers who did not move south in 1974) and Agia Marina. Geographical and religious factors may have played a role, such as the remote location of Kormakitis and its economic independence as a community based on agriculture, and the contacts of residents of Agia Marina with monks of Lebanese origin.

The Sanna-speaking context is clearly different from the Armenian language still spoken in Cyprus, given the rapid decrease of native speakers and the absence of any teaching or other policy intervention to preserve the language for a long period of time. Given the different social conditions of Armenian and Sanna heritage speakers in Cyprus, the effects on today's grammar and child language acquisition are likely to be different in their respective heritage languages, with the dominant languages of (Cypriot) Greek and Turkish as part of their speech communities.

The complexity involved in the creation of contexts where a minority or home (or less used) linguistic variety competes with a more dominant or prestigious language cannot be analyzed in a single way. Different languages found in southeastern Europe, ranging from the well-known members of the Balkan *Sprachbund* to languages spoken in Cyprus, are based on different historical factors that do contribute to our understanding of heritage language as a heterogeneous concept.

3.3   Socio-psychological Factors

Language typically takes different forms among subsequent generations, even within the same speech community. The different forms range from the grammar acquired in the early stages of life, a speaker's first language (L1) to grammars with different properties in speakers of later generations whose dominant language is different from their home-spoken L1; these are typically known as *heritage* speakers. Originally, the term heritage language was used to refer to the development of children's mother tongues in Canada (Cummins 1992); it was only subsequently borrowed for use in other countries and contexts.

Classifying a language as heritage strongly depends on its coexistence with other linguistic varieties in the same context. In this section, we will attempt to discuss the socio-psychological factors that can derive contexts that are typically predicted as heritage language situations and compare the similarities that these show with other contexts that are not identified as such. If a heritage language is compared to the respective native-like language, the latter serves as the baseline and informs our scientific understanding of linguistic innovations in emerging grammars. As a native-like grammar of the heritage language is spoken less and less, it acquires the status of an endangered language. This problem essentially highlights a dimension of minority language acquisition that concerns the input received by younger generations, which could be grammatically divergent from the input received in earlier generations. Heritage language acquisition is characterized by decreased exposure to and use of the heritage language in childhood, when the language is still at an early stage (e.g., Montrul and Polinsky 2011; Benmamoun et al. 2013).

In her analysis of heritage languages, Polinsky (2018) identifies three groups of speakers when it comes to identifying and studying heritage languages. A *heritage* language speaker is defined as a simultaneous or sequential (successive) bilingual whose weaker language is a minority language and whose stronger language is the dominant language of a given society. The notion of a *baseline* – the language of adult first-generation immigrants that serves as the input to heritage learners – is critical for understanding what heritage speakers learn. This diaspora baseline can be compared to the *homeland* language variety, which is the variety spoken in the country or region of origin. The classification of the main players as such describes a clear scenario where all three groups are easily identifiable; however, the need for modifying these definitions becomes more obvious once we consider how the terms apply in the context of Sanna speakers.

With the identification of different groups, they should ideally correspond to linguistic abilities of different scales of multilingualism. This is even more expected, as distinct levels of language acquisition can be observed across speakers in environments of dominant and minority languages. The comparison of linguistic abilities across different populations falls under a specific area of research recently identified as "comparative linguality" (Grohmann and Kambanaros 2016), which explores the linguistic and cognitive abilities of monolingual, bi(dia)lectal, and bi-/multilingual speakers within a gradient spectrum of multilingualism (Grohmann 2014). In this realm of research, different combinations of linguality features, ranging from mono- to multilingualism and from typical development to pathologies, allow us to examine the degrees of variation of speakers.

Within this more general context of comparative lingualities, the social dominance of one linguality over another is seen in different contexts, creating the need for a more specific characterization of the different properties that may identify a speaker as heritage. Taking the existence of a group for comparison purposes (i.e., the *baseline*), it could be argued that the standard or official language can serve as the baseline for comparing varieties closely related to that language and discussing the extent to which the grammar of the latter deviates from the former (see also Kupisch 2013; Aalberse, Backus, and Muysken 2019).

A diglossic context is another situation in which a more dominant or stronger variety is being imposed for use by speakers under certain circumstances and a weaker or home variety is used in contexts in which such circumstances are absent. Those factors defining the use of a sociolinguistically "high" (H) and a "low" (L) variety in diglossic contexts are usually described as reasons of prestige, seen in formal and informal contexts. It would not be unsurprising to find sociolinguistic factors similar to this driving the use of the dominant variety over the weaker minority languages in other contexts, more commonly thought of as a heritage language context. Suarez (2002) identified *linguistic hegemony* for cases when dominant groups convince others to accept a consensus about language norms and usage. In this case, linguistic minorities will believe in the subjugation of the minority language to the dominant, leading to the preservation and establishment of the dominant language. In a similar manner, the dominance of an H variety in a diglossic or bilectal context is reinforced when language policies are such that they guide the speakers to show subjugation toward the L variety.

From the perspective of the minority speaker, a maintenance or presentation attempt may be based on socio-psychological motivation of preserving the language and the culture or feeling of pride and a rather implicit status of belonging as prestige. This still cannot be isolated in instances of minority or heritage languages, as will be further discussed later, and requires a more careful examination of the different conditions involved, for example, in the interaction between CG and SMG as well as between Sanna and CG.

3.3.1 The Case of Cypriot Greek

Following Newton (1972) in his original characterization, Arvaniti (2010) identifies Hellenic Cyprus as diglossic, based on the differences in the functional use of Standard and Cypriot Greek as H and L, respectively. CG and SMG have different functional uses in Cyprus. Demotic Greek, or Modern Greek (which linguists refer to as SMG, as used here throughout), is learned through formal schooling and used in all forms of writing and oral discourse, such as news broadcasting; CG, in turn, is acquired at home and used in informal interactions. Diglossia has been argued to characterize the Greek Cypriot speech community, easily understood by speakers who have a clear sense that certain circumstances require use of CG while other contexts require SMG. These speakers perceive other speakers' use of language according to their skill in using both varieties in an appropriate manner and register.

CG and SMG show differences at all levels of linguistic analysis. Greek Cypriot speakers often do not provide reliable judgments of their own speech, since these are often clouded by sociolinguistic attitudes toward using the non-standard variety. CG lacks official codification; indeed, its status as a distinct language or variety is often denied by Greek Cypriots who ignore the differences between SMG and CG. All CG speakers have exposure to SMG through education and other mediums – it is in this way that they are competent in both varieties to different degrees.

As Rowe and Grohmann (2013) explain, the socio-psychology of speakers in diglossic societies usually centers on the notion of prestige and a negative valuation of the L variety. Since the use of the H variety indicates advanced education, speakers typically want to speak it in order to present themselves as well educated. They further suggest that a *co-overt* prestige of CG has prevented a takeover by SMG or death of CG. This co-overt prestige is not unlikely to be found in more typical scenarios characterized as heritage and especially in minority languages. Minority speakers are very likely to promote the use of their language as a means of resisting the death of the language or the complete assimilation to the dominant context.

3.3.2 The Case of Sanna

The process of Maronite assimilation into mainstream Greek Cypriot culture and language was set in motion by the historical facts of 1974, when they were uprooted from their ethnically homogeneous villages and forced to resettle in towns in parts of the island controlled by the Republic of Cyprus, which were dominated by Greek Cypriot culture and language. Cultural centers such as churches and cafeterias connected to the Cypriot Maronite Arabs could possibly be found in different locations in the southern part of Cyprus following the relocation of large parts of the population – these places are likely to have been reduced in number with the passing of years and the Maronites' assimilation into Cypriot culture.

Through this process, the Maronite population resides all over Cyprus, creating two possible situations: First, all Sanna speakers share the same level of competence in their language independently of their place of residence. Second, those speakers who were exposed to CG as the dominant language due to their move to the south do not share the same competence with the Sanna speakers still residing in northern Cyprus. The current situation is that individuals identifying as Maronites mostly live in the south without any actual reports on their linguistic competence in order to compare them to Sanna speakers living in the north.

With respect to literacy, speakers report that they were never taught Sanna in a classroom setting (but some consultants acknowledge classes in Standard Arabic for a short period of time). It is thus a language acquired only in oral mode as the home language or language of the community. As the group of speakers most competent in Sanna, they are also the most reliable source of native judgments and intuitions about all aspects of the grammar and function as the control group for any comparison with all other groups of speakers of Sanna in other parts of the island. Speakers who reside in the south are expected to have mostly attended Greek-speaking schools, where the H variety of SMG is supposedly imposed by teachers in the classroom (but see Leivada et al. 2020 and references therein). If so, these speakers should be sensitive to the same sociolinguistic factors that account for the use of CG and SMG while also being speakers of the minority language Sanna.

Efforts to use Sanna in written form have been undertaken with the adaptation of the Latin alphabet, which is used in teaching camps targeting the language's revitalization. Two teams of teachers, linguists, and other community members, the Kermia Ztite and Hki fi Sanna, are working toward contributing to revitalization efforts. Currently, Sanna is being taught in adult classes in different cities in the southern part of Cyprus by native speakers with the use of a booklet especially prepared for revitalization purposes.

While the descriptions of the Sanna grammar identify interesting phonological, morphological, and syntactic differences with other varieties of Arabic, the situation described here remains yet to be investigated. That is, the status of Cypriot Maronite Arabs living in different parts of the island and having been exposed to different levels of Sanna, CG, and SMG still needs to be put in perspective with the more appropriate description of these populations as bilingual or heritage – or perhaps something else.

The socio-psychological factor of *covert prestige* (Labov 1972; Trudgill 1972) is still found among Sanna speakers. This may suggest that the community has preserved and protected their minority language from any other contact with the neighboring languages of (possibly Cypriot) Turkish and (Cypriot) Greek as a matter of identity and culture. Even if possibly not being the expected choice for communication in other contexts, Sanna is still used in those places where speakers reside. Regarding CG and SMG, this prestige depends on the appropriate judgment of the context as being formal or not. In contrast, for Sanna speakers this would depend on the existence of other speakers in the same context. Still, the use of CG and Sanna can be seen as a choice by the speakers resisting the use and takeover of the H variety or the dominant language.

3.4 Heritage Grammars and Divergent Attainment

When new concepts or phenomena emerge in heritage speakers compared to the baseline, the grammar is identified as *divergent*. This is possibly one of the factors that cannot overlap in the comparison of CG–SMG and Sanna–CG as discussed previously, or, in other words, the comparison of two closely related varieties in a bilectal setting and the Sanna language spoken by Cypriot Maronite Arabs using a genealogically different language as the dominant. The crucial difference between the two is that in the first pair, the "weaker" variety can diverge in the use of grammar in a substantially different way, as described later, but it can also retain the grammar of the baseline or the standard variety.

Perhaps, then, heritage languages are only restricted to one new, emerged strategy in the use of a linguistic phenomenon that is adopted and produced by the majority of speakers in a given community. In this way, heritage speakers would not only be classified on the basis of socio-psychological and historical factors that characterize that community but also purely linguistic conditions that may be associated with this character-ization. Previous descriptions of this kind have been identified as *speech rate* or *lexical proficiency* (see Polinsky 2008; Benmamoun et al. 2013). In other work, heritage speakers' knowledge of the root and pattern system of Arabic is not target-like, identifying a linguistic diagnostic (Benmamoun et al. 2014). We describe here our observations on grammatical phenomena that may be associated with the emergence of new, divergent patterns that may be a criterion for the heritage grammar.

3.4.1 Heritage Linguistic Issues for Sanna

Identifying a clear case of divergent grammar is not a simple task, as the phenomenon should be different from the "baseline" grammar – in the case of Sanna, possibly other varieties of Arabic. In this section, we present one example of a divergent grammar phenomenon, namely the diminuti-vization strategy in Sanna, while case-marking in reflexivization will be laid out as possible instances of borrowing and language changes.

  Morphosyntactic code-mixing between Sanna and CG appears in spontan-eous productions and elicitations from native speakers living in the village of Kormakitis (northern Cyprus). Code-mixing in the presence of a CG diminutive –*u* shows up with both singular and plural stems (known as "broken plural"; compare McCarthy and Prince 1990) and results in the use of a Sanna stem followed by CG derivational and inflectional suffixes.

(1)   a.   it   –u   –i
           hand   –DIM   –NEUT.SG
      b.* it   –u   –θkja
           hand   –DIM   –NEUT.PL
      c.   ten   –u   –i
           hand   –DIM   –NEUT.SG
      d.* ten   –u   –θkja
           hand   –DIM   –NEUT.PL
           'little hands'

An Arabic stem like *it* 'hand' is followed by the CG diminutive –*u* and both are followed by CG inflectional morphology, as in (1a). The puzzle that arises here is that plural inflectional morphology from CG is ungrammat-ical with a singular Sanna stem, like *it* in (1b), but not with a plural stem that shows a different form (hence, suppletive), as in (1d) – which, as (1c) shows, cannot be combined with singular –*i* (for a discussion of allomorphy conditions, see Pavlou 2018a). The use of diminutives as a suffix to the stem, following CG suffixation of the diminutive head, is an innovation to the common way of observing changes in the root following prosodic morphology patterns (Watson 2006). This, in a sense, creates an innovative way of diminutivization in Arabic which shows that at the morphological level rules of grammar apply between the two languages.

In addition to this paradigm, diminutivization also appears in "sound plurals," that is, stems that do not show any allomorphy in the stem depending on number:

(2) a. xank   −u   −i
         mouth   −DIM   −NEUT.SG
         'little mouth'
     b. xank   −u   −θkja
         mouth   −DIM   −NEUT.PL
         'little mouths'

The diminutivization strategy is extremely productive as a new emerging structure in the morphology of nouns in Sanna (Pavlou 2018a). The extent to which such a productive emerging structure is also acquired by speakers that had a lesser degree of exposure to this language, namely younger speakers currently residing in the southern part of Cyprus and likely to have a different grammar from the baseline speakers, remains a question for future research. If that is the case, the morphological change and borrowing are consistent despite different lingualities in this speech community. If there is a difference, however, it raises questions about the interaction of morphology and acquisition in ways that can inform our understanding of heritage language acquisition and how that variation is shaped by the social conditions in which Sanna is spoken.

In the formation of reflexives, speakers combine the Arabic definite marker with the Greek root "self" plus the Sanna possessor masculine marker *tel–* and the pronominal object. Again, this is viewed as an emerging grammatical phenomenon, as the combination of these elements is characterized as novel and unique to Sanna.

(3) a. l'   eafto   tel   −i
         he   self   POSS.MASC   −1SG
         'myself'
     b. l'   eafto   tel   −on
         the   self   POSS.MASC   −3PL
         'themselves'

Case-marking usually expressed on the borrowed *eafto* in Greek is no longer found in the new form "eafto," which already suggests that some features have been lost in the formation of this structure. In other instances, Sanna speakers who use Greek nouns fully inflect the noun itself with agreement, case, and other features. Further investigation of *eafto* in Sanna will show the extent to which it is used with any case morphology in other structures and whether it appears in other anaphoric contexts as well. If it is restricted with a reflexive use, then this makes reflexivization subject to language contact and borrowing and likely to exhibit a different acquisition by heritage speakers, who admittedly will allow more use of the dominant language.

Other even clearer cases of transfer are found with nouns in possessive structures. Interestingly, with the use of the Greek noun, there is an additional grammatical operation: obligatory agreement between the head noun and the possessive marker. The use of a masculine or feminine possessor morpheme follows the use of the corresponding gender of the head noun in these constructions, even if they are found in different languages.

(4) a.   pappu   tel   –i
          grandfather.MASC   POSS.MASC   –1SG
          'my grandfather'
     b.* pappu   shait   –i
          grandfather.MASC   POSS.FEM   –1SG
     c.   kandila   shait   –i
          glass.FEM   POSS.FEM   –1SG
          'my glass'
     d.* kandila   tel   –i
          glass.FEM   POSS.MASC   –1SG

Agreement between two elements in the clause is a syntactic phenomenon and the extent to which the correct possessive marker will be used by speakers in both populations can show whether this part of grammar is affected in heritage language acquisition. Some of the cases reported here are divergent from the baseline Arabic variety and, to our knowledge, without any option of forming the same structure otherwise. Grammar, in this sense, provides the diagnostics necessary for identifying such a complex linguistic context as heritage and disentangling the application of the different criteria that can be used. In this case, these patterns may be different because the dominant language is different (Albirini et al. 2011; Benmamoun et al. 2014).

3.4.2 Linguistic Questions for Cypriot Greek

When making a careful examination of the grammatical properties that characterize grammars of less used and dominant languages as divergent, differences between CG and SMG at all levels of linguistic analysis are crucial. Such differences can easily be tracked and indeed have been the subject of much previous theoretical and experimental research.

One of the (morpho)syntactic differences between SMG and CG relates to clitic placement. Placement patterns are the same across the two varieties in some environments (e.g., imperatives and negation), but not in others (e.g., declaratives in indicative mood) (see Petinou and Terzi 2002; Grohmann 2011). CG requires enclisis, whereas SMG requires proclisis

(Terzi 1999; Agouraki 2001; Mavrogiorgos 2013). While matrix environments are identified as exhibiting enclisis in CG, embedded environments headed by certain complementizers can show either proclisis or enclisis (Pavlou 2018b).

(5) a. θelo   to.
         want.PRES.1SG   it.NEUT.ACC
     b. to   θelo.
         it.NEUT.ACC   want.PRES.1SG
         'I want it.'

Papadopoulou et al. (2014) argue that this variation relates to the socio-syntactic aspects of language use, such as the implications of the existence of competing grammars and the notion of gradience existent within a dialect–standard continuum.

Another well-known morphological difference between CG and SMG concerns the diminutive morpheme: the CG suffix *–u* vs. SMG *–ak*. The two suffixes have the exact same meaning and function, but they have a slightly different distribution depending on the noun declension class; their only difference is with respect to the variety they belong to. (Just to be clear, the *–u* variant is not an option at all for Hellenic Greek speakers of SMG.)

(6) a. trapez   –u   –i
         table   –DIM   –NEUT.SG
         'little table'
     b. trapez –ak   –i
         table   –DIM   –NEUT.SG

The expectation is that these morphosyntactic differences would be found only when speakers use the corresponding grammars of CG and SMG. Yet, recent findings show that this is not the case. Leivada et al. (2017) report their findings that highlight the presence of variants that belong to different varieties/lects across levels of linguistic analysis. This means that despite clitic placement and diminutives (as well as phonological differences) belonging to different grammars, these variants are present in the speech (and hence in the grammar) of Greek Cypriot speakers using CG. Given that the different varieties are so clearly marked as functionally different according to the socio-psychological basis perceived by speakers, the expectation would be that the two options should not coexist – but a more careful examination of the grammar used shows that they actually do. If, then, both variants appear in a single grammar, however that may be characterized on a language continuum, the criterion of *divergence* as a diagnostic for heritage language grammars does not hold in this case, clearly setting apart the bilectal context of a dominant and an L variety from the heritage language context.

3.4.3 Heritage Speakers and Language Acquisition

In the minority acquisition literature, child bilinguals could acquire the heritage language from the minority community but lose parts of it after entering school on exposure to the dominant language, contrary to the expected outcome that traditional generative acquisition theories on parameter setting early in life might assume. This outcome would then move toward the *contingency hypothesis*, as also discussed by Benmamoun et al. (2013): Learning is contingent upon continued exposure to language throughout the lifespan and any loss of that input causes system optimization.

This conclusion is subject to the study of the different components of grammar and the extent to which they can be subject to change and/or variation. Kupisch et al. (2014) argue that different components of language pose different degrees of difficulty in development. Morphosyntax does not create particular problems in simultaneous bilingual development, since bilingual children develop their two languages separately and show the same developmental stages and patterns as monolinguals. In contrast to their morphosyntactic abilities, bilingual children may have a smaller lexicon than monolinguals, especially in the minority language. Still, previous work may predict that interfaces in grammar would be more problematic than its internal properties, which could also be attested in heritage speakers (Sorace 2004).

The understanding of heritage language acquisition also relates to the use of the term *incomplete acquisition*, as often used in heritage language acquisition contexts (see especially Montrul 2008). Incomplete acquisition is understood in different terms from incomplete grammar as in, for example, the acquisition of relative clauses and postverbal noun phrases in Mandarin proceeded in a typical way (Montrul and Silva-Corvalan 2019). With phenomena like transfer appearing in the grammar of heritage speakers, the age of exposure in the two languages cannot be a determining factor, since the phenomenon itself can appear in simultaneous bilinguals as well as L2 speakers. However, if incomplete acquisition is indeed defined as a developmental effect that results in gaps in grammar, then crucially a bilectal case would differ significantly from heritage speakers in that exposure to a second language comes after any expected age of acquisition of the core grammar of the first language – whether that is assumed to be vocabulary, syntax, or semantics. Note that language *attrition* would also not be a possible explanation for bilectal speakers, who do not show absence of particular grammar phenomena compared to a baseline set of speakers but have continuous access to both (sociolinguistically) L and H varieties.

Our understanding, then, of terms like incomplete acquisition as a developmental pattern cannot be supported from such a hypothesis. In the case of heritage speakers again, a developmental effect that results in grammar gaps while acquiring both languages is a disputable concept with other contexts of simultaneous acquisition of languages being fully acquired in all different components of grammar. In some instances, however, a restricted exposure to the heritage language, when that truly happens, might lead to linguistic gaps. Admittedly, the lack of schooling later on aggravates the situation with heritage speakers not receiving much (if any) literacy education in, for, and about their language (Montrul 2010).

Descriptively, heritage language speakers are L1 learners as they show naturalistic acquisition before the start of any formal education, if that exists. Some characteristics presented in Montrul (2010) include the exposure to the language in the early years as well as developmental patterns and errors. As Montrul notes, heritage speakers cannot be compared to L2 speakers, since L2 acquisition takes place in a classroom – a setting that is often absent in heritage language situations.

A diglossic situation is different from a heritage language context. However, against the background of identifying and comparing different contexts in which two languages coexist as well as are acquired and used by speakers, we can identify the following differences in terms of the acquisition path between CG and Sanna:

Cypriot Greek

a. Acquisition is target-like in the early years, with the dominant language making its appearance at the first stages of schooling (Grohmann et al. 2010).
b. Variation in the use of the "high" and "low" L1 variety remains during adulthood, but with the L variety appearing in a decreased manner and restricted to particular contexts.

Sanna

a. Acquisition of Sanna and Cypriot Greek is likely to take place simultaneously when children are exposed to both languages from their parents.
b. Use of Sanna is restricted only as home language or with other native speaker peers and the dominant language of Cypriot Greek is established, with speakers likely to code-switch between the two.

The crucial difference during acquisition is that in the first case, speakers in the diglossic context are exposed to the H variety only during the first years of schooling (and earlier possibly through multimedia), while in the second case, acquisition is simultaneous given the bilingual parents, as also discussed by Montrul (2010). Like monolingual children, heritage language children acquire the language naturalistically, from the early years of interacting with family members. Minority languages, like Sanna, are primarily spoken at home and acquisition happens in a naturalistic manner from interaction with the family and peers. In all cases, it is predicted that one or both parents also speak the majority or dominant language. This can be associated with the creation of a divergent grammar in the latter case presented in this chapter through the appearance of new, emerging linguistic phenomena that are acquired in the early years of life and become part of the speaker's grammar that is likely to be different from the parents. In bilectal settings, parents can be communicating with their child in the L variety and the child receives care in the H variety later on. Regarding CG and SMG, late exposure of Greek Cypriot children to SMG does not create these patterns in grammar ("Socio-Syntax of Development Hypothesis"; Grohmann 2011), but allows access to the H grammar as well as the appearance of functionally equivalent variants (Leivada et al. 2017), given its prominent use in the society.

3.5   Conclusion

The term "heritage speaker" has not been used in many contexts across the world and is even more rarely found in linguistic descriptions in south-eastern Europe. With various contexts of dominant and minority languages, also found in this region, the definition of heritage speakers as "second generation immigrants, the children of the original immigrants, who live in a bilingual/multilingual environment from an early age" (Benmamoun et al. 2013: 132) cannot apply to cases like the Sanna community. After all, a large number of languages that can still be classified as "heritage" do not conform to this description. Instead, a broader view may cover more relevant cases. For example, a language qualifies as a heritage language "if it is a language spoken at home or otherwise readily available to young children, and crucially this language is not a dominant language of the larger (national) society" (Rothman 2009: 156). Still, though, a critical component of any definition has to do with identifying different levels of competence or lingualities, reflecting the variation in heritage language proficiency. This is one way defining heritage languages that may provide a better description of these grammars. Other approaches are based on social definitions for languages that are acquired in the home as the non-dominant language of the wider society largely acquired naturalistically rather than through instruction (Valdés 2001).

In this sense, future research could focus on identifying particular phenomena that are subject to variation between different generations of heritage speakers and associating those with those parts of grammar that are mostly affected in these situations. This path will enable researchers to develop linguistic diagnostics that can identify, separate, and classify a heritage speaker as such in the socially different contexts revealing the interplay between human faculty and social competence.

References

Aalberse, Suzanne, Ad Backus, and Pieter Muysken. 2019. *Heritage Languages: A Language Contact Approach*. Amsterdam: John Benjamins.

Agouraki, Yoryia. 2001. The Position of Clitics in Cypriot Greek. In Angeliki Ralli, Brian D. Joseph, and Mark Janse (eds.), *Proceedings of the First International Conference of Modern Greek Dialects and Linguistic Theory (Patras, Greece, Oct. 12–14, 2000)*. Patras: University of Patras, 1–17.

Albirini, Abdulkafi, Elabbas Benmamoun, and Eman Saadah. 2011. Grammatical Features of Egyptian and Palestinian Arabic Heritage Speakers Oral Production. *Studies in Second Language Acquisition* 33(2), 273–303.

Arvaniti, Amalia. 2010. Linguistic Practices in Cyprus and the Emergence of Cypriot Standard Greek. *Mediterranean Language Review* 17, 15–45.

Benmamoun, Elabbas, Silvina A. Montrul, and Maria Polinsky. 2013. Heritage Languages and Their Speakers: Opportunities and Challenges for Linguistics. *Theoretical Linguistics* 39, 129–181.

Benmamoun, Elabbas, Abdulkafi Albirini, Silvina A. Montrul, and Eman Saadah. 2014. Arabic Plurals and Root and Pattern Morphology in Palestinian and Egyptian Heritage Speakers. *Linguistic Approaches to Bilingualism* 4, 89–123.

Borg, Alexander. 1985. *Cypriot Arabic: A Historical and Comparative Investigation into the Phonology and Morphology of the Arabic Vernacular Spoken by the Maronites of Kormakiti Village in the Kyrenia District of North-Western Cyprus*. Stuttgart: Deutsche Morgenländische Gesellschaft.

Buschfeld, Sarah. 2013. *English in Cyprus or Cyprus English: An Empirical Investigation of Variety Status*. Amsterdam: John Benjamins.

Cummins, Jim. 1992. Heritage Language Teaching in Canadian Schools. *Journal of Curriculum Studies* 24, 281–286.

Friedman, Victor A. 2017. *Languages of the Balkans: Oxford Research Encyclopedia of Linguistics*. Oxford: Oxford University Press.

Friedman, Victor A. and Brian D. Joseph. 2014. Lessons from Judezmo about the Balkan Sprachbund and Contact Linguistics. *International Journal of the Sociology of Language* 2014(226), 3–23.

Grohmann, Kleanthes K. 2011. Some Directions for the Systematic Investigation of the Acquisition of Cypriot Greek: A New Perspective on Production Abilities from Object Clitic Placement. In Esther Rinke and Tanja Kupisch (eds.), *The Development of Grammar: Language Acquisition and Diachronic Change*. Amsterdam: John Benjamins, 179–203.

Grohmann, Kleanthes K. 2014. Towards Comparative Bilingualism. *Linguistic Approaches to Bilingualism* 4(3), 336–341.

Grohmann, Kleanthes K. and Maria Kambanaros. 2016. The Gradience of Multilingualism in Typical and Impaired Language Development: Positioning Bilectalism within Comparative Bilingualism. *Frontiers in Psychology* 7, 37.

Grohmann, Kleanthes K., Eleni Theodorou, Natalia Pavlou, Evelina Leivada, Elena Papadopoulou, and Silvia Martínez-Ferreiro. 2010. The Development of Object Clitic Placement in Cypriot Greek and the Romance Connection. In Sandrine Ferré, Philippe Prévost, Laurie Tuller, and Rasha Zebib (eds.), *Selected Proceedings of the Romance Turn IV Workshop on the Acquisition of Romance Languages*. Newcastle-upon-Tyne: Cambridge Scholars Publishing, 128–152.

Hadjilyra, Alexander-Michael. 2009. *The Armenians of Cyprus*. Nicosia: Kalaydjian Foundation.

Karoulla-Vrikki, Dimitra. 2001. English or Greek Language? State or Ethnic Identity? The Case of the Courts in Cyprus. *Language Problems and Language Planning* 25, 259–288.

Karyolemou, Marilena. 2010. The Demographics of the Cypriot Maronite Community and of Cypriot Arabic Speakers. In Brian Bielenberg and Costas M. Constantinou (eds.), *The Sanna Project – Empowerment through Language Revival: Current Efforts and Recommendations for Cypriot Maronite Arabic*. Oslo: International Peace Research Institute, 1–6.

Karyolemou, Marilena and Pavlos Pavlou. 2001. Language Attitudes and Assessment of Salient Variables in a Bi-Dialectal Speech Community. In *Proceedings of the 1st International Conference on Language Variation in Europe*. Barcelona: Universitat Pompeu Fabra, 110–120.

Kerswill, Paul. 2013. Koineization. In J. K. Chambers and Natalie Schilling (eds.), *Handbook of Language Variation and Change*, 2nd ed. Oxford: Wiley-Blackwell, 519–536.

Kupisch, Tanja. 2013. A New Term for a Better Distinction? A View from the Higher End of the Proficiency Scale. *Theoretical Linguistics* 39(3–4), 203–214.

Kupisch, Tanja, Tatjana Lein, Dagmar Barton, Dawn Judith Schröder, Ilse Stangen, and Antje Stoehr. 2014. Acquisition Outcomes across Domains in Adult Simultaneous Bilinguals with French as Weaker and Stronger Language. *Journal of French Language Studies* 24, 347–376.

Labov, William. 1972. *Language in the Inner City: Studies in the Black English Vernacular*. Philadelphia: University of Pennsylvania Press.

Leivada, Evelina, Elena Papadopoulou, and Natalia Pavlou. 2017. Functionally Equivalent Variants in a Non-Standard Variety and Their Implications for Universal Grammar: A Spontaneous Speech Corpus. *Frontiers in Psychology* 8, 1260.

Leivada, Evelina, Maria Kambanaros, Loukia Taxitari, and Kleanthes K. Grohmann. 2020. (Meta)Linguistic Abilities of Bilectal Educators: The Case of Cyprus. *International Journal of Bilingual Education and Bilingualism* 23(8), 1003–1018.

Lindstedt, Jouko. 2000. Linguistic Balkanization: Contact-Induced Change by Mutual Reinforcement. *Studies in Slavic and General Linguistics* 28, 231–246.

McCarthy, John J. and Alan S. Prince. 1990. Foot and Word in Prosodic Morphology: The Arabic Broken Plural. *Natural Language and Linguistic Theory* 8, 209–283.

Mavrogiorgos, Marios. 2013. Enclisis at the Syntax–PF Interface. In Christine Meklenborg Salvesen and Hans Petter Helland (eds.), *Challenging Clitics*. Amsterdam: John Benjamins, 27–54.

Montrul, Silvina A. 2008. *Incomplete Acquisition in Bilingualism: Re-Examining the Age Factor*. Amsterdam: John Benjamins.

Montrul, Silvina A. 2010. Current Issues in Heritage Language Acquisition. *Annual Review of Applied Linguistics* 30(3), 3–23.

Montrul, Silvina A. and Maria Polinsky. 2011. Why Not Heritage Speakers? *Linguistic Approaches to Bilingualism* 1(1), 58–62.

Montrul, Silvina A. and Carmen Silvan-Corvalán. 2019. The Social Context Contributes to the Incomplete Acquisition of Aspect of Heritage Languages. *Studies in Second Language Acquisition* 41(2): 269–273.

Newton, Brian. 1972. *Cypriot Greek: Its Phonology and Inflections*. The Hague: Mouton.

Papadopoulou, Elena, Evelina Leivada, and Natalia Pavlou. 2014. Acceptability Judgments in Bilectal Populations: Competition, Gradience and Socio-Syntax. *Linguistic Variation* 14, 109–128.

Pavlou, Natalia. 2018a. Alternations in Contexts of Code-Mixing: Allomorphy, Suppletion and Diminutives. *University of Pennsylvania Working Papers in Linguistics* 24(1), 18.

Pavlou, Natalia. 2018b. Morphosyntactic Dependencies and Verb Movement in Cypriot Greek. PhD dissertation, The University of Chicago.

Pelekani, Chryso. 2018. *Roma and Their Rights*. Nicosia: Mediterranean Migration Network Activities.

Petinou, Kakia and Arhonto Terzi. 2002. Clitic Misplacement among Normally Developing Children and Children with Specific Language Impairment and the Status of Infl Heads. *Language Acquisition* 10, 1–28.

Polinsky, Maria. 2008. Russian Gender under Incomplete Acquisition. *The Heritage Language Journal* 6(1), 40–71.

Polinsky, Maria. 2018. *Heritage Languages and Their Speakers*. Cambridge: Cambridge University Press.

Rothman, Jason. 2009. Understanding the Nature and Outcomes of Early Bilingualism: Romance Languages as Heritage Languages. *International Journal of Bilingualism* 13, 155–163.

Rowe, Charley and Kleanthes K. Grohmann. 2013. Discrete Bilectalism: Towards Co-Overt Prestige and Diglossic Shift in Cyprus. *International Journal of the Sociology of Language* 2013, 119–142.

Sorace, Antonella. 2004. Native Language Attrition and Developmental Instability at the Syntax–Discourse Interface: Data, Interpretations and Methods. *Bilingualism: Language and Cognition* 7, 143–145.

Suarez, Debra. 2002. The Paradox of Linguistic Hegemony and the Maintenance of Spanish as a Heritage Language in the United States. *Journal of Multilingual and Multicultural Development* 23, 512–530.

Terkourafi, Marina. 2011. Thank You, Sorry and Please in Cypriot Greek: What Happens to Politeness Markers When They Are Borrowed across Languages? *Journal of Pragmatics* 43, 218–235.

Terzi, Arhonto. 1999. Clitic Combinations, Their Hosts and Their Ordering. *Natural Language and Linguistic Theory* 17, 85–121.

Trudgill, Peter. 1972. Sex, Covert Prestige and Linguistic Change in the Urban British English of Norwich. *Language in Society* 1. 179–195.

Tsiplakou, Stavroula, Andreas Papapavlou, Pavlos Pavlou, and Marianna Katsoyannou. 2006. Levelling, Koineization and Their Implications for Bidialectism. In Frans Hinskens (ed.), *Language Variation – European Perspectives. Selected Papers from the 3rd International Conference on Language Variation in Europe (ICLaVE 3), University of Amsterdam, 23–25 June 2005*. Amsterdam: John Benjamins, 265–276.

Valdés, Guadalupe. 2001. *Learning and Not Learning English: Latino Students in American Schools*. New York: Teachers College Press.

Watson, Janet C. E. 2006. Arabic Morphology: Diminutive Verbs and Diminutive Nouns in San'ani Arabic. *Morphology* 16(2), 189–204.

4

Heritage Languages in China

Linda Tsung and Lubei Zhang

4.1   Introduction

China is one of the most multilingual countries in the world. With 55 legally recognized ethnic minority groups (about 111 million people in 2018), there are more than 400 languages spoken and used in China. Heritage languages, which we understand as minority languages here, are spoken and used by different ethnic minority groups. In many chapters of the handbook, the heritage language is understood as the weaker language of a bilingual. However, in China a minority language is not necessarily the weaker language; for example, the Uyghur language is the *lingua franca* among minority groups in Xinjiang. While some of these minority languages are greatly endangered and are now on the verge of extinction, some minority languages are still enjoying a high vitality and functioning as regional common languages. Most minority groups in China have at least one spoken language, and thirty have their own written language. Although most young people can speak Chinese *Putonghua*, some old people are monolingual in their own ethnic languages. Since the 1950s the PRC government has not only legally recognized multilingualism but also encouraged and promoted multilingual education with the teaching and learning of a variety of languages in schools and universities. However, multilingual practice and education for some of these heritage languages have faced challenges, particularly as a result of economic reform since the 1980s. In China currently, state regulation provides minority languages with legitimacy in various models of multilingual education, but a clear linguistic hierarchy is evident in terms of language legitimacy in the language market that is largely controlled by the authorities. Minority students have been faced with making choices among their first language, the second and dominant Chinese language, and a third language, English. For larger minority groups such as Tibetans, Uyghurs, Kazakhs, and Koreans, the key issue is whether to choose a school where the medium of instruction is Chinese or a mother tongue. Smaller minority groups such as Salar or Jinuo have no choice; their native language is not offered as the medium of instruction in school or as a subject of study. Many practical factors, including social, political, and economic, have influenced minority students' choice, since they need to not only think about their present studies but also their jobs and long-term future development (Zhang and Tsung 2019b). Being proficient in Chinese *Putonghua* appears to enjoy more political and economic benefits than being proficient in their mother tongue in terms of career development.

This chapter aims to provide a brief background of these heritage languages in China, including the geographical area they are spoken, the size of communities that use them, their distinctive linguistic features, and their social functions. We then discuss historical and current language policies and efforts to maintain and protect these heritage languages. The following questions guide the content of this chapter.

1. What are the heritage languages in China? And what types of heritage languages have been protected?
2. Why are some varieties of heritage languages more prestigious than others? What rights and opportunities do these minorities have to use their languages?
3. How have heritage languages been maintained in recent years?

4.2   Defining Heritage Languages in China

The term "heritage language" is used to identify languages other than the dominant language (or languages) in a given social context. Alternative terms to "heritage language" include "minority language," "community language," "indigenous language," and "home language" (e.g., Baker and Jones 1998; Corson 1999; Yeung et al. 2000; Wiley 2001; Hornberger 2005). Joshua Fishman defines three types of heritage languages in the United States according to their different historical and social conditions relative to English (Fishman 2001). They are immigrant heritage languages, indigenous heritage languages, and colonial heritage languages. In the United States, heritage and modern language discourses remain separated and Spanish has primarily been the target of second language policy (García 2014). While in Australia, where immigrant languages have been referred to as community languages, attention has only recently emerged on the policy agenda (Modood and May 2001).

In China, Chinese (Mandarin) is the dominant language used in government, education, and public communication. Thus, any language other than Chinese can be considered a minority language roughly belonging to what Fishman classified as indigenous heritage languages.

Scholars in China have generally classified the minority/heritage languages of China as belonging to four language families: Sino-Tibetan, Altaic, Indo-European, and Austric. Within these, several branches and sub-branches are also identified. The Sino-Tibetan family, which has the most speakers, has four main branches: Han Chinese, Tibeto-Burman, Thai (Tai), and Miao-Yao (Mai 1954; Bloomfeld 1967; Dai 1994). Many minority languages in northern and western China belong to the Altaic family, with three branches: Turkic, Manchu-Tungusic, and Mongolian. A small number of speakers belong to the Iranian and Slavic branches of the Indo-European family, and Austro-Asiatic and Austronesian branches of the Austric family (see Table 4.1).

Since classification of different types of speech as separate languages or dialects of one language is difficult and somewhat arbitrary, it is hardly possible to state definitively how many indigenous languages are spoken in China. The State Language Commission has officially distinguished 80–120 minority languages (State Language Commission 1995: 159), while Crystal believes there are nearly 300 languages in the Tibetan-Burmese branch alone (Crystal 1987: 310). UNESCO has recognized 144 endangered heritage minority languages spoken within China's borders (Moseley 2010), mostly concentrated in northern, northwestern, southwestern, and southern parts of its territory. While the northern and western languages tend to have agglutinative structure, the minority languages in southern China are more diverse, with a tendency toward

Table 4.1 *Language families in China*

Language families	Sub-branches	Languages
Sino-Tibetan	Chinese	Mandarin/ Wu/ Xiang/ Min (Hokkien)/ Yue (Cantonese)/ Gan / Kejia (Hakka)
	Tibetan-Burmese	Zang (Tibetan)/ Mongba/ Changla/ Lhoba/ Qiang/ Pumi/ Drung/ Jingpo/ Yi/ Lisu/ Hani/ Lahu/ Naxi/ Jinuo/ Nusu/ Nung/ Zauzou/ Tujia/ Zaiwa/ Achang/ etc.
	Miao-Yao	Miao/ Bunu/ Mian/ She/ etc.
	Thai (Tai)	Zhuang/ Buyi/ Thai/ Tong/ Shui/ Mulao/ Maonan/Lakkia/ Li/ Kelao/ etc.
Altaic	Mongolian	Mongolian/ Daur/ Dongxiang/ Tuzu/ Bonan/ Yugur/ etc.
	Turkic	Uyghur/ Kazakh/ Kirgiz/ Uzbek/ Tatar/ Salar/ etc.
	Tungusic	Manchu/ Xibe/ Hezhe/ Oroqen/ Ewenki/ etc.
	Korean	Korean
Indo-European	Iranian	Tajik
	Slavic	Russian
Austric	Austro-Asiatic	Wa (Va)/ Blang/ De'ang/ etc.
	Austronesian	Gaoshan

monosyllabicity and a rich profusion of tones (Ramsey 1987: 164–165). A large number of these languages in the south of China do not have written scripts. For them, Chinese has always been chosen as their written script. Thirty-three minority language scripts are now being used and managed by the government at different levels. Among them, eleven scripts are traditional language scripts that had been developed long before the establishment of the People's Republic of China (PRC) in 1949, fifteen are scripts that were newly created after liberation, and others are modified scripts based on their original ones.

Based on their writing system and access to bilingual education, Yang (2005: 554) categorized heritage minority groups in China into the following three types:

> **Type 1** Minority groups who had functional writing systems that were broadly used before the founding of the People's Republic of China in 1949, and who have had regular bilingual education since then. These groups include the Koreans, the Kazakhs, the Mongolians, the Tibetans, and the Uyghurs, who have a combined population of about 24 million.
>
> **Type 2** Minority groups who had functional writing systems that were in limited use before 1949, and who have had occasional bilingual education since then. This type includes eight groups, the Dai, the Jingpo, the Lisu, the Lahu, the Miao, the Naxi, the Wa, and the Yi, who have a combined population of around 22 million.
>
> **Type 3** Minority groups who had no fully functional writing systems before 1949 and who have had limited or no bilingual education since then. They take Chinese as their primary or only language of instruction. It includes the remaining forty-two minority groups, and they have a total population of about 60 million. (see Table 4.2)

Type 1 heritage minorities, all with a population between 100 million and 900 million, are mostly scattered around the northern parts of China, while Type 2 and Type 3 heritage minorities are mostly from the southern parts of China. Among the forty-two Type 3 minorities, there are five groups with a population of less than 10,000. Without access to mother-tongue education, many of these heritage minorities in Type 3 experience difficulty in maintaining their languages.

4.3   Status of Heritage Languages in China

Throughout the long history of Chinese civilization, minority languages have constituted an important part of the rich Chinese culture heritage. However, with an ever-accelerating rate of economic development in China, these heritage languages, just like many other small languages worldwide,

Table 4.2 *Three types of heritage minorities in China*

Category	Minority Groups	Population	Geographic Distribution
Type 1	Kazakh (哈萨克族)	1,462,588	Xinjing, Gansu, Qinghai
	Korean (朝鲜族)	1,830,929	Jilin, Liaoning, Heilongjiang, Beijing Koreatown
	Mongol (蒙古族)	5,981,849	Inner Mongolia, Liaoning, Jilin, Hebei, Xinjiang, Heilongjian, Qinghai, Henan
	Tibetan (藏族)	6,282,187	Tibet, Qinghai, Sichuan, Gansu, Yunnan
	Uyghur (维吾尔族)	10,069,346	Xinjiang
Type 2	Dai (傣族)	1,261,311	Yunnan
	Jingpo (景颇族)	147,828	Yunnan
	Lahu (拉祜族)	485,966	Yunnan
	Lisu (傈僳族)	702,839	Yunnan, Sichuan
	Miao (苗族)	9,426,007	Guizhou, Hunan, Yunnan, Guangxi, Sichuan, Hainan, Hubei, Guangdong
	Naxi (纳西族)	326,295	Yunnan, Sichuan
	Wa (佤族)	429,709	Yunnan
	Yi (彝族)	8,714,393	Sichuan, Yunnan, Guizhou, Guangxi
Type 3	Achang (阿昌族)	39,555	Yunnan
	Bai (白族)	1,933,510	Yunnan, Guizhou, Hunan
	Blang (布朗族)	119,639	Yunnan
	Bonan (保安族)	20,074	Gansu
	Bouyei (布依族)	2,870,034	Guizhou, Yunnan, Sichuan
	Daur (达斡尔族)	131,992	Inner Mongolia, Heilongjian, Xinjiang
	De'ang (德昂族)	20,556	Yunnan
	Derung (独龙族)	6,930	Yunnan
	Dong (侗族)	2,879,974	Guizhou, Hunan, Guangxi
	Dongxiang (东乡族)	621,500	Gansu, Ningxia, Qinghai, Xinjiang
	Evenki (鄂温克族)	30,875	Inner Mongolia, Heilongjiang
	Gaoshan (高山族)	4,009	Taiwan (population not counted), Fujian
	Gelao (仡佬族)	550,746	Guizhou, Guangxi, Yunnan, Sichuan
	Gin (京族)	28,199	Guangxi
	Hani (哈尼族)	1,660,932	Yunnan
	Hui (回族)	10,586,087	Ningxia, Gansu, Qinghai, Xinjiang, with communities across the country.
	Jino (基诺族)	23,143	Yunnan
	Kyrgyz (柯尔克孜族)	186,708	Xinjiang, Heilongjiang
	Lhoba (珞巴)	3,682	Tibet
	Li (黎族)	1,463,064	Hainan
	Manchu (满族)	10,387,958	Liaoning, Jilin, Heilongjiang, Hebei, Beijing, Inner Mongolia
	Maonan (毛南族)	101,192	Guangxi
	Mongba (门巴族)	10,561	Tibet
	Mulao (仫佬族)	216,257	Guangxi
	Nu (怒族)	37,523	Yunnan
	Oroqen (鄂伦春族)	8,659	Inner Mongolia, Heilongjiang
	Pumi (普米族)	42,861	Yunnan
	Qiang (羌族)	309,576	Sichuan
	Russian (俄罗斯族)	15,393	Xinjiang, Inner Mongolia, Heilongjiang
	Salar (撒拉族)	130,607	Qinghai, Gansu, Xinjiang
	She (畲族)	708,651	Fujian, Zhejiang, Jiangxi, Guangdong, Anhui
	Sui (水族)	411,847	Guizhou, Guangxi
	Tajik (塔吉克族)	51,069	Xinjiang
	Tartar (塔塔尔族)	3,556	Xinjiang
	Tu (土族)	289,565	Qinghai, Gansu
	Tujia (土家族)	8,353,912	Hunan, Hubei, Guizhou, Chongqing
	Uzbek (乌孜别克族)	10,569	Xinjiang
	Wa (佤族)	429,709	Yunnan
	Xibe (锡伯)	190,481	Xinjiang, Liaoning, Jilin
	Yao (瑶族)	2,796,003	Guangxi, Hunan, Yunna, Guangdong, Guizhou
	Yugur (裕固族)	14,378	Gansu
	Zhuang (壮族)	16,926,381	Guangxi, Yunnan, Guangdong, Guizhou, Hunan

Statistics taken from the 6th National Population Census (2010) are facing unprecedented challenges. At least eighty-five of the heritage languages spoken by the 105 million non-Han minorities in China are considered to be endangered (Bradley 2005). Moreover, powerful forces of mandatory use of Putonghua in all public sectors, along with rapid social and demographic changes, all contribute to the decline of many dialects and minority languages. More and more parents are abandoning their native dialects in favor of Putonghua, believing this will give their children better access to education and jobs.

Paradoxically, at the same time, the state has advocated a doctrine of language equality among the classified languages of the officially recognized ethnic groups. Apart from Chinese Putonghua, seven other languages, namely, Mongolian, Tibetan, Uyghur, Kazakh, Korean, Yi, and Zhuang, are granted the right to be used in the major national political conferences.[1] Among these heritage languages, the first five languages are mainly used in the northern parts of China and function as a regional common language. All these languages belong to the Type 1 minority groups, which have their own traditional scripts and enjoy a regular bilingual education since the liberation in 1949. Besides Chinese Putonghua, China's national radio stations broadcast ethnic programs in these five heritage languages on a daily basis. However, as a result of the national promotion of Putonghua and the great impact of economic development, these heritage languages are facing a problem of shrinkage as well. A sampling survey conducted at the end of the last century showed that 60–80 percent of Korean teenagers living in big cities did not speak Korean, and 20–30 percent of those living in the countryside transferred to using Chinese Putonghua as their first language (Xuan 1989). Investigations on Mongolian usage reflected the same trend. The number of ethnic primary schools in Inner Mongolia Autonomous Region had decreased from 4,387 in 1980 to 1,626 in 2001 (Zhou 2015). Tsung's (2014) study in Xinjiang also showed that between 2005 and 2009 student enrolment in Uyghur-instruction primary schools fell from 1,330,065 to 891,977. This trend is also true for other minority groups of this type. Ethnic heritage language instructions are declining steadily under pressure from the national promotion of Putonghua.

Besides the five heritage languages mentioned previously, Yi and Zhuang are also ranked as languages used in major national political conferences. Although having a large population inhabiting the southern parts of China, Yi and Zhuang are not regional common languages but are only used in local communities. With three different scripts (two traditional and one newly created after liberation), respectively, both Yi and Zhuang have many

---

[1] The major national political conferences refer to National congress of the Communist Party of China, National People's Congress, and National People's Political Consultative Conference.

different branches of dialects. Chinese scholars report that 68 percent of Zhuang speak the northern Zhuang dialect, of which there are eight sub-dialects; 32 percent speak the southern Zhuang dialect, of which there are five subdialects (Tsung 2014). Yi, as well, has been recognized by Chinese scholars as having at least six subdialects. These subdialects are all mutually unintelligible, which has impeded their becoming a regional common language. Chinese scholars believe that Zhuang languages in all areas have long been influenced by Chinese. Zhang et al. (1999) state that, when speaking about matters of daily life, the average speaker of Zhuang uses 30–40 percent Chinese loanwords; when speaking about issues of government or economics, the percentage of loanwords rises to 80 percent. Like Type 1 heritage languages, Yi and Zhuang also enjoy equal national status officially. However, literacy practice and mother-tongue instruction in schools are limited compared to the Type 1 minority groups. Although undergoing substantial development since the 1950s, Yi-Han and Zhuang-Han bilingual education implementation is becoming more difficult due to a series of situational and practical reasons. Lacking resources and functional utilities, the literacy practices of Yi and Zhuang languages are mostly confined to political slogans and documents in governments. Even the textbooks in Yi and Zhuang languages are largely translations from mainstream Chinese textbooks. As regard to literacy practice in people's daily lives, Chinese is still their first option (Zhang and Tsung 2019a).

Within other heritage minority languages in China, five more languages (Miao, Buyi, Tong, Hani, and Bai) have over 1 million native speakers and fourteen other languages (Tai, Li, Mian, Lisu, Bunu, Lahu, Wa, Shui, Naxi, Dongxiang, Tujia, Qiang, Kirgiz, Tuzu) have over 100,000 native speakers (Zhou 2015). However, most of these languages are only used in local communities, with little attention paid to their literacy practice. Seven of them lack writing systems, which has made language maintenance especially difficult. Although some of these heritage groups, like Tai, Miao, and Naxi, have had access to bilingual education since the 1980s, opportunities for economic and political expansion of these languages are quite limited in the age of the market economy. In search of a better life, more and more young people leave their hometowns for urban areas and gradually shift their language.

According to UNESCO's *Atlas of the World's Languages in Danger* (Moseley 2010), between the status of safe and extinct, languages can be classified into four levels, namely, vulnerable, definitely endangered, severely endangered, and critically endangered. Among the 144 languages identified by UNESCO in China, 25 are critically endangered, 49 are definitely endangered, 20 are severely endangered, and 41 are vulnerable (Moseley 2010). Sun (2001) also pointed out that in China more than twenty languages are now on the verge of extinction. These languages do not only include languages of small minority groups but also languages of larger ethnic groups, like Manchu, whose population is several million. Now the Manchurian community has only about a dozen elderly native language speakers in Heilongjiang Province. Their own language is retained mostly among these elderly people. The younger generation has shifted to Putonghua. This situation is true for many other minority groups. As Bradley (2001) has observed, in the last millennium many members of minorities in the southwest, including quite a few Yi, have been assimilated into the Chinese population, who speak southwestern Mandarin.

4.4 Protection Measures for Heritage Languages in China

In the last 40 years, we have witnessed the rise of *Putonghua* as a common means of communication: in education, services, employment, media, entertainment, trade, and everyday speech. Its national reach is arguably unprecedented (Tsung 2014). However, languages such as Tibetan, Uyghur, Mongolian, and Zhuang, in spite of having large demographic constituencies, have their status and learning threatened. Some larger minorities have resisted the language challenge inherent in the spread of *Putonghua*, while some minorities have tried to seize the opportunity to protect their heritage. How is China preserving its rich and diversified cultures and languages in its society? What are the government's policies toward heritage languages?

4.4.1 Explicit Policy toward Heritage Languages

For a multiethnic and multilingual country, the Chinese government has one of the best heritage language policies, which advocates a doctrine of language equality among all classified languages of the officially recognized ethnic groups. The Chinese constitution explicitly states that "people of all ethnic groups are equal in the People' Republic of China. The government will guarantee the rights and interests of all minorities, and develop a good relationship between all ethnic groups" (Act 4 of the Constitution of the People's Republic of China 1982). Based on this essential principle, the constitution further stipulates that people of all ethnic groups have the right to use and develop their native language and writing systems. This right to use one's native language is especially guaranteed in ethnic autonomous areas. Act 10 of the Laws of Autonomous Governing of Minority Regions states that "authorities of autonomous minority should guarantee that all ethnic groups are free to use and develop their native languages." Government initiatives to protect minority people and salvage their languages are evident in many of China's policies (Zuo 2007).

Following this general guidance, in the 1950s the central government of China made some efforts to help minority groups without writing systems[2] create their own language scripts, referred to as xinchuang wenzi (newly created scripts). Based on two large-scale investigations undertaken between 1950–1955 and 1956–1959, fourteen Latin alphabetic scripts have been created for ten minority groups in the south, among which Miao has four scripts and Hani has two scripts. Efforts have also been made to help some minority groups modify their existing writing systems, which include Tai, Lahu, and Jingpo in Yunnan, and Uyghur and Kazakh in Xinjiang.

However, the implementation of heritage language scripts has not been successful. Many of the newly created scripts were not welcomed by minority people. For example, the Li did not prefer the Li script at all; they finally decided to use Chinese script instead. Another example is the newly created script for the Yi, which was not accepted by the Yi people. After some work of improvement and standardization, the Yi people picked up the traditional Yi writing system. In 1982, the local government of Xinjiang Uyghur Autonomous Region proclaimed that the traditional Uyghur and Kazakh scripts would be restored due to the impracticality of the new Latin scripts. In 1986 Yunnan also decided to abandon the new Dai in favor of the old Dai script. Lacking domains for these newly created scripts to be used in either private or public contexts, the strategy of script creation has failed.

In 1991, the national congress of China issued *Report on Further Work on Minority Languages*, which pointed out that in the new era the basic principles for minority languages are as follows:

1. Adhere to the principle of equality and safeguard minority people's right to use and develop their own languages;
2. Considering the unity, progress, and prosperity of all ethnic groups, works regarding ethnic heritage languages should adopt the strategy of classified instruction in a cautious and safe way.
3. Language works in the minority areas should serve the all-round area development of political, economic, and cultural undertakings, and promote the socialist modernization of the country.

Until 2013, thirty-two local governments had passed regulations concerning the local heritage languages. A framework legal system regarding the development and protection of heritage languages had been established. Strengthening legal construction, standardization, and digitalization of ethnic heritage languages has become the focus of minority language work in the new era.

---

[2] In some cases, some minority groups have an "old script," which was based on Chinese characters or created by western missionaries. But the "old scripts" were only used in religious domains.

4.4.2 Heritage Languages in Education

Under the guidance of the national explicit language policy, ethnic minorities within the 148 autonomous areas of China enjoy the right to use their own languages. Bilingual education is promoted in many minority areas, including Yunnan, Guangxi, Qinghai, Xinjiang, and Inner Mongolia. Laws and regulations at different levels all seem to guarantee minority children's right to be educated in their own heritage languages (Tsung et al. 2012). For example, Act thirty-seven of the Law of the People's Republic of China on Regional National Autonomy (2001) states that:

> If permitting, schools where the majority of the students are ethnic minority, text books in minority languages should be used and courses should be taught in minority languages. Chinese courses can be offered in the early years or the late years of elementary schools in response to different circumstances in order to spread Putonghua and modern standard Chinese throughout China.

Generally, bilingual education in the compulsory stage in minority areas is carried out following three modes, namely, preservation, transition, or coping (Zhou 2015). With an aim to preserve heritage languages and cultures, schools of the preservation mode are committed to helping students maintain their heritage languages while learning the dominant language. Some of these schools take heritage languages as their instructional language while setting a separate course in Chinese; some take Chinese as their instructional language while setting a separate course in heritage languages; some use heritage language and Chinese as instructional languages for different subjects. Minority groups carrying out preservation in bilingual schools are usually those groups having a common script for their own languages. Due to different circumstances, these bilingual schools adopt different strategies of instruction. Bilingual schools in Inner Mongolia, Xinjiang, Helongjiang, Jilin, Liaoning, Qinhai, and some of the bilingual schools in Tibet, Sichuan, Yunnan, and Guangxi have adopted this mode of bilingual education, covering minority groups of Mongolian, Tibetan, Uyghur, Korean, Kazakh, Zhuang, Yi, etc. Bilingual schools in transitional mode are mainly designed to help minority children who do not speak Chinese in their family situation get accustomed to Chinese instruction in school. Usually, schools of this kind will start with minority language instruction in the early years, and then gradually transition to using both minority language and Chinese at the same time; in the later years of schooling, Chinese will become the only instructional language. As the use of the minority language decreases, Chinese will become more and more important in the child's schooling. Bilingual schools of this kind are generally for minorities who do not have a systematic writing system or whose language scripts are newly created. These minority groups are mainly from south, southwest, or central China, including Wa, Bai, Tai,

Jingpo, and Lisu in Yunnan, and Tong and Miao in Guizhou. In the third kind of bilingual education, coping, bilingual education is actually not implemented in a real sense. Students are educated in Chinese throughout their school years, and heritage languages are only introduced in the last few months before graduation in order to cope with the preferential policy granted to minorities and to save more students from dropping out from school. Heritage languages in these schools are taught at a superficial level. A few minority groups have to take up this mode due to the lack of heritage language teachers and teaching materials.

According to statistics released by the State Council Information Office,[3] there are twenty-one minority groups carrying out mother-tongue or bilingual instruction in more than 10,000 schools in thirteen provinces and autonomous prefectures, using twenty-nine writing scripts and covering a student population of over 6 million. Some areas, such as Mongolia, Jilin, and Xinjiang, have already developed a sound system, whose local bilingual schools can basically meet the needs of minorities; while in some other minority areas, such as Qinghai and Tibet, although the current bilingual school system is already established, it still cannot satisfy local needs and improvement is badly needed; many more minority areas have recently set up experimental sites, which can barely achieve the aim of bilingual education.

Notwithstanding the reality, *Outline of the National Medium- and Long-Term Education Reform and Development (2010–2020)* states that "Bilingual education will be promoted. While Chinese course will be set up to promote the standard common Chinese and Putonghua nationally, minority people's right to be educated in their own heritage languages will be respected and guaranteed." This seemingly preferential policy for the protection of heritage languages and mother-tongue education has encountered many obstacles in the implementation stage. With the overwhelming force of the market economy, heritage bilingual schools have been shrinking remarkably over the last four decades. This trend also applies to groups that boast of having a sound heritage bilingual education system. Take Inner Mongolia, for example; the number of students enrolled in Mongolian primary schools has declined from 283,725 in 1980 to 172,213 in 2001 (Zhou 2015). By 2016, only 449 schools carried out bilingual education, only 15.91 percent of all the schools in the Inner Mongolian region. The number of students enrolled in bilingual schools in 2016 was around 82,900, only 8.63 percent of all students in the Inner Mongolia Region (Sude et al. 2017). Korean schools in the Yanbian Prefecture are also

---

[3] The State Council Information Office (2009): *China's Ethnic Policy and Common Prosperity and Development of All Ethnic Groups*, Retrieved on April 2, 2019 from www.gov.cn/zwgk/2009-09/27/content_1427930.htm

experiencing a similar trend. With more and more Korean teachers moving to big cities, Korean schools in villages are decreasing sharply (Zheng 1999). Nowadays, the situation facing heritage bilingual schools is very serious.

In the last 10 years, the Chinese Government has restated the objectives of bilingual education in Chinese-heritage language in some minority areas. The *Outline of the National Medium- and Long-Term Education Reform and Development Plan (2010–2020)* issued by the Ministry of Education stated that support will be given to teacher training, teaching research, teaching material development, and publication in bilingual teaching. Bilingual education plays an important role in protecting and inheriting heritage language, restraining the decline of heritage languages, reversing language conversion, and protecting endangered languages (Xu 2012). However, the way this policy has been implemented in different regions is to emphasize and promote Chinese language.

4.4.3 Heritage Languages in the Public Sector

As in education, communities are entitled to use heritage languages as official languages in many other social and public sectors. Local government offices, courts, procurator's offices, etc. in minority autonomous areas all use heritage languages. Politically, ever since the first National Peoples' Congress in 1954 there have been simultaneous interpreters for minority representatives. Interpreters of seven heritage languages, namely, Mongolian, Tibetan, Uyghur, Kazakh, Korean, Yi, and Zhuang, are provided in all kinds of important political congresses and activities in national and local governments. The coexistence of heritage languages with standard Chinese can also be found in the seals of ethnic autonomous authorities and organizations, identity cards of minorities, and the names of businesses in ethnic autonomous areas (Zuo 2007). Heritage language versions are provided for important documents, laws, and administrative rules issued by the central government, the State Congress, and various local committees and governments with areas containing multinational populations. As Article 139 of the constitution (2018) states:

> citizens of all ethnic groups are entitled to file suit in their own native language. The people's courts and procuratorates should provide translation for suitors who are not familiar with the common languages. In areas where a minority group lives in a concentrated community or a number of minority groups live together, cases should be tried in the local popular language and all documents concerned with lawsuits including indictments, court verdicts, notices should be written in one or several local popular languages.

In Xinjiang, Language Regulation of Xinjiang Uyghur Autonomous Region (2002) makes it clear that departments of commerce, post and telecommunication, transportation, hospital, finance, tax, industrial and commercial administration, and police should give their staff training in minority languages, ensuring that their staff can serve minority residents in local languages. Moreover, postal departments should help people send and receive mail in minority languages, and financial departments should help minorities make deposits into and borrow money from banks. In Tibet, Regulation for the Learning, Application and Developing of Tibetan in Tibetan Autonomous Region (2002) stipulates that leaders under 45 years old and staff under 40 years old must study Tibetan if they have not mastered the language. When recruiting Tibetan cadres and workers, an adequate educational level in Tibetan should be regarded as necessary. This regulation further points out that in the autonomous region postal departments, banks, and shops that serve local people directly should carry out their business mainly in Tibetan, while also using Chinese. Product names, trademarks, and price tickets in local shops should be bilingual in Tibetan and Chinese. In Inner Mongolia, a similar regulation stipulates that Mongolian and Chinese should both be used for local social life. When serving citizens using Mongolian, public sectors should provide services in Mongolian.

From these examples, it seems that the use of heritage languages in local public sectors is guaranteed by law. However, in reality the effectiveness of the legal protection afforded is limited. In some cases, use of heritage languages is restricted to a very superficial level. By analyzing the linguistic landscape in Liangshan, Zhang and Tsung (2019a) found that the use of Yi in the public space is mainly limited to titles and name plates. All other practical functions of language are realized through Chinese. Language expectations, especially for those small heritage languages, are not optimistic.

4.4.4 Heritage Languages in Publication

Publication in heritage languages in China has passed through three stages since reform in the 1980s, namely, rescue and protection, moving toward market, and public welfare (Zhang 2009). In the last two decades, the Chinese government has adopted a series of measures to support the news and publishing industry in minority languages. Twenty-one publishing houses that can publish in minority languages have been established on top of the previously existing seventeen. The current thirty-eight ethnic publishing houses spread over fourteen provinces can publish in a wide range of heritage minority languages, including Mongolian, Tibetan, Uyghur, Kazakh, Korean, Yi, Zhuang, Xibe, Kirgiz, Tai, Jingpo, Lisu, Wa, Lahu, Hani, Miao, Naxi, Zaiwa, Buyi, Tong, and Man. It is claimed that minority language publications have covered nearly all minority densely inhabited areas. However, among these publications, Mongolian, Tibetan, Uyghur, Kazakh, and Korean make up 97 percent, while other languages only account for 3 percent (Yan and Guo 2004). Until 2007, 5,561 books in minority languages have been published with a circulation of around 644,000. This is double the 1990 figure (Zhou 2015). In 2005, 223 magazines in 10 languages and 99 newspapers in 13 languages were said to have been published (Bai 2018). In a conference held by the Propaganda Department of the Central Committee of the CPC, State Ethnic Affairs Commission and National News Publication Bureau in 1996, a series of special privileges were offered to minority language authors and translators, including no barcode fee, no limit on the use of ISBN, funding to support publication in minority languages, and preferential tax policy. In response to an initiative of the National News Publication Bureau, over 10 million yuan has been raised to support the publication of high quality minority language books. Starting from 2007, a special fund of 30 million yuan per year has been set up by the state finance bureau to support publication in minority languages. However, notwithstanding the great impact of the market economy, the ethnic publication cause has still encountered many difficulties. Because the print circulation of books in minority languages is usually low, few of these publications can make a profit by themselves. Financial aid from government becomes their only investment. Compared with the ever-increasing expense of running a publication operation, the state subsidy is far from enough. Poor economic performance led to the loss of minority language editors, which further increased the difficulties faced by these ethnic publishing houses. Also, as more and more parents choose to enroll their children in Chinese schools, readership of minority languages is shrinking sharply. Thus, due to a lack of readers and profits, few bookstores are willing to engage in the business of minority language books, which, in turn, has further led to the dwindling of publication volume. Take a Mongolian textbook, for example; circulation had decreased from 80,000 in the early 1990s to 37,000 in 2005 (Bai 2007). This vicious circle is hard to break.

4.4.5 Heritage Languages in Mass Media

Founding newspapers, broadcasting companies, and television programs in heritage minority languages is an explicit language policy set by the government to protect minority languages in mass media. The government has issued several rules and regulations to encourage the development of mass media in minority languages (the State Congress 2005, 2009; National Ethnic Committee 2007, 2013), which all emphasize that government will sponsor the press and publishing industries in minority languages and efforts would also be made to support the translation, production, and broadcasting of programs in minority languages. During the past 40 years, mass media in heritage minority languages has made great progress. By the end of the 1990s, there were around 100 newspapers published in 17 minority languages and 73 magazines published in 11 languages in Mainland China (The State Council Information Office of People's Republic of China 1999). Minority languages used in newspapers and magazines include Mongolian, Tibetan, Uyghur, Kazakh, Korean, Yi, Zhuang, Jingpo, Zaiwa, Kirgiz, Xibe, Naxi, Tai, and Lisu. However, more than half of these newspapers and magazines are concentrated in Inner Mongolia and Xinjiang autonomous regions (Zhao 2016). And the majority of them are government bulletins for local CCP committees. In 2009, *Peoples Daily* Tibetan version was published in Lasa, which is the first newspaper in a minority language for the CCP Central Committee. Most of these newspapers are distributed freely through party and state organs.

In addition to newspapers, radio and television broadcasting have also developed substantially in recent decades. Radio programs in Tibetan, Uyghur, Kazak, Mongolian, and Korean have been broadcast by Central People's Broadcasting Station since the 1950s. From 2015, broadcasting times have been extended to 18 hours per day for the first three languages and 9 hours per day for the last two. Now there are more than twenty languages broadcast by over 200 local radio stations and broadcasting rooms (Bai 2012), including Mongolian, Tibetan, Uyghur, Miao, Yi, and Buyi. Benefiting from the Great Western Development Strategy, the broadcasting power of minority languages has been greatly enhanced. A framework of four-level broadcasting, central, provincial, regional, and county, has been established. By 2010, radio and television broadcasting coverage had reached 94.38 percent and 95.511 percent, respectively, in Tibet (Zhao 2016). According to the statistics, by the end of the twentieth century, 10,430 translated movies and TV programs in minority languages had been produced. And more than 3,000 story, documentary, science, and educational films were produced in more than twenty languages (The State Council Information Office of People's Republic of China 1999).

However, entering the new millennium, with the development of internet technology, social media has become more and more popular. The development of websites in minority languages has lagged far behind. According to the *Report on the Development Status and Safety of Websites in China* (Internet Society of China 2016), only a few are in minority languages. Moreover, those websites in minority languages are mainly based on traditional newspapers, radio, and television broadcasting. Although in 2010 news websites in five minority languages, Mongolian, Tibetan, Uyghur, Kazakh, and Korean, were put into operation by the Central People's Broadcasting Station, their influence has been quite limited. However, the popular WeChat account has an instant sound message facility, which allows heritage languages to be recorded for messages.

4.5 Recent Trends and Development for Heritage Languages

4.5.1 Database Construction of Endangered Heritage Languages

Since 2010, China has stepped up efforts to develop audio heritage language files. The Department of Language and Information, Ministry of Education has hosted a Project for the Protection of Language Resources of China. One of its key subprojects, Constructing Chinese Language Audio Database Resources, collects language data using modern information technologies in the hope that language and cultural heritage will be protected in the long run. Related audio or video documents have been processed, by transcribing and marking them, and then classified into storage. Endangered minority languages have been preserved in different databases, websites, museums, language labs, etc., so that in-depth research and effective development and utilization in the future will be possible. At the local level, organizations such as the "Yunnan Minority Language Database," built by Yunnan Minzu University, collect some of the weak and endangered languages in Yunnan. The project, "Construction of Voice Archives of Endangered Languages in Yunnan," hosted by Xu and Bai, has adopted digital voice storage to record and preserve audiovisual materials of various endangered languages in Yunnan, such as Rouruo, Keno, and Sadu.

4.5.2 Protection of Living Heritage Language Use

The protection of current heritage languages and their writing systems is a hot topic in the study of Chinese heritage languages. This concept is based on the living language of intangible cultural heritage.

> 'Living' is the state of language and its writing system. That is to say the spoken and written languages are naturally used in the process of human production and life. 'Protection of living heritage language' is to protect the language that is currently used or endangered, to protect the environment in which the language is used and its survival chain, making it truly and naturally being used by people, and can be passed down from generation to generation. (Luo and Yu 2015)

Xu Xianming (2012) of Yunnan Endangered Language Collection Base advocates that recording the living corpus is "not only to record the language, but also to record the living knowledge and experience carried by the language"; emphasis should be placed on the collection of minority language and cultural materials that can fully reflect the knowledge structures of the traditional culture, such as ethnic language life, ecological environment, social history, religious practices, and so on. Li (2018) believes that it is necessary not only to record the language but also to improve the ecological environment of language use as far as possible, so as to preserve or enhance the vitality of the endangered language. Yang and Yu believe that the geographical environment played a key role in the ecological protection of Yunnan's Pumi language. Based on a case study in Dulong Town and Maguan County in Yunnan Province, Luo and Yu (2015) held that maintaining the scale of ethnic settlements, protecting ethnic culture and traditional customs, and strengthening cross-border ethnic communication and exchange effectively protects and develops the living state of the mother-tongue of endangered ethnic groups. Wu and Wen (2006) believe that the protection of ethnic communities and autonomous regions and the establishment of endangered language protection areas can protect and maintain the survival and development areas of endangered languages.

4.6   Conclusion

As a multiethnic and multilingual country, China's language policy toward its heritage minorities has long adhered to the principle of unity with diversity. On the one hand, the Chinese government has engaged in both corpus and status planning to make Putonghua (common speech, Modern Standard Chinese) the national language for all the ethnic groups of China since the 1950s. The constitution has clearly stated that Putonghua should be promoted nationwide and be used as a common language for interethnic communications. On the other hand, the constitution also guaranteed minorities' freedom to use and develop their own heritage languages. Under the influence of explicit policy and the impact of various social and economic factors, heritage minority languages in China have faced a range of opportunities and challenges.

Within the fifty-five minority groups in China, apart from Hui and Man, which have already adopted Chinese as their communication language, all the other fifty-three minority groups have their own languages for communication. While Chinese Putonghua has seized a dominant position, it is said that heritage languages are protected at different levels. Among these heritage languages, five languages are used as regional common languages, namely, Mongolian, Tibetan, Uyghur, Kazakh, and Korean. With a population of around 24 million, the speakers of these languages are mainly scattered over the northern part of China. With functional writing systems, they are used regularly in various social sectors, education, publication, and mass media. Yi and Zhuang, two heritage languages used in the southern mountainous areas, also have a large population. Although used as official languages in most political conferences at national level, because of their large number of unintelligible dialects, their social functions are greatly limited. According to a UNESCO report, the majority of the other heritage languages in China are now in a status of definitely endangered or critically endangered. Although efforts are being made to protect these heritage languages, their vitality is dwindling as a result of globalization. With China's economic transition to a market economy in recent decades, heritage languages are faced with ever-increasing pressure from the dominant Chinese language. Now, out of consideration for their children's employment prospects and development space, many minority parents choose to send their children to Chinese schools, striking a critical blow to the protection of heritage languages. With more and more minorities becoming bilingual or even monolingual in Chinese, the social functions of these heritage languages are definitely becoming weaker and weaker. There is still a long way to go for the Chinese government at different levels to adopt effective policies to successfully assist minorities to preserve their heritage languages.

References

Bai, L. 2007. Minzu Tushu de Chunban Wenti ji Yingdui Celue [Problems and Solutions for the Publication of Minority Books]. *Journal of Minzu University of China* 2, 140.

Bai, R. 2012. Woguo Shaoshu Minzu Yuyan Guangbo de Lishi Yange, diwei yu Zuoyong [History, Status and Functions of Minority Language Broadcasting in China]. Retrieved on February 22, 2020 from http://media.people.com.cn/n/2012/0926/c349714–19118659.html

Bai, R. 2018. Zhongguo Shaoshu Minzu Wenzi Baokan de Bainian Huiwang [One Hundred Years Introspection on China's Minority Language Newspaper]. Retrieved on March 15, 2020 from http://media.people.com.cn/n1/2018/0806/c420824-30212149.html

Baker, C. and S. P. Jones. 1998. *Encyclopedia of Bilingualism and Bilingual Education*. Clevedon: Multilingual Matters.

Bloomfeld, L. 1967. *Language*. London: Allen & Unwin.

Bradley, D. 2001. Language Policy for the Yi. In S. Harrell (ed.), *Perspectives on the Yi of Southwest China*. Berkeley: University of California Press, 194–198.

Bradley, D. 2005. Sanie and Language Loss in China. *International Journal of the Sociology of Language* 173, 159–176.

Corson, D. 1999. Community-Based Education for Indigenous Cultures. In S. May (ed.), *Indigenous Community-Based Education*. Clevedon: Multilingual Matters, 8–19.

Crystal, D. 1987. *The Cambridge Encyclopedia of Language*. Cambridge: Cambridge University Press.

Dai, Q. 1994. *Yuyan he Minzu [Language and Ethnicity]*. Beijing: Zhongyang Minzu Daxue Chubanshe (The Central University for Nationalities Press).

Fishman, J. 2001. 300-Plus Years of Heritage Language Education in the United States. In J. K. Peyton, D. A. Ranard, and S. McGinnis (eds.), *Heritage Languages in America: Preserving a National Resource*. Washington, DC and McHenry, IL: Center for Applied Linguistics & Delta Systems, 81–89.

García, O. 2014. U.S. Spanish and Education: Global and Local Intersections. *Language Policy, Politics, and Diversity in Education: Review of Research in Education* 38(1), 58–80.

Hornberger, N. H. 2005. Opening and Filling Up Implementational and Ideological Spaces in Heritage Language Education. *Modern Language Journal* 89, 605–612.

Internet Society of China. 2016. Zhongguo Hulianwang Fazhan Zhuangkuang jiqi Anquan Baogao [Report on the Development Status and Safety of Websites in China]. Retrieved on March 15, 2020 from www.isc.org.cn/zxzx/ywsd/listinfo-33676.html

Li, Y. 2018. Languages Pave the Road for the Belt and Road Project, *Guangming Newspaper*, August 12, 2018.

Luo, J. and J. Yu. 2015. Protections of The Living Minority Languages and Bilingual Harmonious Town Construction: A Case Study of Dulong Village, Maguan County, Yunnan. *China Social Sciences*.

Ma, X. 1954. Zhongguo Shaoshu Minzu Yuyan [Minority Languages of China], Zhongguo Jianshe [China Reconstructs], 37–41.

Modood, T. and S. May. 2001. Multiculturalism and Education in Britain: An Internally Contested Debate. *International Journal of Educational Research* 35, 305–317.

Moseley, Christopher (ed.) 2010. *Atlas of the World's Languages in Danger*, 3rd ed. Paris: UNESCO Publishing. Online version: www.unesco.org/culture/en/endangeredlanguages/atlas

Ramsey, R. S. 1987. *Languages of China*. Princeton, NJ: Princeton University Press.

State Language Commission. 1995. *Yuyan Wenzi Gongzuo Baiti (100 Questions in Language Orthography Work)*. Beijing: Yuwen Chubanshe.

Sude, B., M. Yuan, Z. Chen, and J. Zhang. 2017. Neimenggu shuangyu jiaoyu fazhan xianzhuang, wenti yu jianyi [Bilingual Education in Inner Mongolia: Development, Problems and Suggestion]. Zhongguo Minzu Jiaoyu Fazhan Baogao [Report on Minority Education in China]. Retrieved on March 3, 2020 from www.pishu.com.cn/skwx_ps/initDatabaseDetail?contentId=9413507&siteId=14&contentType=literature

Sun, H. 2001. Guanyu Binwei Yuyan Wenti [Concerning the Problem of Endangered Languages]. *Yuyan Jiaoxue yu Yanjiu [Language Education and Research]* 1, 1–7.

The State Council Information Office of People's Republic of China. 1999. Zhongguo de Shaoshu Minzu Zhengce jiqi Shijian [China's Minority Policy and Its Practice]. Retrieved on March 3, 2020 from www.scio.gov.cn/zfbps/ndhf/1999/Document/307953/307953.htm

Tsung, L., G. Wang and Q. Zhang. 2012. Bilingual Education in China: The Case of Yunnan. In G. H. Beckett and G. A. Postiglione (eds.), *China's Assimilationist Language Policy: The Impact on Indigenous/Minority Literacy and Social Harmony*, Abingdon, Oxfordshire: Routledge imprint of Taylor & Francis, 105–120.

Tsung, L. 2014. *Language Power and Hierarchy: Multilingual Education in China*. London: Bloomsbury Publishing Plc.

Wiley, T. G. 2001. On Defining Heritage Languages and Their Speakers. In J. K. Peyton, D. A. Ranard, and S. McGinnis (eds.), *Heritage Languages in*

America: Preserving a National Resource. Washington, DC and McHenry, IL: Center for Applied Linguistics & Delta Systems, 29–36.

Wu, Z. and J. Wen. 2006. The Studies of the Endangered Languages during the Recent 20 Years in China, *Zhangjiang Xueshu*, 3.

Xu, X. 2012. Bilingual Education of the Effect of Protection for Minority Languages. *The Journal of Yuxi Teachers University*, 5.

Xuan, W. 1989. Woguo Chaoxianzu Shuangyu Shiyong Qingkuang Qianxi [Analysis of Bilingualism of China's Korean]. *Minzu Yuwen [Ethnic Language]* 5, 45–48.

Yan, H. and J. Guo. 2004. Woguo Minzu Wenzi Tushu de Chuban Zhuangkuang jiqi Shoucang Fenxi [Analysis of the Publication and Collecting of Ethnic Minority Language Books in China]. *Tushuguan kan [Journal of Library]* 2, 41.

Yang, J. 2005. English as a Third Language among China's Ethnic Minorities. *International Journal of Bilingual Education and Bilingualism* 8(6), 552–567.

Yeung, Y. S., H. W. Marsh, and R. Suliman. 2000. Can Two Tongues Live in Harmony: Analysis of the National Education Longitudinal Study of 1988 (NELS88) Longitudinal Data on the Maintenance of Home Language. *American Educational Research Journal* 37(4), 1001–1026.

Zhang, J., M. Liang, J. Ouyang, Y. Zheng, X. Li, and J. Xie. 1999. *Zhuangyu Fangyan Yanjiu [Zhuang Dialect Research]. Zhongguo Shaoshu Minzu Yuyan Fangyan Yanjiu Congshu [Chinese Minority Language Dialect Research Series]*. Chengdu: Sichuan Ethnic Publishing House.

Zhang, L. and Tsung, L. 2019a. *Bilingual Education and Minority Language Maintenance in China: The Role of Schools in Saving the Yi Language*. Switzerland: Springer.

Zhang, L. and Tsung, L. 2019b. Tibetan Bilingual Education in Qinghai: Government Policy vs Family Language Practice. *International Journal of Bilingual Education and Bilingualism* 22(3), 290–302.

Zhang, Y. 2009. "Gongyixing Dingwei" Cu Minwen Chuban Kuaishu Fazhan [Public Welfare Orientation for the Fast Development of Minority Language Publication]. *Zhongguo Xinwen Chuban Bao [China's News Publication Newspaper]*.

Zhao, L. 2016. Shaoshu Minzu Yuyan Meiti de Fazhan yu Huoli: Falü yu Zhengce de shijiao [Development and Vitality of Minority Language Media: From the Perspective of Law and Policy]. *Zhongguo Guangbo Dianshi Xuekan [China Radio and TV Academic Journal]* 10, 66–68.

Zheng, X. 1999. Zhongguo Chaoxian Renkou Liudong de Zhongda Yingxiang ji Duice [The Great Impact of Population Mobility of Koreans in China and the Countermeasures]. *Journal of Yanbiao University* 3, 69.

Zhou, Q. 2015. *Yuyan Shenghuo yu Yuyan Zhengce: Zhongguo Shaoshu Minzu Yanjiu [Language Life and Language Policy: Studies on China's Ethnic Minorities]*. Beijing: Social Science Publishing House.

Zuo, X. 2007. China's Policy towards Minority Languages in a Globalising Age. *Transnational Curriculum Inquiry* 4 (1), http://nitinat.library.ubc.ca/ojs/index.php/tci

5

Heritage Languages in Japan and Korea

Hyun-Sook Kang and James Hye Suk Yoon

5.1 Introduction

This chapter examines heritage languages in Japan and Korea, two East Asian countries with relatively strict immigration policies. Historically, Japan and Korea have been migrant-sending countries with national discourses centered on monolingual, ethnically homogeneous national identities (see Watson 2012; Fujita-Round and Maher 2017). Due to a significant increase in transnational mobility, migration, and marriage-based immigration in East Asia and around the globe, however, a growing number of foreigners have come to reside in Japan and Korea for various personal and professional reasons. These countries have since made attempts to accommodate the demographic and societal shifts associated with these global trends and to address the looming domestic challenges of historically low birth rates, aging populations, and labor shortages (see Kim and Oh 2012 for a comparative review).

Drawing on existing scholarship on heritage languages and heritage language speakers, this chapter aims to situate these developments in the context of the emerging discourses on multilingualism in Japan and Korea. Debunking the myths of monolingualism and ethnically pure national identities that were largely imposed by central governments, the chapter illuminates the linguistic and cultural diversity of these countries. After discussing Japan's indigenous languages, which include Ainu and Ryukyuan, it categorizes the heritage languages of modern-day Japan as those of *oldcomers* (arrivals during World War II) and those of *newcomers* (arrivals after Japan's economic boom in the 1980s) (see Chapman 2006; Kirkpatrick and Liddicoat 2017 for more details).

Geographically proximate and historically intertwined, Japan and Korea exhibit comparable shifts in demographic composition and cultural and linguistic diversity. Despite the state-sanctioned discourse emphasizing its linguistic and ethnic homogeneity, Korean history is characterized by a degree of ethnic and linguistic diversity, such as the presence of ethnic Chinese residents on the Korean Peninsula (called *hwagyo*). More recently, the Korean government has opened the country's doors to migrant workers and marriage migrants to address the domestic needs and challenges associated with low birth rates, labor shortage, and a disproportionate sex ratio (i.e., the population's ratio of males to females), to name only a few.

Following a descriptive account of the chronological and cultural shifts in the emergence and maintenance of heritage languages in Japan and Korea, the chapter discusses the typological similarity of the Japanese and Korean languages and the effect of that similarity on the maintenance (or loss) of heritage Japanese in Korea and heritage Korean in Japan. Finally, areas of future research in this context are discussed to address theoretical and practical concerns in relation to geopolitics and cultural history in the Far East.

5.2   (Re)Defining Heritage Languages in Japan and Korea

The term, *heritage language* has widely been understood to refer to languages other than the dominant societal language(s) in multi-ethnic and multicultural countries, such as Australia, Canada, the United States, and many European countries. While a heritage language is often associated with the language used in home settings during familial interaction, some scholars take a broader approach, suggesting that a heritage language can be identified as any language, other than a society's official or dominant language, that has personal associations and relevance (Van Deusen-Scholl 2003; King and Ennser-Kananen 2012). Fishman (2001), for instance, identifies three categories of heritage languages: (1) languages spoken by indigenous peoples (e.g., Cherokee in the United States or Inuktitut in Canada), (2) colonial languages (e.g., Dutch or German in the United States), and (3) immigrant and refugee languages (e.g., Spanish or Vietnamese in the United States). These categories of heritage languages, taken together, suggest that, despite family histories and personal connections, a heritage language may not necessarily be a language used on a daily basis in the home and the immediate community. As Van Deusen-Scholl (2003) notes, "The linguistic evidence of that connection may have been lost for generations" (233).

Along with the term *heritage language*, a number of labels have been proposed to describe the diversity of linkages between a language and its speakers. Among them are *primary language*, *home language*, *native language*, and *mother tongue*, which imply "some level of past or current proficiency in the language," as well as labels such as *minority language, indigenous language, immigrant language*, and *ethnic language*, which are "loaded with sociopolitical implications" (Lee and Wright 2014: 139). Despite the varied merits of these terms, *heritage language* has typically been considered to be more inclusive and neutral than the other labels because it embraces speakers of the language who have heritage motivation but little or no fluency in it as well as those who have regular contact with the language and its speakers in the community. For the purposes of this chapter, therefore, we use the term *heritage language* to include the full spectrum of competencies in, and connections to, those languages that are influenced by (im)migration patterns and settlements in Japan and Korea, countries often regarded as linguistically and culturally homogenous in official government discourses.

5.3 (Re)Defining Heritage Language Speakers in Japan and Korea

In line with the multifaceted nature of the term *heritage language*, the related term *heritage language speaker* has gained much traction in the fields of linguistics, language acquisition, and other related disciplines. A relatively narrow definition that is widely accepted in linguistic and language education research on heritage languages identifies heritage language speakers as individuals who were raised in homes in which a language other than the societal language was spoken, typically possessing some degree of bilingualism in the heritage language and the dominant societal language (Valdés 2005). In this view, a heritage language speaker may grow up in an immigrant household, often undergoing a shift from their first language to the dominant language of their host society. The acquisition of the heritage language may take place prior to, or synchronously with, the mastery of the societal language, which in turn may lead to imbalanced bilingualism, generally in favor of the societal language. An emerging and robust body of literature has revealed the linguistic needs and characteristics of heritage language speakers, whose developmental trajectories and outcomes usually differ from those of adult second language learners (see Montrul 2010 for a review). It has further been reported that heritage language speakers' grammars manifest simplification processes often observed in language contact contexts as well as forms that diverge from those used by native speakers of either the heritage or the societal language.

Because of the differences between heritage language speakers and adult second language learners and the wide variability within the heritage language speaker population, many concerns have been raised regarding how to accommodate the needs and challenges that are typical of heritage language speakers (see Lee and Wright 2014 for a review), among which is the mismatch between "age-developmental" and "proficiency-level" needs that is often observed in heritage language speakers (Lee and Wright 2014). It is not uncommon, for instance, for a first-grader to exhibit a more expansive lexicon and complex grammar in the heritage language than a fifth grader or older person from the same household. The traditional criteria of learner profiles, such as age and proficiency, cannot capture the varied characteristics unique to heritage language speakers.

As Hornberger and Wang (2008) note, it is important to consider how speakers perceive themselves and their relationship to the heritage language in addition to examining linguistic proficiency and family connections. This necessitates moving beyond the narrow definition of the term *heritage language speaker* given by researchers, educators, and administrators to a group of students for the purpose of categorizing individual students in classrooms and programs (Leeman 2015). This chapter therefore employs the term *heritage language speaker* to describe individuals with heritage connections and motivations who may or may not have productive skills in the language in question as well as users who have regular contact with the language and its speakers in familial, community, and sometimes professional situations. In line with the way Tsung and Zhang (this volume) considered the historical, cultural, and policy issues in describing heritage languages in China, we drew on research ranging from those dealing with the contributions of immigrant history and policy to the emergence, teaching, and maintenance of heritage languages in Japan and Korea.

5.4   Heritage Languages in Japan: An Overview

Japan has long been perceived as linguistically and culturally homogeneous despite the presence of indigenous minorities (such as the Ainu, the Burakumin, and the Ryukyu Islanders) and various waves of immigrants over time. Although Japanese society is intrinsically diverse, *Nihonjinron* (the thesis of Japanese identity) has undergirded governmental attempts to construct and enforce the unique ideology of a monolithic Japanese national identity, which privileges the main island of Honshu and its Yamato people as the sole representative of Japanese identity (Liddicoat 2007). This ideology of Japanese identity has a strong linguistic component in which the Japanese language is perceived to play a pivotal part in the manifestation of that identity's distinctiveness (Maeda 2003). In other words, the Japanese language contributes to the unique character of the Japanese people due to the close linkages between the language and Japanese identity within *Nihonjinron* discourse.

This ideological position, which espouses a mono-ethnic state and a uniform identity, has led to a policy of assimilating indigenous linguistic minorities, such as the Ainu and the Ryukyu Islanders, into the dominant Yamato group of the main island (see DeChicchis 1995 for the revitalization of the Ainu language; Heinrich 2004 for language retention and shifting in the Ryukyu Islands.) A top-down, assimilationist approach is also observed when it comes to dealing with immigrant groups. Scholars working on this topic (Mori 1997; Chapman 2006; Kirkpatrick and Liddicoat 2017) have categorized the immigrant population into two main groups: (1) *oldcomers* (who arrived in Japan prior to the end of World War II) and (2) *newcomers* (who immigrated to Japan after approximately 1980). The former group largely comprises Chinese and Korean migrants, who often arrived as colonial subjects of the former Japanese Empire, while the latter includes migrant workers and marriage immigrants from South East Asian countries, ethnic Japanese returnees from South America and China, and a new wave of immigrants from China and Korea. The patterns of language maintenance, education, and language shift vary among speakers of indigenous languages, oldcomers, and more recent immigrants in Japanese society.

5.4.1 Indigenous Languages in Japan

The myth of an ethnically homogeneous Japanese identity arose primarily during the emergence of the modern Japanese state after the Meiji Restoration of 1868 (Fujita-Round and Maher 2017). It was during the process of building a nation state that Japan's ideologies of identity were constructed. The core element of that ideology is *Nihonjinron*, which argues that Japan is ethnically, linguistically, and culturally homogeneous (Liddicoat 2007). Intent on nation building and nationalism, a new Japanese government adopted a standard dialect because it was deemed essential to establish a national language. Noteworthy is that the Japanese people, in this homogeneity, comprise members of the Yamato race, which relegated indigenous minorities to the status of ethnic minority groups. Since the mid-eighteenth century, the Japanese government has paid little attention to these ethnic minorities and their languages, which have been overshadowed by the centralist approach of standardization, distinctiveness, and homogeneity.

As a result of globalization and demographic shifts in recent years, however, the treatment of ethnic minorities and their languages and cultures by the Japanese government and public has evolved. The *Atlas of the World's Languages in Danger* (Moseley 2010) lists eight languages in Japan: five definitely endangered (Hachijo, Amami, Kunigami, Okinawan, and Miyako), two severely endangered (Yaeyama and Yonaguni), and one critically endangered (Ainu). The seven languages other than Ainu are considered dialects of the Japanese language, while Ainu is categorized as a distinct language from Japanese (Yotsumoto 2019). In what follows, the cases of Ainu and Okinawan (also known as Ryukyuan in scholarly circles) are described, with an emphasis on language shift and revitalization in relation to history and policy in Japan and beyond.

Historically, the Ainu are residents of Hokkaido, the Kuril Islands, and Sakhalin. Government surveys report 25,000 Ainu living in Japan, but varying sources claim that there may be up to 200,000. It has been reported that the Ainu culture was established around the twelfth and thirteenth centuries and that trade between the Ainu and the mainstream Japanese (*Wajin*) began around the thirteenth and fourteenth centuries (Yotsumoto 2019). The historical relations between the Ainu and Japan's governments may be summarized as an asymmetric trade system in which Japan was interested in exploiting the resources of the Ainu (DeChicchis 1995). During the Meiji era, when soldiers and mainstream Japanese (*Wajin*) immigrants moved to Hokkaido to develop and guard the expanded territory, the Ainu experienced a displacement, and their language and culture were suppressed. For instance, the medium of instruction in formal schools became Japanese, reflecting Japan's policy of assimilating the Ainu during the Meiji period, which eventually led to Ainu being classified as a critically endangered language, only one step before extinction in the list of the *Atlas of the World's Languages in Danger* (Moseley 2010).

Supported by international organizations and initiatives in the 1990s, such as the United Nations' declaration on language rights in 1993 (the International Year of the World's Indigenous Peoples), indigenous Ainu has gained ground in language retention efforts. Universities and community groups began to offer Ainu language classes, and, by 2010, classes funded by the Japanese government were offered in fourteen locations across Hokkaido. Nonetheless, it has been reported that the Ainu people themselves have ceased using the Ainu language in daily life and ceased passing it down to their children, leading *Ethnologue* to categorize it as nearly extinct. It has further been noted that Ainu living outside Hokkaido tend to break away from Ainu communities and instead adopt mainstream Japanese (*Wajin*) lifestyles when they move to cities in Honshu, the main island of Japan. Considering the relatively small size of the Ainu population (0.003 percent of the population in Hokkaido and 0.0001 percent of the population in Japan) and the absence of geographic locations where Ainu are concentrated, it may be impossible to revive the use of the Ainu language in daily life. As Yotsumoto (2019) notes, the only realistic hope of maintaining Ainu may be to continue to expand language course offerings not only for ethnic Ainu but also for mainstream Japanese speakers in connection with the Ainu cultural heritage, such as music and dance.

While Ainu has been viewed as genetically unrelated to Japanese, Ryukyuan and other varieties, spoken in the Okinawa prefecture, have long been considered as historically related to Japanese (Yotsumoto 2019). More recently, Ryukyuan has been treated as a sister language to Japanese while forming a branch of its own (Fujita-Round and Maher 2017). Although Ryukyuan and Japanese share the same parent language, the languages diverged by the seventh century, when the first written evidence is available (Heinrich 2004). What is labeled as Ryukyuan comprises five distinct vernacular language varieties that are spoken in the Ryukyu Islands: Amami-Oshima, Okinawa, Miyako, Yaeyama, and Yonaguni (from north to south). None of these language varieties is mutually intelligible with Standard Japanese. In the Meiji era (1868–1912), a language variety called Okinawan Japanese emerged as a result of increased contact between Ryukyuan and Standard Japanese. The contact variety, perceived as the use of unnatural expressions in Standard Japanese, has undergone phases of "correction" as part of language-planning activities throughout the twentieth century.

The decline of Ryukyuan is intimately linked to the history of Japan. In particular, the return of the islands to Japan from US control in 1972 marks the turning point in the acceleration of the decline of Ryukyuan. While Standard Japanese is employed in the public domain, such as mass media, public signs, and as the medium of instruction in the Ryukyuan school system, Ryukyuan plays no official part in public education. In fact, the use of Ryukyuan has been discouraged in the classroom, as illustrated by the "dialect tag" worn by the student in class who most recently used a "dialect" (Dubinsky and Davis 2013: 5). Thanks to the enhanced awareness of language endangerment through the efforts of international organizations and initiatives, attitudes toward the Ryukyuan varieties are changing, but there is no official policy to integrate Ryukyuan languages into the formal schooling system in the Ryukyuan Islands or anywhere else in Japan.

5.4.2   Languages of the Oldcomers

The so-called oldcomer immigrants are predominantly composed of ethnic Koreans and Chinese who are descended from those who first came to Japan during the period of Japan's colonization of East Asia. In this section, we discuss the Korean and Chinese oldcomer immigrants separately.

Oldcomer Korean immigrants are the descendants of those who moved to or were forcefully relocated to Japan as workers and conscripts starting from Japan's annexation of Korea in 1910 through the end of the World War II in 1945 and prior to the establishment of diplomatic relations between Korea and Japan in 1965. Though many Koreans were repatriated after the end of the war, enough chose to stay to make ethnic Koreans the largest group of postwar immigrants in Japan until recently, when the number of Chinese came to exceed that of Koreans. Current oldcomers are mostly second- and third-generation descendants of the original group, although there are a few first and fourth generations among the oldcomers as well. Oldcomers are divided into two groups that identify politically with North Korea (*Cochongnyen*) and South Korea (*Mindan*), respectively. The year 1965 is used as a conventional date to demarcate the new from the old-comers, but in fact the majority of the newer immigrants arrived after 1980. This group comprises primarily first- and second-generation immi-grants. *Zainichi* ("residing in Japan") *Korean*, or simply *zainichi*, is one of the terms used to refer to ethnic Korean residents of Japan, primarily with respect to the oldcomer group. A 2013 Japanese government survey of oldcomer Koreans in Japan (cited in Lee 2017) estimates that there are around 680,000 people in this group, of whom roughly 540,000 retain citizenship in North or South Korea but have a special residency status in Japan. Another 330,000 have become naturalized Japanese citizens. A South Korean government survey of ethnic Koreans living abroad in the same year found a total of approximately 900,000 ethnic Koreans residing in Japan. These numbers indicate that the majority of ethnic Korean residents in Japan are still oldcomers.

There are interconnected issues of ethnicity, identity, nationality, and assimilation among the oldcomer *zainichi* population (see Chapman 2006 for an illuminating discussion). The complications stem from the dominant societal discourse in Japan (as well as among the *zainichi* population) that equates ethnicity with nationality, which are inextricably linked to the history of the forced annexation of Korea by Japan, when ethnic Koreans were forced to adopt Japanese names (a policy known as *chang-ssi-kay-myeng*). The choice between living as a marginalized, non-naturalized *zaini-chi* and choosing to be a naturalized Japanese is often viewed as a choice between maintaining and giving up one's ethnic identity. Until recently, barriers to naturalization were high in Japan, and the practice, only recently abandoned, of requiring a Japanese name as part of the naturaliza-tion process must have acted as a powerful deterrent to naturalization for many *zainichi*, in light of the historical background of the forced imposition of Japanese names during the colonial period. Nevertheless, there are those who view naturalization as compatible with the maintenance of Korean ethnic identity and advocate this path as a step to changing the dominant discourse that identifies nationality with ethnicity in mainstream Japanese society (Chapman 2006 and reference cited therein).

Understandably, the use of and attitudes toward the teaching and main-tenance of the Korean language vary among members of the oldcomer *zainichi* group. Because language is perhaps the strongest signifier of ethnic identity, both political camps of *zainichi* have established schools where the

Korean language is taught. Jo (2002) reports that in a 1985 survey there were 185 institutions, ranging from elementary to high school, which were run by *zainichi* groups, enrolling roughly 15 percent of school-age ethnic Korean children. But even in these schools, the proportion of classes dedicated to Korean language instruction is rather low, and there is a dearth of quality pedagogical materials. There are also some surveys of language use and attitudes among oldcomers that have found, not surprisingly, both language competency and the desire to maintain the Korean language declining through successive generations of oldcomers when compared to first-generation newcomers (Yim 2013; Lee 2017). Though the maintenance and use of Korean as an ethnic signifier seems stronger among *zainichi* Koreans than in other immigrant groups, such as Korean Americans, among whom the community language (English) usually displaces Korean as the dominant language within a generation, there are inevitable changes in attitudes toward Korean in succeeding generations.

Korean spoken as a heritage language among the oldcomer *zainichi* population displays the usual traits of language contact, such as simplification due to dominant language transfer and the emergence of contact-induced grammatical structures. Based on conversations between the researcher and Korean residents in Japan, Kim (1994), for example, illustrated coding-switching patterns. Among them are the use of the Korean verbalizer *hata*, preceded by Japanese verbal nouns, adjectives, or idiomatic expressions (e.g., *ashitsuke hay-poseyo* [the expression "to season" in Japanese followed by the Korean verbalizer *hata*]), or the use of Japanese verbalizer *suru* after Korean nouns or verbs (e.g., *siksa-suru* ["meal" in Korean plus Japanese verbalizer] and *nwunchi pwa-suru* [the Korean expression "be watchful" plus the Japanese verbalizer]). When compared to the large body of research on heritage Korean among the Korean diaspora in North America (see Kim et al. 2010; Kang 2013, 2015), relatively little work has been done on the linguistic aspects of heritage Korean in Japan. Another obstacle is that the few scholars who work on heritage Korean in Japan tend to publish in venues and in languages (Korean, Japanese) that are not accessible to a wider audience. Sohn (2018) reports an attempt to build a corpus of spoken heritage Korean in Japan, which is a promising development.

5.4.3   Languages of the Newcomers

While Chinese and Korean immigrants comprised the majority of oldcomers, ethnic Japanese who have moved back to Japan from Asia or South America (particularly speakers of Portuguese as the dominant society language) constitute a significant portion of the newcomer population, though the group also includes an increasing number of non-Japanese migrants. Unlike the oldcomer generation, who were forced to move to Japan during the Japanese colonial occupation, the newcomer migrants typically came to Japan for better economic and educational opportunities in the 1980s, when the Japanese economy thrived under the moniker of the "bubble economy." This economic upturn attracted workers to the so-called *san-K* (3-K) jobs that were considered to be of low status, especially in the construction industry. 3-K stands for the following: difficult (*kitsui*), dirty (*kitanai*), and dangerous (*kiken*). A 2014 survey by the Japanese Ministry of Education reports that 29,198 foreign national children in public schools were in need of Japanese language support, showing a significant increase from 19,678 children in 2004 (cited in Fujita-Round and Maher 2017). It was further reported that, in 2014, the first languages of these children were Portuguese (8,340), Chinese (6,410), Filipino (5,153), and Spanish (3,576), respectively.

Despite the recent demographic shifts in Japan, few policies are in place when it comes to accommodating the academic challenges encountered by immigrant children, such as high dropout rates and difficulties with acquiring Japanese (Kirkpatrick and Liddicoat 2017). Existing educational policies are focused mostly on programs for teaching Japanese as a second language, with little attention to the maintenance of heritage languages of immigrants and their children. The only exception is for students of Brazilian origin, whose language classes are subsidized by the Brazilian government. As of 2015, forty-four Portuguese language schools were operated by the Brazilian government with the support of the Japanese government. Of note is that the Brazilian schools, like other ethnic schools in Japan, are not accredited by the Ministry of Education because the use of the Ministry's curriculum, with Japanese as the medium of instruction, is required for private schools to be accredited. This suggests that minority/heritage languages are perceived as being outside the realm of the formal education system in Japan.

In addition to ethnic Japanese returnees, a new wave of Chinese and Korean students and temporary workers came to Japan for economic and educational opportunities in the 1980s, some of whom stayed in Japan (Maher 1997; Fujita-Round and Maher 2017). With regard to the use and retention of heritage languages, these so-called newcomers tended to exhibit perspectives and ideologies that differ from those of the oldcomers who were forced to move to Japan (see Maher 1997 for Chinese, Yim 2013 for Korean, and Kanno 2004 for a comparative perspective on the interplay of bilingualism and student identities shaped by school practices). Thanks to the enhanced stature of countries of origin in the global economy, there is an expressed desire among newer immigrants from these countries to pass down some working knowledge of the heritage language while making efforts to advance in the Japanese system, even among those with no plans to return to their countries of origin.

5.5   Heritage Languages in Korea: An Overview

Notwithstanding the fact that there was a fair share of foreign residents on the peninsula since the early 1880s, Korea has regarded itself as a monolingual and mono-cultural country, an attitude largely derived from ethnic nationalism rooted in the ideal of "five thousand years (of history) as one nation" (Kim and Kang 2007; Park 2014). This section presents an overview of chronological shifts in immigration and settlement patterns in the Korean peninsula, with an emphasis on immigrants' languages and linguistic behaviors. It will first offer a brief overview of ethnic Chinese immigrants and their settlement patterns, which were sometimes resonant with, but at other times at odds with, Korea as a receiving country. Next, recent waves of immigrants and their languages and linguistic settlements will be discussed in relation to linguistic and societal accommodations on the part of the host country.

5.5.1   Hwagyo: Long-term Chinese Immigrants in Korea

Scholars like Kim, Lee, Lee, and Kim (2017) use the term *hwagyo* (*kakyo* in Japanese) to refer only to the original Chinese immigrants who migrated to Korea prior to 1992 and their descendants. The year 1992 is when the Peoples' Republic of China and the Republic of Korea re-established diplomatic relations after a hiatus of several decades. This resulted in an influx of Chinese and ethnic Korean Chinese into (South) Korea, whose numbers now dwarf those of the original *hwagyo* and their descendants. Our discussion of *hwagyo* is restricted to the former group.

The arrival of Chinese merchants on the Korean peninsula dates back to the 1880s, and by the mid-1940s, more than 80,000 Chinese had settled in Korea, most of whom were from Shan-Tung province (Yang and Yeo 2011). Following the liberation of Korea from Japanese rule in 1945, however, the number of *hwagyo* underwent a significant decline. One factor that contributed to the decline is political. The democratic Korean government established in 1945 and the communist Chinese government established in 1949 severed diplomatic relations. Not only did this cut off the flow of migration from China but also resulted in the *hwagyo* in Korea giving up their Chinese citizenship and adopting Taiwanese citizenship instead, even though Taiwan was not the place of origin for the majority of *hwagyo* (Kim et al. 2017). Thus, the current *hwagyo* consist mostly of second- and third-generation descendants of those who came to Korea prior to 1949. Another factor that contributed to the reduction of the *hwagyo* population is the policy enacted by the newly established Korean government to restrict the economic activities of the *hwagyo* (Yeo 2013). These factors contributed to the continued decline of the population and pushed many *hwagyo* to seek immigration to other countries, notably, the United States. Various policies of discrimination and isolation of the *hwagyo* continued through the early 1990s and were reversed only with the dawn of the new era of "multiculturalism," necessitated by economic pressures to bring in migrant workers to fill emerging gaps in the labor force.

As a result of discrimination and societal isolation, *hwagyo* came to constitute a close-knit community, with relatively low rates of marriage outside the group and with their identity anchored on cultural and educational institutions that served to perpetuate and safeguard their cultural and linguistic heritage. As a result, a majority of *hwagyo* children attend *hwagyo* schools, which offer bilingual education. Many of these schools are not accredited by the Korean government, which constitutes an obstacle for those graduating from them to enter Korean universities. The curriculum at *hwagyo* high schools is structured to allow students to choose between tracks geared toward Korean universities or Chinese universities, primarily those in Taiwan in the case of the latter. Many *hwagyo* spend summers, if not longer, with relatives in Taiwan or China, which has a facilitative effect on their linguistic and cultural skills. Like oldcomer Korean residents in Japan, and perhaps more so, the *hwagyo* identity molded by discrimination and isolation has contributed to the maintenance of Chinese in the community through the generations.

The linguistic repertoire of *hwagyo* includes heritage Chinese, Korean, as well as a code-mixed variety with structural modifications of both the host and the target language (*hwagyo-e*, "hwagyo speak") that some consider a unique signature of *hwagyo* linguistic identity (Kim 2017). There are a few studies that have examined the changes in the heritage Chinese varieties spoken by *hwagyo* (Eom et al. 1997 on the simplification of the phonological inventory). A number of publications examine language use, including code-mixing among the *hwagyo* (Son and Seo 2008; Kim 2017). Son and Seo (2008), for instance, analyzed naturally occurring conversations between two friends in their twenties who had been exposed to both Chinese and Korean while growing up in mixed ethnic households in Korea. Among the code-switching patterns identified were the insertion of Chinese words (e.g., proper nouns and common nouns) and phrases (e.g., idiomatic expressions) in Korean matrix sentences, using the Korean verbalizer *hata* or the copula *ita* in code-switched utterances, and the switch from Korean to Chinese to emphasize a speaker's emotive attitudes, indicate topic shift, or clarify a speaker's intent (e.g., a joke). Several studies have further examined language use and attitudes in the *hwagyo* community, mostly based on qualitative interviews (Yeo 2013). The maintenance of Chinese as a heritage language across generations for the *hwagyo* is more successful and somewhat comparable to that of Korean among *zainichi* oldcomer Koreans in Japan. However, as with the literature on oldcomer

Korean residents in Japan, most studies, especially those that focus on structural aspects of the *hwagyo* linguistic repertoire, are written in Korean and published in venues that are not easily accessible to scholars outside Korea.

5.5.2 Migrant Workers and Marriage Migrants in Korea

Since the 1990s, there has been a dramatic demographic shift in South Korea, where the narrative of linguistic and cultural homogeneity had buttressed the thesis of a homogeneous national identity. As of 2017, foreign nationals residing in Korea accounted for 2.9 percent of the population (1.48 million), which is still a small proportion in comparison to immigrant-receiving countries in North America and Europe. However, considering that there was no significant immigration population in Korea until the early 1990s, the increase from roughly 110,000 noncitizen residents in the mid-1990s to approximately 1.5 million in 2017 is remarkable, resulting in a pressing need for policy and cultural accommodations of the new immigrants (Park 2014).

This demographic change has been wrought by two groups of immigrants: (1) labor immigrants and (2) marriage immigrants. Along with an expanding economy, enhanced visibility in international relations, and a decrease in birth rates, Korea in the 1990s began to experience labor shortages, especially in the "3-D" (the rendition of 3-K into English) jobs: difficult, dirty, and dangerous jobs that native-born workers often eschew. The combination of a substantial drop in Korean birth rates and a lopsided sex ratio in the marriage market led to the new reality that Korean men, particularly those with less education residing in rural areas, had a hard time finding wives among Korean women.

To address the emerging demographic changes, the government instituted a policy that welcomed immigrants, mostly from less developed neighboring Asian countries, to move to and settle in Korea as laborers. A recent governmental report (Statistics Korea 2017) shows that these labor migrants come from Southeast Asia and, increasingly, from Central Asian countries, such as Uzbekistan and Mongolia. As for marriages of foreign wives by nationality, Vietnam occupies the largest share (27.7 percent), followed by China (25.0 percent) and Thailand (4.7 percent). What is noteworthy is that more than 80 percent of foreign nationals in Korea came from nearby Asian countries and that, since 2005, approximately 65 percent of Chinese immigrants to Korea have been ethnically Korean, who come with some knowledge of Korean spoken as a heritage language (Kong et al. 2010).

Of further note is that the recent surge in labor and marriage immigrants in Korea has been strategically driven by top-down governmental policies in response to the emerging demographic and cultural shifts in society (see Watson 2012 for a review). In a similar vein, support services for these new members of society, such as Korean language classes offered at community centers, have been implemented based on the emerging needs in line with an assimilationist approach that aims to "Koreanize" foreign migrants and their children, sometimes at the price of abandoning their heritage languages and culture (Kim and Kim 2015; Park 2019). Furthermore, the challenges of maintaining heritage languages that immigrants in Korea face are often multiplied by the interplay of their economic status, countries of origin, race, and gender. As Han and Price (2015) report, immigrants and their languages in Korea are perceived differently depending on the status of their countries of origin; languages of power in the global context (English and Japanese) are more valued and accepted than languages associated with less economically strong countries and people of darker skin (Thai and Vietnamese).

5.6 Conclusions

Despite the state-sanctioned discourses touting national identities as monolingual and ethnically homogeneous countries in the Far East, this chapter laid out the linguistic and cultural diversity that has long been present in Japan and Korea. The diversity stems not just from the presence of indigenous languages, such as Ainu and Ryukyuan in Japan, but also languages of different waves of immigrants, including those of the so-called oldcomers and newcomers in Japan and different generations of Chinese immigrants in Korea. In contrast to historically rigid immigration policies that had been in place, both countries have recently made significant changes to their immigration and immigrant policies and practices in an effort to accommodate domestic shifts, such as low birth rates, aging populations, and labor shortages. The two countries as newly emerging immigrant-receiving countries, however, have consistently taken an assimilationist approach to immigrants and their languages, as well as toward domestic minority groups and their languages. In line with the multi-layered nature of language maintenance and education (or lack thereof), much research has been conducted on various aspects of linguistic diversity, focused on individual languages and ethnic groups in one study at a time. As a result, we still know relatively little about the overarching picture of the driving forces that influence the maintenance and shift of heritage languages across time and geography, which leads to a need for future research in this area. In particular, a need is identified to apply fine-grained linguistic analytic tools to the documentation of heritage languages in contact with the societal languages in Japan and Korea from a comparative perspective.

References

Chapman, D. 2006. Discourses of Multicultural Coexistence (Tabunka Kyōsei) and the "Old-Comer" Korean Residents of Japan. *Asian Ethnicity* 7(1), 89–102.

DeChicchis, J. 1995. The Current State of the Ainu Language. *Journal of Multilingual and Multicultural Development* 16(1–2), 103–124.

Dubinsky, S. and W. D. Davies. 2013. Language Conflict and Language Rights: The Ainu, Ryūkyūans, and Koreans in Japan. *Japan Studies Review* 16, 3–28.

Eom, I. S., J. H. Han, and S. J. Kim. 1997. Sewul ilco-hwakyo pangen-cosapoko [Report of Ilco Dialect of Seoul Hwagyo Speakers]. *Cwungkwuk Emwun Yenkwu [Chinese Language Research]* 5, 191–212.

Fishman, J. A. 2001. 300-Plus Years of Heritage Language in the United States. In J. K. Peyton, D. A. Ranard, and S. McGinnis (eds.), *Heritage Languages in America: Preserving a National Resource.* Washington, DC: Center for Applied Linguistics: 81–97.

Fujita-Round, S. and J. Maher. 2017. Language Policy and Education in Japan. In T. L. McCarty and S. May (eds.), *Language Policy and Political Issues in Education.* New York: Springer, 491–505.

Han, E. J. and P. G. Price. 2015. Uncovering the Hidden Power of Language: Critical Race Theory, Critical Language Socialization and Multicultural Families in Korea. *Journal of Intercultural Communication Research* 44(2), 108–131.

Heinrich, P. 2004. Language Planning and Language Ideology in the Ryūkyū Islands. *Language Policy* 3(2), 153–179.

Heinrich, P. 2015. Japanese Language Spread. In P. Heinrich, S. Miyara, and M. Shimoji (eds.), *Handbook of the Ryukyuan Languages: History, Structure, and Use.* Berlin/Boston/Munich: De Gruyter Mouton, 593–611.

Hornberger, N. H. and S. C. Wang. 2008. Who Are Our Heritage Language Learners? Identity and Biliteracy in Heritage Language Education in the United States. In D. Brinton, O. Kagan, and S. Bauckus (eds.), *Heritage Language Education: A New Field Emerging.* New York: Routledge, 3–35.

Jo, H. H. 2002. Ilpon-eyse hankwuke-uy ene-ciwi hyangsang-ey kwanhan yenkwu [A Study on the Improvement of the Language Status of Korean in Japan]. *Enehak [Korean Linguistics]* 10(2), 111–134.

Kang, H. S. 2013. Korean American College Students' Language Practices and Identity Positioning: "Not Korean, but not American". *Journal of Language, Identity & Education* 12(4), 248–261.

Kang, H. S. 2015. Korean Families in America: Their Family Language Policies and Home-Language Maintenance. *Bilingual Research Journal* 38(3), 275–291.

Kanno, Y. 2004. Sending Mixed Messages: Language Minority Education at a Japanese Public Elementary School. In A. Pavlenko and A. Blackledge (eds.), *Negotiation of Identities in Multilingual Contexts*. Clevedon: Multilingual Matters, 316–338.

Kim, E. M. and J. S. Kang. 2007. Seoul as a Global City with Ethnic Villages. *Korea Journal* 47(4), 64–99.

Kim, H., J. G. Lee, B. C. Lee, and S. Kim. 2017. Understanding the Life of Chinese Immigrants in Korea: Forgotten People in the Land of Multiculturalism. *Asian Social Work and Policy Review* 11(3), 184–192.

Kim, H. R. and I. Oh. 2012. Foreigners Cometh! Paths to Multiculturalism in Japan, Korea and Taiwan. *Asian and Pacific Migration Journal* 21(1), 105–133.

Kim, J. H., S. Montrul, and J. Yoon. 2010. Dominant Language Influence in Acquisition and Attrition of Binding: Interpretation of the Korean Reflexive Caki. *Bilingualism: Language and Cognition* 13(1), 73–84.

Kim, J. J. 1994. Ilpon-nay han-il i-ene pyengyong-hwaca (hankwukin)-uy code-switching-ey tayhaye [On the Code-Switching of Korean-Japanese Bilinguals in Japan]. *Icwung-ene-hakswulci [Bilingualism Studies]* 11, 71–96.

Kim, M. and T. Y. Kim, 2015. A Critical Study of Language Minority Students' Participation in Language Communities in the Korean Context. *Language and Intercultural Communication* 15(2), 224–239.

Kim, S. H. 2017. Hankwuk hwakyo-uy Han-Chwung khotu-cenhwan yuhyeng-kwa pwunpho [Korean-Chinese Code Switching Types and Its Distributions among Overseas Chinese in Korea]. *Emwun-Yenkwu [Bilingual Studies]* 45(2), 36–59.

King, K. A. and J. Ennser-Kananen. 2012. Heritage Languages and Language Policy. In C. Chapelle (ed.), *The Encyclopedia of Applied Linguistics*. Oxford: Wiley-Blackwell, 1–4.

Kirkpatrick, A. and A. J. Liddicoat. 2017. Language Education Policy and Practice in East and Southeast Asia. *Language Teaching* 50(2), 155–188.

Kong, D. S., K. W. Yoon, and S. Y. Yu. 2010. The Social Dimensions of Immigration in Korea. *Journal of Contemporary Asia* 40(2), 252–274, https://doi.org/10.1080/00472331003600473

Lee, J. S. and W. E. Wright. 2014. The Rediscovery of Heritage and Community Language Education in the United States. *Review of Research in Education* 38(1), 137–165.

Lee, S. Y. 2017. Chayil Kholian-uy hankwuke-ey tayhan uysik yenkwu [A study on the Zainichi Korean's Recognition of Language]. *Icwung-Enehak [Korean Bilingualism]* 68, 119–139.

Leeman, J. 2015. Heritage Language Education and Identity in the United States. *Annual Review of Applied Linguistics* 35, 100–119.

Liddicoat, A. J. 2007. Internationalising Japan: Nihonjinron and the Intercultural in Japanese Language-in-Education Policy. *Journal of Multicultural Discourses* 2(1), 32–46.

Maeda, N. 2003. Influence of Kotodamaism on Japanese Journalism. *Media, Culture, and Society* 25, 757–772.

Maher, J. 1997. Linguistic Minorities and Education in Japan. *Educational Review* 49(2), 115–127.

Montrul, S. 2010. Current Issues in Heritage Language Acquisition. *Annual Review of Applied Linguistics* 30, 3–23.

Mori, H. 1997. *Immigration Policy and Foreign Workers in Japan*. Houndsmill: MacMillan.

Moseley, C. (ed.) 2010. *Atlas of the World's Languages in Danger*. Paris: UNESCO Publishing.

Nguyen, T. T. T. and M. O. Hamid. 2018. Bilingualism as a Resource: Language Attitudes of Vietnamese Ethnic Minority Students. *Current Issues in Language Planning* 19(4), 343–362.

Park, K. 2014. Foreigners or Multicultural Citizens? Press Media's Construction of Immigrants in South Korea. *Ethnic and Racial Studies* 37 (9), 1565–1586.

Park, M. Y. 2019. Challenges of Maintaining the Mother's Language: Marriage-Migrants and Their Mixed-Heritage Children in South Korea. *Language and Education* 33(5), 1–17.

Sohn, Y. S. 2018. A Study of Japanese Korean Bilinguals' Use of -hata. *The Journal of Korea Association of Japanology* 115(5), 109–127. https://doi.org/10.15532/kaja.2018.05.115.109

Son, Y. S. 2015. Chayil hankwukin icwung-ene sayongcatul-uy sayong-ene-pyel palhwa-mwuncang pwunpho [The Distribution of Sentences by Language Type among Japanese-Korean Bilinguals]. *Ilpone-Mwunhak [Japanese Literature]* 67, 55–74.

Son, Y. S. 2018. Chayil hankwukin icwung-ene sayongcatul-uy 'suru'/'hata' sayong-silthay yenkwu [A Study of the Use of 'suru'/'hata' among Japanese-Korean Bilinguals]. *Ilpon-Hakpo [Japanese Academic Reports]* 115, 109–127.

Son, H. Y. and S. J. Seo, 2008. Hankwuk hwakyo hwacatul-uy icwung-ene sayong yenkwu [A Research on the Bilingualism of the Overseas Chinese in Korea]. *Sahoy-Enehak [Korean Sociolinguistics]* 16(1), 185–211.

Statistics Korea. 2017. *Current status of married immigrants*. Retrieved from www.index.go.kr/potal/main/EachDtlPageDetail.do?idx_cd=2819

Valdés, G. 2005. Bilingualism, Heritage Language Learners, and SLA Research: Opportunities Lost or Seized?. *The Modern Language Journal* 89 (3), 410–426.

Van Deusen-Scholl, N. 2003. Toward a Definition of Heritage Language: Sociopolitical and Pedagogical Considerations. *Journal of Language, Identity, and Education* 2, 211–230.

Watson, I. 2012. Paradoxical Multiculturalism in South Korea. *Asian Politics and Policy* 4(2), 233–258.

Yang, S. Y. and B. C. Yeo. 2011. A Study for Korea's Multicultural Policy and Overseas Chinese' Social Welfare. *The Societies for Chinese Humanities in Korea* 12, 441–460.

Yeo, B. C. 2013. Hwakyo tiasuphola-uy hanpanto icwu-wa ene-cengchey-seng kochal [An Investigation of the Settlement of the Hwagyo Diaspora on the Korean Peninsula and Their Linguistic Identity]. *Cwungkwumwunhak-Yenkwu [Chinese Cultural Studies]* 52, 263–293.

Yi, J. and G. Jung. 2015. Debating Multicultural Korea: Media Discourse on Migrants and Minorities in South Korea. *Journal of Ethnic and Migration Studies* 41(6), 985–1013.

Yim, Y. C. 2013. Kwukoy tongpho ene silthay cosa-lul wihan kicho-yenkwu – chayil hankwukin-uy ene saynghwal-ey tayhan silthay cosa-lul cwung-sim-ulo [A Basic Study for Research on Korean Language Use of Overseas Koreans – Focusing on the Actual Condition Survey on the Language of Korean Residents in Japan]. *Tongpwuka-Mwunhwa-Yenkwu [North East Asia Cultural Studies]* 34, 129–147.

Yotsumoto Y. 2019. Revitalization of the Ainu Language: Japanese Government Efforts. In S. Brunn and R. Kehrein (eds.), *Handbook of the Changing World Language Map*. Basel: Springer, 1711–1727.

6

Heritage Languages in Israel

A Multilingual Tapestry with Hebrew Threads

Natalia Meir, Susan Joffe, Ronald Shabtaev,
Joel Walters, and Sharon Armon-Lotem

6.1 Introduction

6.1.1 The History of Multilingualism in Israel and Revitalization of Hebrew

Israel's strategic geographic position as a land bridge, connecting Europe, Asia, and Africa, a history of conquest and reconquest, and a meeting ground of three major world religions (Judaism, Christianity, and Islam) have assured a long tradition of complex multilingualism in the geographic territory between Mesopotamia and the Nile (Spolsky 1997). Multilingualism emerged thousands of years ago, with Hebrew, Judeo-Aramaic, and Greek all playing meaningful roles (Spolsky 1983). Multilingualism has been the norm for the Jewish people during most of their dispersion, with separate clearly defined functions for each language: Hebrew (actually Hebrew and Talmudic Aramaic) was used for religious and literacy purposes; Jewish languages like Yiddish, Ladino, Judeo-Arabic, Judeo-French, or Judeo-Tat (Juhuri) were used for most other community and home functions; and one or more "coterritorial vernaculars" were used for communication with non-Jews (Spolsky 1997; Burstein-Feldman et al. 2009). Jewish communities in the diaspora around the world developed a language/dialect distinct from the language of their non-Jewish neighbors when the Jewish language variety initially developed. Jewish languages vary with respect to how similar and/or different they are from their non-Jewish correlates. In some cases, the differences are minor and represented simply by Hebrew or Aramaic words, and, in other cases, the Jewish language variety is unintelligible to their non-Jewish neighbors. Yet, the different Jewish languages are mutually unintelligible as they stem from the non-Jewish neighbors' language rather than from a mutual source (for a detailed information on Jewish languages see Hary and Benor (2018)).

The pattern of modern multilingualism in the region began to take shape with the return of Jews to Palestine toward the end of the nineteenth century (Spolsky 1997). During that period, multilingualism was in flux. Turkish was used by soldiers and officials. Local dialects of Arabic were used by peasants and town-dwellers. Classical Arabic was spoken by educated elites. Judezmo (a Jewish language based on Spanish) was used by Sephardic Jews, who also spoke Arabic. European languages were being introduced and encouraged by missionary churches and foreign consuls. Ashkenazi Jews, who began arriving from Eastern Europe, spoke Yiddish but also brought with them co-territorial vernaculars like Russian, Polish, and Hungarian. Multilingualism was developing and changing rapidly. Arabic words and phrases penetrated Yiddish, the language spoken by Ashkenazi Jews along with other European languages and Hebrew-Aramaic. At the same time, some Arabs were developing spoken proficiency in the Yiddish of those Jews with whom they were doing business (Spolsky 1997).

The end of the nineteenth century was marked by "revival" or "reverna-cularization" or revitalization of Hebrew, as the early teaching of Hebrew at schools began in Palestine. Hebrew became the main language for Zionist socialists (founders of *Kibbutzim* – communal settlements), and proponents of ideological monolingualism in the new "Hebrew" city of Tel Aviv. Hebrew rapidly spread through the entire Jewish *Yishuv* [settlement]. By 1913, supporters of the "revival" were able to succeed in a bitter argument over the language of instruction to be used at the first university, naming it "The Hebrew University of Jerusalem." By the 1920s, Hebrew was a native language for many and the public language of the Jewish community of Palestine, although many leading academic and literary figures were still far from fluent.

The British Mandatory government, appointed by the Council of the League of Nations in 1920, ended 400 years of Ottoman Turkish rule in the region. The British Mandate (1919–1948) bolstered the standing of Hebrew in several ways. The use of German in schools was banned, and teachers of that language interned. Even before the Mandate was formally proclaimed, the British Government had been persuaded that Hebrew was the language of the Jewish population: Hebrew was established as an official language alongside Arabic and English. Second, to minimize its financial commitment to the mandated territory, the British allowed the Jewish community to conduct its own educational system. As the language of instruction in Jewish schools and in the university, Hebrew adapted to modern life and technology. Under British Mandatory rule (1923–1948), English was the main language of government, and Jewish and Arab communities maintained separate school systems.

Contact bilingualism developed, English serving both communities as a potential language of wider communication. And yet, new Jewish immigrants who wished to integrate needed to acquire Hebrew, the language of the workplace, education, and public cultural life. The revival of Hebrew involved decisions about its lexicon, syntax, spelling, etc. by the legendary Eliezer Ben-Yehuda and his circle (*Safah B'rurah*) in the late nineteenth and early twentieth centuries in Jerusalem, by linguistic institutions such as the "Language Committee" (*Va'ad Halashon*), and later on by The Academy of the Hebrew Language established by the Israeli parliament in 1953 (Shur 1996). Modern Hebrew comprises words from different historical periods: Biblical period, Mishnaic period, and Middle Ages (Schwartzwald 1995), including foreign words that entered the language during those periods, e.g., *pitgam* (proverb – Aramaic), *parvar* (suburb – Persian), and *psanter* (piano – Greek). The Academy of the Hebrew Language continues to renew words, and about 50 percent of them are accepted into the language (Nir 2004), yet Israel's multilingualism is a powerful source of Modern Hebrew's lexical enrichment: *puncher* (puncture – English), *ambreksim* (handbrakes – English), *egzoz* (exhaust – English), *dzhiga* (giga – English), *selulari* (cellular – English), *riba* (*muraba* – Arabic), *mabruk* (congratulations – Arabic), etc. (Zuckermann 2003a, b; Henkin-Roitfarb 2011).

Current Multilingualism

By 1948, when the State of Israel was established, Hebrew was the principal language of the bulk of the Jewish population (Bachi 1956). Over the next decade, large numbers of *olim xadashim* "new immigrants" arrived, and the linguistic heterogeneity of their origins (Arabic, German, Romanian, Yiddish) contributed to rapid acceptance of Hebrew by the new arrivals and their children. The indigenous Jewish population and the immigrants, who arrived in Israel between the establishment of the State of Israel and the 1960s, learned Hebrew and began to make it their primary language (Spolsky and Shohamy 1999). Hebrew penetrated immigrant groups, and its ideological revitalization and the implementation of a "one-nation-one-language" ideology asserted the hegemony of Hebrew and led to the disappearance of many immigrant languages: First-generation immigrant parents adopted Hebrew to various degrees, and their children became monolingual in Hebrew (Spolsky and Shohamy 2001). Many languages have failed or did not even try to resist Hebrew. The fate of these languages is in fact the most obvious cost of the success of Hebrew revitalization.

Nevertheless, Israel remains a multilingual state. In 2019, the population of Israel stood at 8.8 million people comprising 79 percent Jews and 21 percent Christian and Muslim Arabs, Druze and Circassians. Indigenous vernaculars of Arabic are spoken by 1.5 million Muslims (17.8 percent of the population), 175,000 Christians (2 percent of the population), 143,000

Druze (1.6 percent of the population), and about a half-million Jewish immigrants of North African, Iraqi, and Yemenite origin (Central Bureau of Statistics 2018).

Besides Hebrew and Arabic, between forty and fifty different HLs are spoken by first-, second-, and third-generation immigrants (Spolsky and Shohamy 1999). Jewish immigrants to Israel brought with them Jewish Languages, i.e., languages/dialects spoken by different Jewish communities: Yiddish, Judezmo (Ladino/Judeo-Spanish), Judeo-Arabic, Judeo-French, Judeo-Tat (Juhuri), Dzidi (Judeo-Persian), and others (for detailed information on Jewish languages, see Hary and Benor 2018). With the revival of Hebrew in the land of Israel, some of the Jewish languages have become endangered and close to extinction, spoken by small numbers of aging individuals. Such is the case of Judeo-Arabic and Judezmo (Ladino/Judeo-Spanish) (Hary 2018). A Hebrew-only ideology has led to gradual attrition of Jewish languages, especially among the younger generations. Arabic-speaking Jews who immigrated to Israel from Arabic-speaking countries dropped Judeo-Arabic in a single generation and adopted Hebrew. Similarly, Judeo-Spanish, which also lacked prestige, was gradually replaced by Hebrew in Israel (Bunis 2018). In this chapter, we focus on two Jewish languages spoken in Israel – Israeli Haredi Yiddish and Juhuri (Judeo-Tat). The two languages differ in numbers of speakers, prestige, and motivation of the community to integrate into Israeli society.

Together with traditional Jewish languages, Jews immigrating to Israel brought languages of the outer communities spoken in the country of origin. More than 1,000,000 native speakers of Russian immigrated to Israel from the former Soviet Union, which today makes Russian the most frequently used HL in Israel. There are more than 200,000 native speakers each of English and Romanian, another half million native speakers of ten different languages (Amharic, Bukharic, Georgian, French, German, Hungarian, Spanish, and Polish), and many other languages with 5–50,000 native speakers (Armenian, Bulgarian, Chinese, Czech, Dutch, Greek, Italian, Portuguese, Tagalog, Thai, Tigrigna, and Turkish) (see Burstein-Feldman et al. 2009).

Many *olim xadashim* "new immigrants" abandoned their diaspora Jewish and non-Jewish languages and gradually switched to Hebrew under the influence of Zionist language policy (Spolsky and Shohamy 1999) and/or for ideological reasons, i.e., memories of the Holocaust period (Rosenhouse 2012). For example, after World War II, the Polish-speaking community in Israel was relatively large; today it is dominated by elderly people who are fluent in Hebrew (Kamusella 2016). The Polish-speaking community has not been replenished by *olim xadashim*, and thus Polish speakers are bound to vanish soon as a linguistically distinctive group. Another example of an aging community in Israel, which has seen only a trickle of recent immigration, is the Hungarian-speaking community. Hungarian-speaking Jewish immigrants, who came to Israel in the 1940–1950s, have acquired Hebrew, and their offspring, from the second generation on, hardly know the parents' mother tongue (Rosenhouse 2012).

Furthermore, the Israeli *Kibbutz* (communal settlements) movement, deeply rooted in Zionist-Socialism, promoted the exclusive use of Hebrew in daily life, together with the renouncement of the immigrants' HL. *Kibbutz* settlements, which began to be established in 1920, by the 1960s had around 90,000 men, women, and children living in 225 communal settlements around the country (Leon 2013). The Kibbutz form of settlement was grounded on collective ownership of all means of production and sharing of profits. Hebrew was encouraged as the prevalent language in daily life and family interaction, even for couples who were both speakers of HLs (see Ben-Rafael and Schmid 2007 for more information on HL French speakers residing on Kibbutzim). With very few exceptions, the parents did not transmit their HL to their children, aspiring to bring up a generation of native speakers of Hebrew.

However, some language communities are interested in maintaining and passing on their HL to children and grandchildren. The success of transmission is related to a number of factors: the size of the language community, desire to foster Israeli identity while maintaining home language identity, the number of additional *olim xadashim*, and bonds with the country of origin. Despite the desire to maintain and transfer the heritage language, many second-generation immigrants do not develop full mastery of their parents' language: They become "dormant" bilinguals, as is the case of many second-generation Spanish-Hebrew immigrants (Spector-Bitan 2012). First-generation Latin American Jews immigrated to Israel in small numbers, developed dual identities (e.g., Jewish/Israeli-Argentinian), and showed high proficiency in Hebrew with nonnative-like speech reflected in their Latin American accents in Hebrew. Even languages of first-generation immigrants, who maintain their native language and try to transmit it to future generations, show evidence of intensive contact with Hebrew, resulting in Hebraized versions of the languages, giving rise to hybrid versions that can be spoken only with bilingual speakers of Hebrew and that language: *Franbreu*/Israeli Jewish French (Ben-Rafael and Ben-Rafael 2018); *Hebrish*/Hebraized English (Ohlstain and Blum-Kulka 1989), *HebRush*/Hebraized Russian (Remennick 2003a, 2003b), Hebraized Amharic (Teferra 2018), and Hebraized Spanish (Berk-Seligson 1986; Kupersmitt and Berman 2001). Code-switching and borrowing from Hebrew are the most salient linguistic characteristics of all HLs in Israel. Constraints due to space do not allow us to distinguish borrowing from code-switching, as has been done in many studies of language contact (e.g., Sankoff and Poplack 1981; Myers-Scotton 1993). In the current chapter, in addition to traditional Jewish languages, we discuss English, Russian, and Amharic, three language communities that enjoy a constant flow *of olim xadashim*, nevertheless differing with respect to language status and the size of the language community.

Along with the diversity of spoken languages, several sign languages are used by members of different deaf communities in Israel. The most common sign language in Israel is Israeli Sign Language (ISL), the language spoken by the Jewish deaf community as well as Muslim and Christian Arabic-speaking deaf communities. Israeli Sign Language emerged in the 1930s, and the language is now in its fourth generation with around 10,000 users. Other known village sign languages are Al-Sayyid Bedouin Sign Language, Kfar-Qasem Sign Language, and a few small village sign languages, e.g., the sign language of Ein Mahel, a Muslim village located in the lower Galilee (Meir, I. et al. 2010). Algerian Jewish Sign Language is currently a disappearing language: It is mainly used together with Israeli Sign Language today (Meir, I. and Sandler 2007). Like Hebrew, which affects many of the spoken heritage languages in Israel, Israeli Sign Language seems to influence and gradually replace sign languages of smaller deaf communities (both Jewish and Arabic-speaking), leading to new varieties emerging in contact situations (Meir, I. and Sandler 2019).

Despite the linguistic diversity, the hegemony of Hebrew is evident in all aspects of life. Today, Hebrew is the only official language (Knesset 2018), after a controversial bill was passed by virtue of which the status of Arabic was downgraded from an official language to "a language with a special status." Despite this linguistic diversity, Israeli pre-school and school-age educational systems are largely monolingual institutions: Jewish students are taught only in Hebrew, while Arab students are taught in Arabic. Hebrew is taught as a compulsory subject in the Arabic school system starting from the second grade. In the Hebrew/Jewish school system, Arabic (mainly Modern Standard Arabic) is taught on a limited basis from seventh to ninth grade (Ram 2015). In both the Hebrew and Arabic systems, all students study English as the principle foreign language. At almost all institutions of higher education, *de facto* language policy requires academic language competence in both Hebrew and English, as a prerequisite for university admission; Arabic has never been required. English is not designated as an official language in Israel, but it is widely used in academia, business, commerce, and technology (see Spolsky and Shohamy 1999). In 1996, the Ministry of Education consolidated first-language education policy in a document that reflected the language diversity of the State of Israel. It encouraged use and teaching of traditional Jewish heritage languages (e.g., Yiddish, Ladino), HLs (e.g., Russian, Amharic), and world languages not necessarily spoken by Jewish immigrants (e.g., German, Spanish, Chinese). Immigrants are encouraged to maintain home languages through special classes, but they are not used as languages of instruction. The language education policy of Israel may seem progressive and pluralistic, yet there are discrepancies between linguistic ideology, management strategies of authorities, and actual language practice (Shohamy 2003). Despite official encouragement to teach home languages in schools, this policy is rarely implemented. HL transmission to the second and third generations is considered to be the parents' responsibility rather than state policy. Non-formal education in private and semi-private schools supported by immigrant communities seems to be more attuned to the needs and distinctive cultural features of the immigrant population.

The scope of this chapter does not allow us to present the entire linguistic diversity of all forty to fifty heritage languages of Israel. Therefore, we discuss English, Russian, Amharic, Yiddish, and Juhuri. These heritage languages vary tremendously in the number of first-, second-, and third-generation speakers; their social status as perceived by members of the immigrant community and their diasporas; the presence and transmission of literacy; and motivation to integrate into Israeli society. Despite all these differences, we will argue that all HLs interact with Hebrew, the official language of the State of Israel, and all are affected to a greater or lesser degree, giving rise to hybrid versions (e.g., *Hebrish*, *HebRush*, *Hebraized Amharic*, Israeli Haredi Yiddish). We will discuss the linguistic properties of HLs that undergo changes in contact situations and whose mechanisms might be potentially associated with these divergences from those of baseline speakers (i.e., speakers of that language in the country of origin or dominant speakers of that language).

6.2 Heritage English in Israel

English has always enjoyed a special status in Israel. With the arrival of the British in Palestine following World War I, English became and remained an official government language throughout the Mandate period (until 1948). Following the establishment of the State of Israel in 1948, English was replaced as Israel's official language by Hebrew and Arabic but continued to be an important language for government and commercial purposes. The importance of English as a language of globalization is strongly reflected in Israel in many sectors of Israeli society. English is one of four compulsory subjects in secondary school matriculation exams; university students must satisfy an English-proficiency requirement at both BA and MA levels. Many employers value, and even require, high proficiency in English. Finally, the Internet and other technological changes have made English a *Lingua Franca*, i.e., the language of music, television, movies, and cross-border communication.

The number of native English speakers in Israel has always been small, both in real numbers and as a percentage of the overall population. By the end of the British mandate period, 6,613 American citizens had immigrated to Israel (Avruch 1981). English speakers continued to immigrate to Israel after 1948. According to The Israeli Central Bureau of Statistics, 33,891 immigrants arrived from the United States, Canada, Australia, the United Kingdom, and South Africa between 1969 and 1971. The number that arrived from English-speaking countries between 1972 and 1979 was 56,068. That number decreased in the next three decades (1980s, 44,531; 1990s, 37,281; 2000s, 42,679). The most recent figures (2000–2015) showed a further decline to 22,535 immigrants. English-speaking immigrants who arrived in Israel prior to 1948, and certainly until the 1980s, tended to exhibit the same transitional bilingualism as immigrants from other language backgrounds (Nadel, Fishman, and Cooper 1977). They made up a very small part of the overall population, and like other immigrants to Israel who were motivated to immigrate for nationalist and religious reasons, they embraced Hebrew as their new primary language and English became secondary if not attrited.

Resistance to maintaining English (due in part to an aversion to British influence) began to change at the end of the 1960s. The increase of English-speaking immigrants that began in 1967 meant that there were larger cohorts of English speakers. But the numbers are not the whole story. The influence of American culture, in the form of commercial news and media, resulted in a more positive attitude toward English on the part of English speakers and non-English speakers alike. English became a compulsory subject in Israeli schools in 1960 as well. A study of English-speaking immigrants who arrived in the 1970s showed that almost all (96.7 percent) spoke English at home, either exclusively or together with Hebrew or Yiddish (Levine 1982). Of those who had children in Israel, one-fifth spoke to them exclusively in Hebrew, almost a third spoke in English, and the rest reported using both languages.

By the early 1970s, the initial effects of globalization were obvious to the Israeli public, and English grew in status (Spolsky and Shohamy 1999: 156–186). The teaching of English moved from pre-1960 concern for literature and culture to a focus on English as an international language of communication. That change has brought increased emphasis on oral proficiency over the years. Cooper (1985) argued that English, as a marker of educational status, became a key determinant of socioeconomic status. The high status of English in Israel has been claimed to be one of the reasons North American immigrants do not attain the same level of Hebrew as former Soviet citizens (Beenstock 1996), since their ability to speak English reduces their need to learn Hebrew.

Since the 1990s, most English-speaking immigrants have worked very hard to ensure that their children maintain a high level of English-language proficiency. It is common for English to be the only language spoken in their homes, and they often enroll their children in after-school English classes to preserve and improve their proficiency. The family language policy of most English-speaking parents in Israel is to speak only English (or predominantly English) in the home (Kayam and Hirsch 2012). This results in linguistic evidence for both L1 preservation and L2 influence on Heritage English. Yet, English-speaking children born in Israel and dominant in Hebrew manifest substantial differences in their spoken English when compared with monolingual English-speaking peers. Children's Heritage English shows the influence of Hebrew in lexicon, morphology, and syntax with asymmetrical development of their two languages in these domains. While syntax is less affected, expressive vocabulary in Heritage English poses a major challenge to these children, with age of exposure to the societal language making a significant contribution (Armon-Lotem et al. 2021).

Describing Heritage English in contact with different majority languages (e.g., French and Hebrew), Polinsky (2018) notes several commonalities. At the level of phonology, Heritage English speakers do not show detectable signs of a Hebrew accent, indicating that segmental phonology is native-like. However, numerous uses of *and then*, frequent silent pauses, repetitions, false starts, repairs, and the use of short segments all signify lexical access difficulties. Code-switching to Hebrew is also characteristic of the speech of Heritage speakers. Another notable component of Heritage English is low lexical density, i.e., the small number of distinct content words (Polinsky 2018). Although English does not have rich morphology, its simple system is reported to undergo changes (see (1)): overgeneralization of irregular verbs (e.g., *goed, speaked, teached, drawed*). Heritage English speakers often omit copula *be*, especially for third-person singular (see (2)). Verb particle combinations also undergo changes (see (3)). Heritage English speakers over-generalize the use of *who* as a general relative pronoun.

(1) [It] just **leaved** him a scar.
(2) There's a hippo who [**auxiliary omitted**] going shopping too.
(3) The police passes away (intended meaning: passed by)
(4) There's a rope **who** has clothes from the washing.

   (see the examples in chapter 2 in Polinsky (2018) from Viswanath and
      Polinsky (2012))

Among adults, there is evidence of Hebrew influence in the use of Hebrew discourse markers in predominantly English conversations. Polinsky (2018) reports that English Heritage speakers occasionally use the Hebrew vocalized pause *eh* rather than the English fillers *um* and *uh*. Use of Hebrew discourse markers increases in the speech of Heritage speakers, as demonstrated by Maschler (2000), who analyzed the discourse of two adults. Twelve years following initial data collection with the same participants, an increased use of Hebrew discourse markers was observed, far more than seen for English discourse markers, as seen in (5).

(5)   Grace: . . . so how can you . . . play the role of counselor?
        Shira: **'az zehu** ('so that's it'), . . .
                   . . . I did it for fifteen minutes,
                   . . . **ve'ad kan** ('and that's that', [lit., 'and up to here'].),
        Grace: . . . are you supposed to do it?!
        Shira: **vegamarnu** ('and that's done').
        (Maschler 2000)

The transition away from the use of the HL to the L2 majority language is often seen as a sign of integration. In the case of English-speaking immigrants to Israel, however, immigrants retain English as their primary language (Joffe 2018) despite very positive attitudes to Israeli/Hebrew speakers, sometimes despite low motivation to speak Hebrew. Still, we see the influence of Hebrew on the Heritage English of English-speaking immigrants. Thus, despite the high prestige that English enjoys in Israel, Hebrew permeates English, giving rise to *Hebrish* (Hebraicized English), which incorporates borrowings and code-switches from Hebrew into English (Olshtain and Blum-Kulka 1989).

6.3   Heritage Russian in Israel

In the early 1990s, Israel experienced a massive immigration wave from the Former Soviet Union (FSU), resulting in an intake of more than one million speakers of Russian, or approximately 15 percent of the total population of Israel (Altman et al. 2014; Yelenevskaya 2015). Immigrants to Israel from the FSU continue to account for the largest proportion of immigrants to Israel: Immigrants from Russia and the Ukraine comprised 57 percent of all immigrants to Israel in 2016 (Konstantinov 2017). This makes Russian the most frequently spoken language in Israel, after Hebrew and Arabic. The mass immigration from the FSU has created a rich ethno-linguistic community with its own economic, social, and political networks based on Russian language and culture, reflecting identity choices ranging from assimilation to separatism (Remennick 2003a).

Many members of the Russian-speaking community in Israel are interested in maintaining the Russian language and culture and transmitting Russian to the next generation (Leshem and Lissak 1999; Ben-Rafael et al. 2006; Schwartz et al. 2011). Many state agencies and commercial companies offer information and services in Russian alongside Hebrew, Arabic, and English. Moreover, there are Israeli radio and TV channels broadcasting exclusively in Russian. There are private Russian-only and bilingual Russian–Hebrew kindergartens for children aged 2–5 as well as afternoon schools for older children (Moin et al. 2013), reflecting the community's strong desire to maintain and transmit Russian to future generations.

Despite an interest in maintenance of the Russian language and cultural heritage, studies show that the ubiquitous presence of Russian vis-à-vis other languages in Israel is gradually decreasing. Kheimets and Epstein (2005) report low interest in the idea of establishing a Russian-speaking university in Israel among immigrant scientists despite university programs conducted entirely in Russian in mathematics in the 1990s.

Another threat to the salience of Russian is posed by a process of rapid linguistic convergence: Hebrew elements penetrate the speech of Russian-Israelis, turning "immigrant Russian" into a contact language comprehensible only to bilinguals (Naiditch 2000; Remennick 2003a; Prashizky and Remennick 2018). Survey data show that only 36 percent of Russian–Hebrew speakers who immigrated to Israel as teenagers report using Russian only at home; 49 percent report that they mix Russian with some Hebrew, and 9 percent report using so-called *HebRush*, the code-switched variety of Hebrew and Russian (Remennick 2003b). Most Russian speakers in Israel borrow nouns that denote concepts particular to life in Israel: *miluim* 'reserve service', *mashkanta* 'bank loan', *pkida* 'female clerk', *mazkira* 'secretary', *mishtara* 'police', *mazgan* 'air conditioner', *bagrut* 'matriculation exam' (Naiditch 2004; Perelmutter 2018a, b). The speech of Russian speakers in Israel is spattered with Hebrew discourse markers, such as *yofi* 'great', *be-seder* 'all right', *beemet* 'really', *xaval al-ha-zman* 'amazing', *derex agav* 'by the way', and Arabic *yalla*, which was borrowed into Hebrew (Niznik 2005; Perelmutter 2018a, b).

Regardless of Hebrew proficiency, immigrants mix languages in the same utterance. In (6), Hebrew, lexical items (in bold) inserted into a Russian sentence are inflected for case following the Russian system of case assignment based on declension classes. Correct assignment of case (even on Hebrew borrowings) is indicative of intact grammatical structure among first-generation immigrant speakers dominant in Russian.

(6) hey, ty   posadil mne **ketem**   na   ***xulcu,***   kakoj   ***tembel!***
     hey   you   set   me stain.ACC   on   shirt.LOC   what.M   fool
     'Hey, you stained my blouse, [you] fool!'
     (Remennick 2003a: 438)

Furthermore, cross-linguistic influence in the form of calques (i.e., loan translations) (7) is observed even among Russian-dominant participants aged 60–89 who report no mastery of Hebrew when compared to monolingual Russian-speaking controls (Baladzhaeva and Laufer 2018). Immigrants' sensitivity to calques decreased in comparison to monolingual controls.

(7)   # **zakroj** *(vykljuchi)*, pozhalujsta, *kondicioner,*   *mne xolodno.*
      # close (turn off), please,   air-conditioning,   I am cold
      'Turn off the air-conditioning, please. I am cold.'
      (Baladzhaeva and Laufer 2018)

The influence of Hebrew is observed at different language levels among HL 1.5 and 2- generation speakers. Generally, the phonology of HL speakers is reported to show less variation and divergence from a monolingual baseline, and their production of the home language sounds is better in comparison to highly proficient L2 learners (Polinsky 2018). However, some studies report that HL speakers have "a foreign accent" in their HL and are identified by "baseline" monolingual speakers as individuals who were born in the country of origin and currently reside in a foreign country (e.g., Kupisch 2020). Asherov, Fishman, and Cohen (2016) compared vowel production of real and nonce words among Hebrew-dominant Heritage Russian speakers residing in Israel and found that HL speakers were comparable to baseline controls for real words but differed for nonce words. Baseline speakers differentiate three underlying variants of /o/ (stressed: *nos* 'nose'; pretonic: *nos ɨ* 'nose pl.'; and antepretonic: *noso ʋoj* 'nasal.'), but Heritage Russian speakers do not make these distinctions, and might be indirectly affected by Hebrew, thus combining phonotactic/phonological features of the HL and the Dominant Language.

With regard to morphosyntax of Russian-speaking immigrants, Meir N. and Polinsky (2021) conducted an auditory acceptability judgment task evaluating sensitivity to ungrammaticalities in adjective–noun and numeral–noun expressions in three groups of adult Russian-Hebrew speakers: Heritage Russian speakers with Age of Onset (AoO) before age 5, HL speakers with AoO from 5 to 13, and Russian-dominant bilinguals. Participants in all three groups had been exposed to Russian from birth and had on average 20 years of residence in Israel. Sensitivity to ungrammaticalities in adjectival phrases (e.g., **mjasn-yje kotlet-a* 'meaty-PL.NOM meatball.F-S.NOM'/**mjasn-aja kotlet-y* 'meaty-S.NOM meatball.F-PL.NOM') and numerical phrases (**tri samoljet-ov* 'three plane.M-PL.GEN' versus **pjat' samoljet-a* 'five plane.M-PAUC') were tested. Findings demonstrated a robust effect for AoO on the development and maintenance of the HL. The group with late AoO (Russian-Dominant bilinguals) showed ceiling-level performance in sensitivity to (mis)matches for both adjective–noun and numeral–noun conditions. HL speakers with earlier AoOs (before age 5 and from 5–13) were less accurate in detecting ungrammaticalities than the Russian-dominant group, thus confirming that Heritage speakers' grammatical representations sometimes diverge from those of Russian-dominant bilinguals. The two groups of

Heritage Russian speakers showed reduced sensitivity to ungrammatical numeral–noun constructions in comparison to adjective–noun constructions, which indicates that properties of the dominant language influence HL restructuring, facilitating reanalysis in the weaker language.

Divergence from baseline Russian in the domain of morphosyntax is observed not only in Hebrew-dominant adults but also in children who are born in Israel (e.g., Gupol et al. 2012; Schwartz and Minkov 2014; Meir, N. and Armon-Lotem 2015; Schwartz et al. 2015; Meir, N. et al. 2016, 2017). Data from these child studies show that the case and aspect systems in child HL grammars undergo representational restructuring. Adjective–noun agreement and subject–verb agreement seem to be better preserved and show similarities to baseline monolingual grammars (Gagarina et al. 2007; Schwartz et al. 2015; Meir, N. et al. 2017).

Despite the ubiquitous presence of Russian in Israel and a strong desire to maintain and transmit Russian to future generations, recent studies show a decline in Russian proficiency among second-generation adult immigrants (Niznik 2011; Meir N. and Polinsky 2021). Russian-speaking children born in Israel and dominant in Hebrew manifest substantial differences in their Russian compared to monolingual Russian-speaking peers (e.g., Meir, N., Walters, and Armon-Lotem 2016, 2017). A recent survey conducted among Russian-speaking mothers in four countries, including Israel, showed that 96 percent of the respondents in Israel indicated that their children can speak and understand Russian. However, 47 percent of the respondents showed dissatisfaction with their children's proficiency in the HL (Otwinowska, Meir, N., Ringblom, Karpava, and La Morgia 2021). Furthermore, the respondents indicated that only 41 percent of children have literacy skills in Heritage Russian.

In summary, despite the high vitality of Heritage Russian in the Russian-speaking community and the desire to transmit Heritage Russian to future generations, Hebrew has penetrated Heritage Russian at different levels, including Hebrew borrowings, calques, and code-switches among Russian-dominant speakers and a general decline in Heritage Russian proficiency in 1.5–2nd generation speakers whose grammars show grammatical restructuring.

6.4   Heritage Amharic in Israel

In 2016, there were approximately 144,100 Ethiopian-Israelis: 85,500 immigrated to Israel from Ethiopia and 56,600 were born in Israel (Central Bureau of Statistics 2017). For the majority of immigrants from Ethiopia, Amharic was their native language, while a small percentage spoke Tigrinya as well as Amharic. The vast majority of immigrants from Ethiopia came with no formal education and were illiterate in the home language (Anteby-Yemini 2005). Due to meaningful cultural, ethnic, social, and literacy differences between Ethiopian immigrants and the host Israeli society (Levin-Rozalis 2000), Amharic is a low prestige language in Israel (Spolsky and Shohamy 1999). However, despite its low perceived social value in Israeli society, Amharic-speaking parents, like other immigrant parents, believe that Amharic should be both used and maintained, since it is the sole language of communication with older members of the extended family (Stavans 2015).

Currently, there is very little research on linguistic changes that Amharic has undergone in contact with Hebrew. A recent study by Teferra (2018) is the first to provide a comprehensive overview of the Amharic language used by immigrants from Ethiopia to Israel. Amharic is reported to be used by older people and its use is more prevalent among those who were illiterate when they immigrated to Israel. Like other HL varieties, among first-generation speakers, Amharic undergoes a number of changes in contact with Hebrew, especially in the lexicon, giving birth to "*Hebraized Amharic*." Sometimes, borrowings simply do not have equivalents in Amharic. Equivalents exist in Modern Standard Amharic, but immigrants do not know these Amharic equivalents, since they immigrated to Israel from rural parts of Ethiopia and were not exposed to those terms in the home country. The borrowings cut across different domains: health (e.g., *kupat xolim* 'health fund', *xom* 'fever', *nituax* 'surgery'), education (e.g., *tixon* 'high school', *xinux* 'education'), social services (e.g., *bitu'ax* 'insurance'), food items (e.g., *tapuwax/tabbuwax* 'apple', *kemax* 'flour'). Borrowings are usually accompanied by phonological changes to comply with the phonetic inventory and phonology of Amharic.

Borrowed lexical items from Hebrew (in bold) are integrated into the grammar of Amharic using grammatical affixes and adpositions (see (8) and (9)).

(8)   suq-*u*   kä-**tahana**   **merkazit**-*u*   at'ägäb näw
       shop-def   from-station   central-def   near cop-3m.sg
       'The shop is near the central bus station'
       Teferra (2018, p.514)

(9)   ləj-e-n   **ahot**-wa   zare   tə-**täpl**-at-alläčč
       child-1:gen-obj   nurse-def   today   3f:imperf-treat-3f:obj-3f:aux
       'The nurse will treat my child today'
       Teferra (2018: 516)

"*Hebraized Amharic*" is reported to be widely used by first generation immigrants (Teferra 2018). Speakers of the 1.5 generation (i.e., those who immigrated at a young age) show mastery of both languages (Amharic and Hebrew), while children who were born in Israel have little (if any) command of Amharic and prefer to use Hebrew among themselves and when they respond to their parents (*A School Guide to Ethiopian Israelis* 2008). Preschool children from Amharic-speaking families display preference for Hebrew and limited abilities in Amharic, i.e., children show poor or no comprehension of simple instructions in Amharic (e.g., "*Move the chair away from the table*") (Ben-Oved and Armon-Lotem 2016). Hebrew proficiency of preschoolers from Amharic-speaking families is comparable to that of monolingual Hebrew-speaking children, reflecting a complete shift toward Hebrew within a single generation (Altman et al. 2018).

With this shift into Hebrew, it is possible that if the immigration of Ethiopian Jews ceases at some point, then "Hebraized Amharic" might gradually be at risk for extinction. Ethiopian immigrant parents are involved in their child's development, socialization, and pre-literacy practices only up to the age of formal education (Stavans et al. 2009). Once schooling begins, parents are less involved in their children's education.

6.5 Heritage Israeli Haredi Yiddish

Yiddish is a language that originated among Ashkenazi Jews from Eastern-Europe from about 1000 CE when Jews settled in Germanic-speaking regions of Central Europe and adopted local Germanic dialects. The Ashkenazi Jews who immigrated to Israel toward the end of the nineteenth century spoke Yiddish but used co-territorial vernaculars like Russian, Polish, and Hungarian (Spolsky 1983). Yiddish (Israeli Haredi Yiddish) is a daily means of communication in rapidly growing Haredi (ultra-Orthodox) communities, mainly in religious neighborhoods in Jerusalem, Bet-Shemesh, Bnei Brak, Betar Illit, and Ashdod (Isaacs 1999a, 1999b; Assouline, 2018a). However, for sizable segments of Israeli Haredi communities, perhaps the majority, Modern Hebrew is the language of wider communication, not Yiddish (Isaacs 1999a, 1999b). The exact number of Yiddish speakers in Israel is unknown due to a rabbinic objection in the Haredi community to participating in the census (Isaacs 1998). Yiddish is acquired as a native tongue and is used as the main language spoken with family and friends and used in communal educational institutions. It is the dominant language in traditional Jewish educational institutions, the Hasidic yeshivas, where it serves as the primary means of oral discourse in the study of sacred Hebrew and Aramaic texts (Isaacs 1999a, 1999b). In this context, Israeli Haredi Yiddish is maintained within a triglossic setting, i.e., Hebrew is used on a daily basis for communicating with the outside community, while *loshn-kóydesh* (literally, Holy Tongue), a mix of Hebrew and Aramaic, is used in specific domains such as prayer and study (Assouline 2014). A sizable proportion of these speakers are also fluent in English.

Maintenance of Israeli Haredi Yiddish is largely driven by its prestigious status in ultra-Orthodox communities: Yiddish is deemed vital in the pursuit of an authentic Hasidic way of life (Isaacs 1999a, 1999b). The language has two main dialects, "Hasidic Yiddish" and "Jerusalemite Yiddish," which today serve as two communal dialects: "Jerusalemite Yiddish," also known as *Litvish* (i.e., Lithuanian Yiddish), is used by members of the distinctive group of non-Hasidic communities; and "Hasidic Yiddish" is used by a range of Hasidic sects such as *Belz, Tzanz, Vizhnitz, Ger, Satmar*, and others (Assouline 2017). Within Yiddish-speaking communities, Yiddish is viewed as a powerful symbol of a sacred Jewish tradition, while Hebrew embodies dangers and temptations of the secular world (Assouline 2017). Israeli Haredi Yiddish is the product of deliberate ideological effort among the Haredi communities (Assouline 2017) in order to maintain their segregation from the outside world.

Despite ideological opposition to Hebrew, there is widespread contact between Yiddish and Hebrew in Israel that is evident at all linguistic levels: phonology, morphology, lexicon, and syntax. Today the phonological system of Israeli Haredi Yiddish is virtually indistinguishable from Hebrew among speakers under age 50, who have no "Yiddish" accent (Assouline 2018b), while there are still distinct phonological differences among those in their 70s, 80s, and 90s. Likewise, few speakers of Yiddish still maintain syllabic consonants [m], [n], and to a lesser extent also [l], e.g., *dortn* 'there', and it should be noted that these consonants are not syllabic in Hebrew. Yet, the majority of speakers consistently avoid such clusters (e.g., *dorten* instead of *dortn* 'there').

For the lexicon, Abugov and Ravid (2014) show from a picture-naming task with adult Yiddish speakers, that 62 percent of the singular nouns were produced in Yiddish (e. g., *ay* 'eye', *tug* 'day', *xasene* 'wedding'), while 38 percent of the nouns were in Hebrew (e.g. *maxshev* for 'computer', *pil* for 'elephant'). Lexical borrowings from Hebrew into Yiddish are so widespread that they are reported to create difficulties in communication between speakers of American Yiddish and Israeli Yiddish (Isaacs 1999a). Lexical borrowing reflects vocabulary gaps in Standard Yiddish but also extensive contact between Hebrew and Yiddish in Israel. For example, the Yiddish word *problém* 'problem' is found to be replaced by the Hebrew word *beayá* (which may or may not be phonologically integrated as *beáye*) (Assouline 2017). Similarly, integrated and non-integrated borrowings from Hebrew are attested (e.g., *bekorét* (non-integrated)/*bekóyres* (integrated) 'criticism'; *misgéret* (non-integrated)/*misgéres* (integrated) 'framework') (Assouline 2017).

At the level of morphology, the inflectional paradigms of Israeli Hassidic Yiddish manifest considerable simplification and variation (Assouline 2014). Plural marking seems to be generally preserved. For example, Abugov and Ravid (2014) show that adult speakers of Israeli Haredi Yiddish remain loyal to the high frequency Standard Yiddish and *Loshn*

Kóydesh plural forms: 95 percent of the responses were target-like (e.g., *kop/ kep* 'head-s', *maranc/n* 'orang-s') or *Loshn Kóydesh* (*bar micve/bar micves* 'bar mitzvah-s', *sayfer/sforim* 'book-s'). Modern Hebrew plural inflections are usually used together with Modern Hebrew lemmas, e.g., *kof-im* 'monkeys' and *vilon-ot* 'curtains. In contrast, another important grammatical category of Yiddish, the case system, has undergone attrition (Assouline, 2014). While the grammatical gender distinction is preserved, case distinctions are eroding: a single form *der gutter mentsh* 'the good man' is used not only in the nominative case but also in the accusative and dative. Furthermore, as a result of erosion of the case system, speakers resort to an analytic construction with the preposition *far* to mark the indirect object, which might be triggered by Hebrew, which marks indirect objects with the preposition *l-* (see (10). Alternatively, it may be due to lack of Yiddish literacy (Assouline 2014).

(10) *er gi-t   a   patsh **far** a   kind.*
      he give.PRS-3sg INDF slap   for INDF   child
      'he slaps a child.'
      (Assouline 2014: 44)

As Yiddish speakers are highly proficient in Hebrew, code-switching to Hebrew and borrowing from Hebrew are extensive in everyday conversation. However, when conversing in public, Yiddish predominates (Assouline 2017). When code-switches to Hebrew occur in public, they are used in order to quote Israeli Hebrew speakers to highlight the language's out-group status in the view of the Yiddish-speaking Haredi community (see (11)).

(11) *de velt   rift   dus **laasot khayim,** ober inz viln take makhn a leybn*
      the world calls this to make life   but we want really to make a life
      'The world calls it to have fun, but we really want to make a life!'
      (Assouline 2018b: 55)

6.6 Heritage Juhuri (Judeo-Tat) in Israel

Juhuri, also known as Judeo-Tat for its origin and likely its relation to the Tat language (a form of Persian), is the traditional language of Mountain Jews from the eastern mountains of the Caucasus. Mountain Jews are an ethno-cultural group, descendants of Persian Jews from Iran (Borjian and Kaufman 2016). Juhuri was maintained in the Caucasus as a heritage language, while the dominant language in the area became Russian when the Soviets came to power in the region. Like Yiddish, Juhuri has been cited as one of the few Jewish languages that has significantly diverged from its non-Jewish counterpart, namely Muslim Tat. Today the number of speakers is estimated at around 200,000 world-wide. According to its speakers, Judeo-Tat is considered a Semitic language which is to be distinguished from the Indo-European Muslim Tat, an offshoot of Persian (Shalem 2018).

This self-designation is sociolinguistically motivated by the preference to call the language Juhuri (simply translated as "Jewish"). Most researchers, however, believe Juhuri and Tat are a single language divided along religious lines with correlated linguistic differences, where Juhuri is essentially a dialect of Tat with a lexicon rich with Hebrew, Aramaic, and Russian words, as well as other Jewish influences. The Juhuri of those who immigrated to Israel in the 1990s bears influences of Russian, which had become dominant long before most had arrived in Israel. Beside the linguistic features that set the two dialects apart, Juhuri has a distinct writing system, also cited in support of its status as a distinct language. The orthographies used for Juhuri have changed over the years. Hebrew script was used until 1929 when the Latin alphabet took over, and Soviet policy instituted Cyrillic script ten years later (Spolsky 2014).

According to the UNESCO *Atlas of the World's Languages in Danger* (Moseley 2010), the vitality of Juhuri is classified as "Definitely Endangered," one level above "Vulnerable," but less endangered than the three lowest categories: "Severely Endangered," "Critically Endangered," and "Extinct." The Endangered Languages Project, however, labels its status as "Vulnerable." Most speakers of Juhuri are multilingual; there are no schools where Juhuri is taught; the language has no official status; no attempts are being made to adapt the language to the challenges of modernity; and documentation is fragmentary at best (Shalem 2018).

During the 1980s and 1990s, Mountain Jews immigrated in vast numbers to the United States and Israel. The demographic estimates for Mountain Jews vary across sources. According to several sources (Minahan 2014; Joshua Project 2019), the number of Mountain Jews, who are presumed to be Juhuri speakers, is estimated at from 70,000 to 140,000 in Israel, from 15,000–24,000 in Azerbaijan, and at about 20,000 in the United States. Estimates in Russia range from 500 to 2,000. The Endangered Languages Project, however, believes that the number of native speakers of Juhuri who make use of the language on a daily basis is roughly 25,000.

Bram (2008) discussed changes in the use of Juhuri among Mountain Jews in Russia and Israel, focusing on differences in how its speakers perceive the language in relation to the surroundings. The first major decrease in the use of Juhuri resulted from intense processes of Russification due to Soviet cultural policy in the Caucasus in the 1920s. Thus, prior to immigration to Israel, Juhuri speakers already used two languages on a daily basis (Russian and Juhuri). In Israel, Russification not only caused a substantial decrease in the use of Juhuri but also brought about a decline in its status even among native speakers, who due to the fact that the Israeli government ignored differences among ethno-cultural communities coming from the FSU, were seen as no less Russian than other former Soviet immigrants. This, in turn, marginalized the Mountain Jews, who were commonly referred to as

Kavkazim (simply translated as "Caucasian," in reference to their ethnic background in the Caucasus), and the specific needs of its members to adapt to their new surroundings (Borjian and Kaufman 2016). Juhuri was granted no official recognition in Israel, Russian being considered the language of immigrants from the Caucasus, leading to a substantial lack of Juhuri communication arenas.

Over the years, mostly since the mass immigration in the 1990s (along with smaller numbers who had arrived two decades earlier), Mountain Jews have gradually come to terms with Juhuri becoming extinct and at times being looked down on as culturally inferior (Bram 2008). This is a prime reason for the failure to promote cultural continuity. As a result, there is almost a complete absence of Juhuri in the public sphere, despite its strong vitality in the inner space of Mountain Jews' everyday life at home and in family and community gatherings and festivities. Even when events dedicated to the absorption of the Mountain Jews' community were organized, discussion of Juhuri as their language was not included as a means of promoting their identity. The younger generation sees Juhuri as having no relevance to their lives in Israel, and thus they do not use it or attempt to learn it. Nevertheless, Juhuri remains a prime component of Mountain Jews' collective identity as evidenced by the fact that it has managed to resist Israeli government neglect of its importance over the years.

First-generation speakers of Juhuri residing in Israel use Hebrew, Russian, and Juhuri in their everyday life. Trilingual code-switching can be seen as a cultural option for many, where the societal language (Hebrew) alternates with the language they grew up with (Russian), and the HL (Juhuri). This can be seen in the following excerpt (12), where all three languages are used in a single utterance. The base language and main propositional content are Russian, with a Hebrew discourse marker (**in bold**) inserted to make a metalinguistic comment, then a switch to Juhuri (underlined) to issue a blessing before returning to Russian to complete the main purpose of the utterance.

(12)   *A, pogulat,*   **nu beseder,**   <u>*xudo kumek eyšmu,*</u>   *da zaberi ix*
       Ah, to-travel,   so okay   God help   to-you.PL   yes take them
       'Ah, to travel, so okay, may God be with you, yes take them.'
       (Shabtaev 2018)

The foregoing example comes from Shabtaev's (2018) MA thesis, which examined differences in language use across three generations of Mountain Jewish immigrants in Israel. The findings revealed significant cross-generational differences, where the use of both Russian and Juhuri decreased across generations, along with an increase in the use of Hebrew. Maintenance of Juhuri was, by and large, observed only among first-generation participants, with second-generation speakers retaining it at the level of comprehension and third-generation speakers abandoning it entirely. While second-generation participants strongly preserved Russian for interactions with their parents, most of them were less inclined to use it with their third-generation children, opting to use Hebrew instead. Thus, Hebrew was dominant for third-generation participants, and only a few were able to speak Russian at all.

6.7 Conclusions

Today's multilingualism of Israel is deeply rooted in the country's complex history. The Jewish people have been multilingual for thousands of years, using Hebrew for religious and literacy purposes, a Jewish language (like Yiddish, Judeo-French, Ladino, or Judeo-Arabic) for most other community and home functions, and one or more "coterritorial vernaculars" for communication with non-Jews. With the establishment of Jewish settlement in Palestine at the end of the nineteenth century and revitalization of Hebrew, the hegemony of Hebrew began, as seen in a policy of one-language-one-nation. This remains evident today in all aspects of life. Hebrew is the only official language of Israel, although Arabic is designated to have a special status.

Today, between 40 and 50 HLs are spoken by first-, second-, and third-generation immigrants. The current chapter has focused on five HLs (English, Russian, Amharic, Yiddish, and Juhuri) in Israel. These languages were selected to show diversity in terms of (a) the number of speakers residing in Israel and in the host country, (b) the social status of the language as perceived by the members of the in-group community and the outside world, (c) the presence and transmission of literacy, and (d) the desire to integrate into Israeli Society. Despite tremendous differences, extensive contact between Hebrew and the HL results in a Hebraized version of that language. Borrowings, calques, and code-switching from Hebrew are observed in the speech of first-generation speakers who are dominant in the HL. These contact phenomena are observed not only in the communities embracing integration but also in the communities that ideologically resist integration into Israeli society, as in the case of Israeli Haredim. Speakers of the 1.5 and second-generations become less proficient in their HL and adopt Hebrew as their primary language. Thus, the transmission of the HL is compromised to the extent that the vitality of some HLs is endangered, as in the case of Juhuri (the language of Mountain Jews), a language that suffers from low prestige in a small community of speakers. To preserve the multilingual landscape of Israel, more practical steps should be taken by policy makers to implement pluralistic education policies that will allow speakers of different HLs access to education in their HL.

References

Abugov, N. and D. Ravid. 2014. Noun Plurals in Israeli Hasidic Yiddish: A Psycholinguistic Perspective. In M. Aptroot and B. Hansen (eds.), *Yiddish Language Structures*. Berlin: Mouton de Gruyter, 9–39.

Altman, C., J. Walters, and S. Armon-Lotem. 2018. The Influence of Bilingualism, Socio-Economic Status and Developmental Language Disorder on Literacy Skills (BLISS-EL) Report. (in Hebrew). Retrieved from http://meyda.education.gov.il/files/LishcatMadaan/AltmanWaltersFINALreport.pdf

Altman, C., Z. Burstein Feldman, D. Yitzhaki, S. Armon Lotem, and J. Walters. 2014. Family Language Policies, Reported Language Use and Proficiency in Russian-Hebrew Bilingual Children in Israel. *Journal of Multilingual and Multicultural Development* 35(3), 216–234.

Anteby-Yemini, L. 2005. From Ethiopian Villager to Global Villager: Ethiopian Jews in Israel. In A. Levy and A. Weingrod (eds.), *Homelands and Diasporas: Holy Lands and Other Places*. Stanford, CA: Stanford University Press, 220–244.

Armon-Lotem, S., Rose, K., and Altman, C. 2021. The Development of English as a Heritage Language: The Role of Chronological Age and Age of Onset of Bilingualism. *First Language*, 41(1), 67–8.

Asherov, D., A. Fishman, and E. G. Cohen. 2016. Vowel Reduction in Israeli Heritage Russian. *Heritage Language Journal* 13(2), 113–133.

Assouline, D. 2014. Language Change in a Bilingual Community: The Preposition Far in Israeli Haredi Yiddish. In M. Aptroot and B. Hansen (eds.), *Yiddish Language Structures*. Berlin: De Gruyter Mouton, 39–61.

Assouline, D. 2017. *Contact and Ideology in a Multilingual Community: Yiddish and Hebrew among the Ultra-Orthodox* (Vol. 16). Boston: De Gruyter Mouton.

Assouline, D. 2018a. Haredi Yiddish in Israel and the United States. B. Hary and S. B. Benor (eds.), *Languages in Jewish Communities, Past and Present*. Boston: De Gruyter Mouton, 472–488.

Assouline, D. 2018b. English Can Be Jewish but Hebrew Cannot: Code-Switching Patterns among Yiddish-Speaking Hasidic Women. *Journal of Jewish Languages* 6(1), 43–59.

Avruch, K. 1981. *American Immigrants in Israel: Social Identities and Change*. Chicago: University of Chicago Press.

Bachi, R. 1956. A Statistical Analysis of the Revival of Hebrew in Israel. *Scripta Hierosolymitana* 2, 179–247.

Baladzhaeva, L. and B. Laufer. 2018. Is First Language Attrition Possible without Second Language Knowledge? *International Review of Applied Linguistics in Language Teaching* 56(2), 103–136.

Beenstock, M. 1996. The Acquisition of Language Skills by Immigrants: The Case of Hebrew in Israel. *International Migration* 34(1), 3–30.

Ben-Oved S. H. and S. Armon-Lotem. 2016. Ethnolinguistic Identity and Lexical Knowledge among Children from Amharic Speaking Families. *Israel Studies in Language and Society* 8(1–2), 238–275.

Ben-Rafael, M. and E. Ben-Rafael. 2018. Jewish French in Israel. In B. Hary and S. B. Benor (eds.), *Languages in Jewish Communities, Past and Present*. Boston: De Gruyter Mouton, 544–580.

Ben-Rafael, M. and M. S. Schmid. 2007. Language Attrition and Ideology: Two Groups of Immigrants in Israel. In B. Köpke (ed.), *Language Attrition: Theoretical Perspectives*. Amsterdam/Philadelphia: John Benjamins Publishing Company, 205–226.

Ben-Rafael, E., M. Lyubansky, O. Glöckner, P. Harris, Y. Israel, W. Jasper, and J. H. Schoeps. 2006. *Building a Diaspora: Russian Jews in Israel, Germany and the USA*. Leiden: Brill.

Berk-Seligson, S. 1986. Linguistic Constraints on Intrasentential Code-Switching: A Study of Spanish/Hebrew Bilingualism. *Language in Society* 15(3), 313–348.

Borjian, H. and D. Kaufman. 2016. Juhuri: From the Caucasus to New York City. *International Journal of the Sociology of Language* 2016(237), 59–74.

Bram, C. 2008. The Language of Caucasus Jews: Language Preservation and Sociolinguistic Dilemmas before and after the Migration to Israel. *Irano-Judaica* 6, 337–351.

Bunis, D. M. 2018. Judezmo (Ladino/Judeo-Spanish): A Historical and Sociolinguistic Portrait. In B. Hary and S. B. Benor (eds.), *Languages in Jewish Communities, Past and Present*. Boston: De Gruyter Mouton, 185–239.

Burstein-Feldman, Z., A. D. Epstein, N. Kheimets, S. Kopeliovich, D. Yitzhaki, and J. Walters. 2009. Israeli Sociolinguistics. In Martin J. Ball and Nicole Muller (eds.), *The Routledge Handbook of Sociolinguistics Around the World*. Amsterdam: Routledge, 226–238.

Central Bureau of Statistics. 2017. *The Population of Ethiopian Origin in Israel*. Retrieved from www.cbs.gov.il/he/mediarelease/DocLib/2018/326/11_18_326e.pdf

Central Bureau of Statistics. 2018. *Israel in Figures*. Retrieved from www.cbs.gov.il/he/publications/DocLib/isr_in_n/isr_in_n18e.pdf

Cooper, R. L. 1985. Fantasti! Israeli Attitudes towards English. In S. Greenbaum (ed.), *The English Language Today*. Oxford: Pergamon Institute of English, 233–241.

Gagarina, G., S. Armon-Lotem, and O. Gupol. 2007. Developmental Variation in the Acquisition of L1 Russian Verb Inflection by Monolinguals and Bilinguals. In H. Caunt-Nulton, S. Kulatilake, and I. H. Woo (eds.), *On-line Supplement to the Proceedings of BUCLD 31*. Somerville, MA: Cascadilla Press, 1–11.

Goldscheider, C. 1974. American Aliyah: Sociological and Demographic Perspectives. *The Jew in American Society* 335–384.

Gupol, O., S. Rothstein, and S. Armon-Lotem. 2012. The Development of L1 Tense-Aspect Morphology in Russian-Hebrew Bilinguals. In E. Labeau and I. Saddour (eds.), *Tense, Aspect and Mood in First and Second Language Acquisition*. Amsterdam; New York: Rodopi, 73–106.

Hary, B. 2018. Hebraized Amharic in Israel. B. Hary and S. B. Benor (eds.), *Judeo-Arabic in the Arabic-Speaking World*. Boston: De Gruyter Mouton, 35–69.

Hary, B. and S. B. Benor (eds.) 2018. *Judeo-Arabic in the Arabic-Speaking World*. Boston: De Gruyter Mouton.

Henkin-Roitfarb, R. 2011. Hebrew and Arabic in Asymmetric Contact in Israel. *Lodz Papers in Pragmatics* 7(1), 61–100.

Isaacs, M. 1998. Yiddish in the Orthodox Communities of Jerusalem. In D.-B. Kerler (ed.), *Politics of Yiddish: Studies in Language, Literature and Society*. Walnut Creek: Altamira Press, 85–96.

Isaacs, M. 1999a. Haredi, haymish and frim: Yiddish Vitality and Language Choice in a Transnational, Multilingual Community. *International Journal of the Sociology of Language* 138(1), 9–30.

Isaacs, M. 1999b. Contentious Partners: Yiddish and Hebrew in Haredi Israel. *International Journal of the Sociology of Language* 138(1), 101–121.

Joffe, S. 2018. Identity, Motivation, Language Shift, and Language Maintenance. Doctoral dissertation, Bar Ilan University.

Joshua Project. 2019. Jewish Tat, Mountain Jews. Retrieved from https://joshuaproject.net/people_groups/10839.

Kamusella, T. 2016. Migration or Immigration? Ireland's New and Unexpected Polish-Language Community. In *The Palgrave Handbook of Slavic Languages, Identities and Borders*. London: Palgrave Macmillan, 524–548.

Kayam, O. and T. Hirsch. 2012. Family Language Policy of the English Speaking Immigrant Community in Israel: Families with Young Children and Their FLP Planning, Management, and Outcomes. *International Journal of Linguistics* 4(4), 622.

Kheimets, N. G. and A. D. Epstein. 2005. Adult Language Education in a Multilingual Situation: The Post-Soviet Immigrants in Israel. *Adult Education in Israel* 8, 40–65.

Knesset. 2018. Basic Law: Israel – the Nation State of the Jewish People. Retrieved from http://knesset.gov.il/laws/special/eng/BasicLawNationState.pdf.

Konstantinov, V. 2017. Quarter Century of the Great Aliya: A Statistical Analysis of Changes. Jerusalem. (in Russian).

Kupersmitt, J. and R. A. Berman. 2001. Linguistic Features of Spanish-Hebrew Children's Narratives. In L. Verhoeven and S. Strömqvist (eds.), *Narrative Development in a Multilingual Context*. Amsterdam: John Benjamins Publishing Company, 277–317.

Kupisch, T. 2020. Towards Modelling Heritage Speakers' Sound Systems. *Bilingualism*, 23(1), 29–30.

Leon, D. 2013. *The Kibbutz: A New Way of Life*. Oxford: Pergamon Press.

Leshem, E. and M. Lissak. 1999. Development and Consolidation of the Russian Community in Israel. In S. Weil (ed.), *Roots and Routes: Ethnicity and Migration in Global Perspective*. Jerusalem: Magnes Press, 136–171.

Levin-Rozalis, M. 2000. Social Representations as Emerging from Social Structure: The Case of the Ethiopian Immigrants to Israel. *Papers on Social Representations* 9, 1.

Levine, H. B. 1982. Toward a Psychoanalytic Understanding of Children of Survivors of the Holocaust. *The Psychoanalytic Quarterly* 51(1), 70–92.

Maschler, Y. 2000. Toward Fused Lects: Discourse Markers in Hebrew English Bilingual Conversation Twelve Years Later. *International Journal of Bilingualism* 4(4), 529–561.

Meir, I. and W. Sandler. 2007. *A Language in Space: The Story of Israel Sign Language*. Mahwah, NJ: Lawrence Erlbaum Associates.

Meir, I. and W. Sandler. 2019. Variation and Conventionalization in Language Emergence. In E.Doron, M. Rappaport Hovav, Y. Reshef, and M. Taube (eds.), *Language Contact, Continuity and Change in the Genesis of Modern Hebrew*. Amsterdam: John Benjamins Publishing Company, 256–337.

Meir, I., W. Sandler, C. Padden, and M. Aronoff. 2010. Emerging Sign Languages. In M. Marschark and P. E. Spencer (eds.), *Oxford Handbook of Deaf Studies, Language, and Education*. Vol. 2. Oxford: Oxford University Press, 267–280.

Meir, N. and S. Armon-Lotem. 2015. Disentangling Bilingualism from SLI in Heritage Russian: The Impact of L2 Properties and Length of Exposure to the L2. In C. Hamann and E. Ruigendijk (eds.), *Language Acquisition and Development: Proceedings of GALA 2013*. Newcastle-upon-Tyne: Cambridge Scholars Publishing, 299–314.

Meir, N. & Polinsky, M. 2021. Restructuring in Heritage Grammars: Adjectival and Numerical Phrases in Israeli Russian. *Linguistic Approaches to Bilingualism, 11*(2), 222–258.

Meir, N., J. Walters, and S. Armon-Lotem. 2016. Disentangling Bilingualism from SLI Using Sentence Repetition Tasks: The Impact of L1 and L2 Properties. *International Journal of Bilingualism* 20(4), 421–452.

Meir, N., J. Walters, and S. Armon-Lotem. 2017. Bi-Directional Cross-linguistic Influence in Bilingual Russian-Hebrew Speaking Children. *Linguistic Approaches to Bilingualism* 7(5), 514–553.

Minahan, J. B. 2014. *Ethnic Groups of North, East, and Central Asia: An Encyclopedia*. California: ABC-CLIO.

Moin, V., L. Schwartz, and M. Leikin. 2013. Immigrant Parents' Lay Theories of Children's Preschool Bilingual Development and Family Language Ideologies. *International Multilingual Research Journal* 7(2), 99–118.

Moseley, C. 2010. *Atlas of the World's Languages in Danger*, 3rd ed. Paris: UNESCO Publishing. Retrieved from www.unesco.org/culture/en/endan geredlanguages/atlas

Myers-Scotton C. 1993. *Social Motivations for Codeswitching. Evidence from Africa*. Oxford: Clarendon Press.

Nadel, E., J. A. Fishman, and R. L. Cooper. 1977. English in Israel: A Sociolinguistic Study. *Anthropological Linguistics* 19(1), 26–53.

Naiditch, L. 2000. Code-Switching and -Mixing in Russian-Hebrew Bilinguals. *Studies in Slavic and General Linguistics* 28, 277–282.

Naiditch, L. 2004. Russian Immigrants of the Last Wave in Israel: Patterns and Characteristics of Language Usage. *Weiner Slawistischer Almanach* 53, 291–314.

Nir, R. 2004. Modern Hebrew Neologisms and Their Application by Speakers of Modern Israeli Hebrew. In Y. Schlesinger and M. Muchnik (eds.), *Lamed-Leilash – Studies on the 30th Anniversary of the Israeli Association of Applied Linguistics*. Tel Aviv: Tzivonim, 185–191.

Niznik, M. 2005. Searching for a New Identity: The Acculturation of Russian-born Adolescents in Israel. In J. Cohen et al. (eds.), *ISB4, Proceedings of the 4th International Symposium on Bilingualism*. Somerville, MA: Cascadilla Press, 1703–1721.

Niznik, M. 2011. Cultural Practices and Preferences of 'Russian' Youth in Israel. *Israel Affairs* 17(1), 89–107.

Olshtain, E. and S. Blum-Kulka. 1989. Happy *Hebrish*: Mixing and Switching in American-Israeli Family Interactions. In S. Gass, S. Madden, D. Preston, and L. Selinker (eds.), *Variations in Second Language Acquisition: Discourse and Pragmatics*. Philadelphia: Multilingual Matters, 37–59.

Otwinowska, A., Meir, N., Ringblom, N., Karpava, S., and La Morgia, F. 2021. Language and Literacy Transmission in Heritage Language: Evidence from Russian-Speaking Families in Cyprus, Ireland, Israel, and Sweden. *Journal of Multilingual and Multicultural Development*, 42(4), 357–382.

Perelmutter, R. 2018a. Globalization, Conflict Discourse, and Jewish Identity in an Israeli Russian-Speaking Online Community. *Journal of Pragmatics* 134, 134–148.

Perelmutter, R. 2018b. Israeli Russian in Israel. B. Hary and S. B. Benor (eds.), *Languages in Jewish Communities, Past and Present*. Boston: De Gruyter Mouton, 520–543.

Polinsky, M. 2018. *Heritage Languages and Their Speakers*. Cambridge: Cambridge University Press.

Prashizky, A. and L. Remennick. 2018. Celebrating Memory and Belonging: Young Russian Israelis Claim Their Unique Place in Tel-Aviv's Urban Space. *Journal of Contemporary Ethnography* 47(3), 336–366.

Ram, D. 2015. Challenges for Hebrew in Higher Education and Research Environments. In F. Xavier Vila and Vanessa Bretxa (eds.), *Language Policy in Higher Education: The Case of Medium-Sized Languages*. Bristol: Multilingual Matters, 103–131.

Remennick, L. 2003a. The 1.5 Generation of Russian Immigrants in Israel: Between Integration and Sociocultural Retention. *Diaspora: A Journal of Transnational Studies* 12(1), 39–66.

Remennick, L. 2003b. From Russian to Hebrew via HebRush: Intergenerational Patterns of Language Use among Former Soviet Immigrants in Israel. *Journal of Multilingual and Multicultural Development* 24(5), 431–453.

Rosenhouse, J. 2012. Two Generations of Hungarian and Hebrew in Israel: A Sociolinguistic Study. *Helqat Lashon* 45, 159–183. (Hebrew).

Sankoff, D. and S. Poplack. 1981. A Formal Grammar for Code-Switching. *Research on Language and Social Interaction* 14(1), 3–45.

Schwartz, M. and M. Minkov. 2014. Russian Case System Acquisition among Russian-Hebrew Speaking Children. *Journal of Slavic Linguistics* 22(1), 51–92.

Schwartz, M., M. Minkov, E. Dieser, E. Protassova, V. Moin, and M. Polinsky. 2015. Acquisition of Russian Gender Agreement by Monolingual and Bilingual Children. *International Journal of Bilingualism* 19(6), 726–752.

Schwartz, M., V. Moin, and M. Leikin. 2011. Parents' Discourses about Language Strategies for Their Children's Preschool Bilingual Development. *Diaspora, Indigenous, and Minority Education* 5(3), 149–166.

Schwartzwald, O. 1995. The Components of the Hebrew Lexicon: The Influence of Hebrew Classical Sources, Jewish Languages and other Foreign Languages on Modern Hebrew. *Hebrew Linguistics* 39, 79–90.

Shabtaev, R. 2018. Cross-generational Differences in Language Use among Mountain Jews in Israel. Unpublished MA thesis, Bar-Ilan University, Ramat Gan, Israel.

Shalem, V. 2018. Judeo-Tat in the Eastern Caucasus. B. Hary and S. B. Benor (eds.), *Languages in Jewish Communities, Past and Present*. Boston: De Gruyter Mouton, 313–356.

Shohamy, E. 2003. Implications of Language Education Policies for Language Study in Schools and Universities. *The Modern Language Journal* 87(2), 278–286.

Shur, S. A. 1996. Modern Hebrew in the Light of Language Planning Terminology, History, and Periodization. *Hebrew Studies* 37(1), 39–54.

Spector-Bitan, G. 2012. Los Muertos que Vos Matáis Gozan de Buena Salud: Changes in Spanish Proficiency in Early Adulthood among the Second Generation of Latin-Americans in Israel. *Israel Studies in Language and Society* 4(1), 73–97.

Spolsky, B. 1983. Triglossia and Literacy in Jewish Palestine of the First Century. *International Journal of the Sociology of Language* 1983(42), 95–110.

Spolsky, B. 1997. Multilingualism in Israel. *Annual Review of Applied Linguistics* 17, 138–150.

Spolsky, B. 2014. *The Languages of the Jews: A Sociolinguistic History.* Cambridge: Cambridge University Press.

Spolsky, B. and E. G. Shohamy. 1999. *The Languages of Israel: Policy, Ideology, and Practice.* Vol. 17. Clevedon: Multilingual Matters.

Spolsky, B. and E. G. Shohamy. 2001. Hebrew after a Century of RLS Efforts. In J. A. Fishman (ed.), *Can Threatened Languages Be Saved?* Clevedon: Multilingual Matters Ltd., 349–362.

Stavans, A. 2015. Enabling Bi-Literacy Patterns in Ethiopian Immigrant Families in Israel: A Socio-Educational Challenge. *International Journal of Multilingualism* 12(2), 178–195.

Stavans, A., E. Olshtain, and G. Goldzweig. 2009. Parental Perceptions of Children's Literacy and Bilingualism: The Case of Ethiopian Immigrants in Israel. *Journal of Multilingual and Multicultural Development* 30(2), 111–126.

Teferra, A. 2018. Hebraized Amharic in Israel. In B. Hary and S. B. Benor (eds.), *Languages in Jewish Communities, Past and Present.* Boston: De Gruyter Mouton, 489–519.

Viswanath, A. and M. Polinsky. 2012. *A Look at Heritage English. In Poster Presented at the Colloquium of Formal Approaches to Heritage Languages.* Amherst: University of Massachusetts.

Yelenevskaya, M. 2015. An Immigrant Language in a Multilingual State: Status and Group Competition (Russian in Israel). *Russian Journal of Communication* 7(2), 193–207.

Zuckermann, G. A. 2003a. *Language Contact and Lexical Enrichment in Israeli Hebrew.* London: Palgrave Macmillan.

Zuckermann, G. A. 2003b. Language Contact and Globalisation: The Camouflaged Influence of English on the World's Languages: With Special Attention to Israeli (sic) and Mandarin. *Cambridge Review of International Affairs* 16(2), 287–307.

7

Heritage Languages in Aotearoa New Zealand and Australia

Corinne A. Seals

7.1 Introduction

In Aotearoa New Zealand, over 160 languages are spoken in a country of between four and five million people, and in Australia, over 360 languages are spoken in a country of between 24 and 25 million people. This proportionally large number of languages in each of the two countries makes each one superdiverse, which is particularly remarkable given the history of prolonged British and European colonization experienced by each country. However, despite New Zealand and Australia's shared geographic region and shared history of colonization, there remain many differences when it comes to heritage languages. These differences include which languages are spoken, what language policies and practices have affected heritage language speakers in each place, and what researchers have looked at in each place. These differences and similarities are the focus of the current chapter.

Furthermore, it is only very recently that either country has begun to use the term "heritage language." The reason for this is twofold. First, "heritage language" is viewed in the Australasian region as a North American and European term. This only changed recently (in the past five years or so) with the movement of more heritage language scholars from North America and Europe to New Zealand and Australia. Since then, the use of the term "heritage language" has become increasingly common, though some still choose not to use it. Second, the term "heritage language" has had undesirable connotations for many in New Zealand and Australia. More specifically, stakeholders have discussed equating the term "heritage language" with a sense of language loss, past but not present importance, and less power and status for communities (Seals and Berardi-Wiltshire 2017). This perception among many policy makers, community leaders, language activists, researchers, and instructors has also restricted the use of this term in the Australasian context. Therefore, it is important to specify that the discussion of heritage languages in this current chapter is in relation to the established North American and European use of the term, not necessarily in all cases that of New Zealand or Australia.

With this established, it is also important to specify that the current use of the term "heritage language" in New Zealand and Australia is used by the majority (of those who subscribe to the term) to refer to both Indigenous and immigrant languages. It is this positioning that influenced the definition used by Seals and Shah (2018: 3) of "heritage languages" and that which I am using in the current chapter, as:

> including Indigenous and immigrant/diaspora community languages, due to the recognition that languages do not have to be *either* one thing *or* the other; they can be both. That is, for example, a language does not have to be either an Indigenous language or a heritage language – it can be, and often is, both at once. We argue that since the term 'heritage language' focuses on identity, agency, and cultural history, it is a self-identifying categorization and one that is up to the individual and/or community to decide upon.

Now that this contextualization has been established, the chapter continues with an overview of heritage language policies and education in Aotearoa New Zealand. This is followed by an examination of key research to date, first focusing on te reo Māori, then New Zealand Sign Language (NZSL), followed by Pasifika languages, and finally additional community-based languages. Following this, the same outline is followed for a discussion of Australia, presenting first relevant policies and a background of heritage languages in Australia, followed by a discussion of research trends with Australian Indigenous and immigrant languages.[1]

7.2 Aotearoa New Zealand

Despite the large number of languages and language varieties spoken in Aotearoa New Zealand (over 160), there is still no national languages policy. This is something that scholars and policy makers in support of minority languages have sought to address several times over the past few decades, with the most recent large-scale renewal attempt taking place in 2015 via the Royal Society of New Zealand (Royal Society of New Zealand 2013). That is not to say that New Zealand has no policies dictating official languages of the country. Rather, there are both official de jure and official de facto

---

[1] As I am a New Zealand-based researcher who works with heritage languages in Aotearoa New Zealand, the New Zealand section will necessarily be more extensive than the Australia section. However, recommendations are made for additional reading of these topics for the Australian context.

languages of the country. Additionally, there are ministries (governing bodies) that support the official languages as well as some of the unofficial languages. This will be discussed in more depth later.

The official *de jure* languages of New Zealand are te reo Māori (named official in 1987) and NZSL (named official in 2006). English also operates as an official *de facto* language of the country, as it has the largest number of speakers, at a rate of 90 percent of the population (Statistics New Zealand 2013). Te reo Māori speakers make up 3 percent of the population, and NZSL speakers make up slightly less than 1 percent of the population (Statistics New Zealand 2013). Additionally, while English is a colonial language, te reo Māori is the Indigenous language of Aotearoa New Zealand, and NZSL is also native to Aotearoa. For reasons of official language status and of indigeneity, these two languages have received increased attention in language-based research within the country in the past few decades.

This focus on heritage language maintenance and language revitalization is fueled in part by New Zealand's history of linguistic oppression following British and European colonization beginning in the seventeenth and eighteenth centuries. In particular, the nineteenth century saw the British introduce mass assimilationist policies for all Māori in New Zealand, which continued until the 1980s (Mikaere 2013; Moon 2013). In the 1970s, all Māori people and all immigrants to New Zealand were expected to replace their native language(s) with English. This had such a strongly negative impact on heritage language maintenance that while 90 percent of Māori children spoke te reo Māori in 1900, this dropped to 2 percent by the 1980s (Ka'ai-Mahuta 2011), leading to language endangerment and the language revitalization efforts that we see today.

7.2.1 Te Reo Māori

In terms of te reo Māori, most research by both Māori and non-Māori researchers has focused primarily on language education, language policy, language rights, and efforts in language revitalization and maintenance. While the account in this current chapter is by no means exhaustive of the research that has been done, it will give an indication of the research trends in this area.

Heritage language research focused on te reo Māori has included that by Durie (1997) looking at Māori–English bilingual education, and by Harrison and Papa (2005) examining the development of an Indigenous knowledge (mātauranga Māori) program in a Māori language immersion school in New Zealand. Also in the language education space, the presence and characteristics of Māori-medium education in New Zealand have been examined (May 2004), as have non-Māori teachers' beliefs and use of te reo Māori in mainstream New Zealand education, as micro-language planners in these contexts (Barr and Seals 2018). In a particularly large-scale study, the language acquisition of over 6,000 two-year-olds was examined, and the researchers determined that te reo Māori acquisition seemed to be occurring within the context of New Zealand English (Reese et al. 2018).

Further research has also looked into opportunities for innovative bilingual education models supported by social justice efforts. In this vein, Tamati (2019) developed and trialed a TransAcquisition Pedagogy, developing students' academic literacy across languages through cross-language tasks. In this particularly groundbreaking research, Tamati worked with students who have te reo Māori as a first language but struggle with the standardized exams in English, particularly in areas to do with literacy. She developed a task-based pedagogy that built upon students' conceptual and abstract knowledge in te reo Māori, building cognitive bridges to connect this knowledge and literary expression in English. Tamati found that this approach of translingual language education is able to contribute to bilingual language proficiency for students, with her student cohort raising their English language exam scores to the same levels as New Zealand's most socioeconomically advantaged students, while still simultaneously valuing and retaining te reo Māori. Similar results have been found and arguments made by Seals and Olsen-Reeder (2020), who analyzed how socially responsive translanguaging (building students' linguistic repertoires up and across languages sustainably and in a culturally responsive way) in the cases of te reo Māori and Samoan can contribute positively to language revitalization and maintenance efforts.

The issue of language rights for speakers of te reo Māori has also been given major consideration by researchers. For example, Kāretu (1994) argued for the rights of Māori language speakers in New Zealand to be brought front and center in language policy. Additionally, an important area of inquiry has been identity and language politics of self-determination for Māori in New Zealand (Durie 1998), as well as relatedly the New Zealand government's approach to a language-in-education policy of teaching te reo Māori to those who do not identify as Māori (De Bres 2011). Much of the discussion of New Zealand's language-in-education policy in relation to te reo Māori has focused on *Tau Mai Te Reo, The Māori Language in Education Strategy 2013–2017* published by the Ministry of Education (2013) and the Māori Language Act 2016, and some research has added to this by examining the current language policies surrounding te reo Māori education through a historical political lens (Seals and Olsen-Reeder 2018).

Relatedly, there have been many critical macro-level discussions of language revitalization efforts for te reo Māori, which have been very important in guiding the focus of researchers in this context. For example, May and Hill (2018) wrote a comprehensive updated account of key work done in the area of language revitalization for te reo Māori in New Zealand. Perhaps even more importantly in framing future research directions, Higgins and Rewi (2014) critically examined the benefits and challenges of repositioning te reo Māori as normalized in New Zealanders' linguistic repertoire in a movement toward sustainability, work which has been significant in strengthening arguments for more active use and public presence of te reo Māori across all domains. Additional research has been carried out looking at the attitudes of New Zealanders broadly toward te reo Māori revitalization efforts (Nicholson and Garland 1992), and the factors influencing language choice and use for bilingual speakers of te reo Māori and English, and the impact that this has on Māori revitalization and maintenance efforts (Olsen-Reeder 2017). Further contributing to the discussion of repositioning te reo Māori for sustainability, Olsen-Reeder (2018) has made a significant argument for moving away from a focus on language death when discussing te reo Māori, as this can actually impede revitalization efforts.

7.2.2 New Zealand Sign Language

The research into NZSL has trended in a different direction from that focusing on te reo Māori. NZSL research has largely focused on sociolinguistic variation, pragmatics, corpus creation, professional interpretation, and issues of wellbeing (particularly looking at access to medical services). However, there has been overlap in some focus areas with te reo Māori, such as identity construction, language maintenance, and language policy.

Looking first at sociolinguistic variation, McKee and McKee (2011) have examined sociolinguistic variation in the NZSL lexicon and how this has changed over time. Additional research in sociolinguistic variation has included that on phonological variation and change (Schembri et al. 2009), and multimodal variation, specifically for fingerspelling in NZSL (Pivac Alexander 2008).

In regard to language maintenance efforts, a new focus involves family language policies within NZSL speaker homes of Deaf children and how this relates to the potential for NZSL vitality in New Zealand (McKee and Smiler 2016). McKee (2017) has also written an updated assessment of the projected vitality of NZSL in New Zealand and the factors contributing to this. These projections are important in connecting language vitality and language rights, as shown in McKee and Manning's (2015) analysis of the causal relationship between the two for NZSL. Additionally, as previously mentioned, a large proportion of research on NZSL language rights has focused on wellbeing and access to healthcare. For example, research has looked specifically at NZSL users' access to healthcare, especially when it comes to readily being able to access interpretation services in this space (Witko et al. 2017).

Identity also arises in NZSL research as another issue connected to well-being. For example, McKee and McKee (2000) studied the name signs that are given by those from within the NZSL community to determine the connection between name signs and identity. Additionally, cross-community membership is acknowledged in the important research by McKee, McKee, Smiler and Pointon (2007) looking at how identity as Māori is constructed by deaf Māori who are users of NZSL.

7.2.3 Pasifika Languages

Aligning with the previously discussed definition of "heritage language," New Zealand researchers, policy makers, and communities further define two groups when discussing heritage languages and their speakers: Pasifika languages and other community-based minority languages. Pasifika languages (the largest groups of which include Samoan, Tongan, Cook Islands Māori, Niuean, and Tokelauan) are not recognized as official languages of New Zealand, but there is a dedicated ministry (Ministry of Pacific Peoples) providing support for these community groups, including the institution and promotion of language weeks. Therefore, the Pasifika languages are unofficial languages of New Zealand but with dedicated governmental support (see Seals and Olsen-Reeder 2018 for more discussion of this). Furthermore, Samoan is the third most spoken language in New Zealand (with 2 percent of the population, [Statistics New Zealand 2013]), and Auckland has the highest concentration of Pasifika language speakers in the world (Komiti Pasifika 2010). As such, research into Pasifika language maintenance, language shift, identity in relation to language, and official recognition of the Pasifika languages have been major areas of focus for heritage language research in New Zealand, especially in recent years.

In particular, a great deal of research in New Zealand focused on Pasifika languages has been in the area of language maintenance and language shift (LMLS). One of the earliest studies in this area focused on Tongan LMLS across New Zealand ('Aipolo and Holmes 1990), but interestingly Tongan is no longer a main focus of Pasifika LMLS research. Instead, Samoan has become a major community of focus, especially in research on the factors affecting Samoan LMLS in New Zealand (Fairburn-Dunlop 1984), including specific focus on Samoan language communities in Auckland (Hoare 1991; Taumoefolau et al. 2002) and in Wellington (Roberts 1999). However, LMLS research has also been conducted recently with some of the smaller Pasifika communities in New Zealand, such as Tokelauan (Pene et al. 2009) and Cook Islands Māori (David and Starks 2005).

In terms of language education, Amosa Burgess and Fiti (2019) looked at the results of implementing a translingual approach to education in a Samoan early childhood center, finding that this offers promise for increasing children's use of Samoan, regardless of the children's individual linguistic backgrounds. Similarly, bilingual literacy and language development for Samoan children in the Auckland area has been studied (McCaffery and Tuafuti 2003), as has LMLS in terms of children's acquisition and use of Samoan and Tongan when growing up in New Zealand (Reese et al. 2015). Finally, a recent comprehensive overview of Pasifika heritage language education and language-in-education policies related to Pasifika languages in New Zealand argues that while in-school language offerings have increased for Samoan, the offerings have not kept up with the demand in any Pasifika language, resulting in language loss across all Pasifika languages (Seals 2017).

Pasifika language and identity research has had a generally broader focus than in the case of te reo Māori or NZSL, looking across Pasifika language communities and speakers to investigate issues of language and identity, both current and projected (Hunkin-Tuiletufugu 2001). Likewise, language as a marker of ethnic identity has also been examined across Pasifika language communities in New Zealand (Starks et al. 2005).

7.2.4   Additional Community-Based Heritage Languages

In addition to the Pasifika languages discussed in the previous subsection, there are heritage languages in New Zealand that do not receive any dedicated governmental resources, and yet these languages make up the majority of 160+ languages being spoken every day in New Zealand. The language with the most speakers in this category is Hindi – the fourth most spoken language in New Zealand at 2 percent of the population (Statistics New Zealand 2013). This is followed by Northern Chinese, French, Yue, Sinitic, German, Tagalog, Afrikaans, Spanish, Korean, and Dutch – each with 1 percent of the population as speakers (Statistics New Zealand 2013). Similar to research into Pasifika heritage languages, research into the additional community-based heritage languages has focused largely on LMLS as well as language and identity. Further areas of particular interest to researchers working with these communities have included family language policy and ethnographic investigations into community-based schools for teaching heritage language speakers.

Looking first at LMLS, LMLS has been robustly examined among Dutch communities living in New Zealand, given the large Dutch communities that historically lived here (Hulsen 2000; De Bres 2004; Crezee 2012). LMLS has also been the focus of studies with the Greek community in Wellington (Verivaki 1990), Spanish speaking communities in New Zealand (Walker 2011; Revis 2015), New Zealand-born Chinese speakers in Auckland (Sun 1999), Japanese speakers in Auckland (Nakanishi 2000), the Chilean community in Auckland (Lee 2013), the Serbo-Croatian community in New

Zealand (Stoffel 1982), Gujarati and Dutch communities in Wellington (Roberts 1999), Polish and Italian communities in Wellington (Neazor 1991, 1994), and Indo-Fijians living in Wellington (Shameem 1994).

Furthermore, an interest in family language policy has seen this research subfield combined with research into LMLS, such as the investigation of the role of families, and particularly fathers, in Arabic language maintenance in New Zealand (Al-Sahafi 2010, 2015). This combined research focus has also led to fascinating studies of the role of fathers in Korean family language policies in bilingual Korean-English speaking homes in New Zealand (Kim and Starks 2010), and children's Afrikaans language use in their homes in New Zealand and their parents' perception of this use for LMLS (Kim and Starks 2010). The role of family language policies in LMLS of heritage language has also been looked at with Persian families (Gharibi and Seals 2019), as well as Spanish speakers in New Zealand (Navarro and Macalister 2016; Berardi-Wiltshire 2017b). Additionally, Revis (2016) investigated the influence of religious ideologies and practices specifically on Ethiopian families' language policies.

Heritage language education has not been researched as extensively as other types of LMLS research, but there are some notable exceptions. These include Berardi-Wiltshire's (2009, 2017a) work with Italian heritage language learners in New Zealand and how this is connected to language and identity, as well as Cui's (2012) work with Chinese parents' and children's attitudes toward Chinese as a heritage language education in New Zealand. When it comes to research into language and identity, Adlam (1987) was one of the first to officially investigate language and identity in this context, looking at the experience of Indonesian speakers living in Wellington. Since then, more work has been done in this area, including narratives of identity, social inclusion, and language maintenance among Afrikaans speakers (Barkhuizen 2013), the role of identity for language use and maintenance within the Wellington Iraqi community (Tawalbeh 2016), and narratives of language and identity for those in the New Zealand Ukrainian community (Seals 2019).

7.3 Australia

While Aotearoa New Zealand and Australia are considered to be in the same region and share a history of British and European colonization, the heritage language speaker populations of each country are distinct. Furthermore, the language policies regarding Indigenous[2] and immigrant heritage languages in each country are also distinct. As previously

---

[2] The term "Indigenous" is used to encompass Aboriginal languages as well as Torres Strait Islander languages.

mentioned, New Zealand has no formal languages policy, though it does recognize te reo Māori and NZSL as official languages. Australia, on the other hand, has had several language policies, all of which have reflected the political priorities of the government in power at the time of each policy's establishment. While these are discussed somewhat below, the reader should refer to Liddicoat (2018) and Hobson, Lowe, Poetsch, and Walsh (2010) for more in-depth coverage of these policies, associated language-in-education policies, and research involving heritage languages in Australia.

In Australia, over 360 languages are spoken, among which at least 160 are Aboriginal languages (Department of Immigration and Border Protection 2014). While 160 Indigenous languages are far more than New Zealand's one, this is still a drastic decline from the more than 250 Indigenous languages that were spoken in Australia before the first European settlers arrived at the end of the eighteenth century (Walsh 1991), showing the severe lack of support for Indigenous language speakers in this country historically and currently. The additional 200 heritage languages that are now in Australia are a result of pull factors such as the Australian gold rushes and push factors such as mass migration from Europe after World War II (Liddicoat 2018).

Like New Zealand, English is the most spoken language in Australia – with over 80 percent of the population classified as only speaking English (Department of Immigration and Border Protection 2014) (note that these statistics are classified differently from New Zealand, where English is classified as one of the possible languages, not the only language). Following this, less than 2 percent of the Australian population speak the following languages – Mandarin, Italian, Arabic, Cantonese, Greek, and Vietnamese. Then, less than 1 percent of Australia's population speak Spanish, Hindi, and Tagalog. All Indigenous languages in Australia are spoken by less than 0.04 percent of the population. The most spoken of these (by more than 0.01 percent of the Australian population) are Kriol (a hybridized creole variety of Aboriginal languages), Torres Strait Creole (Yumplatok), Pitjantjatjara, Warlpiri, Yolngu Matha, Murrinh Pata, and Tiwi (Department of Immigration and Border Protection 2014).

Since British colonization of Australia, Indigenous languages have been actively discouraged or at times banned in education. As an example, in 1845 the Kaurna school in Adelaide was closed and replaced with an English only school (Amery 2013). This has been a historical trend in the Australian school system, with Indigenous language speakers being largely viewed as deficient and needing to "focus on English" in school (Liddicoat 2013). Additionally, following a British colonial educational model, English was enforced in schools for all students, and the heritage languages of immigrant populations were seen as something for children of the elite to be educated in, not something for immigrant populations to keep. Now, there are provisions for specialist heritage language classes, though they are largely taught in after-school programs or community-based schools.

In terms of official language policies, Australia first had the National Policy on Languages in 1987, which focused on heritage language maintenance and bilingual development (Lo Bianco 1987). Then, in 1991, the Australian Language and Literacy Policy was established, shifting the focus from bilingual education to additional language learning, with a movement away from language maintenance in general at this time (DEET 1991). Finally, in 2011, the Australian Curriculum: Languages national language curriculum was established, which created three pathways for language learning: second-language learning; heritage language learning; and first language learning (ACARA 2011), though all three pathways have not been put into effect for the majority of languages in Australia (Liddicoat 2018). These language policies, national curricula, and historical background are reflected in the heritage language research in Australia involving Indigenous and immigrant languages, discussed further in the next section.

7.3.1 Indigenous Languages

Research into Indigenous languages in Australia includes research with Aboriginal communities and Torres Strait Island communities. Research with Indigenous heritage languages in this context has mostly focused on questions of language maintenance and revitalization, language planning in education as well as family language policies, language status in Australian society, and questions of Indigenous identity and wellbeing as tied to language.

First looking at language maintenance, language reclamation and revitalization efforts involving the Kaurna language of South Australia have been investigated (Amery 2000, 2013), as have language maintenance efforts broadly for Australia's native languages (Cavallaro 2005). Looking at more specific language maintenance endeavors, a classic study by Harris (1990) investigated the possibility of two-way Aboriginal schooling as a way to increase language exposure and usage, contributing to maintenance efforts, which importantly was in line with the National Policy on Languages in 1987 and the important maintenance work originally focused on there. Much more recently, Verdon and McLeod (2015) revisited these original maintenance goals in their large-scale analysis of data from 580 children in the Footprint in Time: The Longitudinal Study of Indigenous Children data set. Through this, they were able to identify trends in successful Aboriginal and Torres Strait Islander language maintenance, and how these findings can be applied more broadly in Australian education to support Indigenous heritage language speakers. The challenge now is whether future Australian language policy will take up their recommendations.

Much work has been done examining the shifting language policies, planning, and statuses in Australia, including the perceived competing priorities when it comes to language planning for Aboriginal languages (Black 1990). Simpson, Caffery, and McConvell (2009) also investigated bilingual education in Australia, pointing to important gaps in policy that have provided a disservice to Indigenous speaking children, and what efforts should be made to repair this. Australian researchers have shown how critical it is that the government act on these efforts and also support family language policies and language-in-education policies in favor of Indigenous languages to prevent the prediction that all of Australia's Indigenous languages may be extinct by 2050 (Simpson and Wigglesworth 2008; Forrest 2018).

Finally, regarding questions of identity and wellbeing, Karidakis and Kelly (2018) analyzed 15 years of Australian Census data to uncover that even though more people are self-claiming Aboriginal identity, language use at home continues to decline, which is worrying for the above-mentioned language maintenance efforts. Furthermore, Marmion, Obata, and Troy (2014) found that there is growing recognition of the status of Aboriginal and Torres Strait Islander languages in Australian society, which contributes positively to identity and self-esteem, as well as wellbeing. However, they too found that despite this, language loss is continuing across the country.

As can be seen, many of the same questions and topic areas are investigated for both Australia and New Zealand's Indigenous languages. However, the current successes and prospects for each remain markedly different, largely due to the different histories and different widespread efforts in both places.

7.3.2 Additional Community-Based Languages

Much of the research into heritage languages in Australia has been focused on the languages of immigrant communities who have established Australia as their home. This research has a related, though different, focus to the Indigenous language research. More specifically, heritage language research with immigrant languages in Australia has largely focused on individual language case studies, examining efforts in community-based language maintenance, both in the home and in community-based schools. There has also been a focus on the presence of heritage language education initiatives in mainstream schools throughout different parts of Australia. Finally, a third major focus, similar to New Zealand, has been on the connections between heritage languages and identity.

An example of the first trend comes from a massive amount of research by Clyne and Kipp (1999, 2006), who have profiled multiple heritage language communities in Australia, including speakers of Spanish, Arabic, Chinese, Macedonian, Filipino, and Somali. Also, the role of home and school in heritage language maintenance has been investigated in Japanese communities (Oriyama 2010; Kawasaki 2014; Aiko 2017), Armenian and Ethiopian communities (Debela and Milosh 1995), Tamil communities (Fernandez and Clyne 2007), Italian communities (Finocchiaro 1995), Salvadorian and Spanish communities (Sanchez-Castro and Gil 2008), Chinese families (Tannenbaum and Howie 2002), and Sudanese refugees (Hatoss 2013), among many other case studies. Furthermore, variable issues involved with the enactment of family language policies have been examined by Pauwels (2005), Tekeuchi (2006), Li (2012), and Yates and Terraschke (2013).

Additionally, different school types and levels have also been analyzed independently. For example, logistical issues for community-based heritage language schools have been reported on by Baldauf (2005). Meanwhile, heritage languages in the upper secondary school context have been looked at by Mecurio and Scarino (2005), while Willoughby (2018) has analyzed the presence of heritage languages in the Victorian Certificate of Education. Finally, heritage language education has been examined as a means of community identity building within a Maltese community (Borland 2005), and the role specifically of ethnic and religious identity has been considered for young Indonesian heritage language speakers in Australia (Muslim and Brown 2016).

7.4   What Has Been Done and What Still Needs To Be Done

As discussed throughout this chapter, Aotearoa New Zealand and Australia have had different historical experiences with the treatment of heritage language speakers, and this has led to the many differences in terms of policy, recognition, and access that are seen today. The contemporary challenges faced by heritage languages (including Indigenous, native, and immigrant languages) have been reflected in the trends in research undertaken with communities as well.

Section 7.2 (heritage languages of Aotearoa New Zealand) showed different research trends for te reo Māori, NZSL, Pasifika languages, and additional community-based languages, which are also reflective of current issues in language policy, planning, and education for these languages. Section 7.3 (heritage languages of Australia) showed different research trends between Indigenous languages and additional community-based languages. However, there are some research trends that are shared across the region, as well as some research trends specific to the Indigenous languages of this area.

First, all six categories of heritage languages covered in this chapter show evidence of research trends focusing on language maintenance and language shift (a particular strength of Australasian researchers), heritage language education and associated language policy and planning, heritage language speakers' identities, and more recently family language policy. Research in New Zealand also currently has more discussion of language policy, though Australia has in the past. Wellbeing of heritage language speakers also seems to be an area of interest particularly for NZSL and Indigenous languages of Australia, while language revitalization and language rights are understandably of particular interest to Indigenous languages of both countries.

What research gaps remain? There has not been a strong trend yet toward research into the benefits of technology for this region, though this is understandably new. Additionally, new concepts such as translanguaging, linguistic landscapes, and new speakers bring further dynamism to heritage language discussions. These discussions are beginning to happen in the region, but much more research in these areas can still be done. Furthermore, there should be additional work done longitudinally on the perceptions of heritage language education and policy in this region, as opinion has been shifting among stakeholders and continues to do so. We do ourselves a disservice as researchers if we do not stay on top of these developments. Finally, heritage language literacy is a topic that occasionally surfaces in the Australasia region but deserves further attention. However, these are additional suggestions that should not take away from the fact that a huge amount of work has been done with heritage languages in Aotearoa New Zealand and Australia in a relatively short amount of time, often through the combined efforts of Indigenous and non-Indigenous researchers to promote community voices.

References

'Aipolo, 'Anahina and Janet Holmes. 1990. The Use of Tongan in New Zealand: Prospects for Language Maintenance. *Journal of Multilingual and Multicultural Development* 11(6), 501–521.

ACARA. 2011. *The Shape of the Australian Curriculum: Languages.* Sydney: ACARA.

Adlam, Patrick Lewis. 1987. Language and Identity: A Sociolinguistic Survey of the Indonesian Speech Community in Wellington, New Zealand. Unpublished MA thesis, Victoria University of Wellington.

Al-Sahafi, Morad. 2010. The Dynamics of Language Maintenance among Arabic-Speaking Muslim Immigrant Families in New Zealand. Unpublished PhD thesis, University of Auckland, New Zealand.

Al-Sahafi, Morad. 2015. The Role of Arab Fathers in Heritage Language Maintenance in New Zealand. *International Journal of English Linguistics* 5(1), 73–83.

Amery, Robert. 2000. *Warrabarna Kaurna! Reclaiming an Australian Language.* Lisse: Swets & Zeitlinger.

Amery, Robert. 2013. A Matter of Interpretation: Language Planning for a Sleeping Language, Kaurna, the Language of the Adelaide Plains, South Australia. *Language Problems & Language Planning* 37(2), 101–124.

Amosa Burgess, Feaua'i and Sadie Fiti. 2019. Using both Samoan and English to Shape Understandings, Reasoning and Appreciation during a Book Experience in an A'oga Amata: An Example of Translanguaging. In Corinne A. Seals and Vincent Ieni Olsen-Reeder (eds.), *Embracing Multilingualism across Educational Contexts.* Wellington: Victoria University Press, 23–38.

Baldauf, Richard B. 2005. Coordinating Government and Community Support for Community Language Teaching in Australia: Overview with Special Attention to New South Wales. *International Journal of Bilingual Education and Bilingualism* 8(2–3), 132–144.

Barkhuizen, Gary. 2006. Immigrant Parents' Perceptions of Their Children's Language Practices: Afrikaans Speakers Living in New Zealand. *Language Awareness* 15(2), 63–79.

Barkhuizen, Gary. 2013. Maintenance, Identity and Social Inclusion Narratives of an Afrikaans Speaker Living in New Zealand. *International Journal of the Sociology of Language* 222, 77–100.

Barr, Sophie and Corinne A. Seals. 2018. *He Reo* for Our Future: Te Reo Māori and Teacher Identities, Attitudes, and Micro-Policies in Mainstream New Zealand Schools. *Journal of Language, Identity & Education* 17(6), 434–447.

Berardi-Wiltshire, Arianna. 2009. Italian Identity and Heritage Language Motivation: Five Stories of Heritage Language Learning in Traditional Foreign Language Courses in Wellington, New Zealand. Unpublished PhD thesis, Massey University.

Berardi-Wiltshire, Arianna. 2017a. Identity and Motivation among Heritage Language Learners of Italian in New Zealand: A Social Constructivist Perspective. In Peter Pericles Trifonas and Themistoklis Aravossitas (eds.), *Handbook of Research and Practice in Heritage Language Education.* Cham: Springer.

Berardi-Wiltshire, Arianna. 2017b. Parental Ideologies and Family Language Policies among Spanish-speaking Migrants to New Zealand. *Journal of Iberian and Latin American Research* 23(3), 271–285.

Black, Paul. 1990. Some Competing Goals in Aboriginal Language Planning. In Richard B. Baldauf and Allan Luke (eds.), *Language Planning and*

Education in Australasia and the South Pacific. Clevedon: Multilingual Matters, 80–88.

Borland, Helen. 2005. Heritage Languages and Community Identity Building: The Case of a Language of Lesser Status. *International Journal of Bilingual Education and Bilingualism* 8(2–3), 109–123.

Cavallaro, Francesco. 2005. Language Maintenance Revisited: An Australian Perspective. *Bilingual Research Journal* 29(3), 561–582.

Clyne, Michael and Sandra Kipp. 1999. *Pluricentric Languages in an Immigrant Context: Spanish, Arabic and Chinese*. Berlin/New York: Walter de Gruyter.

Clyne, Michael and Sandra Kipp. 2006. *Tiles in a Multilingual Mosaic: Macedonian, Filipino and Somali in Melbourne*. Canberra: Pacific Linguistics.

Crezee, Ineke. 2012. Language Shift and Host Society Attitudes: Dutch Migrants Who Arrived in New Zealand between 1950 and 1965. *International Journal of Bilingualism* 16(4), 528–540.

Cui, Bao-Hui. 2012. The Differential Attitudes of Parents and Children towards Chinese as a Heritage Language in a New Zealand Context. Unpublished MA thesis, University of Auckland.

Davis, Karen and Donna Starks. 2005. Four Factors for Cook Islands Māori Language Maintenance. In Allan Bell, Ray Harlow, and Donna Starks (eds.), *Languages of New Zealand*. Wellington: Victoria University Press, 298–321.

De Bres, Julia. 2004. Intergenerational Attitudes towards Dutch Language Maintenance in New Zealand. *Wellington Working Papers in Linguistics* 16, 1–20.

De Bres, Julia. 2011. Promoting the Māori Language to Non-Māori: Evaluating the New Zealand Government's Approach. *Language Policy* 10, 361–376.

Debela, Nega Worku and Raykov Milosh. 1995. Language Maintenance and Loss among Armenians and Ethiopians in South Australia. *Educational Practice and Theory* 17(2), 51–61.

DEET. 1991. *Australia's Language: An Australian Language and Literacy Policy*. Canberra: Australian Government Publishing Service.

Department of Immigration and Border Protection. 2014. *The People of Australia: Statistics from the 2011 Census*. Retrieved from www.border.gov .au/ReportsandPublications/Documents/research/people-australia-2013-statistics.pdf

Durie, Arohia. 1997. Maori-English Bilingual Education in New Zealand. In Jim Cummins and David Corson (eds.), *Bilingual Education*. London: Kluwer Academic Publishers, 15–24.

Durie, Mason. 1998. *Te mana, te kāwanatanga: The Politics of Māori Self-determination*. Oxford: Oxford University Press.

Fairburn-Dunlop, Peggy. 1984. Factors Associated with Language Maintenance: The Samoans in New Zealand. *New Zealand Journal of Educational Studies* 20(2), 115–128.

Fernandez, Sue and Michael Clyne. 2007. Tamil in Melbourne. *Journal of Multilingual and Multicultural Development* 28(3), 169–187.

Finocchiaro, Carla. 1995. Intergenerational Language Maintenance of Minority Groups in Australia in the 1990s: An Italian Case Study. *Journal of Intercultural Studies* 16(1–2), 41–54.

Forrest, Walter. 2018. The Intergenerational Transmission of Australian Indigenous Languages: Why Language Maintenance Programmes Should Be Family-Focused. *Ethnic and Racial Studies* 41(2), 303–323.

Gharibi, Khadij and Corinne Seals. 2019. Family Language Policy towards Heritage Language Literacy Acquisition and Maintenance: Iranians in New Zealand. In Seyed Hadi Mirvahedi (ed.), *The Sociolinguistics of Iran's Languages at Home and Abroad*. London: Springer, 109–139.

Harris, Stephen. 1990. *Two-way Aboriginal Schooling. Education and Cultural Survival*. Canberra: Aboriginal Studies Press.

Harrison, Barbara and Rahui Papa. 2005. The Development of an Indigenous Knowledge Program in a New Zealand Maori Language Immersion School. *Anthropology and Education Quarterly* 36(1), 57–72.

Hatoss, Anikó. 2013. *Displacement, Language Maintenance and Identity: Sudanese Refugees in Australia*. Amsterdam: John Benjamins.

Higgins, Rawinia and Poia Rewi. 2014. Right-Shifting: Reorientation towards Normalisation. In Rawinia Higgins, Poia Rewi, and Vincent Olsen-Reeder (eds.), *The Value of the Māori Language: Te Hua o te Reo Māori*. Wellington: Huia, 7–32.

Hoare, Richard David. 1991. Samoan Language Maintenance within the Aukilani (Auckland), Niu Sila (New Zealand) Community. Unpublished MA thesis, University of Otago.

Hobson, John, Kevin Lowe, Susan Poetsch, and Michael Walsh. 2010. *Re-Awakening Languages. Theory and Practice in The Revitalisation of Australia's Indigenous Languages*. Sydney: Sydney University Press.

Hunkin-Tuiletufuga, Galumalemana. 2001. Pasefika Languages and Pasefika Identities: Contemporary and Future Challenges. In Cluni Macpherson, Paul Spoonley and Melani Anae (eds.), *Tangata O Te Moana Nui: The Evolving Identities of Pacific Peoples in Aotearoa/New Zealand*. Palmerston North: Dunmore Press.

Hulsen, Madeleine E. H. 2000. Language Loss and Language Processing: Three Generations of Dutch Migrants in New Zealand. Unpublished PhD thesis, Katholieke Universiteit Nijmegen.

Ka'ai-Mahuta, Rachael. 2011. The Impact of Colonisation on te reo Māori: A Critical Review of the State Education System. *Te Kaharoa* 4(1), 195–225.

Kāretu, Timoti. 1994. Māori Language Rights in New Zealand. In Tove Skutnabb-Kangas and Robert Phillipson (eds.), *Linguistic Human Rights. Overcoming Linguistic Discrimination*. New York: Mouton de Gruyter, 209–218.

Karidakis, Maria and Barbara Kelly. 2018. Trends in Indigenous Language Usage. *Australian Journal of Linguistics* 38(1), 105–126.

Kawasaki, Kyoko. 2014. A Place for Second Generation Japanese Speaking Children in Perth: Can they Maintain Japanese as a Community Language? In Katie Dunworth and Grace Zhang (eds.), *Critical Perspectives on Language Education*. Cham: Springer.

Kim, Sun and Donna Starks. 2010. The Role of Fathers in language Maintenance and Language Attrition: The Case of Korean–English Late Bilinguals in New Zealand. *International Journal of Bilingual Education and Bilingualism* 13(3), 285–301.

Komiti Pasifika. 2010. *'Mind Your Language': Our Responsibility to Protect and Promote Pacific Islands Languages in New Zealand as Part of a National Languages Policy*. Retrieved from www.ppta.org.nz/index.php/resources/publications/doc_download/953-mind-your-language-our-responsibility-to-protect-and-promote-pacific-islands-languages-in-nz

Lee, Sarah. 2013. Spanish Language Maintenance and Shift among the Chilean Community in Auckland. Unpublished PhD thesis, Auckland University of Technology.

Li, Liang. 2012. How Do Immigrant Parents Support Preschoolers' Bilingual Heritage Language Development in a Role-Play Context? *Australasian Journal of Early Childhood* 37(1), 142–151.

Liddicoat, Anthony J. 2013. *Language-in-Education Policies: The Discursive Construction of Intercultural Relations*. Bristol: Multilingual Matters.

Liddicoat, Anthony J. 2018. Indigenous and Immigrant Languages in Australia. In Corinne A. Seals and Sheena Shah (eds.), *Heritage Language Policies around the World*. London: Routledge, 237–253.

Lo Bianco, Joseph. 1987. *National Policy on Languages*. Canberra: Australian Government Publishing Service.

Manuela, Sam and Chris G. Sibley. 2015. The Pacific Identity and Wellbeing Scale-Revised. *Cultural Diversity and Ethnic Minority Psychology* 21(1), 146–155.

Māori Language Act. 2016.

Marmion, Doug, Kazuko Obata, and Jakelin Troy. 2014. *Community, Identity, Wellbeing: The Report of the Second National Indigenous Languages Survey*. Canberra: Australian Institute of Aboriginal and Torres Strait Islander Studies. Retrieved from https://aiatsis.gov.au/publications/products/community-identity-wellbeing-report-second-national-indigenous-languages-survey

May, Stephen. 2004. Māori-Medium Education in Aotearoa/New Zealand. In James W. Tollefson and Amy B. M. Tsui (eds.), *Medium of Instruction Policies. Which Agenda? Whose Agenda?* Mahwah, NJ: Lawrence Erlbaum, 21–41.

May, Stephen and Richard Hill. 2018. Language Revitalization in Aotearoa/New Zealand. In Leanne Hinton, Leena Huss, and Gerald Roche (eds.), *The Routledge Handbook of Language Revitalization*. London: Routledge, 309–319.

McCaffery, John and Patisepa Tuafuti. 2003. Samoan Children's Bilingual Language and Literacy Development. In Richard Barnard and Ted Glynn (eds.), *Bilingual Children's Language and Literacy Development*. Clevedon: Multilingual Matters, 80–107.

McKee, Rachel and David McKee. 2011. Old Signs, New Signs, Whose Signs? Sociolinguistic Variation in the New Zealand Sign Language Lexicon. *Sign Language Studies* 11(4), 485–527.

McKee, Rachel and Kirsten Smiler. 2016. Family Language Policy for Deaf Children and the Vitality of New Zealand Sign Language. In John Macalister and Seyed Hadi Mirvahedi (eds.), *Family Language Policies in a Multilingual World: Opportunities, Challenges, and Consequences*. London: Routledge, 30–55.

McKee, Rachel, David McKee, Kirsten Smiler, and Karen Pointon. 2007. 'Maori Signs': The Construction of Indigenous Deaf Identity in New Zealand Sign Language. In David Quinto-Pozos (ed.), *Sign Languages in Contact*. Washington, DC: Gallaudet University Press, 31–81.

McKee, Rachel L. 2017. Assessing the Vitality of New Zealand Sign Language. *Sign Language Studies* 17(3), 322–362.

McKee, Rachel L. and David McKee. 2000. Name Signs and Identity in New Zealand Sign Language. In Melanie Metzger (ed.), *Bilingualism and Identity in Deaf Communities*. Washington, DC: Gallaudet University Press.

McKee, Rachel L. and Victoria Manning. 2015. Evaluating Effects of Language Recognition on Language Rights and the Vitality of New Zealand Sign Language. *Sign Language Studies* 15(4), 473–497.

Mercurio, Antonio and Angela Scarino. 2005. Heritage Languages at Upper Secondary Level in South Australia: A Struggle for Legitimacy. *International Journal of Bilingual Education and Bilingualism* 8(2–3), 145–159.

Mikaere, Buddy. 2013. *Māori in Aotearoa New Zealand: Understanding the Culture, Protocols and Customs*. Auckland: New Holland.

Ministry of Education. 2013. *Tau Mai Te Reo – The Māori Language in Education Strategy 2013–2017*. Retrieved from https://education.govt.nz/ministry-of-education/overall-strategies-and-policies/tau-mai-te-reo-the-maori-lan guage-in-education-strategy-2013-2017

Moon, Paul. 2013. *Turning Points: Events That Changed the Course of New Zealand History*. Auckland: New Holland.

Muslim, Ahmad Bukhori and Jillian Roberta Brown. 2016. Navigating between Ethnic and Religious Identity Heritage Language Maintenance among Young Australians of Indonesian Origin. *Indonesian Journal of Applied Linguistics* 6(1), 145–155.

Muzie, Aiko. 2017. Learning Japanese as a Heritage Language: The Home School Environment. *European Journal of Foreign Language Teaching* 2(3), 103–130.

Nakanishi, Nobuko. 2000. Language Maintenance and Language Shift in the Japanese Community of Auckland: A Study of the Interaction between the Sojourners and the Immigrants. Unpublished MA thesis, University of Auckland.

Navarro, Diego and John Macalister. 2016. Adrift in an Anglophone World: Refugee Families' Language Policy Challenges. In John Macalister and Seyed Hadi Mirvahedi (eds.), *Family Language Policies in a Multilingual World: Opportunities, Challenges, and Consequences*. London: Routledge, 115–132.

Neazor, Catherine. 1991. Language Maintenance and Shift in the Wellington Polish Community. *Wellington Working Papers in Linguistics* 3, 36–55.

Neazor, Catherine. 1994. Language Maintenance and Shift in the Italian Community in Wellington. *Wellington Working Papers in Linguistics* 6, 83–104.

Nicholson, Rangi and Ron Garland. 1992. New Zealanders' Attitudes to the Revitalisation of the Maori Language. *Journal of Multilingual and Multicultural Development* 12(5), 393–410.

Olsen-Reeder, Vincent. 2017. Kia Tomokia te Kākahu o te Reo Māori: He whakamahere i ngā kōwhiri reo a te reo rua Māori. Unpublished PhD thesis, Victoria University of Wellington.

Olsen-Reeder, Vincent. 2018. Deathly Narratives: Theorising "Reo-Rientation" for Language Revitalisation Discourses. *MAI Journal* 7(2), 203–204.

Oriyama, Kaya. 2010. Heritage Language Maintenance and Japanese Identity Formation: What Role Can Schooling and Ethnic Community Contact Play? *Heritage Language Journal* 7(2), 76–111.

Pauwels, Anne. 2005. Maintaining the Community Language in Australia: Challenges and Roles for Families. *International Journal of Bilingual Education and Bilingualism* 8(2–3), 124–131.

Pene, Gina, Marisa Peita, and Philippa Howden-Chapman. 2009. Living the Tokelauan Way in New Zealand. *Social Policy Journal of New Zealand* 35, 79–92.

Pivac Alexander, Sara. 2008. Sociolinguistic Variation in New Zealand Sign Language Fingerspelling. Unpublished MA dissertation, Victoria University of Wellington.

Reese, Elaine, Elaine Ballard, Mele Taumoepeau, Melenaite Taumoefolau, Susan B. Morton, Cameron Grant, and Lana Perese. 2015. Estimating Language Skills in Samoan- and Tongan-Speaking Children Growing Up in New Zealand. *First Language* 35, 407–427.

Reese, Elaine, Peter Keegan, Stuart McNaughton, Te Kani Kingi, Polly Atatoa Carr, Joahanna Schmidt, Jatender Mohal, Cameron Grant, and Susan Morton. 2018. Te reo Māori: Indigenous Language Acquisition in the Context of New Zealand English. *Journal of Child Language* 45(2), 340–367.

Revis, Melanie. 2015. Family Language Policies of Refugees in New Zealand. Unpublished PhD thesis, Victoria University of Wellington.

Revis, Melanie. 2016. How Religious Ideologies and Practices Impact on Family Language Policy. In John Macalister and Seyed Hadi Mirvahedi (eds.), *Family Language Policies in a Multilingual World: Opportunities, Challenges, and Consequences*. London: Routledge, 135–153.

Roberts, Mary L. 1999. Immigrant Language Maintenance and Shift in the Gujarati, Dutch and Samoan Communities of Wellington. Unpublished PhD thesis, Victoria University of Wellington.

Royal Society of New Zealand. 2013. *Languages in Aotearoa New Zealand*. http://assets.royalsociety.org.nz/media/Languages-in-Aotearoa-New-Zealand.pdf

Sanchez-Castro, Olga and Jeffrey Allan Gil. 2008. Two Perspectives on Language Maintenance: The Salvadorian Community in Queensland and the Spanish Community in South Australia. *The International Journal of Language, Society and Culture* 26(1), 80–92.

Schembri, Adam, David McKee, Rachel McKee, Sara Pivac, Trevor Johnston, and Della Goswell. 2009. Phonological Variation and Change in Australian and New Zealand Sign Languages: The Location Variable. *Language Variation and Change* 21(2), 193–231.

Seals, Corinne A. 2017. Pasifika Heritage Language Education in New Zealand. In Olga Kagan, Maria Carreira, and Claire Chik (eds.), *The Routledge Handbook of Heritage Language Education*. London: Routledge, 298–312.

Seals, Corinne A. 2019. *Choosing a Mother Tongue: The Politics of Language and Identity in Ukraine*. Bristol: Multilingual Matters.

Seals, Corinne A. and Arianna Berardi-Wiltshire. 2017, June 14. An Alternative Perspective to Minority Language Terminology. Paper presented at the 11th International Symposium on Bilingualism. University of Limerick.

Seals, Corinne A. and Sheena Shah (eds.) 2018. *Heritage Language Policies around the World*. London: Routledge.

Seals, Corinne A. and Vincent Olsen-Reeder. 2018. Te Reo Māori, Samoan, and Ukrainian in New Zealand. In Corinne A. Seals and Sheena Shah (eds.), *Heritage Language Policies around the World*. London: Routledge, 221–236.

Seals, Corinne A. and Vincent Olsen-Reeder. (2020). Translanguaging in Conjunction with Language Revitalisation: Where Beliefs Meet Practice. *System* 92, 1–11.

Shameem, Nikhat. 1994. The Wellington Indo-Fijians: Language Shift among Teenage New Immigrants. *Journal of Multilingual and Multicultural Development* 15(5), 399–418.

Simpson, J. and G. Wigglesworth (eds.) 2008. *Children's Language and Multilingualism: Indigenous Language Use at Home and School*. London: Continuum.

Simpson, Jane, Jo Caffery, and Patrick McConvell. 2009. *Gaps in Australia's Indigenous Language Policy: Dismantling Bilingual Education in the Northern Territory*. Canberra: Aboriginal Studies Press.

Starks, Donna, Melenaite Taumoefolau, Allan Bell, and Karen Davis. 2005. Language as a Marker of Ethnic Identity in New Zealand's Pasifika Communities. In James Cohen, Kara T. McAlister, Kellie Rolstad, and Jeff MacSwan (eds.), *Proceedings of the 4th International Symposium on Bilingualism*. Somerville, MA: Cascadilla Press, 2189–2196.

Statistics New Zealand. 2013. *2013 Census Totals by Topic*. www.stats.govt .nz/~/media/Statistics/Census/2013%20Census/data-tables/totals-by-topic/ totals-by-topic-tables.xls

Stoffel, Hans P. 1982. Language Maintenance and Shift of the Serbo-Croatian Language in a New Zealand Dalmatian Community. In Roland Sussex (ed.), *The Slavic Languages in Émigré Communities*. Edmonton: Linguistic Research Inc., 121–139.

Sun, Susan. 1999. The New Zealand-Born Chinese Community of Auckland: Aspects of Language Maintenance and Shift. *Hong Kong Journal of Applied Linguistics* 4(2), 1–14.

Takeuchi, Masae. 2006. *Raising Children Bilingually through the "One Parent-One Language" Approach: A Case Study of Japanese Mothers in the Australian Context*. Bern: Peter Lang.

Tamati, Sophie Tauwehe. 2019. TransAcquisition Pedagogy with Emergent Bilinguals in Indigenous and Minority Groups for Cultural and Linguistic Sustainability. In Corinne A. Seals and Vincent Ieni Olsen-Reeder (eds.), *Embracing Multilingualism across Educational Contexts*. Wellington: Victoria University Press, 69–96.

Tannenbaum, Michal and Pauline Howie. 2002. The Association between Language Maintenance and Family Relations: Chinese Immigrant Children in Australia. *Journal of Multilingual and Multicultural Development* 23(5), 408–424.

Taumoefolau, Melenaite, Donna Starks, Karen Davis, and Allan Bell. 2002. Linguists and Language Maintenance: Pasifika Languages in Manukau, New Zealand. *Oceanic Linguistics* 41(1), 15–27.

Tawalbeh, Ayman Z. 2016. Pre and Post Migration: Identity, Language Use and Attitudes among the Wellington Iraqi Community. Unpublished PhD thesis, Victoria University of Wellington.

Verdon, Sarah and Sharynne McLeod. 2015. Indigenous Language Learning and Maintenance among Young Australian Aboriginal and Torres Strait Islander Children. *International Journal of Early Childhood* 47 (1), 153–170.

Verivaki, Maria. 1990. Language Maintenance and Shift in the Greek Community of Wellington, New Zealand. Unpublished MA thesis, Victoria University of Wellington.

Walker, Ute. 2011. The Role of Community in Preserving Spanish in New Zealand. In Kim Potowski and Jason Rothman (eds.), *Bilingual Youth: Spanish in English-Speaking Societies*. Philadelphia: John Benjamins, 331–354.

Walsh, Michael. 1991. Overview of Indigenous Languages of Australia. In Suzanne Romaine (ed.), *Language in Australia*. Cambridge: Cambridge University Press, 27–48.

Willoughby, Louisa. 2018. High Stakes Assessment of Heritage Languages: The Case of the Victorian Certificate of Education. In Peter Pericles Trifonas and Themistoklis Aravossitas (eds.), *Handbook of Research and Practice in Heritage Language Education*. Cham: Springer.

Witko, Joanne, Pauline Boyles, Kirsten Smiler, and Rachel L. McKee. 2017. Deaf New Zealand Sign Language Users' Access to Healthcare. *New Zealand Medical Journal* 130(1466), 53–61.

Yates, Lynda and Agnes Terraschke. 2013. Love, Language and Little Ones: Successes and Stresses for Mothers Raising Bilingual Children in Exogamous Relationships. In Mila Schwartz and Anna Verschik (eds.), *Successful Family Language Policy*. Dordrecht: Springer.

8

Heritage Languages in Canada

Naomi Nagy

8.1 Introduction to the Canadian Linguistic Context

"Most readers will know that issues of language and culture are central to current Canadian social and political life," wrote John Edwards (1998: 1) as the opening line of *Language in Canada*, and this still holds true. Much attention is given in daily life and in the media to the languages we speak in Canada. Ricento (2013: 533) notes that language issues are still "front and center" in Canadian politics. As just one example, the importance of Chinese was highlighted by a front page spread in *The Globe and Mail* (a Toronto newspaper) with a large headline consisting of twenty Chinese characters with this English accompaniment: "If you can't read these words, better start brushing up … " (Foreign Affairs Canada 2005: 8).

Why does Canada suggest that its residents need familiarity with multiple languages while its neighbor to the south engages with proposals for English Only legislation? Factors that contribute to supporting multilingualism and language retention are reviewed in this chapter, from the interacting domains of language usage, research, and education. It begins by reporting on the ethnolinguistic vitality of heritage languages (HLs) in Canada, examining their demographics (population sizes, transmission rates), institutional support (via schools, community groups, a museum, and legislation), and status (as portrayed through the media, through socioeconomic indicators, and through attitudes reported by speakers and researchers).

The chapter surveys Canadian HL research, including overviews and surveys; studies from the domain of sociolinguistics (language variation and change, attitudes, and linguistic practices) that rely on spontaneous speech corpora and ethnographic observation; acquisition studies employing experimental methodology as well as elicited speech; and research with pedagogical approaches and applications. Specific information is provided about heritage varieties of Cantonese, German, Greek, Italian, Inuktitut, Korean, Mandarin, Russian, Spanish, Tagalog, and Ukrainian, sampling from coast to coast to coast.

A country with 38 million residents, Canada has speakers of nearly 600 varieties of 70+ indigenous languages, spread across twelve language families (Statistics Canada 2017b); comprising 260,550 speakers of indigenous languages (O'Donnell and Anderson 2017). Additionally, more than 140 immigrant languages are reported in the 2016 census (Statistics Canada 2018). Overall, as of 2016, more than 7 million Canadians speak an immigrant language at home (this number does not include). This is over one-fifth of the population of Canada, representing an increase of almost 15 percent since the 2011 census (Statistics Canada 2017b).

In Canada, the term *heritage language* (HL) refers to mother tongue languages other than the two *official* languages, English and French.[1] This definition appears in the Canadian Heritage Languages Institute Act of 1991 (Government of Canada 1991). In this context, HLs include aboriginal/indigenous languages as well as those brought to Canada by immigrants (except immigrants from English- and French-speaking countries). However, Canadian First Nations communities generally do not see their languages as heritage languages and prefer to use terms such as indigenous or aboriginal language (Cummins 2005: 591).

What these Canadian definitions have in common is that they include no reference to fluency or proficiency. Thus, the focus of this chapter may differ from that of other chapters where the term "HL speaker" refers to speakers who are less than fully proficient (as defined in Benmamoun et al. 2013: 129) or where reference to abilities in an official language form part of the definition of a heritage language speaker (Montrul 2012: 168).

8.2 The Ethnolinguistic Vitality of Heritage Languages in Canada

Ethnolinguistic vitality has been defined by Giles, Bourhis, and Taylor (1977: 308) as "that [which] makes a group likely to behave as a distinctive and active collective entity in intergroup situations." Its three key components are demography, status and institutional support, which are discussed in turn in this section.

---

[1] In 1994, the Ontario government adapted the term "international language" to replace "heritage language"; in Quebec the French terms *langue d'origine* and *langue patrimoniale* were introduced in 1993 (Cummins 1998b: 293).

8.2.1 Demographics

Provinces and territories in Canada range widely in terms of their number of HL speakers, from Nunavut with 67 percent of its people reporting a language other than French or English as their mother tongue (primarily Inuktitut) to Brunswick and Newfoundland and Labrador reporting 3 percent. These percentages include both immigrant and indigenous languages, excluding only French and English. Table 8.1 reports data from Canada's most recent (2016) national census. It compares the number of respondents to the number reporting a mother tongue that is not one of the two federal official languages. Quite a few people report more than one mother tongue, often one official and one non-official. These speakers are primarily in Ontario and Quebec. The number of such speakers is given in the third column of numbers. The final column represents the percentage of speakers who report a non-official language as their mother tongue (with or without an additional mother tongue). Provinces and territories are listed in decreasing order of percentage of people with a heritage language as mother tongue.

Table 8.2 reports the same type of information as Table 8.1, for the "census metropolitan areas" containing Canada's largest cities, where most

Table 8.1 *Density of HL speakers in Canada, by province and territory (Statistics Canada 2017a. Language highlight tables. 2016 census).*

Region	Total	Non-official language	Non-official + official language	% HL as Mother Tongue
Canada	34,767,255	7,321,060	653,305	23
Nunavut	35,690	23,345	710	67
British Columbia	4,598,415	1,267,465	93,360	30
Ontario	13,312,870	3,553,925	311,860	29
Manitoba	1,261,620	288,985	27,140	25
Alberta	4,026,650	870,945	81,845	24
Northwest Territories	41,380	7,625	675	20
Saskatchewan	1,083,235	156,960	16,520	16
Quebec	8,066,560	1,060,830	112,510	15
Yukon	35,560	4,210	450	13
Prince Edward Island	141,020	7,160	510	5
Nova Scotia	912,295	44,550	4,615	5
New Brunswick	736,280	23,150	2,010	3
Newfoundland and Labrador	515,680	11,920	1,115	3

Table 8.2 *(Statistics Canada 2017a. Language highlight tables. 2016 census).*

City	Total	Non-official language	Non-official + official language	% HL as Mother Tongue	% HL used at home
Toronto	5,883,670	2,518,560	222,810	47	34
Vancouver	2,440,145	1,020,250	73,050	45	33
Montréal	4,053,360	910,605	98,700	25	17

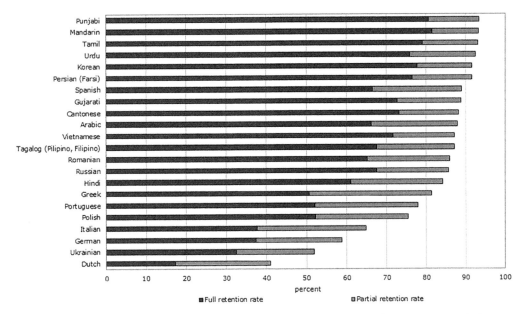

Figure 8.1 Full or partial retention rate for the 22 most common immigrant mother tongues, Canada (LePage 2017)

recent immigrants settle. Additionally, the rightmost column gives the percentage of people who report using an HL (only or in addition to an official language) at home. In each case, the number for home-language use is lower than the number of people who report that their mother tongue is not an official language, reflecting a degree of language shift in the home.

This shift is further reflected by examining retention rates for the twenty-two largest HLs in Canada (see Figure 8.1). This graph shows the percentage of people who speak their mother tongue at home, according to the 2016 census. Sixteen languages have more than 80 percent of their mother tongue speakers using the language at home. In 2016 (as well as in 2011), each of these twenty-two immigrant mother tongues had more than 100,000 speakers.

However, we can also apply the "glass half-full" perspective: In 2016, there were twenty-one heritage languages still being spoken at home by more than half of the people who had acquired them as children. There are several reasons where heritage languages persist in Canada. Immigration continues strong. In fact, Canada has the highest immigration rate among G8 countries, 20.6 percent (2010 data, Di Salvo 2017: 77).

In addition to high immigration rates, another reason that heritage language use continues strongly is high transmission rates. The rate of immigrant-language transmission rose from 41 percent in 1981 to 56 percent in 2006. However, the intensity of intergenerational language transmission moved in the opposite direction from historic transmission:

41 percent of mothers surveyed in 1981 passed on their language, but *their* daughters, 25 years later, only passed on the language 23 percent of the time. Thus only 10 percent (41% × 23%) of the grandchildren of the 1981 first-generation immigrant mothers have the same mother tongue as their mother and grandmother. That is, it is newer immigrant families that are responsible for the historic increase in transmission rates. Unsurprisingly, there is variation in transmission rates across languages. For some languages (Dutch, Italian, Creole, and Tagalog), transmission of the mother's mother tongue to children under 18 years of age was less than 20 percent, while for others (Armenian, Punjabi, Chinese, Persian, Turkish, Bengali, and Urdu) it exceeded 70 percent. Several European languages (Portuguese, Italian, Greek, Czech) decreased (Houle 2011: 5).

The most recent (2016) census reports more than one-third of Canadian children have at least one foreign-born parent. Nearly half of these children have an Asian country of ancestry, while less than 25 percent are from a European country of ancestry or the United States. Seventy-six percent of children who have two foreign-born parents that share the same HL mother tongue speak that language at home (possibly along with an official language). Thirty-four percent of parents who share the same heritage mother tongue as their partner speak that language at home. Thirty-two percent of children with one foreign-born and one Canadian-born parent speak the parent's heritage language at home. Sixty-three percent of children who live with a single parent who speaks a heritage language speak their parent's language at home (Houle and Maheux 2017: 5–6). In some cases, families, of course, do not communicate in the heritage language.

Census data reports on almost seventy indigenous languages spoken in Canada. Eight have more than 5,000 mother tongue speakers. More people report speaking an indigenous language at home (228,770 people) than report having an indigenous mother tongue (213,225 people) (LePage 2017). Retention rates (percent of mother tongue speakers who use the language at home) for these eight most popular indigenous languages are reported in Figure 8.2; all exceed 70 percent.

Census data is restricted to the larger populations. Smaller varieties, often moribund, are not individually represented. In Canada, these include, for example, Germanic languages in Manitoba (Page and Putnam 2015), Faetar[2] (Nagy 2011b; Nagy et al. 2018), and Scandinavian languages (Arnbjörnsdóttir 2006; Johannessen 2015). A list of endangered indigenous languages, with endangerment levels, is provided at https://en.wikipedia .org/wiki/List_of_endangered_languages_in_Canada.

---

[2] Faetar is a Francoprovençal variety spoken in two villages in southern Italy and in an HL diaspora including Canada (Nagy 2017a, 2018). Faetar is also an HL in southern Italy, a result of migration from the French Alps some 800 years ago.

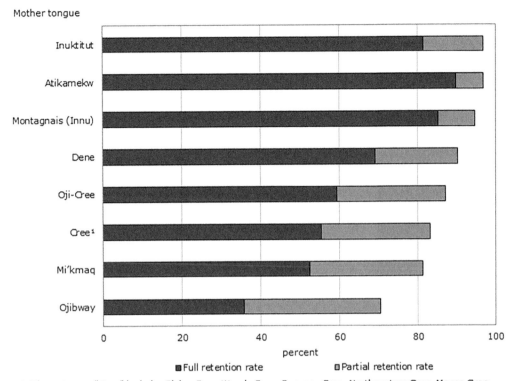

Mother tongue

1. The category "Cree" includes Plains Cree, Woods Cree, Swampy Cree, Northeastern Cree, Moose Cree, Southeastern Cree, and the category "Cree n.o.s." The abbreviation "n.o.s." means "not otherwise specified".
Source: Statistics Canada, Census of Population, 2016.

Figure 8.2 Full or partial retention rate for the eight main Aboriginal mother tongues, Canada, 2016 (LePage 2017)

8.2.2 Status

One reason for these high rates of use of non-official languages may be understood by considering acculturation strategies. Berry (1998: 88) provides a paradigm of possible acculturation strategies, related to orientation to two issues: the value of maintaining one's identity and the value of relationships with the larger society (see Table 8.3). Canadians are quite likely to answer "Yes" to both issues, leading to integration, that is, the maintenance of one's (cultural) identity at the same time as maintenance of relationships with the larger (Canadian) society. We may see this as parallel to additive bilingualism: Canadians are likely to learn English or French without necessarily giving up their heritage mother tongue. Berry (1998: 84) notes that the goals of the official multiculturalism policy are to avoid assimilation while encouraging intergroup harmony and acceptance (which requires learning an official language). His study indicates fairly high levels of acceptance of multicultural ideology and of tolerance and no effect of ethnic origins on either.

Table 8.3 *Acculturation strategies (adapted from Berry 1998: 88).*

		Issue 1: It is considered to be of value to maintain one's identity and characteristics.	
		YES	NO
Issue 2: It is considered to be of value to maintain relationships with larger society.	YES	Integration or "mosaic"	Assimilation or "melting pot"
	NO	Separation/Segregation	Marginalization

This integration option means that

> exposure to one's immigrant language can also occur outside the home, and through contact with other children who are also exposed to those languages and various learning activities organized by language communities, as well as through greater contact with other people with the same mother tongue. (Houle 2011: 3)

The perception of HLs in Canada is partially circumscribed by political actions. In 1971, Prime Minister Pierre Trudeau established the policy of "multiculturalism within a bilingual framework," defining two official languages but no official culture (Cummins and Danesi 1990: 23). Thus, the value of multiple ethnic groups contributing to Canada was recognized, but not at the expense of supporting only the two official languages. In the 1980s, Canada saw discussion of the term "heritage" as a way of subjugating people who were not mother tongue speakers of one of Canada's official languages, but today people are "more familiar [and comfortable] with the *de facto* use of the term for government departments," for example, "Canadian Heritage/*Patrimonie canadien*" (Dressler 2010: 168).

While it is recognized that fluency in at least one official language is necessary for socioeconomic success, Harrison (2000: 14) describes the importance attributed to HL preservation, noting that Canadians value maintaining and transmitting their mother tongue. He points out that many children attend heritage language classes outside of school hours, indicating that parents value this transmission. A positive attitude toward HLs and bilingualism is often noted in research publications. For example, Pérez-Leroux, Cuza, and Thomas (2011b: 168) report that their participants' positive attitude toward their HL and to bilingualism resembles that for Toronto more broadly,

> where languages and diverse ethnic backgrounds are accepted as the norm, and there is an abundance of multilingual media, street signs, language services in government, education and commercial establishments and community support for ethnic celebrations.

Although Canada was the first country to adopt an official policy of *multiculturalism*, in 1969 (Brousseau and Dewing 2009), it maintains a policy of bilingualism, which supports only the two official languages, English and

French. Thus, there is considerably less research published about education in minority, heritage, and indigenous language settings than for French and English (Duff and Li 2009). Canada's policy of multiculturalism symbolizes "Canada's commitment to a society that not only tolerates linguistic and cultural diversity, but strives to preserve, develop and institutionalize it" (Danesi et al. 1993). While the purpose of this policy (and its revision in 1988) is to encourage language maintenance, there is no legislation or funding to implement it. Thus, most heritage language education programs are run by local community groups (Cumming 2014).

In spite of these efforts, income levels, an important marker of status, are uneven among mother tongue groups. The 2016 census shows the Canadian median income to be around $CA35,000 for people whose mother tongue is English or French, around $CA25,000 for mother tongue speakers of immigrant languages and under $CA20,000 for mother tongue speakers of indigenous languages (Statistics Canada 2018).

Yet Canada, and perhaps Toronto in particular, is viewed from the outside as exemplary in terms of strong attention to heritage culture both at an intellectual and a material level (Turchetta and Vedovelli 2018). Supporting this perspective with current data, Di Salvo (2017: 80–81) reports an interview study of twenty Italian immigrants to Toronto, representing two migration waves, the first shortly after World War II, which consists of less educated Italians and a second, university-educated, wave, who arrived between 2000 and 2015 as part of "the new wave of transnational mobility." While the earlier immigration group reported little contemporary connection with Italy and frequently employed English in conversations with Italian interviewers, the more recent immigration group assigned a negative value to English, reporting using it in limited home contexts, particular when they want to "give the impression of harshness and strictness" (Di Salvo 2017: 85–86). The earlier group used English more often with their children to help them integrate, while the second group prioritized passing on Italian to the next generation (Di Salvo 2017: 88–89).

Another marker of the status of languages in Canadian culture is the Canadian Language Museum (www.languagemuseum.ca). It was founded in 2011 with the goal of promoting "an appreciation of all of the languages spoken in Canada, and of their role in the development of the country." It has a home base at York University, and traveling and digital exhibits, including exhibits featuring Cree and Inuktitut, and two on HLs more generally: "Read between the Signs" (Toronto's linguistic landscape) and "A Tapestry of Voices."

8.2.3 Institutional Support

HL programs funded provincially or locally have existed in many areas of Canada for over a hundred years. These reflect immigrant settlement patterns and have primarily supported Arabic, Cantonese, German, Hebrew, Italian, Mandarin, Polish, Punjabi, Spanish, Tamil, Ukrainian, and Urdu (Statistics Canada 2012). The government's policy of "official multiculturalism" supports language programs whose goals are to "encourage cultural retention, particularly identity maintenance, and social integration, involving equitable and respectful interactions among cultural groups" (Noels and Clément 1998: 102). Different methods of HL instruction exist in Canada. Depending on provincial policy and the number of students seeking instruction, transitional, dual track, or heritage language programs might be available in public schools (Babaee 2012: 7; Cummins 1998a, 2005). Primary and secondary school transitional and dual language programs exist in provinces where a heritage language may be used as the medium of instruction, that is, in British Columbia, Alberta, Saskatchewan, and Manitoba. Universities, colleges, and private language schools also teach international languages. Some university courses have sections designated for HL speakers (Oikonomakou et al. 2018; Department of Spanish and Portuguese 2019). Overall, more than 200 languages are taught in Canada.

Canada has no federal mandate to fund HL education (for immigrant languages) with the exception of transitional programs to help students learn an official language. However, in February 2019, the Canadian government brought forward legislation to protect indigenous languages in Canada by providing sustainable funding for the "reclamation, revitalization, strengthening and maintenance of Indigenous languages in Canada" (Bill C-91). The bill establishes the Office of the Commissioner of Indigenous Languages to protect and promote indigenous languages by developing activities, tools, educational materials, and archives; funding immersion programs and interpretation and translation services; and conducting research (Tasker 2019). There have also been recent changes in funding allocations for First Nations education to ensure that students living on reserves are funded in a manner comparable to those in provincial school systems (Canadian Press 2019).

The provincial level provides more support. According to the Canadian Education Association (1991), heritage language programs exist in Ontario, Quebec, Manitoba, Alberta, Saskatchewan, and Alberta. Languages taught include Italian, Greek, Spanish, and Portuguese in Quebec (Canadian Education Association 1991), and Filipino, German, Hebrew, Japanese, Mandarin, Portuguese, Spanish, and Ukrainian in Manitoba (Manitoba Education 2011, cited in Babaee 2012: 8). Ontario has provided funding for HL classes since 1977. It supports up to 2.5 hours per week of class when there are at least twenty-five students in one school requesting a particular language (Canadian Education Association 1991). Today, more than 100 languages are offered (International Languages Educators' Association n.d.).

These include some immersion programs, but most are after school or weekend programs (Cumming 2014: 1). Recently, the Toronto Catholic District School Board voted to continue its HL program with classes taught during the regular school day (Jones 2018).

HL programs tend to be favored by the cultural groups whose languages are taught, but many others oppose the use of public funds to teach heritage languages (Cummins 1998b: 294–295). Thus, there are provinces where heritage language medium instruction has been outlawed. Examples are Prince Edward Island (Canadian Education Association 1991) and Newfoundland and Labrador (Department of Education Newfoundland and Labrador 2011).

Outside the government, community groups have organized and funded non-official languages classes since the nineteenth century. This included publicly supported bilingual schools until the early twentieth century, when provincial education acts forbade them. However, immigrant groups continue to fund HL education.

As heritage language programs offer only a few hours of programming per week, heritage language learners, especially those whose home language is English or French, might receive insufficient language input to develop communicative skills in their heritage languages (Babaee 2012: 10). Due to often limited success of foreign and heritage language programs, and high rates of language shift in immigrant families, some Canadian educators have proposed combining HL and foreign language programs, with multiple goals:

> to promote students developing plurilingual abilities in multiple languages, identities that value cultural diversity and differences, and preparedness for global mobility – through the creation and uses of dual-language books, projects involving sister classes internationally through electronic media, planning and monitoring long-term personal goals for language learning, and facilitating cross-language transfer and intercultural awareness. (Cumming 2014: 1)

For additional recent reviews of language policies and trends in Canada, see Burnaby (2008), Cumming (2014) and references therein, Duff, Brighton, Kagan, and Bauckus (2008), Duff and Li (2009). Drapeau (1998) surveys educational policy related to the teaching of indigenous languages in the late twentieth century, noting little financial investment and the existence of classes primarily for primary school through grade three.

8.3 Examples of Innovative HL Programs

Moving from the above broad-strokes overview, this section summarizes two innovative programs that support indigenous languages and another that supports immigrant heritage languages.

The *Miqqut* ('needle') program is "community-based, non-formal, interge-nerational, safe, healthy, culturally relevant, learner-driven" and embeds language and literacy skill development in the practice of traditional crafts (Ilitaqsiniq n.d.: 3) to support Inuktitut in the territory of Nunavut. Research on the efficacy of the program compared students who partici-pated in two versions of it: one in which "language and literacy skills were not intentionally embedded into [the] program" and one where they were (Ilitaqsiniq n.d.: 9). Sixty-six participants were interviewed and completed questionnaires. Participants improved their abilities in traditional skills and crafts as well as increasing their language skills in both English and Inuktitut; gained comfort with reading, expanding their use of writing skills, and gained confidence in speaking to groups; as well as a number of other positive outcomes. They found that using both Inuktitut and English for learning activities was a productive approach. The report (http://ilitaqsiniq.ca/projects/miqqut-project/) offers a series of recommenda-tions to the Canadian and Nunavut governments and literacy programs on the basis of their research.

Sarkar and Metallic (2009) describe an adult Mi'gmaq education program and participatory action research project. Mi'gmaq is an Algonquian lan-guage that is considered "a 'viable small' language and is far from mori-bund," (Norris 2007) though it has disappeared from many communities where it used to be spoken (Sarkar and Metallic 2009: 50). In the first two years of the program, the community experienced a shift in attitude toward the language, giving hope for the language's future. Success is attributed to the fact that the program was developed by local speakers and is based on a syllabus that "expands on the basic categories found in Mi'gmaq grammar" rather than borrowing methods for other languages.

The University of Toronto's Linguistics Department offers "heritage lan-guage" modules in several sociolinguistics courses (Nagy 2017b). These give students the opportunity to study their own and their peers' experiences as heritage language speakers, supported by academic resources as a means of establishing the academic value of such languages and speakers. Students from first-year undergraduates through PhD participate.

A sample assignment from a first-year course is "Learning about the structure of an HL." Students work in small groups that include at least one student who speaks an HL for which there is transcribed speech in the project's database, one student who is good with computers and learning to use new tools, and one student with strong management skills. The assignment has three purposes: to build and share knowledge about an HL; to learn to transcribe, translate, and annotate linguistic data; and to learn to describe linguistic variation based on empirical evidence. Students are tasked with learning to translate and gloss (a short segment of) a time-aligned transcription, and to find, label, and quantify the distribution of some phonetic and syntactic features of the HL. In a further assignment, students generate hypotheses about types of inter-generational variation they expect to see and then find examples to test their hypothesis. To provide concrete models, previous student-authored research papers are reviewed. This engagement with a language that is normally limited to the home environment is appreciated on many levels by students. For assignment descriptions and student responses, see Nagy (2017b).

8.4   Research on Heritage Languages in Canada

Linguistic studies of heritage languages have increased in Canada over the past decade. This section concentrates on sociolinguistic studies of structural properties of heritage languages, a relatively new approach to HL study in Canada, but also includes a sample of studies of attitude and orientation, experimental studies of structural properties, and studies of pedagogical approaches.

8.4.1   Sociolinguistic Study of Spontaneous Speech

Variationist sociolinguists primarily examine corpora of spontaneously produced speech or sign, recorded in "ecologically valid" contexts, that is, in contexts where speakers regularly use the language under study. The goal is to understand the constraints determining the distribution of competing forms (e.g., different pronunciations, different morphological or grammatical structures, or different lexical items) in terms of their linguistic and social context.

Systematically structured patterns of variation at these different levels "may be indicative of socially salient differences among the participants, and how they understand the speech event they are part of" (Nagy and Meyerhoff 2008: 1). While the field focused primarily on speakers presented as monolingual in its first 50 years, work on the sociolinguistics of language contact is increasing (Meyerhoff and Nagy 2008; Stanford and Preston 2009; Hildebrandt et al. 2017). Heritage language speakers, by definition, live in language contact situations, presenting relatively accessible populations for study. However, there is little overlap in languages spoken natively by professional sociolinguistic researchers and heritage languages. Thus, a key aspect of HL sociolinguistics is the training and involvement of student heritage-language speakers at every level of investigation. One example of such an approach is the Heritage Language Variation and Change Project (HLVC, Nagy 2009, 2011a), a large-scale project investigating variation and change in ten of Toronto's heritage languages. The goals of the project are to:

- Create a corpus of recorded and transcribed speech, accompanied by language use and attitude information for each speaker, available for research of the following heritage languages: Cantonese, Faetar, Hungarian, Italian, Korean, Polish, Portuguese, Russian, Tagalog, and Ukrainian. People interested in conducting academic research with this corpus may find access information at http://ngn.artsci.utoronto.ca/pdf/ HLVC/5_1_opportunities.php.
- Document and describe heritage languages spoken by immigrants and two generations of their descendants.
  - Determine whether (and, if so, what) cross-linguistic generalizations are possible about the types of features, structures, rules, or constraints that are malleable in heritage languages, either through language contact, isolation from standard varieties and standardizing institutions or internal changes.
  - Determine which social factors are correlated to the variation and how, particularly questioning whether the same factors which play important roles in majority languages also do so in minority languages.[3]
- Push variationist sociolinguistic research beyond its monolingually oriented core (and its majority language focus) (Nagy and Meyerhoff 2008).
  - Promote HL vitality through research, training, and "knowledge mobilization" in and out of the classroom, particularly by engaging heritage language speakers as researchers (Nagy 2017b).

Linguistic analysis is based on samples extracted from recordings of conversations among HL speakers in relaxed environments. Evidence for participants' linguistic attitudes and practices is collected through a questionnaire (http://ngn.artsci.utoronto.ca/pdf/HLVC/short_questionnaire_English.pdf). A key finding from these studies of spontaneously produced speech is a lack of connection between linguistic and cultural attitudes (the status element of ethnolinguistic vitality) and structural variation in the language. More specifically:

1. There is no relationship between the strength of out-group ties and linguistic patterns that are, at least conceivably, contact-influenced. In other words, ethnolinguistic vitality is not a predictor of speaker-specific linguistic contact effects in heritage languages. This is a socio-linguistically important finding insofar as many features (e.g.,

---

[3] To this end, efforts have been made to recruit participants broadly, outside the school/university environment.

education, neighborhood) that may correlate to social class are included in the Ethnic Orientation Questionnaire (discussed in Nagy 2018: 434).

2. The status of a heritage variety, in terms of its recognition as a variety that is independent of the homeland variety (by virtue of having its own label[4] and/or institutional supports), does not reliably relate to the degree of difference observed between the heritage and the corresponding homeland or source variety, nor between generations of speakers.

3. For four sociolinguistic variables (null subject, classifiers, case-marking, and voice onset time of voiceless stops) studied in several languages, there is no correlation between individuals' rate of use of more English-like forms and their ethnic orientation.

4. For the three morphosyntactic variables (null subjects, classifiers, and case-marking), there is no consistent difference between heritage and homeland speaker rates, nor between first- and second-generation heritage speakers' rates. In contrast, for voice onset time, there is a heritage–homeland difference in two of the four languages studied and concomitant cross-generational differences (Nagy 2018: 441).

Studies that have contributed to this understanding of Toronto's heritage languages include Kang and Nagy (2016) on Korean aspiration and tonogenesis, Łyskawa (2015) on case-marking in Polish; Łyskawa, Maddeaux, Melara, and Nagy (2016) on word-final devoicing in Polish; Łyskawa and Nagy (2019) on case-marking in Polish, Russian, and Ukrainian; Nagy (2015, 2017a, 2018) and Nagy, Iannozzi, and Heap (2018) on several aspects of voice onset time and null subject variability in Cantonese, Faetar, Italian, Russian, and Ukrainian; Nagy and Kochetov (2013) on voice onset time in Italian, Russian, and Ukrainian; Nodari, Celata, and Nagy (2019) on voice onset time in multiple phonological contexts in Italian; Tse (2016, 2017, 2019) on Cantonese vowel phonology; and Nagy and Lo (2019) on Cantonese classifiers.

The majority of other HL sociolinguistic studies examining the Toronto context focus on Italian and come from a multi-institutional collaboration in Italy, reported in Turchetta and Vedovelli (2018). From this project, Casini (2018) explores the linguistic landscape of Italian in Toronto; and Turchetta and Di Salvo (2018) report on attitudes to the transmission of Italian and shift to English in data collected from interviews and surveys. They report on language preference rates, mother tongue transmission (very low in their sample of students), self-reported ability to understand,

---

[4] For example, the term "Canadian-Ukrainian dialect" has existed at least since used by Sekirin and Courtois (1994) in an article describing features of Ukrainian as used in Canada that differ from the homeland variety.

speak and read, and frequency of interaction with Italian-language media (50 percent report watching Italian TV).

Other sociolinguistic studies of Ontario HLs include an examination of mother–child language usage practices in heritage Ukrainian families (Chumak-Horbatch 1987) and code-switching in heritage German speakers (McKinnie 2000).

Chumak-Horbatch (1987) selected families that report a positive orientation to the Ukrainian language (self-reported "Ukrainian-only" households) and, through participant observation, interviews, and questionnaires, investigated linguistic behavior. She found that English was used in many ways in every household, although the mothers were often not aware of their own, or their preschool children's, use of English. Given these findings, the author was pessimistic about the future of Ukrainian in Toronto, but, 30 years later, the HLVC project has recorded fourth- and fifth-generation heritage Ukrainian speakers and Statistics Canada (2017a) reports 26,550 mother tongue speakers of Ukrainian in Toronto.

McKinnie (2000) reports on code-switching strategies of two heritage German speakers, noting that their degree of cultural integration affects how often (and in what structures) English appears in a German conversation. She notes that "the ability to facilitate both inter- and intra-sentential code-switching is indicative of excellent knowledge of the grammatical systems of both languages and not necessarily a sign of attrition of the mother tongue" (McKinnie 2000: 173), reiterating Poplack's (1980) claim.

Indigenous language studies with a sociolinguistic orientation include the *Algonquian Linguistic Atlas* (Junker and Stewart 2011), an online resource illustrating variation in sixteen varieties; and Carrier's ongoing work on morphosyntactic variation in Inuktitut. Through an examination of the conditioning of ergative and antipassive constructions, Carrier (2017) argues for the formation of a new dialect, with different grammatical constraints, following relocation of speakers from several dialects to the High Arctic (in Nunavut).

In western Canada, there are recent HL studies of Greek (Pappas 2019) and Icelandic (Arnbjörnsdóttir 2006) phonology, and studies of attitudes of German (Dressler 2010) and Spanish (Guardado 2002, 2014) speakers.

Pappas (2019) studied two features in Greek as part of the *Immigration and Language in Canada: Greeks and Greek-Canadians* project (Anastassiadis et al. 2017). Fifty sociolinguistic interviews provided over 2,000 tokens of unstressed high vowels (with variable deletion) and over 3,000 tokens of variable /l/ and /n/ palatalization, supporting an investigation of stigmatized features and of dialect-leveling in the immigration context. The rate of /i/-deletion in HL speakers was much lower than in Homeland speakers, likely due to the majority of HL speakers not being from the region of Greece where the stigmatized variant is prevalent. In contrast, palatalization, which is found in the predominant homeland source variety of Heritage Greek speakers, is widespread among Canadian speakers of heritage Greek (Pappas 2019: 273–274).

Arnbjörnsdóttir (2006) reports on data collected in 1986 in New Iceland, Manitoba (and Mountain, North Dakota). Twenty-one Canadian heritage Icelandic speakers were recorded in sociolinguistic interviews, picture description tasks, and reading lists. Chapter 5 briefly describes the grammar of the language and notes that there is little morphological or syntactic difference between the heritage and homeland varieties, explicitly noting that case-marking variation resembles that in homeland Icelandic. It describes a few phonological features that distinguish the heritage variety, while noting that it does not sound like a learner variety but rather exhibits some evidence of dialect leveling (106). A quantitative analysis of two vowel mergers (I/E; Y/ö, primarily for long vowels) is presented. These raising and lowering processes are collectively known as *Flámæli*, a process that existed in Iceland but was systematically eradicated from the language after migration to Manitoba and North Dakota (85). An analysis of 1,000+ tokens shows that younger speakers, women, and North Dakotan speakers exhibit this merger more than older speakers, men, and Manitoban speakers (135–140).

Through case studies of six heritage language learners of German at the post-secondary level, Dressler (2010) explored self-identification (as HL learners [HLL] or not) and attitudes related to being German HLLs. For most of these university students living in Alberta, their self-identification as heritage German learners rests on their parents' or their grandparents' mother tongue, in spite of not being childhood German speakers themselves (Dressler 2010: 166). One participant points out that Germans felt that "they shouldn't speak German to us because that caused greater ostracism or social penalties at the time" (Dressler 2010). She notes that researchers and teachers should be aware "that not all HLLs will self-identify as such," and decide whether that is essential for research participation or course enrollment (Dressler 2010: 173).

Guardado (2002), in contrast, explored the claim that heritage cultural identity is critical to the maintenance of HLs, and showed that, even in the context of a small community of a particular HL and input from only one parent, HL maintenance is possible. Guardado urges parents to "promote a positive attitude in their children" as key to HL maintenance (Guardado 2002: 341). Guardado (2014) describes ideologies related to maintenance and transmission, as understood through observation of daily interactions in fifteen Spanish-speaking families in Vancouver. Critical discourse analysis was applied to their conversations to understand motivations for HL development. The article concludes by arguing that "making these discourses explicit and public may contribute to the spread of an ideology that ultimately contributes to the promotion of heritage language development and maintenance" (Guardado 2014: 22). This is representative of a popular (if not governmental) Canadian perspective: that heritage languages are worthy of development and maintenance.

I note also the existence of an online searchable corpus of North American Norwegian spontaneous speech that includes data from twenty-four speakers recorded in 2013 in Saskatchewan (Johannessen 2015). They range in age from 43 to 97.

8.4.2 Acquisition/Experimental Research

HLs have also been examined from a developmental perspective. A selection of representative articles that focus on acquisition from an experimental perspective is provided here. These studies examining Inuktitut, Greek, Korean, Mandarin, Spanish, or Tagalog all show differences between monolingual and heritage speakers.

Sherkina-Lieber (and colleagues) conducted studies of many aspects of Inuktitut using comprehension, grammaticality judgment, elicited imitation, and picture-matching tasks. Sherkina-Lieber and Murasugi (2015) investigated noun incorporation among adult speakers of the Baffin dialect and Sherkina-Lieber (2015, also examining tense, aspect, case, and agreement) did the same for receptive bilinguals of a Labrador dialect. Both studies found less fluent HL speakers to be more selective than fluent speakers in their choice between two types of sentences (with and without noun incorporation). They report that speakers do not, overall, prefer non-synthetic over synthetic structures, surprising given other reports of HL preference for analytic forms. Sherkina-Lieber's (2010) study reported that higher-proficiency receptive bilinguals in Nain, Labrador, comprehend time and remoteness features in Inuktitut tense morphemes, while less proficient speakers do not access the remoteness feature. Sherkina-Lieber, Pérez-Leroux, and Johns (2011) used grammaticality judgment tasks to show that receptive bilinguals demonstrate knowledge of the structure and ordering of agreement and case morphemes, although a significant difference from the fluent-speaker group emerged.

Pérez-Leroux, Cuza, and Thomas (2011a) investigate language transfer through an experiment targeting clitic-placement in two groups of second-generation Heritage Spanish speakers in Toronto. They compared simultaneous and sequential bilinguals, aged three to eight. These tests were conducted in the speakers' homes, a Spanish-speaking setting, by a Spanish-speaking tester. A sentence-imitation task revealed that sequential bilinguals accurately reproduced the clitic sequence in the stimulus more frequently than simultaneous bilinguals and, specifically, that sequential bilinguals were more likely than simultaneous bilinguals to reproduce proclisis stimuli (the less English-like form that monolingual Spanish-speaking children favor). To further account for these differences, Pérez-Leroux et al. (2011b) contrast the family environments for simultaneous vs. sequential bilingual children. They report differences in two dimensions: "the proportion of parental conversation initiated in Spanish, and the degree of exposure [to Spanish] outside the home," and find that these differences, though small, have an effect on children's language dominance, particularly for simultaneous bilinguals.

Tagalog voice onset time was examined in Kang, George, and Soo (2016), comparing nine heritage Tagalog speakers to ten native Tagalog speakers and twelve native English speakers in a word-list reading task. Acoustic analysis revealed that heritage speakers "successfully establish separate phonetic categories" for their two languages' voiceless stops, but that voiced stops "exhibit considerable cross-language influence" (Kang et al. 2016: 184).

The speech of heritage Greek children in New York City and Western Canada shows some difference between homeland and heritage subject realization patterns (Daskalaki et al. 2019) and contradicts expectations of the Interface Hypothesis (Sorace 2011) in that only one of two syntax-discourse structures was found to trigger errors (compared to a monolingual sample) and one narrowly syntactic context also triggered errors. This study also revealed a gradient effect of Language Use – more monolingual-like accuracy rates are increasingly prevalent with higher Greek Language Use scores.

Using a story-retelling task, Lin and Nicoladis (2018) compared Heritage Mandarin children in Edmonton, Alberta, to homeland monolingual Mandarin speakers. For 4–6 year olds, no important differences were noted in the means of expressing motion (deictics, simple and complex verb constructions). However, 8–10 year olds showed significant differences from Homeland speakers, suggesting that it is the influence of English rather than differences in early HL input that account for these syntactic differences.

Jia and Paradis (2015) examined narratives in heritage and monolingual Mandarin children and report that "HL children used less adequate referring expressions for first mentions than the monolinguals, mainly due to overgeneralization of classifiers and lack of vocabulary knowledge." In contrast, no significant inter-group differences were found for relative clauses or post-verbal NP placement to mark first mentions. They also showed effects for age of arrival, education level, and "diversity" of the Mandarin home environment.

Jia and Paradis (2018) focused on relative clauses, reporting longitudinal and cross-sectional studies. Here differences between the groups were reported at an early time-point, but became more similar over time. This led them to conclude that "the reduced L1 input HL children receive in the host country does not necessarily lead to deficient acquisition of the L1."

8.4.3   Research on HL education in Canada

Readers in search of more in-depth coverage of Canadian heritage language studies of education policy are referred to two special issues of the *Canadian Modern Language Review* on heritage language education in Canada: first Cummins (1991) and, two decades later, Duff and Li (2009) and references therein, as well as Burnaby (2008). Studies of the HL pedagogical context in Canada include Comanaru and Noels (2009), Goldstein (1997), and Cummins (1998b, 2014, *inter alia*). Trifonas and Aravossitas's (2018) book on heritage language teaching includes a number of chapters about Canadian programs.

Comanaru and Noels (2009) examined university students' motivations to learn Mandarin in Alberta, highlighting differences among types of HL learners who enrolled in university courses. They report:

> few differences between heritage learners who spoke Chinese as a mother tongue and those who spoke English, which suggests that from the standpoint of social psychology, regardless of Chinese proficiency, subgroups of heritage language learners may be more alike than different. (Comanaru and Noels 2009: 131)

Goldstein (1997) reports on benefits of a teacher's use of the students' HL in (limited contexts within) the classroom. She reports that heritage Cantonese-speaking students "achieve academic and social success" through the deployment of multiple languages in the math classroom, but also notes the existence of inter-ethnic tensions around the issues of advantages and disadvantages of this practice.

Foreshadowing this finding, Cummins reported that "many people of diverse backgrounds fear balkanization of school communities, loss of time for core curriculum subjects, undue pressure on children, disruption in school programming and staffing, inadequate preparation for eventual employment, and indeed, a dramatic shift of direction in Canadian society" (Toronto Board of Education, cited in Cummins 1998b: 302). Such attitudes persist despite the research summarized in Cummins (1983, 1998a, b 2014) establishing the benefits of teaching HLs as "support[ing] the educational merits of teaching international languages … No adverse effects on academic attainment in English (or French) have been noted."

8.5   Summary and Conclusion

The benefits of learning, speaking, and understanding HLs have been illustrated through the studies reported here and elsewhere, highlighting how important it is that HL research continue, deepening and broadening our understanding of the features, structures, and malleability of HLs, of the attitudes and practices of HL users, of how these interact, and how our understanding of the HL context may best be applied to education at every level. The studies surveyed here suggest a number of research questions that remain open. We have seen differing effects (including no effect) reported for factors that relate to language use and linguistic attitudes. Do these depend on the linguistic variable being examined? On the speaker sample or the population? On the methodology applied? To answer these questions, it is critical that additional languages and communities be investigated, particularly indigenous communities, which remain under-studied. So far, we know something about less than 10 percent of the HLs spoken in Canada, and a far smaller percentage of the communities. And we need to continue to apply a range of methodologies to understand the structural properties and sociolinguistic ecology of HLs, and the relationship between these. Examples of many methodologies have been reviewed here: surveys (Statistics Canada 2017a, 2017b, 2018), ethnographic observation (Di Salvo 2017; Turchetta and Vedovelli, 2018), sociolinguistic approaches (Section 8.4.1), experimental approaches (Section 8.4.2), and pedagogical projects (Section 8.4.3).

Canada, with its rich variety of indigenous languages and its history of many layers of immigration, is an excellent site for such research. The high rate of multilingualism and HL retention and use may be attributed to the attitudes of its residents, the political actions of its government, including the welcoming of immigrants, community and provincial support for HL maintenance, and its policy of official multiculturalism, which leads to high rates of acculturation and, as a frequent result, multilingualism rather than HL loss.

References

Anastassiadis, A., R. Ralli, A. Gekas, P. Pappas, C. Papangiotou, A. Siotou, C. Tsimbouris, and S. Tsolakidis. 2017. Immigration and language in Canada: Greeks and Greek Canadians. [Electronic Database]. https://immigrec.com/en

Arnbjörnsdóttir, Birna. 2006. *North American Icelandic: The Life of a Language*. Winnipeg: University of Manitoba Press.

Babaee, N. 2012. Heritage language learning in Canadian public Schools: Language rights challenges. Manitoba: http://umanitoba.ca/faculties/education/media/Babaee12.pdf

Benmamoun, E., S. Montrul, and M. Polinsky. 2013. Heritage Languages and Their Speakers: Opportunities and Challenges for Linguistics. *Theoretical Linguistics* 39(3–4), 129–181.

Berry, J. 1998. Official Multiculturalism. In J. Edwards (ed.), *Language in Canada*. New York: Cambridge, 84–101.

Brousseau, L. and M. Dewing. 2009. Canadian Multiculturalism. Library of Parliament. Publication No. 2009-20-E.

Burnaby, B. 2008. Language Policy and Education in Canada. In S. May and N. H. Hornberger (eds.), *Encyclopedia of Language and Education (2nd ed.): Vol. 1. Language Policy and Political Issues in Education*. New York: Springer, 331–341.

Canadian Education Association. 1991. *Heritage Language Programs in Canadian School Boards*. Toronto.

Canadian Press. 2019. Liberals Taking New Approach for First Nations On-Reserve Education Funding. *CBC News*, January 21, 2019. www.cbc.ca/news/indigenous/first-nations-on-reserve-school-funding-1.4987134

Carrier, J. 2017. The Ergative-Antipassive Alternation in Inuktitut: Analyzed in a Case of New-Dialect Formation. *Canadian Journal of Linguistics/Revue canadienne de linguistique* 62(4), 661–684.

Casini, S. 2018. Italianismi e pseudoitalianismi a Toronto: tra valori simbolici e prospettive di apprendimento [Italianisms and Pseudoitalianisms in Toronto: Between Symbolic Value and Acquisition Perspectives]. In B. Turchetta and M. Vedovelli (eds.), *Lo spazio linguistico italiano globale: il caso dell'Ontario [The Global Italian Linguistic Space: The Case of Ontario]*. Pisa: Pacini, 225–253.

Chumak-Horbatsch, R. 1987. Language Use in the Ukrainian Home: A Toronto Sample. *International Journal of the Sociology of Language* 63, 99–118.

Comanaru, R. and K. Noels. 2009. Self-Determination, Motivation, and the Learning of Chinese as a Heritage Language. *Canadian Modern Language Review* 66(1), 131–158.

Cumming, A. 2014. *Programs for Education in Immigrant, Heritage, or International Languages in Canada*. Toronto: CERLL (Centre for Educational Research on Languages and Literacies), OISE, University of Toronto. www.oise.utoronto.ca/cerll1/wp-content/uploads/sites/49/2018/02/A

Cummins, J. 1983. *Heritage Language Education: A Literature Review*. Toronto: Ministry of Education.

Cummins, J. (ed.) 1991. Heritage Languages [Special Issue]. *The Canadian Modern Language Review* 47(4).

Cummins, J. 1998a. Language Issues and Educational Change. In A. Hargreaves, A. Lieberman, M. Fullan, and D. Hopkins (eds.), *International Handbook of Educational Change*. Dordrecht, Boston, London: Kluwer Academic Publishers, 440–459.

Cummins, J. 1998b. The Teaching of International Languages. In J. Edwards (ed.), *Language in Canada*. New York: Cambridge, 293–304.

Cummins, J. 2005. A Proposal for Action: Strategies for Recognizing Heritage Language Competence as a Learning Resource within the Mainstream Classroom. *The Modern Language Journal* 89(4), 585–592.

Cummins, J. 2014. To What Extent Are Canadian Second Language Policies Evidence-Based? Reflections on the Intersections of Research and Policy. *Frontiers in Psychology: Language Sciences* 5 (article 358), 1–10. https://doi.org/10.3389/fpsyg.2014.00358

Cummins, J. and M. Danesi. 1990. *Heritage Languages: The Development and Denial of Canada's Linguistic Resources.* Toronto: James Lorimer.

Danesi, M., K. McLeod, and S. Morris. 1993. *Heritage Languages and Education: The Canadian Experience.* Oakville, ON: Mosaic. www.mosaic-press.com/product/heritage-languages-and-education-the-canadian-experience/

Daskalaki, E., V. Chondrogianni, E. Blom, F. Argyri, and J. Paradis. 2019. Input Effects across Domains: The Case of Greek Subjects in Child Heritage Language. *Second Language Research* 35(3), 421–445.

Department of Education Newfoundland and Labrador. 2011. www.ed.gov.nl.ca/edu/

Department of Spanish and Portuguese. 2019. Undergraduate Programs in Spanish: Language sequence. www.spanport.utoronto.ca/undergraduate/spanish

Di Salvo, M. 2017. Heritage Language and Identity in Old and New Italian Migrants in Toronto. In M. Di Salvo and P. Moreno (eds.), *Italian Communities Abroad: Multilingualism and Migration.* Newcastle-upon-Tyne: Cambridge Scholars, 74–95.

Drapeau, L. 1998. Aboriginal Languages: Current Status. In J. Edwards (ed.), *Language in Canada.* New York: Cambridge, 144–159.

Dressler, R. 2010. "There Is No Space for Being German": Portraits of Willing and Reluctant Heritage Language Learners of German. *Heritage Language Journal* 7(2), 162–182.

Duff, P. and D. Li (eds.) 2009. Indigenous, Minority, and Heritage Language Education in Canada: Policies, Contexts, and Issues. *Canadian Modern Language Review* 66(1). https://doi.org/10.3138/cmlr.66.1.001

Duff, P., D. Brinton, O. Kagan, and S. Bauckus. 2008. *Heritage Language Education: A New Field Emerging.* New York: Routledge, 71–90.

Edwards, J. (ed.) 1998. *Language in Canada.* New York: Cambridge.

Feuerverger, G. 1997. "On the Edges of the Map": A Study of Heritage Language Teachers in Toronto. *Teaching and Teacher Education* 13(1), 39–53.

Foreign Affairs Canada. 2005. Asia in Focus. *Canada World View* 25, 5–9.

Giles, H., R. Bourhis, and D. Taylor. 1977. Toward a Theory of Language in Ethnic Group Relations. In H. Giles (ed.), *Language, Ethnicity and Intergroup Relations.* New York: Academic, 307–348.

Goldstein, T. 1997. Bilingual Life in a Multilingual High School Classroom: Teaching and Learning in Cantonese and English. *The Canadian Modern Language Review/La Revue canadienne des langues vivantes* 53(2), 356–372.

Government of Canada. 1991. Canadian Heritage Languages Institute Act (S.C. 1991, c. 7). Justice Laws website. https://laws-lois.justice.gc.ca/eng/acts/C-17.6/

Guardado, M. 2002. Loss and Maintenance of First Language Skills: Case Studies of Hispanic Families in Vancouver. *Canadian Modern Language Review* 58(3), 341–363.

Guardado, M. 2014. The Discourses of Heritage Language Development: Engaging Ideologies in Canadian Hispanic Communities. *Heritage Language Journal* 11(1), 1–28.

Harrison, B. 2000. Passing on the Language: Heritage Language Diversity in Canada. *Canadian Social Trends* 58, 14–19.

Hildebrandt, Kristine A., C. Jany, and W. Silva (eds.) 2017. *Documenting Variation in Endangered Languages. Language Documentation & Conservation* Special Publication no. 13. Honolulu: University of Hawai'i Press.

Houle, R. 2011. Recent Evolution of Immigrant-Language Transmission in Canada. *Canadian Social Trends* 11-008-X No. 92 2011002. Statistics Canada.

Houle, R. and H. Maheux. 2017. Census in Brief: Children with an Immigrant Background: Bridging Cultures. Statistics Canada. www12 .statcan.gc.ca/census-recensement/2016/as-sa/98-200-x/2016015/98–200-x2016015-eng.cfm

Ilitaqsiniq. *no date*. The Miqqut Project: Joining Literacy, Culture and Well-being through Non-formal Learning in Nunavut. Summary of the Research Report. Nunavut Literacy Council.

International Languages Educators' Association. *no date*. About ILP [International Languages Program]. https://ilea.ca/news-2/ilp/

Jia, R. and J. Paradis. 2015. The Use of Referring Expressions in Narratives by Mandarin Heritage Language Children and the Role of Language Environment Factors in Predicting Individual Differences. *Bilingualism: Language and Cognition* 18(4), 737–752.

Jia, R. and J. Paradis. 2018. The Acquisition of Relative Clauses by Mandarin Heritage Language Children. *Linguistic Approaches to Bilingualism* 18, 737–752.

Johannessen, J. B. 2015. The Corpus of American Norwegian Speech (CANS). In Béata Megyesi (ed.), *Proceedings of the 20th Nordic Conference of Computational Linguistics, NODALIDA 2015, May 11–13, 2015, Vilnius, Lithuania. NEALT Proceedings Series 23.* http://tekstlab.uio.no/norskiamer ika/english/corpus.html

Jones, R. 2018. TCDSB Opts to Keep Popular Program That Teaches Students Heritage Languages. CBC, Jul 13, 2018. www.cbc.ca/news/canada/toronto/tcdsb-opts-to-keep-popular-program-that-teaches-students-heritage-lan guages-1.4747074

Junker, M.-O. and T. Stewart. 2011. A Linguistic Atlas for Endangered Languages: www.atlas-ling.ca. In *Proceedings of EDULEARN 11: International Conference on Education and New Learning Technologies* (3366–3377).

Kang, Y., S. George, and R. Soo. 2016. Cross-Language Influence in the Stop Voicing Contrast in Heritage Tagalog. *Heritage Language Journal* 13(2), 184–218.

Kang, Y.-J. and N. Nagy. 2016. VOT Merger in Heritage Korean in Toronto. *Language Variation and Change* 28(2), 249–272. https://doi.org/10.1017/S095439451600003X

LePage, J.-F. 2017. Census in Brief: Linguistic Diversity and Multilingualism in Canadian Homes. Statistics Canada. www12.statcan.gc.ca/census-recen sement/2016/as-sa/98-200-x/2016010/98–200-x2016010-eng.cfm

Lin, Y. and E. Nicoladis. 2018. Motion Lexicalization in Chinese among Heritage Language Children in Canada. *Heritage Language Journal* 15(3), 272–296.

Łyskawa, P. 2015. Variation in Case Marking in Heritage Polish. MA Thesis, Linguistics Department, University of Toronto. http://ngn.artsci.utoronto .ca/pdf/Lyskawa_2015_Variation in case marking in Heritage Polish.pdf

Łyskawa, P., R. Maddeaux, E. Melara, and N. Nagy. 2016. Heritage Speakers Follow All the Rules: Language Contact and Convergence in Polish Devoicing. *Heritage Language Journal* 13(2), 219–244.

Manitoba Education. 2011. International and Heritage Languages. www.edu .gov.mb.ca/k12/cur/languages/

McKinnie, M. 2000. What Do You Want Me To Say, in Deutsch oder in English?: Code-Switching and Borrowing Strategies for Two Post–World War II German-Speaking Immigrants in Edmonton. In L. Zimmerman and H. Froeschle (eds.), *German-Canadian Yearbook*. Vol. XVI. Toronto: Historical Society of Mecklenburg Upper Canada, 171–188.

Meyerhoff, M. and N. Nagy (eds.) 2008. *Social Lives in Language – Sociolinguistics and Multilingual Speech Communities*. Amsterdam: John Benjamins.

Montrul, S. 2012. Bilingualism and the Heritage Language Speaker. In T. K. Bhatia and W. C. Ritchie (eds.), *The Handbook of Bilingualism and Multilingualism*. Chichester and Malden, MA: Blackwell, 168–189.

Nagy, N. 2009. Heritage Language Variation and Change in Toronto. http:// ngn.artsci.utoronto.ca/HLVC/1_5_publications.php

Nagy, N. 2011a. A Multilingual Corpus to Explore Geographic Variation. *Rassegna Italiana di Linguistica Applicata* 43(1–2), 65–84.

Nagy, N. 2011b. Lexical Change and Language Contact: Faetar in Italy and Canada. *Journal of Sociolinguistics* 15, 366–382.

Nagy, N. 2015. A Sociolinguistic View of Null Subjects and VOT in Toronto Heritage Languages. *Lingua* 164B, 309–327.

Nagy, N. 2017a. Documenting Variation In (Endangered) Heritage Languages: How and Why? *Language Documentation and Conservation* SP13. http://nflrc .hawaii.edu/ldc/latest-posts/special-publications/#thirteen

Nagy, N. 2017b. Heritage Language Speakers in the University Classroom, Doing Research. In P. Trifonas and T. Aravossitas (eds.), *International Handbook on Research and Practice in Heritage Language Education*. Cham:

Springer. https://link.springer.com/referenceworkentry/10.1007%2F978-3-319-38893-9_41-1

Nagy, N. 2018. Linguistic Attitudes and Contact Effects in Toronto's Heritage Languages: A Variationist Sociolinguistic Investigation. *International Journal of Bilingualism* 22(4), 429–446. https://doi.org/10.1177/1367006918762160

Nagy, N. and A. Kochetov. 2013. Voice Onset Time across the Generations: A Cross-Linguistic Study of Contact-Induced Change. In P. Siemund, I. Gogolin, M. Schulz, and J. Davydova (eds.), *Multilingualism and Language Contact in Urban Areas: Acquisition – Development – Teaching – Communication*. Amsterdam: John Benjamins, 19–38.

Nagy, N. and S. Lo. 2019. Variation and Change in Heritage and Hong Kong Cantonese Classifiers. *Asia-Pacific Language Variation* 5(1), 84–108.

Nagy, N. and M. Meyerhoff. 2008. The Social Lives of Linguistics. In M. Meyerhoff and N. Nagy (eds.), *Social Lives in Language – Sociolinguistics and Multilingual Speech Communities*. Amsterdam: John Benjamins, 1–17.

Nagy, N., M. Iannozzi, and D. Heap. 2018. Faetar Null Subjects: A Variationist Study of a Heritage Language in Contact. *International Journal of the Sociology of Language* 249, 31–47.

Nodari, R., C. Celata, and N. Nagy. 2019. Socio-Indexical Phonetic Features in the Heritage Language Context: VOT in the Calabrian Community in Toronto. *Journal of Phonetics* 73, 91–112. https://doi.org/10.1016/j.wocn.2018.12.005

Noels, K. and R. Clément. 1998. Language in Education: Bridging Educational Policy and Social Psychological Research. In J. Edwards (ed.), *Language in Canada*. New York: Cambridge, 102–124.

Norris, M. J. 2007. Aboriginal Languages in Canada: Emerging Trends and Perspectives on Second Language Acquisition. *Canadian Social Trends* 83, 19–27. Statistics Canada catalogue no. 11-008.

O'Donnell, V. and T. Anderson. 2017. Census in Brief: The Aboriginal languages of First Nations people, Métis and Inuit. Statistics Canada. www12.statcan.gc.ca/census-recensement/2016/as-sa/98-200-x/2016022/98–200-x2016022-eng.cfm

Oikonomakou, M., T. Aravossitas, and E. Skourtou. 2018. Heritage Language Learners in Mixed University Classes: Language Skills, Attitudes, and Implications for Curriculum Development. In P. Trifonas and T. Aravossitas (eds.), *Handbook of Research and Practice in Heritage Language Education*. Cham: Springer, 75–113.

Page, B. R. and M. T. Putnam (eds.) 2015. *Moribund Germanic Heritage Languages in North America: Theoretical Perspectives and Empirical Findings*. Leiden: Brill.

Pappas, P. A. 2019. Stigmatized Dialectal Features in the Greek of Greek-Canadians. In J. J. Pennington, V. A. Friedman, and L. A. Grenoble (eds.),

And Thus You Are Everywhere Honored: Studies Dedicated to Brian D. Joseph. Bloomington, IN: Slavica Publishers, 267–282.

Pérez-Leroux, A.-T., A. Cuza, and D. Thomas. 2011a. Clitic Placement in Spanish–English Bilingual Children. *Bilingualism: Language and Cognition* 14(2), 221–232.

Pérez-Leroux, A.-T., A. Cuza, and D. Thomas. 2011b. From Parental Attitudes to Input Conditions. In Kim Potowski and Jason Rothman (eds.), *Bilingual Youth: Spanish in English-Speaking Societies*. Philadelphia: John Benjamins, 149–176.

Poplack, S. 1980. Sometimes I'll Start a Sentence In Spanish y Termino en Espanol: Toward a Typology of Code-Switching. *Linguistics* 18(7–8), 581–618.

Ricento, T. 2013. Language Policy, Ideology & Attitudes in English-Dominant Countries. In R. Bayley, R. Cameron, and C. Lucas (eds.), *The Oxford Handbook of Sociolinguistics*. Oxford: Oxford University Press, 525–544.

Sarkar, M. and M. A. Metallic. 2009. Indigenizing the Structural Syllabus: The Challenge of Revitalizing Mi'gmaq in Listuguj. *Canadian Modern Language Journal* 66(1), 49–71. https://doi.org/10.3138/cmlr.66.1 .049

Sekirin, P. and J. Courtois. 1994. Endangered Dialect: Sociolinguistic Study of the Ukrainian Language in Canada. In A. Boudreau and L. Dubois (eds.), *Sociolinguistique et aménagement des langues/Sociolinguistic Studies and Language Planning*. Moncton, NB: Centre de recherche en linguistique appliquée, Université de Moncton, 145–153.

Sherkina-Lieber, M. 2010. Comprehension of Functional Morphemes by Labrador Inuttitut Receptive Bilinguals. In *Proceedings of the Annual Boston University Conference on Language Development* 34, 351–362.

Sherkina-Lieber, M. 2015. Tense, Aspect, and Agreement in Heritage Labrador Inuttitut: Do Receptive Bilinguals Understand Functional Morphology? *Linguistic Approaches to Bilingualism* 5(1), 30–61.

Sherkina-Lieber, M. and K. Murasugi. 2015. Noun Incorporation and Case in Heritage Inuktitut. *Proceedings of the 2015 Annual Conference of the Canadian Linguistic Association*. www.academia.edu/download/39937714/ SherkinaLieber_Murasugi-2015.pdf

Sherkina-Lieber, M., A. T. Pérez-Leroux, and A. Johns. 2011. Grammar without Speech Production: The Case of Labrador Inuttitut Heritage Receptive Bilinguals. *Bilingualism: Language and Cognition* 14(3), 301–317.

Sorace, A. 2011. Pinning Down the Concept of "Interface" in Bilingualism. *Linguistic Approaches to Bilingualism* 1(1), 1–33.

Stanford, J. N. and D. R. Preston (eds.) 2009. *Variation in Indigenous Minority Languages*. Vol. 25. Philadelphia: John Benjamins.

Statistics Canada. 2012. *Linguistic Characteristics of Canadians: Language, 2011 Census*. Ottawa: Ministry of Industry. http://www.publications.gc.ca/site/ eng/9.696712/publication.html

Statistics Canada. 2017a. *Toronto [Census Metropolitan Area], Ontario and Canada [Country]* (table). *Census Profile*. 2016 Census. Statistics Canada Catalogue no. 98-316-X2016001. Ottawa. https://www12.statcan.gc.ca/census-recensement/2016/dp-pd/index-eng.cfm

Statistics Canada. 2017b. 2016 Census: Immigrant Languages in Canada. www12.statcan.gc.ca/census-recensement/2016/dp-pd/prof/index.cfm?Lang=E

Statistics Canada. 2018. Data Tables, 2016 Census. Catalogue number 8-400-X2016199. https://www150.statcan.gc.ca/n1/en/catalogue/98-400-X2016199

Tasker, J. 2019. Ottawa Tables Legislation to Protect and Promote Indigenous Languages, Inuit Call It 'Colonial'. *CBC News*, February 5, 2019. www.cbc.ca/news/politics/ottawa-indigenous-languages-legislation-1.5006504

Trifonas P. and T. Aravossitas (eds.) 2018. *Handbook of Research and Practice in Heritage Language Education*. Cham: Springer International Handbooks of Education.

Tse, H. 2016. Contact-Induced Splits In Toronto Heritage Cantonese Mid-Vowels. *Linguistica Atlantica* 35(2), 133–155.

Tse, H. 2017. Variation and Change in Toronto Heritage Cantonese: An Analysis of Two Monophthongs across Two Generations. *Asia Pacific Language Variation* 2(2), 124–156.

Tse, H. 2019. Beyond the Monolingual Core and Out into the Wild: A Variationist Study of Early Bilingualism and Sound Change in Toronto Heritage Cantonese. Doctoral Dissertation, University of Pittsburgh.

Turchetta, B. and M. Di Salvo. 2018. Analisi dei dati quantitativi [Quantitative Data Analysis]. In B. Turchetta and M. Vedovelli (eds.), *Lo spazio linguistico italiano globale: il caso dell'Ontario [The Global Italian Linguistic Space: The Case of Ontario]*. Pisa: Pacini, 121–170.

Turchetta, B. and M. Vedovelli (eds.) 2018. *Lo spazio linguistico italiano globale: il caso dell'Ontario [The Global Italian Linguistic Space: The Case of Ontario]*. Pisa: Pacini.

9

Asian Heritage Languages in the United States

Chinese and Hindi Language Communities

Shereen Bhalla, Na Liu, and Terrence G. Wiley

9.1   Introduction

This chapter provides a brief overview of efforts to promote heritage and community language education among two of the fastest growing newly emerging minority populations in the United States, that is, those who fall broadly under the labels of "Chinese" and "Indian" language communities in the United States. Each of these two ethnolinguistic communities in the United States are not homogenous because they reflect the linguistic, ethnic, and cultural diversities of their respective homelands. Beyond their importance in the United States, the primary heritage languages of these communities, Mandarin and Hindi, are among the most widely spoken languages in the world and tied to two of the fastest growing economies of the twenty-first century. Thus, they are important for their heritage speakers in the United States and for the country as a whole. From a policy perspective, it is important to build on the multilingual resources of these communities. As the chapter demonstrates, the United States would be missing an opportunity to not build on its community-based linguistic resources, both for the benefit of these communities themselves and to further promote bi-/multilingualism within the country as a whole. The chapter also shows that some federally sponsored projects have demonstrated the potential for integrating an HL–CL learner focus. The responsibility for promoting these programs, however, has fallen largely to the efforts of these communities themselves. Thus, there is much that can be learned by studying these communities and their efforts to maintain and promote their heritage languages. In selecting the greater DC area and San Francisco, we have chosen communities that are among the fastest growing and to which we as scholars have had personal connections.

Throughout much of US history, attention to immigrant language diversity has focused primarily on European languages. This is largely the result of immigration policies, which were favorable to European immigration and overtly racially restrictive or discriminatory toward those from other parts of the world. In the wake of the civil rights movement, which peaked in the 1960s, racially restrictive immigration policies were liberalized under the Johnson Administration. Since the suspension of racially selective immigration policies in 1965, the ethnolinguistic diversity of the United States has increased rapidly to levels not seen since the early decades of the 1900s. Although national-origins criteria have been racially liberalized, there remain considerable social and economic class differences among immigrants who have come into the United States, particularly in terms of their levels of education and literacy in the major national languages of their countries of origin ('). This is also true for those of Chinese and Indian origin, although their education and literacy levels generally tend to be higher than those, for example, of Central American origin.

During the early decades of the twentieth century, anti-immigrant activity and the Americanization Movement (1914–1925) had a negative impact on language education, and accelerated language shift to English. Xenophobia led to restrictions on the use of foreign languages in schools, churches, and the public sphere in many parts of the country. The effects of these restrictions impacted both public and private spheres of language use, which then resulted in a decline in bilingualism and intergenerational language shift. During the era of Americanization, many states outlawed or restricted instruction in languages other than English. Rapid loss of immigrants' first languages has been seen to negatively impact their social cohesion during the processes of integration into the new society and represents the loss of an important linguistic resource (Rumbaut 2009). The negative consequences of the loss of first languages have been underscored by a number of scholars. For example, Lomawaima and McCarty (2006) note the psychological consequences, such as feelings of guilt, for the loss of indigenous languages among American Indian youth.

In terms of the right to learn one's heritage language, two major Supreme Court decisions are noteworthy. In 1923 the Supreme Court (in *Meyer v. Nebraska*) ruled against a Nebraska English-Only law that targeted the teaching of German and other foreign languages in schools. Similarly, in Hawaii and California there were attempts to restrict Asian languages, particularly Japanese and Chinese, even in private schools. Again, the Supreme Court, based on *Meyer*, upheld the right to private foreign language instruction in *Farrington v. Tokushige*, 1927.

In the years since 1965, the Chinese, and, more recently, South Asian and Indian immigrant populations have grown dramatically. Although some Federal programs have promoted Mandarin as a "strategic" language, most of the growth of Mandarin language education in the United States has largely resulted from community-based efforts organized by immigrants from Mainland China, Taiwan, Hong Kong, as well as the greater global Chinese diaspora. Similarly, the growth in Indian and South Asian languages has resulted from the efforts of parents and communities. The importance of Mandarin as both a community and heritage language will likely continue to grow, unless there is a major political rift between the United States and China, which could echo the more restrictive climate of the era of Americanization. Similarly, with the rising economic and political clout of India, we may expect to see the continued promotion of Hindi and certain larger languages of South Asia.

The success of these efforts to promote Mandarin and South Asian languages draws on the high levels of homeland literacy that parents bring with them, as well as their strong motivations to maintain ties with the homeland and instill a sense of heritage identity among their raised-in-America children. Heritage or community-based schools are essential for this purpose, but so too is the local community's linguistic landscape (see de Klerk and Wiley 2010), which includes the visible presence of languages in not only schools, sometimes connected with places of worship, but also commercial sites, market places, apothecaries, and community or cultural centers where members of the community shop, gather, and congregate. The visible use of languages in these places can be seen to a certain extent as reflecting the linguistic vitality of the social networks that energize and maintain heritage and community languages. The brief discussions of the two communities that follow underscore the importance of community-based analysis in understanding these dynamic, growing, ethnolinguistic populations.

9.2 The Case of Chinese Language Communities in the San Francisco Bay Area

9.2.1 A Historical Sketch of Chinese Immigrants in the United States and Chinese Community Language Education

As of the 2010 Census, the population of immigrants of Chinese-origin and those of Chinese heritage residing in the United States had reached 3.14 million (American Fact Finder 2010). The number was estimated to be 3.71 million in the 2010–2014 American Community Survey 5-year Estimates. Chinese immigration to the United States has primarily consisted of two waves (Hooper and Batalova 2015). The first wave occurred in the mid-1800s gold rush era and continued with the building of railroads on the west coast but was later halted by the Chinese Exclusion Act enacted in 1882. This first wave of Chinese immigrants arrived in San Francisco in 1848 and eventually established the first Chinatown. As of today, San Francisco still has the largest Chinatown outside Asia (Sanfranciscochinatown n.d.). The first-wave Chinese immigration comprised mostly poor peasants from Guangdong Province, a province in southern China (Chang 2003). The majority of them spoke Cantonese (Wong and Lopez 2000) and tended to reside in Chinatown. The second wave of immigration started in the late 1970s after the abolition of the Chinese Exclusion Act in 1965 and the normalization of US–China relations in 1972. These second-wave immigrants have mainly consisted of highly educated and wealthy Chinese. Most of them speak Mandarin Chinese, can speak fluent English, and reside in suburbs or near research centers rather than in city-center Chinatowns.

Over half of Chinese immigrants reside in California and New York. Out of the 12 US counties with the most Chinese immigrants, four of them (San Francisco County, Santa Clara County, Alameda County, and San Mateo County) are in the Metropolitan San Francisco Bay Area, which is the focus of this discussion (US Immigrant Population by State and County 2017). According to Zhang and Slaughter-Defoe (2009), the majority of Chinese immigrants have a common desire over generations, which is to maintain Chinese language and culture among their children. While this effort articulated with a desire to keep the door back to China open for the first-wave immigrants who might wish to return to China, it has become more closely linked with questions of identity formation and heritage continuation for the second-wave immigrants.

The mastery of the Chinese language might also boost job opportunities with the rising economic power of China in the past decade. This pragmatic lens became more prominent, especially since China's President Xi visited the United States in September, 2015, and President Obama announced the "One Million Strong" initiative to increase the number of K-12 students studying Mandarin Chinese to one million by 2020 (Yap 2015). To achieve the goal of Chinese heritage maintenance, Chinese community language schools were established to support the learning of the Chinese language and culture, with the first one created in San Francisco in 1859 (Sanfranciscochinatown n.d.). As stated in the introduction, Chinese immigrant communities are ethnically, culturally, and linguistically heterogeneous. When Chinese is used to refer to language, it includes language varieties other than Mandarin. Even though the majority of Chinese community language schools teach Mandarin, some teach Cantonese in communities with large numbers of immigrants from Hong Kong and Guangdong province of China (Wiley et al. 2008). Therefore, Chinese in this chapter mainly refers to Mandarin, but can also mean any other language varieties. These schools primarily offer classes on weekends, during after-school hours, or over the summer. In weekend schools, classes are held for two to four hours once per week to teach Chinese language and culture, such as drawing, calligraphy, martial arts, and Chinese dancing. Some larger Chinese schools even offer leadership classes, or advanced placement (AP) physics or calculus. After-school Chinese classes meet every weekday at the end of the school day, from 3:00 PM until 6:00 PM. Since after-school classes meet more frequently than weekend schools, after-school classes are generally viewed as a more effective program model in terms of maintaining Chinese. Summer camps are offered in areas like San Francisco and Maryland, which are often more densely populated by Chinese immigrants and Chinese-Americans. These kinds of summer camps provide a period of intensive time for students to learn Chinese, sometimes coupled with the opportunities to visit places of interest in China.

Two national organizations were formed in the 1990s to support Chinese schools: NCACLS (National Council of Associations of Chinese Language Schools), primarily established and operated by immigrants from Taiwan, and CSAUS (Chinese School Association in the United States), primarily organized by immigrants from the People's Republic of China (Mainland). Determining the current number of students served by Chinese schools nationally is difficult. McGinnis (2005) estimated that there were 140,000 students enrolled in over 1,000 Chinese schools across the United States. Given the increases in Chinese immigration since then, the number is likely much higher now.

9.2.2 Demographic Analysis of the Current Chinese Community in the San Francisco-San Jose-Oakland Bay Area

California has an estimated total population of 38 million (ACS Demographic and Housing Estimates, 2017), out of which 5.13 million are of Asian descent (13.5 percent of the total population) and 1.35 million are of Chinese descent in particular (3.6 percent of the total population). If we strictly define the San Francisco Bay Area in Northern California, it comprises nine counties: Alameda, Napa, Santa Clara, Contra Costa, San Francisco, Solano, Marin, San Mateo, and Sonoma (see Figure 9.1). In this section, we will focus on four counties in the Bay Area, San Francisco, San Mateo, Santa Clara, and Alameda, because these are where Asians and the population of those of Chinese-origin tend to reside. Asians alone (1.5 million) comprise one-third of the total population in the Bay Area. Chinese is the biggest ethnicity among Asians, with a population of 563,950, representing 11.3 percent of the total Bay Area population. As Lam (2012) claimed,

> San Francisco is now part of a statewide trend that has resulted in majority becoming minority, with minority continuing to surge and multiply. The latest census showed that whites have slowly shrunk to 48 percent of the population in San Francisco, becoming another minority in a city that has

Figure 9.1 Nine counties in the San Francisco Bay Area
Source: Bay Area Census by Metropolitan Transportation Commission February 13, 2017

no majority. The city's Asian population, on the other hand, has risen above the 33 percent mark. That is, one in three San Francisco residents has an Asian face.

The city of San Francisco represents a special and unique case in Chinese immigration history because it accommodated the first wave of Chinese immigrants in the mid-1800s and hosted the first Chinatown and Chinese school. Even in this modern era, those of Chinese-origin still comprise a notable segment of the population in the city, rising from 19.6 percent in the 2000 US Census to 21.4 percent in the 2010 Census. Chinese Americans have gradually come to constitute both a numerical and political force in the Bay Area, not only population-wise but also in terms of political influence. More and more Chinese Americans have actively gotten involved in community services and politics in recent decades. In 2011, for example, Edwin Lee was elected as the first Chinese-American mayor in San Francisco's history (Sanfranciscochinatown n.d.). Additionally, as Chinese-American voter participation has increased, this group has gained more political power and attention (Romney 2004).

The increased population of Chinese-origin in the San Francisco Bay Area has resulted in an enormous demand for Chinatowns, Chinese supermarkets, churches/temples, language schools, newspapers, and even radio stations, all of which are social networking sites and resources essential for maintaining the linguistic vitality of Chinese among Chinese immigrants and their descendants. The lists of Chinese supermarkets, churches/temples, language schools, and newspapers in the next section were identified through Google searches using keywords, and thus cannot be considered exhaustive in any way.

9.2.3 Chinatowns, and Suburban Chinese Spaces in the Bay Area Landscape

There are two Chinatowns in the Bay Area: one in San Francisco and the other in Oakland. The one in San Francisco, as stated previously, is the oldest Chinatown in the United States and the largest one outside Asia. Both Chinatowns host many Chinese businesses, stores, restaurants, and markets, as well as Chinese cultural performances, such as lion dancing. In addition, San Francisco's Chinatown also serves as a famous tourist spot for millions of visitors each year.

Figure 9.2 plots many of the larger Chinese supermarkets in the Bay Area (approximately thirty markets), including chain stores of 99 Ranch Market, Marina Food Market, and Lion Food Market. There are also many smaller markets, which are not identified on this map.

Chinese churches and temples serve as an important hub for Chinese immigrants in the Bay Area. A non-exhaustive list of Chinese churches identified on the Bay Area Chinese Resources website includes over thirty churches (Chinese Churches n.d.).

9.2.4 Educational Institutions That Teach Chinese

Chinese language education in the Bay Area exists in a variety of program models: Chinese community language schools (primarily operated by Chinese immigrants), Chinese immersion schools/programs, and Chinese

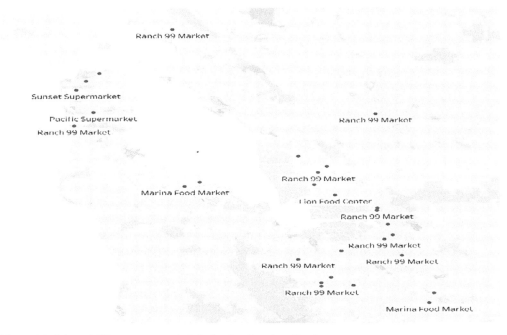

Figure 9.2 Selected Chinese supermarkets in the San Francisco Bay Area

Figure 9.3 Chinese community language schools in the Bay Area

classes in public schools. As stated previously, the first Chinese community language school was established in San Francisco in 1859 in order to maintain future generations' Chinese (Cantonese at that time). Figure 9.3 maps a number of Chinese community language schools in the Bay Area, though this list is far from exhaustive.

A "full US Chinese immersion school list" shared information about approximately forty Chinese (including thirty-plus Mandarin and approximately ten Cantonese schools) immersion schools in the Bay Area (2016). Some of these schools were established as private international schools, such as the Chinese American International School (opened in 1981) and the International School of the Peninsula, while others are either public charter schools or immersion programs hosted in regular public schools, such as Yu Ming Charter School in Oakland and Azevada Elementary School in Fremont, CA. These schools are open to all students and adopt a variety of immersion program models, with the mission of educating bilingual and bicultural American citizens.

In addition to Chinese community language schools and immersion schools, Chinese classes can also be found in regular public schools. Chinese is offered in most junior and senior high schools in the Bay Area, alongside Spanish and French. Moreover, many California community colleges and universities also offer Chinese classes to undergraduate students.

9.2.5 Chinese Newspapers and Radio Station

In San Francisco, *Sing Tao Daily* is the most popular Chinese language newspaper, followed by *Chinese Daily News* (also known as *World Journal*) and *China Press*. Sing Tao Chinese Radio, which was started about 20 years ago in the San Francisco Bay Area and broadcasts in both Cantonese and Mandarin Chinese, is one of the few Chinese radio programs in the United States.

9.2.6 The Current Successes, Challenges and Prospects of Chinese Community Language Education in the Bay Area

As described in the previous section, there are many Chinese community language schools in the San Francisco Bay Area. These schools are independent educational institutions but do connect with each other through organizations such as the ANCCS (Association of Northern California Chinese Schools) or through area-wide student contests. In addition to teaching the Chinese language, another important function of Chinese community language schools is to help children of Chinese heritage form a sense of community (You and Liu 2011). Chinese community language schools provide a unique and special place for students of Chinese heritage to mingle with friends from similar backgrounds: Not only do they share similar physical features, but they also share similar cultural stories and customs. Such experiences found outside the mainstream public school system hopefully assist with their identity formation – a combination of bilingual and bicultural Chinese American identity (Lu 2010).

The San Francisco Bay Area can be viewed as a role model in Chinese community language education not only because it has numerous Chinese language schools (weekend, afterschool, and summer) but also because this is the place where well-known and widely used Chinese textbooks and readers have been produced. For instance, the textbook series "Maliping Chinese" was compiled and published by Dr. Liping Ma in the late 1990s after she established the Stanford Chinese School. This series is well-known for character recognition and the inclusion of intriguing traditional Chinese stories in its texts. Another textbook series is called "Shuangshuang Chinese," created by Ms. Shuangshuang Wang, who established the Shuangshuang Chinese School in the Bay Area. Both textbook series are now widely used across the United States and around the world. "Better Chinese" is a company that was founded by educators from Columbia University and the United Nations in 1997 and is anchored in the Bay Area, with a mission of developing the best materials and programs for teaching the Chinese language and culture to nonnative speakers (Better Chinese n.d.). "Better Chinese" offers six programs that are now widely used in Chinese immersion programs, including *My First Chinese Words*, *My First Chinese Reader*, and *Modern Chinese*.

Despite such success stories of Chinese schools and textbook editors, Chinese community language schools face certain challenges, including low teacher quality, high teacher turn-over rates (You and Liu 2011), and a lack of coordination with public schools and university programs (Liu et al. 2011). Most Chinese teachers in Chinese community language schools are not certified to teach Chinese and may not have any background or experiences in education at all. In order to support Chinese schools and keep them running, however, Chinese parents or volunteers are called on to serve as Chinese teachers. As this is a part-time job or a week-end position, teachers' turnover rates are very high, for a variety of reasons, from teachers' finding full-time jobs to family relocation. While some Chinese schools can apply for public school foreign language credit, most of them cannot. The curriculum in Chinese schools is independent of that in public schools and thus is hard to articulate with public schools or university programs. Other challenges include a lack of stable meeting spaces, the diversity of students' language skills and backgrounds, high student turn-over rates, a lack of parental support, and a lack of public awareness and support (Liu et al. 2011).

Though there are challenges, Chinese community language education still holds great promise in the San Francisco Bay Area. First, the Asian population, and especially that of individuals of Chinese descent, is on the rise and will continue increasing in the coming decade. The booming population will in turn boost local Chinese businesses, markets, and language schools, which provide occasions and opportunities for using Chinese as well as motivations for learning the language. The promising future of Chinese community language education is also related to Chinese parents' positive attitudes toward Chinese language maintenance among their children. As Wiley et al. (2008) found in their survey on language attitudes, Mandarin Chinese was regarded by survey respondents as a resource to be maintained. In addition, as the status of Chinese rises in the world overall and in the United States more specifically, proficiency in Chinese will yield more benefits, both academically and pragmatically. Compared to decades or centuries ago, Chinese language learners now have a wide range of both opportunities and resources for learning and using Chinese, and motivation for learning the language. This statement holds especially true in the San Francisco Bay Area.

9.3 Investigating Hindi Language Communities in Greater Washington, DC

9.3.1 A Historical Sketch of South Asian Immigrants in the United States and of Hindi Community Language Education

The rising population of South Asians[1] in the United States has, like that of the Chinese-origin population, been remarkable. According to the 2010 US Census, over 3.4 million South Asians live in the United States (US Census 2010). When comparing data from the 2000 US Census, which reported 1.9 million South Asians in the United States, this indicates an 81 percent rise in population, with Indians comprising the largest segment of the South Asian American community (SAALT 2012). Along with this rise in immigration, South Asian languages have also been experiencing high levels of growth in language use since 2011, particularly Hindi, which grew by 105 percent (Ryan 2013).

Now the second-largest immigrant group in the country (Zong and Batalova 2015), the current South Asian population can be traced back to the waves of immigration dating back to the 1820s, when many South Asians began arriving in California to work agricultural jobs (Lee 2015). However, the restrictions of the Immigration Acts of 1917 and 1924 effectively banned immigration from Asia and halted migration from India to the United States (Lee 2015). As of the 1960s, there were only 12,000 immigrants from India residing in the United States, representing less than 0.5 percent of the 9.7 million immigrants documented in 1960 (Zong and Batalova 2015).

The 1965 Immigration and Nationality Act, which ended the system of racially based origin-country quotas, led to immigration avenues that were employment-based. This was a result of subsequent legislation, which called for highly skilled immigration and resulted in an entry pathway for a growing number of professionals and students from India (Kulkarni 2013), as well as from other countries. The Immigration Act of 1990 supplemented and advanced temporary skilled worker categories, leading to an increase in the number of permanent work-based visas and contributed to an increase in the population of Indian-born residents in the United States (Kulkarni 2013). One contrast between the waves of immigration following the Immigration and Nationality Act of 1965 and the Immigration Act of 1990 was that many of the migrants were young, educated, and looking to move to urban areas rather than farming communities, and brought strong English skills with them.

---

[1] We will use the term South Asian to refer to individuals who trace their ancestry to Bangladesh, Bhutan, India, the Maldives, Nepal, Pakistan, and Sri Lanka, as well as members of the South Asian Diaspora. When referring specifically to individuals from India, the term Indian or Indian Americans will be used.

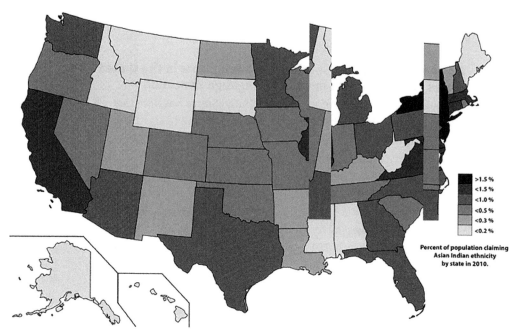

Figure 9.4 Percentage of South Asian population by state in 2010
Source: Zifan, A. (2015), https://commons.wikimedia.org/w/index.php?curid=42766147

From 1980 to 2013, the Indian immigrant population increased tenfold from 206,000 to 2.04 million, and it has approximately doubled every decade since (Zong and Batalova 2015). Today, Indian citizens are the top recipients of the temporary high-skilled worker visa category H-1B, accounting for almost 70 percent of the H-1B visas approved by the United States Citizenship and Immigration Services (USCIS) in 2014 (Zong and Batalova 2015). India is also the second most important sending country of international students to the United States, with nearly 103,000 Indian-born students enrolled in US educational institutions in the 2013–14 academic year (Zong and Batalova 2015).

The five states with the largest South Asian populations are California, New York, New Jersey, Texas, and Illinois (SAALT 2012). The New York City metropolitan area is home to the largest concentration of South Asians in the United States, with Chicago, Los Angeles, San Francisco-Oakland, and Washington, DC making up the rest of the list of top cities for South Asians (SAALT 2015). Figure 9.4 demonstrates the percentage of the United States population claiming South Asian ethnicity by state in the United States 2010 Census.

9.3.2   Who Are Hindi Heritage Language Learners?

What makes the heritage language experience unique for South Asians is the combination of the complicated colonial history of English in India and the linguistic diversity of the region. This is prevalent in India's language policies, where English is considered the associate official language, next to Hindi, which is India's national language (Sedlatschek 2009). Elements of India's national language policy have also impacted the waves of South Asian immigration to the United States, as many of these settlers had come with a strong understanding of English. The Three Language Formula of India, originally set out in the 1968 National Policy Resolution, encourages the study of Hindi, English, and a modern Indian language (preferably one of the southern languages) in the Hindi speaking states and Hindi, English, and regional language in the non-Hindi speaking states (Weinstein 1990). The goal of this education policy is to have Indian students leave secondary school with proficiency in their mother tongue, English, and another Indian dialect.

Unlike many other immigrant groups, South Asians tend to arrive in the United States with a strong command of the English language. Approximately 90 percent of Hindi-Urdu speakers in the United States say that they speak English well or very well (Shin and Kominski 2010). Although many 1.5 and 2.0 generation South Asians are exposed to the Hindi language on a regular basis, they may hear English spoken more frequently in their homes. However, it has been found that these younger generations still feel a strong connection to the South Asian culture and traditions, even if they are considered and/or self-identify as native English speakers (Nijhawan 2011; Kulkarni 2013). Therefore, for this chapter, we will use Gambhir's (2008) pedagogical definition of a heritage learner of Hindi as:

> A heritage learner of Hindi is a student whose family may speak Hindi or another Indian language at home. The student may or may not be able to speak or understand Hindi but is familiar with the Hindi language and its culture through his or her connection with the heritage land (1).

This definition of a Hindi heritage speaker helps clarify the fluidity of this position and those that self-identity as one, as well as providing insight into the "the status of the learners" (Wiley et al. 2014). In the next section, we will examine the Hindi-speaking population in the combined metropolitan area of Washington, DC (DC), Maryland (MD), and Virginia (VA).

9.3.3 Demographic Analysis of the Current Hindi Speaking Community in the DMV Area

According to the 2014 US Census Bureau, the population of the Washington metropolitan area is estimated to be roughly 6 million (US Census Bureau 2015). Over the past ten years, the DC–VA–MD metropolitan area has overtaken the Los Angeles metropolitan area as the area with the third largest South Asian population (SAALT 2012). In this chapter, we will focus on the metropolitan area of the District of Columbia, Virginia, and

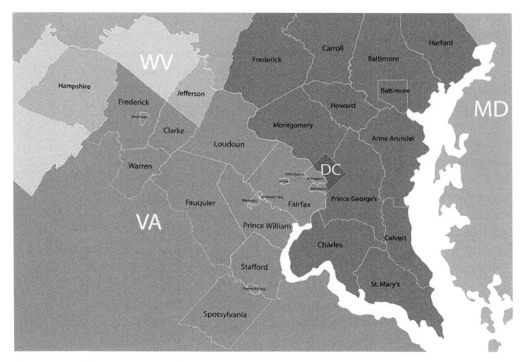

Figure 9.5 Washington, DC Metropolitan Area
Source: Encore Global (http://encoreeb5.com/eb-5-regional-centers/washington-d-c/)

Maryland as a metropolitan region. We use the popular acronym "DMV" to refer to the combined areas of Washington, DC, Maryland, and Virginia, as this term is also used by different United States government extensions when directly referencing this area. The counties of the two states and the District of Columbia are labeled in Figure 9.5.

As the South Asian population has spread across the 68.25 square miles of the DC Metropolitan area, the demand for specialized grocery stores, temples and religious community centers, language schools, cultural entertainment, and networking opportunities has notably increased. As with many other ethnic groups in the United States, the DMV South Asian community has responded to this landscape by organizing existing, and creating new, local resources to meet the needs of language maintenance and cultural preservation. The following description of resources available to South Asians in the DMV area provides an example of a social network for language maintenance and linguistic vitality.

9.3.4   Indian Grocery Stores

Across the DMV area, there are approximately forty Indian supermarkets and grocery stores. Many of these grocery stores are locally owned and sell items such as clothing, prayer books, and cooking utensils in addition to food items. This list of Indian markets does not include the availability of Indian ingredients found in retail chains such as Safeway, Food Lion, and Wegmans, nor does it include general Asian stores, which carry ingredients from all over the Asian continent.

Additionally, there are over fifty South Asian restaurants in the DMV area. Many of them specialize in Indian cuisine, including a variety of vegetarian and non-vegetarian restaurants. Many of the vegetarian restaurants adhere to the food principles that derive from the Jain religion, which derives from Hinduism and is largely prevalent throughout India. Many of the non-vegetarian restaurants do not offer beef or pork options to accommodate Hindu and Muslim South Asians. This is noteworthy, as the Hindi language is not intrinsically tied to the Hindu religion and the Hindi heritage speaker may not be a practicing Hindu.

9.3.5 Temples and Religious and Community Centers

Hindu temples and other religious community centers serve as anchors for the South Asian immigrant community in the DMV area. Figure 9.6 demonstrates the wide variety of religious temples and churches that service the South Asian population in this region. South Asian temples and religious centers offer the community a space where heritage speakers can perform their linguistic and cultural practices (Pennycook 2010) and serve as a social nuclei for South Asians (Shohammy and Durk 2009). In Figure 9.6, a search of South Asian religious centers in the DMV area found that there are ten registered places of worship that incorporate South Asian culture.

Since 2015, the DC Mayor's Office on Asian and Pacific Islander Affairs (APIA) has hosted a Diwali reception, celebrating the festival of lights. Diwali is one of the more, if not most, widely celebrated Hindu festivals around the world. The APIA has worked in conjunction with the Hindu community to perform a ceremony and host a social event that honors the religious traditions and provides South Asians a chance to showcase their culture. In the 2016 event, a local South Asian comedian performed a stand-up set, a *Bhangra*[2] troupe danced, and a traditional Indian dinner was catered by a local Indian restaurant. At this event, a proclamation that November 9, 2016 was Diwali Day in the District of Columbia was declared (Wilson 2016). An official Diwali stamp was developed by the United States Postal Service and unveiled on that day (Wilson 2016).

---

[2] *Bhangra* is a dance style popular in the Punjab region of Indian.

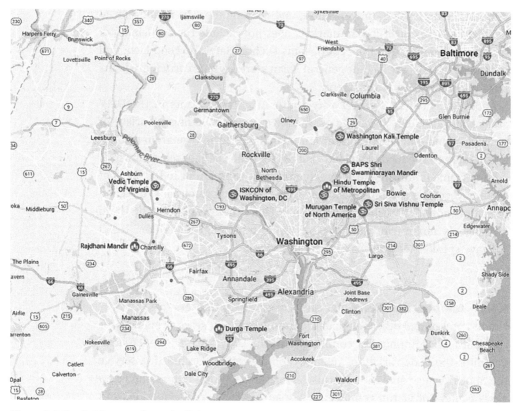

Figure 9.6 South Asian temples and religious centers in the DMV area
Source: Google Maps

9.3.6   Hindi Language Schools

Applied linguistics research on intergenerational transmission and language loss has argued that without active intervention, languages can be lost over time on both an individual and community level, essentially dying out within three generations (Wiley 1996). This is, of course, if language and culture maintenance are actively sought. Many South Asians wish to maintain their language and culture. In the DMV area, there are several schools that offer courses for Hindi heritage speakers. In this region, Hindi language learning opportunities are found mostly in the states of Maryland and Virginia and are integrated with other South Asian cultural offerings such as Indian arts, dancing, culture, vocal and instrumental music, and yoga. Several South Asian ethnic communities around the United States have organized well-developed weekend or evening schools that offer Hindi for heritage learners. Additionally, the University of Virginia hosts a South Asia Center to promote the study of South Asian languages and culture.

9.3.7 Networking Opportunities

There are several large South Asian networking groups in the DMV area, including the Network for South Asian Professionals (NetSAP), the South Asian Leaders of Tomorrow (SAALT), South Asian Bar Association (SABA), South Asian Psychological Networking Associations, Asian American Leadership Empowerment and Development (AALED), the South Asian Women's Network, and the American India Foundation (AIF), which also hosts a second chapter dedicated to Young Professionals (AIF-YP). While these organizations are structured as networking establishments, they offer the South Asian community opportunities for social interaction and community building. Although these organizations do not insist that members be of South Asian origin, their membership is predominantly composed of individuals from India and Bangladesh.

Within the political sphere of DC, there are several lobbying and advocacy groups that strive to enhance and promote South Asian culture, religion, and language. The Hindu American Foundation is a national organization that educates non-Hindus and advocates on behalf of the language and religion. The Embassy of India in Washington, DC regularly disseminates information on local and national happenings through a series of open events and briefings.

9.3.8 The Current Successes, Challenges, and Prospects of Hindu Community Language Education in the Greater Washington, DC Area

Although Hindi has been recognized as the third most commonly spoken language at home in the United States, it does not figure as one of the top foreign languages studied in K-12 schools (Wiley and Bhalla 2019). Therefore, many of the Hindi language learning opportunities are part of community-based efforts that are committed to supporting the emergence of bilingual generations of young South Asian Americans. As documented previously, the vast array of South Asian ethnic and cultural organizations provide numerous possibilities for educating the younger generations in Hindi. Within the South Asian DMV community, local organizations have extensively worked in ways that offer and provide a broad range of cultural and education activities and opportunities, often while incorporating heritage language learning. Like many other cultural groups within the United States, South Asian immigrant parents often have a strong desire for their children to retain these traits while concurrently acclimating to American culture (Warsi 2003).

Despite the consistent and substantial waves of South Asian immigration, Hindi is still classified as a less commonly taught language by the National Security Education Program (NSEP) (Gambhir 2001), and this is reflected in the lack of curriculum materials and instructional resources available in

Table 9.1 *Speakers in the United States of the scheduled languages of India, 2009–2013.*

	Scheduled language of India	Number of speakers in the United States
1	Assamese	1,305
2	Bengali	257,740
3	Gujarati	373,253
4	Hindi	643,337
5	Kannada	48,620
6	Kashmiri	1,775
7	Malayalam	146,310
8	Marathi	73,630
9	Nepali	94,220
10	Oriya	5,385
11	Sindhi	8,965
12	Tamil	190,685
13	Telugu	247,760
14	Urdu	397,502
15	Konkani	The US Census did not include data for 32 languages, likely
16	Manipuri	out of concern that the number would be so small that
17	Punjabi	anyone may be able to deanonymize the data. Additionally,
18	Sanskrit	61,385 individuals were identified as speakers of "Indian
19	Bodo	languages, not classified." Therefore, we believe that the
20	Santhali	lack of data for these languages may fall under one of these
21	Maithili	two categories.
20	Dogri	

Sources: (Sharma 2012; Sonnad 2015)

K-12 schools in the United States. Similarly, in the university setting many of the professors that teach Hindi courses do not have formalized training (Gambhir 2001). These issues are not specific to Hindi heritage language programs, as advanced professional development for teachers, funding opportunities, and infrastructure are often lacking in all language programs. However, progress has been made by programs such as STARTALK[3] and the National Security Language Initiative, which have helped broaden the scope and quality of Hindi courses offered to primary, secondary, and university-level students (Kulkarni 2013).

Additionally, while Hindi is designated as the official language of the Government of India, India has recognized twenty-one other languages as scheduled languages. Scheduled languages are entitled to representation on the Official Languages Commission and receive funding and benefits to enrich the education of these languages, as well as being seen as a base that would be drawn upon to enrich Hindi, the official language of India (Sharma 2012). Therefore, speakers of these scheduled languages may feel a strong connection to Hindi, as their own respective languages provide a base for Hindi language enrichment. Table 9.1 demonstrates the number of

---

[3] STARTALK is a program aimed at increasing speakers of critical languages such as Hindi and Urdu among others.

speakers of these scheduled languages in the United States. Therefore, contributing to the argument that South Asians who do not come from homes where Hindi is spoken still contribute to the Hindi heritage language speaker population.

As illustrated by Table 9.1, it is noticeable that Hindi has the largest number of speakers in the United States, with Urdu, Guajarati, Bengali, and Telugu rounding out the top five most commonly spoken Indian languages. Polinsky and Kagan (2007) explain "the definition of a heritage speaker in general and for specific languages continues to be debated" (3). The debate is of particular significance for such languages as Chinese, Arabic, and the languages of India and the Philippines, where speakers of multiple languages or dialects are seen as heritage speakers of a single standard language taught for geographic, cultural, or other reasons (Mandarin Chinese, Classical Arabic, Hindi, or Tagalog, respectively). Therefore, many South Asians within the United States may not have direct ties to the Hindi language, but still identify Hindi as the language of their heritage.

9.4 Conclusion

In summary, the remarkable growth of Mandarin, and to a lesser extent other major Chinese dialects such as Cantonese, as well as that of Hindi and other major South Asian languages over the past several decades has in large part been the result of the liberalized immigration laws that have been in place since 1965. This growth has also been stimulated by the increase in global immigrant flows and the rising economic positions of both China and India. The rise of these two economic powers has been accompanied by large numbers of international students, who have come to the United States in search of educational opportunities, and many of these individuals have sought avenues for remaining in the country after graduation. Adult immigrants from both countries, moreover, have immigrated to the United States in search of economic opportunities. The rising numbers of Chinese and Indian language speakers are also largely the result of parental and community-based efforts such as those promoted through weekend schools in many communities across the country that are supported by the social, cultural, economic, and – to some extent – faith-based networks that are evident in the linguistic landscapes of strip malls and local shopping areas embedded in these communities (de Klerk and Wiley 2010).

Despite dramatic increases in the number of speakers of Mandarin and Hindi in particular, these languages tend to be underrepresented in schools both in terms of the number of schools offering Mandarin Chinese or Hindi and in terms of the number of students who live in households where these languages are spoken (Fee et al. 2014; see also Wiley et al. 2016).

The result is often rapid language loss among the second generation. Based on the results of a number of longitudinal studies, Rumbaut (2009) has noted that even among much larger heritage and community languages such as Spanish, the languages are rapidly being lost by the second and third generations in the United States:

> The analysis showed that even among those of Mexican origin, the Spanish language "died" by the third generation; all other languages died between the second and third generations. The death of languages in the United States is not only an empirical fact, but can also be considered as part of a larger and widespread global process of "language death" … [A] foreign language represents a scarce resources in a global economy, [and] immigrants' efforts to maintain that part of their cultural heritage and to pass it on to their children certainly seem worth supporting. Indeed the United States finds itself enmeshed in global economic competition … [t]he second generation, now growing up in many American cities, could fulfill such as a need. (64)

Thus, as Wiley et al. (2016) have noted; "It is evident that, if we are to reverse this tremendous loss of languages across generations, there is a need to dramatically improve the opportunities to study languages other than English in school" (9).

From a policy perspective, to the extent that building on the multilingual resources of the United States remains a goal, the United States is missing an opportunity to build on its community-based linguistic resources and further promote bi-/multilingualism within the country. Some federal projects such as STARTALK and Flagship programs have demonstrated the potential for integrating an HL-CL learner focus. Nevertheless, the responsibility for promoting these programs has fallen largely to community-based efforts. There is much that can be learned by studying these efforts through qualitative methodologies and the use of linguistic landscape analyses.

Meanwhile, there is also much that can be done to support community-based efforts. A number of collaborative efforts between universities and heritage-community scholars have been successful in linking university-based educators and non-professionally trained teachers from minority communities across the United States. The efforts of UCLA's National Heritage Language Resource Center are particularly exemplary in this regard. As another example, similar efforts by Loyala Marymount University in Los Angeles to provide summer professional development institutes for teachers of Mandarin have also been noteworthy in providing professional development for non-professional heritage language teachers. Such programs have demonstrated that community-based capacities can be increased. We need to continue to build on similar university–community collaborations. Without these efforts there is much to lose, but with them there is even more to gain for the next generation of heritage learners.

References

ACS Demographic and Housing Estimates: 2010–2014 American Community Survey 5-Year Estimates. n.d. Retrieved from https://factfinder.census.gov/faces/tableservices/jsf/pages/productview.xhtml?pid=ACS_14_5YR_DP05&prodType=table

American Fact Finder. 2010. Community Facts – Find Popular Facts and Frequently Requested Data about Your Community. Retrieved from https://factfinder.census.gov/faces/tableservices/jsf/pages/productview.xhtml?src=CF

Bay Area Census. 2017. Retrieved from www.bayareacensus.ca.gov/counties/counties.htm

Better Chinese. n.d. "About us." Retrieved from www.betterchinese.com/pages/about-us

Bhalla, S. and T. G. Wiley. 2018. Research on Heritage, Community, and Indigenous Languages. In A. Phakiti, P. I. De Costa, L. Plonsky, and S. Starfield (eds.), *The Palgrave Handbook of Applied Linguistics Research*. London: Palgrave Macmillan, 741–760.

Chang, I. 2003. *The Chinese in America*. New York: The Penguin Group.

Chinese Churches. n.d.. Retrieved from www.valleywalk.com/list/html/chinese_churches.html

de Klerk, G. and T. G. Wiley. 2010. Linguistic Landscapes as Multi-Layered Representation: Suburban Asian Communities in the Valley of the Sun. In E. Shohamy, E. B. Rafael, and M. Barni (eds.), *Linguistic Landscapes in the City*. Bristol: Multilingual Matters, 307–325.

Farrington v. Tokushige, 273 U.S. 284 1927.

Fee, M., N. C. Rhodes, and T. G. Wiley. 2014. Demographic Realities, Challenges, and Opportunities. In T. G. Wiley, J. K. Peyton, D. Christian, S. K. Moore, and N. Liu. (eds.), *Handbook on Heritage, Community, and Native American Language Education in the United States: Research, Policy and Practice*. London: Routledge, 6–18.

Full US Mandarin Immersion School List. 2016. Retrieved from https://miparentscouncil.org/full-mandarin-immersion-school-list/

Gambhir, S. 2001. Truly Less Commonly Taught Languages and Heritage Language Learner in the United States. In J. K. Peyton, D. A Ranard, and S. McGinnis (eds.), *Heritage Languages in America: Preserving a National Resource*. McHenry, IL: Center for Applied Linguistics, 207–228.

Gambhir, S. 2009. *Heritage Voices: Hindi*. Washington, DC: Center for Applied Linguistics. Retrieved from www.cal.org/heritage/pdfs/voices-hindi-language.pdf

Gambhir, V. 2008. The Rich Tapestry of Heritage Learners of Hindi. *South Asia Language* Pedagogy and Technology, 1. Retrieved from www.international.ucla.edu/media/files/salpat.pdf

Hooper K. and J. Batalova. 2015. Chinese Immigrants in the United States. Retrieved from www.migrationpolicy.org/article/chinese-immigrants-united-states

Kulkarni, R. 2013. *Hindu-Urdu Heritage Language Schools in the United States*. Washington, DC: Center for Applied Linguistics. Retrieved from www.cal .org/heritage/pdfs/briefs/hindi-urdu-heritage-language-schools-in-the-united-states.pdf

Lam, A. 2012. Welcome to San Francisco, the Asian City by the Bay. Retrieved from www.huffingtonpost.com/andrew-lam/asian-americans-san-francisco_b_2167539.html

Lee, E. 2015, October 1. Legacies of the 1965 Immigration Act. Retrieved December 1, 2016, from www.saada.org/tides/article/20151001-4458

Liu, N. 2013. Linguistic Vitality of Chinese in the United States. In J. Lo Bianco and J. K. Peyton (eds.), Special Issue of the *Heritage Language Journal* 10(3) on Language Vitality. www.heritagelanguages.org/

Liu, N., A. Musica, S. Koscak, P. Vinogradova, and J. López. 2011. *Challenges and Needs of Community-Based Heritage Language Programs and How They Are Addressed*. Heritage Brief. www.cal.org/heritage/research/briefs.html

Lomawaima, T K. and T. L. McCarty. 2006. *To Remain an Indian: Lessons in Democracy from a Century of Native American Education*. New York: Teachers College Press.

Lu, X. 2010. Bicultural Identity Development and Chinese Community Formation: An Ethnographic Study of Chinese Schools in Chicago. *Howard Journal of Communications* 12(4), 203–220.

Lynch, A. 2008. The Linguistic Similarities of Spanish Heritage and Second Language Learners. *Foreign Language Annals* 41(2), 252–281.

McGinnis, S. 2005. From Mirror to Compass: The Chinese Heritage Language Education Sector in the United States. In D. M. Brinton, O. Kagan, and S. Bauckus (eds.), *Heritage Language Education: A New Field Emerging*. London & New York: Routledge Taylor & Francis Group, 229–242.

Meyer v. Nebraska 262 U.S. 390 (1923).

Nijhawan, S. 2011. 'I Got the Point Across and That Is What Counts.' Transcultural versus (?) Linguistic Competence in Language Teaching. *Journal of the National Council of Less Commonly Taught Languages* 9(1), 59–81.

Pennycook, A. D. 2010. *Language as a Local Practice*. London: Routledge.

Polinsky, M. and O. Kagan. 2007. Heritage Languages: In the "Wild" and in the Classroom. *Language and Linguistics Compass* 1(5), 368–395.

Romney, L. 2004. Chinese Americans Emerge as a Political Power in S.F. Retrieved from http://articles.latimes.com/2004/feb/01/local/me-sfchinese1

Ruggles, S., J. T. Alexander, K. Genadek, R. Goeken, M. B. Schorder, and M. Sobek. 2010. *Integrated Public Use Microdata Series: Version 5.0* [Machine-readable database]. Minneapolis: University of Minnesota.

Rumbaut, R. G. 2009. A Language Graveyard? The Evolution of Language Competencies, Preferences and Use among Young, Adult Children of Immigrants. In T. G. Wiley, J. S. Lee, and R. Rumberger (eds.), *The*

Education of Language Minority Immigrants in the United States. Bristol: Multilingual Matters, 35–71.

Ryan, C. 2013. Language Use in the United States: 2011 (American Community Survey Reports). Retrieved from www.census.gov/content/dam/Census/library/publications/2013/acs/acs-22.pdf

SAALT. 2012, July. A Demographic Snapshot of South Asians in the United States. Retrieved December 1, 2016, from http://saalt.org/wp-content/uploads/2012/09/Demographic-Snapshot-Asian-American-Foundation-2012.pdf

SAALT. 2015, December. A Demographic Snapshot of South Asians in the United States. Retrieved December 1, 2016, from http://saalt.org/wp-content/uploads/2016/01/Demographic-Snapshot-updated_Dec-2015.pdf

Sanfranciscochinatown n.d. History. Retrieved from www.sanfranciscochinatown.com/history/index.html

Sedlatschek, A. 2009. *Contemporary Indian English: Variation and Change*. Amsterdam: John Benjamins Publishing Company.

Sharma, D. 2012. English in India. In A. Bergs and L. J. Brinton (eds.), *English Historical Linguistics*. Berlin: De Gruyter, 2077–2092.

Shin, H. B. and R. A. Kominski. 2010. *Language Use in the United States: 2007* (American Community Survey Reports, ACS-12). Washington, DC: US Census Bureau.

Shohamy, E. and G. Durk. 2009. *Linguistic Landscape: Expanding the Scenery*. New York and London: Routledge.

Sonnad, N. 2015, November 5. All 300-plus Languages Spoken in American Homes, and the Number of People Who Speak Them. Retrieved June 25, 2017, from https://qz.com/541479/all-300-plus-languages-spoken-in-american-homes-and-the-number-of-people-who-speak-them/

U. S. Census. 2010. *2010 Census*. Web. January 1, 2013 www.census.gov/2010census/data/.

US Census Bureau. 2015. *American Community Survey 1-year estimates. Retrieved from Census Reporter Profile page for Washington-Arlington-Alexandria, DC-VA-MD-WV Metro Area* https://censusreporter.org/profiles/31000US47900-washington-arlington-alexandria-dc-va-md-wv-metro-area/

US Citizenship and Immigration Services (USCIS). 2015. *Characteristics of H-1B Specialty Occupation Workers: Fiscal Year 2014 Annual Report to Congress*. Washington, DC: USCIS. Retrieved December 2, 2016 from www.uscis.gov/sites/default/files/USCIS/Resources/Reports%20and%20Studies/H-1B/h-1B-characteristics-report-14.pdf

US Immigrant Population by State and County. 2017. Retrieved from www.migrationpolicy.org/programs/data-hub/charts/us-immigrant-population-state-and-county

Warsi, M. J. 2003. Heritage Language Teaching: Issues Regarding Hindi-Urdu in the United States. *South Asian Language Review* 13(1–2), 137–145.

Weinstein, B. 1990. *Language Policy and Political Development*. Greenwood Publishing Group.

Wiley, T. G. 1996. *Literacy and Language Diversity in the United States*. Washington, DC and McHenry, IL: Center for Applied Linguistics & Delta Systems.

Wiley, T. G. 1998. The Imposition of World War I Era English-Only Policies and the Fate of German in North America. In T. Ricento and B. Burnaby (eds.), *Language and Politics in the United States and Canada*. Mahwah, NJ: Lawrence Erlbaum, 211–241.

Wiley, T. G. 2007. Immigrant Minorities: USA. In M. Hellinger and A. Pauwels (eds.), *Handbooks of Applied Linguistics, Vol. 9: Language and Communication: Diversity and Change*. Berlin: Mouton de Gruyter, 53–85.

Wiley, T. G. and S. Bhalla. 2019. The Demographics of Heritage and Community Languages in the United States. In O. Kagan, M. Carreira, and C. Chik (eds.), *A Handbook on Heritage Language Education: From Innovation to Program Building*. New York: Routledge.

Wiley, T. G., M. B. Arias, J. Renn, and S. Bhalla. 2016. *Language and the Fulfillment of the Potential of all Americans. Commissioned Paper for the American Academy of Arts and Sciences*. Commission on Language Learning. Washington, DC: Center for Applied Linguistics. Retrieved from www.cal.org/resource-center/publications-products/aaas-language-fulfillment

Wiley, T. G., D. Christian, J. Peyton, S. Moore, and N. Liu (eds.) 2014. *Handbook on Heritage, Community, and Native American Language Education in the United States: Research, Policy and Practice*. London: Routledge.

Wiley, T. G., G. Klerk, M. Li, N. Liu, Y. Teng, and P. Yang. 2008. Attitudes toward Mandarin, Heritage Languages, and Dialect Diversity among Chinese Immigrants and International Students in the United States. In A. W. He and Y. Xiao (eds.), *Chinese as Heritage: Fostering Rooted Worldcitizenry*. Honolulu: University of Hawai'I Press, 67–87.

Wilson, B. L. 2016, November 11. GW Cohosts a D.C. Diwali Celebration. Retrieved December 12, 2016, from https://gwtoday.gwu.edu/gw-cohosts-dc-diwali-celebration

Wong, S. C. and M. G. Lopez. 2000. English Language Learners of Chinese Background. In S. L. Mckay and S. C. Wong (eds.), *New Immigrants in the United States*. Cambridge: Cambridge University Press, 263–305.

Yap, A. C. 2015. The Changing Face of America's Chinese Schools: Non-Asian Students Are Increasingly Spending Their Saturdays Immersed in China's Language and Culture. Retrieved from www.theatlantic.com/education/archive/2015/11/chinese-schools-in-america/417027/

You, B. K. and N. Liu. 2011. Stakeholder Views on the Roles, Challenges, and Future Prospects of Korean and Chinese Heritage Language-Community Language Schools in the Phoenix Metropolitan Area: A Comparative

Study. *Heritage Language Journal* 8(3), 67–92. http://hlj.ucla.edu/Journal
.aspx

Zhang, D. and D. T. Slaughter-Defoe. 2009. Language Attitudes and Heritage
Language Maintenance among Chinese Immigrant Families in the USA.
Language, Culture and Curriculum 22(2), 77–93.

Zifan, A. 2015. Percent of Population Claiming Asian Indian Ethnicity by
State in 2010. Retrieved from https://commons.wikimedia.org/w/index
.php?curid=42766147

Zong, J. and J. Batalova. 2015, May 6. Indian Immigrants in the United
States. Retrieved December 1, 2016, from www.migrationpolicy.org/art
icle/indian-immigrants-united-states

10

The Vitality of Spanish as a Heritage Language in the United States

Maria M. Carreira

10.1 Introduction

Among this country's heritage languages, Spanish stands in a class of its own. It is the longest-spoken European language in what is now the United States, predating the arrival of English (Carreira and Beeman 2014). Today, the United States is home to the fifth-largest population of Spanish speakers in the world, after Mexico, Columbia, Argentina, and Spain. By 2060, this population is projected to become the second-largest Spanish-speaking country in the world, surpassed only by Mexico (Instituto Cervantes 2019).

The story of US Spanish is one of shifting contours, with immigration ebbs and flows and shifting social, economic, and political winds. Accordingly, the first section of this chapter presents up-to-date information on these topics and considers what this means for the vitality of Spanish as a heritage language (HL) in the United States.

Against this backdrop, the second section looks at Spanish-language education, focusing on how various instructional options and programs fare with respect to addressing the needs of Spanish heritage language speakers (SHLSs) and supporting Spanish language vitality.

Following Valdés (2001), we consider heritage speakers (HLSs) as individuals "who were raised in homes where a language other than the dominant community language was spoken, resulting in some degree of bilingualism in the heritage language and the dominant language." In the educational context, HLSs that are studying their home language in an academic setting are called heritage language learners (HLLs). Delving into a burgeoning line of research referred to as "heritage linguistics" the next section considers links between this field, teaching and learning, and language vitality to address a critical gap in the field of HL studies. Finally, the last section of this chapter looks at US Spanish from the related concepts of *superdiversity* and linguistic *contact zones* (Canagarajah 2017). These constructs raise important questions about what competencies make for effective communication in this country, what strategies should drive teaching and learning, and what all of this means to the vitality of US Spanish.

10.2   The State of US Spanish

10.2.1   Latino Demographics and Immigration

Spanish speakers make up over 13 percent of the US population, including 41 million home speakers and an additional 16 million with some knowledge of the language (Instituto Cervantes 2019; U.S. Census Bureau 2018).

Behind these numbers are two remarkable features of Spanish in the United States (1) that it is by far the most spoken language other than English (LOTE). Indeed, Spanish speakers account for more than 60 percent of all speakers of LOTEs and (2) that the number of US Spanish speakers is at an all-time high, having increased with every census since 1980, the year the currently used question about home language was first introduced (Hernández-Nieto and Gutiérrez 2017).

However, these numbers alone do not paint a complete picture of the vitality of Spanish in the United States. Despite the existence of large numbers of speakers, a well- developed body of research indicates that like other immigrant groups, Latinos are undergoing linguistic assimilation to English with concomitant loss of Spanish (Hernández-Nieto and Gutiérrez 2017; Jenkins 2018). Census figures are telling in this regard. Among US-born Latinos – a population that is particularly susceptible to language loss – the use of Spanish in the home has declined from 67 percent in 1980 to 59.5 percent in 2016 (Krogstad et al. 2015). This suggests that a sizable number of US born Latinos are not engaging in intergenerational transmission of Spanish.

In the past, high levels of immigration have offset the generational loss of speakers (Bills et al. 1999). However, there is no telling whether this will continue. Immigration from Latin America began declining in the early 2000s and actually dipped below zero starting in 2004, as more immigrants from Mexico left the United States than Mexican immigrants came to the United States (González Barrera 2015). But this has changed recently with so-called migrant caravans. As of the writing of this paper, border crossings have hit 13-year highs, with as many as four thousand immigrants entering the country per day fleeing poverty and violence in Central America (Jordan 2019). However, this trend may or may not continue at the same rate in the future. Whatever the case may turn out to be, if intergenerational transmission and immigration cannot be counted on to maintain Spanish are there other mechanisms that can do the job? The next section takes up this question.

10.2.2 Sustaining Language Vitality

A framework developed by Joseph Lo Bianco and others posits three key conditions that in synergy support language vitality, namely, capacity development, opportunity creation, and desire (Lo Bianco 2008, 2009). The "COD" framework has been used to support revitalization efforts on behalf of regional and minority languages like Welsh, Basque, Irish, and Maori. It has also been used to evaluate the vitality of HLs, including Spanish (Lo Bianco and Peyton 2013).

Capacity refers to personal language proficiency, that is, what speakers can do with their language and how well they can do it. Capacity is essential to vitality because it makes language use possible. In the US, Spanish-language capacity is relatively high in terms of sheer numbers of speakers with the facility to use the language at home and in informal contexts. Opportunity refers to the existence of a range of domains where language use is "natural, welcome, and expected" (LoBianco and Peyton 2013: iv). For HL learners, such opportunities are vital to expanding the depth and breadth of linguistic encounters beyond the home and informal contexts. Finally, desire refers to learner investment to learn and use a language.

Desire - or lack thereof - has a direct bearing on capacity development and opportunity creation. Illustrating this and exemplifying a common experience that undermines desire for Spanish, the U.S. Latino cited below has developed... that could further develop his capacity.

> I wish my Spanish was better. When I go to Mexico, my cousins laugh at me; they know I speak mocho. I should know more words, so sometimes I don't want to talk. (Sánchez-Muñoz 2016: 213).[1]

HLLs also encounter criticism in Spanish classes, where they are frequently compared unfavorably with native speakers as well as L2 learners (Beaudrie et al. 2014). In the wider school context, experiences that convey that knowing Spanish is incompatible with knowing English and attaining academic success are particularly harmful to the concept of desire (Carreira and Beeman 2014).

Also undermining desire are hostile societal attitudes toward Latinos and the Spanish language. Two recent incidents widely reported in the media serve by way of example. The first of these involved two women who were stopped by a Border Patrol agent in Montana and detained when they were heard speaking Spanish at a gas station. The second took place at a restaurant in New York City, where a lawyer threated to call Immigration and Customs Enforcement (ICE) because workers were speaking Spanish to each other (Romero 2017).

---

[1] With a literal meaning of "mutilated," "mocho" is often used as a derogatory term to refer to the Spanish of Mexican-Americans.

Coexisting with these and other negatives are significant positives. In the area of stances that favor language maintenance and use are US Latinos' high rates of language loyalty (Jenkins 2018). Also important are the many social and professional opportunities available to Spanish-English bilinguals. For example, in the professional domain, online job postings for Spanish speakers grew by 150 percent between 2010 and 2015, going from 178,320 to 454,771. By comparison, the number of job postings for Chinese, the second most in-demand language, increased by 45.5 percent, from 11,100 to 36,582 (New American Economy 2017). Similarly, Spanish was the most in-demand language in a recent survey of US employers, with 85 percent of respondents reporting a need for Spanish speakers, followed by Chinese (34 percent), French (22 percent), and Japanese (17 percent). Furthermore, Spanish was the only language for which employers' domestic needs matched international needs. In all other languages, the latter needs exceeded the former (American Council on the Teaching of Foreign Languages 2018).

The demand for Spanish-speaking workers reflects the widespread societal use of this language in the United States, which besides the workplace and institutions of learning, includes countless transactional interactions, participation in local clubs and societies, religious organizations, and social media as well as the consumption of traditional media (Carreira 2013). Altogether, these opportunities widen SHLSs' exposure to Spanish beyond the home and foster social interactions that promote a sense of community and shared identity among US Latinos.

To summarize, in terms of vitality, Spanish presents a mixed picture. On the positive side is the presence of large numbers of speakers with a wide range of opportunities to use the language and significant social and professional rewards for doing so. However, negative societal attitudes and school experiences, as well as generational language shift, undercut vitality. The next section looks at one of the most important engines of language vitality, namely formal education.

10.3 Spanish-Language Education

At its best, formal instruction develops HL learners' linguistic capacity by complementing and expanding on the informal transmission process of the home as well as by stimulating and preparing students to use their HL as widely as possible. In addition, education immerses students in larger speech communities beyond those of the home and its immediate surroundings, thereby supporting group identify among SHLSs from diverse backgrounds (Rivera-Mills 2012). This section reviews three categories of educational efforts that are promotive of vitality (1) HL instruction, (2)

Dual-language immersion education, and (3) the Seal of Biliteracy and the Global Seal of Biliteracy.

10.3.1   HL Instruction

What is now known as the field of heritage languages has its origins in the mid to late 1970s in Spanish in the pioneering work of Guadalupe Valdés and others (Valdés-Fallís 1978). In its early stages of development, issues of capacity dominated those of desire and opportunity. For example, Valdés-Fallís (1978) lays out the following objectives for a first year course:

(a) to learn to spell correctly, (b) to develop basic reading skills, (c) to develop basic composition skills, (d) to introduce students to traditional grammar terminology, and (e) to expose the student to standard spoken Spanish.

Still in the domain of capacity, Valdés (1995) sets forth the following goals for instruction, which were highly influential in Spanish HL teaching, curriculum development, and the design of pedagogical materials. (1) Spanish-language maintenance, (2) the acquisition of a prestige variety of Spanish, (3) the transfer of literacy skills from English to Spanish, and (4) the expansion of the bilingual range.

Though present to some extent in Valdés's early work, issues of desire come into focus in the late 1990s, particularly the importance of fostering HL learners' linguistic self-esteem and developing strategies for dealing with the type of negative experiences described earlier that undermine desire (see, for example, Colombi and Alarcón 1996). In line with this, Critical Language Pedagogy has emerged as a powerful tool for fostering linguistic empowerment in HL learners and preparing them to contest negative constructs about local uses of Spanish (Leeman 2014). Attitudes about local norms matter greatly for vitality, for the reasons given here.

For community languages of immigrant origin, homeland institutions sometimes repudiate or repress these norms, or are condescending toward them, or embarrassed by them, or regard them as comical, quaint, or antiquated. The extent to which these characterizations are resisted suggests the level of local vitality, or the possibility of the emergence of a local variety based on such norms that might seek eventually to be codified in a set of authoritative local depictions of the community language (Lo Bianco 2009: 13).

Straddling issues of desire and opportunity are HL learners' motivations for studying Spanish. These include finding identity and cultural connections, communicating more effectively with family and friends in the United States and abroad, and developing professional-level skills (Carreira and Kagan 2011). Recent efforts to address these goals have focused on integrating formal learning and experiential learning. With this work, HL instruction can be said to have entered a third phase focused on opportunity. Key exemplars of this include Martínez and Schwartz's (2012) project on medical Spanish for HL learners, Leeman, Rabin, and

Román-Mendoza's (2011) after-school academic enrichment program, Hartfield-Méndez's (2013) program in bilingual assistance in social service agencies, and Lowther Pereira's (2016) work on community service learning. These types of learning experiences offer many benefits to HL learners such as supporting positive identity development, fostering relationships with local communities, raising sociolinguistic awareness, developing skills for real-world language use, and furthering career goals (Fairclough 2016).

Unfortunately, many Spanish HLSs do not have access to HL instruction, let alone these experiences. The most comprehensive and up to date study of the availability of SHL instruction is Beaudrie (2012), which reports on a nationwide survey of Spanish programs in four-year universities with a Latino student population of 5 percent. Of 422 such institutions, 60 percent did not offer specialized Spanish HL courses (see Beaudrie, this volume). Furthermore, most departments that have an HL track offer one or two levels of HL instruction, typically at the intermediate level (Beaudrie 2012; Carreira 2013). At the secondary level, the situation is more worrying. In 2008, the latest year for which this information is available, only 8 percent of high schools reported having an HL program (Rhodes and Pufahl 2010). Several factors are believed to limit the availability of HL courses at both levels; in particular, uneven access to professional development in HL pedagogy for teachers and, more fundamentally, a lack of awareness on the part of some teachers and administrators of the need for HL instruction (Beaudrie et al. 2014).

Summing up, a COD-based analysis identifies *opportunity* as a relatively new area of development in HL pedagogy, following steady development in earlier years on issue of capacity first, followed by desire. Innovations that forge connections between formal instruction and language use in naturalistic settings stand out for their potential to address the language needs of SHL speakers and respond to their goals for studying Spanish, and ultimately, for their potential to support Spanish-language vitality. With capacity, desire, and opportunity now integrated into the principles and best practices of SHL teaching, it's time to focus on increasing the availability of high-quality SHL instruction to U.S. Latinos.

10.3.2   Dual-Language Immersion Programs

This type of bilingual education provides general academic instruction in two languages to English proficient students and English learners (ELLs). Typically, instruction starts in kindergarten or first grade and continues through elementary school, in various configurations. The goals are the same for both populations of students (1) to develop high levels of bilingualism and biliteracy, (2) to perform at academic grade level or above, and (3) to develop cross-cultural awareness (DeLeon 2016). To this end, both populations of students contribute to learning: The ELLs help with the second language and the English proficient students help with the development of English (see Potowski, this volume).

In the year 2000, there were some 260 dual language immersion programs in the United States, most, but not all, in Spanish. Today, in California alone there are 475 dual language immersion programs, according to the national self-registry DuallanguagePrograms.org., New York has 389 such schools, Texas has 319, and Florida has 119. Among the thirty or so languages taught in these programs, Spanish is by far the most widely available. In 2012–2013, the latest year for which national figures are available, thirty-five states and the District of Columbia had dual language programs in Spanish.

One of the main reasons behind the astonishing growth of these programs is that they succeed at accomplishing two objectives that are frequently viewed by the general public as being incompatible. These are, on the one hand, teaching English to ELLs and supporting their academic achievement, and, on the other, developing their home language (Tse 2001). Belying the incompatibility view and in so doing dismantling one of the many sources of opposition to bilingual education, an extensive body of research shows that ELLs in dual language immersion programs actually outperform their peers in English-medium programs with respect to English, reading, some content areas of the curriculum, and the partner language (Genesse et al. 2005; Lindholm-Leary, 2014). Furthermore, Thomas and Collier (2003) found that dual-language programs are particularly effective at closing the academic achievement gap between ELLs and their peers, as compared to other types of programs for ELLs. These and other outcomes, including significant benefits for English-proficient students, make dual-language programs highly attractive to policymakers, administrators, educators, and families (Steele et al. 2018).

In fact, the enormous popularity of dual language immersion programs among English-dominant families has given rise to the so-called gentrification problem, whereby "English-dominant families use hot housing markets, clever leveraging of lottery systems, and aggressive school district advocacy to ensure that their children gain access to these programs. Unsurprisingly, this reduces access for EL students" (Williams 2019). For all the problems with gentrification, it speaks to the fact that bilingualism can become a coveted goal of mainstream students and their families under particular conditions. Dual-language immersion programs provide a roadmap for achieving those conditions.

Unfortunately, as is the case with HL instruction, the large majority of Spanish-speaking children do not have access to dual-language immersion programs (Potowski 2016). Limited federal and state funding and a shortage of qualified teachers and supportive administrators have much to do with this (Lindholm-Leary 2013; Gándara and Escamilla 2017). There are other models of bilingual education as well as programs that offer native language support to ELLs in content area instruction, but the vast majority of these are designed to transition students to all-English instruction, rather than help them develop age-appropriate skills in their home language (Gándara & Escamilla 2017).

10.3.3 The Seal of Biliteracy and the Global Seal of Biliteracy

The Seal of Biliteracy (SB) is an official award by a school, district, or state to students who have attained a certain level of proficiency in the four skills in English and another language by high school graduation. Proficiency in the foreign language can be established through multiple criteria designed to align with the Intermediate-Mid level of the ACTFL Proficiency Guidelines.[2] The SB is available in many languages, but Spanish is by far the most common. In the Los Angeles Unified School District alone, over 4,000 such awards were awarded in Spanish in 2017–2018 (The Seal of Biliteracy 2019). In terms of outcomes associated with the SB, a study of one Los Angeles high school found higher enrollments in Spanish courses and greater demand for more advanced courses (Castro Santana 2014). Similarly, a study of three Illinois high schools also found increased enrollments in language study as well as an instructional shift "to a setting where students read, view, and listen to authentic texts from target cultures and communicate with their peers, teachers, and heritage and native speakers in the target language" (Davin et al. 2018: 273).

Overall, mirroring the situation of dual language immersion programs, David and Heineke (2017) describe the SB as having "the potential to change world language education in the United States, to make the public aware of the many benefits of multilingualism, and to provide a platform from which practitioners and researchers can advocate for additional resources as well as extended sequences of study for all students" (497).

Also supporting multilingualism is the Global Seal of Biliteracy (GSB). Like the SB, this is an official certification of proficiency in two or more languages, including English. However, unlike the SB, it is not just for high school students in participating schools. Rather, it is available to anyone, regardless of how they acquired their language skills, including HL speakers of any age who have developed such skills outside of the school context (The Global Seal 2019). The GSB certifies proficiency at two levels: the ACTFL Intermediate-Mid level (the level certified by the SB) as well as the Advanced-low level, which is the level associated with many professions (The Global Seal 2019). This makes the GSB an asset for job seekers and a valuable tool for employers looking to hire bilingual workers. The ACTFL

---

[2] The ACTFL proficiency levels are subdivided into three sublevels low, mid, and high.

Proficiency Guidelines are particularly apropos for this purpose, as they put the focus on functional skills for real-world language use, rather than on accuracy and/or explicit linguistic knowledge. As such, the GSB plays to the strengths of HLSs. Furthermore, by making proficiency certification accessible to the general public and useable in a wide range of settings, the SB and the GSB create mutually supportive links between capacity and opportunity.

To summarize, the three categories of models discussed in this section – HL teaching, dual-language immersion, and the two seals – represent some of the most impactful efforts in the area of language education for SHLSs. In terms of noteworthy contributions to the area of language vitality, HL instruction is at the forefront of forging connections between formal and informal learning by tapping into the myriad opportunities for using Spanish in naturalistic settings. Dual language immersion has found the key to generating wide societal support for bilingual education by putting the focus on the academic and linguistic benefits for ELLs and native English speakers. And the SB and the GSB are making certification widely available, thereby operationalizing language proficiency in the workplace and other settings, with potentially positive outcomes in the areas of desire and opportunity.

Unfortunately, at current rates of availability none of these efforts by themselves is likely to make a major difference in the overall vitality of US Spanish. In combination, however, they may tip the scales in favor of improving access to instruction in Spanish, with great potential for vitality. Speaking to this potential is California Global 2030. This is an ambitious initiative to have half of all K–12 students develop proficiency in two or more languages by the year 2030. To this end, California is investing in dual language immersion programs, the Seal of Biliteracy, and HL instruction, among other efforts (California Department of Education 2018a). Why does a California initiative matter to the vitality of Spanish in the nation as a whole? One reason is that the state's 6 million public school students make up 12 percent of the nation's public school students. Specifically to Spanish, California public schools educate 24 percent of the nation's Latino children in K-12 (California Department of Education 2018b). Thus, an increase in capacity and desire on the part of California students translates into a significant net increase in Spanish language vitality in the nation as a whole. Another reason is that if successful, Global California 2030 could become a model for other states.

Before closing this discussion it is important to note the absence of community-based programs from this overview. The Center for Applied Linguistics' self-registry, http://webapp.cal.org/Heritage/, lists a total 520 community-based programs in 49 different languages. Among these, only nine are in Spanish. By comparison, the database lists 191 such programs in Chinese, 38 programs each in Hindi and German, 34 in Korean, and 22 in Persian, among other languages (see Lee and Chen, this volume) Thus, community language programs are arguably the weakest link in in the chain of SHL education as well as being the only area of education where Spanish underperforms relative to other HLs.

Continuing with education, the next section considers advances in heritage linguistics and their connection to teaching and learning.

10.4 Spanish Heritage Speakers' Linguistic Knowledge and Skills

10.4.1 General Remarks

The aforementioned advances in education have been accompanied by remarkable developments in the field of Spanish heritage linguistics. Yet, as Polinsky (2016) notes, teaching and research remain largely disconnected from each other. Why is this? One reason is that the two fields have seemingly incompatible aims and stances with respect to language. Specifically, linguistic research is premised on a "narrow" definition of proficiency, which focuses on grammatical competence or mental representations of language, while teaching assumes a broad-based definition of proficiency, where what matters most is communicative competence (Zyzik 2016). Furthermore, while the point of reference or baseline population of linguistic research is native speakers, comparisons to native speakers in instructional contexts can undermine HL learners' desire to use their HL and exacerbate their linguistic insecurities (Sánchez-Muñoz 2016).

The ACTFL Proficiency Guidelines serve to illustrate the extent to which the two fields diverge with respect to their perspectives on proficiency. Widely used in instructional contexts, these guidelines represent a broad-based approach to measuring proficiency. The following paragraph describes some skills associated with the Advanced-high level of speaking, which is the level typically achieved by learners with a graduate degree in the language and extensive time in a target environment. Crucially, native or even near-native levels of grammatical competence are not expected even at this very high level of proficiency.

> Advanced High speakers may demonstrate a well-developed ability to compensate for an imperfect grasp of some forms or for limitations in vocabulary by the confident use of communicative strategies, such as paraphrasing, circumlocution, and illustration. (American Council on the Teaching of Foreign Languages 2012)

Notwithstanding the above, heritage linguistics has important contributions to make to HL pedagogy. Addressing Polinsky's cited observation, the discussion that follows identifies four categories of contributions along with takeaways on how to build bridges between research and teaching. Given the limitations of space, only a small number of research findings are offered by way of illustration. For a comprehensive overview of the findings of Spanish heritage linguistics, readers should consult Montrul (2018).

Some areas of linguistic research have a direct bearing on the development of broad-based proficiency by virtue of their connection to the ACTFL Proficiency Guidelines. Research on vocabulary provides a good example of this. Fairclough and Belpoliti (2016) investigated the writing of college-level SHSs at the lower end of the bilingual continuum for Spanish. Evidencing a low degree of lexical variation and originality, these students' writing was found to consist almost exclusively of the 1,000 most frequently used words in Spanish. Interestingly, despite these limitations, the authors note:

> the majority of the study participants (78%) were able to write an essay about 'Privacy and the Internet' and argue a good case. Although their spelling reflected lack of formal education in the HL and thus the strong influence of oral discourse in their written production, the texts could be understood. (197)

This comment, along with the sample writings and the student descriptions provided, suggests that the students in this study are somewhere at the Intermediate level of the Proficiency Guidelines for Writing. At this level, the vocabulary, grammar, and style of writing align with the oral register and content is mostly comprehensible to those "accustomed to the writing on non-natives." Intermediate-level vocabulary is "basic" and suffices to meet "practical everyday needs" (American Council on the Teaching of Foreign Languages 2012).

In terms of the vocabulary size associated with this level, research by Santos Palmou (2017) indicates that it is around 3,000 words, including the 2,000 most frequently used words in Spanish and an additional 1,000 words from availability lists from different notional classes.[3]

Thus, if Fairclough and Belpoliti's (2016) subjects are indeed at the Intermediate level, they fell short of using their full lexical repertoire in their writing. It follows that besides teaching new vocabulary, a promising pedagogical intervention for these learners might involve helping them access more of their lexical knowledge, including their receptive vocabulary. What does it take to get to the next ACTFL level of proficiency? Advanced level writers have "fairly wide general vocabulary" that enables them to "meet a range of work and/or academic writing needs." According to Santos Palmou (2017) this requires knowledge of the 5,000 most frequent words plus 2,000 other words from the availability lists.[4]

---

[3] Santos Palmou's estimate is for the A2 level of European Framework, which corresponds roughly to an ACTFL Intermediate Level (American Council on the Teaching of Foreign Languages (n.d.)).

[4] This estimate is for the B1 Level in the European Framework, which corresponds to ACTFL Intermediate High to Advanced Low.

Summarizing, this discussion illustrates a specific teaching application of linguistic research on vocabulary and makes a larger point about the relationship between research and practice. Regarding the larger point, the contributions of linguistic research typically come in the way of supplying the "what" of HLLs' knowledge. Operationalizing this information requires answering the question "so what" – that is, figuring out how research findings connect to the development of broad-based proficiency, which is the focus of instruction.[5] As illustrated here, connecting linguistic research with the ACTFL Proficiency Guidelines and other widely used pedagogical models, can prove valuable in this regard. Other topics of research that figure in one way or another in these guidelines and are therefore ripe for consideration along the lines suggested here include tense/aspect, the subjunctive, and pragmatics.

10.4.2 Linguistic Research Can Help Instantiate Core Principles and Practices of HL Teaching

Polinsky (2016) posits that one way that linguistic research can contribute to teaching is by "helping to categorize and even to predict errors, which in turn leads to more effective teaching" (329). Though accurate and sensible, this observation is likely to be of limited interest to teachers because of its focus on error correction. A preferable formulation is one that conforms to the schemas of HL teaching, i.e. the principles and practices that guide the work of HL teachers. One such principle is that students do not need comprehensive grammar instruction in the manner that L2 learners do. Rather, they benefit from a targeted approach to grammar instruction that addresses their knowledge gaps (Kagan and Dillon 2001). Another principle is that instruction should be differentiated, rather than one size fits all, as is the case with L2 teaching. This is because HL learners in a typical class present a wide range of linguistic needs (Carreira and Hitchins Chik 2018).

Montrul (2009) serves by way of example of how linguistic research that is predictive of errors can be reframed in terms of these principles. This research shows that the subjunctive presents more difficulty than the preterit/imperfect in oral and written production, as well as interpretation. Within the subjunctive, non-obligatory contexts are more affected than obligatory ones, with many SHSs producing only indicative forms in the former context. Regarding aspect, the imperfect proves to be more difficult to acquire than the preterit. Furthermore, non-prototypical combinations, such as achievement verbs in the imperfect (e.g., *llegaba*) are more

---

[5] For a good example of this, see Polinsky's (2006) discussion of how vocabulary tests can be used for placement purposes.

challenging than prototypical combinations, such as achievement verbs in the preterit (e.g., *llegó*).

Connecting this information to the aforementioned principles, these findings indicate, for example, that learners with a fairly good command of the subjunctive in non-obligatory contexts are not likely to need extensive instruction on obligatory contexts. For their part, learners that are struggling with the preterit are also likely to need help with the imperfect. Implicational hierarchies with similar applications to teaching also exist in the area of agreement (see, for example, Polinsky 2018).

Once again, this discussion offers a particular application of linguistic research to HL teaching as well as a larger point. The particular application involves the use of linguistic research to support targeted and differentiated instruction. The larger point is that the findings of linguistic research are rendered most meaningful to educators when framed in terms of the schemas of HL teaching. In the same manner, educators' considerable experiential knowledge of HL learners' capabilities - a valuable resource for linguistic research - is best communicated to researchers in terms of the schemas of narrow-based proficiency. There is a critical need for individuals that can broker this type of communication between the two fields.

10.4.3   Linguistic Research Provides a Foundation for Methodologies of Teaching

Though mixed classes (classes with HL and L2 learners) are the most common instructional setting in which HLLs study their home language, pedagogies and materials for this setting remain underdeveloped. Recent efforts to address this situation have benefitted greatly from linguistic research comparing HL and L2 learners. A pedagogy for the mixed context is emerging that is premised on two tasks (1) addressing issues that undercut learning for each learner type in the mixed context and (2) leveraging the complementary linguistic knowledge and skills of HL and L2 learners for reciprocal learning (Carreira 2016)

Undergirding this pedagogy is research on instructed HL acquisition, a new subfield of HL studies (Bowles 2018; Bowles & Torres, this volume). Instructed HL acquisition constitutes an important step toward bridging the gap between linguistic research and teaching. Key contributions include Potowski, Jegerski, and Morgan-Short (2009); Montrul and Bowles (2010); Bowles (2011); Henshaw (2015). But even this is not enough to operationalize pedagogical advancements. Expertise on classroom management is also needed, for example, to create a protocol for managing complex group work in mixed classes. Beyond the confines of the classroom, institutional expertise is needed to align research and teaching with the larger structures and practices of the foreign-language education system.

The essential point is that solving complex pedagogical problems, such as designing a comprehensive methodology for mixed classes, requires input from many areas of expertise. HL teachers and researchers alone are not likely to advance this goal.

10.4.4 Heritage Linguistics Can Inform the Teaching of Critical Language Awareness.

As discussed earlier, immigrants' ways of speaking are often subject to criticism. Resisting this criticism and embracing local norms as markers of linguistic identity is important for language vitality. Research on the personal "a" offers an example of a marker of linguistic identity with potentially valuable pedagogical implications. Used to mark animate, specific direct objects in all monolingual varieties of Spanish, the personal "a" is often omitted by SHLSs, including advanced speakers. But it's not just SHLSs: Montrul (2014) shows that some immigrants who came to this country as adults also omit this particle (see also Montrul, Bhatt, and Girju 2015). Polinsky (2018) posits that the lack of auditory salience of the "a" diminishes its learnability and renders it vulnerable to loss. But for both Montrul and Polinksy, this is more than about omission of a particle; it is a change at the level of mental representation, leading to coexisting options in US Spanish, one with marked direct objects and one without it. In effect, this is an example of an emerging local norm. Heritage phonology offers other such examples (see, for example, Ronquest and Rao 2018).

Crucially, these findings can alert teachers to the existence of forms that should not be treated as mistakes, but rather as valid local variants and should be embraced for their potential to enhance vitality. More broadly, this discussion speaks to the fact that the contributions of linguistic research to teaching are not confined to issues of grammar, but in some cases can also be applied to attending to students' socio-affective needs. To wrap up this section, the four categories of contributions discussed speak to a variety of ways in which linguistic research can contribute to HL teaching. A common thread to the analysis of each category is that operationalizing the findings of heritage linguistics for teaching purposes is not a straightforward or simple task, but rather requires the integration of different areas of knowledge and consideration of a wide range of factors.

10.5 Spanish for the Contact Zones

The term US Spanish, widely used in the research literature, including in this chapter, is deceptive in the sense that it suggests the existence of a unitary dialect. In fact, the United States is the most linguistically diverse

Spanish-speaking country in the world. Represented here are monolingual and contact variants of Spanish from every corner of the world, as well as a wide range of homegrown variants, heritage, as well as L2.

What competencies make for effective communication in this complex linguistic landscape? Polinsky (2018) posits that the coexistence of many dialects and levels of ability in Spanish has resulted in the development of new community standards that are more tolerant of divergence from monolingual structures. This observation aligns with a larger pattern of interactions and communication associated with places of linguistic super diversity and so-called contact zones, i.e. places that involve interactions between linguistically and culturally diverse people. According to Canagarajah (2017), communication in such places is facilitated by an ethics of cooperation and the deployment of a variety of strategies for negotiating meaning, such as paraphrasing and checking for comprehension. When misunderstandings arise, they are resolved "on equal terms" and with "mutual attentiveness," rather than based on native speaker norms (73). In keeping with this, the emphasis is on the co-construction of norms and the expansion of repertoires (Canagarajah 2013).

The co-construction of norms, which results in a fluidity of forms, co-exists with the seemingly opposite practice of taking strong ownership of local as well as individual forms, the latter being a process we have identified as supporting language vitality. However, in combination, these two processes have the synergistic effect of maximizing communication while also affirming "an egalitarian right to speak in ways that meet diverse local needs" (Rubdy 2009: 163). What does this mean for this chapter as a whole? It means that Spanish in the United States is not just a heritage language but also a language in the contact zones.

Accordingly, beyond studying language maintenance – a concept premised on preserving fixed, native norms – it makes sense to also consider how Spanish is being remade; not in opposition to or deviation from native-speaker norms, but in the context of superdiversity. This line of inquiry stands to yield new insights into the nature of variation in US Spanish, both at the societal and individual levels. In line with this, Toribio and Bullock (2016) underscore the need to document and study the existence of competing language forms within the same modality. Rather than just resulting from grammatical instability, it is conceivable that these competing forms may also serve to facilitate communication in the context of superdiversity.

With respect to instruction, viewing Spanish as a contact language, and not just a heritage language, underscores the importance of teaching strategies for negotiating diversity and navigating unpredictability. Lo Bianco (2014) and Toribio and Durán (2018) offer insights on what such instruction might look like. None of this is to say that native-speaker norms have no place in HL curricula, but rather that instruction should also focus on the full range competencies that make for effective communication in the contact zones of the United States.

10.6   Conclusions

This overview has sought to summarize the state of the field of Spanish as an HL in the United States, as well as to offer new perspectives on long-standing issues and point to directions for future work. The COD framework reveals strengths and weaknesses in the area of vitality, in society at large, as well as in the area of education. Addressing the need to build bridges between HL research and teaching, advances in Spanish heritage linguistics have been reviewed in terms of what they mean for instruction. Lastly, it has been argued that analyzing Spanish in the United States from the perspective of contact linguistics can enrich the study and teaching of this language.

References

American Council on the Teaching of Foreign Languages. 2012. *ACTFL Proficiency Guidelines 2012*. Retrieved from www.actfl.org/publications/guidelines-and-manuals/actfl-proficiency-guidelines-2012

American Council on the Teaching of Foreign Languages. 2018. Making Languages our Business: Addressing Foreign Language Demands among U.S. Employers. Retrieved from www.leadwithlanguages.org/wp-content/uploads/MakingLanguagesOurBusiness_FullReport.pdf

American Council on the Teaching of Foreign Languages. n.d. Assigning CEFR Ratings to ACTFL Assessments. Retrieved from www.actfl.org/sites/default/files/reports/Assigning_CEFR_Ratings_To_ACTFL_Assessments.pdf

Beaudrie, S. M. 2011. Spanish Heritage Language Programs: A Snapshot of Current Programs in the Southwestern United States. *Foreign Language Annals* 44(2), 321–337.

Beaudrie, S. M. 2012. Research on University-Based Spanish Heritage Language Programs in the United States: The Current State of Affairs. In S. Beaudrie and M. Fairclough (eds.), *Spanish as a Heritage Language in the United States: The State of the Field*. Washington, DC: Georgetown University Press, 203–221.

Beaudrie, S., C. Ducar, and K. Potowski. 2014. *Heritage Language Teaching: Research and Practice*. New York: McGraw-Hill Education.

Bills, G. D., A. Hudson, and E. H. Chávez. 1999. Spanish Home Language Use and English Proficiency as Differential Measures of Language Maintenance and Shift. *Southwest Journal of Linguistics* 19(1), 11–27.

Bowles, M. 2018. Outcomes of Classroom Spanish Heritage Language Instruction. In K. Potowski (ed.), *The Routledge Handbook of Spanish as a Heritage Language*. London: Routledge, 331–344.

Bowles, M. A. 2011. Measuring Implicit and Explicit Linguistic Knowledge: What Can Heritage Language Learners Contribute? *Studies in Second Language Acquisition* 33(2), 247–271.

California Department of Education. 2018a. *Global California 2030. Speak. Learn. Lead: An Initiative of State Superintendent of Public Instruction Tom Torlakson*. Retrieved from www.cde.ca.gov/eo/in/documents/global ca2030report.pdf

California Department of Education. 2018b. Fingertip Facts on Education in California. Retrieved from www.cde.ca.gov/ds/sd/cb/ceffingertipfacts.asp

Canagarajah, S. 2013. Introduction. In *Literacy and Translingual Practice: Between Communities and Classrooms*. Florence, KY: Routledge, 1–10.

Canagarajah, S. 2014. Theorizing a Competence for Translingual Practice at the Contact Zone. In Stephen May (ed.), *The Multilingual Turn: Implications for SLA, TESOL, and Bilingual Education*. New York: Routledge, 78–102.

Canagarajah, S. 2017. A Competence for Negotiating Diversity and Unpredictability in Global Contact Zones. In *Diversity and Super-Diversity: Sociocultural Linguistic Perspectives*. Washington, DC: Georgetown University Press, 65–79.

Carreira, M. 2013. Evaluating Spanish-Language Vitality in the United States from a Capacity, Opportunity and Desire Framework. *Heritage Language Journal* 10(3), 396–413.

Carreira, M. 2016. Approaches and Strategies for Teaching Heritage Language Learners: Focus on Mixed Classes. In D. Pascual y Cabo (ed.), *Advances in Spanish as a Heritage Language*. Amsterdam: John Benjamins [Studies in Bilingualism Series], 159–176.

Carreira, M. and T. Beeman. 2014. *Voces: Latino Students on Life in the United States*. Westport, CT: Praeger.

Carreira, M. and C. Hitchins Chik. 2018. Making the Case for Heritage Language Instruction: A Guide to Meeting the Needs of Learners in the Classroom and Beyond. In S. Bauckus and S. Kresin (eds.), *Connecting across Languages and Cultures: A Heritage Language Festschrift in Honor of Olga E. Kagan*. Bloomington, IN: Slavica.

Carreira, M. and O. Kagan. 2011. The Results of the National Heritage Language Survey: Implications for Teaching, Curriculum Design, and Professional Development. *Foreign Language Annals* 44(1), 40–64.

Castro Santana, A. C. 2014. Herencia y legado: Validating the Linguistic Strengths of English Language Learners via the LAUSD Seal of Biliteracy Awards Program. Unpublished doctoral dissertation, California State University, Long Beach.

Colombi, M. C. and F. X. Alarcón (eds.) 1996. *La enseñanza del español a hispanohablantes: Praxis y teoría*. Series on Foreign Language Acq.

David, K. and A. Heineke. 2017. The Seal of Biliteracy: Variations in Policy and Outcomes. *Foreign Language Annals* 50(3), 486–499.

Davin, K. J., A. J. Heineke, and L. Egnatz. 2018. The Seal of Biliteracy: Successes and Challenges to Implementation. *Foreign Language Annals* 51 (2), 275–289.

DeLeon, T. M. 2016. The New Ecology of Biliteracy in California: An Exploratory Study of the Early Implementation of the State Seal of Biliteracy. Unpublished doctoral dissertation, Loyola Marymount University. Retrieved from http://digitalcommons.lmu.edu/etd/197

Fairclough, M. 2016. Emerging Trends with Heritage Language Instructional Practices: Advances and Challenges. In D. Pascual y Cabo (ed.), *Advances in Spanish as a Heritage Language*. Amsterdam: John Benjamins [Studies in Bilingualism Series], 221–236.

Fairclough, M. and F. Belpoliti. 2016. Emerging Literacy in Spanish among Hispanic Heritage Language University Students in the USA: A Pilot Study. *International Journal of Bilingual Education and Bilingualism* 19(2), 185–201.

Gándara, P. 2014. The Value of Bilingualism and the Seal of Biliteracy in the California Labor Market. Retrieved from www.calsa.org/wp-content/uploads/2014/10/Value-of-Bilingualism-UCLA.pdf

Gándara, P. and K. Escamilla. 2017. Bilingual Education in the United States. *Bilingual and Multilingual Education* 1–14.

Genesee, F., K. Lindholm-Leary, W. Saunders, and D. Christian. 2005. English Language Learners in US Schools: An Overview of Research Findings. *Journal of Education for Students Placed at Risk* 10(4), 363–385.

The Global Seal. 2019. About the Global Seal of Biliteracy. Retrieved from https://theglobalseal.com/the-global-seal

Gómez, L., D. Freeman, and Y. Freeman. 2005. Dual Language Education: A Promising 50-50 Model. *Bilingual Research Journal* 29(1), 145–165.

González-Barrera, A. 2015. *More Mexicans Leaving and Coming to the U.S.* Washington, DC: Pew Research Center.

Hartfield-Méndez V. 2013. Community-Based Learning, Internationalization of the Curriculum and University Engagement with Latino Communities. *Hispania* 96, 355–368.

Henshaw, F. G. 2015. Learning Outcomes of L2-Heritage Learner Interaction: The Proof Is in the Posttests. *Heritage Language Journal* 12(3), 245–270.

Hernández-Nieto, R. and M. Gutiérrez. 2017. Hispanic map of the United States. Instituto Cervantes at FAS, Harvard University. Retrieved from http://cervantesobservatorio.fas.harvard.edu/sites/default/files/hispanic_map_2017en.pdf

Instituto Cervantes. 2019. El español: Una language viva. Retrieved from https://cvc.cervantes.es/lengua/espanol_lengua_viva/pdf/espanol_lengua_viva_2019.pdf

Jenkins, D. 2018. Spanish Language Use, Maintenance, and Shift in the United States. In K. Potowski (ed.), *The Routledge Handbook of Spanish as a Heritage Language*. 67–79. London: Routledge.

Jordan, M. 2019, March 5. More Migrants Are Crossing the Border This Year. What's Changed? *The New York Times*. Retrieved from www.nytimes.com/2019/03/05/us/crossing-the-border-statistics.html

Kagan, O. and K. Dillon. 2001. A New Perspective on Teaching Russian: Focus on the Heritage Learner. *The Slavic and East European Journal* 45(3), 507–518.

Krogstad, J. M. and A. Gonzalez-Barrera. 2015. *A Majority of English-Speaking Hispanics in the US are Bilingual*. Washington, DC: Pew Research Center. Retrieved from http://pewrsr.ch/19MGhgV

Krogstad, J. M., R. Stepler, and M. H. López. 2015. *English Proficiency on the Rise among Latinos*. Washington, DC: Pew Research Center. Hispanic Trends. Retrieved from www.pewresearch.org/hispanic/2015/05/12/english-proficiency-on-the-rise-among-latinos/

Leeman, J. 2014. Critical Approaches to the Teaching of Spanish as a Local-Foreign Language. In M. Lacorte (ed.), *The Handbook of Hispanic Applied Linguistics*. New York: Routledge, 275–292.

Leeman, J., L. Rabin, and E. Román-Mendoza.. 2011. Critical Pedagogy beyond the Classroom Walls: Community Service-Learning and Spanish Heritage Language Education. *Heritage Language Journal* 8(3), 1–22.

Lindholm-Leary, K. 2013. Education: Dual Language Instruction in the United States. *Americas Quarterly* 7(4), 97.

Lindholm-Leary, K. 2014. Bilingual and Biliteracy Skills in Young Spanish-Speaking Low-SES Children: Impact of Instructional Language and Primary Language Proficiency. *International Journal of Bilingual Education and Bilingualism* 17(2), 144–159.

Lo Bianco, J. 2008. Policy Activity for Heritage Languages: Connections with Representation and Citizenship. In D. M. Brinton, O. Kagan, and S. Bauckus (eds.), *Heritage Language Education: A New Field Emerging*. New York: Routledge, 53–69.

Lo Bianco, J. 2009. Organizing for Multilingualism: Ecological and Sociological Perspectives. In a TESOL symposium *Keeping Language Diversity Alive*. Alexandria, VA: Teachers of English to Speakers of Other Languages, 1–18.

Lo Bianco, J. 2014. Domesticating the Foreign: Globalization's Effects on the Place/s of Languages. *The Modern Language Journal* 98(1), 312–325.

Lo Bianco, J. and J. K. Peyton (eds.) 2013. Vitality of Heritage Languages in the United States. Special issue of the *Heritage Language Journal* 10(3). Retrieved from http://hlj.ucla.edu/Journal.aspx

Lowther Pereira, K. 2016. New Directions in Heritage Language Pedagogy: Community Service-Learning for Spanish Heritage Speakers. In D. Pascual y Cabo (ed.), *Advances in Spanish as a Heritage Language*. Amsterdam: John Benjamins [Studies in Bilingualism Series], 237–258.

Martínez, G. and A. Schwartz. 2012. Elevating "Low" Language for High Stakes: A Case for Critical, Community-Based Learning in a Medical Spanish for Heritage Learners Program. *Heritage Language Journal* 9(2), 37–49. Retrieved from http://hlj.ucla.edu/Journal.aspx

Montrul, S. 2009. Incomplete Acquisition of Tense-Aspect and Mood in Spanish Heritage Speakers. Special issue of *The International Journal of Bilingualism* 13(2), 239–269.

Montrul, S. 2014. Structural Changes in Spanish in the United States: Differential Object Marking in Spanish Heritage Speakers across Generations. *Lingua* 151, 177–196.

Montrul, S. 2018. Morphology, Syntax, and Semantics in Spanish As a Heritage Language. In K. Potowski (ed.), *The Routledge Handbook of Spanish as a Heritage Language*. London: Routledge, 145–163.

Montrul, S. and M. Bowles. 2010. Is Grammar Instruction Beneficial for Heritage Language Learners? Dative Case Marking in Spanish. *Heritage Language Journal* 7(1), 47–73. Retrieved from http://hlj.ucla.edu/Journal .aspx

Montrul, S., R. Bhatt, and R. Girju. 2015. Differential Object Marking in Spanish, Hindi, and Romanian as Heritage Languages. *Language* 91(3), 564–610.

New American Economy. 2017. *Not Lost in Translation*. Retrieved from http:// research.newamericaneconomy.org/wp-content/uploads/2017/03/NAE_ Bilingual_V9.pdf

Polinsky, M. 2006. Incomplete Acquisition: American Russian. *Journal of Slavic Linguistics* 14, 161–219.

Polinsky, M. 2016. Looking Ahead. In D. Pascual y Cabo (ed.), *Advances in Spanish as a Heritage Language*. Amsterdam: John Benjamins Publishing Company, vol. 49, 325–345.

Polinsky, M. 2018. *Heritage Languages and Their Speakers*. Vol. 159. Cambridge: Cambridge University Press.

Potowski, K. 2016. Current Issues in Heritage Language Education. In D. Pascual y Cabo (ed.), *Advances in Spanish as a heritage language*. Amsterdam: John Benjamins [Studies in Bilingualism Series], 127–142.

Potowski, K., J. Jegerski, and K. Morgan-Short. 2009. The Effects of Instruction on Linguistic Development in Spanish Heritage Language Speakers. *Language Learning* 59(3), 537–579.

Rhodes, N. C. and I. Pufahl. 2010. *Foreign Language Teaching in US Schools: Results of a National Survey*. Washington, DC: Center for Applied Linguistics.

Rivera-Mills, S. V. 2012. Spanish Heritage Language Maintenance. In S. Beaudrie and M. Fairclough (eds.), *Spanish As a Heritage Language in the United States: The State of the Field*. Washington, DC: Georgetown University Press, 21–42.

Romero, S. 2017, August 23. El español florece en Estaods Unidos a pesar de todo. *The New York Times*. Retrieved from www.nytimes.com/es/2017/08/ 23/el-espanol-florece-en-estados-unidos-a-pesar-de-todo/

Ronquest, R. and R. Rao. 2018. Heritage Spanish Phonetics and Phonology. In K. Potowski (ed.), *The Routledge Handbook of Spanish as a Heritage Language*. London: Routledge, 164–277.

Rubdy, R. 2009. Reclaiming the Local in Teaching EIL. *Language and Intercultural Communication* 9(3), 156–174.

Sánchez-Muñoz, A. 2016. Heritage Language Healing? Learners' Attitudes and Damage Control in a Heritage Language Classroom. In D. Pascual y Cabo (ed.), *Advances in Spanish as a Heritage Language*. Amsterdam: John Benjamins Publishing Company, 205–220.

Santos Palmou, X. 2017. El Vocabulario Fundamental: historia, definición y nuevas propuestas aplicadas a la enseñanza de ELE. *E-AESLA* 3, 110–120.

The Seal of Biliteracy. 2019. Level of Language Proficiency Required. Retrieved from https://sealofbiliteracy.org/state-guidelines/level-language-proficiency-required/

Steele, J. L., R. O. Slater, J. Li, G. Zamarro, T. Miller, and M. Bacon. 2018. Dual- Language Immersion Education at Scale: An Analysis of Program Costs, Mechanisms, and Moderators. *Educational Evaluation and Policy Analysis* 40(3), 420–445. Retrieved from https://doi.org/10.3102/0162373718779457

Thomas, W. P. and V. P. Collier. 2003. The Multiple Benefits of Dual Language. *Educational Leadership* 61(2): 61–64. Retrieved from www.ascd.org/ASCD/pdf/journals/ed_lead/el200310_thomas.pdf

Toribio, J. and B. Bullock, B. 2016. A New Look at Heritage Spanish and Its Speakers. In D. Pascual y Cabo (ed.), *Advances in Spanish as a Heritage Language*. Vol. 49. Amsterdam: John Benjamins Publishing Company, 27 –50).

Toribio, J. and L. Durán. 2018. Understanding and Leveraging Spanish Heritage Speakers' Bilingual Practices. In K. Potowski (ed.), *The Routledge Handbook of Spanish as a Heritage Language*. London: Routledge, 190–202.

Torres, J. (2013). Heritage and Second Language Learners of Spanish: The Roles of Task Complexity and Inhibitory Control. Unpublished PhD dissertation, Georgetown University, Washington, DC.

Torres, J. 2018. The Effects of Task Complexity on Heritage and L2 Spanish Development. *Canadian Modern Language Review* 74(1), 128–152.

Tse, L. 2001. *"Why Don't They Learn English?" Separating Fact from Fallacy in the US Language Debate*. Language and Literacy Series. New York: Teachers College Press.

US Census Bureau. 2017. *Language Spoken at Home by Ability to Speak English for the Population 5 years and over* (Table No. B16001). Retrieved from https://factfinder.census.gov/faces/tableservices/jsf/pages/productview.xhtml?pid=ACS_17_1YR_B16001&prodType=tabl

US Census Bureau. 2018. Language Spoken at Home (Table No. S1601). Retrieved from https://data.census.gov/cedsci/table?q=Spanish%20speakers&hidePreview=false&tid=ACSST1Y2018.S1601&vintage=2018

Valdés, G. 1995. The Teaching of Minority Languages as Academic Subjects: Pedagogical and Theoretical Challenges. *The Modern Language Journal* 79(3), 299–328.

Valdés, G. 2001. Heritage Language Students: Profiles and Possibilities. In J. K. Peyton, D. A. Ranard, and S. McGinnis (eds.), *Heritage Languages in America: Preserving a National Resource.* McHenry, IL: Center for Applied Linguistics, 37–77.

Valdés-Fallís, G. 1978. A Comprehensive Approach to the Teaching of Spanish to Bilingual Spanish-Speaking Students. *The Modern Language Journal* 43(3), 101–110.

Villa, D. J. and S. V. Rivera-Mills, 2009. An Integrated Multi-Generational Model for Language Maintenance and Shift: The Case of Spanish in the Southwest. *Spanish in Context* 6(1), 26–42.

Williams, C. 2019, February 7. Making Dual Language Schools Work for English-Learners, Too. *The Century Foundation.* Retrieved from https://tcf .org/content/commentary/making-dual-language-schools-work-english-learners/?agreed=1

Zyzik, E. 2016. Toward a Prototype Model of the Heritage Language Learner: Understanding Strengths and Needs. In M. Fairclough and S. Beaudrie (eds.), *Innovative Strategies for Heritage Language Teaching: A Practical Guide for the Classroom.* Washington, DC: Georgetown University Press, 19–38.

11

Germanic Heritage Varieties in the Americas

Social and Linguistic Perspectives

Janne Bondi Johannessen and Joseph Salmons

11.1 Introduction[*]

This chapter focuses on a set of heritage languages where groups of immigrants settled together up to the early twentieth century and continued to speak these languages in the Americas. Germanic heritage languages in the western hemisphere include Yiddish, Dutch, West Frisian, Afrikaans, German, and other closely related Continental West Germanic varieties, as well as North Germanic languages: Icelandic, Danish, Norwegian, and Swedish. Some varieties, like Pennsylvania Dutch, developed into new languages in the western hemisphere. While we cover a broad range of places and varieties, this chapter reflects the languages and communities where the most historical and heritage language research has been done, mainly North America and especially the American Midwest. (See Lipski, Chapter 13, for more on Germanic heritage languages in South America.)

The Americas have long had large immigrant populations who did not and/or do not speak the dominant language(s). These populations have often been in the majority locally or even regionally, e.g., regionally for Pennsylvania Dutch in southeastern and south central Pennsylvania, and locally for Norwegian and Swedish in the Upper Midwest in communities scattered from Wisconsin through the Dakotas. Non-English immigrant languages have almost universally lacked official status and governmental support, with only modest exceptions. At the same time, in the United States, there is no official language, though various cities, counties, and

[*] We thank the editors for the opportunity to write this chapter. In addition to feedback from the editors we are grateful for suggestions and commentary on this topic and earlier versions of this manuscript from Joshua Bousquette, Josh Brown, Sam[antha] Litty, Monica Macaulay, Laura Moquin, David Natvig, and Mike Putnam. We alone are responsible for remaining errors.

states have passed legislation making English official, often – though hardly always – to the exclusion of other languages. Historically, there have been many flare-ups of acute xenophobia and Nativism, which typically involve and often focus directly on language, and many policy restrictions on languages other than English have been aimed at schools, in particular. Crawford (2000) offers an accessible historical perspective on issues of policy, and primary materials are available in Crawford (1992).

The goal of this chapter is to present a broad survey of Germanic heritage languages in North America, sketching historical and social context, particularly important examples of structural change in these languages and with some attention to language maintenance and shift. This allows us, along the way, to draw attention to stark contrasts between these languages and their speakers with most other heritage languages discussed in this volume. For example, because these communities were founded a century or more ago and language shift is far advanced, most speakers we work with represent the third to sixth generation after migration, and most are elderly. We first introduce the social and historical context of these heritage communities (Section 11.2), and then dedicate the bulk of the paper to structural phenomena and change in several domains: phonetics and phonology, morphology, syntax, pragmatics, and the lexicon (Section 11.3). We touch on language maintenance and shift (Section 11.4) and conclude in Section 11.5.

11.2 Social and Historical Context

Germanic heritage languages exist in a remarkably broad set of circumstances in terms of past and present community structure. We survey some examples here, but emphasize that these matters were and are extremely local, as particular groups have built and maintained communities over generations.

11.2.1 Varieties

Issues of linguistic variation in Germanic heritage languages are deep and wide, including bilingualism, matters of dialect vs. language, and the emergence of new varieties in the heritage setting.

Many Germanic-speaking immigrants were monolingual on arrival, but these communities eventually became bilingual, acquiring the majority language(s) in addition to the heritage language, sometimes only after two or more generations. Yet others arrived multilingual. Often, people spoke dialects or varieties not mutually intelligible with the relevant standard language from their country of origin, e.g., Low German rather than

German. Some countries had established standards for written and even spoken language, while others lacked these or developed them only later. Where standards existed, communities varied in their command and use of them. Much work, like virtually every reference in this chapter, has treated communities in terms of "named languages," abstract varieties associated with particular groups; the reality is more complex and interesting, with various configurations of standard, dialect, and closely related but distinct languages. Calling something "Yiddish" or "Swedish" or "Dutch" reifies highly variable ways of speaking. In the Wisconsin town of Belgium, for example, the 1910 U.S. Census lists what were clearly Letzebuergish speakers as speaking "German." In a migration setting, such status is subject to change in new ways. What were once "dialects" of German in Europe often came into intense new patterns of contact: Where speakers might have commanded a range from Rhenish dialect to a standard-like German, they found themselves now living next to speakers of Low German and southern dialects. For Plautdietsch or Mennonite Low German, spoken from Canada to Mexico to Paraguay, Siemens (2012: 231–239) discusses pros and cons, including political ones, of languagehood for a language without a nation state, roots in several European nations, and speaker populations literally around the world.

Such contact led to various patterns of levelling, and often to koiné development or new dialect formation, where new varieties emerge from contact among various earlier dialects (Kerswill 2002; Kerswill and Trudgill 2005, for instance). This sometimes meant moving closer to standard varieties, like in many German-American communities (Nützel and Salmons 2011; Bousquette 2020), or the partial adoption of a demographically dominant dialect with some koinéization, as with the East Norwegian dialect spectrum in some western Wisconsin communities (Hjelde 2015). That is, the most salient regional features from different dialects were lost and a somewhat more uniform variety emerged from a mix of features already present in some varieties but also including novel ones. Such processes typically take generations to complete and in many heritage communities, a single relatively homogenous variety never fully developed. For Dutch in Pella, Iowa, Webber (1988: 88–92) describes "vestiges of dialect," where he found numbers of speakers with features of assorted regional varieties all in the same small community. In contrast, some more homogenous communities did retain the originally imported dialects to a striking extent, as described for Indiana East Franconian by Nützel (2009) or East Norwegian in Wisconsin (Hjelde 2015). Similar patterns of leveling and new dialect formation are ubiquitous in heritage and colonial settings, e.g., in the rich contact among varieties of Spanish in New York City (e.g., Otheguy and Zentella 2011) but reaching back to the earliest history of how Spanish evolved in the western hemisphere (like Sanz-Sánchez 2013).

11.2.2 Learning Other Languages

One of the most pervasive and politically powerful misconceptions, one being exploited politically today in the United States, is that earlier immigrants learned English quickly. The 1910 U.S. Census asked whether an individual was able to speak English and, if not, to give the language they did speak. Drawing on this data, together with various kinds of qualitative data, Wilkerson and Salmons (2008, 2012) and much work since shows that in heavily German-speaking areas, people often remained monolingual for two or more generations before learning English. In many communities, around one third of the population was non-English monolingual in 1910, sometimes mostly American born. In many communities, non-English speakers held the full range of jobs available in the community and participated actively in a full range of local institutions, including press, religious institutions, and schools. But not all communities followed such a path. Natvig (forthcoming) documents that in heavily Norwegian Ulen, Minnesota, in 1910 only 17 of 313 people reported being monolingual Norwegian speakers. People apparently acquired English fast, but remained bilingual, and the community still has heritage speakers today. Indeed, authors like Kellogg (1918: 23) portray Scandinavian immigrants as "eager for the Americanization of their children," including in schools.

We know little about multilingualism in these communities, aside from contemporary comments and anecdotes. Occasionally, though, we have some examples. Einar Haugen recorded Norwegian speakers in the Upper Midwest from 1935 on. In a recording with Waldemar von Ruden from western Wisconsin, Haugen asked about the speaker's family. Von Ruden responded in native-like eastern Norwegian that his father was from Germany and his mother was from Waukesha County, a largely English-speaking area of Wisconsin. In response to a question about what language they spoke at home, he says German, but that they learned English. When he went to school, he learned Norwegian, because they lived in a "Norwegian settlement," where children only spoke Norwegian. In other settings, communities were more generally multilingual, like the small Sorbian-speaking community in Texas, which existed within a larger German-speaking belt (Olesch 1970). Yiddish speakers often arrived with knowledge of other languages, such as Slavic languages. In some situations of a minority within a minority, languages were essentially invisible to outsiders; even the large Low German-speaking communities in Wisconsin were made invisible.

In a country where inexorable movement toward English is regularly seen as the only relevant dynamic, the learning of immigrant languages by Anglo-Americans or speakers of other languages is often overlooked. Wilkerson and Salmons (2008) present some evidence of such learning of German by Anglo-Americans in Wisconsin and anecdotal reports of this are widespread, but we lack quantitative evidence and further research is needed.

11.2.3 Language Ideology

Language ideology is rarely discussed with regards to these communities, especially historically, and warrants some attention. Lippi-Green (2012: 64) defines Standard Language Ideology as follows:

> ... a bias toward an abstracted, idealized homogenous spoken language which is imposed and maintained by dominant bloc institutions and which names as its model the written language, but which is drawn primarily from the spoken language of the upper middle class.

While discussions of language or dialect contact and history routinely invoke the notion of "prestige" as a factor in maintenance and change in varieties, we follow Milroy's admonition to "avoid relying on the notion of prestige and focus more on the indexicality of linguistic variables as used by social groups independently of the social status of such groups" (2014: 575). That said, how people saw the status of their heritage languages is often surprising from today's perspective, where English is seen as the obvious point of linguistic reference in the United States. Koerner (1890: 9, cited also in Salmons 2017: 317, our translation) asks "why is it not enough that children learn to read and write English?" He goes on to answer his own question in terms of Nativist (anti-immigrant) hatred of German and the Anglo-American drive to suppress German. He argues that it should be enough to learn to read and write English, implying that learning to speak it is not necessary, continuing:

> We are by no means enemies of the English language. But we do not concede that our German language is a foreign language in this country. For centuries it has been spoken here, many millions of inhabitants use it today – in this regard it is surely just as little a foreign language as English, which was just as little spoken and understood by the Indigenous peoples of this country, but was likewise imported from foreign lands. And if we do not count the German language as a foreign language, we admit without hesitation that the English language is the official language of this country, ... Where it is possible, we certainly do not let our children grow up without good English instruction. On the contrary, wherever we can, we introduce English instruction in our community schools.

Leaving aside the fact that English was not and is not an official language, this is a striking statement about the relative positions of German and English in the late nineteenth century. English instruction is presented as desirable but hardly central or necessary to education. Most broadly, English is in no way better than or preferable to German. Such sentiments are widespread in writings of the nineteenth and early twentieth centuries, and they were seen with alarm by some Anglo-Americans, as part of the wave of broad xenophobia beginning in the nineteenth century and culminating with World War I. Kellogg (1918: 9), for instance, stresses the resistance to learning English (emphasis added), specifically among North German immigrants in Wisconsin:

> They desired Americanization, only in so far as it was necessary to make a living. Settled in German communities, they came in slight contact with Americans. They clung with much tenacity to the habits, customs, and language of the fatherland, and their purpose was to keep their children in the same social structure and under the same regime of isolation and tutelage in which they were themselves. Thus grew up a "Germandom" in the heart of Wisconsin – **a body of people speaking only the German language**, maintaining the customs and culture of their first home, and supporting at least a sentimental and spiritual connection with European Germany.

She continues (11, again with emphasis added):

> These communities, both urban and rural, were settled around a church and a parochial school, conducted largely in German. That language was the habitual one. German books alone were read, German songs were constantly sung, and the newspapers read by the people were printed in German. As distance lent enchantment to the scenes of early life, Wisconsin Germans dwelt with ever-increasing fondness upon the ways of the fatherland; their dearest hopes were to rear their children with a similar attachment, and **to impress them with the superiority of things German over things American**.

Such a mindset is hard for many Americans to imagine today among immigrants, even those whose own grandparents were these very German Americans. While members of some immigrant groups did prefer their community languages and were not terribly concerned about learning English, as already hinted, attitudes appear to have differed in other groups. Nearing the mid-twentieth century, writing in the Norwegian newspaper *Reform* (February 5, 1931), Louis Kvalsten argues for learning Norwegian at home and English at school:[1]

> The use of the Norwegian language in speech and writing is necessary for the preservation of *Norskdommen* [Norwegiandom]. It is therefore valuable when Norwegian parents speak Norwegian themselves, and raise their children in this language. The best time is in the childhood years, as soon as they acquire the skill of speech, until that time when they will start English school. What they learn then isn't forgotten so easily and one

---

[1] We are grateful to Laura Moquin for sharing excerpts from Norwegian-American newspapers and allowing us to use her translations (see Moquin 2019).

shouldn't believe that it is to the detriment of their ability to learn the English language; on the contrary, it has turned out, that these children, as a rule, become the smartest also in the English language. Let them learn their mother tongue whether it is in a dialect or in *Riksmaal* [Dano-Norwegian].

Many Germanic-speaking immigrants arrived with some command of standard languages, at least literacy, while large numbers of Anglo-Americans and did not attend school in the nineteenth century. (Kellogg 1918: 3 estimated that 40,000–50,000 children aged between seven and fourteen did not attend school in Wisconsin in the late 1880s.) This situation came with a powerful Standard Language Ideology, commonly expressed in contemporary non-English newspapers. Impressionistically, early twentieth century German newspapers often used styles that surpassed the formal and complex styles of European papers of the time.[2] For Norwegian papers, language reforms underway in Norway at the time posed a particular challenge. Waldemar Ager, editor of *Reform* and a noted Norwegian-American writer, argued (February 6, 1930) the following:

The reasons that have made language change in Norway such a powerful political question, and created some fanaticism about it, are about getting as far away from the Danish language as possible. It has been associated with the perception of "real" patriotism in the same way that opposition and ill-will against people of other races than the Anglo-Saxon has become in this country. We, as Norwegian-Americans, find it difficult to under-stand. The language reform of 1907 is something of a middle road and it wouldn't do much neither here nor there, if we amended and stretched ourselves so much as the reformed language that "The Lutheran" uses.

Ager understands this in the broader context of rapid shift to English:

Incidentally, the issue here seems to resolve itself; the Norwegian language here in this country, many believe, is going to die off anyway. And there are very few who will go through the torments of getting old, but useful, teeth removed, and take on the costs of a new row of teeth to become better-looking when the doctor has told you that you don't have long to live anyway.

Such sentiments are easy enough to find from the nineteenth century on, if seldom recalled as such today.

This section illustrates the variability across communities in what range of varieties were present, including standard ones, and how people negoti-ated linguistic life in new societies after migration. Heritage communities

---

[2] This was not the case everywhere. Brown (2019) shows that Pennsylvania newspapers often used "Pennsylvania High German."

have had widely variable views of and experiences with dominant culture languages. Research is just beginning on issues of language ideology, past and present, an area where more work will bear fruit. For now, we suggest that historical research should move beyond simply framing things in terms of bare "language maintenance" to seeing these heritage languages as having had explicit and institutional roles in their communities, with associated language ideologies.

11.3   Structural Phenomena and Change

Having considered some aspects of the social and ideological issues, we turn now to how immigrant languages changed structurally. Heritage languages exist in a society very different from that in the homeland, as they live side by side with other dialects and languages, surrounded by a majority language whose institutions (schools and other public institutions), where heritage languages typically develop away from their "hearth" varieties.

Linguistic aspects of heritage languages represent a burgeoning research field (see Benmamoun, Montrul, and Polinsky 2013a, b). A vast body of work on structural issues in Germanic heritage languages in the Americas reaches back decades. The last ten years have seen a surge of such work – from edited volumes like Putnam (2011); Johannessen and Salmons (2015); Page and Putnam (2015); Brown and Bousquette (2018); Heegård Petersen and Kühl (2018); and Brown and Biers (2019) to overview articles like Johannessen (2018) – partly triggered by the annual Workshop on Immigrant Languages in the Americas,[3] which since 2010 has brought together researchers in many areas and theoretical frameworks across the Germanic languages and has today grown to include work on many other languages. Much work at WILA treats structural properties, comparing heritage language with "hearth" or base varieties, change in heritage varieties over time and, increasingly, broad comparison across heritage languages. Since the Germanic languages share many grammatical features but vary on others, Germanic heritage languages provide a natural laboratory for micro-comparison. In this section we briefly note a few key examples from phonetics and phonology, morphology, syntax, pragmatics, and the lexicon.

11.3.1   Phonetics and Phonology

The sound systems of Germanic heritage languages in the Americas are relatively understudied and heritage language phonetics and phonology

---

[3] www.workshoponimmigrantlanguages.org/.

generally are among their "least understood properties" (Polinsky 2018:162). In segmental systems, the varieties we are looking at tend, broadly, to have some phonetic but little phonological deviation from their base varieties. This has been found for Voice Onset Time in Wisconsin German (Litty 2017) and Portuguese-German Misiones bilinguals (Klosinski 2019). Ehresmann and Bousquette (2015) report both retention of the native system alongside English-like patterns in the obstruents of Wisconsin West Frisian speakers. Some phonetic contact effects have also been found for the position of vowels within the vowel space for Minnesota Norwegians (Natvig 2016). Occasionally, phonetic changes can be extremely salient even without many phonological consequences, as in the replacement of various rhotics with an American English [ɹ] in German and other immigrant languages (Natvig and Salmons 2020), and in changes in quality of front, close vowels in a heritage Norwegian dialect (Hjelde 1992).

Intonation and prosody have barely been studied in these communities, though Coetzee et al. (2015) provide important experimental results from Afrikaans speakers in Patagonia (Argentina), concluding that "bilingual speakers' L1 (Afrikaans) was rhythmically influenced by their L2 (Spanish), but their L2 showed less evidence for influence from their L1." (See Moen 1988 for related discussion on Norwegian in North America.)

The most investigated issue in this realm is the loss of front rounded vowels in German varieties. The waters are muddied here, though, by the fact that many dialectal and colloquial varieties of German long ago unrounded these vowels. Pierce et al. (2015) argue that a range of factors beyond base dialect, including that English does not have front rounded vowels, contribute to the absence of these vowels in Texas German. Webber (1988: 96) reports a pattern otherwise unknown to us, namely the importation of front rounded vowels into English, where expected /u:/ can be realized as /y:/ in the Dutch heritage community of Pella, Iowa. Variable unrounding is also reported in Trønder dialects of Norwegian by Hjelde (1996: 288–289), where European *by* 'town' [by can be realized as [bɪː] and *dyrt* 'expensive' [dyːʈ] as [dɪːʈ]. This is not attributable to base dialects.

11.3.2 Morphology

Morphology is "one of the most vulnerable areas for heritage attrition" (Polinsky 2018: 164) and the patterns clearly hold for Germanic heritage languages. The most studied structural issue in Germanic heritage languages, in the Americas and beyond, is case marking, especially reductions and loss of case distinctions. While we discuss West Germanic here, note that some Norwegian heritage varieties have dative marking, which has receded or been lost in some communities but also maintained where speakers shared a base dialect (Hjelde 2015). In Icelandic, which has a complex four-case system, Arnbjörnsdóttir (2015) notes that heritage speakers show "some variability in overt marking of case" and that proper names of people and places no longer inflect.

Standard German has four cases – nominative, accusative, dative, and genitive, marked overwhelmingly on determiners and adjectives rather than the nouns themselves – but regional and colloquial varieties make limited use of the genitive in general and many dialects distinguish only nominative versus oblique or nominative-accusative vs. dative. In heritage settings, the use of genitive beyond fixed expressions and personal names is generally a reflection of Standard German education and the dative is not used in communities whose hearth varieties (largely or entirely) lacked it for similar reasons. While the role of Standard German in such communities has been contested in the past, Bousquette (2020) provides solid evidence for standard-like patterns far beyond the educated urban elite.

Some studies have traced the advancing loss of dative case in real and apparent time, e.g., Salmons (1994) for Texas German, where there are other, highly variable innovations in case marking. Strikingly, for example, there is variable but explicit accusative marking on neuter determiners where the standard language uses *das* for nominative and accusative, e.g., *durch den Fenster* "through the window" for standard *durch das Fenster*.

The retreat of case is more complex and orderly than has sometimes been recognized. Marking is often lost in nouns before pronouns (Rosenberg 2005; Yager et al. 2015), parallel to what happened in the history of English. Yager et al. (2015) present evidence that some Wisconsin heritage speakers have not so much lost dative marking as restricted the dative to Differential Object Marking contexts, e.g., definite rather than indefinite Noun Phrases.

The intuitively appealing notion that the lack of case marking in English or Spanish contributes to this where those are the dominant languages does not bear weight, given that loss of dative is found also in German varieties spoken in contact with Slavic languages (Rosenberg 2005). And O'Neil (1978) long ago pointed to a more general correlation: More language contact correlates closely with the reduction of nominal morphology. (For a broad account of case loss, see Barðdal and Kulikov 2008.)

11.3.3 Syntax

All Germanic languages except English share a common word order in declarative matrix clauses: The finite verb has to be in second position, a pattern known as V2. Most also share a second notable feature, that the verb in subordinate clauses is in a different position than in matrix clauses. In West Germanic (apart from English) the finite verb sits in clause-final position, while in North Germanic languages (apart from Icelandic) the finite verb is in third position, after the subject and possible adverbial(s) (see among others Holmberg and Platzack (1995) and Vikner (1995).) The matrix order is illustrated in (1) for baseline European Norwegian: Whatever constituent appears in first position, the finite verb will be second.

(1) a. **Jon kjøpte** litt mer land i går (= target)
         Jon bought little more land in.yesterday
         'Jon bought some more land yesterday.'
     b. **I går kjøpte** Jon litt mer land (= target)
         in.yesterday bought Jon little more land
         'Yesterday Jon bought some more land.'   (Eide and Hjelde 2015a: 68)

Since English does not have matrix V2 or the North and West Germanic subordinate word order patterns described here, one might hypothesize that these word orders would change or disappear from heritage varieties. Many researchers have investigated the word order of these varieties. Declarative matrix V2 in heritage settings has been studied by Eide and Hjelde (2015a, 2018: Leiden: Brill), Johannessen (2015), and Westergaard and Lohndal (2019) for Norwegian, Kühl and Heegård Petersen (2018) for Danish, Larsson et al. (2015) for Swedish, Arnbjörnsdóttir et al. (2018) for Icelandic in Canada and the United States, Page and Brown (2006) for Pennsylvania Dutch, and Kahan Newman (2015) for Hasidic Yiddish. All these studies have found, contrary to the hypothesis, that the V2 requirement is generally kept across heritage language populations, though individual speakers, often less fluent (or attrited) ones may violate it. In the latter cases it may seem that heavy, fronted adverbials (long prepositional phrases or adverbial clauses) trigger the non-target non-V2 order, in contrast to light adverbials (short adverbs including in Norwegian the resumptive element *så* 'so'), which generally trigger target V2. An example of such non-target V3 word order in a matrix sentence uttered by a speaker of a heritage Norwegian variety is given in (2).

(2) **I skolen vi snakte** bare engelsk (target: I skolen snakte vi. . .)
     in school we talked only English
     'At school we only spoke English.' (Chicago_Il_01gk, Johannessen 2015:
        60–62)

The standard subordinate word order is illustrated for North Germanic by a Swedish relative clause in (3): When there is a sentential adverbial in the clause (here: the negation *inte* 'not'), the verb is no longer in the second position, but third (V3). The expected subordinate order for West Germanic is illustrated by a relative clause in an American German variety (Moundridge Schweitzer German, see below), (4): the finite verb is in the clause final position.

(3) tröjan som **han inte köpte** (= target)
     shirt.DEF that he not bought
     'the shirt that he didn't buy'   (Larsson and Johannessen 2015a: 243)

(4)   ... die wo in die Schul jetzt **sin(d)**. (= target)
        those there in the school now are
        'those that are in school currently.'   (Hopp and Putnam 2015: 195–196)

In both Germanic subgroups certain subordinating conjunctions allow V2 word order, as in matrix clauses, sometimes regulated by pragmatic or other factors. In North Germanic, the subordinating conjunction *at* 'that' gives this option (Julien 2008, 2015), and in West Germanic, *weil* 'because' does. However, in hearth varieties, other subordinating conjunctions require the strict order of verb third and verb last, respectively. Learning structures that are rare takes time for any child, but in heritage languages where the children are also subject to much and increasing input in a dominant language, a rare structure may be even rarer in the input to children. Heritage Swedish speakers have been shown to have a lower frequency of relative clauses than European speakers (Karstadt 2003: 105). This leads us to expect that relative clause word order would be vulnerable due to lack of input for learners. For North Germanic heritage varieties one would expect even more non-target word order, given that the special subordinate clauses need a sentential adverbial for the order to be visible. This prediction turns out to be supported. Larsson and Johannessen (2015a, b) investigated subordinate clauses in Heritage Norwegian and Heritage Swedish. They found that non-target V2 order was as frequent as the target V3 order. An example of the non-target V2 (with the adverbial following the verb) from Heritage Norwegian is given in (5).

(5)   ... som **forstår ikke** så mye norsk (target: ikke forstår)
        who understands not so much Norwegian
        'who doesn't understand much Norwegian.'   (zumbrota_MN_01gk,
            Larsson and Johannessen 2015a: 248)

Hopp and Putnam (2015) investigated a South Central Kansas heritage German variety, Moundridge Schweitzer German (MSG). These speakers actually prefer V2 order for the subordinating conjunctions *dass* 'that' and *weil* 'because' in recorded production data, as well as in subsequent judgment tasks, as in (6).

(6)   ... dass da lieber Gott **hot** uns auch net alles genomm (target:
            genomm hot)
        that the dear God has us also not everything taken
        'that dear God hasn't taken everything away from us"   (MSG
            Participant 102, Hopp and Putnam 2015: 195—196)

Clearly, the asymmetry between matrix and subordinate clause word order in European Germanic languages is not retained to the same extent in such heritage varieties. Larsson and Johannessen (2015a, b) discuss possible explanations such as transfer from English, or overgeneralization of V2, but conclude that it must be due to incomplete acquisition, given that subordinate word order develops at a late age even in European Scandinavian, and that in America this development would be hindered by the massive exposure to English from school age onward. Hopp and Putnam (2015) lean toward a complexification effect, arguing that the change is not necessarily a simplification (see also Johannessen and Putnam 2020).

Summing up this section, we have seen that all Germanic languages apart from English have an asymmetry between matrix and subordinate clauses, and also have stricter principles for the word order of mix clauses than English has. However, we do not see direct transfer from English in the Germanic heritage language word orders. The heritage languages have changed somewhat in the system of subordinate clauses, but the matrix clauses remain largely stable, save for individual speakers who can be argued to be attrited in their heritage language.

We have focused on the word order of matrix and subordinate clauses in this section, as an issue widely studied across these languages, but there have also been studies on noun phrases and other structures, illustrated by many chapters in the edited volumes cited in this chapter.

11.3.4 Pragmatics

Pragmatics is not among the most studied areas of Germanic heritage languages, but discourse markers provide a relatively well-studied example of pragmatic research. Using data from German dialects in Texas and Indiana, Salmons (1990) argued that discourse marking systems of bilinguals tend to converge in these settings with English markers like *well* and *you know* largely (though not entirely) replacing the native system of modal particles, like *ja*, *aber*, *doch*. A large body of work since has presented closely similar patterns in bilingual settings around the world and they are robust in Germanic heritage languages in the Americas, including in Nordic languages. Fuller (2001) accounts for this propensity for borrowing of discourse markers in terms of "pragmatic detachability," with Pennsylvania Dutch data.

For Danish in Argentina, Heegård Petersen and Kühl (2017) examine some discourse markers – approximative adverbials – in free conversation and compared them with patterns in Denmark Danish. Looking at markers such as *nesten* 'almost', *omkring* 'approximately' and *mere eller mindre* 'more or less,' they found that especially the latter was used more in Argentina than in hearth varieties. They see this as a calque from Spanish, *más o menos*. *Mere eller mindre* occurs in one syntactic position where it is much less frequently used in Denmark. Semantically, too, the marker is different, occurring in Argentinian Heritage Danish frequently with amounts or time expressions, which are hardly ever thus expressed in Denmark Danish.

These markers are by far the most frequent loanwords in Argentinian Danish, while Spanish loans are surprisingly infrequent (Heegård Petersen and Kühl 2017: 243).

More complex patterns have been found as well. Kahan Newman (2015) finds English discourse markers like *anyway*, *so*, and *you know* among Hasidic Yiddish speakers in New York City but also documents the rise of a new, native marker, *shoyn*, grammaticalized from an adverb. (She also connects such markers with the compromise of V2 patterns in Yiddish, see Section 11.3.4.) Moving beyond discourse marking narrowly, Eide and Hjelde (2015b) describe the borrowing of a modal verb from English into Heritage Norwegian (*spost* 'supposed to').

11.3.5 Lexicon

One immediately obvious difference between Germanic heritage languages and European varieties is the lexicon, which tends to be influenced by the majority language, both in terms of inventory and lexical semantics. This has been studied especially for the North Germanic languages in numerous works, going back almost 200 years, starting from the pastor Duus (1855–1858 [1958]), Flom (1901, 1926), Flaten (1901), and Haugen (1950, 1953), up to today. Consider a few examples from North Germanic.

Annear and Speth (2015) tested Matras's (2009) claim that languages in contact tend toward lexical overlap (convergence) as this will mean a smaller cognitive burden on the speakers. Lexical transfer (loanwords) gives full overlap, so this is predicted to be very common, which is confirmed by Annear and Speth (2015) for Heritage Norwegian, for example, *army* and *acre*. Semantic transfer and phonological transfer are also mechanisms that will bring two languages closer together, and they find examples like *grad* 'grade', which in English mostly means levels at school, while in European Norwegian it means degrees of temperature. In Heritage Norwegian the word has undergone lexical-semantic shift, now meaning level at school, converging in meaning with the English cognate. Phonemic transfer is more difficult to identify, since it could also be categorized as lexical transfer. One example is Norwegian *kaffe/kaffi*, which they find is pronounced [kåffi] in Heritage Norwegian, like English *coffee*.

Hjelde and Johannessen (2017, following Hjelde 1992 and Johannessen and Laake 2017) give evidence that the lexicon can reveal the extent of contact between heritage speakers over a vast area and over time. Haugen (1953) found both words that replace earlier words, like *kas'n* 'cousin' (Norw. *kusine/fetter/søskenbarn*), *fens* 'fence' (Norw. *gjerde*), and *kårne* 'corner' (Norw. *hjørne*) and words for new concepts, like *æker* 'acre', *kaonti* 'county,' and *gråsseri* 'grocery.' Many of these words were documented by Flom (1901, 1926), Haugen (1953), and Hjelde (1992) as well as Johannessen and

Laake (2017), showing stability of the heritage Norwegian lexicon over a hundred years across the Midwest. Hjelde and Johannessen (2017) further argue that words with an unpredictable meaning, such as Heritage Norwegian *travle* 'walk' (rather than 'travel') and *portrett* 'photograph' (rather than 'portrait') have been found, respectively, in the earliest sources and documented in an area stretching from Wisconsin to Saskatchewan, and in many locations in Wisconsin and Minnesota. The heritage Norwegian verb *gå* with its new meaning 'go' rather than the original European Norwegian meaning 'walk' has also been documented for Heritage Swedish (Hasselmo 1974) and Heritage Danish (Kjær and Baumann Larsen 1987), suggesting that Scandinavian heritage speakers had enough contact with each other using their respective languages that their vocabularies have changed in parallel ways.

11.4   Language Maintenance and Shift

Germanic-speaking communities sometimes lost their languages within the first generation born in their new home, while other languages have been actively maintained for centuries and to the present day. Most communities are undergoing shift to the dominant language of the country or region today. A growing body of work – culminating in Brown (forthcoming) – has argued recently that shift in these situations reflects "verticalization." That is, into the twentieth century these communities were heavily "horizontally" organized, with strong local control of key institutions – education, press, religion, economy – and tight connections among those local institutions. In industrial societies, the last century or more has seen a powerful shift toward vertical organization, where control of those institutions has shifted to powers beyond the community, whether regional, national, or international.

Exceptions – communities that are maintaining Germanic heritage languages – are typically religious minorities, e.g., Old Order Amish (Louden 2016), Hutterites (Brown 2018), or Hasidim (Abramac 2014, 2017). In such communities, horizontal control over key institutions is maintained, even within extremely verticalized societies. These groups continue to transmit their languages to children.

Shift to English does not end the story of these languages, though, in at least three ways. First, there is a struggle over the public understanding of the history of these languages, which have undergone a process sometimes called invisibilization (Skutnabb-Kangas 2000). For a language like German, its presence is widely acknowledged across the Midwest and other regions, but the presence of a standard, institutional language has been widely erased (Macaulay and Salmons 2019). Second, many of these languages are enjoying what Shandler (2006) calls a "postvernacular" life, where people can have a powerful "affective or ideological relationship" with a language "without having a command of the language" (4). Shandler's case study is Yiddish and he sees current discussions around postvernacularity as not only allowing a renegotiation of "the distance between [Yiddish's] past and one's present" but also "opening up prospects for more adventures with Yiddish in the future" (201). Brown and Hietpas (2019) have applied this concept to the very different case of Dutch in the Upper Midwest. Third, these languages have continuing impact through their effects on regional and social varieties of English spoken in North America, contributing to the current diversification of English (Salmons and Purnell 2020; Wilkerson and Salmons 2019) and even leading to new bidialectalism, as with "Dutchified English" in Pennsylvania (Anderson 2014).

11.5 Conclusion

Immigrants and refugees formed literally thousands of communities across North and South America where countless (and to an extent unknown) Germanic varieties were and often continue to be spoken.

Some communities have shifted to the relevant dominant (usually national) language or are in the last stages of shift, while others continue to pass their heritage languages on to learners today. As diverse as their histories are, we, interestingly, find many of the same basic patterns of structural change across many of these languages that belong to the same language family, e.g., reduction or loss of case marking and V2 patterns.

These settings provide opportunities to observe change over multiple generations, including where we see the rise of new dialects and often with effects on the majority language they are in contact with. Some pattern of variability in a first-generation heritage community may unfold over several generations and the communities we have discussed allow us to see full paths and trajectories of change.

Where language shift is advanced, these communities provide additional opportunities and real challenges. We have sketched here how research has been anchored in linguistic theory, historical linguistics, sociolinguistics, and the study of language shift. This chapter also shows that work has begun in earnest on issues of corpus linguistics (Yager et al. 2015; Larsson and Johannessen 2015a, 2015b; Kühl and Heegård Petersen 2016, 2018; Hjelde and Johannessen 2017; Eide and Hjelde 2018; Westergaard and Lohndal 2019; Bousquette 2020) and historical sociolinguistics (Litty 2017; Salmons 2017; Hoffman and Kytö 2018; Peterson 2018; Moquin 2019; Bousquette 2020). Experimental psycholinguistic studies are still in their beginnings as researchers work to address particular challenges of the relevant speaker population (Sewell and Salmons 2014; Hopp and Putnam

2015; Rødvand 2017, 2018; Lykke 2018; van Baal 2018, 2019). Other kinds of work have not yet really begun. Notably, Pichler et al. (2018) rightly describe older adults (65+) as "the invisible age group in variationist socio-linguistics" and aim to "confront variationist ageism." The type of heritage speakers we work with are, as should be clear from this, overwhelmingly in this age group, yet we understand far too little what impact age has on the speech patterns we study. Even basic comparison to other elderly and similar but distinct populations is needed, e.g., Schmid (2002) on German-speaking Jewish refugees in English-speaking countries or Levine (2015) on Yiddish speakers in the United States. Both groups speak West Germanic languages but have acquired and use them (or not) in very different contexts. In short, there is a lot of basic work to be done.

References

Abramac, Gabi. 2014. Between Two Worlds: Language and Culture in the Ultra-Orthodox Jewish Communities in New York City and in Upstate New York. *Studii de Ştiinţăşicultură* 10, 13–20.

Abramac, Gabi. 2017. Language Choices and Language Ideologies among Hasidic Jews in New York. Paper presented at the 8th Annual Workshop on Immigrant Languages in the Americas (WILA8). University of Copenhagen, October 12–14, 2017.

Anderson, Vicki M. 2014. *Bidialectalism: An Unexpected Development in the Obsolescence of Pennsylvania Dutchified English*. Durham, NC: Duke University Press.

Annear, Lucas and Kristin Speth. 2015. Maintaining a Multilingual Repertoire: Lexical Change in American Norwegian. In Janne Bondi Johannessen and Joseph Salmons (eds.), *Germanic Heritage Languages in North America: Acquisition, Attrition and Change*. Amsterdam: John Benjamins, 201–216.

Arnbjörnsdóttir, Birna. 2015. Reexamining Icelandic as a Heritage Language in North America. In Janne Bondi Johannessen and Joseph Salmons (eds.), *Germanic Heritage Languages in North America: Acquisition, Attrition and Change*. Amsterdam: John Benjamins, 72–93.

Arnbjörnsdóttir, Birna, Höskuldr Thráinsson, and Iris Nowenstein. 2018. V2 and V3 Orders in North American Icelandic. *Journal of Language Contact* 11, 379–412.

Barðdal, Jóhanna and Leonid Kulikov. 2008. Case in Decline. In A. Malchukov and A. Spencer (eds.), *The Oxford Handbook of Case*. Oxford: Oxford University Press, 470–478.

Benmamoun, Elabbas, Silvina Montrul, and Maria Polinsky. 2013a. Keynote Article. Heritage Languages and Their Speakers: Opportunities and Challenges for Linguistics. *Theoretical Linguistics* 39, 129–181.

Benmamoun, Elabbas, Silvina Montrul, and Maria Polinsky. 2013b. Defining an "Ideal" Heritage Speaker: Theoretical and Methodological Challenges. Reply to Peer Commentaries. *Theoretical Linguistics* 39, 259–294.

Bousquette, Joshua. 2020. From Bidialectal to Bilingual: Oblique Case Marking in Lester W. J. "Smoky" Seifert's 1946–1949 Wisconsin German Recordings. *American Speech* 95, 486–532.

Brown, Joshua R. 2018. Language Maintenance among the Hutterites. *Yearbook of German-American Studies* 52, 1–18.

Brown, Joshua R. 2019. Civil War Writings of the Pennsylvania Dutch. *Journal of Historical Sociolinguistics*, special issues on *Heritage Language Ego-Documents: From Home, from Away, and from Below*, ed. Joshua R. Brown.

Brown, Joshua R. (ed.) Forthcoming. *Verticalization: A Model for Language Shift*. Oxford: Oxford University Press.

Brown, Joshua R. and Joshua Bousquette (eds.) 2018. Heritage and Immigrant Languages in the Americas: Sociolinguistic Approaches, special issue of the *Journal of Language Contact* 11(2) 201–371.

Brown, Joshua R. and Kelly Biers (eds.) 2019. *Selected Proceedings of the 9th Annual Workshop on Immigrant Languages in the Americas (WILA 9)*. Somerville, MA: Cascadilla Press. www.cascadilla.com/wila.html

Brown, Joshua R. and Rachyl Hietpas. 2019. Postvernacular Dutch in Wisconsin. In Joshua R. Brown and Kelly Biers (eds.), *Selected Proceedings of the 9th Annual Workshop on Immigrant Languages in the Americas (WILA 9)*. Somerville, MA: Cascadilla Press.

Coetzee, Andries W., Lorenzo García-Amaya, Nicholas Henriksen, and Daan Wissing. 2015. Bilingual speech rhythm: Spanish-Afrikaans in Patagonia. *International Congress of Phonetic Sciences*.

Crawford, James (ed.) 1992. *Language Loyalties: A Source Book on the Official English Controversy*. Chicago: University of Chicago Press.

Crawford, James. 2000. *At War with Diversity: US Language Policy in an Age of Anxiety*. Clevedon: Multilingual Matters.

Duus, Olaus Fredrik. 1855–1858 [1958]. Frontier Parsonage: The Letters of Olaus Fredrik Duus. Norwegian Pastor in Wisconsin, 1855–1858. NAHA, Northfield 1947. In Theodore C. Blegen (ed.), *Amerikabrev*. Oslo: H. Aschehoug & Co.

Ehresmann, Todd and Joshua Bousquette. 2015. Phonological Non-Integration of Lexical Borrowings in Wisconsin West Frisian. In Janne Bondi Johannessen and Joseph Salmons (eds.), *Germanic Heritage Languages in North America: Acquisition, Attrition and Change*. Amsterdam: John Benjamins, 234–255.

Eide, Kristin Melum and Arnstein Hjelde. 2015a. Verb Second and Finiteness Morphology in Norwegian Heritage Language of the American Midwest. In Richard Page and Michael T. Putnam (eds.), *Moribund Germanic Heritage Languages in North America: Theoretical Perspectives and Empirical Findings*. Leiden: Brill, 64–101.

Eide, Kristin Melum and Arnstein Hjelde. 2015b. Borrowing Modal Elements into American Norwegian: The Case of Suppose(d). In Janne Bondi Johannessen and Joseph Salmons (eds.), *Germanic Heritage Languages in North America: Acquisition, Attrition and Change.* Amsterdam: John Benjamins, 256–282.

Eide, Kristin Melum and Arnstein Hjelde. 2018. Om verbplassering og verbmorfologi i amerikanorsk. *Maal og Minne* 110, 25–69.

Flaten, Nils. 1901. Notes on the American-Norwegian with Vocabulary. *Dialect Notes* 2, 115–126.

Flom, George. T. 1901. English Elements in Norse Dialects of Utica, Wisconsin. *Dialect Notes* 2, 1900–1904.

Flom, George. T. 1926. English Loanwords in American Norwegian: As spoken in the Koshkonong Settlement, Wisconsin. *American Speech* 1, 541–558.

Fuller, Janet M. 2001. The Principle of Pragmatic Detachability in Borrowing: English-Origin Discourse Markers in Pennsylvania German. *Linguistics* 39, 351–370.

Hasselmo, Nils. 1974. *Amerikasvenska: En bok om språkutvecklingen i Svensk-Amerika.* (Skrifter utg. av Svenska språknämnden 51). Lund: Esselte.

Haugen, Einar. 1950. The Analysis of Linguistic Borrowing. *Language* 26, 210–231.

Haugen, Einar. 1953. *The Norwegian Language in America.* 2 vols. Philadelphia: University of Pennsylvania Press.

Heegård Petersen, Jan and Karoline Kühl. 2017. Argentinadansk: Semantiske, syntaktiske og morfologiske forskelle til rigsdansk. *Nydanske Sprogstudier NyS* 52–53, 231–258.

Heegård Petersen, Jan and Karoline Kühl (eds.) 2018. *Selected Proceedings of the 8th Workshop on Immigrant Languages in the Americas (WILA 8).* Somerville, MA: Cascadilla Proceedings Project.

Hjelde, Arnstein. 1992. *Trøndsk talemål i Amerika.* Trondheim: Tapir.

Hjelde, Arnstein. 1996. Some Phonological Changes in a Norwegian Dialect in America. In Sture Ureland (ed.), *Language Contact across the North Atlantic: Proceedings of the Working Groups Held at the University College, Galway (Ireland), 1992 and the University of Göteborg (Sweden).* Berlin: de Gruyter, 283–295.

Hjelde, Arnstein. 2015. Changes in a Norwegian Dialect in America. In Janne Bondi Johannessen and Joseph Salmons (eds.), *Germanic Heritage Languages in North America: Acquisition, Attrition and Change.* Amsterdam: John Benjamins, 283–298.

Hjelde, Arnstein and Janne Bondi Johannessen. 2017. Amerikanorsk: Orda vitner om kontakt mellom folk. In Terje Mikael Hasle Joranger (ed.), *Norwegian-American Essays 2017.* Oslo: Novus, 257–282.

Hoffman, Angela and Merja Kytö. 2018. Heritage Swedish, English, and Textual Space in Rural Communities of Practice. In Jan Heegård

Petersen and Karoline Kühl (eds.), *Selected Proceedings of the 8th Workshop on Immigrant Languages in the Americas (WILA 8)*. Somerville, MA: Cascadilla Proceedings Project, 44–54.

Holmberg, Anders and Christer Platzack. 1995. *The Role of Inflection in Scandinavian Syntax*. New York and Oxford: Oxford University Press.

Hopp, Holger and Michael T. Putnam. 2015. Restructuring in Heritage Grammar: Word Order Variation in Heritage German. *Linguistic Approaches to Bilingualism* 5(2), 180–203.

Johannessen, Janne Bondi. 2015. Attrition in an American Norwegian Heritage Language Speaker. In Janne Bondi Johannessen and Joseph Salmons (eds.), *Germanic Heritage Languages in North America: Acquisition, Attrition and Change*. Amsterdam: John Benjamins, 46–71.

Johannessen, Janne Bondi. 2018. Factors of Variation, Maintenance and Change in Scandinavian Heritage Languages. In Jonathan Kasstan, Anita Auer, and Joe Salmons (eds.), Special Issue on 'Heritage-Language Speakers: Theoretical and Empirical Challenges on Sociolinguistic Attitudes and Prestige', *International Journal of Bilingualism* 22, 447–465.

Johannessen, Janne Bondi and Joseph Salmons (eds.) 2015. *Germanic Heritage Languages in North America: Acquisition, Attrition and Change*. Amsterdam: John Benjamins.

Johannessen, Janne Bondi and Michael Putnam. 2020. Heritage Germanic Languages in North America. In Michael Putnam and Richard Page (eds.), *Handbook of Germanic Languages*. Cambridge: Cambridge University Press, 783–806.

Johannessen, Janne Bondi and Signe Laake. 2017. Norwegian in the American Midwest: A Common Dialect? *Journal of Language Contact* 10, 1.

Julien, Marit. 2008. Så vanleg at det kan ikkje avfeiast: om V2 i innføydde setningar. In Janne Bondi Johannessen and Kristin Hagen (eds.), *Språk i Oslo. Ny forskning om talespråk*. Novus Forlag. Online https://portal.research .lu.se/portal/en/publications/saa-vanleg-at-det-kan-ikkje-avfeiast-om-v2-i-innfoeydde-setningar(90e9f8e1-8829-4336-8e35-7ea64a42be2f).html

Julien, Marit. 2015. The Force of V2 Revisited. *Journal of Comparative Germanic Linguistics* 18, 139–181.

Kahan Newman, Zelda. 2015. Discourse Markers in the Narratives of New York Hasidim. In Janne Bondi Johannessen and Joseph Salmons (eds.), *Germanic Heritage Languages in North America: Acquisition, Attrition and Change*. Amsterdam: John Benjamins, 178–197.

Karstadt, Angela. 2003. *Tracking Swedish-American English: A Longitudinal Study of Linguistic Variation and Identity*. Uppsala: Acta Universitatis Upsaliensis.

Kellogg, Louise Phelps. 1918. The Bennett Law in Wisconsin. *Wisconsin Magazine of History* 2, 3–25.

Kerswill, Paul. 2002. Koineization and Accommodation. In J. K. Chambers, Peter Trudgill, and Natalie Schilling-Estes (eds.), *The Handbook of Language Variation and Change*. Oxford: Blackwell, 669–702.

Kerswill, Paul and Peter Trudgill. 2005. The Birth of New Dialects. In Peter Auer, Frans Hinskens, and Paul Kerswill (eds.), *Dialect Change: Convergence and Divergence in European Languages*. Cambridge: Cambridge University Press, 196–220.

Kjær, Iver and Mogens Baumann Larsen. 1987. A Study of the Vocabulary in an American-Danish Community. In Steffen E. Jørgensen, Lars Scheving, and Niels Peter Stilling (eds.), *From Scandinavia to America: Proceedings of a Conference Held at Gl. Holtegaard*. Odense: Odense University Press, 265–266.

Klosinski, Robert. 2019. Partial Phonetic Convergence in Misionero German-Portuguese Bilinguals. In Joshua R. Brown and Kelly Biers (eds.), *Selected Proceedings of the 9th Annual Workshop on Immigrant Languages in the Americas (WILA 9)*. Somerville, MA: Cascadilla Press.

Koerner, Christian. 1890. *Das Bennett-Gesetz und die deutschen protestantischen Gemeindeschulen in Wisconsin*. Milwaukee: Germania.

Kühl, Karoline and Jan Heegård Petersen. 2016. Ledstillingsvariation i amerikadanske hovedsætninger med topikalisering. *Ny forskning i grammatik* 23, 161–176.

Kühl, Karoline and Jan Heegård Petersen. 2018. Word Order in American Danish Declaratives with a Non-Subject Initial Constituent. *Journal of Language Contact* 11, 413–440.

Kvalsten, Louis. 1931. Article in *Reform*. February 5. 46(6), 3. Waldemar Ager Association. The Ager Museum Collection: Reform. [Online database]. https://rescarta.apps.uwec.edu/Ager-Web/jsp/RcWebBrowse.jsp

Larsson, Ida and Janne Bondi Johannessen. 2015a. Embedded Word Order in Heritage Scandinavian. In Martin Hilpert, Jan-Ola Östman, Christine Mertzlufft, Michael Riessler, and Janet Duke (eds.), *New Trends in Nordic and General Linguistics*. Berlin: De Gruyter, 239–266.

Larsson, Ida and Janne Bondi Johannessen. 2015b. Incomplete Acquisition and Verb Placement in Heritage Scandinavian. In Richard S. Page and Michael T. Putnam (eds.), *Moribund Germanic Heritage Languages in North America: Theoretical Perspectives and Empirical Findings*. Leiden: Brill Academic Publishers, 153–189.

Larsson, Ida, Sofia Tingsell, and Maia Andréasson. 2015. Variation and Change in American Swedish. In Janne Bondi Johannessen and Joseph Salmons (eds.), *Germanic Heritage Languages in North America: Acquisition, Attrition and Change*. Amsterdam: John Benjamins, 359–388.

Levine, Glenn S. 2015. *Incomplete L1 Acquisition in the Immigrant Situation: Yiddish in the United States*. Berlin: Walter de Gruyter.

Lippi-Green, Rosina. 2012. *English with an Accent: Language, Ideology, and Discrimination in the United States*. 2nd ed. London: Routledge.

Litty, Samantha. 2017. We Talk German Now Yet: The Sociolinguistic Development of Voice Onset Time & Final Obstruent Devoicing in Wisconsin German & English varieties, 1863–2013. PhD dissertation, University of Wisconsin–Madison.

Louden, Mark. 2016. *Pennsylvania Dutch: The Story of an American Language.* Baltimore: Johns Hopkins University Press.

Lykke, Alexander K. 2018. The Relation between Finiteness Morphology and Verb-Second: An Empirical Study of Heritage Norwegian. In Jan Heegård Petersen and Karoline Kühl (eds.), *Selected Proceedings of the 8th Workshop on Immigrant Languages in the Americas (WILA 8).* Somerville, MA: Cascadilla Proceedings Project, 71–79.

Macaulay, Monica and Joseph Salmons. 2019. Differential Invisibilization and Its Aftermath: Menominee and German in Wisconsin. *Taal en Tongval* 71(2). 187–207.

Matras, Yaron. 2009. *Language Contact.* Cambridge: Cambridge University Press.

Milroy, James. 2014. Sociolinguistics and Ideologies in Language History. Juan Manuel Hernández-Campoy and Juan Camilo Conde-Silvestre (eds.), *The Handbook of Historical Sociolinguistics.* Oxford: Blackwell, 571–584.

Moen, Per. 1988. The English Pronunciation of Norwegian-Americans in Four Midwestern States. *American Studies in Scandinavia* 20, 105–121.

Moquin, Laura. 2019. Language and Morality in Norwegian-American Newspapers: Reform in Eau Claire, WI. In Joshua R. Brown and Kelly Biers (eds.), *Selected Proceedings of the 9th Annual Workshop on Immigrant Languages in the Americas (WILA 9).* Somerville, MA: Cascadilla Press, 64–71.

Natvig, David. 2016. Heritage Norwegian Vowel Phonology and English Dialect Formation. *Heritage Language Journal* 13, 245–274.

Natvig, David. 2017. A Model of Underspecified Recognition for Phonological Integrations: English Loanwords in American Norwegian. *Journal of Language Contact* 10(1), 22–55.

Natvig, David. 2019. Levels of Representation in Phonetic and Phonological Contact. In Jeroen Darquennes, Wim Vandenbussche, and Joseph Salmons (eds.), *Contact Linguistics.* Vol. 1. Berlin: de Gruyter Handbooks, 88–99.

Natvig, David. Forthcoming. 'The Great Change' and the Shift from Norwegian to English in Ulen, Minnesota. In Joshua R. Brown (ed.), *Verticalization: A Model for Language Shift.* Oxford: Oxford University Press.

Natvig, David and Joseph Salmons. 2020. Fully Accepting Variation in (Pre) History: The Pervasive Heterogeneity of Germanic Rhotics. In Patricia C. Sutcliffe (ed.), *The Polymath Intellectual: A Festschrift in Honor of Professor Robert D. King.* Dripping Springs, TX: Agarita Press, 81–101.

Nützel, Daniel. 2009. *The East Franconian Dialect of Haysville, Indiana: A Study in Language Death / Die ostfränkische Mundart von Haysville, Indiana: Eine Untersuchung mit ausgewählten morphologischen und syntaktischen Phänomenen.* Regensburger Dialektforum, vol. 15. Regensburg: Edition Vulpes.

Nützel, Daniel and Joseph Salmons. 2011. Structural Stability and Change in Language Contact: Evidence from American German. *Language and Linguistics Compass* 5, 705–717.

Olesch, Reinhold. 1970. The West Slavic Languages in Texas with Special Regard to Sorbian in Serbin, Lee County. In Glenn Gilbert (ed.), *Texas Studies in Bilingualism*. Berlin: Walter de Gruyter, 151–162.

O'Neil, Wayne. 1978. The Evolution of the Germanic Inflectional Systems: A Study in the Causes of Language Change. *Orbis* 27, 248–286.

Otheguy, Ricardo and Ana Celia Zentella. 2011. *Spanish in New York: Language Contact, Dialectal Leveling, and Structural Continuity*. Oxford: Oxford University Press.

Page, B. Richard and Joshua R. Brown. 2006. From V2 to SVO? A Quantitative Analysis of Word Order in Pennsylvania German. Paper presented at the Germanic Linguistics Annual Conference 12, University of Illinois at Urbana-Champaign.

Page, Richard and Michael T. Putnam (eds.) 2015. *Moribund Germanic Heritage Languages in North America: Theoretical Perspectives and Empirical Findings*. Leiden: Brill.

Peterson, Elizabeth. 2018. Coffee and Danish in Sanpete County, Utah: An Exploration of Food Rituals and Language Shift. In Jan Heegård Petersen and Karoline Kühl (eds.), *Selected Proceedings of the 8th Workshop on Immigrant Languages in the Americas (WILA 8)*. Somerville, MA: Cascadilla Proceedings Project, 80–87.

Pichler, Heike, Suzanne Evans Wagner, and Ashley Hesson. 2018. Old-age Language Variation and Change: Confronting Variationist Ageism. *Language and Linguistics Compass* 12(6): 1–22.

Pierce, Marc, Hans Boas, and Karen Roesch. 2015. The History of Front Rounded Vowels in New Braunfels German. In Janne Bondi Johannessen and Joseph Salmons (eds.), *Germanic Heritage Languages in North America: Acquisition, Attrition and Change*. Amsterdam: John Benjamins, 117–131.

Polinsky, Maria. 2018. *Heritage Languages and Their Speakers*. Cambridge: Cambridge University Press.

Putnam, Michael (ed.) 2011. *Studies on German Language Islands*. Amsterdam: John Benjamins.

Putnam, Michael and Richard Page (eds.) 2020. *Handbook of Germanic Languages*. Cambridge: Cambridge University Press.

Rødvand, Linn Iren Sjånes. 2017. Empirical Investigations of Grammatical Gender in American Heritage Norwegian. MA thesis, Oslo: University of Oslo, Department of Linguistics and Scandinavian Studies.

Rødvand, Linn Iren Sjånes. 2018. Systematic Variation in the Gender System in American Norwegian. In Jan Heegård Petersen and Karoline Kühl (eds.), *Selected Proceedings of the 8th Workshop on Immigrant Languages in the Americas (WILA 8)*. Somerville, MA: Cascadilla Proceedings Project, 89–95.

Rosenberg, Peter. 2005. Dialect Convergence in the German Language Islands (Sprachinseln). In P. Auer, F. Hinskens, and P. Kerswill (eds.), *Dialect Change: Convergence and Divergence in European Languages*. Cambridge: Cambridge University Press, 221–235.

Salmons, Joseph. 1990. Bilingual Discourse Marking: Codeswitching, Borrowing and Convergence in Some German-American Dialects. *Linguistics* 28, 453–480.

Salmons, Joseph. 1994. Naturalness and Morphological Change in Texas German. In N. Berend and K. J. Mattheier (eds.), *Sprachinselforschung: Eine Gedenkschrift für Hugo Jedig*. Frankfurt: Peter Lang, 59–72.

Salmons, Joseph. 2017. Keineswegs Feinde der englischen Sprache: Deutsch, Englisch und Schulpolitik in Wisconsin. *Muttersprache*, special issue, "Zur Soziolinguistik regionaler Mehrsprachigkeit im deutschsprachigen Raum" (ed.) Nils Langer. 2017(4), 310–323.

Salmons, Joseph and Thomas Purnell. 2020. Language Contact and the Development of American English. In Raymond Hickey (ed.), *The Handbook of Language Contact*. Oxford: Blackwell, 2nd ed., 361–383.

Sanz-Sánchez, Israel. 2013. Dialect Contact as the Cause for Dialect Change: Evidence from a Phonemic Merger in Colonial New Mexican Spanish. *Diachronica* 30, 61–94.

Schmid, Monika. 2002. *First Language Attrition, Use and Maintenance: The Case of German Jews in Anglophone Countries*. Amsterdam: John Benjamins.

Sewell, Alyson and Joseph Salmons. 2014. How Far-Reaching Are the Effects of Contact? Parasitic Gapping in Wisconsin German and English. In Robert Nicolai (ed.), *Questioning Language Contact: Limits of Contact, Contact at its Limits*. Leiden: Brill, 217–251.

Shandler, Jeffrey. 2006. *Adventures in Yiddishland: Postvernacular Language and Culture*. Berkeley: University of California Press.

Siemens, Heinrich. 2012. *Plautdietsch: Grammatik Geschichte Perspektiven*. Bonn: Tweeback.

Skutnabb-Kangas, Tove. 2000. *Linguistic Genocide in Education – or Worldwide Diversity and Human Rights?* Mahwah, NJ: Erlbaum.

van Baal, Yvonne. 2018. Compositional Definiteness in Heritage Norwegian: Production Studied in a Translation Experiment. In Jan Heegård Petersen and Karoline Kühl (eds.), *Selected Proceedings of the 8th Workshop on Immigrant Languages in the Americas (WILA 8)*. Somerville, MA: Cascadilla Proceedings Project, 9–17.

van Baal, Yvonne. 2019. Compositional Definiteness in American Heritage Norwegian. PhD thesis, Oslo: University of Oslo, Department of Linguistics and Scandinavian Studies.

Vikner, Sten. 1995. *Verb Movement and Expletive Subjects in the Germanic Languages*. New York and Oxford: Oxford University Press.

Webber, Philip E. 1988. *Pella Dutch: The Portrait of a Language and Its Use in One of Iowa's Ethnic Communities*. Ames: Iowa State University Press.

Westergaard, Marit and Terje Lohndal. 2019. *Verb Second Word Order in Norwegian Heritage Language: Syntax and Pragmatics*. Washington, DC: Georgetown University Press.

Wilkerson, Miranda and Joseph Salmons. 2008. "Good Old Immigrants of Yesteryear" Who Didn't Learn English: Germans in Wisconsin. *American Speech* 83, 259–283.

Wilkerson, Miranda and Joseph Salmons. 2012. Linguistic Marginalities: Becoming American without Learning English. *Journal of Transnational American Studies* 4(2) acgcc_jtas_7115. www.escholarship.org/uc/item/5vn092kk.

Wilkerson, Miranda and Joseph Salmons. 2019. Leaving Their Mark: How Wisconsin Came to Sound German. In Raymond Hickey (ed.), *English in the German-speaking World*. Cambridge: Cambridge University Press, 362–384.

Yager, Lisa, Nora Hellmold, Hyoun-A Joo, Michael T. Putnam, Eleonora Rossi, Catherine Stafford, and Joseph Salmons. 2015. New Structural Patterns in Moribund Grammar: Case Marking in Heritage German. *Frontiers in Psychology* 6. http://journal.frontiersin.org/article/10.3389/fpsyg.2015.01716/full

12

Arabic in North America

Abdulkafi Albirini

12.1 The Arabic Language

Arabic is a Semitic language that is spoken natively by more than 300 million speakers centered mainly in the Near East and North Africa. It is also the official language or one of the official languages in the twenty-two countries comprising the Arab League (Algeria, Bahrain, Comoros, Djibouti, Egypt, Iraq, Jordan, Kuwait, Lebanon, Libya, Mauritania, Morocco, Oman, Palestine, Qatar, Saudi Arabia, Somalia, Sudan, Syria, Tunisia, the United Arab Emirates, and Yemen). Arabic is the main language of Islamic texts and liturgy, and therefore many Muslims around the world learn Arabic mainly to be able to read and understand Islamic texts that are written in the standard variety of Arabic. Arabic is also spoken outside the Arab region by millions of Arabic speakers who live in the diaspora, but particularly in North America, Europe, and Australia. It is also recognized as an official, national, or regional language in countries like Niger, Senegal, Mali, Turkey, and Iran.

Arabic is a diglossic language in the sense that two varieties of the same language coexist in the same speech communities. The two varieties are Colloquial Arabic (CA) and Standard Arabic (SA). Although the two varieties of Arabic are structurally and historically related, they display differences in their acquisition, structure, functions, and sometimes context of use (Ferguson 1959). CA is the language variety that Arab children acquire from birth through their parents and family members. It is used in everyday life conversations, casual communications (e.g., at work), and other informal domains. SA is used for formal functions, such as news reports, political speeches, religious sermons, newspapers, literary writings, and so on. It is also the variety associated with reading and writing because, unlike CA, it is codified and standardized. Although Arab children do not typically learn SA from parents and family members, they are often exposed to it via television, media, religious texts and sermons, children's stories, and other communication channels (Albirini, 2019).

SA and CA share a number of structural properties and features, but they also differ in a number of ways. Structurally, both use the SVO and VSO word orders and allow the omission of subjects in tensed clauses (i.e., the pro-drop strategy). Both use concatenative and non-concatenative morphology to form plurals, verbal nouns, and other word categories, even though they may use different morphemes. They both may form dual nouns and adjectives by a single morpheme, although again they use dissimilar morphemes. They show other similarities, as in the use of the definite article, subcategorization rules, and relativization (Benmamoun 2000; Aoun et al. 2010). However, SA and CA also exhibit many differences. In terms of morphology, for example, case and mood markings in SA are not used in CA. Similarly, the complex verb agreement paradigms in SA are severely reduced in most CA dialects. Likewise, whereas SA uses different negation particles, most colloquial varieties deploy mainly two negation particles (Aoun et al. 2010; Benmamoun et al. 2014). With respect to syntax, the unmarked word order in SA is the VSO pattern, whereas it is SVO in CA (Shlonsky 1997).

To illustrate the similarities and differences between SA and CA, consider the following examples from SA and the Levantine dialect:

(1)   a.   rama   l-hadaaya   ʕala l-ʔarḍ(i)   (SA)
      b.   rama   l-hadaaya   ʕala l-l-ʔarḍ   (Levantine)
           threw.3MS   the-gifts   on   the-floor
           'He threw the gifts on the floor.'

(2)   a.   ar-rajulu   lan   ya-ðhab-a   ila l-maqha   (SA)
           the-man-Nom   Fut.Neg   3-go-MS.Subj to   the-coffee shop
      b.   z-zalame   maa   raḥ   y-ruuḥ   ʕala   l-ʔahwe   (Levantine)
           the-man   Neg   Fut   3-go.MS   onto   the-coffee shop
           'The man will not go to the coffee shop.'

In (1a, b), the two sentences from SA and the Levantine dialect are almost indistinguishable in the sense that they use the same verb *rama* 'threw' whose subject is not expressed overtly, the same plural noun-object *hadaaya* 'gifts,' which is derived non-concatenatively from the root *hdy* and pattern *CaCaaCaa*, and the same prepositional phrase *ʕala l-ʔarḍ* 'on the floor.' In (2a, b), however, the SA and CA sentences are dissimilar lexically and morphosyntactically. For example, the words for *man, go,* and *coffee shop* are not the same in SA and CA. Moreover, the subject of the SA sentence *ar-rajul* 'the man' is marked for the nominative case by the morpheme *–u*, whereas its counterpart *z-zalame* has no case marking. Similarly, the SA verb *yaðhab* 'goes' is marked for the subjunctive mood by the morpheme -*a*[1], whereas its Levantine counterpart *yruuḥ* lacks mood inflection. In addition, whereas tense and negation in the SA sentence are merged and realized as a single particle *lan* 'will.not,' the CA sentence expresses negation and tense by two independent particles, *maa* 'not' and *raḥ* 'will.'

   SA is structurally uniform across the Arab region. By contrast, there are various CA varieties that share similarities but also exhibit differences among them. Similarities and differences exist in the lexicon, phonetics/phonology, morphology, and syntax, but these are beyond the scope of this chapter (see Benmamoun 2000; Brustad 2000; Aoun et al. 2010). This is true given the geographic spread of where Arabic is spoken, making Arabic varieties physically distant from one another.

12.2   Brief History of Arabic and Arabic Speakers in North America

The earliest presence of Arabic is North America is far from clear. According to one account, Arabic existed at least five hundred years before Columbus began his first voyage across the Atlantic Ocean in 1492 (e.g., Von Wuthenau 1975; Fell 1983; Van Sertima 2003; Ahmad 2014). For example, Fell (1983) found Arabic texts, diagrams, and charts inscribed on rocks that date back to around 800 C.E. These inscriptions were about different school subjects, such as mathematics, history, geography, and sea navigation. Similarly, Ahmad (2014) points to Arabic documents, coins found in the southern Caribbean region off the coast of Venezuela, and names of indigenous cities to suggest possible trade relations between Arabs in North Africa and the indigenous American people. These and similar accounts indicate that Arabic speakers may have been in contact with the indigenous American population and Arabic may have been known to the indigenous people long before Columbus.

   According to a different account, the Arabic language arrived in North America through African slaves who were transported from West Africa in the seventeenth and eighteenth centuries (Osman and Forbes 2004; Alford 2007). Some of these slaves were Muslims. Although Arabic was not their mother tongue, they might have learned Arabic for religious purposes or for reading and writing. The existing records show that some of them, such as Omar Ibn Said and Abdulrahman Ibrahim Ibn Sori, used Arabic to write letters and diaries about their experiences in the New World (Osman and Forbes 2004; Alford 2007). However, there is little evidence to suggest that

---

[1] The subjunctive mood occurs in restricted contexts, including after the particle *lan*. The *lan* + *subjunctive* sequence renders a future negative.

they may have used Arabic in oral communication. It is also not clear whether their Arabic-language skills were transmitted to their children or grandchildren.

In the post-Columbian era, the early immigrants of Arab descent came mostly from Greater Syria (i.e., the Levant) in the nineteenth century and settled in major cities in the United States (Suleiman 1999; Abdelhady 2014). These immigrants were unified in their common endeavor for better living conditions and/or political stability. Because they had to work mostly in low-wage jobs or small businesses, most of the early Arab immigrants found themselves compelled to learn English to survive economically. It is not surprising that most of them assimilated culturally and linguistically within the American culture quickly because they were few in numbers and dispersed geographically (Orfalea 2006). Their linguistic and cultural assimilation is also related to their detachment from other Arabic speakers and Arab social organizations inside and outside the United States. This continued to be the common trend among Arab immigrants until World War II (Abdelhady 2014).

In the second half of the twentieth century, Arab immigrants started to come from different Arab countries, particularly Lebanon, Palestine, Syria, Iraq, and Yemen due to lenient immigration policies in the United States after World War II (Suleiman 1999; Orfalea 2006; Abdelhady 2014). Unlike their predecessors, most of these immigrants were highly educated individuals and professionals (physicians, engineers, professors, etc.) who were able to thrive in American society while still maintaining links with their linguistic and cultural background (Orfalea 2006). Their economic success helped in the creation of educational and social institutions (e.g., schools and mosques/churches) that provide second- and third-generation Arabs with opportunities to learn about their heritage culture.

Since September 11, 2001, there have been various restrictions on immigration from a number of Arab countries. Consequently, the number of regular Arab immigrants has declined in the United States. Since 2001, most Arab incomers came as graduate students from the Gulf region, Egypt, Jordan, and the Maghreb. Some found jobs after graduation and settled with their families in their new milieu (Rouchdy 2013). A new wave of immigrants started after the Gulf War II, particularly from Iraq and more recently from Syria following the so-called Arab Spring. Most of these immigrants are less educated and less economically stable than immigrants from other Arab nationalities and previous Arab immigrants.

The Arab Community Survey estimates the number of Americans with Arab descent to be around 3.7 million (The Arab American Institute 2012). The majority of them come from Lebanon, Iraq, Egypt, Syria, and Palestine. Arab Americans are found in all fifty states, but are mostly concentrated in California, New York, Michigan, Florida, Texas, New Jersey, Ohio, Massachusetts, Pennsylvania, and Virginia. More than 90 percent live in metropolitan areas, such as Los Angeles, Detroit, New York, Chicago, and Washington DC. According to the US Census Bureau (2003), most second- or third-generation Arab Americans speak English even at home. Forty-five percent of Arab American adults have a bachelor's degree or higher and 18 percent have a graduate degree. In terms of occupation, about 65 percent of Arab American adults are in the labor force; with 5 percent unemployed. Of working Arab Americans, 88 percent work in the private sector and 12 percent as government employees. Whereas 73 percent are employed in managerial, professional, technical, or sales fields, 14 percent work in service jobs. The mean income for Arab American households was $56,331 in 2008, compared to $51,369 for an average national household.

Arab immigration to Canada is relatively recent. According to the statistics of the Canadian government, the number of Arab immigrants reached 350,000 in 2001. More than 80 percent of them live in Ontario and Quebec. Arab immigration to Canada may have been affected by the Canadian immigration policies, which, in Quebec for example, have a French language requirement. More than half of Arab Canadians come from Lebanon (41 percent) and Egypt (12 percent). The remaining immigrants come from Morocco, Syria, Iraq, Algeria, and other Arab countries. However, these numbers may have changed after the Arab Spring. In 2001, 96 percent of the Arab Canadian population reported that they could converse in English and/or French, the two official languages. With respect to education, 30 percent of adult Arab Canadians had either a bachelor's or post-graduate degree, compared to 15 percent of all Canadian adults. Similarly, 10 percent of Arab Canadians had a graduate degree, compared to 5 percent of the overall adult population. In terms of employment, 56 percent of adult Arab Canadians were employed, compared to 62 percent of all Canadian adults.

12.3   Acquisition of Colloquial Arabic

Most heritage speakers of Arabic (henceforth HSAs) are exposed to the colloquial Arabic varieties (CA/L1) spoken by their parents at home. However, they have limited L1 input opportunities outside their homes because their L1 is not used in the societies in which they live. In fact, some may be exposed regularly to the L2 even at home, especially from television and older siblings who may have already learned the L2 (Albirini 2018). By school age, they typically shift to L2 as the primary means of communication outside and sometimes even inside the home (Shiri 2010). Eventually, HSAs become unbalanced bilinguals in the sense that their L2 becomes stronger than their L1.

The existing research suggests that HSAs have a unique L1 system when compared to non-heritage speakers of Arabic (NHSAs, henceforth). NHSAs constitute the baseline against which HSAs are compared in terms of L1 development, ultimate attainment, and aspects of maintenance or attrition. The baseline is also important for any meaningful discussion on L1 acquisition contexts, input and use opportunities, and factors influencing attainment (e.g., L2 transfer). It is difficult to pinpoint the specific properties of their unique L1 system because HSAs vary widely in their language abilities and experiences. Still, the uniqueness of their L1 system is generally based on the fact that they rarely attain native-like proficiency in L1 and on common patterns that characterize some key areas in their L1 systems, including phonetics/phonology, lexicon, morphology, syntax, and sociolinguistic competence, as will be explained in the following subsections.

12.3.1   Phonetics/Phonology and Lexicon

In phonetics/phonology, HSAs may "sound" like NHSAs because of their early exposure to their L1 phonetic and phonological systems. However, existing studies point to subtle differences between HSAs and NHSA. Saadah (2011) examined HSAs' ability to produce vowels situated within monosyllabic words of the pattern CVC, particularly focusing on vowel height and vowel frontness/backness. Both the Arabic short vowels /i, u, a/ and their long counterparts /i:, u:, a:/ were examined. These can be divided into three groups: front vowels /i, i:/, back vowels /u, u:/, and low vowels /a, a:/. Saadah compared vowel production in HSAs versus L2 learners of Arabic and NHSAs. She found that HSAs articulate Arabic vowels in ways distinct from both L2 learners and NHSAs; they developed a hybrid phonetic system. The HSAs' front and back vowels were similar to NHSAs and their low vowels were similar to L2 learners in vowel height. In terms of vowel backness, HSAs were more similar to L2 learners for back vowels and to NHSAs for low vowels.

With respect to the lexicon, the lexical knowledge of HSAs does not seem to be as rich as that of NHSAs. This is critical because our mental lexicons store information that relate to other aspects of language. For example, our information of the verb *put* in English includes knowing that it requires two complements, an NP and PP (e.g., He put the pen in the bag). Albirini (forthcoming) used a picture-naming task to evaluate pre-school heritage children's knowledge of forty common lexical items from their immediate environment. He found that the heritage children who were regularly exposed to English early in their childhood – i.e., before 4 years of age – were able to retrieve significantly fewer words than their monolingual age-matched counterparts. Similar findings were reported by Albirini and Benmamoun (2014), who provided adult HSAs with a list of thirty high-frequency words. The HSAs were able to name only 62 percent of the nouns in the pictures, unlike the NHSAs who performed at ceiling. It is not clear whether these patterns are caused by gaps in lexical knowledge or are merely due to lexical retrieval issues.

HSAs also have difficulties with gender assignment to new/borrowed lexical items.[2] Gender assignment is believed to impact the structure of the lexicon and has implications for lexical representation and processing (see Corbett 1991 for a review). In Arabic, gender assignment for animate nouns (i.e., humans and animals) is largely predictable. An animate noun is masculine or feminine based on its biological sex. Animate singular masculine nouns are not marked for gender, whereas animate singular feminine nouns are usually marked with the –*a(t)* ending,[3] as the contrast between example (3a) and (3b) demonstrates. Unlike animate nouns, inanimate nouns, including abstract nouns, are semantically neither male nor female. Therefore, the gender of inanimate nouns is largely arbitrary. Inanimate singular masculine nouns are not marked for gender, as in (3c). Inanimate singular feminine nouns, however, may or may not have the –*a(t)* ending. When they do, they are called canonical feminine nouns, as in (3d). But when they do not, they are noncanonical feminine nouns, as in (3e).

(3) a. mumarriḍ 'nurse.M'
    b. mumarriḍa 'nurse.F'
    c. baab 'door'
    d. sayyara 'car'
    e. šams 'sun'

Ibrahim (2016) examined gender assignment only to inanimate singular loanwords by three groups: (1) a control group of NHSAs, (2) a first group of HSAs who were either born in Canada or arrived at or before the age of four, and (3) a second group of HSAs who arrived in Canada after the age of four. The participants completed an oral production task (where they had to use borrowed words in sentences), a grammaticality judgment task, a metalinguistic task (where they had to explain their choices), and a translation task. The two groups of HSAs differed from the controls on all tasks. In addition, they demonstrated a strong tendency toward assigning the masculine gender to loanwords, particularly when morphophonological cues were missing (e.g., the feminine ending). The findings also revealed a positive correlation between HSAs' performance and their age of arrival in Canada; those who came late performed better than those who were born or arrived early in Canada.

HSAs also display difficulties in word selection (Albirini et al. 2011; Albirini 2014). For example, possession in Arabic is frequently expressed with various prepositions, including ʕind 'at' and maʕ 'with.' However, whereas ʕind 'at' is used to express a general sense of possession of things and humans, as in (4a), maʕ 'with' is often used to express specific possession of things carried at the

---

[2] Grammatical gender is discussed in this section for organization purposes.
[3] Some singular feminine nouns end in /a:/ or /a:ʔ/.

time of speech, as in (4b). HSAs are not always aware of these subtle distinctions and therefore are not always able to select the correct preposition to reflect the intended meaning (Albirini et al. 2011). For example, in (5), the speaker infelicitously indicates general possession by using the preposition *maʕ* 'with,' which denotes a specific meaning of possession.

(4) a. ʕind-e ʔax
         at-me brother
         'I have a brother.'
     b. maʕ-e daftar
         with-me notebook
         'I have a notebook [on me]'

(5) huwwa   *maʕ-u   matʕam   hoon
     he   *with-him   restaurant here
     "He has a restaurant here." (Albirini et al. 2011: 294)

Difficulties with word selection are sometimes due to the influence of L2 (Albirini and Benmamoun 2014). This appears particularly in the selection of words that have certain uses/meanings in their L2 that are not compatible with their usage in their L1. In (6), for example, the speaker replaces the default relative complementizer *lli* 'that' with the *wh*-word *ween* 'where' after the relativized noun *l-ʕamaara* 'the building.' This sequence results in an ungrammatical sentence because only a relativizer can be used in this case; this sequence is equivalent to the English sentence *Many of my friends live in the building where I live now*. This sentence is not well-formed because *ween* cannot serve as a relativizer in Arabic; it is only a question word, unlike its English equivalent *where*, which can be both a relativizer and a question word.

(6) ktiir min ʔaṣhaab-i ʕaayšiin bi-l-ʕamaara *ween ʔana ʕaayeš halla?
     many of friends-my living   in-the-building where I   living now
     "Many of my friends live in the building where I live now" (Albirini and
     Benmamoun 2014: 264)

Similarly, HSAs face challenges in observing the subcategorization requirements for different lexical items[4] (Albirini et al. 2011; Albirini 2014; Albirini et al. 2019). Verbs, for example, subcategorize for different complements in different languages, and that is why subcategorization rules have been found challenging for heritage and L2 learners cross-linguistically (Albirini et al. 2011; Khatib and Ghannadi 2011; El-Dakhs 2015). A major challenge is the ability to identify whether a noun phrase or prepositional phrase serves as a verb complement. Even when a prepositional phrase is used, it may not be always clear which preposition to use. This is because

---

[4] Although they focus on the syntactic requirements of syntactic categories, subcategorization rules are discussed in this section for organization purposes.

preposition selection is not uniform across languages. In (7), the speaker incorrectly uses a prepositional-phrase argument for the verb *kaabal* 'met,' which requires a noun-phrase complement in Palestinian Arabic.

(7) kaabalt *maʕ ktiir naas . . . ktiir ṭəllaab ʕarab w-məslimiin. . .
     met.1S with many people many students Arab and-Muslim . . .
     "I met with many people . . . many Arab and Muslim students . . . "
     (Albirini, 2014: 743)

Overall, it is clear that HSAs differ from NHSAs in terms of their phonetics/phonology, lexical knowledge, word selection, and word subcategorization requirements.

12.3.2 Morphology and Syntax

Morphology is another area that demonstrates the uniqueness of HSAs' L1 system. Arabic has a rich morphological system in its derivation and inflectional forms. Arabic morphology utilizes two strategies, concatenative and non-concatenative. The concatenative strategy involves the affixation of morphemes to a stem, as in (8) where the plural suffix *–iin* is attached to the right edge of the singular stem *mudarres* 'teacher' to generate the plural noun *mudarresiin* 'teachers.' Unlike the concatenative strategy, the non-concatenative mode involves significant internal modifications in the stem. It is widely believed that it requires isolating a consonantal root and then mapping it on a vocalic template (McCarthy and Prince 1990). In (9), the plural noun *quluub* 'heart' is derived from the singular stem *qalb* by identifying the root *qlb* and then mapping it on the template CuCuuC.

(8) *mudarres* 'teacher.m' → *mudarresiin* 'teachers.m'
(9) *qalb* 'heart' → *quluub* 'hearts'

With respect to inflectional morphology, the existing studies suggest that HSAs diverge from NHSAs in the areas of agreement morphology, plural morphology, and dual morphology (Albirini et al. 2011; Albirini et al. 2013; Albirini and Benmamoun 2014; Albirini 2015, 2018). Arabic verb agreement is complex as it involves person (realized as a prefix) and gender and number (realized as a suffix), whereas adjectival agreement is less complex because it involves the addition of a single gender-number suffix, as examples (10a, b) illustrate.

(10) a. l-ulaad   yi-sbaḥ-o
          the-children 3.swim.MP
          "The children swim.'
      b. wlaad   sariiʕ-iin
          children   fast.MP
          'fast children.'

Albirini, Benmamoun, and Chakrani (2013) found that subject–verb agreement morphology is more maintained in HSAs than noun–adjective morphology. They attributed this asymmetry to various factors, including the early age of acquiring verbs, their high frequency, and their centrality to the sentence. The participants did particularly well on morphologically simple agreement paradigms, such as the singular masculine, but did not perform as well on semantically marked forms, such as inanimate plurals. This suggests that morphological and semantic factors are also involved in the attrition of agreement morphology in HA. Subject–verb agreement seems to be more challenging for HSAs in the VSO word order in particular, possibly because this word order is not employed in their dominant L2 (Albirini et al. 2011).

Benmamoun, Albirini, Montrul, and Saadah (2014) report that HSAs are not as accurate as NHSAs in plural formation. Arabic plurals can be *sound/regular* or *broken/irregular* depending on whether they are formed through concatenative or non-concatenative morphology (as in (8) and (9), respectively). HSAs have greater difficulty with broken plurals than with sound plurals. Moreover, they extend representationally simple and frequent plurals – such as sound feminine plurals – to other plural forms. The overgeneralization of representationally simple and unmarked morphemes is a strategy often observed in monolingual Arabic-speaking children (Clyne 1992; Omar 1973; Ravid and Farah 1999; Albirini 2015). Regarding dual morphology, Albirini (2014) reports that many HSAs form dual nouns not by the suffix *–een*, as NHSAs do, but by a "number + noun" construction, as in (11). This pattern is attributed to transfer effects from English, the dominant language.

(11)   ʕindi *tnein zamiil   fi nafs   š-ša??a
        at-me two roommate in same the-apartment
        "I have two roommates in the same apartment." (Egyptian speaker,
        Albirini 2014: 741)

Derivational morphology is more complex because it involves generating open-class words through numerous roots and patterns (Wright 1988; Ratcliffe 1998). For example, the *masdar* – often translated as 'verbal nouns' – can be derived from the most basic verb pattern CaCaCa using more than forty templates[5] (Wright 1988). Derivational morphology is therefore more challenging to HSAs. Albirini and Benmamoun (2014) tested HSAs' ability to derive verbal nouns from verbs and vice versa, using two sentence-completion tasks. They focused on four common verb patterns (CaCaCa; CaCCaCa; CaaCaCa; and CiCCaCaCa) and their corresponding nominal templates. The selected verb patterns differed in their frequency and predictability. The authors found that HSAs were better at deriving verbs from verbal nouns than deriving verbal nouns from verbs, possibly because verbs are more frequent yet representationally less complex.

---

[5] Much of the existing work on derivational morphology has focused on SA because of its rich morphological system, but most of these patterns also exist in CA.

Frequency was a better predictor of the participants' accuracy scores on both tasks than predictability.

As for syntax, the literature suggests that HSAs possess robust knowledge of certain core aspects of their L1 syntax, such as word order (Bos 1997; Albirini et al. 2011; Albirini and Benmamoun 2014, 2015). However, they still find difficulties with other syntactic structures as well as interface relations between syntax and other domains. For example, Albirini et al. (2011) report that HSAs rely heavily on the SVO word order in their narratives even when the VSO is contextually and pragmatically more appropriate. This could be due to the influence of English, which deploys the SVO order exclusively. Similarly, Al Qahtani and Sabourin (2015) compared HSAs in Ottawa (Canada) to their parents and a group of NHSAs from Saudi Arabia with respect to their preference of SVO and VSO word orders. Significant differences were found among the three groups, with the HSAs having the least preference for the VSO order, which the author attributes to L2 effects.

HSAs are reported to use overt pronominals in sentences that pragmatically prefer a pro-drop strategy, unlike NHSAs who opt for drop pronominals extensively (Albirini et al. 2011). This again may be attributed to L2 effects, because English is an overt-pro language. HSAs also face challenges in establishing long-distance dependencies between antecedents and their location in restrictive relative clauses (Albirini and Benmamoun 2014). In (12), for instance, a resumptive pronoun is missing after the verb *saʔal* 'ask,' where it is required to mark the position of the antecedent *l-təlaati* 'the three' in the relativized clause.

(12)   miš mətzakkr-a   šu   hummi l-təlaati   lli   saʔal__
        Neg. remembering. SF what they   the-three that asked. 3SM
        "I do not remember what the three things that he asked [for] are"
        (Albirini and Benmamoun 2014: 266)

Albirini and Benmamoun (2014) examined sentential negation in Egyptian HSAs. Egyptian Arabic deploys two negation forms: the discontinuous *maa-š*, which merges with the verbal head, and the non-discontinuous *miš*, which is realized as an independent negation particle. The discontinuous form *maa-š* is used in present tense, past tense, and imperative sentences, whereas the non-discontinuous *miš* is used in verbless and future-tense sentences. The authors found that HSAs had a strong command of the location of negation and its configurational properties, but encountered difficulties in specific aspects of sentential negation, such as merger with lexical heads and dependency relations. In (13), for example, the speaker infelicitously uses the non-discontinuous particle *miš* instead of the discontinuous *ma-š*, which requires merger of sentential negation with the verbal head in this past tense sentence.

(13)   huwwa *miš raaḥ l-kaftiria
       He   Neg went the-cafeteria
       "He did not go to the cafeteria." (Albirini and Benmamoun,
       2015: 483)

In general, HSAs seem to have clear gaps in their inflectional and derivational morphology, and these gaps become more visible in forms that are
derived non-concatenatively. Their syntax seems to be more maintained,
but gaps still appear in complex relations (e.g., dependencies & mergers)
and syntax interfaces with other domains.

12.3.3 Sociolinguistic Competence

Sociolinguistic competence refers to the ability to use language in socially
appropriate ways. Proper language usage requires observing key dimensions of context, such as the background of the interlocutor/audience,
type of interaction, setting, occasion, and relevant social norms. For
Arabic speakers, it also involves the ability to use CA and SA for their
socially acceptable functions and within their commonly acceptable
contexts.

 Research analyzing adult HSAs' connected speech suggests that they
encounter difficulties in producing extended stretches of discourse in CA/
L1, particularly in tasks involving narratives and story-telling (Elsaadany
2003; Othman 2006; Albirini et al. 2011; Benmamoun et al. 2013; Albirini
2014; Albirini and Chakrani 2017). Thus, they may switch to English and
occasionally SA to be able to complete such tasks. However, they are
generally successful in inserting the switched elements using CA as the
matrix language. In (14), for example, the speaker embeds the noun–
adjective combination *high school* felicitously after the determiner *el* 'the'
to create a complete DP and then correctly places this DP, that is *el high
school*, in an argument position for the transitive verb *baḥib* 'I like.' The fact
that the switched elements are often embedded correctly in CA-structured
sentences shows that HSAs have good command of the basic structure of
their L1.

(14)   kint   baḥib   el ...   baḥib   el *high school*
       was.1S.   ASP-like.1S. the   ASP-like.1S. the high school
       "I used to like the high school." (Albirini et al. 2011: 296)

(15)   ḥadθə-t   l-ʔəṣṣa   ʔabl   sini   taʕriiban
       occurred.3S   the-story   before   year   almost
       "The story occurred almost a year ago." (Albirini and Chakrani 2017:
       325)

(16)   bazuur   ʔusrit-i   f-Cleveland,   bas   miš   frequently
       visit.1s   family-my   in-Cleveland,   but   Neg   frequently
       "I visit my family in Cleveland, but not frequently." (Albirini, 2014: 744)

HSAs differ from NHSAs in an important respect, namely, their codeswitching does not seem to fulfil well-defined social or pragmatic purposes. For example, when they switch to SA, HSAs sometimes use SA elements that are both thematically and situationally inappropriate to informal narratives (Albirini 2014; Albirini and Chakrani 2017). In (15), the speaker starts the sentence with the SA verb ḥadθət 'occurred.3S' and completes the sentence in CA. Although the verb is inserted felicitously within the CA sentence, the introduction of the SA verb does not serve clear sociolinguistic or pragmatic functions in this sentence. This pattern of codeswitching is uncharacteristic of NHSAs, who switch from CA to SA to attain specific social and pragmatic goals (see Holes 1993; Saeed 1997; Albirini 2011). In addition, HSAs incorporate technical and nontechnical terms from English, which is uncharacteristic of NHSAs. In (16), a heritage Egyptian speaker resorts to the English word *frequently*, although its CA equivalent kətiir is common and nontechnical. Thus, the purpose of this switch is not clear. Moreover, the combination of elements from CA, SA, and English in short pieces of discourse is somewhat unique to HSAs. It seems that switching to English or SA allows HSAs to overcome processing delays or to retrieve lexical items that are infrequent or less accessible. This may explain the fact that HSAs typically shift to English or SA at the sub-word, word, or phrase levels (as in the examples in this section), whereas NHSAs switch more often at the sentence and discourse levels.

Albirini and Chakrani (2017) explored HSAs' ability to use CA, SA, and English in the construction of narratives of personal experience. This study compared and contrasted HSAs' narratives with respect to codes, registers, and functions. Fifteen Arabic and fifteen English narratives from five participants, fluent in both Arabic and English, were examined. The results revealed that, despite their fluency, the participants lacked the sociolinguistic competence to socially and pragmatically deploy CA and SA appropriately in their narratives. In the Arabic narratives, respondents alternated between CA and SA, but they were not always able to maintain the asymmetrical functions of CA and SA. English was used mainly as a compensation strategy. In the English narratives, participants switched parsimoniously to Arabic for fillers and culturally specific terms and expressions. Moreover, they displayed a greater register control based on the events in their narratives. This indicates that HSAs are more sociolinguistically skilled in narrating in English than in CA.

Overall, HSAs' L1 use in connected discourse is different from that of NHSAs. The patterns they display in language use may be due to the fact that they are removed from the diglossic context and Arab speech communities that may act as points of reference for sociolinguistically proper language use, as will be explained in Section 12.5.

12.4   Acquisition of Standard Arabic

As noted earlier, Arabic is a diglossic language in the sense that it has two language varieties that are historically linked yet are different in some respects related to social functions, contexts of use, and structure. This means that speakers of Arabic should know the two varieties of Arabic to be fully functional users of Arabic. Their competencies in both CA and SA would allow them to interact with other speakers of Arabic on a daily basis; read and write about different topics; listen and understand news reports; and engage in a wide array of communicative, functional, and social activities. Unlike the NHSAs in the Arab region, however, HSAs are not as familiar with SA as they are with CA due to factors surrounding its use and status in the communities in which they live (Albirini et al. 2019). First, SA is not a language to which they are exposed naturally from their parents early in childhood. Second, it is not used in everyday interactions and communications inside or outside the home, which means that their chances of getting exposed to SA are minimal. Third, it lacks any official status in the societies in which they live, and thus it is not used in social institutions, official communications, publications, or media. This means that HSAs have far fewer opportunities for SA input inside and outside the home. Thus, acquiring SA is not supported by naturalistic exposure, contextual factors, or societal demands.

Because it is not acquired naturally in the home or in other societal domains, SA is typically learned as a new language, typically after HSAs have already learned the colloquial varieties of their parents (L1) and the socially dominant language (L2). In other words, SA represents an L3 for HSAs; it is usually learned formally through dedicated study. This may explain why many HSAs come to college SA classrooms to learn or enhance their abilities in SA. However, this presents a challenge to many HSAs and teachers for various reasons (Alabd 2016; Habbal 2017). For one, many HSAs underestimate the differences between SA and CA and/or overestimate the overlap between SA and CA. At the same time, they often feel anxious due to teacher expectations; some teachers assume that HSAs are not very different from NHSAs because they may sound like them and/or because of their cultural background (Alghothani 2010).

One of the questions often raised with regard to learning SA is whether HSAs are (dis)similar to L2 learners. The existing studies suggest that HSAs have an advantage over L2 learners in certain areas of SA. Albirini and Benmamoun (2015) report that both HSAs and L2 learners had better knowledge of sound than broken plural morphology. Sound plurals are simpler because they are formed by attaching a plural morpheme to the right edge of the singular stem (e.g., *muhandis* 'engineer' ➔ *muhandisiin* 'engineers'), whereas the formation of broken plurals typically involves internal changes to the singular stem using different templates (e.g., *kitaab* 'book' ➔ *kutub* 'books'). However, whereas L2 learners had unbalanced performance on sound versus broken plurals, the HSAs displayed difficulties mainly with forms that are acquired late by monolingual children, such as plurals with geminated and defective roots (e.g., θawr ➔ θiiraan 'bulls' and ṣaff ➔ ṣufuuf 'classes'). With regard to the default strategy, HSAs resorted to the language-specific default form, namely the sound feminine, whereas L2 learners opted for the sound masculine, which is likely a case of adhering to a universal tendency.

HSAs' SA phonetics/phonology is also superior to that of L2 learners. Sanker (2016) compared HSAs' perception of SA consonants to L2 learners of SA and NHSAs. SA consonants were placed in stimuli of two forms: CV and ʔVC. Masking noise was introduced simultaneously with the stimuli. The findings revealed that HSAs possessed better mean accuracy than L2 learners with respect to identifying the correct sound segments, particularly those involving pharyngeals. They did better than their L2 counterparts even on sounds with English analogs (e.g., /da:/). However, HSAs and L2 learners did worse than the NHSAs on gutturals. Expectedly, there was much variability in the accuracies of the HSAs and L2 learners but not the NHSAs.

HSAs appear to have an edge over L2 learners of SA even in areas with no surface overlap between SA and CA, such as sentential negation. Albirini (2015) examined the acquisition of sentential negation by beginner- and advanced-level HSAs and L2 learners of SA. Sentential negation is an area where SA and CA differ noticeably. To illustrate the difference, whereas SA uses five different negation particles, including *laa, maa, lam, laysa,* and *lan,* most CA dialects use only two, such as *maa-š* and *miš*. Whereas SA negation cannot merge with the verbal head, it does so in CA negation involving *maa-š*. Albirini found that HSAs have stronger command of SA sentential negation than L2 learners only in beginner SA courses. This means that they enter SA classrooms with an edge over their L2 counterparts, which may be due to their incidental exposure to SA through Sunday school, electronic media, print media, and other informal venues. However, the advanced HSAs did not perform significantly better than their L2 counterparts. The fact that they were not able to retain the advantage they had in beginner SA courses may be due to the lack of learning materials and strategies targeting HSAs in particular and taking their linguistic background into account.

A second question focuses on the impact of CA and English on the acquisition of SA. The main line of inquiry here is whether and how HSAs are influenced negatively or positively by their previous linguistic experiences. Albirini, Saadah, and Alhawary (2019) addressed this question by comparing HSAs and L2 learners with respect to three linguistic areas:

definite article use, verb subcategorization rules, and negation of verbless, present tense and past tense sentences. They also investigated the role of typological and structural proximity in transfer from these two previously acquired languages. The participants completed three written tasks, each focusing on one of the researched areas. The study reports that CA plays a positive role in HSAs' acquisition of SA, particularly in forms shared by SA and CA. For example, HSAs benefited from their previous knowledge of CA in terms of definite-article and verb-subcategorization use. The negative influence of CA was limited to specific forms in which SA and CA diverge, such as verbless negation. By contrast, English seemed to play largely a negative role for both the HSAs and L2 learners. The researchers argue that typological and structural proximity plays a positive role in transfer to SA.

A third question relevant to HSAs' acquisition of SA concerns the role of Arabic programs in enhancing HSAs' literacy skills in SA. Abu Rabia and Siegel (2002) examined the reading and language skills of Arab-Canadian children aged between 9 and 14 years. The participants had English as the language of instruction at school, but they also attended a Heritage Language Program where they were taught to read and write in SA for 3 hours weekly. The children completed word and pseudo-word reading tests as well as spelling, orthographic, cloze, and visual tests in Arabic and English. Most of the participants showed "adequate proficiency" in SA in the sense that they did not encounter major difficulties in reading in SA. No significant differences were found between the HSAs and monolingual English-speaking children with respect to English language skills. This shows that HSAs may benefit from programs focusing on reading and writing in SA without affecting their English language skills.

Overall, the existing studies reveal that HSAs enter beginner SA classes with an advantage over L2 learners, particularly in areas shared by CA and SA. However, they lose this advantage as they advance in their study of SA, possibly because the learning materials and teaching methods are targeted primarily to L2 learners. Heritage language programs may help advance HSAs' literacy skills in SA without affecting their skills in L2.

12.5   Factors Affecting the Acquisition, Development, and Loss/Maintenance of Heritage Arabic

The study of factors at play in Heritage Arabic (HA) acquisition, development, and maintenance/attrition is an integral part of the study of HA as it is necessary to explain the notable variability in the attainment of HSAs. For organizational purposes, I classify these factors into three main categories: (1) sociolinguistic, (2) socio-contextual, and (3) socio-affective. Sociolinguistic factors here refer mainly to linguistic input and use opportunities and the coexistence of a dominant language.[6] Socio-contextual factors highlight issues related to the social context and communities in which HSAs live. Socio-affective factors have to do with affective factors that are held commonly by speech communities rather than by individual speakers, such as language attitudes and identity sentiments.

12.5.1 Sociolinguistic Factors

HA is influenced by its status as a minority language. In the United States and Canada, Arabic lacks official status or social support, unlike English/French, which is required for educational and economic success and is used in various social spheres. It is not surprising, therefore, that most HSAs rely heavily on L2 due to its social and functional importance. Because Arabic is neither needed nor required in the public domain, many HSAs and their parents prioritize the acquisition and use of L2 over Arabic (Martin 2009).

Although most HSAs may start using L2 outside the home (e.g., at school), their use of English/French eventually leaks into the home, possibly because it becomes cognitively more accessible to them. Suleiman (1999) reports that 75 percent of all Arab Americans speak English "very well," and the majority of them use it regularly inside and outside their homes. The fact that L2 replaces Arabic in everyday interactions even with parents and family members is a factor in L1 attrition among HSAs. Albirini (2014) examined factors that may be responsible for HSAs' variable proficiency levels in HA, including L1 use, L1 input, language attitudes, ethnic identity sentiments, family role, community support, school experience, and demographics. Proficiency in HA was found to correlate positively with L1 use, L1 input, family role, community support, and parents' L1. However, language use (in terms of frequency, range, and contexts) was the main predictor of the variability in HA proficiency.

The onset age of L2 acquisition plays a critical role in the maintenance or attrition of HA. Heritage children who are systematically exposed to L2 at a very early age are less likely to develop/maintain their L1 than those who are exposed to L2 later in their childhood. Albirini (2018) investigated the impact of exposure to English on the development of HA as an L1. Three groups of HA children aged between 5;3 and 5;9 years were compared to age-matched monolingual Arabic-speaking children. All children were exposed to Arabic from birth. However, the first group was also exposed systematically to English before the age of 3 years, and the second group between the ages of 3 and 5, whereas the third group were not exposed to

---

[6] In its most common use, the term "sociolinguistic factors" refers to a wide array of social and contextual factors that are associated with language and its various uses. However, as indicated in this section, here it is used to refer to specific aspects related to the status, acquisition, and use of language.

English at the time of data collection. Systematic exposure referred to hearing L2 on a regular basis from a source with which heritage children have direct daily contact, such as parents, siblings, relatives, caregivers, teachers, and peers. The participants completed three oral tasks targeting subject–verb agreement, plural morphology, and relative clauses. The findings revealed significant differences among the groups, except between the NHSAs and the group of HSAs that had not been exposed to English at the time of the study. Multiple regression analysis pointed to age of L2 exposure as a significant predictor of L1 accuracy.

The attrition of HA has also to do with the limited L1 input that HSAs receive on daily basis. For example, Albirini (2015a) investigated the role of variable input in the acquisition of subject–verb and adjective–noun agreement morphology by HA children. Input was quantified by a questionnaire focusing on the amount, richness, and sources of input HA children receive from (1) family members, (2) peers, (3) community, (4) television, (5) electronic media, and (6) print media (e.g., stories). The author found that HA children receive their L1 input mainly from parents. HA children varied in their command of verbal and adjectival morphology, and this variability was positively correlated with the amount of input they had from different input sources. However, input affected the linguistic forms differently. Forms that are marked, less frequent, and morphologically complex were negatively more influenced by input limitations than unmarked, frequent, and morphologically simple ones. This indicates that input alone does not explain language attrition and therefore other factors seem also to be at play.

Overall, it seems that the maintenance or attrition of HA is influenced by its status as a minority language, which means that HSAs feel no pressure or need to use it on regular basis. The limited input and use opportunities that HSAs receive in L1 are another factor in its maintenance or attrition.

12.5.2 Socio-contextual Factors

Six interrelated socio-contextual dimensions need to be considered when examining the maintenance and attrition of HA: (1) the sociopolitical situation of Arabic speakers in North America, (2) the reduced social value of Arabic, (3) the diglossic situation of Arabic, (4) the lack of close-knit and strong Arabic-speaking communities, (5) the role of family, and (6) the lack of community support.

HA is influenced by the sociopolitical situation of Arabic speakers in North America. In the aftermath of the September 11 tragedy, people of Arab descent have endured assaults, vandalism, threats, hate speech, ethnic slurs, harassment, and discrimination. In some cases, they were discriminated against merely because they spoke Arabic or read Arabic books

(Suleiman 2016). These struggles may deter some HSAs from using Arabic in public.

Arabic lacks the global value and appeal that English/French has in North America and worldwide. Although Arabic ranks sixth among world languages in terms of the number of native speakers, its use is significantly limited outside the Arabic region. Some HSAs may not need to use Arabic even when communicating with relatives in their parents' countries (Albirini 2014). The fact that Arabic has less utilitarian value than English/French may make it less appealing to HSAs, and this often translates into less motivation to learn or maintain it. This is compounded by the fact that Arabic is often perceived to be difficult to learn, which further lessens its appeal to them (Shiri 2010).

The fact that Arabic is a diglossic language impacts its maintenance. HSAs who may be interested in developing proficiency in Arabic have to divide their learning efforts between SA and CA. Even if they decide to learn the two varieties of Arabic, HSAs live in a context where diglossia does not materialize functionally in their daily social lives because the range of contexts in which CA and SA are used is limited. Thus, the social environment in which they live puts socio-contextual constraints on their Arabic-learning experience.

Another factor affecting HA maintenance or attrition is the lack of close-knit and strong Arabic-speaking communities in North America. A speech community is a group of individuals who share a language and rules for its use and interpretation in context (Gumperz 1972; Hymes 1972). A speech community serves as both a source of language input and a platform for language use for its members. HSAs do not live in unified Arabic-speaking communities. Arab speakers are scattered and separated not only by geographical distance but also by their diverse dialects, dissimilar backgrounds, and degree of assimilation into their broader North American societies (Sarroub 2005). The communities in which HSAs live may not serve as bases for Arabic input and use or for learning the norms of language use. It is not surprising therefore that HSAs often use English, rather than Arabic, in their interpersonal and social interactions (Shiri 2010).

North American Arab communities generally lack institutions that support the learning and use of Arabic. Sunday school is the main community-based venue where HSAs may have the chance to interact in HA (Albirini 2016; Shalaby 2017). However, HSAs rarely use or learn HA in Sunday schools because these schools are designed for both Arab and non-Arab Muslim children. In most Sunday schools, Classical Arabic is taught mainly to give Muslim children the ability to read the Qur'an, the Muslim holy book (Jaspal and Coyle 2010). However, existing research shows that Sunday school experience has little impact on HSAs' L1 skills (Albirini 2014). Private

"Arabic schools" exist in some large cities, but ironically the language of instruction is English. Classical Arabic is taught in most of these schools, with reading religious texts being the main focus of study. HSAs may meet in religious centers (mosques and churches). But, again, English remains the main medium of communication in these meeting places because of the diverse linguistic backgrounds of the attendees.

The negative effect of socio-contextual factors on HA maintenance is mitigated by the role of HSAs' families. The literature suggests that the majority of Arab parents view Arabic as an asset that connects HSAs to their parents' culture and history. For example, Martin (2009) reports that parents engage in various practices to retain Arabic in their children. Racism was not found to be significantly associated with the parents' language maintenance efforts. Similar results were reported by Rouchdy (2013), who indicated that her participants viewed their parents' support as a main motive for studying and speaking Arabic. Likewise, Seymour-Jorn (2007) found that the majority of heritage students were learning Arabic under pressure from their families.

In general, HSAs do not have access to the diglossic context and speech communities that NHSAs have. They are also influenced by the lack of social institutions that support Arabic. While these socio-contextual factors play a detrimental role in maintaining HA, Arab parents provide support that helps in limiting the attrition of HA among their children.

12.5.3 Socio-affective Factors

Three socio-affective factors are here considered in relation to the maintenance and attrition of HA, including HSAs' (1) attitudes toward HA, (2) identity sentiments, and (3) religious affiliation and practices.

Language attitudes have been widely recognized as an important indicator of language maintenance or loss in language contact situations (Fishman 1991; Crawford 2000; Ricento 2005; Wilson 2013). People's positive attitudes toward their language often motivate them to acquire it and put it to use in their social lives. By contrast, negative attitudes lead to indifference to the language in terms of acquisition, use, and status. Existing studies on HSAs show that they have favorable attitudes toward Arabic more for its symbolic value than for its communicative or utilitarian value. Rouchdy (2013) reports that out of seventy-nine participants in her study, seventy-four indicated that "Arabic is very important to them" (145). In Kenny (1992), HSAs ascribe their positive attitudes to the importance of Arabic for reading religious texts, understanding Arabic culture and literature, and interacting with family and community members. HSAs' attitudes toward Arabic have been found to correlate positively with their proficiency in L1; those with favorable attitudes toward their L1 have higher proficiency than those who do not, and vice versa (Albirini 2014).

HA is also influenced by identity dynamics in the societies where HSAs live. Since 2001, the consistent negative stereotyping of Arabs by media and politicians has prompted many Arab Americans/Canadians to recall their Arab identity (Haddad 2004; Abdelhady 2014). This has led many HSAs to re-establish the link between the Arabic language and their cultural and historical roots, which is apparent in the sharp increase in the number of HSAs taking college-level Arabic courses since 2001 (Husseinali 2006; Allen 2007; Almubayei 2007; Seymour-Jorn 2007; Carreira and Kagan 2011). The majority of these students take Arabic courses for identity-related reasons (Kenny 1992; Rouchdy 1992, 2013; Seymour-Jorn 2007). Community-focused studies also show that both Arab American parents and children view Arabic as an integral part of their heritage identity (Almubayei 2007; Bitar 2009; Bale 2010). Thus, HSAs and their parents recognize the interdependence of their heritage identity and the preservation of Arabic.

The Arabic language has historically been a symbol of Muslim identity because it is the language of Qur'an and Islamic liturgy (Rouchdy 2013). The religious significance of Arabic in the daily lives of practicing Muslims creates an aura of veneration to the Arabic language among people of this faith, including many HSAs. This impels many practicing Muslims to learn Arabic, particularly Classical Arabic, the language of the Qur'an. Based on her study of first and second-generation Arab Americans in Arizona, Almubayei (2007) identified religion as the main motive for learning Arabic among HSAs. Seymour-Jorn (2004) and Temple (2013) found that many of their participants embrace Arabic as a marker of their religious identity and display its value for them by using it within their families and communities.[7] Non-Muslim Arabs, however, may be less emotionally attached to Arabic as it is not integral to their religious texts and practices. For example, Dweik (1997) reports a notable shift away from the use of Arabic in the social life of Christian Lebanese in Buffalo, New York. In explaining this shift, Dweik suggests that "it had no religious or nationalistic value for these Lebanese" (117).

HSAs' awareness of the link between the Arabic language and their Arab roots and Muslim affiliation increases their desire to learn Arabic and maintain a functional proficiency in it (Seymour-Jorn 2007; Almubayei 2007; Bale 2010; Gogonas 2011; Gomaa 2011; Rouchdy 2013). Studies have shown that the language–identity nexus correlates positively with HSAs' L1 abilities and use. For example, Qawasmeh (2011) reports that Arabic speakers in Vancouver (Canada) use Arabic in various social spheres, thus

---

[7] Similar findings were reported about HSAs in Europe (García-Sánchez 2010; Gogonas 2011; Ouassini 2013).

showing the vitality of Arabic in their lives. This is attributed to their sense of Arab identity and positive attitudes toward Arabic. Albirini (2014a) found that HSAs' attitudes toward Arabic and feelings of heritage identity were positively related to HA input, which correlated with both their HA usage and proficiency. Bitar (2009) indicates that Palestinian HSAs consider Palestinian Arabic as an important marker of their identity, which explains their keenness to acquire Arabic, use it, and pass it from one generation to another.

Overall, HSAs' favorable attitudes toward Arabic may be critical for limiting the attrition of their HA. Another socio-affective factor that plays a positive role in HA maintenance is Arab speakers' strong sense of Arab and Muslim identity. Religious practices also contribute to the maintenance of HA.

12.6   Conclusion and Future Directions

Due to the complex situation of Arabic in North America, HSAs develop a unique L1 system that differs from that of NHSAs in various aspects, including phonetics/phonology, lexicon, morphology, syntax, and proper language use. HSAs' L1 system also appears to be influenced in certain respects by the dominant L2. Moreover, unlike NHSAs, HSAs acquire SA as an L3, usually in formal settings after they have already acquired CA in the home and English from school and peers. Nonetheless, HSAs display an edge over L2 learners of SA because of their incidental exposure to SA and the overlap between SA and CA.

The evolution of HSAs' L1 system is influenced by different sociolinguistic, socio-contextual, and socio-affective factors. Arabic coexists with English, the dominant language in North America and worldwide, which puts Arabic at a disadvantage with respect to societal value and use. HSAs grow up in societies where diglossia and Arabic-speaking communities are lacking and firsthand experience with L1 use in context is restricted. These sociolinguistic and socio-contextual limitations affect HSAs' ability to hear and use HA, which in turn impacts their ultimate attainments in L1. However, HA is sustained by important factors, including HSAs' positive attitudes toward Arabic, family support, and the link between their L1 and Arab and Muslim identities. It is because of these factors that Arabic is likely to persist in the sociolinguistic lives of HSAs in North America (Bale 2010; Rouchdy 2013).

While the literature on HSAs has been growing significantly, there are, as this overview suggests, a few understudied areas in HA research. One area that needs further investigation is phonetics/phonology. HSAs are typically able to understand their parents and sometimes sound like NHSAs, but how much they understand Arabic and how phonetically and phonologically close they are to NHSAs is not entirely clear. The literature also lacks in-depth studies on the role of specific social factors in the maintenance or attrition of HA among different HA groups. For example, little is known about the impact of Arabic schooling on the maintenance of Arabic in HSAs. Another area that merits investigation is classroom research on HSAs. Most of the existing studies on HA learners of SA have focused on the acquisition of the formal features of SA. More studies are needed to examine the dynamics of classrooms containing both HSAs and L2 learners and how this affects their SA-learning experiences.

References

Abdelhady, D. 2014. The Sociopolitical History of Arabs in the United States: Assimilation, Ethnicity, and Global Citizenship. In S. C. Nassar-McMillan, K. J. Ajrouch, and J. Hakim-Larson (eds.), *Biopsychosocial Perspectives on Arab Americans*. New York: Springer, 17–43.

Abu-Rabia, S. and L. S. Siegel. 2002. Reading, Syntactic, Orthographic, and Working Memory Skills of Bilingual Arabic-English Speaking Canadian Children. *Journal of Psycholinguistic Research* 31(6), 661–678.

Ahmad, N. B. 2014. The Islamic Influence in (Pre-)Colonial and Early America: A Historico-Legal Snapshot. *Seattle Journal for Social Justice* 12(3), 919–945.

Alabd, A. 2016. Heritage Language Learners in L2 Arabic Classes: Challenges and Instructional Strategies. Doctoral thesis, The American University in Cairo.

Albirini, A. 2011. The Sociolinguistic Functions of Codeswitching between Standard Arabic and Dialectal Arabic. *Language in Society* 40, 537–562.

Albirini, A. 2014a. Toward Understanding the Variability in the Language Proficiencies of Arabic Heritage Speakers. *International Journal of Bilingualism* 18(6), 730–765.

Albirini, A. 2014b. The Socio-Pragmatics of Dialectal Codeswitching by the Al-'Keidaat Bedouin Speakers. *Intercultural Pragmatics* 11(1), 121–147.

Albirini, A. 2015a. The Role of Varied Input in the Divergent Outcomes of Heritage Language Acquisition. In E. Grillo and K. Jepson (ed.), *The 39th Annual Boston University Conference on Language Development*. Somerville, MA: Cascadilla Press, 27–39.

Albirini, A. 2015b. The Role of the Colloquial Varieties in the Acquisition of The Standard Variety: The Case of Arabic Heritage Speakers. *Foreign Language Annals* 47(3), 447–363.

Albirini, A. 2015c. Factors Affecting the Acquisition of Plural Morphology in Jordanian Arabic. *Journal of Child Language* 42(4), 734–762.

Albirini, A. 2016. *Modern Arabic Sociolinguistics: Diglossia, Codeswitching, Attitudes, and Identity*. London: Routledge.

Albirini, A. 2018. The Role of Exposure to English in the Development of Arabic as a Heritage Language. *Language Acquisition* 25(2), 178–196.

Albirini, A. Forthcoming. *The Acquisition of Arabic as a First Language*. London and New York: Routledge.

Albirini, A. 2019. Why Standard Arabic Is Not a L2 for Arabic Speakers. *Al-Arabiyya* 52, 49–71.

Albirini, A. and E. Benmamoun. 2014. Aspects of Second Language Transfer in the Oral Production of Egyptian and Palestinian Heritage Speakers. *International Journal of Bilingualism* 18(3), 244–273.

Albirini, A. and E. Benmamoun. 2015. Factors Affecting the Retention of Sentential Negation in Heritage Egyptian Arabic. *Bilingualism: Language and Cognition* 18(3), 470–489.

Albirini, A. and B. Chakrani. 2017. Switching Codes and Registers: An Analysis of Heritage Arabic Speakers' Sociolinguistic Competence. *International Journal of Bilingualism* 21(3), 317–339.

Albirini. A., E. Benmamoun, and B. Chakrani. 2013. Gender and Number Agreement in the Oral Production of Arabic Heritage Speakers. *Bilingualism: Language and Cognition* 16(1), 1–18.

Albirini, A., E. Benmamoun, and E. Saadah. 2011. Grammatical Features of Egyptian and Palestinian Arabic Heritage Speakers' Oral Production. *Studies in Second Language Acquisition* 33, 273–303.

Albirini, A., E. Saadah, and M. Alhawary. 2019. L1 and L2 Transfer to L3 in L3 and L2 Learners of Standard Arabic. *Linguistic Approaches to Bilingualism*. Published online first: https://benjamins.com/online/lab/articles/lab.18013.alb.

Alford, T. 2007. *Prince among Slaves*. Oxford: Oxford University Press.

Alghothani, D. 2010. Foreign Language Anxiety in an Intermediate Arabic Reading Course: A Comparison of Heritage and Foreign Language Learners. Doctoral thesis, The Ohio State University.

Allen, R. 2007. Arabic – "Flavor of the Moment": Whence, Why, and How? *Modern Language Journal* 91(2), 258–261.

Almubayei, D. 2007. Language and the Shaping of the Arab-American Identity. *UTA Working Papers in Linguistics* 2, 91–119.

Al Qahtani, S. and L. Sabourin. 2015. Syntactic Processing of Subjects in Different Word Orders in Arabic: Do Arabic Heritage Speakers Differ from Native Speakers When Processing SVO/VSO? *Proceedings of the 2015 Annual Conference of the Canadian Linguistic Association*. Retrieved from http://cla-acl.ca/wp-content/uploads/AlQahtani_Sabourin-2015.pdf

Aoun, J., E. Benmamoun, and L. Choueiri. 2010. *Arabic Syntax*. Cambridge: Cambridge University Press.

Bale, J., 2010. Arabic as a Heritage Language in the United States. *International Multilingual Research Journal* 4(2), 125–151.

Benmamoun, E. 2000. *The Feature Structure of Functional Categories*. New York: Oxford University Press.

Benmamoun, E., S. Montrul, and M. Polinsky. 2013. Defining an "Ideal" Heritage Speaker: Theoretical and Methodological Challenges. Reply to Peer Commentaries. *Theoretical Linguistics* 39(3–4), 259–294.

Benmamoun, E., A. Albirini, S. Montrul, and E. Saadah. 2014. Arabic Plurals and Root and Pattern Morphology in Palestinian and Egyptian Heritage Speakers. *Linguistic Approaches to Bilingualism* 4(1), 89–123.

Benmamoun, E., M. Abu Nasser, R. Al-Sabbagh, A. Bidaoui, D. Shalash. 2014. The Location of Sentential Negation in Arabic Varieties. *Brill's Annual of Afroasiatic Languages and Linguistics* 5, 83–116.

Bitar, S. 2009. Palestinian-Levantine Dialect Diaspora: Exploring Its Role in Maintaining Palestinian Cultural Heritage & Identity. Master's thesis, The University of Montana, Missoula.

Bos, P. 1997. *Development of Bilingualism: A Study of School-Age Moroccan Children in the Netherlands*. Tilburg: Tilburg University Press.

Brustad, K. 2000. *The Syntax of Spoken Arabic: A Comparative Study of Moroccan, Egyptian, Syrian, and Kuwaiti Dialects*. Washington, DC: Georgetown University Press.

Carreira, M. and O. Kagan. 2011. The Results of the Heritage Language Survey: Implications for Teaching, Curriculum Design, and Professional Development, *Foreign Language Annals* 44(1), 40–64.

Clyne, M. G. (ed.) 1992. *Pluricentric Languages: Differing Norms in Different Nations*. Berlin: Mouton.

Corbett, G. 1991. *Gender*. Cambridge: Cambridge University Press.

Crawford, J. 2000. *At War with Diversity: US Language Policy in an Age of Anxiety*. Clevedon: Multilingual Matters.

Dweik, B. S. 1997. Attitudes of Arab Students towards al-Fusha wal-Ammiyya. *Al-'Arabiyya* 30, 48–131.

El-Dakhs, D. 2015. The Lexical Knowledge and Avoidance of Phrasal Verbs: The Case of Egyptian Learners of English. *International Journal of Applied Linguistics & English Literature* 5(1), 132–144.

Elsaadany, K. 2003. Code-alternation among Arab Speakers in America. *Journal of Educational, Social Sciences and Humanities* 15(2), 67–92.

Fell, B. 1983. *Saga America*. New York: Three Rivers Press.

Ferguson, C. 1959. Diglossia. In D. Hymes (ed.) (1964), *Language in Culture and Society*. New York: Harper and Row, 429–439. Reprinted from Ferguson, C. A. (1959). Diglossia. *Word* 15, 325–340.

Fishman, J. A. 1991. *Reversing Language Shift*. Clevedon: Multilingual Matters.

García-Sánchez, I. M. 2010. The Politics of Arabic Language Education: Moroccan Immigrant Children's Language Socialization into Ethnic and Religious Identities. *Linguistics and Education* 21, 171–196.

Gogonas, N. 2011. Religion as a Core Value in Language Maintenance: Arabic Speakers in Greece. *International Migration* 50(2), 113–126.

Gomaa, Y. A. 2011. Language Maintenance and Transmission: The Case of Egyptian Arabic in Durham, UK. *International Journal of English Linguistics* 1(1), 46–53.

Gumperz, J., 1972. The Speech Community. In P. P. Giglioli (ed.), *Language and Social Context: Selected Readings, 9*. Baltimore: Penguin Books, 219–231.

Habbal, M. 2017. Classroom Discourse in an Arabic Foreign Language Classroom and the Perceived Benefits of Interactions among Learners: A Case Study of College-Level Heritage Language Learners (HLLs) and Foreign Language Learners (FLLs). Doctoral thesis, The Ohio State University.

Haddad, Y. Y. 2004. *Not Quite American? The Shaping of Arab and Muslim Identity in the US*. Waco, TX: Baylor University Press.

Holes, C. 1993. The Use of Variation: A Study of the Political Speeches of Gamal Abd al-Nasir. In *Perspectives on Arabic Linguistics, V*. Amsterdam: John Benjamins, 13–45.

Husseinali, G. 2006. Who Is Studying Arabic and Why? A Survey of Arabic Students' Orientations at a Major University. *Foreign Language Annals* 39(3), 395–412.

Hymes, D. 1972. On Communicative Competence. In J. Pride and J. Holmes (eds.), *Sociolinguistics*. Harmondsworth: Penguin, 269–293.

Ibrahim, I. 2016. Gender Assignment to Lexical Borrowings by Heritage Speakers of Arabic. *Western Papers in Linguistics/Cahiers linguistiques de Western* 1, 1–20.

Jaspal, R. and A. Coyle. 2010. Arabic Is the Language of the Muslims – That's How It Was Supposed to Be: Exploring Language and Religious Identity through Reflective Accounts from Young British-born South Asians. *Mental Health, Religion & Culture* 13(1), 17–36.

Kenny, K. D. 1992. Arab-Americans Learning Arabic: Motivations and Attitudes. In A. Rouchdy (ed.), *The Arabic Language in America*. Detroit: Wayne State University Press, 119–161.

Khattab, G. 2002. VOT Production in English and Arabic Bilingual and Monolingual Children. In D. Parkinson and E. Benmamoun (eds.), *Perspectives on Arabic Linguistics*. Amsterdam: John Benjamins, 1–38.

Khatib, M. and M. Ghannadi. 2011. Interventionist (Explicit And Implicit) versus Non-Interventionist (Incidental) Learning of Phrasal Verbs by Iranian EFL Learners. *Journal of Language Teaching and Research* 2(3), 537–546.

Martin, N. 2009. Arab American Parents' Attitudes toward Their Children's Heritage Language Maintenance and Language Practices. Master's thesis, University of North Carolina at Chapel Hill.

McCarthy, J. and A. Prince. 1990. Foot and Word in Prosodic Morphology: The Arabic Broken Plural. *Natural Language and Linguistic Theory* 8, 209–283.

Omar, M. 1973. *The Acquisition of Egyptian Arabic as a Native Language*. The Hague: Mouton.

Orfalea, G. 2006. *The Arab Americans: A History*. New York: Olive Branch Press.

Osman, G. and C. Forbes. 2004. Representing the West in the Arabic Language: The Slave Narrative of Omar Ibn Said. *Journal of Islamic Studies* 15(3), 331–343.

Othman, M. 2006. Language Choice among Arabic-English Bilinguals in Manchester, Britain. Master's thesis, University of Manchester.

Ouassini, A. 2013. Between Islamophobia and the Ummah: How Spanish Moroccans Are Negotiating Their Identities in Post 3-11 Madrid. Doctoral thesis, University of Nevada.

Qawasmeh, R. 2011. Language Use and Language Attitudes among the Muslim Arabs of Vancouver/ Canada: A Sociolinguistic Study. Master's thesis, Middle East University, Beirut.

Ratcliffe, R. R. 1998. *The 'Broken' Plural Problem in Arabic and Comparative Semitic: Allomorphy and Analogy in Non-concatenative Morphology*. Amsterdam: John Benjamins.

Ravid, D. and R. Farah. 1999. Learning about Noun Plurals in Early Palestinian Arabic. *First Language* 19, 187–206.

Ricento, A. 2005. Problems with the 'Language-As-Resource' Discourse in the Promotion of Heritage Languages in the U.S.A. *Journal of Sociolinguistics* 9(3), 348–368.

Rouchdy, A. 1992. Borrowing in Arab-American Speech. In: A. Rouchdy (ed.), *The Arab Language in America*. Detroit: Wayne State University Press, 36–49.

Rouchdy, A. 2013. Language Conflict and Identity: Arabic in the American Diaspora. In A. Rouchdy (ed.), *Language Contact and Language Conflict in Arabic: Variations on a Sociolinguistic Theme*. New York: Routledge, 133–148.

Saadah, E. 2011. The Production of Arabic Vowels by English L2 Learners and Heritage Speakers of Arabic. Doctoral thesis, University of Illinois, Urbana-Champaign.

Saeed, A. 1997. The Pragmatics of Codeswitching Fusha Arabic to Aammiyyah Arabic in Religious Oriented Discourse. Doctoral thesis, Ball State University.

Sanker, C. 2016. Patterns of Misperception of Arabic Guttural and Non-Guttural Consonants. Doctoral thesis, University of Cornell, New York.

Sarroub, L. 2005. Discontinuities and Differences among Muslim Arab-Americans: Making It at Home and School. In M. L. Dantas and P. C. Manyak (eds.), *Home-School Connections in a Multicultural Society: Learning from and with Culturally and Linguistically Diverse Families*. New York: Routledge, 76–93.

Seymour-Jorn, C. 2007. Arabic Language Learning among Arab Immigrants in Milwaukee, Wisconsin: A Study of Attitudes and Motivations. *Journal of Muslim Minority Affairs* 24(1), 109–122.

Shalaby, R. 2017. An Exploration of Heritage Language Maintenance among Arabic Speakers in Montreal, Quebec. Master's thesis, McGill University, Montreal.

Shiri, S. 2010. Arabic in the United States. In K. Potowski (ed.), *Linguistic Diversity in the United States*. New York: Cambridge University Press, 206–222.

Shlonsky, U. 1997. *Clause Structure and Word Order in Hebrew and Arabic: An Essay in Comparative Semitic Syntax*. Oxford: Oxford University Press.

Statistics Canada. 2007. *The Arab Community in Canada*. Retrieved from www150.statcan.gc.ca/n1/en/catalogue/89-621-X2007009

Suleiman, M. 1999. Introduction: The Arab Immigrant Experience. In M. Suleiman (ed.), *Arabs in America: Building a New Future*. Philadelphia: Temple University Press, 1–24.

Suleiman, Y. 2003. *The Arabic Language and National Identity*. Edinburgh: Edinburgh University Press.

Suleiman, Y. 2016. After Islamophobia Comes the Criminalisation of Arabic. Aljzaeera.net retrieved from www.aljazeera.com/indepth/opinion/2016/03/islamophobia-criminalisation-arabic-160320073445033.html

Temples, A. 2013. Constructing Arabic as Heritage: Investment in Language, Literacy, and Identity among Young U.S. Learners. Doctoral thesis, Georgia State University.

The Arab American Institute. 2012. *National Arab American Demographics*. Retrieved from www.aaiusa.org/demographics

US Census Bureau. 2003. *Statistical Abstract of the United States: 2003*. Retrieved from www.census.gov/library/publications/2003/compendia/statab/123ed.html

Van Sertima, I. 2003. *They Came before Columbus: The African Presence in Ancient America*. New York: Random House Trade Paperbacks.

Von Wuthenau, A. 1975. *Unexpected Facts in Ancient America*. New York: Crown Publishers.

Wilson, D. 2013. The Intersection of Identity, Gender, and Attitudes toward Maintenance among Beginning Spanish as a Heritage Language Students. *Southwest Journal of Linguistics* 31(1), 177–198.

Wright, W. 1988. *A Grammar of the Arabic Language* (3rd ed.) Cambridge: Cambridge University Press.

13

Heritage Languages in South America

John M. Lipski

13.1 Introduction

Latin America has received immigrants – voluntary and involuntary – for more than five centuries, and for at least the past century many immigration scenarios are reflected in the survival of heritage language speakers and speech communities. This chapter gives a representative cross-section of heritage languages, in Spanish-speaking South American nations and in Brazil, with occasional reference to other Latin American nations. Primary emphasis falls on situations in which the heritage languages are maintained in cohesive speech communities, and for which at least some linguistic documentation is available. Due to limitations of space, the full spectrum of heritage languages – at least one hundred in number and found in every Latin American nation – cannot be included.

The presentation is organized by the circumstances that gave rise to heritage language enclaves: voluntary immigration, including recruitment efforts by Latin American governments, immigration of religious minorities. immigration resulting from contract labor, and continent-internal migration, often resulting from economic hardship. None of the heritage languages enjoys nationwide official recognition, but some encompass entire communities, while others have dwindled to small groups of speakers. Attitudes toward heritage languages as well as linguistic self-esteem of speakers are equally diverse, ranging from ethnic pride to scorn. With very few exceptions, the heritage languages are not being actively taught, although earlier generations of immigrants sometimes were able to implement some language maintenance instruction.

13.2   Heritage Languages Resulting from Voluntary Immigration

From the beginning of the colonial period in Latin America, there has been considerable immigration from countries where languages other than Spanish or Portuguese are spoken. In most instances, this immigration was motivated by economic stress in the countries of origin together with the promise of expanded opportunities in the Americas. In urban settings, the heritage languages frequently disappeared after a generation or two, while in rural regions there was a greater probability for ethnic language enclaves to survive for longer periods. Immigrants often settled in areas where previous arrivals from their home countries could provide a support network, but in most cases there was no intervention by the Latin American host nations. In a few instances, targeted recruitment efforts brought new settlers who may otherwise not have emigrated. The reasons for such deliberate recruitment included homesteading in sparsely populated territories and neo-eugenic racial "improvement."

The long-term survival of some immigrant languages over others has depended on several factors, the intersection of which was different for each speech community. The most robust heritage language communities are found in the largest nations, which welcomed European immigration, particularly from northern and central-eastern countries characterized by lighter complexions. Within the immigrant communities, there were varying levels of mini-nationalism as regards marriage outside of the ethnic group, as well as the cohesive maintenance of cultural practices and traditions from the countries of origin. Heritage language maintenance has also been bolstered as ethnic neighborhoods become more heterogeneous, and residents spend more time daily speaking the national languages. Finally, attitudes by speakers of the national languages toward immigrants' languages vary across time and space, and are closely tied to issues of social and racial identity, with northern and central European languages generally faring better than languages arriving from southern Europe, Africa, the Caribbean, and Asia.

13.2.1   German Varieties

German – with numerous dialectal variants – is the heritage language most robustly represented in contemporary South America. German immigration to the continent began in the second half of the nineteenth century, with more substantial numbers of immigrants arriving in the first decades of the twentieth century. The aftermath of World War II brought a further group of German-speaking immigrants, many of whom had ties to the defeated Third Reich; unlike the previous arrivals, these individuals did not generally coalesce into German speech communities. Heritage varieties of German have been maintained in several South American nations, due both to the rural surroundings of many speech communities and the tendency for descendants of German immigrants to marry within the same ethnic group. During most of the period of German immigration, the settlers lived in German-speaking colonies, some of which are still in existence. Since much of the immigration occurred before the consolidation of modern Germany and the general acceptance of a High German (*Hochdeutsch*) standard, South American heritage German is in reality based on regional Germanic dialects.

The largest number of heritage German speakers is found in Brazil, primarily concentrated in the southern states of Santa Catarina, Espírito Santo, and Rio Grande do Sul (Rost 2008; Maltzahn 2013). São Paulo state also contains many German-speaking communities (Silva 2010). These speech communities are based on Hunsrückisch from the Rhineland Palatinate area (Altenhofen 1996; Damke 1997; Altenhofen and Frey 2006; Leão 2007; Meyer 2009; Barros and Philippsen 2013), Pomeranian, from a European region now part of Poland (Vandresen and Corrêa 2008; Höhmann and Savedra 2011; Blank and Miranda 2012; Schaeffer 2012; Schneider 2012; Beilke 2013a, 2013b; Bremenkamp 2014), and Westfalian (Luersen 2009). Several Brazilian communities have adopted German varieties as co-official languages; for Hünsruckisch this includes some cities in Santa Catarina and Rio Grande do Sul, and for Pomeranian some localities in Espírito Santo, Minas Gerais, Santa Catarina, and Rio Grande do Sul. The states of Espírito Santo and Rio Grande do Sul officially acknowledge German varieties as part of the states' linguistic heritage.

Many Brazilian German speakers, including some linguists, have identified a Portuguese-influenced Germanic koiné popularly referred to as *Brasildeutsch* (e.g., Damke 2008; Souza 2014), as well as code-switching (e.g., Altenhofen 1996; Rosenberg 2002, 2003a, 2003b, 2012; Schaumloeffel 2003; Fritzen 2007; Meyer 2009) and Germanic influence on local varieties of Portuguese (e.g., Vandresen 2006). Most such influence is confined to the domain of phonetics. For example, Bandeira and Zimmer (2012) and Zimmer, Bandeira, and Blank (2009) study the voice onset timing (VOT) of Pomeranian-Portuguese bilinguals, which are typically longer than those of Portuguese monolinguals (in general, VOT values are lower for Portuguese than for Germanic languages). VOT is the "aspiration" of voiceless stops such as /p/, /t/, and /k/, i.e., the time between the release of the stop consonant and the onset of the following vowel, Lara and Battisti (2014) provide similar data on the VOT of Hunsrückish-Portuguese bilinguals. Beninca (2009) and Rodrigues (2009) provide additional observations of Pomeranian-Portuguese bilingualism, including voiceless articulation of syllable-initial voiced obstruents in Portuguese, e.g., a[p]elha for abelha 'bee,' [p]rasil for Brasil, [k]arfo for garfo 'fork.'

In contemporary Argentina, the greatest number of German speakers (Stößlein 2009) are found in the province of Misiones, in the extreme northeast. After World War I many German settlers arrived in Misiones, attracted by German-owned businesses in South America. Most settled along the western edge of the province along the Paraná River (Capaccio 2001). Even more came from neighboring Brazil, which is separated from most of Misiones by the narrow Uruguay River and in a few places only by small creeks; in one area there is a land border with no natural demarcation. They are descendants of German immigrants to southern Brazil, who during the period 1937–1945 were forced out of Brazil by the ultranationalist government of Getúlio Vargas. The Vargas regime prohibited the teaching or public use of the German language and was alarmed by rumors that German settlers in Brazil intended to form a separatist state (Zubaran 1994; Campos 2006). Although tri-lingual German-Portuguese-Spanish speakers can be found along the entire eastern corridor of Misiones province, the highest concentration is found along the upper Uruguay River region.

Heritage German speakers in eastern Misiones speak several regional dialects, including Hunsrück, Swabian, Plattdeutsch (Low German), and Pomeranian, and given the diversity of these dialects, some of which are barely mutually intelligible, most heritage German speakers in Misiones have developed a sort of koiné German that allows for inter-dialectal communication (Putnam and Schwarz 2014; Putnam and Lipski 2016). Along the western edge of the province, heritage German speakers mostly speak Hunsrück. These speakers descend from immigrants who arrived directly from Germany, and there is little or no contact with Portuguese in this region (Gallero 2005, 2009, 2010; Huber 2010). There are also speakers of Swiss German dialects in western Misiones (Micolis 1973; Gallero and Krautstofl 2010 ; Gallero 2018), but there are no linguistic studies of this variety.

A much smaller group of heritage German speakers is found in the Argentine province of Entre Ríos, being descendants of the "Volga Germans" who emigrated first to Russia, then to Argentina toward the end of the nineteenth century (Hipperdinger 2017). The last vestiges of this archaic German variety are still to be found, and ethnic revival movements may ensure the survival of at least some rudiments of the language (Hipperdinger 1994, 2017; Cipria 2007; Ladilova 2013, 2015). In the city of Buenos Aires, especially in the Belgrano neighborhood, a German-Spanish hybrid, considered by some to be a pidgin, was once prevalent, and was known colloquially as Belgrano-Deutsch (Schirp 2001). The writer Jorge Luis Borges – also an avid philologist – collected specimens of this speech. The reported examples seem to reflect fluent German, with Spanish lexical replacements, e.g.,

(1) "Der *Tipo* hatte ein schwarze *Pedo* y Nach wir *Truco* spielen, *rajieren* wir zum *Quilombo*" 'That guy had a drinking spree, and after we played *truco* [a card game], we split for a brothel'. (De Torre Borges 2004: 230)

Other unsubstantiated examples can be found at https://es.wikipedia.org/wiki/Belgranodeutsch

In Chile, German immigration began in the mid-nineteenth century as part of an effort by the Chilean government to "Europeanize" the southern regions of the country. In the late nineteenth and early twentieth centuries, larger groups of immigrants arrived, mostly in the far-southern region of Llanquihue. A regional Hispanized German variety, known as Launa-Deutsch "lake-region German," continues to be spoken in this area (Deutsche Welle n.d.; Ziebur 2000; Demel 2013; Rojas Marquez 2013; Wolff 2017). A more recently transplanted variety of German is also spoken in the village of Villa Baviera, formerly known as Colonia Dignidad, a community with a troubled history (Basso 2002; Cassigoli 2013).

As in other Southern Cone nations, German immigration to Paraguay began in the second half of the nineteenth century, and several predominantly German communities were founded, among them San Bernardino, Altos, Obligado, Bella Vista, and Hohenau. The most significant German colony was Nueva Germania, where the German language continues to survive (Kurzwelly 2017).

With the exception of the anti-German sentiments during the Getúlio Vargas government in twentieth-century Brazil and during the Argentine military dictatorship, there is no documentation of negative sentiments toward the use of heritage German in South America. In some communities, e.g., Blumenau in Brazil and Puerto Rico and Eldorado in Misiones province, Argentina, German-speaking descendants of immigrants celebrate regionally popular German cultural events such as Oktoberfest, which reinforces neutral to positive reactions to German in these regions. German-language teaching was once prevalent in many of the German immigrant communities, often in church-affiliated institutions, and at least one community (Blumenau, Brazil) is implementing a city-wide bilingual education program, and the nearby city of Pomerode has been teaching German in schools for more than a decade (Fritzen 2012).

13.2.2 Ukrainian and Polish in Brazil

Although a large number of Ukrainian and Polish immigrants to South America settled in northeastern Argentina (Gerus 1986; Lehr and Cipko 2000), only in Brazil have these heritage languages survived. Brazil has received considerable immigration of Ukrainian speakers, particularly in the state of Paraná, and is home to the third largest group of Ukrainians in the Americas (more than 500,000). Immigration began toward the end of the nineteenth century, accelerated following World War I, and reached its peak in the aftermath of World War II (Boruszenko 1981; Garcia 2009; Lemke 2010). The first generations maintained the Ukrainian language and instituted classes in Ukrainian, but a shift to Portuguese has generally occurred in urban areas (Mezavila 2008), while Ukrainian continues to be spoken in many of the rural *colônias* of Paraná (Semechechem 2016). Garcia (2009) provides sociophonetic data on the realization of the Portuguese nasal diphthong –*ão* [ɐ̃w̃] among rural Ukrainian-Portuguese bilinguals, where older bilinguals use the variants [õw̃] and [ɔ̃w̃] to a greater extent than Portuguese monolinguals. Lemke (2010) analyzes the acquisition of Spanish by Portuguese-Ukrainian bilinguals; only Portuguese influence in their Spanish is evident.

Polish immigration to Brazil followed similar patterns to those of Ukrainians, beginning in the late nineteenth century but intensifying after 1920. Currently there are some 1.8 million Polish-Brazilians, mainly concentrated in the state of Paraná, where more than 700,000 are found. The Polish language has not been maintained as extensively as Ukrainian but continues to survive in some villages and rural areas near Curitiba (Miodunka 2003; Ferraz 2007; Malczewski 2010; Dvorak 2013). There is no literature on the characteristics of heritage Polish in Brazil, and little documentation on Polish influence on local varieties of Portuguese; in one study, Druszcz (1984) found subtle phonetic and morphosyntactic traits such as variable word order, inconsistent gender and number agreement, lack of determiners, neutralization of /ɾ/ and /r/, and over-differentiation of the Portuguese vowel system. Portuguese influence has also been detected among heritage Polish speakers (Costa and Gielinski 2014).

Both Ukrainian and Polish immigrants in Brazil migrated to ethnically homogeneous communities, generally devoted to agriculture, and this contributed to the retention of the heritage languages. Brazil's generally favorable response to European immigrants, their cultures, and their languages is a key factor in accounting for the resilience of these Slavic languages.

13.2.3 Italian Varieties

After Spain and Portugal, Italy provided the largest number of immigrants to Latin America, particularly the nations of the Southern Cone (see articles in Patat 2012). The bulk of the immigration occurred during the late nineteenth and early twentieth centuries, and Italian language and culture substantially transformed Argentina and Uruguay, and to some extent also Brazil. Most Italian immigrants came from impoverished regions of southern Italy, speaking regional dialects that contributed many lexical items to the *Lunfardo* slang of Buenos Aires and Montevideo. Although during the height of the immigration period entire neighborhoods of Buenos Aires, Montevideo, and other cities were populated entirely by Italians, recent arrivals frequently took advantage of lexical and morpho-syntactic similarities between Italian and Spanish and developed a transitory interlanguage often referred to colloquially as *Cocoliche* (Meo Zilio 1955c, 1956, 1964; Rosell 1970; Lavandera 1984: 61–75; Aimasso 2016). At the same time, the Italian spoken by these immigrants became increasingly influenced by Spanish (Meo Zilio 1955a, 1955b). After the first generation, most Italians in Argentina and Uruguay switched entirely to Spanish (Italiano-McGreevy 2013), although Italian influence on the intonational patterns of Buenos Aires Spanish are plausible (Colantoni and Gurlekian 2004).

Currently, there are no Italian-speaking communities in Argentina or Uruguay, although individual heritage speakers can be found in many regions (e.g., Misiones province, Argentina), and the speech of some elderly immigrants who arrived in Montevideo during the 1950s provides a glimpse into earlier periods of language contact (Barrios and Mazzolini, 1994; Barrios et al. 1994; Barrios 1999, 2003). Surviving Italian speech communities are found in Brazil and Mexico, and represent immigration from northern Italy, frequently the result of recruitment efforts.

Italian immigration to Brazil was massive, particularly in the final decades of the nineteenth century, when more than one million Italians settled, mainly in the southern region (Cenni 2003), at a time when the total population of Brazil was between ten and fifteen million. The Italian population was most concentrated in São Paulo state (where Italian varieties have influenced the vernacular Portuguese of the city of São Paulo: Castro 1997; Alves and Maroneze 2004; Caprara and Mordente 2004), followed by Rio Grande do Sul and Minas Gerais. Subsequent internal migration resulted in significant Italian communities in the neighboring states of Santa Catarina and Paraná. The greatest proportion of Italian immigration came from the northern region, especially during the first decades, especially areas where the northern Italian language is spoken. The Veneto language continues to be spoken in some areas of Rio Grande do Sul and Santa Catarina (Peres 2011; Dal Picol 2013), and was once prominent in São Paulo as well (Vieira 2010). Veneto and other northern Italian dialects, e.g., Trentino (Boso 1991; Schissatti 2014) are often known as *Talian* in Brazil (Pertile 2009; Armilato 2012. The municipality of Serafina Corrêa (Rio Grande do Sul) has adopted *Talian* as a co-official language, and the states of Rio Grande do Sul and Santa Catarina officially acknowledge *Talian* as integral components of the states' linguistic heritage. Estimates of the current number of *Talian* speakers range from 500,000 to more than three million, with the latter figure undoubtedly including heritage speakers with less than total fluency. The northern Italian Tirolean dialect is also spoken in some communities (Leopoldino 2009, 2014).

Mexico was also the scene of considerable Italian immigration, with most of the immigrants rapidly assimilating to Mexican life without leaving linguistic traces (Zilli Manica 1981). In some parts of Mexico, Italian immigrant colonies maintained their linguistic and cultural integrity; for example, a group of Trentinos founded the cooperative La Estanzuela in 1924. This colony did not prosper as its founders had hoped, but it reproduced in miniature the contact situations found in such Italo-Hispanic communities as the Rio de la Plata. Some Italian communities are still found in northern Mexico, based on agriculture and cattle raising, and regional Italian languages still survive (Zilli Manica 1997, 1998). The best-known case is the town of Chipilo, near Puebla, where the Veneto language brought in the nineteenth century by immigrants from Segusino, Italy, still coexists with Spanish, and where a number of interesting cross-linguistic phenomena have occurred in both languages (Zago Bronca 1982; Santor and Ursini 1983; Ursini 1983; MacKay 1984, 1992, 1993, 1995; Meo Zilio 1987, 1989; Romani 1992). Veneto is closer to Spanish than standard Italian; for example, first conjugation verbs end–ar instead of –are, and past participles end in –á instead of –ato/-ata, which sounds very much like the colloquial reduction of ada to a in Spanish (e.g., nada > na 'nothing'). These similarities have facilitated the interweaving of Spanish and Veneto, for example use of the pronoun nos 'we' instead of ci/noi. Veneto also has influenced local Spanish, for example the neutralization of /ɾ/-/r/ (areglao for arreglado 'arranged'), Veneto plurals (añi for años 'years' [anni in Veneto], aseitune for aceitunas 'olives' [olive in Veneto]), and verbal suffixes (acepten for aceptabábamos '[we] accepted' [az^eten in Veneto], establesesti [the Veneto form] for establecidos 'established'). During the first years of the 2000s the Chipilo community has established a Yahoolist-serv, with many postings, all in Veneto (Barnes 2009, 2017), while more recently, Chipileño Veneto has begun to be used in social media groups such as Facebook.

The Veneto language has been maintained steadfastly by the descendents of northern Italian immigrants to Brazil and Mexico, with at least three factors contributing to the ongoing vitality of this heritage language. First is the fact that these communities are largely the result of official recruitment in past generations, by governments who regarded northern Italians as desirable colonists with superior agricultural skills. Second, these Italian ethnic communities are prosperous and admired by residents of surrounding communities, with relatively little incentive to move outside of the ethnic enclaves. A third factor is the strong preference for marriage within the ethnic group, or for non-Italian marriage partners to accept and even learn Veneto to be fully accepted. Although Veneto is not taught in these communities, some members have traveled to Italy and learned standard Italian, which has the indirect effect of bolstering Veneto usage.

Following World War II and the accompanying economic devastation of Italy, many Italians emigrated to Venezuela. Most settled in large cities such as Caracas and Maracaibo, and did not form cohesive speech communities (Grau 1994), but continued to speak Italian as a home language. There may still be as many as 600,000 heritage Italian speakers in Venezuela (Bondarenko 2012: 177; also Bondarenko 2010), and Spanish-influenced Italian has been documented for Venezuela La Manna (1967). The long-term survival possibilities of Italian in Venezuela are not clear, due both to the potential for morphosyntactic and phonetic convergence with Spanish, as happened in Argentina and Uruguay, and to the massive exodus of Venezuelans of all backgrounds due to the ongoing economic and political crisis.

13. 2.4 Japanese in Brazil

The largest population of Japanese origin outside of Japan is found in Brazil, with numbers approaching two million, of which an estimated 380,000 still speak at least some Japanese. Japanese immigration to Brazil began in 1908 and reached its peak in the period 1910–1940, with another spike occurring in the late 1950s. Japanese immigrants were often viewed with ambivalence in Brazil, which together with Japanese cultural pride resulted in the tenacious retention of the Japanese language beyond the first generation (Smith 1979; Mase 1987; Kanazawa and Loveday 1988; Adachi 2001; Suda and de Souza 2006; Saito 2011), although during the nationalistic Getúlio Vargas regime, public use of Japanese and other "foreign" languages was prohibited. As is the case of many other immigrant groups, descendents of Japanese immigrants in Brazil generally speak regional vernacular dialects of Japanese rather than standardized urban varieties (Ota 2009). Brazilian Portuguese has definitively influenced the Japanese spoken in Brazil, while Brazilian Portuguese shows little influence of Japanese, beyond the L2 approximations to Portuguese produced by first-generation Japanese immigrants (Kanazawa and Loveday, 1988: 430; Fuchs 1996). Lingering traces of Portuguese interference can be found in some Brazilian-Japanese communities (e.g., Ota and Gardenal 2006; Ota 2009; Saiki 2013; Fujiwara 2014; Gibo 2014). For example, Brazilian Portuguese typically inserts [i] to break up disallowed consonant sequences (e.g., *ad [i]vogado* 'lawyer'), while Japanese speakers insert [u] or (after dental stops) [o] under the same circumstances (e.g., English *fight* > J. *fait[o]*, Eng. *sphinx* > J. *sufinksu*; Dupoux et al. 1999). Parlato-Oliveira et al. (2010) demonstrate that when hearing nonce words with no epenthetic vowels, Japanese-Brazilian Portuguese bilinguals perceive illusory or "ghost" vowels /i/ or

/u/ non-permissible phonotactic sequences, in accordance with their degree of bilingualism. There is also an attenuation in the use of formulas of courtesy in heritage Japanese in Brazil (Suzuki 1986), possibly due to the relatively low frequency of similar expressions in Portuguese.

Japanese-Brazilians tend to marry and form social networks within their own ethnic group, thereby reinforcing the retention of the Japanese language. The teaching of Japanese to the descendants of immigrants is another contributing factor (Doi 2006; but compare Usarski 2008). Traditional and modern Japanese religious practices have also been implicated in the maintenance of the language in Brazil (Tomita and Santiago 2004). In the largest cities there are Japanese-language schools for the children of Japanese expatriates, also attended by some Japanese-Brazilians; many of these schools are at least partially financed by the Japanese government.

13.2.5 Welsh in Argentina

An exemplary case of heritage language retention in isolated settings is the Welsh community in Argentina, spread among several towns in the southern provinces, especially Chubut (Martínez Ruíz 1977; Jones 1993; Matthews 1995; Rhys 2000). The Welsh presence in Argentina dates from around 1865, when the first Welsh colony was founded in Patagonia, in the modern province of Chubut. From this point until 1914, Welsh immigration was constant, with more than 3,000 Welsh arriving in this sparsely populated area. Until the end of the nineteenth century, the proportion of these communities who spoke Welsh (and often no Spanish) was between 87and 98 percent. By the time of the 1972 census, among the population under 20 years of age, only 5 percent of men and only 3.5 percent of women had any proficiency in Welsh; among the population older than 60, these figures rose to 25 percent for men and 41 percent for women. These data reveal the rapid erosion of the language, due to greater social and economic integration of the Welsh enclaves, new immigration, mixed marriages, and a more effective school system and mass media. Welsh is currently on the wane in Patagonia, but there are signs of a partial reversal of this trend. Ethnic pride, geographical isolation, internet connectivity, and recent support from the Welsh government (e.g., Kiff 2016) may ensure the survival of the Welsh language in succeeding generations (Virkel 1999, 2000; Jones and Sager 2001; Agozzino 2006; Johnson 2007, 2009; Coupland and Garrett 2010; Harris 2018; Zamarreño 2018).

13.2.6 Heritage British and United States English in Latin America

Linguistic and cultural links between Great Britain and Argentina are long-standing, and in addition to the Welsh-speaking communities in Chubut, a number of heritage speakers of British English are found in Buenos Aires. Although English immigrants in Argentina were found during the colonial period and immediately following independence in 1816, the majority of British English settlers arrived between 1860 and 1930 (Cortes Conde 2007; Silveira 2014). Many were involved in the industrial revolution or large-scale agriculture, and were well-received in Buenos Aires society until the ultra-nationalist government of Juan Perón just after World War II. Following the Falklands Islands War of 1982 (known in Argentina as the Guerra de las Malvinas), resentment toward English-speaking Anglo-Argentines increased. Cortés Conde (1994, 2007) has documented the slow decline in the use of heritage English among Anglo-Argentines in the greater Buenos Aires area, although British and – increasingly – United States English as foreign languages are considered desirable in Argentina.

In the aftermath of the United States Civil War (1861–1865), as many as 20,000 individuals from the defeated secessionist southern states (especially Georgia, Alabama, and Texas) emigrated to Brazil, welcomed by the Brazilian emperor Dom Pedro II, who wanted to expand cotton production in Brazil. The descendents of these "Confederados," especially in the communities of Americana and Santa Bárbara d'Oeste near São Paulo, continue to speak a southern US variety of English as a heritage language, increasingly influenced by Portuguese through borrowing and code-switching (Weaver 1961; Medeiros 1982; Montgomery and Melo 1990, 1995; Lownes 2018; Pérez Gómez 2018), but still retaining the phonetic patterns of the "Deep South." Some of the Confederados have visited the United States and many maintain correspondence with post-Confederacy organizations in the southern United States. While he was still governor of Georgia, former US President Jimmy Carter visited the community in 1972 and spoke English with many of the residents. Within Brazil there is an American Descendents' Association (*Associação Descendência Americana*) and an annual Confederada festival.

Another group of heritage United States English speakers is found in the Samaná Peninsula, on the northern coast of the Dominican Republic (Rodríguez Demorizi 1945; Puig Ortiz 1978; Smith 1989; Tejeda Ortiz 1984). In 1821, the "Estado Independiente del Haití Español," the future Dominican Republic, declared its independence from Spain, but the freedom was short-lived. The following year, following an initially peaceful gambit by Haitian president Jean-Pierre Boyer, Haiti invaded the eastern part of the island, remaining until 1844. It was during this period that more than 6,000 African Americans from the United States, many of whom had formerly been enslaved, were recruited and settled in Samaná and other regions, part of an ambitious plan by Boyer to create a settler-state of dispossessed and formerly enslaved Africans and Afro-descendants from throughout the Americas, who would owe unswerving allegiance to the Haitian revolution. Today, many of the descendants of these *Americanos* continue to speak an archaic form of nineteenth-century African American English, which some scholars have regarded as proof that United States Black English was not formerly creolized (Poplack and Sankoff 1980, 1987; DeBose 1983; Tagliamonte and Poplack 1988; Tagliamonte 1991, 1997; Hannah 1997). Using Samaná English as a linguistic time capsule is not without problems, since the contemporary speech appears to contain traces of West Indian English varieties, which is not surprising considering the comomunities' location near the Caribbean coast.

13.3   Heritage Languages Resulting from Immigration of Religious Minorities

Throughout the history of the Americas, religious groups seeking to escape persecution or shield themselves from outside influences considered as corrupt have established close-knit colonies. Currently, two heritage languages predominate among religion-based communities in Latin America: Mennonite Low German and United States English.

13.3.1   Mennonite Low German

Mennonite Low German, or *Plautdietsch*, continues to be spoken in several Mennonite communities in Latin America (Kaufmann 2007; Cox 2015), where the close-knit character of the faith-based society as well as the strong link between the traditional language and the religious practices encourage language maintenance. Low German-speaking Mennonites originally arrived from Russia beginning in the 1920s. Some also came from Canada, after the teaching of Mennonite Low German was prohibited in that country. One stronghold of Mennonite Low German is the remote Chaco region of Paraguay and Bolivia (Hernández Medina 2004; Bottos 2008; Ostendorf 2018). In the Chaco communities, some speakers of indigenous languages have adopted the Mennonite faith as well as the Low German language. Brazil is also home to several Plautdietsch-speaking Mennonite communities (Dück 2005, 2011, 2012; Drozdowska-Broering 2016). Another large community is found in Mexico, especially in the northern state of Chihuahua (Hedges 1997; Salinas et al. 2014; Klassen 2016), whence many have emigrated to Kansas in the United States as well as to the Canadian province of Manitoba. The Mexican film *Luz silenciosa/ Silent Light/Stellet Licht* (Reygadas 2007) is narrated in *Plautdietsch* and documents the life of Mennonites in Chihuahua.

13.3.2 United States English in Quaker Communities

A number of United States religious communities have established villages in Mexico and Central America (Masing 1964); the best known community is Monteverde in Costa Rica, founded by Quakers beginning in 1950, when a handful of families from the Society of Friends abandoned their native Alabama and headed for the Costa Rican rain forest (Watts 1999; Harwood and Zapata 2006). Other English-speaking Quaker communities are found in Mexico. These communities have existed for less than a century, and the limited Spanish competence of the founders has been replaced by total fluency in Spanish among later generations; the linguistic effects on local Spanish dialects are relatively small in comparison with other language contact zones in Latin America, but given the independent life style of these communities, these microdialects are likely to survive for some time. Monteverde, in particular, has become a popular site for international ecotourism, as the religious community has purchased a large segment of the rainforest to safeguard against unrestrained land development, and contact with thousands of tourists, many of whom speak English, continues to reinforce the use of English in Monteverde.

13.4 Heritage Speakers of Languages from Other Latin American Countries

Throughout Latin America, intra-continental migration is a constant phenomenon, and in some cases heritage language communities from neighboring countries have been formed. The reasons vary, but nearly always involve economic factors, ranging from the search for more available land and job opportunities to the desperation of refugees. Spanish, Portuguese, and Haitian Creole are most significantly represented in heritage language communities, but a number of Native American languages and Afro-Atlantic creoles can also be included.

13.4.1 Brazilian Portuguese in Misiones, Argentina

Brazil, the largest nation in South America, shares a common border with every Spanish-speaking country in South America except for Chile and Ecuador, and in every Spanish-speaking nation bordering on Brazil there are one or more communities located on the border, nearly always paired off with a corresponding community on the Brazilian side. These border communities are far from the respective national capitals, in regions that historically have been slow to be populated and were beyond the reach of national television and radio stations. At the same time, the burgeoning economy of Brazil has resulted in favorable currency exchange values for

Brazilians, resulting in the presence of businesses and duty-free zones in many of these communities. Brazilians in border regions usually do not use Spanish, while residents of border communities in Spanish-speaking nations have considerable passive knowledge of Portuguese and use this language (with varying degrees of proficiency) when speaking with Brazilians and, under some circumstances, with one another.

In addition to the many border regions where native Spanish speakers learn Portuguese as a second language to speak to Brazilians, there are two dialect zones where vernacular Portuguese is spoken consistently in speech communities outside the borders of Brazil: northern Uruguay and the Argentine province of Misiones. Given the demographic and sociolinguistic history of northern Uruguay, Uruguayan Portuguese (sometimes referred to as *Fronterizo* 'border') is best regarded as a national language and not a heritage language (Elizaincín 1973, 1976, 1979; Elizaincín et al. 1987; Carvalho 2003).

In the Argentine province of Misiones, in addition to the arrival of many European immigrants, more settlers came from neighboring Brazil, which is separated from most of Misiones by the narrow Uruguay River and in a few places only by small creeks; in one area there is a land border with no natural demarcation. Most descendants of Brazilians in Misiones work in agriculture, on small farms producing tea, yerba mate, tobacco, and aromatic plants such as citronella and mint, from which the essential oils are extracted in distilleries, and to this day more Portuguese than Spanish is spoken in the rural *colonias* surrounding the cities and towns in eastern Misiones. In a few towns along the Uruguay River (most notably El Soberbio and Santa Rita), Portuguese (or Portuguese-Spanish hybrids) predominate even in urban areas.

The Portuguese spoken in Misiones bears the mark of rural vernacular Brazilian Portuguese of the neighboring states and has little resemblance to urban standardized Portuguese. Basic descriptions can be found in Lipski (2011a, 2011b, 2015, 2017, 2018) and Maia (2004); Misiones Portuguese is also mentioned by Daviña (2003) and Sturza (1994). Notwithstanding the fact that most residents of the *chacras* (small farms) of eastern Misiones listen to Brazilian Portuguese media, there is no attempt to emulate prestigious Brazilian varieties, unlike the situation in northern Uruguay (Carvalho 2004). As in northern Uruguay, the massive presence of Spanish in Misiones arrived with immigrants from more populated regions of the country. The principal difference is that in Misiones the use of Portuguese never provoked the harsh rejection found in northern Uruguay. Although most of the schools in the Portuguese-speaking communities in Misiones do not offer classes in Portuguese, and children from Portuguese-speaking households frequently experience language difficulties in the first years of school, there has never been a campaign to eradicate Portuguese, or to label rural vernacular speech with terms like *rompe-idioma* 'language-breaker,' as used in Uruguay. Misiones Portuguese is frequently referred to informally as *Portuñol* (in Portuguese, *Portunhol*), by speakers and outside observers alike, but in fact there is little convergence with Spanish except for lexical borrowing (Lipski 2017), and more often than not, *Portuñol* carries only the connotation of a quaint regional phenomenon (often mentioned in travel and tourism documents), but not undesirable or to be avoided. Speaking Portuguese is not publicly criticized or explicitly correlated with working-class or rustic speech as in Uruguay. The fact that Portuguese is most frequently spoken in rural regions contributes to its tenacity. Unlike in urban areas, where interaction with Spanish speakers inevitably results in language mixing and ultimately in the displacement of Portuguese by Spanish, on the small farms of Misiones residents spend most days speaking to one another only in Portuguese. This fact, combined with the relatively low sociolinguistic stigmatization of Portuguese/Portuñol, results in Misiones Portuguese having comparatively fewer Spanish incursions than Uruguayan *Fronterizo*. In a few rural schools in Misiones, Portuguese is taught, using pedagogical materials developed in Brazil, and there is one bilingual school (in Bernardo de Irigoyen), where all classes are taught in both Spanish and Portuguese on an alternating basis, and with teachers from each country crossing the dry land border to teach in their respective languages (Prytz Nilsson 2011; Bianchezzi et al. 2012).

13.4.2 Spanish as a Heritage Language in Brazil

Along Brazil's border with its Spanish-speaking neighbors, Spanish speakers are found, although in most border communities Portuguese predominates even on the nominally Spanish-speaking side. In the interior of Brazil, migratory trends from economically stressed Spanish-speaking nations have resulted in groups of Spanish heritage speakers. The largest group is from Bolivia, with significant numbers of Bolivian Spanish speakers found in São Paulo and other Brazilian cities (Silva 2005, 2006; Cymbalista 2007; Souchaud and Baeninger 2008; Souchaud 2010; Simai and Baeninger 2012). These immigrants are immediately distinguishable linguistically and phenotypically, and their low socioeconomic level and frequently undocumented status make them the object of discrimination and exploitation. Under the circumstances, retaining Spanish can be a form of mutual protection in a sometimes hostile environment. More recently, the economic collapse of Venezuela has driven thousands of Venezuelans across the southern border into Brazil, where nuclei of Venezuelan Spanish speakers have already emerged (Cotinguiba and Cotinguiba 2014; Pimentel and Cotinguiba 2014; Santos and Vasconcelos 2016; Simões 2017; Almeida and Santi 2018).

13.4.3 Brazilian Portuguese as a Heritage Language in Paraguay

Since the 1960s, the eastern region of Paraguay has received considerable immigration from Brazil, and the total number of "Brasiguaios" is estimated to be around 500,000. Frequently exploited and marginalized, these descendants of Brazilians continue to speak Portuguese, as well as acquiring Spanish and Guaraní. The linguistic profile of these displaced immigrants reflects the general level of marginalization, both in Paraguay and – when returning – in Brazil (Santos 2004, 2008; Blanc 2015; Albuquerque 2009). From a sociolinguistic perspective, the Brasiguaios in Paraguay speak "nobody's" Spanish, while those who return to Brazil speak "nobody's" Portuguese, which has the effect of hiving off the immigrants' language from the surrounding national languages (Berger 2011).

13.4.4 Haitian Creole throughout Latin America

One of the most dramatic examples of heritage language enclaves results from the Haitian diaspora in the Americas. Haitian immigrants tend to live together, which reinforces the maintenance of Haitian *Kreyòl* past the first generation. Social discrimination and racism, frequently combined with undocumented immigrant status, further isolates Haitians in many countries, and also contributes to heritage language survival.

Haitians in the neighboring Dominican Republic typically migrate between the two nations, and are not readily classified as heritage speakers, although some descendents of Haitians – known as *pichón de haitiano*, literally "Haitian chicks" – retain Haitian Creole as well as Spanish (Ortiz López 2010). An enclave in the Samaná Peninsula also contains a few remaining speakers of an archaic variety of Haitian Creole (Jacobs 2013). A few remaining heritage speakers of Haitian Creole are also found in eastern Cuba (Ortiz López 1998, 1999a, 1999b, 2001).

Haitian immigration in contemporary South America is considerable, and with each natural or political crisis in Haiti, the numbers continue to grow (Audebert 2017). Haitians have formed immigrant communities in Argentina (De Heusch 2016; Duffard 2016; Del Águila 2018), Brazil (Godoy 2011; Alessi 2013; Moraes 2013; Cogo 2014; Nieto 2014), Ecuador (Ceja Cárdenas 2014, 2015; Burbano Alarcón 2015), Chile (Cosgaya 2008; Maza Espinoza and Santibáñez Gaete 2015; Toledo Vega 2016; Guerrero Lacoste 2017; Rojas Pedemonte et al. 2017; Campos-Bustos 2018, 2019; Sumonte et al. 2018), Peru (Vásquez et al. 2014), and Venezuela (Bermúdez 2017). Even in nearby Mexico, where Haitians were virtually unknown, there is a growing Haitian population (Menchaca 2018). To date, there are no reports of Haitian Creole being taught in any of these countries, although at the local level some de facto bilingual education may occur, as Haitian immigrants are incorporated into classroom activities.

13.5 Heritage Languages Resulting from Contract Labor

A major source of heritage language communities – particularly in the Caribbean and Central America – is contract labor recruitment in previous generations. From the construction of the Panama Canal and Central American railroads to the labor needs of sugar cane and banana plantations, recruited workers from creole-speaking Caribbean islands arrived by the thousands, and lived together in communities in which their languages survived. Most spoke some variety of West Indian Creole English; in some cases, French Creole from the Lesser Antilles was also present. The recruited laborers were almost always racially and culturally distinct from the dominant populations in the countries that had recruited them, which combined with their subaltern status and the concomitant social and economic discrimination contributed to retention of heritage languages in successive generations. Currently, lesser Antilles French Creole has all but disappeared, with a few speakers found in the Venezuelan mining town of El Callao and more in Paria, on the Güiria Peninsula near Trinidad (Ferreira and Holbrook 2002; Ferreira 2009, 2010). Various forms of West Indian Creole English continue to be spoken in Central America, as well as in Cuba, the Dominican Republic, and Puerto Rico.

13.5.1 West Indian Creole English

All along the Caribbean coast of Spanish-speaking Central America, from Guatemala to the Panama Canal, the majority population is of Afro-Antillean origin, and speaks varieties of West Indian Creole English. The origins of these creole English-speaking communities are as varied as the areas in which they live, although most arrived during the late nineteenth and early twentieth centuries (Avella 2002). In Costa Rica, Antillean workers were imported to build the railroad, then to work in the expanding banana industry. In Bocas del Toro in northwestern Panama, as well as in Honduras and Guatemala, Afro-Antilleans worked in fruit plantations and railroads, while in Colón, Panama, most creole English speakers are descendants of workers who constructed the Panama Canal. Panamanian Creole English has been studied by Aceto (1995, 1996, 1998), Bishop (1976), Cohen (1976), Herzfeld (1980), Justavino de López (2008), Snow (2000, 2007), and Thomas-Brereton (1993), among others. The creole English of Limón Costa Rica has been documented by such scholars as Chaves (1993, 1995, 2005), Herzfeld (1980, 1994, 2003, 2004), Portilla (1997), Sharpe (1997, 1998), Winkler (2000), and Zimmer (2007), among others. There is little information on the linguistic structure of Creole English along the Caribbean coast of Guatemala and Honduras, where attention is more frequently directed at the Garifuna communities (in some of which Creole English is also spoken).

Nicaragua's Miskito Coast is home to speakers of a variety of Creole English that antedates contract labor, having originated in earlier colonial times (Holm 1978), and as such is more properly classified as a regional non-heritage language, which only recently has come into contact with the national language, Spanish. Substantially, the same is true for the creole and non-creole English varieties spoken on the Honduras Bay Islands (Warantz 1986; Graham 1997, 2005, 2010), and on the Colombian islands of San Andrés and Providencia (Parsons 1956; Dittmann 1992, 2008; Arbeláez 2006; Flórez 2006; Bartens 2013; Calabresi 2014; Chaves 2014n).

The largest population of Creole English speakers in the Spanish-speaking Caribbean nations is found in the Dominican Republic, where descendants of Jamaican laborers, known as *Cocolos*, continue to speak the language and maintain Jamaican customs (Mota Acosta 1977; Walcot 1998; Inoa 2005). Creole English-speaking laborers from Jamaica and other British Caribbean islands were also present in large numbers in Cuba beginning in the twentieth century (Sánchez Guerra 2004; Graham 2013; Howard 2015). In some communities, Creole English and West Indian customs continue to flourish, as documented in the film *My Footsteps in Baraguá* (Rolando 1996). In Puerto Rico, thousands of creole English speakers have arrived from the neighboring Virgen Islands, and more recently Santurce, in metropolitan San Juan, has become home to a large community of workers from all of the Anglophone Caribbean, mostly undocumented workers. Creole English is the lingua franca of this neighborhood; St. Thomas, St. Croix, St. Kitts, St. Lucia, Antigua, Barbuda, and St. Barts are among the many islands represented in this speech community. Most of the linguistic studies of these Creole English speakers, as well as numerous literary imitations, focus on their approximations to Spanish (e.g., Lipski 2004a, 2004b, 2005, 2007; D'Arpa, 2015); there are as yet no linguistic studies of these displaced varieties of Creole English.

Creole English has never been taught in any of these communities, but some teaching of (standard American) English has occurred from time to time, with little consideration for the mismatch between the languages (e.g., Abouchaar 2013 for San Andrés; Bogarin and Ross 1980 for Costa Rica; Ministry of Education 1980 for Nicaragua).

13.6 Conclusions

The continuing existence of heritage languages throughout Latin America is sustained by ongoing immigration as well as by tenacious cultural maintenance in many communities. Among the heritage languages not included in this survey, Arabic and Chinese varieties are present throughout the Americas (Akmir 2009; Cesarín 2010). The Afro-Colombian creole

Palenquero, spoken in the village of San Basilio de Palenque, is present as a heritage language in the large Palenquero diasporic communities in the Colombian cities of Cartagena, Barranquilla, and Valledupar, as well as in western Venezuela (Camargo González 2004; Canavate 2010; Salgado Reyes 2011). The migration of Native Americans from traditional communities to urban settings, often in countries other than their own, is resulting in heritage speakers of Quechua, Aymara, Wayuunaiki, Mapudungun, Mixtec, and Mayan languages, among others. Additional heritage language clusters are the result of migration from West African nations such as Cape Verde, Senegal, and Nigeria to Argentina and Brazil. These and many other linguistic nuclei further highlight the rich tapestry of heritage languages in Latin America, the number and diversity of which provides both challenges and opportunities for linguistic analysis.

References

Abouchaar, A. 2013. Educación bilingüe en San Andrés, Providencia y Santa Catalina, y la revitalización del continuo del creole [Bilingual Education in San Andrés, Providencia and Santa Catalina, and the Revitalization of the Creole Continuum]. In L. Ochoa Sierra (ed.), *Investigación e innovación educativa: panorama general [Educational Research and Innovation: Overview]*. Bogotá: National University of Colombia, Facultad de Ciencias, Instituto de Investigación en Educación [Faculty of Sciences, Institute for Research in Education], 41–60.

Aceto, M. 1995. Variation in a Secret Creole Language of Panama. *Language in Society* 24(4), 537–560.

Aceto, M. 1996. Variation in a Variety of Panamanian Creole English. Doctoral dissertation, University of Texas at Austin.

Aceto, M. 1998. A New Creole Future Tense Marker Emerges in the Panamanian West Indies. *American Speech* 73(1), 29–43.

Adachi, N. 2001. Japanese Brazilians: The Japanese Language Communities in Brazil. *Studies in the Linguistic Sciences* 31(1), 161–178.

Agozzino, M. T. 2006. Transplanted Traditions: An Assessment of Welsh Lore and Language in Argentina. *E-Keltoi: Journal of Interdisciplinary Celtic Studies* 1, 39–67.

Aimasso, A. 2016. Cocoliche. Necesidad, esfuerzo, identidad y, quizá, un idioma [Cocoliche. Need, Effort, Identity and, Perhaps, a Language]. Bachelor's thesis, Venice: Ca'Foscari University.

Akmir, A. (ed.) 2009. *Los árabes en América Latina: historia de una emigración [Arabs in Latin America: History of an Emigration]*. Madrid: Siglo XXI de España Editores.

Albuquerque, J. L. C. (2009). A dinâmica das fronteiras: deslocamento e circulação dos" brasiguaios" entre os limites nacionais [The Dynamics of Borders: Displacement and Circulation of "brasiguaios" between National Limits]. *Horizontes Antropológicos [Anthropological Horizons]* 15 (31), 137–166.

Alessi, M. L. B. 2013. A Migração de Haitianos para o Brasil [Migration of Haitians to Brazil]. *Conjuntura Global [Global Environment]* 2(2), 82–86.

Altenhofen, C. V. 1996. *Hunsrückisch in Rio Grande do Sul: ein Beitrag zur Beschreibung einer deutschbrasilianischen Dialektvarietät im Kontakt mit dem Portugiesischen [Hunsrückisch in Rio Grande do Sul: A Contribution to the Description of a German-Brazilian Dialect Variety in Contact with Portuguese].* Stuttgart: Franz Steiner Verlag.

Almeida, T. A. de and V. J. Santi. 2018. Somos migrantes: o uso das redes sociais na produção midiática alternativa sobre a migração venezuelana em Roraima [We Are Migrants: The Use of Social Networks in Alternative Media Production on Venezuelan Migration in Roraima]. *Aturá-Revista Pan-Amazônica de Comunicação [Aturá-Pan-Amazonian Journal of Communication]* 2(1), 136–156.

Altenhofen, C. V. and J. Frey. 2006. Das bresilionische Deitsch unn die deitsche Bresilioner: en Hunsrickisch Red fo die Sprocherechte. *Revista Contingentia [Contingentia Magazine]* 1(1), 39–50.

Alves, I. M. and B. O. Maroneze. 2004. Italianismos na língua portuguesa contemporânea [Italianisms in Contemporary Portuguese]. *Revista de Italianistica [Italianistica Magazine]* 9, 29–36.

Arbeláez, J. A. 2006. Estudio sociolingüístico de San Andrés, isla: un aporte a la cultura sanandresana [Sociolinguistic Study of San Andrés Island: A Contribution to the Culture of San Andrés]. *Cuadernos del Caribe [Caribbean Notebooks]* 4(8), 42–55.

Armilato, T. G. 2010. A comunicação no rádio e a preservação de uma identidade lingüística regional: o Italian [Radio Communication and the Preservation of a Regional Linguistic Identity: Italian]. Master's thesis, Caixas do Sul: Universidade de [University of] Caixas do Sul.

Audebert, C. 2017. The Recent Geodynamics of Haitian Migration in the Americas: Refugees or Economic Migrants? *Revista Brasileira de Estudos de População [Brazilian Journal of Population Studies]* 34(1), 55–71.

Avella, F. 2002. La diáspora creole anglófona del Caribe Occidental [The Anglophone Creole Diaspora of the Western Caribbean]. *Jangwa Pana* 2 (1), 3–16.

Bandeira, M. T. and M. C. Zimmer. 2012. The Dynamics of Interlinguistic Transfer of VOT Patterns in Multilingual Children. *Linguagem & Ensino [Language and Teaching]* (Pelotas) 15(2), 341–364.

Barnes, H. 2009. A Sociolinguistic Study of Sustained Veneto-Spanish Bilingualism in Chipilo, Mexico. Doctoral dissertation, The Pennsylvania State University.

Barnes, H. 2017. Language Ideologies in an Immigrant Language Setting: The Case of a European Language in Mexico. *Caribbean Studies* 45, 21–41.

Barrios, G. 1999. Etnicidad y lenguaje: la aculturación sociolingüística de los inmigrantes italianos en Montevideo [Ethnicity and Language: The Sociolinguistic Acculturation of Italian Immigrants in Montevideo]. Doctoral dissertation, Bahia Blanca: Universidad Nacional del Sur [National University of the South].

Barrios, G. 2003. Mantenimiento y cambio de lengua en los inmigrantes italianos residentes en Montevideo [Maintenance and Language Change in Italian Immigrants Living in Montevideo]. In G. Barrios (ed.), *Aspectos de la cultura italiana en el Uruguay [Aspects of Italian Culture in Uruguay]*. Montevideo: Ministerio de Educación y Cultura [Ministry of Education and Culture], 43–87.

Barrios, G. and S. Mazzolini. 1994. El proceso de acomodación lingüística en los migrantes italianos residentes en Montevideo [The Process of Linguistic Accommodation in Italian Migrants Residing in Montevideo]. In A. Elizaincín and I. Madfes (eds.), *Analis del discurso [Discourse Analysis]*. Montevideo: Facultad de Humanidades y Ciencias de la Educación [Faculty of Humanities and Educational Sciences], 57–69.

Barrios, G., S. Mazzolini, and V. Orlando. 1994. Lengua, cultura e identidad: los italianos en el Uruguay actual [Language, Culture and Identity: Italians in Today's Uruguay]. In S. Álvarez de Lasowski (ed.), *Presencia italiana en la cultura uruguaya [Italian Presence in Uruguayan Culture]*. Montevideo: Facultad de Humanidades y Ciencias de la Educación [Faculty of Humanities and Educational Sciences], 97–115.

Barros, F. H. T. de and N. I. Philippsen. 2013. O hunsrückisch: entre o hochdeutsch e o português brasileiro: o caso do rádio na comunidade teuto-gaúcha norte mato-grossense [Hunsrückisch: Between Hochdeutsch and Brazilian Portuguese: The Case of Radio in the Teuto-Gaúcha Community in Northern Mato Grosso]. *Revista de Letras Norte@ mentos* 6(12), 111–132.

Bartens, A. 2013. San Andres Creole English. In S. M. Michaelis, P. Maurer, M. Haspelmath, and M. Huber (eds.), *The Survey of Pidgin and Creole Languages, vol. 1*. Oxford: Oxford University Press, 101–114.

Basso, C. 2002. *El último secreto de Colonia Dignidad [The Last Secret of Colonia Dignidad]*. Santiago de Chile: Editorial Mare Nostrum.

Beilke, N. S. V. 2013a. Pomerano: uma variedade germânica em Minas Gerais [Pomeranian: A Germanic Variety in Minas Gerais]. *Anais do SILEL [Annals of SILEL]* 3(1), 1–14.

Beilke, N. S. V. 2013b. Do nativo ao pomerano: as línguas, os dialetos e falares vivos de um Brasil pouco conhecido [From Native to Pomeranian: Languages, Dialects and Living Words of a Little-Known Brazil]. *Domínios de Lingu@gem* 7(1), 263–283.

Benincá, L. R. 2009. Dificuldade no domínio de fonemas do português por crianças bilíngues de português e pomerano [Difficulty Mastering Portuguese Phonemes by Bilingual Portuguese and Pomeranian

Children]. *Revista (Con) textos Lingüísticos [Journal (With) Linguistic Texts]* 3.3(1), 53–70.

Berger, I. R. 2011. Por políticas linguístico-educacionais sensíveis ao contexto da Tríplice Fronteira Argentina-Brasil-Paraguai [For Linguistic-Educational Policies Sensitive to the Context of the Argentina-Brazil-Paraguay Triple Border]. *Ideação [Ideation]* 13(2), 33–44.

Bermúdez, C. R. 2017. "Voy después de ti." Aproximación etnográfica a las redes migratorias de haitianos en Venezuela ["I'm Going after You." Ethnographic Approach to the Migratory Networks of Haitians in Venezuela]. *Espacio abierto: cuaderno venezolano de sociología [Open Space: Venezuelan Sociology Notebook]* 26(3), 139–163.

Bianchezzi, C., D. M. Machiavelli, L. L. Bertuzzi, and M. S. C. Kophal. 2012. A construção e a prática do programa bilíngue em região de fronteira internacional Brasil-Argentina [The Construction and Practice of the Bilingual Program in a Brazil-Argentina International Border Region]. *Revista Cadernos do Ceom [Cadernos do Ceom Journal]* 25(37), 17–37.

Bishop, H. A. 1976. Bidialectal Traits of West Indians in the Panama Canal Zone. Ed. D. dissertation, Columbia University Teachers College.

Blanc, J. 2015. Enclaves of Inequality: Brasiguaios and the Transformation of the Brazil-Paraguay Borderlands. *Journal of Peasant Studies* 42(1), 145–158.

Blank, M. T. and A. R. M. Miranda. 2012. Aspectos fonético-fonológicos da aquisição da escrita do português por crianças bilingües (pomerano/português) [Phonetic-Phonological Aspects of the Acquisition of Portuguese Writing by BILINGUAL CHILDREN (Pomeranian / Portuguese)]. *Anais do X Encontro do CELSUL-Círculo de Estudos Linguísticos do Sul UNIOESTE [Proceedings of the 10th CELSUL Meeting: Circle of Linguistic Studies of the South UNIOESTE]*. Cascavel: Universidade Estadual do Oeste do Paraná, 466–477.

Bogarín, J. and D. Ross. 1980. Limón: educación y bilingüismo [Limón: Education and Bilingualism]. *Letras [Letters]* 2(6), 205–257.

Bondarenko, N. V. 2012. Lenguas minoritarias de Venezuela: consideraciones desde la perspectiva ecolingüística [Minority Languages of Venezuela: Considerations from the Ecolinguistic Perspective. *Revista de Filología y Lingüística de la Universidad de Costa Rica [Journal of Philology and Linguistics of the University of Costa Rica]* Vol. 36, 1, 175–189.

Bondarenko Pisemskaya, N. 2010. Situación ecolingüística venezolana contemporánea [Contemporary Venezuelan Ecolinguistic Situation]. *Papeles de Trabajo [Working Papers]*, no. 20, diciembre [December] 2010, 22–35. Rosario, Argentina: Universidad de Rosario, Centro de Estudios Interdisciplinarios en Etnolingüística y Antropología Socio-Cultural [University of Rosario, Center for Interdisciplinary Studies in Ethnolinguistics and Socio-Cultural Anthropology].

Boruszenko, O. 1981. *A imigração ucraniana no Paraná [Ukrainian Immigration in Paraná]*. Munich: Wirtschaftskraften und Wirtschaftswege.

Boso, I. M. 1991. Entre passado e futuro: bilingüismo em uma comunidade trentino-brasileiro [Between Past and Future: Bilingualism in a Trentino-Brazilian Community]. Master's thesis, Florianópolis: Universidad Federal de [Federal University of] Santa Catarina.

Bottos, L. C. 2008. *Old Colony Mennonites in Argentina and Bolivia: Nation Making, Religious Conflict and Imagination of the Future*. Leiden: Brill.

Bremenkamp, E. S. 2014. Análise sociolingüística da manutenção da língua pomerana em Santa Maria de Jetibá, Espírito Santo [Sociolinguistic Analysis of the Maintenance of the Pomeranian Language in Santa Maria de Jetibá, Espírito Santo]. Master's thesis, Santa Maria de Jetibá: Universidade Federal do [Federal University of] Espírito Santo.

Burbano Alarcón, M. 2015. Las asociaciones de migrantes haitianos en el Ecuador: entre debilidad y resistencia [Haitian Migrant Associations in Ecuador: Between Weakness and Resistance]. *REMHU: Revista Interdisciplinar da Mobilidade Humana [Interdisciplinary Journal of Human Mobility]* 23(44), 207–220.

Calabresi, G. 2014. Religión, etnicidad raizal y educación trilingüe: un estudio de caso en la Isla de San Andrés (Colombia) [Religion, Raizal Ethnicity and Trilingual Education: A Case Study in the Island of San Andrés (Colombia)]. *Gazeta de Antropología [Anthropology Gazette]* 30 (1), article 05. Retrieved from http://digibug.ugr.es/bitstream/handle/10481/30311/GA%2030-1-05%20Gloria%20Calabresi.pdf?sequence=6&isAllowed=y

Camargo González, M. 2004. Palenqueros en Barranquilla. Construyendo identidad y memorias urbanas [Palenqueros in Barranquilla. Building Identity and Urban Memories]. *Memorias. Revista Digital de Historia y Arqueología desde el Caribe [Memories. Digital Magazine of History and Archeology from the Caribbean]* 1(1).

Campos, C. M. 2006. *A política da língua na era Vargas: proibação do falar alemão e resistências no Sul do Brasil [Language Policy in the Vargas Era: Prohibition of Speaking German and Resistance in Southern Brazil]*. Campinas: Editora da UNICAMP.

Campos-Bustos, J. L. 2018. Diálogo intercultural en las aulas: El caso chileno haitiano [Intercultural Dialogue in the Classroom: The Chilean Haitian Case]. *REXE. Revista de Estudios y Experiencias en Educación [REXE. Journal of Studies and Experiences in Education]* 17(35), 155–166.

Campos-Bustos, J. L. 2019. Estudiantado haitiano en Chile: aproximaciones a los procesos de integración lingüística en el aula [Haitian Students in Chile: Approaches to the Processes of Linguistic Integration in the Classroom]. *Revista Educación [Education Journal]* 43(1), 433–450.

Canavate, D. L. 2010. Negras, palenqueras y afrocartageneras. Construyendo un lugar contra la exclusión y la discriminación [Blacks, Palenqueras and Afrocartageneras. Building a Place against Exclusion and Discrimination]. *Reflexión política [Political Reflections]* 12(23), 152–166.

Capaccio, N. (ed.) 2001. *La colonización alemana en Misiones [German Colonization in Misiones]*. Posadas: Editorial de la Universidad Nacional de Posadas.

Caprara, L. de S. and O. A. Mordente. 2004. Panorama dell´ italiano in San Paolo nel contesto plurilinguistico brasiliano [Panorama of Italian in Sao Paulo in the Brazilian Multilingual Context]. *Revista de Iitalianistica* 9, 101–112.

Carvalho, Ana Maria. 2003. Rumo a uma definição do Português Uruguaio [Toward a Definition of Uruguayan Portuguese]. *Revista Internacional de Lingüística Iberoamericana [International Journal of Ibero-American Linguistics]* 1(2), 125–149.

Carvalho, A. M. 2004. I Speak Like the Guys on TV: Palatalization and the Urbanization of Uruguayan Portuguese. *Language Variation and Change* 16, 127–151.

Cassigoli, R. 2013. Sobre la presencia nazi en Chile [On the Nazi Presence in Chile]. *Acta Sociológica* 61, 157–177.

Castro, G. M. de 1997. Pedrinhas Paulista: Comunidade italiana que ainda permanece ligada à língua maternal [Pedrinhas Paulista: Italian Community That Still Remains Linked to the Mother Tongue]. *Revista de Italianistica* 5(5), 275–280.

Ceja Cárdenas, I. 2014. Negociación de identidades de los migrantes haitianos en Quito. Master's thesis, Quito: Facultad Latinoamericana de Ciencias Sociales sede Ecuador [Negotiation of Identities of Haitian Migrants in Quito. Quito: Latin American Faculty of Social Sciences, Ecuador headquarters].

Ceja Cárdenas, I. 2015. Migraciones haitianas en la región andina [Haitian Migrations in the Andean Region]. *Andina Migrante [Andean Migrant]* 19, 2–13.

Cenni, F. 2003. *Italianos no Brasil: "andiamo in 'Merica" [Italians in Brazil: "Let's Go to 'Merica"]*. São Paulo: Editorial da Universidade de São Paulo.

Cesarín, S. 2010. Las comunidades chinas en América Latina [Chinese Communities in Latin America]. *Nueva sociedad [New Society]* 228, 100–115.

Chaves, D. S. M. 2014. La situación sociolingüística de la lengua creole de San Andrés Isla: el caso de San Luis [The Sociolinguistic Situation of the Creole Language of San Andrés Island: The Case of San Luis]. *Colombian Applied Linguistics Journal* 16(1), 55–66.

Chaves, M. P. 1993. Fonemas segmentales en el criollo inglés de Limón [Segmental Phonemes in the English Creole of Limón]. *Revista de Filología y Lingüística de la Universidad de Costa Rica [Journal of Philology and Linguistics of the University of Costa Rica]* 19(2), 89–97.

Chaves, M. P. 1995. Tono en el criollo inglés de Costa Rica [Tone in English Creole from Costa Rica]. *Revista de filología y lingüística de la Universidad de Costa Rica [Journal of Philology and Linguistics of the University of Costa Rica]* 21(1), 135–139.

Chaves, M. P. 2005. Cláusulas relativas en el inglés criollo de Costa Rica [Relative Clauses in the Creole English of Costa Rica]. *Revista de Filología y Lingüística de la Universidad de Costa Rica [Journal of Philology and Linguistics of the University of Costa Rica]*, 251–266.

Cipria, A. 2007. A 250 años de la primera migración: Lealtad y auto-estima lingüísticas en comunidades de alemanes del Volga en Entre Ríos [250 Years after the First Migration: Linguistic Loyalty and Self-Esteem in Communities of Volga Germans in Entre Ríos]. *Southern Journal of Linguistics* 31, 1–19.

Cogo, D. 2014. Haitianos no Brasil. Comunicação e interação em redes migratórias transnacionais [Haitians in Brazil. Communication and Interaction in Transnational Migratory Networks]. *Chasqui. Revista Latinoamericana de Comunicación [Latin American Journal of Communication]* 125, 23–32.

Cohen, P. (ed.) 1976. *Primeras jornadas lingüísticas: el inglés criolllo de Panamá [First Linguistic Sessions: Creole English from Panama]*. Panama: Editorial Universitaria.

Colantoni, L. and J. Gurlekian. 2004. Convergence and Intonation: Historical Evidence from Buenos Aires Spanish. *Bilingualism: Language and Cognition* 7(2), 107–119.

Cortés Conde, F. 1994. English as an Instrumental Language: Language Displacement in the Anglo-Argentine Community. *Bilingual-Review / La revista-bilingüe* 19(1), 25–38.

Cortes Conde, F. 2007. *Los angloargentinos en Buenos Aires. Lengua, identidad y nación antes y después de Malvinas [Anglo-Argentines in Buenos Aires. Language, Identity and Nation before and after Malvinas]*. Buenos Aires: Editorial Biblos.

Cosgaya, T. P. 2008. Fronteras imaginarias en América Latina: La experiencia migratoria de haitianos en Chile [Imaginary Frontiers in Latin America: The Migration Experience of Haitians in Chile]. *Revista Rumbos TS. Un espacio crítico para la reflexión en Ciencias Sociales [Rumbos TS Magazine. A Critical Space for Reflection in Social Sciences]* 3, 69–82.

Costa, L. T. da and M. I. Gielinski. 2014. Detalhes fonéticos do polonês falado em Mallet [Phonetic Details of Polish Spoken at Mallet]. *Revista (Con) textos Linguísticos [Journal (with) Linguistic Texts]* 8(10), 159–174.

Cotinguiba, M. L. P. and G. C. Cotinguiba. 2014. Imigração haitiana para o Brasil: os desafios no caminho da educação escolar [Haitian Immigration to Brazil: The Challenges Facing School Education]. *Pedagógica: Revista do programa de Pós-graduaçao em Educaçao-PPGE [Pedagogical: Magazine of the Postgraduate Program in Education-PPGE]* 16(33), 61–88.

Coupland, N. and P. Garrett. 2010. Linguistic Landscapes, Discursive Frames and Metacultural Performance: The Case of Welsh Patagonia. *International Journal of the Sociology of Language* 2010(205), 7–36.

Cox, C. 2015. The Resilient Word: Linguistic Preservation and Innovation among Old Colony Mennonites in Latin America. *Journal of Mennonite Studies* 31, 50–74.

Cymbalista, R. 2007. A comunidade boliviana em São Paulo: definindo padrões de territorialidade [The Bolivian Community in São Paulo: Defining Territoriality Patterns]. *Cadernos Metrópole [Metropolis Notebooks]* 17, 119–133.

Dal Picol, G. 2013. A morfossintaxe na oralidade do vêneto sul-rio-grandense: perfil dialetal de comunidades rurais da região da 4ª légua [Morphosyntax in the Orality of the Veneto sul Rio Grande Region: Dialectal Profile of Rural Communities in the Region of the 4th League]. Master's thesis, Caixas do Sul: Universidade de [University of] Caxias do Sul.

Damke, C. 1997. *Sprachgebrauch und Sprachkontakt in der deutschen Sprahinsel in Südbrasilien [Language Use and Language Contact in the German Sprahinsel in Southern Brazil]*. Frankfurt am Main: Peter Lang.

Damke, C. 2008. O Brasildeutsch como fator da conservação da língua alemã no Brasil [Brasildeutsch as a Factor in the Conservation of the German Language in Brazil]. *Revista Trama [Trama Journal]* 4(7), 115–123.

D'Arpa, D. S. 2015. Dominican Spanish in Contact with St. Thomas English Creole: A Sociolinguistic Study of Speech Variation on St. Thomas, US Virgin Islands. Doctoral dissertation, Temple University.

Daviña, L. S. 2003. Fronteras discursivas en una región plurilingüe: español y portugués en Misiones [Discursive Frontiers in a Multilingual Region: Spanish and Portuguese in Misiones]. Master's thesis, Buenos Aires: Universidad de Buenos Aires.

DeBose, C. E. 1983, June. Samana English: A Dialect That Time Forgot. In *Annual Meeting of the Berkeley Linguistics Society* (Vol. 9, 47–53).

De Heusch, F. 2016. "Amo a mi pais, sigo hablando en creole, pero tomo el fernet con coca y como el asado": Un etnografia de los migrantes haitianos y de la venta de "bijouteria" en la ciudad de Córdoba, Argentina ["I love My Country, I Still Speak in Creole, but I Take the Fernet with Coca and Eat Barbecue": An Ethnography of Haitian Migrants and the Sale of "Bijouteria" in the City of Córdoba]. Bachelor's thesis, Córdoba: Universidad Nacional de [National University of] Córdoba.

De Torre Borges, M. 2004. Jorge Luis Borges (1899–1986). *Variaciones Borges [Borges Variations]* 18, 229–252.

Del Águila, Á. 2018. *Estudio exploratorio sobre las trayectorias socio-educativas y socio-laborales de migrantes haitianos, senegaleses y ucranianos en la ciudad de Buenos Aires [Exploratory Study on the Socio-educational and Socio-labor Trajectories of Haitian, Senegalese and Ukrainian Migrants in the City of Buenos Aires]*. Buenos Aires: Organización Internacional para las Migraciones (OIM) / Fundación Comisión Católica Argentina de Migraciones (FCCAM)

[International Organization for Migration (IOM) / Argentine Catholic Migration Commission Foundation (FCCAM)].

Demel, E. 2013. Sprachinselminderheiten in Argentinien und der Provinz Llanquihue, Chile [Language Island Minorities in Argentina and the Province of Llanquihue, Chile]. Doctoral dissertation, University of Vienna.

Deutsche-Welle (n.d.) El alemañol del sur de Chile [The German from Southern Chile]. https://p.dw.com/p/1JzXI

Dittmann, M. L. 1992. *El Criollo Sandresano, Lengua Y Cultura [Sandresan Creole, Language and Culture]*. Cali: Universidad del Valle [Valley University].

Dittmann, M. L. 2008. El criollo sanandresano: lengua y cultura raizal en el Archipiélago de San Andrés [Creole from San Andres: Raizal Language and Culture in the Archipelago of San Andrés]. In C. Tello (ed.), *Lenguas y tradición oral, memorias IX encuentro para la promoción y difusión del patrimonio inmaterial de los países iberoamericanos [Languages and Oral Tradition, Memories IX Meeting for the Promotion and Dissemination of the Intangible Heritage of the Ibero-American Countries]*. Bogotá: Corporación para la Promoción y Difusión de la Cultura, 138–159.

Doi, E. T. 2006. O ensino de japonês no Brasil como língua de imigração [Japanese Teaching in Brazil as an Immigration Language]. *Estudos Lingüísticos [Linguistic Studies]. XXXV. Campinas*, 66–75.

Drozdowska-Broering, I. 2016. De Sproak, det is miene kleine Heijmat. Mennonitengemeinden in Südbrasilien [The Language, that's My Little Heijmat. Mennonite Communities in Southern Brazil]. *Studia Germanica Gedanensia* 35, 78–88.

Druszcz, A. M. 1984. O bilingüismo em Araucária: A interferência polonesa na fonologia portuguesa [Bilingualism in Araucária: Polish Interference in Portuguese Phonology]. Master's thesis, Curitiba: Universidade Católica do Paraná [Catholic University of Paraná].

Dück, E. S. 2005. Witmarsum, uma comunidade trilíngüe: Plautdietsch, Hochdeutsch e portuguęs [Witmarsum, a Trilingual Community: Plautdietsch, Hochdeutsch and Portuguese]. Master's thesis, Curitiba: Universidade Fedral de Paraná [Federal University of Paraná].

Dück, E. S. 2011. Vitalidade linguística do 'Plautdietsch' em contato com variedades 'Standard' faladas em comunidades menonitas no Brasil [Linguistic Vitality of "Plautdietsch" in Contact with "Standard" Varieties Spoken in Mennonite Communities in Brazil]. Porto Alegre: Universidade Federal do [Federal University of] Rio Grande do Sul, Doctoral dissertation.

Dück, E. S. 2012. Vitalidad lingüística do Plautdietsch no Brasil [Linguistic Vitality of Plautdietsch in Brazil]. *Anais do X Encontro do CELSUL – Círculo de Estudos Lingüísticos do Sul UNIOESTE[Annals of the X CELSUL Meeting – Southern Linguistic Studies Circle UNIOESTE]*. Cascavel: Universidade Estadual do Oeste do Paraná [State University of Western Paraná], 1–12.

Duffard, I. 2016. Del Caribe haitiano a la Argentina: Trayectorias de cuerpos en movilidad humana pos terremoto 2010 [From the Haitian Caribbean to Argentina: Trajectories of Bodies in Human Mobility after the 2010 Earthquake]. Buenos Aires: CLACSO. DGCIN (2013). Cooperación Sur-Sur: República Argentina. Catálogo de Proyectos [South-South Cooperation: Argentine Republic. Project Catalog].

Dupoux, E., K. Kakehi, Y. Hirose, C. Pallier, and J. Mehler. 1999. Epenthetic Vowels in Japanese: A Perceptual Illusion? *Journal of Experimental Psychology: Human Perception and Performance* 25(6), 1568–1578.

Dvorak, A. 2013. A Hidden Immigration: The Geography of Polish-Brazilian Cultural Identity. Doctoral dissertation, University of California Los Angeles.

Elizaincín, A. 1973. *Algunos aspectos de la sociolingüística del dialecto Fronterizo* [Some Aspects of the Sociolinguistics of the Border Dialect]. Montevideo: Universidad de la República [University of the Republic].

Elizaincín, A. 1976. The Emergence of Bilingual Dialects on the Brazilian-Uruguayan Border. *International Journal of the Sociology of Language* 9, 123–134.

Elizaincín, A. 1979. *Algunas precisiones sobre los dialectos portugueses en el Uruguay* [Some Details about the Portuguese Dialects in Uruguay]. Montevideo: Universidad de la República [University of the Republic].

Elizaincín, A., L. Behares, and G. Barrios. 1987. *Nos falemo brasilero [Let's Talk Brazilian]*. Montevideo: Editorial Amesur.

Ferraz, A. P. 2007. O panorama lingüístico brasileiro: a coexistência de línguas minoritárias com o português [The Brazilian Linguistic Panorama: The Coexistence of Minority Languages with Portuguese]. *Filologia e Linguística Portuguesa [Philology and Portuguese Linguistics]* 9, 43–73.

Ferreira, J. A. S. 2009. The History and Future of Patuá in Paria: Report on Initial Language Revitalization Efforts for French Creole in Venezuela. *Journal of Pidgin and Creole Languages* 24(1), 139–158.

Ferreira, J. A. S. 2010. La historia y el futuro del patuá en Paria: Informe de los esfuerzos iniciales en la revitalización del criollo francés en Venezuela. *Romanitas, lenguas y literaturas romances* 4(2), 3–11. [See above reference for translation].

Ferreira, J. A. and D. Holbrook. 2002. The Case of Some French-lexifier Creoles. *La Torre: Revista de la Universidad de Puerto Rico [La Torre: Journal of the University of Puerto Rico]* 7(25), 367–398.

Flórez, S. 2006. A Study of Language Attitudes in Two Creole-Speaking Islands: San Andres and Providence (Colombia). *Ikala, Revista de lenguaje y cultura [Ikala, Journal of Language and Culture]* 11(17), 119–147.

Fritzen, M. P. 2007. "Ich kann mein Name mit letra junta und letra solta schreib": Deutsch-portugiesisches Code-Switching in einer Grundschule im südbrasilianischen Immigrationsgebiet ["I can write my name with letra junta and letra solta": German-Portuguese Code Switching in a Primary School in the Immigration Region of Southern Brazil]. *Pandaemonium Germanicum. Revista de Estudos Germanísticos* 11, 125–156.

Fritzen, M. P. 2012. Desafios para a educação em contexto bilíngue (alemão/ português) de língua minoritária [Challenges for Education in a Bilingual (German / Portuguese) Minority Language Context]. *Educação Unisinos [Education Unisinos]* 16(2), 161–168.

Fuchs, C. Y. M. 1996. Interferências fonológicas nos falantes bilingües do português e do japonês: fatores socio e psicolingüísticos [Phonological Interference in Portuguese and Japanese Bilingual Speakers: Socio and Psycholinguistic Factors]. Master's thesis, Curitiba: Universidade Federal do [Federal University of] Paraná.

Fujiwara, E. Y. 2014. A criação de neologismos de base japonesa por falantes de português [The Creation of Japanese-Based Neologisms by Portuguese Speakers]. Master's thesis, Três Lagoas: Universidade Federal de Mato Grosso do Sul [Federal University of Mato Grosso do Sul].

Gallero, M. C. 2005. Alemanes-brasileños en Misiones. Identidad en un contexto de frontera [Germans-Brazilians in Misiones. Identity in a Border Context]. *Actas IV Congreso Argentino de Inmigración. Santa Fe [Proceedings IV Argentine Congress of Immigration].* Esperanza, Santa Fe: Asociación Amigos del Archivo General de la Provincia [Friends of the General Archive of the Province Association].

Gallero, M. C. 2009. *Con la patria a cuestas: La inmigración alemana-brasileña en la Colonia Puerto Rico, Misiones [With the Homeland in Tow: German-Brazilian Immigration in Colonia Puerto Rico, Misiones].* Buenos Aires: Araucaria Editora.

Gallero, M. C. 2010. La territorialización de la germaneidad en los alemanes-brasileños de Misiones, Argentina [The territorialization of Germaneity in the German-Brazilians of Misiones, Argentina]. *Iberoamericana (2001-)*, Nueva época, Año 10, No. 39 (Septiembre de 2010) [*Iberoamericana* (2001–), New epoch, Year 10, No. 39 (September 2010)], 77–103.

Gallero, M. C. 2018. La cartografía etnográfica: una metodología para el estudio del poblamiento de Misiones, Argentina [Ethnographic Cartography: A Methodology for the Study of the Settlement of Misiones, Argentina]. *Vivência: Revista de Antropologia [Experience: Journal of Anthropology]* 52, 13–37.

Gallero, M. C. and E. M. Krautstofl. 2010. Proceso de poblamiento y migraciones en la Provincia de Misiones, Argentina: (1881–1970) [Process of Settlement and Migration in the Province of Misiones, Argentina: (1881–1970)]. *Avá. Revista de Antropología [Avá. Journal of Anthropology]* 16, 245–264.

Garcia, N. M. Z. 2009. Estudo linguístico-etnográfico em comunidade paranaense de imigrantes ucranianos: do passado ao presente [Linguistic-Ethnographic Study in a Paraná Community of Ukrainian Immigrants:

from the Past to the Present]. *Signum: Estudos da Linguagem [Signum: Language Studies]* 12(1), 163–189.

Gerus, W. 1986. Ukrainians in Argentina: A Canadian Perspective. *Journal of Ukrainian Studies* 11(2), 3–18.

Gibo, L. E. 2014. O contato lingüístico na comunidade okinawana do Brasil e o portugus falado pelos okinawanos [Linguistic Contact in the Okinawan Community in Brazil and the Portuguese Spoken by the Okinawan People]. *Encontros Lusófonos [Lusophone Meetings]* 16, 5–20.

Godoy, G. G. 2011. O caso dos haitianos no Brasil e a via da proteção humanitária complementar [The Case of Haitians in Brazil and the Path of Complementary Humanitarian Protection]. In A. de C. Ramos, G. Rodrigues, and G. A. de Almeida (eds.), *60 anos de [years of the] ACNUR*. São Paulo: Editora CLA Cultural, 45–68.

Graham, R. 1997. Bay Islands English: Linguistic Contact and Convergence in the Western Caribbean. Doctoral dissertation, University of Florida.

Graham, R. 2005. Partial Creolization, Restructuring and Convergence in Bay Islands Englishes. *English World-Wide* 26(1), 43–76.

Graham, R. 2010. Honduras/Bay Islands English. In D. Schreier, P. Trudgill, E. Schneider, and J. Williams (eds.), *The Lesser-Known Varieties of English: An Introduction*. Cambridge: Cambridge University Press, 92–135.

Graham, T. 2013. Jamaican Migration to Cuba: 1912–1940. Doctoral dissertation, University of Chicago.

Grau, P. C. 1994. 7: Italian Presence in Modern Venezuela: Socioeconomic Dimension and Geo-cultural Changes, 1926–1990. *Center for Migration Studies Special Issues* 11(3), 152–172.

Guerrero Lacoste, C. 2017. Inmigrantes en una escuela multicultural en Santiago de Chile: estudio antropológico-lingüístico de representaciones sociales en torno a variedades lingüísticas en contacto/conflicto: un estudio exploratorio [Immigrants in a Multicultural School in Santiago de Chile: An Anthropological-Linguistic Study of Social Representations Around Linguistic Varieties in Contact / Conflict: An Exploratory Study]. Bachelor's thesis Santiago: Universidad de [University of Chile].

Hannah, D. 1997. Copula Absence in Samaná English: Implications for Research on the Linguistic History of African-American Vernacular English. *American Speech* 72, 339–372.

Harris, T. 2018. The Welsh Language in Patagonia: Evolution and Adaptation. *European Journal of Language Policy* 10(2), 277–295.

Harwood, S. A. and M. Zapata. 2006. Preparing to Plan: Collaborative Planning in Monteverde, Costa Rica. *International Planning Studies* 11 (3–4), 187–207.

Hedges, K. L. 1997. "Plautdietsch" and "Huuchdietsch" in Chihuahua: Language, Literacy, and Identity among the Old Colony Mennonites in Northern Mexico. Doctoral dissertation, Yale University.

Hernández Medina, J. J. 2004. *Los Menonitas germanoparlantes en Paraguay: su lengua, literatura y forma de vida [The German-Speaking Mennonites in Paraguay: Their Language, Literature and Way of Life]*. Almería: Universidad de [University of] Almería.

Herzfeld, A. 1980. Limon Creole and Panamanian Creole: Comparison and Contrast. *Mid-America Linguistics Conference* 218–242.

Herzfeld, A. 1994. Language and Identity: The Black Minority of Costa Rica. *Revista de filología y lingüística de la Universidad de Costa Rica* 20(1), 113–142.

Herzfeld, A. 2003. El multilingüismo y la identidad de los afro-limonenses de Costa Rica [Multilingualism and the Identity of Afro-Limonenses in Costa Rica]. *Memoria y sociedad [Memory and Society]* 7(15), 165–175.

Herzfeld, A. 2004. *Mekaytelyu: la lengua criolla de Limón [Mekaytelyu: the Creole language of Limón]*. San José: Editorial de la Universidad de [of the University of] Costa Rica

Hipperdinger, Y. 1994. *Usos lingüísticos de los Alemanes del Volga [Linguistic Uses of the Volga Germans]*. Bahía Blanca: Universidad Nacional del Sur, Dpto. de Humanidades [National University of the South, Department of Humanities].

Hipperdinger, Y. 2015. Ethnic Revival: Actitudes, políticas y usos lingüísticos de los alemanes del Volga en la Argentina [Attitudes, Policies and Linguistic Uses of the Volga Germans in Argentina]. *Lengua y migración/Language and Migration* 7(2), 7–27.

Hipperdinger, Y. 2017. Las lenguas inmigratorias en la Argentina: El caso de los alemanes del Volga [Immigration Languages in Argentina: The Case of the Volga Germans]. *Sociedad y Discurso [Society and Speech]* 30, 92–114.

Höhmann, B. and M. M. G. Savedra. 2011. Das Pommerische in Espírito Santo: Ergebnisse und Perspektiven einer soziolinguistischen Studie [The Pomeranian in Espírito Santo: Results and Perspectives of a Sociolinguistic Study]. *Pandaemonium* (São Paulo), no. 18, 283–300.

Holm, J. A. 1978. The Creole English of Nicaragua's Miskito Coast: Its Sociolinguistic History and a Comparative Study of Its Lexicon and Syntax. Doctoral dissertation, University of London.

Howard, P. 2015. *Black Labor, White Sugar: Caribbean Braceros and Their Struggle for Power in the Cuban Sugar Industry*. Baton Rouge: Louisiana State University Press.

Huber, Alicia. 2010. *Diversidad lingüística en una comunidad altoparanaense [Linguistic Diversity in an Alto Paraná Community]*. Posadas: Editorial de la Universidad Nacional de Misiones [Editorial of the National University of Misiones].

Inoa, O. 2005. *Los cocolos en la sociedad dominicana [Cocolos in Dominican Society]*. Santo Domingo: Helvetas.

Italiano-McGreevy, M. 2013. The Linguistic Experience of Italians in Buenos Aires, Argentina, 1890–1914: Language Shift As Seen through Social Spaces. Doctoral dissertation, Temple University.

Jacobs, B. 2013. Research in Progress: Cuban and Samaná Haitian as Windows on Creole Genesis. *JournaLIPP* 2, 109–116.

Johnson, I. 2007. Subjective Ethnolinguistic Vitality of Welsh in the Chubut Province, Argentina. Doctoral dissertation, Cardiff University.

Johnson, I. 2009. How Green Is Their Valley? Subjective Vitality of Welsh Language and Culture in the Chubut Province, Argentina. *International Journal of the Sociology of Language* 2009(195), 141–171.

Jones, L. 1993. *La colonia galesa: historia de una Nueva Gales en el territorio del Chubut en la República Argentina, Sudamérica [The Welsh Colony: History of a New Wales in the Territory of Chubut in the Argentine Republic, South America]*. Rawson, Chubut: Editorial El Regional.

Jones, V. N. and C. M. Sager. 2001. Convergencia multilingüística en un campo lexical. El habla en una provincia de la Patagonia argentina: Chubut [Multilingual Convergence in a Lexical Field. He Speaks in a Province of Argentine Patagonia: Chubut]. *Escritos: Revista del Centro de Ciencias del Lenguaje [Writings: Journal of the Language Science Center]* 24, 85–97.

Justavino de López, N. 2008. Los dialectos de inglés en Panamá: un enfoque histórico, social y lingüístico [The Dialects of English in Panama: A Historical, Social and Linguistic Approach]. *Revista de Ciencias Sociales y Humanísticas Universidad de Panamá [Journal of Social and Humanistic Sciences University of Panama]* 10(2), 7–29.

Kanazawa, H. and L. Loveday. 1988. The Japanese Immigrant Community in Brazil: Language Contact and Shift. *Journal of Multilingual and Multicultural Development* 9, 423–435.

Kaufmann, G. 2007. The Verb Cluster in Mennonite Low German: A New Approach to an Old Topic. *Linguistische Berichte* 2007(210), 147–207.

Kiff, G. 2016. *Welsh Language Project in Chubut: Annual Report 2015*. Cardiff: British Council.

Klassen, J. 2016. The Politics of Pronunciation among German-Speaking Mennonites in Northern Mexico. In J. Dueck and S. A. Reily (eds.), *The Oxford Handbook of Music and World Christianities*. Oxford: Oxford University Press, 208–227.

Kurzwelly, J. 2017. Being German and Being Paraguayan in Nueva Germania: Arguing for "Contextual Epistemic Permissibility" and "Methodological Complementarity." Doctoral dissertation, University of St Andrews.

La Manna, C. 1967. *El habla de los italianos en Venezuela [He Speaks of Italians in Venezuela]*. Maracaibo: Universidad del Zulia, Facultad de Humanidades y Educación [University of Zulia, Faculty of Humanities and Education].

Ladilova, A. 2013. *Kollektive Identitätskonstruktion in der Migration: Eine Fallstudie zur Sprachkontaktsituation der Wolgadeutschen in Argentinien [Collective Identity Construction in Migration: A Case Study on the Language Contact Situation of Volga Germans in Argentina]*. Frankfurt am Main: Peter Lang.

Ladilova, A. 2015. Language and Identity of Migrants: The Role of the Heritage Language in the Process of Collective Identity Construction in a Migration Situation. *Language and Dialogue* 5(1), 176–193.

Lamy, D. S. 2012. A Variationist Account of Voice Onset Time among Bilingual West Indians in Panama. Doctoral dissertation, University of Florida.

Lara, C. C. and E. Battisti. 2014. O Voice Onset Time das plosivas do português brasileiro em contato com o Hunsrückisch e seu desvozeamento variável [The Voice Onset Time of Brazilian Portuguese Stops in Contact with Hunsrückisch and Its Variable Deviation]. *Fórum Linguístico* [*Linguistic Forum*] 11(1), 39–50.

Lavandera, B. 1984. *Variación y significado* [*Variation and Meaning*]. Buenos Aires: Hachette.

Leão, P. B. 2007. Transmissão intergeracional do alemão em contato com o português em Vale Real – RS [Intergenerational Transmission of German in Contact with Portuguese in Vale Real – RS]. Master's thesis, Porto Alegre: Universidade Federal do [Federal University of] Rio Grande do Sul.

Lehr, J. C. and S. Cipko. 2000. Contested Identities: Competing Articulations of the National Heritage of Pioneer Settlers in Misiones, Argentina. *Prairie Perspectives: Geographical Essays* 3, 165–180.

Lemke, C. K. 2010. A língua espanhola entre o português e o ucraniano: um estudo sobre a aprendizagem de terceiras línguas [The Spanish Language between Portuguese and Ukrainian: A Study on Third Language Learning]. *Revista Iberoamericana de Educación* [*Journal of Ibero-American Education*] 52, 1–11.

Leopoldino, E. A. 2009. A fala dos tiroleses de piracicaba: um perfil linguístico dos bairros Santana e Santa Olímpia [The Speech of the Piracicaba Tyroleans: A Linguistic Profile of the Santana and Santa Olímpia Neighborhoods]. Master's thesis, São Paulo: Universidade de [University of] São Paulo.

Leopoldino, E. A. 2014. A fala dos tiroleses de piracicaba: um perfil linguístico dos bairros Santana e Santa Olímpia [The speech of the Piracicaba Tyroleans: A Linguistic Profile of the Santana and Santa Olímpia Neighborhoods]. Doctoral dissertation, São Paulo: Universidade de [University of] São Paulo.

Lipski, J. 2004a. El español de América y los contactos bilingües recientes: apuntes microdialectológicos [The Spanish of America and Recent Bilingual Contacts: Microdialectological Notes]. *Revista Internacional de Lingüística iberoamericana* [*International Journal of Ibero-American Linguistics*] 4, 89–103.

Lipski, J. 2004b. El español de América: los contactos bilingües [The Spanish of America: Bilingual Contacts]. In R. Cano (ed.), *Historia de la lengua Española* [*History of Spanish Language*]. Barcelona: Ariel, 1117–1138.

Lipski, J. 2005. El español en el mundo: frutos del último siglo de contactos lingüísticos [Spanish in the World: Fruits of the Last Century of Linguistic

Contacts]. In L. Ortiz López and M. Lacorte (eds.), *Contactos y contextos lingüísticos: el español en los Estados Unidos y en contacto con otras lenguas [Contacts and Linguistic Contexts: Spanish in the United States and in Contact with other Languages]*. Frankfurt and Madrid: Vervuert/Iberoamericana, 29–53.

Lipski, J. 2007. El español de América en contacto con otras lenguas [The Spanish of America in Contact with other Languages]. In M. Lacorte (ed.), *Lingüística aplicada del español [Applied Spanish Linguistics]*. Madrid: Arco Libros, 309–345.

Lipski, J. 2011a. Um caso de contato de fronteira: o sudoeste [A Case of Border Contact: The Southwest]. In H, Mello, C. Altenhofen, and T. Raso (eds.), *Os contatos linguísticos no Brasil [Linguistic Contacts in Brazil]*. Belo Horizonte: Editora UFMG, 349–368.

Lipski, J. 2011b. Encontros linguísticos fronteiriços [Border Linguistic Meetings]. *Ideação* 13(2), 83–100. Retrieved from http://e-revista.unioeste .br/index.php/ideacao/article/viewArticle/6109

Lipski, J. 2015. Portuguese/portuñol in Misiones, Argentina: Another Fronterizo? In S. Sessarego and M. González (eds.), *New Perspectives on Hispanic Contact Linguistics*. Frankfurt and Madrid: Vervuert/ Iberoamericana, 253–281.

Lipski, J. 2017. Portuguese or Portuñol? Language Contact in Misiones, Argentina. *Journal of Linguistic Geography* 4, 47–64.

Lipski, J. 2018. La interfaz portugués-castellano en Misiones, Argentina: zona de prueba para la alternancia de lenguas [The Portuguese-Spanish Interface in Misiones, Argentina: A Test Zone for the Alternation of Languages]. *Estudios Filológicos [Philological Studies]* 60, 169–190.

López, E. 2001: Lealtad lingüística en inmigrantes árabes e italianos [Linguistic Loyalty in Arab and Italian Immigrants]. Master's thesis, Caracas: Universidad Pedagógica Experimental Libertador [Libertador Experimental Pedagogical University].

Lownes, S. P. 2018. Johnny Joãozinho Reb: The Creation and Evolution of Confederate Identity in Brazil. Doctoral dissertation, The Ohio State University.

Luersen, R. W. 2009. A situação de contato plurilíngue no sul do Brasil [The Plurilingual Contact Situation in Southern Brazil]. *Visões. Revista Científica da Faculdade Salesiana Maria Auxiliadora [Visions. Scientific Journal of the Salesian Faculty Mary Saviour of Christians]* 7, 70–87.

MacKay, C. 1984. The Veneto Dialect of Chipilo, México. *Texas Linguistic Forum* 23, 123–133.

MacKay, C. 1992. Language Maintenance in Chipilo: A Veneto Dialect in Mexico. *International Journal of the Sociology of Language* 96, 129–145.

MacKay, C. 1993. *Il dialetto veneto di Segusino e Chipilo [The Venetian Dialect of Segusino and Chipilo]*. Cornuda, Treviso: Grafiche Antiga.

MacKay, C. 1995. *A Veneto Lexicon: The Dialect of Segusino and Chipilo*. Cornuda, Treviso: Grafiche Antiga.

Maia, I. C. da. 2004. Intercambios lingüísticos de frontera: incidencia el el hablar de los alumnos del profesorado en portugués de la UNAM [Border Language Exchanges: Incidence of Portuguese Speaking in Students and Teaching Staff of the UNAM]. Master's thesis, Posadas: Universidad Nacional de [National University of] Misiones.

Malczewski, Z. 2010. *Polonii Brazylijskiej Obraz Wlasny [The Polish Diaspora's Self-Image]*. Warsaw, Biblioteka Iberyjska.

Maltzahn, P. C. 2013. Construção e Formação da identidade étnica do imigrante alemão no Rio Grande do Sul (BRASIL): A Língua Alemã como marcador importante de etnicidade [Construction and Formation of the Ethnic Identity of the German Immigrant in Rio Grande do Sul (BRAZIL): The German Language as an Important Marker of Ethnicity]. Retrieved from www.abrapa.org.br/cd/pdfs/Maltzahn-S1-Paulo-korr.pdf

Martínez Ruíz, B. 1977. *La colonización galesa en el Valle del Chubut [Welsh Colonization in the Chubut Valley]*. Buenos Aires: Editorial Galerna.

Mase, Y. 1987. A língua japonesa dos imigrantes japoneses e seus descendentes no Brasil [The Japanese Language of Japanese Immigrants and their Descendants in Brazil]. *Estudos Japoneses [Japanese Studies]* 7, 137–146.

Masing, U. 1964. Foreign Agricultural Colonies in Costa Rica: An Analysis of Foreign Colonization in a Tropical Environment. Doctoral dissertation, University of Florida.

Matthews, A. 1995. *Crónica de la colonia galesa de la Patagonia [Chronicle of the Welsh Colony of Patagonia]*. Buenos Aires: Ediciones Alfonsina.

Maza Espinoza, C. M. and G. P. Santibáñez Gaete. 2015. Ser niño haitiano (que no habla español) en una escuela chilena. Doctoral dissertation, Santiago: Universidad Academia de Humanismo Cristiano [Being a Haitian Child (Who Does Not Speak Spanish) in a Chilean School. Santiago: University Academy of Christian Humanism].

Medeiros, R. D. N. 1982. American Brazilian English. *American Speech* 57, 150–152.

Menchaca, T. R. 2018. Migrantes haitianos en México: un nuevo escenario migratorio [Haitian Migrants in Mexico: A New Migration Scenario]. *Huellas de la Migración [Traces of Migration]* 3(6), 133–156.

Meo-Zilio, G. 1955a. Fenomeni lessicali dell'italiano rioplatense [Lexical Phenomena of Rioplatense Italian]. *Lingua Nostra [Our Language]* 16, 53–55.

Meo-Zilio, G. 1955b. Influenze dello spagnolo sull'italiano parlato nel Rio de la Plata [Influences of Spanish on Italian Spoken in the Rio de la Plata]. *Lingua Nostra [Our Language]* 16, 16–22.

Meo-Zilio, G. 1955c. Contaminazioni morfologiche nel cocoliche rioplatense [Morphological Contamination in the Copliche Rioplatense]. *Lingua Nostra [Our Language]*, 16, 112–117.

Meo-Zilio, G. 1956. Interferenze sintattiche nel cocoliche rioplatense [Syntactic Interference in Cocoliche Rioplatense]. *Lingua Nostra [Our Language]* 17(54–59), 88–91.

Meo-Zilio, G. 1964. El [The] 'Cocoliche' Rioplatense. *Boletín de filología* *[Bulletin of Philology]* 16, 61–119.

Meo-Zilio, G. 1987. Lingue in contatto: interferenze fra veneto e spagnolo in Messico [Languages in Contact: Interference between Venetian and Spanish in Mexico]. In G. Meo Zilio (ed.), *Presenza, cultura, lingua e tradizioni dei veneti nel mondo, parte I: America Latina [Presence, Culture, Language and Traditions of the Venetians in the World, Part I: Latin America].* Regione Veneto [Veneto Region]: Centro Interuniverisario di Studi Veneti [Interuniverisary Center of Venetian Studies], 237–263.

Meo-Zilio, G. 1989. *Estudios hispanoamericanos: temas lingüísticos [Hispanic American Studies: Language Issues].* Rome: Bulzoni.

Meyer, M. 2009. Deitsch ou deutsch? macroanálise pluridimensional da variação do hunsrückisch rio-grandense em contato com o português [Deitsch or deutsch? Multidimensional Macroanalysis of the Variation of Hunsrückisch Rio-Grandense in Contact with Portuguese]. Undergraduate thesis Porto Alegre: Universidade Federal de [Federal University of] Rio Grando do Sul.

Mezavila, A. 2008. Bilingüismo e as redes de comunicação na comunidade ucraniana de Cascavel [Bilingualism and Communication Networks in the Ukrainian Community of Cascavel]. *Línguas e Letras [Languages and Letters]* 9(17), 289–304.

Micolis, M. 1973. *Une communauté allemande en Argentine: Eldorado (Problèmes d'intégration socio-culturelle) [A German Community in Argentina: Eldorado (Problems of Socio-cultural Integration)].* Quebec: Centre International de Recherches sur le Bilinguisme [International Center for Research on Bilingualism].

Ministry of Education. 1980. *The Sunrise of the People. A Sandinista Education Workbook for Reading and Writing.* Managua: Ministry of Education, National Literacy Crusade Heroes and Martyrs for Nicaragua's Liberation.

Miodunka, W. 2003. *Bilingwizm polsko-portugalski w Brazylii. [Polish-Portuguese Bilingualism in Brazil.]* Krakow: Universitas.

Montgomery, M. and C. A. Melo. 1990. The Phonology of the Lost Cause: The English of the Confederados in Brazil. *English World-Wide* 11(2), 195–216.

Montgomery, M. and C. A. Melo. 1995. The Language: The Preservation of Southern Speech among the Colonists. In C. B. Dawsey and J. M. Dawsey (eds.), *The Confederados: Old South immigrants in Brazil.* Tuscaloosa: University of Alabama Press, 176–190.

Moraes, I. A. 2013. A imigração haitiana para o Brasil: causas e desafios [Haitian Immigration to Brazil: Causes and Challenges]. *Conjuntura Austral [Southern Conjuncture]* 4(20), 95–114.

Mota Acosta, J. C. 1977. *Los cocolos en Santo Domingo [The Cocolos in Santo Domingo].* Santo Domingo: Editorial "La Gaviota."

Nieto, C. 2014. *Migración haitiana a Brasil: Redes migratorias y espacio social transnacional [Haitian Migration to Brazil: Migration Networks and Transnational Social Space].* Buenos Aires: CLACSO.

Ortiz López, L. 1998. *Huellas etno-sociolingüísticas bozales y afrocubanas [Ethno-sociolinguistic Footprints of bozales and Afro-Cubans]*. Frankfurt: Vervuert.

Ortiz López, L. 1999a. El español haitiano en Cuba y su relación con el habla bozal [Haitian Spanish in Cuba and Its Relationship with Muzzle Speech]. In K. Zimmermann (ed.), *Lenguas criollos de base lexical española y portuguesa [Creole Languages of Spanish and Portuguese Lexical Base]*. Frankfurt: Vervuert, 177–203.

Ortiz López, L. 1999b. La variante hispánica haitianizada en Cuba: otro rostro del contacto lingüístico en el Caribe [The Haitianized Hispanic Variation in Cuba: Another Face of Linguistic Contact in the Caribbean]. In A. Morales (ed.), *Estudios de lingüística hispánica: homenaje a María Vaquera [Hispanic Linguistics Studies: Tribute to María Vaquera]*. Río Piedras: Editorial de la UPR, 428–456.

Ortiz López, L. 2001. El sistema verbal del español haitiano en Cuba: implicaciones para las lenguas en contacto en el Caribe [The Verbal System of Haitian Spanish in Cuba: Implications for Languages in Contact in the Caribbean]. *Southwest Journal of Linguistics* 20(2), 175–192.

Ortiz López, L. 2010. *El español y el criollo haitiano: contacto lingüístico y adquisición de segunda lengua [Spanish and Haitian Creole: Linguistic Contact and Second Language Acquisition]*. Frankfurt and Madrid: Vervuert/Iberoamericana.

Ostendorf, K. 2018. Zwischen Plautdietsch, Hochdeutsch und Spanisch: Dreisprachigkeit von in Paraguay und Bolivien lebenden Mennoniten und ihre Auswirkung auf die spanische Lernersprache [Between Plautdietsch, Standard German and Spanish: Trilingualism of Mennonites Living in Paraguay and Bolivia and Their Impact on the Spanish Learner Language]. Doctoral dissertation, Bochum: Ruhr-Universität.

Ota, J. 2009. A língua falada nas comunidades rurais nipo-brasileiras do estado de São Paulo – considerações sobre koronia-go [The Language Spoken in Japanese-Brazilian Rural Communities in the State of São Paulo – Considerations about koronia-go]. *Synergies Brésil [Brazilian Synergies]* 7, 49–56.

Ota, J. and L. M. S. Gardenal. 2006. As línguas japonesa y portuguesa em duas comunidades nipo-brasileiras: a relação entre os domínios e as gerações [Japanese and Portuguese Languages in Two Japanese-Brazilian Communities: The Relationship between Domains and Generations]. *Estudos Lingüísticos [Linguistic Studies]* 35, 1062–1071.

Parlato-Oliveira, E., A. Christophe, Y. Hirose, and E. Dupoux. 2010. Plasticity of Illusory Vowel Perception in Brazilian-Japanese Bilingual. *The Journal of the Acoustical Society of America* 127(6), 3738–3748.

Parsons, J. J. 1956. *San Andrés and Providencia: English-Speaking Islands in the Western Caribbean*. Berkeley: University of California Press.

Patat, A. (ed.) 2012. *Vida nueva: la lingua e la cultura italiana in America Latina [New Life: The Language of Italian Culture in Latin America]*. Macerata: Quodlibet.

Peres, E. P. 2011. Aspectos da imigração italiana no Espírito Santo: a língua e cultura do Vêneto em Araguaia [Aspects of Italian Immigration in Espírito Santo: The Language and Culture of Veneto in Araguaia]. *Dimensões [Dimensions]* 26, 44–59.

Pérez Gómez, R. 2018. Un caso de emigración cultural? Los sudistas confederados y el Brasil de su llegada (1860–1870) [A Case of Cultural Emigration? The Confederate Southerners and the Brazil of Their Arrival (1860–1870)]. *Procesos Históricos [Historical Processes]* 34, 88–106.

Pertile, M. T. 2009. O talian entre o italiano-padrão e o português brasileiro: manutenção e substituição no Alto Uruguai gaucho [Talian between Standard Italian and Brazilian Portuguese: Maintenance and Replacement in Alto Uruguai Gaúcho]. Doctoral dissertation, Porto Alegre: Universidade Federal do [Federal University of] Rio Grande do Sul.

Pimentel, M. L. and G. C. Cotinguiba. 2014. Wout, raketè, fwontyè, anpil mizè: reflexões sobre os limites da alteridade em relação à imigração haitiana para o Brasil [Wout, raketè, fwontyè, anpil mizè: Reflections on the Limits of otherness in Relation to Haitian Immigration to Brazil]. *Universitas: Relações Internacionais [Universitas: International Relations]* 12(1), 73–86.

Poplack, S. and D. Sankoff. 1980. El inglés de Samaná y la hipótesis del origen criollo [The English of Samaná and the Hypothesis of the Creole Origin]. *Boletín de la Academia Puertorriqueña [Bulletin of the Puerto Rican Academy]* 8, 103–121.

Poplack, S. and D. Sankoff. 1987. The Philadelphia Story in the Spanish Caribbean. *American Speech* 62(4), 291–314.

Portilla, M. 1997. Tiempo-aspecto-modo en el criollo inglés de Costa Rica [Time-Aspect-Mode in the English Creole of Costa Rica]. *Revista de filología y lingüística de la Universidad de Costa Rica [Journal of Philology and Linguistics of the University of Costa Rica]* 23(2), 161–172.

Prytz Nilsson, L. S. 2011. Planificación y gestión del programa de educación intercultural bilingüe de frontera en el Mercosur educativo: su aplicación en la provincia de Misiones [Planning and Management of the Border Bilingual Intercultural Education Program in the Educational Mercosur: Its Application in the Province of Misiones]. *Ideação [Ideation]* 13(2), 21–32.

Puig Ortiz, J. A. 1978. *Emigración de libertos norteamericanos a Puerto Plata en la primera mitad del siglo XIX [Emigration of North American Freedmen to Puerto Plata in the First Half of the 19th Century]*. Santo Domingo: Editorial Alfa y Omega.

Putnam, M. T. and J. Lipski. 2016. Null Arguments in Transitional Trilingual Grammars: Field Observations from Misionero German. *Multilingua* 35(1), 85–104.

Putnam, M. T. and L. Schwarz. 2014. How Interrogative Pronouns Can Become Relative Pronouns: The Case of Was in Misionero German. *STUF-Language Typology and Universals* 67(4), 613–625.

Reygadas, C. 2007. *Luz silenciosa/Silent Light/Stellet Licht*, co-produced by J. Romandia. DVD edition New York: Palisades Tartan, 2009.

Rhys, W. C. 2000. *La Patagonia que canta: memorias de la colonización galesa [The Patagonia That Sings: Memories of the Welsh Colonization]*. Buenos Aires: Emecé.

Rodrigues, C. V. 2009. Bilinguismo no Espírito Santo: reflexos no português de adultos e crianças [Bilingualism in Espírito Santo: Reflexes in Portuguese of Adults and Children]. *Signum: Estudos da Linguagem [Signum: Language Studies]* 12(1), 293–316.

Rodríguez Demorizi, E. 1945. *Samaná, pasado y porvenir [Samaná, Past and Future]*. Ciudad Trujillo [Santo Domingo]: Montalvo.

Rojas Marquez, I. 2013. *Launa-Deutsch. Sprachkontakt und die Verwendung der deutschen Sprache in Chile [Launa German. Language Contact and the Use of the German Language in Chile]*. Munich: GRIN Verlag.

Rojas Pedemonte, N., N. Amode, and J. Vásquez. 2017. Migración haitiana hacia Chile: origen y aterrizaje de nuevos proyectos migratorios [Haitian Migration to Chile: Origin and Landing of New Migration Projects]. In N. Rojas Pedemonte and J. Koechlin (eds.), *Migración haitiana hacia el sur andino [Haitian Migration to the Southern Andes]*. Lima: Universidad Antonio Ruiz de Montoya, 65–172.

Rolando, G. 1996. *My Footsteps in Baraguá*. Havana: Mundo Latino [film].

Romani, P. 1992. *Conservación del idioma en una comunidad italo-mexicana [Language Preservation in an Italian-Mexican Community]*. Mexico: Instituto Nacional de Antropología e Historia [National Institute of Anthropology and History].

Rosell, A. 1970. *Cocoliche*. Montevideo: Distribuidora Ibana.

Rosenberg, P. 2002. Deutsche Minderheiten in Lateinamerika [German Minorities in Latin America]. In H. Donato, R. S. G. Kutschat, and J. Tiemann (eds.), *Institut Martius-Staden Jahrbuch [Yearbook] 2001–2002*, Nr. 49. São Paulo: Instituto Martius-Staden, 9–50.

Rosenberg, P. 2003a, Vergleichende Sprachinselforschung: Sprachwandel in deutschen Sprachinseln in Russland und Brasilien [Comparative Language Island Research: Language Change in German Language Islands in Russia and Brazil]. In E. Hentschel (ed.), *Particulae collectae. Festschrift für Harald Weydt zum 65. Geburtstag [Particulae Collectae. Festschrift for Harald Weydt on his 65th Birthday]* (= LinguistikOnline 13, 1/03). Frankfurt: Europa-Universität Viadrina, Fakultät für Kulturwissenschaften [European University Viadrina, Faculty of Cultural Studies], 273–323. Retrieved from https://bop.unibe.ch/linguistik-online/issue/view/205

Rosenberg, P. 2003b. Comparative Speech Island Research: Some Results from Studies in Russia and Brazil. In W. Keel and K. J. Mattheier (eds.), *Deutsche Sprachinseln weltweit: Interne und externe Perspektiven. German Language Varieties Worldwide: Internal and External Perspectives*. Frankfurt am Main: Peter Lang, 199–238.

Rosenberg, P. 2012. Regularität und Irregularität in der Kasusmorphologie deutscher Sprachinselvarietäten (Russland, Brasilien) [Regularity and Irregularity in the Case Morphology of German Language Island Varieties (Russia, Brazil)]. In K.-M. Köpcke and A. Bittner (eds.), *Regularität und Irregularität in Phonologie und Morphologie [Regularity and Irregularity in Phonology and Morphology]*. Berlin: Mouton de Gruyter, 177–217.

Rost, C. A. 2008. A identidade do teuto-brasileiro na região sul do Brasil [The Identity of the German-Brazilian in the Southern Region of Brazil]. *Interdisciplinar-Revista de Estudos em Língua e Literatura, Ano 3 [Interdisciplinary-Journal of Studies in Language and Literature, Year 3]* 5(5), 215–234.

Saiki, R. A. U. 2013. Esboço sobre o ritmo do português-brasileiro / japonês: um estudo experimental [Sketch on the Rhythm of Brazilian Portuguese / Japanese: An Experimental Study]. Undergraduate thesis, Florianópolis: Universidade Federal de [Federal University of] Santa Catarina.

Saito, C. N. I. 2011. O imigrante e a imigração japonesa no Brasil e no Estado de Goiás [The Immigrant and Japanese Immigration in Brazil and in the State of Goiás]. *Revista UFG [UFG Journal]* 13(10), 57–61.

Salgado Reyes, N. 2011. *Migración palenquera a la ciudad de Cartagena: 1960–2000 [Palenquera migration to the city of Cartagena: 1960–2000]*. Undergraduate thesis, Universidad de [University of] Cartagena.

Salinas, P. I., M. O. T. Nevárez, F. A. P. Piñón, and A. H. Torres. 2014. La identidad cultural de los menonitas mexicanos [The Cultural Identity of Mexican Mennonites]. *IE Revista de Investigación Educativa de la REDIECH [IE Journal of Educational Research of REDIECH]* 5(9), 69–76.

Sánchez Avendaño, C. 2014. "Ticos auténticos … que no hablan español" Ideologías sobre las lenguas minoritarias y la diversidad lingüística de Costa Rica ["Authentic Ticos … Who Do Not Speak Spanish" Ideologies on Minority Languages and Linguistic Diversity in Costa Rica]. *Revista de Filología y Lingüística de la Universidad de Costa Rica [Journal of Philology and Linguistics of the University of Costa Rica]* 39(2), 191–218.

Sánchez Guerra, J. 2004. *Los anglo-caribeños en Guantánamo, 1902–1950 [The Anglo-Caribbean in Guantánamo, 1902–1950]*. Guantánamo: Editorial El Mar y la Montaña.

Santos, F. N. Z. P. and T. M. Vasconcelos. 2016. Venezuelanos no Brasil: da crise econômica para a crise política e midiática [Venezuelans in Brazil: From the Economic Crisis to the Political and Media Crisis]. *XVII Encontro de História da Anpuh-Rio [XVII Anpuh-Rio History Meeting]* 1–16.

Santos, M. E. P. 2004. O cenario multilingue, multidialetal, multicultura de fronteira e o processo identitario brasiguaio na escola e no entorno social [The Multilingual, Multidialetal, Multicultural Frontier Scenario and the Brazilian Identity Process at School and in the Social Environment]. Doctoral dissertation, Campinas: Universidade Estadual de Campinas [Campinas State University].

Santos, M. E. P. 2008. Identidades híbridas, língua (gens) provisórias–alunos "brasiguaios" em foco [Hybrid Identities, Provisional Language (Genes) – "Brasiguaio" Students in Focus]. *Trabalhos em Linguística Aplicada [Applied Linguistics Employment]* 47(2), 429–446.

Sartor, M. and F. Ursini. 1983. *Cent'anni di emigrazione: una comunita veneta sugli altipiani del Messico [One Hundred Years of Emigration: A Venetian Community on the Mexican Highlands]*. Cornuda, Treviso: Grafiche Antiga.

Schaeffer, S. C. B. 2012. Descrição fonetica e fonológica do pomerano falado no Espírito Santo [Phonetic and Phonological Description of the Pomeranian Spoken in Espírito Santo]. Master's thesis, Vitória: Universidade Federal do Espírito Santo [Federal University of Espirito Santo].

Schaumloeffel, M. A. 2003. Estudo da interferência do português da variedade dialetal Hunsrück falada em Boa Vista do Herval [Study of Portuguese Interference in the Hunsrück Dialectal Variety Spoken in Boa Vista do Herval]. Master's thesis, Curutiba: Universidade Federal de Paraná [Federal University of Paraná].

Schirp, Kerstin E. 2001. *Die Wochenzeitung "Semanario Israelita": Sprachrohr der Deutsch-jüdischen Emigranten in Argentinien [The Weekly Newspaper "Semanario Israelita": Mouthpiece for German-Jewish Emigrants in Argentina]*. Berlin-Hamburg-Münster: LIT Verlag.

Schissatti, L. C. S. 2014. Interrogativas – WH no dialeto trentino de Rodeio [Interrogatives – WH in the Trentino Dialect of Rodeio]. Doctoral dissertation, Florianópolis: Universidade Federal de Santa Catarina [Federal University of Santa Catarina].

Schneider, M. N. 2012. A manutenção do Hunsrückisch e do pomerano e o ensino de alemão em comunidades teuto-brasileiras no Rio Grande do Sul [Maintaining Hunsrückisch and Pomeranians and Teaching German in German-Brazilian Communities in Rio Grande do Sul]. *Anais do X Encontro do CELSUL – Círculo de Estudos Linguísticos do Sul UNIOESTE [Annals of the 10th CELSUL Meeting – Linguistic Studies Circle of the South UNIOESTE]*. Cascavel: Universidade Estadual do Oeste do Paraná, 1–15.

Semechechem, J. 2016. O multilinguismo na escola: práticas linguísticas uma comunidade de imigração ucraniana no Paraná [Multilingualism At School: Linguistic Practices in a Ukrainian Immigration Community in Paran]. Maringá: Universidade Estadual de Maringá [State University of Maringá], doctoral dissertation.

Sharpe, M. S. 1997. A Case Study of Language Shift in Progress in Port Limon, Costa Rica. *Revista de filología y lingüística de la Universidad de Costa Rica [Journal of Philology and Linguistics of the University of Costa Rica]* 23(1), 225–234.

Sharpe, M. S. 1998. Language Attitudes of Limon Creole Speakers. *Revista de filología y lingüística de la Universidad de Costa Rica [Journal of Philology and Linguistics of the University of Costa Rica]* 24(1), 101–112.

Silva, F. R. de. 2010. A educação alemã na colônia riograndense [German Education in the Rio Grande do Norte Colony]: 1922–1938 (Maracaí/Cruzália-SP). Master's thesis, São Paulo: Universidade Estadual Paulista UNESP de Presidente Prudente [Paulista State University UNESP of Presidente Prudente].

Silva, S. A. D. 2005. A migração dos símbolos: diálogo intercultural e processos identitários entre os bolivianos em São Paulo [The Migration of Symbols: Intercultural Dialogue and Identity Processes among Bolivians in São Paulo]. *São Paulo em perspectiva [São Paulo in Perspective]* 19(3), 77–83.

Silva, S. A. D. 2006. Bolivianos em São Paulo: entre o sonho e a realidade [Bolivians in São Paulo: Between Dream and Reality]. *Estudos avançados [Advanced Studies]* 20(57), 157–170.

Silveira, A. 2014. Ingleses y escocesess en Buenos Aires: movimientos poblacionales, integración y prácticas asociativas (1800–1880) [English and Scots in Buenos Aires: Population Movements, Integration and Associative Practices (1800—1880)]. Doctoral thesis, Buenos Aires: Universidad de [University of] San Andrés.

Simai, S. and R. Baeninger. 2012. Discurso, negação e preconceito: bolivianos em São Paulo [Discourse, Denial and Prejudice: Bolivians in São Paulo]. In R. Baeninger (ed.), *Imigração boliviana no Brasil [Bolivian Immigration in Brazil]*. Campinas: NEPO/UNICAMP, 195–210.

Simões, G. da F. (ed.) 2017. *Perfil Sociodemográfico e Laboral da Imigração Venezuelana no Brasil [Sociodemographic and Labor Profile of Venezuelan Immigration in Brazil]*. Curitiba: Editora CRV.

Smith, E. V. 1989. A Merging of Two Cultures: The Afro-Hispanic Immigrants of Samaná, Dominican Republic. *Afro-Hispanic Review* 8(1–2), 9–14.

Smith, R. J. 1979. The Ethnic Japanese in Brazil. *Journal of Japanese Studies* 5 (1), 53–70.

Snow, P. 2000. The Case for Diglossia on the Panamanian Island of Bastimentos. *Journal of Pidgin and Creole languages* 15(1), 165–169.

Snow, P. 2007. Vernacular Shift: Language and the Built Environment in Bastimentos, Panama. *Identities: Global Studies in Culture and Power* 14(1–2), 161–182.

Souchaud, S. 2010. A imigração boliviana em São Paulo [Bolivian Immigration in São Paulo]. In A. P. Ferreira, C. Vainer, H. Póvoa Neto, and M. de O. Santos (eds.), *Deslocamentos e reconstruções da experiência migrante [Displacements and Reconstructions of the Migrant Experience]*. Paris: Garamond, 267–290.

Souchaud, S. and R. Baeninger. 2008. Collas e cambas do outro lado da fronteira: aspectos da distribuição diferenciada da imigração boliviana em Corumbá, Mato Grosso do Sul [Collas and Cambas across the Border: Aspects of the Different Distribution of Bolivian Immigration in

Corumbá, Mato Grosso do Sul]. *Revista Brasileira de Estudos de População [Brazilian Journal of Population Studies]* 25(2), 271–286.

Souza, A. C. 2014. Crenças e atitudes lingüísticas: a língua alemã, a língua portuguesa e o Brasildeutsch [Linguistic Beliefs and Attitudes: German, Portuguese and Brasildeutsch]. *III CIELLI: Colóquio de Estudos Lingüísticos e Literários, Universidade Estadual de Maringá, agosto 2014* (1–12). Anais electrónicos [Colloquium on Linguistic and Literary Studies, State University of Maringá, August 2014 (pp. 1–12). Electronic Proceedings] ISSN 2177-6350. Retrieved from https://drive.google.com/file/d/0B0BzcWVyuWkVVklBdkIwQ1dTWXc/view

Stößlein, H. 2009. *Deutsch-spanischer Sprachkontakt am Rio de la Plata: eine Untersuchung am Korpus deutsch-argentinischer Zeitungssprache [German-Spanish Language Contact on the Rio de la Plata: An Investigation into the Corpus of German-Argentine Newspaper Language]* (Vol. 3). Bamberg: University of Bamberg Press.

Sturza, E. R. 1994. O espanhol do cotidiano e o espanhol da escola: um estudo de caso na fronteira Brasil-Argentina [Everyday Spanish and School Spanish: A Case Study on the Brazil-Argentina Border]. Master's thesis, Santa Maria: Universidade Federal de Santa Maria [Federal University of Santa Maria].

Suda, J. R. and L. de Souza. 2006. Identidade social em movimento: a comunidade japonesa na Grande Vitória (ES) [Social Identity on the Move: The Japanese Community in Grande Vitória (ES)]. *Psicologia & Sociedade [Psychology & Society]* 18(2), 72–80.

Sumonte, V., S. Sanhueza, M. Friz, and K. Morales. 2018. Inmersión lingüística de comunidades haitianas en Chile: Aportes para el desarrollo de un modelo comunicativo intercultural [Linguistic Immersion of Haitian Communities in Chile: Contributions for the Development of an Intercultural Communicative Model]. *Paples de Trabajo* 35, 68–79. Rosario: Universidad Nacional de Rosario, Centro de Estudios Interdisciplinarios en Etnolingüística y Antropología Socio-Cultural [National University of Rosario, Center for Interdisciplinary Studies in Ethnolinguistics and Socio-Cultural Anthropology].

Suzuki, T. 1986. As expressões de tratamento da língua japonesa no Brasil: uso e processo de aculturação [Japanese Language Treatment Expressions in Brazil: Use and Acculturation Process]. *Estudos Japoneses [Japanese Studies]* 6, 89–154.

Tagliamonte, S. A. 1991. A Matter of Time: Past Temporal Reference Verbal Structures in Samana English and the Ex-Slave Recordings. Doctoral dissertation, University of Ottawa.

Tagliamonte, S. A. 1997. Obsolescence in the English Perfect? Evidence from Samaná English. *American Speech* 72, 33–68.

Tagliamonte, S. and S. Poplack. 1988. How Black English Past Got to the Present: Evidence from Samaná. *Language in Society* 17(4), 513–533.

Tejeda Ortiz, D. (ed.) 1984. *Cultura y folklore en Samaná [Culture and Folklore in Samaná]*. Santo Domingo: Editorial Alfa y Omega.

Thomas-Brereton, L. C. 1994. An Exploration of Panamanian Creole English: Some Syntactic, Lexical and Sociolinguistic Features. Doctoral dissertation, New York University.

Toledo Vega, G. 2016. Propuesta didáctica para la enseñanza de español como segunda lengua a inmigrantes haitianos en Chile [Didactic Proposal for Teaching Spanish as a Second Language to Haitian Immigrants in Chile]. *Lengua y Migración [Language and Migration]* 8(1), 81–103.

Tomita, A. G. S. and G. Santiago. 2004. As Novas Religiões Japonesas como instrumento de transmissão de cultura japonesa no Brasil [The New Japanese Religions as an Instrument for Transmitting Japanese Culture in Brazil]. *Revista de Estudos da Religião [Journal of Religious Studies]* 3, 88–102.

Ursini, F. 1983. Trevigiani in Messico: riflessi linguistici di una dialettica tra conservazione ed assimilazione [Trevigiani in Mexico: Linguistic Reflections of a Dialectic between Conservation and Assimilation]. In M. Cortelazzo (ed.), *Guida ai dialetti veneti 5 [Guide to Venetian dialects 5]*. Padova [Padua]: CLEUP, 73–84.

Usarski, F. 2008. Declínio do budismo "amarelo" no Brasil [Decline of "Yellow" Buddhism in Brazil]. *Tempo Social: revista de sociologia da USP [Tempo Social: Sociology Journal of USP]* 20(2), 133–153.

Vandresen, P. (ed.) 2006. *Variação, mudança e contato lingüístico no português da região sul [Variation, Change and Linguistic Contact in Southern Portuguese]*. Pelotas: EDUCAT.

Vandresen, P. and A. R. Corrêa. 2008. O bilingüismo Pomerano-Português na região de Pelotas [Pomeranian-Portuguese Bilingualism in the Pelotas Region]. In C. Roncarati and J. Abraçado (eds.), *Português brasileiro II: contato linguístico, heterogeneidade e história [Brazilian Portuguese II: Linguistic Contact, Heterogeneity and History]*. Niterói, EdUFF, 39–51.

Vásquez, T., E. Busse, and L. Izaguirre. 2014. La migración haitiana en Perú y su tránsito hacia Brasil [Haitian Migration in Peru and Its Transit to Brazil]. *La migración haitiana hacia Brasil: características, oportunidades y desafíos [Haitian Migration to Brazil: Characteristics, Opportunities and Challenges]*. Buenos Aires: Organización Internacional para las Migraciones (OIM), Cuadernos Migratorios No. 6 [International Organization for Migration (IOM), Migratory Notebooks No. 6], 83–105.

Vieira, M. M. 2010. Para um estudo das influências fonológicas do italiano no português falado na cidade de São Paulo [For a Study of the Phonological Influences of Italian in Portuguese Spoken in the City of São Paulo]. Master's thesis, São Paulo: Universidade de [University of] São Paulo.

Virkel, A. E. 1999. Contactos lingüísticos en Trelew. El bilingüismo español-galés [Linguistic Contacts in Trelew. Spanish-Welsh Bilingualism]. *Anclajes* 3(3), 123–139.

Virkel, A. E. 2000. El español hablado en Chubut: aportes para la definición de un perfil sociolingüístico [The Spanish Spoken in Chubut: Contributions to the Definition of a Sociolinguistic Profile]. Doctoral dissertation, Valladolid: Universidad de [University of] Valladolid.

Walcot, N. 1998. *Los Cocolos*. Santo Domingo: Consejo Presidencial de Cultura, Instituto Dominicano de Folklore, Editora Alfa y Omega [Presidential Council of Culture, Dominican Institute of Folklore, Editora Alfa y Omega].

Warantz, E. 1986. The Bay Islands English of Honduras. In J. Holm (ed.), *Central American English*. Heidelberg: Julios Groos Verlag, 71–94.

Watts, Keith. 1999. English Maintenance in Costa Rica? The Case of Bilingual Monteverde. Doctoral dissertation, University of New Mexico.

Weaver, B. H. C. 1961. Confederate Emigration to Brazil. *The Journal of Southern History* 27, 33–53.

Winkler, E. G. 2000. Cambio de códigos en el criollo limonense [Change of Codes in Limonense Creole]. *Revista de filología y lingüística de la Universidad de Costa Rica [Journal of Philology and Linguistics of the University of Costa Rica]* 26(1), 189–196.

Wolff, L. K. 2017. *Die Entwicklung und aktuelle Lage der deutschen Sprache und der deutschstämmigen Minderheit in Chile. Das" Launa"-Deutsch [The Development and Current Situation of the German Language and the Ethnic German Minority in Chile. The "Launa" German]*. Munich: GRIN Verlag

Zago Bronca, J. A. 1982. *Breve historia de la fundación de Chipilo [Brief History of the Founding of Chipilo]*. Chipilo, Puebla: Imprenta Venecia.

Zamarreño, S. A. 2018. La lengua galesa y su mantenimiento en Chubua: el Eisteddfod en el marco del dominio de las actividades culturales [The Welsh Language and Its Maintenance in Chubua: The Eisteddfod within the Framework of the Domain of Cultural Activities]. *E-AESLA* 4, 331–338.

Ziebur, U. 2000. Die soziolinguistische Situation von Chilenen deutscher Abstammung [The Sociolinguistic Situation of Chileans of German Descent]. *Linguistik Online,* 7. Retrieved from https://bop.unibe.ch/linguistik-online/article/download/987/1646?inline=1

Zilli Manica, J. B. 1981. *Italianos en México: documentos para la historia de los colonos italianos en México [Italians in Mexico: Documents for the History of Italian Settlers in Mexico]*. Xalapa: Ediciones San José.

Zilli Manica, J. B. 1997. *La Villa Luisa de los italianos: un proyecto liberal [The Villa Luisa of the Italians: A Liberal Project]*. Xalapa: Universidad [University] Veracruzana.

Zilli Manica, J. B. 1998. *La estanzuela: historia de una cooperativa agrícola de italianos en México [La Estanzuela: History of an Italian Agricultural Cooperative in Mexico]*. Xalapa: Editora del Gobierno del Estado de Veracruz-Llave [Editor of the Government of the State of Veracruz-Llave].

Zimmer, M., M. Bandeira, and C. A. Blank. 2009. A dinâmica do multilingüismo na transferência de padrões de aspiração de obstruintes iniciais entre o pomerano (L1), o português (L2) e o inglês (L3) [The Dynamics of Multilingualism in the Transfer of Aspiration Patterns of Initial Obstruents between Pomeranian (L1), Portuguese (L2) and English (L3)]. In V. Borba, M. L. G. C. Carvalho, and G. O. S. Lima (eds.), *Contribuições para a pesquisa em linguística nas diferentes áreas: partilhando reflexões e resultados [Contributions to Linguistic Research in Different Areas: Sharing Reflections and Results]*. Maceió: EDUFAL, 57–72.

Zimmer, T. 2007. La expresión de la identidad lingüística y cultural en el caribe costarricense [The Expression of Linguistic and Cultural Identity in the Costa Rican Caribbean]. *Signo y seña [Sign and Signal]* 18, 139–168.

Zubaran, M. A. 1994. Os teuto-rio-grandenses, a escravidão e as alforrias [Teuto-rio-grandenses, Slavery and Manumission]. In C. Mauch and N. Vasconcellos (eds.), *Os alemães no sul do Brasil: cultura-etnicidade-história [Germans in Southern Brazil: Culture-Ethnicity-History]*. Porto Alegre: Ulbra, 65–74.

14

Language Attrition and Heritage Language Reversal in Returnees

Cristina Flores and Neal Snape

The desire to return is a sentiment almost always present
in the minds and hearts, and often rhetoric, of those
who find themselves displaced from their country of origin.

Sardinha, 2011

14.1 Introduction

The present chapter discusses effects of input changes on the language competence of a particular case of bilingual speakers, namely returnees. Returnees are second- (or third-) generation speakers who grew up in a migration setting with exposure to the language of their homeland, their first language (L1) or heritage language (HL), mainly spoken within the family, and to the language of the wider community, which may be a second language (L2) or one of two first languages (2L1) (see Section 14.2). After living for a certain period of time in the immigration setting, during childhood, adolescence or early adulthood, these speakers move (back) to their parents' country of origin (Seliger 1991; Daller 2005; Flores 2010). Thus, what characterizes this population is the reversal of the dominant environmental language after their return. The language that used to be the speaker's HL becomes (again) the language of the wider community, while the former majority language (of the wider community during migration) becomes a minority or a second language in the country of origin (Flores 2019a). This change raises interesting questions that can offer profound insights not only into the processes of language acquisition and attrition but also with respect to social and educational implications of remigration movements. This chapter discusses these questions with a main focus on linguistic aspects but sliding also into nonlinguistic issues.

We start by critically discussing the term *heritage language reversal*. Montrul (2015, 2016a) has proposed the term to encompass the linguistic changes that occur in both directions in situations of return of heritage speakers to their homeland:

> ... return marks a reversal of the sociopolitical and functional status of the languages: what used to be the heritage language now becomes the societal majority language, and the L2 learned in the host country, even when it is not the primary language of the parents, becomes a heritage language of the child in the new environment. It would be considered a heritage language because in addition to having high proficiency in the language, the child still has a connection with the culture. The language and the culture were part of the child's upbringing and socialization. (Montrul 2015: 15)

From Montrul's (2016a) perspective, the reversal of the L1 and L2 and subsequent reduction of L2 input " ... are often described as L2 attrition, but in fact it is attrition of a heritage language of the child. (37)." In assuming that both languages of an immigrant child, the home language and the societal language, are in fact HLs, Montrul adopts a broad definition of the term *heritage language*. This definition is based on the idea that the close cultural connection to one's childhood language suffices to classify a language as HL, even if it is not a language spoken by parents in the home. From this perspective, L2 attrition may, indeed, be considered HL attrition. Conversely, a more restricted definition of the term *heritage language*, which classifies the HL as family language that is not the language of the dominant environment (see, for instance, Rothman 2009), takes issue with the L2 characterized as an HL, particularly in the case of sequential bilingual children, who acquire the majority language after age 4, when they enter the majority language school system. In order to account for the diverse types of returnees (simultaneous and sequential bilinguals), in the present chapter we adopt a restricted definition of *heritage language* as the language that is not the dominant language of society. In this sense, we use the term *heritage language reversal* to specifically describe the change that occurs in one direction only: When the HL, acquired in the context of a minority language during migration, becomes the language of the wider community after return. In fact, what happens in this situation is a change of the sociopolitical and functional status of the family language, as stated by Montrul (2015, 2016a). The HL reverses from a minority language into the majority language of the home country, where it is, commonly, the high-prestige national language. As a consequence, after returning, the bilingual returnee, who usually had reduced contact to his/her L1/HL, will be exposed to greater amounts and, importantly, more diversified input, which includes formal instruction and exposure to standard registers of the target language. The changes that may affect the returnees' L1/HL competence after their return raise interesting questions related to the permeability of the language faculty, which are still under-investigated (Flores 2019b).

Although newly introduced into the field of HL development, the term *language reversal* is a longstanding concept in the field of ethnolinguistics (Paulston et al. 1993). Subsumed under the broader concept of *language regenesis*, "language reversal implies the turning around of existing trends in language usage" (Paulston et al. 1993: 281), focusing specifically on sociopolitical situations in which one of the (several) languages spoken in a state starts to become more prominent and to widen the social contexts where it is used.[1] This is exactly what happens in the case of HL reversal, though at an individual level, i.e., it is not the language community that expands the use of the target language but the individual speaker.

The other side of the coin is related to the change that may affect the language that was the dominant environmental language before the moment of return and becomes a minority language in the returnee's country of origin. Naturally, the status of this "minority" language in the country of origin may vary significantly depending on the language in question. In particular, if the returnee returns from an English-speaking country, the prestige and status of English as lingua franca may affect its maintenance differently than in the cases of return from Germany or France. Still, the existing research on this particular situation almost consensually describes cases of language attrition or interrupted acquisition of the once dominant language, particularly if the return occurs in childhood, roughly until 12 years of age (Seliger 1991), even in the case of English. Common effects of attrition are due to an almost complete loss of daily exposure to this language after return, especially when it occurs in childhood because the returnee speaker has limited opportunities to engage with the previous dominant language. In many cases, contact is maintained only through schooling (e.g., special English language maintenance classes for returnees in Japan, Kubota 2018; Taura 2008, 2019) and is not spoken within the family, contradicting, thus, the (more restricted) definition of the HL as home language. For this reason, we propose to reserve the term *heritage language reversal* for the changes affecting the L1/HL (which reverses from a minority language to an environmental language) and *first/second language attrition* for the changes affecting the once dominant language (which usually loses the status of a daily language). We acknowledge that this choice of terminology follows from a particular definition of *heritage language*, which, in our view, best fits the returnee population targeted in this chapter.

The following sections discuss the diverse profiles of returnees by distinguishing between simultaneous and sequential bilingual returnees. We

---

[1] From an ethnolinguistic perspective, the concept of *language reversal* has to be distinguished from other processes of language regenesis like *reversing language shift* (Fishman 1990) or *language revitalization*.

then summarize the main findings of the still scarce research on language change in returnee populations, mainly from a linguistic, developmental perspective. This chapter concludes with an overview of social, cultural, and pedagogical dimensions of return migration.

14.2 Who Are Returnees?

Who are returnees? Before we attempt to answer this question, it is important to understand who bilinguals are. Bilingual speakers can be categorized as the following:

i.   Heritage speakers (generational status and dominance of the language)
ii. Balanced and nonbalanced bilinguals (relative proficiency in each language).

A number of studies have looked at bilingual speakers and what the potential cognitive benefits are of acquiring two languages (Bialystok and Feng 2009; Antoniou et al. 2016; Blom et al. 2017). Typically, bilingual studies are concerned with factors such as age of onset, exposure to input, languages used inside and outside of the home, minority and majority languages, and proficiency of the two languages in question. However, one branch of bilingualism that is not listed is on *returnees*, in particular, returnee children. Returnees are often children who start life as monolingual, but at some point, early on in their development, they move to another country and start to acquire a second language (this is known as sequential bilingualism). It also refers to children from immigrant families who were born in the host country and grew up with exposure to their family language and to the language of the environment (simultaneous bilinguals). There are, of course, many reasons for a family to move to an L2 speaking environment, the most common being economic reasons. One case, discussed in more detail in the following section, is that of parents being assigned to a post abroad for a short or long period of time, and returning to their country of origin after finishing this post. Other cases are that of immigrant families who wish to return to their homeland because they have reached financial stability and have the desire to live back in the country of origin. There are also many cases of forced return due to deportation or family reasons. We also look at the implications of these situations for language development.

14.2.1 Sequential Bilinguals
Sequential bilinguals or child L2 learners are children who acquire the first language and then go on to acquire the second. In most cases, the child will fully acquire the L1 grammar before L2 acquisition begins or may be in the

process of acquiring the L1 when L2 acquisition begins. In Japan, for instance, many parents are Japanese nationals who speak Japanese in the home with their children. However, when a Japanese family migrates to the United States, for example, the children have a chance to start to acquire English as a second language. On return to Japan, in the majority of cases, the path of L2 acquisition of English may continue as the children receive their ongoing education through the school system, and predictably, the children will receive little input in an English as a Foreign Language (EFL) setting since, in regular Japanese schools, English classes take place once a week (Kubota 2018).

Sequential returnee bilinguals are children who move to a foreign country with their parents for a number of diverse reasons (e.g., parents who migrate because they are unemployed), but others move abroad because one of the parents is required by the company they work for to represent the company abroad for a fixed period of time. The job posting abroad can be anywhere between one year to many years (Goodman 1993; Kanno 2003). Children may have started to acquire a second language in their homeland before moving abroad, but in most cases, L2 acquisition starts effectively once a family has relocated to the L2 speaking country. In the previous example, when a family moves from Japan to the United States, as the children and parents settle into their new surroundings, the children have to start attending school. Since all school subjects are taught in English, the children must quickly adjust and adapt to the L2 environment in order to keep up with their peers and be able to communicate with teachers and students alike. The exposure to and use of the L2 on a daily basis is likely to lead to an increase in proficiency in the L2, despite it not being the home language, as many immigrant parents wish to maintain the L1 by using it in the home (see Montrul 2008, 2016b; Unsworth 2019). If we take the Japanese community as an example, in fact, many Japanese parents elect to send their children to a Japanese school at weekends in order to help them maintain the L1 for when they finally return to Japan and enter the Japanese school system (Goodman 1993; Rose and Fujishima 1994). Nevertheless, there are exceptions to these examples because the path of L2 acquisition is anything but predictable for sequential returnee bilinguals.

In cases of working immigration that is limited in time, this path of L2 acquisition can only be maintained for a certain amount of time before family members return to their homeland. This may happen, for instance, in the case of Japanese families who had a temporary contract abroad and it has come to an end. Upon return, the L2 takes a back seat because now the L1 is once again the majority language. It does not necessarily mean that the L2 is no longer used. It simply means that before returning, the L2 was used every day, but now the situation is reversed because the L1 (e.g.,

Japanese) is the language the child is exposed to inside and outside of the home. In other words, the L1 once again becomes the dominant language in the child's life, whereas before, living abroad, the L2 was the dominant language (Tomiyama 2000). This reversal from L2 to L1 may have large implications for the child because there is likely to be less use of the L2 in regular daily life.

Up to this point, we have focused on sequential bilingual children at a young age, but there are also those sequential bilinguals who are already older before they go to live in an L2 environment. One study by Snape et al. (2014a) looked at four returnee Japanese children, one of whom was 11 years of age (referred to as CS) when the family moved from Japan to the United States and lived there for eight years. CS had already been through the Japanese educational system and therefore had acquired and was literate in Japanese. CS started to acquire L2 English once the family's life began in the United States. Snape et al. found that CS's performance on an English tense and aspect acceptability judgment task was similar to her younger siblings, one of whom is a simultaneous bilingual. Perhaps due to age of arrival in the United States, CS was still within the critical period to acquire the L2 (see Johnson and Newport 1989; White 2003), "as age of arrival is the best predictor of successful L2 acquisition" (Montrul 2008: 46).

In the cases discussed so far, the HL is likely to be spoken within the home, but otherwise input is greatly reduced. However, when children return to the L1-speaking country, the language situation is essentially reversed, as we discussed earlier. The L1 now becomes (again) the dominant language for sequential bilinguals who started to acquire the L1 before living in the L2-speaking community. The reversal means that whereas the L1 was once the minority language, it is now again the majority language. The implications of the switch from the L2 being the dominant language to the L1 becoming the dominant language can, in some cases, lead to *second language attrition*, which is explored further in Section 14.3.

14.2.2 Simultaneous Bilinguals

The previous section focused on children who started to acquire their L1 in the homeland before immigration. In this case, the return means re-immersion in the L1-setting, where the speaker already lived in early childhood. It is, therefore, a "real" return. However, in many cases, immigrant children are born in the host country. In these situations, the bilingual speakers have contact with two languages from very early on. Typically, they are exposed to their family language from birth and to the majority language, either from birth, too, if the majority language is spoken within the family, or more intensively when the child enters kindergarten or pre-school, at the latest. In both cases, the child has very early exposure to two languages and can be considered a simultaneous bilingual. These are the circumstances where scholars unambiguously define the family language as an HL and the children as HSs (cross-reference to chapters of this handbook). These cases of children who are born in the host country and move to their parents' homeland are somehow distinct from the situations described in the previous section, starting with the validity of the term "returnee." In fact, when these speakers move to the country of origin of their families, they are not really returning because they never lived in the families' homeland. What actually happens is that they move to a country that they know from holidays and temporary stays and where a part of their families live (e.g., grandparents). There is, though, a strong cultural and often emotional bond to the parents' home country, which is felt as being indeed a "homeland." Therefore, it is very common to apply the term *returnee* also to those simultaneous bilinguals, who were not born in the country of origin, but moved there at a certain time in their life (Flores 2019a). To be more precise, this population can be defined as *returnee heritage speakers* (Flores 2019b).

The particular situation of returnee HSs raises particular questions. The first question, which studies on sequential bilingual returnees typically do not address, is related to the development of the HL. As discussed in Section 14.4, this language was acquired under circumstances of reduced input in the migration setting and may (or not) change on immersion in the homeland society. The second question is related to the status of the language of the host country. Contrary to sequential language acquisition, where the language of the host country is acquired as an L2, in the case of simultaneous bilinguals this language is acquired as a native language. Consequently, the loss of daily exposure to this language on return is an instance of native language deprivation. To be exact, in this situation, we are not referring to L2 attrition, but rather *native language attrition*. The difference between both types of attrition rests mainly in the "age of onset of acquisition" of the language that will be attrited (birth *vs* later in childhood). Eventually, the amount of exposure to this language may be similar in both types of bilinguals, for instance, the language of the host country may become (or not) a language of communication within the family during migration. Furthermore, it may become the speakers' dominant language regardless of whether it is acquired simultaneously or sequentially. This means that, ultimately, native and second language attrition in contexts of return may be similar processes that lead to identical effects of competence changes. We therefore refer to this process as dominant language attrition in the following section.

14.3   Research on Dominant Language Attrition

The term *dominant language attrition* applies to those bilingual speakers (children or adults) who are returnees. We may further distinguish between native language and L2 attrition as discussed in the previous sections. On return to the L1/HL homeland, the previous majority language is no longer the dominant language for the bilingual speaker, and as a result, the L2/2L1 may start to attrite.

2L1/L2 attrition may be the gradual decline in use and fluency, even though there is ongoing exposure to the previous dominant language, but limited, or in more extreme cases, it may be that the L2/other L1 is no longer used at all, in which case the attrition process may be more pronounced. Although research on returnee populations is very promising, it is also extremely scarce. Still, the limited number of studies focused on returnees' language competence have looked at a range of linguistic phenomena including frequency of input, loss of morphological complexity, phonetic and phonological processing, lexical and morphosyntactic influence from the dominant language, and a reduction in registers of use (Yoshitomi 1992, 1999; Reetz-Kurashige 1999; Tomiyama 1999, 2000; Taura and Taura 2000; Flores 2010, 2012, 2015; Snape et al. 2014b; Matthews 2016; Snape 2016; see also the overview by Bardovi-Harlig and Stringer 2010, and suggestions on the way forward on how to conduct future returnee studies). Many of these studies are, however, case studies with a limited number of participants.

Tomiyama (2009) conducted a study that included two Japanese siblings. The older sibling was 5;8 and the younger one was 2;8 when they both moved with their family to the United States. The children were both born in Japan to Japanese native speaker parents, which means that they started to acquire Japanese as the L1 before they started to acquire L2 English. They lived and attended a school in the United States for four years. Japanese was spoken at home during the period in the United States except for the time when they were in the company of monolingual English speakers. On the children's return to Japan, Tomiyama (2009) examined their L2 grammatical complexity, grammatical accuracy, lexical complexity, and lexical productivity by administering a storytelling task. The task was retelling Mayer's (1971) frog series. The participants were given a few minutes each to look over the pictures before they started to narrate a story based on the pictures. The task was not timed. Data was collected over a period of 31 months in total. Tomiyama (2009) found that overall both children showed similar L2 attrition patterns. Grammatical complexity was well maintained as they both used main clauses with subordinate clauses, e.g., the child seemed to get confused because all of a sudden the turtle is back alive. This is counted as one T-unit with two clauses. However,

Tomiyama (2009) found some L2 attrition in the area of lexical complexity, whereas lexical productivity was well maintained by both children. For grammatical accuracy, the older child managed to keep the same level throughout the study, but the younger child's grammatical accuracy peaked in session 6 when her grammatical complexity was at its minimum. Tomiyama (2009) describes the young child's performance in grammatical accuracy as a trade-off with grammatical complexity as she was only able to maintain one, grammatical complexity, and not the other, grammatical accuracy. Tomiyama's (2009) findings could support the possibility that gaining a high proficiency level in the L2 before returning to the home country might reduce the degree of attrition. It seems that both children had passed the critical threshold level: "beyond that threshold, they become immune to interference or decay" (Neisser 1984: 33).

In a recent study, Kubota (2018) examined thirty-six bilingual returnee children's lexical access, measured by a verbal fluency task. The aim of the study was to uncover what the effects of individual variables are such as age of L2 onset, age of return to the home country, length of L2 residence, L2 exposure since return, and proficiency. The findings show that the age of L2 onset and/or the length of L2 residence, but not proficiency or L2 exposure, correlate with the degree of L2 lexical maintenance: Children with an earlier age of L2 onset and a longer length of L2 residence were able to maintain and even improve their L2 verbal fluency performance on their return to the L1 environment. Kubota (2018) argues that the results are partially in line with the maturational account: Children require some time to consolidate their language knowledge for it to become resistant to input reduction.

The idea that language may need to stabilize in the bilingual mind in order to become resistant to effects of attrition is also proposed by Flores (2010, 2019b), based on research on Portuguese returnees from Germany/ Switzerland. In a corpus study that analyzes oral speech of fourteen return- ees, Flores (2019b) shows that the length of exposure to German during migration predicts the speakers' accurate production of German morphology on return. Bilingual speakers who had been exposed to German for less than 10 years show high rates of erosion, whereas return- ees who lived in the migration context for more than 10 years demon- strated very robust knowledge, even after a long-term stay back in Portugal. Flores argues that it is length of exposure that predicts the returnees' language development after return and not the age of onset of bilingualism. This could indicate that returnees who had not enough time to stabilize their bilingual competence due to an early return (and subse- quent loss of regular language exposure) may show eroded knowledge of their once dominant language, even if this language was acquired as a native language since birth. Some longitudinal case studies, with one or two participants, suggest that, in situations of very restricted or complete loss of contact with the once dominant language, returnee children, who returned before the age of 10 years, may show severe effects of language loss up to two years after returning (Kuhberg 1992; Flores 2015).

The relatively limited number of studies so far do not allow us to draw precise conclusions regarding the degree of attrition in situations of return. The age of the speaker's return, the age of acquisition of the majority language and the length of residence in the migration setting, as well as the degree of contact with that language after return to the homeland appear to be relevant predictors; however, more studies with a higher number of participants are needed to confirm these hypotheses.

In addition, many known studies report on the return from English-speaking countries (Berman and Olshtain 1983; Yoshitomi 1992, 1999; Taura 2008; Snape et al. 2014a/b; Snape 2016; Kubota et al. 2020). The fact that English is taught as a foreign language in almost all countries world-wide and is a high-prestige language may further blur this picture. On the one hand, parents may invest more in ensuring that their children continue to have daily contact with English after the return (e.g., making an effort to use English at home or enrolling their children in English complement classes). On the other hand, children will most probably have contact with English as a school subject, even though not necessarily on a daily basis. In addition, nowadays English is present in almost all children's lives, world-wide, through social networks, media, songs, and films. The same is not true for other languages like German or French. Although these are also high-prestige languages, having access to these languages abroad is much more difficult than compared to English.

We now turn to the definition of HL reversal we adopt throughout this paper in Section 14.4.

14.4   Research on Heritage Language Reversal

As discussed previously, a consequence of the return is not only the change that may affect the language that ceases to be the majority language (see previous section) but also the alterations related to the HL. In the home country, the HL, which had been acquired as a minority language within the family, with reduced exposure to formal input, becomes the dominant environmental language. Thus, a reversal of the language's status occurs from minority to majority language.

A crucial question that derives from this sociolinguistic change is whether this reversal affects the returnee's HL at the linguistic level, namely if linguistic traces that are typical of HLs (Montrul 2016a/b; Polinsky and Scontras 2020) are overcome if the HS becomes immersed in an environment where the HL is no longer a minority language. Several further questions are related to this main question: Does competence reversal affect all domains of linguistic knowledge? Do extra-linguistic factors such as age of return, length of emigration, length of residence in the home country, or age of onset of bilingualism predict the outcome of linguistic reversal? How does the return impact the development of academic language skills in the HL?

Research into HL reversal may contribute to inform psycholinguistic, theoretical, and pedagogical linguistics; however, the body of research in this area of investigation is even scarcer than on 2L1/L2 attrition. Thus, in this section, we summarize some preliminary results from a few studies and outline some hypotheses and predictions, which need to be verified and complemented by future research.

A language domain that is known to be shaped in early stages of language development and to be vulnerable to input and age effects is the phonological domain (Bever 1981). The phonological competence of returnees is, therefore, a good candidate to test for effects of language reversal. It has been widely demonstrated that HSs may show particularities in their HL accent that distinguish them from monolinguals, but also from late second language learners (Godson 2004; Ronquest 2013; Kupisch, Barton et al. 2014). Lloyd-Smith, Einfeldt and Kupisch (2019), for instance, argue that traces of nonnative pronunciation in the HL are caused by HSs' reduced exposure to the HL, i.e., early exposure to this language does not guarantee a native accent if exposure is limited over time (see also Rao 2014). This implies that the input factor overrides the age factor, i.e., according to this argument, it is reduced input that shapes the accent of bilingual speakers and not the age of onset of bilingualism. In the case of returnee HSs, we have a population with exposure to the HL, generally, since birth, who receive reduced input until a certain moment followed by a significant increase in exposure to the HL after return. Research on returnee populations may, therefore, shed some further light on the development of HL pronunciation. If it is mainly the input factor that shapes HL accent, immersion in the HL environment after return will re-shape the HS's phonological competence. This means that the particular nonnative features of HL accent will be lost after some time and the returnee's phonological system will, ultimately, converge toward the homeland accent. If this re-shaping is independent from the returnee HSs' age at return, this would be evidence against the hypothesis that pronunciation is constrained by maturational factors (Moyer 2014). It would mean that accent may change at any age if input conditions are favorable to invoke change. This has been shown for L1 attrition in the inverse direction, i.e., adult bilinguals' L1 accent may gain nonnative traces after long-term emigration (Hopp and Schmid 2013). What about losing nonnative phonological traces in the HL?

One study that addresses this question is Flores and Rato's (2016) research on twenty Portuguese HSs, who grew up in a German-speaking environment and returned to Portugal at 11–29 years of age. This study fails to show an association between the age at which they returned to the homeland and their perceived Portuguese accent. Also, the length of stay in Portugal does not predict HSs pronunciation, rated by a group of thirty Portuguese monolingual speakers in a foreign accent rating task. Instead, the study finds an association, even though marginal, between their age of onset of bilingualism (i.e., the age of acquisition of German) and their HL accent. The later the speakers started to acquire their L2 German (between 0 and 7 years), the more native-like they were perceived in Portuguese. Flores and Rato interpret these results as evidence in favor of age effects in early stages of language acquisition, i.e., phonological competence is predominantly shaped in the early years of development. If a HS develops nonnative traces in the HL, these may last over a lifetime, even if the speaker returns to the homeland. However, the Portuguese HSs investigated had intensive contact with Portuguese in their daily lives, even when they lived in Germany. Therefore, no conclusion can be put forward with respect to the role of input. HSs with less exposure to their HL during migration may, in fact, benefit from the return and show stronger signs of accent change in their HL after living for some time (back) in the home country. This and other questions related to the sample, different methodologies, and different language pairs may be answered in future research.

The question of whether HSs' competence converges toward that of monolinguals after being (re)immerged in the HL environment has been addressed in studies on Turkish HSs who returned to Turkey after spending their childhood and adolescence in Germany (Daller and Yıldız 1995; Daller et al. 2011; Treffers-Daller et al. 2016). Daller and Yıldız (1995), for instance, measured returnee HSs' overall language proficiency in Turkish by means of a C-test. They show that the returnees' scores were significantly lower than the monolinguals' results two years after returning to Turkey, but monolinguals' and returnees' scores were statistically comparable when the returnee group was tested eight years after return. This shows that, in some linguistic domains (e.g., lexical knowledge), HL competence is mainly shaped by reduced input and develops positively if exposure increases as a consequence of immersion in the HL environment.

14.5   Social, Cultural, and Pedagogical Dimensions of Second Generation/Young Return Migration

Even though the present chapter focuses mainly on the development of the linguistic knowledge of returnees, social, cultural, and pedagogical dimensions of young immigrants' return to the parents' homeland also play a crucial role in the remigration process. This last section gives an overview of some central questions related to the return of second- (seldom third-) generation migrants, discussed from a sociolinguistic, pedagogical, and anthropological perspective. We cover mainly, but not exclusively, work on returnees to Mexico, Portugal, Turkey, and Japan, although the questions discussed are global issues that affect returnees all over the world.

A first relevant point, already mentioned, is related to the term *return*. Although we use the terms "return" and "returnees" to describe the remigration of second (third) generations settling in their ancestral homelands, the use of this terminology does not apply to all cases of returnee HSs. Many returnees were born in the emigration country and know their parents' country of origin only from vacations. In their cases, the settlement in the homeland is not a real return, since they never lived there and have never experienced a previous migration (Sardinha 2011). Nevertheless, the term is commonly used as an umbrella concept for the movement back from a migrant families' host to the home country (Flores 2019a), affecting all kinds of individuals at different ages: older migrants who are (close to be) retired, middle-age adults, young adults about to enter the labor market, high-school adolescents, and school-age children (Mar-Molinero 2018).

A crucial question targets the motivation for the return to the homeland (Sardinha 2011; Borjian et al. 2016; Hazán 2017). Much of the focus has been directed at sociological work on return migration, but the reasons for return migration are various, depending on a diversity of experiences. These largely derive from economic, political, and social situations of the migrant family and the societies they return into. In general, economic reasons (e.g., unemployment in the host country), retirement, family- and health-related motivations, or even racism are the top causes (Házan 2017). In the particular case of Mexican returnees from the United States, deportation is a further relevant cause for the return of undocumented migrants (Zúñiga and Hamann 2006). Even though the desire to return (the "return ideology", Sardinha 2011) is strongly anchored in migrants' lives, for the vast majority of migrant populations, the effective return is a personal commitment, not planned from the onset of migration. In this case, strategies are set out after years of living abroad (Klimt 2000). For others, e.g., Japanese workers who are sent by their Japanese companies, migration is limited to the duration of the working contract and the return is foreseen from the onset of migration (Kanno 2003).

Particularly relevant for the present chapter are the causes for the return of second generations, which never lived in their homeland (or did so only as infants). Most second-generation returnees move to their ancestral homeland with their family, but there is also a considerable number of children and adolescents that return without their parents (Schmitz-Bewyl 1983; Abali and Widman 1990; Schäfer 1995; Daller 2005; Zúñiga and Hamann 2006; Borjian et al. 2016). Distinct motivations underlie this particular case of child remigration. First, children are sent back to the homeland to live with relatives for educational reasons (Daller 2005). Parents believe that an early enrollment in the homeland school system will promote their children's success in school, which could be at risk in the emigration setting. In addition, religious and ethnic reasons influence parental decisions to send children to the country of origin, e.g., the fear that, particularly daughters, may marry outside the ethnic community and constitute binational families (see Santos 2005, for the importance of wedding rites transmitted to Portuguese-descendant second generations). However, in many cases the decision to return is made by the descendants themselves, with the goal of finishing high school, to pursue university studies, or to enter the labor market in the homeland. This decision echoes a strong return ideology (Sardinha 2011), i.e., a long-lasting desire of homecoming (Brettell 1979), which is consciously harbored by first-generation parents and transmitted to their children, who develop a sense of ethnic belonging and the desire of "returning to one's roots" (see also Wessendorf 2007).

Two major issues arise from the return of younger populations (i.e., child and adolescent HSs), namely their integration in the homeland's school system (Schmitz-Bewyl 1983) and their adjustment to various dimensions of a society that they experienced from vacations and ethnicity within the family, but where they never resided (Klimt 2000).

Taking Mexico as a case in point, several authors have described the difficulties that many child and adolescent returnees face when trying to integrate into the homeland's school system (Zúñiga and Hamann 2006; Borjian et al. 2016; Mar-Molinero 2018). Many factors contribute to initial negative and unwelcome school experiences, starting with curricular differences between the school systems of the host and the home country, which often force returnee children to delay one school year. Further difficulties arise from administrative requirements related to lack of documentation (especially in cases of undocumented migrants, Borjian et al. 2016). In fact, what many studies show is that the school systems of the countries that cyclically receive return migration are not adjusted to receiving HSs and to give special attention to their educational and specific linguistic needs (Zúñiga and Hamann 2006; Sanchez-Garcia et al. 2012; Daller and Treffers-Daller 2014). As stated by Zúñiga and Hamann (2006: 51), they "compose a classic hidden population."

It is now common sense to acknowledge that bilingual speakers have a particular linguistic competence that does not equate two monolingual systems as one (Grosjean 1982). As addressed in previous chapters of this handbook, this is particularly true for HSs, who normally are unbalanced bilingual speakers and show a particular development of their HL, which is predominantly shaped by exposure to colloquial language registers. Especially in monolingual-oriented societies such as Mexico (Zúñiga and Hamann 2006) and Portugal (Koven 2004; Keating and Solovova 2011), divergent linguistic competence is very often conceived as a social and educational barrier and may impact negatively on the way schoolmates and even teachers perceive returnee students. To overcome educational barriers in the homeland, many parents (who can afford it) enroll their children in private schools (Mar-Molinero 2018). As Zúñiga and Hamann (2006) warn, public schooling systems mostly fail in taking advantage of the linguistic and cultural capital of returnee students, whose bilingual language skills are ignored or confined to classes where the former emigration language is taught as a foreign language.

There are some countries that support specific schools aimed at receiving returnee children, for instance, the bilingual Turkish-German or Turkish-English *Anadolu*-high schools in Turkey (Schäfer 1995; Tapan and Hatipoğlu 2016) and international, private, and some public schools in Japan (Goodman 1993). The primary aim of these schools is, however, not to foster the students' HL, but mainly to support the former majority language, preventing the onset of attrition. Nevertheless, returnees frequently report self-perceived language loss and failure to maintain the former emigration language as the daily language of communication within the family, despite their efforts to maintain frequent contact with the former emigration language, through institutional support or/and bilingual language habits at home. Many returnees acknowledge shifting their preferred language of communication with their siblings, from the previous language of migration to the homeland (=heritage) language within one or two years of their return (Flores 2010).

The lack of institutional support for returnees in public schools entails that normally they have to fend for themselves and catch up on their own. This means that some students will perform well in school and overcome disadvantages, for instance, related to low academic language skills and lexical competence, and others will fail to catch up (e.g., Daller 2005). Consequently, the reported outcomes of young returnees' immersion in the homeland society (at school, university, or in the labor market) are mixed. Many returnees label themselves as "semilingual" and perceive their HL as a long-term handicap, which is associated with sentiments of uncertainty. They self-question their language ability even after years of living (back) in the homeland (Daller 2005; Koven 2013). Others characterize their bilingualism as capital that enabled them to get good jobs or pursue successful academic careers (see, for instance, the typical biography of the Pizarro family presented by Mar-Molinero 2018).

To sum up, it is very common that, after their remigration, second generation returnees question their sense of belonging to the homeland society and experience multiple ambiguities toward their bilingual identity (Klimt 2000; Koven 2004; Santos 2005; Sardinha 2011; Afonso 2017). What characterizes remigration experiences is a dual sense of belonging that crosses national borders and expresses strong transnational feelings and relations (Koven 2004). To best capture these multiple sentiments of belonging, ethnographic and sociolinguistic research on returnee HSs has consensually adopted the concept of *transnationalism* (Basch, Schiller, and Blanc 1994; Levitt 2001), which has been used to describe migrants' simultaneous participation in their sending and receiving societies (Koven 2004; Sardinha 2011). In fact, "(r)eturn is not necessarily the end of the migration cycle but in many cases only a stage as the person may choose to re-emigrate, or move back and forth between the two countries" (Házan 2017: 11).

14.6   Conclusion

To conclude, we have provided a broad overview of the main topics investigated in research on bilingual returnees. On the one hand, it involves research on dominant language attrition, and on the other hand, it may focus on L1/HL development after immersion in the L1/HL environment. Also, pedagogical and sociological implications of return were briefly discussed, which go hand in hand with language development.

When discussing dominant language attrition, "dominant" can refer to the first or the second language of returnee bilinguals – those children or adolescents who return to their homeland after many years either due to necessity or choice. The dominant language may start to attrite in settings where it is used less frequently and there is limited exposure to it on a daily basis. It seems that an important factor to mitigate attrition is to reach a level of attainment in the L1, L2, or 2L1 where the language or languages in question have stabilized and are not vulnerable to effects of erosion. Still more research is needed to better understand the role of extra-linguistic variables such as quantity and quality of exposure, age, and literacy skills in maintaining a language that ceases to be the majority language.

So far, research on returnees has demonstrated that the language competence of bilingual returnees is malleable in many domains. This competence tends to develop positively as far as the L1/HL is concerned, due to reinforced exposure to this language in the homeland. However, if one looks at the language that ceases to be the dominant language of the environment, it may develop negatively, particularly in cases of early return and very restricted exposure to the target language.

The overview of the research questions that arise from studies on returnee populations highlights the research potential of this field, which should be further explored in future investigations.

References

Abali, Ü. and H. Widman. 1990. Zur Reintegration türkischer Migrantenkinder. Versuch einer Übersicht (Reintegration of Turkish children. An Overview). In W. Steinig (ed.), *Zwischen den Stühlen. Schüler in ihrer fremden Heimat.* Munich: Waxmann, 17–37.

Afonso, S. 2017. Regresso como exercício de desdobramento de pertença ["Returning Home" Is Not Like Being Home. Return as an Exercise of Expanding Sense of Belonging]. *População e Sociedade* 27, 110–125.

Antoniou, K., K. Grohmann, M., Kambanaros, and N. Katsos. 2016. The Effect of Childhood Bilectalism and Multilingualism on Executive Control. *Cognition* 149, 18–30. https://doi.org /10.1016/j.cognition.2015 .12.002

Bardovi-Harlig, K. and D. Stringer. 2010. Variables in Second Language Attrition: Advancing the State of the Art. *Studies in Second Language Acquisition* 32(1), 1–45.

Basch, L., N. G. Schiller, and C. S. Blanc. 1994. *Nations Unbound: Transnational Projects, Post-Colonial Predicaments, and Deterritorialized Nation-States.* Amsterdam: Gordon and Breach.

Berman, R. A. and E. Olshtain. 1983. Features of First Language Transfer in Second Language Attrition. *Applied Linguistics* 4, 222–234.

Bever, T. G. 1981. Normal Acquisition Processes Explain the Critical Period. In K. C. Diller (ed.), *Individual Differences and Universals in Language Learning Aptitude.* Rowley, MA: Newbury House, 176–198.

Bialystok, E. and X. Feng. 2009. Language Proficiency and Executive Control in Proactive Interference: Evidence from Monolingual and Bilingual Children and Adults. *Brain and Language* 109(2–3), 93–100. https://doi .org/10.1016/j.bandl.2008.09.001

Blom, E., T. Boerma, E. Bosma, L., Cornips, and E. Everaert. 2017. Cognitive Advantages of Bilingual Children in Different Sociolinguistic Contexts. *Frontiers in Psychology: Cognition* 8(552), 1–12. https://doi.org/10.3389/fpsyg .2017.00552

Borjian, A., M. L. Muñoz deCote, S. van Dijk, and P. Houde. 2016. Transnational Children in Mexico: Context of Migration and Adaptation. *Diaspora, Indigenous, and Minority Education* 10(1), 42–54.

Brettell, C. 1979. Emigrar para voltar: A Portuguese Ideology of Return Migration. *Papers in Anthropology* 20, 1–20.

Daller, H. and C. Yıldız. 1995. Die türkischen Sprachfähigkeiten von Rückkehrern aus Deutschland (The Langauge Proficiency of Turkish

Returnees from Germany). In J. Treffers-Daller and H. Daller (eds.), *Zwischen den Sprachen. Sprachgebrauch, Sprachmischung und Sprachfähigkeiten türkischer Rückkehrer aus Deutschland. [Between the Languages. Language Use, Language Mixing and Language Proficiency of Turkish Returnees from Germany]*. Vol. 2. Bogaziçi University, Turkey: The Language Center, 83–94.

Daller, M. H. 2005. Migration und bilinguale Sprachentwicklung. Türkische Rückkehrer aus Deutschland [Migration and Bilingual Language Development. Turkish Returnees from Germany]. In V. Hinnenkamp and M. Meng (eds.), *Sprachgrenzen überspringen. Sprachliche Hybridität und polykulturelles Selbstverständnis [Crossing Language Boundaries. Linguistic Hybrids and Poly-Cultural Identities]*. Vol. 32. Tübingen: Narr, 325–345.

Daller, M. H. and J. Treffers-Daller. 2014. Moving between Languages: Turkish Returnees from Germany. In B. Menzel and C. Engel (eds.), *Rückkehr in die Fremde? Ethnische Remigration russlanddeutscher Spätaussiedler. Ost-West- Express. Kultur und Übersetzung (21)*. Berlin: Frank & Timme, 185–212.

Daller, M. H., J. Treffers-Daller, and R. Furman. 2011. Transfer of Conceptualization Patterns in Bilinguals: The Construal of Motion Events in Turkish and German. *Bilingualism: Language and Cognition* 14 (1), 95–119. https://doi.org/10.1017/S1366728910000106

Fishman, J. 1990. What Is Reversing Language Shift (RLS) and How Can It Succeed? *Journal of Multilingual and Multicultural Development* 11(1–2), 5–36.

Flores, C. 2010. The Effect of Age on Language Attrition: Evidence from Bilingual Returnees. *Bilingualism: Language and Cognition* 13(4), 533–546.

Flores, C. 2012. Differential Effects of Language Attrition in the Domains of Verb Placement and Object Expression. *Bilingualism: Language and Cognition* 15(3), 550–567.

Flores, C. 2015. Losing a Language in Childhood: A Longitudinal Case Study on Language Attrition. *Journal of Child Language* 42(3), 562–590.

Flores, C. 2019a. Language Development of Bilingual Returnees. M. Schmid and B. Köpke (eds.), *Oxford Handbook of Language Attrition*. Oxford: Oxford University Press, 493–501.

Flores, C. 2019b. Attrition and Reactivation of a Childhood Language: The Case of Returned Heritage Speakers. *Language Learning*. https://doi.org/10.1111/lang.12350

Flores, C. and A. Rato. 2016. Global Accent in the Portuguese Speech of Heritage Returnees. *Heritage Language Journal* 13(2). Special Issue on Heritage Phonetics and Phonology, edited by R. Rao, 161–183.

Godson, L. 2004. Vowel Production in the Speech of Western Armenian Heritage Speakers. *Heritage Language Journal* 2(1), 44–69. http://doi.org/10.1121/1.3569736

Goodman, R. 1993. *Japan's International Youth: The Emergence of a New Class of School Children*. Oxford: Clarendon.

Grenoble, L. A. and J. W. Lindsay. 2006. *Saving Languages: An Introduction to Language Revitalization*. Cambridge: Cambridge University Press.

Grosjean, F. 1982 *Life with Two Languages: An Introduction to Bilingualism*. Cambridge, MA: Harvard University Press.

Hazán, M. 2017. *Understanding Return Migration to Mexico: Towards a Comprehensive Policy for the Reintegration of Returning Migrants*. San Diego: Center for Comparative Immigration Studies. Retrieved from https://escholarship.org/uc/item/5nd4q6n3

Hopp, H. and M. S. Schmid. 2013. Perceived Foreign Accent in First Language Attrition and Second Language Acquisition: The Impact of Age of Acquisition and Bilingualism. *Applied Psycholinguistics* 34(2), 361–394. https://doi.org/(. . .)17/S0142716411000737

Johnson, J. S. and E. L. Newport. 1989. Critical Period Effects in Second Language Learning: The Influence of Maturational State on the Acquisition of English as a Second Language. *Cognitive Psychology*, 21(1), 60–99. https://doi.org/10.1016/0010-0285(89)90003-0

Kanno, Y. 2003. *Negotiating Bilingual and Bicultural Identities: Japanese Returnees Betwixt Two Worlds*. Mahwah, NJ: Lawrence Erlbaum.

Keating, M. C. and O. Solovova. 2011. Multilingual Dynamics among Portuguese Based Migrant Contexts in Europe. *Journal of Pragmatics* 43, 1251–1263.

Klimt, A. 2000. European Spaces. Portuguese Migrant's Notions of Home and Belonging. *Diaspora* 9, 259–285.

Koven, M. 2004. Transnational Perspectives on Sociolinguistic Capital among Luso-descendants in France and Portugal. *American Ethnologist* 31, 270–290.

Koven, M. 2013. Speaking French in Portugal: An Analysis of Contested models of Emigrant Personhood in Narratives about Return Migration and Language Use. *Journal of Sociolinguistics* 17(3), 324–354.

Kubota, M. 2018. Language Change in Bilingual Returnee Children: Mutual Effects of Bilingual Experience and Cognition. Unpublished PhD thesis, Edinburgh: University of Edinburgh.

Kubota, M., N. Chevalier, and A. Sorace. 2020. How Bilingual Experience and Executive Control Influence Development in Language Control among Bilingual Children. *Developmental Science* 23, e12865. https://doi.org/10.1111/desc.12865

Kuhberg, H. 1992. Longitudinal L2-attrition versus L2-acquisition in Three Turkish Children: Empirical Findings. *Second Language Research* 8(2), 138–154. https://doi.org/10.1177/026765839200800203

Kupisch, T., D. Barton, E. Klaschik, T. Lein, I. Stangen, and J. van de Weijer. 2014. Foreign Accent in Adult Simultaneous Bilinguals. *Heritage Language Journal* 11(2), 123–150.

Kupisch, T., T. Lein, D. Barton, D. J. Schröder, L. Stangen, and A. Stoehr. 2014. Acquisition Outcomes across Domains in Adult Simultaneous

Bilinguals with French as Weaker and Stronger Language. *Journal of French Language Studies* 24(3), 347–376.

Levitt, P. 2001. *The Transnational Villagers*. Berkeley: University of California Press.

Llanes, À. 2011. The Many Faces of Study Abroad: An Update on the Research on L2 Gains Emerged during a Study Abroad Experience. *The International Journal of Multilingualism* 8(3), 189–215.

Llanes, À. and C. Muñoz. 2009. A Short Stay Abroad: Does It Make a Difference? *System* 37(3), 353–365.

Lloyd-Smith, A., M. Einfeldt, and T. Kupisch. 2019. Italian-German Bilinguals: The Effects of Heritage Language Use on Accent in Early-acquired Languages. *International Journal of Bilingualism*. https://doi.org/10.1177/1367006919826867

Mar-Molinero, C. 2018 Language Issues for US-raised 'Returnees' in Mexico. In K. Potowski (ed.), *The Routledge Handbook of Spanish as a Heritage Language*. London: Routledge, 555–568.

Matthews, J. 2016. Phonological Processing under Conditions of Reduced Input: Do Child Returnees Suffer L2 Phonological Attrition? In K. Horie, T. Suzuki, and W. Suzuki, *Studies in Language Sciences: Journal of the Japanese Society for Language Sciences*, 15. Tokyo: Kaitakusha, 47–70.

Mayer, M. 1971. *A Boy, a Dog, a Frog, and a Friend*. New York: Dial.

Montrul, S. 2008. *Incomplete Acquisition in Bilingualism: Re-examining the Age Factor*. Amsterdam: John Benjamins.

Montrul, S. 2015. Language Attrition and Heritage Language Reversal. *Studies in Language Sciences: Journal of the Japanese Society for Language Sciences* 14, 1–28.

Montrul, S. 2016a. *The Acquisition of Heritage Languages*. Cambridge: Cambridge University Press.

Montrul, S. 2016b. Heritage Language Development. Connecting the Dots. *International Journal of Bilingualism* 22(5), 530–546.

Moyer, A. 2014. What's Age Got to Do with It? Accounting for Individual Factors in Second Language Accent. *Studies in Second Language Learning and Teaching* 4(3), 443–464.

Neisser, U. 1984. Interpreting Harry Bahrick's Discovery: What Confers Immunity against Forgetting? *Journal of Experimental Psychology: General* 113(1), 32–35.

Paulston, C. B., P. C. Chen, and M. C. Connerty. 1993. Language Regenesis: A Conceptual Overview of Language Revival, Revitalisation and Reversal. *Journal of Multilingual and Multicultural Development* 14(4), 275–286, https://doi.org/10.1080/01434632.1993.9994535

Polinsky, M. and G. Scontras. 2020. Understanding Heritage Languages. *Bilingualism: Language and Cognition* 23(1), 4–20. https://doi.org/10.1017/S1366728919000245

Rao, R. 2014. On the Status of the Phoneme /b/ in Heritage Speakers of Spanish. *Sintagma* 26, 37–54.

Reetz-Kurashige, A. 1999. Japanese Returnees' Retention of English-speaking Skills: Changes in Verb Usage over Time. In L. Hansen (ed.), *Second Language Attrition in Japanese Contexts*. Oxford: Oxford University Press, 21–58.

Ronquest, R. E. 2013. An Acoustic Examination of Unstressed Vowel Reduction in Heritage Spanish. In C. Howe, S. E. Blackwell, and M. Quesada (eds.), *Selected Proceedings of the 15th Hispanic Linguistics Symposium*. Somerville, MA: Cascadilla Press, 157–171.

Rose, R. R. and N. K. Fujishima. 1994. English-Speaking Returnees in Japan: An Exploratory Study at One University. *JALT Journal* 6(2), 179–194.

Rothman, J. 2009. Understanding the Nature and Outcomes of Early Bilingualism: Romance Languages as Heritage Languages. *International Journal of Bilingualism* 13(2), 155–163.

Sanchez-Garcia, J., E. T. Hamann, and V. Zuñiga. 2012. What the Youngest Transnational Students Have to Say about Their Transition from U.S. Schools to Mexican Ones. *Diaspora, Indigenous, and Minority Education* 6, 157–171.

Santos, I. dos 2005. Being a Part of Several "Worlds": Sense of Belonging and Wedding Rites among Franco-Portuguese Youth. *Croatian Journal of Ethnology and Folklore Research* 42, 25–45.

Sardinha, J. 2011. 'Returned' Second-generation Portuguese-Canadians and Portuguese-French: Return Motivations and Sense of Belonging. *Journal of Mediterranean Studies* 20(2), 231–254.

Schäfer, H. 1995. Sprach- und andere Probleme bei Schülern der deutsch-sprachigen Anadolu-Schulen. In J. Treffers-Daller and M. H. Daller (eds.), *Zwischen den Sprachen: Sprachgebrauch, Sprachmischung und Sprachfähigkeiten türkischer Rückkehrer aus Deutschland*. (Vol. 2). Istanbul: Boğaziçi University, 47–56.

Schmitz-Bewyl, L. 1983. Studie zur schulischen Reintegration zurückgekehrter türkischer Jugendlicher. *Info DaF* 10(2), 25–35.

Seliger, H. W. 1991. Language Attrition, Reduced Redundancy and Creativity. In H. W. Seliger and R. M. Vago (eds.), *First Language Attrition*. New York: Cambridge University Press, 227–240.

Snape, N. 2016. Judgments of Articles in L2 English by a Child Returnee: A Case Study. *Studies in Language Sciences: Journal of the Japanese Society for Language Sciences* 15, 71–95.

Snape, N., J. Matthews, M. Hirakawa, Y. Hirakawa, and H. Hosoi. 2014a. Aspect in L2 English: A Longitudinal Study of Four Japanese Child Returnees. In L. Roberts, I. Vedder, and J. H. Hulstijn (eds.), *EUROSLA Yearbook, 14*. Amsterdam: John Benjamins, 79–110.

Snape, N., J. Matthews, M. Hirakawa, Y. Hirakawa, and H. Hosoi. 2014b. L2 English Generics: Japanese Child Returnees' Incomplete Acquisition or

Attrition? In R. T. Miller, K. I. Martin, C. M. Eddington, A. Henery, N. M. Miguel, A. Tseng, A. Tuninetti, and D. Walter (eds.), *Selected Proceedings of the 2012 Second Language Research Forum: SLA in Many Contexts*. Somerville, MA: Cascadilla Proceedings Project, 155–169.

Tapan, N. and S. Hatipoğlu. 2016. Grenzen überschreiten durch Sprachen: Interkulturelle Begegnungen an deutschsprachigen Schulen in der Türkei. In Almut Küppers, Barbara Pusch, and Pinar Uyan Semerci (eds.), *Bildung in transnationalen Räumen*. Berlin: Springer, 231–240.

Taura, H. 2008. *Language Attrition and Retention in Japanese Returnee Students*. Tokyo: Akashi Shoten.

Taura, H. 2019. Attrition Studies on Japanese Returnees. In M. S. Schmid and B. Köpke (eds.), *The Oxford Handbook of Language Attrition*. Oxford: Oxford University Press. https://doi.org/10.1093/oxfordhb/9780198793595.013.31

Taura, H. and A. Taura. 2000. Reverse Language Attrition Observed in Japanese Returnee Students' English Productive Skills. *Journal of Fukui Medical University* 1, 535–543.

Tomiyama, M. 1999. The First Stage of Second Language Attrition: A Case Study of a Japanese Returnee. In L. Hansen (ed.), *Second Language in Japanese Contexts*. Oxford: Oxford University Press, 59–79.

Tomiyama, M. 2000. Child Second Language Attrition: A Longitudinal Case Study. *Applied Linguistics* 21(3), 304–332.

Tomiyama, M. 2009. Age and Proficiency in L2 Attrition: Data from Two Siblings. *Applied Linguistics* 30(2), 253–275. https://doi.org/10.1093/applin/amn038

Treffers-Daller, J., M. Daller, R. Furman, and J. Rothman. 2016. Ultimate Attainment in the Use of Collocations among Heritage Speakers of Turkish in Germany and Turkish–German Returnees. *Bilingualism: Language and Cognition* 19(3), 504–519.

Unsworth, S. 2019. Quantifying Language Experience in HL Development. In M. S. Schmid and B. Köpke (eds.), *The Oxford Handbook of Language Attrition*. Oxford: Oxford University Press. https://doi.org/10.1093/oxfordhb/9780198793595.013.34

Wessendorf, S. 2007. "Roots Migrants": Transnationalism and "Return" among Second-Generation Italians in Switzerland. *Journal of Ethnic and Migration Studies* 33(7), 1083–1102, https://doi.org/10.1080/13691830701541614

White, L. 2003. *Second Language Acquisition and Universal Grammar*. Cambridge: Cambridge University Press.

Yoshitomi, A. 1992. Towards a Model of Language Attrition: Neurobiological and Psychological Contributions. *Issues in Applied Linguistics* 3, 293–318.

Yoshitomi, A. 1999. On the Loss of English as a Second Language by Japanese Returnee Children. In L. Hansen (ed.), *Second Language in Japanese Contexts*. Oxford: Oxford University Press, 80–113.

Zúñiga, V. and E. T. Hamann. 2006. Going Home? Schooling in Mexico of Transnational Children. *CONfines* 2, 41–57.

Part II

Research Approaches to Heritage Languages

15

Heritage Language Research and Theoretical Linguistics

Elabbas Benmamoun

15.1   Introduction

Research on formal aspects of natural language has traditionally had two main goals. One goal has been to uncover the properties of natural language and the underpinnings of those properties, through their systems of primitives, rules, and principles. An essential component of this goal has been the quest for aspects that are shared by all languages and aspects that vary. The second major goal has been to determine the cognitive aspects of linguistic knowledge and how it relates to other domains of human cognition and the properties of the domains with which language interfaces. To make progress toward these goals, linguistic research started by focusing on native speakers who acquire their native language from birth through uninterrupted and sustained exposure to the native language and in various settings where the language can be acquired and used. Though there is still a great deal we do not understand about how language evolved, the relation between language and general cognition, and aspects that are exclusive to language, at least on heuristic grounds this approach yielded significant empirical results and uncovered many important aspects of the structure of natural languages; the primitives that go into building that structure and their properties; the interaction and mapping between different components; and the extents and limits of linguistic variation. Thanks to the generative enterprise, linguists have been able to identify significant numbers of generalizations about the phonology, morphology, syntax, and semantics of natural languages. All theories and approaches have to contend, for example, with the inventory and nature of lexical and functional categories, agreement and agreement asymmetries, word order and word order alternations, locality conditions that govern syntactic relations, binding, scope phenomena, displacement properties, and reduced or truncated structures that display properties of their fully realized counterparts, among many others. All the languages that have been carefully studied so far display many of these properties, which in turn raises questions about how to account for them in ways that allow for capturing the parts that hold across languages and the parts where languages may diverge. In addition to providing a framework for describing and analyzing aspects of linguistic form, the generative enterprise has spurred research on language acquisition, the role of input, stages of acquisition, the issue of the critical period, and how different linguistic structures are processed, among many others.

While the acquisition of native languages has formed the empirical base of linguistic theory over the last six decades, it is becoming increasingly evident that languages acquired under conditions that are different from those of native languages can be enormously valuable. This research territory is enormous and includes research on pidgins, creoles, selective language impairment, bilingualism and code-switching, and second and third language acquisition, to mention a few. However, one group of speakers that is now considered equally vital is heritage speakers. Heritage speakers, typically, though not exclusively, are second-generation immigrants who are born and raised in societies where their parents' first language is a minority language. Unlike typical second language learners, they are usually exposed to their parents' language (L1) in the early stages of their lives in the home and in the community. However, exposure to the dominant language limits their acquisition of their heritage language in significant ways. Eventually, heritage speakers become "unbalanced bilinguals" in the sense that their L1 becomes less dominant than their L2. Comparisons among heritage speakers, native speakers, and L2 learners have led researchers to revisit a number of key issues in L1 development research, including the idea of L1 stability, the role of input, linguistic areas of vulnerability to constrained input or to attrition, and the social factors that shape the contexts where heritage languages are acquired and used.

One consistent finding in the research on the phonological, morphological, and syntactic aspects of heritage languages is that heritage speakers pattern with both native speakers and L2 speakers. Thus, heritage speakers may have good mastery of the phonetic inventory of their heritage languages and solid perceptive command, though by no means in a similar way to that of native speakers. However, they differ from native speakers when one looks at the metrical and prosodic aspects of their languages (Au et al. 2002; Oh et al. 2003; Godson 2003; Oh et al. 2010; Saadah 2011). Similarly, in morphology, heritage speakers display native-like knowledge of certain areas of morphology while differing in other areas from native speakers (see Putnam, Schwarz, and Hoffman, this volume). For example, in research on heritage Arabic, Albirini and Benmamoun, in a series of papers, report that heritage speakers of Arabic do show knowledge of the root and pattern systems of Arabic, but their knowledge is different from that of native speakers and L2 learners.

In this chapter, I will focus on key syntactic aspects of heritage languages, covering areas that have proved fruitful for research on non-heritage languages, such as phrase structure, word order, and word order alternations, negation, and head movement. The implications of heritage language research on debates about major issues in theoretical syntax will be discussed.

15.2 Relevance of Heritage Language Data to Theoretical Syntax

In the last few years, there has been significant attention devoted to the syntax of heritage languages (Polinsky 2018; Lohndal, this volume). The common thread in this research is the extent to which heritage grammar is similar to or different from the syntax of non-heritage native speakers and of second language learners (L2), particularly those who acquire the second language as adults. The intuition behind this research is that heritage speakers do not fall neatly into one of the two groups. Rather, their syntax seems to pattern in some ways with non-heritage natives and in other ways with L2 speakers. This finding about heritage grammars has significant implications for syntactic theory and for the debate about language acquisition and particularly the role of input.[1] For example, areas where heritage grammar patterns with non-heritage native syntax could point to syntactic knowledge that does not require intensive and sustainable input for the child to converge on (assuming that no transfer effects are at work). This may be the case, for instance, with phrase structure and word order. By contrast, areas where heritage speakers differ from non-heritage native speakers and instead pattern with L2 speakers may have to do with parts of syntax that require intensive and sustainable input within a particular age window. This may reveal itself, for example, in the tendency of heritage speakers to use unmarked syntactic forms, such as nominative case, where a marked form may be required in the non-heritage language, or not deploy movement in contexts where it is expected in the baseline. If it can be demonstrated that this pattern is consistently manifested in typologically

---

[1] See Benmamoun et al. (2013) and Polinsky (2018) for an overview of the debate about the notion of native speakers and relevance of heritage language search to the debate. Heritage language research is, of course, part of the vast area of research on bilingualism and multilingualism and the various issues that that research has been engaging, including the role of input; the interaction between the languages that the learner is exposed to; and issues of transfer, contact, maintenance and attrition. See Yip and Mathews (2007) for an overview of the main issues and in-depth study of bilingual children exposed to Cantonese and English. See also Montrul (2016), which focuses on the acquisition of heritage languages and compares heritage speakers to native speakers and L2 learners.

different heritage languages, it could have important consequences for syntactic theory. Therefore, if we just focus on the empirical value of heritage language syntax, the opportunities for deepening our understanding of how syntax is acquired and the role of the environment in determining and shaping the outcome are substantial. Linguistics has benefited enormously from extending its empirical coverage beyond Germanic and Romance languages and by also incorporating results from research on language impairment and pidgins and creoles. Heritage languages add another empirical angle to enrich the debate because of the nature of the data they bring to the table. In the sections that follow, I will focus on some properties of heritage grammar as they relate to key aspects of syntax and morphosyntax.

15.3   Generative and Minimalist Approaches

Within the generative framework, and certainly within its minimalist versions, one core assumption is that significant generalizations about phrasal and sentential aspects of natural languages can be captured in a system that consists of primitives, rules, and principles that govern how a structure is built and the local and nonlocal relations between the different components of the structure (Chomsky 1995; Chomsky 2000; Chomsky 2019).[2] Though minimalist approaches to language are still taking shape, the consensus is that some properties such as External Merge, which usually combines simple units in an asymmetric fashion to form even more complex units, and Internal Merge, which, at the risk of gross simplification, moves syntactic units from one position to another within the syntactic phrase marker, are core and universal aspects of language.[3] For example, it is assumed that verbs and nouns are composites of features (phonological, formal, and semantic) and that when the two externally merge, say to form the traditional VP that consists of a verb and its complement, that merger is asymmetric, resulting in a complex linguistic expression that is verbal in nature.[4] After merger with the verb to form a phrasal complex (VP), the complement may move (undergo internal merge) from the complement position and merge with a higher unit in the structure such as tense (possibly in the case of passives and subject-to-subject raising)

---

[2] Hornstein (2018) provides an evaluative perspective on the last 25 years of the Minimalist Program and the main ideas that have animated the debate.

[3] The other fundamental assumption of the generative enterprise since its inception is structure dependence, namely, that important generalizations can be captured by referencing properties of and hierarchical relations within the phrase marker.

[4] The verb itself may be the result of the merger of a root, devoid of category features, and functional heads. See Section 15.6.

or the complementizer (possibly in the case of questions and relative clauses). In addition to structure building operations, relations between the members of the phrase marker are constrained by rules and principles that govern their interdependencies. These interdependencies may be manifested, for example, as case, agreement, and polarity licensing. The syntactic component that governs the merger of the members of the phrase marker and regulates their dependencies in turn interfaces with the semantic and phonological components, which also impose their constraints. Thus, knowledge of the syntax of a language entails knowledge of how linguistic expressions of that language are put together, the relationships between the members of the phrase marker and the principles that govern those relationships, and the correspondence relations or mapping between syntax and the semantic and phonological interfaces. The debate is ongoing about the nature of the syntactic component, its core primitives and operations, and principles and rules that belong in syntax proper and properties that seem to be driven by the exigencies of the interfaces, particularly the PF interface.[5] Research on heritage languages can significantly contribute to this debate and help expand the empirical base to advance our understanding of some of its key dimensions. For example, if there are structural aspects of language that are readily acquired and retained by heritage speakers in the context of constrained input and pressure from more dominant languages that could imply that those aspects are part of core syntax, compared to other aspects that require more extensive input and are more vulnerable to attrition.

15.4   Phrase Structure and Word Order

Phrase structure and word order are areas where heritage speakers' grammar patterns closely with the grammar of native speakers. Heritage speakers seem to acquire the word order of the heritage language early and they do not seem to deviate from the dominant and default order in the baseline. Thus, heritage Swedish speakers have been shown to adhere to the verb second pattern that some Germanic languages are known for Håkansson (1995). In the two examples in (1a) and (1b) from Albirini et al. (2013), the heritage speaker follows the order of Arabic with the verb preceding the object and the adjective following the noun it modifies. In

---

[5] The debate is ongoing about what belongs in the so-called core syntax and what belongs in other components that interface with syntax. The core idea of structural dependence and of the relevance of features of words and phrases to capturing generalizations about categorization, word order, and dependencies remain central, though articulated in different ways.

both examples, there are "errors" in the concord between the noun and its adjective but the word order is the same as in the native language.

(1a)   laʔa   l-DifDaʕ   maʕ   ʕaaʔila   w-ʔawlaad   Saʁiir*
       found.3s.m   the-frog   with   family   and-children   little.ms
       '[The boy] found the frog with its family and little children.'

(1b)   l-walad   simiʕ   ʔiši   žanb   l-šažra   l-waaʔiʕ
       the-boy   heard   thing   beside   the-tree.f   the-falling.m.*
       'The boy heard something beside the falling tree [log].'

The same results obtain in more complex forms such as the famous Semitic Construct State, where two nouns in a genitive relationship are combined without an intervening preposition, as shown in (2a) and (2b)[6]:

(2a)   ʔana   ba-šuuf-hum   ʕind   l-ʕamaaraat   l-žaamʕa
       I   ASP-see-them   at   the-buildings   the-university
       'I saw some in the university buildings.' (Palestinian heritage speaker)

(2b)   huwwa   raaħit   l-beit   r-raʔiis
       he   went   the-house   the-president
       'He went to the house of the president [king].' (Egyptian heritage speaker)

Again, the heritage speakers deploy the same word order of the genitive construction as native speakers of the baseline. What is different about the forms used by heritage speakers in (2a) and (2b) is that the first member of the Construct State also carries the definite article when none is expected in the native language. Interestingly, semantically, the first noun is interpreted as definite when the second one carries the definiteness marker, so in this respect the heritage language is more transparent in that it does not rely on definiteness spreading or agreement in definiteness between the two nouns but on overt morphological marking on the head that is interpreted as definite. Word order and phrase structure are intact in the heritage language but the definiteness feature is realized differently, which may have more to do with the interaction between syntax and the PF interface and the prosodic properties of the Construct-State complex, as argued in Benmamoun (2000).

Heritage speakers also have relatively comparable knowledge of the functional structure of the phrase marker. Though agreement may be different from the baseline and some morphosyntactic markers may be absent, the word order and the sequencing of aspectual markers is close to the baseline. In the sentence in (3) from Albirini et al. (2011), the heritage speaker is adhering to the expected word order within the functional structure of the clause, with the auxiliary carrying tense information at the highest position

---

[6] The Construct State is a highly complex construction. The members of the Construct State enter into a grammatical dependency where the head assigns genitive case to its complement. The entire construction is interpreted as definite or indefinite depending on the (in)definiteness marking on the last member of the Construct State. Finally, the members of the Construct State form a prosodic unit. See Benmamoun (2000) for details.

followed by the main predicate, which in turns selects a stative verb.[7] To generate a sentence such as (3), which is very close to the baseline, one needs to acquire the functional structure of the sentence, how the different heads are sequenced and how that sequence is derived, and the dependency relation between the different heads of the phrase marker.

(3)　huwwa　kan　ʕayez　yebʔa　raagel　maʕa　fluus　kitiir
　　　He　　was　wanting　become　man　with.him　money　plenty
　　　'He wanted to be a man who possesses a lot of money.' (reference)

　Narratives from Egyptian Arabic heritage speakers and Palestinian Arabic speakers studied by Albirini (2011) indicate that the former produce more SVO orders, while the latter showed no difficulty with the VSO order. As discussed in Aoun et al. (2010) and widely known in the literature, Arabic varieties display both the SVO and VSO orders. Curiously, the rate of SVO and VSO orders among the heritage speakers was higher relative to the baseline speakers. Thus, Egyptian heritage speakers produced the SVO order at a higher rate than their baseline counterparts and, similarly, Palestinian heritage speakers produced more VSO orders than their baseline counterparts. In both populations, however, it is clear that one word order predominates, the SVO order in Egyptian Arabic, and the VSO order in Palestinian Arabic, a finding that is consistent with the current understanding about word order in the two Arabic varieties.

　It is then reasonable to tentatively conclude that heritage speakers have no significant problems with acquiring the basic word order and phrase structure of their heritage language. While one cannot readily dismiss the possibility of transfer from English in the Egyptian Arabic variety spoken by heritage speakers, this seems unlikely, as the data from Palestinian heritage speakers where the VSO order predominates show.[8]

　We saw in (3) how heritage speakers have facility with the functional structure of the clause, particularly the sequencing of key elements of the functional and lexical domains and the selectional relationships between them. Formation of relative clauses seems to confirm the same finding. Though heritage speakers may diverge from the grammar of the baseline in their interpretation of relative clauses (Polinsky 2011) and in the realization of the relative markers, the ability to generate relative clause structures seems to remain resilient. This is particularly the case in Arabic, as shown

---

[7] See Polinsky (2018) for an overview of morphosyntax in heritage languages. Not all functional categories behave the same way in heritage grammars. Tense, for example, seems to be more resilient than agreement, which is more resilient than concord (such as concord between a noun and an adjective). The results have been consistent across a number of languages, as discussed in Polinsky (2018) and the references cited therein.

[8] The question does arise, however, about the derivations of the SVO and VSO orders. Though there is a debate about the status of the subject in the SVO order in Arabic and whether it is a genuine subject or rather a topic (Soltan 2007), there is more consensus that the VSO order involves the movement of the verb (Aoun et al. 2010 and Benmamoun 2017).

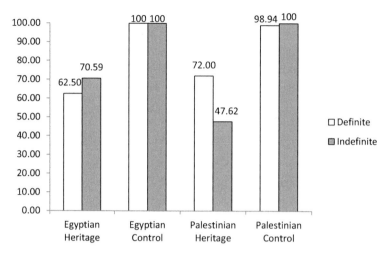

Figure 15.1 Percentage accuracy on definite and indefinite relative clauses (Albirini et al. 2011)

in Albirini et al. (2011). The relative clauses in the narratives collected from twenty heritage speakers of Egyptian and Palestinian Arabic did not show any problems with word order but only with the baseline rule that requires an overt marker with definite relatives and no overt marker with indefinite relatives, as shown in Figure 15.1 from Albirini et al. (2011).

In (4a), there is a definite noun phrase *l-ʔasbaab* that requires an overt relative marker but the speaker does not use one. By contrast, (4b) has an indefinite noun phrase that does not require a relative marker but the speaker uses the marker that is usually only expected in definite relative clauses in the baseline. The absence of the relative marker in (4a) could be a case of transfer from English, whereas transfer effects seem unlikely in (4b). Note that everything else about the word order in these two clauses matches the order in the baseline, including the use of the resumptive pronoun in (4b) because Arabic varieties do not allow preposition stranding, unlike English.

(4a)   Dimn l-ʔasbaab ʕalaaʔ d-diin kaan   ʕaayez ykuun ʔamiir ʕašaan yiggwwiz
        among the reasons Aladdin   was.3s.m wanting be.3s.m. prince because marry.3s.m
        ʔamiira
        princes
        'Among the reason that made Aladdin want to become a prince is to marry a princess.' (Egyptian heritage speaker)

(4b)   Tələʕ   min maħall lli   kaan   fi-i
        left.3s.m from place   that was.3s.m in-it
        'He left from the place in which he was' (PHS)

Polinsky (2011) provides comprehension data that also demonstrate that heritage speakers of Russian do relatively well on relative clauses, particularly relativization of subjects and objects, with stronger performance on the former, which is consistent with the prediction of Keenan and Comrie's

Accessibility Hierarchy (Keenan and Comrie 1977) that states that if a language allows extraction of the object, for example, then we expect that language to also allow extraction of the subject. Polinsky's study, however, is more nuanced in a very critical way. Heritage children do better on both subjects and objects than heritage adults. Heritage children are closer to the native baseline than the heritage adults, particularly with regard to the relativization of the object in Russian. The reasonable conclusion that Polinsky draws from this contrast between heritage children and heritage adult speakers is that as English becomes dominant and there is less input from Russian, coupled with other attrition factors that affect the morphological cues for grammatical function, the heritage grammar is restructured to basically allow for relativization of the highest member of the Accessibility Hierarchy, which is the subject. Thus, the heritage Russian data show that relativization as a construction is learned early but that the type of relativization that is maintained may be sensitive to input (and possibly other cues within the language). In addition, Polinsky provides compelling evidence that it is not an issue of transfer from English, as word order does not seem to matter regardless of whether the order is similar to English. In other words, the change in the grammar seems to be due to factors other than influence from English.

One question that arises is why the subject is given this privileged status. Within generative grammar, subjects have always had a prominent role. For example, while the presence of complements, including oblique arguments, depends on the thematic properties of the predicate and its valence, the presence of the subject seems to be required independently and purely on formal grounds. This insight has allowed the theory to capture a number of generalizations that cut across constructions such as the presence of expletives in subject positions, passives, subject-to-subject raising, unaccusative constructions, and control, among others. The heritage Russian data are consistent with the status of the subject, or rather the structural position that the subject occupies, in the theory. The subject, thanks to its hierarchical position and its features, is an essential element of the clause and is relevant to a number of constructions in the language, so that its syntactic distribution may not require significant input for it to be acquired by heritage speakers.

Before closing this discussion on relative clauses in heritage languages, I would like to discuss another area where heritage grammar may help shed critical light on current syntactic debates. Relative clauses are highly complex structures because they involve both local and nonlocal dependencies. Consider a simple relative clause such as (5):

(5)   I read the book [that you recommended].

In (5), the noun phrase *the book* is interpreted as a complement of the main verb *read* and of the embedded verb *recommended*. To capture these multiple dependencies, the dominant analysis within generative grammar (Chomsky 1977) assumes that the overt NP *the book* is generated in the matrix clause and that the embedded complex NP is the residue of a null operator that moves from the complement position to the left periphery of the relative clause that modifies the matrix complement *the book*. There is, however, an alternative analysis that originated with Brame (1968) and Vergnaud (1974) and was updated in Kayne (1994) that posits a competing analysis (Promotion Analysis), whereby the head noun *book* itself is generated in the embedded clause and moved to the higher clause. There are arguments on both sides of the debate that we don't have room to get into, and it is plausible that languages may deploy both relativization options (Åfarli 1994). However, given that heritage speakers seem to acquire the phrase structure of relative clauses without significant difficulties and given that dependencies do provide some challenges for heritage speakers, it would be appropriate to ask the question as to which approach is more consistent with what we know about heritage speakers' knowledge of relative clauses. Consider how the two competing approaches generate the relative clause in (5):

(5)   Promotion Analysis: $[_{DP}$ the $[_{CP}$ book$_i$ $[_{TP}. \ldots \ldots t_i \ldots]]]$
       Matching Analysis: $[_{DP}$ the book$_i$ $[_{CP}$ OP$_i$ $[_{TP} \ldots . t_i \ldots]]]$

The details of the two approaches are more nuanced but the two representations above illustrate their main imports, namely whether the relativized noun is generated in the lower clause and raised to the main clause or whether the lower position is occupied/licenced by an abstract operator. Both analyses are highly complex and require movement and some mechanism to establish the semantic dependency between the noun *book* and the embedded complement position. This semantic dependency is established directly under the Promotion Analysis via the copy of the noun and via the operator in CP under the Matching Analysis. The data we have from heritage language grammars on relative clauses is too rudimentary but the fact that heritage speakers show vulnerabilities in establishing dependencies at a distance, including anaphoric dependencies (Kim et al. 2009), may argue for the Matching Analysis for relatives in heritage grammar.

The same question arises about complex movement approaches that have been proposed for word order in the Semitic Construct State (Shlonsky 2004) and other constructions such as verbal complexes in Dutch and Hungarian (Koopman and Szabolcsi 2000). Those approaches assume highly complex movement operations that deploy multiple iterations of phrasal movement. Similarly, within the Antisymmetry program of Kayne (1994), which has been able to derive some significant generalizations about phrase structure and word order in natural language, head final orders require complex movement operations that involve movement of large constituents.[9] Given that heritage speakers show no significant problems acquiring and generating the basic word order of unmarked constructions in their heritage language while showing vulnerabilities in cases where dependencies between different positions in the phrase marker need to be established, it would be relevant to ask whether approaches that posit universal order schemas and deploy highly complex movement operations to derive different word order alternations and sequences of morphemes on heads are consistent with the existing findings in heritage language syntax.[10]

The members of the phrase marker can have a phonological matrix or none, i.e., they can be realized as overt or silent in the phonological component. A consistent result reported in heritage language research is the overuse of overt pronouns when both the overt and null options are available. This has been reported in a number of languages as discussed in Polinsky (2018) and Lohndal (this volume). The same results obtain in the study of heritage Arabic speakers conducted by Albirini et al. (2011), where heritage speakers produce more overt pronouns than their baseline counterparts. We have, however, to be careful not to overstate the significance of this finding because heritage Arabic speakers still use null pronouns at a very high rate. This, in turn, could be taken to indicate that the issue at stake is not phrase structure per se or problems associating null forms with the relevant grammatical function in the sentence but could be due to other factors, such as transfer from English or pragmatics, which would make it an interface issue. There is, however, one area where heritage speakers diverge from the baseline grammar, which is in how they establish dependencies between null subjects and other overt arguments in the sentence. Heritage speakers seem to opt for establishing a referential dependency between pronouns and arguments in prominent positions in the phrase marker

The pattern that emerges from research on phrase structure and word order in heritage grammar is that heritage speakers are usually able to converge on the baseline grammar, particularly with regard to basic structures such as simple sentences and phrases, regardless of whether the phrase structure and word order patterns are similar or different from

---

[9] One challenge for these types of movement operations, and admittedly for even some simpler forms of movement, is independently establishing the syntactic motivation for the movement. In many instances, features are posited to drive movement to a particular position without providing independent motivations for the feature. This is not a problem exclusive to these approaches but it does raise the question of how learners, including heritage speakers, learn those (abstract and non-interpretable) features.

[10] It is, of course, possible that the problem in heritage grammars may have to do with the cues associated with dependencies such as morphosyntactic and prosodic cues. However, given the prevalence of the findings across languages with different morphosyntactic cues, that may not be the full story. See Polinsky and Scontras (2020) for an overview of syntactic vulnerabilities in heritage grammars, including silent or null elements in the context of ellipsis.

the dominant language with which the heritage language is in contact. This is not meant to imply that transfer from the dominant language does not play a role in the acquisition and maintenance of phrase structure and word order. The grammar of the dominant language may impact and shape choices when the heritage grammar provides the learners with different options, some of which may be close to the patterns in the dominant language. However, as we saw with heritage speakers of Arabic, they are able to acquire the VSO order, the noun adjective order, the sequencing of verbal heads in the sentence, and the noun and noun order that we find in genitive constructions. Likewise, heritage speakers of V2 languages are able to acquire the V2 construction. Similar findings have been reported with regard to the acquisition of relative clauses.

Putting these findings about phrase structure and word order in heritage grammar together with the findings about phonology and morphology, it seems that heritage speakers do better on the acquisition of rules and principles that combine small units to form complex units, particularly those considered canonical in the language. This is the case in phonology, morphology, and syntax. In phonology, heritage speakers do relatively better on the acquisition of the sounds of the language and on how to combine phonemes to form syllables. They do equally well on the acquisition of the morphological building blocks of the heritage language, even when those building blocks involve units below the word level such as consonantal roots, syllables, and prosodic feet. Heritage speakers may diverge from the baseline in their knowledge of individual morphemes but generally have little difficulty converging on how words are put together. The findings from research on the syntax of heritage languages seem to point in the same direction. The conclusion may not be surprising in a model that assumes that linguistic generalizations at different levels of language are better captured by referring to units such as phonemes, prosodic units, words, phrases, and sentences, which makes acquisition of the combinatorial rules and processes essential. These results from heritage grammars are important because of the relatively constrained input that heritage speakers receive. It could be taken to indicate that acquiring phrase structure and canonical word order does not require the same amount of input that is needed to acquire other patterns such as referential dependencies and interpreting quantifier scope, for example. Can one go as far as to conclude from the existing data that operations such as (External) Merge that are posited to build structure are specific to language and are part of UG, and therefore only require minimal input for their acquisition? It is premature, perhaps, to venture an answer to that question but the facts available to us so far from research on heritage languages seem to suggest that a positive answer may not be unreasonable.

15.5   Head Movement

Assuming a relatively simple phrase marker like in (6), where the clause consists of a lexical layer headed by the verb and a functional layer that contains tense and other functional categories, one area of debate within syntactic theory is how to capture the relationship between the functional domain and the lexical domain and whether operations over the phrase marker can account for word order alternations such as the relative order of the verb, functional categories, the subject, and other members of the clause.

(6)

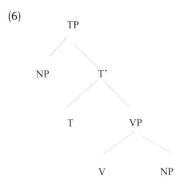

For example, Pollock (1989) posits a negative projection between TP and VP and argues that the difference in the placement of the main verb in English and French has to do with the availability of verb movement to T in French and the lack of that movement in English, and hence the need for Do-support in English in the context of negation and the inability of adverbs to split the verb and object. The well-known verb-second phenomenon in Germanic languages has been accounted for by positing verb movement to a higher functional domain such as CP, and thus allowing for matrix verbs to occur higher in the clause. In Arabic, head movement has been posited to account for the VSO order by moving the verb to a position higher than the subject. This has been considered an improvement over an analysis that assumes a flat basic VSO structure where the subject and object are in a symmetric relationship, a structure that has proven to be inadequate on various empirical grounds.[11]

The status of head movement is still a matter of debate within the Minimalist Program, whether it is a syntactic operation or post-syntactic operation and whether the movement in question involves the head or the entire phrase that contains the verbal head. What is significant for our present purpose is how the phenomena that fall under the head movement

---

[11] See Aoun et al (2010) for an overview. For details see Mohammad (1988), Fassi Fehri (1993), Shlonsky (1997), and Benmamoun (2000).

label operate in heritage languages. Research on V2 in heritage language points to the relative resiliency of the construction as reported and discussed by Lohndal (this volume) but in more nuanced ways than we expect.[12] Heritage grammar allows for head movement but its domains and reach may be different.

Albirini and Benmamoun (2015) come to the same conclusion based on their study of heritage Egyptian negation. In Egyptian Arabic, as in many other varieties of Arabic (Aoun et al. 2010; Benmamoun et al. 2013), sentential negation is realized either as a discontinuous marker with a negative proclitic and a negative enclitic on the host or as a non-discontinuous combination of the proclitic and enclitic. For example, in (7a) and (7b), the negative is realized as one unit located between the subject, on one hand, and, on the other, the nominal predicate or the verb carrying the future marker, respectively:[13]

(7) a. huwwa   miš   muhandis
         he   neg   engineer
         'He is not an engineer.'

     b. huwwa   miš   ħa-yigi
         he   neg   fut-3.come
         'He will not come.'

In the past tense, on the other hand, the discontinuous negative is required.[14]

(8) ma-gat-š
     neg-came.3f-neg
     'She didn't come.'

The discontinuous negative is also required in existential constructions and imperatives as shown in (9a) and (9b):

(9) a. ma-fii-š   kitab   ʕa-l-maktab
         neg-there-neg   book   on-the-desk
         'There is no book on the desk.'

     b. ma-t-ruħ-š
         neg-2-go-neg
         'Don't go.'

---

[12] See Larsson and Johannessen (2015) for a very insightful account of heritage Norwegian where head movement seems to have been maintained (which indicates lack of influence from English) but in a different way from the baseline. Head movement seems to have survived in the language but works differently from the baseline.

[13] All the data in this section are from Albirini and Benmamoun (2015) and the references cited there.

[14] The non-discontinuous form has been reported to occur in the past tense in some varieties but we don't have sufficient information and analyses from those varieties to determine the nature of the data and their semantic and pragmatic properties. Our data from the speakers of the baseline and the performance of the heritage speakers on past tense negation are consistent with the assumption that discontinuous negation is required in past tense sentences.

Interestingly, in the present tense in Egyptian Arabic both negation patterns are available (Jelinek 1981):

(10)   a.   ma-b-yi-ktib-š
              neg-asp-3m-write-neg
              'He isn't writing.'

       b.   miš   b-yi-ktib
              Neg   asp-3m-write
              'He isn't writing.'

(11)

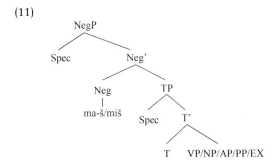

Assuming a structure of negative sentences as in (11), Albirini and Benmamoun adopt the consensus analysis that discontinuous negation is due to head movement.[15] Thus, in the past tense, the verb moves to the tense head and then to the negative head to merge with it. In imperatives and existential constructions, movement and merger with negation are also obligatory. By contrast, when the predicate is an NP, AP, or PP or when the head of T is the future marker, no movement or merger with negation takes place. The present tense strikes the middle ground and allows for movement and merger with negation to be optional, though with movement as the preferred option. These are very complex patterns to acquire because they require knowledge of the phrase marker and the position of negation relative to the other syntactic projections in the clause and also the lexical and featural properties of the heads that drive their interaction with negation. Egyptian children, studied by Omar (1973), master the non-discontinuous form before the discontinuous form, and the errors they make involve generalizing the non-discontinuous form or using a completely different negative (the holophrastic negative).

    Albirini and Benmamoun studied the above patterns in the heritage speech of thirty-five Arabic heritage speakers in the United States and compared them to sixteen speakers of the baseline.

---

[15] See Benmamoun et al. (2014) for several arguments for the structure in (11), particularly the argument that negation is higher than tense, which makes Arabic different from English, where negation seems to be located below T (Pollock 1989).

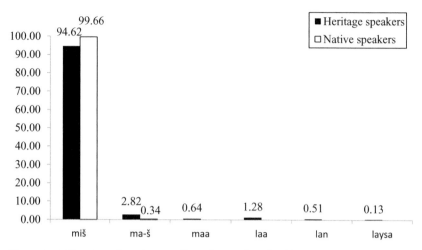

Figure 15.2 Negation when the non-discontinuous form is obligatory in future tense and non-verbal predicates (Albirini and Benmamoun 2015)

Overall, the results show that heritage speakers have strong command of the functional structure of negative clauses. They position the projection of negation higher than tense as it is in the baseline. They also deploy the non-discontinuous form of negation in the context where it is expected in the baseline as shown in Figure 15.2.[16]

The heritage speakers also deployed the discontinuous form at a higher rate in contexts where it is expected to occur in the baseline, which are the past tense, existential, and imperative constructions as shown in Figure 15.3. Since the discontinuous is taken as a reliable indicator of movement, the results in Figure 15.3 show strong presence of movement but not to the same extent as in the baseline, which is consistent with the findings about head movement in other heritage languages.[17]

Interestingly, in negative sentences in the present tense the picture is mixed but could be revealing about the nature of heritage grammar. Recall that in the baseline, both forms of the negative are possible in the present tense, though there is preference for the discontinuous form. In Figure 15.4, the preference for the discontinuous form is quite clear in the baseline, but notice that heritage speakers prefer the non-discontinuous form over the discontinuous form.

One plausible interpretation of these results is that heritage speakers opt for the non-movement option when they have the choice. They tend to

---

[16] There were also negligible instances where the subjects used negatives from Standard Arabic (such as *maa, lan* and *laysa*) or the holophrastic negative *laa*.

[17] Sherkina-Lieber and Murasugi (2015) show that Heritage Inuktitut maintains Noun Incorporation, though not at the same level as speakers of the baseline. If Noun Incorporation is derived by head movement as in Baker (1988), then this is another instance of head movement in heritage grammar.

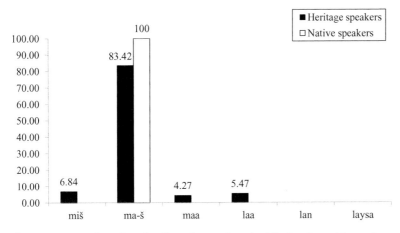

Figure 15.3 Negation when the discontinuous form is obligatory in past tense, imperative, and existential sentences Albirini and Benmamoun (2015)

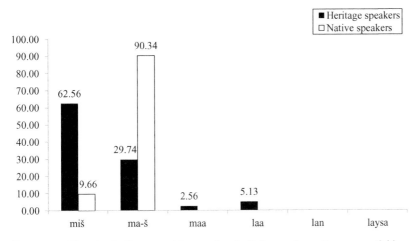

Figure 15.4 Negation in the present tense when both forms of negation are available (Albirini and Benmamoun 2015)

deploy movement when they have to (Figure 15.3) but prefer the non-movement strategy when the grammar allows it. Albirini and Benmamoun suggest a possible explanation based on markedness for the present tense results, but what is also important is that heritage speakers recognize that the present tense verb is different from the past tense verb and has a different syntax (Benmamoun 2000). In other words, whatever abstract features drive movement to tense and then to negation, it appears that heritage speakers have converged on that knowledge. In short, these results confirm the understanding that we have about heritage languages, namely that movement, including head movement, is maintained in heritage grammar. This conclusion may have far-reaching consequences with regard to how movement is acquired and the cues that learners need to converge on it. Benmamoun (2000) argues that both past and present tense verbs in Arabic carry only overt agreement but not overt tense. To motivate movement, he relies on the categorical features of Chomsky (1995), like the EPP features that have been used in recent versions of Minimalism. However, even if we cannot pin down the abstract features that drive movement, the fact that heritage speakers acquire movement even when overt triggers are absent implies that the abstract features that drive movement are present in their grammars, which is significant.

15.6   Roots and Lexical Categories

One idea within Minimalist approaches that has gained a lot of attention concerns the structure and derivation of so-called lexical categories, such as nouns and verbs. Rather than treating lexical categories as primitives, in a number of approaches, lexical categories are derived through processes that combine roots, which carry the basic lexical meaning, and other functional categories such as tense and aspect (Halle and Marantz 1993; Arad 2003; Borer 2005a, b, 2013). Under these approaches, the basic units of syntactic derivations are roots that are acategorial, i.e., do not come pre-specified for category labels, and functional categories such as aspect, tense, negation, number, definiteness, etc. The roots combine with functional categories through movement processes and the output is transferred to the PF interface, which, subject to its own rules and constraints, yields the complex words that we usually associate with verbs, nouns, and adjectives. While the morphophonological arguments for the notion of root, or equivalent basic unit below the word level, are not straightforward in a language such as English, Semitic languages, such as Arabic, do provide such arguments in a compelling way, which makes them good testing grounds for exploring heritage speakers' knowledge of the notion of root.

As is well known, Arabic words are formed in two ways, concatenatively and non-concatenatively (McCarthy 1979, 1981). Concatenative word formation is similar to word formation in many languages where a morpheme marking a grammatical category, such as number or tense, is attached at the right or left edge of the word or stem. Non-concatenative morphology deploys a different mechanism, which consists of mapping a consonantal root onto a template. The process is complex in that it requires (1) the ability to isolate and extract the root from the base word, (2) knowledge of the appropriate template for the relevant derivation, such as the causative or plural, and (3) the rules that govern the mapping of the root onto the template. In addition, not all the roots are equal: While some roots consist of three consonants with no glides or geminates, other roots may have them, in which case the derivation is even more complex and may require recovering or deleting the glide and breaking up the geminate. Benmamoun, Albirini, Montrul, and Saadah (2014) argue that heritage Arabic speakers have native-like knowledge of the root, but they differ from native speakers in their treatment of roots that contain geminates and glides. Somewhat like L2 learners, they opt for the concatenative form when the non-concatenative pattern is required, but unlike L2 learners they choose the pattern that is considered default in the language, which is remarkable given the complexity of the morphology and its prosodic structure. L2 learners tend to choose the concatenative masculine plural as default pattern but heritage speakers, like baseline speakers, are more likely to use the feminine plural, which is the concatenative default pattern in the language. Equally striking is the fact that, even when they deviate from the baseline in non-concatenative morphology, heritage speakers deploy the iambic pattern, which is the dominant pattern in non-concatenative plural formation (McCarthy and Prince 1990). In short, heritage speakers exhibit a highly sophisticated knowledge of the root and pattern morphological system that relies on a complex set of building blocks (consonantal roots, vocalic melodies, and templates) and mapping conventions. The grammar is not identical to the baseline grammar but it patterns with it in fundamental ways, particularly with regard to processes that build word structure and the rules that govern them. Thus, even with constrained input, heritage speakers' grammar does contain the notion of root as basic building block, which is consistent with many current (derivational) approaches to the syntax and morphology of natural language. The difference between heritage speakers and the native speakers of the baseline is in the overt realization of the roots and the phonological constraints that govern their realization. In other words, the difference has more to do with the interface between syntax and PF, where, as expected, heritage grammar shows vulnerabilities.

15.7 Conclusion

In this chapter, I have discussed some syntactic findings from research on the syntax of heritage languages. I focused mostly on phrase structure, word order, head movement, and the root as primitive building blocks of the syntax. The picture that emerges from research on these aspects of heritage languages is that heritage learners are able to converge on core areas of the grammar of the baseline. Heritage speakers seem to be able to learn the basic phrase structure of the heritage language, word order, and dependencies between the members of the phrase marker, including head movement. In this respect, knowledge of these areas is markedly different from their knowledge of the morphosyntax, such as agreement, aspect, case, and phonological realization of the root, where they display vulnerabilities (Polinsky 2018). Other areas of vulnerabilities have been identified in patterns where syntax interfaces with the semantic component (binding and quantifier scope). One tentative conclusion that can be drawn from these results is that phrase structure, word order, head movement, and the root as basic unit of derivation do not require extensive input and extended exposure to the language. As we have seen, heritage speakers of Arabic display the Arabic VSO order, place negation above tense, which is opposite to the order in English, and deploy verb movement, which English restricts to modals and auxiliaries in matrix clauses. They are also able to isolate the consonantal root and combine it with other elements.

The question for theoretical linguistics is why some syntactic aspects, such as phrase structure, word order, and movement, are relatively easier to acquire and maintain in heritage languages. The opposite question arises about areas of the heritage language grammar that display vulnerabilities. For example, heritage grammars display vulnerabilities in case and agreement and also in establishing dependencies that are not local. It is tempting to attribute the difference to the operation that is critical to phrase structure, word order, and movement, namely Merge, both Internal Merge and External Merge. On the other hand, it is plausible that the key factor in the vulnerabilities of agreement, case, and other dependencies at a distance is that they involve mapping between syntax and the two interfaces, the semantic and the morphophonological components.[18] Mapping between components requires knowledge of the properties of each component and the mapping conventions or correspondence rules and is also subject to performance factors. It would be reasonable, then, to expect interface phenomena to require more extensive and rich input, and thus to be more vulnerable when acquired under constrained conditions. The results so far from heritage language research appear to be consistent with this view of the syntax of natural language.

Minimalism, with its stated goal to significantly narrow down the core aspects of the language faculty, provides a roadmap to engage findings from research on heritage languages. It may well turn out that those core aspects of grammar, such as Merge, are what is acquired early and maintained under constrained language acquisition and use conditions. That makes it worthwhile for theoretical linguists to incorporate heritage languages in their empirical base as they continue their efforts to understand what it means to know a language.

---

[18] There is extensive psycholinguistic and syntactic research that shows that agreement is susceptible to interface effects. Phenomena such as agreement attraction (Bock 1999) and some cases of close conjunct agreement (Benmamoun et al. 2013) are sensitive to linear order and adjacency effects, which are not syntactic in nature.

References

Åfarli, T. 1994. A Promotion Analysis of Restrictive Relative Clauses. *The Linguistic Review* 11, 81–100.

Aoun, J., E. Benmamoun, and L. Choueiri. 2010. *The Syntax of Arabic*. Cambridge: Cambridge University Press.

Albirini, A. 2014. Toward Understanding the Variability in the Language Proficiencies of Arabic Heritage Speakers. *International Journal of Bilingualism* 18(6), 730–765.

Albirini, A. and E. Benmamoun. 2015. Factors Affecting the Retention of Sentential Negation in Heritage Egyptian Arabic. *Bilingualism: Language and Cognition* 8(3), 470–489.

Albirini, A., E. Benmamoun, and B. Chakrani. 2013. Gender and Number Agreement in the Oral Production of Arabic Heritage Speakers. *Bilingualism: Language and Cognition* 16, 1–18.

Albirini, A., E. Benmamoun, and E. Saadah. 2011. Grammatical Features of Egyptian and Palestinian Arabic Heritage Speakers' Oral Production. *Studies in Second Language Acquisition* 45, 273–303.

Arad, M. 2003. *Roots and Patterns*. Dordrecht: Springer.

Au, T., L. Knightly, S. Jun, and J. Oh. 2002. Overhearing a Language during Childhood. *Psychological Science* 13, 238–243.

Baker, M. 1988. *Incorporation: A Theory of Grammatical Function Changing*. Chicago: University of Chicago Press.

Benmamoun, E. 2000. *The Feature Structure of Functional Categories: A Comparative Study of Arabic Dialects*. New York: Oxford University Press.

Benmamoun, E. 2017. *VSO Word Order, Primarily in Arabic Languages. The Wiley Blackwell Companion to Syntax*.

Benmamoun, E., A. Bhatia, and M. Polinsky. 2009. Closest Conjunct Agreement in Head Final Languages. In Jeroen van Craenenbroeck (ed.), *Linguistic Variation Yearbook*. Amsterdam: John Benjamins, 67–88.

Benmamoun, E., S. Montrul, and M. Polinsky. 2013. Heritage Languages and Their Speakers: Opportunities and Challenges for Linguistics. *Theoretical Linguistics* 39, 129–181.

Benmamoun, E., A. Albirini, S. Montrul, and E. Saadah. 2014. Arabic Plurals and Root and Pattern Morphology in Palestinian and Egyptian Heritage Speakers. *Linguistic Approaches to Bilingualism* 4(1), 89–123.

Benmamoun, E., M. Abunasser, R. Al-Sabbagh, A. Bidaoui, and D. Shalash. 2014. The Location of Sentential Negation in Arabic Varieties. *Brill's Annual of Afroasiatic Languages and Linguistics* 5, 83–116.

Bock, J. K., J. Nicol, and J. C. Cutting. 1999. The Ties That Bind: Creating Number Agreement in Speech. *Journal of Memory and Language* 40, 330–346.

Bolonyai, A. 2007. (In)vulnerable Agreement in Incomplete Bilingual L1 Learners. *The International Journal of Bilingualism* 11, 3–21.

Borer, H. 2005a. *Structuring Sense: Vol. 1. In Name Only*. Oxford: Oxford University Press.

Borer, H. 2005b. *Structuring Sense: Vol. 2. The Normal Course of Events*. Oxford: Oxford University Press.

Borer, H. 2013. *Structuring Sense: Vol. 3. Taking Form*. Oxford: Oxford University Press.

Brame, M. 1968. *A New Analysis of the Relative Clause: Evidence for an Interpretive Theory*. Unpublished ms., MIT.

Chomsky, N. 1977. 'On wh-Movement.' In P. Culicover et al. (eds.), *Formal Syntax*. New York: Academic Press, 71–132.

Chomsky, N. 1981. *Lectures on Government and Binding*. Dordrecht: Foris.

Chomsky, N. 1995. *The Minimalist Program*. Cambridge: MIT Press.

Chomsky, N. 2000. Minimalist Inquiries: The Framework. In R. Martin et al. (eds.), *Step by Step. Essays on Minimalist Syntax in Honor of Howard Lasnik*. Cambridge, MA: MIT Press, 89–155.

Chomsky, N. 2019. Some Puzzling Foundational Issues: The Reading Program. *Catalan Journal of Linguistics Special Issue*, 263–285.

Fassi Fehri, A. 1993. *Issues in the Structure of Arabic Clauses and Words*. Dordrecht: Kluwer Academic Publishers.

Godson, L. 2004. Phonetics of Language Attrition: Vowel Production and Articulatory Setting in the Speech of Western Armenian Heritage Speakers. Ph.D. dissertation, UCSD.

Håkansson, G. 1995. Syntax and Morphology of Language Attrition: A Study of Five Bilingual Expatriate Swedes. *International Journal of Applied Linguistics* 5, 153–171.

Halle, M. and A. Marantz. 1993. Distributed Morphology and the Pieces of Inflection. In K. Hale and S. J. Keyser (eds.), *The View from Building 20*. Cambridge, MA: MIT Press, 111–176.

Hornstein, N. 2018. The Minimalist Program after 25 Years. *Annual Review of Linguistics* 4, 49–65.

Jelinek, E. 1981. On Defining Categories: Aux and Predicate in Egyptian Colloquial Arabic. Ph.D. dissertation, University of Arizona.

Kayne, Richard S. 1994. *The Antisymmetry of Syntax*. Cambridge, MA: MIT Press.

Keenan, E. and B. Comrie. 1977. Noun Phrase Accessibility and Universal Grammar. *Linguistic Inquiry* 8, 63–99.

Kim J.-H., S. Montrul, and J. Yoon. 2009. Binding Interpretations of Anaphors by Korean Heritage Speakers. *Language Acquisition* 16, 3–35.

Koopman H. and A. Szabolcsi. 2000. *Verbal Complexes*. Cambridge, MA: MIT Press.

Larsson, I and J. B. Johannessen. 2015. Embedded Word Order in Heritage Scandinavian. In M. Hilpert, J.-O. Östman, C. Mertzlufft, and M. Riessler (eds.), *New Trends in Nordic and General Linguistics*. Berlin: Mouton de Gruyter, 239–267.

McCarthy, J. 1979. Formal Problems in Semitic Phonology and Morphology. Ph.D. dissertation, Massachusetts Institute of Technology.

McCarthy, J. 1981. A Prosodic Theory of Nonconcatenative Morphology. *Linguistic Inquiry* 12(3), 373–418.

McCarthy, J. and A. Prince. 1990. Foot and Word in Prosodic Morphology: The Arabic Broken Plural. *Natural Language and Linguistic Theory* 8, 209–283.

Mohammad, M. 1988. On the Parallelism between IP and DP. In H. Borer (ed.), *Proceedings of WCCFL VII*. Stanford, CA: Center for the Study of Language and Information, 241–254.

Montrul, S. 2008. *Incomplete Acquisition in Bilingualism: Re-examining the Age Factor*. Amsterdam: John Benjamins.

Montrul, S. 2010. How Similar are L2 Learners and Heritage Speakers? Spanish Clitics and Word Order. *Applied Psycholinguistics* 31, 167–207.

Montrul, S. 2016. *The Acquisition of Heritage Languages*. Cambridge, MA: Cambridge University Press.

Oh, J. S., T. K.-F. Au, and S.-A. Jun. 2010. Early Childhood Language Memory in the Speech Perception of International Adoptees. *Journal of Child Language* 37, 1123–1132.

Oh, J., S. Jun, L. Knightly, and T. K.-F. Au. 2003. Holding on to Childhood Language Memory. *Cognition* 86, B53–B64.

Omar, M. 1973. *The Acquisition of Egyptian Arabic as a Native Language*. The Hague: Mouton.

Polinsky, M. 2011. Reanalysis in Adult Heritage Language: A Case for Attrition. *Studies in Second Language Acquisition* 33, 305–328.

Polinsky, M. 2018. *Heritage Languages and Their Speakers*. Cambridge: Cambridge University Press.

Polinsky, M. and G. Scontras. 2020. Understanding Heritage Languages. *Bilingualism: Language and Cognition* 23, 4–20.

Pollock, J.-Y. 1989. Verb Movement, Universal Grammar, and the Structure of IP. *Linguistic Inquiry* 20, 365–424.

Saadah, E. 2011. The production of Arabic Vowels by English L2 Learners and Heritage Speakers of Arabic. Ph.D. dissertation, University of Illinois at Urbana-Champaign.

Sherkina-Lieber, M. and K. Murasugi. 2015. Noun Incorporation and Case in Heritage Inuktitut. In S. Vinerte (ed.) *Proceedings of the 2015 Canadian Linguistic Association Annual Conference*.

Shlonsky, U. 1997. *Clause Structure and Word Order in Hebrew and Arabic: An Essay in Comparative Semitic Syntax*. Oxford: Oxford University Press.

Shlonsky, U. 2004. The Form of Semitic Noun Phrases. *Lingua* 114(12), 1465–1526.

Soltan, U. 2007. On Formal Feature Licensing in Minimalism: Aspects of Standard Arabic Morphosyntax. Ph.D. dissertation, University of Maryland at College Park.

Sorace, A. 2004. Native Language Attrition and Developmental Instability at the Syntax-Discourse Interface: Data, Interpretations and Methods. *Bilingualism: Language and Cognition* 7(2), 143–145.

Unsworth, S. 2016. Quantity and Quality of Language Input in Bilingual Language Development. In E. Nicoladis and S. Montanari (eds.), *Lifespan Perspectives on Bilingualism*. Berlin: Mouton de Gruyter, 136–196.

Vergnaud, J. R. 1974. French Relative Clauses. Ph.D. dissertation, Massachusetts Institute of Technology.

Yip, V. and S. Mathews. 2007. *The Bilingual Child: Early Development and Language Contact*. Cambridge: Cambridge University Press.

16

The Emergence of Heritage Language
A Case Study from Korean[*]

William O'Grady and Chae-Eun Kim

16.1 Introduction

The single most important point of consensus in the study of heritage languages is that they are *languages*: They have their own lexicon, their own phonology, and their own system for combining words to create sentences. Moreover, and perhaps above all, they are acquired by children without the benefit of instruction. These facts call for analysis and explanation that can incorporate the study of heritage languages into the larger study of the language faculty – the uniquely human ability to acquire and use a system of communication that permits strings of articulated sounds to express complex meanings. The challenge is daunting.

Despite the progress that has been made in the last half century of scholarship, the field of linguistics remains deeply divided over the nature of the language faculty. Most attempts to explore this issue are based on two competing ideas. A first view, strongly associated with the generative framework, appeals to an inborn Universal Grammar (UG), whose formal constraints and parametric options offer a partial blueprint for language development. In contrast, usage-based approaches focus on the role of input in shaping the acquisition of language through a gradual process of generalization and abstraction. Rothman and Slabakova (2018) offer a recent summary and comparison of the two perspectives.

We focus here on a third possibility for approaching the study of heritage languages, which draws its inspiration from the study of complex systems in fields ranging from astronomy to cognitive science. The key feature of this approach, often dubbed "emergentist," is that complexity arises from

[*] We thank the editors and referees for their helpful comments and advice, and Gyu-Ho Shin for providing valuable data on the frequency of reflexive pronouns in Korean caregiver speech.

the interaction of forces that are far simpler than the system they ultimately produce. The next section of this chapter explores this idea in more detail by focusing on two major factors whose interaction shapes the properties of language in general, setting the stage for the investigation of two phenomena in heritage Korean – the acquisition and use of reflexive pronouns and of relative clauses, to which we turn in Section 16.3. We offer a brief set of concluding remarks in Section 16.4.

16.2   The Emergentist Program

Writing in 1843 about the nature of scientific explanation, the British philosopher and economist John Stuart Mill reminded his readers that many things in nature cannot be construed as the sum of their parts.

> The chemical combination of two substances produces, as is well known, a third substance with properties different from those of either of the two substances separately, or both of them taken together. Not a trace of the properties of hydrogen or oxygen is observable in those of their compound, water. (Book III, ch. 6)

The phenomenon described by Mill is a simple example of what we today call "emergence," the process whereby the interaction of simple parts, forces, and events produces a more complex system with its own novel properties.

Emergence is now recognized as an essential feature of complex systems of all sorts: city traffic, baseball games, the global economy, the weather, human history – and, arguably, language too. The case for an emergentist approach to linguistic inquiry lies in the idea that the key properties of language and their seemingly effortless acquisition by children can be traced to the interaction of factors that include cognition, physiology, perception, memory, processing, and experience.

It is relatively easy to see how factors such as physiology and perception might, at least in principle, help shape various aspects of a language's phonology, but it is considerably more challenging to show how the properties of syntactic phenomena might fall out from emergentist principles. We will outline here an approach to this challenge that is rooted in the importance of processing pressures and, to a lesser extent, experience.

16.2.1   The Role of Processing

Because emergentist work within linguistics is typically put forward as an alternative to Universal Grammar, it makes sense to begin our discussion by considering a phenomenon for which there is a well-established and widely accepted UG analysis. A case in point involves the syntax of anaphora, for which there is also interesting data from heritage languages (see Section 16.3.1).

Anaphoric dependencies, which typically involve the relationship between a reflexive pronoun and its antecedent, are subject to intriguing constraints, one of which is illustrated in the following pair of sentences.

(1) a. **Mary** pinched **herself**.
     b. ***Mary's** brother pinched **herself**.

This contrast is often attributed to a core principle of Universal Grammar.

(2) Principle A
     An anaphor (reflexive pronoun) must have a c-commanding antecedent in its minimal domain.

In nontechnical terms, Principle A requires that a reflexive pronoun be matched with a structurally higher antecedent in the same clause. The (heavily simplified) syntactic representations below help illustrate how this works.

(3)   a. Acceptable pattern   b. Unacceptable pattern

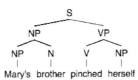

In the acceptable (3a) the intended antecedent (the NP *Mary*) is both higher than the reflexive pronoun and in the same clause. In the unacceptable (3b), in contrast, the antecedent lies in the same clause, but is not higher than the pronoun, in violation of Principle A.

The explanatory scope of UG goes beyond an account of the syntactic facts to include issues in language acquisition, psycholinguistics, and typology (e.g., Rothman and Chomsky 2018: 767). For example, the existence of an inborn grammatical system that includes Principle A offers a plausible explanation for why even very young children who have had little exposure to reflexive pronouns can interpret them with ease (Chien and Wexler 1990). Access to UG also explains why reflexive pronouns are instantly interpreted in the course of comprehending a sentence (Nicol and Swinney 1989; Clackson et al. 2011). Moreover, flexibility in what counts as a minimal domain (in some languages it is just a clause; in others it is the entire sentence) explains variation in how anaphora works across languages: English allows only the pattern in (4a), whereas Chinese allows the equivalent of both (4a) and (b).

(4)   a.   **Mary** pinched **herself**.
     b.   **Mary** said that [I pinched **herself**].

The emergentist program for syntax embraces the same set of challenges, seeking a unified account for the facts of acquisition, processing, and typology, but without a commitment to inborn grammatical principles or even to traditional syntactic representations. A common explanatory strategy in emergentist work, as represented in proposals by Hawkins (2004, 2014) and O'Grady (2015a,b), attributes key properties of language to the effect of processing pressures that seek to increase the ease and efficiency of language acquisition. These pressures have the effect of directing language learners and language users down particular paths, creating the processing routines that are responsible for the association between form and meaning in acceptable sentences. To see how this works, let us reconsider the contrasts that we have been discussing.

The mapping from form to meaning in the course of processing proceeds one word at a time, from left to right. In the case of a sentence such as *Mary pinched herself*, the relevant steps can be characterized as follows for comprehension.

(5)   a.   The first word in the sentence (*Mary*) is encountered and interpreted (*m* stands for the referent of *Mary*).
         Mary
         m

     b.   The transitive verb *pinch* is encountered, allowing *Mary* to be identified as its first argument.
         Mary pinched
         PINCH
         $<m...>$

     c.   The reflexive pronoun *herself* is encountered and identified as the verb's second argument, which we represent as the variable x to indicate that its referent is yet to be determined.
         Mary pinched herself
         PINCH
         $<m\ x>$

     d.   The reflexive pronoun *herself* is interpreted with the help of its immediately available co-argument, *Mary*.
         Mary pinched herself
         PINCH
         $<m\ x>$
           ↳ *m*

Two types of processing operations or "routines" are required in a case such as this – one associated with word order (SVO in the case of English, independently of whether the direct object is a reflexive pronoun) and the other with the interpretation of the anaphor. We focus here on the latter routine, which can be stated as follows for our purposes.

(6)　Resolve the anaphoric dependency immediately.

$< \alpha \; x>$

$\llcorner \alpha$

By choosing an immediately available local referent to resolve anaphoric dependencies, this routine minimizes the burden on working memory, a major factor in processing cost. Moreover, in addition to predicting the acceptability of *Mary pinched herself*, it correctly rules out (7) by forcing an interpretation in which the reflexive pronoun is associated with *Mary's brother* (the verb's first argument), thereby creating a gender clash that renders the sentence unacceptable. (*m-b* = *Mary's brother*)

(7)　Mary's brother pinched herself.
　　　PINCH

$<m\text{-}b \; x>$

$\llcorner {}^{*}m\text{-}b$

On this view, then, there is no grammatical principle per se for interpreting anaphors and, of course, no UG either.[1] Instead, a processing routine emerges in response to the pressure to resolve anaphoric dependencies as quickly and efficiently as possible. This in turn helps explain why even very young children interpret reflexive pronouns correctly, why the interpretive process unfolds so quickly in the course of comprehension, why this pattern of anaphora is instantiated so commonly in languages of the world, and why any language that allows a more distant antecedent for its reflexive (e.g., Chinese) must also allow a local interpretation as well.

Emergentism offers an account for many other puzzles that have been discussed in the UG literature. One such phenomenon involves the notorious constraint on *want to* contraction illustrated as follows.

(8)　a.　Contraction allowed:
　　　　　Tell me if they want to stay here. (cf. They want to stay here.)
　　　　　　　　　wanna
　　　b.　Contraction prohibited:
　　　　　Tell me who they want to stay here. (cf. They want Mary to stay here.)
　　　　　　　　*wanna

Jaeggli (1980) proposes that contraction is blocked in (8b) by the presence of an invisible Case-marked trace between *want* and *to* – a classic example of a UG-based analysis.

(9)　Tell me who they want *t* to stay here.

<hr />

[1] In recent years, the idea of UG has evolved in a curious way and is now treated by some scholars as simply "the collection of factors that underlies the uniquely human capacity for language whatever they may turn out to be" (Nevins et al. 2009:357). We use the term here in its original sense, as exemplified by Crain et al.'s claim that "children are born with a set of universal linguistic principles … many aspects of adult grammar are innate." (2006: 31)

In contrast, O'Grady (2008) outlines a processing-based alternative that turns on the interplay between two pressures:

(i)   In order to minimize the burden on working memory, filler-gap dependencies such as the one involving *who* in (9) are best resolved at the first opportunity (Clifton and Frazier 1989).

(ii) For articulatory reasons, contraction is most likely when *want* and *to* combine with each other without delay.

Matters are straightforward in (8a), where the transition from *want* to *to* is seamless, opening the door to contraction.

(10) The trajectory of incremental processing in *Tell me if they want to stay here*:
      Tell me ...
      Tell me if ...
      Tell me if they ...
      Tell me if they want ...
      Tell me if they want to ...
                            ↓
                        wanna

The situation is very different in (8b), in which the transition from *want* to *to* is interrupted by the need to promptly resolve the filler-gap dependency by associating the *wh* word with *want* (compare with *They want **who** to stay*). As illustrated next, the resulting delay compromises the naturalness of contraction.[2]

(11) The trajectory of incremental processing in *Tell me who they want to stay*

      here:
      Tell me ...
      Tell me who ...
      Tell me who they ...
      Tell me who they want ...
      Tell me who they want
                |_____| ⇐ *Resolution of the filler-gap dependency*
      Tell me if they want ... to
                        ↓   ⇐ *Delayed attempt at contraction*
                    *wanna

Processing effects such as these are ubiquitous in language, but they are not sufficient in and of themselves to ensure a language's acquisition. Input too is necessary. As we will see next, it interacts with processing in important ways.

---

[2] A further side-effect, noted by Warren et al. (2003), involves lengthening of the verb *want* itself.

16.2.2 The Role of Input

An important strand of emergentist thought focuses on usage – the speech of those in the learner's environment. The effect of this factor on the emergence of a first language is evident in well-established correlations between a pattern's frequency in caregiver speech and the timing and ease of its acquisition.[3] Ambridge and Kidd (2015) offer a helpful survey of this work and of its potential importance; see also Gülzow and Gagarina (2007) and Ellis (2016), among many others.

It is not unusual to see competing usage-based and processing-based analyses for the same phenomenon. Indeed, one case in point involves *want-to* contraction, for which a usage-based analysis has been put forward by Ellis (2002: 331–32). The key idea is that there are two *want to* patterns: a highly frequent one in which there is no direct object (e.g., *They want to stay here*) and a much less frequent one with a displaced direct object – typically a *wh* word (e.g., *Tell me* **who** *they want to stay here*). Crucially, *wanna* is permitted only in the first pattern, consistent with the idea that contraction is made possible by frequent usage (Bybee 2002: 112).

Is it possible to choose between this analysis and the processing-based analysis sketched in Section 16.2.1? Perhaps. A key clue comes from the fact that contraction contrasts occur in verbs other than *want*. A case in point involves the participial form of *expect* as it is used in patterns such as the following.

(12) a. Contraction allowed:
          Tell me if they were expecting to stay here.
                          expectin'na
      b. Contraction prohibited:
          Tell me who they were expecting to stay here.
                          ?*expectin'na

It is easy to extend the processing approach to these patterns, since the need to associate the displaced direct object with *expect* in (12b) disrupts the flow of processing at a crucial point, blocking contraction.

(13)   Ask who they were expecting ... to stay there.
       |_____|

In contrast, frequency of occurrence in the input is of little help in this case. Unlike *want to*, which occurs frequently in natural speech, *expecting to* is far less common. Indeed, whereas there are a few hundred instances of *want to* in maternal speech to Adam, Eve, and Sarah in the CHILDES data base, there are no examples at all of *expecting to* (O'Grady 2008). Yet we find a

---

[3] This proposal raises many issues that cannot be discussed here, including the question of the level of generality at which frequency should be calculated (e.g., syntactic categories, lexical items, types, tokens, and so on). For discussion, see Ambridge (2010).

Table 16.1 *Scenarios relevant to the use of a particular pattern or operation*

Internal	External
+	+
+	−
−	+
−	−

parallel contrast in the possibility of contraction, just as the processing-based analysis would predict.

Disputes like this notwithstanding, the two lines of emergentist inquiry can and should be unified within a processing-based framework. The key to this rapprochement lies in the recognition of two types of processing pressures – one internal and the other external. Internal pressures are prototypically instantiated by a preference for operations that minimize the burden on working memory, as illustrated in Section 16.2.1. In contrast, external pressures arise from factors manifested in experience, including the relative frequency of particular items and patterns in caregiver input, as just noted. Taken together, the two types of processing pressure create the four potential scenarios summarized in Table 16.1. (A plus sign indicates that processing considerations favor a particular pattern or operation; a minus sign indicates that they work against it.)

Not surprisingly, there is a tendency for the two pressures to be aligned. In particular, the forms that occur most frequently in the input tend to be those that maximize processing efficiency, which is arguably why they are preferred in the first place. To take an example involving the first scenario in Table 16.1, active-voice patterns not only occur far more frequently in speech than their passive counterparts, they also enjoy a processing advantage thanks to the occurrence of the semantically prominent animate agent in initial position, reflecting its role as initiator of the event (Bornkessel-Schlesewsky and Schlesewsky 2009).

(14) a. Active (agent-initial):
          A newcomer wrote that book.
     b. Passive (non–agent-initial):
          That book was written by a newcomer.

Consistent with the joint effect of both types of processing pressure, active patterns are easier to elicit and to understand than their passive counterparts (Townsend and Bever 2001: 119). They are less likely to undergo attrition in the case of aphasia (Grodzinsky 2000), and are mastered earlier in the course of acquisition (e.g., Deen 2011).

An example of the second scenario in Table 16.1 comes from children's early success at interpreting reflexive pronouns (*himself*, *herself*) compared to plain pronouns (*him*, *her*). As illustrated by the second example below, plain pronouns differ from their reflexive counterparts in allowing a distant antecedent, including one not even mentioned in the same sentence.

(15)   a.   Mickey thought [Donald scratched **himself**].
            (himself = Donald)
       b.   Mickey thought [Donald scratched **him**].
            (him = Mickey or someone not mentioned in the sentence)

Here, internal and external pressures appear to be in conflict. Although reflexive pronouns can be processed with maximal efficiency (for the reasons we have already seen), plain pronouns occur *100 times* more frequently in the input (O'Grady 2015a). Crucially, internal processing factors appear to be paramount, as reflexive pronouns are mastered earlier and interpreted faster than their plain-pronoun counterparts (Conroy et al. 2009; van Rij et al. 2010).

Are there cases of the reverse type in which external forces override internal pressures so that a computationally more demanding pattern is more accessible than a less costly alternative, simply because it occurs more frequently (the third option in Table 16.1)? Or, even more extremely, are there cases where the accessibility of a particular pattern or operation enjoys a developmental advantage even though both internal and external pressures favor an alternative (the fourth option)? It is our contention that neither of these possibilities is commonly attested, if at all.

As is often noted (e.g., Scontras et al. 2015; Rothman & Slabakova 2018; Lohndal et al. 2019), the study of heritage languages offers a new and promising testing ground for theories of language acquisition (for comprehensive overviews, see Montrul 2016 and Polinsky 2018). In the prototypical case, children begin to acquire their heritage language in infancy at home, only to have their linguistic development disrupted and diverted by the onset of schooling in the community's dominant language, with the opportunities for frequent use outside the home.

The importance of reduced usage cannot be underestimated. There is general agreement that large amounts of sustained input are crucial to linguistic development and that children learning their first language in a monolingual setting typically hear thousands of utterances every day (Wells 1985; Hart and Risley 1995 Van de Weijer; 2002; Roy 2009). In the case of bilingual children, including of course heritage learners, the input is divided between the two languages. This has the effect of slowing the developmental trajectory to some degree (e.g., Hoff et al. 2012), with the possibility of even more dire consequences if an appropriate balance between the two languages is not maintained. This is no trivial matter, as current estimates suggest that a ratio greater than 70/30 seriously undermines the likelihood that the weaker language can be fully acquired and maintained (Pearson et al. 1997; Genesee 2007; Baker 2014).

Because access to the heritage language typically diminishes dramatically once children enter school, development and maintenance of the language is often compromised. Some words and patterns are lost through attrition, and others are not learned at all or are encountered for the first time in adolescence, at a time normally associated with second language learning. Nonetheless, if the central thesis of the emergentist approach is correct, heritage languages should be the product of the same forces that produce a first language in a monolingual situation. We will seek to explore this matter in more detail by considering processing-related effects in two patterns in heritage Korean, one involving reflexive pronouns and the other focusing on relative clauses.

16.3   An Emergentist Perspective on Heritage Korean

As just noted, a defining feature of heritage language acquisition is the reduced opportunity to hear and use the family language, especially after children commence their schooling – often at age 4 or 5 in communities where pre-school and kindergarten programs are the norm. In the absence of ample input, it is common for children's grasp of their heritage language to exhibit significant gaps, as frequently noted in the literature (Montrul 2016; Polinsky 2018; Polinsky and Scontras 2019). We will consider a first such case in the next subsection by examining reflexive pronouns in heritage Korean from the emergentist perspective outlined in Section 16.2.

16.3.1   Reflexive Pronouns in Heritage Korean

Korean has at least four reflexive pronouns for use with a third-person antecedent – *caki-casin, caki, casin,* and *ku casin,* each with its own unique conditions of use (see Kim et al. 2009 for a review). Matters are further complicated by the fact that the use of these pronouns is rare in caregiver speech, even in monolingual settings. Indeed, in a study of the CHILDES database for Korean, which contains a total of 81,526 caregiver utterances (produced by nine different speakers), Gyu-Ho Shin (pers. comm.) found just 101 instances of *caki,* 27 of *casin* and one of *caki-casin.* (There were no instances at all of *ku-casin.*) It seems reasonable to suppose that substantially less exposure to these forms is available to children being raised in a home where exposure to a heritage language diminishes progressively as they grow older.

A suggestive piece of evidence in this regard comes from a pilot study by Song et al. (1997) of twelve Korean heritage learners aged 6 to 14, all living in America. In an initial survey, the children demonstrated an unfamiliarity with the two reflexive pronouns under investigation (*caki-casin* and *caki*),

Figure 16.1 *Holangi-ka caki-casin-ul kalikhinta* 'The cat is pointing to herself'

indicating that they knew neither word when directly asked about them, in contrast to other words on which they were queried. This created the opportunity to pursue an "intervention" study, in which the children were exposed (without instruction) to a small number of sentences (five in all) in which the form was used in an appropriate way – for example, to describe a situation in which a mother cat is pointing to herself rather than to a nearby baby cat (Figure 16.1).

Song et al. then tested the children's understanding of *caki-casin* in a picture-selection test involving a variety of monoclausal and biclausal sentences, including those that follow. (NOM = nominative, ACC = accusative, GEN = genitive, PST = past, DECL = declarative, Q = question, COMP = complementizer)

(16)   a. Koyangi-uy   emma-ka   cakicasin-ul   kaliki-ni?
           cat-GEN   mother-NOM   self-ACC   point-Q
           'Is the cat's mother pointing to herself?'

       b. Cwi-nun   [wensungi-ka cakicasin-ul manci-ess-   sayngkakha-ni?
                                                 ta-ko]
           mouse-TOP monkey-   self-ACC   touch-PST-   think-Q
                       NOM   DECL-
                                                    COMP
           'Does the mouse think [that the monkey touched himself]?'

Despite the lack of explicit instruction and prior input, the children selected a co-argument antecedent for *caki-casin* within the same clause about three-quarters of the time. This fits well with the idea that this interpretation is brought to the fore by processing pressures that help shape the course of learning in all languages.[4]

---

[4] The possibility that the developmental pattern observed in heritage learners might be a "transfer effect" from English cannot be ruled out. However, as explained in O'Grady (2013: 271ff), transfer is itself regulated by considerations of processing cost.

Further support for this perspective comes from Kim et al.'s (2009) study of fifty-one adult heritage learners of Korean (aged 19–27). Based on a picture-based truth value judgment test involving both monoclausal and biclausal test items, Kim et al. reported a strong preference for the co-argument (same-clause) interpretation of *caki-casin*. Moreover, they note (pp. 31–32) that the heritage learners in their study favored this type of interpretation even for *caki*, which permits a long-distance antecedent; see also Polinsky and Scontras (2019: 7).

In sum, we see here two manifestations of processing pressure in the acquisition of heritage Korean. On the one hand, the advantage of a "local" antecedent is strong enough to facilitate immediate learning of a reflexive form (*caki-casin*) by children who received very minimal exposure to it (the Song et al. study). On the other hand, the results of the Kim et al. study suggest that the processing effect is also strong enough to *undermine* mastery of a different form (*caki*) even in adult heritage speakers, who resist its (legitimate) use with a long-distance antecedent.

There is never a single possible explanation for anything, of course. Nonetheless, we see here a pattern of partial acquisition that fits well with the idea that language and learning are shaped by the interaction of processing pressures with the available input, as an emergentist account of acquisition proposes. The study of relative clauses provides a further opportunity to explore this perspective.

16.3.2   Relative Clauses in Heritage Korean

Both Korean and English have relative clauses (RCs), sentence-like constructions that can be used to narrow down the reference of the NP in which they occur. (ADN = adnominal)

(17)   English:
       the man [RC that/who Mary met _ yesterday]

(18)   Korean:
       [RC Mary-ka   ecey   _ manna-n]   namca
       Mary-NOM   yesterday   meet-PST.ADN   man
       'the man Mary met yesterday'

As these examples help illustrate, Korean RCs differ from their English counterparts in at least three ways: they occur to the left rather than the right of the noun they modify, their internal order is verb-final rather than verb-medial, and they rely on case rather than word order to distinguish between subject and direct object NPs.

Since the pioneering work of Keenan and Comrie (1977), a major concern of research on the syntax and acquisition of relative clauses has been the claimed universality of a preference for subject relative clauses, both across languages and across types of learners, with a possible further asymmetry between direct object relative clauses and other relative-clause types. Hawkins (2004: 177) summarizes the full set of preferences with the help of an "accessibility hierarchy."[5]

(19)   Subject > Direct Object > Indirect Object/Oblique

The accessibility hierarchy originated as a typological generalization: If a language allows an RC type that is lower in the hierarchy, it necessarily also allows higher RC types. The motivation for the particular asymmetries that make up the hierarchy, which were initially quite mysterious, is now widely believed to involve processing factors (e.g., Hawkins 2004; Yun et al. 2015; and the references cited there). In support of this idea, numerous studies have shown that subject relative clauses are easier to process than their direct object counterparts in both English (e.g., Traxler et al. 2002 and the references cited there) and Korean (e.g., Kwon et al. 2006, 2010), among many other languages. If this line of thinking is on the right track, as we will assume, then – on an emergentist account – there should be similar asymmetries in the difficulty of RCs for all types of learners, whether they are acquiring a first language, a second language, or a heritage language.

This prediction is especially interesting in the case of heritage learners of Korean whose dominant language is English, since relative clause patterns in the two languages differ in fundamental ways, as noted above. Any similarities that arise in the difficulty of RC types across the two languages are therefore unlikely to be the result of transfer or analogy. Rather, they should reflect a fundamental similarity in the processing-related factors that are responsible for the typological asymmetries noted by Keenan and Comrie.

A subject advantage has been documented for monolingual child learners of Korean in both comprehension (Cho 1999:65ff) and production (Kim and O'Grady 2016). Parallel observations have been made for adult second language learners, also in both comprehension (O'Grady, Lee, and Choo 2003) and production (Kim and O'Grady, in preparation). The search for a similar asymmetry in adult heritage learners goes back at least to O'Grady, Lee, and Choo (2001), who examined the ability of sixteen speakers of this type to comprehend relative clauses in a picture selection task. The heritage

---

[5] RC type is determined by identifying the missing element inside the relative clause, represented in the examples below by a gap (_).

  (i)   Subject RC: the boy [that _ gave a bag to the girl]
  (ii)   Direct object RC: the book [that the boy put _ on the box]
  (iii) Indirect object RC: the girl [that the boy gave a bag to _]
  (iv)   Oblique RC: the box [that the boy put the book on _]

learners did significantly better on subject relative clauses (SRCs), respond-ing correctly 65 percent of the time, compared to just 41.3 percent for object relative clauses (ORCs). Moreover, 23.75 percent of their responses to the ORC patterns involved interpreting them as if they were SRCs. (In contrast, SRCs were interpreted as ORCs just 13.75 percent of the time.) This result has been replicated a number of times for Korean (e.g., Kim 2005) as well as for other languages, as noted by Lee-Ellis (2011: 82–83) and Polinsky (2011: 308).[6]

A shortcoming of these studies and others like them is that they concen-trate on the contrast between subject and direct object RCs, ignoring the predictions that are made for indirect object and oblique RCs. In an attempt to address this gap in the literature, we conducted a study involving all four major RC types with a view to determining whether their degree of diffi-culty aligns with the predictions of the accessibility hierarchy.

Participants

Twenty English-dominant learners of Korean as a heritage language partici-pated in our study (mean age = 21.9). All had grown up in the United States in homes where the parents were first-generation immigrants whose native language was Korean. At the time of testing, the participants were either enrolled in a Korean language program at a US university or were studying at a university in Korea as international students. A control group of twenty-one adult native speakers of Korean (fourteen females and seven males; mean age 21.5) also participated in the experiment.

A Korean C-test consisting of 125 items (Lee-Ellis 2009) was used to divide the participants into a higher-proficiency group consisting of six males and four females (mean score = 186) and an intermediate-proficiency group consisting of three males and seven females (mean score = 82.3).

Materials and Procedure

Our study consisted of two parts, one involving a contrast between subject and indirect object relative clauses, and the other focusing on a contrast between direct object and oblique RCs. All four sentence types involve three arguments, one of which is relativized. In order to ensure that arguments cannot be mapped onto grammatical relations based solely on meaning, both the subject and the indirect object are animate (and hence "revers-ible") in the first contrast, and both the direct object and the oblique are inanimate in the second contrast. (DAT = dative, ASP = aspect, PRS = present)

---

[6] Elicited production studies by Jeon and Kim (2007) and Lee-Ellis (2011) report less conclusive results, but both studies included "non-reversible" RC patterns with an animate subject and inanimate patient (e.g., the equivalent of *the cookie that the boy ate*), which minimize the need to draw on the language's syntactic resources since semantic and pragmatic clues determine whether arguments are encoded as subjects or direct objects (a boy can eat a cookie, but a cookie cannot eat a boy).

(20) a. Subject RC:
          [_ sonye-eykey   kapang-ul   cwu-koiss-nun]   sonyen
             girl-DAT   bag-ACC   give-ASP-ADN.PRS   boy
          'the boy that is giving a bag to the girl'

      b. Indirect object RC:
          [sonye-ka _   kapang-ul   cwu-koiss-nun]   sonyen
           girl-NOM   bag-ACC   give-ASP-ADN.PRS   boy
          'the boy that the girl is giving a bag to _'

(21) a. Direct object RC:
          [sonyen-i   sangca-ey   _   noh-un]   chayk
           boy-NOM   box-on   put-ADN.PRS   book
          'the book that the boy is putting _ on the box'

      b. Oblique RC:
          [sonyen-i _ chayk-ul   noh-un]   sangca
           boy-NOM   book-ACC   put-ADN.PRS   box
          'the box that the boy is putting the book on _'

RCs were elicited with the help of a production task based on the one employed by Cho (1999); Goodluck and Stojanovic (1996); Hsu et al. (2009); Zukowski (2009); and Kim and O'Grady (2016). Participants were told that they would see a series of pictures on a computer screen and that a (pre-recorded) woman's voice would describe each picture. They then heard the following instructions (in Korean):

> After listening to what [the woman] says, you will hear a beep sound and see an arrow mark. I would like you to describe the person (or thing) that has the arrow mark. Can you do it?

An example of the protocol used to elicit a subject RC appears in Figure 16.2.

Because there are two different boys in the test pictures, description of the boy singled out by the arrow requires participants to provide additional information – such as the fact that he is the boy who is handing a bag to the girl (a relative clause).

Indirect object RCs were elicited in a parallel way: the participant saw the same initial pair of pictures (with two different boys) and heard the same background description. However, in this case, an arrow appeared over the boy on the right in the second set of pictures (Figure 16.3).

Comparable test items were prepared for direct object and oblique relative clauses; for a sample, see Kim and O'Grady (2016).

All participants were tested individually in a quiet setting. Half of the participants were tested on the subject RC items first, and the other half on the indirect object RC items. Items within each block were randomized. At the end of the session, the participants filled out a background information questionnaire and were given the C-test described earlier. The entire session lasted approximately 40 minutes.

Step 1: Prompt: "In the first picture, a boy is giving a bag to a girl. In the second picture, a girl is giving a bag to a boy."

Step 2: An arrow appears over the boy in the picture on the left.
Targeted description: "the boy [that_is giving a bag to the girl] (see [20a])"

Figure 16.2 Sample protocol used to elicit a subject RC

Testing on the direct object and oblique RCs took place a week later, under similar conditions and following a similar protocol (except for the C-test), with half the participants tested on the randomly ordered direct object RC items first and the other half on oblique RC items first.

Results

The participants' responses were recorded in Audacity, transcribed by one of the authors, and entered onto a spreadsheet for coding and analysis. If more than one response was given for a particular test item, only the first one was considered. Tables 16.2 and 16.3 summarize our results.

The predominance of subject RCs in this comparison is overwhelming. In contrast, as the data in Table 16.3 reveals, direct object RCs manifest a more modest advantage compared to their oblique counterparts. All three groups of participants produced targeted direct object RCs at a significantly higher

Table 16.2 *Percentage of target-like responses in the subject and indirect object RC conditions*

Group	Subject RCs (%)	Indirect object RCs (%)[7]
Intermediate proficiency HL learners	92	0
High proficiency HL learners	100	18
Native speakers of Korean	100	7.6

Step 1: Prompt: "In the first picture, a boy is giving a bag to a girl. In the second picture, a girl is giving a bag to a boy."

Step 2: An arrow appears over the boy in the picture on the right.
Targeted description: "the boy [that the girl is giving a bag to_] (see [20b])"

Figure 16.3 Sample protocol used to elicit an indirect object RC

---

[7] The rate of production for indirect object RCs is surprisingly low, including for the native-speaker participants. Interestingly, however, avoidance of indirect object RCs is widespread in non-experimental contexts as well. Kang (2014) reports no examples in the 1,383 relative clauses in his newspaper-based corpus study, and we found none in the 768 relative clauses used by caregivers in our examination of the CHILDES data base; see Section 16.4. The most straightforward way to interpret these findings is to conclude that indirect object RCs are avoided for two reasons: they are difficult, and they can often be recast as subject RCs by changing the verb (e.g., 'the girl that the boy gave a book to _' > 'the girl that _ got a book from the boy').

Table 16.3 *Percentage of target-like responses in the direct object and oblique RC conditions (KSL)*

Group	Direct Object RCs (%)	Oblique RCs (%)
Intermediate proficiency HL learners	76	36
High proficiency HL learners	92	68
Native speakers of Korean	82.85	68.57

rate than oblique RCs (76% vs. 36% [$p < 0.001$] for intermediate-proficiency learners, 92% vs. 68% [$p < 0.001$] for high-proficiency learners, and 82.85% vs. 68.57% [$p < 0.05$] for native speakers).

Discussion

In sum, our results point to two very robust asymmetries for all three groups of participants: Subject RCs are favored over indirect object RCs by a wide margin, and direct object RCs are preferred to their oblique counterparts. Our results therefore appear to support a set of production asymmetries that aligns well with the accessibility hierarchy, which assigns the highest preference to subject relative clauses, followed by direct object relative clauses, and then indirect object and oblique RCs.

(22)   Subject > Direct Object > Indirect Object/Oblique

Importantly, exactly the same asymmetries show up in studies of child first language learners of Korean (Kim and O'Grady 2016) and in adult second language learners (Kim and O'Grady, in preparation). These parallels are just what one would expect if (a) RC asymmetries are motivated by differences in processing difficulty, and (b) those same processing pressures shape development in all types of acquisition, as an emergentist approach to this phenomenon would predict.

Our findings also align well with asymmetries in language use. Indeed, Kang (2014: 18) reports an order of frequency for Korean relative clauses that exactly mirrors the accessibility hierarchy (Table 16.4). (Kang's data come from newspaper stories that make up one part of the Sejong Corpus.)

We have found similar asymmetries in maternal speech to four Korean children aged 2;0–3;6 in the CHILDES data base (Table 16.5). Not surprisingly, the same asymmetry shows up in the speech of the four Korean children (Table 16.6). Huh (2015: 858) report similar contrasts in speech samples from adult learners of Korean as a second language.

All of this makes sense. Frequency effects, whether in the speech of adults or children, arise because of the attractiveness of patterns that are

Table 16.4 *Frequency of relative clause types in a portion of the Sejong corpus*

Relative clause type	Number of instances
Subject	521
Direct object	136
Indirect Object/Oblique	58

Table 16.5 *Frequency of relative clause types in maternal speech in the CHILDES corpus*

Relative clause type	Number of instances
Subject	483
Direct object	205
Indirect Object/Oblique	80

Table 16.6 *Frequency of relative clause types in the speech of four children aged 2;0–3;6*

Relative clause type	Number of instances
Subject	28
Direct object	7
Indirect Object/Oblique	0

easy to process. And ease of processing reflects the cost associated with different types of relative clause patterns.

16.4 Concluding Remarks

Input is crucial to the acquisition of any language under any conditions. An intriguing question that arises in the study of heritage languages has to do with what happens when the input is too sparse to support children's full acquisition of their parents' language. There is reason to think that under those circumstances, children have recourse to options that minimize processing cost. In particular, in the absence of ample opportunities to hear and use particular patterns (reflexive pronouns, certain types of relative clause, and so on), learners opt for strategies that place the least demand on their processing resources. In some cases, this yields the right result – the association of *caki-casin* with a "local" antecedent, discussed in Section 16.3.1, is one such example. However, in other cases, the strategy leads to a different result that is also characteristic of heritage language learning – partial acquisition, as illustrated by the resistance of even adults to a long-distance interpretation for *caki* and their retreat from the full range of relative clause patterns permitted by Korean, among the many other shortfalls documented in the literature (see also Scontras et al. 2015: 17).

The relevance of heritage languages to linguistic inquiry, to which the literature often alludes, is thus borne out. Heritage languages do in fact offer a valuable perspective on the development and use of language, and there is good reason to think that their study can contribute to a more comprehensive understanding of the forces that shape language in general. What we seek in this line of research, though, is not a unique type of linguistic competence or an unsuspected mode of acquisition. Rather, as illustrated in the findings reported here, what we hope to find in heritage languages is evidence of the same set of simple forces whose interaction shapes language in all its other manifestations.

References

Ambridge, B. 2010. Review of *Frequency Effects in Language Acquisition: Defining the Limits of Frequency as an Explanatory Concept*, ed. by I. Gülzow & N. Gagarina. *Journal of Child Language* 37, 453–475.

Ambridge, B. and E. Kidd. 2015. The Ubiquity of Frequency Effects. *Journal of Child Language* 42, 239–273.

Baker, C. 2014. *A Parents' and Teachers' Guide to Bilingualism*. Clarendon: Multilingual Matters.

Bornkessel-Schlesewsky, I. and M. Schlesewsky. 2009. The Role of Prominence Information in the Real-Time Comprehension of Transitive Constructions: A Cross-Linguistic Approach. *Language and Linguistics Compass* 3, 19–58.

Bybee, J. 2002. Sequentiality as the Basis of Constituent Structure. In T. Givón and B. Malle (eds.), *The Evolution of Language Out of Pre-Language*. Amsterdam: Benjamins, 109–134.

Chien, Y.-C. and K. Wexler. 1990. Children's Knowledge of Locality Conditions in Binding as Evidence for the Modularity of Syntax and Pragmatics. *Language Acquisition* 1, 225–295.

Cho, S. 1999. The Acquisition of Relative Clauses: Experimental Studies on Korean. Unpublished PhD dissertation, Department of Linguistics, University of Hawaii at Manoa.

Clackson, K., C. Felser, and H. Clahsen. 2011. Children's Processing of Reflexives and Pronouns in English: Evidence for Eye-Movements during Listening. *Journal of Memory and Language* 65, 128–144.

Clifton, C. and L. Frazier. 1989. Comprehending Sentences with Long-distance Dependencies. In G. Carlson and M. Tanenhaus (eds.), *Linguistic Structure in Language Processing*. Dordrecht: Kluwer, 273–317.

Conroy, A., E. Takahashi, J. Lidz, and C. Phillips. 2009. Equal Treatment for All Antecedents: How Children Succeed with Principle B. *Linguistic Inquiry* 40, 446–486.

Crain, S., T. Goro, and R. Thornton. 2006. Language Acquisition Is Language Change. *Journal of Psycholinguistic Research* 35, 31–49.

Deen, K. 2011. The Acquisition of the Passive. In J. de Villiers and T. Roeper (eds.), *Handbook of Generative Approaches to Language Acquisition*. New York: Springer, 155–187.

Ellis, N. 2002. Reflections on Frequency Effects in Language Processing. *Studies in Second Language Acquisition* 24, 297–339.

Ellis, N. 2016. Frequency in Language Learning and Language Change. In H. Behrens and S. Pfänder (eds.), *Experience Counts: Frequency Effects in Language*. Berlin: de Gruyter, 239–256.

Genesee, F. 2007. A Short Guide to Raising Children Bilingually. *Multilingual Living Magazine* 2, 18–21.

Goodluck, H. and D. Stojanovic. 1996.The Structure and Acquisition of Relative Clauses in Serbo-Croatian. *Language Acquisition* 5, 285–315.

Grodzinsky Y. 2000. The Neurology of Syntax: Language Use without Broca's Area. *Behavioral and Brain Sciences* 23, 1–71.

Gülzow, I. and N. Gagarina. 2007. *Frequency Effects in Language Acquisition: Defining the Limits of Frequency as an Explanatory Concept*. Berlin: Mouton de Gruyter.

Hart, B. and T. Risley. 1995. *Meaningful Differences in the Everyday Experience of Young American Children*. Baltimore: Paul H. Brookes.

Hawkins, J. 2004. *Efficiency and Complexity in Grammars*. Oxford: Oxford University Press.

Hawkins, J. 2014. *Cross-linguistic Variation and Efficiency*. Oxford: Oxford

Hoff, E., C. Core, S. Place, R. Rumiche, M. Señor, and M. Parra, 2012. Dual Language Exposure and Early Bilingual Development. *Journal of Child Language* 39, 1–27.

Hsu, C.-C., G. Hermon, and A. Zukowski. 2009. Young Children's Production of Head-Final Relative Clauses: Elicited Production Data from Chinese Children. *Journal of East Asian Linguistics* 18, 323–360.

Huh, Sorin. 2015. A Corpus Study of L2 Korean Relative Clause Development. *Language Research* 51, 845–868.

Jaeggli, O. 1980. Remarks on *to*-contraction. *Linguistic Inquiry* 11, 239–245.

Jeon, K. S. and H.-Y. Kim. 2007. Development of Relativization in Korean as a Foreign Language: The Noun Phrase Accessibility Hierarchy in Head-internal and Head-external Relative Clause. *Studies in Second Language Acquisition* 29, 253–276.

Kang, S. 2014. The Role of Syntactic and Semantic Information in the Frequency Distribution of Relative Clauses in Korean: A Corpus-based Analysis. *Language Information* 19, 5–32.

Keenan, E. and B. Comrie. 1977. Noun Phrase Accessibility and Universal Grammar. *Linguistic Inquiry* 8, 63–100.

Kim, C.-E. and W. O'Grady. 2016. Asymmetries in Children's Production of Relative Clauses: Data from English and Korean. *Journal of Child Language* 42, 1038–1071.

Kim, H.-S. 2005. Processing Strategies and Transfer of Heritage and Non-heritage Learners of Korean. Unpublished PhD dissertation, Department of East Asian Languages and Literatures, University of Hawaii at Manoa.

Kim J.-H., S. Montrul, and J. Yoon. 2009. Binding Interpretations of Anaphors by Korean Heritage Speakers. *Language Acquisition* 16, 3–35.

Kwon, N., M. Polinsky, and R. Kluender. 2006. Subject Preference in Korean. In D. Baumer, D. Montero, and M. Scanlon (eds.), *Proceedings of the 25th West Coast Conference on Formal Linguistics*. Somerville, MA: Cascadilla Proceedings Project, 1–14.

Kwon, N., Y. Lee, P. Gordon, and R. Kluender. 2010. Cognitive and Linguistic Factors Affecting Subject/Object Asymmetry: An Eye-tracking Study of Prenominal Relative Clauses in Korean. *Language* 86, 546–582.

Lee-Ellis, S. 2009. The Development and Validation of a Korean C-Test Using Rasch Analysis. *Language Testing* 26, 245–274.

Lee-Ellis, S. 2011. The Elicited Production of Korean Relative Clauses by Heritage Speakers. *Studies in Second Language Acquisition* 33, 57–89.

Lohndal, T., J. Rothman, T. Kupisch, and M. Westergaard. 2019. Heritage Language Acquisition: What It Reveals and Why It Is Important for Formal Linguistic Theories. *Language and Linguistics Compass* 13, https://doi.org/10.1111/lnc3.12357

Mill, J. S. 1843. *A System of Logic Ratiocinative and Inductive*. London: Longmans, Green and Co..

Montrul, S. 2016. *The Acquisition of Heritage Languages*. Cambridge: Cambridge University Press.

Nevins, A., D. Pesetsky, and C. Rodrigues. 2009. Pirahã Exceptionality: A Reassessment. *Language* 85, 355–402.

Nicol, J. and D. Swinney. 1989. The Role of Structure in Coreference Assignment during Sentence Comprehension. *Journal of Psycholinguistic Research* 18, 5–19.

O'Grady, W. 2008. Does Emergentism Have a Chance? In H. Chan, H. Jacob, and E. Kapia (eds.), *Proceedings of the 32nd Annual Boston University Conference on Language Development*. Somerville, MA: Cascadilla Press, 16–35.

O'Grady, W. 2013. The Illusion of Language Acquisition. *Linguistic Approaches to Bilingualism* 3, 253–285.

O'Grady, W. 2015a. Anaphora and the Case for Emergentism. In B. MacWhinney and W. O'Grady (eds.), *The Handbook of Language Emergence*. Boston: Wiley-Blackwell, 100–122,

O'Grady, W. 2015b. Processing Determinism. *Language Learning* 65, 6–32.

O'Grady, W., M. Lee, and M. Choo. 2001. The Acquisition of Relative Clauses by Heritage and Non-heritage Learners of Korean as a Second Language: A Comparative Study. *Journal of Korean Language Education* 12, 283–294.

O'Grady, W., M. Lee, and M. Choo. 2003. A Subject-Object Asymmetry in the Acquisition of Relative Clauses in Korean as a Second Language. *Studies in Second Language Acquisition* 25, 433–448.

O'Grady, W., M. Lee, and H. Kwak. 2009. Emergentism and Second Language Acquisition. In W. Ritchie and T. Bhatia (eds.), *The New Handbook of Second Language Acquisition*. Bingley: Emerald Press, 69–88.

Pearson, B., S. Fernández, V. Lewedeg, and D. Oller. 1997. The Relation of Input Factors to Lexical Learning by Bilingual Infants. *Applied Psycholinguistics* 18, 41–58.

Polinsky, M. 2011. Reanalysis in Adult Heritage Language. *Studies in Second Language Acquisition* 33, 305–332.

Polinsky, M. 2018. *Heritage Languages and Their Speakers*. Cambridge: Cambridge University Press.

Polinsky, M. and G. Scontras. 2019. Understanding Heritage Languages. *Bilingualism: Language and Cognition* 22, in press.

Rothman, J. and N. Chomsky. 2018. Towards Eliminating Arbitrary Stipulations Related to Parameters: Linguistic Innateness and the Variation Model. *Linguistic Approaches to Bilingualism* 8, 764–769.

Rothman, J. and R. Slabakova. 2018. The Generative Approach to SLA and Its Place in Modern Second Language Studies. *Studies in Second Language Acquisition* 40, 417–442.

Roy, D. 2009. New Horizons in the Study of Child Language Acquisition. Proceedings of Interspeech 2009. Brighton. Retrieved from http://dkroy.media.mit.edu/publications/

Scontras, G., Z. Fuchs, and M. Polinsky. 2015. Heritage Language and Linguistic Theory. *Frontiers in Psychology: Language Sciences* 6, 1–20.

Song, M., W. O'Grady, S. Cho, and M. Lee. 1997. The Learning and Teaching of Korean in Community Schools. In Y.-H. Kim (ed.), *Korean language in America* 2. American Association of Teachers of Korean, 111–127.

Townsend, D. and T. Bever. 2001. *Sentence Comprehension: The Integration of Habits and Rules*. Cambridge, MA: MIT Press.

Traxler, M., R. Morris, and R. Seely. 2002. Processing Subject and Object Relative Clauses: Evidence from Eye Movements. *Journal of Memory and Language* 47, 69–90.

Van de Weijer, J. 2002. How Much Does an Infant Hear in a Day? Proceedings of the GALA2001 Conference on Language Acquisition, 2002. Retrieved from http://person2.sol.lu.se/JoostVanDeWeijer/Texts/gala01.pdf

van Rij, J., J. van Rijn, and P. Hendriks. 2010. Language Acquisition: A Case Study in Pronoun Comprehension. *Journal of Child Language* 37, 731–766.

Warren, P., S. Speer, and A. Schafer. 2003. *Wanna*-contraction and Prosodic Disambiguation in US and NZ English. *Wellington Working Papers in Linguistics* 15, 31–49.

Wells, C. 1985. *Language Development in the Pre-school Years*. Cambridge: Cambridge University Press.

Yun, J., Z. Chen, T. Hunter, J. Whitman, and J. Hale. 2015. Uncertainty in Processing Relative Clauses across East Asian Languages. *Journal of East Asian Linguistics* 24, 113–148.

Zukowski, A. 2009. Elicited Production of Relative Clauses in Children with Williams Syndrome. *Language and Cognition Processes* 24, 1–42.

17

Sociolinguistic Approaches to Heritage Languages

Andrew Lynch and Netta Avineri

17.1 Introduction: The Social Dimensions of Heritage Language Studies

The contemporary field of Heritage Language Studies possibly finds its origins in the social movements of the 1960s and 1970s. With the evolution of the post-World War II political order and the advent of economic globalization, the notion of borders fell increasingly under social scrutiny. Western post-structuralist thought began to contest the structuralist principle of binary oppositions and the concept of static, bounded entities. Scholars such as Michel Foucault, Pierre Bourdieu, and Jacques Derrida presented a sort of social exegesis or epistemic archaeology that exposed the ideological and historical basis of institutional and political constructs like social class, race, gender, sexuality, and even the notions of "history" and "knowledge" themselves. Within this political and social context, the concepts of periphery and minority came to the intellectual forefront, concomitant with the discussion of minority languages. At that time, some four decades ago, those whom we now refer to as "heritage speakers" were termed "bilinguals" or "native speakers," as commonly understood in linguistic research (e.g., Weinreich 1953; Fishman 1966). Advocating for "native" Spanish language education for US Chicanos/as, Valdés affirmed in 1978 that: "defining native language instruction for the profession ... is simply a question of deciding exactly what teaching a standard dialect of a language involves" (103). She urged that learners must hone "a dedication to bringing about the acquisition of 'educated' language use to include an overall development of total proficiency as characteristic of educated speakers of any language" (106). The term "heritage language" would not come into currency in the United States until the late 1990s, having been borrowed from the Canadian context, where it had emerged in the late

1970s during the inception of the Ontario Heritage Languages programs (Cummins and Danesi 1990; see Nagy, this volume). In addition, the notion of "heritage" can itself be an ideology to which individuals may or may not orient based on their own experiences (Avineri 2019). Depending on the context, different terminologies are used to describe the "same" or similar languages or language situations (e.g., community language, minority language, endangered language, heritage language). This demonstrates how important context and ideology are to the discourses of heritage languages themselves.

As academic and institutional usage of the term continues to expand and evolve, concomitant with a growing knowledge of the language systems of those whom we now consider heritage language (henceforth HL) speakers (Polinsky 2018), inquiry regarding the societal configurations and sociolinguistic profiles of HL populations has proliferated. In this chapter, we provide an overview of the main topics of that line of inquiry. We first discuss methodological approaches to understanding the social and affective dimensions of HL acquisition and use, taking macro, meso, and micro levels of analysis into account. We then turn to the contextual factors inherent in HL research, highlighting political and ideological dimensions of HL use, concepts of "community," and the important distinction between national and local spheres as well as public and private settings. The key social variables of research on HL speakers and their communities are discussed next. Then we provide a brief synthesis of principal areas of research on HL variability. In conclusion, we offer some suggestions for future research.

17.2 Methodological Approaches

As Montrul (2015) notes, researchers' theories of language underpin their methodological approaches to HLs. Sociolinguistic and sociocultural (Lantolf 2000) perspectives on HLs foreground the role of context to gain an understanding of individual and community language use. It is therefore essential for research methodologies to capture macro-level context (e.g., nation, region), meso-level context (e.g., schools, other institutions), and micro-level context (e.g., family, interpersonal language use) for HLs and their users. There are a range of methodologies that researchers use to shed light on these aspects of HLs and their users.

Variationist sociolinguistics is a methodological perspective that seeks to discover how social variables condition language variability (see Nagy, this volume). We consider some of the key social variables in HL research in a later section. A historical approach to HLs provides researchers, teachers, and students with material that is relevant to their present-day engagement with the language. This history can be about the language, immigration patterns, and demographic shift in communities as well as about individuals' histories as they relate to the language. Case studies (Duff 2018) provide researchers with in-depth knowledge about a particular individual or family (Yazan and Ali 2018), context (Willoughby 2014), or language situation. Elements of these case studies may be generalizable to other HL situations, therefore illuminating key aspects relevant in a range of contexts. Critical discourse analysis (CDA) "draws connections between the structure of written and spoken texts and the multiple layers of discursive practices and social contexts to illuminate connections between discourse and power" (Johnson et al. 2017: 10). This methodology is relevant in HL contexts since power, dominance, and hegemony are so crucial to our understanding of HLs. For example, Burns and Waugh (2018) conducted CDA on Spanish textbooks to reveal ideologies and tensions that underpin materials development as it relates to HL learners. Narrative inquiry (Barkhuizen 2015; He, this volume) provides analytical tools for investigating personal and communal narratives (Avineri 2019 for "heritage narratives" about Yiddish and Goble 2016 for third-generation Mexican-Americans' narratives about Spanish). Interviews, questionnaires, focus groups, and reflections (Avineri 2017) are also used to explore HL users' perspectives and life experiences as they relate to the language. Ethnography, the "written description of the social organization, social activities, symbolic and material resources, and interpretive practices characteristic of a particular group of people" (Duranti 1997: 85), is a fruitful methodological approach for HLs since it can provide multi-layered perspectives on the experiences of individuals and groups. For example, Guardado (2014) engaged in a 1.5 year ethnography in Western Canada focused on the experiences of Hispanic communities. Many HL ethnographies take a language socialization approach, examining the connections between sociolinguistic and cultural learning in a particular context (Avineri 2012 for Yiddish "metalinguistic community" members; Chen, Zhou, and Uchikoshi 2018 for Chinese immigrant families; Garcia-Sanchez 2010 for Moroccan immigrant children in Spain; Klein 2013 for Punjabi Sikh religious education; Lo 2009 for Korean HL education; Moore 2014 for Russian HL and religious education). This range of methodological approaches provides valuable sociolinguistic and sociocultural perspectives that highlight the complexity of HL users, interactions, and contexts.

17.3 Context, Community, and Culture

HLs, their users, and contexts have inherent political aspects to them. By virtue of a language being considered "heritage" it is juxtaposed against other languages that have more or less power and (perceived) dominance in a multilingual context. This political component has implications for the languages that individuals and communities maintain and why. For example, in the US context, Arabic is connected to aspects of religion, family, immigration, discrimination, and other political features (Bale 2010). Explicit and implicit language policies at macro (large), meso (institutional), and micro (interpersonal) scales have an impact on HL users' linguistic choices and practices.

The role of context is crucial in understanding HL communities. In Fishman's (2001) typology of immigrant, indigenous, and colonial languages, context is implicit in every case – immigrant languages are those used by communities that have moved from one context to another; indigenous languages are those used by communities that are native to a particular land (see Stanford and Preston 2009); and colonial languages are those used in contexts that have been directly impacted by colonialism. For immigrant languages one can consider the context where the language has historically been used as well as the new contexts in which it has relevance for immigrant communities. One can also consider how national context (e.g., Yeh et al. 2015 in Taiwan; Willoughby 2014 in Australia; Creese 2009 and Weekly 2018 in the United Kingdom) manifests in the particulars of a local context (regions, states, cities, communities, schools, classrooms). One can also consider public contexts of HL use such as schools (Chinese, Pu 2012; Hebrew, Avni 2012; Lithuanian, Tamošiūnaitė 2013; Vietnamese, Maloof et al. 2006), workplaces, religious settings, and media (Szecsi and Szilagyi 2012), as well as private contexts such as homes, family interactions (Melo-Pfeifer 2015), and other interpersonal relationships.

How "community" is conceptualized may vary for different HL situations. In fact, in some literature, HLs are seen as "community languages." It is fruitful to explore the juxtaposition between the communities where the HL is used and the broader communities where a dominant language may be valued. As described in Avineri and Kroskrity (2014: 1–2), notions of language and community have shifted over time. The "speech community" concept (Gumperz 1968) emphasized shared norms and "regular and frequent interaction" (43). Newer conceptualizations (Duranti 1997; Silverstein 1998; Morgan 2006; Jaffe 2007) highlight the dynamic nature of practices, ideologies, and interactions in different contexts. The concept of "communities of practice" (Lave and Wenger 1991) highlights "complementary interactional practices, the social distribution of knowledge, the creation of group identities through activities, and an interest in evolving cultural reproduction" (Avineri and Kroskrity 2014: 2). Polinsky and Kagan (2007) provide both narrow and broad definitions of HLs; the broad definition "emphasizes possible links between cultural heritage and linguistic heritage" (369). Building on this broad definition, "metalinguistic community" (Avineri 2019) is a community of positioned social actors engaged in practices that position language as an object. This conceptualization highlights the affective and ideological orientations that community members may experience, whether or not they are proficient in the language. In addition, many HL users orient toward an "imagined community" (Anderson 1983) of which they wish to be a part in the present or future.

The role of culture in HL learning has been explored by numerous scholars interested in the culture(s) students are learning about and becoming a part of. This cultural and intercultural learning may happen in communities and/or in classrooms. Oh and Au (2005) demonstrate the importance of cultural identification and participation in students' mastery of Spanish as HL. Beaudrie, Ducar, and Relaño-Pastor (2009) have explored the ways that culture and identity are taught in Spanish HL curricular materials, and Demuro and Gurney (2018) discuss how culture is framed in foreign language instruction. Kagan (2012) highlighted the "intrinsically intercultural attitude" of HL learners, particularly "1) their language proficiencies; 2) their reasons for studying their home language in the formal setting of a foreign language classroom; 3) their perception of themselves as hyphenated Americans, or, if we use Kipling's wording, as 'we' and 'they' at the same time." For HL learners, culture is central to their sense of identity.

17.4   Identity, Investment, and Ideology

Identity is a central area of inquiry within the field of HLs (see He, this volume), since the language is intimately connected with individuals' life experiences and sense of self (Lee 2002; He 2010; Shin 2010; Leeman et al. 2011; Leeman 2015; Anya 2016; Seal 2017). The notion of situated identities (Bucholtz and Hall 2005) is especially relevant since it highlights the role of context in processes of meaning-making for HL users. For example, Leeman (2015) has explored the notion of "HL learner" itself as an identity to which individuals may or may not orient. He (2010), in her exploration of Chinese HL users, demonstrates the "sociocultural complexity" inherent in identity practices. Identity approaches recognize the relationships between individual understandings of self and identities at the community level. This focus on "social factors" is key to making sense of the complex experiences of HL users of different backgrounds. Heritage language users' positionalities impact "how one's identities, experiences, and history shape interactions with others" (Avineri 2019: 7). It is essential to recognize intersectionality (Crenshaw 1989) in relation to HL learners, as well as how different aspects of their identities (e.g., race, class, gender) connect in one's life experience. Considering how HL learners may be perceived by others (including their own teachers) also means that language-based discrimination (Roman et al. 2019) must be acknowledged.

Investment (Norton Peirce 1995), a dynamic view of motivation that acknowledges the roles of identity and context in language learning, is central for our understanding of HL users. This moves away from considering motivation to be static. For HL learners there may be instrumental or integrative motivations. However, for others, there may not be communities to engage with or concrete outcomes associated with learning the language. For example, Harasta (2017) explored adult motivations for learning Cornish in the United Kingdom despite its perceived "uselessness." This more ecological view of motivation is therefore a fruitful one in HL situations. Motivations and attitudes regarding the language are intricately connected, as demonstrated by Kurata (2015) for Japanese HL speakers in Australia and Oh and Nash (2014) for adult Spanish HL learners.

Language ideologies, a "mediating link between social structures and forms of talk" (Woolard and Schieffelin 1994: 55), is another fruitful area of inquiry in HL studies (see King, this volume). The belief systems associated with an HL, held by those in the dominant group as well as the community members themselves, impact language policies and individuals' language use. As Avineri and Kroskrity (2014) note, "from language ideological approaches springs the openings of such considerations as the role of a local metasemiotics and other language beliefs and feelings that underlay the very construction of community and one's place in it" (2). King (2000), in her examination of conflicting language ideologies in an Ecuadorian community, underscores the complex relationships among language shift, ideologies, and use. Avineri (2017), in her discussion of "contested stance practices" in Yiddish metalinguistic communities, highlights the inherent tensions in HL contexts – where language ideologies connect with standard forms, teachers' life experiences, and students' "nostalgia socialization" practices. As Kroskrity (2004) emphasizes, language ideologies are complex and "represent the perception of language and discourse that is constructed in the interest of a specific social or cultural group" (501). Processes of language loss, shift, assimilation, and abandonment at both individual and community levels are inextricably linked with language ideologies (e.g., values, prestige, multilingualism, codeswitching/translanguaging, borrowing) about the HL and its users (Carreira and Beeman 2014).

17.5   Key Social Variables

17.5.1   Generation

Of all the variables usually taken into account by HL scholars, generation is undoubtedly the most fundamental. In contexts of (im)migration, generations are conceptualized according to time spent in the host country: "first generation" (G1) speakers arrive as adults; "second generation" (G2) speakers immigrate as small children or are born in the host country to G1 parents; "third generation" (G3) speakers are the children of G2 speakers, and so on. Typically, proficiency in the HL diminishes across generations, with the most complex bilingual repertoires observable among G2 speakers and the least extent of HL abilities in G3 and G4 individuals (Silva-Corvalán 1994; Carreira and Kagan 2011; Montrul 2015). Although some studies have documented cross-generational continuity in some linguistic domains (e.g., Nagy 2015 on HL speakers of Cantonese, Russian, and Italian in Toronto), the majority of studies suggest a lack of social and linguistic continuity in successive generations. In urban immigrant settings, it is rare to find G4 speakers with high degrees of productive ability in the HL; many are passive bilinguals and still many others do not even understand the HL beyond very basic or simplified discourse. The explanation for lack of cross-generational continuity or intergenerational transmission is, in essence, sociopolitical. Montrul (2015) explains the inextricable relationship between the social, psychological, and linguistic as follows:

> the sociopolitical status of the language (majority versus minority status) affects the attitudes and beliefs of its speakers toward the language, as well as the availability of the education in that language, and its degree of public use, for example. Language attitudes, in turn, affect language practices and patterns of language use: if a language is not used in education and outside of the home, it will not be heard and used as much by its speakers because they may not see its value. Input and use affect, in turn, grammatical and communicative competence, as manifested in particular linguistic features that are now part of the psycholinguistic representation of the speaker. (10)

Although there is a prevalent negative correlation between generation in the host country and linguistic proficiency in the HL, there are multiple scenarios in which G3 or G4 speakers might attain stronger levels of ability than G2 speakers due to formal study, time spent in a country where the HL is spoken, or recontact with the HL via close relationships with G1 speakers. The latter is especially true for individuals who live in so-called borderlands or in areas with high rates of (im)migration. From the perspective of the US–Mexico border region, Villa and Rivera-Mills (2009) observe that: "It is the need to connect with a particular speech community that requires a change in the traditional unidirectional, linear pattern of change to a more circular one, in which at any given point and with any generation there is the opportunity to recapture the HL, thereby promoting a more stable bilingualism" (30). HL "reversal" is a rather particular exception to cross-generational language reduction. In these cases, the HL (i.e., minority language) becomes the socially dominant (i.e., majority) language due to return migration (Vilar Sánchez 2003; Tomiyama 2008; Flores 2010; Mar-Molinero 2018).

Different than in studies of language change conducted in language majority settings, generation is not synonymous with age in studies of HL variability. In other words, G1 speakers in (im)migrant settings are not necessarily older than G2 or G3 speakers. In borderlands and global cities where rates of immigration tend to be high and the influx of G1 speakers is continual (see Lynch 2019), it is quite common to find G3 speakers who are much older in age than recent arrivals. However, in non-immigrant HL settings, it is common that older speakers possess greater levels of oral proficiency in the HL than those of the younger generations. Such tends to be the case of historically minoritized languages, for example, Basque, Igbo, Irish, Nahuatl, or Quechua. Sibling order has proven to be an important variable in some HL studies, with older siblings demonstrating greater awareness and a stronger command of the HL than younger siblings (Lambert and Taylor 1996; Anderson 1999; Silva-Corvalán 2014). First-born offspring often have a longer period of sustained exposure to the HL through parents and grandparents, but input for second-, third- and fourth-born children is curtailed by use of the majority language with older siblings.

17.5.2   Social Class

The concept of social class or socioeconomic status has been fundamental to the field of contemporary sociolinguistics. Several now classic arguments come to mind: Bernstein's (1971) proposal regarding the "restricted code" of children of working-class families vs. the "elaborated code" of middle-class children[1] (cf. Valdés and Geoffrion-Vinci 1998), as well as Brice Heath's (1983) ethnographic research on the effect of social class in child literacy development; Labov's (1972) pioneering variationist studies of English in New York City and Trudgill's (1974) studies of English in Norwich, England, in which the occurrence of particular phonological and grammatical variants appeared stratified according to the social class of the speakers; Bourdieu's (1979, 1991) proposals regarding the linguistic marketplace and language as symbolic capital that is embodied and enacted in cultural practice; and Sánchez's (1983) Marxist treatise on the effects of upward mobility on Spanish language use among US Chicanos in relation to migration and urbanization. Yet despite its centrality to sociolinguistics and educational linguistics (see Guy 2011 and Stroud and Heugh 2011), social class or socioeconomic status has gone largely unaddressed in HL

---

[1] The notion of restricted and elaborated codes as associated with class (and implicitly, race) has been problematized in recent literature (Johnson, Avineri, and Johnson 2017).

studies. As Nagy (2018) rightly points out, "Social class ... is not straight-forward in instances of migration. People's class and status may change dramatically upon immigration and it is not clear whether pre- or post-immigration status is more predictive of linguistic patterns, nor is it clear how to compare (pre-immigration) class across diverse countries of origin" (433). It is noteworthy that among successive immigrant waves and US-born generations of Cubans in Miami, constructs of social class (pre- and post-Castro) appear to play a vital role in the perception and production of particular phonological and lexical variants in Spanish (Lynch 2009, 2017).

The bulk of HL research has been based on data taken from young adult university students in the United States, Canada, and Europe. There has been extremely little research into the plight of HL speakers in impover-ished regions of the world, for example, sub-Saharan Africa, Central America, South Asia, and even parts of China. The same can be affirmed in relation to creole languages; there is a dearth of research regarding the sociolinguistic situation of creole varieties vis-à-vis standard French in Haiti, Guadeloupe, and Martinique, for example. The great privilege ascribed to French in these settings is indisputably linked to socioeconomic status and symbolic capital, and these values are reterritorialized in the diasporic contexts of the United States, Canada, and France where creole is positioned as HL (Zéphir 1997; Pégram 2005). Lacking extensive documen-tation or empirical evidence, it is nonetheless safe to assume that socio-economic status exerts a crucial influence on the perception and use of HLs.

For middle- and upper-income earners and those with higher levels of formal education, the HL is likely to have more positive social value than for those who occupy the lower social classes, and certain HLs or varieties of the HL are likely to have higher social prestige than others (Urciuoli 1996). A study carried out by Zhang (2012) among Chinese-origin immigrants in Philadelphia is highly illustrative. Zhang compared the HL outcomes of children in middle-class Mandarin-speaking families who lived in the uni-versity area or the suburbs with those of children in working-class Fujianese-speaking families who lived in Chinatown. Parents of the former had high levels of formal education (in some cases, doctoral degrees), while parents of the latter had only completed primary or secondary schooling in China. Zhang observed that even though the middle-class children faced immense social pressure to speak only English, particularly given their minority status at school and in their respective communities, their fam-ilies possessed strong co-ethnic networks in Philadelphia, and they traveled to China, affording the children immersive exposure to Mandarin. The Fujianese, on the other hand, remained largely confined to Philadelphia's Chinatown and did not maintain meaningful connections to China, that is, they did not have transnational ties. Despite their dense social networks and the numerous opportunities that the Fujianese children and their families had to socialize with one another, they resisted use of the HL more strongly than their middle-class Mandarin-speaking counterparts and tended to relegate it to older people and newcomer children who were placed in bilingual education programs. Lambert and Taylor (1996) made a similar finding among Spanish-speaking Cuban-American families in Miami, that is, parents of middle-class backgrounds encouraged additive bilingualism for their children while those of lower socioeconomic standing favored English dominance (i.e., subtractive bilingualism). Interestingly, a study by Moore et al. (2014) based on US Census Bureau American Community Survey data revealed a significant earnings advantage for literate US Spanish-English bilinguals aged 30+ (in comparison with English-dominant and Spanish-dominant respondents) at middle (versus lower) income levels, but not at upper income levels (64–65). Literacy in either language (Spanish or English) yielded significant income advantages for respondents of all age groups.

In Philadelphia, Zhang (2012) affirmed that: "Unlike the well-educated bilingual Mandarin adults, the lower-class Fujianese parents had little understanding of their children's school life and could provide no learning support at home. At the same time, lacking the transnational view of the Chinese language(s) among the Mandarin parents, they failed to recognize the importance of HLM [HL maintenance] in their children" (218). The author thus concluded by characterizing co-ethnic networks – which were actually more dense for the Fujianese and hence more propitious to HL maintenance – as a "double-edged sword that works differently on children from different social classes" (219). Constrained by economic circumstances, confined to Chinatown, and concomitantly excluded from transnational activities, the Fujianese parents regarded their HL as unviable in US society and their children tended to regard it as "inferior and degrading" (220). Zhang's (2012) study thus not only points to the importance of socioeconomic status but the influence of the ways in which middle- and upper-income families experience the forces of globalization and transnationalism. It also reminds us that global flows favor some languages and varieties (e.g., Mandarin or Modern Standard Arabic) over others that are perceived as more local (e.g., Cantonese, Fujianese, or other Min varieties in China, or the so-called colloquial varieties of the Arab World such as Darija or Levantine). This brings us to the matter of ethnicity and race in HL studies.

17.5.3 Ethnicity and Race

In the context of London, one of the world's most "global" cities, Bloch and Hirsch (2017) observed that: "Heritage languages did not simply correspond to a 'standard' language but were more dynamic and hybrid with mixtures of languages being used and incorporated into everyday life" (2459). Their inquiry focused on the adult children of refugees who were also ethnic minorities in their respective countries of origin: Tamils from Sri Lanka, Kurds from Turkey, and Chinese from Vietnam. They noted that despite their higher pre-migration education levels and English language ability, second-generation Tamils faced pressure to assimilate to "British values" (i.e., abandon use of the HL) and experienced racial "othering" in equal measure to the children of less-educated Chinese- and Kurdish-speaking refugees. Personal significance of the HL appeared greatest among the latter, perhaps because parents insisted more on speaking the language as a reaction to having been prohibited from using it in Turkey (2459). Once in London, Kurdish refugees faced the difficult dynamic of reconciliation with Turkish, which had been the language of the oppressor in their homeland: "refugees were often faced with hostility towards their language, with problems arising as the UK government provided Turkish interpreters for Kurdish asylum seekers who were often antagonistic towards asylum seekers … Different waves of Turkish migration to the UK coalesced around a commonality of a Turkish language" (2449). In other words, a language of antagonism (Turkish) in the country of origin is reworked as a language of solidarity in the host country, where both Turkish and Kurdish become objects of Islamophobic sentiment. This sort of social "rescaling" of languages is highly characteristic of HL situations, as orders of indexicality vary across geopolitical spaces (Blommaert 2010). As a further example, Andean migrants from Peru will experience the racialization and social stigmatization of their dialect of Spanish in its relation to HL Quechua in different ways, and according to different scales, as they first migrate to Lima (see Back and Zavala 2019), then to Spain and ultimately Italy (Klee and Caravedo 2019).

As in the context of Great Britain, in the United States, commonly spoken HLs such as Spanish, Chinese, and Arabic (in its multiple varieties) are often racialized. By "racialization of language," we refer to the fact that language, like phenotype, can be a key feature of the construct of race in lived sociopolitical reality. In the process of "othering" racial and ethnic minorities, their ways of speaking are oftentimes also "othered," be it through exoticizing or commodifying their identities or through culturally stigmatizing and in some cases repudiating their participation in mainstream society, matters that are key to the field of raciolinguistics (Alim et al. 2016). Latinxs in the United States confront and at times contest political and institutional discourses that have historically linked Spanish language ability to *Latinidad* as a social construct (Lynch 2018a) and have served to commodify the language within the postmodern framework of economic neoliberalism (Del Valle 2007; Leeman and Martínez 2007; Lynch 2018b). Those same discourses work to racialize Spanish in the US context by particularizing it along identity lines and, in some respects, portraying it as inferior

(Zentella 1995; Hill 2008); in this way, as Zentella explains, language "profiling" happens (2014). This tendency is pervasive in US educational settings (Urciuoli 2008; Rosa 2018; Chaparro 2019). In Japan, Okubo (2010) described HL education as a sort of double-edged sword for Chinese return-migrant children and Japan-born Vietnamese children, in the sense that while HL learning should empower minority students, it simultaneously works to maintain a social boundary between those students and Japanese students, becoming an ethnic marker. These HL studies expose the reality of race as an educational and cultural construct as much as a biological one, and point to the inextricable relationship between racial and ethnic categories, social class configurations, and notions of citizenship and national belonging. It is worth noting that, in the context of the Heritage Language Variation and Change Project in Toronto, ethnic orientation has not been found to correlate significantly with linguistic microvariation (Nagy, this volume). On the other hand, Potowski (2016) cogently shows how ethnic identity concepts condition patterns of lexical and phonological variability among HL Spanish speakers of mixed Mexican and Puerto Rican origins (i.e., "MexiRicans") in Chicago. Studies of Judeo-Spanish and Ladino usage in Los Angeles, New York, and South Florida highlight the roles of diglossia and lexical variation within these ethnically affiliated communities (Kirschen 2015, 2016 2019, 2020). Language variation (Bleaman 2018) and case syncretism (Nove 2018) in contact situations is central to language maintenance in New York Yiddish-speaking Jewish communities as well. The connections among language variation, ethnicity, affiliation, and "heritage" are also evident among Jewish language users in diverse Latino populations in Mexico and Argentina (Dean-Olmsted 2012; Skura and Dean-Olmsted 2018).

17.5.4 Gender and Sexuality

Research on gender-based language variation has a solid tradition in sociolinguistics, beginning with Lakoff's (1975) classic proposals regarding "women's language" and Labov's (1972) empirically based conclusion that women tend to use more standard phonological and morphosyntactic variants than men, especially among middle socioeconomic class speakers and in more formal speech styles. Later research questioned the notion of gender as a dichotomous variable (Bucholtz 1999; Eckert 2000) and introduced identity-based dimensions of gender and sexuality (Leap 1996; Livia and Hall 1997; Cameron and Kulick 2003). Schilling (2011) affirms that even though sociolinguistics researchers recognize the fluidity of gender and sexuality as well its discursively co-constructed nature, "… they cannot ignore the pervasiveness of the dominant gender order, or the fact that expectations for appropriate or normal gender and sexual identities and behaviors often serve to perpetuate normative and even hyper-normative (i.e. stereotypical) performances" (236–237).

In studies of bilingualism, gender has proven to be a crucial variable in some settings. Tannenbaum and Abugov (2010) highlighted the social significance of Yiddish over Hebrew among girls in a Jewish ultra-Orthodox community in Israel. Preece (2008) observed the family pressures that young British Asian and African-origin women in London faced to know and use their respective HLs, which were linked to structures of traditional marriage and childrearing, that is, being the "dutiful daughter." The author cited numerous examples of discursive strategies for establishing female friendships and resolving conflicting subject positions, characterized by Coates (1996) as "exchanged vulnerable talking." Preece explained that:

> [T]he British-born female participants frequently co-construct a floor in which it is normal for parents to expect their children to learn their heritage language and usual for children not to live up to these expectations. Underlying the 'embarrassment' that they associate with this situation is a heteronormative discourse in which they are positioned as future wives and mothers with responsibility for transmitting heritage practices to their children. While there is some resistance to this positioning, it is often difficult to sustain, suggesting that some of the participants are uncomfortable with subverting doing being a "dutiful daughter." (14)

Studies of Spanish in the United States have offered interesting insights into gender-based patterns of language use and variation. In a widely cited longitudinal study of Puerto Ricans in New York, Zentella (1997) found that girls tended to use Spanish more actively and have higher levels of ability in the language than boys, principally because of domestic roles and caregiver responsibilities, and the fact that boys were given freedom to leave the neighborhood much more than girls, where they interacted in English. Girls also regularly watched *telenovelas* (soap operas) in Spanish. Zentella (1997) noted that one of the adolescent males in her study who participated more actively in female social networks and was believed to be gay spoke much more Spanish than his "male-bonded" brother (52). Similarly, Hidalgo (1993) observed that young female Mexican-Americans in Chula Vista (San Diego), California reported using Spanish more frequently than young males. Potowski (2016) noted the important influence of mothers' Spanish variety in the linguistic repertoires of "MexiRicans" in Chicago. A matched guise study conducted by Chappell (2019) revealed that HL Spanish speakers positively attributed social status and confidence to female voices in which the non-standard labiodental variant of /b/ was heard; yet this same variant [v] was perceived negatively when they heard it in male voices. Chappell noted that HL speakers' judgments appeared to align with tendencies among monolingual Mexican Spanish speakers. In terms of sexual identity, Peña (2013) analyzed the semantic function and social significance of Spanish in drag queen performances and the labeling of gay identities among Cuban-origin males in Miami, and Torres (2016) observed the social divisions that sometimes emerge in relation to Spanish and English language preferences among first- and second-generation bilinguals in Latina lesbian organizing in Chicago. Cashman's (2018) groundbreaking study of LGBT Mexicans/Latinxs in Phoenix demonstrates how both language proficiency and practice are conditioned by the intersectionality of ethnicity, sexuality, and (im)migrant identities. Importantly, in Cashman's study, the choice to speak Spanish or not was oftentimes influenced by familial pressures regarding sexual identity and efforts to silence or oppress LGBT speakers. In sum, Smith's (2008) argument that "heritage is gendered" and that "gender identities are constructed and naturalized through 'heritage', but also ultimately contested and negotiated within the heritage process" (159) seems quite convincing.

17.6   Heritage Language Variability

A prominent perspective in studies of HL acquisition is that the apparently simplified or partial grammars and discursive repertoires of HL speakers in comparison with those of monolingual or language-dominant speakers can be attributed to "reduced input" in the HL, leading to what has been termed "incomplete acquisition" (Silva-Corvalán 2014; Montrul 2015; Polinsky 2018; among others). While quantity of input or exposure is highlighted in some studies, other scholars emphasize "quality" of input (Schwartz et al. 2014), variety of sources of input (Kupisch et al. 2014), and the creation of form-meaning mappings through productive use of the HL, i.e., not just exposure to it (O'Grady et al. 2011). Putnam and Sánchez (2013) affirmed that "claims of low frequency in the input as the sole or dominant source of 'incomplete acquisition' are insufficient" (480) and suggested that process rather than result of grammar development should take focus in HL research. While input leads to very strong comprehension or receptive abilities for most HLs, productive abilities will not develop without agency or willful effort on the part of the HL speaker to put the language into actual social practice (i.e., output). This argument regarding the relative weight of input on one hand, and the lack of what Putnam and Sánchez term "activation of functional features" on the other, is reminiscent of the debate that took place in the field of SLA during the 1990s between proponents of input as the key ingredient in L2 acquisition and those who, like Swain (1985), wagered that output must receive equal if not greater consideration in the acquisition equation. In general, the acquisitional processes of HL output have received little attention to date.

Montrul (2011) clarified that HL grammars have "... certain structural characteristics that differ from those of fully fluent bilinguals and monolinguals of the same variety. But these characteristics are most likely due to an interruption in the normal transmission of the language in childhood, rather than to exposure to a different language variety spoken by parents and siblings or their immediate network of heritage speakers" (iii–iv). This brings us to the matter of language variability in HL studies. One must not confound the role of dialectal variation in HL acquisition and those aspects of HL grammars or discourse that reflect differential outcomes due to restricted social use of the HL in minority (or minoritized) language settings (cf. Nagy 2016; Otheguy 2016). In other words, HL speech is often characterized by differential features that cannot be attributed to dialectal varieties that have been the source of input in HL acquisition.

There is a wealth of research on morphosyntactic features that reflect differential processes of acquisition among HL speakers (see Montrul 2015 and Polinsky 2018 for detailed overviews). Published research on phonological and pragmatic variability is less abundant, but numerous scholars have concluded that HL speakers differ from monolinguals, first-generation bilinguals, and L2 users in important ways. For example, Łyskawa, Maddeaux, Melara, and Nagy (2016) observed convergence of English and "homeland" Polish patterns of word-final obstruent devoicing among second-generation Polish HL speakers in Toronto, and Dao and Nguyen (2017) documented the confusion of same-register tones among English-dominant HL Vietnamese speakers in Australia. Kang and Nagy (2016) demonstrated that a female-led change in progress affecting voice onset time (VOT) of aspirated and lenis voiceless stops in Seoul Korean appears to be reversed among young HL Korean speakers in Toronto. Alvord and Rogers (2014) observed the centralization of unstressed vowels among Miami Cubans, and Ronquest (2016) noted the effect of speech style on vowel space among Mexican-Americans. In a comparative study of /b d g/ spirantization among US Spanish HL speakers, Rao (2015) concluded that the most native-like patterns were observed among participants who "... used and felt a connection with Spanish in various domains of life as children, as well as throughout all their years of schooling, and maintained a connection with the language as young adults," pointing to the importance of social and affective factors in HL proficiency (66). Similarly, in a study of tone production by HL Mandarin speakers in the United States, Chang and Yao (2016) concluded that: "early heritage language experience can, but does not necessarily, result in a phonological advantage over L2 learners ... [H]eritage speakers are language users distinct from both native and L2 speakers" (134).

Studies at the pragmatic level have yielded similar conclusions. For example, Li, Zhang, and Taguchi (2017) observed that Chinese HL learners in general had better control of mitigation devices than intermediate and advanced Chinese L2 learners, particularly in the use of sentence-final particles in speech acts that reflected low degrees of power difference and social distance (e.g., suggestions to friends). However, they reflected a limited pragmatic function of particles (e.g., *ba* and *ne*) in comparison with Chinese mainlanders, suggesting that: "... home language exposure available to Chinese HLs promotes the development of heritage learners' pragmatic competence [but]... home language exposure alone might not be sufficient to develop Chinese HLs' complete pragmatic knowledge of Chinese-specific features" (167). In a study of speech acts produced by Miami Cubans, Gutiérrez-Rivas (2011a, 2011b) noted the influence of dominant-language discourse patterns. She found that second- and third-generation Miami Cubans tended to calque the English-based patterns of negative politeness in the formulation of requests (2011a), and she noted a greater reliance on strategies of indirectness in the speech of third-generation Cuban-American females than among their male counterparts, a tendency that she attributed to Anglophone cultural and discursive influences (2011b).

17.7   Directions for Future Research

Some areas of valuable future research include a consideration of HL learners and service-learning (see *Heritage Language Journal* 2016 special issue on the topic), as this integrates relevant sociocultural and sociolinguistic perspectives on community, context, culture, and language varieties. This focuses also on HL learners' strengths (DuBord and Kimball 2016), as opposed to deficit models focused on what these learners are perceived to be unable to do. Further research on curriculum development as it relates to sociocultural topics (Leeman and Martinez 2007; Curdt-Christiansen 2008; Pascual y Cabo 2016) could also be relevant, to see how these manifest in course planning and pedagogical approaches. Additional research that more explicitly connects HL learning with social justice would be a meaningful contribution to the field as well (Leonard 2017; Avineri 2019; Ortega 2020). Finally, additional research that compares HL learners with other learners (e.g., second, foreign language) would be of interest, especially in relation to topics like investment, intersectionality, and discrimination. Overall, much could be gained from continued exploration of the complexities of sociolinguistic and sociocultural concerns in relation to HLs and their users.

References

Alim, H. S., J. Rickford, and A. Ball (eds.) 2016. *Raciolinguistics. How Language Shapes Our Ideas about Race*. Oxford: Oxford University Press.

Alvord, S. and B. Rogers. 2014. Miami Cuban Spanish Vowels in Contact. *Sociolinguistic Studies* 8(1), 139–170.

Anderson, B. R. 1983. *Imagined Communities: Reflections on the Origin and Spread of Nationalism.* London: Verso.

Anderson, R. 1999. Loss of Gender Agreement in L1 Attrition: Preliminary Results. *Bilingual Research Journal* 23(4), 389–408.

Anya, U. 2016. *Realized Identities in Second Language Learning: Speaking Blackness in Brazil.* New York: Routledge.

Avineri, N. 2012. Heritage Language Socialization Practices in Secular Yiddish Educational Contexts: The Creation of a Metalinguistic Community. Doctoral Dissertation, UCLA. Retrieved from www.bjpa.org/content/upload/bjpa/c__c/Avineri-%20Heritage%20Language%20Socialization.pdf.

Avineri, N. 2017. Contested Stance Practices in Secular Yiddish Metalinguistic Communities: Negotiating Closeness and Distance. *Journal of Jewish Languages* 5(2), 174–199.

Avineri, N. 2019. The 'Heritage Narratives' of Yiddish Metalinguistic Community Members. In E. Falconi and K. Garber (eds.), *The Tales We Tell: Storytelling and Narrative Practice.* Leiden: Brill Publishers.

Avineri, N. and P. V. Kroskrity. 2014. On the (Re-)Production and Representation of Endangered Language Communities: Social Boundaries and Temporal Borders. In N. Avineri and P. V. Kroskrity (eds.), Reconceptualizing Endangered Language Communities: Crossing Borders and Constructing Boundaries. [Special Issue]. *Language & Communication* 38(1), 1–7.

Avni, S. 2012. Hebrew as Heritage: The Work of Language in Religious and Communal Continuity. *Linguistics and Education* 23(3), 323–333.

Back, M. and V. Zavala (eds.) 2019. *Racialization and Language: Interdisciplinary Perspectives from Peru.* London: Routledge.

Bale, J. 2010. Arabic As a Heritage Language in the United States. *International Multilingual Research Journal* 4(2), 125–151.

Barkhuizen, G. 2015. Narrative Inquiry. In B. Paltridge and A. Phakiti (eds.), *Research Methods in Applied Linguistics: A Practical Resource.* London: Bloomsbury, 169–185.

Beaudrie, S., C. Ducar, and A. M. Relaño-Pastor. 2009. Curricular Perspectives in the Heritage Language Context: Assessing Culture and Identity. *Language, Culture and Curriculum* 22(2), 157–174.

Bernstein, B. 1971. *Class, Codes and Control.* Vol. I. London: Routledge.

Bleaman, I. L. 2018. Outcomes of Minority Language Maintenance: Variation and Change in New York Yiddish (Publication No. 10824723). Doctoral dissertation, New York University. ProQuest Dissertations Publishing.

Bloch, A. and S. Hirsch. 2017. "Second Generation" Refugees and Multilingualism: Identity, Race and Language Transmission. *Ethnic and Racial Studies* 40(14), 2444–2462.

Blommaert. J. 2010. *The Sociolinguistics of Globalization.* Cambridge: Cambridge University Press.

Bourdieu, P. 1979. *La distinction: Critique sociale du jugement*. Paris,FR: Éditions de Minuit.

Bourdieu, P. 1991. *Language and Symbolic Power*. Cambridge, MA: Harvard University Press.

Brice Heath, S. 1983. *Ways with Words. Language, Life, and Work in Communities and Classrooms*. Cambridge: Cambridge University Press.

Bucholtz, M. 1999. 'Why Be Normal?': Language and Identity Practices in a Community of Nerd Girls. *Language in Society* 28(2), 203–223.

Bucholtz, M. and K. Hall. 2005. Identity and Interaction: A Sociocultural Linguistic Approach. *Discourse Studies* 7(4–5), 585–614.

Burns, K. E. and L. R. Waugh. 2018. Mixed Messages in the Spanish Heritage Language Classroom: Insights from CDA of Textbooks and Instructor Focus Group Discussions. *Heritage Language Journal* 15(1), 1–24.

Cameron, D. and D. Kulick. 2003. *Language and Sexuality*. Cambridge: Cambridge University Press.

Carreira, M. and T. Beeman. 2014. *Voces: Latino Students on Life in the United States*. Santa Barbara, CA: Praeger Publishers.

Carreira, M. and O. Kagan. 2011. The Results of the National Heritage Language Survey: Implications for Teaching, Curriculum Design, and Professional Development. Retrieved from the National Heritage Language Resource Center website: www.nhlrc.ucla.edu/surveyreport/paper.pdf

Cashman, H. 2018. *Queer, Latinx, & Bilingual: Narrative Resources in the Negotiation of Identities*. London: Routledge.

Chang, C. and Y. Yao. 2016. Toward an Understanding of Heritage Prosody: Acoustic and Perceptual Properties of Tone Produced by Heritage, Native, and Second Language Speakers of Mandarin. *Heritage Language Journal* 13(2), 134–160.

Chaparro, S. 2019. *But Mom! I'm Not a Spanish Boy*: Raciolinguistic Socialization in a Two-way Immersion Bilingual Program. *Linguistics and Education* 50, 1–12.

Chappell, W. 2019. The Sociophonetic Perception of Heritage Spanish Speakers in the United States: Reactions to Labiodentalized <v> in the Speech of Late Immigrant and U.S.-born Voices. In W. Chappell (ed.), *Recent Advances in the Study of Spanish Sociophonetic Perception*. Amsterdam: John Benjamins, 240–264.

Chen, S., Q. Zhou, and Y. Uchikoshi,. 2018. Heritage Language Socialization in Chinese American Immigrant Families: Prospective Links to Children's Heritage Language Proficiency. *International Journal of Bilingual Education and Bilingualism* 21(1), 1–18.

Coates, J. 1996. *Women Talk: Conversation between Women Friends*. Oxford: Blackwell.

Creese, A. 2009. Building on Young People's Linguistic and Cultural Continuity: Complementary Schools in the United Kingdom. *Theory Into Practice* 48(4), 267–273.

Crenshaw, K. 1989. Demarginalizing the Intersection of Race and Sex: A Black Feminist Critique of Antidiscrimination Doctrine, Feminist Theory and Antiracist Politics. *University of Chicago Forum* 89(1), 139–167.

Cummins, J. and M. Danesi. 1990. *Heritage Languages: The Development and Denial of Canada's Linguistic Resources*. Toronto: Our Schools/Our Selves and Garamond Press.

Curdt-Christiansen, X. 2008. Reading the World through Words: Cultural Themes in Heritage Chinese Language Textbooks. *Language and Education* 22(2), 95–113.

Dao, M. D. and A. T. Nguyen. 2017. Vietnamese Tones Produced by Australian Vietnamese Speakers. *Heritage Language Journal* 14(3), 224–247.

Dean-Olmsted, E. M. 2012. Speaking Shami: Syrian Jewish Mexican Language Practices as Strategies of Integration and Legitimation (Publication No. 3509907). Doctoral dissertation, Indiana University. ProQuest Dissertations Publishing.

Del Valle, J. (ed.) 2007. *La lengua, ¿patria común? Ideas e ideologías del español*. Madrid: Vervuert/Iberoamericana.

Demuro, E. and L. Gurney. 2018. Mapping Language, Culture, Ideology: Rethinking Language in Foreign Language Instruction. *Language and Intercultural Communication* 18(3), 287–299.

DuBord, E. and E. Kimball. 2016. Cross-language Community Engagement: Assessing the Strengths of Heritage Learners. *Heritage Language Journal* 13(3), 298–330.

Duff, P. A. 2018. Case Study Research in Applied Linguistics. In L. Litosseliti (ed.), *Research Methods in Linguistics*. London: Bloomsbury, 305–330.

Duranti, A. 1997. *Linguistic Anthropology*. Cambridge: Cambridge University Press.

Eckert, P. 2000. *Linguistic Variation As Social Practice*. Oxford: Blackwell.

Fishman, J. A. 1966. *Language Loyalty in the United States: The Maintenance and Perpetuation of Non-English Mother Tongues by American Ethnic and Religious Groups*. The Hague: Mouton.

Fishman, J. A. 2001. 300-Plus Years of Heritage Language Education in the United States. In J. K. Peyton, D. A. Ranard, and S. McGinnis (eds.), *Heritage Languages in America: Preserving a National Resource*. McHenry, IL: Center for Applied Linguistics, 81–97.

Flores, C. 2010. The Effect of Age on Language Attrition: Evidence from Bilingual Returnees. *Bilingualism: Language and Cognition* 13(4), 533–546.

García-Sánchez, I. M. 2010. The Politics of Arabic Language Education: Moroccan Immigrant Children's Language Socialization into Ethnic and Religious Identities. *Linguistics and Education* 21(3), 171–196.

Goble, R. A. 2016. Linguistic Insecurity and Lack of Entitlement to Spanish among Third-generation Mexican Americans in Narrative Accounts. *Heritage Language Journal* 13(1), 29–54.

Guardado, M. 2014. The Discourses of Heritage Language Development: Engaging Ideologies in Canadian Hispanic Communities. *Heritage Language Journal* 11(1), 1–28.

Gumperz, J. J. 1968. The Speech Community. In D. L. Sills (ed.), *International Encyclopedia of the Social Sciences*. New York: Macmillan, 381–386.

Gutiérrez-Rivas, C. 2011a. Variación y cambio pragmático en el español de los cubanos en Miami: el efecto de la generación en el discurso bilingüe. In C. García and M. E. Placencia (eds.), *Estudios de variación pragmática en español*. Buenos Aires: Dunken, 167–183.

Gutiérrez-Rivas, C. 2011b. El efecto del género en el discurso bilingüe. Un estudio sobre peticiones. *Estudios de Lingüística Aplicada* 54, 37–59.

Guy, G. 2011. Language, Social Class, and Status. In R. Mesthrie (ed.), *The Cambridge Handbook of Sociolinguistics*. Cambridge: Cambridge University Press, 159–185.

Harasta, J. 2017. 'Because They Are Cornish': Four Uses of a Useless Language. *Heritage Language Journal* 14, 248–263.

He, A. W. 2010. The Heart of Heritage: Sociocultural Dimensions of Heritage Language Learning. *Annual Review of Applied Linguistics* 30, 66–82.

Hidalgo, M. 1993. The Dialectics of Language Maintenance and Language Loyalty in Chula Vista, CA: A Two-Generation Study. In A. Roca and J. M. Lipski (eds.), *Spanish in the U.S.: Language Contact and Diversity*. Berlin: Mouton, 47–71.

Hill, J. 2008. *The Everyday Language of White Racism*. Malden, MA: Wiley Blackwell.

Jaffe, A. 2007. Discourses of Endangerment: Contexts and Consequences of Essentializing Discourses. In A. Duchene and M. Heller (eds.), *Discourses of Endangerment: Ideology and Interest in the Defence of Languages*. London: Continuum International Publishing Group, 57–75.

Johnson, E. J., N. Avineri, and D. C. Johnson. 2017. Exposing Gaps in/ between Discourses of Linguistic Deficits. *International Multilingual Research Journal* 11(1), 5–22.

Kagan, O. 2012. Intercultural Competence of Heritage Language Learners: Motivation, Identity, Language Attitudes, and the Curriculum. *Proceedings of Second Intercultural Competence Conference* 2, 72–84.

Kang, Y. and N. Nagy. 2016. VOT Merger in Heritage Korean in Toronto. *Language Variation and Change* 28(2), 249–272.

King, K. A. 2000. Language Ideologies and Heritage Language Education. *International Journal of Bilingual Education and Bilingualism* 3(3), 167–184.

Kirschen, B. 2020. Intergenerational Transmission of Ladino: Three Generations of Speakers in the Twenty-First Century. *Heritage Language Journal* 17(1), 70–91.

Kirschen, B. 2015. Judeo-Spanish Encounters Modern Spanish: Language Contact and Diglossia among the Sephardim of Los Angeles and New York City. Doctoral dissertation, UCLA.

Kirschen, B. 2016. Diglossic Distribution among Judeo-Spanish-Speaking Sephardim in the United States. In S. Ross, S. Soomekh, and L. Ansell (eds.), *Sephardi and Mizrahi Jews in America: The Jewish Role in American Life*. West Lafayette, IN: Purdue University Press, 25–52.

Kirschen, B. 2019. Lexical Variation among South Florida's Judeo-Spanish-speaking Sephardim. *Journal of Jewish Languages* 7(1), 53–84.

Klee, C. and R. Caravedo. 2019. Migration and Orders of Indexicality in Lima. In A. Lynch (ed.), *The Routledge Handbook of Spanish in the Global City*. London: Routledge, 176–203.

Klein, W. 2013. Speaking Punjabi: Heritage Language Socialization and Language Ideologies in a Sikh Education Program. *Heritage Language Journal* 10(1), 36–50.

Kroskrity, P. V. 2004. Language Ideologies. In A. Duranti (ed.), *A Companion to Linguistic Anthropology*. Malden, MA: Blackwell, 496–517.

Kupisch, T., D. Barton, K. Hailer, E. Klaschik, I. Stangen, T. Lein, and J. van de Weijer. 2014. Foreign Accent in Adult Simultaneous Bilinguals. *Heritage Language Journal* 11(2), 123–150.

Kurata, N. 2015. Motivational Selves of Japanese Heritage Speakers in Australia. *Heritage Language Journal* 12(2), 110–131.

Labov, W. 1972. *Sociolinguistic Patterns*. Philadelphia: University of Pennsylvania Press.

Lakoff, R. 1975. *Language and Woman's Place*. New York: Harper & Row.

Lambert, W. and D. Taylor. 1996. Language in the Lives of Ethnic Minorities: Cuban American Families in Miami. *Applied Linguistics* 17(4), 477–500.

Lantolf, J. P. 2000. *Sociocultural Theory and Second Language Learning*. Oxford: Oxford University Press.

Lave, J. and E. Wenger. 1991. *Situated Learning: Legitimate Peripheral Participation*. Cambridge: Cambridge University Press.

Leap, W. 1996. *Word's Out: Gay Men's English*. Minneapolis: University of Minnesota Press.

Lee, J. S. 2002. The Korean Language in America: The Role of Cultural Identity in Heritage Language Learning. *Language, Culture, and Curriculum* 15(2), 117–133.

Leeman, J. 2015. Heritage Language Education and Identity in the United States. *Annual Review of Applied Linguistics* 35, 100–119.

Leeman, J. and G. Martínez. 2007. From Identity to Commodity: Discourses of Spanish in Heritage Language Textbooks. *Critical Inquiry in Language Studies* 4(1), 35–65.

Leeman, J., L. Rabin, and E. Román-Mendoza. 2011. Critical Pedagogy beyond the Classroom Walls: Community Service-learning and Spanish Heritage Language Education. *Heritage Language Journal* 8(3), 481–495.

Leonard, W. Y. 2017. Producing Language Reclamation by Decolonising 'Language'. In W. Y. Leonard and H. De Korne (eds.), *Language Documentation and Description*. London: EL Publishing, 15–36.

Li, Q., H. Zhang, and N. Taguchi. 2017). The Use of Mitigation Devices in Heritage Learners of Chinese. *Heritage Language Journal* 14(2), 150–170.

Livia, A. and K. Hall (eds.) 1997. *Queerly Phrased: Language, Gender and Sexuality.* Oxford: Oxford University Press.

Lo, A. 2009. Lessons about Respect and Affect in a Korean Heritage Language School. *Linguistics and Education* 20(3), 217–234.

Lynch, A. 2009. A Sociolinguistic Analysis of Final /s/ in Miami Cuban Spanish. *Language Sciences* 31(6), 767–790.

Lynch, A. 2017. The Social Diffusion of English-based Lexical Innovations in Miami Cuban Spanish. In A. Cuza (ed.), *Cuban Spanish Dialectology: Variation, Contact and Change.* Washington, DC: Georgetown University Press, 165–187.

Lynch, A. 2018a. A Historical View of US *Latinidad* and Spanish as Heritage Language. In K. Potowski (ed.), *The Routledge Handbook of Spanish as a Heritage Language.* London: Routledge, 17–35.

Lynch, A. 2018b. Spatial Reconfigurations of Spanish in Postmodernity: The Relationship to English and Minoritized Languages. In J. King and S. Sessarego (eds.), *The Dynamics of Language Variation and Change: Varieties of Spanish across Space and Time.* Amsterdam: John Benjamins, 11–34.

Lynch, A. (ed.) 2019. *The Routledge Handbook of Spanish in the Global City.* London: Routledge.

Łyskawa, P., R. Maddeaux, E. Melara, and N. Nagy. 2016. Heritage Speakers Follow All the Rules: Language Contact and Convergence in Polish Devoicing. *Heritage Language Journal* 13(2), 219–244.

Maloof, V. M., D. L. Rubin, and A. N. Miller. 2006. Cultural Competence and Identity in Cross-Cultural Adaptation: The Role of a Vietnamese Heritage Language School. *International Journal of Bilingual Education and Bilingualism* 9(2), 255–273.

Mar-Molinero, C. 2018. Language Issues for US-raised 'Returnees' in Mexico. In K. Potowski (ed.), *The Routledge Handbook of Spanish as a Heritage Language.* London: Routledge, 555–567.

Melo-Pfeifer, S. 2015. The Role of the Family in Heritage Language Use and Learning: Impact on Heritage Language Policies. *International Journal of Bilingual Education and Bilingualism* 18(1), 26–44.

Montrul, S. 2011. Spanish Heritage Speakers: Bridging Formal Linguistics, Psycholinguistics and Pedagogy. *Heritage Language Journal* 8(1), 1–6.

Montrul, S. 2015. *The Acquisition of Heritage Languages.* Cambridge: Cambridge University Press.

Moore, E. 2014. "You Are Children But You Can Always Say …": Hypothetical Direct Reported Speech and Child–Parent Relationships in a Heritage Language Classroom. *Text & Talk* 34(5), 591–621.

Moore, S. C., M. Fee, J. Ee, T. Wiley, M. B. Arias. 2014. Exploring Bilingualism, Literacy, Employability and Income Levels among Latinos in the United States. In R. Callahan and P. Gándara (eds.), *The Bilingual Advantage: Language, Literacy and the US Labor Market*. Bristol: Multilingual Matters, 45–76.

Morgan, M. 2006. Speech Community. In A. Duranti (ed.), *A Companion to Linguistic Anthropology*. Malden, MA: Blackwell, 3–22.

Nagy, N. 2015. A Sociolinguistic View of Null Subjects and VOT in Toronto Heritage Languages. *Lingua* 164, 309–327.

Nagy, N. 2016. Heritage Languages as New Dialects. In M.-H. Côté, R. Knooihuizen, and J. Nerbonne (eds.), *The Future of Dialects: Selected Papers from Methods in Dialectology XV*. Berlin: Language Science, 15–34.

Nagy, N. 2018. Linguistic Attitudes and Contact Effects in Toronto's Heritage Languages: A Variationist Sociolinguistic Investigation. *International Journal of Bilingualism* 22(4), 429–446.

Norton Peirce, B. 1995. Social Identity, Investment, and Language Learning. *TESOL Quarterly* 29(1), 9–31.

Nove, C. R. 2018. Social Predictors of Case Syncretism in New York Hasidic Yiddish. *University of Pennsylvania Working Papers in Linguistics* 24(2), 87–95.

O'Grady, W., O. S. Lee, and J. H. Lee. 2011. Practical and Theoretical Issues in the Study of Heritage Language Acquisition. *Heritage Language Journal* 8(3), 315–332.

Oh, J. S. and T. K. Au. 2005. Learning Spanish As a Heritage Language: The Role of Sociocultural Background Variables. *Language, Culture and Curriculum* 18(3), 229–241.

Oh, J. S. and B. A. Nash. 2014. Attitudes and Motivations of Adult Spanish Language Learners: A Comparison of Heritage Language Learners and Second Language Learners. *Heritage Language Journal* 11(1), 29–44.

Okubo, Y. 2010. Heritage: Owned or Assigned? The Cultural Politics of Teaching Heritage Language in Osaka, Japan. *Critical Asian Studies* 42(1), 111–138.

Ortega, L. 2020. The Study of Heritage Language Development from a Bilingualism and Social Justice Perspective. *Language Learning* 70(S1), 15–53.

Otheguy, R. 2016. The Linguistic Competence of Second-Generation Bilinguals: A Critique of 'Incomplete Acquisition'. In C. Tortora, M. den Dikken, I. Montoya, and T. O'Neill (eds.), *Romance Linguistics 2013*. Selected papers from the 43rd Linguistic Symposium on Romance Languages. Amsterdam: John Benjamins, 301–319.

Pascual y Cabo, D. (ed.) 2016. *Advances in Spanish as a Heritage Language*. Amsterdam: John Benjamins.

Pégram, S. 2005. Being Ourselves: Immigrant Culture and Self-identification among Young Haitians in Montreal. *Ethnic Studies Review* 28(1), 1–20.

Peña, S. 2013. *¡Oye loca! From the Mariel Boatlift to Gay Cuban Miami*. Minneapolis: University of Minnesota Press.

Polinsky, M. 2018. *Heritage Languages and Their Speakers*. Cambridge: Cambridge University Press.

Polinsky, M. and O. Kagan. 2007. Heritage Languages: In the 'Wild' and in the Classroom. *Languages and Linguistics Compass* 1(5), 368–395.

Potowski, K. 2016. *Inter-Latino Language and Identity: MexiRicans*. Amsterdam: John Benjamins.

Preece, S. 2008. Multilingual Gendered Identities: Female Undergraduate Students in London Talk about Heritage Languages. *Journal of Language, Identity & Education* 7(1), 41–60.

Pu, C. 2012. Community-based Heritage Language Schools: A Chinese Example. *Kappa Delta Pi Record* 48(1), 29–34.

Putnam, M. and L. Sánchez. 2013. What's So Incomplete about Incomplete Acquisition? A Prolegomenon to Modeling Heritage Language Grammars. *Linguistic Approaches to Bilingualism* 3(4), 478–508.

Rao, R. 2015. Manifestations of /bdg/ in Heritage Speakers of Spanish. *Heritage Language Journal* 12(1), 48–74.

Roman, D., A. Pastor, and D. Basaraba. 2019. Internal Linguistic Discrimination: A Survey of Bilingual Teachers' Language Attitudes toward Their Heritage Students' Spanish. *Bilingual Research Journal* 42(1), 6–30.

Ronquest, R. 2016. Stylistic Variation in Heritage Spanish Vowel Production. *Heritage Language Journal* 13(2), 275–297.

Rosa, J. 2018. *Looking Like a Language, Sounding Like a Race. Raciolinguistic Ideologies and the Learning of Latinidad*. Oxford: Oxford University Press.

Sánchez, R. 1983. *Chicano Discourse*. Rowley, MA: Newbury House.

Schilling, N. 2011. Language, Gender, and Sexuality. In R. Mesthrie (ed.), *The Cambridge Handbook of Sociolinguistics*. Cambridge: Cambridge University Press, 218–237.

Schwartz, M., B. Nir, M. Leiken, R. Levie, and D. Ravid. 2014. The Acquisition of Noun Plurals among Early Sequential Russian-Hebrew Speaking Bilinguals. *Heritage Language Journal* 11(2), 151–185.

Seal, C. A. 2017. Positive and Negative Identity Practices in Heritage Language Education. *International Journal of Multilingualism* 15(4), 329–348.

Shin, S. J. 2010. "What about Me? I'm Not Like Chinese but I'm Not Like American": Heritage-Language Learning and Identity of Mixed-Heritage Adults. *Journal of Language, Identity, and Education* 9(3), 203–219.

Silva-Corvalán, C. 1994. *Language Contact and Change. Spanish in Los Angeles*. Oxford: Clarendon Press.

Silva-Corvalán, C. 2014. *Bilingual Language Acquisition: Spanish and English in the First Six Years*. Cambridge: Cambridge University Press.

Silverstein, M. 1998. Contemporary Transformations of Local Linguistic Communities. *Annual Review of Anthropology* 27, 401–426.

Skura, S. and E. M. Dean-Olmsted. 2018. Jewish Spanish in Mexico City and Buenos Aires. In B. Hary and S. Benor (eds.), *Languages in Jewish Communities, Past and Present*. Berlin: De Gruyter Mouton, 383–413.

Smith, L. 2008. Heritage, Gender and Identity. In B. Graham and P. Howard (eds.), *The Ashgate Research Companion to Heritage and Identity*. Farnham: Ashgate, 159–179.

Stanford, J. N. and D. Preston (eds.) 2009. *Variation in Indigenous Minority Languages*. Amsterdam: John Benjamins.

Stroud, C. and K. Heugh. 2011. Language in Education. In R. Mesthrie (ed.), *The Cambridge Handbook of Sociolinguistics*. Cambridge: Cambridge University Press, 413–429.

Swain, M. 1985. Communicative Competence: Some Roles of Comprehensible Input and Comprehensible Output in Its Development. In S. Gass and C. Madden (eds.), *Input in Second Language Acquisition*. Rowley, MA: Newbury House, 235–253.

Szecsi, T. and J. Szilagyi. 2012. Immigrant Hungarian Families' Perceptions of New Media Technologies in the Transmission of Heritage Language and Culture. *Language, Culture and Curriculum* 25(3), 265–281.

Tamošiūnaitė, A. 2013. Lithuanian Saturday Schools in Chicago: Student Proficiency, Generational Shift, and Community Involvement. *Heritage Language Journal* 10(1), 108–133.

Tannenbaum, M. and N. Abugov. 2010. The Legacy of the Linguistic Fence: Linguistic Patterns among Ultra-Orthodox Jewish Girls. *Heritage Language Journal* 7(1), 74–90.

Tomiyama, M. 2008. Age and Proficiency in L2 Attrition: Data from Two Siblings. *Applied Linguistics* 30(2), 253–275.

Torres, L. 2016. Building a Translengua in Latina Lesbian Organizing. *The Journal of Lesbian Studies* 21(3), 272–288.

Trudgill, P. 1974. *The Social Differentiation of English in Norwich*. Cambridge: Cambridge University Press.

Urciuoli, B. 1996. *Exposing Prejudice: Puerto Rican Experiences of Language, Race, and Class*. Boulder, CO: Westview Press.

Urciuoli, B. 2008. Whose Spanish? The Tension between Linguistic Correctness and Cultural Identity. In M. Niño-Murcia and J. Rothman (eds.), *Bilingualism and Identity: Spanish at the Crossroads with other Languages*. Amsterdam: John Benjamins, 257–277.

Valdés, G. 1978. A Comprehensive Approach to the Teaching of Spanish to Bilingual Spanish-Speaking Students. *Modern Language Journal* 62(3), 102–110.

Valdés, G. and M. Geoffrion-Vinci. 1998. Chicano Spanish: The Problem of the 'Underdeveloped' Code in Bilingual Repertoires. *Modern Language Journal* 82(4), 473–501.

Vilar Sánchez, K. 2003. *La remigración en la adolescencia. Aspectos sociolingüísticos, psicológicos y sociolaborales*. Granada: Editorial Universidad de Granada.

Villa, D. and S. Rivera-Mills. 2009. An Integrated Multi-generational Model for Language Maintenance and Shift: The Case of Spanish in the Southwest. *Spanish in Context* 6(1), 26–42.

Weekly, R. 2018. Attitudes, beliefs and responsibility for heritage language maintenance in the UK. *Current Issues in Language Planning*. Retrieved from https://doi.org/10.1080/14664208.2018.1554324

Weinreich, U. 1953. *Languages in Contact: Findings and Problems*. New York: Linguistic Circle of New York.

Willoughby, L. 2014. Meeting the Challenges of Heritage Language Education: Lessons from One School Community. *Current Issue in Language Planning* 15(3), 265–281.

Woolard, K. A. and B. B. Schieffelin. 1994. Language Ideology. *Annual Review of Anthropology* 23(1), 55–82.

Yazan, B. and I. Ali. 2018. Family Language Policies in a Libyan Immigrant Family in the U.S.: Language and Religious Identity. *Heritage Language Journal* 15(3), 369–388.

Yeh, Y. C., H. J. Ho, and M. C. Chen. 2015. Learning Vietnamese as a Heritage Language in Taiwan. *Journal of Multilingual and Multicultural Development* 36(3), 255–265.

Zentella, A. C. 1995. The *"Chiquita-fication" of U.S. Latinos and Their Languages, or Why We Need an Anthro-political Linguistics. SALSA III: The Proceedings of the Symposium about Language and Society at Austin (1–18)*. Austin, TX: Department of Linguistics.

Zentella, A. C. 1997. *Growing Up Bilingual*. Malden, MA: Blackwell.

Zentella, A. C. 2014. TWB (Talking While Bilingual): Linguistic Profiling of Latin@s, and other Linguistic *Torquemadas. Latino Studies* 12(4), 620–635.

Zéphir, F. 1997. The Social Value of French for Bilingual Haitian Immigrants. *The French Review* 70(3), 395–406.

Zhang, D. 2012. Co-ethnic Network, Social Class, and Heritage Language Maintenance among Chinese Immigrant Families. *Journal of Language, Identity, and Education* 11(3), 200–223.

18

The Psycholinguistics of Heritage Languages

Jill Jegerski and Irina A. Sekerina

18.1 Introduction

Psycholinguistics is an interdisciplinary field that studies linguistic behavior and the cognitive processes that underlie it. There is a great deal of overlap with the field of linguistics, but in psycholinguistics the cognitive perspective on language is fundamental. For instance, current theoretical issues that have motivated research in mainstream psycholinguistics include the role of prediction in sentence processing (e.g., Kuperberg and Jaeger 2016; Pickering and Gambi 2018) and whether comprehension and production rely on the same underlying cognitive mechanisms (e.g., Momma and Phillips 2018). Language acquisition is a key area of study in psycholinguistics (along with language comprehension, production, and disorders), so there is a natural affinity between psycholinguistics and the study of heritage languages. Psycholinguistics generally employs technologically advanced methods for empirical language research, which may be particularly useful for research on heritage speakers because a lack of formal education in the heritage language (i.e., underdeveloped literacy) means that some empirical tests can put them at a disadvantage relative to other populations to which they are frequently compared (Benmamoun et al. 2013; Montrul 2016, chapter 6; Jegerski 2018a).

The goal of this chapter is to provide a review of psycholinguistic research on adult heritage speakers. The review is fairly comprehensive, especially with regard to studies that used real-time experimental measures (e.g., eye-tracking, self-paced reading, and other reaction time methods), but we have not included unpublished work, our coverage of research using offline methods such as judgments is selective, and there is much greater emphasis on comprehension than on production. The chapter is organized by area of language, starting with speech perception and production, followed by lexical and morphological processing, sentence processing, and processing at levels beyond the sentence. Despite the separation into distinct sections here, there are some overarching issues that are relevant to much of the research in this chapter, including cross-linguistic influence between the two languages of a heritage bilingual and the role of language background variables like age of acquisition, early exposure, and proficiency level.

To our knowledge, this is the first review of psycholinguistic work with heritage speakers that includes all languages (but see Jegerski 2018a, for a selective review for Spanish). For this reason, we have tried to make this chapter inclusive, covering a range of both linguistic domains – from phonology to discourse – and research methods, which are described in Table 18.1. All of these experimental methods are administered via

Table 18.1 *Experimental methods used in psycholinguistics of heritage languages*

Linguistic domain: Method	Description	Measures
Psychophonology: (1) AXB discrimination	Participants hear three sounds in a row and have to decide if the middle sound (X) is the same as the first sound (A) or the third sound (B). Variants include ABX, XAB, and AB (same or different?).	Accuracy Sometimes RTs
(2) Sound identification	Participants identify a particular sound (e.g., the final sound in an auditory stimulus word) from multiple options presented on the screen.	Accuracy RTs
Mental lexicon: (3) Lexical decision (4) Lexical priming	Participants make a decision whether a string of letters is a word of the language or not. Exposure to one word (the prime) can facilitate or inhibit some type of response to a second word (the target) because of cognitive relationship between the two.	Accuracy RTs
(5) Picture naming (6) Picture matching	Participants are shown a picture of an object or concept and asked to name it out loud. Participants choose a name for the picture from options provided.	Accuracy Sometimes RTs
Syntax: (7) Acceptability judgment task (AJT)	Participants indicate their personal evaluation of a sentence with regard to a linguistic feature of interest, such as grammaticality or semantic plausibility	Ratings (binary or Likert scale) sometimes RTs
(8) Self-paced reading	Participants use a button to advance through written sentences one word or phrase at a time, with the previous words getting covered by a mask (moving window) or remaining visible (cumulative)	RT for each word or phrase
Multiple domains: (9) Eyetracking in reading	Participants' eye movements (saccades and fixations) across a written sentence or paragraph are recorded by one or more small cameras	Fixation durations, word skipping rates, regressive saccades, total gaze time
(10) Visual World	Participants listen to an auditory stimulus while their eye movements across an array of pictures or physical objects related to the stimulus are recorded	Proportions of looks to pictures averaged across the trial or moment-by-moment

computer and require specialized software and, in many cases, hardware as well. For further information on psycholinguistic research methods, we refer the reader to practical guides by Jegerski and VanPatten (2014); Keating and Jegerski (2015); and Sekerina, Fernández, and Clahsen (2008).

18.2   Speech Perception and Production

We start with speech perception and production, the lower-level processes involved in using sounds to convey linguistic meaning. The auditory signal of speech is messy – a stream of overlapping units, each of which varies widely in how it is produced from one moment to the next – and yet knowledge of a language allows the user to effortlessly perceive individual sounds. A further complication is that most speech variables change along a continuum, but they are perceived as belonging to distinct categories. In addition, the perceived categories are language-specific. Hence, key approaches to the study of speech perception and production with heritage speakers have included investigating whether such categorical distinctions are maintained in the heritage language, whether between-language distinctions hold for heritage language sounds that are acoustically close to majority language sounds, and how heritage speakers compare to L2 learners and prototypical native speakers on both counts.

So far, research in this area has been limited, but results suggest that this is a domain of particular strength for heritage speakers, especially in perception. For instance, Lukyanchenko and Gor (2011) found that heritage speakers of Russian in the United States were better able to perceive the difference between hard and soft consonants than were L2 learners, and they were very nearly the same as prototypical native speakers (i.e., adult immigrants who were raised abroad in a Russian-speaking society and who completed their schooling in the language before becoming bilingual). Heritage speakers of Russian also performed better than L2 learners on sound discrimination and word recognition under noisy conditions, and those with high proficiency were close to native speakers (Gor 2014). In another example, heritage speakers of Korean in the United States performed as well as native speakers raised abroad in the identification of Korean unreleased final stops (Chang 2016).

Observations from speech production studies have suggested that the advantage holds there as well, although heritage speakers tend not to be quite the same as prototypical native speakers. Several studies (Chang, Haynes, Yao, and Rhodes 2009; Chang, Haynes, Yao, and Rhodes 2010; Chang, Yao, Haynes, and Rhodes 2011) found that heritage speakers of Mandarin in the United States were more similar to prototypical native speakers raised and formally educated in a Chinese-speaking society than were L2 learners with regard to the production of back vowels and post-alveolar fricative consonants. They also maintained the between-language distinction when producing these two classes of sounds, plus stop consonants, and similar sounds in English. Still, there is evidence that heritage speakers' production tends to be not quite as developed as their perception, even when both exceed the performance of L2 learners, at least with a suprasegmental feature like lexical stress (Kim 2015). Furthermore, it appears that the production of sounds that are similar to those of the majority language can shift and become even more similar to them, at least in some cases (Godson 2004; Hrycyna et al. 2011), so even in this domain the heritage language is not immune to the influence of the majority language.

18.3   Lexical and Morphological Processing

Lexical processing involves accessing words in memory while a language user is engaged in the comprehension or production of one or more words. The speed of lexical access for individual words is most often used as an experimental measure because it is thought to indicate how developed the representations are for different words in memory and to reflect the connections between words and the concepts they represent. For instance, a response involving the word *elephant* might generally be faster than for *pachyderm* because *elephant* is encountered more frequently and thus has a more robust representation in memory.

Lexical processing among heritage speakers has not been the object of much research so far, but one general observation is that the lexical knowledge of heritage speakers is typically less developed, with a smaller vocabulary and slower lexical access than in the majority language or as compared to prototypical native speakers of the heritage language, in both production and comprehension. For word production, Hulsen (2000) asked three sociolinguistic generations of Dutch immigrants in Australia (i.e., first generation immigrants, children of first generation immigrants, and grandchildren of first generation immigrants) to name pictures in Dutch and match Dutch words with pictures. Each successive generation of participants showed slower and less accurate responses than the previous generation. In a study that used a timed paragraph read aloud measure, heritage speakers of Spanish in the United States were found to read more quickly in English than in Spanish (Gollan et al. 2014). O'Grady, Schafer, Perla, Lee, and Wieting (2009) found a slower speech rate in Korean versus English for highly proficient heritage speakers, even with high frequency words well known to the participants, such as body parts. Polinsky (2008) also found that the speech rate of heritage speakers of Russian in the United States was slower than that of monolingual native speakers of Russian, although the highest performing participants in the study were nearly as fast as the comparison group.

Similarly, for word comprehension, heritage speakers seem to not perform quite the same as other native speakers in lexical decision experiments (Table 18.1, (3)), or as compared to their own lexical processing in the majority language (Basnight-Brown and Altarriba 2007), but they often appear to have stronger lexical knowledge than L2 learners. For instance, the lexical decision times of heritage speakers have been found to be slower than those of prototypical native speakers with Spanish in the United States (Davis et al. 2010) and with Turkish in Germany (Jacob et al. 2019), although the heritage speakers were similar to prototypical native speakers in a study of Russian in the United States (Gor and Cook 2010). It is also a common finding that heritage speakers are faster than L2 learners: with Spanish in the United States (Davis et al. 2010), and with Russian in the United States (Gor and Cook 2010). Or they can be of similar speed but more accurate than L2 learners (Gor 2018). Nevertheless, Montrul and Foote (2014) found that heritage speakers of Spanish in the United States were actually slower than L2 learners, and Gor et al. (2019) observed the same with Russian in the United States, so there are some exceptions to the overall trends.

In sum, research has shown that heritage speakers often know fewer words in the heritage language and generally have weaker representations of the words they do know (in line with the Weaker Links Hypothesis of Gollan, Montoya, Cera, and Sandoval 2008), as shown by slower access times. These trends can be explained by limited exposure to the heritage language in childhood (Jacob et al. 2019; O'Grady et al. 2009), as reduced exposure to words means that the effective frequency of many words is lower in a heritage language versus a majority language, and frequency effects are a widespread finding in lexical processing research in general (i.e., RTs decline and accuracy improves as word frequency increases), even with prototypical native speakers and L2 learners. In addition, the speed of lexical access is so fundamental that it has been used to gauge language loss among different speech communities (O'Grady et al. 2009) and it has been employed as a global proficiency measure with heritage speakers (e.g., Polinsky and Kagan 2007; see Montrul 2016: 181–186, for an overview), as it correlates with at least some types of grammar knowledge in the heritage language (e.g., grammatical gender, Polinsky 2008).

In addition to these basic questions regarding the production and comprehension of words in the heritage language, another fundamental issue in the broader field of bilingualism is the organization of two languages and especially two mental dictionaries, or *lexicons*, in the mind of the bilingual. The potential for connections between the two languages is key, which dovetails with the heritage language issue of cross-linguistic influence from the majority language. Other heritage language issues that have been addressed in research on lexical processing pertain to ways that heritage speakers might differ from prototypical native speakers, with special attention to cross-linguistic influence in morphology and whether complex words are processed via their component morphemes or as whole forms.

18.3.1 Cross-Linguistic Influence and the Heritage Bilingual Lexicon

At least four lexical processing studies have investigated the connections between words in the two mental lexicons of heritage speakers, all with heritage Spanish in the United States. Silverberg and Samuel (2004) conducted an early unidirectional study using a primed lexical decision task with visible primes (350, 500, or 650 milliseconds) (Table 18.1 (4)). A group of heritage speakers showed between-language semantic priming, meaning faster lexical decision times for written Spanish target words that followed a semantically related English word versus an unrelated English word (e.g., *nail – tornillo* 'screw' as opposed to *bark – tornillo*), but no form priming when the prime and target shared the same first three letters (e.g., *torture – tornillo* 'screw'). An L1 Spanish – L2 English group, on the other hand, showed the opposite pattern, form priming without semantic priming. The researchers concluded that the two languages of (early) heritage bilinguals are linked at the conceptual level and that with adult L2 learners the two languages are linked primarily at the level of lexical form.

Another type of between-language priming (Table 18.1 (4)) that has been documented with heritage speakers of Spanish is with noncognate translation pairs (e.g., *luna – moon*). Basnight-Brown and Altarriba (2007) found translation priming effects in both directions, Spanish to English and English to Spanish, both with and without a *mask* (the non-alphabetic characters "########" appeared before the 100 ms prime, making it even harder to perceive). They also replicated the semantic priming effect previously observed by Silverberg and Samuel (2004), but it only occurred with unmasked priming and only from English to Spanish. This asymmetry was taken as evidence that heritage speakers have stronger mental representations for words in the majority language than for those in the heritage language.

Davis et al. (2010: Experiment 1) also examined between-language translation priming in heritage speakers of Spanish, comparing cognates to noncognates. This time, only the prime-target pairs that were cognates (e.g., *rich-rico* but not *cola-tail*) showed priming effects, which likely occurred because cognate pairs have a larger amount of overlap in their lexical entries, meaning that they are similar in terms of form and meaning, whereas noncognate translation pairs are only similar in terms of meaning. Also, the primes in this study appeared for only 57 ms (vs. 100 ms in the study by Basnight-Brown and Altarriba 2007), so there was less time for words related to the prime to be activated. As with the prior investigation, priming effects were observed in both directions, Spanish to English and English to Spanish, among heritage speakers plus two groups of proficient L2 learners, which suggests a certain degree of balance between their two languages. On the other hand, a group of L2 English learners with lower proficiency only showed priming in one direction, from their L1 to their L2, which likely reflects stronger mental representations for L1 words than for L2 words.

Thus, research on the bilingual mental lexicon of heritage speakers has shown that words in their two languages are most clearly linked at the conceptual level and that form-based connections can further facilitate lexical processing, as with cognate translation pairs (Basnight-Brown and Altarriba 2007; Davis et al. 2010), although form-based priming may not always work on its own (Silverberg and Samuel 2004). Still, in a related study using eye-tracking (Table 18.1 (10)) rather than lexical priming, also with heritage speakers of Spanish in the United States, Canseco-Gonzalez et al. (2010) observed phonological influence from Spanish on their comprehension of words in English, which shows that the two languages are also cognitively connected at the level of sound, so lexical connections between languages are not exclusively semantic. Additionally, one study observed an asymmetry in priming (Basnight-Brown and Altarriba 2007) – with stronger effects from the majority language to the heritage language than in the other direction because of stronger representations in the mental lexicon for words in the majority language – but the other study testing priming in both directions found no asymmetry (Davis et al. 2010: Experiment 1), so there is no consensus so far.

18.3.2 Functional Morphology in Lexical Processing

One common approach to the role of functional morphology in lexical processing is to examine morphological decomposition, which has been the objective of three studies of heritage speakers so far (Gor and Cook 2010; Jacob and Kirkici 2016; Jacob et al. 2019). Such research is based on dual mechanism or dual route theories of lexical access, which posit that morphologically complex words can be accessed either as a whole word form stored in the lexicon, or via the component morphemes that comprise the word. There is evidence that morphological decomposition occurs efficiently among native speakers (Marslen-Wilson 2007), but it has been proposed that adult L2 learners rely more on the storage of whole words (Clahsen, Felser, Neubauer, Sato, and Silva 2010).

Gor and Cook (2010: Experiment 1) investigated the potential for morphological decomposition among heritage speakers in the auditory processing of Russian verbs (Table 18.1 (4)), comparing them to prototypical native speakers and L2 learners. All three groups exhibited priming effects, with faster lexical decision times for infinitive verb forms that were preceded by an inflected form of the same verb (e.g., *noshu – nosit'* 'I carry' – 'to carry'), which was taken as a sign that the inflected verb forms were indeed broken down into their component morphemes during lexical access. Similarly, two studies also documented morphological priming with heritage speakers of Turkish, but with written rather than auditory stimuli and with 50 ms primes that are typically not consciously noticed by participants (Jacob and Kirkici 2016: Experiment 1; Jacob et al. 2019). Response facilitation occurred with both inflected primes (e.g., *sorar–sor* 'asks' – 'to ask') and derived primes (e.g., '*sağlık–sağ*' 'health' – 'healthy'), similar to prototypical native speakers. This suggested the heritage speakers engaged in very rapid morphological decomposition of the primes.

A second approach to the processing of functional morphology is to examine the role of case inflections in lexical processing. For example, Gor et al. (2019) reported faster lexical decisions for (written) nouns with nominal case than genitive or instrumental case, among heritage speakers of Russian in the United States, L2 learners, and prototypical native speakers, an effect referred to as the *citation form advantage* (also with nominative vs. oblique case, Gor et al. 2018). However, a second, frequency-based effect occurred with the other two groups but not with the heritage speakers: Faster RTs were seen with genitive inflected nouns than with instrumental ones. Gor and colleagues proposed that this was due to a lack of formal instruction in Russian, because the case system is more ambiguous in speech than in writing. In a related study, Gor et al. (2018) found that both heritage speakers and L2 learners of Russian were inclined to accept nonwords that were created by illegally combining a real noun from one declension with a case inflection from another declension as words. Error rates were over 50 percent, although the performance of the highest proficiency participants was similar to that of the prototypical native speakers. Thus, even though heritage speakers appear able to decompose morphologically complex words into parts during processing, they can still be lacking in their knowledge of functional morphology, particularly with lower proficiency.

18.4   Sentence Processing

Sentence processing, or parsing, is a general process of identification of the component elements of a sentence and their grammatical relation to one another in language comprehension. HL bilingual sentence processing, a field that is still in its infancy, focuses on the changes that happen in the comprehension of a heritage L1 in comparison to monolingual processing, and factors that cause these changes, of which competition from the dominant language is just one. From the point of view of methodology, HL sentence processing is dominated by the *acceptability judgment task* (Table 18.1 (8)), whose suitability for HL speakers is debated (Orfitelly and Polinsky 2017). The AJT constraints – engaging in metacognition regarding one's linguistic performance, a written modality that requires literacy, and complex and lengthy materials – may put HL speakers at a disadvantage, particularly those with lower proficiency in the language or with limited literacy. There is also a small, but growing number of reaction time, self-paced reading, and eye-tracking studies of HLs, and little neuroimaging research so far.

In the remainder of this chapter, we will sample HL sentence processing studies of morphosyntax of nominal (i.e., gender and case) and verbal categories (aspect) (Section 18.4.1) and related syntactic phenomena of long-distance dependencies and word order (Section 18.4.2). We will complete the chapter by illustrating the interaction between linguistic domains at interfaces and in discourse (i.e., evidentiality, definiteness, negation, scope, and topic/focus) (Section 18.5).

18.4.1 Processing of Morphosyntax

Errors in production and misinterpretation of morphosyntactic information in comprehension are pervasive in many HLs, from morphologically impoverished ones like English (omission of number and overproduction of past tense, Polinsky 2018) to the ones with a fair amount of morphological complexity (e.g., Spanish, German, Korean), to morphologically rich and complex ones (e.g., Russian, Hindi, Inuttitut). Difficulties are found in nominal and verbal morphology, but, interestingly, not every grammatical category is equally affected.

Grammatical gender has been an especially fertile ground, with many experimental studies conducted in Spanish, Italian, and Russian. These languages differ in their gender assignment systems and gender agreement between the noun and articles and adjectives. For Spanish (Montrul 2011; Montrul and Foote 2014; Montrul et al. 2014) and Italian as HLs (Bianchi 2013), the acceptance of sentences with gender agreement violations have been attributed to extra-linguistic factors, such as age of acquisition, proficiency, language experience, literacy, metalinguistic awareness, and methodological tasks. For Russian as an HL, Polinsky (2008, 2018) proposed that heritage speakers make gender errors as a consequence of the linguistic (re)structuring of the Russian HL grammar from the 3-gender baseline to the 2-gender system. Proficiency, however, can protect from this structural shrinkage: Advanced Russian HL speakers in Laleko's (2018) study provided acceptability judgments that were indistinguishable from the native speakers. For Spanish as an HL, Polinsky and colleagues (Scontras et al. 2017) argue that errors are explained by the fact that MASC becomes the default gender, making it a single-valued system; Spanish number is also restructured to a single value. Thus, there is a general tendency for simplification in HL grammars in favor of single-valued grammatical categories in which gender and number systems are then bundled together.

While gender errors are characteristic of many Romance HLs, case in the nominal system is a fundamental grammatical category in a wide variety of typologically diverse languages. Polinsky (2011, 2018) has described shrinkage of the 6-case Russian system to two cases (NOM and ACC) in intermediate Russian HL speakers' production. However, in comprehension, the picture is more nuanced. Montrul and colleagues (Montrul, Bhatia, Bhatt, and Puri 2019) described unstable acceptability judgments for two case markers -ne and -ko in Hindi, which has a complex split-ergativity case system. Because heritage Hindi speakers seemed unsure about the effects of numerous constraints on the distribution of these case markers, the authors suggested that the uncertainty in acceptability judgments revealed the differential effects of language dominance; amount of exposure and current use of Hindi; syntactic and semantic complexity; and transfer from the dominant English, which does not have case.

Erosion of case markers can have serious implications for sentence processing, as the two closely interact with each other. For instance, in Spanish, indirect objects of ditransitive verbs, animate and specific direct objects, and objects of *psych*-verbs must be marked with the preposition *a*, a phenomenon referred to as *Differential Object Marking (DOM)*. In a written AJT, Montrul and Bowles (2009) found that Spanish HL speakers judged all types of the ungrammatical sentences with the omitted DOM as grammatical significantly more than the native speakers regardless of their proficiency level. An AJT, however, does not tell us much about whether HL speakers actually notice the missing DOM *a* as they are reading the sentence. After all, acceptability judgments are rendered offline, after the processing of a sentence is completed.

To test the potential dissociation between online and offline processing of DOM, Jegerski (2018b) used a self-paced reading task (Table 18.1 (8)) and tested three types of Spanish sentences similar to the ones from Montrul and Bowles (2009), i.e., ditransitive and transitive with inanimate or animate direct objects. While the timed but offline grammaticality judgments replicated the previous AJT findings (sensitivity to the marking of indirect objects in ditransitive sentences vs. a lack thereof in DOM constructions), reading times (RTs) revealed a more nuanced differentiation, with a robust grammaticality effect (i.e., longer RTs) for the ungrammatical segment in ditransitive sentences, a weaker effect for DOM with inanimate direct objects, and no effect for DOM with animate direct objects. Jegerski and Sekerina (2020), who employed Visual World eye-tracking (Table 18.1 (10)), demonstrated that Spanish HL speakers could actually notice the DOM *a* on animate objects if the modality of presentation is auditory, and the stimuli are questions that attract the participants' attention to the marker *a*, which appears at the beginning.

As far as verbal morphosyntax is concerned, there are a few pockets of resilient knowledge of such grammatical categories as tense and person (Polinsky 2018) and considerable variability with others like aspect and voice. In a rare empirical study of heritage Labrador Inuttitut, an Eskimo-Aleut language spoken in Canada, Sherkina-Lieber (2015) tested receptive Inuttitut adults and found that highly proficient participants were indistinguishable from a control group of balanced bilinguals in their knowledge of tense (although a special feature of remoteness of the described event was less target-like). Surprisingly, they also showed a relatively good comprehension of pluractional and ingressive aspectual forms, as well as object–verb person agreement in the indicative mood. These results were unexpected given that in well-studied Russian as an HL, aspect is more vulnerable; several comprehension studies of aspect with Russian HL speakers revealed a range of differences in processing of imperfective, perfective, and secondary imperfective forms (*šil* 'sewed-IMP'– *zašil* 'sewed-PERF' – *zašival* 'was sewing-IMP'), with different methods and diverse HL groups.

For instance, Pereltsvaig (2005) found that for low-proficiency HL speakers, most verbs were frozen in either imperfective or perfective forms, demonstrating loss of productivity in the aspectual system. In contrast, Laleko's (2011) high-proficiency speakers judged the perfective form as significantly better than the native speakers, who preferred the general-factual imperfective form with completed events. Laleko took this as evidence of restructuring of the aspectual system from the baseline single-valued [+aspect] to a less ambiguous two-valued [+/-aspect]. Mikhaylova (2018) discovered many subtle differences between her advanced HL and native speakers in two tasks, selecting a continuation for a sentence and the stop-making-sense task. HL speakers found the imperfective forms less preferred and less noticeable than the perfective ones. Finally, Dragoy, Virfel, Yurchenko, and Bastiaanse (2019) tested Russian-German bilinguals, with either an earlier age of onset of 6–10 years or a later one of 12–15, on the detection of aspect violations. The later bilinguals were indistinguishable from native speakers, whereas the early bilinguals detected significantly fewer violations. Thus, regardless of the manipulation, task, and group, all the reviewed studies on the processing of aspect in Russian HL confirmed both the general tendency of the imperfective being a more vulnerable form than the perfective, and the effect of input quantity.

18.4.2 Processing of Syntactic Dependencies

Syntactic dependencies are relations between elements in a clause or across clauses, determined by the syntactic properties of those elements and the structures in which they occur. In syntactic dependencies with movement, also known as *filler–gap dependencies*, one element called *a filler* appears to have moved to a position in the sentence different from where it originated, referred to as *a gap*. Filler–gap dependencies that have been studied in HL processing include, but are not limited to, relative clauses, *wh*-questions, and islands in Spanish, Korean, Russian, and Dutch. Interestingly, in contrast to the vulnerability of morphology in HLs, filler–gap dependencies are much more resilient, especially in the cases when they are similar in the HL and the dominant language.

The difference in processing between subject and object relative clauses (RC) has been long established for many languages and methods, with subject RCs being easier to process. In Korean (O'Grady et al. 2011) and Russian, the correct interpretation of subject and object RCs depends on knowledge of case and word order, and the former is vulnerable in HLs. Polinsky (2011) found that while Russian HL adults of intermediate proficiency interpreted 90 percent of subject RCs correctly in a sentence–picture matching test, it happened only on 44 percent of trials with object RCs, regardless of word order. She argued that this lack of word order effect is evidence against transfer from the dominant language (English). Polinsky instead suggested once again (as in the case of grammatical gender) that there is restructuring of the HL system in which, in contrast to the native Russian, only subject arguments can undergo relativization.

Absence of transfer from the dominant English in HL sentence processing has been found with two other syntactic phenomena, namely, RC attachment ambiguity in Spanish as an HL and island constraints in Korean as an HL. Globally ambiguous Spanish sentences of the type *Alguien disparó contra el criado de la actriz que estaba en el balcón* 'Somebody shot the servant$_{MASC}$ of the actress who was on the balcony' demonstrate an NP1 (high) RC attachment preference. If a pragmatically disambiguating PP *con su marido* 'with her husband' is added, RC attachment has to change to NP2 (low). This construction occupies a unique place in sentence processing as it is the only known one in which universal low attachment (Frazier and Fodor 1978) differs cross-linguistically: Spanish is high- while English is low-attaching. However, the high attachment preference in late Spanish L1-English L2 bilinguals can become low if their Spanish becomes less dominant and the amount of exposure to English supersedes that of Spanish (Dussias 2003; Dussias and Sagarra 2007).

Jegerski, Keating, and VanPatten (2016) asked high proficiency Mexican Spanish HL speakers to read sentences disambiguated for high or low attachment using self-paced reading (Table 18.1 (8)) and found that their offline comprehension was better and their RTs were faster for the high-attaching than low-attaching conditions. Even Spanish HL speakers with intermediate proficiency tested by Jegerski (2018c) preferred high attachment, although only in offline comprehension. Korean HL speakers from Kim and Goodall's (2016) study also behaved just like native speakers: They accepted extraction out of adjunct islands as grammatical and rejected extraction out of *wh*-islands as ungrammatical even though the former are not allowed in English. In contrast, Cuza (2012) showed that Spanish HL speakers can experience difficulties in several types of *wh*-questions whose formation in Spanish is different from English. Thus, most studies (e.g., RC attachment ambiguity and island constraints vs. *wh*-questions formation) confirm the possible absence of transfer of processing strategies from the dominant English and suggest that processing of some syntactic dependencies can be preserved in HLs (Polinsky and Scontras 2020).

18.5   Beyond the Sentence: Semantics, Discourse, and Interfaces

When language is mapped onto a conceptual system, the resulting semantic representations correspond to words or sentences (or larger units of language). In this final section, we focus on processing that involves the construction of semantic representations and interface-based phenomena by heritage speakers. While the review of the published research on heritage languages has revealed vulnerability in the area of functional morphology (Section 18.4.1) and relative resilience in the domain of syntax (Section 18.4.2), very little is known whether heritage speakers maintain the semantic, discourse, and interface distinctions between their HL and the dominant language. In her review, Polinsky (2018) notes that research on HL above the sentence level is rather limited. Thus, our description will by necessity be limited to empirical studies of selected topics, such as definiteness, negation, anaphora, evidentiality, focus, quantifiers, and contrastiveness.

18.5.1   Definiteness, Negation, and Anaphora

Kupisch et al. (2017) investigated knowledge of the definiteness effect in HL Turkish-German speakers. Turkish negative existential sentences with verb *yok* 'not.exist' allow definitive DPs, but the equivalent German sentences do not. HL Turkish participants' accuracy in judging German sentences was indistinguishable from the control native speakers and there was no transfer of the restriction on definite DPs from German to HL Turkish.

Nonetheless, their acceptance of such DPs in Turkish was lower, demonstrating that HL speakers did experience some cross-linguistic influence. This suggests that HL speakers' semantic knowledge can be quite stable. However, when definiteness interacts with another semantic feature such as specificity, the complexity that results from this interaction may lead to difficulty in the acquisition of definiteness, as Montrul and Ionin (2012) demonstrated. They found that HL Spanish participants incorrectly accepted bare plural subjects in generic contexts and preferred specific interpretation of definite plurals in HL Spanish as a result of transfer from their dominant English (Table 18.1, (6)–(7)). Variability in the knowledge of definiteness was also reported by Chung (2018) in a study of case marker omission by HL Korean speakers.

Albirini and Benmamoun (2015) investigated difficulties HL speakers experience in their heritage language at the syntax–semantics interface, in addition to the well-established factors of age of acquisition and proficiency. In their AJT study of sentential negation in heritage Egyptian Arabic (Exp. 3), HL Arabic speakers correctly accepted the grammatical word order variations and rejected the ungrammatical ones in sentences with the discontinuous negation marker *ma-š*, but they accepted significantly more ungrammatical sentences with the two-part negation with the enclitic *š* than the native speakers. The authors attributed this unstable performance to the complexity of negation in Arabic and to the participants' switch to English dominance before some types of negation had a chance to be acquired.

The acquisition and processing of anaphoric expressions such as reflexive and personal pronouns is yet another area where HL speakers exhibit large variability. Kim and colleagues (2009) tested the knowledge of three types of Korean reflexive pronouns and their combinations and showed that early and late HL Korean participants' preferences for local or long-distance binding varied depending on the type of the pronoun, age of arrival, and proficiency level, with early HL speakers clearly differing from the native and late HL groups. In this case, the standard three-way contrast among *caki, casin*, and *caki+casin* was reduced to only two, similar to the restructuring of the grammatical gender system found in HL Spanish and Russian (Polinsky 2018). In a self-paced reading study (Table 18.1, (7)), Keating, Jegerski, and VanPatten (2016) investigated the antecedent assignment strategies that HL Spanish used for ambiguous overt and null subject pronouns, which are subject to different discourse constraints. Both Mexican Spanish native and HL Spanish readers preferred and were faster in linking null pronouns in one clause to a subject antecedent in the previous clause. In contrast, only native controls were faster in assigning overt pronouns to object antecedents and heritage speakers appeared to follow the subject bias from their dominant English.

18.5.2 Interfaces: Evidentiality, Quantifiers, Focus, and Contrastiveness

Interface phenomena, namely, phenomena whose acquisition requires simultaneous application of knowledge from the linguistic system and cognitive domains (e.g., syntax/discourse) or between different linguistic levels (e.g., syntax/semantics) (White 2011) have been claimed to be problematic for bilinguals. Similar observations have been made in first language acquisition (Grinstead 2010), leading perhaps to noticeable deficits in this area in HL speakers for whom HL development slowed down in childhood.

Turkish encodes the evidentiality of events with a special suffix on the verb, i.e., -*DI* when somebody witnessed an event first-hand or -*mIş* when the event is indirectly reported. Arslan et al. (2015) investigated the processing of evidentiality in HL Turkish speakers using the Visual World eye-tracking paradigm (Table 18.1, (10)). Previous offline studies had revealed insensitivity to evidentiality in this population. In offline and online measures, both early and late HL Turkish speakers were less accurate, slower in selecting the target picture, and looked at it less in the direct evidentiality condition with -*DI* than the native controls. No such differences were found among the three groups in the indirect evidentiality condition. The authors' proposed explanation was a restructuring of the evidentiality system in HL Turkish, in which the direct evidential suffix has become a marker of both types of evidentiality contexts.

Quantification presents yet another interface-based phenomenon associated with variability. Lee (2011) and Fukuda (2017) tested whether HL speakers of Japanese and Korean, respectively, knew the differences in licensing of float quantifiers by unaccusative and unergative verbs. The former participants were indistinguishable from native speakers, whereas the HL Korean ones showed an age of acquisition effect, with only the late group being close to the native controls. HL Mandarin speakers accepted the inverse scope interpretation for sentences with quantifier-scope ambiguities such as *A shark attacked every pirate* at rates different from either of the two native groups: higher than the Mandarin natives that did not allow it and lower than the English native controls that did. Scontras and colleagues (2017) concluded that it was a yes-bias rather than cross-linguistic influence that explained the HL speakers' acceptance of inverse scope stems. Ronai (2018) also showed absence of the inverse scope, not only in HL Hungarian speakers (as expected because Hungarian, like Mandarin, does not allow scope ambiguities) but also in HL English speakers, who lost the inverse scope available in native English.

Finally, Sekerina and Sauermann (2015) compared the processing of sentences with the quantifier *every* (e.g., *Every alligator is in a bathtub*) in native Russian adults, children, and HL Russian adults using the Visual World eye-tracking paradigm. Participants saw pictures of three pairs of alligators in bathtubs with either two elephants (control condition) or two extra bathtubs (overexhaustive condition). Although the children made many more errors in the overexhaustive condition known as *q-spreading* (35 percent), HL Russian adults were closer to them (20 percent errors) than to the native adults (at ceiling). Eye-movement analysis revealed that both groups looked more to the extra bathtubs, possibly as a result of processing overload as they struggled to integrate the spoken sentences in their weaker HL and an attention-demanding visual context.

Our final example of how HL speakers deal with interface-based phenomena comes from the area of information structure, namely, focus and contrastiveness. Hoot (2017, 2019) investigated knowledge of presentational focus in HL Spanish and narrow identificational focus in HL Hungarian and showed a proficiency effect, with no difference between the high proficiency HL speakers and the native controls, and some variability in AJT results for the low proficiency HL speakers. In general, regardless of proficiency, the HL speakers patterned with the native speakers with regard to acceptability judgments of focus realization in syntax, but low-proficiency ones differed slightly in focus interpretation. Interestingly, in both studies, the HL participants were especially sensitive to the prosodic realization of focus with emphatic stress. However, in Sekerina and Trueswell's (2011) Visual World eye-tracking study, HL Russian listeners were much slower than native listeners to look at the target noun with color adjective-noun phrases embedded in split-constituent constructions like *Krasnuju položite zvezdočku...* 'Red put star...'. The inherent contrastiveness of this construction requires the integration of multiple sources of information (i.e., word order, prosody, and visual context) and the HL participants were unable to rapidly take notice of all of them to engage in predictive processing.

18.6   Conclusion and Future Directions

This chapter has provided a selective review of psycholinguistic research on heritage languages in the areas of speech perception and production, lexical and morphological processing, sentence processing, and processing at levels higher than the sentence. We have seen that heritage speakers are relatively understudied in psycholinguistics, compared to other populations of language users, so there are many possible avenues for future research. One notable gap was in the area of lexical and morphological processing, where we are aware of fewer than ten published studies that go beyond global lexical access, and some of these included heritage speakers only incidentally in research that was not explicitly focused on heritage language. There have also been very few studies so far using real-time psycholinguistic and neurolinguistic research methods like eye-tracking, self-paced reading, and

EEG (electroencephalography). Scholars have begun to recognize that some of the more traditional research methods may not be optimal for heritage speakers, yet very little research has been conducted to compare different methods to each other (e.g., Montrul et al. 2014; Jegerski and Keating 2018). In addition to these gaps in the current body of research, some current theoretical questions from mainstream and L2 psycholinguistics that might be worth exploring with heritage speakers include predictive processing (Kaan 2014), cue-based memory retrieval (Cunnings 2017), and the impact of the bilingual mental lexicon on morphosyntax and other sentence-processing phenomena (Hopp 2017). As we hope has been evident in this chapter, the fields of psycholinguistics and heritage languages fit well together and future research that combines the two has the potential to inform both areas.

References

Albirini, A. and E. Benmamoun. 2015. Factors Affecting the Retention of Sentential Negation in Heritage Egyptian Arabic. *Bilingualism: Language and Cognition* 18(3), 470–489.

Arslan, S., R. Bastiaanse, and C. Felser. 2015. Looking at Evidence in Visual World: Eye-movements Reveal How Bilingual and Monolingual Turkish Speakers Process Grammatical Evidentiality. *Frontiers in Psychology* 6, Art. 1387. https://doi.org/10.3389/fpsyg.2015.01387

Basnight-Brown, D. M. and J. Altarriba. 2007. Differences in Semantic and Translation Priming across Languages: The Role of Language Direction and Language Dominance. *Memory and Cognition* 35(5), 953–965.

Benmamoun, E., S. Montrul, and M. Polinsky. 2013. Heritage Languages and Their Speakers: Opportunities and Challenges for Linguistics. *Theoretical Linguistics* 46, 129–181.

Bianchi, J. 2013. Gender in Italian-German Bilinguals: A comparison with German L2 Learners of Italian. *Bilingualism: Language and Cognition* 16(3), 538–557.

Canseco-González, E., L. Brehm, C. A. Brick, S. Brown-Schmidt, K. Fischer, K. Wagner. 2010. Carpet or Cárcel: The Effect of Age of Acquisition and Language Mode on Bilingual Lexical Access. *Language and Cognitive Processes* 25(5), 669–705.

Chang, C. B. 2016. Bilingual Perceptual Benefits of Experience with a Heritage Language. *Bilingualism: Language and Cognition* 19(4), 791–809.

Chang, C. B., E. F. Haynes, Y. Yao, and R. Rhodes. 2009. A Tale of Five Fricatives: Consonantal Contrast in Heritage Speakers of Mandarin. *University of Pennsylvania Working Papers in Linguistics* 15, 37–43.

Chang, C. B., E. F. Haynes, Y. Yao, and R. Rhodes. 2010. The Phonetic Space of Phonological Categories in Heritage Speakers of Mandarin. In M. Bane,

J. Bueno, T. Grano, A. Grotberg, and Y. McNabb (eds.), *Proceedings from the 44th Annual Meeting of the Chicago Linguistic Society: The Main Session.* Chicago: Chicago Linguistic Society, 31–45.

Chang, C. B., E. F. Haynes, Y. Yao, and R. Rhodes. 2011. Production of Phonetic and Phonological Contrast by Heritage Speakers of Mandarin. *Journal of the Acoustical Society of America* 129(6), 3964–3980.

Chung, E. S. 2018. Second and Heritage Language Acquisition of Korean Case Drop. *Bilingualism: Language and Cognition* 21(1), 63–79.

Clahsen, H., C. Felser, K. Neubauer, M. Sato, and R. Silva. 2010. Morphological Structure in Native and Nonnative Language Processing. *Language Learning* 60, 21–43.

Cunnings, I. 2017. Parsing and Working Memory in Bilingual Sentence Processing. *Bilingualism: Language and Cognition* 20(4), 659–678.

Cuza, A. 2012. Cross-Linguistic Influence at the Syntax Proper: Interrogative Subject-Verb Inversion in Heritage Spanish. *International Journal of Bilingualism* 17(1), 71–96.

Davis, C., R. Sánchez-Casas, J. E. Garcia-Albea, M. Guasch, M. Molero, and P. Ferré. 2010. Masked Translation Priming: Varying Language Experience and Word Type with Spanish–English Bilinguals. *Bilingualism: Language and Cognition* 13(2), 137–155.

Dragoy, O., E. Virfel, A. Yurchenko, and R. Bastiaanse. 2019. Aspect and Tense Attrition in Russian-German Bilingual Speakers. *International Journal of Bilingualism* 23(1), 275–295.

Dussias, P. E. 2003. Syntactic Ambiguity Resolution in Second Language Learners: Some Effects of Bilinguality on L1 and L2 Processing Strategies. *Studies in Second Language Acquisition* 25, 529–557.

Dussias, P. E. and N. Sagarra. 2007. The Effect of Exposure on Parsing in Spanish-English Bilinguals. *Bilingualism: Language and Cognition* 10, 101–116.

Frazier, L. and J. D. Fodor. 1978. The Sausage Machine: A New Two-Stage Parsing Model. *Cognition* 6(4), 291–325.

Fukuda, S. 2017. Floating Numeral Quantifiers as an Unaccusative Diagnostic in Native, Heritage, and L2 Japanese Speakers. *Language Acquisition* 24(3), 169–208.

Godson, L. 2004. Vowel Production in the Speech of Western Armenian Heritage Speakers. *Heritage Language Journal* 2, 44–69.

Gollan, T. H., R. I. Montoya, C. Cera, and T. C. Sandoval. 2008. More Use Almost Always Means a Smaller Frequency Effect: Aging, Bilingualism, and the Weaker Links Hypothesis. *Journal of Memory and Language* 58, 787–814.

Gollan, T. H., E. R. Schotter, J. Gomez, M. Murillo, and K. Rayner. 2014. Multiple Levels of Bilingual Language Control: Evidence from Language Intrusions in Reading Aloud. *Psychological Science* 25, 585–595.

Gor, K. 2014. Raspberry, Not a Car: Context Predictability and a Phonological Advantage in Early and Late Learners' Processing of Speech in Noise. *Frontiers in Psychology* 5, Art. 1449.

Gor, K. 2018. Yes to the King, and No To the ship: Heritage Speakers Differ from Late Second Language Learners in Word Recognition. In S. Kresin and S. Baukus (eds.), *Connecting across Languages and Cultures: A Heritage Language Festschrift in Honor of Olga Kagan*. Bloomington, IN: Slavica Publishers, 163–172.

Gor, K. and S. Cook. 2010. Nonnative Processing of Verbal Morphology: In Search of Regularity. *Language Learning* 60(1), 88–126.

Gor, K., A. Chrabaszcz, and S. Cook. 2018. Early and Late Learners Decompose Inflected Nouns, but Can They Tell Which Ones Are Inflected Correctly? *Journal of Second Language Studies* 1, 113–147.

Gor, K., A. Chrabaszcz, and S. Cook. 2019. A Case for Agreement: Processing of Case Inflection by Early and Late Learners. *Linguistic Approaches to Bilingualism* 9(1), 6–41.

Grinstead, J. 2010. Linguistic Interfaces and Child Spanish. In L. Domínguez and P. Guijarro-Fuentes (eds.), *Proceedings of the Romance Turn 3*. Newcastle: Cambridge Scholars Publishing, 189–218.

Hoot, B. 2017. Narrow Presentational Focus in Heritage Spanish and the Syntax–Discourse Interface. *Linguistic Approaches to Bilingualism* 7, 63–95.

Hoot, B. 2019. Focus in Heritage Hungarian. *Language Acquisition* 26(1), 46–72.

Hopp, H. 2017. Individual Differences in L2 Parsing and Lexical Representations. *Bilingualism: Language and Cognition* 20(4), 689–690.

Hrycyna, M., N. Lapinskaya, A. Kochetoz, and N. Nagy. 2011. VOT Drift in 3 Generations of Heritage Language Speakers in Toronto. *Canadian Acoustics* 39, 166–167.

Hulsen, M. 2000. Language Loss and Language Processing: Three Generations of Dutch Migrants in New Zealand. Doctoral Dissertation, University of Nijmegen, The Netherlands.

Jacob, G. and B. Kirkici. 2016. The Processing of Morphologically Complex Words in a Specific Speaker Group: A Masked-priming Study with Turkish Heritage Speakers. *The Mental Lexicon* 11(2), 308.

Jacob, G., D. F. Safak, O. Demir, and B. Kikici. 2019. Preserved Morphological Processing in Heritage Speakers: A Masked Priming Study on Turkish. *Second Language Research* 35(2), 173–194.

Jegerski, J. 2018a. Psycholinguistic Perspectives on Spanish as a Heritage Language. In K. Potowski (ed.), *Routledge Handbook of Spanish as a Heritage/ Minority Language*. New York: Routledge, 221–234.

Jegerski, J. 2018b. The Processing of the Object Marker *a* by Heritage Spanish Speakers. *International Journal of Bilingualism* 22(6), 585–602.

Jegerski, J. 2018c. Sentence Processing in Spanish as a Heritage Language: Relative Clause Attachment in Early Bilinguals. *Language Learning* 68(3), 598–634.

Jegerski, J. and G. D. Keating. 2018, October. *Processing Difficulty in Heritage Bilingual Sentence Comprehension: A Comparison of Self-Paced Reading and*

Eyetracking. Paper presented at the Bilingualism Forum, University of Illinois at Chicago.

Jegerski, J. and B. VanPatten (eds.) 2014. *Research Methods in Second Language Psycholinguistics*. New York: Routledge.

Jegerski, J. and I. A. Sekerina. 2020. The Processing of Input with Differential Object Marking by Heritage Spanish Speakers. *Bilingualism: Language and Cognition* 23(2), 274–282.

Jegerski, J., G. D. Keating, and B. VanPatten. 2016. On-line Relative Clause Attachment Strategy in Heritage Speakers of Spanish. *International Journal of Bilingualism* 20(3), 254–268.

Kaan, E. 2014. Predictive Sentence Processing in L2 and L2. What Is Different? *Linguistic Approaches to Bilingualism* 4, 257–282.

Keating, G. D. and J. Jegerski. 2015. Experimental Designs in Sentence Processing Research: A Methodological Review and User's Guide. *Studies in Second Language Acquisition* 37(1), 1–32.

Keating, G. D., J. Jegerski, and B. VanPatten. 2016. Online Processing of Subject Pronouns in Monolingual and Heritage Bilingual Speakers of Mexican Spanish. *Bilingualism: Language and Cognition* 19(1), 36–49.

Kim, B. and G. Goodall. 2016. Islands and Non-islands in Native and Heritage Korean. *Frontiers in Psychology* 7, Art. 134. https://doi.org/10.3389/fpsyg.2016.00134

Kim, J.-Y. 2015. Perception and Production of Spanish Lexical Stress by Spanish Heritage Speakers and English L2 Learners of Spanish, In E. Willis, P. Martín Butragueño, and E. Herrera Zendejas (eds.), *Proceedings of the 6th Conference on Laboratory Approaches to Romance Phonology*. Somerville, MA: Cascadilla Press, 106–128.

Kim, J.-H., S. Montrul, and J. Yoon. 2009. Binding Interpretation of Anaphors by Korean Heritage Speakers. *Language Acquisition* 16, 3–35.

Kuperberg, G. R. and T. F. Jaeger. 2016. What Do We Mean by Prediction in Language Comprehension? *Language, Cognition and Neuroscience* 31(1), 32–59.

Kupisch, T., A. Belikova, Ö. Özçelik, I. Stangen, and L. White. 2017. Restrictions on Definiteness in the Grammars of German-Turkish Heritage Speakers. *Linguistic Approaches to Bilingualism* 7, 1–32.

Laleko, O. 2011. Restructuring of Verbal Aspect in Heritage Russian: Beyond Lexicalization. *International Journal of Language Studies* 5(3), 13–26.

Laleko, O. 2018. What Is Difficult about Grammatical Gender? Evidence from Heritage Russian. *Journal of Language Contact* 11, 233–267.

Lee, T. 2011. Grammatical Knowledge of Korean Heritage Speakers. Early vs. Late Bilinguals. *Linguistic Approaches to Bilingualism* 1, 149–174.

Lukyanchenko, A. and K. Gor. 2011. Perceptual Correlates of Phonological Representations in Heritage Speakers and L2 Learners. In *Proceedings of the 35th Annual Boston University Conference on Language Development*. Somerville, MA: Cascadilla Press, 414–426.

Marslen-Wilson, W. 2007. Morphological Processes in Language Comprehension. In G. Gaskell (ed.), *The Oxford Handbook of Psycholinguistics*. Oxford: Oxford University Press, 175–193.

Mikhaylova, A. 2018. Morphological Bottleneck: The Case of Russian Heritage Speakers. *Journal of Language Contact* 11, 268–303.

Momma, S. and C. Phillips. 2018. The Relationship between Parsing and Generation. *Annual Review of Linguistics* 4, 233–254.

Montrul, S. 2011. Morphological Errors in Spanish Second Language Learners and Heritage Speakers. *Studies in Second Language Acquisition* 33 (2), 155–161.

Montrul, S. 2016. *The Acquisition of Heritage Languages*. Cambridge: Cambridge University Press.

Montrul, S, and M. Bowles. 2009. Back to Basics: Differential Object Marking under Incomplete Acquisition in Spanish Heritage Speakers. *Bilingualism: Language and Cognition* 12(4), 363–383.

Montrul, S. and R. Foote. 2014. Age of Acquisition Interactions in Bilingual Lexical Access: A Study of the Weaker Language of L2 Learners and Heritage Speakers. *The International Journal of Bilingualism* 18(3), 274–303.

Montrul, S. and T. Ionin. 2012. Dominant Language Transfer in Spanish Heritage Speakers and L2 Learners in the Interpretation of Definite Articles. *The Modern Language Journal* 96(1), 70–94.

Montrul, S., A. Bhatia, R. Bhatt, and V. Puri. 2019. Case Marking in Hindi as a Weaker Language. *Frontiers in Psychology* 10, Art. 461. doi: 10.3389/fpsyg .2019.00461.

Montrul, S., J. Davidson, I. de la Fuente, and R. Foote. 2014. Early Language Experience Facilitates Gender Agreement Processing in Spanish Heritage Speakers. *Bilingualism: Language and Cognition* 17(1), 118–138.

O'Grady, W., A. Schafer, J. Perla, O.-S. Lee, and J. Wieting. 2009. A Psycholinguistic Tool for the Assessment of Language Loss: The HALA Project. *Language Documentation and Conservation* 3, 100–112.

O'Grady, W., H.-Y. Kwak, O.-S. Lee, and M. Lee. 2011. An Emergentist Perspective on Heritage Language Acquisition. *Studies in Second Language Acquisition* 33, 223–245.

Orfitelly, R. and M. Polinsky. 2013. Is It All Processing All the Way Down? *Linguistic Approaches to Bilingualism* 3(3), 335–340.

Pereltsvaig, A. 2005. Aspect Lost, Aspect Regained. Restructuring of Aspectual Marking in American Russian. In P. Kempchinsky and R. Slabakova (eds.), *Aspectual Inquiries*. Berlin: Springer, 369–395.

Pickering, M. J. and C. Gambi. 2018. Predicting While Comprehending Language: A Theory and Review. *Psychological Bulletin* 144(10), 1002–1044.

Polinsky, M. 2008. Russian Gender under Incomplete Acquisition. *Heritage Language Journal* 6(1), 40–71.

Polinsky, M. 2011. Reanalysis in Adult Heritage Language. *Studies in Second Language Acquisition* 33, 305–328.

Polinsky, M. 2018. *Heritage Languages and Their Speakers*. Cambridge: Cambridge University Press.

Polinsky, M. and O. Kagan. 2007. Heritage Languages: In the 'Wild' and in the Classroom. *Language and Linguistics Compass* 1(5), 368–395.

Polinsky, M. and G. Scontras. 2020. Understanding Heritage Languages. *Bilingualism: Language and Cognition* 23, 4–20.

Ronai, E. 2018. Quantifier Scope in Heritage Bilinguals: A Comparative Experimental Study. In S. Hucklebidge and M. Nelson (eds.), *NELS 48: Proceedings of the 48th Annual Meeting of the North East Linguistic Society*. Vol. 2. 29–38. GLSA, 29–38.

Scontras, G., M. Polinsky, C.-Y. E. Tsai, and K. Mai. 2017. Cross-Linguistic Scope Ambiguity: When Two Systems Meet. *Glossa* 2(1), 36, 1–28.

Sekerina, I. A. and A. Sauermann. 2015. Visual Attention and Quantifier-Spreading in Heritage Russian Bilinguals. *Second Language Research* 31(1), 75–104.

Sekerina, I. A. and J. C. Trueswell. 2011. Processing of Contrastiveness by Heritage Russian Bilinguals. *Bilingualism: Language and Cognition* 14(3), 280–300.

Sekerina, I. A., E. M. Fernández, and H. Clahsen (eds.) 2008. *Developmental Psycholinguistics: Online Methods in Children's Language Processing*. Amsterdam: John Benjamins.

Sherkina-Lieber, M. 2015. Tense, Aspect, and Agreement in Heritage Labrador Inuttitut. Do Receptive Bilinguals Understand Functional Morphology? *Linguistic Approaches to Bilingualism* 5(1), 30–61.

Silverberg, S. and A. G. Samuel. 2004. The Effect of Age of Second Language Acquisition on the Representation and Processing of Second Language Words. *Journal of Memory and Language* 51, 381–398.

White, L. 2011. Second Language Acquisition at the Interfaces. *Lingua* 121, 577–590.

19

Contact Linguistics and Heritage Languages

Itxaso Rodríguez-Ordóñez and Lorena Sainzmaza-Lecanda

19.1 Introduction

Uriel Weinreich, along with Joshua Fishman and Einar Haugen, sparked an interest in the study of heritage languages along with their speakers, forging the path of understanding language from a multilingual angle. Weinreich, the grandfather of contact linguistics, argued that the locus of language contact is the bilingual individual[1] and that theorizing about the behavior of such speakers needs to consider the interplay between "purely structural considerations [...] psychological reasons [...] and socio-cultural factors" (Weinreich 1953: 44). The bilingual individual is, nonetheless, a social creature who lives as part of a much larger network of social interactions and it is through these interactions that contact phenomena diffuse.

Among subsequent theorizations of language contact, Thomason and Kaufman (1988) presented a typology of borrowability based on two general kinds of language contact situations: *language maintenance* and *interference via language shift*. Heritage speakers,[2] broadly defined as individuals who are exposed to a minoritized language at home and who subsequently become dominant in the majority language of their social environment, do not clearly fit this shift vs. language maintenance dichotomy. Despite showing patterns of language shift to the dominant language, they also possess

---

[1] The same applies to the multilingual speaker. Here, both terms are used interchangeably.

[2] Debates still abound regarding what it means to be a heritage speaker. Some authors consider the minority status of the language as a principal criterion, including thus, speakers of national minoritized languages (i.e., Basque in Spain and France, Welsh in Wales) or indigenous languages (i.e. Nahuatl in Mexico, Navajo in the United States, Dyirbal in Australia) (Montrul 2016). In this chapter, we assume a narrower definition of heritage languages in reference to second-generation speakers (and beyond) but also bring a few examples from other minoritized languages. For a discussion see Valdés (2000), Benmamoun et al. (2013), Putnam and Sánchez (2013).

rule-governed repertoires that may allow them to achieve communicative goals in their respective communities. Like in any other contact situation, heritage speakers' linguistic repertoires change over time and are governed by the myriad factors that come with living in any society (i.e., amount and type of input, onset of bilingualism, degree of literacy in the heritage language, complexity of linguistic material, subjective factors, etc.).

Within the bilingualism literature, two approaches have dominated in explaining the linguistic behavior of heritage speakers, whose patterns have been categorized into three types: (a) *cross-linguistic-influence* (CLI) or *dominant-language transfer*, (b), *attrition*, and (c) *divergent attainment*.[3] On the one hand, formal generative approaches to language acquisition often focus on the linguistic knowledge that the individual speaker possesses and how such knowledge develops or changes across their lifespan (Montrul 2008; Benmamoun et al. 2013; Scontras et al. 2015; Polinsky 2018). On the other hand, variationist sociolinguists embrace the inherent variability of language and theorize about the mechanisms that may induce linguistic change, either by examining it at a given point in time (synchronically) or throughout time (diachronically) (Nagy, this volume; Silva-Corvalán 1994; Otheguy and Zentella 2012). These two seemingly incommensurable approaches, however, converge in one common tenet, namely, that linguistic vulnerability or permeability is contingent on some sort of optionality or variation. That is, a speaker may use two variants to say the same thing, or a categorical rule may become optional for some speakers, who use it invariably in a given context. A key question in contact linguistics is which factors (linguistic, social, and psychological) constrain such variability, and this question has been at the forefront of the field of contact linguistics, which studies the linguistic outcome of linguistic systems in contact.

A unified theory of contact linguistics that would predict all heritage speakers' linguistic behaviors seems far-fetched, at least given our current knowledge (Thomason 2001; Scontras et al. 2015). However, we believe that recent usage-based approaches to contact linguistics, also known as "Cognitive Sociolinguistics," may be in the right direction in bridging the gap between an understanding of heritage speakers' linguistic outcomes both at the individual and social level. Such approach, based on the works of usage-based scholars (Croft 2000; Tomasello 2008; Bybee 2010), is presented in Backus (2014) and more recently in Aalberse et al. (2019), who seek to understand the synchronic and diachronic processes of contact phenomena in bilinguals. A basic tenet of usage-based approaches is that grammar emerges from social interaction; "entrenchment," understood as

---

[3] Such term was proposed by Scontras and colleagues (2015) in order to address the controversies raised by the notion of *incomplete acquisition* (Montrul 2008) For a discussion on this critique see Otheguy (2016) and Kupisch and Rothman (2018).

the degree to which form-meaning representations are stored in the individual mind depend on the individuals' usage patterns – which through interactions with other members of the speech community – may lead to conventionalization or shared societal norms within such community. Heritage speakers represent an ideal kind of bilingual to examine how variable linguistic behavior is an interplay between cognitive entrenchment and societal conventionalization, given the rapid linguistic and social changes that may occur throughout their lifespan; heritage speakers may introduce new elements to their linguistic inventory, replace older elements, or merely lose them.[4]

In the present chapter, we follow this approach by focusing on heritage speakers' morphosyntactic outcomes, a linguistic domain that has received more attention in the literature. This attention stems from the fact that this domain of language presents a wider range of variation in heritage grammars, and can therefore provide theoretical contributions for understanding language change or cognitive flexibility in acquiring language. In doing so, our goal is to review this literature with the hope that it will shed light on some longstanding questions in contact linguistics. In Section 19.2, we address the following questions: What are the mechanisms of contact-induced change in heritage grammars? What domains of language are more transferrable in heritage grammars and with what other learning or borrowing mechanisms do they interact? Section 19.3 delves into mechanisms of simplification and complexification in heritage grammars and Section 19.4 calls for a more direct examination of intersubjective factors in understanding the linguistic structures of heritage grammars.

19.2 Mechanisms of Contact-Induced Phenomena in Heritage Languages

Previous work has shown that heritage languages may converge toward – become structurally closer to – their dominant language. While early work on contact linguistics described patterns of structural convergence as a *product*, work in the past decade has taken a more prominent role in understanding convergence as a *process*. This shift was primarily sparked by the overwhelming evidence that not all initial stages of convergence (process) lead to propagation (product) (Doğruöz and Backus 2009; Poplack et al. 2010). However, other queries remain: (a) what is the role of transfer in patterns of convergence? (b) how do mechanisms of borrowing interact with internal changes? (c) What is the role of cross-linguistic structural

---

[4] A challenge for this approach is to explain data entrenched in the mind of the heritage speaker irrespective of use (Montrul 2016), as discrepancies between perception and production have been found (Kim 2019).

priming in contact-induced changes? In this section, we will review some literature on heritage grammars that has shown that syntactic material rarely gets transferred; that changes in the amount and type of input in heritage grammars halt certain processes of grammaticalization; and that the role of cross-linguistic priming in linguistic change is subject to the social dynamics of the heritage community.

Before we provide evidence for these questions, two cautionary theoretical challenges are in order. The first one pertains to the lack of terminological consensus in describing processes of language contact with terms such as "transfer," "borrowing," "shift-induced interference," "copying," "replication," "calque," or "loan-translation," often being used interchangeably (see Sankoff (2002) for a review). In this chapter, we will be using "transfer" for elements that are directly being incorporated in the source language. Because converging grammatical structures are hardly ever identical to the replicating structure in the source language we will refer to these patterns as "pattern-replication" (Matras and Sakel 2007: 829–830) to describe the re-distribution of formal-syntactic arrangements that are modelled from an external source.

The second challenge, related to the first, is defining "contact-induced change." While the notion of linguistic change is relatively well-understood in the sociolinguistic literature – operationalized here as the propagation (and conventionalization) of an altered replication (Croft 2000) – establishing criteria for what constitutes "contact-induced" is still a recurrent theme in the literature. Certain theorists within the variationist sociolinguistic approach still insist on finding strictly internal or external motivations of linguistic change (Poplack and Levey 2010) even if the field of contact linguistics is principled in deciphering explanations of "multiple causations" in linguistic change, whereby both internal and external causal factors interact with one another (Thomason 2001). Thomason's (2001: 62) broader definition of contact-induced change, "any change that would be less likely to occur outside the contact situation" is understood to embrace these multifaceted explanations of contact, and therefore, it is the one we adopt here.

19.2.1 The Role of Transfer in Contact-Induced Change

The role that linguistic transfer plays in converging heritage grammars is not a straightforward matter. Despite considerable advancement in understanding cross-linguistic permeability, debates exist around which linguistic domains are actually transferrable. The "anything-goes" argument postulates that any linguistic material can be borrowed given the right social circumstances (Thomason and Kaufman 1988: 14). However, what those "right" social circumstances are is far from clear. Alternatively, it has been argued that many of the structural changes that we see in heritage languages are not the result of direct syntactic transfer, but are more likely the result of the vulnerability found in semantic or discourse-pragmatic interfaces (Sorace 2011; Benmamoun et al. 2013). While evidence showing the low permeability of syntax comes from a number of heritage language communities, here we focus on two particular cases, namely Spanish-English bilinguals in the United States and Turkish-Dutch bilinguals in the Netherlands.

Spanish-English bilingualism in the United States is characterized both in terms of language shift toward the dominant language and subsequent contact with more recent immigration waves from different parts of the Spanish-speaking world. Silva-Corvalán (1994, 2008) surveyed a number of cases of convergence among Spanish-English bilinguals in Los Angeles. Her results indicate that most of the transfer effects from English are attributed to lexicon-semantics or pragmatic uses, whereby an English expression is semantically or pragmatically matched with a Spanish word or meaning, and subsequently adapted to the syntax of the non-dominant language. For instance, the use of *como* in (1a) used in the sense of 'to what extent' may be considered an extension of an already *cómo X gustar Y* in Spanish, and the innovative pragmatic usage is copied from English.

(1a)   Y   tu   carro   que   compraste,   ¿cómo   te   gusta?
       and   your   car   that   (you).bought, how   to.you   pleases
       'And the car that you bought, how do you like it?' (Silva-Corvalán 2008: 218)

Similarly, Doğruöz and Backus (2009) examined a number of innovations in the speech of Turkish heritage speakers in the Netherlands. They followed a construction-based theory that assumes that the lexicon and the syntax form a continuum of specificity; specific constructions are situated within the lexical end of the continuum, whereas schematic ones are located in the syntactic end of the continuum. Their results indicated that the large majority of copying strategies were located at the maximally specific side (lexical) or partially schematic side (morphosyntax) of the continuum (i.e., verb–object collocations, compound verbs, the extension of indefinite *bir* 'one' (based on the Dutch model)). Other examples included a number of omissions, as is commonly found in heritage grammars wherein the dominant language may not mark a distinction. The loss of accusative marking, for instance, appeared to be more common in certain mental verbs (*like, read, think, know*), which by virtue of being considered low in transitivity, are less likely to be differentially marked and, therefore, prone to more variability. For these omission cases, transfer from Dutch does not seem an obvious explanation and, instead, a multiple-causation explanation is proposed: The inherently variable cases of marking in low transitive verbs are vulnerable to loss under the influence of the speakers' dominant language when the latter does not mark such distinction.

The first conclusion that can be drawn from these studies is that although morphosyntactic aspects can be adopted from the dominant language, these are rarely the result of direct transfer from maximally specified structures (i.e., syntax). Instead, transfer effects are the result of the perceived degree of semantic equivalence between common shared structures, whereby speakers perceive a transparent connection between form and meaning representations in their respective languages. The second conclusion is that cross-linguistic morphosyntactic influence is determined by two general principles: first, cross-linguistic material is more common if both languages share a particular structure and, second, if such structure is already variable in the non-dominant language. A possible explanation behind these findings could be attributed to the fact that variable material requires larger amount of input in order for certain structures to get entrenched in heritage grammars. Disruptions to such input thus increase variability and, therefore, linguistic permeability.

19.2.2 Contact-Induced Grammaticalization

Less transparent cases of transfer effects at the morphosyntactic level in heritage grammars could be explained through patterns of grammaticalization. Historically, grammaticalization was strictly treated as an internal motivation of language change, whereby a lexical item becomes more obscure and begins to serve a grammatical function (Hopper and Traugott 2003: 18). Because grammaticalization is derivative of processes that can take multiple paths (Bybee et al. 1994: 240), it allows us to examine the role of contact and the interaction between other internal factors in the developments of heritage grammars. A model that explains the not-so-mutually-exclusive underpinnings of internal and external factors in grammaticalization has been presented in the works of Heine and Kuteva (2005, 2010), who propose two types of contact-induced grammaticalization: *ordinary contact-induced grammaticalization* and *replica grammaticalization*. Both processes are similar in that speakers create a new pattern or category that is equivalent in the model language, but differ in the paths they take; the former is explained in terms of universal principles of grammaticalization, whereas the latter is ascribed to grammaticalization patterns that were assumed to have occurred in the source language and adapt to the linguistic constraints of the replica language.

In language contact studies, patterns of both types of grammaticalization have been extensively described, especially in the development of pidgins and creoles (Siegel 2008; Bruyn 2009) as well as contact scenarios of language revitalization (Rodríguez-Ordóñez 2017). Within heritage language studies, contact-induced patterns of grammaticalization have been reported in the development of new varieties (i.e., "New Mexican Spanish") of communities with a relatively high maintenance of the heritage language (Torres-Cacoullos 2000; Vergara-Wilson and Dumont 2015) or in the descriptions of the early development of a contact variety among children with simultaneous bilingual acquisition. For instance, Matthews and Yip (2009) investigate the grammatical development of two properties in the English of Cantonese-English bilingual children in Hong Kong: *already* as a tense/aspect marker and passive *give*. Their results indicate that English *already* is following a pattern of ordinary grammaticalization in its development as a marker of perfective aspect based on the model of Cantonese particles [V saai3] and [V laa3]. With respect to passive *give* (2c), it is argued that it is an extension from lexical *give* (2a) and permissive *give* (2b), which correspond to the grammaticalization process that occurred in Cantonese. In this respect, it is argued that these innovative constructions of *give* represent a process of replica grammaticalization in the incipient stages of their bilingual development.

Lexical 'give' (age 2;01)
(2a)   I give you. I want to watch this one.

Permissive 'give' (3;03)
(2b)   You open give me see.

Passive 'give' (3;04-4;11)
(2c)   Daddy I give you see.

In subsequent work, Szeto et al. (2017) demonstrate that once children begin literacy in English, they replace uses of the perfective marker *already* in auxiliary constructions with *have*, and suggest that the transient nature of grammaticalization processes emerges due to a change in the sociolinguistic ecology in which English develops. The radical change on the source of the input among these Cantonese-English bilinguals is thus responsible to halt such grammaticalization process.

Similar results have been found among second generation adult Ambon Malay heritage speakers in the Netherlands. In their study, Aalberse and Moro (2014) examine the grammaticalization process of enclitic *punya* in Malay, which shares functional properties with the definite article *de* or *het* 'the' in Dutch. Their results indicate that while baseline speakers in the homeland preferred phonetically reduced forms such as *pung, pu,* or *ng,* heritage speakers in the Netherlands have halted the grammaticalization process in favor of forms such as *punya* and *pung.* Alberse and Moro (2014: 157) propose that the interruption of this grammaticalization process is the result of reduced input in the heritage language, which is necessary to promote later stages of a grammaticalization process. This study shows that language contact does not always promote language change or loss, but some kind of grammatical stability, especially if the dominant language has an equivalent structure.

An example of ongoing contact-induced grammaticalization has been more recently found in the encoding of tense/aspect among the same Ambon Malay heritage speakers (Moro 2017). Ambon Malay does not mark tense, but aspect is analytically expressed through the progressive marker *ada* or perfective *su* (perfectivity often translated as English 'already'). Additionally, Ambon Malay uses reduplication to mark iterative aspect. In contrast, Dutch marks both aspect and tense obligatorily in the verbal inflection. Moro found that both reduplication and *su* are losing ground, but the use of *ada* is not only being retained as a progressive marker but it is also being extended as a marker of present tense in the model of Dutch. Moro (2017) argues that this extension is an example of contact-induced replica grammaticalization, whereby the extension in the use of *ada* is brought by the influence of Dutch in combination with internal paths of grammaticalization.

The relatively low cases of grammaticalization in heritage grammars can be linked to the fact that, in order for contact-induced grammaticalization to occur, prolonged and frequent exposure and use of the language are necessary, which heritage speakers tend to lack. Despite these conditions, cases of contact-induced grammaticalization can and do emerge but they have shown slightly different patterns from other contact scenarios where revitalization efforts have led to widespread bilingualism (Rodríguez-Ordóñez 2017). Because patterns of grammaticalization are intrinsically connected to use, the working hypothesis would be that these patterns will be more likely to evolve among speakers with higher rates of heritage language use or maintenance, with subsequent generations either slowing down the process if patterns of shift interfere or advancing it along increased use. Further work on incipient stages of contact-induced grammaticalization patterns in heritage language grammars is a promising avenue to disentangle long-term contact effects from individual variation. If the current hypothesis is on the right track, it could also provide evidence against the argument that social factors play a minimal role in these processes (Heine and Kuteva 2010: 101).

19.2.3   The Role of Cross-Linguistic Priming in Contact-Induced Change

In contact linguistics, it is generally argued that speakers create some sort of equivalence between the structures they speak (Matras 2009). The question is how those formulas of equivalence are established, especially in cases of pattern replication (Silva-Corvalán 2008). This question requires that we resort to the understanding of processing mechanisms among bilinguals. One such mechanism is (cross-linguistic) priming, which has been extensively examined in the psycholinguistic literature. In the present section, we describe work looking at the role of cross-linguistic priming with implications for contact-induced change.

Cross-linguistic structural priming is defined as speakers' tendency to re-use syntactic structures from a recently processed structure in a different language (Loebell and Bock 2003; Kootstra and Doedens 2016). Cross-linguistic priming effects are taken as evidence of bilinguals' coactivation of syntactic structures at the processing level (Kootstra and Muysken 2017). It has been especially found to occur in structures with high vulnerability for cross-linguistic influence such as pronominal subjects. Previous work has shown that in languages that allow null subjects, heritage speakers tend to show higher rates of overt pronouns than their baseline counterparts (Montrul 2004; Doğruöz and Backus 2009; Sorace 2011). Recently, Sodaci et al. (2019) examined whether higher rates of overt subject expression among Turkish heritage speakers in the Netherlands were due to cross-linguistic priming effects, and whether such effects could lead to long-term convergence. In their study, twenty-eight Turkish-Dutch bilinguals, who represented a continuum of Turkish or Dutch dominance, listened to a series of stories that ended with an instruction prime sentence, which was produced either with an overt or null subject. Results indicated that participants were more likely to use an overt subject pronoun after being primed with an overt subject pronoun only in the bilingual condition, with a marginally significant stronger effect for Dutch-dominant Turkish speakers. Assuming that priming effects are reflective of a cumulative effect of language learning, this cross-linguistic priming effect was interpreted as a potential factor driving language change in heritage Turkish.

Contrary evidence comes from Torres-Cacoullos and Travis (2018), who examined cross-linguistic structural priming effects among Spanish-English bilinguals in New Mexico, United States. These effects were examined through patterns of English-to-Spanish code-switching to test whether code-switches from English increased the rates of subject pronoun *yo* 'I' in Spanish. Results indicated that two kinds of priming are at play: Spanish-English bilinguals tended to use higher rates of Spanish *yo* if the previous sentence contained an overt English subject (22 percent) (cross-linguistic priming), but much higher rates if the previous subject was Spanish *yo* (38 percent) (intra-linguistic priming). Additionally, they showed that these priming effects were short-lived, that is, they didn't extend to more than three subjects. Importantly, they also found that the linguistic constraints governing the use of Spanish *yo* among these bilinguals were the same as those found in monolingual varieties.

The differences found in the Turkish and Spanish data can be adduced to two factors. First, the data collection techniques differed vastly; while the Turkish study was conducted in a laboratory setting with highly controlled stimuli, the observations in the Spanish data came from naturalistic data with rigorous constraint analysis common in the variationist sociolinguistic tradition. These differences in data-collection settings could unequivocally alter the kind of linguistic knowledge that is being examined, given that different production tasks differ in cognitive demands, with further consequences in speech production to adapt to the communicative needs or demands of the interlocutor (Lively et al. 1993; Abel and Babel 2017). Second, and importantly, the social dynamics in the two communities vary dramatically; the speakers in the New Mexican English Spanish Corpus comprise highly proficient bilinguals who report using both languages on a regular basis with patterns of language transmission up to eight generations. In contrast, Turkish immigrants are relatively recent in the Netherlands (since the 50s) and most of the data are representative of first- or second-generation speakers with clear signs of language shift. While all speakers interact in their least dominant languages to carry out a number of social tasks, the relative stability of overt subjects in New Mexican Spanish may be representative of a prolonged stable bilingual community. Ideally, future comparative analysis from diverse social contexts would benefit from combining different methodological tools as a way to assess the role of priming in contact-induced change.

19.3   Simplification and Complexification

An important debate in contact linguistics concerns the questions of whether language contact leads to *simplification* or *complexification* as well as deciphering the social conditions in which these processes tend to occur. The contact-induced mechanisms described in Section 19.2 are not unique to heritage grammars as they are common in any living language. However, many heritage speaker communities are often characterized by language attrition (here understood as the loss of linguistic structures).[5] Thomason (2001: 320) predicts that attrition, understood as a form of simplification, is the only type of contact-induced change that is exclusively linked to language shift and such cases have been widely reported in the heritage language acquisition literature (Silva-Corvalán 1994, 2014; Montrul 2008, 2016; Benmamoun et al. 2013; Polinsky 2018). Patterns of contact-induced complexification, on the contrary, have been linked to stable child bilingualism with tight social networks in high contact situations (Trudgill

---

[5] For recent debates on "language attrition" see Schmid and Köpke (2017) and articles therein.

2011). Cases of complexification have been found in heritage grammars, but these tend to occur among reasonably fluent speakers in communities in which the language is used for a number of social functions. Overall, these findings tend to suggest that patterns of simplification and complexification are intrinsically linked to usage. In this section, we outline some common mechanisms of simplification as well as complexification found in heritage grammars with a brief note addressing the challenges in studying these processes.

The major challenge in examining simplification and complexification processes rests in how each is defined, operationalized, and theorized. The *absolute* approach, also known as the "objective" approach, defines complexity based on description length or the amount of linguistic description that is necessary to account for the differences that a particular language makes to encode particular meaningful information (McWhorter 2001; Dahl 2004). For instance, a language with more phonemic distinctions is generally understood to have a more complex phonemic sound inventory. The *relative* approach, also known as the "subjective" one, defines complexity in terms of cost or difficulty to process a particular linguistic material. That is, a structure will be considered more complex if it is also costlier to process (Kusters 2003; Hawkins 2004). Thus, those embracing an absolutive approach focus on output material, whereas the relative approach targets processing. This distinction is relevant because not all complex structures are difficult to process (Dahl 2004) nor do all patterns of simplification in processing lead to simplified outputs (Rodríguez-Ordóñez and Sainzmaza-Lecanda 2018; Jacob et al. 2019). Ideally, studies should include both types of analysis, but these hybrid approaches are scant at the moment. For now, we will assume an absolutive approach in the remaining of the chapter, mainly because more research exists from this view.

19.3.1 Mechanisms of Simplification

In the absolute approach, two general principles inform mechanisms of simplification or complexification (Miestamo 2008). The *Principle of Fewer Distinctions* suggests that fewer distinctions require shorter linguistic descriptions. The *Principle of One-Meaning-One Form* is intimately linked to the notion of transparency, whereby form-meaning correspondences are made on a one-to-one basis; adhering to these principles would constitute simpler structures, whereas violations of these principles are argued to increase complexity. With these principles in mind, three broad mechanisms have been described to support linguistic simplification: a) regularization / overgeneralizations, b) increase in transparency, and c) loss of redundancy (Trudgill 2011: 20–26). The first two meanings are intrinsically related, as regularization of irregular forms tends to show less allomorphy and more transparency. Examples of regularization in heritage grammars are plentiful and have been reported for a myriad of languages and linguistic domains.

Patterns *of regularization / overgeneralizations* have been found for gender assignment, whereby the unmarked forms are often generalized to the marked one. That is, for languages that only have a masculine-feminine distinction, feminine objects tend to be marked with default masculine (Montrul et al. 2008). For languages with three-way distinctions (masculine, feminine, neuter) such as Russian, Greek, or Norwegian, the neuter is treated as feminine, whereas some feminine nouns may also be treated as masculine, which often leads to two-way distinctions (Polinsky 2008; Lohndal and Westergaard 2016; Rodina and Westergaard 2017). Within the domain of verbal morphology, regularization patterns seem to be prevalent with respect to Tense, Aspect, Mood, or a combination of all three; in heritage Spanish, the use of indicative verbal forms is rapidly being overgeneralized into the subjunctive forms (Silva-Corvalán 1994; Montrul and Perpiñán 2011; Irizarri von Schulten 2016) as well as over-extensions of the preterit in contexts where the imperfect would be expected (Montrul 2009). While regularizations of tense are scarcely reported, they nonetheless exist in heritage grammars. For instance, in Netherlands Turkish, instead of resorting to verbal morphology, temporal deitics such as *o zaman* 'then' or *ondan sonra* 'and then' are used to mark temporality, leading to more analytic structures with respect to verbal morphology (Rehbein and Karakoç 2004: 142).

Patterns of *transparency* beyond morphology are rarely reported. An exception to this trend is found in Rakhilina et al. (2016), who examined the heritage Russian speakers' mechanisms behind the use of certain idiomatic structures that deviate from baseline Russian speakers. Idiomatic expressions tend to be less transparent and, hence, more complex. In their study, they found that Russian heritage speakers resorted to universal strategies to produce compositional structures by decomposing some of the complex meanings into simpler units. An example is provided with the expression *učit'sja na ošibkax* 'learn from one's mistakes' (literally 'to learn on mistakes'), the meaning of which was decomposed by heritage speakers, producing a semantically more transparent utterance ('for us to learn and develop as we explore and follow the example of our ancestors'). In order to account for these innovative uses, Rakhilina et al. (2016: 6) rely on the notion of *conceptual structure*, which is understood as a cognitive feature that allows the speaker to "build semantic categories by combining functions and arguments" yielding a more transparent way to express the desired idiomatic expression.

In some way, overgeneralizations are linked to transparency in that less transparent or irregular forms tend to be the first to overgencralize in situations of reduced-input. While these overgeneralizations are often attributed to "incomplete acquisition," usage-based approaches instead explain these uses as remaining lexically specific within a lexicon–syntax continuum. Zyzik (2019) examines Spanish-English bilinguals' acceptability of certain creative overgeneralized constructions in Spanish (i.e., *amarguez* instead of *amargura* 'bitterness', *profundez* as opposed to *profundidad* 'depth') and shows that heritage speakers are more likely to accept those constructions, even if unattested in production. The acceptance of these innovations was argued to be the result of pressures of conventionality, whereby expectations of communal norms are reinforced in the school setting, leading to higher set expectations in adult monolinguals.

Loss of redundancy is another common mechanism of simplification found in heritage speakers. Trudgill (2011) distinguishes two types of redundancy: syntagmatic, or the repetition of the same linguistic material (i.e., agreement), and paradigmatic, the morphological expression of grammatical categories (i.e., gender, case, mood, aspect, etc). Trudgill suggests that in cases of language shift or death, syntagmatic redundancy is lost before paradigmatic redundancy. While there is no doubt that inflectional morphology is a vulnerable area prone to simplification in heritage grammars, research that has simultaneously examined both gender agreement (syntactic redundancy) and assignment (paradigmatic redundancy) has shown that Trudgill's claim may not be entirely accurate. For instance, Montrul et al. (2013) found higher rates of deviations with respect to gender assignment (84 percent) than agreement (15 percent). These deviations were more common in noncanonical feminine nouns. Similarly, Kupisch et al. (2013) examined gender marking and agreement among heritage speakers of French in Germany and, although speakers were highly accurate with respect to gender, they were more deviant in gender assignment than agreement. In Russian, Polinsky (2008) found an overall reduction of three-way gender distinction into a binary one, but agreement mismatches were largely confined to noun classes that showed variable agreement patterns (Laleko 2018). Other work has shown evidence that gender agreement is more prone to variability, but such variability is not equated to loss. For instance, Johannessen and Larsson (2015) examined gender agreement and noun declension in heritage US-Norwegian and found that while declension patterns were quite robust, 12 percent were target-deviant DP-internal agreement patterns. In a follow-up study, they also found evidence that gender assignment is completely target-like in the pronominal domain both in heritage Norwegian and Swedish (Johannessen and Larsson 2018). These seemingly conflicting results suggest that loss of redundancy largely depends on how grammatical categories are encoded cross-linguistically, whereby less transparent form-meaning matches are prone to loss. These findings, thus, suggest that the loss of redundancies as a mechanism of simplification is language-specific and intrinsically related to the second mechanism outlined earlier, namely, transparency.

19.3.2 Mechanisms of Complexification

Patterns of complexification are often described in terms of the following four mechanisms: (a) increase in opacity, (b) irregularization, (c) growth in morphological categories/distinctions, and (d) increase in sintagmatic redundancy (Trudgill 2011). Increase in opacity is understood as the reduction of transparent form-meaning representations. For instance, agglutinative languages like Turkish and Finish are considered more transparent than a fusional language like Spanish, given the one-meaning-one-form mappings in the former. Irregularization occurs when regular forms are disrupted, say through analogy, yielding less transparent forms (i.e., past tense *lit* vs. *lighted*). The growth of morphological categories involves using a new morpheme to encode new grammatical relations or meanings. Increase in syntagmatic redundancy happens when new patterns of agreement emerge.

The overwhelming literature on heritage grammars has mainly focused on the "gaps" that these speakers present, leaving little room to an understanding of potential cases of complexification.

Despite this gap, recent work has shown that cases of complexification do arise among heritage speakers, most of which pertain to the third mechanism: reallocations and rearrangement of morphological material leading to further grammatically meaningful distinctions. The addition of these distinctions, often referred to as "additive patterns," do not necessarily involve language transfer (additive borrowing) but may be the result of internally motivated changes. For instance, Yager et al. (2015: 2) examined the rearrangement of the dative case in different dialects of heritage German (Wisconsin, Texas, and Misionero German in Northeast Argentina and Uruguay) and show that, despite some patterns of loss, the dative case has also adopted a new function that closely relates to patterns of Differential Object Marking (DOM). DOM languages often use the dative case to mark objects based on semantic factors or information structure (specially animacy, specificity, or definiteness). In heritage German, a new dative form *in + den* competes with invariant Standard German *im* to mark third person singular pronouns and definite NPs (5b). Such development is argued to have developed internally, and not through transfer, given that all the Heritage German varieties examined in their study show similar patterns, regardless of whether they are in contact with a canonically DOM language (Spanish) or a non-DOM language (English, Portuguese).[6] This study thus

---

[6] The status of DOM in Portuguese has been raised in Schwenter (2014), who provides evidence for a clear-cut DOM system, albeit different from Spanish.

shows that linguistic complexification can be a byproduct of internally motivated rearrangement of case marking in heritage grammars.

Standard German

(4a) im   Baun
      in.the.$_{DAT}$ tree
      'In the tree'

(4b) im   Haus
      in.the.$_{DAT}$ house
      'In the house'

Wisconsin Heritage German (WGS)

(5a) im   Boom
      in.the.$_{DAT}$ tree
      'In the tree'

(5b) es war in den   Haus
      It was in the.$_{ACC}$ house
      'It was in the house'

A site for cross-linguistic influence that may lead to complexification is the use of subject pronoun expression (SPE). While the use of more overt subjects may give the impression of increased redundancy, such uses have often been linked to alleviation of processing costs in bilingual speakers (Sorace 2011). Using methods in variationist sociolinguistics, Shin (2014) examines the internal configuration of subject pronoun expression (SPE) among Spanish-English heritage bilinguals in New York City. Her results show that second generation Spanish-English bilinguals have developed a novel constraint in the use of overt subjects in Spanish, a pattern not found in the first gener-ation: The increased uses of overt subjects with the imperfect forms was adduced to a possible disambiguation strategy between first and third person imperfect forms (*el/ella cantaba* 's/he used to sing' ~ *yo cantaba* 'I used to sing'). The emergence of a new linguistic factor (tense-aspect-mood) in accounting for the variability in Spanish SPE is concluded to be an additive pattern and, therefore, a case of complexification.

A final example of additive complexification is explored in Adamou (2013), who examines copula choice in heritage Romani in contact with Spanish in Oaxaca, Mexico. Her results indicate that contrary to the single copula forms in European Romani, heritage Romani has developed a two-way copula distinction under the influence of a two-way copula distinction in Spanish (*ser* and *estar*). Spanish *ser* is commonly used for permanent states whereas *estar* is generally used for temporary entities. Mexican Romani follows a similar distinction through [*si* + adjective] ('is/are' + adjective) (6a) and [adjective + 3rd person clitic *lo*] (6b). This latter pattern has been attributed as a replication of *estar* uses in Spanish and argued to increase structural complexity in the grammar of Mexican Romani.

(6a) le   ʃave   muʁa   bibiake   **si**   barbale
      def.pl   children poss.1sg aunt.dat be.3pl   rich
      'My aunt's children are rich.'

(6b) o   ɣadʒo   tsulo   **lo**
      def.m   man   fat   3sg.m
      'The non-Gypsy man is fat.'   Adamou (2013:1085)

The first conclusion that can be gathered from this section is that mechanisms of simplification in heritage grammars seem more prevalent and significantly affect inflectional morphology. The difficulty of acquiring inflectional morphology is no news. Dahl (2004) attributes this difficulty to inflection as being an archetypal exemplar of "mature phenomena," which are referred to as linguistic features that imply a lengthy period of historical development. The acquisition stages of mature phenomena can be then described as a synchronic process, which require more time (higher frequency of input and language usage) in order to be acquired. Heritage speakers' tendency for regularization, overextensions, and loss of paradigmatic redundancies, especially in inflectional morphology, can be attributed to the disruption in the amount of input and shifts in the heritage language use. The patterns of complexification reported here lead to the conclusion that, like simplification, complexification can arise in situations of language obsolescence, but such cases are not always associated with language contact, as predicted by Thomason (2001). The social conditions in which patterns of complexification arise in heritage speakers are less understood; given the evidence, it is not unsafe to claim that patterns of complexification are more likely to be introduced by relatively fluent speakers of the language (as in the case of Spanish in New York City) or in close-knit communities (Roma speakers in Mexico or heritage German speakers explored previously). Further studies would be needed to test this prediction so that we can better understand the consequences, limits, and relationship between patterns of socialization and linguistic complexification.

19.4 Intersubjective Factors in Heritage Grammars

Usage-based approaches to contact linguistics place emphasis on the intrinsic relationship between patterns of use of language and the social dynamics of a community in fostering the development of linguistic knowledge. Although early theorizations of contact linguistics argued that the locus of language contact is the individual speaker, it is now generally acknowledged that language contact is also a social phenomenon mediated through linguistic interaction between speakers, whose linguistic behaviors can promote certain contact-induced changes. This means that the study of language contact should be undertaken hand-in-hand with the immediate context and the social significance of language.

The importance of the immediate context, understood as socio-cultural factors, has been couched ever since Weinreich, and yet remains the least understood aspect in the field (Thomason 2001: 82; Rodríguez-Ordóñez 2019). A reason could be attributed to the difficulty of operationalizing the complexity that entails examining macro aspects of language, and linking them to linguistic patterns at the micro level. Despite these challenges, socio-cultural approaches to sociolinguistics have made numerous advancements in understanding language as part of a semiotic system, or the way particular sings (a way of pronouncing a word, a morpheme, ways of behaving, dressing, etc.) are connected to social groups or particular identities (Irvine and Gal 2000). Ultimately, it is language ideologies, or the cultural system of ideas about linguistic and social relationships that are responsible for how speakers operate in the social space. This is particularly relevant for heritage language studies, given that the reduced use of the language is often attributed to its minority status, which, in turn, can be argued to be shaped by the wider ideologies of the sociopolitical contexts in which they are spoken.

An important aspect of language ideologies is that they are characterized by their multiplicity, that is, they interact with a wide range of other social divisions (class, race, ethnicity) giving rise to often contradictory ideas about language (Kroskrity 2004). For instance, Babel (2018) shows how the incorporation of Quechua contact features in certain skillful Spanish speakers may contribute to oratory ability of these speakers, whereas the same features used by Quechua-dominant speakers may be regarded as "backward" and "rural." In minority language revitalization contexts, Rodríguez-Ordóñez (2021) similarly shows that the contact phenomenon of Basque DOM is regarded as both "authentic" and "non-legitimate," depending on who uses it, and while these meanings are representative of further social divisions within the Basque-speaking contexts, the phenomenon is being diffused not necessarily by means of claiming a particular "Basque" identity.

This seemingly contradictory relationship among attitudes, identities, and language use becomes even more complex in contexts of rapid social change, such as those in which heritage speakers operate. As a way to understand these complexities, Avineri (2017) proposes a "metalinguistic community" framework to understand the multiple, sometimes overlapping, reasons as to why and how heritage speakers of Yiddish in California experience both closeness to or distance from the language or speakers. Similarly, Showstack (2017) examines how Spanish heritage speakers take various affective and epistemic stances through uses of "Spanglish" in the classroom. While socio-cultural approaches of heritage languages have provided an understanding of how language may be used to construct multiple identities (see He, this volume), the gap often resides in assessing how these processes and practices have longstanding effects in heritage speakers' linguistic structures at the micro level.

Contact linguistic approaches to heritage language acquisition have attempted to address this relationship more recently, by examining the social meaning of language through the lenses of identity and attitudes. In their 2010 report, Hoffman and Walker developed an Ethnic Orientation Questionnaire to quantitatively and comparatively examine attitudinal factors in the development and diffusion of contact phenomena in a number of heritage groups in Toronto, Canada. Using this questionnaire, Nagy (2018) shows no direct correlation between ethnic orientation and the adopting of more English-like patterns. Moro (2018) examined the interactions between three psychosocial factors (onset of bilingualism, social networks, and overall attitudes toward the heritage language) as predictors of more Dutch-like features in six morphosyntactic features among speakers of Ambon Malay in the Netherlands (aspectual marker *ada*, the definite marker =*nya*, the double object (DO) construction, the prepositional phrase and adjectival phrase in resultative constructions, the pre-nominal order for the demonstrative *itu* 'that', and the numeral *satu* 'one'). Overall results indicated that attitudes only played a role in two of the linguistic features examined: Speakers with mild positive attitudes toward their heritage language showed more Dutch-like uses of double object construction and adjectival phrases.

One reason for these conflicting results is that overall attitudes toward the heritage language are not sufficient to capture changes at the micro-level. The key, we argue, is that wider linguistic ideologies give rise to multiple social meanings of linguistic variables, and ultimately, it is the semiotic processes of these variables that need to be more examined as a way to understand patterns of cross-linguistic influence. Such approach is taken in Erker (2017), who examines the role that salience – understood as the relative perceptual or cognitive prominence of the linguistic feature – has in contact-induced changes in Spanish. The linguistic variables of interest were weakening of coda /s/ (such as *mismo* [mihmo] or [mimo] 'same'), voseo (*vos hablás* 'you speak'), and subject pronoun expression (SPE) (*tú hablas* vs. ø *hablas* 'you speak') among twenty speakers from the *Otheguy-Zentella Corpus of Spanish in New York* (Otheguy and Zentella 2012). Erker shows that the relatively high salience of /s/ coda weakening and *voseo* in the Spanish-speaking world lead speakers to lower their usage rates on these features, resulting in dialectal leveling (i.e., erosion of differences within a speech community), whereas the higher rates in SPE are argued to be the result of language contact with English, leading to convergence due to the relatively low salience of the feature.

Erker's (2017) study provides an empirical basis from which we could make certain predictions to understand linguistic behavior and cross-linguistic permeability in heritage grammars: High salience features lead to feature loss, whereas low salience features promote convergence with the dominant language. Salience, understood as "the property of a linguistic item or feature that makes it in some way perceptually and cognitively prominent" (Kerswill and Williams 2002: 81) is a widely examined phenomenon. Despite challenges in operationalizing it, it is generally agreed that linguistic salience is a cognitive component that is mediated in society, which leads to another kind of salience, namely *social salience* or "the ability of listeners [. . .] to [also] associate that form with a given social group or personality trait" (Rácz 2013; Levon and Buchstaller 2015: 322). The role that cognitive salience plays in the acquisition process of heritage grammars has been previously examined (O'Grady et al. 2011), but the mediating role between cognitive and social salience in understanding cross-linguistic influence in bilingual populations in general, and heritage grammars in particular, is relatively scarce. The relationship between the two are not ephemeral, that is, social meanings of linguistic phenomena emerge from context and use, and these meanings can also affect how speakers may, consciously or unconsciously, adopt certain features in their multilingual repertoires. Ultimately, this approach has the potential to shed light on (1) whether or not variation constitutes a separate domain of linguistic knowledge (Preston 2004); (2) whether variation at different linguistic interfaces is processed differently; and (3) how linguistic variation mediates between abstract linguistic knowledge and societal norms.

19.5 Conclusions

The inclusion of linguistic, psychological, and cultural factors in the understanding of the outcomes of linguistic contact forms the foundation of contact linguistic theory. The social realities of heritage speakers along with the changes that these speakers experience throughout their lifespan constitute an opportunity to understand language as an interplay of human faculty and social competence.

By focusing on a small aspect of linguistic material (i.e., morphosyntactic variation), usage-based approaches to contact linguistics have uncovered that the outcomes in heritage grammars are largely not unique to them, but speak to wider processes of how linguistic material may adapt to the sociolinguistic environments where bilinguals or multilinguals operate. Like many other bilinguals, heritage speakers create formulas of equivalence between languages in reallocating innovative forms into their less-dominant heritage language. The converging grammars of heritage speakers are rarely an exact replica of the dominant language and such similarities rarely involve the adoption of direct borrowing of highly schematic material (i.e., syntax). Importantly, cross-linguistic material is more permeable if both languages share a particular structure and if such structure is already variable in the non-dominant language. These formulas of equivalence are also a prerequisite for the emergence of contact-induced changes, some of which may follow grammaticalization processes whose paths and stages will be largely determined by the social dynamics of the heritage community at hand. In what follows, we close with a brief reflection on a few venues of research in heritage language grammars.

Heritage speakers, like many other bilinguals, could be arguably conceived as agents of linguistic change; as some heritage speakers' input may be reduced during the lifespan, their patterns of use demonstrate that the use of language occurs within particular social environments that foster certain patterns to become more variable, to stabilize, or ultimately get lost. It is clear that not all outcomes could be directly linked to the dominant language, but instead interact with other cognitive processes, such as priming. While numerous works exist on priming, the role that cross-linguistic priming plays on heritage speakers' contact-induced changes is less understood; in some cases, priming has been argued to be a precondition for linguistic change, while in other cases it is merely shown to be a short-lived mechanism with no bearing on convergence. It is quite possible that the strength of cross-linguistic priming is not only task-based but also highly dependent on the dynamics of the community, and the extent to which speakers use their languages to achieve their various communicative goals. We believe that more cross-linguistic comparative work within and across heritage communities to determine which social conditions are more likely to favor change as a result of cross-linguistic priming is necessary.

The structural changes in heritage speakers' weaker language have often been argued to exhibit systematic simplification, especially when compared to counterpart monolinguals. However, it has been shown that heritage speakers also resort to unique cognitive processes to construct grammatical knowledge, sometimes bringing additive patterns of variation that may lead to more complex structures in absolutive terms. Assuming that language is an adaptive system of the social ecology in which it is spoken, it requires that mechanisms of simplification and/or complexification are understood as part of this ecology. In this regard, another venue of research involves examining how differing mechanisms may be interrelated, that is, how certain losses may result in further structural reorganizations leading to complexification. The vast majority of cases of simplification and complexification in heritage grammars focus on language output, and therefore can only inform absolutive approaches. Ideally, future studies will adopt more hybrid approaches as a way to comprehensively uncover the complexities that arise in the interactions between production and processing in context.

An area of focus that remains particularly open for further inquiry is the linguistic development throughout the school age years (6–17 years old), a critical time in which changes in the kind of input that bilinguals receive contribute to the changes in these structures. Existing work has shown that school age children tend to behave closer to monolinguals than adult heritage speakers in certain domains (O'Grady et al. 2011), while other work has demonstrated that children could also influence their parents' linguistic output (Montrul and Sánchez-Walker 2013; Montrul 2018). While this work continues to inform developmental patterns throughout a critical period in language development, it is largely assumed that the household or caregivers are the main source of input of the minoritized language (understood as *transmission*). Sociolinguistic theory, however, has shown that as children grow and expand their socialization networks, peer influence or orientation largely override caregiver influence. While evidence to this generalization is attested in some language-minoritized contexts (Mayr et al. 2017; Nance 2020), other work has shown that certain changes are more gradual, showing robust bi-dialectalism and, therefore, question mutually exclusive accounts of cognitive or socially oriented explanations of language variation (Sharma and Sankaran 2011). As this transmission–diffusion dichotomy becomes more complex in situations of rapid social change, heritage language contexts constitute ideal candidates for future exploration on this matter.

We conclude by foregrounding the important roles that intersubjective factors play in language variation and change, especially in contact situations as well as in heritage grammar development, a field ripe for further study. We believe that studying overall attitudes toward the heritage language may not suffice to understand the multiplicity of outcomes among heritage language speakers. Instead, we propose that a cognitive sociolinguistic approach to language variation may be a more fruitful outlook to explore the role that social meaning plays in the permeability of cross-linguistic material (Zenner et al. 2019). How is sociolinguistic information processed and stored among heritage speakers? What linguistic aspects are prone to frequency distribution effects in storing socially meaningful information? How do those processing mechanisms get reflected in output? Addressing these questions seems a necessary step to help elucidate whether variation constitutes a separate domain of linguistic knowledge and how it allows for linguistic material to become more entrenched. Undoubtedly, heritage speakers hold the key to answering these and other unexplored questions of contact linguistics in the years to come.

References

Aalberse, S. and F. R. Moro. 2014. Stability in Chinese and Malay Heritage Languages as a Source of Divergence. In Kurt Braunmüller, Steffen Höder, and Karoline Kühl (eds.), *Stability and Divergence in Language Contact. Factors and Mechanisms*. Amsterdam: John Benjamins, 141–161.

Aalberse, S., A. Backus, and P. Myusken. 2019. *Heritage Languages: A Language Contact Approach*. Amsterdam: John Benjamins.

Abel, J. and M. Babel. 2017. Cognitive Load Reduces Perceived Linguistic Convergence between Dyads. *Language and Speech* 60(3), 479–502.

Adamou, E. 2013. Replicating Spanish estar in Mexican Romani. *Linguistics* 51(6), 1075–1105.

Avineri, N. 2017. Contested Stance Practices in Secular Yiddish Metalinguistic Communities: Negotiating Closeness and Distance. *Journal of Jewish Languages* 5(2), 174–199.

Babel, A. (ed.) 2016. *Awareness and Control in Sociolinguistic Research*. Cambridge: Cambridge University Press.

Babel, A. 2018. *Between the Andes and the Amazon: Language and Social Meaning in Bolivia*. Tucson: The University of Arizona Press.

Backus, A. 2014. Towards a Usage-Based Account of Language Change: Implications of Contact Linguistics for Linguistic Theory. In Robert Nicolaï (ed.), *Questioning Language Contact*. Leiden: Brill, 91–118.

Benmamoun, E., S. Montrul, and M. Polinsky. 2013. Heritage Languages and Their Speakers: Opportunities and Challenges for Linguistics. *Theoretical Linguistics* 39(3–4), 129–181.

Bruyn, A. 2009. Grammaticalization in Creoles: Ordinary and Not-so-ordinary Cases. *Studies in Language* 33(2), 312–337.

Bybee, J. 2010. *Language, Usage and Cognition*. Cambridge: Cambridge University Press.

Bybee, J., R. Perkins, and W. Pagliuca. 1994. *The Evolution of Grammar: Tense, Aspect and Modality in the Languages of the World*. Chicago: The University of Chicago Press.

Croft, W. 2000. *Explaining Language Change: An Evolutionary Approach*. Harlow: Longman.

D'Alessandro, R. 2015. Null Subjects. In Antonio Fábregas, Jaume Mateu, and Michael Putnam (eds.), *Contemporary Linguistic Parameters*. London: Bloomsbury Press, 201–226.

Dahl, O. 2004. *The Growth and Maintenance of Linguistic Complexity*. Amsterdam: Benjamins.

Doğruöz, A. S. and A. Backus. 2009. Innovative Constructions in Dutch Turkish: An Assessment of Ongoing Contact-induced Change. *Bilingualism: Language and Cognition* 12(1), 41–63.

Erker, D. 2017. The Limits of Named Language Varieties and the Role of Social Salience in Dialectal Contact: The Case of Spanish in the United States. *Language and Linguistics Compass* 11(1), 1–20.

Hawkins, J. A. 2004. *Efficiency and Complexity in Grammars*. Oxford: Oxford University Press.

Heine, B. and T. Kuteva. 2005. *Language Contact and Grammatical Change*. Cambridge: Cambridge University Press.

Heine, B. and T. Kuteva. 2010. Contact and Grammaticalization in Raymond Hickey (ed.), *The Handbook of Language Contact*. Oxford: Wiley-Blackwell, 86–105.

Hoffman, M. F., and Walker, J. 2010. Ethnolects and the city: Ethnic orientation and linguistic variation in Toronto English. *Language variation and change* 22 (1), 37–67.

Hopper, P. J. and E. C. Traugott. 2003. *Grammaticalization*. Cambridge: Cambridge University Press.

Irizarri von Schulten, P. 2016. Spanish as a Heritage Language in the Netherlands: A Cognitive Linguistic Exploration. PhD dissertation, Utrecht: LOT.

Irvine, J. and S. Gal. 2000. Language Ideology and Linguistic Differentiation. In P. V. Kroskrity (ed.), *Regimes of Language: Ideologies, Polities, and Identities*. Santa Fe: School of American Research Press, 35–83.

Jacob, G., D. F. Safak, O. Demir, and B. Kirkici. 2019. Preserved Morphological Processing in Heritage Speakers: A Masked Priming Study on Turkish. *Second Language Research* 35(2), 173–194.

Johannessen, J. B. and I. Larsson. 2015. Complexity Matters: On Gender Agreement in Heritage Scandinavian. *Frontiers in Psychology* 6, 1842.

Johannessen, J. B. and I. Larsson. 2018. Stability and Change in Grammatical Gender: Pronouns in Heritage Scandinavian. *Journal of Language Contact* 11(3), 441–480.

Kerswill, P. and A. Williams. 2002. "Salience" as an Explanatory Factor in Language Change: Evidence from Dialect Levelling in Urban England. In M. Jones and E. Esch (eds.), *Language Change: The Interplay of Internal, External and Extra-linguistic Factors*. Berlin: Mouton de Gruyter, 81–110.

Kim, J. Y. 2019. Discrepancy between Heritage Speakers' Use of Suprasegmental Cues in the Perception and Production of Spanish Lexical Stress. *Bilingualism: Language and Cognition* 1–18.

Kootstra, G. J. and W. J. Doedens. 2016. How Multiple Sources of Experience Influence Bilingual Syntactic Choice: Immediate and Cumulative Cross-language Effects of Structural Priming, Verb Bias, and Language Dominance. *Bilingualism: Language and Cognition* 19(4), 710–732.

Kootstra, G. J. and P. Muysken. 2017. Cross-Linguistic Priming in Bilinguals: Multidisciplinary Perspectives on Language Processing, Acquisition, and Change. *Bilingualism: Language and Cognition* 20(2), 215–218.

Kroskrity, P. V. 2004. Language Ideologies. In A. Duranti (ed.), *A Companion to Linguistic Anthropology*. Oxford: Wiley-Blackwell, 496–517.

Kupisch, T. and J. Rothman. 2018. Terminology Matters! Why Difference Is Not Incompleteness and How Early Child Bilinguals Are Heritage Speakers. *International Journal of Bilingualism* 22(5): 564–582.

Kupisch, T., D. Akpinar, and A. Stöhr. 2013. Gender Assignment and Gender Agreement in Adult Bilinguals and Second Language Learners of French. *Linguistic Approaches to Bilingualism* 3(2), 150–179.

Kusters, W. 2003. *Linguistic Complexity, the Influence of Social Change on Verbal Inflection*. Leiden: Leiden University Press.

Laleko, O. 2018. What Is Difficult about Grammatical Gender? Evidence from Heritage Russian. *Journal of Language Contact* 11(2), 233–267.

Levon, E. and I. Buchstaller. 2015. Perception, Cognition, and Linguistic Structure: The Effect of Linguistic Modularity and Cognitive Style on Sociolinguistic Processing. *Language Variation and Change* 27(3), 319–348.

Lively, S., D. Pisoni, V. Summers, and R. Bernacki. 1993. Effects of Cognitive Workload on Speech Production: Acoustic Analyses and Perceptual Consequences. *Journal of the Acoustical Society of America* 93(5), 2962–2973.

Loebell, H. and K. Bock. 2003. Structural Priming across Languages. *Linguistics* 41(5), 791–824.

Lohndal, T. and M. Westergaard. 2016. Grammatical Gender in American Norwegian Heritage Language: Stability or Attrition? *Frontiers in Psychology* 7, 344.

Matthews, S. and V. Yip. 2009. Contact-induced Grammaticalization: Evidence from Bilingual Acquisition. *Studies in Language* 33(2), 366–395.

Matras, Y. 2009. *Language Contact*. Cambridge: Cambridge University Press.

Matras, Y. and J. Sakel. 2007. Investigating the Mechanisms of Pattern Replication in Language Convergence. *Studies in Language* 31(4), 829–865.

Mayr, R., J. Morris, I. Mennen, and R. Williams. 2017. Disentangling the Effects of Long-term Language Contact and Individual Bilingualism: The Case of Monophthongs in Welsh and English. *International Journal of Bilingualism* 21(3), 245–267.

McWhorter, J. 2001. The World's Simplest Grammars Are Creole Grammars. *Linguistic Typology* 5(2–3), 125–166.

Miestamo, M. 2008. Grammatical Complexity in a Cross-Linguistic Perspective. In M. Miestamo, K. Sinnemäki, and F. Karlsson (eds.), *Language Complexity: Typology, Contact, Change*. Amsterdam: John Benjamins, 23–41.

Montrul, S. 2004. Subject and Object Expression in Spanish Heritage Speakers: A Case of Morphosyntactic Convergence. *Bilingualism: Language and Cognition* 7(2), 125–142.

Montrul, S. 2008. *Incomplete Acquisition in Bilingualism: Re-examining the Age Factor*. Amsterdam: John Benjamins.

Montrul, S. 2009. Knowledge of Tense-Aspect and Mood in Spanish Heritage Speakers. *International Journal of Bilingualism* 13(2), 239–269.

Montrul, S. 2016. *The Acquisition of Heritage Languages*. Oxford: Oxford University Press.

Montrul, S. 2018. Heritage Language Development: Connecting the Dots. *International Journal of Bilingualism* 22(5), 530–546.

Montrul, S. and S. Perpiñán. 2011. Assessing Differences and Similarities between Instructed Heritage Language Learners and L2 Learners in Their Knowledge of Spanish Tense-Aspect and Mood (TAM) Morphology. *Heritage Language Journal* 8(1), 90–133.

Montrul, S. and N. Sánchez-Walker. 2013. Differential Object Marking in Child and Adult Spanish Heritage Speakers. *Language Acquisition* 20(2), 109–132.

Montrul, S., R. Foote, and S. Perpiñán. 2008. Gender Agreement in Adult Second Language Learners and Spanish Heritage Speakers: The Effects of Age and Context of Acquisition. *Language Learning* 58(3), 503–553.

Montrul, S., I. de la Fuenta, J. Davidson, and R. Foote. 2013. The Role of Experience in the Acquisition and Production of Diminutives and Gender in Spanish: Evidence from L2 Learners and Heritage Speakers. *Second Language Research* 29(1), 87–118.

Moro, F. R. 2017. Aspectual Distinctions in Dutch-Ambon Malay Bilingual Heritage Speakers. *International Journal of Bilingualism* 21(2), 178–193.

Moro, F. R. 2018. Divergence in Heritage Ambon Malay in the Netherlands: The Role of Social-Psychological Factors. *International Journal of Bilingualism* 22(4), 395–411.

Nagy, N. 2018. Linguistic Attitudes and Contact Effects in Toronto's Heritage Languages: A Variationist Sociolinguistic Investigation. *International Journal of Bilingualism* 22(4), 429–446.

Nance, C. 2020. Bilingual Language Exposure and the Peer Group: Acquiring Phonetics and Phonology in Gaelic Medium Education. *International Journal of Bilingualism* 24(2), 360–375.

O'Grady, W., H-Y. Kwak, O.-S. Lee, and M. Lee. 2011. An Emergentist Perspective on Heritage Language Acquisition. *Studies in Second Language Acquisition* 33(2), 223–245.

Otheguy, R. 2016. The Linguistic Competence of Second-Generation Bilinguals: A Critique of "Incomplete Acquisition." In C. Tortora, M. den Dikken, I. Montoya, and T. O'Neill (eds.), *Romance Linguistics 2013: Selected Papers from the 43rd Linguistic Symposium on Romance Languages*. Amsterdam: Benjamins, 301–329.

Otheguy, R. and A. C. Zentella. 2012. *Spanish in New York: Language Contact, Dialectal Leveling, and Structural Continuity*. Oxford: Oxford University Press.

Polinsky, M. 2008. Russian Gender under Incomplete Acquisition. *The Heritage Language Journal* 6(1), 40–71.

Polinsky, M. 2018. *Heritage Languages and Their Speakers*. Cambridge: Cambridge University Press.

Poplack, S. and S. Levey. 2010. Contact-Induced Grammatical Change: A Cautionary Tale. In Peter Auer and Jürgen Enrich Schmidt (eds.), *Language and Space – An International Handbook of Linguistic Variation: Volume 1 – Theories and Methods*. Berlin: Mouton de Gruyter, 391–419.

Preston, D. 2004. Three Kinds of Sociolinguistics: A Psycholinguistic Perspective. In C. Fought (ed.), *Sociolinguistic Variation: Critical Reflections.* New York: Oxford University Press, 140–158.

Putnam, M. T. and L. Sánchez. 2013. What's So Incomplete about Incomplete Acquisition?: A Prolegomenon to Modeling Heritage Language Grammars. *Linguistic Approaches to Bilingualism* 3(4), 478–508.

Rácz, P. 2013. *Salience in Sociolinguistics.* Berlin: De Gruyter.

Rakhilina, E., A. Vryenkova, and M. Polinsky. 2016. Linguistic Creativity in Heritage Speakers. *Glossa: A Journal of General Linguistics* 1(1), 1–29.

Rehbein, J. and B. Karakoç. 2004. On Contact-induced Change of Turkish Aspects: Languaging in Bilingual Discourse. In Christine Dabelsteen and Normann Jogersen (eds.), *Languaging and Language Practices* (Copenhagen Studies in Bilingualism 36). Copenhagen: University of Copenhagen, 125–149.

Rodina, Y. and M. Westergaard. 2017. Grammatical Gender in Bilingual Norwegian-Russian Acquisition: The Role of Input and Transparency. *Bilingualism: Language and Cognition* 20(1), 197–214.

Rodríguez-Ordóñez, I. 2017. Reexamining Differential Object Marking as a Linguistic Contact-phenomenon in Gernika Basque. *Journal of Language Contact* 10(2), 318–352.

Rodríguez-Ordóñez, I. 2019. The Role of Linguistic Ideologies in Language Contact Situations. *Language and Linguistic Compass*: e12351.

Rodríguez-Ordóñez, I. (2021). The Role of Social Meaning in Contact-Induced Variation among New Speakers of Basque. *Journal of Sociolinguistics* [Online first].

Rodríguez-Ordóñez, I. and L. Sainzmaza-Lacanda. 2018. Bilingualism Effects in Basque Subject Pronoun Expression: Evidence from L2 Basque. *Linguistic Approaches to Bilingualism* 8(5), 523–560.

Sankoff, G. 2002. Linguistic Outcomes of Language Contact. In J. K. Chambers, Peter Trudgill, and Natalie Schilling-Estes (eds.), *Handbook of Language Variation and Change.* Oxford: Blackwell, 338–368.

Schmid, M. and B. Köpke. 2017. The Relevance of First Language Attrition To Theories of Bilingual Development. *Linguistic Approaches to Bilingualism* 7(6), 637–667.

Schwenter, S. 2014. Two Kinds of Differential Object Marking in Portuguese and Spanish. In P. Amaral and A. M. Carvalho (eds.), *Portuguese–Spanish Interfaces: Diachrony, Synchrony and Contact.* Amsterdam: Benjamins, 237–260.

Scontras, G., M. Fuchs, and M. Polinsky. 2015. Heritage Language and Linguistic Theory. *Frontiers in Psychology* 6, 1545.

Sharma, D. and L. Sankaran. 2011. Cognitive and Social Forces in Dialect Shift: Gradual Change in London Asian Speech. *Language Variation and Change* 23(3), 399–428.

Shin, N. 2014. Grammatical Complexification in Spanish in New York: 3sg Pronoun Expression and Verbal Morphology. *Language Variation and Change* 26(3), 303–330.

Showstack, R. 2017. Stancetaking and Language Ideologies in Heritage Language Learner Classroom Discourse. *Journal of Language, Identity and Education* 16(5), 271–294.

Siegel, J. 2008. *The Emergence of Pidgins and Creole Languages*. Oxford: Oxford University Press.

Silva-Corvalán, C. 1986. Bilingualism and Language Change: The Extension of estar in Los Angeles Spanish. *Language* 62, 587–608.

Silva-Corvalán, C. 1994. *Language Contact and Change: Spanish in Los Angeles*. Oxford: Clarendon.

Silva-Corvalán, C. 2008. The Limits of Convergence in Language Contact. *Journal of Language Contact* 2(1), 213–224.

Silva-Corvalán, C. 2014. *Bilingual Language Acquisition Spanish and English in the First Six Years* (Cambridge Approaches to Language Contact). Cambridge: Cambridge University Press.

Sodaci, H., A. Backus, and G. J. Kootstra. 2019. Role of Structural Priming in Contact-Induced Change: Subject Pronoun Expression in L1 Turkish by Turkish-Dutch Bilinguals. *PsyArchiv*. https://doi.org/10.31234/osf.io/2uxej

Sorace, A. 2011. Pinning Down the Concept of "Interface" in Bilingualism. *Linguistic Approaches to Bilingualism* 1(1), 1–34.

Szeto, P. Y., S. Matthews, and V. Yip. 2017. Multiple Correspondence and Typological Convergence in Contact-Induced Grammaticalization: Evidence from Cantonese-English Bilingual Development. *Journal of Language Contact* 10(3), 485–518.

Thomason, S. G. 2001. *Language Contact: An Introduction*. Washington, DC: Georgetown University Press.

Thomason, S. G. and T. Kaufman. 1988. *Language Contact, Creolization and Genetic Linguistics*. Berkeley: University of California Press.

Tomasello, M. 2008. *Origins of Human Communication*. Cambridge, MA: MIT Press.

Torres-Cacoullos, R. 2000. *Grammaticization, Synchronic Variation, and Language Contact*. Amsterdam/Philadelphia: John Benjamins.

Torres-Cacoullos, R. and C. Travis. 2018. *Bilingualism in the Community: Code-switching and Grammars in Contact*. Cambridge: Cambridge University Press.

Trudgill, Peter. 2011. *Sociolinguistic Typology: Social Determinants of Linguistic Complexity*. Oxford: Oxford University Press.

Valdés, G. 2000. Introduction. *Spanish for Native Speakers, Volume I. AATSP Professional Development Series Handbook for teachers K-16*. New York: Harcourt College, 1–20.

Vergara-Wilson, D. and J. Dumont. 2015. The Emergent Grammar of Bilinguals: The Spanish Verb *hacer* 'do' with a Bare English Infinitive. *International Journal of Bilingualism* 19(4), 444–458.

Weinreich, U. 1953. *Languages in Contact: Findings and Problems*. The Hague: Mouton.

Yager, L., N. Hellmold, H-A. Joo, M. Putnam, E. Rossi, C. Stafford, and J. Salmons. 2015. New Structural Patterns in Moribund Grammar: Case Marking in Heritage German. *Frontiers in Psychology* 6, 1716.

Zenner, E., A. Backus, and E. Winter-Froemel (eds.) 2019. *Cognitive Contact Linguistics: Placing Usage, Meaning and Mind at the Core of Contact-Induced Variation and Change*. Berlin: DeGruyter.

Zyzik, E. 2019. Creativity and Conventionality in Heritage Speaker Bilingualism. *Language Learning* 70(1), 157–187.

20

A Narrative-Ethnographic Approach to Research on Heritage Language Development

Agnes Weiyun He

"Heritage languages," whether deemed a blessing or a burden by their speakers, are at the same time both valuable and vulnerable linguistic resources in an age of global, multidirectional flow of languages and lives. The "time-space compression" (Harvey 1990) brought forth by globalization and digitization has made it mandatory for us to cope with shifting and sometimes conflicting linguistic and cultural identities; to redefine our sense of linguistic integrity and cultural cohesiveness; to navigate and negotiate communicative borders both real and imagined; and to rethink what it means to acquire or abandon a language, and more fundamentally, what it entails to be a productive participant in the socio-cultural space that both unites and transcends the country/culture of our birth and that of our choice. Understanding such complex human conditions requires a kind of research perspective that is naturalistic, observational, and descriptive; that traces language and life in time and space; that contextualizes the notion of "heritage language" in the histories and contexts of its use; and that fundamentally assumes that language should be examined as both the venue and the vehicle for human development.

In this chapter, I present a qualitative approach to research on heritage language development – narrative ethnography, which integrates text-based methods of narrative analysis with field-based, interaction-enriched methods of linguistic anthropology. I will begin with an overview of its epistemological orientations and an exploration of its usefulness for HL research before discussing its methodological orientations. I will argue that such an approach is particularly productive for a context-dependent field such as heritage language development. I will conclude with a consideration of the merits and challenges of this approach and its potential to advance knowledge about heritage language development and learning.

20.1   Epistemological Orientations: Narrative Knowing and/as Scientific Understanding

A narrative, in this chapter, refers to an account of a series of related events or experiences across a significant span of life that either have taken place (i.e., true) or the speaker would like to see happen (i.e., aspirations and hopes). Broadly speaking, narrative analysis refers to a wide spectrum of research traditions that focus on formal, semantic, or interactional structures of narratives (Labov and Waletzky 1967/1997; Labov 1972; van Dijk 1977; de Beaugrande 1982; Fillmore 1982; Sacks 1992), or on the ways in which we use narratives to construct meanings such as personhood, identities, relationships, and communities (Scollon and Scollon 1981; Heath 1983; Polanyi 1989; Daiute and Lightfoot 2004). This current chapter focuses on the latter. It explores a research perspectives within the broader field of qualitative research, which uses stories, interviews, autobiography, journals, field notes, letters, conversations, family histories, and stated and observed life experience as bases of analyses to understand the way people make sense of their lives. This type of "narrative inquiry" has been applied in different ways in a wide range of fields including sociology, anthropology, sociolinguistics, history, literary criticism, philosophy, communication studies, and education research, among others. In these social science and humanities disciplines, "narrative" has been both the phenomenon being studied, such as a narrative of immigration and language adjustment, and the method used in the study, as a way of knowing and understanding (Polkinghorne 1988).

The construction of narrative involves postulating relatively speculative causal connections between well-observed, well-established events/phenomena. A narrative framework and scaffold can help us determine what to include as new, relevant events/phenomena. Where formal theories achieve precision and accuracy, narratives obtain richness as they track complex processes (twists, turns, constraints, possibilities, alternative paths, and opportunities taken or forsaken) in a developmental trajectory over time. However, narrative knowing and scientific understanding need not be antithetical to each other. In combination, they both enable us to understand and explain highly complex phenomena such as heritage language development. A robust scientific theory does not substitute for a rich narrative; conversely, a well-grounded narrative may well lead to a robust theory. What is measurable in quantifiable parameters may not be the same as what is meaningful to the participants. Whereas quantitative data at a large scale involves technologies to capture, store, and analyze and requires normalizing, standardizing, defining, and clustering (thus often stripping the data set of context, meaning, and stories), thick narrative-ethnographic data have the capacity to map unknown territory, thereby providing insight and inspiration. The two forms of knowing are not mutually exclusive and may well reinforce each other. Ultimately, explanations derived from rich, deep, significant (but seemingly anecdotal) narratives should complement theories generated by highly structured, formal scientific experiments and inferences.

Narratives in this sense, then, are not merely events strung together. They can serve as the medium for presenting evidence, or a mode for articulating concepts. They are not merely events/phenomena themselves, but become the means of bringing connection and coherence to otherwise disparate, random events and fragmented, chaotic phenomena, and become the path for unfolding or revealing events/phenomena. Such "narrative knowing" (Polkinghorne 1988) has the potential to integrate theories of heritage language development, to identify or fill in gaps between theories, thereby proving complementary to existing theories. It enables us to account for phenomena that can only be revealed, or best understood, in rich contexts and from multiple perspectives.

Narrative-ethnographic inquiry as a qualitative method in language development research integrates text-based methods of narrative analysis with field-based methods of ethnography. The term "narrative ethnography" is relatively new (Tedlock 1991), but the practice has long been employed by researchers of second language acquisition (see early work by Bailey (1980) using learner diaries as data) and has gained renewed attention in recent years (Pavlenko 2007; Benson 2014; De Fina and Georgakopoulou 2015). In language learning research, narrative data are typically collected through interviews, diaries and journals, semi-structured interviews, or e-mail exchanges – sources that are likely to provide the researcher with participant-based, subjective experiences and emic perspectives (Longhini 2002; Barkhuizen 2015). In this context, the narrative approach has been used as a framework to tell the stories of learners regarding their language learning experiences. Such stories reveal both actual events as experienced by learners and their reactions to these experiences in the process of learning a new language as well as learners' aspirations and expectations. As an emic approach, narratives explain how the language learners themselves make sense of their language development (Duff et al. 2013) and have the power and potential to explain the key constructs in language development such as motivation across the lifespan (Simon-Maeda 2011; Choi 2017) and changes over multiple scales of micro moments, speech events, and longitudinal time He (2016).

This approach becomes most productive when the phenomena in question involve complexity, variety, and contingency, and when events/phenomena need to be carefully "storied" in order to make sense. Heritage language development is one such case. To gain a full picture of HL development, we need to unravel the complex forces that shape the trajectory of acquisition/attrition/maintenance, the relationship between home language and mainstream societal language, the relationship between different participation structures and interactional routines when HL is used, the relationship between different communicative needs, choices and styles of different generations, as well as the relationship between different speech roles (e.g., speaker, hearer, eavesdropper, bystander) required for the same participants in different, sometimes simultaneous, sometimes consecutive, discourse contexts. HL research lends itself naturally to a narrative-ethnographic approach.

20.2   Uses of Narrative-Ethnography Approach for HL Research

Although not without conceptual difficulties (see Blackledge and Creese 2008; García et al. 2012; He 2013a; Mufwene 2016), the term *heritage language* (hereafter HL), has conventionally referred to an immigrant, indigenous, or ancestral language that a speaker personally finds relevant and desires to (re)connect with (Fishman 1991). In the United States, Canada, and the United Kingdom, the term has often been used synonymously with *community language*, *home language*, *native language*, and *mother tongue* to refer to a language other than English used by immigrants and their children (Valdés 2001; Wiley 2001;Van Deusen-Scholl 2003; He 2010). Accordingly, heritage speakers have most likely been exposed to the HL since birth and may have used the HL during the initial years of their life and on and off subsequently, but have never developed the full range of phonological, morphological, syntactic, pragmatic, and discourse patterns that will enable them to use it with the scope and sophistication characteristic of and comparable to native speakers' usage (Benmamoun et al. 2013). Having evolved historically into an ecology of extensive linguistic diversity as a result of immigration, the United States has become a milieu of massive language shift. Even though immigrant cultures may survive in some form into the third and fourth generations, immigrant languages generally experience rapid attrition, if not loss (Potowski 2013; Rumbaut and Massey 2014). Most intriguingly, given the largely voluntary nature of immigration, the shift from immigrant languages cannot be adequately explicated by external macro societal forces and pressures only; internal individual agency – the micro-level, evolving, context-specific purposes and significance that speakers attach to their immigrant languages – appears to play a significant role (Li 1994; Zentella 1997; Lo 2004; Zhu 2008; Tsu 2010; Fader 2011; Klein 2013; Avineri 2014; Yang and Wong 2014; He 2015). Current work on HL use and HL developmental trajectory thus challenges existing research on language shift that has generally evoked broadly conceived macro-level variables (such as colonization, industrialization, immigration, globalization, urbanization, assimilation, and national identity formation) that may accompany and correlate with language shift but are yet to sufficiently explain, let alone predict, when language shift will occur, as has long been noted by scholars such as Gal (1979), Kulick (1997), Mufwene (2017), Makihara & Schieffelin (2007), and Sankoff (1980, 2001).

A narrative-ethnographic approach enables us to focus on a small group of individuals and their families that have experienced changes in their language choices and language uses, over a sustained period of time and in a nonlinear manner. It approaches language development and language shift through a micro, interactional lens. It refrains from attributing heritage language shift directly (and, perhaps, simplistically) to immigration and globalization, from isolating language attitude (Gardner, 1985) as an exclusively psychological construct, and from abstracting language development from situated interpersonal engagement. Instead, it explores how macro-level social changes such as immigration and globalization have come to be lived everyday communicative experiences in the lives of individual persons and their families. Rather than using census data, questionnaires, or surveys covering large populations, a narrative-ethnographic approach relies on intensive analyses of language use by a small number of speakers that takes place in specific settings. It delineates the relationship between the ways in which speakers frame their lives and enact their identities, as well as the kinds of decisions they make about their languages, viz., whether to replace one language with another in daily communication or to oscillate along a bilingual continuum. In other words, a narrative-ethnographic approach enables us to present a study of language development and language change that is grounded in the shift of the speakers' projected and perceived identities as their immigration experiences unfold. It enables us to make sense of how those projections and perceptions are both codified in and mediated through dynamic language choices and language use.

The narratives we collect from HL learners at different life stages are intended to give prominence to the interconnected and collective meanings of life histories and life experiences of HL speakers with respect to their language trajectories. It is not our goal to capture and describe every possible kind of HL speaker. In fact, research has shown that using an ethnic language takes on different meanings for ethnic groups of different social statuses (de Fina 2007; Blommaert 2010; Pennycook 2010; Canagarajah 2013) and functions differently for different purposes, even for the same speakers at different stages of life (He 2011). Every diasporic experience creates a pattern of its own. No single experience can be conveniently mapped onto another, regardless of origin. By providing narratives of the lives of HL learners, our goal is to examine how the acquisition, attrition, re-acquisition, and maintenance of an HL take place at different times and in different settings so that researchers, educators, parents, and HL speakers themselves may find resonance and relevance to their own circumstances. In some sense, this approach parallels a number of efforts in applied linguistics and linguistic anthropology, including research on identity investment and language learning over time and space (Rampton, 2006; Norton 2013), the examination of socialization across speech events (Li 1994; Zentella 1997; Wortham 2005; Fader 2009), and the tracking of speakers' behavioral change across interactions (Markee, 2008; Choi 2017). When applied appropriately, this approach may shed unique light on both HLs and HL learners.

20.2.1 Continual Unfolding: Narratives of Languages

A narrative-ethnographic approach considers micro, discursive processes as underlying language choice in immigrant communities that can lead ultimately to the abandonment or attrition of heritage languages. To an individual, an HL may provide valuable personal and familial resources, or it can become a linguistic and cultural liability. There have been substantive debates at social and political as well as cultural and linguistic levels on whether HLs should be maintained and whether the loss of HLs is part of the price to be paid for becoming acculturated into mainstream society (Fishman 1991; Wong-Fillmore 1991; Hornberger 2004). Some communities and individuals have taken active and proactive measures to ensure that their HL is passed down from one generation to the next, while others have let theirs disappear gradually or almost abruptly.

What are the decisive factors for the success of HL development and maintenance? How do learner attitude, motivation, and social network enhance or hinder HL development? Why is it that we often witness a resistance to HL learning when speakers are young but subsequently an embrace of HL after they come of age? What is the impact of speaker identity (projected as well as perceived, interactional as well as developmental) on the HL learning process? How do the political history, geography, demography, and social status of the HL impact its maintenance or attrition? What is the role of classroom cultural and interactional practices in shaping the HL development trajectory? Which factors (e.g., amount of input, years of schooling, parental educational levels, and gender) determine whether HL speakers are literate in the HL? Should variation among the speakers' home varieties of their HLs be revitalized or eradicated? How do language ideologies interact with particular pedagogical objectives? A narrative-ethnographic approach enables us to elucidate these complexities and to situate the HL learning process in a learner-centered, context-enriched, humanistic dimension.

For some, *heritage* as a noun may denote something of the past, something that has a fixed, static, essential property. However, like all languages, HLs change over time. HLs are fluid and always in flux with respect to evolving social and cultural conditions; as such, they provide a critical lens that facilitates our understanding of the construction and reconstruction of identities, communities, and cultures in human diaspora. As immigrant experience unfolds, the language used in immigrant households changes in sound and significance. As parents' (and grandparents') exposure to the societal mainstream language increases and intensifies, as digital communication becomes more common, as immigrants from specific regions with specific dialects/languages get into more frequent contact with those from other regions with other dialects/languages, the home language may undergo changes in lexis, phonology, morphology, syntax, and certainly in discourse and interactional patterns in the form of multiple-sourced language use, known as multi-performance (He 2013b) or translanguaging (Li 2011). The HL that is initially used by necessity (due to parents' inadequate proficiency in the mainstream language) may eventually become a language used in the household by choice (as parents' bilingual repertoire expands). The use of HL that is initially meant to preserve the home culture may evolve to be viewed as a means toward greater career options in the increasingly globalized world. The motivation for using HL may also evolve from nostalgia of the past to aspirations for the future.

In the age of immigration and globalization, given the inevitable language contact and competition between the HL and mainstream language and between different dialects/languages that immigrants bring to the United States, there are bound to be hierarchical orders of languages and dialects, which in turn may lead to concerns and challenges regarding the status or even the legitimacy of some languages or some varieties of a certain language. Canagarajah's (2013) examination of Tamil as a diasporic, heritage language in Sri Lanka, for example, suggests that, even though the participants in his study speak a hybrid Tamil that is not equivalent to the language used by fully proficient Tamil speakers, they still believe that their heritage language is intact, except that it has gone through transformation triggered by contact with other languages. This leads Canagarajah to conclude that heritage languages within diasporic communities go through redefinition as their practitioners negotiate the place of their ethnic identities in the host societies and cultures.

Because language indexes culture and identity, as culture and identity acquire newer forms, language also transforms in order to acquire new indexicality, hence, creating new values. Fader's (2009) research on heritage language use by Hasidic Jews in New York City is a case in point. Fader (2009: 91–107) documented a specific kind of "Hasidic multilingualism," where the emphasis is not on how speakers distinguish between English and Yiddish, but rather on the simultaneous use of two languages through interweaving features of phonology, lexis, syntax, and speech genres from both languages in order to both preserve the past and incorporate modernity. As a result, children in this community are socialized to speak syncretic forms of Hasidic Yiddish and Hasidic English, with the goal of not merely maintaining the heritage language but also maintaining the Hasidic Jewish identity.

A narrative-ethnographic approach highlights the fact that the heritage culture has a complex, developing, transnational, intercultural, cross-linguistic, and hybrid life. It also treats an HL as an emergent story that undergoes deconstruction and reconstruction processes, as a result of its usage by HL speakers and their interlocutors (He 2011). As such, instead of reinforcing or endorsing the idea of heritage language and culture as a set of essentialized practices and concepts, a narrative-ethnographic approach explores the *transformative* potential of HLs (He 2006) – how they enable speakers to actively (re)construct themselves as members of a particular ethnicity, nationality, speech community, social rank, and profession, and to (re)create a new set of familiar and familial, ethnolinguistic indexicalities, while at the same time being transformed through the evolving practices of their speakers.

20.2.2   Complex Shifts: Narratives of Learners

Human beings are primarily *homo narrans* (Niles 1999). Narrative is the main form of social life because it is the main device for making sense of social action. All HL learners have a narrative about themselves that they tell themselves and others in order to bring coherence and continuity and to make sense of cross-cultural, cross-linguistic lives. Each of them possesses, constructs, and lives an unfolding narrative, which constitutes the core of their identities. In this context and for this reason, it is imperative for HL development to be understood in terms of the HL speaker's identity construction process, and it is necessary to appreciate the identity formations and transformations as inseparable from various trajectories of language development. Viewing identity as a process of constructing a lifespan narrative rather than as a specific developmental stage or a static category enables us to see identity as inherently dynamic and consistently open to re-enactment, revision, and re-presentation.

For illustrative purposes, let us consider the linguistic auto-ethnography by Julie Choi (2017). In this work, Choi examines her own multilingualism (what she terms "multivocality") across the lifespan. She was born and raised in New York, living largely within a Korean-American community and speaking Korean as a heritage language at home, English at school, and a mix of Korean and English in the Korean-American community. Despite New York being the place of birth and upbringing and Korea being her ancestral homeland where she has strong familial ties, she did not have a strong sense of identity either as an American or as a Korean. Subsequently, she spent equal numbers of years in Beijing and Tokyo, from which she found a meaningful identity in Japanese but not in Chinese and acquired a stronger command of Japanese through schooling and work than her heritage language Korean. The work was completed and presented as "work in progress" (xxi) as the researcher continues to experience and explore a multilingual life.

In order to make sense of her complex and dynamic changes in life and language, Choi combines narrative studies with ethnography and gathered two major types of data – external and personal (74–75). The external includes diaries, photos, letters, cards, teachers' notes, classroom handouts, song lyrics, screen shots of TV shows, plots of popular dramas, paintings, and content and images of books read from the different places where she lived for extended periods of time – New York, Seoul, Beijing, Tokyo, Sydney – which corresponded to the major stages of her life from childhood, to adolescence, youth, and adulthood. The personal includes memories in the form of reconstructed dialogues, commentaries, reflections, and analyses. She uses the aforementioned data as "texts of personal experience" (xxxiv) to examine "the multiple forces that crisscross particular events, explore what lies at the intersections, and find ways of broadening possibilities for identity development" (xxxv). Her goal is to explore the "multiple meanings, interpretations, histories, social conditions, dimensions of affect and creative energy" (xxix) that have shaped the trajectory of her language choice and language use. Situating Korean, her heritage language, in the context of a whole range of linguistic resources at her disposal (including also English, Chinese, and Japanese) and documenting and reflecting on the responses and reactions to her language and cultural backgrounds from her peers, friends, teachers, family members, and strangers, Choi argues that her language choices (whether HL or non-HL) and her projected and perceived identity options (whether as American, Korean, Japanese, Chinese, or any form of combination of these) are highly susceptible to the historical, political, social, and cultural stance, the embodiment of which ranges from macro-level ideologies concerning immigration and globalization to micro-level everyday practices such as different pronunciations of spellings of the "same" name in different spaces by different interlocutors.

As Choi's work illustrates, the multiple dimensions to HL speakers' lives are open to multiple interpretations. Consequently, the HL speaker's life history is highly unpredictable. Unpredictability does not, however, imply inexplicability. The sense of purpose of a story is not determined *a priori*, but emerges as the narrative takes shape and the meaning and purpose of the linguistic repertoire is reshaped. A speaker's life history involves not only searching for the significance of the HL but also creating it. A lifespan narrative approach instates the meaning and significance of HL as both the results and the antecedents of linguistic practice. In this sense then, HL learner development is understood as a form of narrative, a form of social life, a form of knowledge and knowing, and a form of communication.

Such a sociocultural view of narrative life history and identity construction enables us to realize that the lifespan narratives we study and portray are always and forever a part of other narratives. As such, their origins are not assignable to a single time or place. The lifespan narratives through which we make sense of HL development are not researchers' introspection or imagination but participants' lived and reflected experiences. Like identity, instead of being reducible to an essence, lifespan narratives emerge only as we focus our attention on not only the public but also the private; not only the communal and familial but also the individual; not only the past but also the present and the future. The value of such a perspective is that one individual's lifespan narratives can be other individuals' mirror and metaphor. Through a lifespan narrative lens, we may vicariously insert ourselves into the life of others to seek relevance and references. Next, I turn to methodological matters.

20.3   Methodological Considerations: Doing Narrative-ethnography

The process of engaging in research guided by narrative research typically includes the following steps: (1) focusing on a small number of individuals; (2) gathering various forms of data (stories, documents, conversations, interviews, observations, etc.) about the individuals' lived and told experiences across a significant span of life; (3) shaping the data into a chronological and logical order; (4) analyzing the themes of the data and ways in which data are produced (the telling of stories, the manner of conversations, etc.); (5) locating turning points (Denzin 1989) in the data; (6) drawing inferences and significances. It involves a sewing together of events, stories, interactions, conversations, and interviews for purposes of meaning-making and identity construction (Tedlock 1991, 2004; Atkinson and Hammersley 1994; Holstein and Gubrium 2000a, 2000b; Barkhuizen 2015). Throughout the process, we need to pay particular attention to issues concerning the nature of research questions, the role of theories, the role of the researcher, field methods, the kinds of data, and the ways in which results are presented.

The research questions in a narrative-ethnographic approach have a dynamic nature that contrasts with the predetermined, fixed nature of questions found in studies in the hypothesis-testing paradigm. Whereas researchers conducting correlational or experimental studies spell out their questions and hypotheses in advance and adhere to them throughout the study (when they modify their questions, they do so for subsequent studies), narrative-ethnographic researchers pose broad questions at the onset of the study, but they refine and refocus their questions in the field as the study evolves. The reason is that some of the issues that are important only come to light in the field and cannot be predetermined or be foreseen. Hence a good part of narrative-ethnographic work is hypothesis-generating rather than hypothesis-testing.

Since new and refined/refocused questions emerge as field research proceeds, the theory or theories guiding the study may also shift or expand. Theories that are most foundational for narrative-ethnography of HL development typically address socio-cultural processes and interactional structures, including language socialization (Schieffelin and Ochs 1986, 1996; Ochs and Schieffelin 2008; Duranti et al. 2011), interactional sociolinguistics (Hymes 1972; Gumperz 1982), participation structures in learning environments (Heath 1983; Cazden 1988), language attitudes and motivations (Gardner 1985; Schumann 1986), language and identity (Norton 2013), individual differences in language learners (Dörnyei 2005), and ethical considerations in language learning research (Ortega 2005). Part of the goal of doing narrative-ethnography is to expand the scope suggested by prior theory in order to identify what may be missing or misleading in existing theory and to search for patterns of language use and their meanings/significance that is specific to the situation under study (Copland et al. 2015).

In the ethnographic tradition of research on language learning/use (Barkhuizen et al. 2013; Duff 2021), the researcher plays a dual role, both as a keen observer and reflective participant (the extreme case of which would be Choi (2017), where the researcher herself becomes the object of study), and as the narrator providing explanations of events/phenomena in natural settings. While the researcher is a key instrument for data collection, the researcher–narrator dual status affords the researcher space to establish her/his credibility and enables the reader to experience complexity, unpredictability, surprise, or difficulty about her/his field work vicariously.

To accomplish the goal of discovering and presenting the participant's view (the emic view), researchers reply primarily on observation and interview as field methods (e.g., Fader 2009). Researchers spend a great deal of time observing what actually, naturally happens in the field as they collect and make sense of the participants' narratives. Observation may (but does not have to) take place while the researcher herself/himself also participates in the events being observed (participant observation). For example, an HL researcher may also serve as a volunteer teacher in community-based heritage language schools. Narrative-ethnographers also go beyond naturalistic observation to intrude on the natural setting and obtain particular information directly from the participants through various interviews, including life history interviews and key informant (e.g., our target HL learner and his/her family members) interviews, ranging in style from highly structured to very informal. Given the emic goal of the research, the interview should be conducted in a way that promotes the natural unfolding of the participant's narratives and their meanings and perspectives.

In terms of the kinds of data, besides observation and interview data, the researcher may also gather a variety of hand-written and digital materials such as diaries, letters, samples of learners' homework, family correspondences (either hand-written or digital), community demographic data, audio- and video-recordings of actual interactions in the home and in the classroom, photos, etc., as richly illustrated by Choi (2017). However, the data themselves do not make the study narrative-ethnographic; it is the fact that the researcher attends to the context in gathering, interpreting, and reporting narratives that does. As Choi observes (131), the narratives are not just told; they are "always told within a specific set of conditions and fused by a practice of certain kind of telling." The context can be the "culture" of the family, the community, or the classroom, or the larger context of immigration history, language ideology, and language policy. The analysis of narrative ethnographic data is necessarily inductive, comprehensive, recursive, and interpretative, with the end products being descriptions and interpretations of HL learning and HL use that are grounded in both micro and macro contexts.

A few guidelines are useful for the presentation of results of narrative-ethnographic analyses. First, sequentiality. Narratives would appear to follow chronological sequences. After all, they tell stories over time. However, much is to be said about the kinds of chronology. Since language development is necessarily longitudinal, involving change over time, some narratives are certainly presented in the sequence of real time events, such as the developmental narratives of the (heritage) language learner from infanthood to adulthood, the big societal narratives of immigration and language contact across generations, or perhaps the micro narratives of turn-by-turn, moment-by-moment interaction over a sustained period of time. But some narratives can order events/phenomena in logical sequence as well: The sequencing of events/phenomena is determined by the logical relationships between them, such as cause-effect, condition-outcome, circumstances/constraints. Ethnographic details, for instance, would be one example of narrating the interconnectedness between events/phenomena that is not exactly temporal in nature. Hence, while narratives often present accounts over time, they are not a mere temporal sequence of events/ phenomena; rather, they are also organized around a specifiable, non-temporal connection.

Second, explicability. Since narratives present events/phenomena related to one another in a sequence beyond a temporal listing of events/phenomena, they have the power and/or potential not merely to document and describe but also to explain such events/phenomena. Narratives give shape, structure, and significance to the seemingly fragmented events/phenomena and make sense of them in scientific terms. For example, what sets of conditions collectively create the likelihood of HL maintenance in the household? Is the family language policy sufficient to give a credible account of language dynamics or do we need also to take into consideration the societal attitudes to the specific HL in order to have a narrative that fully explains the variable outcomes of HL? Narratives attempt to figure how things fit together, how they relate to one another, what effect some cause might have, what cause might have produced this effect.

Third, coherence. As narratives strive to establish relations between events/phenomena from various sources and settings that are within the scope of what is to be described or explained, they must also meet the criterion of "coherence." The narrativizing process may involve different pieces of theories or different conceptual elements. It is a process of coherence making, of showing how disparate elements interrelate, so as to make an account that is coherent in itself, thereby enabling integration and synthesis. This process of narrativization may serve to identify gaps in evidence that might then be filled through the search for further, additional pieces of evidence. The piecing together may also serve to delineate where and why the different accounts and different elements fit or do not fit together. Constructing narratives thus becomes a natural conduit for bringing related, relevant elements into order and for making meaning out of otherwise fragmented events and experiences.

Fourth and finally, perspective. Narrative perspective refers to a set of features shaping a story: What is being told? What information is included and what left out? Who is the story teller? Who is the story about? From whose point of view is the story told? What are the broad sociopolitical discourses, local contexts of participants' lives, and the immediate situational contexts of story-telling? Given that stories of heritage language development are inevitably stories about the quest for identity and about growth and change across languages, lives, geographies, and generations and given that language development, affect, community, and communicative engagement are inseparable from one another, there are bound to be multiple participants, multiple perspectives, and therefore multiple versions of the "same" story. A clear sense of perspective gives meaning and significance to narratives and narrativizing.

20.4   Merits and Challenges

The goal of using a narrative-ethnographic approach is to draw large conclusions from small but chronologically/logically related and densely textured events/experiences and to support broad assertions about the role of context and culture in the development of heritage language by situating language and life in complex, concrete specifics. As is the case with any other analytic perspective, however, a narrative-ethnography approach to research on HL learning certainly faces its own challenges, the greatest of which is the validity of this line of work. Are the narratives collected valid? Is the process of narrativization valid? In narrative-ethnographic research, what is the narrativized text intended to represent? Are the narratives and narrativized accounts valid representations of the participant's life and language? Are they the co-constructions jointly produced by the researcher and the participant? Are they exact or modified recounts about past events and happenings, considered or off-the-cuff projections of the future? To make claims supported by the narrative textual evidence, the researcher needs to understand and make clear the nature of her/his collected and (re-)constructed narratives, addressing challenges with regard to the degree of participants' disclosure, the limits imposed by language itself and by the level of participants' language proficiency, the influence of the researcher on participants' responses, and the gap between small stories and large issues.

Not necessarily all HL learners and their interlocutors are naturally, readily "narrative." Participants may be reluctant to reveal or resistant to revealing self-explorations of their experiences and understandings. Furthermore, participants' descriptions may be selective, leaving out those parts they for whatever reason do not wish to share. What does get included may be somewhat *ad hoc*, partial or piecemeal, or a compromise of rigor for the sake of the greater meaning (Creswell 2013). It requires a certain degree of familiarity with and a certain degree of trust in the researcher for the participant to open up fully.

As the philosopher Wittgenstein observed, the language we use (including the language we use when we narrate ourselves and others) can be limiting or even distorting. Our experiences and reflections on experiences are inevitably more complicated and more intricate than the categories and generalizations that are conveyed through the lexico-grammar of any given language, and certainly even more so if the narrative interviews are conducted in a language that is not the participant's dominant language (for some, the dominant language may be the HL; for others, it may be the mainstream language).

Furthermore, the final narratives generated from interviews and observations are not merely data gathered from participants; they embody as well the researcher's objectives and preferences. Briggs (1986) noted that the very ways in which we ask questions may impose limitations on or suggest directions for answers. Researcher attributes such as language choice/language style, immigrant experience (or lack thereof), socio-culture status, gender, and nonverbal behavior may all contribute to participants' choice of responses.

The final challenge comes from the interpretation of narratives. Ultimately, on the basis of participants' narratives, the researcher is to interpret and clarify the meanings of the narratives and to make connections between narrativized texts and the interpretations of those texts so as to deepen the reader's understanding of the meaning conveyed through the narrative. S/he also infers implications in the narrative for understanding other narratives, taking into account the impact of the social and cultural contingencies. The challenge for future work here is to ensure the credibility of the connection we make between small stories of mundane interaction in everyday life and big stories of language development and language change and to ensure the credibility of the link between a collection of remarks and anecdotes and linguistic/cultural landscapes of the family, the community, and even the country.

20.5   Acknowledgment

This chapter benefited from constructive comments by Hongyin Tao, an anonymous reader, as well as the editors of the volume. I alone am responsible for any remaining errors and deficiencies.

References

Atkinson, P. and M. Hammersley. 1994. Ethnography and Participant Observation. In N. K. Denzin and Y. S. Lincoln (eds.), *Handbook of Qualitative Research*. Thousand Oaks, CA: Sage, 248–261.

Avineri, N. 2014. Yiddish: A Jewish Language in the Diaspora. In T. Wiley, J. Kreeft-Peyton, D. Christian, S. K. Moore, and N. Liu (eds.), *Handbook of Heritage, Community, and Native American Languages in the United States: Research, Educational Practice, and Policy*. New York: Routledge, 263–271.

Bailey, K. 1980. An Introspective Analysis of an Individual's Language Learning Experience. In R. Scarcella and S. Krashen (eds.), *Research on Second Language Acquisition*. Rowley, MA: Newbury House, 58–65.

Barkhuizen, G. 2015. Narrative Knowledging in Second Language Teaching and Learning Contexts. In A. De Fina and A. Georgakopoulou (eds.), *The Handbook of Narrative Analysis*. Hoboken, NJ: John Wiley & Sons, 97–115.

Barkhuizen, G., P. Benson, and A. Chik. 2013. *Narrative Inquiry in Language Teaching and Learning Research*. London: Routledge.

Bell, S. 1988. Becoming a Political Woman: The Reconstruction and Interpretation of Experience through Stories. In A. D. Todd and S. Fisher (eds.), *Gender and Discourse: The Power of Talk*. Norwood, NJ: Ablex, 97–123.

Benmamoun, E., M. Silvina, and M. Polinsky. 2013. Heritage Languages and Their Speakers: Opportunities and Challenges for Linguistics. *Theoretical Linguistics* 39(3–4), 129–181.

Benson, P. 2014. Narrative Inquiry in Applied Linguistics Research. *Annual Review of Applied Linguistics* 34, 154–170.

Blackledge, A. and A. Creese. 2008. Contesting 'Language' as 'Heritage': Negotiation of Identities in Late Modernity. *Applied Linguistics* 29(4), 533–554.

Blommaert, J. 2010. *The Sociolinguistics of Globalization*. Cambridge: Cambridge University Press.

Briggs, C. 1986. *Learning How to Ask*. Cambridge: Cambridge University Press.

Bruner, J. 1991. The Narrative Construction of Reality. *Critical Inquiry* 18(1), 1–21.

Canagarajah, S. 2013. Reconstructing Heritage Language: Resolving Dilemmas in Language Maintenance for Sri Lankan Tamil Migrants. *International Journal of the Sociology of Language* 222, 131–155.

Cazden, C. B. 1988. *Classroom Discourse: The Language of Teaching and Learning*. Portsmouth, NH: Heinemann.

Choi, J. 2017. *Creating a Multivocal Self: Autoethnography as Method*. New York: Routledge.

Copland, F. and A. Creese, with F. Rock and S. E. Shaw. 2015 *Linguistic Ethnography: Collecting, Analysing and Presenting Data*. London: Sage.

Creswell, J. W. 2013. *Qualitative Inquiry and Research Design*. Los Angeles: Sage.

Daiute, C. and C. Lightfoot (eds.) 2004. *Narrative Analysis: Studying the Development of Individuals in Society*. Thousand Oaks, CA: Sage.

De Beaugrande, R. 1982. The Story of Grammars and the Grammar of Stories. *Journal of Pragmatics* 6(5–6), 383–422.

De Fina, A. 2007. Code-switching and the Construction of Ethnic Identity in a Community of Practice. *Language in Society* 36, 371–392.

De Fina, A. and A. Georgakopoulou (eds.) 2015. *The Handbook of Narrative Analysis*. Hoboken, NJ: John Wiley & Sons.

Denzin, N. K. 1989. *Interpretive Biography*. Newbury Park: Sage.

Dörnyei, Z. 2005. *The Psychology of the Language Learner: Individual Differences in Second Language Acquisition*. New York: Routledge.

Duff, P. 2021. *Ethnographic Research in Applied Linguistics: Exploring Language Teaching, Learning, and Use in Diverse Communities*. London: Routledge.

Duff, P., T. Anderson, R. Ilnyckyj, E. van Gaya, R. T. Wang, and E. Yates. 2013. *Learning Chinese*. Berlin: De Gruyter Mouton.

Duranti, A., E. Ochs, and B. Schieffelin (eds.) 2011. *The Handbook of Language Socialization*. Oxford: Blackwell.

Fader, A. 2009. *Mitzvah Girls*. Princeton, NJ: Princeton University Press.

Fader, A. 2011. Language Socialization and Morality. In A. Duranti, E. Ochs, and B. Schieffelin (eds.), *The Handbook of Language Socialization*. Oxford: Blackwell, 321–340.

Fillmore, C. J. 1982. Towards a Descriptive Framework for Spatial Deixis. In R. J. Jarvella and W. Klein (eds.), *Speech, Place and Action: Studies in Deixis and Related Topics*. New York: John Wiley & Sons, 31–59.

Fishman, J. A. 1991. *Reversing Language Shift: Theoretical and Empirical Foundations of Assistance to Threatened Languages*. Clevedon: Multilingual Matters.

Harvey, D. 1990. *The Condition of Postmodernity: An Enquiry into the Origins of Cultural Change*. Cambridge, MA: Blackwell.

Gal, S. 1979. *Language Shift: Social Determinants of Linguistic Change in Bilingual Australia*. San Francisco: Academic Press.

García, O., Z. Zakharia, and B. Otcu (eds.) 2012. *Bilingual Community Education and Multilingualism: Beyond Heritage Languages in a Global City*. Clevedon: Multilingual Matters.

Gardner, R. C. 1985. *Social Psychology and Second Language Learning: The Role of Attitudes and Motivation*. London: Edward Arnold.

Gumperz, J. 1982. *Discourse Strategies*. New York: Cambridge University Press.

He, A. W. 2006. Toward an Identity-based Model for the Development of Chinese As a Heritage Language. *The Heritage Language Journal* 4(1), 1–28.

He, A. W. 2010. The Heart of Heritage: Sociocultural Dimensions of Heritage Language Learning. *Annual Review of Applied Linguistics* 30, 66–82.

He, A. W. 2011. Heritage Language Socialization. In A. Duranti, E. Ochs, and B. Schieffelin (eds.), *The Handbook of Language Socialization*. Oxford: Blackwell, 587–609.

He, A. W. 2013a. Language of the Heart and Heritage: A Tangled Tale. Plenary Address Delivered at the Annual Meeting of the American Association for Applied Linguistics (AAAL). March 16–19, Dallas, Texas.

He, A. W. 2013b. The Wor(L)D Is a Collage: Multi-performance by Chinese Heritage Language Speakers. *The Modern Language Journal* 97(2), 304–317.

He, A. W. 2014. Heritage Language Development and Identity Construction throughout the Life Cycle. In T. G. Wiley, J. K. Peyton, D. Christian,

S. C. K. Moore, and N. Liu (eds.), *Handbook of Heritage, Community, and Native American Languages in the United States: Research, Policy, and Educational Practice*. New York: Routledge, 324–332.

He, A. W. 2015. Chinese as a Heritage Language. In W. Wang and C. Sun (eds.), *Oxford Handbook of Chinese Linguistics*. Oxford: Oxford University Press, 578–589.

He, A. W. 2016. Heritage Language Learning and Socialization. In P. A. Duff and S. May (eds.), *Language Socialization, Encyclopedia of Language and Education*. Berlin: Springer. https://doi.org/10.1007/978-3-319-02327-4-14-1

Heath, S. B. 1983. *Ways with Words*. Cambridge: Cambridge University Press.

Holstein, J. A. and J. F. Gubrium. 2000a. *Constructing the Life Course*. Lanham, MD: AltaMira Press.

Holstein, J. A. and J. F. Gubrium. 2000b. *The Self We Live by: Narrative Identity in a Postmodern World*. New York: Oxford University Press.

Hornberger, N. 2004. The Continua of Biliteracy and the Bilingual Educator: Educational Linguistics in Practice. *International Journal of Bilingual Education and Bilingualism* 7(2–3), 155–171.

Hymes, D. 1964. The Ethnography of Communication. *American Anthropologist* 66, 6–56.

Hymes, D. 1972. What Is Ethnography? in P. Gilmore and A. A. Glatthorn (eds.), *Children In and Out of School: Ethnography and Education*. Washington, DC: Centre for Applied Linguistics, 21–32.

Kellman, S. G. 2000. *The Translingual Imagination*. Lincoln: University of Nebraska Press.

Klein, W. 2013. Heritage Language Socialization and Language Ideologies in a Sikh Education Program. *Heritage Language Journal* 10(1), 36–50.

Kramsch, C. 2010. *The Multilingual Subject*. New York: Oxford University Press.

Kulick, D. 1997. *Language Shift and Cultural Reproduction: Socialization, Self and Syncretism in a Papua New Guinean Village*. Cambridge: Cambridge University Press.

Labov, W. 1972. The Transformation of Experience in Narrative Syntax. In *Language in the Inner City*. Philadelphia: University of Pennsylvania Press, 354–396.

Labov, W. and J. Waletzky. 1967. Narrative Analysis. In J. Helm (ed.), *Essays on the Verbal and Visual Arts*. Seattle: University of Washington Press, 12–44. Reprinted in *Journal of Narrative and Life History* 7, 3–38, 1997.

Li, Wei. 1994. *Three Generations, Two Languages, One Family*. Clevedon: Multilingual Matters.

Li, Wei. 2011. Moment Analysis and Translanguaging Space. *Journal of Pragmatics* 43(5), 1222–1235.

Lindenfeld, J. and G. Varro. 2008. Language Maintenance among Fortunate Immigrants: The French in the United States and Americans in France. *International Journal of the Sociology of Language* 189, 115–131.

Lo, A. 2004. Evidentiality and Morality in a Korean Heritage Language School. *Pragmatics* 14(2–3), 235–256.

Longhini, A. 2002. Focusing on Learning Styles and Strategies: A Diary Study in an Immersion Setting. *Language Learning* 52, 401–438.

Makihara, M. and B. Schieffelin (eds.) 2007. *Consequences of Contact*. Oxford: Oxford University press.

Markee, N. 2008. Toward a Learning Behavior Tracking Methodology for CA-for-SLA. *Applied Linguistics*, 1–24.

McKay, S. L. and S. C. Wong. 1996. Multiple Discourses, Multiple Identities. *Harvard Educational Review* 66(3), 577–608.

Mufwene, S. S. 2016. A Cost-and-Benefit Approach to Language Loss. In L. Filipović and M. Pütz (eds.), *Endangered languages and languages in Danger*. New York: John Benjamins, 115–143.

Mufwene, S. S. 2017. Language Vitality: Weak Theoretical Underpinnings of What Can Be an Exciting Research Area. *Language* (Perspectives, February 2017).

Niles, J. D. 1999. *Homo Narrans: The Poetics and Anthropology of Oral Literature*. Philadelphia: University of Pennsylvania Press.

Norton, B. 2013. *Identity and Language Learning: Extending the Conversation*. Bristol: Multilingual Matters.

Ochs, E. and B. Schieffelin. 2008. Language Socialization: An Historical Overview. In P. Duff and N. Hornberger (eds.), *Encyclopedia of Language and Education, Vol. 8, Language Socialization*. New York: Springer, 3–15.

Ortega, L. 2005. For What and for Whom Is Our Research? The Ethical As Transformative Lens in Instructed SLA. *Modern Language Journal* 89(3), 427–443.

Pavlenko, A. 2007. Autobiographic Narratives as Data in Applied Linguistics. *Applied Linguistics* 28(2), 163–188.

Pennycook, A. 2010 *Language as a Local Practice*. New York: Routledge.

Polanyi, L. 1989. *Telling the American Story*. Cambridge, MA: The MIT Press.

Polkinghorne, D. 1988. *Narrative Knowing and the Human Sciences*. Albany, NY: SUNY Press.

Potowski, K. 2013. Language Maintenance and Shift. In R. Bayley, R. Cameron, and C. Lucas (eds.), *The Oxford Handbook of Sociolinguistics*. https://doi.org/10.1093/oxfordhb/9780199744084.013.0016

Rampton, B. 2006 *Language in Late Modernity: Interaction in an Urban School*. Cambridge: Cambridge University Press.

Riessman, C. K. 1993. *Narrative Analysis*. Newbury Park: Sage Publications.

Rumbaut, R. G. and D. S. Massey. 2014. Immigration and Language Diversity in the United States. *Daedalus* 2013 Summer 142(3), 141–154. Retrieved from www.ncbi.nlm.nih.gov/pmc/articles/PMC4092008/

Sacks, H. (1992). Lectures 1–8, Part IV, Spring 1970. In G. Jefferson (ed.), *Lectures on Conversation*. Vol. II, Harvey Sacks. Oxford: Blackwell, 215–288.

Sankoff, G. 1980. Introduction. In G. Sankoff (ed.), *The Social Life of Language*. Philadelphia: University of Pennsylvania Press, ix–xxii.

Sankoff, G. 2001. Linguistic Outcomes of Language Contact. In Peter Trudgill, J. Chambers, and N. Schilling-Estes (eds.), *Handbook of Sociolinguistics*. Oxford: Basil Blackwell, 638–668.

Schieffelin, B. and E. Ochs (eds.) 1986. *Language Socialization across Cultures*. New York: Cambridge University Press.

Schieffelin, B. and E. Ochs. 1996. The Microgenesis of Competence. In D. Slobin, J. Gerhardt, A. Kyratzis, and J. Guo (eds.), *Social Interaction, Social Context, and Language*. Mahwah, NJ: Lawrence Erlbaum, 251–264.

Schumann, J. 1986. Research on the Acculturation Model for Second Language Acquisition. *Journal of Multiligual and Multicultural Development* 7, 379–392

Scollon, R. and S. Scollon. 1981. *Narrative, Literacy and Face in Interethnic Communication*. Norwood, NJ: Ablex.

Simon-Maeda, A. 2011. *Being and Becoming a Speaker of Japanese: An Autobiographic Account*. Buffalo, NY: Multilingual Matters.

Tan, E. K. 2017. A Rhizomatic Account of Heritage Language. In S. Canagarajah (ed.), *The Routledge Handbook of Migration and Language*. New York: Routeledge, 468–485.

Tedlock, B. 1991. From Participant Observation to the Observation of Participation: The Emergence of Narrative Ethnography. *Journal of Anthropological Research* 47, 69–94.

Tedlock, B. 2004. Narrative Ethnography as Social Science Discourse. *Studies in Symbolic Interaction* 27, 23–31.

Tsu, J. 2010. *Sound and Script in Chinese Diaspora*. Cambridge, MA: Harvard University Press.

Valdés, G. 2001. Heritage Language Students. In J. K. Peyton, D. A. Ranard, and S. McGinnis (eds.), *Heritage Languages in America. Preserving a National Resource*. McHenry, IL: CAL, 37–80.

Van Deusen-Scholl, N. 2003. Toward a Definition of Heritage Language: Sociopolitical and Pedagogical Considerations. *Journal of Language, Identity, and Education* 2(3), 211–230.

Watson, C. 2007. Small Stories, Positioning Analysis, and the Doing of Professional Identities in Learning to Teach. *Narrative Inquiry* 17, 371–389.

Watson-Gegeo, K. A. 2004. Mind, Language, and Epistemology: Toward a Language Socialization Paradigm for SLA. *The Modern Language Journal* 88 (3), 331–350.

Wiley, T. G. 2001. On Defining Heritage Languages and Their Speakers. In J. K. Peyton, D. A. Ranard, and S. McGinnis (eds.), *Heritage Languages in America: Preserving a National Resource*. Washington, DC: Delta Systems/Center for Applied Linguistics, 29–36.

Wong, K. F. and Y. Xiao. 2010. Diversity and Difference. *Heritage Language Journal* 7(2), 153–187.

Wong Fillmore, L. 1991. When Learning a Second Language Means Losing the First. *Early Childhood Research Quarterly* 6, 323–346.

Wortham, S. 2005. Socialization beyond the Speech Event. *Journal of Linguistic Anthropology* 15(1), 95–112.

Yang, X. and K. F. Wong. 2014. Exploring Heritage Language Anxiety. *The Modern Language Journal* 98(2), 589–611.

Zentella, A. C. 1997. *Growing up Bilingual: Puerto Rican Children in New York.* Malden, MA: Blackwell.

Zhu, H. 2008. Duelling Languages, Duelling Values: Codeswitching in Bilingual Intergenerational Conflict Talk in Diasporic Families. *Journal of Pragmatics* 40(10), 1799–1816.

21

Corpus-Based Methodologies in the Study of Heritage Languages

Olesya Kisselev

21.1 Introduction

Over the course of the past few decades, the study of heritage languages has evolved as a truly interdisciplinary field spanning linguistics, language acquisition, psycholinguistics, educational policy, and identity studies. Given the large number of associated fields, it is only natural to find a diversity of theoretical and methodological approaches adopted and applied to the study of heritage languages. The current chapter explores one particular methodological approach, that of corpus linguistics. Originating in the 1970s and gaining full speed in the 1990s with the advancement of computer technology, corpus linguistics has gained prominence in the study of language, both of standard and learner varieties. This new set of methodologies involving computer-aided analyses of large principled collections of authentic texts, known as language corpora, brought about new insights into the nature of language and afforded a more nuanced understanding of linguistic structure, language change, and language development.

While corpus methodologies have had a significant impact on theoretical linguistics, second language acquisition theory and second language learning and teaching, the same cannot be said of the field of heritage languages. Despite the fact that the professional community has been engaged in discussion of the potential of corpus methods in the study of heritage languages, the ambition of creating a robust repertoire of corpus-based heritage language research has not been fully realized. In the current chapter, I hope to foster a conversation about the benefits of applying corpus linguistics methods to the study of heritage languages and issue a call to the heritage language community for better utilization of the available corpus techniques and instruments.

The chapter is divided into six parts. It opens (Section 21.2) with a brief introduction of the key concepts and principles crucial to corpus linguistics methods and a description of some frequently used corpus instruments and procedures. Section 21.3 reviews the benefits of the application of corpus linguistics methods and instruments to the study of non-standard language varieties, including second and heritage languages. Section 21.4 offers an overview of the existing heritage language corpora and reviews pertinent issues in heritage corpora design, compilation, and annotation. In Section 21.5, I call on the heritage language community to invest in the development of heritage language corpora and to make better use of the existing computational tools in the study of heritage languages. A conclusion follows in Section 21.6.

21.2 Defining Corpus Linguistics and the Nature of Corpus-Based Language Research

Defining *corpus linguistics* is not as simple a task as it is with many more traditional areas of language study. Corpus linguistics has been described as a methodology and a method (McEnery et al. 2006; Gries 2009), a practice, a "philosophical approach" (Leech 1992), and a theory. Although the latter is a contentious assertion and not many corpus researchers ascribe to this position (Gries 2011; McEnery and Hardie 2012), most corpus linguists will likely agree that corpus linguistic methods are particularly compatible with a certain set of linguistic theories, more specifically, usage-based, emergentist, and cognitive linguistics models (Barlow and Kemmer 2000; Gries 2009; Gries 2011). As Gries (2009) points out, this compatibility is based on the fact that "corpus linguistic analyses are always based on the evaluation of some kind of frequencies, and frequency as well as its supposed mental correlate of cognitive-entrenchment is one of several key explanatory mechanisms within cognitively motivated approaches" (2). Yet, unlike more traditional subfields that study particular aspects of language (such as semantics, syntax, or pragmatics) or major theoretical approaches (such as the ones described in this volume), the focus of corpus-based studies has been largely on the thorough *description* of large machine-readable sets of authentic data obtained through the application of a set of computational procedures, or methods (McEnery and Hardie 2012: 1).

A (somewhat) a-theoretical nature of corpus linguistics should not be interpreted as a weakness; in fact, the utmost empirical nature of corpus-based research allows testing of linguists' intuitions, hypotheses, and linguistic theories in an objective manner. Thus, corpus linguistics constitutes a method(ology), "no more, but also no less" (Gries 2009: 1; Gries 2011: 83). The "no less" part of this definition refers to the fact that corpus linguistics has matured significantly in recent decades, both methodologically and conceptually, and has grown into a diverse field with a wide range of research agendas and, consequentially, methods and tools developed to answer various research questions. Within this conceptual and methodological diversity, however, certain key assumptions, or generalizations, about what constitutes specifically *corpus* methods and procedures still stand (Biber 2004; McEnery and Hardie 2012). These generalizations are briefly described next and revisited in Section 21.5.

21.2.1 Corpus Compilation

First and foremost, corpus methods and procedures include a set of specific principles for collecting and processing the data, which can then be analyzed with the help of corpus tools. These principles are, *systematic data selection, representativeness and balanced-ness of data, size, and authenticity*. Briefly, the principle of systematic, or principled, data selection presupposes a thorough advance corpus design and ensures that data sampling is not random and is clearly relevant to research questions. Representativeness, achieved through the sheer size of data but also, and often crucially, through careful selection of maximally diverse data, warrants the fact that the data found in a corpus represents a specific mode, variety, or genre of a language as fully as possible. This principle is inherently tied into the principle of *balanced-ness* of data entered in a corpus, which accounts for the fact that no one type of text is over-represented (and skews the results of a corpus-analysis as a consequence), and the principle of large corpus *size* which allows to generalize findings. Finally, historically, corpora were based on data that occurred naturally in authentic settings and *not* created for research purposes. Engaging with authentic language is thought to overcome the potential biases that encroach data collected in experimental settings. Most importantly, authenticity allowed the inclusion of contextual and situational aspects into analysis. However, as discussed later, many contemporary corpora, especially those collected for specific purposes, effectively represent elicited data, although these normally come in the form of elicited narratives, interviews, and other types of situationally grounded discourses.

Based on these principles, *language corpora* are defined as such not only on the basis of being *large* and *machine-readable* but as *systematically* compiled *balanced* collections of *authentic* texts that are *representative* of a language or a specific language variety. Examples of corpora include large national corpora (such as the Corpus of Contemporary American English, the British National Corpus, German Reference Corpus, and so on), which amount to many millions of words and whose representativeness is achieved by including texts from multiple modes of communication (written, spoken, multimodal, and intermediary modes such as text messaging) of various genres, and by different authors representing diverse regional and historical varieties. Not every corpus is or needs to be as large as a national corpus; in fact, most corpora are smaller and have a narrower specific focus. For instance, a set of classroom essays collected throughout an academic year from the same group of students constitutes a corpus that aims to be a basis of student assessment and/or of assessment of instructional approaches in this specific instructional context (Biber et al. 2004).

21.2.2 Corpus Annotation

The next set of methods and procedures applied to corpora involve systematic description of corpus data. The description is provided in a form of *meta-tags*, which must accompany each text entered in the corpus and provide pertinent information about each text (e.g., genre, mode, date of creation) and the text creator (gender, age, etc.). Another layer of description may be added to a corpus not at the level of each text but at the level of textual units, such as words, sentences, and any longer or shorter meaningful units of text. This type of labelling is called annotation (or mark-up) and it can provide morphological and morphosyntactic information (e.g., Parts of Speech notation) or any other information about the linguistic units in the texts themselves that can be used to analyze the texts in research. This additional information is "attached" to relevant linguistic units in the form of *tags*, which is why annotation is often referred to as *tagging*.

21.2.3 Corpus Tools and Corpus Analysis

A principally designed and well-annotated corpus is available for an array of possible statistical procedures, which largely present some variation of data retrieval, obtaining frequencies, and statistical analysis. These analyses require the use of special corpus-analytic software. These software programs can be standalone or web-based. Standalone corpus-analytic packages can be installed on one's personal computer; the most commonly used such programs are license-based WordSmith Tools (Scott 2016) and the freely available AntConc (Anthony 2019). Web-based tools are available online and typically provide tools for building smaller custom-built corpora and some tools for annotating and analyzing the data (e.g., IntelliText at http://corpus.leeds.ac.uk/it/). These various programs vary in functionality and user-friendliness but they all "share the essential properties of facilitating quantitative analysis and enabling analysts quickly and easily collect, sort, and manipulate the linguistic data contained in a corpus." (Schlitz 2010: 92).

21.3   What Corpora Are For?

Standard corpora, and the accompanying software that can quickly and efficiently analyze vast quantities of data, have given rise to many exploratory and data-driven studies that have so far resulted in development of new corpus-based dictionaries, more nuanced descriptive grammars, as well as new language textbooks and reference materials based on the examination of learner corpora. The impact of the rapidly developing field of corpus linguistics has reached beyond applied language study and it has been described as revolutionary on theoretical and applied linguistics (Hunston 2002; Kopotev and Mustajoki 2008; Gries 2011). Corpus linguistics has provided answers that were previously only hypothesized and theorized, tested theories, obtained evidence, and supported (or, at times, contradicted) previously held ideas about certain linguistic facts. For instance, corpora of historic English, annotated and parsed, led to radical reexamination of processes driving English language change (Kroch and Taylor 2000; Kroch et al. 2004; Taylor and Pintzuk 2012; Hilpert 2013); the same is true for historic Spanish (Torres Cacoullos et al. 2017; Torres Cacoullos and Bauman 2018). In socio- and contact linguistics, corpus approaches have helped unearth new evidence of strong interdependence between linguistic behaviors and sociodemographic characteristics (Torres Cacoullos and Berry 2018; Nagy and Lo 2019). Corpora as collections of authentic texts have been crucial to sociolinguistic research and variationist studies since "the vernacular – the unreflecting use of language in the absence of the observer, when minimum attention is paid to monitoring speech – is the style that is most regular in structure (Labov 1972:112)" (Torres Cacoullos and Berry 2018: 2).

Corpora were instrumental in bringing major advances in understanding child language acquisition, both monolingual and bilingual. In fact, creating corpora in first (monolingual and bilingual) language acquisition has been a staple practice for decades (MacWhinney 2000). Child Language Data Exchange System (CHILDES, MacWhinney 2000) is the largest collection of naturally occurring child language data, consisting of more than thirty corpora, many of them grammatically tagged. Exploration of such corpora accrued a large body of evidence that children develop language structures from positive input. In other words, children repeat and reuse high frequency chunks afforded to them in the linguistic environment, accumulate exemplars in multiple usage events, and in this manner move toward greater schematicity and creativity in language usage (Tomasello 2003; Goldberg 2005; Lieven and Tomasello 2008; Bannard and Lieven 2012; Ellis 2012).

Corpus linguistics methods have been crucial in contributing to the study of non-compositionality in language. Statistical analyses of various corpora corroborated the argument of omnipresence of non-compositionality (formulaicity) in naturally occurring language (Pawley and Snyder 1983; Wray 2002; Biber et al. 2004; Biber 2009; Herbst et al. 2014; inter alia). Corpus linguistics methods have also aided in understanding distributional "preferences" of specific formulaic expressions, as well as other, rule-based linguistic structures, which show particular distribution across specific registers, genres, and modalities (Biber et al. 2004; Biber and Conrad 2009; Yagunova and Pivovarova 2014).

The application of corpus linguistics methods to the study of Second and Foreign language acquisition (SLA) has also resulted in significant shifts in SLA theories and approaches. The approach was pioneered in the 1990s through such projects as the Longman Learners' Corpus (LLC, http://global .longmandictionaries.com/longman/corpus#aa) and the Cambridge Learners' Corpus (CLC, www.cambridge.org/elt/corpus), and Sylvain Granger's groundbreaking work on The International Corpus of Learner English (ICLE). Whereas the overarching goal of the two former (commercial) corpora was to produce research-informed language learning reference materials and learner dictionaries (Carter and McCarthy 2006), ICLE, as well as a generation of learner corpora that followed, set out to contribute to a better understanding of the universal, as well as language- and group-specific, patterns of second/foreign language acquisition. Within a very short period of time, a new area of language research known as *learner corpus linguistics* (Granger 1996, 2004) emerged. Today, a survey of learner corpora reveals a fruitful line of research into the nature of language development: learner corpus research seeks to identify general patterns of language development by groups of learners of various first languages (L1); to develop linguistic portraits of nonnative speakers of various proficiency levels and various L1s; to compare patterns of errors produced by different learner groups; to study the effectiveness of pedagogical intervention by analyzing linguistic progress over time; and more (Granger 1996; Dagneaux et al. 1998; Granger 1999; Hinkel 2001; Nesi 2004; Nesselhauf 2005; Paquot and Granger 2012; Vyatkina 2012, 2013; Gries and Wulff 2013; Kisselev and Alsufieva 2017; Xiao-Desai and Wong 2017; inter alia). Corpus-based SLA research has also accumulated a growing body of evidence that adult second language learners do, in fact, follow the developmental path from item-specific to generalized (Eskildsen and Cadierno 2007; Eskildsen 2009; Li et al. 2014).

In sum, corpus linguistics methods have significantly contributed to the study of language and to gaining a greater understanding of the very nature of language, language development, and language change.

21.4 Corpus Linguistics Methodologies in Heritage Language Research

The field of heritage language and heritage language development stands to similarly benefit from the application of corpus tools and methods and from the triangulation of the more traditional to the field experimental, psycholinguistic, and sociolinguistic methods and corpus linguistics approaches.

The number of heritage language corpora at this point in time, however, is rather small, despite the fact that the first attempts to apply corpus linguistics methods to heritage data are over a decade old. One of the pioneer heritage language corpus projects is the Heritage Language Documentation Corpus (HerLD Corpus, http://projects.chass.utoronto.ca/ngn/HLVC/1_4_corpus.php). HerLD Corpus aims to systematically describe and track changes in the usage of six heritage languages spoken in Toronto, Canada; more specifically, Cantonese, Faetar, Italian, Korean, Russian, and Ukrainian. The project has to date produced more than thirty published papers spanning such topics as phonology and phonetics, morphology and syntax, as well as identity and attitudes (Nagy et al. 2011; Iannozzi, 2015; Nagy et al. 2018; Nagy and Lo 2019; Tse 2019). The overarching goal of this project is to track stable variation and change over time in grammars of heritage speakers over three generations of contact with the dominant societal language.

Other projects that record data for sociolinguistic research, such as the Corpus of Spanish in Southern Arizona (https://cesa.arizona.edu) and The New England Corpus of Heritage and Second Language Speakers (https://digitalhumanities.umass.edu/projects/new-england-corpus-heritage-and-second-language-speakers) may contain data collected from heritage language speakers of various languages and can be a valuable resource for researchers of heritage language.

Another type of project where heritage language varieties have found a place is learner corpora. Some learner corpora are specifically designed to compare learner groups that differ in language learning histories, i.e., post-adolescent second language speakers and heritage language speakers. For example, the *Russian Learner Corpus of Academic Writing* (RULEC, Alsufieva et al. 2012), a longitudinal corpus of approximately 450,000 tokens of advanced-level writing includes data from second language and heritage students of Russian, who were enrolled in the same advanced language courses. The context of data collection in the case of RULEC allowed for a balanced distribution of data across language learning backgrounds, with nineteen of the thirty-six authors in the corpus representing heritage speakers of Russian. As such, the corpus allows for a systematic comparison of developmental patterns in the language of heritage and non-heritage instructed learners (Apresjan 2017; Kisselev and Alsufieva 2017; Peirce 2018).

Another example of a learner corpus that comprises both heritage and non-heritage texts is a corpus of Korean collected by Lee and colleagues (Lee et al. 2009) with the aim of developing an error annotation schema, specifically for particle errors, the most frequent errors in Korean second language and Korean heritage language speech. The end goal of the study was to help train computational tools in automatic detection of learner errors in language production; however, the description of error patterns in and of itself is a worthwhile endeavor, especially in the absence of much (or any) previous research in this area. Thus, Lee et al. (2009) found a specific pattern of distribution of the types of particle errors, which differs depending on the language acquisition background (heritage vs non-heritage) but not on language proficiency (beginner vs intermediate). Such results invite further theoretical interpretations, on the one hand, and, at the same time, can immediately inform classroom practices.

Other corpora collected in the instructional settings that include second and heritage language data is the Arabic Learners Written Corpus (www .arabiclearnercorpus.com) and the Multilingual Academic Corpus of Assignments – Writing and Speech (MACAWS), which is currently under development and will include such heritage languages as Portuguese and Russian (for more information refer to https://sites.google.com/email .arizona.edu/macawswebinar/home). These corpora are becoming an important tool for heritage language researchers and, more importantly, heritage language teachers, as they promise to help uncover similarities and differences in the developmental trajectories in heritage and non-heritage learners, who, these days, populate most college-level classes (Montrul 2010; Kisselev et al. 2020).

Larger heritage languages, such as Mandarin Chinese (at least in the context of the U.S.) stand to benefit from the creation of corpora that specifically set out to track the development of heritage language skills, such as the Chinese Heritage Language Corpus (Ming and Tao 2008) and the Chinese Heritage Learner Blog Explorer (CHLBE, Xiao-Desai and Wao 2017).

The CHLBE was collected longitudinally and focuses on one genre of learner writing, that of blog writing; CHLBE is large; it contains approximately 1.5 million characters produced by 266 heritage speakers of four different developmental levels. It is fully segmented and tagged for parts-of-speech (POS). The Chinese Heritage Language Corpus is smaller; it contains 2,000 texts of different genres, adding up to 460,000 characters. The corpus is also POS-tagged and, crucially, a small portion of the corpus is manually error annotated. A sample study by Ming and Tao (2008) provides an example of advantages in utilizing error-tagged data. Using the error-tagged part of the Chinese Heritage Language Corpus, Ming and Tao compared the use of two specific types of errors, namely, the over-production and under-production of the perfective aspect particle *le*. The results of the study indicate that the heritage learners significantly under-use the particle *le* in contexts where it is required and often supply the particle in contexts where it is not expected. However, when comparing the results of their study to a similar type of corpus-based research conducted with second language data, Ming and Tao find that heritage speakers have an advantage over second language learners of Chinese, who, unlike the heritage speakers, conceptualize the particle *le* as a tense marker rather than an aspect marker. The results, however descriptive, present an important piece of evidence that the nature of language knowledge in heritage and second language speakers is, indeed, different in at least some aspects of linguistic competence.

Finally, heritage language data is found in projects devoted to examining bilingual language development. In fact, creating corpora in first (monolingual and bilingual) language acquisition has been a staple practice for decades (MacWhinney 2000). Unsurprisingly, many of the bilingual databases contain data for speakers who will grow up to be heritage speakers of one (or more) of their languages. Among the more recent child corpora that specifically contribute to the agenda of heritage language research are the Child Heritage Chinese Language corpus (CHCC, Mai and Yip 2017) and the Corpus of Bilingual Russian Child and Child-directed Speech (BiRCh, Malamud et al. 2013–2019; Malamud et al. 2017–2019). The CHCC (available through CHILDES, https://childes.talkbank.org/access/Biling/CHCC .html) is a longitudinal study of three Chinese heritage children living in the United States; it provides rich multi-modal data for children's language development covering the age range of 1.7–4.11 years. The BiRCh corpus, currently under construction, provides comparable longitudinal data for three Russian-English and four Russian-German bilingual children, as well as three Russian monolingual children (ages of the subjects range from 18 months to 6 years, with the bulk of the data collected for children between 3 and 5 years of age, http://birch.ling.brandeis.edu/). Importantly, the goal of the project is to make the data available to researchers in technologically advantageous forms, such as searchable digital recording time-aligned with transcripts and grammatically annotated transcribed data. The combination of dense, longitudinal, grammatically parsed data with a searchability component can serve as a powerful tool for investigating language development in Russian-speaking heritage children in the context of different dominant languages.

Research into child language acquisition has been greatly aided in recent years by important technological developments. Dense input and output data can be easily collected with the help of such systems as the Language Environment Analysis System (LENA™, Richards et al. 2008), which allows measurement of early linguistic development in children of aged 2–48 months, as well as the linguistic environment afforded to these children by their caregivers. LENA™ software parses the data collected in the natural environment of the child into Adult Word Counts, Child Vocalizations, and Conversational Turns between adults and the child, and can automatically provide counts of these speech units in large swaths of data.

21.5 A Call for Advancement of Corpus Methodologies in the Field of Heritage Language Research

Although the efforts of the projects described in the previous section are laudable, the shortage of heritage corpora or corpora including heritage data is disconcerting. Such a deficit is not surprising; the development of corpora, as discussed earlier, is not a simple endeavor. To create a viable heritage corpus, not only does one need access to a sufficiently large number of learners and learner texts (whether written or oral) but also one has to contend with the inherent complexity and heterogeneity of heritage language datasets compared to data representing standard linguistic varieties.[1] This means that all corpus procedures – from compilation to analysis – require more human resources and innovative technological solutions. Still, the potential advantages of corpus-based approaches to the study and teaching of heritage languages are significant enough to outweigh the inherent challenges of corpus work and are well worth the investment.

In what follows, I outline several considerations and practical steps in creating and utilizing heritage language corpora.

21.5.1 Compiling Heritage Corpora: Principles and Considerations

First, at the stage of corpus compilation, a heritage corpus designer has to carefully consider the principled approach to corpus building outlined in Section 21.2, namely, authenticity, size, representativeness, and balancedness.

Authenticity. Most standard corpora represent collections of texts produced for authentic (i.e., non-research) purposes such as writing an email to a friend or presenting a lecture. Learner corpora, on the other hand, often contain elicited texts created for specific research purposes; yet, these normally represent the so-called situationally grounded discourses such as narratives, interviews, and the like. Learner corpora also often include classroom-based data, i.e., authentic texts created by second language learners as homework assignments, research papers, or even global proficiency tests.

Heritage language corpus research so far has followed the model of learner corpora, drawing on the tradition of elicited narrative methodology in experimental research and utilizing convenience data such as classroom-produced texts. Looking ahead, heritage corpus research needs to expand

---

[1] A similar notion is expressed in Barlow (2005: 335) in regard to the nature of second language; however, heritage languages may be even more variable due to the multitude of factors that impact heritage language development.

both in the now traditional "elicited speech" direction, as well as in currently unexplored routes of collecting such authentic genres, such as naturally occurring speech in different settings, diaspora media, and the like.

Size. Although corpora are generally large, compiling heritage language corpora comprising millions of words may be unfeasible for individual researchers due to such practical reasons as labor-intensiveness of data processing, lack of access to quality data, lack of readily-available language-specific software, etc. Thus, a more productive approach may be working in research teams or contributing to existing projects that have established protocols for data collection and processing in place and, more importantly, have technological capabilities of data storage, retrieval, and analysis. Such efforts in creating large multi-contributor corpora of heritage languages are currently underway. For example, the project titled The Heritage Language Data Repository (Polinsky et al. 2020, https://international.ucla.edu/helada) aims to create a comprehensive, user-friendly, and searchable platform for ethically shared heritage language data. Created under the auspices of the National Heritage Language Resource Center (https://nhlrc.ucla.edu/nhlrc), the Repository is envisioned as a large principled and searchable collection of heritage language samples of various languages collected for various research projects; as such, the platform will host different types of data, including oral and written speech, in monologic and dialogic mode, collected in various settings. Ideally, any researcher will be able to create comparable sub-corpora of significant size using the metatags available in the platform and move beyond the constraints of small sample studies that are still over-represented in our field.

With regard to *representative* and *balanced selection*, a heritage corpus designer has to consider the notorious, in heritage language study, issue of language proficiency. With the field still struggling to create solid approaches to evaluating language proficiency of heritage speakers, the question of how to account for different levels in language command of speakers is significant. Ideally, information on proficiency levels (either in the form of global proficiency ratings such as OPI or CEFR or in the form of some proxy measure such as number of words per minute) should be available to the researcher and form a basis for organizing data within a corpus. A corpus compiler will then balance out the number of texts representing each sub-group. For example, given that fluency, i.e., the number of linguistic units per a measured period of time, is related to proficiency, one might choose to include more lower-level speakers in the corpus and fewer higher-level speakers to counterbalance the average number of words per sub-corpus. Crucially, each sub-corpus must include sufficient speakers to ensure powerful and valid statistical analyses. Additionally, the sub-groups should be ideally balanced across all other parameters included in meta-annotation; for example, if task conditions for various texts in the corpus are different, then the texts should be more or less equally distributed across these task conditions.

Other parameters, such as age of exposure to the dominant language, amount of exposure to the heritage language, literacy skills in the heritage language, contexts of acquisition and current use, attitudes, and other factors that have been shown to have a strong impact on the general level of proficiency, also need to be considered at the stage of corpus compilation. Even if a perfect balance of data across all the parameters is not feasible, corpus data must be systematically organized to ensure rigorous corpus design.

Overall, adherence to the principles of corpus compilation ensures the quality of corpora as language databases capable of providing important insights into the nature of language they claim to represent. Rigorous corpus design, when considerations of balancedness, representativeness, diversity, size, etc. are well-thought through, ensures that the subsequent statistical analyses applied to the corpora texts can be meaningfully interpreted.

21.5.2 Annotation of Heritage Corpora

The next step in heritage corpus compilation involves systematic description of the data. This description is provided in the form of *meta-tags*, which must accompany each text entered in the corpus and provide pertinent information about each text and the text creator. Meta-tags must include the name of the text author (or any unique text ID such as a pseudonym or a number) and biodata, i.e., information about the age and gender of the speaker, age of their exposure to the dominant language, dominant language(s), literacy skills, proficiency level, amount of exposure to the heritage language, and/or other available information pertinent to the questions raised in heritage language research. The information about the texts may include the date of creation/occurrence, genre of the text, and any other metadata that is deemed (potentially) important to the purposes of the corpus.

It may be useful to think about metadata descriptors as variables in the subsequent analyses of the corpus data; meta-tags effectively allow researchers to "pick and choose" texts from a corpus and pull the data into customized sub-corpora, principally organized along such parameters as age, gender, dominant language, and proficiency level. The sub-corpora can then be meaningfully compared with regards to whatever linguistic structures the researcher is interested in. (Samples of meta-tags are available in Lee, Jang, and Seo's (2009) cross-sectional corpus of learner writing and Kisselev and Alsufieva's (2017) longitudinal corpus of academic writing.)

Another layer of additional information that may be added to a heritage corpus involves annotation (or mark-up) of lexical units in the texts; and it can provide:

- morphological information (e.g., inflection, derivation),
- morpho-syntactic information (such as commonly used Parts of Speech notation, as well as person, number, gender, case, voice, tense, aspect),
- syntactic information (e.g., phrasal chunking, sentence parsing),
- semantic information (e.g., word-sense disambiguation, anaphora resolution),
- discoursal information (e.g., speech acts),
- information about erroneous or infelicitous forms (e.g., minimally, a provision of the correct or intended form plus a description of structural and/or functional properties of the error), and/or
- any other information needed for a research-specific corpus.

This additional information is "attached" to the relevant linguistic units in the form of *tags*, which is why annotation is often referred to as *tagging*.

Why and how is this additional information about linguistics helpful in a corpus study? Some of these annotations are an important first step in conducting more sophisticated procedures, e.g., a text needs to be first lemmatized and POS-tagged in order to be then subjected to syntactic parsing. But tags, of course, are not a means to an end, but rather, they offer a researcher an opportunity to look at the data from different perspectives; for example, even simple frequency counts of POS tags in texts of various genres/registers can yield useful information on the variable distribution of parts of speech across genres and registers and help researchers describe characteristics of written and spoken registers (Biber 1991; Leech 2000) or formal and conversational styles (Biber 1991). A morphologically tagged corpus may allow testing of morphological productivity in language learner data as shown, for instance, in Lüdeling, Hirschmann, and Shadrova (2017). Syntactically parsed corpora allow investigation of the usage of different types of structures and their distributional patterns, including type-token frequency distributions of various structures, as well as their prototypicality, semantic cohesion, polysemy, and the like (see, for example, Ellis 2002; Ellis et al. 2016 for a review); and corpora annotated for discourse functions, such as rhetorical moves, can be analyzed with an eye toward which discourse functions are most frequently realized through which linguistic structures (Cortes 2013; Mizumoto et al. 2017; Lu et al. 2020). Yet, it is important to understand that tagging corpora is not a type of analysis per se, rather, it is a way to prepare the data for subsequent analyses.

Annotation is considered to be an interpretative layer, since the type of information provided through annotation necessarily presupposes some level of analysis, as well as making certain choices such as the use of one theoretical model over another as a basis of annotation (Leech 2005; Gries, 2009). Indeed, if some types of annotation may be considered uncontroversial (e.g., *lemmatization*, which simply implies that each word in a corpus is provided a tag with a lemma), such annotation as syntactic parsing or error tagging necessarily requires a choice of theoretical model that drives the procedure.

Another issue concerning annotation, of heightened importance for the discussion of heritage corpora, is annotation of non-standard language varieties and the reliability of automatic algorithms that tag and parse texts containing unexpected or non-standard forms. Such linguistic varieties as learner languages, heritage languages, lingua francas, and language varieties making use of code-mixing or code-switching may be difficult to annotate using computational tools that are trained on standard, rather than "noisy," data. Fortunately, many researchers are now turning to the methodological issue of working with such data and focus their efforts on developing programs that can recognize, tag, and automatically correct errors as well as tag and parse the corrected version of the corpus (Rosen et al. 2014; Rozovskaya and Roth 2014, 2019; Zaghouani et al. 2014 inter alia). Naturally, the quality of annotation will affect what types of further analyses may be available to the researcher.

Regardless of whether certain levels of annotation are too interpretative or theoretically incompatible with a researcher's stance, they do not render a corpus automatically useless. A corpus can always be returned to its "raw," or un-annotated, form, and/or provided different or additional tagging. As long as the user is made aware of the specifics of annotation schema applied to the data, annotation is a useful tool to be used – or not – at the researcher's discretion (Leech 2005).

Far more challenging at this point in time are the considerations of automated and semi-automated annotation of heritage language. As mentioned previously, most programs developed for automatic grammatical tagging of corpora are trained on native speaker data and produce unsatisfactory results for non-standard, "noisy," texts full of unpredictable and non-standards forms and combinations. Nonetheless, a growing number of computational linguistics studies is devoted to the development of such programs (Rosen et al. 2014; Rozovskaya and Roth 2014, 2019; Zaghouani et al. 2014 inter alia). Rozovskaya and Roth (2019) bring up an important point; the more non-standard data computational linguists have access too, the better their computational tools are becoming. In other words, if heritage language scholars desire to have better computational and corpus tools, it is in their interest to develop corpora for training.

Raw corpora, i.e., texts that have not yet undergone grammatical tagging, can still be used in corpus analysis with some research questions in mind.

Moreover, certain research questions necessitate manual tagging of data. For instance, most corpus-based error analyses require either manual tagging or extensive human rater checking of (semi)automated error identification algorithms. In a corpus-based study that analyzes patterns of misspellings typical to heritage speakers of Spanish, Beaudrie (2012) compiled a corpus of written essays collected at the beginning of a semester from heritage students enrolled in a heritage Spanish course, and then conducted a semi-automatic extraction of misspelled words followed by a manual annotation for types of errors in spelling. The study allowed the teacher-researcher to tailor her instruction based on the results of the corpus-based study of her learners and to preempt this specific gap in the learner's knowledge rather than rely on ad hoc remediation of issues.

In another study that focused on a specific type of error (such as genitive case errors in Russian), Peirce (2018) opted for human rater identification and tagging of inflectional morphology on all nouns, adjectives, and determiners using oXygen XML Editor software. These tags were applied "to each error to show the correct grammatical case, gender and number and to indicate whether the author used an incorrect grammatical case, gender and/or number, or whether the type of error could not be determined" (Peirce 2018: 103). The study utilized the meta information available in the corpus, specifically time constraint in the writing of text and the language learning history of the corpus authors, as independent variables; comparing the rate and types of errors by group and by time constraint allowed the author to discuss the results in light of what role early/late exposure to language plays both on possible representations of nominal functional features in two groups of learners and on processing constraints that the two groups of learners may be subject to in timed task conditions.

The potential for error-tagged heritage corpora on heritage language development research and teaching cannot be overstated. Systematic errors when grouped by frequency, by group characteristics (such as proficiency levels, age, or parental involvement), and by structural and functional properties can shed light on developmental processes of heritage language development or attrition. Error analysis can also help test hypotheses about dominant language influence, understand the impact of instructional practices and different learning histories, and answer many other important questions largely under-researched in heritage language acquisition.

21.5.3 Corpus Analyses

A carefully designed and well-annotated corpus can be used for numerous research studies and answer multiple research questions. With the help of corpus-analytic software programs (such as AntConc (Anthony 2019) or

WordSmith Tools (Scott 2016)), a researcher will be able to run various corpus-analytic procedures, most common of which are the following:

Compilation of word lists. This procedure extracts and sorts all the lexical items in the corpus either by lemma or by unique form found in a corpus; the sorting effectively builds a kind of "dictionary" of the entire corpus or "dictionaries" by sub-corpora/sub-groups, which can be ordered either alphabetically or by frequency.

Obtaining descriptive statistics. These tools allow the researcher to obtain general descriptive statistical information about the corpus (and/or the sub-corpora), such as the number of words and word tokens, number of sentences, number of paragraphs, length of these linguistic units, etc.

Concordancing. The term *concordance* or a *concordance line* in corpus linguistics describes a language sample of pre-determined length, which contains the search term, usually a word, a phrase, or a grammatical pattern. Concordancing refers to automatic extraction of such samples, as well as automatic sorting of the extracted concordances in different ways: alphabetically, by the first word to the left/right of the search term, by second/third/etc. word to the left/right, etc. Such automatic sorting allows the user to identify different patterns in the data.

Keyword analysis, i.e., identifying particular words in one or more texts in the corpus, whose frequency is unusually high relative to some "norm" (typically a baseline corpus). This type of analysis is helpful when examining the unique features of a particular genre or mode.

Collocation, i.e., retrieving lists of *collocates* (lexical units or strings that co-occur with the search term more frequently than would be expected by chance). Relatedly, *colligation* refers to this phenomenon but with grammatical, rather than lexical, constructions.[2]

By and large, these procedures allow a researcher to extract and examine multiple samples of linguistic units produced by the speakers and writers of the language varieties under study in authentic settings. Extracting and sorting the linguistic structures chosen for analysis in varying ways helps the researcher look for regularities, or patterns, in the usage of these structures, which often escape the intuition of native speakers and trained linguists.

As indicated, even analyses of raw corpora can yield interesting results. For instance, corpus analytic software designed for corpus research, such as WordSmith Tools 7.0 (Scott 2016), automatically provide general statistical information on word tokens and types, sentences, paragraphs, as well as

---

[2] The number of procedures available to corpus linguists today is continuously expanding as tools and lines of inquiry rapidly develop (McEnery and Hardie 2012).

type/token ratio (TTR) and mean length of a word, sentence, or paragraph. Given that differences in word token counts (as well as in the number of words per sentence, number of word types per essay, and TTR counts) between different groups of heritage speakers might index qualitative differences in language proficiency (Lee et al. 2009; Kisselev and Alsufieva 2017), such automated analyses can be used to quickly sub-group participants into proficiency levels. In addition to these descriptors, a researcher can quickly assess lexical sophistication (i.e., the proportion of more frequent words to less frequent words) by compiling a word list of the heritage corpus and then comparing this list with similar frequency lists based on native or other standard corpora.

Wordlists may be useful for many different research purposes. To illustrate, in a study of epistemic stance in Chinese heritage wiring, Xiao-Desai and Wong (2017) compared a full word list extracted from their learner corpus to a predetermined comprehensive list of standard means of epistemic candidates. Although the authors followed this procedure with an additional manual analysis of concordances to ensure maximal extraction of all qualifying candidates, they found that the additional analysis of a concordance line did not impact the results, proving that even a relatively simple procedure of word list creation can be a powerful tool in data analysis.

Kisselev and Alsufieva's (2017) study of complex sentences with subordinating conjunctions in the writing of heritage and non-heritage learners of Russian similarly started with word list examination. Using information from the word lists as a guiding tool, Kisselev and Alsufieva then conducted a comprehensive analysis of concordance lines containing all the conjunctions in question. Having analyzed and categorized the concordance lines, Kisselev and Alsufieva were able to assess the quantitative changes in the structural and functional use of complex sentence structures with different conjunctions, as well as the rates of accuracy and the types of error patterns across heritage and non-heritage groups at intermediate and advanced language proficiency.

Apart from descriptive text statistics, word lists, and concordancing, the other types of corpus-based analyses, specifically, collocational and colligational analyses, have not been reported yet. Although collocational and colligational knowledge of heritage speakers presents an interesting area of research, the relatively small sizes of the available heritage language corpora prevent researchers from engaging in this type of statistical analysis. However, manual examination of corpus data reveals great potential for this line of inquiry. For example, in a study of collocations in heritage Russian, Kopotev, Kisselev, and Polinsky (2020) examine collocations by structural types and find that heritage learners engage in a number of different collocational strategies, with calquing (or word-by-word borrowing of collocations from the dominant language) being the least preferred strategy, contrary to predictions. The heritage speakers in this study appear to rely on *amalgaming*, or concatenating structures from both languages available to them, indicating that the linguistic knowledge of a heritage speaker is better interpreted as a result of **interaction** between languages, rather than of one-language dominance.

The small number of corpus-based heritage language studies available today suggests that the field of heritage language research is only beginning to explore the full potential of corpus linguistics methods. However, with the development of heritage corpora well underway, more and more heritage language researchers are using and will continue to use corpus data and corpus methods in their research, addressing both global and local questions of heritage language change, development, and maintenance.

21.6 Conclusions

The bread and butter of language researchers is in trying to understand the mental processes that underlie language production and language development; the crucial source of evidence that allows for interpretation of these mental processes is language produced by speakers of the language variety (Myles 2005: 374). Language corpora represent an invaluable resource for such evidence in the form of valid, reliable, representative, and large databases. Coupled with technologically advanced instruments that allow for fast and reliable statistical analyses of data, language corpora have proved to be an indispensable tool in linguistic research. The field of heritage language stands to benefit tremendously from embracing corpus linguistic methods and creating more and better heritage speaker corpora. These resources will ultimately help advance our understanding of the nature of (heritage) language, and (heritage) language development and maintenance.

As the field grows the number of corpus-based heritage language studies, it also has to move these studies beyond the largely descriptive agenda. Although a thorough description of heritage language varieties is a substantial and important contribution in and of itself, more interpretative and theory-driven corpus-based studies are needed.

Corpus linguistics overall has recently begun to "look beyond the confines of the texts or discourses and contribute to, and interface with, neighboring fields" (Gries 2011). As many social and behavioral studies move toward better practices of triangulating results of different methods, the field of heritage languages, too, stands to benefit from triangulating the heavily empirical, quantitative corpus methods with the explanatory power of traditionally theory-driven fields such as theoretical linguistics, psycholinguistics, and the study of bilingualism.

References

Alsufieva, A., O. Kisselev, and S. Freels. 2012. Results 2012: Using Flagship Data to Develop a Russian Learner Corpus of Academic Writing. *Russian Language Journal* 62, 79–105.

Anthony, L. 2019. AntConc (Version 3.5.8) [Computer Software]. Tokyo, Japan: Waseda University. Available from www.laurenceanthony.net/software

Apresjan, V. Yu. 2017. Russkie possessivnye konstrukcii s nulevym i vyraženynnym glagolom: pravila i ošibki [Russian Possessive Constructions with Null Predicate: Rules and Errors]. *Russkij jazyk v naučnom osvesčenii [Russian Language in Light of Scientific Description]* 33, 86–116.

Bannard, C. and E. Lieven. 2012. Formulaic Language in L1 Acquisition. *Annual Review of Applied Linguistics* 32, 3–16.

Barlow, M. 2003. *Concordancing and Corpus Analysis Using MP 2.2.* Houston: Athelstan.

Barlow, M. 2005. Computer-Based Analyses of Learner Language. In R. Ellis and G. Barkhuizen (eds.), *Analysing Learner Language.* Oxford: Oxford University Press, 335–369.

Barlow, M. and S. Kemmer. (eds.) 2000. *Usage-Based Models of Language.* Stanford, CA: CSLI Publications.

Beaudrie, S. M. 2012. A Corpus-Based Study on the Misspellings of Spanish Heritage Learners and Their Implications for Teaching. *Linguistics and Education* 23(1), 135–144.

Biber, D. 1991. *Variation across Speech and Writing.* Cambridge: Cambridge University Press.

Biber, D. and S. Conrad. 2009. *Register, Genre, and Style.* Cambridge: Cambridge University Press.

Biber, D. and S. Conrad. 2010. *Corpus Linguistics and Grammar Teaching.* White Plains, NY: Pearson Education.

Biber, D. and C. Vásquez. 2009. Writing and Speaking. In *Handbook of Research on Writing: History, Society, School, Individual, Text.* London and New York: Taylor and Francis, 657–672.

Biber, D., S. Conrad and G. Leech. 2002. *The Longman Student Grammar of Spoken and Written English.* London: Longman.

Biber, D., S. Conrad and R. Reppen. 2004. *Corpus Linguistics: Investigating Language Structure and Use.* Cambridge: Cambridge University Press.

Carter, R. and M. McCarthy. 2006. *Cambridge Grammar of English.* Cambridge: Cambridge University Press.

Centre for English Corpus Linguistics. 2019. Learner Corpora around the World. Retrieved May 2, 2019, from https://uclouvain.be/en/research-insti tutes/ilc/cecl/learner-corpora- around-the-world.html

Conrad, S. 1999. The Importance of Corpus-Based Research for Language Teachers. *System* 27(1), 1–18.

Conrad, S. and D. Biber. 2009. *Real Grammar: A Corpus-Based Approach to English*. New York: Pearson/Longman.

Cortes, V. 2013. The Purpose of This Study Is To: Connecting Lexical Bundles and Moves in Research Article Introductions. *Journal of English for Academic Purposes* 12, 33–43.

Coxhead, A. 2000. A New Academic Word List. *TESOL Quarterly* 34(2), 213–238.

Dagneaux, E., S. Denness, and S. Granger. 1998. Computer-Aided Error Analysis. *System* 26, 163–174.

Dubinina, I., S. A. Malamud, and E. Denisova-Schmidt. 2013–present. Audio-aligned Longitudinal Corpus of Bilingual Russian Child and Child-directed Speech (BiRCh Longitudinal).

Ellis, N. C. 2002. Frequency Effects in Language Processing: A Review with Implications for Theories of Implicit and Explicit Language Acquisition. *Studies in Second Language Acquisition* 24(2), 143–188.

Ellis, N. C. 2012. Formulaic Language and Second Language Acquisition: Zipf and the Phrasal Teddy Bear. *Annual Review of Applied Linguistics* 32, 17–44.

Ellis, N. C. 2017. Cognition, Corpora, and Computing: Triangulating Research in Usage-Based Language Learning. *Language Learning* 67(S1), 40–65.

Ellis, N. C., U. Römer, and M. B. O'Donnell. 2016. *Usage-Based Approaches to Language Acquisition and Processing: Cognitive and Corpus Investigations of Construction Grammar* (The Language Learning Monograph Series). Hoboken, NJ: Wiley-Blackwell.

Eskildsen, S. W. 2009. Constructing another Language: Usage-Based Linguistics in Second Language Acquisition. *Applied Linguistics* 30(3), 335–357.

Eskildsen, S. W. and T. Cadierno. 2007. Are Recurring Multi-Word Expressions Really Syntactic Freezes? Second Language Acquisition from the Perspective of Usage-Based Linguistics. *Collocations and Idioms* 1, 19–20.

Flowerdew, L. 2012. *Corpora and Language Education*. Basingstoke: Palgrave Macmillan.

Goldberg, A. E. 2005. *Constructions at Work: The Nature of Generalizations in Language*. Oxford: Oxford University Press.

Granger, S. 1996. From CA to CIA and Back: An Integrated Approach to Computerized Bilingual and Learner Corpora. In K. Aijmer, B. Altenberg, and M. Johansson (eds.), *Languages in Contrast. Papers from a Symposium on Text-Based Cross-Linguistic Studies. Lund 4–5 March 1994*. Lund, Sweden: Lund University Press, 37–51.

Granger, S. 1999. Use of Tenses by Advanced EFL Learners: Evidence from an Error-Tagged Computer Corpus. In H. Hasselgard and S. Oksefjell (eds.), *Out of Corpora. Studies in Honour of Stig Johansson*. Amsterdam: Rodopi, 191–202.

Granger, S. 2004. Computer Learner Corpus Research: Current Status and Future Prospects. In U. Connor and T. A. Upton (eds.), *Applied Corpus Linguistics: A Multidimensional Perspective*. Amsterdam: Brill Rodopi, 123–145.

Granger, S. 2009. The Contribution of Learner Corpora to Second Language Acquisition and Foreign Language Teaching. In K. Ajmer (ed.), *Corpora and Language Teaching*. Philadelphia/Amsterdam: John Benjamins, 1332.

Gries, S. 2009. What Is Corpus Linguistics? *Language and Linguistics Compass* 3(5), 1225–1241.

Gries, S. 2011. Methodological and Interdisciplinary Stance in Corpus Linguistics. In G. Barnbrook, V. Viana, and S. Zyngier (eds.), *Perspectives on Corpus Linguistics: Connections and Controversies*. Philadelphia/Amsterdam: John Benjamins, 81–98.

Gries, S. and S. Wulff. 2013. The Genitive Alternation in Chinese and German ESL Learners: Towards a Multifactorial Notion of Context in Learner Corpus Research. *International Journal of Corpus Linguistics* 18(3), 327–356.

He, A. W. and Y. Xiao (eds.) 2008. *Chinese as a Heritage Language: Fostering Rooted World Citizenry* (Vol. 2). Honolulu, HI: National Foreign Language Resource Center.

Herbst, T., H-J. Schmid, and S. Faulhaber. 2014. From Collocations and Patterns to Constructions: An Introduction. In T. Herbst, H-J. Schmid, and S. Faulhaber (eds.), *Constructions Collocations Patterns*. Berlin: Walter de Gruyter, 1–9.

Hilpert, M. 2013. *Constructional Change in English: Developments in Allomorphy, Word Formation, and Syntax*. Cambridge: Cambridge University Press.

Hinkel, E. 2001. Matters of Cohesion in L2 Academic Texts. *Applied Language Learning* 12 (2), 111–132.

Hunston, S. 2002. *Corpora in Applied Linguistics*. Cambridge: Cambridge University Press.

Iannozzi, M. 2015 Pro-drop in Faetar in Canada: A Study of a Heritage Language in Contact. *Western Papers in Linguistics* 1(2), 1–11.

Kisselev, O. and A. Alsufieva. 2017. The Development of Syntactic Complexity in the Writing of Russian Language Learners: A Longitudinal Corpus Study. *Russian Language Journal* 67, 27–53.

Kisselev, O. and E. Furniss. forthcoming. Corpus Linguistics and Russian Language Pedagogy. In E. Dengub, I. Dubinina, and J. Merill (eds.) *The Art of Teaching Russian*. Washington, DC: Georgetown University Press, 307–332.

Kisselev, O., I. Dubinina, and M. Polinsky. 2020. Form-Focused Instruction in the Heritage Language Classroom: Toward Research-Informed Heritage Language Pedagogy. In *Frontiers in Education* (Vol. 5). Switzerland: Frontiers, 53.

Kopotev, M. 2008. Ispol'zovanie èlektronnyx korpusov v prepodavanii russkogo jazyka [The Use of Electronic Corpora in the Teaching of the Russian Language]. In J. Lindstedt et al. (eds.), *SLAVICA HELSINGIENSIA 35, S ljubov'ju k slovu, Festschrift in Honour of Professor Arto Mustajoki on the Occasion of his 60th Birthday*. Helsinki, 110–118.

Kopotev, M. and A. Mustajoki. 2008. Sovremennaja korpusnaja rusistika [Contemporary Corpus Linguistics]. In A. Mustajoki, M. Kopotev, L. Birjulin, and Ju. Protasova (eds.), *Instrumentarij rusistiki: Korpusnye podxody [Instruments for Russian Studies: Corpus Approaches]*. Helsinki: Helsinki University Press, 7–24.

Kopotev, M., O. Kisselev, and M. Polinsky. 2020. Lexical Strategies of Heritage Speakers: Collocations in Heritage Russian. In H. Halmari and A. Backus (eds.), *Balancing Bilingualism: Linguistic Implications of Input Limitations*. Special Issue for the *International Journal of Bilingualism*.

Kroch, A. and A. Taylor. 2000. Verb–Object Order in Early Middle English. In S. Pintzuk, G. Tsoulas, and A. Warner (eds.), *Diachronic Syntax: Models and Mechanisms*. Oxford: Oxford University Press, 132–163.

Kroch, A., B. Santorini, and L. Delfs. 2004. *The Penn-Helsinki Parsed Corpus of Early Modern English (PPCEME)*. Department of Linguistics, University of Pennsylvania. CD-ROM, First Edition, Release 3 (www.ling.upenn.edu/ppche-release-2016/PPCEME-RELEASE-3).

Lee, S. H., S. B. Jang, and S. K. Seo. 2009. Annotation of Korean Learner Corpora for Particle Error Detection. *CALICO Journal* 26(3), 529–544.

Leech, G. 1992. Corpora and Theories of Linguistic Performance, Directions in Corpus Linguistics. *Proceedings of Nobel Symposium 82*. Berlin, New York: Mouton de Gruyter, 105–122.

Leech, G. 2000. Grammars of Spoken English: New Outcomes of Corpus-Oriented Research. *Language Learning* 50(4), 675–724.

Leech, G. 2005. Adding Linguistic Annotation. In M. Wynne (ed.), *Developing Linguistic Corpora: A Guide to Good Practice*. Oxford: Oxbow Books, 17–29.

Li, P., S. W. Eskildsen, and T. Cadierno. 2014. Tracing an L2 Learner's Motion Constructions Over Time: A Usage-Based Classroom Investigation. *The Modern Language Journal* 98(2), 612–628.

Lieven, E. and M. Tomasello. 2008. Children's First Language Acquisition from a Usage-Based Perspective. In P. Robinson and N. C. Ellis (eds.), *Handbook of Cognitive Linguistics and Second Language Acquisition*. New York: Routledge, 168–196.

Lozano, C. and A. Mendikoetxea. 2013. Learner Corpora and Second Language Acquisition. *Automatic Treatment and Analysis of Learner Corpus Data* 59, 65–100.

Lu, X., J. Yoon, and O. Kisselev. 2018. A Phrase-Frame List for Social Science Research Article Introductions. *Journal of English for Academic Purposes* 36, 76–85.

Lüdeling, A., H. Hirschmann, and A. Shadrova. 2017. Linguistic Models, Acquisition Theories, and Learner Corpora: Morphological Productivity in SLA Research Exemplified by Complex Verbs in German. *Language Learning* 67(S1), 96–129.

MacWhinney, B. 2000. *The CHILDES Project: Tools for Analyzing Talk: Transcription Format and Programs* (3rd ed.) Mahwah, NJ: Lawrence Erlbaum Associates Publishers.

Malamud, S. A., I. Dubinina, A. Luu, and N. Xue. 2017–present. Parsed and Audio-aligned Corpus of Bilingual Russian Child and Child-directed Speech (Parsed BiRCh).

Mayer, M. 1969. *Frog, Where Are You?* New York: Dial Books for Young Readers.

McEnery, T. and A. Hardie. 2012. *Corpus Linguistics: Method, Theory and Practice*. Cambridge: Cambridge University Press.

McEnery, T., R. Xiao, and Y. Tono. 2006. *Corpus-Based Language Studies: An Advanced Resource Book*. New York: Routledge.

Ming, T. and H. Tao. 2008. Developing a Chinese Heritage Language Corpus: Issues and a Preliminary Report. In A. W. He and Y. Xiao (eds.), *Chinese as a Heritage Language: Fostering Rooted World Citizenry*. Honolulu, HI: National Foreign Language Resource Center, 167–188.

Mizumoto, A., S. Hamatani, and Y. Imao. 2017. Applying the Bundle–Move Connection Approach to the Development of an Online Writing Support Tool for Research Articles. *Language Learning* 67(4), 885–921.

Montrul, S. 2010. Current Issues in Heritage Language Acquisition. *Annual Review of Applied Linguistics* 30, 3–23.

Montrul, S. 2016. *The Acquisition of Heritage Languages*. Cambridge: Cambridge University Press.

Myles, F. 2005. Interlanguage Corpora and Second Language Acquisition Research. *Second Language Research* 21(4), 373–391.

Nagy, N. and S. Lo. 2019. Variation and Change in Heritage and Hong Kong Cantonese Classifiers *Asia-Pacific Language Variation* 1(5), 84–108.

Nagy, N., M. Iannozzi, and D. Heap. 2018. Faetar Null Subjects: A Variationist Study of a Heritage Language in Contact. *International Journal of the Sociology of Language*, 249.

Nagy, N., N. Aghdasi, D. Denis, and A. Motut. 2011. Pro-drop in Heritage Languages: A Cross-Linguistic Study of Contact-Induced Change. *Penn Working Papers in Linguistics* 17, 2.

Nesselhauf, N. 2005. *Collocations in a Learner Corpus*. Phildelphia/Amsterdam: John Benjamins.

Nesi, H., G. Sharpling, and L. Ganobcsik-Williams. 2004. Student Papers across the Curriculum: Designing and Developing a Corpus of British Student Writing. *Computers and Composition* 21, 439–450.

Paquot, M. and S. Granger. 2012. Formulaic Language in Learner Corpora. *Annual Review of Applied Linguistics* 32(1), 130–149.

Pawley, A. and F. H. Snyder. 1983. Two Puzzles for Linguistic Theory: Nativelike Selection and Nativelike Fluency. In J. C. Richards and R. W. Schimdt (eds.), *Language and Communication*. New York: Longman, 191–226.

Peirce, G. 2018. Representational and Processing Constraints on the Acquisition of Case and Gender by Heritage and L2 Learners of Russian: A Corpus Study. *Heritage Language Journal* 15(1), 95–111.

Polinsky, M., M. Kopotev, and O. Kisselev. 2020. *Heritage Language Data Repository*. National Heritage Language Resource Center, UCLA https://international.ucla.edu/helada

Rebuschat, P. E., M. Detmar, and T. McEnery. 2017. Language Learning Research at the Intersection of Experimental, Computational and Corpus-Based Approaches. *Language Learning* 67(S1), 6–13.

Richards, J. A., J. Gilkerson, T. Paul, and D. Xu. 2008. The LENATM Automatic Vocalization Assessment. LTR-08-1. Retrieved from www.lenafoundation. org/wp-content/uploads/2014/10/LTR-08-1_Automatic_Vocalization_Assessment. pdf

Römer, U. 2011. Corpus Research Applications in Second Language Teaching. *Annual Review of Applied Linguistics* 31, 205–225.

Rosen, A., J. Hana, B. Štindlová, and A. Feldman. 2014. Evaluating and Automating the Annotation of a Learner Corpus. *Language Resources and Evaluation* 48(1), 65–92.

Rozovskaya, A. and D. Roth. 2014. Building a State-of-the-Art Grammatical Error Correction System. *Transactions of American Computational Linguistics* 2, 419–434.

Rozovskaya, A. and D. Roth. 2019. Grammar Error Correction in Morphologically Rich Languages: The Case of Russian. *Transactions of the Association for Computational Linguistics* 7, 1–17.

Schlitz, S. 2010. Introduction to the Special Issue: Exploring Corpus-Informed Approaches to Writing Research. *Journal of Writing Research* 2(2), 91–98.

Schmitt, D. and N. Schmitt. 2005. *Focus on Vocabulary: Mastering the Academic Word List*. White Plains, NY: Longman.

Scott, M. 2016. WordSmith Tools version 7 [Computer Program]. Stroud: Lexical Analysis Software.

Taylor, A. and S. Pintzuk. 2012. Verb Order, Object Position and Information Status in Old English. *York Papers in Linguistics* Series 2, 29–52.

Taylor, C. 2008. What Is Corpus Linguistics? What the Data Says. *ICAME Journal* 32, 179–200.

Taylor, L. and F. Barker. 2008. Using Corpora in Language Assessment. In E. Shohamy and N. H. Hornberger (eds.), *Encyclopedia of Language and Education* (2nd ed.): *Volume 7: Language Testing and Assessment*. New York: Springer, 241–254.

Tomasello, M. 2003. The Key is Social Cognition. In D. Gentner and S. Goldin-Meadow (eds.), *Language in Mind: Advances in the Study of Language and Thought*. Cambridge: MIT Press, 47–57.

Torres Cacoullos, R. and J. Bauman. 2018. Allative to Purposive Grammaticalization: A Quantitative Story of Spanish Para. *Studies in Historical Ibero-Romance Morpho-Syntax* 16, 165.

Torres Cacoullos, R. and G. Berry 2018. Language Variation in US Spanish: Social Factors. K. Potowski (ed.), *Handbook of Spanish as a Minority/Heritage Language*. London/New York: Routledge.

Torres Cacoullos, R., D. LaCasse, M. Johns, and J. De la Rosa Yacomelo. 2017. El subjuntivo: hacia la rutinización. *Moenia* 23.

Tse, H. 2019. Beyond the Monolingual Core and out into the Wild: A Variationist Study of Early Bilingualism and Sound Change in Toronto Heritage Cantonese. Doctoral dissertation, University of Pittsburgh.

Vyatkina, N. 2012. The Development of Second Language Writing Complexity in Groups and Individuals: A Longitudinal Learner Corpus Study. *Modern Language Journal* 96(4), 572–594.

Vyatkina, N. 2013. Discovery Learning and Teaching with Electronic Corpora in an Advanced German Grammar Course. *Die Unterrichtspraxis/ Teaching German* 46(1), 44–61.

Vyrenkova, A. S., M. S. Polinskaja, and E. V. Raxilina. 2014. Grammatika ošibok i grammatika konstrukcij: "Èritažnyj" ("unasledovannyj") russkij jazyk. *Voprosy Jazykoznanija* 3, 3–19.

Wray, A. 2002. *Formulaic Language and the Lexicon*. Oxford: Oxford University Press.

Xiao-Desai, Y. and K. F. Wong. 2017. Epistemic Stance in Chinese Heritage Language Writing: A Developmental View. *Chinese as a Second Language Research* 6(1), 73–102.

Yagunova, E. V. and L. M. Pivovarova. 2014. Ot Kollokacij k Konstrukcijam [From Collocations to Constructs]. S. S. Saj, M. A. Ovsyannikova, and S. A. Oskol'skaja (eds.), *Russkij Yazyk: Grammatika Konstrukcij i Leksiko-Semnaticeskie Podkhody [Russian Language: Grammar of Constructions and Lexico-Semmatic Approaches]*. St. Petersburg: Nauka, 568–5617.

Yu, L. C., L. H. Lee, and L. P. Chang. 2014, November. Overview of Grammatical Error Diagnosis for Learning Chinese As a Foreign Language. *Proceedings of the 1st Workshop on Natural Language Processing Techniques for Educational Applications* 42–47.

Zaghouani, W., B. Mohit, N. Habash, O. Obeid, N. Tomeh, A. Rozovskaya, N. Farra, S. Alkuhlani, and K. Oflazer. 2014. Large Scale Arabic Error Annotation: Guidelines and Framework. *Proceedings of LREC*.

22

Current Trends and Emerging Methodologies in Charting Heritage Language Grammars[*]

Fatih Bayram, Grazia Di Pisa, Jason Rothman,
and Roumyana Slabakova

22.1 Introduction

The field of heritage language (HL) acquisition has emerged in earnest over the past two decades as part of a wave of expansion in investigating bilingual language scenarios beyond the two previously widely studied cases: (i) simultaneous child bilingual (2L1) development and (ii) nonnative adult second language (L2) acquisition. Whereas 2L1 development tends to follow qualitatively similar paths and developmental milestones to monolingual children (see e.g., de Houwer 1990; Meisel 2011; Serratrice 2013; Kupisch 2006 for review), adult L2 learners are often significantly different in developmental sequencing and outcomes (see White 2003; Ortega 2014; Slabakova 2016 for review). This juxtaposition seemed to offer solid argumentation in favor of the Critical Period Hypothesis (CPH) (Lenneberg 1967) application to adult bilingual language learning.[1] Must such differences mean that age is deterministic for one's potential to employ domain-specific mechanisms for acquiring language in a truly native manner? Most relevant for the present handbook, how can the study of heritage

[*] The work was funded by grants from the *European Union's Horizon 2020 research and innovation programme under the Marie Skłodowska Curie grant agreements No 799652 and 765556*; and the *Tromsø Forskningsstiftelse (TFS) starting grant (2019–2023)*.

[1] See du Plessis, Solin, Travi, and White (1987) and Schwartz (1992) for early on argumentation related to concerns with using comparative developmental sequencing data to make such claims.

speaker (HS) bilinguals help adjudicate between the various positions argued on the basis of this juxtaposition?

Definitive claims based on these observations suffered in the 1980s and 1990s from a lack of data from other populations, arguably needed to understand the overall picture. Child L2 acquirers,[2] L1 attriters,[3] and especially adult HS bilinguals were studied in increasing numbers starting in the mid-1990s, changing what we now see as a much wider picture. The developmental trajectories and outcomes of these then understudied populations had something relevant to contribute to the CPH debate in adult bilingualism. For example, if asymmetries in developmental sequencing or outcome differences from monolingual baselines indicate a fundamental difference between child and adult acquisition, then, distinctly from what is expected of adult L2 learners, one would predict child L2 acquisition to approximate somewhat faithfully child L1 development; and early native bilingual speakers to wind up with grammars falling within the range of monolingual variation. As it turns out, neither of these predictions obtain straightforwardly. Child L2 acquisition shows very similar degrees of transfer as adult L2 acquisition, whereby developmental trajectories are distinct from monolingual children even if, on average, ultimate attainment is more convergent in the case of L2 children (see Haznedar and Gavruseva 2008; Haznedar 2013 for review). HS bilinguals tested in early adulthood, despite being naturalistic L1 or 2L1 native speakers of their home language (Rothman and Treffers-Daller 2014), present competencies and performances[4] across a wide spectrum of differences as compared to monolingual natives (see Polinsky 2018 for review). Both of these facts challenge the claim that similar differences seen in adult L2 acquisition must be taken as evidence for a fundamental difference in mechanisms between children and adults for language learning overall. Apparently, early exposure before puberty does not guarantee a monolingual-like path or outcomes.

As Polinsky and Scontras (2020: 2) put it, "heritage speakers constitute an outcome often assumed to be impossible outside of pathology or trauma: children exposed to a language from birth who nevertheless appear to deviate from the expected native-like mastery in pronounced and principled ways." Understanding how and why heritage grammars develop the way they do, inclusive of what variables predict outcomes at the

---

[2] Sequential learners of a second language in early childhood after an L1 is established but not yet completely acquired (see e.g., Haznedar 2013)

[3] Native speaker individuals, typically immigrants, who experience significant shift in exposure to and opportunities for use of their L1, resulting in changes in competence and/or ways in which they process their L1 (see e.g., Schmid and Köpke 2017),

[4] By competence and performance, we refer to the distinction between one's underlying system of the mental representation of grammar versus the way in which this knowledge system is used. The latter can be affected by memory limitations, attention, and other filtering issues (e.g., Chomsky 1964).

individual level, can offer profound insights for linguistic theory in general (e.g., Scontras et al. 2015; Lohndal et al. 2019) as well as for challenges related to language maintenance, contact, policy and more (e.g., Suarez 2002; Valdés 2005; Brinton et al. 2017). However, capturing what HSs actually know about (one of) their native grammar(s) is especially challenging for various reasons (see Polinsky 2018 for comprehensive review) related to their experiences with their HL, how we test such knowledge, and the interface of the two.

HSs are typically not trained, literate readers of their HL. For many HSs, the language is imparted and used almost exclusively orally. Thus, even in the case that the HL and the majority language share the same script and overlap in phoneme-to-grapheme correspondence, HSs are likely to be slower in reading the HL. HSs experience, on a continuum, reduced quantities of input as well as contexts in which they are likely to hear/use the HL. This reality, in turn, affects knowledge of particular vocabularies and discourse conventions pertaining to distinct registers. These facts, of course, bring much to bear on the appropriateness of particular experimental designs/choices, depending on the questions one seeks to address. In general, tasks that assume some level of literacy competence/experience, specific vocabulary knowledge, and/or are likely to hinge to some degree on metalinguistic training that formal education imparts are best avoided. Moreover, HSs can simply be reluctant or anxious for a multitude of reasons to offer definitive judgments on their HL (Polinsky 2016). As a result, some tasks widely used with other sets of speakers such as Grammaticality Judgement Tasks and Acceptability Judgement Tasks are either best avoided or need to be modified with the above in mind.

Depending on the research question, for example, seeking to tap the status of a morphosyntactic or phonological representation in the HS mental grammar becomes more appropriate than testing whether or not, and if so under what conditions, HSs produce morphosyntactic reflexes or phonological exponents. Consequently, methodologies that probe comprehension offline and related online processing reflexes (e.g., prediction/facilitation) versus production come to the fore. Comprehending/processing (some of) the manifold implications of functional morphology and/or perceiving phonological contrasts that are not consistently produced, if at all, by the HSs offers insight into competence that would go unnoticed via production alone. For example, if a HS of Cantonese has apparent issues in the production of lexical tones but shows via perception experimentation that such differences are more quantitative than qualitative in nature (Lam 2018), such experimentation reveals knowledge that is not easy to intuit from her use of the language.

At the end of the day, we seek to understand HL grammars fully, which entails studying both comprehension and production and, more to the point, reconciling what we take the relationship between the two to be. We know from the rather limited work on receptive or passive heritage bilinguals – heritage bilinguals that seemingly have much greater comprehension skills in the HL than production abilities – that production can lag far behind the ability to understand the HL (e.g., Sherkina-Lieber 2015; Holmes 2017). There is clearly not a one-to-one relationship between comprehension and production abilities. The exact relationship between the two and how they inform each other are a matter of perspective, if not debate; however, what is uncontroversial is that they both relate to an underlying language system. Although in dominant native speakers, comprehension and production have much greater overlap, studying HSs reminds us that while both relate to each other and to a common source of mental competence, they are distinct and diverge in their involvement/dependence on other mechanisms. Various traditions of linguistics place more or less emphasis on the two: Experimental acquisitionists and psycholinguists tend to be more interested in comprehension/perception, whereas sociolinguists and more applied linguists have a greater tendency to focus on production, especially what conditions the production of language in various contexts. Comprehension/perception and related processing in real-time experimentation might offer the most straightforward glimpses into more automatic underlying processes. Production, alternatively, offers greater, more ecologically valid insights into how the HL is used in sociolinguistic patterns and/or can be exploited as a path to capturing the status of the underlying mental grammar.

Given that it is not clear what can be concluded based on testing HSs in the "traditional" ways used with subjects trained in the target language, be it an L1 or L2, experimentation that is able to neutralize or circumvent these challenges is especially welcome and on the rise. In this chapter, we take stock of where we are at methodologically. We place special emphasis on newer methods to the domain of HL bilingualism that we believe are particularly suited to uncovering the underlying basis of individual differences in HS outcomes as well as on methods that capture more automatic indexes of processing.

22.2   Offline Studies

To date, most studies interested in tapping the nature of HL competence have used offline methods, for example, acceptability judgment tasks, comprehension tasks, production (elicitation tasks and natural corpora) and recognition tasks (e.g., Montrul 2002, 2011; Rothman 2007; Montrul et al. 2008; Isurin and Ivanova-Sullivan 2008; Polinsky 2008, 2011; Pires and Rothman 2009; Lee-Ellis 2011; Silva-Corvalán 2014; Lohndal and

Westergaard 2016; Bayram et al. 2017; Hopp et al. 2019; Johannessen 2018; Kim et al. 2018; Lloyd-Smith et al. 2021; Pascual y Cabo 2020). By their nature, offline tasks do not offer direct access to one's mental processes as they unfold in real time. They are an outcome measure of the linguistic and/or cognitive processes that took place before a production, judgment, or comprehension index is recorded, together with (potentially) conscious, metalinguistic knowledge. Having a look at how grammatical gender has been typically studied in HL affords us the opportunity to examine a range of typical offline experimental tasks. We thus turn to this property now as an exemplar.

It is well established that in languages where it is a grammatical category, gender is an inherent lexical feature on nouns (Corbett 1991), while determiners and adjectives may exhibit gender agreement with the head noun. The former constitutes lexical knowledge, i.e., one-to-one for each noun, while the latter, gender as expressed via systematic agreement within noun phrases (e.g., on determiners and adjectives), does not require one-to-one learning and constitutes syntactic knowledge.[5] A clever experimental paradigm to tap knowledge of the gender system has been used to examine the status of gender agreement within the determiner phrase without the appearance/suppliance of the lexical noun itself. Nominal ellipsis, noun-drop in Spanish, *la roja* 'the red [one],' is the example. The identification of the missing noun in context crucially depends on the gender and number valuation of the elided noun in the mental lexicon. And so, examining noun-drop gives one simultaneously insight into the gender assignment for specific lexical items as well as one's ability to use the morphosyntactic agreement cues in real-time comprehension. In a well-known study following White et al. (2004), Montrul, Foote, and Perpiñán (2008) used a noun-drop task to compare knowledge of gender agreement in the performance of Spanish L2 learners and HSs, ranging from low to advanced levels of proficiency. L2 speakers showed an advantage over HSs for this particular task (90 percent versus 80 percent). Montrul, Foote, and Perpiñán's participants were given a choice of three common objects in three pictures. In one experimental item, the three pictures showed a suitcase, a book, and a pair of socks. The stimulus sentence was *María contesta: "Sí, claro, va a hacer mucho sol. Ponlas ahí cerca de la roja."* (Maria answers: "Yes, of course, it is going to be very sunny. Put them over there by the red [one]"). The phrase *la roja* points to a missing nominal, which is feminine and singular, as indicated by the determiner *la* and the morphological ending in the adjective *roja*. If

---

[5] We do not mean to suggest that gender is literally learned in a one-to-one manner for each word for all speakers of all languages. The need for doing so depends on the relative transparency of the system, for example, we might expect differences between Spanish, which has highly transparent patterns, and Dutch, which is highly opaque, regardless of the type of learner.

learners compute gender agreement, they can use it to pick the picture of the suitcase (*la maleta*), whose gender is feminine. The book (*el libro*) should not be selected, since it is masculine. The third picture contains a foil (*los calcetines*) that is masculine and plural. Participants are engaged in a puzzle-like task, and their comprehension rather than production indicates whether abstract features are functional in their grammars.

Generally speaking, how do we know whether HSs have monolingual-like gender assignment, i.e., have the same gender class assignment for each noun compared to native monolinguals? How much emphasis should we even be placing on gender assignment "correctness" if agreement is our real object of inquiry? These are crucial questions if one wishes to shed light on the status of the HL syntax of gender, precisely because it manifests as an agreement system dependent on the lexical assignment of the nouns, even if "wrong." One potential contributor for divergence noted in work like Montrul, Foote, and Perpiñán could have as much or more to do with HL differences in gender assignment at the lexical level than be indicative of anything askew in the HL syntactic agreement system. Such a possibility gains credence in light of later work by Hopp (2013), which highlights the inherent nature between lexical and syntactic variability in this domain, and recent eye-tracking work by Fuchs (2019), showing that when one corrects for assignment, HSs of Spanish show the exact same qualitative patterns in processing gender and using it facilitatively. Hopp's work calls for a leveling of the playing field (so to speak) when comparing monolinguals to bilinguals of all sorts: Agreement should be evaluated in direct proportion to the lexical assignment an individual has for the set of nouns used in experimentation. In other words, if a noun is demonstrated to be feminine in the mental grammar of HS X, whether or not it is in other speakers' grammars, then agreement is evaluated as correct on the basis of what X's assignment is established to be. Of course, we are also interested in understanding how and why individual HSs might wind up with distinct lexical gender assignments, but that is a different question, one of learning, as opposed to our main question that seeks to uncover the status of the mental representation of gender as an operative functional category in HL grammars.

Other offline tasks abound in the literature. For example, Polinsky (2008) tested Russian heritage speakers' knowledge of gender categorization. In two experiments, she combined nouns with well-known adjectives and possessive pronouns. The participants' task was to produce a phrase with the adjective *bol'š-* 'big' or the pronoun *tv-* 'your' after hearing each noun. In a second experiment, participants heard recordings of congruent and incongruent combinations of the same adjectives with various nouns, and had to indicate whether the combination was acceptable. The findings allowed the researcher to conclude that half of her participants had a two-gender system instead of a three-gender one, as in baseline monolingual Russian. Such exemplary work allows for documenting and understanding the systematic nature of HL systems, in this case gender, even when they are distinct from the monolingual baseline. Polinsky (2008) thus demonstrates that HL Russian in the United States is distinct from monolingual Russian, but in a way that shows an intact gender system in its own right, albeit one that deviates from the standard variety.

Undoubtedly, chapters in this handbook will have looked into offline methods in much greater detail. The remit of this chapter is not to delve into the details of such research but to highlight three points relevant for our assigned task of discussing and encouraging innovation in HL research methodologies: (a) establish what has been done in an effort to (b) highlight the inherent methodological challenges in order to (c) promote research methods that circumvent these challenges. With notable exceptions we will discuss in detail, experimental tasks to date have tended to range from more metalinguistic, classroom-style tasks such as forced choice of morphological endings or free morphemes, through oral picture description tasks to written comprehension tasks such as White et al.'s (2004) noun-drop experiment adopted to HL Spanish in Montrul, Foote, and Perpiñán (2008) described earlier. There is relative consensus (Montrul 2015) that experimental tasks and groups (HSs and L2ers) interact in this type of research. L2 learners typically perform better than HSs in highly metalinguistic written tasks. On the other hand, HSs perform more monolingual-like than L2 learners in oral production tasks and in phonology discrimination tasks (Au, Knightly, Jun, and Oh 2002). In sum, offline methods of studying HL have closely replicated those used in L2 acquisition research, both because the experiments are known to be tried and true from decades of use and for the purposes of comparing these two populations. The variety of tasks has uncovered both similarities and significant distinctions between HL development/outcomes and those of typical adult L2 learners (Montrul 2008, 2012).

While HL studies as a cohort have documented time and again differences from the expected baselines of monolinguals, the field has yet to uncover with the same precision and replication what variables prove predictive (related to input exposure, patterns of use and more) to path and outcome, at the group or individual level (see Polinsky and Scontras 2020 for steps in this direction). Moreover, a critical mass of research on HL processing is not yet available to meaningfully test if there is a convergence between offline and online data in general, much less fully understand the consequences of what it would mean to show qualitatively more convergent processing by the same HS participants that can diverge so much in offline task performances. We do not yet have the data needed to fully chart heritage language development to see, longitudinally or via carefully constructed cross-sections, what the dynamic course of development and maintenance of HLs are over the lifespan, despite compelling reasons to believe that a lot would be gained by focusing on filling these gaps. As Scontras, Fuchs, and Polinsky (2015) note: "[w]hile these practices necessitate a good deal of time and care on the part of the researcher, we have seen that they pay off, both by answering the specific questions targeted by the given study, and by raising additional questions central to any theory of grammar." In the remainder of this chapter, we focus on research that attempts to fill these gaps, since we see these as integral to the future of HL studies on HS competence.

22.3   Online Research Methods

22.3.1   Why Do We Need Online Methods in HL Studies?

As established in the previous section, offline measures seeking to tap HS competence represent, by far, the largest portion of available data sets. While this literature has produced a wealth of high quality research and knowledge, there are at least two important issues related to the use of offline methods that can affect conclusions drawn almost exclusively from them: (i) the kind of knowledge that they require from participants and (ii) the granularity and purity of what is (sometimes) captured by offline performances alone.

In untimed offline tasks, participants have the space to think before they offer an answer. This can mean that metalinguistic consciousness and potentially other affective factors become difficult to tease apart from underlying competence, with only the former being the actual object of inquiry in the relevant HL literature. Whether formally trained in their HL or not, HSs are likely to have various types of explicit knowledge related to their HL (either specifically learned or what they have deduced themselves) and regarding language in general. Conscious explicit knowledge in the case of HSs is, potentially, distinct from what educated dominant-native speakers have. HSs often have the impression that their knowledge and use of the HL is prescriptively "wrong," often viewed negatively by themselves and by various members of their communities. How does this affect how they perform on offline tasks? Do (all) offline methods (equally) ensure that such factors (and other potential noise) do not obscure ensuing data? Unlike native-dominant speakers of the same language, HSs typically do not have the same common formal experiences with their home language such as schooling in the standard variety. What is the effect of this in offline tasks (Rothman 2009; Bayram et al. 2017)? Both native-dominant L1 and adult L2 speakers are exposed to the formal standard variety in school settings and purposefully develop literacy and metalinguistic skills in that language.

Recall that many HSs have little or no literacy experience in their L1, at least until adult age if they endeavor to re-learn their heritage language in a formal setting (Polinsky and Kagan 2007; Polinsky 2015). HSs are well-known to be conservative in judgment tasks (effectively not using the absolute ends of Likert scales, for example, Polinsky 2018). This is potentially, at least in part, due to the formality of being tested in a language they are (typically) not dominant or balanced in and has not been the language in which they would have done other types of testing throughout childhood and adolescence. As discussed in the introduction, specific tasks requiring or easily impacted by any experience-based and affective factors are not ideal, on their own, to study HLs and their speakers (Bolger and Zapata 2011; Polinsky 2018).

Without doubt, there are very carefully designed studies tapping into HL comprehension that are not easily affected by the above factors and/or production-based work showing clear patterns of underlying HL competence. However, efforts in recent years to assess HL knowledge while bypassing some of these concerns have turned the field more and more to online research methods, such as self-paced reading tasks, masked priming tasks, eye-tracking, and electroencephalography (EEG) methodology (e.g., self-paced reading task: Foote 2011; Keating et al. 2016; Jegerski 2018a, 2018b; Puig-Mayenco et al. 2018; Villegas 2018; eye-tracking: Sekerina and Trueswell 2011; Villegas 2014; Arslan et al. 2015; Sekerina and Sauermann 2015; van Rijswijk et al. 2017; Jegerski and Sekerina 2019; masked priming task: Jacob and Kırkıcı 2016; Jacob et al. 2019; EEG methodology: van Rijswijk 2016; Martohardjono et al. 2017).

Online tasks measure participants' automatic responses to language stimuli, giving us a more direct access to *how* language processing unfolds in real time. To be fair, all measures, offline and online alike, record types of performances and are, thus, subject to extraneous, interceding factors. Each, albeit differentially, tap into unconscious knowledge while measuring linguistic behavior (White 2018). However, online measures capturing automatic processes are not affected by having time to ponder metalinguistic knowledge. Automatic reactions measured with high temporal resolution can be taken to indicate underlying knowledge more reliably. In doing so, online methods provide a path to test whether or not HSs process their HL qualitatively differently from other sets of speakers of the same language. If they perform like dominant-native speakers, for example, this could indicate that HL grammars are more like native-dominant ones than differences in production, judgments, and/or comprehension offline methods have suggested (Villegas 2014). Alternatively, even if HSs process some domains of grammar qualitatively distinctly, online measures can help us to better understand and describe the coherent nature of their underlying grammars in their own right.

22.3.2 Online Methods in HL Studies

To date, the most widely used online methods have been self-paced reading, eye-tracking, and masked priming tasks. In a *self-paced reading task*, participants are asked to read sentences on the screen presented one word (or phrase) at a time, pressing a button to move onto the next. The main assumption behind self-paced reading is that the amount of time taken to read a word reflects the amount of time needed to process that word. Thus, longer reading times mean processing difficulty, while faster reading times could be interpreted as a sign that facilitation occurred (Jegerski 2014). Self-paced reading could be seen as a more implicit measure of grammatical competence, compared to offline judgments, because its time constraints prevent relying on explicit grammar rules. At first glance, the use of self-paced reading could seem problematic in and of itself, at least for certain groups of HSs, given the previously discussed concerns related to literacy effects. In studies using self-paced reading, however, it should be said that the focus is not (or should not be) on comparing overall reading times to dominant-native speakers. Rather, the goal is to understand whether HSs have qualitatively similar reactions to ungrammaticality, irrespective of overall speed. In other words, do HSs' reading times slow down after ungrammaticalities, relative to sentences with no violations, independent of how long they take to read overall? The differences between scripts across the languages can have obvious effects as well. And so, an alternative way to effectively accomplish the same goals would be to use self-paced listening.

Eye-tracking measures where one focuses visual attention and eye movements. It is widely used in language processing, monolingual and bilingual alike, as it is argued that it offers a window into the mind and, as such, an automatic measure into how language comprehension unfolds in real time (uses of cues for parsing, prediction/facilitation, etc., Traxler and Pickering 1996; Rayner 1998; Demberg and Keller 2008; Dussias 2010; Holmqvist et al. 2011). Although it is typically done with a task from which an accuracy measure can be derived, it does not require nor is it dependent on a secondary task, thus providing rich temporal data in and of itself. The eye-tracking methodology uses two main approaches: (i) recording the eyes' fixation patterns as a sentence is read, analyzing the time spent on each word/phrase; and (ii) the visual world paradigm in which participants' patterns of eye movements are tracked while they listen to phrases/sentences that correspond to one (or more) of the pictures they see on the screen. Both approaches have proven very informative tools for investigating sentence comprehension processes.

The *masked priming paradigm* (Foster and Davis 1984; Kinoshita and Lupker 2003) has been extensively used to study the online processing of a variety of lexical and morphosyntactic phenomena in different languages, in order to tap into the earliest stages of visual-word recognition. In the experiment, the prime (stimulus) is typically presented for a very short time (~50 ms) between a mask (≲500 ms) and a target (≲500 ms), making it virtually invisible and consciously unnoticeable. This presentation allows for investigating the effect of the prime–target relationship at an unconscious level. For example, participants can be presented with a morphologically complex prime word like *walk* quickly enough that it is typically not noticed at the conscious level. They are then asked to perform a speeded lexical decision for a morphologically related target word (e.g., *walk-er*). Identification times to a target word are consistently faster when it has been preceded by a related word than an unrelated one such as *key* (within the same language and even across languages).

By comparison to other online methods, there have been fewer studies applying *electroencephalography (EEG) methods* to HL bilingualism (van Rijswijk 2016; Martohardjono et al. 2017), despite the fact that they have been used increasingly in other bilingualism scenarios (see for review Roberts et al. 2018). EEG is a non-invasive electrophysiological method that is particularly well-suited for examining online language processing. EEG records electrical activity at the scalp level. When time-locked to a stimulus of interest and averaged over numerous similar trials, this is referred to as event related potential (ERP). ERP brain signals and their characteristic negative and positive deflections produced, known as components (see Luck 2014 for an overview of the ERP technique), have been found to be modulated by different linguistic processes, making this technique suitable to examine the qualitative nature of language processing. Because there is a relatively well-established literature on dominant-native language processing using EEG/ERP, we can predict the brain signatures of how various types of grammatical violations are processed (e.g., early negativity for lexical semantic violations (N400), late positivities for syntactic violations (P600)) in what has been the typical baseline comparison for HSs. In the case that one is more interested in revealing the underlying nature of HS individual differences, with large enough samples one could examine how individual HS brains react in terms of ERP components (e.g., Tanner 2019) to the same phenomena or how amplitudinal differences within the same component might be differentially modulated by a set of linguistic factors (e.g., relative markedness: Alemán Bañón and Rothman 2016, 2019) and/or experiential variables that distinguish HSs from one another. Like other online methods, EEG/ERP provides a real-time measure of automatic language processing that is not subject to introspection like offline measures can be. What is gained in temporal resolution and measuring of automatic responses comes with some trade-offs. There are limitations to what can be done with ERPs related to how stimuli sentences need to be constructed and counterbalanced (ERP components themselves are the differences between a grammatical baseline and an ungrammatical counterpart) as well as the number of exemplars required (at least thirty per condition if not more, because the data are collapsed into grand averages needed to capture the subtle effects). As a result, not all linguistic properties are (as) easily tested with ERPs.

To date, of the relatively few studies using online methods, some, which we detail in the following subsections, have found differences between online and offline data, suggesting that online research methods, requiring less explicit knowledge, are more successful in revealing the underlying nature of HS grammars. Given that such methods are less subject to undesirable mitigation of various external factors, they might be most appropriate for studying HS knowledge. Minimally, the combination of online methods in complement to offline ones offers a very promising and powerful battery to test HL competence. In an effort to understand how and why it is important to combine online data with offline data, we briefly review the main findings of exemplar studies in relation to various online methodologies used. We also describe some in-progress studies building on the very limited work adopting an EEG/ERP approach, suggesting that this method is ripe for expansion in HL studies.

22.3.2.1　Self-paced Reading Studies

Jegerski (2018a) investigated the real-time processing of Differential Object Marking (DOM) in Spanish HSs compared to late Spanish-English bilinguals using an offline acceptability judgment task and an online self-paced reading task. Previous offline studies showed a consistent variability with DOM in Spanish HSs (Montrul and Bowles 2009; Montrul and Sánchez-Walker 2013; Montrul 2014). Jegerski (2018a) is the first study investigating the processing of sentences with DOM in Spanish HSs using an online measure. Results showed that both groups were sensitive to DOM marking of indirect objects with inanimate direct objects, but not to DOM marking with animate direct objects. Moreover, although there were no significant differences between the HSs and the late bilinguals for the online experiment, the HSs gave fewer determinate judgments during the offline task. The online results are important because they show that variability with DOM is not only limited to HSs but is also present in native-dominant speakers of Spanish who are late bilinguals of English, where the construct of incomplete acquisition does not apply. The qualitative similarity in the two groups' online performances, in combination with indeterminacy in offline judgments for the HSs, seems to indicate that online measures can capture key information that is not reliably documented in offline performance.

In another example study, Keating, Jegerski, and VanPatten (2016) used a phrase-by-phrase self-paced reading task to investigate anaphora resolution in Spanish HSs of Mexican descent compared to monolingual Mexican

Spanish speakers. The online data results showed that HSs responded in a different way to null vs. overt pronouns, following a similar pattern to monolingual controls. These findings run in contrast to a prior investigation (Keating et al. 2011), where the same authors used an offline interpretation method, that showed that HSs processed null and overt pronouns in the same way. Keating, Jegerski, and VanPatten (2016) highlight the importance of using online methods, such as self-paced reading, to get a more informative picture of linguistic phenomena investigated so far only with offline methods.

22.3.2.2 Eye-Tracking Studies

Sekerina and Trueswell (2011) investigated the processing of contrastive constituents in Russian HSs compared to monolinguals in two eye-tracking experiments using a visual world paradigm. The authors used color adjective–noun phrases embedded into the split-constituent construction. Contrastiveness results from integration of multiple sources of information, e.g., word order, prosody, and visual context. Their results showed that while monolingual controls rapidly used word order and visual context (but not prosody) to compute the contrast, Russian HSs of low proficiency were very slow, both in performing the task and in eye-movements. Moreover, to compute the contrast, HSs made use of multiple sources of information. Possible explanations for this slowdown might be that bilinguals in general are slower in verbal tasks (Bialystok 2009). Another could be that bilinguals have slower reading times because of their tendency to re-read, to re-analyze what they just read (Frenck-Mestre 2002). The authors suggested instead that the slowdown in Russian HSs might reflect covert competition between their two languages starting at the level of spoken word recognition.

Jegerski and Sekerina (2019), following a prior investigation (Jegerski 2018a), investigated auditory comprehension of DOM in Spanish HSs compared to adult immigrant bilinguals. In this study, the authors used a visual world eye-tracking paradigm, where participants were listening to *wh*-questions with the DOM particle *a* (*quién*/*a quién* 'who/whom') while their eye movements were recorded across four referent pictures. Results for verbal responses to the questions (offline method) showed that the HSs were less accurate but the online eye-tracking data revealed that both groups, HSs and native Spanish late English bilinguals, started to look at the correct picture at the same point in the question, suggesting that the two were similar in real-time processing for comprehension. Once again, results from the offline data differ from the online data in the same experiment. The difference is also in the direction that suggests online methods can capture a distinct level of granularity and showcase more convergent HL competence.

Van Rijswijk, Muntendam, and Dijkstra (2017) used an eye-tracking reading experiment to explore whether the Dutch prosody of Turkish HSs living in the Netherlands differs from that of Dutch native-speakers who do not speak Turkish, and whether observed differences could be attributed to an effect of Turkish. Focus marking is different in Dutch and Turkish: Dutch mainly uses prosody to indicate focus, while Turkish uses both prosody and word order. In written sentences, no explicit prosody is available, which likely enhances the role of syntactic cues in interpreting focus. The authors found a difference in the total fixation durations between the HSs and controls. This result is in contrast with a previous study (van Rijswijk et al. 2017) that investigated focus marking in Dutch involving the same type of Turkish-Dutch HSs using an offline production task that revealed no difficulties in the HSs using prosody to mark focus. The differences in interpretations between HSs and controls in the eye-tracking experiment suggest that HSs relied on word order cues from their L1 (Turkish) to determine focus structure. This indeed showed an effect of Turkish L1 on Dutch L2, even though as HSs of Turkish they are overall more dominant in Dutch. These findings indicate that difficulties at the syntax-discourse interface are not necessarily visible in all modalities (i.e., speaking vs reading) and that some linguistic phenomena should be investigated using both offline and online methods in an effort to better explain variance in HSs' knowledge and performance.

In a final example study, Villegas (2014) investigated possible effects of immersion on comprehension and production in the linguistic representations of the Spanish subjunctive using online and offline methods. In the online comprehension experiment, the author used eye-tracking methodology to investigate whether native speakers of Spanish with different immersion experiences in the L2 (non-immersion, L1 native-late bilingual immersion, heritage speakers) differ in their ability to predict upcoming information while they read sentences in their L1. Overall, the results showed no significant differences between groups, suggesting that immersion did not affect speakers' predictive strategies during comprehension. The second experiment focused on the production of the subjunctive mood using an offline sentence completion task. The author wanted to determine whether there was a difference in the production of the subjunctive mood compared to comprehension. Interestingly, in this study HSs revealed significantly higher error rates in the production of the subjunctive mood compared to the non-immersed and the immersed L2 learner groups. These results suggest that HSs had difficulties in the production of the subjunctive mood but not during comprehension, pointing to complete grammatical representation. Villegas (2014) reports another case where HSs performed differently in the online task compared to the offline one, raising awareness for future research to address *what* underlies the differences between production versus comprehension in online versus offline tasks in HSs.

The question of what would explain the distinct behaviors with different methodologies and which result should be taken to best index knowledge comes to the fore. The answer is not straightforward and any attempt at an answer is likely to meet with some reasonable counter argumentation. However, the relevant point in a chapter like this one is to highlight that some linguistic phenomena should be investigated using both offline and online methods in an effort to better explain variance in HSs' knowledge and performance.

22.3.2.3 Masked Priming Studies

Jacob and Kırkıcı (2016) investigated the processing of morphological decomposition of complex words in Turkish HSs raised and living in Germany. The authors used materials and experimental design of a previous study (Kırkıcı and Clahsen 2013) on morphological processing in Turkish native speakers and L2 learners, allowing for a comparison across the three groups. The study used two masked-priming experiments. The first experiment investigated priming effects for morphologically related prime–target pairs. HSs showed significant priming effects for prime–target pairs with inflected and derived primes, a pattern of results similar to the native-speaker comparison group. In the second experiment, the authors wanted to check whether the priming effects from the first experiment could be explained on the basis of orthographic overlap or not. HSs showed significant priming effects also in this experiment, unlike both L1 speakers raised in Turkey and highly proficient L2 learners. In sum, Turkish HSs were found to rely less on morpho-orthographic decomposition, while focusing mainly on the orthographic surface form. Their results stress how the HSs are a highly unique population, different from both native speakers and L2 learners, that could give us insights into how some linguistic phenomena undergo universal processing mechanisms, or whether they are shaped by the way the language has been acquired.

Jacob, Şafak, Demir, and Kırkıcı (2019) compared the processing of derived and inflected morphologically complex Turkish words in Turkish HSs compared to Turkish native speakers, using a masked morphological priming experiment. Their results showed similar effects in the two groups, suggesting that morphological processing in HSs is based on the same processing mechanisms as in dominant-native Turkish speakers. Previous offline studies on morphology in HSs (e.g., Montrul et al. 2008; Polinsky 2008) have reported differences between HSs and native-dominant speakers, claiming signs of attrition or incomplete acquisition in the HSs output. Jacob and colleagues' (2019) results show instead that HSs can develop monolingual-like processing mechanisms for complex words, even though they were exposed to a limited amount of input. Again, another exemplar study stressed the importance of using online research methods in the field of HLs, in order to shed some light on what might cause variance within the HS population.

22.3.2.4 EEG/ERP

Van Rijswijk (2016) compared the Dutch of Turkish HSs to the Dutch of L1 speakers in the Netherlands, covering language production (speaking) and comprehension (both listening and reading). Combining different research methods, both offline and online, the author investigates the use of prosody, and the encoding and decoding of information structure. The main aim of the thesis is to shed some light on the processing mechanisms that underlie the specific interactions between the HL and the dominant L2. The author used a production task to investigate prosody in the speaking modality, an eye-tracking experiment focused on prosody at the sentence level monitoring reading behavior (see van Rijswijk, Muntendam, and Dijkstra 2017), and finally an auditory lexical decision task with reaction times (RTs) and EEG to measure prosody at the word level studying the process of listening. In the auditory lexical decision experiments with RTs and EEG, van Rijswijk investigated various factors that might play a role in auditory cognate processing and the role of stress position in Turkish-Dutch cognates in Turkish HSs. Findings showed a cognate effect in both languages, Turkish and Dutch, but the direction of the effect (facilitation or inhibition) was different. For Dutch, the RTs revealed cognate facilitation that was supported by the EEG data, with a larger N400 for control words than for cognates, thus smaller lexical-semantic integration difficulties for cognates than for control words. By contrast, for Turkish, the RTs indicated cognate inhibition in all conditions. The nonsignificant difference between the N400 for cognates and control words pointed to a lack of cognate effect. In sum, van Rijswijk's (2016) study showed that language dominance, the status of the L1, and stress position all have an impact on auditory word processing in the HSs, providing evidence that linguistic transfer can also occur in the other direction (i.e., from the weaker L1 Turkish to the dominant L2 Dutch).

Martohardjono, Phillips, Madsen, and Schwartz (2017) used a comprehensive methodology combining different experimental approaches, both online (ERP) and offline (acceptability judgments), with a sociolinguistic questionnaire probing proficiency, literacy, use, and exposure to both the HL and the dominant L2. The authors compared Spanish HSs and late bilinguals in an ERP experiment with auditorily presented stimuli seeking to show whether the two groups process in a similar or distinct way syntactically anomalous sentences in Spanish. To investigate the processing of Spanish sentences with grammatical structures that are anomalous in both Spanish and English, the participants listened to *wh*-questions containing a complex noun–phrase violation like (1a), and their grammatically correct counterparts like (1b). In both Spanish and English, sentences like (1a) are not grammatically correct due to the presence of the head noun in the complex noun phrase.

1a.   *Qué vecino contó Juan ||el chisme que robó el carro anoche?
      What neighbor told Juan the rumor that robbed the car last night
      'What neighbor did Juan say the rumor that robbed the car last night?'

1b.   Qué vecino contó Juan Ø ||que robó el carro anoche?
      What neighbor told Juan that robbed the car last night
      'What neighbor did Juan say robbed the car last night?'

To investigate the processing of Spanish sentences with grammatical structures that are anomalous in Spanish but not in English, the participants listened to *wh*-questions with a missing complementizer *que* like (2a), and their grammatically correct counterparts like (2b). In Spanish, the absence of the complementizer *que* introducing the subordinate clause is not grammatically correct. This is in contrast to English, where the sentences with the presence of the complementizer *that* are instead ungrammatical.

2a.   *Qué hermana confesó Inés Ø ||había comdio la tarta?
      What sister confessed Inés had eaten the cake
      'What sister did Inés confess had eaten the cake?'

2b.   Qué hermana confesó Inés ||que había comdio la tarta?
      What sister confessed Inés that had eaten the cake
      'What sister did Inés confess had eaten the cake?'

In the EEG experiment, half of the trials contained ungrammatical *wh*-questions, like (1a) and (2a); and half contained grammatical *wh*-questions, like (1b) and (2b), that were used as controls and provided a baseline for EEG processing purposes.

The ERP data were then analyzed with linear mixed-effects models using responses collected in the linguistic background questionnaire as individual-level predictor variables in the model. Results showed that the two groups reacted the same, in terms of implicit responses. The authors found an N400 and a P600 in both late bilinguals and HSs. In the acceptability judgment (AJ) task, participants were asked to judge a subset of the items presented in the ERP task, using a five-point Likert scale. While for late bilinguals, data from online and offline tasks aligned well, the explicit results for the HSs are in contrast with the implicit ERP data. In the AJ task, HSs showed less accuracy compared to late bilinguals, pointing again in the direction of a clear discrepancy in HSs' performance using offline and online measures. This study confirms again that measures requiring reflection and conscious manipulation of the language can underestimate HS competencies and result in a skewed picture when such results are generalized.

Unlike the other online methods where we presented exemplar studies from a larger cohort of available ones, on a continuum depending on the method, the two EEG studies presented here are the only ones, to our knowledge, that have been completed to date. Van Rijswijk (2016) and Martohardjono et al. (2017) are a good starting point, but nevertheless they present some limitations. Van Rijswijk's (2016) study is an interesting attempt to examine prosody in HSs; unfortunately, in the EEG study there was no control group because the focus was on L1 (Turkish) influence in the L2 (Dutch) of Turkish HSs living in the Netherlands. Nevertheless, they did compare their results with previous studies done on L1 and L2 populations, the result of which tentatively suggests that HSs performance shows a similar pattern as late L2 speakers. Furthermore, the language history questionnaire data were not correlated with the EEG measures. In HL studies, the weight of extra-linguistic factors, such as age of L2 onset, quantity and quality of exposure, formal vs. non-formal education in the HL, and more, might contribute to explaining differences in performance between HSs and native-dominant speakers, as well as individual differences among the HSs themselves.

Conversely, Martohardjono et al. (2017) is the first study attempting to employ EEG/ERP to investigating HL proper. Combining different research methodologies (offline and online) and administering a language and social background questionnaire to identify those extra-linguistic factors that are most predictive of variance within the HS population, the study is a huge step in the right direction. The main criticism with the Martohardjono et al. (2017) study is related to some methodological issues: the number of items per condition used in the EEG experiment (N = 15 items in condition 1 and N = 20 items in condition 2) and the number of participants (late bilinguals N = 20 and heritage speakers N = 18). In EEG/ERP studies, due to signal to noise ratios and the very nature of how ERP components are derived (via grand averaging), these technical details can have an influence on the reliability of the data. To ensure that enough data after artifact rejection survives into the grand averaging analysis, it is crucial to have at least 20–25 participants and around 30–40 items per condition (less than .5 SD from the mean) to have confidence in what the analysis shows (e.g., Molinaro et al. 2011). And so, while the Martohardjono et al. study is very promising, further work is needed to see if what they show can be replicated and expanded under better normative conditions for EEG/ERP research.

Our work in progress combines offline linguistic testing, EEG (time-frequency oscillation and resting state), and ERP with in depth sociolinguistic background questionnaires and measures of cognitive functions such as working memory, inhibitory control, and pattern detection capacity. In line with the general trends we have seen in studies that combine offline and online measures or compare online ones with previous offline measures, the emerging interest in EEG/ERP studies promises to help us better understand the dynamic nature of HL competence and processing via methods that can capture involuntary, automatic responses to stimuli and probe correlations of variation. Given the nature of EEG/ERP and the level of granularity it can potentially access, it stands out as a good method to combine in a battery of HS experimentation that we hope will become more mainstream in the near future.

22.4   Variation, Correlation, and Complex Statistical Modelling

While the previous two sections relate to empirical testing methods proper, this section highlights how and why more fine-grained language background/language experience data collection in combination with more appropriate statistical modeling techniques can and should be used as an additional methodological innovation. Doing so is critically relevant to HS studies in general, since the methods typically used to date, with few exceptions, have not been ideal for understanding the dynamic relationship and directionality of influence that key variables have for explaining HS outcomes. We believe that the field will not only engage more and more with underused statistical methods in the immediate future, but that it is imperative that we do so.

Over the last 20 plus years, descriptive studies have revealed a lot about the nature of HL grammars, but as is to be expected in a relatively new field, they have also left us with more questions than answers. There is a dearth of studies, much less bespoke HL theories themselves, offering testable and generalizable predictions for HL grammars in their own right. Such theories need to provide ways of predicting and accounting for at least two continua of variation across HL grammars, (i) the domains of grammar that are more and less vulnerable (and why) and (ii) the variables and their weighting that conspire to explain individual difference outcomes among HSs themselves.

In recent years, preliminary attempts at theories addressing, at least partially, (i) and (ii) are emerging, including work by Putnam and Sánchez (2013) and Polinsky and Scontras (2020). As part of this general trend, we wish to highlight work in this final section that has shifted away from HS-to-monolingual differences toward HS-to-other bilingual and/or HS-to-HS comparisons in recent years. For certain questions, the HS-to-monolingual comparison is valid. Our intention is not to suggest otherwise. That said, this comparison is not always the ideal one, hence the work we focus on herein is being understood as increasingly more needed and welcome in the field.

While there certainly is individual variation in paths and outcomes for child L1 acquisition scenarios (see, e.g., de Houwer 1995, 2007; Meisel 2004, 2011; Snyder 2007; Haznedar 2013; Serratrice 2013; Grüter and Paradis 2014; Nicoladis and Montanari 2016; Guasti 2017), the range of individual variation in HS grammar far exceeds the ranges of other native-language acquisition scenarios, be it monolingual or bilingual. Nevertheless, as pointed out by Flores and Rinke (2019) and Kupisch and Rothman (2018), general statements that characterize HL bilingualism as "differ[ing] from the baseline language that served as the input for acquisition" (Polinsky and Scontras 2020: 2) must be qualified and taken with caution. While we are all interested in unpacking what variables predict and explain deviations, it is not always the case that HSs differ (see work reviewed in Kupisch and Rothman 2018) and even when they do, some cases seem to show HSs' overextending (not reducing or simplifying) licit constructions (Rinke et al. 2018) or reflecting variation that, while lacking in the so-called standard, exists in colloquial monolingual varieties (Rinke and Flores 2014). And so, the range of HS outcomes (property-by-property in grammatical terms or overall fluency/proficiency in holistic terms) encompasses passive bilingualism with severely limited oracy ability to some individuals that are (nearly) indistinguishable from monolingual counterparts. It is not new to claim that the qualitative shape of input, from quantity reductions to the qualitative nature of it, should explain (some of) the differences between HSs and monolinguals, as well as capture some of the variance across the HS individual differences continuum (e.g., Montrul 2004; Sorace 2004; Rothman 2007, 2009). However, very few attempts to actually model this have been undertaken.

Who would deny the veracity of the general statement claiming the input of HSs has consequences for their path and outcome? After all, no theory or hypothesis across paradigms denies that input is deterministic for all acquisition and, therefore, what is reasonable to expect as grammatical representational outcomes. Such statements made over the years by many, ourselves included, are too simplistic. As always, the devil is in the detail. What do we mean by reduction in input and how can we proxy this in measurement (as direct measurement is typically impossible) for means of modeling it meaningfully? What do we mean by quality of the input, beyond the obvious, which of course relates to honing in increasingly on appropriate baselines for HSs? What do we mean when we speak of opportunities for specific types of exposure, such as schooling or otherwise engagement with literacy in the HL? Until recently, and for very good reasons in the proper context, investigations of HL development and its outcomes had deemphasized the role of individual language experiences, or, better said, not considered them in the dynamic ways we are starting to do now. There is a general ethos in the field; HL studies have reached a level of maturity and critical mass of empirical work where transitional, predictive theories proper are ripe for creation. We have already discussed recent advances in this regard (e.g., Polinsky and Scontras 2020). Now we turn our focus to work, and specifically methods that can afford predictions for individual differences among HSs to understand how experiential factors relate to outcomes and what is the directionality of influence as variables interact.

To date, most of the HL literature has traditionally used *means-based* statistical techniques such as ANOVAs and *t*-tests. This is partially because early studies started with investigations into HS-to-L2 speaker comparisons (Montrul 2012). Doing so has effectively reduced the range of variability in the HL performance data (e.g., accuracy) into factorial categories juxtaposed against proficiency measured by self-evaluation or some type of standardized language tests. Information regarding individual experiences with one's languages, if collected at all, was used for achieving homogenous participant groups and/or accounting for potential outliers and variance of error in statistical (descriptive) analyses. Under this scenario, *reduced input conditions* often served as *catchall* explanations for HS-to-monolingual difference outcomes when on average HS performance was lower than that of monolinguals, rather than unpacking these *conditions* to account for the gamut of individual variation existing within HS group. In a way, this is similar to stating that more than 20 percent of the Polar Ice Cap has melted since 1979 as a result of warmer air and ocean temperatures (aka, global warming) (NRDC 2005) without explaining what has actually caused (and is causing) this change in the air and ocean temperatures. The observation alone is true and potentially enough for general consumption, but of course scientists and their vested stakeholders need to know why the general observation obtains. Today, thanks to advanced data collection and statistical modeling techniques, not only do we know the key factors that have contributed to the increase in air and ocean temperatures and thus global warming in general but also how these individual factors interact with each other and the environment in different parts of the world, so we can also predict the current path and future outcome of this process (Parmesan and Yohe 2003; Mora et al. 2017). Complex data-driven approaches are also becoming more and more widespread in linguistics applying more advanced modeling techniques, such as fixed- and mixed-effects regression modeling as well as other predictive modeling techniques such as discriminant function analysis (structural equation modeling), moderation modeling, classification/conditional inference trees, and (random) forests (e.g.,

Baayen et al. 2008; Quené and van den Bergh 2008; Cunnings 2012; Gries 2013, 2018; Baayen et al. 2018; Pouplier et al. 2017; Coupé 2018).

Within the HS research context, however, such progress has been slow. Although it is only logical to assume that *reduced input conditions* lead to the observed divergence of HS grammatical competence from monolingual baselines, implementing advanced regression models and more rigorous data collection techniques (to get the data necessary for such analyses) is the next logical step. Below we review some recent studies that have made preliminary steps forward at trying to unpack experience-based variables that potentially correlate to individual differences in HS performances.

Bayram et al. (2017), for instance, looked at the production of passives in the Turkish and German of young Turkish heritage speakers (age 9–15) in Germany, comparing them with age-matched monolingual speakers of Turkish and German. Differently from previous studies though, they focused on understanding the relative weight of key language experience factors (age at time of testing, immigration status of the Turkish parents [first or second generation], and literacy engagement with the HL) that might predict individual variation in HS performance. Data for factors such as degree of exposure to and engagement with the standard variety, parental immigration status, age of testing, etc. were collected and used as regressors in the analysis. The data were analyzed using a logistic mixed model, a type of Generalized Linear Mixed Model (Breslow and Clayton 1993) that incorporates both fixed and random effects of factors (see Jaeger 2008; Cunnings 2012; Coupé 2018 for a discussion). The descriptive results show that all HSs used passives in both German and Turkish without being exposed to the structure/morphology in the experiment (this means producing unique morphology for passives in Turkish and changing case morphology), indicating that they have the underlying representation for passives in both Turkish and German. However, the aggregate results showed highly significant differences between the HS and the native Turkish controls in terms of proportional use, but not from the German controls. In other words, HSs use passives in German like German monolinguals but do not use passives in Turkish like monolinguals in Turkish. So far, the story aligns nicely with the previously documented HS-to-monolingual differences. That is, on average, HS performance was distinct from that of monolinguals. Was this, however, true of all individuals? Did any fall within the range of Turkish monolinguals? If so, what might predict which HSs did and did not? The logistic mixed model showed a significant effect of *literacy level* (see Bayram et al. 2017 for how this was quantified) with no other significant main effects or interactions. Whether or not and for how long HSs had been in Sunday school classes provided by the Turkish government in its diaspora correlated nicely with individual HS performances; the more they had, the more likely they were to fall in the monolingual range.

In a similar vein, Gharibi and Boers (2017) used two vocabulary tests (verbal fluency test and auditory picture-word matching test) to investigate the vocabulary knowledge of simultaneous and sequential Persian-Iranian heritage speakers (age 6–18) in New Zealand, compared to their matched monolingual peers. They also utilized a detailed language background questionnaire to collect information about factors (age, age at emigration, length of emigration, frequency of heritage language use, and parents' attitude toward heritage language acquisition and maintenance) that were used in linear regression models to predict variation within the HS group. While the between-group comparisons were in line with previous research – that monolinguals outperformed the HS group – different demographic and sociolinguistic factors predicted different outcomes for each group. For instance, while the frequency of use of the HL was the second strongest predictor for both groups, age of arrival was the strongest predictor for the sequential HSs' performance, and parental attitude toward the HL was the strongest predictor for the simultaneous HS group.

Most recently, Schmid and Karayayla (2020) looked at the productive use of various lexical and morphosyntactic structures (e.g., embedded clauses, evidentiality) by ninety-two Turkish-English adult bilinguals living in the United Kingdom with age of onset (AoO) varying from birth to adulthood (age 0 to 42), as well as a control group of forty-four Turkish monolinguals. Importantly, they investigated the extent to which external language background factors (e.g., AoO, experience, exposure, attitudes toward the HL) predicted bilingual participants' proficiency in Turkish. They adapted Yilmaz's (2013) Personal Background Questionnaire for external language data and employed a number of tasks (e.g., semi-structured interview, picture description task, verbal fluency task, C-Test, evidentiality experiment) to test participants' proficiency in Turkish. Their group comparison results are in line with previous research in that Turkish-English bilinguals' overall performance was degraded in comparison to their monolingual peers in all proficiency measures (lexical access, morphosyntactic complexity, and formal accuracy). In an attempt to account for the variation within the bilingual group, Schmid and Karayayla (2020) looked at the interaction between the proficiency measures and language background data. Moving away from the traditional regression models that were not able to capture the effect of these fine-grained and complex interactions, Schmid and Karayayla (2020) used Structural Equation Modelling (SEM), which, in a nutshell, is a flexible multivariate statistical approach that can assess unobservable latent constructs using one or more observed and measured variables. Their model measured the extent to which the outcome components (lexical access, morphosyntactic complexity, formal accuracy) weigh into *proficiency* (a latent construct), and finally tested the predictive relationship between the *background* construct and the *proficiency* construct. The results from the SEM analyses showed that exposure-related factors (e.g., use, exposure, AoO) played a significant role in determining L1 (Turkish) proficiency in speakers who were exposed to English before age 10 (clear cases of HSs), while this effect disappeared with speakers who started learning English after age 10. We concur with Schmid and Karayayla's (2020) call for using more advanced statistical models that are capable of identifying the complex relationships between multiple variables and providing comprehensive explanations for the ways in which these (cause and effect) relationships obtain.

A crucial part of the HL bilingualism methodology equation that remains largely underdeveloped is the charting of input quantities and qualities as well as the usage patterns and domain distributions of the heritage and majority language. The idea is that, as is the case for other populations of bilinguals, understanding the linguistic experiences of HSs would, at least in part, serve to explain some of the characterizing outcome variation. No one denies, nor should anyone be surprised, that HSs almost always deviate at the group level from L1-dominant natives. We, however, still know far too little about how much and, crucially, why HSs (can) differ from one another so much. In an ideal world, one would observe, record, and analyze all (or most) of the interactions of HSs within their environment from birth up to young adulthood to shed light on answers to these questions. One potential and promising way to circumvent the impracticality of doing so is increasing our use of standardized questionnaires widely used with other populations of bilinguals and able to measure in detail one's social experiences with their languages (e.g. LEAP-Q: Marian et al. 2007; BILEC: Unsworth 2013; LSBQ: Anderson et al. 2018).

These questionnaires offer composite scores that can be used as proxies for quantifying and qualifying input HSs receive, how they engage with and distribute use and function of the HL, relative dominance in one or the other language, and more. Ideally, composite scores are backed up by significant norming and principled factor analyses that render the question sets used to derive relative scores more reliable than binary questions of self-reflection (e.g., relative self-assessment for proficiency). These scores can be used as regressors, much like common variables such as Age-of-Acquisition is, in an effort to see how experiential factors explain variance at the individual level. Doing so entails a shift in focus toward treating bilingualism in general, but specifically HLB, as a continuous construct, unpacking the dynamic nature of bilingualism as a spectrum of experiences and their correlations to (linguistic) outcomes. This, of course, does not mean that experiential factors alone neatly explain linguistic outcomes. However, we believe that the observable facts of HL bilingualism themselves highlight the inseparability of the social milieu of language at multiple levels (society and individual) and the outcomes of its acquisition. Of course, to do this meaningfully we will need to develop new questionnaires or sub-versions of existing ones that are tailored specifically for HSs and their spectrum of realities with bilingual experiences. The desire is an end result where we have instruments able to record relevant information that is meaningful enough to distinguish types of HL bilinguals and reliably predict outcomes a priori.

22.5 Conclusions

What the discussions and studies in this chapter have in common is that all are pieces of a complex puzzle that come together to offer deeper insights and answers to complex questions pertaining to HL bilingualism. They reveal that the competence/performance variation within HS populations is not random; certain modalities might be more useful in capturing what heritage speakers know; combining online and offline measures might provide a more complete picture; and variation in individual experiences with the HL plays specific deterministic roles that can be successfully modeled. We submit that HL bilingualism studies will benefit from more work with research designs that include inter and within group investigations: (i) across various age groups and linguistic domains, (ii) with increasingly larger numbers of participants for more reliable estimate effect sizes (Kidd et al. 2018), (iii) using questionnaires that can capture experience factors (from issues pertaining to input to language use and attitudes) made specifically for HSs, (iv) use the information gathered in (iii) to probe what factors correlate to outcomes at the individual level, and finally (v) combine methods of empirical testing to gauge competence and processing at the same time. Doing all of this will help achieve a fuller picture of variation at all levels: internal to a single HS's grammar and comparatively between HSs and whatever other populations are appropriate for any specific comparisons.

References

Alemán Bañón, J. and J. Rothman. 2016. The Role of Morphological Markedness in the Processing of Number and Gender Agreement in Spanish: An Event-Related Potential Investigation. *Language, Cognition and Neuroscience* 31, 1273–1298.

Alemán Bañón, J. and J. Rothman. 2019. Being a Participant Matters: Event-Related Potentials Show That Markedness Modulates Person Agreement in Spanish. *Frontiers in Psychology* 10, 746.

Anderson, J. A., L. Mak, A. K. Chahi, and E. Bialystok. 2018. The Language and Social Background Questionnaire: Assessing Degree of Bilingualism in a Diverse Population. *Behavior Research Methods* 50(1), 250–263.

Arslan, S., R. Bastiaanse, and C. Felser. 2015. Looking at the Evidence in Visual World: Eye-Movements Reveal How Bilingual and Monolingual Turkish Speakers Process Grammatical Evidentiality. *Frontiers in Psychology* 6, 1387.

Au, T. K. F., L. M. Knightly, S. A. Jun, and J. S. Oh. 2002. Overhearing a Language during Childhood. *Psychological Science* 13(3), 238–243.

Baayen, R. H., D. J. Davidson, and D. M. Bates. 2008. Mixed-Effects Modeling with Crossed Random Effects for Subjects and Items. *Journal of Memory and Language* 59(4), 390–412.

Baayen, R. H., J. van Rij, C. de Cat, and S. Wood. 2018. Autocorrelated Errors in Experimental Data in the Language Sciences: Some Solutions Offered by Generalized Additive Mixed Models. In D. Speelman, K. Heylen, and D. Geeraerts (eds.), *Mixed Effects Regression Models in Linguistics*. Berlin: Springer, 49–69.

Bayram, F., J. Rothman, M. Iverson, T. Kupisch, D. Miller, E. Puig-Mayenco, and M. Westergaard. 2017. Differences in Use without Deficiencies in Competence: Passives in the Turkish and German of Turkish Heritage Speakers in Germany. *International Journal of Bilingual Education and Bilingualism*, 1–21.

Bialystok, E. 2009. Bilingualism: The Good, the Bad, and the Indifferent. *Bilingualism: Language and Cognition* 12(1), 3–11.

Bolger, P. A. and G. C. Zapata. 2011. Psycholinguistic Approaches to Language Processing in Heritage Speakers. *Heritage Language Journal* 8(1), 1–29.

Breslow, N. E. and D. G. Clayton. 1993. Approximate Inference in Generalized Linear Mixed Models. *Journal of the American Statistical Association* 88(421), 9–25.

Brinton, D. M., O. Kagan, and S. Bauckus (eds.) 2017. *Heritage Language Education: A New Field Emerging*. New York: Routledge.

Chomsky, N. 1964. *Current Issues in Linguistic Theory*. The Hague: Mouton.

Corbett, G. G. 1991. *Gender*. Cambridge: Cambridge University Press

Coupé, C. 2018. Modelling Linguistic Variables with Regression Models: Addressing Non-Gaussian Distributions, Non-independent Observations and Nonlinear Predictors with Random Effects and Generalized Additive Models for Location, Scale and Shape. *Frontiers in Psychology* 9, 513.

Cunnings, I. 2012. An Overview of Mixed-Effects Statistical Models for Second Language Researchers. *Second Language Research* 28(3), 369–382.

De Houwer, A. 1990. *The Acquisition of Two Languages from Birth: A Case Study*. Cambridge: Cambridge University Press.

De Houwer, A. 1995. Bilingual Language Acquisition. In P. Fletcher and B. MacWhinney (eds.), *The Handbook of Child Language*. Cambridge: Blackwell, 219–250.

De Houwer, A. 2007. Parental Language Input Patterns and Children's Bilingual Use. *Applied Psycholinguistics* 28(3), 411–424.

Demberg, V. and F. Keller. 2008. Data from Eye-Tracking Corpora As Evidence for Theories of Syntactic Processing Complexity. *Cognition* 109 (2), 193–210.

Du Plessis, J., D. Solin, L. Travis, and L. White. 1987. UG or not UG, That Is the Question: A Reply to Clahsen and Muysken. *Interlanguage Studies Bulletin (Utrecht)* 3(1), 56–75.

Dussias, P. E. 2010. Uses of Eye-Tracking Data in Second Language Sentence Processing Research. *Annual Review of Applied Linguistics* 30, 149–166.

Flores, C. and E. Rinke. 2019. The Relevance of Language-Internal Variation in Predicting Heritage Language Grammars. *Bilingualism: Language and Cognition* 1–2.

Foote, R. 2011. Integrated Knowledge of Agreement in Early and Late English–Spanish Bilinguals. *Applied Psycholinguistics* 32(1), 187–220.

Forster, K. I. and C. Davis. 1984. Repetition Priming and Frequency Attenuation in Lexical Access. *Journal of Experimental Psychology: Learning, Memory, and Cognition* 10, 680–698.

Frenck-Mestre, C. 2002. An On-line Look at Sentence Processing in the Second Language. In R. R. Heredia and J. Altarriba (eds.), *Advances in Psychology: Vol. 134. Bilingual Sentence Processing*. Amsterdam: North-Holland/Elsevier Science Publishers, 217–236.

Fuchs, Z. 2019. Gender in the Nominal Domain: Evidence From Bilingualism and Eye-Tracking. Doctoral dissertation, Harvard University, Cambridge, MA.

Gharibi, K. and F. Boers. 2017. Influential Factors in Incomplete Acquisition and Attrition of Young Heritage Speakers' Vocabulary Knowledge. *Language Acquisition* 24(1), 52–69.

Gries, S. T. 2013. *Statistics for Linguistics with R: A Practical Introduction*. Berlin/Boston: Walter de Gruyter.

Gries, S. T. 2018. Mechanistic Formal Approaches to Language Acquisition. *Linguistic Approaches to Bilingualism* 8(6), 733–737.

Grüter, T. and J. Paradis (eds.) 2014. *Input and Experience in Bilingual Development*. Vol. 13. Amsterdam: John Benjamins Publishing Company.

Guasti, M. T. 2017. *Language Acquisition: The Growth of Grammar*. Cambridge, MA: MIT press.

Haznedar, B. 2013. Child Second Language Acquisition from a Generative Perspective. *Linguistic Approaches to Bilingualism* 3(1), 26–47.

Haznedar, B. and E. Gavruseva (eds.) 2008. Current Trends in Child Second Language Acquisition: A Generative *Perspective*. Vol. 46. Amsterdam: John Benjamins Publishing.

Holmes, B. C. 2017. "I Understand Everything You Say, I Just Don't Speak It": The Role of Morphology in the Comprehension of Spanish by Receptive Heritage Bilinguals. PhD Dissertation, University of Arizona.

Holmqvist, K., M. Nyström, R. Andersson, R. Dewhurst, H. Jarodzka, and J. Van de Weijer. 2011. *Eye Tracking: A Comprehensive Guide to Methods and Measures*. Oxford: Oxford University Press.

Hopp, H. 2013. Grammatical Gender in Adult L2 Acquisition: Relations between Lexical and Syntactic Variability. *Second Language Research* 29(1), 33–56.

Hopp, H., M. T. Putnam, and N. Vosburg. 2019. Derivational Complexity vs. Transfer Effects: Long-Distance wh-Movement in Heritage and L2 Grammars. *Linguistic Approaches to Bilingualism* 9(3), 341–375.

Isurin, L. and T. Ivanova-Sullivan. 2008. Lost in between: The Case of Russian Heritage Speakers. *Heritage Language Journal* 6(1), 72–104.

Jacob, G. and B. Kırkıcı. 2016. The Processing of Morphologically Complex Words in a Specific Speaker Group. *The Mental Lexicon* 11(2), 308–328.

Jacob, G., D. F. Şafak, O. Demir, and B. Kırkıcı. 2019. Preserved Morphological Processing in Heritage Speakers: A Masked Priming Study on Turkish. *Second Language Research* 35(2), 173–194.

Jaeger, T. F. 2008. Categorical Data Analysis: Away from ANOVAs (Transformation or not) and Towards Logit Mixed Models. *Journal of Memory and Language* 59(4), 434–446.

Jegerski, J. 2014. Self-Paced Reading. In J. Jegerski and B. VanPatten (eds.), *Research Methods in Second Language Psycholinguistics*. New York: Routledge, 20–49.

Jegerski, J. 2018a. The Processing of the Object Marker *a* by Heritage Spanish Speakers. *International Journal of Bilingualism* 22(6), 585–602.

Jegerski, J. 2018b. Sentence Processing in Spanish as a Heritage Language: A Self-Paced Reading Study of Relative Clause Attachment. *Language Learning* 68(3), 598–634.

Jegerski, J. and I. A. Sekerina. 2019. The Processing of Input with Differential Object Marking by Heritage Spanish Speakers. *Bilingualism: Language and Cognition* 1–9.

Johannessen, J. B. 2018. Factors of Variation, Maintenance and Change in Scandinavian Heritage Languages. *International Journal of Bilingualism* 22(4), 447–465.

Keating, G. D., J. Jegerski, and B. Vanpatten. 2016. Online Processing of Subject Pronouns in Monolingual and Heritage Bilingual Speakers of Mexican Spanish. *Bilingualism: Language and Cognition* 19(1), 36–49.

Keating, G. D., B. VanPatten, and J. Jegerski. 2011. Who Was Walking on the Beach? Anaphora Resolution in Spanish Heritage Speakers and Adult Second Language Learners. *Studies in Second Language Acquisition* 33(2), 193–221.

Kırkıcı, B. and H. Clahsen. 2013. Inflection and Derivation in Native and Non-native Language Processing: Masked Priming Experiments on Turkish. *Bilingualism: Language and Cognition* 16(4), 776–791.

Kidd, E., S. Donnelly, and M. H. Christiansen. 2018. Individual Differences in Language Acquisition and Processing. *Trends in Cognitive Sciences* 22(2), 154–169.

Kim, K., W. O'Grady, and B. D. Schwartz. 2018. Case in Heritage Korean. *Linguistic Approaches to Bilingualism* 8(2), 252–282.

Kinoshita, S. and S. J. Lupker. 2003. *Masked Priming: State of the Art*. New York: Psychology Press.

Kupisch, T. 2006. The Acquisition of Determiners in Bilingual German-Italian and German-French Children. Doctoral dissertation, Hamburg University. Munich: Lincom Europa.

Kupisch, T. and J. Rothman. 2018. Terminology Matters! Why Difference Is Not Incompleteness and How Early Child Bilinguals Are Heritage Speakers. *International Journal of Bilingualism* 22(5), 564–582.

Lam, W. M. 2018. Perception of Lexical Tones by Homeland and Heritage Speakers of Cantonese. Doctoral dissertation, University of British Columbia.

Lee-Ellis, S. 2011. The Elicited Production of Korean Relative Clauses by Heritage Speakers. *Studies in Second Language Acquisition* 33(1), 57–89.

Lenneberg, E. H. 1967. The Biological Foundations of Language. *Hospital Practice* 2(12), 59–67.

Lloyd-Smith, A., H. Gyllstad, T. Kupisch, and S. Quaglia. 2021. Heritage Language Proficiency Does not Predict Syntactic CLI into L3 English. *International Journal of Bilingual Education and Bilingualism* 24(3), 435–451, DOI: HYPERLINK "https://doi.org/10.1080/13670050.2018.1472208" 10.1080/13670050.2018.1472208.

Lohndal, T. and M. Westergaard. 2016. Grammatical Gender in American Norwegian Heritage Language: Stability or Attrition? *Frontiers in Psychology* 7, 344.

Lohndal, T., J. Rothman, T. Kupisch, and M. Westergaard. 2019. Heritage Language Acquisition: What It Reveals and Why It Is Important for Formal Linguistic Theories. *Language and Linguistics Compass* 13(12), 1–19

Luck, S. J. 2014. *An Introduction to the Event-Related Potential Technique*. Cambridge, MA: MIT Press.

Marian, V. and H. K. Blumenfeld, and M. Kaushanskaya. 2007. The Language Experience and Proficiency Questionnaire (LEAP-Q): Assessing Language Profiles in Bilinguals and Multilinguals. *Journal of Speech, Language, and Hearing Research* 50, 940–967.

Martohardjono, G., L. Phillips, C. N. Madsen II, and R. G. Schwartz. 2017. Cross-Linguistic Influence in Bilingual Processing: An ERP Study. In *Proceedings of the 41st Boston University Conference on Language Development*. Vol. 2. Somerville, MA: Cascadilla Press, 452–465.

Meisel, J. M. 2004. The Bilingual Child. In T. K. Bhatia and W. C. Ritchie (eds.), *The Handbook of Bilingualism*. Oxford: Blackwell, 91–113.

Meisel, J. M. 2011. *First and Second Language Acquisition: Parallels and Differences*. Cambridge: Cambridge University Press.

Molinaro, N., H. A. Barber, and M. Carreiras. 2011. Grammatical Agreement Processing in Reading: ERP Findings and Future Directions. *Cortex* 47(8), 908–930.

Montrul, S. 2002. Incomplete Acquisition and Attrition of Spanish Tense/Aspect Distinctions in Adult Bilinguals. *Bilingualism: Language and Cognition* 5(1), 39–68.

Montrul, S. 2004. Subject and Object Expression in Spanish Heritage Speakers: A Case of Morphosyntactic Convergence. *Bilingualism: Language and Cognition* 7(2), 125–142.

Montrul, S. 2008. *Incomplete Acquisition in Bilingualism: Re-examining the Age Factor*. Vol. 39. Amsterdam: John Benjamins Publishing.

Montrul, S. 2011. Morphological Errors in Spanish Second Language Learners and Heritage Speakers. *Studies in Second Language Acquisition* 33(2), 163–192.

Montrul, S. 2012. Is the Heritage Language Like a Second Language? *Eurosla Yearbook* 12(1), 1–29.

Montrul, S. 2014. Structural Changes in Spanish in the United States: Differential Object Marking in Spanish Heritage Speakers across Generations. *Lingua* 151, 177–196.

Montrul, S. 2015. *The Acquisition of Heritage Languages*. Cambridge: Cambridge University Press.

Montrul, S. A. and M. A. Bowles. 2009. Back to Basics: Differential Object Marking under Incomplete Acquisition in Spanish Heritage Speakers. *Bilingualism* 12(3), 363–383.

Montrul, S. and N. Sánchez-Walker. 2013. Differential Object Marking in Child and Adult Spanish Heritage Speakers. *Language Acquisition* 20(2), 109–132.

Montrul, S., R. Foote, and S. Perpiñán. 2008. Gender Agreement in Adult Second Language Learners and Spanish Heritage Speakers: The Effects of Age and Context of Acquisition. *Language Learning* 58(3), 503–553.

Mora, C., B. Dousset, I. R. Caldwell, F. E. Powell, R. C. Geronimo, C. R. Bielecki, and M. P. Lucas. 2017. Global Risk of Deadly Heat. *Nature Climate Change* 7(7), 501.

Nicoladis, E. and S. Montanari (eds.) 2016. *Bilingualism across the Lifespan: Factors Moderating Language Proficiency*. Berlin: de Gruyter Mouton

The Natural Resources Defense Council (NRDC) (2005). Arctic Sea Ice Continues to Decline, Arctic Temperatures Continue to Rise in 2005. Retrieved from www.nasa.gov/centers/goddard/news/topstory/2005/arctice_decline.html

Ortega, L. 2014. *Understanding Second Language Acquisition*. Oxford: Routledge.

Parmesan, C. and G. Yohe. 2003. A Globally Coherent Fingerprint of Climate Change Impacts across Natural Systems. *Nature* 421(6918), 37.

Pascual y Cabo, D. 2020. Examining the Role of Cross-Generational Attrition in the Development of Spanish as a Heritage Language: Evidence from Gustar-Like Verbs. *Linguistic Approaches to Bilingualism* 10(1), 86–108.

Pires, A. and J. Rothman. 2009. Disentangling Sources of Incomplete Acquisition: An Explanation for Competence Divergence across Heritage Grammars. *International Journal of Bilingualism* 13(2), 211–238.

Polinsky, M. 2008. Gender under Incomplete Acquisition: Heritage Speakers' Knowledge of Noun Categorization. *Heritage Language Journal* 6(1), 40–71.

Polinsky, M. 2011. Reanalysis in Adult Heritage Language: New Evidence in Support of Attrition. *Studies in Second Language Acquisition* 33(2), 305–328.

Polinsky, M. 2015. When L1 Becomes an L3: Do Heritage Speakers Make Better L3 Learners? *Bilingualism: Language and Cognition* 18(2), 163–178.

Polinsky, M. 2016. Structure vs. Use in Heritage Language. *Linguistics Vanguard* 2(1), 1–14.

Polinsky, M. 2018. *Heritage Languages and Their Speakers*. Cambridge: Cambridge University Press.

Polinsky, M. and O. Kagan. 2007. Heritage Languages: In the 'Wild' and in the Classroom. *Language and Linguistics Compass* 1(5), 368–395.

Polinsky, M. and G. Scontras. 2020. Understanding Heritage Languages. *Bilingualism: Language and Cognition*, 23(1), 4–20.

Pouplier, M., J. Cederbaum, P. Hoole, S. Marin, and S. Greven. 2017. Mixed Modeling for Irregularly Sampled and Correlated Functional Data: Speech Science Applications. *The Journal of the Acoustical Society of America* 142(2), 935–946.

Puig-Mayenco, E., I. Cunnings, F. Bayram, D. Miller, S. Tubau, and J. Rothman. 2018. Language Dominance Affects Bilingual Performance and Processing Outcomes in Adulthood. *Frontiers in Psychology* 9, 1–16.

Putnam, M. T. and L. Sánchez. 2013. What's So Incomplete about Incomplete Acquisition? A Prolegomenon to Modeling Heritage Language Grammars. *Linguistic Approaches to Bilingualism* 3(4), 478–508.

Quené, H. and H. Van den Bergh. 2008. Examples of Mixed-Effects Modeling with Crossed Random Effects and with Binomial Data. *Journal of Memory and Language* 59(4), 413–425.

Rayner, K. 1998. Eye Movements in Reading and Information Processing: 20 Years of Research. *Psychological Bulletin* 124(3), 372.

Rinke, E. and C. Flores. 2014. Morphosyntactic Knowledge of Clitics by Portuguese Heritage Bilinguals. *Bilingualism: Language and Cognition* 17(4), 681–699.

Rinke, E., C. Flores, and P. Barbosa. 2018. Null Objects in the Spontaneous Speech of Monolingual and Bilingual Speakers of European Portuguese. *Probus* 30(1), 93–119.

Roberts, L., J. González Alonso, C. Pliatsikas, and J. Rothman. 2018. Evidence from Neurolinguistic Methodologies: Can It Actually Inform Linguistic/Language Acquisition Theories and Translate to Evidence-Based Applications? *Second Language Research* 34(1), 125–143.

Rothman, J. 2007. Heritage Speaker Competence Differences, Language Change, and Input Type: Inflected Infinitives in Heritage Brazilian Portuguese. *International Journal of Bilingualism* 11(4), 359–389.

Rothman, J. 2009. Understanding the Nature and Outcomes of Early Bilingualism: Romance Languages as Heritage Languages. *International Journal of Bilingualism* 13(2), 155–163.

Rothman, J. and J. Treffers-Daller. 2014. A Prolegomenon to the Construct of the Native Speaker: Heritage Speaker Bilinguals Are Natives Too! *Applied Linguistics* 35(1), 93–98.

Schmid, M. S. and T. Karayayla. 2020. The Roles of Age, Attitude, and Use in First Language Development and Attrition of Turkish–English Bilinguals. *Language Learning* 70, 54–84.

Schmid, M. S. and B. Köpke. 2017. The Relevance of First Language Attrition to Theories of Bilingual Development. *Linguistic Approaches to Bilingualism* 7(6), 637–667.

Schwartz, B. D. 1992. Testing between UG-Based and Problem-Solving Models of L2A: Developmental Sequence Data. *Language Acquisition* 2(1), 1–19.

Scontras, G., Z. Fuchs, and M. Polinsky. 2015. Heritage Language and Linguistic Theory. *Frontiers in Psychology* 6, 1545.

Sekerina, I. A. and A. Sauermann. 2015. Visual Attention and Quantifier-Spreading in Heritage Russian Bilinguals. *Second Language Research* 31(1), 75–104.

Sekerina, I. A. and J. C. Trueswell. 2011. Processing of Contrastiveness by Heritage Russian Bilinguals. *Bilingualism: Language and Cognition* 14(3), 280–300.

Serratrice, L. 2013. Cross-Linguistic Influence in Bilingual Development: Determinants and Mechanisms. *Linguistic Approaches to Bilingualism* 3(1), 3–25.

Sherkina-Lieber, M. 2015. Tense, Aspect, and Agreement in Heritage Labrador Inuttitut: Do Receptive Bilinguals Understand Functional Morphology? *Linguistic Approaches to Bilingualism* 5(1), 30–61.

Silva-Corvalán, C. 2014. *Bilingual Language Acquisition: Spanish and English in the First Six Years.* Cambridge: Cambridge University Press.

Slabakova, R. 2016. *Second Language Acquisition.* Oxford: Oxford University Press.

Sorace, A. 2004. Native Language Attrition and Developmental Instability at the Syntax-Discourse Interface: Data, Interpretations and Methods. *Bilingualism: Language and Cognition* 7(2), 143–145.

Suarez, D. 2002. The Paradox of Linguistic Hegemony and the Maintenance of Spanish As a Heritage Language in the United States. *Journal of Multilingual and Multicultural Development* 23(6), 512–530.

Snyder, W. 2007. *Child Language: The Parametric Approach.* Oxford: Oxford University Press.

Tanner, D. 2019. Robust Neurocognitive Individual Differences in Grammatical Agreement Processing: A Latent Variable Approach. *Cortex* 111, 210–237.

Traxler, M. J. and M. J. Pickering. 1996. Plausibility and the Processing of Unbounded Dependencies: An Eye-Tracking Study. *Journal of Memory and Language* 35(3), 454–475.

Unsworth, S. 2013. Assessing the Role of Current and Cumulative Exposure in Simultaneous Bilingual Acquisition: The Case of Dutch Gender. *Bilingualism: Language and Cognition* 16(1), 86–110.

Valdés, G. 2005. Bilingualism, Heritage Language Learners, and SLA Research: Opportunities Lost or Seized? *The Modern Language Journal* 89 (3), 410–426.

Van Rijswijk, R. 2016. The Strength of a Weaker First Language: Language Production and Comprehension by Turkish Heritage Speakers in the Netherlands. Doctoral dissertation, Radboud University, Nijmegen, The Netherlands. Utrecht: LOT.

Van Rijswijk, R., A. Muntendam, and T. Dijkstra. 2017. Focus in Dutch Reading: An Eye-Tracking Experiment with Heritage Speakers of Turkish. *Language, Cognition and Neuroscience* 32(8), 984–1000.

Villegas, Á. 2014. The Role of L2 English Immersion in the Processing of L1 Spanish Sentence Complement/Relative Clause Ambiguities. Doctoral dissertation, Pennsylvania State University. Retrieved from https://etda .libraries.psu.edu/catalog/21436.

Villegas, Á. 2018. Bilingual Processing of Comparative Structures in Spanish. *Languages* 3(3), 35.

White, L. 2003. Fossilization in Steady State L2 Grammars: Persistent Problems with Inflectional Morphology. *Bilingualism: Language and Cognition* 6(2), 129–141.

White, L. 2018. Formal Linguistics and Second Language Acquisition. In Miller, D., F. Bayram, J. Rothman, and L. Serratrice (eds.), *Bilingual Cognition and Language: The State of the Science across Its Subfields*. Amsterdam: John Benjamins Publishing Company, 57–78.

White, L., E. Valenzuela, M. Kozlowska–Macgregor, and Y. K. I. Leung. 2004. Gender and Number Agreement in Non-native Spanish. *Applied Psycholinguistics* 25(1), 105–133.

Winter, B. and M. Wieling. 2016. How to Analyze Linguistic Change Using Mixed Models, Growth Curve Analysis and Generalized Additive Modeling. *Journal of Language Evolution* 1(1), 7–18.

Yilmaz, G. 2013. Bilingual Language Development among the First Generation Turkish Immigrants in the Netherlands. Doctoral dissertation, Groningen: University of Groningen.

Part III

Grammatical Aspects of Heritage Languages

23

Phonetics and Phonology of Heritage Languages

Charles B. Chang

23.1 Introduction

What do adult heritage speakers know about the sound system of their heritage language (HL), their first-acquired, yet weaker, language? Conversely, how do heritage speakers pattern in the sound system of their dominant language, which, despite currently being their stronger language, was not the one they were exposed to first? This chapter examines these two interrelated questions by surveying the state of the science in HL phonetics and phonology, with a view toward outlining directions for future research in this burgeoning field (Polinsky and Kagan 2007; Montrul 2015; Rao 2016a; Polinsky 2018).

First, let me start with some notes about terminology. The term "heritage speakers" can be (and has been) used to refer to diverse (sub)populations of language users that share the core characteristic of an "interrupted" trajectory of exposure to their first language (L1), where the discontinuity is brought about by intensive exposure to a second language (L2).[1] Intensive L2 exposure, however, may occur due to a variety of life events (e.g., volitional immigration, forced migration, international adoption), which differ in their effect on HL acquisition. For example, international adoptees generally receive less initial, as well as intermittent, exposure to their HL

---

[1] The use of scare quotes here to describe the onset of L2 exposure as an "interruption" is intentional, because this description may imply that continuous, monolingual exposure to a target language is, or should be, the norm. On the contrary, many languages do not develop, and are not used, in a monolingual ecology (see, e.g., Lüpke and Storch 2013); in fact, the majority of language users across the world can be described as bilingual or multilingual (Tucker 2001). Thus, it is worth bearing in mind that, when monolinguals are identified as a baseline or standard of comparison in the literature, this is not necessarily because monolinguals should be considered normal or even the most common type of user of the given language. Rather, they provide a useful picture of what the language (and grammar) *can* look like, when the intricacies of language contact at both individual and societal levels are removed from the equation.

compared to second-generation immigrant bilinguals raised in HL-speaking households. In what follows, I will use the term "heritage speaker" (HS) loosely, to refer to any bilingual whose L1 (HL) was learned primarily at home as a minority language and whose L2 was learned primarily outside the home as the societal (majority) language, and will use more specific descriptors (e.g., "overhearer," "listener," "talker") when fine-grained distinctions in the nature of HSs' experience with the HL are necessary. That said, the focus of this chapter is on HSs who continued to use and/or hear their HL during childhood (as opposed to HSs who were cut off from their HL, and may not even have any conscious memory of it; compare Choi et al. 2017), because these HSs exemplify the most common situation of language shift within migratory contexts. Related to this, the nature of the minority language context means that the HS populations under discussion will usually comprise switched-dominance bilinguals (i.e., L2-dominant speakers), but this will not always be the case.

Much of the research into HL phonetics and phonology has been spurred by two recurrent observations about HSs. The first is that, even if they may have significant gaps in their vocabulary or grammar of the HL, HSs may have little to no trouble with aural comprehension and, when they speak the HL, can sound very much like a "native" speaker (i.e., an "expert" speaker who has reached some notional peak level of proficiency, generally due to having been immersed in the language from birth to adulthood). The second observation is that, even though their listening and pronunciation skills may be strong, HSs tend to differ subtly from L1-dominant native speakers, such that they can be readily identified by native speakers as not exactly "native." The themes of similarity and difference vis-a-vis native speakers of the HL, as well as late-onset L2 learners, are thus pervasive in the literature on HL phonetics and phonology.

Following from these themes, the majority of studies of HL phonetics and phonology to date has focused on HSs' knowledge and performance in their HL and has devoted little attention to examining HSs' dominant L2, which often appears to be native-like. Increasingly, however, researchers are carrying out systematic investigations of HSs' dominant language as well, treating HSs as the bilinguals they are. This development is consistent with a "multicompetence" view of the L2 user, which predicts bilingual–monolingual differences at a number of levels (Cook 1997, 2003), as well as with mounting evidence that a bilingual's divergence from monolingual norms may begin to occur early in bilingual development and, furthermore, persist despite weak proficiency in and infrequent use of the other language (Chang 2012, 2013, 2019a; Cho and Lee 2016). In short, the assumption that HSs do not differ from monolingual native speakers in their dominant language has become more questionable, thus increasing the impetus to directly test both languages in HSs. Accordingly, this chapter addresses the existing research on HSs' dominant language along with the research on their HL.

The rest of the chapter is organized as follows. I begin in Section 23.2 by reviewing the research examining HL production at a holistic level, including accent, intelligibility, and identifiability. I then delve into specific properties of segmental (23.3) and suprasegmental production (23.4), as well as salient patterns in speech perception (23.5). Throughout this discussion, I consider the evidence for maintenance (or loss) of phonemic contrasts, phonological alternations and processes, and phonotactic constraints. In Section 23.6, I provide a synthesis of these findings, including their implications for theories of bilingualism, and conclude with comments on future directions.

23.2 Global Qualities of Speech Production

Impressionistically, HSs often seem to sound similar to native speakers (NSs) when speaking the HL, yet not quite the same. This impression of a high quality, albeit not exactly native-like, accent in the HL has been reflected in several different studies examining NSs' perception of HSs' speech, as well as their ability to classify HSs socio-demographically.

To take one example, a series of studies on Spanish HSs in the United States who were engaged in learning their HL in college reported a significant advantage of HSs over late-onset L2 learners (L2ers) in terms of holistic accent in Spanish (Au et al. 2002; Knightly et al. 2003). In these studies, accent was measured in terms of subjective ratings from NSs (using a five-point Likert scale with "5" indicating the most native-like) and on two types of speech samples: (1) longer samples from a semi-spontaneous narrative and (2) shorter samples – namely, target phonemes within a carrier sentence. HSs showed a sizable advantage over L2ers on both the narrative accent ratings (M_{HS} = 3.0; cf. M_{L2er} = 2.4) and the phoneme accent ratings (M_{HS} = 3.4–3.6; cf. M_{L2er} = 2.8–3.0). At the same time, HSs' accents were rated clearly below NSs' accents (M_{NS} = 4.4–5.0, depending on sample type). However, note that the HSs in these studies comprised "childhood overhearers" (i.e., HSs with early experience hearing the HL, but little to no early experience producing it). A later study using a similar design thus included a group of "childhood speakers" with early experience producing the HL as well (Au et al. 2008). These HSs were rated closer to NSs, but still not the same (M_{HS} = 3.4–3.8; cf. M_{NS} = 4.4–5.0); a separate study on Korean HSs in the United States showed this pattern as well (Oh et al. 2003).

Work on European Portuguese HSs has produced similar results. For example, a study comparing Portuguese HSs raised in a majority German language environment with L1 German L2ers and monolingual Portuguese

NSs found that the HSs obtained holistic accent ratings (of semi-spontaneous speech samples from various production tasks) in between the L2ers' and the NSs' (on a nine-point scale where "1" represents the most native-like: $M_{HS} = 1.79$, $M_{L2er} = 7.24$, $M_{NS} = 1.11$; Flores and Rato 2016). The majority of the HSs in this study were "returnees" living in Portugal at the time of the study; thus, recent immersion experience with the HL could be responsible for the closer patterning of these HSs vis-a-vis NSs (at a group level) as compared to the Spanish HSs discussed previously. Interestingly, however, when various possible predictors of accent ratings, including length of residence (LOR) in Portugal before and after migration, were investigated statistically, only age of emigration/arrival (to the German-speaking host country, i.e., AOA) was found to be a significant predictor. This result echoes a pattern found in earlier research on accentedness among Korean-English bilinguals in the United States (Yeni-Komshian et al. 2000), which also reported the strongest predictiveness for AOA and little predictive value of LOR (but compare Kupisch et al. 2014). An additional point of similarity with the Korean-English bilinguals in Yeni-Komshian et al. (2000) pertains to variability: like Korean-English bilinguals, the Portuguese HSs in Flores and Rato (2016) were observed to be much more variable in their accent ratings compared to NSs (as well as L2ers), and follow-up work by Flores et al. (2017) showed the same pattern, with some HSs receiving accent ratings in the range of NSs but others not. I return to the matter of variability among HSs in §3.

The intermediate nature of HSs' HL production – at once closer to native-like than L2ers' yet not exactly the same – is also apparent in research that examined accent using categorical classification judgments rather than Likert-scale ratings. For example, on the basis of naturalistic speech samples, French, German, and Italian HSs were classified as "foreign" (as opposed to "native") by NSs of the respective language approximately 67 percent of the time on average, less often than L2ers were (>80 percent of the time) yet more often than monolingual NSs were (10 percent of the time) (Kupisch et al. 2014). Echoing findings based on scale ratings, Kupisch et al. (2014) also found that HSs were the most variable in terms of classification: In contrast to the NSs and L2ers, the vast majority of whom were consistently classified (correctly) as "native" and "foreign," respectively, only about half of the HSs tended to be classified as "foreign," while the other half tended to be classified as "native" or classified inconsistently. Furthermore, the classification of HSs was associated with the most uncertainty, with NS judges reporting being "uncertain" or only "semi-certain" of their classification of HSs nearly 40 percent of the time. Related findings on Italian HSs in Germany were reported by Lloyd-Smith et al. (2020), who also observed stronger predictiveness of a composite Italian use score (including several dimensions of Italian experience, including size of the social network and formal education in the language) than of age of acquisition of the majority language (cf. Yeni-Komshian et al. 2000; Flores and Rato 2016).

Classification data on Western Armenian, Russian, and Mandarin Chinese HSs in the United States, collected with slightly different methods but the same basic metric of NS judgments, add to a picture in which HSs' accent in the HL is perceived as more ambiguous than L1-dominant NSs' and L2ers', at least by NSs. On the one hand, Western Armenian NSs were able to identify HSs as US-born speakers (as opposed to NSs raised in a Western Armenian language environment) with little difficulty, even on the basis of short (word-length) speech samples (Godson 2003, 2004). On the other hand, Russian NSs had quite a lot of difficulty correctly classifying HSs as individuals who were not born in Russia, even given a sizable (seven-second) speech sample (Polinsky 2018: 118–121). This apparent socio-demographic ambiguity is reflected in a pattern documented for Mandarin HSs in which HSs as a group were more difficult to classify correctly (as "American-born Chinese"[2]) than NSs or L2ers were (Chang and Yao 2016; see also Kupisch et al. 2014). This pattern was highly consistent, holding for every type of speech sample included in that study: monosyllabic samples carrying each of the four lexical tones, as well as multisyllabic samples ranging from two to four syllables in length (Figure 23.1). Moreover, an additional analysis of confidence ratings given

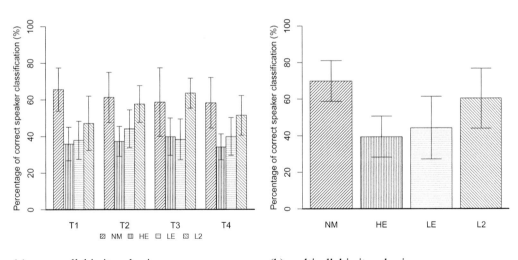

(a) monosyllabic item basis   (b) multisyllabic item basis

Figure 23.1 Demographic classifiability of the groups in Chang and Yao (2016), averaged over talkers. Panel (a) shows classifiability on the basis of monosyllabic items (separated by tone); panel (b), based on multisyllabic items. Groups are Mandarin NSs (NM), HSs with high exposure (HE) and low exposure (LE) to Mandarin, and L2ers (L2). Error bars show standard error

---

[2] Note that this was the label offered for the HS category because it was more likely to be familiar to the NS judges than the term "heritage speaker"; however, not all the HSs evaluated in this study were literally born in the United States.

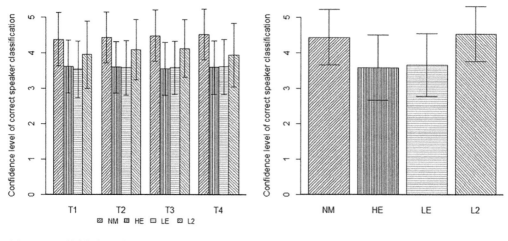

(a) monosyllabic item basis   (b) multisyllabic item basis

Figure 23.2 Confidence levels associated with correct demographic classifications in Chang and Yao (2016), by talker group. Panel (a) shows confidence ratings (on a 1–5 scale; 5 = most confident/certain) from classifications based on monosyllabic items (separated by tone); panel (b), based on multisyllabic items. Groups are Mandarin NSs (NM), HSs with high exposure (HE) and low exposure (LE) to Mandarin, and L2ers (L2). Error bars show standard error

on target classification judgments replicated the result reported in Kupisch et al. (2014), wherein listeners were the least confident about their classifications of HSs (Figure 23.2). Although the source of this pattern – which may be due to NSs having a lower degree of exposure to and/or familiarity with HSs, to HSs showing a wide range of pronunciation patterns, or to some combination of these factors – is not entirely clear, it is a striking pattern supporting the view that HSs are language users distinct from both L2ers and L1-dominant (i.e., "uninterrupted") NSs.

Whether HSs also differ from "uninterrupted" NSs in the majority language has been less studied, but some results suggest that, insofar as differences in accent and/or intelligibility exist, they tend to be much less detectable in the majority language than the HL. For example, the US-based Korean-English bilinguals in Yeni-Komshian et al. (2000) with an AOA of 1–5 years, though sometimes rated as more foreign-accented in English than English NSs, received English accent scores that, as a group, were overlapping with those of English NSs (whereas their Korean accent scores generally did not fall within the range of Korean NSs'; see Yeni-Komshian et al. 2000: 138–139). Additionally, Kupisch and colleagues (Kupisch et al. 2014; Lloyd-Smith et al. 2020) tested HSs in their majority language (either French, German, or Italian) and, using the same methodology of accent measurement as for the HL, found that, with very few exceptions, HSs' accent in their majority language was perceived on par with monolingual NSs'. As for intelligibility, Spanish HSs in the United States were found, at a challenging signal-to-noise ratio, to be less intelligible in Spanish than Spanish NSs but just as intelligible in English as English NSs (Blasingame 2018). Thus, at the level of holistic accent as well as intelligibility, the current evidence points to the conclusion that, in their (dominant) majority language, HSs tend to be largely indistinguishable from NSs.

23.3   Segmental Production

Findings on perceived accent in HSs suggest that, at a global level, HSs tend to differ in their production of the HL from L2ers and L1-dominant NSs, but leave open the question of which aspects of their production give rise to this impression of difference. A growing body of research, however, has been contributing acoustic phonetic data to address this question, with targeted studies comparing HSs, L2ers, and NSs on their realization of specific segmental properties such as voice onset time (VOT) and vowel formants (most often, F_1 and/or F_2). Much of this research has been based on specific theories of L2 phonetic and phonological acquisition (for a recent review, see Chang 2019b). For example, the Perceptual Assimilation Model (PAM; Best 1994, 1995) and Perceptual Assimilation Model-L2 (PAM-L2; Best and Tyler 2007), as theories that typologize nonnative phonological contrasts in terms of their perceptual mapping to L1 contrasts, have influenced studies testing perception, especially the discrimination of L2 contrasts. Production studies, on the other hand, have often been framed in terms of the Speech Learning Model (SLM; Flege 1995, 1996, 2007), a theory of L2 phonetic development in both perception and production that differentiates L2 sounds in terms of being "new," "similar," or "identical" vis-a-vis the L1 inventory. Among the tenets of the SLM, three are particularly relevant to HL sound systems: (1) coexistence of L1 and L2 sounds in a shared mental phonetic space, with bilinguals striving to maintain contrast between them, (2) an increasing likelihood of perceptually conflating L2 sounds with L1 counterparts with a later age of L2 acquisition, and (3) bidirectionality of influence between perceptually linked L1 and L2 sounds. Note that the third tenet, by allowing for L2 influence on the L1, does not grant the L1 a special status, at least with respect to susceptibility to crosslinguistic influence, and is instead consistent with the occurrence of "incomplete acquisition" and/or attrition of the HL/L1 in different contexts of bilingualism (Montrul 2008; Schmid 2013). This contrasts with another kind of view of the L1 (in particular, early linguistic exposure) as privileged (e.g., leading to a "neural commitment" to L1 sounds that differs qualitatively from L2 outcomes; Kuhl 2000).

Whether oriented toward one of these theories or not, several studies of segmental production in the HL have focused on or included analyses of oral stop consonants (i.e., plosives). In the work on Spanish HSs discussed earlier (Au et al. 2002; Knightly et al. 2003), the speech samples submitted to perceptual evaluation (in particular, word-initial and -medial tokens of the Spanish voiced and voiceless stops produced intervocalically within a frame sentence) were also submitted to acoustic analysis of several properties: VOT (i.e., the latency between a stop's release burst and the onset of voicing) and closure duration of voiceless stops, and the degree of voicing (binned into three categories of "voiceless," "partial voicing," and "full voicing") and lenition of voiced stops. Although there were no significant differences among groups with respect to closure duration, HSs approximated the short VOTs of NSs much more closely than L2ers, who produced (English-influenced) longer VOTs; in fact, HSs' VOTs did not differ significantly from NSs' in either initial or medial position (compare Kim 2011). HSs also showed a tendency to produce partial voicing and full voicing of voiced stops (i.e., to approximate Spanish norms for implementation of voiced stops) and to apply intervocalic voiced stop lenition at rates in between NSs' and L2ers' (for evidence of further differences in lenition among "regular speakers," "childhood speakers," and "childhood addressees" and depending on age of onset of the majority language, see Rao 2015, and Amengual 2019). Similar results were reported for German HSs in France, who produced the canonically long-lag German voiceless stops with slightly shorter VOTs than monolingual NSs and German-French bilinguals in Germany, but still within NS ranges (van de Weijer and Kupisch 2015; Lein et al. 2016).

Acoustic studies of HLs in Canada have also addressed HSs' stop production, including the role of sociolinguistic, typological, and phonological factors. For example, cross-generational comparisons of VOT in the canonically short-lag voiceless stops of Italian, Russian, and Ukrainian showed a tendency for first-generation immigrants to diverge from homeland norms (in terms of longer VOTs) only slightly, whereas second-, third-, and fifth-generation HSs tended to show more divergence from these norms; however, there was variation across the different HL groups, with Italian HSs showing less divergence from homeland norms than Russian or Ukrainian HSs (Hrycyna et al. 2011; Nagy 2015; for similar cross-generational data on UK-based Sylheti HSs' stop production, see Mayr and Siddika 2018). Although this variation could be due to differences in sociocultural dimensions, including the size and cohesiveness of the HL community and attitudes toward cultural integration into the host country, correlations with the construct of "ethnic orientation," including "speakers' self-identified ethnicity and exposure to their HL, and attitudes toward the heritage language and culture" (Hrycyna et al. 2011: 167) were weak or not significant (compare Oh and Au 2005). On the other hand, work on Calabrian Italian HSs also examined VOT – specifically, in relation to the socio-indexical feature of voiceless stop aspiration – and found effects of speaker generation (which were not always linear) as well as of speaker sex (Nodari et al. 2019), while work on Polish HSs showed a positive correlation of Polish stop devoicing with rates of code-switching with English (Łyskawa et al. 2016). A study of Tagalog HSs explored the possible influence of phonological markedness as well, finding that HSs produced the canonically short-lag voiceless stops of Tagalog with VOTs showing little influence from English's voiceless (phonologically marked) stops (including with respect to effects of lexical stress), but the voiced stops, which are canonically lead-voiced, with more apparent influence from English's voiced (phonologically unmarked) stops (Kang et al. 2016). These findings thus contradicted the hypothesis that influence from the majority language would be stronger from marked, as opposed to unmarked, categories (Newlin-Łukowicz 2014).

Research on stop production in heritage Korean has additionally provided compelling evidence of conservatism in HSs (Kang and Nagy 2016). In this work, Korean HSs in Toronto were compared to Korean NSs in Seoul with respect to an ongoing sound change in the implementation of the lenis and aspirated stop series, which have become less distinct in terms of VOT and more distinct in terms of onset fundamental frequency (f_0) over time. This change has rapidly progressed in the homeland (Seoul) variety, led by young females, and consistent with other studies, Kang and Nagy observed young female NSs in Seoul to rely almost entirely on f_0 to distinguish these stops. On the other hand, young HSs in Toronto continued to rely on VOT to produce this contrast, and there was little evidence of a sex difference in their reliance on VOT. That is, younger HSs showed a pattern of stop production reminiscent of an older stage of Seoul Korean and did not appear to be innovating in the manner of younger homeland NSs, which Kang and Nagy speculated may be due to the dominant role of VOT in the voiced–voiceless stop contrast in English. Converging results were reported for second-generation Korean HSs in California as well; interestingly, however, "1.5 generation" HSs (i.e., late childhood arrivals to the United States) patterned more like homeland NSs than like second-generation HSs (Cheng 2019b). Taken together, these findings highlight the relevance of three considerations in the analysis of HL sound systems: (1) the fundamental differences in target language input and exposure between a diaspora (HL) context and the homeland context, (2) linguistic aspects of HSs' specific brand of bilingualism, and (3) the continuity and variability inherent in the demographic variable of speaker generation, often treated as categorical in research on HSs.

Apart from stops, other consonant types, such as fricatives, taps, trills, and approximants, have also been investigated in acoustic studies of HL production. For example, research on Mandarin HSs in the United States analyzed aspects of sibilant fricatives – in particular, the centroid and peak amplitude frequency of Mandarin alveolar /s/ and postalveolar /ʂ ɕ/ – finding that HSs tended to be better than both L2ers and NSs (who were L2 learners of English) at distinguishing these fricatives from similar English fricatives (Chang et al. 2009, 2011); moreover, there was no evidence of HSs having lost (or failed to acquire) any of the HL phonemic contrasts tested. Studies of Spanish HSs' production of the Spanish tap–trill contrast and lateral approximants additionally showed effects of both language dominance and language mode: HSs were less likely to approximate canonical production in terms of number of occlusions in the trill /r/ and F_2 - F_1 values for the lateral /l/ when they were dominant in English and/or put into bilingual mode, and these effects for /l/ were clearest for the combination of English dominance and bilingual mode (Amengual 2016, 2018; see Kim and Repiso Puigdelliura 2020, for data on frequency of lingual constriction in HSs' production of the tap). Despite these effects, however, the tap–trill contrast was maintained by most HSs, if by greater use of duration vis-a-vis NSs, thus converging with the results of Chang et al. (2011).

Complementing data on consonantal production, other studies of HL production have focused on vowels, demonstrating the relevance of factors such as phonological environment, phonetic distance between crosslinguistically corresponding vowels, and the precise comparison group. For Western Armenian HSs in the United States, for example, the influence of English was evident for vowels acoustically close to English vowels (/i ɛ a/), but not for the back rounded vowels /o u/ that lie farther from English counterparts (Godson 2003, 2004), consistent with the SLM's prediction that L2 sounds distant from L1 sounds are likely to be perceived as different (and are thus likely to motivate formation of a separate L2 category that resists assimilatory crosslinguistic influence from the L1). Along similar lines, Mandarin HSs in the United States produced back rounded vowels of Mandarin (characterized by lower F_2 values) as clearly distinct from those of English (characterized by higher F_2 values), and were also found to outperform L2ers and L1-dominant NSs in terms of establishing crosslinguistic distance between corresponding vowels in the two languages (Chang et al. 2010, 2011; see Figure 23.3). This advantage for HSs in making crosslinguistic distinctions at a phonetic (i.e., non-contrastive) level is also in line with the SLM's prediction that systematic phonetic differences between L1 and L2 sounds will be better perceived by early than late L2 acquirers. As for the role of phonological environment, this was predictive of Toronto-based Cantonese HSs' production of mid /ɛ ɔ/, which showed an allophonic split conditioned by a velar context; consequently, the split could be attributed in large part to majority language influence (Tse 2016a,b, 2019). On the other hand, majority language influence is often much less clear when HSs are compared to L1-dominant,

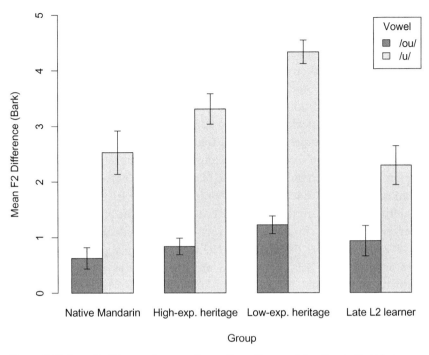

Figure 23.3 Acoustic distances (in mean F_2 over the entire vowel duration, in Bark) between corresponding Mandarin and English back rounded vowels in Chang et al. (2011), by group. Groups are (from left to right) Mandarin-dominant NSs, HSs with high or low exposure to Mandarin, and L2ers. Error bars show standard error

but not homeland monolingual, NSs (i.e., a group better approximating the HL input to HSs; Solon et al. 2019).

Studies of HL vowel production have also addressed the role of demographics, dialectal and stylistic variation, language mode, code-switching, dominance, and proficiency. A recent study of Spanish HSs in the North Midland dialect region of the United States, for instance, tested the hypothesis that the North Midland feature of fronted /u/ would cause HSs to produce Spanish /u/ also as fronted (Cummings Ruiz 2019). Contrary to this hypothesis, however, HSs actually produced Spanish /u/ as even more back (i.e., with lower F_2 values) than monolingual NSs. As an instance of cross-linguistic dissimilation (namely, from the more front English /u/), this production pattern is consistent with the SLM's hypothesis that new category formation in early L2 acquirers may lead to dissimilation of nearby sounds in order to maximize contrast within the shared mental phonetic space. In other work examining vowel quality and duration across different tasks, HSs' Spanish vowel production was also observed to show similar patterns of stylistic variation as monolingual NSs' and other bilinguals' and to be influenced by code-switching with English as well as the presence of lexical stress (Ronquest 2016; Elias et al. 2017). In the case of Cantonese HSs in Toronto, speaker generation and sex showed an interaction in predicting conversational vowel production in the HL (Tse 2016b, 2019), while for Shanghainese HSs in China, speaker generation, language mode, and cross-linguistic similarity (with the dominant societal language, Mandarin Chinese) were all found to significantly modulate the intrusion of Mandarin into Shanghainese vowel production (Yao and Chang 2016). Additionally, statistical modeling of Spanish HSs' normalized vowel production data (in comparison to those for Spanish NSs and L1 English L2ers) provided support for examining both dominance and proficiency as "separate but related constructs" related to HSs' linguistic behavior (Shea 2019). Even so, it is clear that individual dominance in the HL does not rule out majority language influence on the HL, as shown by the Spanish-influenced merger of Galician mid-vowel contrasts in Galician-dominant HSs (Mayr et al. 2019), nor does dominance in the majority language rule out target-like acquisition of HL phonological processes such as unstressed vowel reduction (Amengual and Simonet, 2020; but compare Asherov et al. 2016, for evidence of hybridized vowel reduction in HL Russian in Israel).

As alluded to in Section 23.1, studies of HSs' production of the majority language remain less common than studies focusing on the HL, but the available acoustic data support the view that HSs as a group are often indistinguishable from NSs of the majority language and, where there is a detectable difference from NSs, this difference tends to be quite subtle (Section 23.2). For example, the California-based Spanish HSs in Au et al. (2002) produced mean VOTs for English voiced and voiceless stops that were "comparable to published results from monolingual native English speakers" (fn. 5, 241), such that they did not differ significantly from the L1 English NS group (for converging results on Spanish HSs in the Midwest, see Kim 2011). Along similar lines, second- and third-generation Sylheti HSs in London and Cardiff produced English stops, vowels, and approximants in a manner resembling NSs (McCarthy et al. 2011, 2013; Mayr and Siddika 2018), while Korean HSs in California, both second-generation and "1.5 generation" HSs, showed evidence of having acquired the local dialect features in their English vowel production (Cheng 2019a). On the other hand, Tagalog HSs in Canada produced English voiced stops with apparent influence from the lead-voicing characteristic of Tagalog (Kang et al. 2016; for similar data on US-based Polish HSs, see Newlin-Łukowicz 2014), and non-standard or non-monolingual-like properties have been observed in the English vowels of Norwegian HSs in the United States and the English interdental fricatives of Dutch HSs in Canada (Natvig 2016; Cornwell and Rafat 2017). In these latter cases, however, the divergence from majority language norms is small and/or involves variability, such that it is often not clear whether it is consequential – namely, reliably perceptible to listeners of the majority language.

23.4   Suprasegmental Production

The literature on HSs' production of suprasegmental properties is considerably smaller than that focusing on segmental properties, but there are now several different studies addressing aspects of HL prosody such as stress, voice quality, lexical tone, and intonation. For example, research on US-based Spanish HSs by Kim (2020) found that HSs' production of lexical stress contrasts between words bearing penultimate vs. final stress differed significantly from monolingual NSs', especially in the use of duration, showing a similarly large amount of overlap between the two word types as in L2ers' production. Additional work on Spanish HSs' production of focus revealed that HSs tended to use a mix of strategies for expressing focus, including both the non-prosodic (i.e., syntactic) strategies favored by NSs and the prosodic strategies (e.g., post-focal deaccenting) favored by L2ers, suggesting that "heritage speakers are flexible in their use of linguistic strategies as they are able to extract resources from their two language systems" (Kim 2019). Spanish HSs' production of voice quality (as reflected in spectral tilt measures) was also found to differ from NSs' in that, like L2ers (L1 English speakers), HSs, especially female HSs, often produced utterance-final creaky voice in Spanish, consistent with influence from voice quality variation in the majority language (Kim 2017).

Adding to this picture have been studies of tone production by Mandarin Chinese HSs in the United States (Chang and Yao 2016, 2019). In this work, HSs as a group were observed to approximate NSs' production of Mandarin's four main tones (T1–T4) more closely than L2ers in a number of ways: the pitch contour of T3 (a low-falling tone), durational shortening of tones in connected speech, and rates of T3 reduction in non-final contexts. In other respects, however, HSs' tone production tended to resemble L2ers'. For instance, HSs' tones in isolation were not generally more intelligible to NSs than were L2ers'. In connected speech, by contrast, HSs' tones were significantly more intelligible than L2ers'. As for perceived goodness, HSs' intelligible tones, both in isolation and in connected speech, were rated as higher quality than L2ers', although not as good as NSs'. Thus, given the limited consistency in between-group patterning observed across different tones, contexts, and measures, these findings on Mandarin HSs suggested that "early heritage language experience can, but does not necessarily, result in a phonological advantage over L2 learners" (Chang and Yao 2016: 134).

In addition to production of T1–T4, production of Mandarin's "neutral" tone (T0, a short tone surfacing on weak syllables) was also examined in this research, in both obligatory contexts (i.e., where a target item must be pronounced with T0 as opposed to some other tone) and non-obligatory contexts (Chang and Yao 2019). Like the data on T1–T4, data on T0

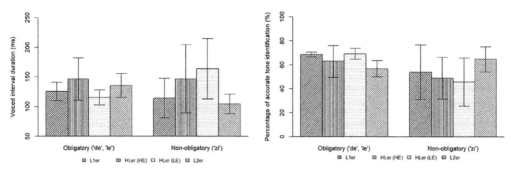

(a) duration of T0   (b) intelligibility of T0

Figure 23.4 Acoustic and perceptual properties of Mandarin's neutral tone (T0) as produced in Chang and Yao (2019), averaged over talkers and separated by context. Panel (a) shows duration (in ms); panel (b), intelligibility (i.e., percent of time the tone was correctly identified as T0 by native listeners). Groups are Mandarin NSs (L1ers), HSs with high exposure (HE) and low exposure (LE) to Mandarin, and L2ers. Error bars show standard error

production showed significant between-group variation in duration; however, the nature of this variation differed from that observed for T1–T4. In contrast to the shorter durations they produced for T3 in non-final contexts, HSs produced T0 in non-obligatory contexts with significantly *longer* durations than did L2ers (see Figure 23.4a). To put it another way, in the case of non-obligatory T0, L2ers, rather than HSs, were more successful at approximating the short durations of NSs. Consequently, L2ers' production of T0 was also more intelligible as T0 compared to HSs' (Figure 23.4b), although HSs nevertheless received higher goodness ratings for their intelligible T0 tokens than L2ers did. These results thus converged with those on T1–T4 in indicating that differences between HSs and L2ers "are not unidirectional, but instead vary across aspects of the language" (Chang and Yao 2019: 2291).

A central factor related to the directionality of between-group patterning (e.g., whether, for a given variable, HSs or L2ers will be closer to NSs) is speakers' linguistic experience with the HL – in particular, their dialectal exposure and experience with standards and norms that are reinforced by formal education in the target language. Thus, in Chang and Yao (2016), L2ers were found to produce overly long durations for T3 in connected speech, ostensibly because their initial exposure to T3 in the classroom had consisted of focused productions in isolation, where T3 is standardly produced with a long contour including not only a pitch fall but also a final rise; this pattern for T3 was much less apparent in HSs. On the other hand, HSs were found to produce T3 reduction (i.e., "half Tone 3") at rates exceeding even NSs', which could be attributed in part to a greater percentage of the HS group having been exposed to southern dialects of Mandarin in which T3 reduction is frequent across contexts. Along the same lines, in

Chang and Yao (2019), it was HSs – not L2ers – who were found to produce overly long durations for T0 in non-obligatory contexts. Like the HS–L2er disparity in T3 reduction rates, this result could also be explained in terms of differences in dialectal and educational exposure: Whereas at least some HSs were primarily exposed to southern dialects in which T0 may alternate with another tone (e.g., T3) in non-obligatory contexts, L2ers were primarily exposed to standard Mandarin, which is based on northern Mandarin varieties in which T0 is typically realized even in non-obligatory contexts.

Taken together, these findings highlight the importance of considering the details of HSs' experience with their HL and the manner in which HSs' experience may diverge from that of the NSs and/or L2ers under study. In particular, the likelihood of variation and divergence in experience poses a major challenge for a group-based approach to studying HL sound systems. For example, Mandarin HSs in Chang and Yao (2016) showed, as a group, higher levels of acoustic variability in production of T1–T4 than both NSs and L2ers; however, as pointed out in that study, this higher variability cannot be attributed to HS status per se, as it may be due in part to a higher degree of variation in dialectal exposure and/or educational experience with Mandarin within the HS group compared to the NS and L2er groups. While one approach to addressing variability is, of course, to attempt to control dialect and/or educational experience more strictly, in some cases this may not be entirely feasible, due to fundamental experiential differences between two populations (e.g., limiting a HS group to those formally educated in the HL may leave one with very few HSs, who are not necessarily representative of the population at large). Therefore, future research on HL sound systems stands to benefit from more individual-centric analyses, where variability is not reduced but rather accounted for statistically, such as the modeling approach taken in recent work (e.g., Shea 2019).

With regard to intonation, there has long been interest in HSs' intonation as a possible contributor to a "heritage accent," but systematic empirical research documenting the properties of HSs' intonation in the HL is relatively scarce. This may be due in part to a methodological challenge for crosslinguistic intonation research: the lack of broad consensus on analytical conventions that can be used across languages. In the case of Russian HSs in the United States, for example, "[a]ny comparison of English and Russian intonation is made more difficult by conflicting methods of describing intonational form" (Andrews 1993: 165). Nevertheless, such HSs have been described impressionistically as producing English-influenced intonation in the HL – in particular, with "the substitution of American-English intonational patterns for standard Russian ones in neutral declarative utterances and in yes/no questions" (Andrews 2001: 528; see also Polinsky 2018: 120–121). More recent studies of US-based HSs' intonation in HLs such as French (Bullock 2009), Korean (Shin 2005), Norwegian

(Dehé 2018), and Spanish (Zárate-Sández 2015; Colantoni et al. 2016; Rao 2016b) have brought quantitative and/or acoustic data to bear on the issue of HL intonation, leading to a nuanced picture. The recurring theme in these studies is indeed one of crosslinguistic influence from the majority language (English) but also clear, if not always native-like, acquisition of some HL-specific intonational features (e.g., accentual phrase-initial tone height, prenuclear peak alignment). For example, in a small-scale study using acoustic analysis as well as perceptual evaluation of low-pass filtered speech, Shin (2005) found that Korean HSs produced intonation closer to NSs' than did L2ers, such that the prosody in HSs' filtered speech was perceived as "Korean" by NSs much more often (58–75 percent of the time) than L2ers' (11–19 percent); nevertheless, HSs' prosody was still frequently perceived as nonnative-like.

Work on HL intonation has pointed out a number of factors that influence the observed intonation patterns of HSs, including task type (Colantoni et al. 2016) and utterance type (Rao 2016b), and cautioned against interpreting majority language influence in terms of a deficit model. Indeed, the specific conditions under which HSs are asked to produce HL intonation (in particular, the degree to which HSs may be familiar or comfortable with a task such as free narration vs. reading) has a significant effect on their production, leading Colantoni et al. (2016) to recommend that "metalinguistic tasks, such as reading aloud, should be implemented with caution" (1). Furthermore, the fact that divergence in HL intonation patterns associated with specific syntactic patterns may occur in spite of apparent control of the syntax raises the possibility that "contact-influenced prosodic innovations among heritage speakers may serve as additional communication resources for the expression of discourse-pragmatic distinctions rather than as mere replacement strategies" (Bullock 2009: 165), echoing the sentiments of Kim (2019) regarding Spanish HSs' mixed strategies for the expression of focus and of Nagy (2016) on viewing HSs' language varieties as "new dialects." Certainly, it is clear that more research remains to be done on HL intonation, and as the field converges on analysis standards for more languages (see Hualde and Prieto 2016), one can expect that this will lead to increased research activity in the study of HL intonation.

To close this section, it is worth mentioning that there is very little research on HSs' suprasegmental production in the majority language, thus leaving open a clear path for future research in this area. In one of the few studies on this topic, Turkish HSs in the Netherlands were observed to produce focus prosody in Dutch somewhat differently from Dutch NSs, in a manner consistent with influence from Turkish (van Rijswijk et al. 2017). Norwegian HSs in the United States were also found to produce English polar questions with some apparent intonational influence from the HL (Dehé 2018). On the other hand, Mandarin-dominant Southern Min HSs in

China produced focus prosody in Mandarin with no apparent influence from the HL (Chen et al. 2014). In addition, US-based Korean HSs produced English-specific syllable structures (e.g., coda consonants disallowed in Korean) in code-switched contexts with no apparent phonotactic influence from the HL, in contrast to the pattern observed for Korean NSs (Kim 2010). As for younger HSs, a recent study of kindergarten-age Urdu HSs' production of Cantonese tones in Hong Kong found that, in comparison to age-matched Cantonese NSs, the HSs produced Cantonese tones with lower intelligibility and greater confusion between tones, which could be attributed in part to influence from the HL (Yao et al., 2020). However, given that lexical tone can show a protracted trajectory of development even for NSs (e.g., Wong and Strange 2017), this snapshot of early divergence between HSs and NSs may or may not be reflected in how HSs produce the majority language in adulthood. In short, work on HSs' suprasegmentals in the majority language is in its nascent stages, and much more research is needed to understand when and to what degree HSs may pattern uniquely in this regard.

23.5 Speech Perception

The depth of perceptual advantages that accrue to HSs, even those who may not have actively used the HL for many years, has been the subject of a great deal of research examining HSs across a continuum of HL experience, ranging from international adoptees with no conscious memory of the HL to second-generation immigrant bilinguals who continue to use the HL regularly. Although this literature contains some examples of apparent "forgetting" of the HL (Pallier et al. 2003; Ventureyra et al. 2004), the bulk of the studies in this area evince a significant impact of early linguistic experience on speech perception, both in the HL and in the majority language. Indeed, this pattern should not be surprising, given theoretical claims about the transformative, and lasting, impact of early linguistic exposure. For example, the theory of "automatic selective perception" (Strange 2011) posits that L1 experience tunes the perceptual mechanism to be maximally efficient for the L1 (i.e., sensitive to only those cues important for perceiving L1 contrasts), leading to difficulties in perception of an L2 that requires sensitivity to different cues, while the "native language magnet" theory argues for a "neural commitment" to the L1 that affects the perception of other languages (Kuhl 2000; Zhang et al. 2005).

Accordingly, several studies focusing on segmental contrasts have documented a perceptual advantage of HSs over L2ers and, under certain conditions, perceptual abilities for HSs that are on par with NSs'. For example, Hindi HSs with minimal HL exposure after age 2 outperformed L2ers in perception of the Hindi /ʈ/-/t̪/ place contrast and /t̪ʰ/-/d̪ʰ/ voicing contrast (Tees and Werker 1984), while Korean HSs, including Korean adoptees with minimal HL exposure prior to relearning their HL in adulthood, outperformed L2ers in perception of Korean stop laryngeal contrasts, rate of perceptual learning of these contrasts, and/or transfer of perceptual learning to production of these contrasts (Oh et al. 2010; Cheon and Lee 2013; Choi et al. 2017). These and other studies used a variety of experimental methods differing in terms of task demands, which have revealed the task- and stimulus-dependent nature of HSs' perceptual performance. Using the AX discrimination paradigm as well as a sequence recall task taxing working memory, for instance, Lee-Ellis (2012) tested US-based Korean HSs on perception of the Korean-specific /s/-/s*/ contrast and found that HSs were significantly more accurate than L2ers across tasks, but resembled NSs only in the perceptually easiest task (discrimination with no talker variability). Along similar lines, US-based Russian HSs outperformed L2ers in perception of Russian palatalization contrasts across different sound pairs, contexts, and tasks, often with native-like levels of accuracy, but were significantly less accurate than NSs on the less acoustically distinct (and less frequent) pair of word-final /p/-/pʲ/ (Lukyanchenko and Gor 2011).

The perceptual advantage of HSs is found in perception of suprasegmental properties of the HL as well. In the case of lexical stress in Spanish, HSs outperformed L2ers in perceiving penultimate vs. final stress contrasts and in fact resembled monolingual NSs in this respect; however, there was also a significant effect of generation, whereby later generations of US-born HSs patterned more like L2ers in terms of a bias toward penultimate stress (Kim 2014, 2015). Echoing a pattern seen in other combined perception-production studies (e.g., Oh et al. 2003), Spanish HSs' advantage on stress contrasts was larger in perception than production, where they showed a strong resemblance to L2ers (Kim 2019; see Section 23.4). Other studies have similarly suggested that HSs have a perceptual advantage in perception of prominence and intonation in the HL (Zárate-Sández 2015; Laleko and Polinsky 2017). As for lexical tone, Mandarin HSs showed an advantage over L2ers in the categoricalness and stability of their tone perception and resembled NSs in their ability to recognize the starting pitch level of a tone, while at the same time resembling L2ers in their overreliance on pitch level (Yang 2015). Perceptual divergence from homeland NSs was also reported for young US-based Cantonese HSs' perception of both acoustically similar and distinct tone contrasts, although HSs performed much better on distinct tone contrasts (Kan and Schmid 2019). Much as in segmental perception, however, in tone perception the impact of early HL exposure can be quite long-lasting, as evidenced by the significant advantage in perceptual learning of Hokkien tone contrasts shown by Singapore-based HSs with no conscious memory of the HL (Singh and Seet 2019).

Apart from task type, HS generation, and acoustic similarity of HL contrasts, several other variables have emerged as predictors of HSs' perceptual behavior in the HL, including age of onset of the majority language (i.e., age of reduced contact with the HL) and assimilability of a given HL contrast to contrasts of the majority language/L2 (Ahn et al. 2017), age of testing and degree of literacy, especially in a developmental context (Kan and Schmid 2019), language mode (Antoniou et al. 2012), and proficiency level (Gor 2014), and the usefulness of a multivariate approach in particular is evident in the increasing number of studies that apply a sociolinguistic lens to HSs' linguistic behavior (e.g., Nagy 2016; Tse 2019). For example, Escalante (2018) found that Spanish HSs who traveled to coastal Ecuador were not necessarily more successful at perceiving the local dialect feature of /s/-aspiration than L2ers; although the most accurate participant was indeed a HS, more predictive of perceptual accuracy overall than HS status were the factors of phonological context, prior exposure to /s/-aspirating dialects, and proficiency level. Recent findings on perceptual adaptation by Mandarin HSs in Australia further pointed out the relevance of the social context of HL use (Cutler et al. 2019). In this work, Mandarin HSs who used the HL regularly were found to retune phonemic boundaries in accordance with exposure to unfamiliar talkers in the majority language (English), but not in the HL – a disparity that mirrored the much smaller number of interlocutors the HSs reported for the HL compared to the majority language. In other words, the social context of HL use, which involved regular exposure to a limited, and largely unchanging, set of talkers, apparently did not promote the development of perceptual adaptation mechanisms in the HL. An interesting avenue for future research, therefore, would be to test the degree to which these perceptual adaptation mechanisms may develop in HSs in response to changes in the context of HL use (e.g., study abroad in a HL-dominant language environment).

As for HSs' perception of the majority language, there is, again, less research on this topic in comparison to research focusing on HL perception, but existing studies, which generally focus on English as a majority language, have shown little evidence of a perceptual deficit vis-a-vis NSs of the majority language and, instead, evidence of perceptual benefits for the majority language. For example, the Hokkien HSs examined by Singh and Seet (2019) showed no significant differences from English NSs in a battery of grammatical, semantic, and sound-based English tasks, which included discrimination of English-specific phoneme contrasts (e.g., /z/ vs. /ð/, /d/ vs. /ð/). Similarly, the Korean HSs examined by Lee-Ellis (2012) showed no significant differences from English NSs in perception of the English-specific phonotactic contrast between word-medial consonant clusters and consonant–vowel sequences (e.g., /kasta/ vs. /kasuta/), across tasks; in fact, there was a nonsignificant tendency for the HSs to outperform the English

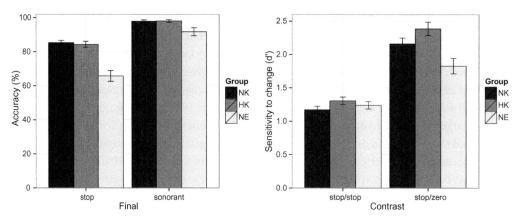

(a) Korean stop perception   (b) English stop perception

Figure 23.5 Perception of unreleased stops in Chang (2016) averaged over listeners and separated by item type. Panel (a) shows percent accuracy in identifying the final sound of stop-final (left) and sonorant-final (right) Korean nonce items. Panel (b) shows sensitivity to a change (*d'*) in English minimal pairs differing in final stop identity (left) or in presence/absence of a final stop (right). Groups are Korean NSs (NK), HSs (HK), and English NSs (NE). Error bars show standard error

NSs on discrimination of this English contrast. This apparent perceptual advantage over monolingual English NSs came out to be statistically significant in a study of US-based Korean HSs' perception of unreleased stops in both the HL and the majority language (Chang 2016). In this study, not only did HSs' perception of Korean resemble Korean NSs', their perception of English surpassed English NSs' (see Figure 23.5). Crucially, both in Chang's and in Lee-Ellis's studies, listeners who shared the same L1 background as the HSs but did not receive as early and as extensive exposure to English (i.e., Korean NSs) performed significantly worse on English perception than English NSs did; that is, there was a clear potential for HSs' experience with the HL to have a negative effect on their English perception. Despite this possibility, however, in both of these cases HL experience had either no such effect or even a beneficial effect, an outcome described by Chang (2016: 805) as a "best-case scenario" for early bilingual experience. The generalizability of this outcome to other HS communities and to other linguistic features awaits further investigation.

23.6   General Discussion

Research on HL sound systems is notable for its breadth (including work on diverse HLs, majority language contexts, and phonetic and phonological features) but also for several recurring themes that have emerged out of the specific cases examined to date. Perhaps the most abundantly attested is the finding that early exposure to a HL, even if relatively brief, leads to significant phonetic and/or phonological learning, although the depth and the accessibility of acquired HL knowledge show considerable variation related to structural linguistic factors (e.g., phonological environment, proximity to aspects of the majority language), demographic and sociolinguistic factors (e.g., HSs' age of reduced contact with the HL, immigrant generation, gender, size of the HL social network), input and usage-based factors (e.g., education, dialectal exposure, rate of code-switching, language dominance, proficiency), and methodological factors (e.g., task type and difficulty, language mode, dependent measure). Other frequently observed outcomes include intermediate patterning between NSs and L2ers (e.g., Knightly et al. 2003; Chang and Yao 2016), a wide range of individual variability (e.g., Kupisch et al. 2014; Flores and Rato 2016), and a relatively higher level of performance in perception as compared to production (e.g., Kim 2019), consistent with the interconnected, yet staggered, development of perception and production observed in monolingual L1 acquisition. In addition, although a broad comparison between segmental and suprasegmental production is limited by the smaller number of findings on suprasegmentals, it appears that suprasegmentals – at least certain global prosodic features such as intonation – may evince more frequent divergence from NS norms compared to segmentals. Viewed in relation to the early onset of exposure to HL prosody *in utero*, this disparity may seem surprising; however, given the oftentimes long developmental trajectory of L1 prosodic features, this should not be very surprising at all. Notably, such innovations at a suprasegmental level provide an explanation for why HSs who look similar to NSs at a segmental level may nevertheless be perceived by NSs as having a "heritage accent" in the HL.

For HSs to show, broadly, some degree of convergence or integration of the HL and the majority language is in fact expected under a "multicompetence" view of bilinguals, and as alluded to in Sections 3–5, several findings concerning adult HSs' phonetic and phonological systems are consistent with predictions of theoretical models such as Flege's SLM and Best's PAM. For example, degrees of crosslinguistic similarity between contrasts, which play a central role in PAM, were indeed predictive of perceptual discrimination of HL contrasts (Ahn et al. 2017), while HSs' successful maintenance of both within- and between-language contrasts, variability in behavior related to crosslinguistic proximity between the HL and the majority language, and closer patterning to NSs relative to L2ers (e.g., Au et al. 2008; Chang et al. 2011) followed from the shared L1–L2 phonetic space, the preference to maximize contrast within this space, and the inverse correlation between age of L2 onset and phonetic sensitivity that are posited in the SLM. However, although there are some studies directly investigating the early stages of HL development in childhood, which can already show divergence from NS norms (e.g., Cho and Lee 2016; Kan and Schmid 2019), it remains a largely theoretical question how the ostensible advantage of early HL exposure leads to the specific profile of HSs' linguistic knowledge in adulthood (e.g., it is often ambiguous whether development involves attrition and/or "incomplete acquisition" per se). Thus, longitudinal research tracking HSs over time in comparison to relevant peer groups would make significant contributions to our understanding of the lifespan development of HSs' phonetic and phonological systems (for an example concerning the majority language of UK-based Sylheti HSs, see McCarthy et al. 2014).

Besides widening their temporal scope, another way in which future studies are likely to improve our understanding of HL phonetics and phonology is by strengthening connections to two different literatures: the cognitive science literature on bilingualism and the sociolinguistic literature on indexicality and persona construction. In regard to the first, numerous researchers have argued for the existence of bilingual advantages in a range of domains (e.g., Bialystok et al. 2004; Antoniou et al. 2015; de Leeuw and Bogulski 2016), yet few have focused on HSs per se (compare Gabriel et al. 2018, who found Russian and Turkish HSs in Germany showed an advantage over monolingual German NSs in production of French voiceless stops). As for the sociolinguistic literature, a challenge, and an opportunity, for future research on HSs will be to grapple with the reality that an observed divergence of HSs from monolingual NS norms, which can often appear to reflect a passive "interference" of the majority language, may not be passive at all, but rather sociolinguistically motivated, under control, and deployed strategically as a flexible resource for constructing one's social identity and signaling group membership (Alam and Stuart-Smith 2011; D'Onofrio 2018). Naturally, this latter possibility raises an important question: When are HSs' non-monolingual-like behaviors (especially at the phonetic and phonological levels, which are typically salient loci of sociolinguistic variation) sociolinguistically motivated, and when are they not? It will be crucial for future research to approach HSs' linguistic data with this question in mind, in order to be able to give them the properly nuanced interpretation that they deserve.

While diversifying conceptual approaches to studying HSs will surely enrich the field of HL phonetics and phonology, it is also worth mentioning the empirical gaps in this area that are clear directions for future research. As discussed in Section 23.4, studies focusing on HL suprasegmentals are relatively sparse, and in particular there is a need for more work on HL intonation and rhythm, including in widely studied HLs such as Spanish (Rao and Ronquest 2015; Yakel 2018) and in intonational perception (Laleko and Polinsky 2017). Moreover, whereas a considerable number of studies discussed in Section 23.3–5 have addressed implicit phonological knowledge (pertaining to aspects such as phonemic contrasts, phonological processes, and phonotactic constraints), few have examined highly abstract or metalinguistic dimensions of phonological knowledge such as syllabification (Shelton et al. 2017). Studies investigating these facets of linguistic knowledge will provide valuable insights into HL sound systems.

In addition, work on HSs' majority language is currently lacking, yet very much needed to round out the picture of HSs' unique profile of bilingualism. For example, given HSs' bilingual experience, one question that arises is whether HSs might differ in intelligibility in their majority language compared to monolingual NS peers. On the one hand, as discussed in Section 23.2–4, there are occasional hints in the (small) literature on HSs' majority language that HSs may acoustically diverge, if ever so slightly, from their monolingual NS peers, but whether these differences negatively affect intelligibility – or, for that matter, are reliably perceptible at all – is typically unclear. On the other hand, it has also been suggested that, perhaps due to greater experience speaking the majority language to non-native speakers (e.g., family members from the first generation of immigration), HSs might tend to produce the majority language in a clearer or more enunciated fashion than NS peers (see Polinsky 2018: 141–144, for data on final stop realization in English as the majority language of US-based HSs from a variety of HL backgrounds); this would predict that HSs would be generally *more* intelligible in the majority language than NS peers. Interestingly, findings on US-based Spanish HSs do not show such an intelligibility advantage, although, crucially, they also show no disadvantage (Blasingame 2018). However, much more research – ideally, in a variety of majority language contexts – will be required to formulate any general principles underlying the phonetics and phonology of HSs' majority language.

In closing, I would like to end on a methodological note. To produce a full, richly elaborated picture of adult HSs' phonetic and phonological knowledge, it will be crucial to expand the scope of individual studies in two ways. First, more bilingual studies (i.e., studies examining both languages within the same sample of HSs), as opposed to studies examining only the HL or only the majority language, are needed to understand the dynamics of crosslinguistic interaction within HSs' linguistic repertoire. Second, more combined, and longitudinal, studies of both perception and production, as opposed to studies targeting one modality, are needed to understand how perception and production may lead, lag, or otherwise support each other over the course of HL development. In short, there is room in the study of HL sound systems not only for theoretical and conceptual diversification, but also for methodological innovation, both of which hold the potential to deepen the insights about HL sound systems to be gained in the years to come.

References

Ahn, S., C. B. Chang, R. DeKeyser, and S. Lee-Ellis. 2017. Age Effects in First Language Attrition: Speech Perception by Korean-English Bilinguals. *Language Learning* 67(3), 694–733.

Alam, F. and J. Stuart-Smith. 2011. Identity and Ethnicity in /t/ in Glasgow-Pakistani High-School Girls. In W.-S. Lee and E. Zee (eds.), *Proceedings of the 17th International Congress of Phonetic Sciences*. Hong Kong: City University of Hong Kong, 216–219.

Amengual, M. 2016. Acoustic Correlates of the Spanish Tap–Trill Contrast: Heritage and L2 Spanish Speakers. *Heritage Language Journal* 13(2), 88–112.

Amengual, M. 2018. Asymmetrical Interlingual Influence in the Production of Spanish and English Laterals as a Result of Competing Activation in Bilingual Language Processing. *Journal of Phonetics* 69, 12–28.

Amengual, M. 2019. Type of Early Bilingualism and Its Effect on the Acoustic Realization of Allophonic Variants: Early Sequential and Simultaneous Bilinguals. *International Journal of Bilingualism* 23(5), 954–970.

Amengual, M. and M. Simonet. 2020. Language Dominance Does Not Always Predict Cross-linguistic Interactions in Bilingual Speech Production. *Linguistic Approaches to Bilingualism* 10(6), 847–872.

Andrews, D. R. 1993. American Intonational Interference in Emigré Russian: A Comparative Analysis of Elicited Speech Samples. *Slavic and East European Journal* 37(2), 162–177.

Andrews, D. R. 2001. Teaching the Russian Heritage Learner: Socio- and Psycholinguistic Perspectives. *Slavic and East European Journal* 45(3), 519–530.

Antoniou, M., M. D. Tyler, and C. T. Best. 2012. Two Ways to Listen: Do L2-dominant Bilinguals Perceive Stop Voicing According to Language Mode? *Journal of Phonetics* 40(4), 582–594.

Antoniou, M., E. Liang, M. Ettlinger, and P. C. M. Wong. 2015. The Bilingual Advantage in Phonetic Learning. *Bilingualism: Language and Cognition* 18(4), 683–695.

Asherov, D., A. Fishman, and E.-G. Cohen. 2016. Vowel Reduction in Israeli Heritage Russian. *Heritage Language Journal* 13(2), 113–133.

Au, T. K., L. M. Knightly, S.-A. Jun, and J. S. Oh. 2002. Overhearing a Language during Childhood. *Psychological Science* 13(3), 238–243.

Au, T. K., J. S. Oh, L. M. Knightly, S.-A. Jun, and L. F. Romo. 2008. Salvaging a Childhood Language. *Journal of Memory and Language* 58(4), 998–1011.

Best, C. T. 1994. The Emergence of Native-Language Phonological Influences in Infants: A Perceptual Assimilation Model. In J. C. Goodman and H. C. Nusbaum (eds.), *The Development of Speech Perception: The Transition from Speech Sounds to Spoken Words*. Cambridge, MA: MIT Press, 167–224.

Best, C. T. 1995. A Direct Realist View of Cross-language Speech Perception. In W. Strange (ed.), *Speech Perception and Linguistic Experience: Issues in Cross-Language Research*. Baltimore, MD: York Press, 171–204.

Best, C. T. and M. D. Tyler. 2007. Nonnative and Second-Language Speech Perception: Commonalities and Complementarities. In O.-S. Bohn and M. J. Munro (eds.), *Language Experience in Second Language Speech Learning: In Honor of James Emil Flege*. Amsterdam: John Benjamins Publishing, 13–34.

Bialystok, E., F. I. M. Craik, R. Klein, and M. Viswanathan. 2004. Bilingualism, Aging, and Cognitive Control: Evidence from the Simon Task. *Psychology and Aging* 19(2), 290–303.

Blasingame, M. 2018. Early versus Extended Exposure in Speech and Vocabulary Learning: Evidence from Switched-Dominance Bilinguals. PhD thesis, Northwestern University, Evanston, IL.

Bullock, B. E. 2009. Prosody in Contact in French: A Case Study from a Heritage Variety in the USA. *International Journal of Bilingualism* 13(2), 165–194.

Chang, C. B. 2012. Rapid and Multifaceted Effects of Second-Language Learning on First-Language Speech Production. *Journal of Phonetics* 40(2), 249–268.

Chang, C. B. 2013. A Novelty Effect in Phonetic Drift of the Native Language. *Journal of Phonetics* 41(6), 491–504.

Chang, C. B. 2016. Bilingual Perceptual Benefits of Experience with a Heritage Language. *Bilingualism: Language and Cognition* 19(4), 791–809.

Chang, C. B. 2019a. Language Change and Linguistic Inquiry in a World of Multicompetence: Sustained Phonetic Drift And Its Implications for Behavioral Linguistic Research. *Journal of Phonetics* 74, 96–113.

Chang, C. B. 2019b. The Phonetics of Second Language Learning and Bilingualism. In W. F. Katz and P. F. Assmann (eds.), *The Routledge Handbook of Phonetics*. Abingdon: Routledge, 427–447.

Chang, C. B. and Y. Yao. 2016. Toward an Understanding of Heritage Prosody: Acoustic and Perceptual Properties of Tone Produced by Heritage, Native, and Second Language Speakers of Mandarin. *Heritage Language Journal* 13(2), 134–160.

Chang, C. B. and Y. Yao. 2019. Production of Neutral Tone in Mandarin by Heritage, Native, and Second Language Speakers. In S. Calhoun, P. Escudero, M. Tabain, and P. Warren (eds.), *Proceedings of the 19th International Congress of Phonetic Sciences*. Canberra, Australia: Australasian Speech Science and Technology Association Inc., 2291–2295.

Chang, C. B., E. F. Haynes, Y. Yao, and R. Rhodes. 2009. A Tale of Five Fricatives: Consonantal Contrast in Heritage Speakers of Mandarin. *University of Pennsylvania Working Papers in Linguistics* 15(1), 37–43.

Chang, C. B., E. F. Haynes, Y. Yao, and R. Rhodes. 2010. The Phonetic Space of Phonological Categories in Heritage Speakers of Mandarin. In Bane, M., J. Bueno, T. Grano, A. Grotberg, and Y. McNabb (eds.),

Proceedings from the 44th Annual Meeting of the Chicago Linguistic Society: The Main Session. Chicago: Chicago Linguistic Society, 31–45.

Chang, C. B., Y. Yao, E. F. Haynes, and R. Rhodes. 2011. Production of Phonetic and Phonological Contrast by Heritage Speakers of Mandarin. *Journal of the Acoustical Society of America* 129(6), 3964–3980.

Chen, Y., Y. Xu, and S. Guion-Anderson. 2014. Prosodic Realization of Focus in Bilingual Production of Southern Min and Mandarin. *Phonetica* 71(4), 249–270.

Cheng, A. 2019a. Age of Arrival Does Not Affect Childhood Immigrants' Acquisition of Ongoing Sound Change: Evidence from Korean Americans. In S. Calhoun, P. Escudero, M. Tabain, and P. Warren (eds.), *Proceedings of the 19th International Congress of Phonetic Sciences*. Canberra: Australasian Speech Science and Technology Association Inc., 2213–2217.

Cheng, A. 2019b. VOT Merger and f0 Contrast in Heritage Korean in California. *University of Pennsylvania Working Papers in Linguistics* 25(1), 69–77.

Cheon, S. Y. and T. Lee. 2013. The Perception of Korean Stops by Heritage and Non-heritage Learners: Pedagogical Implications for Beginning Learners. *The Korean Language in America* 18, 23–39.

Cho, M.-H. and S. Lee. 2016. The Impact of Different L1 and L2 Learning Experience in the Acquisition of L1 Phonological Processes. *Language Sciences* 56, 30–44.

Choi, J., A. Cutler, and M. Broersma. 2017. Early Development of Abstract Language Knowledge: Evidence from Perception–Production Transfer of Birth-Language Memory. *Royal Society Open Science* 4(1), 160660.

Colantoni, L., A. Cuza, and N. Mazzaro. 2016. Task-Related Effects in the Prosody of Spanish Heritage Speakers and Long-Term Immigrants. In M. E. Armstrong, N. Henriksen, and M. M. Vanrell (eds.), *Intonational Grammar in Ibero-Romance: Approaches across Linguistic Subfields*. Amsterdam: John Benjamins Publishing, 1–24.

Cook, V. 1997. The Consequences of Bilingualism for Cognitive Processing. In A. M. B. de Groot and J. F. Kroll (eds.), *Tutorials in Bilingualism: Psycholinguistic Perspectives*. Mahwah, NJ: Lawrence Erlbaum Associates, 279–300.

Cook, V. 2003. The Changing L1 in the L2 User's Mind. In V. Cook (ed.), *Effects of the Second Language on the First*. Clevedon: Multilingual Matters, 1–18.

Cornwell, S. and Y. Rafat. 2017. English Interdental Fricative Production in Dutch Heritage Speakers Living in Canada. *Ilha do Desterro* 70(3), 95–115.

Cummings Ruiz, L. D. 2019. North Midland /u/-fronting and Its Effects on Heritage Speakers of Spanish. In S. Calhoun, P. Escudero, M. Tabain, and P. Warren (eds.), *Proceedings of the 19th International Congress of Phonetic Sciences*. Melbourne, Australia: Australasian Speech Science and Technology Association Inc., 1099–1103.

Cutler, A., L. A. Burchfield, and M. Antoniou. 2019. A Criterial Interlocutor Tally for Successful Talker Adaptation? In S. Calhoun, P. Escudero, M. Tabain, and P. Warren (eds.), *Proceedings of the 19th International Congress of Phonetic Sciences*. Melbourne, Australia: Australasian Speech Science and Technology Association Inc., 1485–1489.

de Leeuw, E. and C. A. Bogulski. 2016. Frequent L2 Language Use Enhances Executive Control in Bilinguals. *Bilingualism: Language and Cognition* 19(5), 907–913.

Dehé, N. 2018. The Intonation of Polar Questions in North American ("Heritage") Icelandic. *Journal of Germanic Linguistics* 30(3), 213–259.

D'Onofrio, A. 2018. Personae and Phonetic Detail in Sociolinguistic Signs. *Language in Society* 47(4), 513–539.

Elias, V., S. McKinnon, and Á. Milla-Muñoz. 2017. The Effects of Code-Switching and Lexical Stress on Vowel Quality and Duration of Heritage Speakers of Spanish. *Languages* 2(4), 29.

Escalante, C. 2018. ¡Ya pué[h]! Perception of Coda-/s/ Weakening among L2 and Heritage Speakers in Coastal Ecuador. *EuroAmerican Journal of Applied Linguistics and Languages* 5(1), 1–26.

Flege, J. E. 1995. Second Language Speech Learning: Theory, Findings, and Problems. In W. Strange (ed.), *Speech Perception and Linguistic Experience: Issues in Cross-Language Research*. Baltimore: York Press, 233–272.

Flege, J. E. 1996. English Vowel Productions by Dutch Talkers: More Evidence for the "Similar" vs "New" Distinction. In A. James and J. Leather (eds.), *Second-Language Speech: Structure and Process*. Berlin: Mouton de Gruyter, 11–52.

Flege, J. E. 2007. Language Contact in Bilingualism: Phonetic System Interactions. In J. Cole and J. I. Hualde (eds.), *Laboratory Phonology 9*. Berlin: Walter de Gruyter, 353–382.

Flores, C. and A. Rato. 2016. Global Accent in the Portuguese Speech of Heritage Returnees. *Heritage Language Journal* 13(2), 161–183.

Flores, C., E. Rinke, and A. Rato. 2017. Comparing the Outcomes of Early and Late Acquisition of European Portuguese: An Analysis of Morphosyntactic and Phonetic Performance. *Heritage Language Journal* 14(2), 124–149.

Gabriel, C., M. Krause, and T. Dittmers. 2018. VOT Production in Multilingual Learners of French As a Foreign Language: Cross-Linguistic Influence from the Heritage Languages Russian and Turkish. *Revue Française de Linguistique Appliquée* 23(1), 59–72.

Godson, L. 2003. Phonetics of Language Attrition: Vowel Production and Articulatory Setting in the Speech of Western Armenian Heritage Speakers. PhD dissertation, University of California, San Diego, San Diego, CA.

Godson, L. 2004. Vowel Production in the Speech of Western Armenian Heritage Speakers. *Heritage Language Journal* 2(1), 44–69.

Gor, K. 2014. Raspberry, Not a Car: Context Predictability and a Phonological Advantage in Early and Late Learners' Processing of Speech in Noise. *Frontiers in Psychology* 5, 1449.

Hrycyna, M., N. Lapinskaya, A. Kochetov, and N. Nagy. 2011. VOT Drift in 3 Generations of Heritage Language Speakers in Toronto. *Canadian Acoustics* 39(3), 166–167.

Hualde, J. I. and P. Prieto. 2016. Towards an International Prosodic Alphabet (IPrA). *Laboratory Phonology* 7(1), 5.

Kan, R. T. Y. and M. S. Schmid. 2019. Development of Tonal Discrimination in Young Heritage Speakers of Cantonese. *Journal of Phonetics* 73, 40–54.

Kang, Y. and N. Nagy. 2016. VOT Merger in Heritage Korean in Toronto. *Language Variation and Change* 28(2), 249–272.

Kang, Y., S. George, and R. Soo. 2016. Cross-Language Influence in the Stop Voicing Contrast in Heritage Tagalog. *Heritage Language Journal* 13(2), 184–218.

Kim, J.-Y. 2010. Phonological Effect of Single-Word Insertion by Korean Heritage Speakers: Vowel Epenthesis in Word-Final Position. *Korean Journal of Linguistics* 35(1), 49–70.

Kim, J.-Y. 2011. L1–L2 Phonetic Interference in the Production of Spanish Heritage Speakers in the US. *The Korean Journal of Hispanic Studies* 4, 1–28.

Kim, J.-Y. 2014. Use of Suprasegmental Information in the Perception of Spanish Lexical Stress by Spanish Heritage Speakers of Different Generations. In N. Campbell, D. Gibbon, and D. Hirst (eds.), *Proceedings of the 7th International Conference on Speech Prosody*. Dublin: International Speech Communication Association, 453–456.

Kim, J.-Y. 2015. Perception and Production of Spanish Lexical Stress by Spanish Heritage Speakers and English L2 Learners of Spanish. In E. W. Willis, P. Martín Butragueño, and E. Herrera Zendejas (eds.), *Selected Proceedings of the 6th Conference on Laboratory Approaches to Romance Phonology*. Somerville, MA: Cascadilla Proceedings Project, 106–128.

Kim, J.-Y. 2017. Voice Quality Transfer in the Production of Spanish Heritage Speakers and English L2 Learners of Spanish. In S. Perpiñán, D. Heap, I. Moreno-Villamar, and A. Soto-Corominas (eds.), *Selected Proceedings of the 44th Linguistic Symposium on Romance Languages*. Amsterdam: John Benjamins Publishing, 191–207.

Kim, J.-Y. 2019. Heritage Speakers' Use of Prosodic Strategies in Focus Marking in Spanish. *International Journal of Bilingualism* 23(5), 986–1004.

Kim, J.-Y. 2020. Discrepancy between Heritage Speakers' Use of Suprasegmental Cues in the Perception and Production of Spanish Lexical Stress. *Bilingualism: Language and Cognition* 23(2), 233–250.

Kim, J.-Y. and G. Repiso Puigdelliura. 2020. Deconstructing Heritage Language Dominance: Effects of Proficiency, Use, and Input on Heritage Speakers' Production of the Spanish Alveolar Tap. *Phonetica* 77(1), 55–80.

Knightly, L. M., S.-A. Jun, J. S. Oh, and T. K. Au. 2003. Production Benefits of Childhood Overhearing. *Journal of the Acoustical Society of America* 114(1), 465–474.

Kuhl, P. K. 2000. A New View of Language Acquisition. *Proceedings of the National Academy of Sciences of the United States of America* 97(22), 11850–11857.

Kupisch, T., D. Barton, K. Hailer, E. Klaschik, I. Stangen, T. Lein, and J. van de Weijer. 2014. Foreign Accent in Adult Simultaneous Bilinguals. *Heritage Language Journal* 11(2), 123–150.

Laleko, O. and M. Polinsky. 2017. Silence Is Difficult: On Missing Elements in Bilingual Grammars. *Zeitschrift für Sprachwissenschaft* 36(1), 135–163.

Lee-Ellis, S. 2012. Looking into Bilingualism through the Heritage Speaker's Mind. PhD thesis, University of Maryland, College Park.

Lein, T., T. Kupisch, and J. van de Weijer. 2016. Voice Onset Time and Global Foreign Accent in German–French Simultaneous Bilinguals during Adulthood. *International Journal of Bilingualism* 20(6), 732–749.

Lloyd-Smith, A., M. Einfeldt, and T. Kupisch. 2020. Italian-German Bilinguals: The Effects of Heritage Language Use on Accent in Early-Acquired Languages. *International Journal of Bilingualism* 24(2), 289–304.

Lukyanchenko, A. and K. Gor. 2011. Perceptual Correlates of Phonological Representations in Heritage Speakers and L2 Learners. In N. Danis, K. Mesh, and H. Sung (eds.), *Proceedings of the 35th Annual Boston University Conference on Language Development*. Somerville, MA: Cascadilla Press, 414–426.

Lüpke, F. and A. Storch. 2013. *Repertoires and Choices in African Languages*. Boston: Walter de Gruyter.

Łyskawa, P., R. Maddeaux, E. Melara, and N. Nagy. 2016. Heritage Speakers Follow All the Rules: Language Contact and Convergence in Polish Devoicing. *Heritage Language Journal* 13(2), 219–244.

Mayr, R. and A. Siddika. 2018. Inter-generational Transmission in a Minority Language Setting: Stop Consonant Production by Bangladeshi Heritage Children and Adults. *International Journal of Bilingualism* 22(3), 255–284.

Mayr, R., L. López-Bueno, M. Vázquez Fernández, and G. Tomé Lourido. 2019. The Role of Early Experience and Continued Language Use in Bilingual Speech Production: A Study of Galician and Spanish Mid Vowels by Galician-Spanish Bilinguals. *Journal of Phonetics* 72, 1–16.

McCarthy, K., B. G. Evans, and M. Mahon. 2011. Detailing the Phonetic Environment: A Sociophonetic Study of the London Bengali Community. In W.-S. Lee and E. Zee (eds.), *Proceedings of the 17th International Congress of Phonetic Sciences*. Hong Kong, China: City University of Hong Kong, 1354–1357.

McCarthy, K., B. G. Evans, and M. Mahon. 2013. Acquiring a Second Language in an Immigrant Community: The Production of Sylheti and

English Stops and Vowels by London-Bengali Speakers. *Journal of Phonetics* 41(5), 344–358.

McCarthy, K. M., M. Mahon, S. Rosen, and B. G. Evans. 2014. Speech Perception and Production by Sequential Bilingual Children: A Longitudinal Study of Voice Onset Time Acquisition. *Child Development* 85(5), 1965–1980.

Montrul, S. 2015. *The Acquisition of Heritage Languages*. Cambridge: Cambridge University Press.

Montrul, S. A. 2008. *Incomplete Acquisition in Bilingualism: Re-examining the Age Factor*. Amsterdam: John Benjamins Publishing.

Nagy, N. 2015. A Sociolinguistic View of Null Subjects and VOT in Toronto Heritage Languages. *Lingua* 164(B), 309–327.

Nagy, N. 2016. Heritage Languages as New Dialects. In M.-H. Côté, R. Knooihuizen, and J. Nerbonne (eds.), *The Future of Dialects*. Berlin: Language Science Press, 15–35.

Natvig, D. 2016. Heritage Norwegian Vowel Phonology and English Dialect Formation. *Heritage Language Journal* 13(2), 245–274.

Newlin-Łukowicz, L. 2014. From Interference to Transfer in Language Contact: Variation in Voice Onset Time. *Language Variation and Change* 26(3), 359–385.

Nodari, R., C. Celata, and N. Nagy. 2019. Socio-indexical Phonetic Features in the Heritage Language Context: Voiceless Stop Aspiration in the Calabrian Community in Toronto. *Journal of Phonetics* 73, 91–112.

Oh, J. S. and T. K. Au. 2005. Learning Spanish as a Heritage Language: The Role of Sociocultural Background Variables. *Language, Culture and Curriculum* 18(3), 229–241.

Oh, J. S., T. K. Au, and S. A. Jun. 2010. Early Childhood Language Memory in the Speech Perception of International Adoptees. *Journal of Child Language* 37(5), 1123–1132.

Oh, J., S.-A. Jun, L. Knightly, and T. Au. 2003. Holding on to Childhood Language Memory. *Cognition* 86(3), B53–B64.

Pallier, C., S. Dehaene, J.-B. Poline, D. LeBihan, A.-M. Argenti, E. Dupoux, and J. Mehler. 2003. Brain Imaging of Language Plasticity in Adopted Adults: Can a Second Language Replace the First? *Cerebral Cortex* 13(2), 155–161.

Polinsky, M. 2018. *Heritage Languages and Their Speakers*. Cambridge: Cambridge University Press.

Polinsky, M. and O. Kagan. 2007. Heritage Languages: In the 'Wild' and in the Classroom. *Language and Linguistics Compass* 1(5), 368–395.

Rao, R. 2015. Manifestations of /bdg/ in Heritage Speakers of Spanish. *Heritage Language Journal* 12(1), 48–74.

Rao, R. 2016a. Introduction to Special Issue on Heritage Phonetics and Phonology. *Heritage Language Journal* 13(2), i.

Rao, R. 2016b. On the Nuclear Intonational Phonology of Heritage Speakers of Spanish. In D. Pascual y Cabo (ed.), *Advances in Spanish as a Heritage Language*. Amsterdam: John Benjamins Publishing, 51–80.

Rao, R. and R. Ronquest. 2015. The Heritage Spanish Phonetic/Phonological System: Looking Back and Moving Forward. *Studies in Hispanic and Lusophone Linguistics* 8(2), 403–414.

Ronquest, R. 2016. Stylistic Variation in Heritage Spanish Vowel Production. *Heritage Language Journal* 13(2), 275–297.

Schmid, M. S. 2013. First Language Attrition. *Wiley Interdisciplinary Reviews: Cognitive Science* 4(2), 117–123.

Shea, C. 2019. Dominance, Proficiency, and Spanish Heritage Speakers' Production of English and Spanish Vowels. *Studies in Second Language Acquisition* 41(1), 123–149.

Shelton, M., D. Counselman, and N. Gutiérrez Palma. 2017. Metalinguistic Intuitions and Dominant Language Transfer in Heritage Spanish Syllabification. *Heritage Language Journal* 14(3), 288–306.

Shin, E. 2005. The Perception of Foreign Accents in Spoken Korean by Prosody: Comparison of Heritage and Non-heritage Speakers. *The Korean Language in America* 10, 103–118.

Singh, L. and S. K. Seet. 2019. The Impact of Foreign Language Caregiving on Native Language Acquisition. *Journal of Experimental Child Psychology* 185, 51–70.

Solon, M., N. Knarvik, and J. DeClerck. 2019. On Comparison Groups in Heritage Phonetics/Phonology Research: The Case of Bilingual Spanish Vowels. *Hispanic Studies Review* 4(1), 165–192.

Strange, W. 2011. Automatic Selective Perception (ASP) of First and Second Language Speech: A Working Model. *Journal of Phonetics* 39(4), 456–466.

Tees, R. C. and J. F. Werker. 1984. Perceptual Flexibility: Maintenance or Recovery of the Ability to Discriminate Non-native Speech Sounds. *Canadian Journal of Psychology* 38(4), 579–590.

Tse, H. 2016a. Contact-Induced Splits in Toronto Heritage Cantonese Mid-vowels. *Linguistica Atlantica* 35(2), 133–155.

Tse, H. 2016b. Variation and Change in Toronto Heritage Cantonese: An Analysis of Two Monophthongs across Two Generations. *Asia-Pacific Language Variation* 2(2), 124–156.

Tse, H. 2019. Beyond the Monolingual Core and out into the Wild: A Variationist Study of Early Bilingualism and Sound Change in Toronto Heritage Cantonese. PhD thesis, University of Pittsburgh, Pittsburgh, PA.

Tucker, G. R. 2001. A Global Perspective on Bilingualism and Bilingual Education. In J. E. Alatis and A.-H. Tan (eds.), *Language in Our Time: Bilingual Education and Official English, Ebonics and Standard English, Immigration and the Unz Initiative*. Washington, DC: Georgetown University Press, 332–340.

van de Weijer, J. and T. Kupisch 2015. Voice Onset Time in Heritage Speakers and Second-Language Speakers of German. In E. Babatsouli and D. Ingram (eds.), *Proceedings of the International Symposium on*

Monolingual and Bilingual Speech 2015. Chania: Institute of Monolingual and Bilingual Speech, 414–420.

van Rijswijk, R., A. Muntendam, and T. Dijkstra. 2017. Focus Marking in Dutch by Heritage Speakers of Turkish and Dutch L1 Speakers. *Journal of Phonetics* 61, 48–70.

Ventureyra, V. A. G., C. Pallier, and H.-Y. Yoo. 2004. The Loss of First Language Phonetic Perception in Adopted Koreans. *Journal of Neurolinguistics* 17(1), 79–91.

Wong, P. and W. Strange. 2017. Phonetic Complexity Affects Children's Mandarin Tone Production Accuracy in Disyllabic Words: A Perceptual Study. *PLoS ONE* 12(8), e0182337.

Yakel, A. N. 2018. Rhythmic Variation in Speakers of Spanish as a Heritage Language. PhD thesis, University of Houston, Houston, TX.

Yang, B. 2015. *Perception and Production of Mandarin Tones by Native Speakers and L2 Learners*. Berlin: Springer Verlag.

Yao, Y. and C. B. Chang. 2016. On the Cognitive Basis of Contact-Induced Sound Change: Vowel Merger Reversal in Shanghainese. *Language* 92(2), 433–467.

Yao, Y., A. Chan, R. Fung, W. L. Wu, N. Leung, S. Lee, and J. Luo. 2020. Cantonese Tone Production in Pre-school Urdu-Cantonese Bilingual Minority Children. *International Journal of Bilingualism* 24(2), 767–782.

Yeni-Komshian, G. H., J. E. Flege, and S. Liu. 2000. Pronunciation Proficiency in the First and Second Languages of Korean-English Bilinguals. *Bilingualism: Language and Cognition* 3(2), 131–149.

Zárate-Sández, G. A. 2015. Perception and Production of Intonation among English-Spanish Bilingual Speakers at Different Proficiency Levels. PhD thesis, Georgetown University, Washington, DC.

Zhang, Y., P. K. Kuhl, T. Imada, M. Kotani, and Y. Tohkura. 2005. Effects of Language Experience: Neural Commitment to Language-Specific Auditory Patterns. *NeuroImage* 26(3), 703–720.

24

Morphology of Heritage Languages

Michael T. Putnam, Lara Schwarz, and Andrew D. Hoffman

24.1 Introduction

The morphology and morphosyntax of heritage languages have been the focus of numerous studies and have arguably been the domain of grammar that has received the majority of attention in this literature to date. Unlike phonology (see Chang (this volume)) and most elements of syntax (see Lohndal (this volume)), heritage morphology displays a high degree of variability when compared with baseline standards. The fact that morphology represents one of the most vulnerable domains to change and loss in these populations should not come as a major surprise, since morphology is generally considered a complex system consisting of a substantial number of paradigmatic irregularities that confound ontological and phylogenetic acquisition and development (Carstairs-McCarthy 2010). This chapter surveys observed developmental trends in heritage morphology, focusing on its acquisition, maintenance, and attrition across the lifespan. Although there are differences in the morphological systems of child, adult, and late-stage/moribund HSs, there are noted similarities across these varieties as well Putnam, Pascual y Cabo, and Kupisch's (2018). With that being said, the majority of our discussion here centers on data from late-stage and moribund HSs.

Before starting with this empirical survey, three additional confounds need to be acknowledged. The first matter concerns the problem of defining the boundaries of "morphology." Although it is accepted practice to assume that the study of morphology concerns notions of "wordhood" and inflections, the definition of these concepts remains nonetheless elusive (Di Sciullo and Williams 1987; Dixon and Aikhenvald 2002). Some morphologists working within anti-lexicalist paradigms such as *Distributed Morphology* (Marantz 1997) and related models (Borer 2013) deny the existence of "word" as an analytical or metalinguistic concept altogether. Newell

et al. (2017: 1) summarize this paradoxical situation as follows: "the concept of 'word' is arguably one of the most intuitive constructs in language
as far as speakers are concerned; every child and adult is aware that there is
a unit that correlates to word. And yet, from a theoretical point of view,
there is no consensus on the definition of word." Haspelmath (2011) and
Svenonius (2016) point out along the same lines that although a host of
phonological analyses make reference to lexical items, i.e., "words," this is
often carried out in the absence of clear delineating criteria of these objects
of study. Similar difficulties exist in establishing boundaries between
morphology and syntax (see Lohndal (this volume) for a discussion). It
remains a mystery which sorts of phonological, structural (i.e., morphological), and semantic criteria are recruited to determine wordhood in a
given language (see Bauer (2017: ch.2) for an overview of these issues),
leading to the question of whether all languages have structural units
classified as *words* (Dixon and Aikhenvald 2002). This issue is even more
poignant when linguistic typology is concerned; see Section 24.3. We therefore readily acknowledge that we must tolerate some degree of overlap and
intersection with phonology and syntax when investigating the morphological properties of languages. Ironically, although morphology is notoriously unstable and highly vulnerable to change and loss in heritage
contexts, it is situated between two largely stable domains of grammar;
namely, phonology and syntax. In Section 24.5 we discuss how these findings impact theoretical treatments of heritage languages.

The second issue concerns the persistent problem of "monolingual bias"
in the study of bi- and multilingual grammars. Research on bilingual
grammars tends to be "deficit"-oriented (Ortega 2014), and, unfortunately,
research on aspects of heritage languages is not immune to this noted
pitfall. Polinsky (2018) refers to this as the "glass-half-empty" approach.
Neurocognitive and psycholinguistic research on bilingualism confirms
that elements of both source grammars can be simultaneously active, thus
leading to the possibility that continued competition for limited processing
resources may lead to a restructuring of "weaker," or "less actively used"
grammars. Therefore, viewing the competence of one source grammar in
the bi/multilingual mind as being "deficient" can be considered erroneous
and hinders progress on efforts to better understand both the processes
that shape these grammars and their underlying structure (for an overview
of this literature, see Kroll and Gollan (2014) and Putnam, Carlson, et al.
(2018)).[1] Although heritage grammars may exhibit some of the developmental trends discussed in Section 24.2, aspects of grammar successfully

---

[1] As a point of clarification, we are not arguing for an abandonment of the widely accepted practice of comparing the
production and performance of bi/multilinguals with baseline standards. This method is especially effective when
longitudinal data exist for communities and speakers under investigation.

acquired in childhood remain fundamentally intact (Montrul 2008, 2016; Bousquette and Putnam 2020).[2]

Third, we recognize the difficulty in defining which individuals and populations count as *heritage speakers* (HSs). Although heritage language speakers are L1 speakers (Rothman and Treffers-Daller 2014), there none-theless exist notable differences between (predominantly) monolinguals and these individuals due to myriad factors (literacy, differences in quanti-tative and qualitative linguistic input, sociolinguistic factors, etc.). In spite of the high degree of individual variation among heritage speakers' linguis-tic ability (as is common in bi/multilingual populations), their grammars display certain common traits in speakers of various ages and backgrounds (Putnam, Pascual y Cabo, and Kupisch 2018). Furthermore, the "errors" that heritage speakers produce when compared with baseline standards may differ in rate and form from L2-learners (Montrul 2008), but not always (Montrul et al. 2019). These factors coalesce in the *Heritage Bilingual Paradox* (Bayram et al. 2019), which attempts to come to grips with how naturalistic child acquisition in heritage speakers results in disparities in grammatical competence between (predominantly) monolingual and other heritage speaker populations.

In spite of these noted challenges, we review and discuss observable trends in heritage morphology. Due to space constraints, we cannot adequately address the vast literature on this topic; therefore, we will restrict our treat-ment of heritage morphology to these larger themes: In Section 24.2 we highlight general properties exhibited in heritage morphology, focusing primarily on inflectional morphology, while giving a secondary nod to deriv-ational morphology. We turn our focus to typological distinctions (e.g., agglutinative, polysynthetic, fusional, and isolating) in Section 24.3 to explore whether the tendencies introduced in the previous section hold across these different types of languages or whether more specific and localized trends are observed. In Section 24.4 we turn our attention to additional factors (matur-ational effects, typological proximity, etc.) that may impact the development of heritage morphology. This chapter concludes in Section 24.5 with a discus-sion of under-researched empirical domains of heritage morphology and their potential theoretical importance moving forward.

24.2 Structural Tendencies in Heritage Morphology

Collectively, heritage language morphology displays a certain number of structural tendencies. This section uses Polinsky (2018: ch. 5) as a

---

[2] Bousquette and Putnam (2020) provide additional evidence of the retention of relatively complex morphosyntax phenomena, such as complementizer agreement, in moribund varieties of heritage German spoken in Wisconsin.

foundation and expands on this seminal treatment. There is a strong degree of overlap and interrelatedness between these trends, which is expected to some degree. What emerges from this picture is a general overarching tendency to establish direct one-structure-to-one meaning mappings in heritage morphology.

24.2.1 Frequency and Salience of Forms and Structures

Forms that are frequent and salient/transparent are easier to detect in complex paradigms (such as morphology), when compared with infrequent ones. Therefore, it comes as little surprise that the transparency of morphological units plays a central role in heritage languages. Polinsky (2018: 166) discusses two particular scenarios where transparency comes into play in the development of morphology in heritage languages. Here, we understand transparency and salience to be near-synonymous and the two terms are often used interchangeably in the literature. The first involves the conflict between two or more non-silent (i.e., overt) forms, and the second involves the perception and production of a single overt exponent. In the first scenario, it is hypothesized that the most perceptually salient/transparent form will eventually win out, while in the second, an individual exponent will be lost or extended to other contexts.[3] This is referred to as *simplification*, in which a competing structure is eliminated or reanalyzed (Romaine 1995). For instance, in Italian and Spanish, monolingual speakers drop subject pronouns, and reserve overt subject pronouns for the discourse-pragmatic function of topic change or focus (Laleko this volume). HSs of these languages have reanalyzed overt pronouns to be used even in discourse-neutral contexts, eliminating the competition between the null and overt pronouns (Sorace and Filiaci 2006). This process is also attested in heritage language acquisition; for example, in the acquisition of gender, HL learners tend to struggle assigning the correct gender to non-transparent nouns (Montrul et al. 2008; Laleko 2018, 2019). Another strategy is *reduction* (Mühlhäuser 1974), through which structural elements are lost without compensation by other elements from a recessive language. In recent literature this process is commonly referred to as *attrition*.

Theoretical analyses of the internal structure (i.e., grammar) of heritage languages often make some reference to the notion of *complexity* (Culicover 2013). Proposals by Amaral and Roeper (2014) and Scontras et al. (2015, 2018) appeal to the notion that less dominant grammars (i.e., heritage and L2 varieties) often show reduced complexity. Invoking the notion of complexity comes with the responsibility of defining the heuristic of standards

---

[3] Polinsky (2018) rightly notes that the second scenario technically involves competition between two forms; i.e., an overt one and a zero/non-overt form.

and structures that are (more) simplistic or complex in relation to others. For example, are we comparing structures and paradigms observed in natural data, abstract theoretical rules and representations, or a combination of both? We return to this discussion in Section 24.2.5.

24.2.2 Overregulation and Overmarking

The tendency to regularize paradigms in heritage morphology is further attested in instances where heritage speakers *overuse*, or hyperextend, highly transparent and regularized forms and patterns. This practice is referred to as **overregulation**. This process is observed in child acquisition, where Fernández-Dobao and Herschensohn (2019) note the overregulation of stem vowels in the verbal system of Heritage Spanish for person agreement and the marking of tense, mood, and aspect. This pattern is also found in adult HSs; Johnson (2016) reports overapplication of the nominative case in Heritage Finnish spoken in northern Wisconsin. The nominative form in Finnish is unmarked and occurs most frequently. Over the course of time it is foreseeable that such a situation could lead to a loss of features for other case distinctions in language contact situations, reinforcing the cognitively salient nature of the nominative form.

A higher frequency of input does not always lead to *intake*; a perfect example of this is agreement in languages that have rich agreement systems. Even though agreement is robust in input, agreement represents a domain of grammar that is vulnerable in heritage language acquisition and maintenance, for case marking in Heritage Hindi (Section 24.3.3.3). A closely related phenomenon known as **overmarking** represents a special case of overregulation in which highly systematic morphology is overapplied. In her treatment of the properties of heritage English, Polinsky (2018) cites the excessive application of the weak past tense -*ed* marker, resulting in overmarking on English weak (e.g., *dresseded, walkeded*) and strong verbs (e.g., *sanged, wented*).

Polinsky (2018) highlights an important contrast between elements that are frequent targets for overmarking (such as strong past tense verbs) and those that are seldom if ever attested forms. For example, verbal forms displaying excessive marking of the -*ing* in English present progressives do not occur (**runninging*) nor do we find an overmarking of plurality on forms such as plural English count nouns (**shoeses*). Polinsky appeals to the theoretical axiom of **structural salience** to explain this dichotomous behavior. Appealing to a hierarchy of functional projections (Cinque 1999; Ramchand and Svenonius 2014; Wiltschko 2014),[4] structural salience in this context

---

[4] Functionalist, usage-based approach to language emergence and its resulting structure also support such a layered design of functional elements (see Bybee et al. (1994)).

predicts that functional heads in a higher position are more salient than the other functional heads that they dominate. Structural salience thus predicts why the overmarking of aspectual -*ing* is absent in heritage English since it is dominated by a functional head responsible for tense (e.g., [TP T [MoodP [Aux/AspP -ing …]]]]). Along these same lines, the absence of overmarking on plural forms is due to the functional category of Number appearing in the middle of Determiner Phrases (DPs) (e.g., [DP D-article [NumP [GenP [*n*P NP]]]]). Based on the two structures provided immediately above, we can offer two additional predictions based on the notion of structural salience: (i) heritage language speakers should have strong control of functional elements such as tense (T) and determiners (D) and (ii) elements such as mood and gender should be vulnerable targets for attrition effects. Both of these predictions are strongly supported, with mood (Putnam and Árnbjörnsdóttir 2015) and gender (Polinsky 2018: §5.3.2.1) being notoriously difficult for heritage speakers.

As pointed out to us by Maria Polinsky (p.c.), the structural position of functional heads in the syntactic spine does not mean that structural salience does not have any effect on the morphological system in an HL. As we saw with the case of **overmarking**, tense forms were targeted for doubling; however, the category of Tense (with regard to its semantics) remains unaltered. Conversely, a vulnerable category such as aspect, which is regarded to be structurally dominated by Tense and Mood (e.g., [TP T [MoodP M [AspP Asp …]]]) is more likely to undergo restructuring via attrition than Tense due to its structural position (see Laleko (2008, 2010) and Polinsky (2008) for examples of aspect in Heritage Russian.) Polinsky (2018: 63) suggests that since tense is inherently indexical (i.e., it relates the moment of speech to some other moment in time) it is perceptually salient, and hence more resilient to attrition.

24.2.3   Preference for Analytical Forms

Heritage language speakers show an overwhelming preference for analytical and periphrastic forms and constructions when compared with more synthetic ones. One of the key factors behind this *increased analyticity* (Polinsky 2018: 183) observed in heritage morphology is the tendency to establish one-to-one mappings between form and meaning.[5] The drive for transparency and perceptual salience in form-to-meaning mappings predicts that analytical forms are more preferable than synthetic ones (Section 24.2.1).

---

[5] This proposal also accounts for the difficulty in producing "null elements" (i.e., phonologically overt) such as null subjects. Laleko and Polinsky (2017) refer to this as the **silent problem** (see Polinsky (2018): ch. 6.5 for a summary and key references).

An example of this is changes in the marking of direct and indirect objects, including the rise of adpositions in heritage case systems. In Heritage Russian, speakers use a marked vs. unmarked paradigm to distinguish between indirect and direct objects respectively (1a), rather than the less salient dative/accusative marking system (1b).

Changes to the case marking system in Heritage Russian (Polinsky 2018: 186:(28))

(1) a. pokazal devočk-u   mašinka
         showed girl-MARKED toy.car.UNMARKED
         'showed the girl a toy car'
     b. pokazal devočk-e mašink-u
         showed girl-DAT toy.car-ACC
         'showed the girl a toy car'

24.2.4 Avoidance of Ambiguity and Underspecification

A grammar that consists predominantly of one-to-one form-meaning mappings is also designed to avoid structural ambiguities, i.e., situations in which one form may be associated with two (or more) different meanings. In the nominal domain, the restructuring of form-meaning associations involving dative case represents an ideal example of this phenomenon. Cross-linguistically dative case can involve multiple functions, such as representing experiencer subjects and recipient objects (indirect objects). In languages such as German and Russian, certain prepositions assign dative case to the elements they govern. The multiple mappings of dative case to (at least) two different syntactic positions and contrasting thematic interpretations make dative case a paragon candidate for restructuring. Keine (2007) and Montrul et al. (2019) point out that there is a hierarchy that determines which dative arguments are most likely to restructure: Whereas dative experiencer subjects and DOM-marked objects are more susceptible to restructuring, indirect objects are least likely to be affected. This state of affairs is confirmed cross-linguistically in languages such as Heritage German (Yager et al. 2015; Schwarz 2019), Heritage Hindi (Montrul et al. 2015), and Heritage Spanish (Pascual y Cabo 2013). The restructuring strategies vary, with some languages, such as Heritage Hindi, Spanish, Russian, and Turkish (Pfaff 1993; Anstatt 2011; Pascual y Cabo 2013; Montrul et al. 2015) showing a reduction of differential object markings (DOM), while some varieties of Heritage German actually show the rise of DOM (Yager et al. 2015).

Another commonly attested attribute of heritage morphology is the dispreference of underspecification for two or more linguistic segments from a paradigmatic opposition. Laleko (2010) captures the shift in preference from a singleton feature opposition to an equipollent one in Heritage Russian, where all members of a contrastive set are fully valued with the feature(s) in question (Polinsky 2018: §5.2.2).[6] Feature contrasts that exist in equipollent opposition to one another may lead to a stronger resistance of underspecification in morphology. Many linguists working on Russian aspect agree that the perfective and imperfective form a privative, singled-valued opposition (Binnick 1991; Filip 1999), where "the perfective is specified with respect to the completion of an event, whereas the imperfective is not. Since the imperfective is not specified for event completion or the absence of such completion, it can be used to encode completed events, resulting in competition" (Polinsky 2018: 192). Laleko (2008, 2010) conducted a series of comprehension experiments involving baseline and heritage speakers of Russian, showing that even highly proficient Heritage Russian speakers fail to interpret the imperfective as denoting a completed event. The Heritage Russian speakers struggled to interpret imperfective aspect with completed events even in the presence of contextual pragmatic information. In her analysis, Laleko proposes that Heritage Russian speakers have replaced a privative opposition with an equipollent one with respect to aspect and that this restructuring is primarily due to difficulties interfacing morphosyntax and contextual/pragmatic information.

(2)   a.   perfective aspect: [+completive]   Aspect in Heritage Russian
      b.   imperfective aspect: [-completive] or [+ongoing]
           (Polinsky 2018: 194)

24.2.5   Minimal Domains

The culmination of these aforementioned factors results in a grammatical system that exhibits reduced complexity when compared with baseline standards and the grammar of previous generations of heritage speakers. Following Hawkins (2004), we refer to this as the preference of **Minimal Domains** in language production. This preference for minimal domains of computation leads to structural preferences in heritage languages such as: (i) the reduction in paradigmatic irregularities and (ii) adjacent forms being preferred over those separated by other elements. If the domains of computation in heritage grammars face an increasing danger of "shrinking," this provides a potential account as to why case morphology is often particularly difficult for heritage speakers to master (Montrul 2016).

---

[6] Polinsky's (2018) review and assessment of the general properties of heritage phonology suggests that the restructuring of privative oppositions for equipollent ones is not observed, making this a phenomenon restricted to the morphological domain based on extant studies and evidence.

Scontras et al.'s (2018) argument is that the pressures to establish minimal domains explains the coalescence of gender and number morphology in English-dominant speakers of Heritage Spanish. Their primary results show that their informants have restructured their agreement options, favoring fewer exponents to represent number and gender marking for morphophonologically transparent inanimate nouns with uninterpretable gender. Scontras et al. (2018) capture this restructuring by proposing that the syntactic projections responsible for number and gender have been conjoined, resulting in a "minimal domain," which restricts morphological agreement options.

The reduction or elimination of categories of inflectional morphology can also signal the reduction of syntactic properties of heritage grammars. Putnam and Árnbjörnsdóttir (2015) argue that the loss of inflectional morphology indicating subjunctive mood in Heritage Icelandic also reflects a loss in long-distance (logophoric) binding. In Icelandic, subjunctive mood must be marked on the verb in the subordinate clause in order to establish a long-distance binding relationship (3a). Árnbjörnsdóttir (2006) documents that North American Icelandic appears to have lost the allomorphy associated with the subjunctive mood (3b), resulting in the loss of long-distance binding. This situation affirms the close relationship between morphological and syntactic components of grammar, and suggests that any appeal to minimizing computational domains of heritage grammars will have a direct impact on both.

(3)   Loss of subjunctive mood; North American Icelandic, Canada
       (Putnam and Árnbjörnsdóttir 2015)

    a. þeir vildu nú trúa ekki mér að ég kæmi frá Kanada.
        they would really not believe me that I **come.SBJV** from Canada
        'They would not believe me that I came from Canada.'

    b. þeir vildu nú ekki trúa mér að ég kom frá Kanada.
        they would really not believe me that I **come.IND** from Canada
        'They would not believe me that I came from Canada.'

The structural tendencies of heritage morphology just summarized yield a set of hypotheses that allow comparisons between baseline standards – be they idealized standard grammars or data elicited from previous generations of immigrants – and heritage language speakers. Another attractive feature of employing these standards in the study of heritage morphology is that they provide a standard of comparison across typologically distinct languages, which is a point explored in more detail in the next section.

24.3 Typological Considerations

In this section we explore to what extent these observed tendencies of heritage morphology are present in typologically diverse languages. We restrict our investigation to a limited number of token examples of *isolating* and *synthetic* (e.g., *agglutinating, fusional,* and *polysynthetic*) structures. Controversy surrounds the partitioning of languages along these lines (see Croft (2003: 45–48) and Bauer (2017: ch.2.6)). A fundamental issue with this classification system is that an individual language may license structures of multiple kinds. For example, consider the English sentence *The babysitter waits for the grandparents to return*, in which *babysitter* is arguably polysynthetic (as a nominalized form of a verb with an incorporated noun), *grandparents* is agglutinative (semantically transparent morpheme concatenation), *waits* is fusional (the *-s* morpheme encodes tense, person, and number), and the remaining elements are isolating (example from Bauer (2017: 14).

While this is a simplistic schematization of typologically motivated morphosyntactic structure types, it serves to highlight the fact that no one language may be defined exclusively by any of these individual types. It should be noted that while this schematization reflects traditional descriptions of these types, there are competing conceptualizations thereof. Baker (1996), for example, views polysynthesis as a morphological system of encoding participants based on "pronominal arguments" and noun incorporation, as opposed to the more traditional notions outlined in Section 3.4. See also Fortescue (1994) and Evans and Sasse (2002) for critical remarks on the usefulness of the classification of languages as *polysynthetic*. These caveats notwithstanding, we adopt these traditional typological classifications while acknowledging that it is more appropriate to recognize that languages exist on a gradient continuum with respect to these morphological properties.

24.3.1 Isolating

Isolating morphology typically involves more direct correspondence between form and function, where each individual "word" consists of a single morpheme. Polymorphemic compounds may exist in these languages due to the presence of derivational morphology. At first glance, it would appear that heritage languages that (primarily) license isolating morphology may be largely immune to the restructuring process commonly attested in synthetic languages (see 2). Polinsky (2018: §5.3.3) discusses a handful of studies that show that heritage languages that predominantly employ isolating morphology are also susceptible to restructuring processes that result in grammars that differ from baseline standards.

Isolating languages such as Cantonese, Mandarin, and Vietnamese use classifiers in the presence of numeral and demonstratives in the nominal domain. Heritage speakers of Mandarin find it difficult to assign the appropriate classifier to nominal elements. The examples in (4) are spontaneously produced elements from a heritage speaker of Mandarin. Example (4a) illustrates an unacceptable omission of a classifier and (4b) shows the use of an incorrect classifier (the general classifier *ge* is produced rather than the more specific *ke*).

(4)　Heritage Mandarin (Ming and Tao 2008: 173)

　　a.　women　cong　yi*(-ge)　guoji　　dao　bie　　de　　guojia　jiu　　zuo　huoche.
　　　　we　　　from　one-CLF　country　to　　other　ADN　country　then　sit　train
　　　　'We take the train from one country to another.'

　　b.　Xiangzhang　dui-mian　　you　yi-ge　si　de　　shu.
　　　　XZ.　　　　　opposite-face　have　one-CLF　die　ADN　tree
　　　　'There is a dead tree opposite Xiaozhang.'

Examples such as those in (4) demonstrate that the association of classifiers to nominal elements is analogous to other restructuring processes observed in synthetic languages. Additional evidence can be found in a corpus study of English-dominant Cantonese-heritage speaking children in the United Kingdom conducted by Wei and Lee (2001). With respect to nominal classifiers, the researchers discovered that the number of classifiers correlated with the child's proficiency in Cantonese.

Difficulties with classifiers are not only found in language production but are also observed in language comprehension. Benmamoun et al. (2013) report on the results of a language comprehension (auditory) study that confirms this. In this study, classifier phrases (underlined) and their associated nouns (**boldfaced**) were separated by one content word and the adnominal marker *de*; see (5).

(5)　Matching condition: appropriate classifier (Mandarin) (Benmamoun et al. 2013: 145–46)

　　a.　Laozhang　ba　na-yi-liang　　hen-kuan-chang　de　　**qiche**　songgei　le
　　　　Mr.Zhang　BA　DEM-one-CLF　very-wide-open　ADN　car　　give　　PFV
　　　　Laowang.
　　　　Mr.Wang
　　　　'Mr. Zhang gave a very big car to Mr.Wang.'

　　b.　Nonmatching condition: inappropriate classifier
　　　　*Laozhang　　ba　na-yi-suo　　hen-kuan-chang　de　　**quiche**　songgei　le
　　　　Mr.Zhang　　BA　DEM-one-CLF　very-wide-open　ADN　car　　give　　PFV
　　　　Laowang.
　　　　Mr.Wang
　　　　'Mr. Zhang gave a very big car to Mr. Wang.'

When compared with a monolingual control group, the HSs' acceptability judgments were notably higher, suggesting that they overlooked the classifier–noun mismatches. The addition of lexical material, such as the adnominal *de*, presented an additional confound for the HSs in noticing the classifier–noun mismatches (Benmamoun et al. 2013: 146).

In addition to the omission of elements, other studies focusing on isolating heritage morphology have found the overregularization of prepositions

(Ming and Tao 2008: 173). In the verbal domain, Jia and Bailey (2008) and Ming and Tao (2008) note the omission or incorrect use of the perfective aspectual marker *le*. Although the number of studies focusing on isolating heritage morphology are few to date when compared with those targeting fusional languages, these extant investigations suggest that heritage varieties of these languages are equally susceptible to the restructuring trends outlined in the previous section.

24.3.2 Agglutinative

As indicated by their descriptive designation, agglutinative languages employ the extensive use of morpheme concatenation to create larger morphological units. Lexical elements may consist of many morphemes, which remain essentially unchanged from their base form even in more complex units. As expected, agglutinative languages tend to have a high morpheme-to-word ratio, where each morpheme is assigned to one grammatical category. This contrasts with fusional languages, which allow one morpheme to be associated potentially with many grammatical categories. Here we consider data from Heritage Hungarian (Fenyvesi 2000; Tóth 2007) and Heritage Turkish (Arslan et al. 2015; Karayayla 2018) as representative samples.

Although agglutinative languages adhere to a strict one-form (morpheme)-to-one grammatical category mapping (essentially differing from analytic constructions only in the degree to which the morphemes are phonologically integrated into the greater morphological whole), evidence from American Hungarian shows a trend toward producing analytical forms (Section 24.2.3). In the examples in (6a) and (6b), the morphemes that mark number are accompanied by pronouns, resulting in redundancy that is not required in European Hungarian.

(6)   Additional elements, American Hungarian (Tóth 2007: 169)

   a. Én nem tud-<u>om</u>,   mért ő   nem men-t-Ø   haza.
      I   not   know-1SG why he   not   went-PST-3SG home
      'I don't know why he went home.'

   b. Ők   tud-t-ák   hogy őneki   rossz kedve   volt.
      they know-PST-3PL that   him.DAT bad   his.mood   was
      'They knew that he was in a bad mood.'

Another feature of European Hungarian is a complex system of definiteness marking that involves separate person, number, and definiteness markers. In European Hungarian, the use of a prenominal definite determiner does not necessarily license the definite verbal suffix (see 7a), e.g., intransitive verbs do not receive definite marking. In American Hungarian, however, this system has been simplified, with determiner and verbal suffix definiteness necessarily mirroring one another (see 7b) (Fenyvesi 2000).[7]

(7)   Definite instead of indefinite marking, American Hungarian (Fenyvesi 2000: 97)

 a. European Hungarian
  az öreg-ek meg-hal-t-ak
  the old-PL PVB-**die-PST-3PL.INDEF**
  'the old people died'
 b. American Hungarian
  az öreg-ek meg-hal-t-ák
  the old-PL PVB-**die-PST-3PL.DEF**
  'the old people died'

Tóth (2007) cites additional trends in his extensive study of Heritage Hungarian in America, such as the extension (*overmarking*) of the *ik*-morpheme to verbs not originally included in this class (4.6.14), missing verb conjugations (4.6.10), and incorrect and inconsistent case marking on nouns (4.6.1.1). Bolonyai (2007) reports similar findings regarding the production of possessive and verbal inflection in a child heritage speaker of Hungarian.

Heritage Turkish in contact with other European languages such as Dutch, English, French, and German has been extensively studied in both child and adult populations. With respect to morphology, the consensus in the literature is that Heritage Turkish relies on more analytical structures (Huls and van de Mond 1992; Pfaff 1993; Treffers-Daller et al. 2007) displays reductions in past tense and narrative structures (Aarssen 2001; Akıncı 2003; Arslan et al. 2015; Karayayla 2018) and exhibits changes with derivational nominal morphology and null pronouns (Pfaff 1993). An example of such morphological reduction can be found in the morphological marking of evidentiality in Turkish.

(8)   Turkish evidential forms (Arslan et al. 2015: 459)

 a. Adam yemeği ye-**di**
  man food.ACC eat-DIRECTEVID.3SG
  'The man ate the food.' [witnessed past]
 b. Adam yemeği ye-**miş**
  man food.ACC eat-INDIRECTEVID.3SG
  'The man ate the food.' [reported/inferred past]

The use of the direct evidential inflection -DI in (8a) indicates that the speaker witnessed the entire eating event from start to finish. In contract, when the indirect evidential -(I)MIŞ is used as in (8b), the speaker either

---

[7] Hungarian <a> = /ɒ/ and <á> = /aː/.

infers the event took place or has heard about it from someone else. Studies by Arslan et al. (2015) and Karayayla (2018) confirm that Heritage Turkish speakers face difficulties processing forms marked for indirect evidentiality. The indirect evidential form is semantically complex, including epistemic modality (Aksu-Koç 1998, 2000), and as a result, the morphology associated with the direct evidentiality represents the unmarked form.

24.3.3 Fusional

Fusional languages are characterized by morphemes that can encode multiple meanings (Payne 1997: 28). For instance, the verbal inflection morpheme *-st* in German encodes morphosyntactic information about person (2nd) and number (singular), as well as discourse-pragmatic information about formality. In fusional heritage languages, there are frequent reports of simplification (Montrul 2016), in particular where the meaning behind the inflectional morphology is not salient and can be expressed through alternative means. Heritage German features prominently in this literature, characterized by a collapse of grammatical gender and a loss of grammatical case marking, e.g., marked alternatively by word order rather than with case endings (Eikel 1949; Gilbert 1965; Boas 2009). More detailed information on Heritage German can be found in Johannessen and Salmons (this volume). Heritage Spanish is another widely cited fusional heritage language, again with gender and case morphology being affected (Montrul 2004; Montrul et al. 2008; Montrul & Bowles 2009; Montrul et al. 2015; Scontras et al. 2018). More information on Heritage Spanish can be found in Lipski (this volume).

Icelandic

North American Icelandic (NAIce) is described as not much different from Icelandic (Ice), in particular regarding case, gender, and number morphology (Árnbjörnsdóttir 2006, 2015). Nevertheless, a recent investigation into gender and case in NAIce showed that there are some trends that align with changes in Ice, but some that do not (Schwarz 2019). This is best illustrated on Quirky Case impersonal verbs; verbs that assign accusative case to an experiencer subject (9a). Typically, experiencer subjects receive dative case in Icelandic, so the use of accusative is unexpected (i.e., quirky). In Ice, these verbs are undergoing what is called Dative Sickness: instead of marking the arguments with accusative case, speakers use dative case analogous to non-quirky verbs of a similar semantic class (Árnbjörnsdóttir 2006). In NAIce, speakers exhibit Dative Sickness (Árnbjörnsdóttir 2006, 2015; Schwarz 2019), but, uniquely, they also apply nominative case to the subjects of these verbs (9b).

(9) Instability in quirky case, NAIce (Schwarz 2019)
a. stelp-una   langar   a   eiga   rau-tt   hjól-Ø.
    girl.the-ACC wants   to   have   red-ACC   bike-ACC
    'The girl wants a red bike.'

b. stelpa-n   langar   a   eiga   rau-tt   hjól-Ø.
    girl.the-NOM wants   to   have   red-ACC   bike-ACC
    'The girl wants a red bike.'

Leveling is characteristic of NAIce morphology. In a picture-naming task, speakers exhibited variability most specifically in assigning gender morphology to strong masculine nouns, omitting the expected nominative ending -*ur* in favor of a bare, unmarked noun (example: *ost-ur* vs. *ost-* 'cheese'), the marking strategy traditionally employed by feminine and neuter nouns in this context (Schwarz 2019). Schwarz (2019) hypothesizes that this is an effect of the frequency of the form: Feminine and neuter strong nouns appear as bare, unmarked nouns in both nominative and accusative cases (and for all cases with strong neuter nouns), whereas masculine strong nouns only surface without case marking in the accusative case. The objectively more frequent and transparent form lacking overt marking then becomes an attractive "marking" strategy in expanded domains.

Russian

Like many fusional languages, Heritage Russian exhibits a loss of grammatical case distinctions on pronominal forms, but the degree of loss depends on the fluency of the speaker (Polinsky 2006). Interestingly, Heritage Russian speakers introduce positional restrictions on dative case marking in perception and psychological verbs (Polinsky 2006), limiting the use of dative case in these contexts to pre-verbal noun phrases (10a) while post-verbal noun phrases are marked differently (10b).

(10) Positional restriction on the dative case, Heritage Russian (Polinsky 2006)
a. Vsegda   tebe   nravitsja   takie   ljudi
    always   **you.DAT** like   such.UNM   people.UNM
    'One always likes such people.' (lit: you always like such people)

b. prosit' u   moi   roditeli   neprijatn[ə]   menja
    to ask from my.UNM   parents.UNM   unpleasant   **me.2NDOBJ**
    'I don't like to ask my parents (for money)'

Another interesting development in Heritage Russian is the change to aspectual marking. Heritage Russian speakers exhibit three different strategies when marking aspect that differ from baseline L1 Russian speakers (Laleko 2008). In some instances, HSs use an opposite aspect marker than would be expected from monolingual speakers, or they use a form with the same aspectual meaning, but a different morphological form, or they use an analytical construction to express the meaning. In baseline Russian (11a), aspect is marked on the verb to make a distinction between the perfective or imperfective aspect. Heritage Russian (11b) instead introduces an aspectual verb "begin" and the entire construction can carry either an imperfective or perfective mood, despite being morphologically marked as imperfective.

(11) Compositional aspect, Heritage Russian (Polinsky 2008)
    a. on   sxvatil/xvataet   olenja   za   roga.
       he   seized.PERF/seizes.IMPF   deer.ACC   by   horns.ACC.PL
       'He grabbed/grabs the deer by the antlers.'

    b. on   načinaet/deržit   olen'   roga.
       He   begins.IMPF/holds.IMPF   deer.NOM horns.UNM.PL
       'He grabbed the deer by the antlers.'

Hindi

In Hindi, case markers and verb agreement appear in complementary distribution. Subjects marked with the ergative morpheme *-ne* block agreement on the verb, and as a result the verb agrees with the object. Conversely, animate person objects or specific inanimate objects marked with the dative morpheme *-ko* block agreement, so the verb agrees with the subject. If both nouns are marked, the verb receives default agreement. Heritage speakers of Hindi, in production tasks, omit both of these case markers frequently (Montrul et al. 2012), and accept the omission of the case markers more than native speakers of Hindi (Montrul et al. 2015).

(12) Ergative marking omission; Hindi, United States (Montrul et al. 2012)
    a. laRkii-ne uskii naanii   dekhii.
       girl-ERG her   grandmother saw
       'The girl saw her grandmother.'

    b. laRkii   uskii   naanii   dekhii.
       girl-Ø   her   grandmother saw
       'The girl saw her grandmother.'

(13) Dative marking omission; Hindi, United States (Montrul et al. 2012)
    a. thoRii sii Dar ho gayaa   naaniijii-ko.
       little   bit fear happened **grandmother-DAT**
       'Grandmother got frightened a little.'

    b. thoRii sii Dar ho gayaa   naaniijii.
       little   bit fear happened grandmother-Ø
       'Grandmother got frightened a little.'

Summary

In fusional languages, there are two main trends. First, we observe the simplification of inflectional paradigms. Fusional heritage languages consolidate overlapping form-meaning pairs, or eliminate redundancy. Second is a shift toward analytical forms. Whether as a result of simplification, the impetus for simplification, or just a parallel process, heritage speakers of fusional languages prefer compositional constructions over morphological markers.

24.3.4 Polysynthetic

Fortescue (1994) recognizes several linguistic features or structures that may be termed "polysynthetic" (cited from Gruzdeva and Vakhtin (2017: 428–9): (i) numerous morphological "slots" and a large inventory of bound morphemes, (ii) verbal forms typically contain pronominal markers and integrated adverbial elements, allowing verbal forms to be used as sentence equivalents, (iii) adjectives are incorporated into nominal forms and nouns are incorporated into verbal forms. Though not a requirement for poly-synthesis, many polysynthetic languages also exhibit a fourth feature, productive morphophonemics and complex allomorphy of bound and free morphemes. We will also restrict our discussion here to polysynthetic *structures* rather than to polysynthetic *languages* as a whole, in acknowledgment of the problems associated with such typological categorization. There are obvious similarities between agglutinative and polysynthetic languages. However, the presence of allomorphic variation in the latter is a distinguishing characteristic.

Based on these characteristics, the following examples from Onondaga, Central Alaskan Yupik, and Chukchi serve to highlight these polysynthetic traits, as each shows elements of complex morphological structure, head-marking, and incorporation (e.g., noun incorporation).

(14)   Onondaga, Canada/United States (Woodbury 1975: 10)
         Waʔ-ha-yɛʔkw-ahnínu-ʔ
         PST-3SG.M-tobacco-buy-ASP
         'He bought tobacco.'

(15)   Central Alaskan Yupik, United States (Woodbury 2002: 91–93)
         Mallu-ssu-tu-llini-luni=gguq
         beached.whale-hunt-always-apparently-3SG.APP=REP
         'S/he is apparently always hunting beached whales, it is said.'

(16)   Chukchi, Russia (Spencer 1995: 481)
         a-taŋ=caat-kə-lʔə=ʔaacek-etə
         NEG-good=lasso-NEG-PTCPL=youth-DAT
         'to the youth who does not have a good lasso.'

Polysynthetic languages in heritage language contexts display a number of similar traits with other types of languages mentioned earlier, for instance instability in both nominal and verbal inflectional morphology. Other typical features of polysynthesis, e.g., incorporation and complex allomorphy, are similarly affected in heritage language contexts. The tendencies presented in the following sections are not representative of all contexts. Due to a limited number of studies on heritage polysynthetic languages, much of the following discussion draws from investigations of language obsolescence.

Nominal Inflection

Gruzdeva and Vakhtin (2017: 440) note that nominal morphology is particularly susceptible to "obsolescence-induced changes" in head-marked possessor constructions (see also Gruzdeva and Vakhtin (2017) for discussion of the effects on nominal derivational morphology). Such morphological encoding of possession is frequently lost to some extent. This has been the case, for example, with Nivkh, a Paleosiberian isolate of the Russian Far East. In the traditional variety of the language, kinship terms (i.e., nouns) were obligatorily marked. If the "possessor" was a singular person, the noun would be marked with a reduced form of the corresponding personal pronoun, e.g., ñ-ətk 'my father' and ṭ'-əmk 'your.sg mother.' If, however, the possessor was dual or plural, a full form of the personal pronoun was used in preposition to the noun, e.g. ṭ'in-aqi 'your.pl elder brother' or in-asq 'their junior brother.' This pattern, however, has begun to vanish, perhaps due to the influence of Russian (Gruzdeva 2015: 166).

Verbal Inflection

Gruzdeva and Vakhtin (2017: 434) note that verbal morphology is the most vulnerable domain in polysynthetic languages. Complex verb structures may be restructured, including the reduction of morphological "slots," especially when the same category is doubly marked. In Tlahuica, an Oto-Manguean language of Mexico, grammatical number is marked by both prefixes and suffixes on the verb. Speakers who are not dominant in Tlahuica, however, may eliminate such double marking, as shown in example (17) (elided forms shown in parentheses) (Campbell and Muntzel 1989).

(17)   Tlahuica, Mexico (Campbell and Muntzel 1989: 191–192)
    a. kiat-kwe-p-tyɨ̈(-nkwe(-βi))
        FUT-1PL-EXCL-sing(-DU(EXCL))
        'We (two, but not you) will sing.'

    b. kiat-kwe-p-tyɨ̈ (-hñə(-βi))
        FUT-1PL-EXCL-sing(-PL(-EXCL))
        'We (all, but not you) will sing.'

The morphological reduction seen in Heritage Tlahuica is exceptional, in that person and number marking tends to be stable in baseline polysynthetic languages. Gruzdeva and Vakhtin (2017: 434–435) argue that such stability is the consequence of the fact that person marking in polysynthetic languages is found on verbs alone, whereas it is also marked on NPs in non-polysynthetic languages, i.e., in non-polysynthetic languages, it is an agreement feature rather than a essential structural feature, as it is in polysynthetic languages. Loss of such marking would instantiate a loss of a core feature, rather than the loss of a peripheral morphological feature. Example (17) shows that it is only the redundant marking that is lost, rather than the entire, core person-marking feature.

In Kabardian (a Northwest Caucasian language of the North Caucasus in Russia), for example, subjects, direct objects, and indirect objects are all marked on the verb by bound morphemes, meaning that the sentence in (18a) may serve as a full clause. Speakers of "reduced" Kabardian, however, restore overt pronouns or full NPs in such situations (18b), and do not accept utterances such as (18a) as full clauses, despite continuing to mark the relevant relations on the verb. In general, however, loss of person/ number marking on verbs is rare in heritage polysynthetic languages Gruzdeva and Vakhtin (2017: 436)

18   (Kabardian, Russia (Polinsky 1995: 97)
  a. Ø-zə–yə-t+a-ŝă
      3SG.OBJ-to-1SG-3SG.SBJ-give+PRF-DEC
      'She/he gave me that/it.'

  b. abə   s   q°ə   mər Ø-zə-yə-t+a-ś
      3SG.ERG 1SG to/for it 3SG.OBJ-1SG-3SG.SBJ-give+PRF-DEC
      'She/he gave me that/it.'

Tense, mood, and aspect may be similarly affected in polysynthetic heritage language scenarios. Here, there is a clear tendency toward greater analyticity. Mithun (1989: 248–249) notes that while the most fluent Oklahoma Cayuga speaker could use all the appropriate tma affixes, there was hesitation to combine several within a single word. When there were few prepronominal prefixes, both Ontario and Oklahoma Cayuga speakers would, for example, use the repetitive aspect prefix *s-* with the particle *é:?* 'again' (19). When more prepronominal prefixes were present, however, the Oklahoma Cayuga speaker relied on the particle *é:?* alone to carry the meaning, whereas an Ontario speaker would have simply combined the prefixes ((20) (Mithun 1989: 248–249).

(19) a.   aǫtati?anyú?uh 'she beat her up'
      b.   saǫtati?tanyú *é:?* 'she beat her up again'

(20) a.   Ontario Cayuga
           tǫsasatkahaté:nih
           DUALIC.REPETITIVE.2SG.SEMIREFLEXIVE.turn.around
           'turn back around, re-turn'

      b.   Oklahoma Cayuga
           teskạa:té:ni   é:?
           DUALIC.2SG.AG.SEMIREFLEXIVE.turn.around again
           'turn around again'

Sherkina-Lieber (2015) investigated the grammatical knowledge of *receptive bilinguals* (RBs, i.e., individuals who report they can understand but not speak their heritage language) of Labrador Inuttitut. Her study focused on their knowledge of functional morphemes (e.g., tense, aspect, and agreement markers) and whether or not these elements were accessible and understood in comprehension tasks. The results of this study show many

English dominant-RB Heritage Labrador Inuttitut comprehenders have baseline-like comprehension of aspectual suffixes, the distinction between past vs. future contrasts in tense suffixes, and subject–object–verb agreement suffixes. Most participants, however, struggled to identify remoteness degrees in tense suffixes. The lowest proficiency RBs in this study failed to show any knowledge of the morphology of Labrador Inuttitut. Two important takeaways from this study are that RBs with high proficiency (in comprehension) still have knowledge of the morphology of this language, but simply exhibit difficulties in accessing it. Second, tense, in spite of its indexical nature and high structural position, can be vulnerable in some contexts of heritage language development.

Noun Incorporation

Noun incorporation is a "morphological construction where a nominal lexical element is added to a verbal lexical element; the resulting construction being a verb and a single word" (De Reuse 1994: 200). Example (21) shows propositionally equivalent utterances with syntactically independent arguments (21a) and a morphologically incorporated object (21b). Gruzdeva and Vakhtin (2017: 442) note that this type of noun incorporation appears to be a common "early victim" in cases of polysynthetic language obsolescence.

(21)   Chukchi, Russia (Muravyova 2004: 116, cited in Gruzdeva and Vakhtin (2017: 442))
    a.   gəm-nan jəkərgə-n tə-lwə-gʔe
         I-1SG.ERG mouth-NOM.SG 1SG.SBJ-burn-PST.3SG.OBJ
         'I burned my mouth.'

    b.   gəm tə-jəkərgə-lwə-gʔek
         I.NOM 1SG.SBJ-mouth-burn-PST.1SG.SBJ
         'I burned my mouth.'

In heritage varieties of polysynthetic languages, reduction in the productivity of (noun) incorporation appears to often progress with speakers incorporating increasingly fewer nouns, especially in novel combinations. Early stages of this process may see speakers' frequent use of noun incorporation to background discourse arguments (the traditional purpose of noun incorporation). However, this is only productive for nouns and verbs that speakers have already heard in combination. With greater time depth, native lexical items are replaced with borrowings, and the stock of nouns and verbs that lend themselves to incorporation decreases, leading to ever fewer instances of noun incorporation (Mithun 1984: 880–881).

Cayuga is an Iroquoian language originally spoken in New York state. Historical circumstances following the American Revolution, however, led to many Cayuga moving to Ontario and Oklahoma. The language continues in Ontario, but has been receding in Oklahoma over the last 30 years (Mithun 1989: 243–244). In Oklahoma, noun incorporation has ceased to be productive; only the most frequent noun-verb combinations are used.

The relatively common collocation in example (22) is therefore produced similarly in the Ontario and Oklahoma varieties of Cayuga, with comparable levels of morphological complexity. However, in rarer combinations (as in example (23)), Oklahoma Cayuga speakers prefer the construction with a simplex verb and unincorporated noun (Mithun 1989: 249–250).

(22)   Ontario Cayuga
      a.   konǫhsowá:neh
         F.SG.PAT.house.large.STATIVE
         'She has a big house/her house is big.'

      b.   Oklahoma Cayuga
         kanǫhsuwá:nęh
         N.house.large.STATIVE
         'She has a big house/her house is big.'

(23)   a.   Ontario Cayuga
         ko-ʔnǫhs-owanę
         F.SG.PAT-onion-large.STAT
         'She has a big onion'

      b.   Oklahoma Cayuga
         k-uwane   ʔnǫhs-aʔ
         N-big.STAT onion-NOMINAL.SUFFIX
         'The onion is big'

24.3.5 Summary

Our review of the various types of morphological processes reveals that the structural trends found in heritage morphology outlined in Section 24.2 are present to varying degrees in all typological types. Morphological systems trend toward perceptually salient forms, with a preference for analytic over synthetic forms that involve minimal domains of computation when compared with baseline standards. In addition, nominal morphology appears to be more affected than verbal morphology, and, in a similar stripe, inflectional morphology more so than derivational morphology. The crucial distinction between verbs and nouns that is likely responsible for this asymmetry is that verbs are inherently predicative, whereas nouns are sortal (Polinsky 2018: 227).

24.4 Additional Factors

The previous section confirms the existence of many of the structural trends in heritage morphology outlined in Section 24.2. The development of heritage morphology is principally analytic in nature. What remains an area of debate is the motivation behind these deviations from baseline standards. An additional controversy that we do not pursue in detail here concerns whether these trends represent a mapping (or processing) difficulty or whether they are a sign of a true representational deficit (Putnam and Sánchez 2013; Montrul 2016). Extant research strongly supports maturational constraints on the quality of linguistic representations, with those structures acquired pre-puberty exhibiting a stronger propensity to remain in the heritage grammar throughout the lifespan (Montrul 2008). These effects of maturational constraints on language acquisition obviously do not infer that all aspects of linguistic knowledge are locked into place throughout the lifespan; there are countless examples of transfer, attrition, and divergence attainment that refute this. Rather, the existence of maturational constraints makes a strong case for the guiding hand of universal principles that anchor and aid in the acquisition process.

There are two additional factors that we have not discussed previously that may impact the development of heritage morphology. Both involve the simultaneous activation of elements of bilingual grammars (for an overview of this literature, see Putnam, Carlson, et al. (2018)). The presence of mixed forms (Riksem 2017) provides a clue that these observed systemic trends are primarily the result of the conflict between two (or more) grammatical systems.

(24)   Mixed Determiner Phrases, American Norwegian (Riksem 2017: 2)
   a. det   andre **crew**-et
      the.N other crew-DEF.SG.N
      'the other crew'

   b. eg fekk arbeid på **railroad**-en
      I got work at railroad-DEF.SG.M
      'I got a job at the railroad.'

The examples in (24) represent mixed determiner phrases attested in American Norwegian. In both examples the nouns are of English-origin modified by a Norwegian-origin determiner. The existence of mixed structures such as these supports the hypothesis that bilingual linguistic representations are gradient, at least to some degree. Any account of restructuring processes in heritage morphology must also take structures such as these into account.

A second factor related to an integrated architecture of bilingual grammars has to do with the typological profiles of both source grammars. Schwarz (2019) explores the role of typological proximity and distance in the retention of case morphology in North American Icelandic (see also Polinsky (2018: ch. 5: table 5.5) for an overview of the development of heritage case systems when both source grammars are typologically distinct from one another). Her results suggest that one of the key factors preventing, or at the very least impeding, paradigmatic case erosion resides in the specific exponents and the composition of their two grammars, especially with regard to their connection with event semantics and thematic interpretation. The case systems of English and German share more commonalities than English and Icelandic with respect to their mapping to event semantics, leading to a strengthening of these commonalities, which are similar in structure and appear English on the surface. English and Icelandic, on the other hand, share fewer commonalities, facilitating the separation of the Heritage Icelandic case system from the English during acquisition and maintenance.

24.5 Conclusion and Future Directions

Our review of the general properties of heritage morphology shows that the structural tendencies outlined in Section 24.2 are strongly attested. The evidence to date obtained from heritage speakers promotes a model in which most syntactic and phonological properties of heritage grammars are largely invulnerable to significant restructuring. This state of affairs supports a view of morphological properties of language being the result of computational processes that follow, rather than precede, those responsible for generating syntactic structure (i.e., exocentric architecture; see Borer (2013); Lohndal (2014); Ramchand and Svenonius (2014)). Additionally, production–comprehension asymmetries and the fact that some aspects of heritage grammar can be reestablished in the case of returnees Flores (2015, 2020) further suggest that these combinatorial distinctions are not completely lost, but rather suggest an architecture in which representations exist along a gradient continuum (Gollan et al. 2008). Flores (2020) discusses the morphology of heritage speakers of Portuguese who grew up in Germany but moved to Portugal later in their childhood/adolescence. One of the datasets in this study takes a detailed look at the oral production of one returnee who was re-immersed in a German-speaking environment after living in Portugal for 4 years. A comparative analysis of this speaker's performance 13 months after leaving Germany and 11 months after returning to Germany reveals a significant decrease of inaccurate case, gender, and plural marking. This finding is consistent with other contemporary work on the grammar of returnees, which demonstrates that target-like morphology with a high degree of accuracy can be reestablished under appropriate conditions.

There are a host of unanswered questions and under-researched empirical domains that will ultimately lead us to a better understanding of the motivation behind the structural tendencies in Section 24.2. Empirically, additional studies focusing on the derivational morphology of fusional languages along the lines of Zyzik (2020) will fill a noticeable gap in the literature to date. The morphological properties of heritage varieties of isolating languages (see Section 24.3.1) represent an under-researched domain for future studies. Moving forward, the inclusion of more diverse groups of heritage speakers who differ from one another with respect to various extralinguistic factors such as (but not limited to) (i) age of acquisition of the HL, (ii) age of exposure to the non-HL (iii), opportunities to use the HL throughout the lifespan, and (iv) the age of the speaker stands to reveal more details related to maturational effects and their impact on heritage morphology.

Finally, perhaps the most intriguing research question that emerges from this review is the following: Given the rather robust support from the structural tendencies outlined in Section 24.2 in heritage morphology, what factors are responsible for instances in which complex morphology is acquired and maintained in heritage grammars (Nützel and Salmons 2011; Schwarz 2019; Bousquette and Putnam 2020; Łyskawa and Nagy 2020)? These situations involve the retention of complex agreement paradigms, such as complementizer agreement in varieties of Heritage German (see Bousquette and Putnam (2020)). Although it is common for heritage grammars to retain certain "archaic" structures, the presence of these complex elements in heritage grammars, with some of them being moribund, warrants further investigation. An important point that cannot be overstated is that the restructuring of heritage morphology does not equate with language loss. Rather, we observe the establishment of new, innovative patterns. In closing, although heritage morphology represents one of the domains of grammar studied most extensively to date, there remains much important research to be carried out in the years to come.

24.6 Acknowledgements

Thanks to Maria Polinsky and Silvina Montrul for the invitation to contribute to this volume. Thanks to Joshua Bousquette, Oksana Laleko, Terje Lohndal, Silvina Montrul, Richard Page, Maria Polinsky, Robert Klosinski, Liliana Sánchez, and Joe Salmons, for comments on an earlier draft of this paper and stimulating discussions. The usual disclaimers apply.

Abbreviations used

1. Ø = null morpheme
2. acc = accusative
3. adn = adnominal
4. app = appositional
5. asp = aspect
6. clf = classifier
7. dat = dative
8. dec = declarative
9. def = definite

10. du = dual
11. erg = ergative
12. excl = exclusive
13. f = feminine
14. fut = future
15. m = masculine
16. n = neuter
17. neg = negative
18. nom = nominative
19. obj = object
20. pat = patient
21. pl = plural
22. prf = perfective
23. pst = past
24. ptcpl = participle
25. pvb = preverb
26. rep = reportative
27. sbj = subject
28. sbjv = subjunctive
29. sg = singular
30. stat = stative
31. unm = unmarked

References

Aarssen, J. 2001. Development of Temporal Relations in Narratives by Turkish-Dutch Bilingual Children. In L. Verhoeven and S. Stömqvist (eds.), *Narrative Development in a Multilingual Context*. Amsterdam: John Benjmains, 209–232.

Akıncı, M. 2003. Temporal Anchoring of Texts in Turkish of First and Second Generation Turkish Immigrants in France. In S. Ozsoy, D. Akar, N. Nkipoglu-Demiralp, A. Erguvanli-Taylan, and A. Aksu-Koç (eds.), *Studies in Turkish Linguistics*. Istanbul: Boğaziçi University Press, 289–297.

Aksu-Koç, A. 1998. *The Acquisition of Aspect and Modality: The Case of Past Reference in Turkish*. Cambridge: Cambridge University Press.

Aksu-Koç, A. 2000. Some Aspects of the Acquisition of Evidential in Turkish. In L. Johnson and B. Utas (eds.), *Evidential: Turkic, Iranian and Neighbouring Languages*. Berlin: Mouton de Gruyter, 15–28.

Amaral, L. and T. Roeper. 2014. Multiple Grammars and Second Language Representation. *Second Language Research* 30(1), 3–36.

Anstatt, T. 2011. Sprachattrition: Abbau der Erstsprache bei russisch-deutschen Jugendlichen. *Wiener Slawistischer Almanach* 67, 7–31.

Árnbjörnsdóttir, B. 2006. *North American Icelandic: The Life of a Language.* Manitoba: University of Manitoba Press.

Árnbjörnsdóttir, B. 2015. Reexamining Icelandic as a Heritage Language in North America. In J. B. Johannessen and J. C. Salmons (eds.), *Germanic Heritage Languages in North America: Acquisition, Attrition and Change.* Amsterdam: John Benjamins, 72–93.

Arslan, S., D. DeKok, and R. Bastiaanse. 2015. Processing Grammatical Evidentiality and Time Reference in Turkish Heritage and Monolingual Speakers. *Bilingualism: Language and Cognition* 20(5), 457–472.

Baker, M. 1996. *The Polysynthesis Parameter.* Oxford: Oxford University Press.

Bauer. L. 2017. *Compounds and Compounding.* Cambridge: Cambridge University Press.

Bayram, F., D. Pascual y Cabo, and J. Rothman. 2019. Intra-generational Attrition: Contributions to Heritage Speaker Competence. In M. Schmid and B. Köpke (eds.), *The Oxford Handbook of Language Attrition.* Oxford: Oxford University Press, 446–457.

Benmamoun, E., S. Montrul, and M. Polinsky. 2013. Heritage Languages and Their Speakers: Opportunities and Challenges for Linguistics. *Theoretical Linguistics* 39, 129–181.

Binnick. R. I. 1991. *Time and the Verb: A Guide to Tense and Aspect.* Oxford: Oxford University Press.

Boas H. C. 2009. Case Loss in Texas German: The Influence of Semantic and Pragmatic Factors. In J. Barðdal and S. L. Chelliah (eds.), *The Role of Semantics, Pragmatic, and Discourse Factors in the Development of Case.* Amsterdam: John Benjamins, 347–373.

Bolonyai, A. 2007. (In) Vulnerable Agreement in Incomplete Bilingual L1 Learners. *International Journal of Bilingualism* 11(1), 3–23.

Borer H. 2013. *Structuring Sense: Volume III: Taking Form.* Oxford: Oxford University Press.

Bousquette, J. and M. T. Putnam. 2020. Reassessing Language Death: Evidence from Moribund Grammars. *Language Learning* 70(S1), 188–225.

Bybee, J. L., R. D. Perkins, and W. Pagliuca. 1994. *The Evolution of Grammar: Tense, Aspect, and Modality in the Languages of the World.* Chicago: University of Chicago Press.

Campbell, L. and M. C. Muntzel. 1989. The Structural Consequences of Language Death. In *Investigating Obsolescence: Studies in Language Contraction and Death.* Cambridge: Cambridge University Press, 181–196.

Carstairs-McCarthy, A. 2010. *The Evolution of Morphology.* Oxford: Oxford University Press.

Cinque, G. 1999. *Adverbs and Functional Heads: A Cross-Linguistic Perspective.* Oxford: Oxford University Press.

Croft, W. 2003. *Typology and Universals*, 2nd edition. Oxford: Oxford University Press.

Culicover. P. 2013. *Grammar & Complexity: Language at the Intersection of Competence and Performance*. Oxford: Oxford University Press.

De Reuse, W. J. 1994. Noun Incorporation in Lakota (Siouan). *International Journal of American Linguistics* 60(3), 199–260.

Dixon, R. M. and A. Y. Aikhenvald. 2002. Word: A Typological Framework. In R. M. Dixon and A. Y. Aikhenvald (eds.), *Word: A Cross-Linguistic Typology*. Cambridge: Cambridge University Press, 1–41.

Di Sciullo, A. M. and E. Edwin Williams. 1987. *On the Definition of Word*. Cambridge, MA: MIT Press.

Eikel, F. 1949. The Use of Cases in New Braunfels German. *American Speech* 24(4), 278–281.

Evans, N and H.-J. Sasse. 2002. *Problems of Polysynthesis*. Berlin: Akademie Verlag.

Fenyvesi, A. 2000. The Affectedness of the Verbal Complex in American Hungarian. In *Language Contact and the Verb Complex of Dutch and Hungarian*. Szeged: University of Szeged, 94–107.

Fernández-Dobao, A. and J. Herschensohn. 2019. Present Tense Verb Morphology on Spanish HL and L2 Children in Dual Immersion: Feature Reassembly Revisited. *Linguistic Approaches to Bilingualism*. Online First.

Filip, H. 1999. *Aspect, Eventuality Types, and Noun Phrase Semantics*. New York: Routledge.

Flores, C. 2015. Losing a Childhood Language: A Longitudinal Study on Language Attrition. *Journal of Child Language* 42, 562–590.

Flores, C. 2020. Attrition and Reactivation of a Childhood Language: The Case of Returnee Heritage Speakers. *Language Learning* 70(S1), 85–121.

Fortescue, M. 1994. Morphology Polysynthetic, In R. E. Asher (ed.), *The Encylopedia of Language and Linguistics*. Oxford: Pergamon, 2600–2602.

Gilbert, G. G. 1965. Dative vs. Accusative in the German Dialects of Central Texas. *Zeitschrift für Dialektologie und Linguistik* 32(3), 288.

Gollan, T. H., R. I. Montoya, C. Cera, and T. C. Sandoval. 2008. More Use almost always Means a Smaller Frequency Effect: Aging, Bilingualism, and the Weaker Links Hypothesis. *Journal of Memory and Language* 58(3), 787–814.

Gruzdeva, E. 2015. Sociolinguistic and Linguistic Outcomes of Nivkh-Russian Language Contact. *Language Empires in Comparative Perspective* 6, 153–181.

Gruzdeva, E. and N. Vakhtin. 2017. Language Obsolescence in Polysynthetic Languages. In M. Fortescue, M. Mithun, and N. Evans (eds.), *The Oxford Handbook of Polysynthesis*. Oxford: Oxford University Press, 428–448.

Haspelmath, M. 2011. The Indeterminacy of Word Segmentation and the Nature of Morphology and Syntax. *Folia Linguistica* 45(1), 31–80.

Hawkins, J. A. 2004. *Efficiency and Complexity in Grammars*. Oxford: Oxford University Press.

Huls, E. and A. van de Mond. 1992. Some Aspects of Language Attrition in Turkish Families in the Netherlands. In W. Fase, K. Jaspaert, and

S. Kroom (eds.), *Maintenance and Loss of Minority Languages*. Amsterdam: John Benjamins, 99–117.

Jia, L. and R. Bailey. 2008. The (re)acquisition of Perfective Aspect Marking by Chinese Heritage Language Learners. In A. W. He and Yun Xiao (eds.), *Chinese as a Heritage Language: Fostering Rooted World Citizenry*. Honolulu: University of Hawaii Mànoa, 205–224.

Johannessen, J. B. and J. C. Salmons, Forthcoming. Heritage Germanic. In M. Polinsky and S. Montrul (eds.), *The Cambridge Handbook of Heritage Languages*. Cambridge: Cambridge University Press.

Johnson, M. 2016. Object case assignment in heritage Finnish. Presentation. 7th Annual Workshop on Immigrant Languages in the Americas, Oct 2016.

Karayayla, T. 2018. Turkish as an Immigrant and Heritage Language in the UK: Effects of Exposure and Age at Onset of Bilingualism on Grammatical and Lexical Development of the First Language. PhD thesis, University of Essex.

Keine, S. 2007. Reanalyzing Hindi Split-Ergativity as a Morphological Phenomenon. *Linguistische Arbeitsberichte* 85, 73–127.

Kroll, J. F. and T. H. Gollan. 2014. Speech Planning in Two Languages: What Bilinguals Tell Us about Language Production. In M. Goldrick, V. Ferreira, and M. Miozzo (eds.), *The Oxford Handbook of Language Production*. Oxford: Oxford University Press, 165–181.

Laleko, O. 2008. Compositional Telicity and Heritage Russian Aspect. *Proceedings of the Thirty-Eighth Western Conference on Linguistics (WECOL)* 19, 150–160.

Laleko, O. 2010. The Syntax-Pragmatics Interface in Language Loss: Covert Restructuring of Aspect in Heritage Russian. PhD thesis, University of Minnesota.

Laleko, O. 2018. What Is Difficult about Grammatical Gender? Evidence from Heritage Russian. *Journal of Language Contact* 11(2), 233–267.

Laleko, O. 2019. Resolving Indeterminacy in Gender Agreement: Comparing Heritage Speakers and L2 Learners of Russian. *Heritage Language Journal* 16(2), 151–182.

Laleko, O. and M. Polinsky. 2017. Silence Is Difficult: On Missing Elements in Bilingual Grammars. *Zeitschrift für Sprachwissenschaft* 36(1), 135–163.

Lohndal, T. 2014. *Phrase Structure and Argument Structure: A Case Study of the Syntax-Semantics Interface*. Oxford: Oxford University Press.

Łyskawa, P. and N. Nagy. 2020. Case Marking Variation in Heritage Slavic Languages in Toronto: Not So Different. *Language Learning* 70(S1), 122–156.

Marantz, A. 1997. No Escape from Syntax: Don't Try Morphological Analysis in the Privacy of Your Own Lexicon. *University of Pennsylvania Working Papers in Linguistics* 4(2), 200–225.

Ming, T. and H. Tao. 2008. Developing a Chinese Heritage Language Corpus: Issues and a Preliminary Report. In A. W. He and Y. Xiao (eds.), *Chinese as a Heritage Language: Fostering Rooted World Citizenry*. Honolulu: University of Hawaii Mànoa, 167–188.

Mithun, M. 1984. The Evolution of Noun Incorporation. *Language* 60(4), 847–894.

Mithun, M. 1989. The Incipient Obsolescence of Polysynthesis: Cayuga in Ontario and Oklahoma. In N. C. Dorian (ed.), *Investigating Obsolescence: Studies in Language Contraction and Death*. Cambridge: Cambridge University Press, 243–257.

Montrul, S. 2004. Subject and Object Expression in Spanish Heritage Speakers: A Case of Morpho-syntactic Convergence. *Bilingualism: Language and Cognition* 7, 125–142.

Montrul, S. 2008. *Incomplete Acquisition in Bilingualism: Re-examining the Age Factor*. Amsterdam: John Benjmains.

Montrul, S. 2016. *The Acquisition of Heritage Languages*. Cambridge: Cambridge University Press.

Montrul, S. and M. A. Bowles. 2009. Back to Basics: Differential Object Marking under Incomplete Acquisition in Spanish Heritage Speakers. *Bilingualism: Language and Cognition* 12(3), 363–383.

Montrul, S. and K. Potowski. 2007. Command of Gender Agreement in School-Age Spanish-English Bilingual Children. *International Journal of Bilingualism* 11(3), 301–328.

Montrul, S., R. M. Bhatt, and A. Bhatia. 2012. Erosion of Case and Agreement in Hindi Heritage Speakers. *Linguistic Approaches to Bilingualism* 2(2), 141–176.

Montrul, S., R. M. Bhatt, and R. Girju. 2015. Differential Object Marking in Spanish, Hindi, and Romanian as Heritage Languages. *Language* 91(3), 564–610.

Montrul, S., R. Foote, and S. Perpiñán. 2008. Gender Agreement in Adult Second Language Learners and Spanish Heritage Speakers: The Effects of Age and Context of Acquisition. *Language Learning* 58(3), 503–553.

Montrul, S., A. Bhatia, R. M. Bhatt, and V. Puri. 2019. Case Marking in Hindi as the Weaker Language. *Frontiers in Psychology* 10(461).

Mühlhäuser, P. 1974. *Pidginization and Simplification of Language*. Canberra: Austrailian National University.

Muravyova, I. A. 2004. Tipologija Incorporatsii [The Typology of Incorporation]. Habilitationsschrift (MS). University of Moscow.

Newell, H., M. Noonan, G. Piggott, and L. D. Travis. 2017. Introduction. In H. Newell, M. Noonan, G. Piggot, and L. D. Travis (eds.), *The Structure of Words at the Interfaces*. Oxford: Oxford University Press, 1–19.

Nützel, D. and J. Salmons. 2011. Language Contact and New Dialect Formation: Evidence from German in North America. *Language and Linguistics Compass* 5(10), 705–717.

Ortega, L. 2014. Ways Forward for a Bi/Multilingual Turn in SLA. In S. May (ed.), *The Multilingual Turn: Implications for SLA, TESOL, and Bilingual Education*. New York: Routledge, 32–53.

Pascual y Cabo, D. 2013. Agreement Reflexes of Emerging Optionality in Heritage Speaker Spanish. PhD thesis, University of Florida.

Payne, T. E. 1997. *Describing Morphosyntax: A Guide for Field Linguists*. Cambridge: Cambridge University Press.

Pfaff, C. W. 1993. Turkish Language Development in Germany. In G. Extra and L. T. Verhoeven (eds.), *Immigrant Languages in Europe*. Bristol: Multilingual Matters, 119–146.

Polinsky, M. 1995. Cross-Linguistic Parallels in Language Loss. *Southwest Journal of Linguistics* 14(1–2), 87–123.

Polinsky, M. 2006. Incomplete Acquisition: American Russian. *Journal of Slavic Linguistics* 14(2), 161–219.

Polinsky, M. 2008. Without Aspect. In G. Corbett and M. Noonan (eds.), *Case and Grammatical Relations*. Oxford: Oxford University Press, 263–282.

Polinsky, M. 2018. *Heritage Languages and Their Speakers*. Cambridge: Cambridge University Press.

Polinsky, M. and G. Scontras. 2020. Understanding Heritage Languages. *Bilingualism: Language and Cognition* 23(1), 4–20.

Putnam, M. T. and B. Árnbjörnsdóttir. 2015. Minimizing (Interface) Domains: The Loss of Long-Distance Binding in North American Icelandic. In B. R. Page and M. T. Putnam (eds.), *Moribund Germanic Heritage Languages in North America*. Leiden: Brill, 203–223.

Putnam, M. T. and L. Sánchez. 2013. What's So Incomplete about Incomplete Acquisition? A Prolegomenon to Modeling Heritage Language Grammars. *Linguistic Approaches to Bilingualism* 3(4), 478–508.

Putnam, M. T., M. Carlson, and D. Reitter. 2018. Integrated, Not Isolated: Defining Typological Proximity in an Integrated Multilingual Architecture. *Frontiers in Psychology* 8(2212).

Putnam, M. T., D. Pascual y Cabo, and T. Kupisch. 2018. Different Situations, Similar Outcomes: Heritage Grammars across the Lifespan. In F. Bayram, N. Denhovska, D. Miller, J. Rothman, and L. Serratrice (eds.), *Bilingual Cognition and Language: The State of the Science across Its Subfields*. Amsterdam: John Benjamins, 251–279.

Ramchand, G. and P. Svenonius. 2014. Deriving the Functional Hierarchy. *Language Sciences* 46, 152–174.

Riksem, B. R. 2017. Language Mixing and Diachronic Change: American Norwegian Noun Phrases Then and Now. *Languages* 2(3).

Romaine, S. 1995. *Bilingualism*, 2nd edition. Oxford: Blackwell.

Rothman, J. and J. Treffers-Daller. 2014. A Prolegomenon to the Construct of the Native Speaker: Heritage Speaker Bilinguals Are Natives Too! *Applied Linguistics* 35(1), 93–98.

Schwarz, L. S. 2019. (In)Stability in Heritage Germanic: Examining the Role of Form and Function. PhD thesis, Penn State University.

Scontras, G., M. Polinsky, and Z. Fuchs. 2015. Heritage Language and Linguistic Theory. *Frontiers in Psychology* 6(1545).

Scontras, G., M. Polinsky, and Z. Fuchs. 2018. In Support of Representational Economy: Agreement in Heritage Spanish. *Glossa* 3(1), 1–29.

Sherkina-Lieber, M. 2015. Tense, Aspect, and Agreement in Heritage Labrador Inuttitut: Do Receptive Bilinguals Understand Functional Morphology? *Linguistic Approaches to Bilingualism* 5(1), 30–61.

Silva-Corvalán, C. 1994. *Language Contact and Change: Spanish in Los Angeles*. Oxford: Oxford University Press.

Silva-Corvalán, C. 2014. *Bilingual Language Acquisition: Spanish and English in the First Six Years*. Cambridge: Cambridge University Press.

Sorace, A. and F. Filiaci. 2006. Anaphora Resolution in Near-Native Speakers of Italian. *Second Language Research* 22(3), 339–368.

Spencer, A. 1995. Incorporation in Chukchi. *Language* 71(3), 439–489.

Svenonius, P. 2016. Spans and Words. In D. Siddiqi and H. Harley (eds.), *Morphological Metatheory*. Amsterdam: John Benjamins, 201–222.

Tóth, G. 2007. *Linguistic Interference and First-Language Attrition: German and Hungarian in the San Francisco Bay Area*. Frankfurt: Peter Lang.

Treffers-Daller, J., A. S. Ozsoy, and R. van Hout. 2007. (In)complete Acquisition of Turkish among Turkish-English Bilinguals in Germany and Turkey: An Analysis of Complex Embeddings in Narratives. *International Journal of Bilingual Education and Bilingualism* 10(3), 248–276.

Wei, L. and S. Lee. 2001. L1 Development in an l2 Environment: The Use of Cantonese Classifiers and Quantifiers by Young British-Born Chinese in Tyneside. *International Journal of Bilingual Education and Bilingualism* 4, 359–382.

Wiltschko, M. 2014. *The Universal Structure of Categories: Towards a Formal Typology*. Cambridge: Cambridge University Press.

Woodbury, A. C. 1975. Onondaga Noun Incorporation: Some Notes on the Interdependence of Syntax and Semantics. *International Journal of American Linguistics* 41(1), 10–20.

Woodbury, A. C. 2002. The Word in Cup'ik. In R. M. W. Dixon and A. Aikhenvald (eds.), *Word: A Cross-linguistic Typology*. Cambridge: Cambridge University Press, 79–99.

Yager L., N. Hellmold, H.-A. Joo, M. T. Putnam, E. Rossi, C. Stafford, and J. Salmons. 2015. New Structural Patterns in Moribund Grammar: Case Marking in Heritage German. *Frontiers in Psychology* 6(1716).

Zyzik, E. 2020. Creativity and Conventionality in Heritage Language Bilingualism. *Language Learning* 70(S1), 157–187.

25

Syntax of Heritage Languages

Terje Lohndal

25.1 Introduction[*]

The topic of the present chapter is the syntax of heritage languages. Heritage speakers are native speakers with grammatical representations based on the same principles as all other languages (Rothman 2009: 156; Rothman and Treffers-Daller 2014: 95; Polinsky 2018: 9). That is, even though the representational outcomes may be different,[1] we expect that the grammatical competence of heritage speakers is based on the same principles and constraints as the grammatical competence of all other native speakers: Their grammars are construed along the same principles that enable humans to acquire language (often called Universal Grammar in formal approaches to language; see, e.g., Chomsky 1972, 1975). This requires a broader concept of nativeness than the standard monolingual speaker (as, e.g., defined in Chomsky 1965; see Lohndal 2013 and Polinsky 2018: 27 for discussion). Nevertheless, the fact that these speakers are bilinguals with a clearly defined dominant language suggests that their grammars may exhibit certain hallmarks. A lot of research into the syntax of heritage speakers has been and is concerned with these hallmarks and how they differ from a given baseline. The fact that these speakers are

[*] I am grateful to Maria Polinsky and Silvina Montrul for the invitation to contribute to this volume, and for their comments and stimulating discussions. I am also grateful to Artemis Alexiadou and Merete Anderssen for comments on previous versions. Special thanks to Tania Ionin and Michael T. Putnam for extensive and very helpful comments. This chapter was completed as part of the international research project *MultiGender* at the Centre for Advanced Study at the Norwegian Academy of Science and Letters during the academic year 2019–2020.

[1] Polinsky (2018) shows that there are instances where heritage speakers more strongly resemble L2 speakers than L1 speakers. Montrul, Bhatia, Bhatt, and Puri (2019) also argue that it is not always straightforward to distinguish heritage grammars from the grammar of L2 speakers in the domain of morphosyntax. But facts like these do not mean that heritage speakers are not native speakers of their heritage language, it just means that their representations in some cases resemble L1 speakers and in others L2 speakers.

native speakers of their variety does not prevent comparisons with such a baseline, as we will discuss in more detail in Section 25.2.1.

Polinsky (2018: 222–223) highlights two main observations when it comes to the syntax of heritage languages. The first is that certain properties are resilient, whereas others are quite vulnerable, compared to a given baseline. The second is that there is a substantial amount of uniformity in the syntax across heritage languages, and these languages seem to differ "from their respective baseline grammars in comparable ways" (Polinsky 2018: 223). We will see this quite clearly when we turn to the case studies in Sections 25.3 and 25.4. As such, heritage grammars provide a different kind of testing ground for studying the relationship between nature and nurture, in particular in developing better models of universal aspects of language design and the relationship between input quantity and quality (Lohndal, Rothman, Kupisch, and Westergaard 2019).

The structure of this chapter is as follows. Section 25.2 is a preamble that discusses certain theoretical issues that are necessary to clarify before we look at some hallmarks of the syntax of heritage speakers and their languages. There are many ways in which one can structure such an overview. Here, we follow Polinsky and Scontras (2020) who divide the domains of interest into two categories: Resilient and vulnerable. We look at resilient syntactic rules in Section 25.3 before turning to vulnerable rules in Section 25.4, while keeping in mind that this two-way distinction is not always clear-cut. Section 24.5 provides a summary and concluding remarks.

25.2 Preamble: Baseline, Differences, and Syntax vs. Morphology

Before we can embark on a discussion of the central issues concerning the syntax of heritage speakers, we need to consider several theoretical questions. One concerns the question of what the appropriate baseline is, that is, what we compare the syntax of heritage speakers against. The other is whether and how to distinguish between syntax and morphology.

25.2.1 The Question of Baseline and Linguistic Differences

A lot of work on heritage languages and heritage speakers has tended to emphasize the ways in which these are different from a baseline. That is also the case for syntax: Most papers have focused on whether or not heritage speakers are similar to the baseline, mostly finding that they are different, raising the question of how and why they differ. However, the question of the baseline is extremely important in work on heritage speakers. Often, scholars compare the linguistic competence of a heritage

Table 25.1 *Relevant groups of comparison for studying heritage language speakers (Polinsky 2018: 16).*

	Immigrant setting	Homeland (if available)
Baseline	First-generation immigrants/ monolingual speakers in diaspora	Age-matched homeland speakers or age-matched speakers at the time of emigration
Adult heritage speakers	Second- and subsequent-generation bilinguals	NA
Child heritage speakers	Second- and subsequent-generation bilinguals	Age-matched and younger homeland speakers

speaker against that of a monolingual speaker of the same variety as the heritage speaker. If the heritage language is Spanish, the comparison would then be monolingual speakers of Spanish. However, this is inadequate (Bley-Vroman 1983; Cook 1997), since the input to the heritage speaker typically would not be monolingual Spanish. Rather, the baseline should be the input provided to the heritage speakers, be it the diaspora baseline (the language of first-generation immigrants) or the language spoken by later generations of immigrants. Put simply, the baseline is the language that serves as the input to the child acquiring the language (Benmamoun et al. 2013; Polinsky 2018; Madsen 2018). Polinsky (2018) provides a helpful table of the relevant comparison groups (Table 25.1).

Compared to a relevant baseline, for a given linguistic property there are at least four possible outcomes, listed in (1) (from Polinsky 2018: 18).

(1)　　a.　No difference
　　　　b.　Transfer from the dominant language
　　　　c.　Attrition across the lifespan
　　　　d.　Divergent attainment

Let us consider each of these in turn, albeit only briefly as they will all resurface in discussions of individual phenomena. The case of no difference at all is rare in heritage speakers, although as we will see in later sections, whether or not there is a difference depends on the domain of the grammar being investigated. It is impossible to make an overarching claim regarding difference as this has to be relativized to specific linguistic properties (Polinsky 2018: 18). Transfer (or cross-linguistic influence) are cases where a pattern from the dominant language is used in another language that does not exhibit the same pattern (in the same way; see also Aboh 2015).[2] In general, transfer has mostly been seen in individuals whose dominant language is English, although this is arguably due to transfer mostly being

---

[2] Rothman, Gonzalez Alonso, and Puig-Mayenco (2019) argue that transfer and cross-linguistic influence should be separated. Since such a distinction won't matter much for what follows, the text will treat them as equivalent for present purposes. See also Muysken (2019) on the role of transfer in heritage languages.

studied in individuals with English as their dominant language. Attrition is defined as follows by Seliger (1996: 616): "the temporary or permanent loss of language ability as reflected in a speaker's performance or in their inability to make grammaticality judgments that would be consistent with native speaker monolinguals of the same age and stage of language development." If adult heritage speakers do not have a property that younger bilingual children have, attrition or loss is often invoked (de Bot 1990; Yukawa 1997; Köpke 1999, 2004, 2007; Isurin 2000; Sorace 2000; Montrul 2002, 2008, 2016; Tsimpli et al. 2004; Tsimpli 2017; Schmid and Köpke 2007, 2017; Bylund 2009; Polinsky 2011, 2016, 2018; Schmid 2011; Iverson 2012, Pascual y Cabo and Rothman 2012; Montrul and Sánchez-Walker 2013; Putnam and Sánchez 2013).[3] Lastly, we have the concept of divergent attainment or arrested development. Polinsky (2006) and Montrul (2008) originally developed this idea under the rubric of "incomplete acquisition" (see also Silva-Corvalán 2018), which means that the reason for a different end-state grammar is that a pattern was not fully acquired (especially so for patterns that were known to be late-acquired by monolinguals). However, this term has been widely criticized for a variety of reasons (see Pascual y Cabo and Rothman 2012; Putnam and Sánchez 2013; Kupisch, Lein, Barton, and Schröder 2014; Kupisch and Rothman 2018; Otheguy 2016; Polinsky 2018). The term is discussed more fully in the Preface to this handbook and the reader is referred to this discussion. Here it is important to highlight that "the grammar heritage speakers come up with is internally consistent, and, as such, complete, yet in a number of ways different from the grammar of the baseline" (Polinsky 2018: 28). Put differently, the grammar is systematic, and a divergent pattern is also systematic. This relates to a proposal by Lohndal and Westergaard (2016), who suggest that divergence is systematic and attrition may be unsystematic. The latter may also suggest that attrition is more directly associated with performance-type issues. Crucially, looking for differences between a heritage grammar and some relevant baseline does not at all entail a deficiency-based approach to heritage speakers and their languages.

25.2.2   Syntax vs. Morphology and How to Tease Them Apart

Distinguishing between syntax and morphology is not a trivial task. Various theories of syntax and morphology take different stands on how they relate to each other (e.g., Carstairs-McCarthy's 1992 overview, the

---

[3] Bylund (2009) highlights the ways in which attrition in adults and in children may behave differently. In adults, attrition is primarily seen in syntactic violations (Schmid 2002), whereas in children, attrition affects the linguistic system more generally: case marking (Polinsky 1997), verb morphology (Seliger 1991; Turian and Altenberg 1991), disintegration of aspectual contrasts (Montrul 2002), and the syntax-morphology of mood selection (Perez-Cortes 2016; Perez-Cortes, Putnam and Sánchez 2019).

contributions to Spencer and Zwicky 1998; Hippisley and Stump 2014, and the discussion in Ackema and Neeleman 2004; Julien 2002; Borer 2005a, b; Caha 2009; Embick 2010, 2015; Matushansky and Marantz 2013). Space does not allow us to consider these here; rather the purpose is to show that it may sometimes be difficult to diagnose whether or not a particular linguistic property belongs to syntax or to morphology (compare also Polinsky 2008: 222).[4]

Let us consider the following case study. Riksem (2017) discusses changes in the grammar of heritage speakers of American Norwegian, the heritage language stemming from Norwegians who moved to the United States generally in the nineteenth century (see Haugen 1953). Riksem looks at nominal morphology and she compares data from the speakers in Haugen (1953) with a subset of the speakers in the Corpus of American Nordic Speech (CANS; Johannessen 2015b). She finds two main patterns: (i) Omission of functional suffixes, both in plural and/or definite noun phrases (ii) an increased usage of functional exponents from English. Two main hypotheses are presented in order to account for these changes: The syntactic structure could be intact and the changes are due to a change in the morphophonological exponents. Alternatively, the syntactic structure itself may have changed. The former analysis relies on a model within second language acquisition called the Missing Surface Inflection Hypothesis (MSIH), proposed by Lardiere (2000, 2009) and Prévost and White (2000); see also Putnam, Perez-Cortes, and Sánchez (2019). This model holds that there is no one-to-one relationship between overt morphological exponents and the underlying syntactic heads. Rather, there can be discrepancies, either because the learner has not acquired the relevant exponents, or because the matching conditions between the syntactic structure and the exponents are not met. A fundamental claim is that a learner would rather omit a form than produce the wrong form (Lardiere 2000). However, as Riksem (2017: 21) discusses, the MSIH does not make clear predictions concerning where and how inflection may go missing, making it possible for avoidance to explain any instance where the syntax and the morphophonology do not align according to a given baseline. For this reason, and due to properties of the data, Riksem (2017) favors the second hypothesis whereby the syntactic structure itself is the culprit for the diachronic changes. It should be noted, though, that the two hypotheses are not mutually exclusive, again demonstrating how difficult it can be to claim that the locus of a given change toward a baseline is squarely within syntax or squarely within morphology. For that reason, the reader should consult Putnam, Schwarz, and Hoffman (2021) alongside the present chapter. As

[4] The same argument can be made concerning syntax and information structure, see Laleko (2021) for a comparable discussion.

much as possible, we will try to only focus on core syntactic phenomena in what follows, but as the reader will see in the next section, it is not always straightforward to locate the true source of the behavior.

25.3   Resilient Syntactic Properties

In general, core syntax is resilient toward change across heritage languages. Benmamoun, Montrul, and Polinsky (2013: 148) put it as follows:

> Syntactic knowledge, particularly the knowledge of phrase structure and word order, appears to be more resilient to incomplete acquisition under reduced input conditions than inflectional morphology is. There is a tendency for heritage language speakers to retain the basic, perhaps universal, core structural properties of their language.

What the "basic, perhaps universal, core structural properties" of language are is an ongoing research topic. Nevertheless, the fact that some areas are highly resilient despite reduced access to input can be used to probe the nature of these core properties of language. The distinction between the core and the periphery originates with Chomsky (1981). Here, core rules of grammar are determined by principles and parameters, themselves part of Universal Grammar. The periphery consists of "marked" phenomena, such as irregularities and exceptions more generally. As Chomsky and Lasnik (1993: 510) put it: "A reasonable approach would be to focus attention to the core system, putting aside phenomena that result from historical accident, dialect mixture, personal idiosyncrasies, and the like." Currently, the core consists (at least) of syntactic features and syntactic operations (e.g., Merge, Agree, Spell-Out). As Lohndal, Rothman, Kupisch, and Westergaard (2019) point out, research on heritage grammars has contributed a range of important results when it comes to core properties. Notably, across the literature, there is an adherence to what we may label "default" strategies in the acquisition and development of heritage grammars (Polinsky 2018). For example, the basic word order is mostly robust, whereas the noncanonical ones are not (Montrul 2016). We still need a better understanding what a default pattern is, including the cross-linguistic ramifications of default patterns (see Polinsky and Scontras 2020 and Putnam 2020).

Looking beyond core syntax, work on first language attrition has shown that, whereas syntactic features are intact, semantic and/or pragmatic features are vulnerable (Tsimpli et al. 2004).[5] In general, the syntax–semantics interface is considered to be less vulnerable than the

---

[5] However, Iverson and Miller (2017) argue that syntactic features also can be affected by reduced exposure. Furthermore, similar effects are seen for word order in general, to which we return in Section 25.4.

syntax–pragmatics interface (Sorace 2011; Polinsky 2018). However, not that much research has been done on the syntax–semantics interface. In reviewing this literature, Polinsky (2018: 270–273) shows that those heritage speakers who have been studied appear to observe the binding principles (Chomsky 1981; Büring 2005) pretty much like the baseline speakers. However, unlike the baseline, the structural and linear distance between the binder and the anaphor matters for how well they observe the principles (see also Ionin 2021). Greater distance means that they are less target-like, which is an effect that we also see in the area of agreement and morphological dependencies more generally (see Montrul 2016; Polinsky 2018; Putnam, Schwarz, and Hoffman 2021).

Summarizing, the general picture is that core syntax is quite resilient toward change. In what follows, we will look more closely at a few examples of this. We will first consider parts of speech, then passivization, before turning to a more extended discussion of Verb Second.

25.3.1 Lexical Categories

Polinsky (2018) argues that the distinctions between various parts of speech, notably verbs, nouns, and adjectives, are relatively stable across heritage languages. Heritage speakers do not, say, collapse everything into one lexical category. Rather, they maintain the distinctions that are in the baseline. However, that is not to say that they maintain the distinctions *in the same way*. Polinsky (2005) argues that nouns and verbs are represented and also maintained differently. She conducted a lexical decision-task whereby both heritage speakers and speakers of the baseline Russian heard items from the three lexical categories: verbs, nouns, and adjectives. These were distributed across three frequency ranges based on the frequency dictionary by Brown (1996). Eleven items from each range were selected for each class, yielding thirty-three items across three classes that were all matched in frequency and word length. Unsurprisingly, Polinsky found that the baseline speakers were faster and they had the same response times across the three classes. There was no significant effect of frequency. The heritage speakers behaved quite differently: They were much faster for verbs than for the two other classes, adjectives being the weakest class. Polinsky argues that heritage speakers have selective control of word classes, and in particular, they show a clear verb bias. This is not surprising given that we know that nominal morphology generally is less resilient than verbal morphology in heritage languages (Benmamoun et al. 2013; Polinsky 2018: ch. 5). Polinsky (2018: 227) shows that a frequency explanation for the verb bias does not work; rather, the size of the word classes may be a more essential part of the explanation: About 18 percent of the Russian lexicon consists of verbs, whereas 48 percent is made up of nouns. Such factors also clearly suggest that different heritage languages may have different biases, and so far, too little work has been done on this to provide robust cross-linguistic generalizations.

25.3.2   The Passive

Turning from lexical categories to another area of grammar, Putnam and Salmons (2013) study how heritage speakers in Kansas use the German passive (see Polinsky 2018: 237–238 for a comparable study of heritage Russian speakers). Their variety is labeled Moundridge Schweitzer German (Eastern Palatinate in origin), and the variety was established by migrants settling in Freeman, South Dakota, and Moundridge, Kansas, starting in 1874. This is a small population, consisting of roughly fifty remaining speakers, and Putnam and Salmons (2013) study ten of them. These ten speakers did not produce passives spontaneously, but by using a translation task it was possible to elicit them. Importantly, in a comprehension experiment, speakers accepted the relevant passive constructions, suggesting that the knowledge of the passive is indeed present in these heritage speakers (Putnam and Salmons 2013: 239) as a grammar that generates the relevant structural representations (Putnam and Salmons 2013: 245). If so, then heritage speakers are able to retain the rules underlying the passive, but "[t]heir poor performance has to do with morphological difficulties, not ignorance of the operations involved in A-chains" (Polinsky 2018: 238). This general observation may extend to A-movement more generally, as Polinsky and Scontras (2020) speculate.

25.3.3   Verb Second

The last example of a resilient property is Verb Second (V2), which is to say that the finite verb has to appear in the second position (Holmberg and Platzack 1995; Vikner 1995; Holmberg 2015). Ever since Håkansson's (1995) seminal study, V2 has been a favorite topic when it comes to work on Germanic heritage languages. Håkansson studied five bilingual expatriate (heritage) speakers who all had slightly different backgrounds. Three of them grew up in the United States using English at school and Swedish or Norwegian at home. One grew up in France learning Swedish and French, and lastly, one grew up in both Sweden and France acquiring both Swedish and French. These speakers were studying Swedish as a second language in Sweden at the time they were tested. The main finding is that, whereas noun phrase morphology has undergone attrition, word order has not. One of the areas Håkansson investigated is V2. She labeled V2 errors "XSV patterns," that is, patterns whereby an initial constituent is followed by the subject and then the verb. In her study, she compared the heritage speakers to L2 learners of Swedish, and a striking difference emerged: The

L2 learners frequently made V2 mistakes, whereas only one of the heritage speakers made one such mistake. Håkansson (1995: 160) argues that her findings suggest that "the V2 rule resists attrition."

Additional evidence for the resilience of V2 comes from Schmid's (2002) study. She studied the grammar of fifty-four German Jews. During the Nazi regime, they emigrated to England and the United States. Schmid's corpus has 5050 sentences requiring V2 word order, and only 2 percent (102/5050) displayed an error in V2. However, the total number of subject-initial sentences is not provided, and we also do not know if some of the speakers displayed a more English-like word order.

Another study by Hopp and Putnam (2015) investigates word order in Moundridge Schweitzer German, the same population as discussed in Section 25.3.2. Hopp and Putnam (2015) collected both production data and acceptability judgment data. They find that in both production and acceptability judgments, V2 is retained in matrix clauses. Interestingly, in embedded clauses, there is more variation. In particular, in embedded clauses introduced by the complementizer *dass* 'that' (2) and by *weil* 'because' (3), the word order is predominantly V2.

(2)   ... dass da Lieber Gott hot uns auch net alles   genomm wie dat in
      Oklahoma
      that the dear   God has us   also not everything taken   like there in O.
      'that the dear God hasn't taken everything away from us like in
      Oklahoma.' (Participant 102; Hopp and Putnam 2015: 195)

(3)   ... weil ich duh   net Hochdeutsch redde
      because I   do/can not High.German talk
      'because I can't speak standard German'   (Participant 103; Hopp and
      Putnam 2015: 195)

Hopp and Putnam (2015: 203) argue that there "is little to no evidence in the production data that English SVO word order has affected [Moundridge Schweitzer German]." Rather, they argue that "the combination of lesser use or activation of [Moundridge Schweitzer German] and cross-linguistic influence from English which does not instantiate asymmetric word order in main and subordinate clause contexts leads to a particular type of leveling of word order distinctions across clause types within the constraints afforded by German syntax" (Hopp and Putnam 2015: 206). They also speculate that the changes in Moundridge Schweitzer German may be an instance of what they call "typological drift" – since modern German is also developing options for licensing V2 in certain embedded clauses.

It should be noted that similar asymmetries are also observed in other heritage varieties, notably heritage Norwegian and Swedish. See Larsson and Johannessen (2015a,b) and Johannessen and Salmons (2021) for further discussion. More generally, there has recently been a lot of research into V2 in Germanic heritage varieties. Strømsvåg (2013), Eide and Hjelde (2015, 2018), Johannessen (2015a), Khayitova (2016), Alexiadou and Lohndal (2018), and Westergaard and Lohndal (2019) look at Norwegian (based on the Corpus of American Nordic Speech (CANS); Johannessen 2015b), Kühl and Heegård (2018) consider Danish, Larsson and Johannessen (2015a and b) Swedish, and lastly, Arnbjörnsdottir, Thrainsson, and Nowenstein (2018) study Icelandic. Generalizing across these languages, the main finding aligns with Håkansson (1995) and Hopp and Putnam (2015): V2 is generally intact in matrix clauses. Individual speakers may occasionally violate it, and some may also violate it more generally, which tends to align with fluency (Johannessen and Salmons, 2021). Westergaard and Lohndal (2019) find that the number of contexts for V2 word order also may be severely reduced, where the relevant context is non–subject-initial declaratives like in (4a), as opposed to subject-initial clauses, which structurally overlap with SVO (4b).

(4)   a.   På mandag kjøpte John mange bøker.   Norwegian
           on Monday bought John many books
           'On Monday, John bought many books.'

      b.   John kjøpte mange bøker på mandag.
           John bought many books on Monday
           'John bought many books on Monday.'

Typically, V2 languages have a higher degree of non–subject-initial declaratives in spontaneous speech, whereas languages like English mostly have subject-initial declaratives. Westergaard and Lohndal find that there is a correlation between the loss of V2 and the loss of contexts that trigger V2: the fewer the contexts a speaker produces, the less V2 the speaker produces. Furthermore, they argue, like Hopp and Putnam (2015), that a likely reason for this development is cross-linguistic influence from the speaker's dominant language, English. The pragmatic structure of English is more deeply entrenched, leading the speakers to let it override the acquired structure for Norwegian. However, as Westergaard and Lohndal point out, another possible analysis is that SVO order "is chosen because it is less complex than non–subject-initial declaratives and also leads to greater word order rigidity" (Westergaard and Lohndal 2019: 98). Scholars have suggested that there is such a "default strategy" in Russian and Spanish (Benmamoun et al. 2013; Scontras et al. 2015; Polinsky and Scontras 2020). In these cases, the dominant language is also English, making it impossible to argue in favor of one or the other account.

   Taken together, even though V2 is remarkably stable, we see that whatever syntactic feature is responsible for deriving V2 (see Holmberg 2015 for comprehensive discussion; see also Johannessen and Salmons, 2021, for additional discussion of V2 in heritage grammars), this feature can be attrited, most likely due to reduced exposure. The outcome may in part be determined either through cross-linguistic influence or through heritage speakers resorting to default strategies.

25.4   Vulnerable Syntactic Rules

Even though heritage speakers are able to retain a lot of core grammatical properties, there are also properties that are retained to a lesser degree. For example, even though they maintain abstract knowledge of A-bar movement, notably *wh*-question formation and relativization, this knowledge is rather limited. In this section, we will look at examples of syntactic rules that are vulnerable, in particular, word order, long-distance dependencies, and discontinuous elements. Other phenomena that have a clear syntactic component can also be vulnerable, but these are discussed elsewhere in this handbook: See Laleko (2021) on null forms, and Ionin (2021) on quantifier raising and quantifier ambiguities.

25.4.1   Word Order

Polinsky (2018: 273) argues that "[. . .] word order appears to be a more vulnerable domain, subject to general change and sometimes to transfer [. . .]." Languages that allow multiple word orders generally allow fewer possibilities in the heritage language. However, many studies investigate speakers whose dominant language is English, which has rather strict restrictions on word order, and they often find that there is transfer of word order properties from English. However, there are also cases demonstrating that transfer is not the entire answer. Let us look at one of these in some detail.

   Albirini, Benmamoun, and Saadah (2011) report on a production study of SVO versus VSO in two groups of heritage speakers of Egyptian and Palestinian Arabic, each consisting of ten participants. The groups were somewhat heterogeneous in terms of the background of the participants and which language they self-identified as their L1. For example, all of the Palestinian heritage speakers still speak Arabic at home, whereas eight of the Egyptian heritage speakers do the same. The heritage speakers were compared to ten native speakers of Egyptian Arabic and Palestinian Arabic, respectively, who all came to the United States as adults. For word order, Albirini, Benmamoun, and Saadah (2011) find that the heritage speakers were split in their behavior: The Egyptian heritage speakers predominantly use SVO (77.65 percent), and they use it more than the native speaker baseline (52.24 percent). However, the Palestinian heritage speakers are different: They use SVO less than the baseline speakers, 19.73 percent compared to 29.34 percent, although this difference is not statistically significant. The authors speculate that "The prevalence of SVO in the speech of the Egyptian groups versus the Palestinian groups may be attributed to word order differences between the Egyptian and Palestinian dialects of Arabic" (Albirini et al. 2011: 281). However, as the authors also say, it may also be that the Egyptian heritage speakers somehow are more prone to transfer from English.

The Egyptian heritage speakers seem to avoid using VSO, which can be seen by speakers shifting to SVO after they have started a sentence with a verb. The example in (5) illustrates this (Albirini et al. 2011: 281).

(5) marra   laʔi   laʔeit ... huwwa   laʔi   ʔizaz   ʔaw   ħaga   zay   kida
     Once   found   found.1s   he   found   bottle   or   thing   like   that
     'One time he found ... found ... he found a bottle or something like that.'

This example also illustrates the speaker's uncertainty about verbal inflection or about subject–verb agreement. In (5), the correct form is not used the first time, and then the speaker replaces it with another incorrect form, before repeating the first form when using SVO word order. For Palestinian heritage speakers, the extensive use of VSO cannot be attributed to transfer from English. Presumably, VSO is dominant in baseline Palestinian Arabic, in which case overgeneralization or cross-linguistic overcorrection (Kupisch 2014) may account for heritage speakers' tendency to over-use VSO. However, additional studies on different language pairs, notably with a different dominant language, are sorely needed to better understand exactly when and how word order may be vulnerable in heritage speakers.

25.4.2 Long-Distance Dependencies

Heritage speakers often struggle with long-distance dependencies, such as antecedent-gap relations in the case of *wh*-movement or relative clauses. Relative clauses are one of the most heavily studied A-bar dependencies and there is no space here to do justice to the rich literature on the topic; see Polinsky (2018: 241–248 for a thorough review). Here we will consider an example based on Polinsky's (2011) study of the comprehension of relative clauses in monolingual and bilingual children (ages 6;0–7;0) and adults. She investigates English and Russian, where relative clauses in both languages are formed by creating an antecedent-gap relation. In Russian, there is a relative pronoun *kotor-*, which agrees with the extracted constituent in gender and number. Furthermore, this pronoun exhibits case concord with the gap site. Examples of a subject gap and an object gap are provided in (6) and (7) (setting aside different possible word order permutations).

(6)   sobak-a₁ [kotor-aja __₁ ukusila košk-u] SUBJECT GAP
        dog-NOM which-NOM   bit   cat-ACC
        'the dog that bit the cat.'

(7)   sobak-a₁ [kotor-uju __₁ukusila košk-a] OBJECT GAP
        dog-NOMwhich-ACC   bit   cat-NOM
        'the dog that the cat bit.'   (Polinsky 2018: 245)

Both the child-language groups and the monolingual adults achieved more than 90 percent accuracy on both subject and object relative clauses. However, the adult heritage group struggled, and they struggled with object relatives. Rather than associating the antecedent with an object gap, the speakers treated these clauses as subject relatives. Polinsky argues that what we see in the adult heritage speakers is not a result of a fossilized pattern; rather, it is the result of attrition in the course of their lifespan. This attrition is due to less input, which in turn means that heritage speakers are less sensitive to case morphology, which dovetails with findings from the morphology of heritage speakers more generally (Montrul 2016; Polinsky 2018; Putnam, Schwarz and Hoffman, 2021).[6] In addition, "the universal preference for subject relative interpretation kicks in, causing heritage speakers to perform perfectly on subject relatives and at chance on object relatives" (Polinsky 2018: 246).

   This preference for subject relative clauses is supported by O'Grady, Lee, and Choo's (2001) study of adult Korean heritage speakers. They contrast patterns like the one shown in (8).

(8)   a. [__ namca-lul cohaha-nun] yeca   SUBJECT RELATIVE CLAUSE
           man-ACC   like-PRS   woman
           'the woman who likes the man'
       b. [namca-ka __ cohaha-nun] yeca   DIRECT OBJECT RELATIVE CLAUSE
           man-NOM   like-PRS   woman
           'the woman who the man likes'

As (8) shows, case markers and the adnominal suffix -nun on the verb are essential in order to master the difference between subject and direct object relative clauses. To test heritage speakers' knowledge of relative clauses, O'Grady, Lee, and Choo conducted a comprehension experiment based on the contrast in (8). The experiment had three groups of participants: sixteen heritage learners attending an accelerated second-semester university course in Korean, twenty-five non-heritage learners enrolled in the same course, and twenty non-heritage learners in a fourth-semester university course. There were no significant differences between the three groups, and

---

[6] The importance of language use and proficiency can also be seen through cross-linguistic differences: Sánchez-Walker (2012) does not find that her heritage speakers of Spanish struggle with object relative clauses, which is arguably due to these speakers being more proficient and less subject to attrition than the Russian heritage speakers in Polinsky's (2011) study.

importantly, all groups did much better on subject relative clauses compared to their direct object counterparts. An important reason why the heritage speakers and non-heritage speaker learners do so poorly, the authors argue, lies in their poor ability to make use of the morphosyntactic cues.

Polinsky and Scontras (2020) argue that the difficulty with object relative clauses is an example of a more general difficulty, namely that of long-distance dependencies. As they put it: "Object-gap dependencies are reanalyzed as subject-gap ones, which is a manifestation of the need to shorten the distance in the long-distance dependency" (Polinsky and Scontras 2020: 10). As we will see next, the difference between subject and object relatives fits well into a general pattern in heritage speakers.

When it comes to other types of long-distance dependencies, there is not much work done on, say, *wh*-questions. As Polinsky (2018: 249) puts it: "there is no evidence that heritage speakers lack the ability to form A-bar dependencies in principle." The general finding, as summarized by Hopp, Putnam, and Vosburg (2019), is that long-distance *wh*-movement is difficult to produce and comprehend, and they cite the following studies, which more or less represent an exhaustive list when it comes to this area of the grammar: O'Grady, Lee, and Choo (2001), Polinsky and Kagan (2007), Montrul, Foote, and Perpiñán (2008), Polinsky (2011), Gürel (2015) Pascual y Cabo and Gómez Soler (2015), and Bousquette, Frey, Nützel, Putnam, and Salmons (2016). Here we will consider Hopp, Putnam, and Vosburg's (2019) study of *wh*-questions in heritage Low German (and L2 English) speakers. They show that in order to avoid complex ("longer") dependencies, these speakers often use the so-called medial-*wh* construction, which is to say that a copy of the *wh*-constituent surfaces overtly at the left edge of the embedded clause (see Lohndal 2010 and references therein for more on these constructions). An example is provided in (9) from Mennonite Low German, or Plautdietsch, as it is often called.

(9)   Wua   denkjst du   **wua**   John sien Jeburtsdach fiert?   Plautdietsch
       where think   you where   John his   birthday   celebrates
       'Where do you think that John celebrates his birthday?'   (Hopp et al. 2019: 355)

Hopp, Putnam, and Vosburg (2019) find that only heritage speakers produce this medial-*wh* pattern, which arguably also has been part of their input. They argue that the Derivational Complexity Hypothesis (Jakubowicz 2005; Jakubowocz and Strik 2008), which holds that more syntactic Merge and Move operations create greater derivational complexity, can illuminate these findings since this medial-*wh* strategy can be viewed as a way of avoiding derivational complexity.

When it comes to the question of whether or not heritage speakers obey constraints on *wh*-movement (i.e., whether or not they obey island constraints), there is really only one study that addresses this issue. Kim and Goodall (2016) investigate *wh*-islands (10) and adjunct islands (11) in homeland speakers of Korean compared to heritage speakers of Korean in the United States.

(10)   *Who₁ do you wonder [whether Sue saw __₁]?   WH-ISLAND

(11)   *Who₁ did Jason cry [when Nat kissed __₁]?   ADJUNCT ISLAND

Interestingly, Korean does not display overt *wh*-movement, and importantly, the language only observes *wh*-islands; it does not have adjunct islands. It may be expected that heritage speakers may transfer island properties from their dominant language into their heritage language, meaning that they show an island effect for adjuncts in Korean. However, that is not what Kim and Goodall (2016) find. Rather, they find that the homeland group and the heritage speaker group are very similar. They rejected *wh*-islands and they also accepted adjunct islands. Kim and Goodall argue that this supports previous claims that island phenomena by and large are immune to environmental influences and that input may not be as important as some have argued (e.g., Culicover and Jackendoff 2005; Pearl and Sprouse 2013). However, given recent findings of cross-linguistic variation, e.g., between English and Norwegian (Kush et al. 2018, 2019), the field needs additional studies of how heritage speakers navigate island constraints in the face of variation.

25.4.3 Discontinous Elements

We have seen that long-distance dependencies pose problems for heritage speakers. However, similar problems emerge in discontinuous relationships, for instance between verbs and functional heads, or between nouns and classifiers. Here we will consider nouns and classifiers. Studies show that classifiers are vulnerable in heritage speakers, in the sense that speakers may have a reduced inventory of classifiers, they may not produce them, or they may produce the wrong ones (Wei and Lee 2001; Ming and Tao 2008). It has also been demonstrated that the number of classifiers can correlate with proficiency (see Wei and Lee 2001 on Cantonese heritage speakers). In addition to these findings, the distance between the classifier and the noun also matters. Benmamoun, Montrul, and Polinsky (2013: 145–146) report on an auditory comprehension experiment involving Mandarin Chinese. Here classifier phrases and their associated nouns are separated by one content word and the adnominal marker *de* (12). The classifier phrase and the content word are both underlined.

(12)   Laozhang ba na-yi-liang   hen-kuan-chang de   qiche songgei le   Laowang
        Mr.Zhang BA DEM-one-CLF very-wide-open ADN car give   PERF Mr.Wang
        'Mr. Zhang gave a very big car to Mr. Wang.' (Polinsky 2018. 217)

Sentences like (12) are compared to instances where the wrong classifier is used (13).

(13) *Laozhang ba na-yi-suo   hen-kuan-chang de   qiche songgei le   Laowang
       Mr.Zhang BA DEM-one-CLF very-wide-open   ADN car   give   PERF Mr.Wang
       Intended: 'Mr. Zhang gave a very big car to Mr. Wang.' (Polinsky 2018: 217)

Baseline speakers rated sentences with classifier–noun mismatches significantly lower compared to those with classifer–noun matches. Heritage speakers, on the other hand, do not distinguish between matching and mismatching conditions: They rate both conditions very highly, suggesting that they are not sensitive to the mismatch. This suggests that the distance between two discontinuous elements matters, quite similarly to what is known from morphology and agreement-dependencies (see Putnam, Schwarz, and Hoffman 2021).

25.5 Conclusion

In this chapter, we reviewed some of the main findings stemming from work on the syntax of heritage grammars. The core properties of syntax are relatively resilient, although this is not the case when additional factors come into play, as in the case of long-distance dependencies (where speakers seek to reduce the distance as much as possible) or certain aspects of word order (where the possible options are reduced or eliminated). More generally, studying the syntax of heritage speakers allows us to probe the nature of grammatical representations and better understand the plasticity of such representations, which in turn contributes valuable data to linguistic theorizing (Lohndal et al. 2019). In particular, the resilience of syntax can be modeled by adopting an exoskeletal approach to grammar (Borer 2005 a, b; Lohndal 2014; Grimstad 2018; Riksem 2018), whereby syntactic structures are independent of morphological exponents. As Putnam, Schwarz, and Hoffman (2021) highlight, the structural tendencies in heritage morphology also support an architecture whereby morphological processes follow those that generate syntactic structures. Taken together, studying the grammar of heritage languages offers exciting avenues for improving our theoretical models of possible human languages.

References

Aboh, Enoch. 2015. *The Emergence of Hybrid Grammars: Language Contact and Change.* Cambridge: Cambridge University Press.

Ackema, Peter and Ad Neeleman. 2004. *Beyond Morphology.* Oxford: Oxford University Press.

Albirini, Abdulkafi, Elabbas Benmamoun, and Eman Saadah. 2011. Grammatical Features of Egyptian and Palestinian Arabic Heritage Speakers' Oral Production. *Studies in Second Language Acquisition* 33, 273–303.

Alexiadou, Artemis and Terje Lohndal. 2018. V3 in Germanic: A Comparison of Urban Vernaculars and Heritage Languages. *Linguistische Berichte Sonderheft* 25, 245–263.

Arnbjörnsdóttir, Birna, Höskuldur Thráinsson, and Iris Edda Nowenstein. 2018. V2 and V3 Orders in North-American Icelandic. *Journal of Language Contact* 11, 379–412.

Benmamoun, Elabbas, Silvina Montrul, and Maria Polinsky. 2013. Heritage Languages and Their Speakers: Opportunities and Challenges for Linguistics. *Theoretical Linguistics* 39, 129–181.

Bley-Vroman, Robert. 1983. The Comparative Fallacy in Interlanguage Studies: The Case of Systematicity. *Language Learning* 33, 1–17.

Borer, Hagit. 2005a. *Structuring Sense, Volume 1: In Name Only*. Oxford: Oxford University Press.

Borer, Hagit. 2005b. *Structuring Sense, Volume 2: The Normal Course of Events*. Oxford: Oxford University Press.

Bousquette, Joshua, Ben Frey, Daniel Nützel, Michael T. Putnam, and Joseph Salmons. 2016. Parasitic Gapping in Bilingual Grammar: Evidence from Wisconsin Heritage German. *Heritage Language Journal* 13, 1–28.

Brown, Nicholas J. 1996. *Russian Learners' Dictionary: 10,000 Russian Words in Frequency Order*. London: Routledge.

Büring, Daniel. 2005. *Binding Theory*. Cambridge: Cambridge University Press.

Bylund, Emanuel. 2009. Maturational Constraints and First Language Attrition. *Language Learning* 59, 687–715.

Caha, Pavel. 2009. The Nanosyntax of Case. Doctoral dissertation, University of Tromsø.

Carstairs-McCarthy, Andrew. 1992. *Contemporary Morphology*. London: Routledge.

Chomsky, Noam. 1965. *Aspects of the Theory of Syntax*. Cambridge, MA: MIT Press.

Chomsky, Noam. 1972. *Language and Mind*. New York: Harcourt Brace Jovanovich.

Chomsky, Noam. 1975. *Reflections on Language*. New York: Pantheon.

Chomsky, Noam. 1981. *Lectures on Government and Binding*. Dordrecht: Foris.

Chomsky, Noam and Howard Lasnik. 1993. The Theory of Principles and Parameters. In Joachim Jacobs, Arnim von Stechow, Wolfgang Sternefeld, and Theo Venneman (eds.), *Syntax: An International Handbook of Contemporary Research*. Berlin: Mouton de Gruyter, 506–569.

Cook, Vivian. 1997. Monolingual Bias in Second Language Acquisition Research. *Revista Canaria de Estudios Ingleses* 34, 35–50.

Culicover, Peter and Ray Jackendoff. 2005. *Simpler Syntax*. Oxford: Oxford University Press.

De Bot, Kees. 1990. Language Attrition, Competence Loss or Performance Loss. In B. Spillner (ed.), *Sprache und Politik: Kongressbeiträge zur 19. Jahrestagung der Gesellschaft für Angewandte Linguistik*. Frankfurt: Peter Lang, 63–65.

Eide, Kristin Melum and Arnstein Hjelde. 2015. Verb Second and Finiteness Morphology in Norwegian Heritage Language of the American Midwest. In B. Richard Page and Michael T. Putnam (eds.), *Moribound Germanic Heritage Languages in North America Theoretical Perspectives and Empirical Findings*. Leiden: Brill, 64–101.

Eide, Kristin Melum and Arnstein Hjelde. 2018. Om verbplassering og verbmorfologi i amerikanorsk [On verb placement and verbal morphology in American Norwegian]. *Maal og Minne* 1, 25–69.

Embick, David. 2010. *Localism versus Globalism in Morphology and Phonology*. Cambridge, MA: MIT Press.

Embick, David. 2015. *The Morpheme: A Theoretical Introduction*. Berlin: De Gruyter.

Grimstad, Maren Berg. 2018. Language Mixing in American Norwegian Noun Phrases: An Exoskeletal Analysis of Synchronic and Diachronic Patterns. Doctoral dissertation, NTNU Norwegian University of Science and Technology.

Gürel, Ayşe. 2015. First Language Attrition of Constraints on Wh-scrambling: Does the Second Language Have an Effect? *International Journal of Bilingualism* 19, 75–91.

Haugen, Einar. 1953. *The Norwegian Language in America: A Study in Bilingual Behavior*. Philadelphia: University of Philadelphia Press.

Hippisley, Andrew and Gregory Stump (eds.), 2014. *The Cambridge Handbook of Morphology*. Cambridge: Cambridge University Press.

Holmberg, Anders. 2015. Verb Second. In Tibor Kiss and Artemis Alexiadou (eds.), *Syntax – Theory and Analysis*. Berlin: Mouton de Gruyter, 342–383.

Holmberg, Anders and Christer Platzack. 1995. *The Role of Inflection in Scandinavian Syntax*. New York and Oxford: Oxford University Press.

Hopp, Holger and Michael T. Putnam. 2015. Syntactic Restructuring in Heritage Grammars: Word Order Variation in Moundridge Schweitzer German. *Linguistic Approaches to Bilingualism* 5, 180–214.

Hopp, Holger, Michael T. Putnam, and Nora Vosburg. 2019. Derivational Complexity vs. Transfer Effects: Long Distance *Wh*-movement in Heritage and L2 Grammars. *Linguistic Approaches to Bilingualism* 9, 341–375.

Håkansson, Gisela. 1995. Syntax and Morphology in Language Attrition: A Study of Five Bilingual Expatriate Swedes. *International Journal of Applied Linguistics* 5, 151–171.

Isurin, Ludmila. 2000. Deserted Islands or a Child's First Language Forgetting. *Bilingualism: Language and Cognition* 3, 151–166.

Iverson, Mike B. 2012. Advanced *Language Attrition of Spanish in Contact with Brazilian Portuguese*. Doctoral dissertation, University of Iowa.

Iverson, Mike B. and David Miller. 2017. Language Attrition and Maintenance: Two Sides of the Same Coin? *Linguistic Approaches to Bilingualism* 7, 704–708.

Jakubowicz, Celia. 2005. The Language Faculty: (Ab)Normal Development and Interface Constraints. Paper presented at Generative Approaches to Language Acquisition, University of Siena.

Jakubowicz, Celia and Nelleke Strik. 2008. Scope-Marking Strategies in the Acquisition of Long-Distance *Wh*-questions in French and Dutch. *Language and Speech* 51, 101–132.

Johannessen, Janne Bondi. 2015a. Attrition in an American Norwegian Heritage Language Speaker. In Janne B. Johannessen and Joseph Salmons (eds.), *Germanic Heritage Languages in North America: Acquisition, Attrition and Change*. Amsterdam: John Benjamins, 21–45.

Johannessen, Janne Bondi. 2015b. The Corpus of American Norwegian Speech. In B. Megyesi (ed.), *NEALT Proceedings Series Vol. 23, Proceedings of the 20th Nordic Conference of Computational Linguistics (NoDaLiDa 2015)*. Stockholm: ACL Anthology, 297–300.

Johannessen, Janne Bondi and Joseph Salmons. 2021. Germanic Languages in America. In Silvina Montrul and Maria Polinsky (eds.), *The Cambridge Handbook of Heritage Languages and Linguistics*. Cambridge: Cambridge University Press.

Julien, Marit. 2002. *Syntactic Heads and Word Formation*. Oxford: Oxford University Press.

Khayitova, Sofiya. 2016. V2 i amerikanorsk – ufullstendig innlæring eller språkforvitring? [V2 in American Norwegian – Incomplete Acquisition or Attrition?]. MA thesis, University of Oslo.

Kim, Boyoung and Grant Goodall. 2016. Islands and Non-islands in Native and Heritage Korean. *Frontiers in Psychology* 7, 134. https://doi.org/10.3389/fpsyg.2016.00134

Köpke, Barbara. 1999. *L'attrition de la première langue chez le bilingue tardif: implications pour l'étude psycholinguistique du bilinguisme*. Doctoral dissertation, Université de Toulouse-Le Mirail.

Köpke, Barbara. 2004. Neurolinguistic Aspects of L1 Attrition. *Journal of Neurolinguistics* 17, 1–28.

Köpke, Barbara. 2007. Language Attrition at the Crossroads of Brain, Mind, and Society. In Barbara Köpke, Monika S. Schmid, Merel Keijzer, and Susan Dostert (eds.), *Language Attrition. Theoretical Perspectives*. Amsterdam: John Benjamins, 9–38.

Kühl, Karoline and Jan Heegård Petersen. 2018. Word Order in American Danish Declaratives with a Non-subject Initial Constituent. *Journal of Language Contact* 11, 413–440.

Kupisch, Tanja. 2014. Adjective Placement in Simultaneous Bilinguals (German-Italian) and the Concept of Crosslinguistic Overcorrection. *Bilingualism: Language and Cognition* 17, 222–233.

Kupisch, Tanja and Jason Rothman. 2018. Terminology Matters! Why Difference Is Not Incompleteness and How Early Child Bilinguals Are Heritage Speakers. *International Journal of Bilingualism* 22, 564–582.

Kupisch, Tanja, Tatjana Lein, Dagmar Barton, and Dawn Judith Schröder. 2014. Acquisition Outcomes across Domains in Adult Simultaneous Bilinguals with French as a Weaker and Stronger Language. *French Language Studies* 24, 347–376.

Kush, Dave, Terje Lohndal, and Jon Sprouse. 2018. Investigating Variation in Island Effects: A Case Study of Norwegian Wh-Extraction. *Natural Language and Linguistic Theory* 36, 743–779.

Kush, Dave, Terje Lohndal, and Jon Sprouse. 2019. On the Island Sensitivity of Topicalization in Norwegian: An Experimental Investigation. *Language* 95, 393–420.

Laleko, Oksana. 2021. Discourse and Information Structure in Heritage Languages. In Silvina Montrul and Maria Polinsky (eds.), *The Cambridge Handbook of Heritage Languages and Linguistics*. Cambridge: Cambridge University Press.

Lardiere, Donna. 2000. Mapping Features to Forms in Second Language Acquisition. In John Archibald (ed.), *Second Language Acquisition and Linguistic Theory*. Malden: Blackwell, 102–129.

Lardiere, Donna. 2009. Some Thoughts on the Contrastive Analysis of Features in Second Language Acquisition. *Second Language Acquisition* 25, 173–227.

Larsson, Ida and Janne Bondi Johannessen. 2015a. Incomplete Acquisition and Verb Placement in Heritage Scandinavian. In B. Richard Page and Michael T. Putnam (eds.), *Moribound Germanic Heritage Languages in North America: Theoretical Perspectives and Empirical Findings*. Leiden: Brill, 153–189.

Larsson, Ida and Janne Bondi Johannessen. 2015b. Embedded Word Order in Heritage Scandinavian. In Martin Hilpert, Jan-Ola Östman, Christine Mertzlufft, and Michael Riessler (eds.), *New Trends in Nordic and General Linguistics*. Berlin: Mouton de Gruyter, 239–267.

Lohndal, Terje. 2010. Medial-*wh* Phenomena, Parallel Movement, and Parameters. *Linguistic Analysis* 34, 245–270.

Lohndal, Terje. 2013. Generative Grammar and Language Mixing. *Theoretical Linguistics* 39, 215–224.

Lohndal, Terje. 2014. *Phrase Structure and Argument Structure: A Case Study of the Syntax Semantics Interface*. Oxford: Oxford University Press.

Lohndal, Terje and Marit Westergaard. 2016. Grammatical Gender in American Norwegian Heritage Language: Stability or Attrition? *Frontiers in Psychology* 7. https://doi.org/10.3389/fpsyg.2016.00344

Lohndal, Terje, Jason Rothman, Tanja Kupisch, and Marit Westergaard. 2019. Heritage Language Acquisition: What It Reveals and Why It Is Important for Formal Linguistic Theories. *Language and Linguistics Compass*. https://doi.org/10.1111/lnc3.12357

Madsen, Christen N. 2018. De-centering the Monolingual: A Psychophysiological Study of Heritage Speaker Language Processing. Doctoral dissertation, CUNY Graduate Center.

Matushansky, Ora and Alec Marantz (eds.) 2013. *Distributed Morphology Today*. Cambridge, MA: MIT Press.

Ming, Tao and Hongyin Tao. 2008. Developing a Chinese Heritage Language Corpus: Issues and a Preliminary Report. In Agnes Weiyun He and Yun Xiao (eds.), *Chinese as a Heritage Language: Fostering Rooted World Citizenry*. Honolulu: University of Hawaii Mañoa, 167–188.

Montrul, Silvina. 2002. Incomplete Acquisition and Attrition of Spanish Tense/Aspect Distinctions in Adult Bilinguals. *Bilingualism: Language and Cognition* 5, 39–68.

Montrul, Silvina. 2008. *Incomplete Acquisition in Bilingualism: Re-examining the Age Factor*. Amsterdam: John Benjamins.

Montrul, Silvina. 2016. *The Acquisition of Heritage Languages*. Cambridge: Cambridge University Press.

Montrul, Silvina. 2018. Heritage Language Development: Connecting the Dots. *International Journal of Bilingualism* 22, 530–546.

Montrul, Silvina, Archna Bhatia, Rakesh Bhatt, and Vandana Puri. 2019. Case Marking in Hindi as the Weaker Language. *Frontiers in Psychology* 10, 461. https://doi.org/10.3389/fpsyg.2019.00461

Montrul, Silvina and Noelia Sánchez-Walker. 2013. Differential Object Marking in Child and Adult Spanish Heritage Speakers. *Language Acquisition* 20, 109–132.

Montrul, Silvina, Rebecca Foote, and Sílvia Perpiñán. 2008. Knowledge of Wh-movement in Spanish L2 Learners and Heritage Speakers. In Joyce Bruhn de Garavito and Elena Valenzuela (eds.), *Selected Proceedings of the 2006 Hispanic Linguistics Symposium*. Somerville, MA: Cascadilla Proceedings Project, 93–106.

Muysken, Pieter. 2019. The Case for Contact–Induced Change in Heritage Languages. *Bilingualism: Language and Cognition* 23, 37–38. https://doi.org/10.1017/S1366728919000373

O'Grady, William, Miseon Lee, and Miho Choo. 2001. The Acquisition of Relative Clauses by Heritage and Non-heritage Learners of Korean as a Second Language: A Comparative Study. *Journal of Korean Language Education* 12, 283–294.

Otheguy, Ricardo. 2016. The Linguistic Competence of Second-Generation Bilinguals: A Critique of "Incomplete Acquisition". In Christina Tortora, Marcel den Dikken, Ignacio L. Montoya, and Theresa O'Neill (eds.), *Romance Linguistics 2013: Selected Papers from the 43rd Linguistic Symposium on Romance Languages (LSLR), New York, 17–19 April 2013*. Amsterdam: John Benjamins, 301–319.

Pascual y Cabo, Diego and Jason Rothman. 2012. The (Il)Logical Problem of Heritage Speaker Bilingualism and Incomplete Acquisition. *Applied Linguistics* 33, 1–7.

Pascual y Cabo, Diego and Inmaculada Gómez Soler. 2015. Preposition Stranding in Spanish as a Heritage Language. *Heritage Language Journal* 12, 186–209.

Pearl, Lisa and Jon Sprouse. 2013. Syntactic Islands and Learning Biases: Combining Experimental Syntax and Computational Modeling to Investigate the Language Acquisition Problem. *Language Acquisition* 20, 23–68.

Peres-Cortes, Silvia. 2016. Acquiring Obligatory and Variable Mood Selection: Spanish Heritage Speakers and L2 Learners' Performance in Desideratives and Reported Speech Contexts. Doctoral dissertation, Rutgers University.

Polinsky, Maria. 1997. American Russian: Language Loss Meets Language Acquisition. In W. Brown et al. (eds.), *Formal Approaches to Slavic Linguistics*. Ann Arbor: Michigan Slavic Publications, 370–407.

Polinsky, Maria. 2005. Word Class Distinctions in an Incomplete Grammar. In D. Ravid and Z. B. Shyldkrot (eds.), *Perspectives on Language and Language Development*. Dordrecht: Kluwer, 419–434.

Polinsky, Maria. 2006. Incomplete Acquisition: American Russian. *Journal of Slavic Linguistics* 14, 161–219.

Polinsky, Maria. 2008. Gender under Incomplete Acquisition: Heritage Speakers' Knowledge of Noun Categorization. *Heritage Language Journal* 6, 40–71.

Polinsky, Maria. 2011. Reanalysis in Adult Heritage Language: A Case for Attrition. *Studies in Second Language Acquisition* 33, 305–328.

Polinsky, Maria. 2016. Bilingual Children and Adult Heritage Speakers: The Range of Comparison. *International Journal of Bilingualism* 13, 195–201.

Polinsky, Maria. *Heritage Languages and Their Speakers*. Cambridge: Cambridge University Press.

Polinsky, Maria and Gregory Scontras. 2020. Understanding Heritage Languages. *Bilingualism: Language and Cognition* 23(1), 4–20.

Polinsky, Maria and Olga Kagan. 2007. Heritage Languages: In the "Wild" and in the Classroom. *Language and Linguistics Compass* 1, 368–395.

Prévost, Philippe and Lydia White. 2000. Missing Surface Inflection or Impairment in Second Language Acquisition? Evidence from Tense and Agreement. *Second Language Research* 16, 103–133.

Putnam, Michael T. 2020. Separating vs. Shrinking. *Bilingualism: Language and Cognition* 23(1), 41–42.

Putnam, Michael T. and Joseph C. Salmons. 2013. Losing Their (Passive) Voice: Syntactic Neutralization in Heritage German. *Linguistic Approaches to Bilingualism* 3(2), 233–252.

Putnam, Michael T., Lara Schwarz, and Andrew D. Hoffman. 2021. In Silvina Montrul and Maria Polinsky (eds.), *The Cambridge Handbook of Heritage Languages and Linguistics*. Cambridge: Cambridge University Press.

Putnam, Michael T. and Liliana Sánchez. 2013. What's So Incomplete about Incomplete Acquisition? A Prolegomenon to Modeling Heritage Language Grammars. *Linguistic Approaches to Bilingualism* 3, 478–508.

Putnam, Michael T., Silvia Perez-Cortes, and Liliana Sánchez. 2019. Language Attrition and the Feature Reassembly Hypothesis. In Monika S. Schmid and Barbara Köpke (eds.), *The Oxford Handbook of Language Attrition*. Oxford: Oxford University Press, 18–24.

Riksem, Brita Ramsevik. 2017. Language Mixing and Diachronic Change: American Norwegian Noun Phrases Then and Now. *Languages* 2, 3. https: doi.org/10.3390/languages2020003

Riksem, Brita Ramsevik. 2018. Language Mixing in American Norwegian Noun Phrases. An Exoskeletal Analysis of Synchronic and Diachronic Patterns. Doctoral dissertation, NTNU Norwegian University of Science and Technology.

Rothman, Jason. 2007. Heritage Speaker Competence Differences, Language Change, and Input Type: Inflected Infinitives in Heritage Brazilian Portuguese. *International Journal of Bilingualism* 11, 359–389.

Rothman, Jason. 2009. Understanding the Nature and Outcomes of Early Bilingualism: Romance Languages as Heritage Languages. *International Journal of Bilingualism* 13, 155–163.

Rothman, Jason and Jeanine Treffers-Daller. 2014. A Prolegomenon to the Construct of the Native Speaker: Heritage Speaker Bilinguals Are Natives Too! *Applied Linguistics* 35, 93–98.

Rothman, Jason, Jorge González Alonso, and Eloi Puig-Mayenco. 2019. *Third Language Acquisition and Linguistic Transfer*. Cambridge: Cambridge University Press.

Sánchez-Walker, Noelia. 2012. Comprehension of subject and object relative clauses in Spanish heritage speakers and L2 learners of Spanish. Poster presented at the Sixth Heritage Language Institute, UCLA.

Schmid, Monika S. 2002. *Language Attrition, Maintenance and Use. The Case of German Jews in Anglophone Countries*. Amsterdam: John Benjamins.

Schmid, Monika S. 2011. *Language Attrition*. Cambridge: Cambridge University Press.

Schmid, Monika S. and Barbara Köpke. 2007. Bilingualism and Attrition. In Barbara Köpke, Monika S. Schmid, Merel Keijzer, and Susan Dostert (eds.), *Language Attrition. Theoretical Perspectives*. Amsterdam: John Benjamins, 1–7.

Schmid, Monika S. and Barbara Köpke. 2017. When Is a Bilingual an Attriter? *Linguistic Approaches to Bilingualism* 7, 763–770.

Scontras, Gregory, Maria Polinsky, C.-Y. Edwin Tsai, and Kenneth Mai. 2017. Cross Linguistic Scope Ambiguity: When Two Systems Meet. *Glossa: A Journal of General Linguistics* 2(36). http://doi.org/10.5334/gjgl.198

Scontras, Gregory, Zuzanna Fuchs, and Maria Polinsky. 2015. Heritage Language and Linguistic Theory. *Frontiers in Psychology* 6, 1545. https://doi.org/10.3389/fpsyg.2015.01545

Seliger, H. 1991. Language Attrition, Reduced Redundancy, and Creativity. In H. Seliger and R. Vago (eds.), *First Language Attrition*. Cambridge: Cambridge University Press, 227–240.

Seliger, H. 1996. Primary Language Attrition in the Context of Bilingualism. In William C. Ritchie and Tej K. Bhatia (eds.), *Handbook of Second Language Acquisition*. New York: Academic Press, 605–625.

Silva-Corvalán, Carmen. 2018. Simultaneous Bilingualism: Early Developments, Incomplete Later Outcomes? *International Journal of Bilingualism* 22(5), 497–512.

Sorace, Antonella. 2000. Differential Effects of Attrition in the L1 Syntax of Near-Native L2 Speakers. In S. Catherine Howell, Sarah A. Fish, and Thea Keith-Lucas (eds.), *Proceedings of the 24th Boston University Conference on Language Development*. Somerville, MA: Cascadilla Press, 719–725.

Sorace, Antonella. 2011. Pinning down the Concept of "interface" in Bilingualism. *Linguistic Approaches to Bilingualism* 1, 1–33.

Spencer, Andrew and Arnold M. Zwicky (eds.) 1998. *The Handbook of Morphology*. Malden, MA: Blackwell.

Strømsvåg, Sunniva. 2013. Syntaktisk attrisjon i amerikanorsk. [Syntactic Attrition in American Norwegian]. MA thesis, NTNU Norwegian University of Science and Technology.

Tsimpli, Ianthi. 2017. Crosslinguistic Influence Is Not Necessarily Attrition. *Linguistic Approaches to Bilingualism* 7, 759–762.

Tsimpli, Ianthi, Antonella Sorace, Caroline Heycock, and Francesca Filiaci. 2004. First Language Attrition and Syntactic Subjects: A Study of Greek and Italian Near-Native Speakers of English. *International Journal of Bilingualism* 8, 257–277.

Turian, D. and E. Altenberg. 1991. Compensatory Strategies of Child First Language Attrition. In H. Seliger and R. Vago (eds.), *First Language Attrition*. Cambridge: Cambridge University Press, 207–226.

Vikner, Sten. 1995. *Verb Movement and Expletive Subjects in the Germanic Languages*. Oxford: Oxford University Press.

Wei, Li and Sherman Lee. 2001. L1 Development in an L2 Environment: The Use of Cantonese Classifiers and Quantifiers by Young British-Born Chinese in Tyneside. *International Journal of Bilingual Education and Bilingualism* 4, 359–383.

Westergaard, Marit and Terje Lohndal. 2019. Verb Second Word Order in Norwegian Heritage Language: Syntax and Pragmatics. In David Lightfoot and Jonathan Havenhill (eds.), *Variable Properties in Language: Their Nature and Acquisition*. Georgetown: Georgetown University Press, 91–102.

Yukawa, Emiko. 1997. L1 Japanese Attrition and Regaining: Three Case Studies of Two Early Bilingual Children. Doctoral dissertation, Stockholm University.

26

Semantics of Heritage Languages

Tania Ionin

26.1 Introduction

This chapter provides an overview of the research on semantics and related interface phenomena in heritage language (HL) grammars. Semantics is the branch of linguistics that studies meaning, but meaning is always tied to form: Just as lexical semantics studies the meaning of words, compositional semantics studies how the meaning of phrases and sentences is composed from their internal elements. Work that examines the acquisition or attrition of semantics nearly always looks at the relationship between semantics and morphology or syntax: for example, how the meaning of definiteness or plurality is encoded by particular morphemes; how the meaning of aspect or past tense or subjunctive mood is encoded by particular verb forms; what differences in meaning are related to the presence vs. absence of case morphemes; etc. In that sense, nearly all or perhaps all phenomena in the acquisition or attrition of semantics are phenomena at the interface between semantics and morphosyntax: We can ask whether heritage speakers (and other learner populations) successfully map the target form to the target meaning, whether they are influenced by transfer of form/ meaning mappings from another language, whether certain form/meaning mappings serve as defaults, and so on.

In the domain of second language (L2) acquisition, Slabakova (2008) argues that semantics is not subject to critical period effects, and that the challenge for second language learners (L2ers) is in learning which morphological forms encode which aspects of linguistic meaning; Slabakova calls morphology the "bottleneck" of the acquisition process. Extending this proposal to HL grammars, it is reasonable to suppose that semantics is just as acquirable by heritage speakers (HSs) as by L2ers; an empirical question is whether acquiring the target mappings between morphosyntax and semantics is as challenging for HSs as it is for L2-learners, given that HSs, unlike L2ers, are exposed to the target language during the critical period. The studies discussed in this chapter examine a number of phenomena in HL grammars that fall at the interface between semantics and morphosyntax. In each case, the focus is not simply on whether a given form (such as a case marker or an aspectual verb form or a reflexive anaphor) is part of the HL grammar, but on what *meaning* it has in the HL grammar, and on whether the form-meaning mapping diverges from that of the target monolingual grammar.

The research studies discussed in this chapter address one or more of the following questions. First, all of this work addresses the question of whether the phenomena under investigation are subject to incomplete acquisition and/or attrition in HLs (Montrul 2008). Given that all of the studies on semantics in HLs are cross-sectional, they cannot definitively tease apart incomplete acquisition from attrition (though some studies address this issue by looking at cross-age comparisons). In light of this, the present overview focuses on whether HL grammars diverge from monolingual grammars in the domains discussed, rather than on whether the source of the divergence is incomplete acquisition (i.e., the phenomenon was never fully acquired) or attrition (i.e., the phenomenon was acquired and then lost).[1]

The second question addressed by some of the studies on HL semantics is whether HL grammars are subject to cross-linguistic influence from the dominant language. As discussed later, many (but by no means all) of the studies do find patterns of divergence that are consistent with cross-linguistic influence from the dominant language. A limitation of the field is that most studies are conducted with only one dominant language, and furthermore, the vast majority of studies have English as the dominant language. This makes it difficult to definitively establish the role of cross-linguistic influence, and to tease it apart from a general process of grammar simplification or reversion to defaults that is not tied to a specific dominant language.

These two questions (the existence of incomplete acquisition and the role of cross-linguistic influence) are not specific to the study of semantics, and are also investigated in the areas of morphosyntax and phonology (see Chang, this volume, on phonology; Putnam, Schwarz, and Hoffman, this volume, on morphology; and Lohndal, this volume, on syntax). The third question discussed here is more specific: namely, whether interface phenomena are particularly vulnerable to incomplete acquisition and/or attrition. Previous research has proposed that interface phenomena are

---

[1] The studies reported in this chapter generally use monolinguals as the baseline population; for more discussion of what should constitute the baseline population for HL languages, please see Polinsky (2018) and Lohndal (this volume).

more subject to attrition than purely syntactic phenomena (e.g., Sorace 2000a; Montrul 2002). Sorace and Filiaci 2006 began using the term Interface Hypothesis (IH) with regard to advanced, near-native L2ers' difficulty with phenomena falling at the interface between syntax and discourse or pragmatics. Sorace and Serratrice 2009, in a study of bilingual children, compared internal interface phenomena (genericity) and external interface phenomena (discourse conditions on anaphora resolution); they found that the external interface phenomena were vulnerable independently of the language combination, whereas internal interface phenomena were subject to cross-linguistic influence, with vulnerability dependent on language-specific factors. Sorace (2011), updating the IH, proposed that external interface phenomena are vulnerable due to difficulty with processing and resource allocation.

While the IH was formulated for first language (L1) attrition and (advanced) L2 acquisition (but see White 2011), it has also been extended to heritage languages (Rothman 2009; Montrul and Polinsky 2011), and many of the studies discussed here address the question of whether interface phenomena, and specifically external interface phenomena, are particularly vulnerable in HL grammars. As discussed here, the results on this point are fairly mixed, in that vulnerabilities are attested at internal as well as external interfaces. For more discussion of the IH, and criticisms thereof, see the special issue of *Linguistic Approaches to Bilingualism 1:1*. See also Laleko (this volume).

The present chapter focuses on four linguistic domains that fall at the interface between syntax and semantics where there has been a substantial body of research with HSs. First, it discusses work on the semantics of the verbal domain, which includes the semantics of tense, aspect, mood, and evidentiality, as well as the semantics of unaccusatives. The work in this domain addresses the existence of incomplete acquisition, the role of cross-linguistic influence, and – in some cases – the relative difficulty of purely syntactic vs. interface phenomena. Second, the chapter moves onto the semantics of the nominal domain, and considers the status of reference, definiteness, and genericity in HL grammars. The studies in this area have primarily focused on the degree of incomplete acquisition and the possible role of cross-linguistic influence; in some cases, HSs are compared to L2ers.

The third area considered here is the expression of subjects and objects, which includes such topics as case marking and anaphor binding. Subject and object expression involve the interface between syntax and discourse as well as that between syntax and semantics, with many of the studies addressing predictions of the IH, in addition to the questions of incomplete acquisition and cross-linguistic influence. This chapter focuses primarily on those aspects of subject–object expression that involve the syntax–semantics interface and leaves aside the distribution of overt vs. null anaphora, which involves the syntax–discourse interface (see Laleko, this volume, for discussion of this topic).

Finally, the fourth area considered here is the semantics of quantifiers; the (relatively small) body of research conducted on this topic with HSs suggests a lack of cross-linguistic influence in this domain, and instead points toward simplified grammars and the role of processing.

Most of the studies discussed in this chapter were conducted with adult HSs, who were either born or arrived as children into the country where the dominant language (in most cases, English) is spoken. For these HSs, the language of the society is also the language in which they are dominant, whereas their first, family language is the weaker language. In some studies, the HSs are all simultaneous bilinguals, while others also include early sequential bilinguals (who learned the dominant language in the preschool years). Some studies also include comparison groups of late sequential bilinguals (who learned the dominant language during the school years), of adult learners of the target language as an L2, or of adult L1 attriters; these last are individuals who emigrated to the country of the dominant language as adults, with a fully formed L1-grammar, but whose L1 grammars may have undergone attrition due to a lengthy residence into the country of their L2. Following the literature, this chapter uses the term "L1 attriters" for adult immigrants who may have undergone attrition in the target language; the term L2ers is reserved for adult L2-learners of the target language. Finally, some studies were conducted with bilingual children, and do not use the term "heritage speaker" in referring to the children. Unlike the case of adult bilinguals, with children it is not always clear which language is the dominant language, especially since dominance may switch during childhood, as the child becomes less exposed to the heritage language and more exposed to the language of the society (Montrul 2008).

26.2 Semantics of the Verbal Domain

Studies on the semantics of the verbal domain in HL grammars can be divided into two broad types. On the one hand, there are studies that focus on the functional categories of the verbal domain, including tense, aspect, mood, and evidentiality. On the other hand, several studies have addressed the semantics of a particular verb class, unaccusatives.

26.2.1 Tense, Aspect, Mood, and Evidentiality

A number of studies have documented that HSs of Spanish and Russian have difficulty acquiring the distinction between grammatical aspectual forms (preterit vs. imperfect in Spanish; perfective vs. imperfective in Russian). Informally, the preterit/perfective forms denote completed events, whereas the imperfect/imperfective forms denote incomplete events; however, the language-specific distinctions are considerably more subtle and complex (see, e.g., Comrie 1976). The aspectual contrasts of Spanish and Russian have no direct equivalent in English, the dominant language of the HSs in all the studies cited here. The acquisition task is further complicated by the fact that verbal predicates also have different types of lexical aspect (Vendler 1967; Verkuyl 1993). There is some correspondence between lexical aspect and grammatical aspect: for example, *telic* predicates, ones that denote events with an inherent endpoint (e.g., *eat an apple* or *reach the mountaintop*) tend to occur more in the perfective, while *atelic* ones, which denote events without an inherent endpoint (e.g., *drink water* or *know French*), tend to occur in the imperfective. Lexical and grammatical aspect are in principle independent, but associations between the two have been found in both L1 and L2 acquisition (e.g., Antinucci and Miller 1976; Shirai and Andersen 1996).

In the case of heritage Spanish, Silva-Corvalán (1994) noted errors with both preterit and imperfect aspect morphology in the production data of both first-generation HSs (who were born in the United States to Mexican parents, or else arrived in the United States as children), and second-generation ones (children of the first-generation HSs). Montrul (2002) followed up on this finding by examining both production and interpretation of the aspectual forms in Spanish. While there was much individual variation in the data, HSs diverged from monolingual native speakers primarily with regard to use of the preterit with stative verbs, as well as various uses of the imperfect. Divergence was greater among the HSs exposed to English in early childhood, compared to those with later exposure to English (who were monolingual in Spanish until late childhood). In the case of heritage Russian, both Polinsky (2008b) and Laleko (2011) have similarly found much divergence from monolinguals in the use of both perfective and imperfective forms. Laleko (2011) found that grammatical aspect in heritage Russian interacts with lexical aspect, much the same as has been found for Spanish.

A different kind of aspectual contrast was investigated by Sherkina-Lieber (2015) in a study of receptive bilinguals of Labrador Inuttitut, that is, bilinguals who can understand but not speak the language. In addition to marking tense, Labrador Inuttitut marks the degree of remoteness (e.g., whether the event is within the day or beyond the day when the utterance is made). Sherkina-Lieber (2015) found that (compared to a control group of fluent bilinguals), high-proficiency receptive bilinguals performed better on time contrasts than on remoteness contrasts, probably due to English, the dominant language, having no equivalent of the latter. Low-proficiency receptive bilinguals did not exhibit any understanding of tense morphology at all.

Moving beyond aspect, Montrul (2009) examined knowledge of the indicative vs. subjunctive mood in adult Spanish HSs, and compared it to knowledge of grammatical aspect. Montrul (2009) used both elicitation tasks to examine production, and sentence conjunction tasks to examine appropriateness of interpretation. Montrul found that HSs made errors on both mood and aspect, with clear proficiency effects (advanced HSs performed much more like the control group of native speakers than intermediate and low-proficiency HSs). The HSs made errors on all tasks, but when it came to the task tapping into the semantic contrasts, they did better on the preterit–imperfect contrast than on the indicative–subjunctive one. Montrul suggests that this could be an effect of age of acquisition, since mood is acquired later in L1-acquisition than grammatical aspect. Alternatively, she notes that mood may involve greater linguistic complexity than aspect, as it involves the integration of pragmatic knowledge, in addition to the syntax and semantics; the difficulty with mood relative to aspect would be predicted by the IH. Following up on Montrul (2009), Pascual y Cabo, Lingwall, and Rothman (2012) examined mood in Spanish HSs in light of the IH (Sorace 2011), and argued that their findings (more difficulty in contexts where the discourse rather than the syntax determined the choice of indicative vs. subjunctive) are consistent with the predictions of the IH.

Finally, Arslan, De Kok, and Bastiaanse (2017) examined evidentiality as well as tense in HSs of Turkish, using both offline (accuracy) and online (processing time) measures. They found that the HSs were both less accurate and slower than monolinguals with regard to both time-reference and evidentiality, with the latter being particularly affected. Arslan et al. (2017) argue that these findings are consistent with the IH, since evidentiality involves the syntax–pragmatics interface.

To sum up, research on the semantics of the verbal domain in HL grammars shows divergence from monolingual grammars in nearly every area and language tested. There is also suggestive evidence that phenomena involving discourse knowledge (mood and evidentiality, and possibly also remoteness, though Sherkina-Lieber (2015) does not frame her study in terms of interfaces) are more difficult to acquire than grammatical aspect and tense. However, there are other possible explanations for why certain phenomena are especially vulnerable, such as absence of the relevant property in the dominant language, as well as (at least in the case of mood) later age of L1-acquisition.

Unaccusative Verbs

A different area of verbal semantics involves the particular properties of certain verb classes, such as unaccusatives vs. unergatives. In this domain, lexical semantic differences between verb classes correspond to different syntactic behaviors, thus placing the phenomena at the syntax–semantics interface.

The semantic distinction between two types of intransitive verbs, unaccusatives such as *fall* or *arrive* (which take a non-agentive argument) and unergatives such as *laugh* (which take an agentive argument) is considered to be universal. At the same time, languages vary with regard to the syntactic and morphological markers of this distinction (see Perlmutter 1978; Burzio 1981; Levin and Rappaport Hovav 1995; Sorace 2000b, among many others). In the case of Spanish, there are a number of syntactic differences between the two intransitive verb types, such as subject placement and compatibility with the absolutive construction (see Montrul 2005 for an overview and references). Montrul (2005) found that adult Spanish HSs exhibited knowledge of the syntactic reflexes of unaccusativity in Spanish, more so than adult L2-Spanish learners. They furthermore showed sensitivity to the different semantic subclasses of unaccusatives that were consistent with the unaccusativity hierarchy proposed by Sorace (2000b). Overall, the HSs (as well as the L2ers) in Montrul's study exhibited robust knowledge of syntax, but more variability with regard to the semantics of unaccusativity, supporting the view that syntax is stable while interface phenomena are more vulnerable in acquisition and attrition (Sorace 2000a). However, given that unaccusatives arguably involve the internal syntax/semantics interface, the more recent version of the IH (Sorace 2011) would not predict difficulty in this domain.

Zyzik (2014) examined whether Spanish HSs overgeneralize intransitive verbs in causative transitive constructions, as L2-Spanish learners were shown to do in prior studies. Zyzik found that the HSs did indeed overgeneralize, indicating that phenomena at the interface between syntax and lexical semantics are vulnerable in incomplete acquisition. There was also evidence of transfer from English, the dominant language, in that the HSs were most likely to accept incorrect causavization of unaccusative verbs that have transitive uses in English.

Turning to unaccusativity in other languages, in the case of Japanese and Korean, quantifier float is a diagnostic for unaccusativity (Miyagawa 1989; Ahn 1991): The argument of an unaccusative verb can be the antecedent of a floating numeral classifier, unlike the argument of an unergative verb, but just like the object of a transitive verb. T. Lee (2011) found that adult Korean HSs born in the United States did not exhibit knowledge of this distinction, while Korean-born HSs were more target-like, though still not entirely native-like. In contrast, Fukuda (2017) found that Japanese HSs demonstrated knowledge of the floating quantifier diagnostic, behaving similarly to the Spanish HSs in Montrul (2005), who were also sensitive to the syntactic reflexes of unaccusativity.

Thus, some degree of success on unaccusative verbs in HL grammars is attested, at least with regard to the purely syntactic aspects of the knowledge of unaccusatives (for more on the syntax of heritage languages, please see Polinsky 2018 and Lohndal, this volume). At the same time, there is also evidence for incomplete acquisition, which may be due to the influence of the dominant language (English).

26.3 Semantics of the Nominal Domain

There have been a number of investigations of the semantics of nominals in HL grammars, most of which have focused on the interpretations of nominals with vs. without articles.

26.3.1 Definiteness and Genericity

Several recent studies have examined the interpretation of definite and bare (article-less) plural NPs in bilinguals who speak Romance vs. Germanic languages. In English and in Standard German, bare plurals express generic readings (e.g., *Tigers eat meat* is a statement about tigers in general), while definite plurals are restricted to specific (non-generic) readings (e.g., *The tigers eat meat* is a statement about specific tigers). In contrast, in Italian and Spanish, definite plurals have both specific and generic readings, while bare plurals are, depending on the context, either ungrammatical or restricted to existential readings.

Serratrice, Sorace, Filiaci, and Baldo (2009) examined how bilingual Italian-English children in both Italy and the United Kingdom judged bare vs. definite plurals in generic vs. specific contexts. They found that in English, bilingual children performed similarly to monolingual ones (with all child groups being less accurate than monolingual adult controls); in contrast, in Italian, English-Italian bilinguals were much less accurate than Italian monolinguals and also than Spanish-Italian bilinguals (whose two languages behave similarly in this domain). Furthermore, English-Italian bilinguals in Italy (for whom Italian is presumably the stronger language) outperformed those in the United Kingdom (for whom Italian is the weaker, heritage language). Thus, the results suggest that both cross-linguistic influence and input play a role.

Turning to adult bilinguals, Montrul and Ionin (2010, 2012) tested English-dominant Spanish HSs, while Kupisch (2012) tested two groups of Italian-German bilinguals, those dominant in Italian and those dominant in German. Montrul and Ionin (2010) found that Spanish HSs exhibited transfer from English to Spanish, accepting generic readings of Spanish definite plurals less than native speaker controls (similarly to L2-Spanish learners, Montrul and Ionin 2012), while being quite target-like in English. Kupisch (2012) found that Italian-dominant bilinguals were at-ceiling in Italian, while German-dominant bilinguals were less accurate, patterning similarly to L1-German L2-Italian learners.

Taken together, these studies suggest that both cross-linguistic influence and language dominance play a role, so that bilinguals behave similarly to monolinguals when tested on their dominant language, and exhibit transfer from the dominant language to the weaker (heritage) language. At the same time, the findings of Serratrice et al. (2009) with bilingual children indicate cross-linguistic influence only from English to Italian, and not the other way around, regardless of language dominance (however, their findings are somewhat difficult to interpret, given that even monolingual children behaved in a non-target manner when tested on English).

26.3.2   Reference without Articles

Mandarin Chinese is an article-less language, which uses both NP-internal morphology and syntactic placement to signal when an NP conveys new information (see Jia and Paradis 2015, and the references cited therein). Jia and Paradis (2015) found that English-dominant child HSs of Mandarin scored lower than monolingual children in the appropriateness of their first-mention forms; in particular, they overused the general classifier in place of specific classifiers. With regard to other types of first-mention forms, in particular use of the numeral "one," the bilingual children did not differ from the monolinguals. HSs who arrived in Canada (and hence became exposed to English) at a later age were more accurate than HSs who arrived at an earlier age or were born in Canada. Thus, when it comes to reference without articles, some divergence from monolinguals is observed.

26.3.3   Definiteness Effect

In addition to the semantics of different types of nominals, HSs also need to acquire the corresponding syntactic properties. One much-studied property is the *definiteness effect*, a restriction against definites (as well as various strong quantifiers, Milsark 1977) occurring in existential constructions (e.g., *There is a/*the cat in the room*). In English and German, languages that have both definite and indefinite articles, the definiteness effect is present for both affirmative and negative existentials. However, for other languages, such as Russian (which has no articles) and Turkish (which has only an optional indefinite article), the definiteness effect is present only in affirmative existentials but not in negative ones (Enç 1991; White et al. 2012; Kupisch et al. 2017). Prior work on L2-acquisition (White et al. 2012) found that L1-Russian and L1-Turkish L2-English learners are sensitive to the definiteness effect in English, in both affirmative and negative constructions. Kupisch et al. (2017) extended this investigation to German-dominant

HSs of Turkish, testing the bilinguals on both of their languages. The Turkish-German bilinguals were fully target-like with respect to the definiteness effect in German, and also quite target-like in Turkish; this was the case for both simultaneous and sequential bilinguals, though some influence from German was found in the simultaneous bilingual group.

Kupisch et al. (2017) conclude that HSs have no difficulty with the internal syntax–semantics interface involved in the definiteness effect. Comparing their findings to the divergence observed with regard to genericity, it would seem that a purely syntactic reflex (ungrammaticality of definites inside existential constructions) is less vulnerable than semantic distinctions.

26.4   Subject and Object Expression

The expression of subjects and objects is probably one of the most extensively studied areas in research on HL grammars and involves both the internal interface between syntax and semantics, and the external interface between syntax and discourse, thus presenting a testing ground for the IH. In this chapter, we focus on those aspects of subject and object expression that involve the syntax–semantics interface: case marking, case drop, differential object marking, and the binding properties of reflexive pronouns. In all of these domains, there are interpretational differences between different linguistic forms (e.g., different types of reflexive pronouns), or between the presence vs. absence of linguistic forms (e.g., case markers).

One much-studied aspect of subject and object expression that this chapter leaves out is the distribution of overt vs. null anaphora in null-subject languages. This distribution, which is subject to discourse constraints, falls squarely at the syntax–discourse interface, and is discussed at length in Laleko (this volume).

26.4.1   Case Marking and Case Drop

The acquisition of case marking in languages such as Korean or Russian is first and foremost a task involving morphosyntax, as learners map particular morphemes to abstract syntactic concepts as "subject/nominative" or "object/accusative." It is quite well-established that HSs of case-marking languages often have difficulty with the production of case marking (e.g., adult Russian HSs have been found to misuse nominative for other cases and accusative for indirect cases, Polinsky 2007, 2008a).

There are at least two distinct properties of case marking that involve the mapping between morphosyntax and semantics. First, speakers of case-marking languages use case marking rather than word order in order to determine who did what to whom: Case markers play an important (and sometimes crucial) role in the interpretation of a sentence. Second, in languages where case marking is optional (such as Korean), the apparent optionality is in fact governed by semantic as well as discourse-based properties. This section discusses how these two semantic aspects of case marking (the use of case markers for interpretation, and the factors that govern case drop) play out in HL grammars.

With regard to the use of case markers in interpretation, Song, O'Grady, Cho, and Lee (1997) found that child HSs of Korean failed to use case markers to interpret noncanonical order (OSV) sentences in a picture-matching task. Failure to use case-marking cues has also been found to result in the misinterpretation of object relative clauses, in both adult Korean HSs (O'Grady et al. 2001) and adult Russian HSs (Polinsky 2011) (interestingly, the child HSs in Polinsky 2011 were quite target-like, which suggests that attrition rather than incomplete acquisition was at work in this particular case). K. Kim, O'Grady, and Schwartz (2018) followed up the findings of Song et al. (1997) in order to determine whether child HSs of Korean lack knowledge of case marking or whether such knowledge is obscured by other factors. K. Kim et al. (2018) manipulated the prosodic prominence of the case markers and the presence of a context that made OSV order natural. They found that both manipulations led to increased accuracy on OSV sentences by the child HSs, but that they were still much less accurate than monolingual children; proficiency made a difference, so that child HSs of higher proficiency performed in a much more target-like manner. Finally, child HSs were found to be much more accurate on OSV order with dative than with accusative case-marking, again supporting the importance of prosodic prominence, since the Korean dative marker is disyllabic, while the accusative marker is monosyllabic. Thus, in this case, the acquisition of a syntax–semantics mapping (roughly, using the case marker to determine the agent vs. the theme) is also influenced by phonological, and specifically prosodic, characteristics of the case marker.

Failure to correctly use case marking in production and comprehension may be due to transfer from English (the dominant language in all the studies cited), which lacks overt case morphology. It may also be a function of input, given that in Russian, nominative case is the default, and the most frequent, while Korean has case drop. In a recent study of Korean case drop, Chung (2018) examined adult HSs' (as well as L2ers') sensitivity to the semantic and discourse factors behind this phenomenon. Using an oral picture description task as well as a written elicitation task, Chung found that HSs (unlike L2ers) exhibited similar patterns to NSs with regard to the relative strength of factors, and that the differences between HSs and NSs were largely quantitative rather than qualitative. The HSs were particularly similar to NSs with regard to the factors of contrastive focus and animacy, but less consistent with regard to the factor of definiteness. Sensitivity to contrastive focus was also found in the production study in K. Kim et al. (2018), who found that, while child HSs overall dropped case marking in Korean more than monolingual children, they were nevertheless able to use case to signal contrastive focus.

To sum up, while HSs do not always attend to case marking in order to interpret the sentence (overrelying on word order instead), factors such as prosodic prominence and HSs' proficiency in the language affect the degree of accuracy. Furthermore, HSs appear to be sensitive to the discourse factors that govern case marker use vs. omission in a language where such omission is allowed.

26.4.2 Differential Object Marking

A much-studied phenomenon in both L2 and HL acquisition is Differential Object Marking (DOM); in languages which have DOM, only some objects are morphologically marked, those that have higher semantic or pragmatic prominence due to such factors as definiteness, specificity, animacy, etc. (Aissen 2003). In acquisition, DOM has primarily been studied with regard to Spanish, where it takes the form of the occurrence of the dative preposition *a* with direct objects that are animate and specific. (But see also Yager et al. 2015 for evidence that speakers of heritage German reanalyze dative marking as DOM).

Omission of *a*-marking with direct objects has been found in Spanish HSs who had a robust control of accusative and dative clitics (Silva-Corvalán 1994; Montrul 2004). An experimental study by Montrul and Bowles (2009) found that Spanish HSs exhibited incomplete knowledge of DOM as well as of inherent dative marking in both production and judgments. Montrul and Bowles (2010) found that explicit instruction on DOM with Spanish HSs in college classrooms led to improvement. Finally, Montrul and Sánchez-Walker (2013) compared child and young adult Spanish HSs, and found that both groups had difficulty with DOM, but that there was improvement from children to adults, indicating development. There were no differences between simultaneous and sequential bilinguals. Interestingly, Montrul and Sánchez-Walker (2013) also documented some errors with DOM among adult L1 attriters, immigrants from Mexico with several years of residence in the United States (relative to monolingual controls in Mexico), which indicates that DOM is subject to attrition in adults, as well as to incomplete acquisition in bilingual children.

While most studies of DOM in HL grammars have been done on Spanish, Montrul, Bhatt, and Girju (2015) examined DOM in heritage Hindi and Romanian, as well as in Spanish. On the one hand, HSs from all three groups exhibited much omission of DOM, so the phenomenon is clearly not specific to Spanish. On the other hand, there were some cross-linguistic differences. Age of onset made a difference only for Romanian, where sequential bilinguals outperformed simultaneous bilinguals. At the same time, attrition of DOM was documented in adult Spanish-speaking immigrants from Mexico (who omitted DOM more than their monolingual counterparts), but not in adult Romanian and Hindi-speaking immigrants, who performed on a par with monolinguals. Montrul et al. (2015) consider both internal (structural) and external (sociolinguistic) differences among the three languages and populations tested, and ultimately conclude that the structural linguistic differences in the expression of DOM are primarily responsible for the differences among the three language groups tested. They also noted that in the case of the Spanish HSs, the input that they receive, from older immigrants, already has some attrition of DOM, and that this in turn contributes to greater erosion of DOM in Spanish HSs compared to Hindi and Romanian HSs. At the same time, Hindi and Romanian HSs also show incomplete command of DOM, despite input from older immigrants that is not qualitatively different from that of monolinguals. Thus, qualitative differences in the input can account for only some cases of incomplete acquisition in HSs.

26.4.3 Binding and Co-reference

The interpretation of reflexive pronouns is a much-studied topic in L2-acquisition, with most studies focusing on the cross-linguistic variation in the binding domain of reflexives. In particular, while English requires local binding of reflexives, many East Asian languages (Korean, Japanese, Mandarin Chinese) have reflexives that allow long-distance binding as well as those that require local binding. Thus, in a sentence such as "Mary thinks that Sue painted herself," English requires Sue to be the antecedent of *herself*, while Korean, Japanese, and Mandarin have reflexive forms that may take either Mary or Sue as the antecedent.

This topic falls squarely at the interface between syntax and semantics or pragmatics. The binding domain of the reflexive is, on at least some accounts (e.g., Manzini and Wexler 1987), the result of syntactic parametric variation; at the same time, it has direct consequences for interpretation, since the choice of antecedent determines the meaning of the entire sentence. On other accounts (e.g., Huang and Liu 2001 for the reflexive *ziji* in Mandarin), the local vs. long-distance readings of reflexives correspond to a distinction between anaphors and logophors, with the latter subject to pragmatic rather than syntactic constraints. The cross-linguistic differences with regard to the binding domain of reflexives have been investigated with regard to cross-linguistic influence in L2-acquisition (see, e.g., Thomas 1995; White et al. 1996; Yuan 1998), and, more recently, with regard to HL grammars as well.

In Korean, the complex anaphor *caki-casin* requires local binding, while the simplex anaphor *caki* allows both local and long-distance binding. Song et al. (1997) found that child Korean-English bilinguals in the United States were able to distinguish the two anaphors but that they had no preference for the long-distance reading of *caki* over the local one, unlike monolinguals.

J.-H. Kim, Montrul, and Yoon (2009, 2010) tested the interpretation of these reflexive anaphors (as well as a third one, *casin*) in adult Korean HSs. J.-H. Kim et al. (2009) used a truth value judgment task with both early bilinguals (who learned English as well as Korean at birth) and late bilinguals (who learned English only around puberty). They found that early bilinguals correctly treated *caki* as a long-distance anaphor and *caki-casin* as a local one. At the same time, they accepted long-distance readings of *caki* less than monolinguals, and local readings of *caki* more; and they overaccepted long-distance and overrejected local readings of *caki-casin*. The early bilinguals also had the most difficulty with *casin*, a reflexive that allows both local and long-distance readings equally for monolinguals. Late bilinguals, in contrast, were quite similar to monolinguals. Overall, the performance of early bilinguals suggested incomplete acquisition that could be due to both transfer from English and input quality.

J.-H. Kim et al. (2010) further investigated HSs' knowledge of Korean reflexives, comparing HSs with adult L1 attriters, as well as with L2-Korean learners. Focusing on *caki*, they investigated both the binding domain and the ability of a subcommanding antecedent to bind *caki*, something which is not possible in English (*Silvia's pride hurt herself*). The L1 attriters were no different from monolinguals, while the HSs, as well as the L2ers, underaccepted both the long-distance readings of *caki* and the readings that required a subcommanding antecedent (though there was also individual variability).

Chen (2019) conducted a study of Chinese reflexives using a methodology based on J.-H. Kim et al. (2009). In Mandarin Chinese, the complex reflexive *taziji* requires local binding while the simplex reflexive *ziji* allows both local and long-distance binding. Chen (2019) found that adult Mandarin HSs, as well as L2ers, largely rejected long-distance readings of *ziji*, unlike monolinguals. At the same time, HSs were quite target-like on *taziji*; the findings were compatible both with transfer from English, the dominant language, and with local binding being a default option for learners.

In sum, the few studies that have been done on anaphor binding in HLs suggest that HSs have difficulty with reflexives that allow long-distance readings in the heritage language but not in English, the dominant language. While the findings are largely compatible with cross-linguistic influence from the dominant language, other explanations cannot be ruled out.

26.5 Quantifiers

Finally, this chapter considers the interpretation of quantifiers in HL grammars. While this topic is relatively understudied in research with HSs, the few available studies provide evidence that cross-linguistic transfer from the dominant language is not operative in this domain.

26.5.1 Quantifier Scope

The scope of quantifiers has been investigated in several studies with adult L2-learners, which have generally found evidence for cross-linguistic influence in this domain (see, e.g., Marsden 2009; Chung 2013). Two recent studies have looked at quantifier scope in HL grammars. M. Lee, Kwak, Lee, and O'Grady (2010) examined sentences with negation-universal quantifier ambiguity, such as *Mary did not read all the books*. In English, the preferred reading is the one corresponding to the surface scope, *not>every* (it's not the case that Mary read all the books, but she may have read some of the books). In Korean, which has S-O-neg-V order, the preferred reading (corresponding to the surface scope for Korean) is the opposite, *every>not* (for every book, it is not the case that Mary read it, i.e., Mary read none of the books). M. Lee et al. (2010), using a truth-value judgment task, found that adult native Korean speakers tested in Korean nearly always accepted the *every>not* reading but only accepted the *not>every* reading about half the time. Interestingly, both child and adult Korean-English bilinguals in the United States exhibited exactly the same pattern in English as Korean monolinguals did in Korean, differing from what has been found for adult English monolinguals (however, young children acquiring English also exhibit a strong preference for the *every>not* reading, Musolino and Lidz 2006). Thus, the weaker language (Korean) apparently influenced the stronger language (English). A limitation of the M. Lee et al. (2010) study is that the study samples were very small, and no monolingual English control group was tested on the same materials.

O'Grady, Kwak, Lee, and Lee (2011) report on the same two populations (English-dominant Korean HSs, children as well as adults) tested on scope in Korean, and the results are very similar to those of monolingual Korean speakers, and to the results of the HSs tested in English in M. Lee et al. (2010). O'Grady et al. (2011) found that Korean HSs accepted the *not>every* reading more than monolinguals, presumably under the influence of English, but still strongly preferred the *every>not* reading. Thus, negation-universal quantifier scope in Korean appears to be quite robust under conditions of reduced input; O'Grady et al. (2011) argue for a processing explanation, on which the *every>not* reading in Korean is easier to process than the *not>every* reading.

Scontras, Polinsky, Tsai, and Mai (2017) looked at double-quantifier ambiguities in sentences such as *A/one shark attacked every pirate*, in English and in Mandarin Chinese. It is well established that English allows both the surface-scope reading (there is one specific shark that attacked all the pirates) and the inverse-scope reading (for every pirate, there was a shark that attacked it, and the sharks may have been different). In Mandarin, a frozen-scope language, only the surface-scope reading is possible. Scontras et al. (2017) used a sentence-acceptability judgment task with pictures, where the pictures represented either the surface-scope or the inverse-scope reading. As expected, adult monolingual English speakers allowed both readings, while adult monolingual Mandarin speakers allowed only the *one>every* reading. Adult English-dominant Mandarin HSs were tested in both of their languages. In Mandarin, they accepted the inverse-scope reading more than monolinguals did, but overall had low rates of inverse-scope acceptance; in English, they accepted the inverse-scope reading *less* than monolinguals did. Scontras et al. (2017) conclude that there was no cross-linguistic influence, and that the HSs opted for the simplest grammar, one without inverse scope.

26.5.2 Quantifier Spreading

Sekerina and Sauermann (2015) examined a different phenomenon related to quantifiers, namely, quantifier spreading, in HL grammars. There is much literature on child L1-acquisition (starting with Inhelder and Piaget 1964; see Sekerina and Sauermann 2015 for more references) showing that children misinterpret sentences such as "Every alligator is in a bathtub." They make both overexhaustive errors (incorrectly rejecting this sentence when there is one empty bathtub) and underexhaustive errors (incorrectly accepting this sentence when there is an extra alligator not in a bathtub). These errors have also been attested for adult L2ers (Dellicarpini 2003) and for less educated monolingual adults (Street and Dąbrowska 2010). Sekerina and Sauermann (2015) extended the investigation of quantifier spreading to adult English-dominant Russian HSs, using a sentence-picture verification task with eye-tracking. When tested in Russian, the HSs were less accurate than monolinguals in the overexhaustive condition, but were target-like in the underexhaustive condition; they were also at-ceiling when tested in English. Fine-grained eye-movement data revealed that when the HSs were making errors in the overexhaustive condition in Russian, they were looking more at the extra, irrelevant container (e.g., the empty bathtub). Sekerina and Sauermann (2015) suggest that all of the groups who make quantifier-spreading errors, including HSs, have difficulty integrating multiple sources of information at once, because of the pressure being placed on the processor.

Thus, in the case of quantifier spreading, as in the case of quantifier scope, cross-linguistic influence is not attested; instead, divergence from monolinguals is attributed to processing difficulties and/or grammar simplification. However, a word of caution is needed, given that there have been relatively few studies with HSs in this domain.

26.6   Conclusion and Directions for Further Research

The picture painted by the studies discussed in this chapter is quite complicated. Some studies find fairly target-like performance among HSs but most find some degree of divergence. Many of the studies find cross-linguistic influence from the dominant language, but given that only a very small number of dominant languages have been examined, such findings are not definitive, and the divergence could also be due to processing or grammar simplification factors.

Given that the studies differ in the heritage language tested, the HSs' proficiency and experience with the HL, and the methodology used, it is difficult to make any definitive conclusions. However, some trends do arise. Phenomena at the interface with discourse (such as case drop, and also the distribution of overt vs. null anaphora – see the chapter on Discourse and Information Structure) do present difficulty to HSs, consistent with the IH. At the same time, phenomena that are arguably at the internal syntax–semantics interface (such as article semantics, reflexive binding, and grammatical aspect) are also subject to incomplete acquisition. The same phenomena have been found to present difficulty to L2ers as well, and while relatively few studies have compared the two populations directly, it is reasonable to suppose that morphological marking of semantic distinctions is a "bottleneck" in HL as well as L2 grammars (Slabakova 2008).

The effects of age and input on HL grammars seem quite indisputable: Those studies that examine age of onset effects often find that later, sequential bilinguals (who received exposure to the HL prior to acquiring their dominant language) outperform earlier, simultaneous bilinguals. L1 attriters tend to be much more like monolinguals than like HSs, but nevertheless attrition effects are in evidence for this population.

In future research, it would be fruitful to compare multiple phenomena within a single study and with the same population. Some studies have already done this (see, e.g., Montrul 2004 on both DOM and overt vs. null subjects; Serratrice et al. 2009, on genericity, and Sorace, Serratrice, Filiaci, and Baldo 2009, on overt vs. null subjects, compared in Sorace and Serratrice 2009). Rather than focusing on the distinction between internal vs. external interfaces (which is not always clear), it may be fruitful to examine multiple phenomena that all involve syntax–semantics mappings, comparing those that are similarly vs. differently instantiated in the HL and the dominant language. Testing multiple phenomena on the same populations would provide more fine-grained information about what exactly is vulnerable and what is robust in HL grammars.

Another direction is to expand the range of dominant languages that are examined, adding to the body of research on English and other Germanic languages (or Indo-European languages more generally) as the dominant languages. Of course, this research direction applies not only to research on semantics, but to any linguistic domain; in the area of morphosyntax, there is already work on, e.g., Hebrew as the dominant language (Meir and Polinsky 2021). In the research on HL semantics, the range of dominant languages examined seems particularly small. An investigation of different HL/dominant language pairs in which the HL is kept constant would allow for a more definitive conclusion with regard to the role of cross-linguistic influence.

References

Ahn, H. D. 1991. Light Verbs and VP-Movement, Negation and Clausal Architecture in Korean and Japanese. PhD dissertation, University of Wisconsin, Madison.

Aissen, J. 2003. Differential Object Marking: Iconicity vs. Economy. *Natural Language & Linguistic Theory* 21, 435–448.

Antinucci, F. and R. Miller. 1976. How Children Talk about What Happened. *Journal of Child Language* 3, 167–189.

Arslan, S., D. De Kok, and R. Bastiaanse. 2017. Processing Grammatical Evidentiality and Time Reference in Turkish Heritage and Monolingual Speakers. *Bilingualism: Language and Cognition* 20(3), 457–472. https://doi.org/10.1017/S136672891500084X

Burzio, L. 1981. Intransitive Verbs and Italian Auxiliaries. PhD dissertation, MIT.

Chen, C.-Y. 2019. The Acquisition of Mandarin Reflexives by Heritage Speakers and Second Language Learners. In T. Ionin and M. Rispoli (eds.), *Three Streams of Generative Language Acquisition Research: Selected papers from the 7th Meeting of Generative Approaches to Language Acquisition – North America, University of Illinois at Urbana-Champaign.* Amsterdam: John Benjamins, 225–251.

Chung, E. S. 2013. Sources of Difficulty in L2 Scope Judgments. *Second Language Research* 29, 285–310.

Chung, E. S. 2018. Second and Heritage Language Acquisition of Korean Case Drop. *Bilingualism: Language and Cognition* 21(1), 63–79. https://doi.org/10.1017/S1366728916001218

Comrie, B. 1976. *Aspect.* Cambridge: Cambridge University Press.

Dellicarpini, M. 2003. Developmental Stages in the Semantic Acquisition of Quantification by Adult L2 Learners of English: A Pilot Study. In J. Liceras, H. Zobl, and H. Goodluck (eds.), *Proceedings of the 6th Generative Approaches to Second Language Acquisition conference (GASLA 2002): L2 Links*. Somerville, MA: Cascadilla Press, 55–63.

Enç, M. 1991. The Semantics of Specificity. *Linguistic Inquiry* 22, 1–26.

Fukuda, S. 2017. Floating Numeral Quantifiers as an Unaccusative Diagnostic in Native, Heritage, and L2 Japanese Speakers. *Language Acquisition* 24(3), 169–208. https://doi.org/10.1080/10489223.2016.1179742

Huang, C.-T. J. and C.-S. L. Liu. 2001. Logophoricity, Attitudes, and Ziji at the Interface. In P. Cole, G. Hermon, and C.-T. J. Huang (eds.), *Long-Distance Reflexives*. New York: Academic Press, 141–195.

Inhelder, B. and J. Piaget. 1964. *The Early Growth of Logic in the Child*. London: Routledge and Kegan Paul.

Jia, R. and J. Paradis. 2015. The Use of Referring Expressions in Narratives by Mandarin Heritage Language Children and the Role of Language Environment Factors in Predicting Individual Differences. *Bilingualism: Language and Cognition* 18(4), 737–752. https://doi.org/10.1017/S1366728914000728

Kim, J.-H., S. Montrul, and J. Yoon. 2009. Binding Interpretations of Anaphors by Korean Heritage Speakers. *Language Acquisition* 16(1), 3–35.

Kim, J.-H., S. Montrul, and J. Yoon. 2010. Dominant Language Influence in Acquisition and Attrition of Binding: Interpretation of the Korean Reflexive Caki. *Bilingualism: Language and Cognition* 13(1), 73–84. https://doi.org/10.1017/S136672890999037X

Kim, K., W. O'Grady, and B. D. Schwartz. 2018. Case in Heritage Korean. *Linguistic Approaches to Bilingualism* 8(2), 252–282. https://doi.org/10.1075/lab.16001.kim

Kupisch, T. 2012. Specific and Generic Subjects in the Italian of German-Italian Simultaneous Bilinguals and L2 Learners. *Bilingualism: Language and Cognition* 15, 736–756.

Kupisch, T., A. Belikova, Ö. Özçelik, I. Stangen, and L. White. 2017. Restrictions on Definiteness in the Grammars of German-Turkish Heritage Speakers. *Linguistic Approaches to Bilingualism* 7(1), 1–32. https://doi.org/10.1075/lab.13031.kup

Laleko, O. 2011. Restructuring of Verbal Aspect in Heritage Russian: Beyond Lexicalization. *International Journal of Language Studies* 5(3), 13–26.

Lee, M., H.-Y. Kwak, S. Lee, and W. O'Grady. 2010. Processing, Pragmatics, and Scope in Korean and English. In *Proceedings of 19th Japanese-Korean Linguistic Conference*. CSLI Publications.

Lee, T. 2011. Grammatical Knowledge of Korean Heritage Speakers: Early vs. Late Bilinguals. *Linguistic Approaches to Bilingualism* 1(2), 149–174.

Levin, B. and M. Rappaport Hovav. 1995. *Unaccusativity at the Syntax Semantics Interface*. Cambridge, MA: MIT Press

Manzini, M. R. and K. Wexler. 1987. Parameters, Binding Theory, and Learnability. *Linguistic Inquiry* 18, 413–444.

Marsden, H. 2009. Distributive Quantifier Scope in English-Japanese and Korean-Japanese Interlanguage. *Language Acquisition* 16, 135–177.

Meir, N. and M. Polinsky. 2021. Restructuring in Heritage Grammars: Adjective-noun and Numeral-noun Expressions in Israeli Russian. *Linguistic Approaches to Bilingualism*. 11(2), 222–258.

Milsark, G. 1977. Toward an Explanation of Certain Peculiarities of the Existential Construction in English. *Linguistic Analysis* 3, 1–29.

Miyagawa, S. 1989. *Syntax and Semantics: Structure and Case Marking in Japanese*. New York: Academic Press.

Montrul, S. 2002. Incomplete Acquisition and Attrition of Spanish Tense/ Aspect Distinctions in Adult Bilinguals *Bilingualism: Language and Cognition* 5, 39–68.

Montrul, S. 2004. Subject and Object Expression in Spanish Heritage Speakers: A Case of Morpho-syntactic Convergence. *Bilingualism: Language and Cognition* 7, 1–18.

Montrul, S. 2005. Second Language Acquisition and First Language Loss in Adult Early Bilinguals: Exploring Some Differences and Similarities. *Second Language Research* 21(3), 199–249.

Montrul, S. 2008. *Incomplete Acquisition in Bilingualism: Re-examining the Age Factor*. Amsterdam: John Benjamins.

Montrul, S. 2009. Knowledge of Tense-Aspect and Mood in Spanish Heritage Speakers. *International Journal of Bilingualism* 13(2), 239–369.

Montrul, S. and M. Bowles. 2009. Back to Basics: Differential Object Marking under Incomplete Acquisition in Spanish Heritage Speakers. *Bilingualism: Language and Cognition* 12(3), 363–383.

Montrul, S. and M. Bowles. 2010. Is Grammar Instruction Beneficial for Heritage Language Learners? Dative Case Marking in Spanish. *Heritage Language Journal* 7(1), 47–73.

Montrul, S. and T. Ionin. 2010. Transfer Effects in the Interpretation of Definite Articles by Spanish Heritage Speakers. *Bilingualism: Language and Cognition* 13, 449–473.

Montrul, S. and T. Ionin. 2012. Dominant Language Transfer in Spanish Heritage Speakers and L2 Learners in the Interpretation of Definite Articles. *Modern Language Journal* 96, 70–94.

Montrul, S. and M. Polinsky. 2011. Why Not Heritage Speakers? *Linguistic Approaches to Bilingualism* 1(1), 58–62.

Montrul, S. and N. Sánchez-Walker. 2013. Differential Object Marking in Child and Adult Spanish Heritage Speakers. *Language Acquisition* 20(2), 109–132. https://doi.org/10.1080/10489223.2013.766741

Montrul, S., R. Bhatt, and R. Girju. 2015. Differential Object Marking in Spanish, Hindi, and Romanian as Heritage Languages. *Language* 91(3), 564–610.

Musolino, J. and J. Lidz. 2006. Why Children Aren't Universally Successful with Quantification. *Linguistics* 44(4), 817–852. https://doi.org/10.1515/LING.2006.026

O'Grady, W., M. Lee, and M. Choo. 2001. The Acquisition of Relative Clauses by Heritage and Non-heritage Learners of Korean as a Second Language, a Comparative Study. *Journal of Korean Language Education* 12, 283–294.

O'Grady, W., H.-Y. Kwak, O.-S. Lee, and M. Lee. 2011. An Emergentist Perspective on Heritage Language Acquisition. *Studies in Second Language Acquisition* 33(2), 223–245. https://doi.org/10.1017/S0272263110000744

Pascual y Cabo, D., A. Lingwall, and J. Rothman. 2012. Applying the Interface Hypothesis to Heritage Speaker Acquisition: Evidence from Spanish Mood. In A. Biller, E. Chung, and A. Kimball (eds.), *Proceedings of the 36th Annual Boston University Conference on Language Development.* Somerville, MA: Cascadilla Press, 437–448.

Perlmutter, D. 1978. Impersonal Passives and the Unaccusative Hypothesis. In *Proceedings of the Fourth Annual Meeting of the Berkeley-Linguistic Society.* Berkeley, CA: Berkeley Linguistic Society, University of California, 157–189.

Polinsky, M. 2007. Incomplete Acquisition: American Russian. *Journal of Slavic Linguistics* 14, 191–262.

Polinsky, M. 2008a. Heritage Language Narratives. In D. Brinton, O. Kagan, and S. Bauckus (eds.), *Heritage Language Education: A New Field Emerging.* New York: Routledge, 149–164.

Polinsky, M. 2008b. Without Aspect. In G. C. Greville and N. Michael (eds.), *Case and Grammatical Relations.* Amsterdam: John Benjamins, 263–282.

Polinsky, M. 2011. Reanalysis in Adult Heritage Language: A Case for Attrition. *Studies in Second Language Acquisition* 33, 305–328.

Polinsky, M. 2018. *Heritage Languages and Their Speakers.* Cambridge: Cambridge University Press.

Rothman, J. 2009. Understanding the Nature and Outcomes of Early Bilingualism: Romance Languages as Heritage Languages. *International Journal of Bilingualism* 13(2), 155–163.

Scontras, G., M. Polinsky, C.-Y.E. Tsai, and K. Mai. 2017. Cross-Linguistic Scope Ambiguity: When Two Systems Meet. *Glossa* 2(1), 36.1–28.

Sekerina, I. and A. Sauermann. 2015. Visual Attention and Quantifier-Spreading in Heritage Russian Bilinguals. *Second Language Research* 31(1), 75–104. https://doi.org/10.1177/0267658314537292

Serratrice, L., A. Sorace, F. Filiaci, and M. Baldo. 2009. Bilingual Children's Sensitivity to Specificity and Genericity: Evidence from Metalinguistic Awareness. *Bilingualism: Language and Cognition* 12, 239–257.

Sherkina-Lieber, M. 2015. Tense, Aspect, and Agreement in Heritage Labrador Inuttitut: Do Receptive Bilinguals Understand Functional Morphology? *Linguistic Approaches to Bilingualism* 5(1), 30–61. https://doi.org/10.1075/lab.5.1.02she

Shirai, Y. and R. Andersen. 1996. Primacy of Aspect in First and Second Language Acquisition: The Pidgin/Creole Connection. In W. C. Ritchie and T. K. Bhatia (eds.), *Handbook of Second Language Acquisition*. San Diego, CA: Academic Press, 527–570.

Silva-Corvalán, C. 1994. *Language Contact and Change: Spanish in Los Angeles*. Oxford: Oxford University Press

Slabakova, R. 2008. *Meaning in the Second Language*. Berlin: Mouton de Gruyter

Song, M., W. O'Grady, S. Cho, and M. Lee. 1997. The Learning and Teaching of Korean in Community Schools. In Y.-H. Kim (ed.), *Korean Language in America 2*. American Association of Teachers of Korean, 111–127.

Sorace, A. 2000a. Differential Effects of Attrition in the L1 Syntax of Near-Native L2 Speakers. In *Proceedings of the 24th Boston University Conference on Language Development*. Sommerville, MA: Cascadilla Press, 719–725.

Sorace, A. 2000b. Gradients in Auxiliary Selection with Intransitive Verbs. *Language* 76, 859–890.

Sorace, A. 2011. Pinning down the Concept of "Interface" in Bilingualism. *Linguistic Approaches to Bilingualism* 1, 1–33. https://doi.org/10.1075/lab.1.1.01sor

Sorace, A. and F. Filiaci. 2006. Anaphora Resolution in Near-Native Speakers of Italian. *Second Language Research* 22, 339–368. https://doi.org/10.1191/0267658306sr271oa

Sorace, A. and L. Serratrice. 2009. Internal and External Interfaces in Bilingual Language Development: Revisiting the Processing vs. Representation Distinction. *The International Journal of Bilingualism* 13(2), 195–210.

Sorace, A., L. Serratrice, F. Filiaci, and M. Baldo. 2009. Discourse Conditions on Subject Pronoun Realization: Testing the Linguistic Intuitions of Older Bilingual Children. *Lingua* 119, 460–477.

Street, J. A. and E. Dąbrowska. 2010. More Individual Differences in Language Attainment: How Much Do Adult Native Speakers of English Know about Passives and Quantifiers? *Lingua* 120(8), 2080–2094. https://doi.org/10.1016/j.lingua.2010.01.004

Thomas, M. 1995. Acquisition of the Japanese Reflexive Zibun and Movement of Anaphors in Logical Form. *Second Language Research* 11(3), 206–234. https://doi.org/10.1177/026765839501100302

Vendler, Z. 1967. *Linguistics in Philosophy*. Ithaca, NY: Cornell University Press.

Verkuyl, H. 1993. *A Theory of Aspectuality. The Interaction between Temporal and Atemporal Structure*. Cambridge: Cambridge University Press.

White, L. 2011. Second Language Acquisition at the Interfaces. *Lingua* 121, 577–590.

White, L., A. Belikova, P. Hagstrom, T. Kupisch, and Ö. Özçelik. 2012. Restrictions on Definiteness in Second Language Acquisition:

Affirmative and Negative Existentials in the L2 English of Turkish and Russian Speakers. *Linguistic Approaches to Bilingualism* 2(1), 54–89.

White, L., M. Hirakawa, and T. Kawasaki. 1996. Effect of Instruction on Second Language Acquisition of the Japanese Long-Distance Reflexive Zibun. *Canadian Journal of Linguistics* 41, 135–154.

Yager, L., N. Hellmold, H.-A. Joo, M. T. Putnam, E. Rossi, C. Stafford, and J. Salmons. 2015. New Structural Patterns in Moribund Grammar: Case Marking in Heritage German. *Frontiers in Psychology* 6(1716). https://doi.org/10.3389/fpsyg.2015.01716

Yuan, B. 1998. Interpretation of Binding and Orientation of the Chinese Reflexive Ziji by English and Japanese Speakers. *Second Language Research* 14(4), 324–340. https://doi.org/10.1191/026765898670904111

Zyzik, E. 2014. Causative Verbs in the Grammar of Spanish Heritage Speakers. *Linguistic Approaches to Bilingualism* 4, 1–33.

27

Discourse and Information Structure in Heritage Languages

Oksana Laleko

27.1 Introduction

A fundamental function of human language, rooted in its communicative aspect, is to facilitate the exchange of information among discourse participants. It is therefore not surprising that all natural languages have means for organizing sentences into units of information based on the speaker's intent, the addressee's informational needs, and discourse context. The notion of *information structure* subsumes a number of distinct but overlapping concepts related to the distribution of information within and across utterances, often grouped along the binary distinction between *old/given* and *new* information in discourse (Chafe 1976; Lambrecht 1994; Gundel 2003). These two core dimensions of information structure – what is presumed to be known and what is just being introduced – have been recognized in many longstanding linguistic traditions under different terminological labels, such as psychological subject and predicate, theme and rheme, topic and comment, background and focus, presupposition and focus, and, most recently, *topic* and *focus* (see Gundel and Fretheim 2004, for a theoretical overview).

While there is still no agreement among researchers on the exact definitions of the terms "topic" and "focus," some non-overlapping distinctive properties associated with these concepts have been identified. The notion of *topic* seems particularly hard to pin down, as evidenced by a great heterogeneity of the available definitions. In various theoretical approaches, topic has been discussed as what the sentence is about; shared knowledge between the speaker and the addressee; contextual anchoring and boundedness; and old, presupposed, or non-focal information (see Casielles-Suárez 2004). What these different approaches have in common is that the topical part is conceptualized as the relatively less informative part of the utterance that is complemented by another, more informative, part. In terms of their linguistic realization, topic expressions typically surface as deaccented, unstressed, reduced, or phonologically empty elements that may also occupy a specific syntactic position or be marked with a topicalizing morpheme (e.g., *-wa* in Japanese).

Conversely, *focus* is traditionally understood as the non-presupposed or new information in the utterance (Zubizarreta 1998), or "that portion of a proposition that cannot be taken for granted at the time of speech" (Lambrecht 1994: 207). Depending on how much material is being attended to as new, the domain of focus can range from narrow (e.g., a single constituent or part thereof) to broad (e.g., the whole sentence). Within the semantics literature, focus is often discussed in terms of its association with question answering (e.g., *Who came? BILL came*), with its primary function being linked to identifying the presence of alternatives relevant for the interpretation of the expression (Krifka 2008; Rooth 2016). Just like topic expressions, focus expressions may be marked by a variety of different means. Cross-linguistically, the focused constituent usually contains a word that receives a nuclear stress; this prosodic highlighting may apply in the constituent's canonical position (i.e., *in situ*) or in tandem with the syntactic movement of the focal element to a more prominent position, by itself or as part of a conventionalized syntactic construction (e.g., clefting).

The vast theoretical literature identifies a descriptively diverse set of further subtypes of topics and foci. While the full range of these distinctions cannot be adequately encompassed here, one particular subcategory recognized within each of the two notions discussed previously deserves special mention. Both topics and foci may be *contrastive* (Büring 2016; Rooth 2016). In the most basic sense, a contrastive topic establishes or invokes a set of alternatives between presupposed, given, or backgrounded entities (e.g., *A: What did the girls bring? B: Mary brought soup and Sarah brought salad*). The notion of contrastive (also "identificational") focus is less clearly distinguishable from the discourse-new (also "informational" or "presentational") focus discussed earlier, particularly considering the fact that the latter notion is already defined in terms of alternatives. Nevertheless, linguists distinguish between informational and contrastive focus on the basis of their functions: While presentational focus introduces new information, contrastive focus is used for emphasis or correction, often denying part of a previous assertion (*A: Mary made a great salad! B: Actually, it was SARAH who made the salad*). In addition to these semantic distinctions, both contrastive categories, topics and foci, differ from their non-contrastive counterparts in intonation and morpho-syntactic behavior (Rizzi 1997; É. Kiss 1998; Büring 2016).

Research on discourse structure and the expression of information-structural distinctions was slow to enter the realm of Heritage Language

(HL) scholarship. In fact, it is not until now that the various phenomena pertaining to information packaging in discourse in HLs have been brought together under the roof of a single chapter. However, the recent years have seen a flourishing of cross-linguistic investigations in this domain; building on their momentum, this chapter presents a broad overview of the state of the art in the study of the linguistic realization of information structure and discourse organization in HLs. Considering the range of methodological and theoretical approaches to the study of information structure and a diverse set of phenomena that fall under its scope, the overall picture emerging at this juncture is still far from being uniform or complete. Nevertheless, as the following sections show, it is already possible to identify some general patterns in the HL encoding of information structure through morphological (Section 27.2), syntactic (Section 27.3), and prosodic (Section 27.4) means and its role in mediating anaphoric relations in discourse (Section 27.5). As further discussed in Section 27.6, these patterns converge on a set of generalizations that draw attention to language proficiency, degree of literacy, input properties, properties of the dominant language, and bilingual processing effects as factors shaping the resulting HL systems. At the same time, they offer novel insights into these systems by examining the formal and interpretive properties associated with the core categories of information structure in relation to their cognitive import, degree of informational salience, and ways in which they fit into the larger discourse structure.

27.2 Morphological Expression of Information Structure

Many natural languages employ morphological means for the expression of grammatical relations; relatively fewer languages use morphological marking to indicate topic–focus distinctions. In the latter group, Japanese and Korean are perhaps the better known examples of topic-prominent languages, i.e., languages that utilize dedicated morphemes to identify topics (-wa in Japanese, -(n)un in Korean) as distinct from subjects (-ga in Japanese, -i/-ka in Korean). In both languages, topic particles can mark thematic ("aboutness") and contrastive topics, distinguished by prosody and syntactic behavior, and may be omitted under certain grammatical and discourse-pragmatic conditions, particularly in colloquial registers. For topics in particular, particle drop has been analyzed as an important paradigmatic choice linked with the marking of topic continuity and relative prominence of referents in discourse (Shimojo 2006).

Considering the overall rich body of work on HL morphology (see Putnam, Schwartz, and Hoffman, this volume), studies of morphological encoding of information structure in HLs remain surprisingly few. Laleko and Polinsky (2013, 2016) analyzed data from a series of written acceptability judgment tasks with heritage speakers (HSs) of Japanese and Korean and found that while the evaluation of particles employed for the marking of information structure presents relatively more challenges to HSs across the proficiency spectrum than syntactic computation associated with grammatical case marking, not all information-structural distinctions are necessarily or equally problematic for bilinguals. In particular, advanced HSs were successful in conditions targeting overtly expressed case and topic particles, but were less efficient in their evaluation of topic particle omissions. From the processing standpoint, null forms present unique challenges due to their amplified ambiguity: The null form needs to be recovered before it can be interpreted and integrated with context. It is therefore not surprising that difficulty with null forms (the *Silent Problem*) in heritage bilinguals was manifested most strongly in structures that called for a greater degree of contextual embedding (such as anaphoric topics used for continuous reference), compared to the more local restrictions on the realization of grammatical relations through morphological case.

Further evidence of information-structural effects on the HSs' use of particle omission is reported in Chung (2018), who used data from a written elicited production task and an oral picture description task to investigate object case drop in Korean. Based on previous studies showing that case drop in Korean is sensitive to focus, animacy, and definiteness, Chung analyzed these three variables in the use of overt and omitted accusative case particle *-lul/-ul* by early and late bilinguals. With respect to focus, Chung created two conditions with different degrees of predictability from preceding context in order to tease apart strongly contrastive objects, which typically occur with an overt case morpheme, from highly predictable objects, which favor case drop. In written production, both native controls and HSs (but not L2 learners) were sensitive to the effects of focus and judged bare objects as more felicitous in non-contrastive focus contexts. However, in the oral production experiment, HSs diverged from the controls in their use of focus, a result Chung attributed to the blurring of contrast between the two subtypes of focus in the HL. This difference notwithstanding, HSs were overall close to native controls in means, relative strength of factors, and their interactions, with differences between the two groups being quantitative rather than qualitative in nature. In both tasks, HSs demonstrated a consistent significant effect of contrastive focus on their judgments and use of case drop, one that was absent in proficiency-matched L2 learners.

In another study, Laleko and Polinsky (2017) reported a similarly robust effect of contrastiveness in the domain of topic particle ellipsis in heritage Korean. In a written scaled acceptability judgments task, HSs and L2 learners showed a common difficulty in evaluating particle omissions with anaphoric topics, i.e., those forming a referential dependency with an antecedent in preceding discourse. However, the HSs, but not the L2 learners, demonstrated native-like felicity distinctions in their ratings of contrastive topic particles. Taken together with the findings of Chung's (2018) study, these results suggest that the mastery of subtle information-structural cues in bilinguals correlates with the context of acquisition: HSs' early aural naturalistic input boosts their sensitivity to information-structural cues, despite the blurring of some of the more fine-grained distinctions associated with these categories (e.g., subtypes of focus).

The facilitative effects of prosodically rich naturalistic input may be particularly strong for the acquisition of perceptually salient morphological distinctions, such as those associated with contrastiveness (either in topics or foci); Section 27.4 discusses evidence from other studies that parallels these results. Conversely, difficulties with constructing and marking anaphoric dependencies may be relatively more pervasive in the heritage system, particularly when these dependencies are associated with highly underspecified morphologically null forms. As a result, HSs do relatively well with particles that are predominantly overt, local, and predictable in their function, but show a much higher variability in their use and judgments of markers whose surface realization is optional, contextually determined, or associated with larger segments of discourse. Since only a small set of studies have looked at the morphological encoding of information structure distinctions in HLs, with the available data derived from two languages similar in their typology, these preliminary generalizations must be examined more systematically in future work.

27.3 Word Order and Information Structure

In many languages, including the topic-prominent languages discussed previously, the information-structural content of the utterance may be conveyed through the ordering of clausal constituents or dedicated constructions associated with particular topic–focus configurations. While languages differ greatly in their overall word order flexibility, they all seem to provide speakers with at least some syntactic resources to encode information structure (Gundel 2012). Of course, there is considerable variation in terms of how exactly information structure is mapped onto syntactic structure in a given language and to what extent this mapping engages other interface domains. Nevertheless, several broad cross-linguistic generalizations have been drawn. From the information-structural perspective, the relative ordering of constituents in structures that allow multiple order options has been shown to conform to the "given before new" principle, with expressions at the right edge being interpreted as new information, and expressions preceding them as given or old information (Neeleman and van de Koot 2016 and reference therein). Outside of information structure proper, the distribution of clausal constituents has been independently linked to their syntactic weight, with heavy (i.e., longer and more elaborate) constituents typically appearing after light constituents, and to the lexico-syntactic properties of clausal predicates, with unaccusative verbs favoring postverbal subjects in languages where subjects otherwise appear pre-verbally.

Within the HL literature, several studies have reported a tendency toward a reduction of word order flexibility, under-production of the non-default orders, and the increased use of the predominant SVO pattern by HSs (Albirini, Benmamoun, and Saadah 2011 for Egyptian Arabic; Montrul 2005; Zapata, Sánchez, and Toribio 2005 for Spanish; Isurin and Ivanova-Sullivan 2008; Ivanova-Sullivan 2014; Polinsky 1995, 2006 for Russian; see also Lohndal, this volume, for an overview of syntactic phenomena in HLs). Considering that word order in all of these languages is involved in the marking of topic–focus structure, loss of variation in this domain in heritage grammars may be related to changes in the expression of information structure. At the same time, it may also stem from changes in the underlying syntactic, semantic, and lexical properties interacting with discourse-level constraints. To probe into the complex interplay of these factors in HL systems, several researchers have investigated the effects of information structure on HL word order and its interactions with various grammatical principles. For expository purposes, I will first discuss studies that reveal substantial differences between heritage and baseline speakers in the encoding of information structure through word order, followed by studies that point to a relatively more successful acquisition and retention of these distinctions by HSs. A discussion of some possible differences in the observed patterns of results is offered in Section 27.6.

27.3.1   Word Order and Information Structure: What HSs Do Differently

Extending the methodology employed in L2 research to HL acquisition, Zapata et al. (2005) probed into the interpretation and production of word order distinctions in heritage Spanish in the United States in relation to lexical (verb type), discursive (focus), and semantic (definiteness) factors. Drawing on data from a written contextualized forced-choice judgment task, the authors examined the distribution of VS and SV orders with unaccusative and unergative predicates in broad-focus (e.g., *What happened?*) and narrow-focus (e.g., *Who sang?*) contexts. Overall, HSs seemed attuned to the unergative-unaccusative distinction as a trigger of word order variation in Spanish, but were less sensitive to the effects of focus on subject position, selecting SV and VS responses at identical rates under narrow focus with unergative verbs. Apart from focus movement, the study also examined two structures employed for the fronting of topical objects: topicalization, which involves the movement of a bare DP, and clitic left dislocation, which moves a definite DP accompanied by a clitic. The results of the fill-in-the-blank and question-answer tasks pointed to variable performance of HSs on both structures. Only a few instances of the relevant constructions were attested in the data, and the semantic features of the fronted DPs no longer served to distinguish them. Instead, the HSs showed convergence toward English by reinterpreting clause-initial objects as subjects, a finding Zapata et al. attributed to the vulnerability and special permeability of interface domains to cross-linguistic transfer.

Further evidence of differences between the heritage and baseline strategies of marking focused and topical elements through word order comes from studies on heritage Russian in the US context. Laleko (2017) employed a series of written contextualized scaled acceptability ratings tests to investigate the impact of information structure on word order variation in relation to focus (broad vs. narrow), verb type (unaccusative vs. unergative), and object givenness and weight in transitive sentences. Overall, the HSs significantly under-accepted VS orders in all possible contexts and demonstrated a global preference toward SV. In line with Zapata et al.'s findings for Spanish, the HSs' ratings of the VS orders reflected sensitivity to verb type, but there were no statistical effects of subject focus on the occurrence of VS with intransitive verbs.

In transitive subject-focus contexts (e.g., *Who fixed the bicycle?*), inversion in Russian is often accompanied by object fronting, yielding the OVS order as a felicitous response. In these contexts, the HSs showed a strong preference for SVO over OVS structures, whereas the monolinguals rated both orders equally highly. This apparent optionality in the monolingual judgments is not surprising: In addition to movement, focus in languages like Russian can be marked *in situ*, rendering the default SVO order a viable alternative to movement for the expression of subject focus. It is precisely in this condition that the HSs converged with the monolinguals. While compatible with previous accounts that attribute word order changes in the HL to dominant language influence, these results suggest that transfer effects do not have to lead to radical shifts in the heritage grammar or produce ungrammaticality, but may be manifested as more subtle, covert changes that involve the narrowing of the existing options still within the limits of acceptability imposed by the baseline system.

At the same time, when occurring systematically across multiple linguistic domains, even the most subtle changes may accumulate to create effects of occasional pragmatic infelicity or, over time, lead to the rise of novel strategies of discourse organization. Laleko and Dubinina (2018) analyzed oral narratives elicited from HSs of Russian in the United States to investigate the occurrence of canonical and noncanonical word order patterns and evaluate their contextual appropriateness. While HSs seemed generally attuned to the availability of non-SVO orders in Russian (22 percent in the heritage group vs. 32 percent in the monolingual control group), they were not consistent in applying target-like discursive principles in their use. The greatest proportion of infelicitous constructions was attested with structures involving dislocation, the movement of non-subject topical constituents to the left of the verb. In Laleko and Dubinina's account, the observed quantitative differences between the groups stem from different interactions between weight and givenness in the HSs' grammar of dislocations. The HSs adhered more closely to the weight principle in their use of movement than the monolinguals, who in turn were more likely to disregard the "light-before-heavy" principle to achieve information-structural cohesion.

All of the studies reviewed used offline measures; relatively little is known about HSs' processing of word order in online settings. To fill this gap, Sagarra, Sánchez, and Bel (2019) employed a word-by-word non-cumulative self-paced reading task to investigate the effects of word order on the processing and interpretation of Spanish relative clauses, which demonstrate the previously discussed SV/VS variation linked to the information-structural status of the subject. The accuracy results for HSs, advanced L2 learners, and monolinguals were in line with previous studies documenting increased difficulties with VS in bilinguals, with lower accuracy obtained for OVS in both bilingual groups. However, while the HSs patterned with the L2 learners in terms of accuracy, they were closer to monolinguals in their processing patterns and showed faster reaction times with noncanonical orders. These findings attest to the unique status of HSs on the bilingualism continuum and highlight the importance of employing online measures as a window into the strategies utilized by HSs for language comprehension in real time.

27.3.2 Word Order and Information Structure: Where HSs Show Little or No Difference

In contrast to these studies, several researchers reported a relatively more robust knowledge of information-structural principles governing word order variation among HSs across different age groups and levels of proficiency. For child HSs, Jia and Paradis (2015) investigated the use of linguistic devices to signal first mentions in oral narratives produced by school-aged HSs of Mandarin in Canada. While the HSs diverged from the monolingual children in their use of classifiers and vocabulary in introducing new participants or entities, they were successful in placing first-mentioned

NPs postverbally to convey new information and did not differ from the controls in this domain.

Gómez Soler and Pasqual y Cabo (2018) reported a similarly strong control of the correlation between new information focus and word order in adult HSs of Spanish. The study examined word order variation in double object constructions in relation to the end-focus (new information last) and end-weight (the heavier constituent last) principles. The HSs of Spanish tested in the United States demonstrated target-like mastery of both principles in an acceptability judgment task, a result the authors take to indicate an equally robust knowledge of syntactic and discursive word order factors. An earlier study by Prada Pérez and Pascual y Cabo (2012) offers less conclusive results about the distribution of intransitive predicates under broad and narrow subject focus, but supports the overall conclusion that the subject position in heritage Spanish indicates differences in information structure. The HSs at three levels of proficiency were successful in rating postverbal subjects higher in narrow focus than in broad focus with unergative predicates, suggesting good control of the end-focus principle in the HL. However, the HSs showed an overall trend toward preverbal subjects, also attested in the control group of Spanish-dominant speakers tested in the United States. The authors attribute these results to the global effects of language contact, manifested as an extension of SV in both bilingual groups, coupled with the less categorical nature of the rules on subject position in relation to predicate type compared to those related to focus.

Outside of the US context, a number of studies documented successful mastery of information-structural constraints on word order in HSs. Van Osch and Sleeman (2018) used a contextualized scaled acceptability judgment task to examine the effects of verb type, focus, and subject definiteness on word order variation with intransitive verbs in HSs of Spanish with Dutch as their dominant language. The HSs were not sensitive to definiteness, but converged with the controls on both verb type and focus. The fact that focus, an information structure phenomenon, was found to be unproblematic for the HSs in the study may be surprising considering that the participants were not all near-native speakers, occupying a proficiency range from high-intermediate to advanced. The authors link these results to two factors: a categorical nature of focus as a strong word order determiner in Spanish and facilitative effects from Dutch, which also exhibits effects of focus on word order (209). Further evidence for dominant language influence comes from the unexpectedly high ratings for postverbal subjects obtained in the heritage group across the experimental conditions. Contra previous studies pointing to an overgeneralization of SV orders in HLs, including Spanish in particular (Montrul 2005; Zapata et al. 2005), the Spanish HSs in Van Osch and Sleeman's study over-accepted postverbal subjects, possibly due to their frequent occurrence in Dutch.

The reported trend toward the retention or increase of word order flexibility in HLs outside of the English language environment finds further support in several production studies. Based on an analysis of written texts produced by adolescent heritage Russian speakers in Germany, Brehmer and Usanova (2015) concluded that these young bilinguals maintain and even amplify the pragmatic flexibility of verb placement in Russian. While this finding seemingly goes against the typically documented pattern of weakened frequency of noncanonical orders in HLs, it does not constitute direct evidence for target-like application of word order principles in the heritage grammar. Brehmer and Usanova emphasize that it is not clear if all of the attested noncanonical patterns are pragmatically acceptable (183). Thus, the high rates of noncanonical constructions attested in this study may be compatible with results of other studies that report overuse or over-acceptance of infelicitous orders by HSs as a manifestation of systematic differences in the use of rules that determine word order variation in the baseline, their more selective application, or overgeneralization (Laleko 2017; Laleko and Dubinina 2018; Van Osch and Sleeman 2018). Apart from the question of frequency in the use of canonical and noncanonical orders, Brehmer and Usanova also examined potential transfer effects from German on their distribution. The results did not yield a simple answer. In declarative sentences, where German requires a fixed V2 order, HSs did not appear to overuse V2 structures. However, there was a significant increase in V-final orders in subordinate and declarative main clauses, a pattern suggestive of transfer of the German V-final pattern and its subsequent overgeneralization. Brehmer and Usanova attribute the latter tendency to the effects of contact-induced pragmatic unmarking, i.e., the spread of a formerly restricted construction to a wider set of contexts, resulting in the impression of increased flexibility despite the non–target-like application of the relevant principles.

The same pattern of overgeneralization was reported by Albirini et al. (2011) for HSs of Palestinian Arabic, who significantly overused VSO orders in oral narratives. Interestingly, results from HSs of Egyptian Arabic in the same study pointed to a decreased use of VSO and increased use of SVO, a finding the authors attributed to transfer from English. In both varieties of Arabic, both orders are available, distinguished by semantic (definiteness) and information-structural factors. The authors discuss the obtained contrast between the Palestinian and Egyptian HSs as reflective of the degree of language maintenance in the respective speech communities. If these observations are on the right track, they add to the growing body of research pointing to language proficiency as a factor predictive of the extent of transfer effects in the heritage system. While lower-proficiency speakers demonstrate higher levels of dominant language transfer, the grammars of the more proficient speakers tend to show more resilience to direct transfer and rely to a greater extent on the principles operating in the baseline system, perhaps even fully converging with it.

The effects of dominant language transfer on the HL are further examined in Montrul (2010a), who compared HSs and L2 learners of Spanish on their acceptability judgments of clitic left dislocation constructions, employed for the movement of topical objects. Across all proficiency levels, HSs were better at differentiating between acceptable and unacceptable conditions. In fact, the HSs in the advanced group did not differ from the monolinguals, while the advanced L2 speakers never reached the monolingual results. Montrul attributes these patterns to the difference in the mode of acquisition of the target language. Topicalizations are a feature of informal spoken language and rarely occur in written academic settings. The more limited exposure of L2 learners to informal contexts, in contrast to the naturalistic experience of HSs, explains the differential success rates in the acquisition of these constructions.

Montrul (2010b) presents additional experimental data from low-proficiency heritage and L2 speakers of Spanish based on a speeded visual picture–sentence matching task contrasting topicalized and nontopicalized constructions with and without object clitics. Once again, results revealed a difference between the heritage and L2 groups, this time not only in terms of accuracy but also with regard to reaction times, reinforcing the idea that early naturalistic exposure is instrumental for the mastery of structures associated with topicalization. However, since the participant pool specifically excluded advanced speakers, the HSs in this study differed from the controls in both accuracy and processing speed. This result corroborates other studies attesting to the pervasiveness of difficulty with the encoding of topical material in low-proficiency speakers.

Further evidence of successful acquisition of the topic–focus distinction by intermediate and advanced heritage speakers comes from two separate studies of discourse-sensitive movement in Spanish. Leal Méndez, Rothman, and Slabakova (2015) compared the clitic left dislocations discussed previously with fronted focus constructions, in which the moved constituent bears contrastive focus, is marked by emphatic stress, and does not feature a clitic. A web-based audio-visual felicity judgment task was performed with HSs, adult Spanish-dominant bilinguals in the United States, and monolingual Spanish speakers tested in their country of origin. All participants successfully distinguished between felicitous and infelicitous sentences with both constructions, regardless of language dominance and proficiency. However, when the individual results were considered, the monolinguals were more sensitive to the semantic relationship between the antecedent and the topicalized constituent in dislocations. This difference aside, Leal Méndez et al. take the overall results to argue that constructions involving discourse-sensitive movement in Spanish can be successfully acquired by HSs due to their robust and unambiguous presence in the input.

In a related study, Leal, Rothman, and Slabakova (2014) examined clitic right dislocation, a rare topicalization construction that moves deaccented topical material anaphorically linked to an antecedent in prior discourse to the right of the sentence and involves an agreeing clitic. Using an audio-visual web-based acceptability judgment task, the study tested HSs and Spanish-dominant native speakers in the United States based on their ability to differentiate between felicitous and infelicitous constructions, distinguished by the presence or absence of a clitic. Despite the low fre-quency of the construction in Spanish, the HSs at two different proficiency levels demonstrated the relevant felicity contrasts in their judgments. In fact, the grammaticality effects were somewhat stronger in the heritage group, leading Leal et al. to hypothesize that HSs may be less sensitive than the controls to the distance between the topicalized element and its antecedent. This difference notwithstanding, the fact that all groups made similar distinctions suggests that even rare constructions are fully within the grasp of intermediate- and high-proficiency HSs, provided that they are not subject to attrition for L1-dominant speakers.

In summary, while the work reviewed in this section demonstrates a great diversity of theoretical and methodological approaches and yields a complex pattern of results, ranging from virtually target-like attainment of the baseline word order principles by HSs to subtle changes in their inter-pretive nuances to a radical reorganization of the underlying system, it is nevertheless possible to map these findings onto the familiar patterns emerging from prior work. Among these themes, variation in HL profi-ciency and dominant language transfer effects seem particularly robust as factors predicting the degree of mastery of the relevant phenomena and the nature and directionality of the observed changes. Additionally, several studies underscore the key role of early naturalistic exposure in HL acquirers and their high sensitivity to input properties by highlighting similarities in the linguistic behavior of heritage bilinguals and first-generation immigrant speakers.

27.4   Prosody and Information Structure

An association between information structure and prosody seems to hold strongly across languages (Gundel and Fretheim 2004). Regardless of the specific mechanism for their encoding (e.g., pitch, intensity, duration, breaks), focused elements are generally associated with greater prosodic prominence (Selkirk 1995), while elements linked to previously identified or given entities are typically marked by phonological reduction, deaccenting, or "anaphoric destressing" (Reinhart 2006). For English in particular, intonation is commonly identified as the primary marker of information-structural contrasts. Taken together, the status of prosody as a strong cue to information structure in spoken language in general and its central role in marking information structure in English in particular make two predictions for HL research. First, as predominantly spoken varieties, HLs should exhibit some means of utilizing prosodic features to mark distinctions at the level of information structure. Second, considering that the majority of published studies on HLs, including work on prosody, have included English as the dominant language, we may also expect to find evidence of language-specific prosodic patterns from English affecting the use, judgments, or interpretation of the relevant structures in the HL. While research on the supra-segmental properties of HLs is relatively scarce, both predictions appear to be borne out by the empirical evidence available to date.

27.4.1 Prosody and Information Structure: Offline Studies

Bullock (2009) used a corpus of structured naturalistic interviews with HSs of French in a small community of Frenchville, PA, to examine the prosodic marking of focus and left dislocation. The study documented an overall greater range of supra-segmental resources for the expression of information structure in Frenchville French, compared to the relatively more restricted use of prosody for these purposes in standard French. The HSs used pitch accents and tonal contours in ways that were similar to English but not possible in French, pointing to dominant language transfer in this domain. However, rather than replacing the syntactic strategies prevalent in French, these new prosodic means were combined with the existing syntactic resources to reinforce the encoding of information structure in a novel way – as an additional communicative resource and not merely a compensatory strategy designed to fill a grammatical gap.

Kim (2019a) provides further evidence for the creative use of the available linguistic resources by heritage bilinguals in their expression of focus. Using a simulated interactive elicitation task, the study analyzed sentences with different scopes and locations of focus produced by HSs and L2 learners of Spanish in the United States and monolinguals in Mexico. While the monolinguals marked focus predominantly with non-prosodic cues, such as the complementizer *que* 'that' and cleft constructions, the L2 learners relied heavily on the prosodic strategies from their L1, including relative prosodic prominence, early peak alignment, prosodic boundary insertion, and post-focal deaccenting. In contrast, the HSs utilized a mix of strategies attested in the L1 and L2 groups, creatively merging the resources of both of their language systems for the realization of focus in the HL.

Using a different methodology, Hoot (2017) conducted an aural context-ualized acceptability judgment task to examine the interactions between prosody and syntactic movement in the marking of new information focus by HSs of Spanish in the United States. In Spanish, the prosodically marked focused constituents may move to the rightmost position of the sentence or remain *in situ*, while only the latter option is available in English. In transitive sentences with subject focus, all participant groups (including controls) significantly preferred stress *in situ*. High-proficiency HSs con-verged with the monolinguals in their ratings of sentences with movement, while the lower-proficiency speakers rated these sentences significantly higher. According to Hoot, these results suggest optionality in the less proficient speakers' use of focus-marking strategies due to insufficient mastery of discursive restrictions on movement. This conclusion is sup-ported by the observation that both movement and *in situ* marking were rated equally high by all groups in the object focus condition with ditransi-tive sentences. In overextending movement to subject-focus contexts, the low-proficiency HSs displayed the kind of variability that resembles the patterns of overgeneralization reported in other studies (e.g., Brehmer and Usanova 2015). It is significant that the overextended pattern in Hoot's study involved VOS, an order that does not occur in English in these contexts. This finding corroborates the observation that overgeneralization of a language-internal pattern and transfer from the dominant language are distinct factors that may exert independent pressures on the HL system.

Leal, Destruel, and Hoot (2018) provided additional data on the realiza-tion of new information focus by intermediate and advanced HSs of Spanish in the United States, compared to Spanish-dominant late learners of English and monolinguals tested in Mexico and Chile. After watching short video clips, participants answered questions in which either the subject or the direct object was in focus. Once again, speakers in all groups preferred to realize subject focus *in situ*, regardless of language variety, language dom-inance, or proficiency in Spanish. In fact, subject focus realization via movement emerged as the least frequently used strategy in all participant groups. Relatively more movement occurred with object focus, and it was in this condition that the intermediate-proficiency HSs differed from the remaining groups in under-using movement. While these results seem at odds with the findings of Hoot's (2017) study, in which the least proficient HSs over-relied on movement, there are sufficient differences between the studies that make direct comparisons difficult. Crucially, since the partici-pant responses in Leal et al.'s study were not analyzed intonationally, it is impossible to draw conclusions about the specific prosodic means utilized by the HSs for the *in situ* focus marking in comparison to those in Hoot's (2017) acceptability study. Assuming that HSs' strategies for focus realiza-tion via prosody may differ from those employed by the monolinguals and other bilinguals (Kim 2019a), the obtained differences may stem from a reorganization of some of these prosodic preferences and defaults in the HL.

Outside of the Romance languages, Hoot (2019) tested HSs and L1-dominant native speakers of Hungarian in the United States on the realization and interpretation of exhaustive focus, a construction that has received ample attention in the theoretical literature due to the complex interplay of prosodic, syntactic, and semantic-pragmatic factors involved in its use. In addition to carrying emphatic stress, focal constituents in Hungarian move to an immediately preverbal position and trigger inversion of the verb and its particle; the interpretation of the resulting structure yields the reading of exhaustiveness (e.g., *It was X and no one else*). The results did not corroborate previous findings by Fenyvesi (2006), who reported a reduction in preverbal focus movement among speakers of American Hungarian. The HSs in Hoot's study patterned with the Hungarian-dominant bilinguals in rating the felicitous sentences, presented aurally in context, significantly higher than the infelicitous sentences without movement and stress. However, in terms of focus interpretation, neither bilingual group construed focus as semantically exhaustive, a result Hoot attributed to the general effects of bilingualism, typically associated with limited processing resources, manifested in both groups as an overextension of the construction to non-exhaustive contexts. Despite these interpretive differences, the overall results place the study in line with other studies in which HSs demonstrated high levels of mastery in the formal realization of information structure and patterned with monolingually raised speakers in this respect (Leal et al. 2014; Leal Méndez et al. 2015).

27.4.2　Prosody and Information Structure in Real Time

All of the previously discussed studies employed offline tasks to examine the role of prosody in conveying information-structural distinctions; however, several researchers have also looked at the use of prosodic cues for these purposes in real time. Sekerina and Trueswell (2011) used the eye-tracking method in the Visual World paradigm to investigate how HSs of Russian in the United States combine prosody with word order and visual context to compute contrastiveness, i.e., the highlighting of salient information to be evaluated in relation to an explicitly presented or implied contrast set. In particular, the authors tested the so-called split-scrambling constructions, in which an adjective marked with a contrastive pitch accent (H+L* in Russian) scrambles to the sentence-initial position, away from the associated noun. Although these constructions are highly marked and used in restricted contexts, the monolinguals easily perceived contrastive pitch accents on the scrambled adjectives. They were quick to identify the contrast sets presented in the visual context and able to compute the referential implications of the split-constituent construction. While the HSs interpreted all sentences correctly, they were significantly slower in integrating prosodic cues in their processing. According to Sekerina and Trueswell, the observed processing delays in heritage bilinguals is a likely result of the parallel activation of and a covert competition between their two languages, manifested initially as a slowdown at the level of word recognition and subsequently cascading across the entire language processing system.

If the processing mechanism in heritage bilinguals is affected by interlinguistic competition, we may expect to trace the effects of such competition not only in the bilinguals' weaker language but also in their dominant language. In another eye-tracking study, Van Rijswijk, Muntendam, and Dijkstra (2017a) examined whether HSs of Turkish in the Netherlands interpret focus structure differently when reading sentences in Dutch compared to L1 Dutch speakers due to the pressure from their HL. The marking of focus in Dutch and Turkish relies on different linguistic cues. In Dutch, it is expressed prosodically, with the nuclear accent falling on the rightmost constituent in broad-focus contexts. In Turkish, both prosody and word order encode focus: The preverbal area is associated with focused and accented information, whereas the postverbal area is reserved for given and deaccented information. When presented with written sentences in Dutch, the HSs of Turkish and the L1 speakers of Dutch coped differently with the absence of explicit prosody. Unlike the L1 Dutch speakers, the HSs did not associate focus with clause-final constituents and instead interpreted the rightmost position as carrying background information. These results corroborate the idea that heritage bilinguals differ from monolinguals in their processing of information-structural cues but also suggest that, at least in the case of fluent bilinguals, the cues from the weaker L1 may constitute sufficient pressure to affect their online processing of the stronger L2.

Further evidence for this type of "reverse" transfer of prosodic knowledge comes from a separate semi-spontaneous elicited production study by Van Rijswijk et al. (2017b), which examined the prosodic marking of broad and contrastive focus in Turkish-Dutch bilinguals and L1 Dutch speakers. In answering different types of questions based on pictures, speakers in both groups used duration differences to signal informational status and marked contrastive focus by a time-compressed pitch movement. However, the HSs showed differences from the L1 Dutch speakers in terms of peak range, f0, and duration. In tandem with the eye-tracking results discussed earlier, these findings suggest that despite their high proficiency in the societally dominant language, HSs are still influenced by the prosodic characteristics of their weaker L1 in their comprehension and production of focus structures in their L2. According to Van Rijswijk et al., these effects likely stem from early childhood transfer of the prosodic characteristics from their then-dominant HL into the L2.

In summary, the available studies on the prosodic realization of information structure by HSs converge on two common patterns of findings. First, they point to a resilience of the prosodic structures employed for the encoding of topic–focus distinctions, especially those associated with prosodically salient categories such as focus, and a relative advantage of HSs over late bilinguals in the use and comprehension of these structures. Second, several researchers underscore the additive and bidirectional nature of cross-linguistic interactions in this domain by highlighting the multiple ways in which the two coactivated systems can work together in bilinguals. From slowdowns in the processing of the weaker language to an enrichment of the inventory of the available prosodic resources in both languages, including the HSs' dominant language, the observed effects point to complex and multifaceted interactions between sentence-level prosody and other modules of language in the bilingual encoding of information structure.

27.5   Anaphoric Relations

Apart from shaping the morphosyntactic and prosodic structure of sentences, categories of information structure also determine what lexical forms speakers use for introducing new entities or referring back to familiar entities. The effects of information structure on referential form choice are often examined in the context of discourse anaphora, a phenomenon of establishing and maintaining dependencies between a null or overt linguistic form and its antecedent in discourse. In particular, the occurrence of null arguments (pro-drop) in languages in which this option is available has been linked to their informational status: while null forms mark topic continuity across discourse, overt subjects signal a shift in discourse topic (e.g., to introduce a new participant) or convey emphasis. As discussed in greater detail later, this information-structural function has been shown to be weakened or altogether lost in the HL, even when null pronominalization is retained for other purposes, resulting in a greater overlap and interchangeability between the null and overt pronominals in HL production and comprehension.

27.5.1   Pronouns under Pro-Drop

Numerous studies have shown that the division of labor between null and overt pronouns is not carried out in the same way in bilinguals exposed to a non–null-subject language, with a commonly reported trend of overt pronouns being overextended to topic-continuity contexts (Serratrice, Sorace, and Paoli 2004; Sorace and Filiaci 2006; Sorace, Serratrice, Filiaci, and Baldo 2009). This trend has been documented even in speakers of two null-subject languages with similar constraints on pronoun distribution, such as the Spanish-Italian bilingual children in Sorace et al.'s (2009) study, suggesting that cross-linguistic transfer is only one among several factors potentially affecting the production and comprehension of pro-drop in bilinguals.

Research on adult HSs at various proficiency levels has both confirmed and expanded this general trend. For example, Montrul's (2004) oral production study with HSs of Mexican Spanish showed that the advanced HSs performed on par with the monolinguals and produced more null than overt subjects, while the intermediate-proficiency speakers used more overt pronouns across-the-board, with nearly half appearing in pragmatically redundant contexts. Speakers in both groups produced illicit null subjects (e.g., those appearing in change-of-referent contexts). According to Montrul, while the distinction between null and overt subjects is not lost for HSs in either group, their pragmatic distribution does not always adhere to the monolingual principles, either as a result of direct transfer from English or due to a past interference experienced in the formative years of language development.

Using the same narrative task, Montrul (2018) brought in additional data from school-age bilingual and monolingual children, young adult HSs, and adult Mexican immigrants to the United States in an attempt to connect the dots among the different sectors on the bilingual spectrum in the acquisition of pro-drop. In line with the earlier findings, all bilinguals produced more pragmatically illicit null and overt subjects than the monolingual controls. With respect to null subjects, the bilingual speakers performed similarly to the monolingual children; by contrast, redundant overt subjects only occurred in the bilingual groups, with the highest rates attested in child bilinguals. Montrul suggests that while difficulties with null pronouns in HSs may be linked to delays in their acquisition by monolingual children, the increase in the use of overt pronouns by the adult immigrants points to intergenerational attrition as a source of optionality in the overall mastery of the discourse-pragmatic properties of pro-drop by HSs.

Focusing on the interpretation of pro-drop, Keating, VanPatten, and Jegerski (2011) compared heritage and monolingually raised Spanish speakers on their antecedent biases with null and overt pronouns using a written questionnaire. Unlike the monolinguals, who linked null pronouns with subject antecedents, the HSs favored the subject antecedent across the board, effectively treating the null and overt forms as interchangeable. In doing so, the HSs overextended the interpretive scope of the overt pronoun, which did not receive the switch-reference interpretation for the majority of the HSs in the study. The authors attribute this result to insufficient quantity of discourse-level Spanish input combined with the influence of English, in which overt pronouns may occur both in and outside of topic-shift contexts. Despite their early exposure to Spanish, the HSs in the study showed no advantages over L2 learners in the resolution of pronominal ambiguities.

In a later study, Keating, Jegerski, and VanPatten (2016) revisited the question of antecedent biases in the resolution of pronominal anaphora in Spanish by probing into the online processing of null and overt pronouns by monolinguals and advanced HSs. Only the monolinguals demonstrated a consistent referential bias toward non-subject antecedents with overt pronouns in self-paced reading, although the difference between the groups was quantitative rather than representational. When interpreting null pronouns, the two groups were more similar in showing the same subject antecedent bias. The authors suggest that the interpretation of overt pronouns relies on strategies that are more susceptible to variation and are correlated to a greater extent with the amount and type of linguistic exposure, including exposure via reading, which enforces the processing of complex and elaborate planned discourse. Considering the limited access of HL speakers to high-level registers, this account explains why even at high proficiency levels the HSs diverged from baseline speakers in their processing efficiency of the overt forms. Indirectly, it also offers a possible reason why the earlier study did not document any advantage of HSs over L2 learners in this particular domain.

Changes in the distribution and referential properties of pronominals under pro-drop are often linked to the influence of the dominant language; however, few studies have tested this assumption directly. To accomplish this goal, Rinke and Flores (2018) examined the interpretation preferences of null and overt pronominal subjects in topic-shift and topic-continuity contexts in child HSs of Portuguese with distinct dominant languages, German or Spanish/Catalan, contrasting on the pro-drop dimension. The child bilinguals were further compared to monolingual children and adults living in Portugal. All groups interpreted null pronouns in terms of topic continuity and related overt pronouns to topic shift. The bilingual children were sensitive to this distinction regardless of their language combination. However, they also allowed for greater optionality in their interpretations of the target sentences and differed from other groups in the null subject condition. The overt condition proved to be similarly difficult for the bilingual and monolingual children. Building on prior studies, Rinke and Flores attribute this finding to the idea that the overt pronouns show greater interpretive variability in adult grammars, and this makes them intrinsically more challenging in acquisition.

To sum up, evidence from the Romance HLs points to changes in the interpretive properties of the overt forms and their over-extension to topic-continuity contexts as the most common outcomes in the HL acquisition of pro-drop. This trend finds further cross-linguistic support in several studies of typologically different pro-drop HLs, including Arabic, Greek, and Turkish. For example, Albirini et al. (2011) documented an increase in the use of overt pronouns by HSs of Egyptian Arabic in the United States, attributed to transfer from English and to the need to mark subjects overtly due to the weakening of the agreement morphology. Like many other studies reviewed in this chapter, Albirini et al. did not report incomplete knowledge of pro-drop: quantitative differences aside, sentences with null and overt pronouns were generally used appropriately by the HSs in their study. Outside of the US context, Kaltsa, Tsimpli, and Rothman (2015) examined similarities and differences in anaphora resolution of null and overt subject pronouns between L1 attriters and HSs of Greek living in Sweden. Data from a self-paced listening and picture-matching decision task showed that both bilingual groups diverged from the Swedish-speaking monolinguals and patterned together in exhibiting no robust preferences in pronoun resolution and in associating the overt pronoun with both topic-continuity and topic-shift.

Using production data from informal interviews with HSs of Turkish in the Netherlands, Doğruöz and Backus (2009) reported only a very small proportion of redundant overt subjects in the obtained data set, not indicative of a significant influence from Dutch. However, in a variationist study investigating the effects of continuity of reference on the alternation between null and overt subject pronouns in Turkish spoken in New York City, Koban (2011) documented a substantial increase in the use of overt pronouns by second-generation Turkish speakers, corroborating the trend previously reported in Otheguy, Zentella, and Livert (2007) for Spanish. In line with several studies discussed earlier, the findings obtained by Koban also point to a diminished role of reference continuity in determining the choice between the null vs. overt form in heritage Turkish, once again suggesting a weakened information-structural load for this contrast in the HL.

Taking a different approach, Azar, Asli, and Backus (2019) investigated a broader range of reference-tracking strategies employed by highly proficient HSs of Turkish in the Netherlands. In particular, the study examined the distribution of full NPs, overt pronouns, and null pronouns in oral narratives, elicited using silent videos, in relation to the discourse status of the referent (maintained vs. re-introduced) and the larger pragmatic context. Azar et al. analyzed the bilinguals' narratives both in Turkish and Dutch, in comparison to two respective monolingual cohorts. The choice of this language dyad was motivated by the fact that Turkish exhibits typical properties of pro-drop, whereas Dutch, an overt subject language, mediates discourse reference via stress on pronominals. Despite these differences, the bilinguals were very similar to the controls in both languages and followed language-specific strategies of reference maintenance in each language. Contrary to previous studies, Azar et al. did not find an increase in the rate of overt pronouns over null pronouns in heritage Turkish under the influence of Dutch, possibly due to the speakers' very high rates of language attainment. As discussed by the authors, high levels of proficiency may lead to strong entrenchment of mechanisms involved in the integration of syntactic and pragmatic information, leading to a more efficient processing of these structures by HSs. This account predicts that not all bilinguals should exhibit indeterminacy or transfer effects with phenomena at the syntax–discourse interface, including those pertaining to the marking of information-structural distinctions, despite their higher processing costs. Indeed, other studies of near-native speakers in communities with high levels of societal bilingualism seem to support this prediction (see Montrul, 2016: 209; Aalberse, Backus, and Muysken, 2019 and references therein).

27.5.2 Pronouns under Partial Pro-Drop

Similarly to the pro-drop languages discussed in the previous section, mixed pro-drop languages like Russian and Hebrew allow null subjects in certain pragmatically motivated contexts. However, the constraints governing their distribution are less categorical, and the resulting apparent interchangeability of the null or overt forms leads to a much greater optionality in their selection.

Studies of noncanonical pro-drop in HLs remain few and largely limited to Russian. A monograph-length investigation of discourse anaphora by Ivanova-Sullivan (2014) draws on data from a series of oral production and comprehension experiments to offer an extensive analysis of strategies employed by heritage Russian speakers in the United States in their use and identification of null and overt pronouns. In order to identify areas in which HSs differ from monolinguals and determine whether these differences reflect representational or processing problems, Ivanova-Sullivan undertakes a broad investigation of syntactic, semantic, and discourse factors in anaphora resolution, with and without the additional factor of time pressure, in three proficiency-based HS groups. Overall, the results largely corroborate the general patterns reported in the pro-drop HL literature, pointing to some common loci of difficulty in heritage bilinguals in this domain. While the HSs adhered to the syntactic requirements on the use of null pronouns in Russian and used null pronouns at the same rate as the monolinguals in story-telling, they did not exhibit full mastery of the discourse-pragmatic properties associated with null forms, a result Ivanova-Sullivan attributes to the complexity of discourse-based identification of these elements and cross-linguistic influence from English. In a forced-choice aural preference task, both participant groups provided more subject antecedents than object antecedents for null pronouns, pointing to a similar antecedent bias in the two groups; however, while this pattern was categorical for monolinguals, HSs displayed only a gradient trend with increasing preference for subject antecedents along the proficiency continuum.

With respect to overt pronouns, the HSs demonstrated the previously documented pattern of overuse and overextension, resulting in the impression of redundancy in production. According to Ivanova-Sullivan (2014), these results not only signal processing difficulties in contexts requiring a choice between the overt vs. null form but also serve as a reflection of a novel reference-tracking "thematic subject strategy" (105), a tendency to use overt pronouns rather than full noun phrases to mark topical subjects, such as those referring to the main characters of the story. This analysis was further corroborated by the results of the forced choice judgment task, in which the HSs tended to link overt pronouns with subject antecedents, resulting in an inappropriate marking of reference continuity, consistent with the findings by Keating et al. (2011) for Spanish. In accounting for the overall patterns of results across the four experiments, Ivanova-Sullivan appeals to both processing and representational differences between the heritage and monolingual speakers in the use and interpretation of discourse anaphora. While highly proficient HSs employed the same strategies of anaphora resolution as the monolinguals, albeit in a less efficient manner, speakers in the lower proficiency group demonstrated qualitatively different principles of establishing referential dependencies in discourse, suggestive of a higher degree of cross-linguistic influence.

In another study of heritage Russian in the United States, Laleko and Polinsky (2017) examined the use of pronominal forms to mark topical subjects across different sets of contexts. A written scaled acceptability ratings experiment was carried out to compare the occurrence of null and overt subjects in contexts where both options are possible (embedded subjects in neutral indicative sentences) and contexts where only the overt form may occur (embedded subjects under contrastive and subjunctive readings). In the optional contexts, the HSs showed a clear preference for the overt forms, while the monolinguals consistently favored null subjects. The HSs also differed from the L2 learners, who showed indeterminacy in their ratings of both forms. According to Laleko and Polinsky, the fact that the HSs displayed a consistent pattern of judgments, albeit in the opposite direction compared to the monolinguals, signals a qualitative shift indicative of a re-setting of defaults in the heritage grammar. While the null form serves as the more efficient option for marking recently activated and cognitively salient referents in the monolingual system, the overt form appears to have emerged as the more economical alternative for heritage bilinguals, whose cognitive resources are allocated and engaged differently in terms of the pressure on working memory and the cognitive demands needed for resolving anaphoric dependencies in context.

Further differences between the monolinguals and HSs in Laleko and Polinsky's study arose in conditions targeting illicit null subjects. The HSs were not able to identify these forms as unacceptable in subjunctive contexts, but were accurate in rejecting omissions under contrastive readings. This pattern parallels the previously discussed results on topic particle omissions in Korean, where HSs showed some difficulty with illicit null forms but were relatively more successful in contrastive contexts (Laleko and Polinsky 2016, 2017). Taken together with other studies demonstrating differences in the use and construal of null forms in HLs (Montrul 2004; Ivanova-Sullivan 2014), these findings underscore the need for a more systematic investigation of the underlying grammar of silent elements in the heritage system.

27.5.3 Some Common Themes in Pronominal Anaphora Resolution Research

Regardless of the relative prominence and range of pro-drop effects in a given language, these studies point to two overarching factors that appear to affect the resolution of pronominal anaphora across the heritage language landscape. On the one hand, the increased occurrence of overt pronouns is often taken as indirect evidence of cross-linguistic influence from English, discussed by the majority of authors as the underlying force shaping the distribution and functional shifts in the use and interpretation of pronominal forms by HSs. On the other hand, in discussing factors outside of transfer, some researchers also raise the question of input that HSs receive in their home language. While the issues of cross-linguistic transfer and input properties represent two distinct factors in HL development, they are often hard to tease apart in practical terms, considering that speakers in immigrant communities often exhibit some degree of convergence toward the societally dominant language. Looking specifically at pro-drop effects in Émigré varieties, several researchers have reported diminished rates in the use of null pronouns and overuse of overt forms under contact with English (Silva-Corvalán 1994; Otheguy et al. 2007; Dubinina and Polinsky 2013). While this trend is consistent with the transfer hypothesis, Dubinina and Polinsky also observe diminished use of null pronominals in first-generation Russian immigrants to Israel. Since Hebrew does not prohibit pro-drop the way English does, the attested tendencies toward over-marking may turn out to have causes outside of cross-linguistic transfer.

Further evidence against viewing cross-linguistic transfer as a primary or necessary trigger of language change in the domain of pronominals comes from several studies that report robust knowledge of the null–overt contrast in HSs and their L1-dominant parents despite the pressures of a language contact situation. Nagy (2015) provides a comparative variationist analysis of null subjects in the production data elicited from adult speakers of Cantonese, Italian, and Russian representing three generations of immigrants to Canada. The HSs in the study represent the second and third generations (i.e., speakers whose parent or grandparent was an adult immigrant to Canada), analyzed as one group. Contrary to the predominant pattern of results discussed previously, the first generation speakers and the HSs interviewed in Nagy's study had the same rates of null subjects across identical linguistic contexts, showing no inter-generational difference with respect to null subjects. While an increase in raw percentages of null subjects was attested in the first generation of Cantonese speakers, this difference disappeared in the multivariate analysis that took context into account. Thus, while subtle contextual changes emerged between generations with respect to the conditioning constraints on null subject use, none of these effects are taken to constitute evidence of transfer from English or of any substantial changes to the null subject grammar in the three HLs examined in the study.

Within the literature on child HSs, Daskalaki, Chondrogianni, Blom, Argyri, and Paradis (2019) report a similarly robust use of null pronominals by young Greek-English bilinguals with English as a dominant language. The bilingual children were nearly at ceiling in using null forms in topic-continuity contexts in an elicited production task. Even the children with the least amount of HL use (under 25 percent) were very accurate (75 percent correct) in their production of null subjects to mark topic-continuity and did not over-extend overt pronominals to these contexts, contrary to the typically reported trend. According to the authors, a higher frequency of null subjects or the greater referential ambiguity of the overt pronouns in Greek may each serve as a possible explanation for the observed resilience of the null forms in the HL. Under both accounts, the results point to limited effects of transfer and instead shift the focus of future inquiry to language-internal factors involved in shaping the properties of the heritage system during its acquisition and possibly in later stages of attainment.

In sum, empirical studies on pronominal anaphora show that heritage grammars tend to maintain (some aspects of) the null-overt contrast, but that the division of labor between these forms and their association with the particular information-structural functions may not always be carried out the same way in the HL as in the baseline variety. The overt pronouns generally appear in more contexts and exhibit greater interpretive optionality, with HSs often relying on them as defaults in contexts where monolinguals opt for other types of reference tracking markers (e.g., null forms or full NPs). In interpreting these forms, HSs often demonstrate a different referential bias. Null pronouns in baseline grammars are typically linked with topical subject antecedents, and HSs often over-extend overt pronouns to these contexts, preferring to link both pronominal forms to the most salient antecedent (see Polinsky 2018 for further discussion). Several studies also document differences in the use and acceptability of null pronouns, manifested as over-acceptance of illicit null forms and problems in identifying discourse-pragmatic restrictions on their occurrence. Echoing the patterns observed with zero marking in other linguistic domains in the HL, these results may stem from a more global difficulty with deriving and interpreting omitted structures.

27.6 Toward the Big Picture

Despite the significant progress made over the last decade to advance our understanding of discourse-level properties of HLs, there remains a strong need for additional work in this area. This section highlights the major trends emerging from the empirical overviews presented in this chapter, positions them within the larger HL literature, and outlines several ways in which future research could build on these findings.

In broad strokes, the existing research on the encoding of information structure in HLs may be summarized along three dimensions. The first and perhaps most restricted group of studies, including primarily those with high-proficiency speakers, point to areas of convergence between heritage and monolingually raised speakers. In the second and largest group of studies, the results document subtle differences in interpretation or different quantitative preferences between the groups. In some cases, these differences reflect a gradual pattern of change manifested as a reduction of options in the variety undergoing change, rather than (or as a step toward) a fundamental qualitative reorganization of the underlying grammar. Finally, several studies document measurable contrasts between the heritage and baseline speakers suggestive of representational differences due to a qualitative reanalysis of the relevant structures in the HL. This concluding section will attempt to reconcile these findings by relating them to the various dimensions of HL competence that these results bring into focus.

Starting with the literature in the first group, the recurrent finding emerging from these studies – that conformity with the baseline is strongly modulated by proficiency – highlights the idea that heritage bilinguals at high language proficiency rates fall within the native spectrum and can

achieve levels of competence observed in other native speakers. It is particularly notable that many of these studies involve HLs characterized by
high degrees of minority language maintenance in the respective language
communities, e.g., Spanish in the United States or Turkish in the
Netherlands and other European countries. These findings underscore the
importance of community factors in HL maintenance on the societal scale.
However, it is also significant that a great number of studies in which the
HSs demonstrated high levels of mastery of the relevant phenomena
involved written tasks and as such selectively targeted those HSs who were
literate in their home language and thus must have had access to at least
some formal instruction in it (e.g., Brehmer and Usanova 2015). While
literacy in the HL is not in itself a guarantee of target-like performance, it
may serve as an apt marker of the extent to which HSs' language experience
includes the contextually enriched registers argued to facilitate the acquisition of discourse-level competence in language learners (Keating et al. 2016)
and draws the need for more systematic comparisons between HSs "in the
wild" and in the classroom (Polinsky and Kagan 2007).

To approach the issue of convergence between the heritage and baseline
speakers from a different angle, another important consideration concerns
the possible effects of bilingualism in the population of speakers selected as
the baseline against which the performance of HSs is measured. In striving
to understand the mechanism of trans-generational transmission of the HL,
many researchers have argued for the need to include data from first-
generation immigrant speakers, the population that most closely represents the input that HSs receive in their home language (see Pires and
Rothman 2009). While these data are key for answering questions about
the properties of the linguistic systems that HSs set out to acquire, absence
of a monolingual control group may sometimes present its own methodological drawbacks. For one, it makes it difficult to detect changes that may
occur in both populations of speakers simultaneously. For example, the
control group of Hungarian speakers in Hoot's (2019: 10) study, which
found strong convergence effects between the heritage and baseline
speakers, were very fluent speakers of English (mean proficiency score
37.5/40) with a mean length of residence in the United States of 24.9 years.
Considering the scarcity of empirical work on Hungarian, it would be
interesting to contextualize these findings in relation to results from
Hungarian speakers with less extensive exposure to English. A related and
perhaps more serious concern is that absence of a monolingual control
group makes it harder to test specific predictions based on the generalizations discussed in the theoretical literature, as the latter tend to be formulated on the basis of properties observed in the standard varieties of the
languages under investigation. The inherent monolingual bias in the theoretical descriptions of the relevant linguistic phenomena, often reflected in

the experimental conditions and stimuli of studies with bilinguals (under a tacit assumption that the predicted grammaticality or felicity contrasts would hold in this group), may be responsible for some of the unexpected patterns in the results obtained from bilingual controls. For example, nearly 40 percent of the L1-dominant speakers in the control group in Leal et al.'s (2014) study did not make the expected felicity distinctions tested in the experiment; similar "gaps" in the performance of baseline controls with respect to the study's predictions are reported by Prada Pérez and Pascual y Cabo (2012). While there is no question that baseline bilingual data are necessary for understanding the type of input that shapes the grammars that HSs ultimately construct, inclusion of the monolingual baseline group, whenever feasible, could offer significant practical benefits for uncovering the basic descriptive properties of the varieties under investigation in a controlled setting and relating these empirical findings to the existing theoretical generalizations, which for many languages remain based primarily on linguistic introspection.

The quantitative and qualitative properties of the input that HSs receive are often brought forward in "glass-half-empty" contexts, i.e., as a limitation that helps explain why HSs may diverge from the monolingual standard. However, it is worthwhile to bear in mind that input can and should also be considered as an explanatory factor in contexts where HSs perform close to the control group. After all, it is the early and naturalistic exposure to the language that sets heritage bilinguals apart from formally instructed late L2 learners, so it is not surprising that HSs have consistently shown advantages in areas, registers, and modalities associated with such exposure (Montrul 2016). In particular, one recurrent finding within the literature comparing heritage and L2 speakers is that HSs are typically closer to baseline speakers in their knowledge of constructions that occur most frequently in colloquial speech and are relatively more restricted in formal and academic registers. Many of the phenomena discussed in this chapter fall under this umbrella, and this is another reason why the advantages of HSs over L2 learners in the domain of discourse and information structure seem so robust.

At the same time, simple exposure to input is not sufficient for acquiring a stable grammar, and not all exposure involves processing. Putnam and Sánchez (2013) propose a model of heritage bilingual development that is not linked directly to the quantity or quality of the linguistic input that HSs receive. Instead, they emphasize the need to focus on the areas of the input that become *intake* during processing and argue that the composition of lexical items and formal features in heritage grammars reflects fluctuating levels of their activation in processing for comprehension and production purposes. Different levels of activation predict different paths of acquisition, which in turn accounts for differences in the resulting grammatical systems of heritage and baseline speakers regardless of input similarities. Coupled with the effects of attrition and incomplete acquisition documented in various domains of the HL (O'Grady et al. 2011; Polinsky 2011 for evidence of attrition effects; Montrul 2008; Silva-Corvalán 2018 on markers of incomplete acquisition), these differences predict lack of full convergence in domains that involve complex structures, come with higher updating costs of discourse representation, and implicate multiple form-meaning mappings.

With these considerations in mind, it is not surprising that a large number of the reviewed studies do find differences between the heritage and baseline speakers in the marking of information structure. Some of these differences remain pervasive even under the most favorable conditions in HL acquisition. For example, in the study of child HSs of Greek with English as a dominant language, Daskalaki et al. (2019) reported persistent difficulties with subject placement in wide-focus contexts (e.g., *What happened with X?*), which trigger the noncanonical VSO order in Greek. Even the children with the highest proportion of HL use in the home (100 percent) did not reach more than 75 percent accuracy in the use of these constructions, and children with the lowest amount of exposure (less than 25 percent) were on target less than 10 percent of the time. It is also significant that many studies have documented difficulties with the encoding of (at least some of) the information–structural distinctions even in those HSs who perform virtually at ceiling with the morphological or syntactic properties of the target language, such as grammatical constraints on particle use or syntactic restrictions on clitic movement. Whenever these types of asymmetries emerge, greater difficulty typically arises with phenomena that are relatively more heavily discourse-dependent and engage information structure to a larger extent. Whether these difficulties follow from greater computational costs required for structure-building in high syntactic positions or reflect increased processing demands needed for keeping track of contextual information to link elements in discourse (Laleko and Polinsky 2016), these results echo the patterns of the syntax–discourse asymmetry documented in other studies involving bilinguals and monolinguals and bring HL speakers into the realm of the theoretical literature addressing the issues of learnability and complexity in natural language.

Empirical studies of higher-level phenomena in HLs have proven to be a fruitful testing ground for recent proposals aiming to contribute to our understanding of language architecture through identifying its stable and vulnerable domains. To consider one specific example, HL data have now been featured prominently in exploring various tenets of the Interface Hypothesis (Sorace 2011; see Montrul and Polinsky 2011 on extending the proposal to HSs), which claims that properties at the interfaces, and particularly the syntax–discourse interface, may be inherently more complex in bilingual language acquisition and maintenance than non-interface properties (see also Ionin, this volume, for discussion). Further applications and refinements of the hypothesis have generated a rich discussion and produced ample new data for the HL field. In fact, within the literature reviewed here, a significant number of studies were specifically set out to test the particular predictions of the Interface Hypothesis in HSs (e.g., Hoot 2017; Leal et al. 2018; Van Osch and Sleeman 2018). Regardless of the theoretical positions assumed by individual authors or their conclusions, the descriptive data made available through this work have contributed greatly to our understanding of HL properties pertaining to the marking of information structure and discourse relations. In what follows, I will attempt to unify these various findings along some common paths.

Taking stock of the body of empirical evidence presented in this chapter, one overarching pattern of findings reveals a relatively more consistent success of HSs with the *formal integration* of information-structural categories into the linguistic system alongside a seemingly greater difficulty with the *interpretive* aspect of information structure encoding and construal in the HL. A number of studies have uncovered this asymmetry in various domains (e.g., focus realization vs. interpretation; licensing vs. identification of pronominal anaphora), pointing to problems with the mapping of linguistic structure of the relevant categories onto semantic structure even in fairly advanced speakers.

One specific recurrent theme emerging from these studies is the resilient nature of *informationally salient* categories like focus and contrast in heritage grammars across the linguistic subsystems in typologically distinct HLs. This trend has been manifested in different ways at various points on the HL proficiency scale, from target-like use of focusing devices in advanced speakers to an emergence of unique focus-marking strategies that utilize a subset of options provided by the baseline system or draw on the resources of both languages in speakers at lower levels of proficiency. In fact, perhaps it is that very same pressure to mark informationally salient distinctions that accounts for the preservation of these marked structures in the otherwise paradigmatically reduced heritage system, leading at times to an overuse of focusing in pragmatically odd contexts, such as when the referent is already familiar (Dubinina and Polinsky 2013: 173) or, in advanced bilinguals, to transfer of the focusing strategies from the HL to the dominant language (Van Rijswijk et al. 2017a, 2017b). While future experimental work is necessary to validate these preliminary observations, at this juncture I will chart out several possible and non–mutually-exclusive accounts of this trend.

On the surface, the acquisition of focus and contrast, categories invariably expressed by overt linguistic material whose perceptibility is reinforced through prosodic marking, may be aided by their increased phonological prominence. Cross-linguistically, categories associated with the notions of contrast and exhaustiveness in natural languages have been argued to be more formally marked than other concepts associated with information structure (Zimmernann and Onéa 2011). As noted in Laleko and Polinsky (2017), unlike topical elements, which are often marked by deaccentuation or are altogether omitted, focused and contrastive elements cannot be null. "Assuming that the acquisition of contrast is aided by the availability of prosodic cues in the input, HL speakers' relative advantage with contrastive categories may emerge as a result of prosodic bootstrapping …, presumably due to these speakers' early, naturalistic exposure to the language" (157). Recent work on HSs' prosodic skills lends further support to this observation. For example, Kim (2019b) documents a clear advantage of HSs over L2 learners in the use of suprasegmental cues in the perception of Spanish lexical stress, despite the fact that these speakers were less native-like in using these cues in production. Assuming that the degree of intonational marking for a particular linguistic expression is positively correlated with its degree of communicative significance, with the relatively least predictable and most pragmatically informative elements assigned the highest intonational prominence (Beaver-Velleman 2011), further advantages in early bilingual acquirers may come to light in future studies probing into the mechanism of the interaction between prosody and information structure in HLs.

In addition to their higher prosodic salience, contrastive and focused elements are also more constrained in their interpretive range. A fundamental feature of HL grammars is difficulty in resolving ambiguity and dealing with underspecification (Laleko 2010, 2019; Polinsky 2018; Polinsky and Scontras 2020); from this angle, the more rigid semantic structure of contrastive and focused material may turn out to be a strong cue for its successful mastery. In fact, the problem with ambiguity is not unique to HL systems. In the literature on the acquisition of pro-drop, monolingual children typically show protracted delays in the interpretation of overt subjects in ambiguous contexts (Rinke and Flores 2018) but start using overt subjects in contrastive and emphatic contexts at the age of two (Koban 2011 and references therein). Whether a lingering effect from the childhood years or a reflection of particular properties of the adult bilingual system, the amplified difficulty in the evaluation of underspecified elements with a broad interpretive range, constrained primarily by context, can account for the observed differences in the marking of the information-structural distinctions discussed in this chapter.

It is worth noting that in many of the studies reviewed in this chapter, even the baseline controls showed a high degree of gradience, optionality, or below-ceiling performance in their judgments of constructions characterized by a high degree of contextual variation. For example, in the clitic right dislocation constructions discussed by Leal et al. (2014: 424), the felicitous sentences were ranked on average at 2.72 out of 4 by the L1-dominant speakers; similarly, the monolingual ratings of the felicitous topic omissions examined by Laleko and Polinsky (2017: 146) only reached a mean score of 3.9 out of 5. While some of these patterns may reflect independent factors related to the experimental design (e.g., amount of context provided with the experimental stimuli, test modality), they may also be indicative of the type of optionality and gradience in baseline speakers that have been shown to produce a more lasting and categorical indeterminacy in HL acquisition (Prada Pérez 2019).

Yet another dimension that sets topical and anaphoric expressions apart from those associated with focus involves the locality of the domain in which these elements operate. While focus is a property that operates primarily at the level of propositions, topic is a discourse notion (Tomioka 2010). Topical and especially anaphoric elements are likely to straddle larger segments of discourse and thus pose greater demands on working memory compared to expressions with lower degrees of predictability and contextual embedding, such as entities just being introduced into discourse or otherwise highlighted informationally. It has been shown in the processing literature that operations performed at a distance are costly in terms of processing resources (Gibson 1998), while focusing structures increase the availability of the representation in short-term memory and have facilitative effects on processing (Cowles 2012 and references therein). Assuming that the assignment of focus at the level of a proposition or establishing a contrast set between two defined elements are each relatively more local operations than continued topic-maintenance, differential results in the mastery of these categories by HSs may stem from the variable load on the processor involved in the performance of operations based on locality (O'Grady et al. 2011), informativeness, and associated updating costs.

Since all three possible accounts discussed here converge on the general prediction in relation to directionality of difficulty within the topic–focus dichotomy in HLs, future studies should take a closer look at the sub-typology of these notions in order to evaluate each of these possibilities more systematically.

There is no question that research on discourse and information structure in HLs will continue to expand. As the field moves forward, there is a strong need for further experimental and theoretical work to test and build on the existing generalizations and broaden the scope of inquiry to new domains. Among the latter, the cognitive dimensions of information structure focusing on associations between linguistic forms and mental representations of discourse entities (i.e., *referential* givenness-newness in the sense of Gundel 2003), the construal and organization of information-structural relations through discourse particles and other linking devices, and the encoding of information-structural features within individual syntactic projections, such as the DP, are only a few examples of the many areas that still await systematic investigation in heritage linguistics. As early naturalistic bilinguals, HSs seem to present the ideal population to study the effects of reduced input on speakers' ability to construct and evaluate structures with different information-structural configurations and anchor them to context. After all, information structure is encoded in the grammars of all natural languages, and the means for its expression are particularly varied at the level of spoken registers. Building on the momentum and advances of the recent investigations, future work should be well-positioned to formulate more precise questions to be approached from various methodological standpoints and draw generalizations from a more diverse set of language dyads. These data will in turn serve as an excellent testing ground for recent theoretical claims about the cross-linguistic typology and universality of information structure realization, formulated to date primarily on the basis of natural language data outside of the bilingual context.

References

Aalberse, S., A. Backus, and P. Muysken. 2019. *Heritage Languages: A Language Contact Approach*. Amsterdam: John Benjamins.

Albirini, A., E. Benmamoun, and E. Saadah. 2011. Grammatical Features of Egyptian and Palestinian Arabic Heritage Speakers' Oral Production. *Studies in Second Language Acquisition* 33(2), 273–303.

Azar, Z., Ö. Asli, and A. Backus. 2019. Turkish-Dutch Bilinguals Maintain Language-Specific Reference Tracking Strategies in Elicited Narratives. *International Journal of Bilingualism*, 1–34.

Beaver, D. and D. Velleman. 2011. The Communicative Significance of Primary and Secondary Accents. *Lingua* 121(11), 1671–1692.

Brehmer, B. and I. Usanova. 2015. Let's Fix It? Cross-Linguistic Influence in Word Order Patterns of Russian Heritage Speakers in Germany. In H. Peukert (ed.), *Transfer Effects in Multilingual Language Development* 161–188. Amsterdam: John Benjamins.

Bullock, B. E. 2009. Prosody in Contact in French: A Case Study from a Heritage Variety in the USA. *International Journal of Bilingualism* 13(2), 165–194.

Büring, D. 2016. (Contrastive) Topic. In C. Féry and S. Ishihara (eds.), *The Oxford Handbook of Information Structure*. Oxford: Oxford University Press, 65–85.

Casielles-Suárez, E. 2004. *The Syntax-Information Structure Interface: Evidence from Spanish and English*. New York: Routledge.

Chafe, W. 1976. Givenness, Contrastiveness, Definiteness, Subjects, Topics and Point of View. In C. N. Li (ed.), *Subject and Topic*. New York: Academic Press, 27–55.

Chung, E. S. 2018. Second and Heritage Language Acquisition of Korean Case Drop. *Bilingualism: Language and Cognition* 21(1), 63–79.

Cowles, H. W. 2012. The Psychology of Information Structure. In M. Krifka and R. Musan (eds.), *The Expression of Information Structure*. Berlin: Walter de Gruyter, 287–318.

Daskalaki, E., V. Chondrogianni, E. Blom, F. Argyri, and J. Paradis. 2019. Input Effects across Domains: The Case of Greek Subjects in Child Heritage Language. *Second Language Research* 35(3), 421–445.

Doğruöz, S. and A. Backus. 2009. Innovative Constructions in Dutch Turkish: An Assessment of Ongoing Contact-Induced Change. *Bilingualism: Language and Cognition* 12(1), 41–63.

Dubinina, I. and M. Polinsky. 2013. Russian in the USA. In M. Moser and M. Polinsky (eds.), *Slavic Languages in Migration*, 131–60. Wien: University of Vienna.

Fenyvesi, A. 2006. Contact Effects in Toledo, Ohio, Hungarian: Quantitative Findings. In G. Watson and P. Hirvonen (eds.), *Finno-Ugric Language Contacts*. Frankfurt am Main: Peter Lang, 157–177.

Gibson, E. 1998. Linguistic Complexity: Locality of Syntactic Dependencies. *Cognition* 68(1), 1–76.

Gómez Soler, I. and D. Pascual y Cabo. 2018. On Focus and Weight in Spanish as a Heritage Language. *Spanish Journal of Applied Linguistics* 31(2), 437–466.

Gundel, J. 2003. Information Structure and Referential Givenness/Newness: How Much Belongs in the Grammar? *Journal of Cognitive Science* 4, 177–199.

Gundel, J. 2012. Pragmatics and Information Structure. In K. Allan and K. Jaszczolt (eds.), *The Cambridge Handbook of Pragmatics*. Cambridge: Cambridge University Press, 585–598.

Gundel, J. and T. Fretheim. 2004. Topic and Focus. In L. Horn and G. Ward (eds.), *Handbook of Pragmatics*. Oxford: Blackwell Publishing, 175–196.

Hoot, B. 2017. Narrow Presentational Focus in Heritage Spanish and the Syntax-Discourse Interface. *Linguistic Approaches to Bilingualism* 7(1), 63–95.

Hoot, B. 2019. Focus in Heritage Hungarian. *Language Acquisition* 26(1), 46–72.

Isurin, L. and T. Ivanova-Sullivan. 2008. Lost in between: The Case of Russian Heritage Speakers. *Heritage Language Journal* 6(1), 72–104.

Ivanova-Sullivan, T. 2014. *Theoretical and Experimental Aspects of Syntax-Discourse Interface in Heritage Grammars*. Leiden: Brill.

Jia, R. and J. Paradis. 2015. The Use of Referring Expressions in Narratives by Mandarin Heritage Language Children and the Role of Language Environment Factors in Predicting Individual Differences. *Bilingualism: Language and Cognition* 18(4), 737–752.

Kaltsa, M., I. Tsimpli, and J. Rothman. 2015. Exploring the Source of Differences and Similarities in L1 Attrition and Heritage Speaker

Competence: Evidence from Pronominal Resolution. *Lingua* 164(B), 266–288.

Keating, G., B. VanPatten, and J. Jegerski. 2011. Who Was Walking on the Beach: Anaphora Resolution in Spanish Heritage Speakers and Adult Second Language Learners. *Studies in Second Language Acquisition* 33(2), 193–221.

Keating, G. D., J. Jegerski, and B. VanPatten. 2016. Online Processing of Subject Pronouns in Monolingual and Heritage Bilingual Speakers of Mexican Spanish. *Bilingualism: Language and Cognition* 19(1), 36–49.

É. Kiss, K. 1998. Identificational Focus versus Information Focus. *Language* 74(2), 245–273.

Kim, J.-Y. 2019a. Heritage Speakers' Use of Prosodic Strategies in Focus Marking in Spanish. *International Journal of Bilingualism* 23(5), 986–1004.

Kim, J.-Y. 2019b. Discrepancy between Heritage Speakers' use of Suprasegmental Cues in the Perception and Production of Spanish Lexical Stress. *Bilingualism: Language and Cognition*.

Koban, D. 2011. Continuity Reference and Subject Personal Pronoun Variation in the Turkish Spoken in Turkey and New York City. *Australian Journal of Linguistics* 31(3), 351–369.

Krifka, M. 2008. Basic Notions of Information Structure. *Acta Linguistica Hungarica* 55, 243–276.

Laleko, O. 2010. The Syntax-Pragmatics Interface in Language Loss: Covert Restructuring of Aspect in Heritage Russian. Doctoral dissertation, University of Minnesota, Minneapolis.

Laleko, O. 2017. Information Status and Word Order in Heritage and L2 Russian. Paper presented at the Tenth National Heritage Language Research Institute, University of Illinois Urbana-Champaign. May 22–25.

Laleko, O. 2019. Resolving Indeterminacy in Gender Agreement: Comparing Heritage Speakers and L2 Learners of Russian. *Heritage Language Journal* 16(2), 151–182.

Laleko, O. and I. Dubinina. 2018. Word Order Production in Heritage Russian: Perspectives from Linguistics and Pedagogy. In S. Bauckus, and S. Kresin (eds.), *Connecting across languages and Cultures: A Heritage Language Festschrift in Honor of Olga Kagan*. Bloomington, IN: Slavica, 191–215.

Laleko, O. and M. Polinsky. 2013. Marking Topic or Marking Case? A Comparative Investigation of Heritage Japanese and Heritage Korean. *Heritage Language Journal* 10(2), 40–64.

Laleko, O. and M. Polinsky. 2016. Between Syntax and Discourse: Topic and Case Marking in Heritage Speakers and L2 Learners of Japanese and Korean. *Linguistic Approaches to Bilingualism* 6(4), 396–439.

Laleko, O. and M. Polinsky. 2017. Silence Is Difficult. On Missing Elements in Bilingual Grammars. *Zeitschrift für Sprachwissenschaft* 36, 135–163.

Lambrecht, K. 1994. *Information Structure and Sentence Form. Topic, Focus, and the Mental Representation of Discourse Referents*. Cambridge: Cambridge University Press.

Leal, T., E. Destruel, and B. Hoot. 2018. The Realization of Information Focus in Monolingual and Bilingual Native Spanish. *Linguistic Approaches to Bilingualism* 8(2), 217–251.

Leal, T., J. Rothman, and R. Slabakova. 2014. A Rare Structure at the Syntax-Discourse Interface: Heritage and Spanish-Dominant Native Speakers Weigh In. *Language Acquisition* 21(4), 411–429.

Leal Méndez, T., J. Rothman, and R. Slabakova. 2015. Discourse-Sensitive Clitic-Doubled Dislocations in Heritage Spanish. *Lingua* 155, 85–97.

Montrul, S. 2004. Subject and Object Expression in Spanish Heritage Speakers: A Case of Morpho-syntactic Convergence. *Bilingualism, Language and Cognition* 7(2), 125–142.

Montrul, S. 2005. Second Language Acquisition and First Language Loss in Adult Early Bilinguals: Exploring Some Differences and Similarities. *Second Language Research* 22(2), 145–187.

Montrul, S. 2008 *Incomplete Acquisition in Bilingualism: Reexamining the Age Factor*. Amsterdam: John Benjamins.

Montrul, S. 2010a. Dominant Language Transfer in Adult Second Language Learners and Heritage Speakers. *Second Language Research* 26(3), 293–327.

Montrul, S. 2010b. How Similar Are Adult Second Language Learners and Spanish Heritage Speakers? Spanish Clitics and Word Order. *Applied Psycholinguistics* 31(1), 167–207.

Montrul, S. 2016. *The Acquisition of Heritage Languages*. Cambridge: Cambridge University Press.

Montrul, S. 2018. Heritage Language Development: Connecting the Dots. *International Journal of Bilingualism* 22(5), 530–546.

Montrul, S. and M. Polinsky 2011. Why Not Heritage Speakers? *Linguistic Approaches to Bilingualism* 1(1), 58–62.

Nagy, N. 2015. A Sociolinguistic View of Null Subjects and VOT in Toronto Heritage Languages. *Lingua* 164(B), 309–327.

Neeleman, A. and H. van de Koot. 2016. Word Order and Information Structure. In C. Féry and S. Ishihara (eds.), *The Oxford Handbook of Information Structure*. Oxford: Oxford University Press, 383–401.

O'Grady W., H. Y. Kwak, O.-S. Lee, and M. Lee. 2011. An Emergentist Perspective on Heritage Language Acquisition. *Studies in Second Language Acquisition* 33(2), 223–246.

Otheguy, R., A. C. Zentella, and D. Livert. 2007. Language and Dialect Contact in Spanish in New York: Toward the Formation of a Speech Community. *Language* 83(4), 770–803.

Pires, A. and J. Rothman. 2009. Disentangling Sources of Incomplete Acquisition: An Explanation for Competence Divergence across Heritage Grammars. *International Journal of Bilingualism* 13(2), 211–238.

Polinsky, M. 1997. *American Russian: Language Loss Meets Language Acquisition. Proceedings of the Annual Workshop of Formal Approaches to Slavic Linguistics*. Ann Arbor: Michigan Slavic Publications, 370–406.

Polinsky, M. 2006. Incomplete Acquisition: American Russian. *Journal of Slavic Linguistics* 14, 192–265.

Polinsky, M. 2008. Heritage Language Narratives. In D. Brinton, O. Kagan, and S. Bauckus (eds.), *Heritage Language Education. A New Field Emerging*. New York: Routledge, 149–164.

Polinsky, M. 2011. Reanalysis in Adult Heritage Language: A Case for Attrition. *Studies in Second Language Acquisition* 33(2), 305–328.

Polinsky, M. 2018. *Heritage Languages and Their Speakers*. Cambridge: Cambridge University Press.

Polinsky, M. and O. Kagan. 2007. Heritage Languages: In the "Wild" and in the Classroom. *Language and Linguistic Compass* 1(5), 368–395.

Polinsky, M. and G. Scontras. 2020. Understanding Heritage Languages. *Bilingualism: Language and Cognition* 23(1), 4–20.

Prada Pérez, A. de. 2019. Theoretical Implications of Research on Bilingual Subject Production: The Vulnerability Hypothesis. *International Journal of Bilingualism* 23(2), 670–694.

Prada Pérez, A. de and D. Pascual y Cabo. 2012. Interface Heritage Speech across proficiencies: Unaccusativity, Focus, and Subject Position in Spanish. In K. Geeslin and M. Díaz-Campos (eds.), *Selected Proceedings of the 14th Hispanic Linguistics Symposium*. Somerville, MA: Cascadilla, 308–318.

Putnam, M. and L. Sánchez. 2013. What's So Incomplete about Incomplete Acquisition? A Prolegomenon to Modeling Heritage Language Grammars. *Linguistic Approaches to Bilingualism* 3(4), 478–508.

Reinhart, T. 2006. *Interface Strategies*. Cambridge, MA: MIT Press.

Rinke, E. and C. Flores. 2018. Another Look at the Interpretation of Overt and Null Pronominal Subjects in Bilingual Language Acquisition: Heritage Portuguese in Contact with German and Spanish. *Glossa* 3(1), 68.

Rizzi, L. 1997. The Fine Structure of the Left Periphery. In L. Haegeman (ed.), *Elements of Grammar: Handbook in Generative Syntax*. Dordrecht: Kluwer, 281–337.

Rooth, M. 2016. Alternative Semantics. In C. Féry and S. Ishihara (eds.), *The Oxford Handbook of Information Structure*. Oxford: Oxford University Press, 19–40.

Sagarra, N., L. Sánchez, and A. Bel. 2019. Processing DOM in Relative Clauses: Salience and Optionality in Early and Late Bilinguals. *Linguistic Approaches to Bilingualism* 9(1), 120–160.

Sekerina, I. and J. C. Trueswell. 2011. Processing of Contrastiveness by Heritage Russian Bilinguals. *Bilingualism: Language and Cognition* 14(3), 280–300.

Selkirk, E. 1995. Sentence Prosody: Intonation, Stress, and Phrasing. In J. Goldsmith (ed.), *The Handbook of Phonology*. Oxford: Blackwell, 550–569.

Serratrice, L., A. Sorace, and S. Paoli. 2004. Crosslinguistic Influence at the Syntax-Pragmatics Interface: Subjects and Objects in English-Italian Bilingual and Monolingual Acquisition. *Bilingualism: Language and Cognition* 7(3), 183–205.

Shimojo, M. 2006. Properties of Particle "Omission" Revisited. *Toronto Working Papers in Linguistics* 26, 123–140.

Silva-Corvalán, C. 1994. *Language Contact and Change: Spanish in Los Angeles*. Oxford: Clarendon.

Silva-Corvalán, C. 2018. Simultaneous Bilingualism: Early Developments, Incomplete Later Outcomes? *International Journal of Bilingualism* 22(5), 497–512.

Sorace, A. 2011. Pinning down the Concept of "Interface" in Bilingualism. *Linguistic Approaches to Bilingualism* 1(1), 1–33.

Sorace, A. and F. Filiaci. 2006. Anaphora Resolution in Near-Native Speakers of Italian. *Second Language Research* 22(3), 339–368.

Sorace, A., L. Serratrice, F. Filiaci, and M. Baldo. 2009. Discourse Conditions on Subject Pronoun Realization: Testing the Linguistic Conditions of Older Bilingual Children. *Lingua* 119(3), 460–477.

Tomioka, S. 2010. Contrastive Topics Operate on Speech Acts. In M. Zimmermann and C. Féry (eds.), *Information Structure: Theoretical, Typological, and Experimental Perspectives*. Oxford: Oxford University Press, 115–138.

Van Osch, B. and P. Sleeman. 2018. Subject Position in Spanish as a Heritage Language in the Netherlands: External and Internal Interface Factors. In A. Gavarró (ed.), *On the Acquisition of the Syntax of Romance*. Amsterdam: John Benjamins, 187–214.

Van Rijswijk, R., A. Muntendam, and T. Dijkstra. 2017a. Focus in Dutch Reading: An Eye-Tracking Experiment with Heritage Speakers of Turkish. *Language, Cognition, and Neuroscience* 32(8), 984–1000.

Van Rijswijk, R., A. Muntendam, and T. Dijkstra. 2017b. Focus Marking in Dutch by Heritage Speakers of Turkish and Dutch L1 Speakers. *Journal of Phonetics* 61, 48–70.

Zapata, G., L. Sánchez, and A. J. Toribio. 2005. Contact and Contracting Spanish. *International Journal of Bilingualism* 9(3–4), 377–395.

Zimmermann, M. and E. Onéa. 2011. Focus Marking and Focus Interpretation. *Lingua* 121(11), 1651–1670.

Zubizarreta, M. 1998. *Focus, Prosody, and Word Order*. Cambridge, MA: MIT Press.

28

Pragmatics in Heritage Languages

Irina Dubinina

The chapter presents a critical overview of the current state of knowledge regarding the pragmatic competence of heritage speakers (HSs). Although research on heritage language pragmatics is still sparse, it makes an important contribution to the understanding of the linguistic knowledge and abilities of heritage bilinguals. This chapter analyzes currently available studies investigating speech act realizations and normative politeness in heritage languages and provides a description of the emerging profile of HSs' pragmatic competence. It also outlines theoretical frameworks that have been proposed for the investigation of HSs' pragmatic development and abilities, identifies methodological needs of the field, and provides suggestions for future research directions.

28.1 Communicative Competence: Speech Act Pragmatics and Politeness

The field of pragmatics investigates how linguistic forms are used to perform communicative acts in a social context and how the realization of these acts is perceived and evaluated by others in that context. The field covers a vast range of theoretical perspectives and areas of research, but to address all of them in this chapter would not be possible or practical. Instead, the chapter focuses on those areas that have received the most attention in heritage linguistics to date: more specifically, on speech act studies that investigate language use in the performance of social acts and linguistic expressions of deference and politeness, either as part of the performance of speech acts or in the use of forms of address.

The notion of communicative competence, although related to and dependent on grammatical competence, is much broader as it is regulated not only by the knowledge of linguistic rules of grammar and lexicon and the ability to form cohesive and coherent sentences but also by the knowledge of all components of communicative events; attitudes and beliefs about them; norms and rules for turn-taking in a conversation; conventions of language use; communicative norms and strategies associated with particular social contexts; and the sociocultural appropriateness of linguistic forms (Hymes 1974; Swann et al. 2004). Pragmatic competence is a fundamental aspect of the broader notion of communicative competence and incorporates "… the speakers' knowledge and use of rules of appropriateness and politeness which dictate the way the speaker will understand and formulate speech acts" (Koike 1989). Moreover, being pragmatically competent requires both the knowledge of *pragmalinguistic* forms (i.e., linguistic resources available to speakers of a given language to perform communicative functions) and *sociopragmatic norms* (i.e., rules governing the appropriateness of linguistic forms in various social contexts) – a distinction made by Leech (1983) – as well as processing skills that mobilize this knowledge in communication.

An important area of investigation in the pragmatics of speech acts concerns the interrelated notions of (in)appropriateness, (im)politeness, and (in)directness. Several theories have been proposed to explain why speakers use direct or indirect strategies when performing speech acts, but perhaps the most popular one is the politeness theory developed by Brown and Levinson (1987). It is based on the notion that any interaction involves a complex balancing act of attending to one another's positive and negative face needs (Goffman 2005). The choices of (in)directness, (in)appropriateness, and (im)politeness are viewed as strategies to save face and are influenced by three sociocultural variables: the degree of social distance between participants, power hierarchy, and the degree of the imposition on the hearer.

The face-saving theory claims universality; however, some researchers have pointed out that it fails to take into consideration specific sociocultural differences between Western and Asian societies and accounts for only one type of politeness. Ahn (2005), for example, argues that there are in fact two types of linguistic politeness: universal *strategic* politeness, which is situational and controlled by the speaker (e.g., Brown and Levinson's face-saving politeness), and culture-specific *normative* politeness, which is obligatory and is bound by sociocultural norms. While both types of politeness characterize all human societies, normative politeness arguably plays a much more significant role in Asian societies, where the self is defined as highly relational, interpersonal, and collective (Ahn 2005). In Western societies, where the concept of self is viewed as more individualistic and autonomous, the scope of the linguistic systems servicing normative politeness is much smaller and concerns mostly address forms and some aspects of social pleasantries (greetings, opening and closing routines, etc.), which depend on the social factors of age, power relations, social distance, and, sometimes, gender. In comparison, Asian languages require that speakers express their self in relation to others and encode this relational hierarchy with appropriate linguistic forms. For these reasons, some scholars insist that the investigation of normative politeness must be viewed as an important part of pragmatics research.

All these notions of pragmatic competence have been investigated in the field of speech act pragmatics and in its branches – cross-cultural pragmatics, which compares speech acts and politeness/directness in different linguacultures (Blum-Kulka et al. 1989), and interlanguage pragmatics, which focuses on the pragmatic competence and development of second language (L2) learners (Kasper and Blum-Kulka 1993). The third branch, heritage language pragmatics – currently in its nascent stage – investigates the pragmatic competence of HSs of various languages.

28.2 Heritage Language Pragmatics

Scholarship on pragmatic competence of HSs is much smaller than in the general field of heritage linguistics or even in cross-cultural and interlanguage pragmatics. Research in heritage language pragmatics has been developing largely along two directions: the investigation of specific speech act realizations in heritage languages, including strategic politeness, and studies of normative politeness. Currently available studies in both types of research are mostly descriptive in nature, aiming to establish a basic understanding of the pragmatic competence of HSs, and do not cover the array of heritage languages studied by formal linguistics. Some of the studies are difficult to identify as belonging to heritage pragmatics because they do not use the explicit term "heritage" and do not define their participants as "heritage speakers." For the analysis presented in this chapter, much effort was given to identifying heritage pragmatics studies among those that refer to their participants as "English-dominant speakers of language X," "second-generation immigrants," or "L2 learners."

Most research has been carried out on heritage languages in contact with English in the United States, and the majority of this research is focused on Spanish HSs (Pinto and Raschio 2007, 2008; Finestradt-Martínez and Potowski 2016, *inter alia*), but other heritage languages are also represented, e.g., Russian (Dubinina 2013; Dubinina and Malamud 2017), Korean (Ahn 2005; Youn and Brown 2013, *inter alia*), Polish (Wolski-Moskoff 2018), and Chinese (Taguchi et al. 2017, *inter alia*). Although there are many studies on communicative competence of bilingual speakers in Europe, there is a great paucity of published research specifically on the pragmatic abilities of heritage bilinguals. Notable exceptions include the study of Estonian HSs in Sweden (Keevallik 2012), Hungarian in Slovakia (Lanstyák and Szabómihály 2005), and Turkish-Dutch heritage children (Backus and Yağmur 2017).

In experimental studies on HSs' linguistic abilities, these speakers are often compared to two control groups: monolinguals of their home languages (adult and children) and/or L2 learners. These comparisons prove useful for the investigation of HSs' pragmatic knowledge and performance as well. Similar to the measures of other areas of linguistic knowledge, HSs resemble monolingual native speakers (NSs) in that they have early naturalistic exposure to the language and their pragmatic development happens through socialization in the family and community. As a result, they acquire colloquial genres and linguistic forms necessary for interacting in informal settings at home. At the same time, however, HSs share some characteristics with L2 learners, such as varied success in reaching ultimate attainment[1] (as evidenced by HSs' divergence from the monolingual norm) and notable signs of cross-linguistic influence from the dominant language.

It is important to recognize, however, that pragmatic performance of adult HSs has characteristics that distinguish them from either group. Research on speech act realizations in heritage languages indicates that HSs have the knowledge of at least some conventionalized pragmalinguistic forms, especially in informal contexts, and are aware of the sociopragmatic norms governing the production of speech acts as well as of the required expressions of deference even if they do not always pattern with the monolingual group and exhibit their own unique intercultural communicative style. For example, HSs' performance tends to be lacking in interactions taking place in formal settings where the social distance between speakers and power hierarchy are greater. HSs feel more comfortable and more confident performing in informal contexts where they have more experience. They seem to be aware of the sociopragmatic norms of their heritage language, but may not have the linguistic forms required to comply with these norms at their disposal, which leads them to borrowing linguistic material from their dominant language.

Acknowledging these unique features of HSs' pragmatic performance, some researchers have cautioned against unnuanced comparisons between HSs and native speakers or L2 learners and reliance on monolingual norms

---

[1] The ongoing terminological debate over the status of HSs as native speakers and the general concept of native speakerhood (Kupisch and Rothman 2018; Lohndal et al. 2019) makes this statement problematic. At the same time, the plurilingualism and translanguaging frameworks, which have taken hold in linguistics and language education over the past several years, question the established monolingual/ethnocentric paradigm where monolingualism is taken as a norm against which bilingual practices are compared (Arvanitis 2018; Galante 2018; Piccardo 2018). The overwhelming majority of the studies discussed in this chapter, however, were not positioned within these frameworks, nor did they consider the question of native speakerhood in relation to HSs. The overview presented in this chapter reflects this reality.

for comparisons, arguing that the most appropriate frameworks for the study of HSs' pragmatics are the ones that attend to these speakers' bicultural and bilingual experiences (Pinto 2012, 2018; Taguchi and Roever 2017). These researchers point out that studies of HSs' pragmatics must also contextualize HSs' language use differently from L2 pragmatic studies, taking into account the unique sociolinguistic settings of interactions in bilingual/bicultural communities that are affected by linguistic displacement and forces of acculturation.

Because the field of HL pragmatics is still developing, theoretical frameworks that could account for specific features of HSs' pragmatic knowledge, and its development, have not yet been established. Some of the frameworks that are currently being explored were originally proposed for bilingual (L2) and monolingual language experiences. Among them are the intercultural style hypothesis (Blum-Kulka 1991; Cenoz 2003), which argues that bilingual speakers develop special patterns of interaction as a result of their bilingualism, and the language socialization theory (Schieffelin and Ochs 1986; He 2012), which accounts for how children become competent members of their language community and internalize socially constructed patterns of speech. In addition, the "two-dimensional model" (Bialystok 1993), which attempts to explain the acquisition of pragmatics, has also been suggested as being of value to heritage pragmatics (Taguchi 2015), even though it was originally proposed as a way to distinguish between the learning of pragmatics by children and by adult L2 learners. The model specifies that children develop linguistic and pragmatic competences simultaneously, whereas adult learners approach the task of pragmatics learning in L2 after having completed the acquisition of pragmatics in L1, and, therefore, have to rely on different cognitive mechanisms. Taguchi argues that HSs represent both dimensions of this model: "they are similar to children acquiring pragmatics through socialization, but they also represent adults' pragmatics systems because pragmatic socialization occurs in two separate domains ... " (14). While references to these frameworks are made in some studies analyzed in this chapter, they are scarce, and most of the research conducted to date is exploratory and descriptive in nature. The field obviously needs more studies to advance the theoretical understanding of HSs' pragmatic competence and its acquisition.

28.3   Speech Act Studies in Heritage Languages

The most studied speech acts to date in heritage language pragmatics are requests and apologies, which are also the most studied speech acts cross-linguistically (Blum-Kulka et al. 1989). There are also several studies addressing the speech acts of complaints (Pinto and Raschio 2008; Elias

2013), compliments (Bachelor and Barros García 2018), and refusals and suggestions (Ahn 2005; Youn and Brown 2013; Elias 2015; Taguchi et al. 2017). These studies aim to provide a description of HSs' pragmatic abilities through comparisons of their performance either with the monolingual speakers of their home languages and/or with L2 learners. There are, however, some important differences in research using the two control groups, which warrants separate subsections.

Analyses of data from the reviewed studies, which were collected through a variety of instruments, ranging from unstructured and structured interviews to experimental instruments, such as open-ended and multiple-choice discourse completion tasks (DCT) and role plays, indicate several common trends in HSs' performance of speech acts. These trends include evidence of unique intercultural pragmatic norms in heritage languages, a reduced repertoire of conventionalized means to perform various speech acts, novel strategies to compensate for this lack of knowledge, and informal "bias" in HSs' pragmatic abilities as they perform with greater ease and pattern more closely with monolinguals in informal scenarios. Sections 28.3.1 and 28.3.2 present a review of pertinent studies that illustrate these generalizations.

28.3.1 Speech Act Studies: Comparing HSs and Monolingual Groups

Speech act studies across different heritage languages indicate that HSs have a unique intercultural style in performing various speech acts, which is often marked by excessive downgrading, the use of non-conventionalized forms, and cross-linguistic influence from the dominant language. For example, in an investigation of requests for favors made by English-dominant HSs of Spanish, Pinto and Raschio (2007) found that although HSs patterned with monolingual English NSs in avoiding direct requests, they behaved differently from both monolingual English speakers and monolingual Mexican speakers of Spanish on other requestive strategies. Overall, HSs produced grammatically correct utterances, but did not adhere to monolingual pragmatic conventions, using linguistic forms that are not conventionalized in monolingual Spanish as a means to create or mitigate a request. Qualitative description of the differences between the HS group and the two monolingual groups revealed signs of transfer from English, such as multiple downgrading and the use of *if*-clause instead of the canonical past subjunctive in Spanish. The authors suggest that by intensifying downgrading, HSs attempt to compensate for their perceived lack of linguistic abilities, especially when more face work is required, which puts them further apart from the Spanish monolingual norm.

Pinto and Raschio's (2008) study on the speech act of complaint provides more support to their claim that HSs have a unique communicative style.

Compared with monolingual Spanish speakers, HSs used fewer openers (e.g., greetings) and more justifications of the problem, which approximated the monolingual English patterns, and also showed other traces of linguistic transfer from English in their unique use of subjectivizers and consultative devices as mitigation. On the other hand, HSs differed from both monolingual control groups on their use of downgraders. They produced significantly more complaints with zero downgraders than native speakers of English, and at the same time used multiple downgraders even in informal contexts, diverging from monolingual speakers of Mexican Spanish. The authors interpret this clustering of HSs at the opposite ends of the downgrading continuum as a sign of their hybrid communicative style.

Pinto and Raschio's (2008) conclusions regarding the unique intercultural communicative style of Spanish HSs have been supported by studies of pragmatics in heritage Russian in the United States. In this author's investigation of comprehension and production of requests by Russian monolinguals and adult English-dominant HSs (Dubinina 2013), heritage bilinguals differed from NSs not only in their avoidance of direct requests but also in their choices of indirect strategies as well as in the pragmalinguistic rules of forming and mitigating polite requests for favor. In formal contexts when more face work was needed, the differences were more pronounced as HSs relied more on pragmalinguistic forms they transferred from English. Similar to Spanish HSs in Pinto and Raschio's study, Russian HSs used embedded interrogatives (*if*-clauses) as a face management device, a sign of interference from English. In addition, they transferred the co-occurrence rules governing lexical politeness marker *požalujsta* ('please'), which they used in the interrogatives, a pattern not attested to in the NSs data but common in monolingual English. The most dramatic difference between requests made by HSs and NSs was found in the use of modals and the negative particle *ne* ('not'). Dubinina suggests that NSs view the impersonal modal *možno* ('may/can'), which has a strong implicature of permission seeking, as a mitigating device when more face work is needed, while HSs treat the same modal as a generalized marker of any type of request, devoid of its implicature of permission seeking. Russian HSs in this study also failed to use the negative particle *ne*, which serves simultaneously as a marker of the requestive force in indirect requests (yes/no questions) and a mitigating device in monolingual Russian across all social contexts. In the comprehension of requests, HSs too lacked the skills necessary to interpret the nuances of expressing deference through the negative particle: They tended to judge such requests as having a lower politeness value. Together, these differences point to Russian HSs' unique strategies for performing and comprehending requests for favor, which incorporate pragmatic conventions of both of their languages.

As is evident from these studies, one source of the unique communicative style of HSs is cross-linguistic influence from English, the dominant language of heritage bilinguals in the United States and the dominant societal language. Spanish and Russian HSs in the United States seem to borrow English linguistic means to create and mitigate requests. They may borrow specific pragmalinguistic forms (e.g., the *if*-clause) or entire strategies for creating conventionalized indirect requests (e.g., use of multiple levels of downgrading even when addressing peers in the Pinto and Raschio studies, or the use of embedding in the Dubinina study).

Avoidance of direct strategies in making requests has also been proposed to be a sign of cross-linguistic influence. Spanish HSs in the Pinto and Raschio (2007) study of requests avoided using direct strategy, resembling monolingual English NSs (who never used it) and contrasting with monolingual Spanish NSs (who used it 15 percent of the time). Avoidance of direct strategies in making requests was also confirmed for Russian HSs (Dubinina 2013; Dubinina and Malamud, 2017) and Estonian HSs in Sweden (Keevallik 2012). An interesting nuance to the cross-linguistic interference in heritage language pragmatics emerged from research by Finestradt-Martínez and Potowski (2016), who partially replicated and expanded Pinto and Raschio's study on requests by including third-generation speakers of Spanish and testing bilingual participants in both Spanish and English. In general, their results supported the findings of Pinto and Raschio: Monolingual Mexicans used the most direct strategies in requests and monolingual English speakers used the most indirect strategies, while heritage bilinguals placed between the two ends of this continuum in Spanish. However, the study also indicated that bilingual speakers were more indirect when responding in English than they were when responding in Spanish. This, the authors argue, suggests that Spanish HSs may have two overlapping pragmatic systems that they access depending on the context of language use.

A detailed example of the role that cross-linguistic influence plays in forming communicative style in heritage languages comes from the study of Estonian HSs in Sweden. Keevallik (2012) investigated conversation rituals, address forms, as well as speech acts of request, question-asking, proposal/suggestion, compliments, and concessions by World War II Estonian refugees and their decedents in Sweden. The overwhelming majority of participants were second- and third-generation HSs. The study revealed changes not only in pragmalinguistic norms but also in sociopragmatic strategies used by Estonian HSs as a result of intensive language contact in this immigrant community. Swedish Estonians tend to adopt Swedish norms of linguistic behavior in closing and thanking rituals, either using Estonian words in ways that are not conventionalized in full Estonian or calquing Swedish phrases. For example, Swedish Estonians thank their hosts for their time spent together, something that full speakers of

Estonian do not routinely do. Moreover, they use the phrase *aitä tänase eest*, which is a direct translation of the Swedish expression *tak för idag* ('thank you for today'). Swedish Estonians also respond to expressions of gratitude differently, patterning with Swedish monolinguals: In response to a thank-you (*tänan*) they also say *tänan*, whereas in Estonia the word *palun* ('here you are') is normally used.

Furthermore, Keevallik shows that HSs and NSs of Estonian use different syntactic and grammatical means to express polite requests and to mitigate the level of directness. In the study, Estonian HSs avoided imperatives and routinely produced yes/no questions without negation when making requests, patterning with the Swedish monolingual norm. In full Estonian, such questions would be considered rude orders that would normally be addressed to animals. Keevallik points out that, in fact, one and the same grammatical construction has the opposite illocutionary meaning and polite-ness value in full versus heritage varieties of Estonian, which would inevit-ably result in a spectacular pragmalinguistic failure in a conversation between a speaker of full Estonian and a Swedish-Estonian heritage bilingual.

As all of these studies indicate, the intercultural communicative style of HSs is characterized by a lack of conventionalized ways to formulate speech acts and express required levels of politeness that are used in the homeland (i.e., monolingual communities). To compensate for their perceived lack of pragmatic abilities, HSs borrow pragmalinguistic forms from their domin-ant language, such as *if*-clauses, subjectivizers, and semantic formulae (understaters, consultative devices, lexical politeness markers, etc.). As a result, heritage languages may develop their own novel conventions for routine speech acts.

Expanding on the author's 2013 study, Dubinina and Malamud (2017) explore how new pragmatic conventions may be formed in heritage Russian. They analyzed English requests found in the MiCASE corpus and conducted nuanced searches of the Russian National Corpus in order to compare requests produced in full Russian, full English, and heritage Russian in the United States. Based on this analysis, they argue that as a contact language, heritage Russian has developed new conventions for expressing polite requests and hypothesize that these new conventions form a hybrid communicative style under the influence of three factors: (1) transfer from English (the use of *if*-clauses and lexical politeness marker *požalujsta* in interrogatives); (2) possible incomplete acquisition of conven-tionalized forms to express requests (avoidance of the negative particle *ne*); and (3) language internal change (expansion of the use of *možno* to mark any request for favor). Importantly, the new conventions may concern not only pragmalinguistic forms (as is the case with Russian and Spanish in the United States) but may also affect sociopragmatic norms, as Keevallik's (2012) study of Estonian HSs in Sweden indicates.

While the creation of new communicative norms may indicate a certain amount of linguistic resourcefulness, the lack of knowledge of conventionalized pragmalinguistic means, nevertheless, may cause HSs to appear less polite or even rude to monolingual native speakers, as shown, for example, by Keevallik. In a study of requests and apologies produced orally by Korean HSs in role play situations, Koo (2002) also indicates a number of ways in which a reduced repertoire of pragmalinguistic forms affects the politeness value of speech acts produced by heritage bilinguals. In requests, Korean HSs relied on only two conventionalized strategies – mood derivable and preparatory condition – while monolingual NSs exhibited a rich repertoire of strategies, both conventionalized and non-conventional. In addition, HSs used only one supportive move to mitigate the head act, whereas monolingual Korean NSs used a greater number and a wider variety of supportive moves. As a result, requests produced by HSs were much shorter than those produced by NSs. Reliance on mood derivable, lack of supportive moves, and shorter utterances made HS requests more direct and lowered the politeness value of the speech act. In apologies, HSs again produced shorter utterances by using only one formulaic expression with only one or without any intensifying adverbs across all scenarios. By contrast, NSs used a variety of strategies, including explicit formulae and expressions of taking on responsibility, and varied the number of intensifying adverbs, according to the social parameters of the situation. Because HSs did not increase the number of strategies or intensifiers in scenarios involving an older interlocutor or in situations of greater power differential, their apologies had a lower politeness value and could be considered a communicative failure.

Another source of such failure may be a smaller vocabulary size of heritage bilinguals, as a study of sociopragmatic skills of bilingual Turkish-Dutch children indicates (Backus and Yağmur 2017). In this study, thirty bilingual children (third-generation Turkish speakers) in the Netherlands were compared to thirty monolingual Turkish children matched in age (between 5 and 6 years old) and socioeconomic status of their parents. The study analyzed children's ability to carry out basic speech acts, such as voicing opinion, making a request, offering an apology, and expressing a suggestion. The authors note that the bilingual children had much lower active and passive lexicon than their monolingual counterparts, with the difference being more pronounced for the active vocabulary. The smaller active lexicon translated into deficits in children's sociopragmatic knowledge: The bilingual children scored significantly lower on all pragmatics tests in the study, with the majority of them being in the lowest three percentile levels, whereas the monolingual children scored at the two highest levels (75 percent and above). The bilingual children often opted for short utterances and direct strategies, which, in the view of the authors, indicates their struggle to summon up all their linguistic abilities in order to express their communicative intentions despite lexical deficiencies. In scenarios that required more face work, and therefore more lexical knowledge – such as speaking to a teacher – the pragmatic failure of bilingual children who used direct strategies was especially apparent in this study.

At the same time, at least for adult HSs, the observed pragmatic failure is not necessarily connected to their lack of vocabulary or insufficient knowledge of sociopragmatic conventions. In Koo's study of requests and apologies in heritage Korean, participants reflected on their performance in post-task interviews. They indicated that although they were aware of the required politeness levels, they were concerned about grammatical and lexical errors, particularly in the use of honorifics and speech styles, and therefore tried to keep their utterances short for fear of making a mistake. This rare glimpse into HSs' thinking process involved in making linguistic choices shows that HSs may not be able to respond linguistically to the demands imposed by the social context of interaction, even if they *do* understand the sociopragmatic norms, and that avoidance of pragmatic performance, especially in formal contexts, may be practiced by some HSs as one strategy to express politeness.

Finally, all available studies on speech acts in heritage languages point to the informal "bias" of their speakers: HSs feel more comfortable and confident when interacting with peers and in situations unmarked by social hierarchy. In contexts characterized by complications (e.g., a greater degree of imposition or the ambiguity of the hearer's social status) and by larger social distance between interlocutors where more face work is required, HSs' performance diverges more significantly from the monolingual norm. Backus and Yağmur's (2017) study found major differences between the two groups of children concerning the use of colloquial forms (more commonly found in the language of the bilingual participants) and special semantic and syntactic forms expressing politeness (much more common in the data from the monolingual Turkish children). Scenarios that involved talking to an adult with high social power, such as a teacher, proved to be most difficult for the bilinguals. While the monolingual group demonstrated full awareness of the cultural norms required in such interactions (including appropriate forms of address, such as "my teacher"), Turkish-Dutch bilinguals resorted to direct strategies, inappropriate for the situation.

Investigations of speech acts in heritage Korean produce the most dramatic examples of the struggles that HSs experience in formal contexts. Realization of speech acts in Korean is highly complex because of the system of honorifics requiring the speaker to choose between several speech styles contingent on social factors, which include interlocutor's gender, age (younger, older, or of the same age), degree of acquaintance, and power differential. Age considerations play a special part in a Korean speaker's decision to choose a specific level of politeness. In Koo's (2002) study, HSs found scenarios that pinned age against the other social variables (social distance and power differential) particularly challenging and struggled to address this ambiguity through linguistic means. For example, one heritage speaker used honorifics when speaking to a 10-year-old girl who was a stranger (none of the NSs did that). In post-task interviews, participants reported that the production of speech acts felt more automatic in informal situations and involved a lot more preparatory thinking in formal scenarios.

As studies reviewed here indicate, HSs have a hybrid communicative style when performing routine speech acts, which draws on the linguistic systems of both of their languages. They often lack knowledge of monolingual conventionalized means to express communicative intent and mitigate face threats even in informal situations. When HSs are called on to perform speech acts in formal contexts, they experience even greater difficulties in choosing appropriate forms and may use several compensatory mechanisms, which take them further away from the monolingual pragmatic conventions accepted in the homeland. They may rely more on linguistic resources in their dominant language and increase the amount of borrowing from English, as Russian HSs in Dubinina's (2013) study did. They may reduce their output and keep their speech acts short for fear of mistakes, as Koo's (2002) study of Korean HSs showed (a counterproductive strategy that caused their performance to have a lower politeness value). Finally, HSs may over-mitigate and produce longer and wordier utterances, as Pinto and Raschio's (2007, 2008) studies of requests and complaints produced by Spanish HSs indicated.

28.3.2 Speech Act Studies: Comparing HSs and L2 Learners

Studies comparing pragmatic performance of HSs to L2 learners who have no prior experience with the target language provide further details for the emerging profile of HSs' pragmatic competence. In these studies, HSs are usually referred to as heritage language learners (HLLs) to differentiate them from those HSs who may or may not study their heritage language in instructional settings. This division is often blurry, and in many studies the terms "heritage speakers" and "heritage learners" are used interchangeably, making generalizations difficult. In this section of the chapter, the term HLLs will be used consistently to differentiate participants in the studies reviewed in this section from those in the previous section.

Multiple studies where adult HLLs are compared to L2s point to an overwhelming advantage of heritage bilinguals over their L2 counterparts on both the linguistic realization of speech acts and their politeness/appropriateness for the social context, even if they exhibit limited knowledge of monolingual conventionalized forms. Hong (1997) analyzed request strategies produced by HLLs and L2 learners in a second-year Chinese course on two aspects: accessibility (clarity of illocutionary force) and acceptability (appropriateness of request-making expressions in given situations). Both groups were similar in the production of accessible requests, but the rates of acceptable requests were much higher for HLLs (93 percent vs 65 percent). At the same time, HLLs were not on target in their use of formulaic politeness formulas, such as 对不起 (duìbuqǐ 'excuse me') and 劳驾 (láojià 'may I trouble you to'), suggesting their limited experience with these conventionalized mitigating devices.

In an extensive study of pragmatic competence of intermediate and advanced-level Chinese HLLs and L2 learners, Taguchi, Zhang, and Li (2017) examined the production and comprehension of two Chinese pragmalinguistic features – sentence final particles (SFP) and formulaic expressions – which are common in written and oral speech of Chinese NSs. The authors defined formulaic expressions as "fixed or semi-fixed recurrent linguistic strings that are tied to specific situations and used to perform certain communicative functions in a given speech community" (13). The expression 不一定 (bùyídìng 'not necessary'), used as a mitigator in various speech acts, can serve as an example. SFPs, on the other hand, serve as pragmatic devices for saving face as they convey linguistic politeness in social interactions. They can express a variety of functions, such as decreasing the directness level of an imperative and softening a directive speech act: e.g., particles 啊 'a', 吧 'ba', and 呀 'ya'.

Overall, HLLs outperformed their L2 counterparts on both comprehension and written production tasks regardless of the level of instruction – intermediate or advanced. In the comprehension task, HLLs were significantly better at interpreting pragmatic features of utterances in both formal and informal scenarios with a similar effect size. Importantly, however, a post hoc analysis of errors revealed that HLLs sometimes inaccurately interpreted the "pragmatic tone" of the target utterances: for example, missing the mitigating effect of the particle 'ba' in an invitation. By comparison, L2 learners struggled to understand the illocutionary force of the utterance or the utterance itself. In the production task, HLLs also showed advantage over L2 learners, albeit marginally: They used a variety of CFPs and formulaic expressions in both types of scenarios, but not as frequently as NSs would and only slightly more often than L2s. This tendency was especially noticeable in the use of CFPs, which suggests that HSs' high accuracy in the comprehension of the CFPs' pragmatic functions does not necessarily align with their ability to produce these constructions in written speech.

Taguchi, Zhang, and Li point to the amount of interactive language contact (defined as "activity involving face-to-face interactions") as a possible source of HLLs' overall advantage. Significant correlation was found between interactive contact and HLLs' ability to comprehend CFPs and formulaic expressions, and to produce speech acts in formal and informal scenarios. Non-interactive language contact (defined as "media-related activity," such as reading or watching TV) had only one significant, but weak, correlation with the comprehension of CFPs. Due to the naturalistic language acquisition processes, HLLs clearly have a greater exposure to both types of language contact than L2 learners, which allows them to outperform their peers even if they are placed in a same level classroom.

A significant study of pragmatic abilities of Korean HLLs and L2 learners by Youn and Brown (2013) provides further support for the overall HLL advantage but also shows that the advantage is dependent on test modality. Youn and Brown analyzed item difficulty in pragmatic tests of Korean by performing a meta-analysis of two studies that looked at pragmatic competence of adult learners of Korean. One study, by Ahn (2005), involved twenty-one HLLs and thirty-two L2 learners of Korean, while the other, by Youn (2008), tested thirteen HLLs and forty-seven L2 learners with various L1 backgrounds on the production of requests, refusals, and apologies. In both studies HLLs outperformed their non-heritage counterparts on all items regardless of the test type: They showed generally higher average scores than L2s. However, the advantage did not always hold when the modality of the test was taken into consideration. In Youn, there was very little difference between HLLs and L2s on the items of the open-ended written DCT test, and HLLs did not perform on the written tests as well as they did on the spoken tests. Therefore, together with the data from the study by Taguchi, Zhang, and Li (2017), these findings indicate that HLLs' advantage is not uniform across language modalities. The advantage is greatest in oral comprehension, and seems to be weakest in written production.

Another important finding of the Youn and Brown (2013) study reveals that HLLs' advantage is more robust in informal scenarios. The analysis of the data showed that, in general, HLLs did better on test items that involved a lower degree of imposition or lower social hierarchy between interlocutors regardless of the speech act investigated. Items based on situations with a higher degree of imposition or involving someone who had a higher social status were more difficult, and HLLs' advantage over L2 learners was weakened. The authors suggest that such situations require more face work, and, therefore, a better knowledge of complex grammar and Korean speech styles. Thus, they present difficulties for both types of learners and decrease the advantage gap between HLLs and L2 learners. Taguchi, Zhang, and Li (2017) reached similar conclusions in comparing HLLs and L2 performance in formal and informal scenarios on both production and comprehension tasks, noting a smaller effect size for formal situations.

It is important to point out that studies comparing HLLs and L2 learners share two serious shortcomings that cast doubt on the demonstrated HLL advantage: the absence of a full sociolinguistic description of HLL participants, and the lack of proficiency matching between the two groups of learners. Some studies do not provide any sociolinguistic information on HLLs beyond the fact that they are heritage speakers of the language (e.g., Hong 1997). Others provide some information, such as language usage with family and friends, but do not report much more important data on the age of immigration (interruption) or prior formal or informal educational experience (e.g., Barros García and Bachelor 2018). Even more importantly, none of the studies reviewed for this chapter matched the two groups on any objective proficiency measure (such as a standardized written or oral test). Instead, they reported that the two groups of learners were enrolled in the same language course (Taguchi et al. 2017) or that both groups were taking on the target language for the first time at college (Barros García and Bachelor 2018). In addition, these studies tend to treat HLL groups as homogenous in terms of proficiency, which contradicts our knowledge about HSs who exhibit vastly different linguistic abilities even when sociolinguistic characteristics of the acquisitional context are more or less the same. Therefore, the results of studies comparing L2 learners with HLLs outlined in this section must be viewed cautiously until more research taking these factors into consideration becomes available.

28.4   Studies of Normative Politeness in Heritage Languages

Normative politeness is another area in heritage language pragmatics that has received some attention in the United States and in Europe (Wang 1995; Sigüenza-Ortiz 1996; Fenyvesi 2005; Lanstyák and Szabómihály 2005; Park 2006; Wolski-Moskoff 2018). While strategic politeness tied to the notions of (in)directness is studied as part of HSs' performance of speech acts, investigations of normative expressions of deference and politeness in heritage languages focus on the HSs' use of address forms and speech styles, the most vivid example being the use of honorifics in heritage Korean. Unlike strategic politeness, which is situational and depends on the intention of the speaker to maintain face, normative politeness is bound by sociocultural traditions and is obligatory for the speaker (Sohn 1999). It performs the function of social indexing by encoding the hierarchical relationship between the speaker and others in linguistic forms (J. Koo 1995 in Ahn 2005). Because normative politeness is encoded in obligatory linguistic forms, investigating HSs' knowledge and use of these forms is an especially interesting avenue of research in heritage language pragmatics.

The following section reviews available studies that investigate how the linguistic systems of normative politeness may be affected in heritage languages. All of the studies point to severely reduced abilities of HSs to express normative deference appropriately, most likely due to insufficient input during the acquisition of these forms, and to signs of cross-linguistic influence from the societally dominant language.

28.4.1 Normative Politeness in Heritage Languages: Forms of Address

A common finding in studies investigating forms of address in heritage languages indicates the erosion of formal forms of address among HSs and informal "bias" across all social contexts even if heritage bilinguals may be aware of the social norms. One piece of evidence of a restructured normative politeness system in heritage grammars comes from a study of Polish HSs by Wolski-Moskoff (2018). She compared receptive knowledge of formal forms of address by adult Polish HSs who were learning Polish as a heritage language in the United States, L2 learners of Polish, and monolingual speakers in Poland. Her analysis showed that HSs have limited knowledge of these forms and the sociocultural rules governing their usage. Polish forms of address form a complex system that requires both a nuanced morphosyntactic knowledge of the nominal declension system and verb conjugation, and knowledge of sociopragmatic rules dictating what combination of address form (*pan, pani*) and a person's name (first or last) should be used. As a group, Polish HSs understand the general idea of polite forms of address (P forms) in conversations with social superiors, but are not familiar with specific cultural rules affecting their usage. They also do not know the grammatical rules of the Polish system of address, such as the obligatory use of the vocative case for a person's title and name, or the use of the third-person verb form instead of the second-person form. In the study, they routinely failed to recognize the use of a P form as a pronoun (standard in full Polish), ranked sentences with P forms in the nominative higher than in the vocative (violating the obligatory rule in full Polish) – especially for the marked feminine gender – and rejected sentences with the correct third-person verb form in favor of sentences that mixed P forms (*pan, pani*) and the informal pronoun *ty* (T form) or the second-person verb form. This latter pattern suggests that HSs may rely mostly on lexical markers of politeness, rather than grammatical expressions in comprehending forms of address, which may be a pragmalinguistic and sociopragmatic transfer from English.[2] One possible explanation for HSs' limited receptive knowledge of the P forms of address in Polish may be

---

[2] This finding parallels the conclusions in the author's study (Dubinina 2013), where Russian HSs relied on the lexical politeness marker more than on grammatical means of expressing indirectness and communicative intent in both production and comprehension of requests.

the insufficient input they receive during socialization and lack of explicit instruction. Notably, L2 learners of Polish in this study outperformed heritage bilinguals, most likely because they received targeted instruction on the usage and grammar of P forms.

Further evidence of a restructured linguistic system of normative politeness in heritage languages comes from an extensive study of Hungarian speakers outside of Hungary (Fenyvesi 2005). This study shows that HSs in Slovakia (Lanstyák and Szabómihály 2005) and in the United States (Fenyvesi 2005) tend to neglect the formal–informal distinctions in address forms (often referred to as the T–V dichotomy) required in full Hungarian, and exhibit some violations of the co-occurrence rules governing the use of V and T forms with verbs. For example, when some American Hungarians use V pronouns in addressing somebody, they occasionally make errors in pronoun–verb agreement and in the declined forms of the V pronoun. Some Hungarian HSs reported not even being aware of the difference between the T and V address either in the nominal address form or in the verb forms when expressing greetings. In addition, Hungarian HSs in both countries showed divergence from monolinguals in the use of address forms and greeting/closing routines due to cross-linguistic influence from their dominant language. In Slovakia, male Hungarian HSs prefer to greet women according to the time of day (as is done in Slovak) instead of the formulaic *scókolom* (lit., 'I kiss [your hand]') customary in full Hungarian. The authors of the study note that formal address terms in Hungarian are "often clumsy, unsystematic, and ... difficult to use [which] provides a favorable precondition for L2 influence" (Lanstyák and Szabómihály (2005): 84). Instead of using a "clumsy" conventional monolingual formula, such as 'please' plus infinitive or imperative as an address form, HSs often switch to Slovak.

Cross-linguistic influence from HSs' dominant language may serve as one explanation for these speakers' limited knowledge of formal registers requiring polite formal forms. Another possible reason could be the level of heritage language proficiency: the lower it is, the harder it becomes for HSs to attend to the T–V dichotomy in routine social acts. A tendency for the expansion of informal forms of address into all social contexts has been observed in Spanish as a heritage language in the United States. For example, Sigüenza-Ortiz (1996) reported that English-dominant speakers of Spanish in Los Angeles County routinely used *tú* (T form) instead of *usted* (V form) in all social contexts. Although some of the participants self-reported higher use of *usted* at church, indicating that they are at least aware of the social norms requiring this form, observations conducted as part of the study revealed that less proficient HSs still used *tú* more often than *usted*.

In addition to cross-linguistic influence from the dominant language and general proficiency level, the divergent understanding and usage of

V address forms by HSs may be attributed to insufficient input during socialization and the lack of opportunities to use formal address terms. Studies on Polish P forms and on the use of T–V forms by Spanish HSs in the United States indirectly point to this conclusion. Even stronger support comes from the previously mentioned volume on Hungarian outside Hungary (Fenyvesi 2005), as it compares the same heritage language in contact with two different dominant languages: Hungarian in Slovakia and in the United States. Hungarian HSs in both countries deviate from the T–V dichotomy required in full Hungarian, something that cannot be explained solely by cross-linguistic influence from the dominant language because, unlike English, the Slovak language also has a mandatory T–V distinction in address forms. Nevertheless, Hungarian HSs in both countries show the T "bias." For example, Hungarian HSs in Slovakia and the United States initiate the T forms more easily than monolinguals even in formal contexts when speaking with a stranger, regardless of that person's gender (whereas in Hungary some kind of permission would be necessary before a switch from V to T could be made, especially when a male is addressing a female). In addition, Hungarian HSs in the United States reduce the use of the honorary kinship titles *néni* ('aunt') and *bácsi* ('uncle') in combination with a person's first name and V forms when addressing older interlocutors. Fenyvesi argues that these areas of divergence in expression of deference among Hungarian HSs are the result of "incomplete learning of and relatively small range of opportunities to use the complete [full Hungarian] address system ... " (314).

28.4.2 Normative Politeness in Heritage Languages: Honorifics and Speech Styles

A dramatic example of the challenges HSs experience in the acquisition and use of normative politeness systems comes from the study of Korean speech styles. The Korean honorifics system is, arguably, one of the most extensive normative politeness mechanisms, covering lexical, morphological, and syntactic levels of the language. From early childhood, Korean children are exposed to obligatory linguistic markings indicating relational sociocultural status (e.g., generation, age, sex, and social status) across a range of speaker relations, including speaker–addressee, speaker–referent, and addressee–referent. These markings include referent honorifics – address forms, specific kinship terms, different forms of first and second-person pronouns, subject-honorific morphemes, humble forms of nouns, predicates and particles, specialized formulaic expressions for performing a directive act or an apology, etc. In addition, Korean has six sets of sentence final particles for declarative, interrogative, propositive, and imperative utterances for each of the six speech styles – deferential, polite, blunt, familiar, intimate, and plain. The choice of appropriate speech style, level of speech, and specific honorific forms depends on a complex interplay of social factors, with age being the strongest and most important (Ahn 2005). The burden of indicating relational hierarchy is placed on the younger members of society: Younger siblings are expected to use honorific forms, kinship terms, and sentence final particles for different speech styles in interactions with older siblings, parents, and grandparents, but not the other way around. Monolingual Korean children are reportedly aware of two conversation styles used routinely in everyday speech – *panmal* (literally translated as "half-talk") and *jondaemal* ("respect-talk") – as early as the age of two (Park 2006). In the context of heritage language acquisition, where input is less than optimal and the socialization process is inevitably divergent in the absence of the larger speech community, children will most likely struggle to acquire the sociopragmatic and especially the pragmalinguistic norms of expressing normative politeness (He 2003, 2008).

Support for this claim comes from a study on the usage of honorifics by Wang (1995), who measured the rate of honorific usage in oral speech production by adult Korean HLLs in the United States and correlated it with their self-reported language use at home. The analysis indicates that participants have at least partial knowledge of the system and are aware of the importance of honorifics in Korean. Overall, participants produced more honorifics and were more accurate during a face-to-face task of interviewing their instructor (also the study's author) than on an abstract task of narrating about their childhood, which may suggest that their knowledge of honorifics is more developed for personal interactions than for referential usage. The study revealed that home environment is at least partially responsible for the HLLs' knowledge of honorifics. The majority of participants reported that they have not been exposed to different speech levels at home (either between parents or with parents). The majority of them also said that their parents did not emphasize the importance of honorifics because they just wanted them to speak Korean in whatever way possible.

Since the burden of indicating relational hierarchy is placed on younger members of Korean society, it may be assumed that the acquisition of honorifics by Korean children may require even more than rich input and ample opportunities for practice. Modeling and feedback may also play a crucial role. In addition, acquisition of the complex linguistic system of honorifics must be accompanied by the acquisition of the equally complex rules for social interactions.

Two ethnographic and sociolinguistic studies of Korean American families provide detailed insight into the patterns of language socialization and the complex set of social norms governing honorifics and their linguistic representation. Song's (2009) study shows a variety of strategies used by Korean caregivers in the United States to encourage children to use honorific terms of address and reference when speaking to or about older peers. Caregivers modeled correct utterances and then prompted children to produce their own. They also provided feedback in the form of recasts: e.g., repeating children's utterances with another child's name followed by an honorific term meaning "older brother/sister."

Park (2006) examined the transmission of ideologies and linguistic practices that surround politeness in six Korean American families consisting of three generations. Combined data from audio- and video-recorded family conversations, onsite observations, and interviews revealed that the grandparents' role was critical in children's socialization into social and linguistic norms of politeness. The study shows how grandparents modeled and explicitly instructed children to use verbal suffixes and proper honorifics for greetings, farewells, and conversations during meals. By observing the practice of giving priority of eating first to the oldest person, children are socialized to learn the age-based hierarchy among family members and ways to express it linguistically.

Interestingly, both studies on language socialization also indicate that Korean American children do not always conform to explicit instruction, exercising creative agency in using honorifics. In Song's study, a child invented hybrid English-Korean forms to refer to and address a close friend, and in Park's study, some children refused to repeat grandparents' models. Their parents did not always insist, perhaps trying not to overburden their children, which made the grandparents' role in the pragmatic development of children even more important.

As with terms of address, the acquisition and knowledge of honorifics in Korean seems to be affected by a lack of contexts in which they can be practiced, and there is also some indication that they are related to the development of overall linguistic proficiency and fluency. Wang (1995) reported that study participants who were most accurate in their use of honorifics had lower fluency[3] than those who were less accurate in honorific use. This may indicate that HSs have to sacrifice a certain amount of their speech tempo in order to adhere to all the requirements of normative politeness. Participants in the Koo (2002) study commented in post-task interviews that they were uncertain of their linguistic abilities, while at the same time being aware of the importance of correct honorifics use. One strategy to mitigate the fear of grammatical and lexical mistakes these participants used was to produce shorter utterances, which may have lowered the perceived level of their proficiency in the language while simultaneously influencing the politeness value of their requests. Finally, Park (2006) points out that if children are corrected and chastised all the

---

[3] However, Wang did not clarify how she defined fluency. It appears to be an impressionistic measure of participants' speaking tempo.

time for not being proper, they may not want to speak Korean at all, and some parents opt to sacrifice the acquisition of honorifics for the sake of overall proficiency of their children. This also seems to be the reason why participants in the Wang study report that their parents did not insist they use proper honorifics.

28.5   The Emerging Profile of Heritage Speakers' Pragmatic Competence

The investigation of HSs' pragmatic competence, as limited as it is, has allowed the drawing of a more nuanced picture of their linguistic competence precisely because the focus of pragmatics is on language use in social situations. The dramatic reduction of language input at the onset of schooling or at the age of immigration that characterizes heritage language acquisition has consequences not only for lexical and morphosyntactic knowledge (Rothman 2007, 2009; Benmamoun et al. 2010; Montrul 2015; Polinsky 2018) but also affects HSs' pragmatic abilities. Home environment alone does not provide equal and ample opportunities to practice communication in both formal and informal contexts (Lynch 2003), and as a result, HSs grow up with lopsided exposure to and experience of language use in their two languages, and accumulate different pragmatic practices as they move across social contexts. These contexts involve mostly informal but limited interactions at home in the heritage language, and rich experiences in both formal and informal contexts in the dominant language. This asymmetry is known as "immigrant diglossia," when genres, participant relationships, registers, topics, communicative functions, levels of politeness, and the amount of required face work differ a great deal depending on whether interactions take place inside or outside the home (Biber 1994; Valdés 2000; Achugar 2003). As a result of these experiences, HSs grow up as unequally skilled members of two speech communities and often face challenges when attempting to perform communicative functions in social contexts with greater social distance and power hierarchy in their heritage language, even if they are capable of expressing meaning linguistically. To compensate for both the lack of language-specific tools in their home language to express nuances in deference and politeness, and for the reduced repertoire of conventionalized ways to express speech acts, HSs resort to various non-conventional strategies to communicate with others. The source of such strategies may be their dominant language (which is also the societally dominant language), in which they have more experience, revealing the workings of language contact and cross-linguistic influence (Benmamoun et al. 2010; Dubinina and Malamud 2017), linguistic creativity (Polinsky 2018), translanguaging (García and Wei 2014; Wei 2018), or a combination of factors, including independent language-internal processes.

As a result, HSs' pragmatic competence exists as a hybrid system, incorporating features of full varieties of the home language and the societally dominant language, and influenced heavily by cross-linguistic interference from the dominant language. Since pragmatic realizations are based on the social norms for interacting shared by a speech community, HSs' pragmatic competence is inevitably shaped by these speakers' unequal experiences in two different language communities and reflects their knowledge of conventions practiced in both home and public contexts in two different languages. At the same time, bilingual immigrant communities in which HSs grow up may already use new conventionalized ways of performing routine social interactions, which will cause further divergence of HSs' pragmatic competence from the monolingual baseline.

HSs tend to be more capable interlocutors in informal interactions and often exhibit informal "bias" in normative politeness. Possible sources of divergence in the use of the T–V dichotomy include transfer from the dominant language, overt lexical borrowings, and incomplete learning due to lack of exposure to formal contexts where politeness considerations are increased. HSs' socialization into the rules of normative politeness is challenged by the lack of a larger language community that would support and enforce the acquisition of these norms. Where expressions of deference and normative politeness are marked by morphosyntactic complexity (as in Polish forms of address) and also governed by complex social rules (as in Korean system of honorifics and speech styles), their acquisition requires not only rich input but also, possibly, extensive targeted instruction and modeling.

HSs who are also learners of their home languages have measurable advantages over their L2 counterparts, especially in interpreting and producing pragmatic meanings in informal scenarios. However, these advantages do not always hold across language modalities during production (HLLs do not perform as well on written pragmatic tests as they do on oral tasks) and social contexts (HLLs' advantage is greater in informal contexts). Frequent exposure to informal contexts of social interaction at home and a significant amount of interactional language contact result in HSs' greater competence in formulating and comprehending communicative intent, especially in informal contexts.

28.6   Conclusions and Future Directions

The branch of heritage pragmatics is in its developmental stage, and only a handful of studies focus specifically on HSs or HLLs, as a subset of HSs.

Nevertheless, the analysis of available studies can provide useful suggestions for overcoming limitations of the past and indicate opportunities for further research. First and foremost, more research is needed to get a fuller and more nuanced picture of HSs' pragmatic knowledge. The field would benefit greatly from more studies that investigate a greater variety of heritage languages in different language contact situations and a broader group of HS speakers, including adults, children, and adolescents with diverse sociolinguistic backgrounds (e.g., age of arrival and family language policy). In order to be more robust, comparisons between HSs and monolingual NSs or L2 learners need to be more nuanced and must include proficiency measures, discussions of heterogeneity of the HS group in terms of their proficiency, and analysis of the baseline to which HSs are exposed. Investigations of pragmatic development of HSs need to include studies of the role of targeted instruction, which can be critical in the acquisition of complex pragmatic forms. Since cross-linguistic influence has been identified as a characteristic feature of HSs' pragmatic knowledge, research focus should also be directed at investigating bi-directional transfer in the speech of both adult and child heritage bilinguals.

Heterogeneity of HS populations should be accounted for in any study regardless of the comparison groups. HSs exhibit tremendous interindividual variation not only in their linguistic abilities but also in their backgrounds, including exposure to formal or informal instruction, age of interruption, family compositions, and family language ideologies, all of which affect their abilities and performance. When finding an experimental group of the same proficiency level is not logistically possible, analysis should include discussions of differences in performance between subgroups formed on the basis of one or several of the sociolinguistic factors.

Studies that compare HSs and L2 learners should include proficiency measurements and attempt to match the two groups as closely as possible. It may not always be easy to find a good match in terms of oral proficiency, especially for languages that are difficult for acquisition (e.g., Korean or Chinese for native speakers of English), because it usually takes years of instruction to achieve comparable levels of proficiency for L2 learners of these languages. In such cases, other tools to measure linguistic competence of the two groups could be used. Such measurements can be as simple as words per minute in spontaneous speech, or more elaborate, such as vocabulary knowledge. If that is not possible, conclusions that HSs outperform their L2 counterparts should be accompanied by a discussion of the possible effect proficiency may have on the pragmatic advantages exhibited by HSs.

One important question that has not been addressed by the field is the establishment of a baseline to which HSs are exposed during socialization. Paralleling studies on the morphosyntax of heritage languages, future research should investigate communicative norms that exist in the HSs' bilingual homes and communities to which HSs are exposed as children. Both pragmalinguistic and sociopragmatic knowledge of the parent generation need to be explored (see Laleko 2010 and 2011 for an example of such research concerning verbal aspect and information structure) in order to have more nuanced comparison between HSs and monolingual groups. It is also important to conduct comparative studies of two or more pairs of heritage languages in contact with the same majority language in order to uncover how the range of input interlocutors may affect HSs' pragmatic development. For example, Russian and Spanish immigrant communities in the United States offer different opportunities for language socialization to their youngest members: Spanish HSs, as a result of the demographic realities, are more likely to be exposed to a distinct community-level variety as their baseline than Russian HSs who may have very limited contexts of language use in the community outside their homes, with the notable exception of the Brighton Beach area in New York.

At the same time, the field needs to investigate the pragmatic development of bilingual children in immigrant contexts. We know that early exposure to the home language gives HSs an advantage in speaking and listening comprehension abilities. Interactional experiences at home may give them an additional advantage in pragmatic competence. However, more qualitative research is needed to better understand how *specifically* the context of language use at home and family language policies contribute to HSs' pragmatic development. In addition, the role of modeling, feedback, and explicit instruction by family members in this development needs to be investigated. Language socialization framework may be the most effective approach for the exploration of these questions. The framework would allow accounting for many different features of the context in which pragmatic development occurs, including its bicultural/bilingual nature (see He 2012 for a review).

The analysis of the context of HSs' pragmatic development should also include the role of formal instruction. Wolski-Moskoff (2018) suggests that HSs can benefit from focused instruction on Polish polite address forms. The fact that HSs in the study were outperformed by L2 learners of Polish with lower proficiency suggests that targeted instruction can help learners acquire the system of Polish P forms despite its complexity. Potowski (2007) showed that HLLs in a dual immersion school in Chicago performed better on both oral and written tasks that elicited requests and exhibited higher sensitivity to the difference between formal and informal registers. More studies on the effect of instruction will help improve understanding of possible trajectories of HS pragmatic development.

Many studies position HSs' pragmatic abilities on a continuum between the home and societally dominant language and reveal transfer of pragmatic forms and meanings from the dominant language, especially in situations that require more face work. Future research should also investigate evidence of bi-directional transfer, especially from the home to the dominant language in situations of close social distance. In addition, as Pinto (2012) indicates, studies that investigate influence from the dominant language should include a monolingual control group in that language. A potentially promising and new direction in HL pragmatics with regard to cross-linguistic influence concerns the investigation of differences in speech act repertoires between monolingual and heritage bilingual communities. As the study of several generations of Estonian immigrants in Sweden (Keevallik 2012) indicates, HSs may borrow entire speech acts from the dominant language: e.g., thanking others for spending time with them after visiting, a speech act borrowed from Swedish and nonexistent in Estonian.

Importantly, the plurilingualism (Galante 2018) and translanguaging frameworks (Wei 2018) that have gained popularity in the past several years can help advance future studies by encouraging researchers to question the monolingual bias in the understanding and representation of HSs' pragmatic abilities. The debate on the status of HSs with regard to their native speakerhood has important consequences for research in both morphosyntax and pragmatics, as it requires researchers to rethink the appropriateness of comparing HSs' abilities to monolingual norms and to account for the specific characteristics of the contexts in which heritage languages are used.

Finally, the study of pragmatic competence of HSs must view pragmatic norms as fluid and subject to changes in culture and society. For example, the use of the impersonal modal *možno* in combination with the lexical marker 'please' in the Dubinina study as a form of polite request for favor is now becoming a norm in Russian society, something unimaginable only a decade ago. In today's world, even patterns of language use become objects of globalization. Wang (1995) and Ahn (2005) both mention changes in Korean society that affect the use of honorifics: e.g., familiar and blunt speech levels may be disappearing, especially among the younger generation, and children are now using fewer honorifics with their mothers for the sake of maintaining intimacy. Pinto (2018) also mentions subtle English influence on world Spanishes on the global scale through television and multi-media, which makes it hard to distinguish the difference in pragmatic norms between contact and noncontact varieties of Spanish.

Bibliography

Achugar, M. 2003. Academic Registers in Spanish in the US: A Study of Oral Texts Produced by Bilingual Speakers in a University Graduate Program.

In A. Roca and M. Cecilia Colombi (eds.), *Mi lengua: Spanish as a Heritage Language in the United States, Research and Practice*. Washington, DC: Georgetown University Press, 213–234.

Ahn, R. C. 2005. Five Measures of interlanguage Pragmatics in KFL (Korean as Foreign Language) Learners. Doctoral dissertation. Retrieved from ProQuest Dissertations & Theses Global (Accession Order No. 3198341).

Arvanitis, E. 2018. Culturally Responsive Pedagogy: Modeling Teachers' Professional Learning to Advance Plurilingualism. In P. Trifonas and T. Aravossitas (eds.), *Handbook of Research and Practice in Heritage Language Education*. Berlin: Springer, 245–262.

Bachelor, J. and M. Barros García. 2018. A Comparison of Heritage Learners and L2 Learners of Spanish: A Study on Compliment Sequences in the Classroom. *Journal of Foreign Language Education and Technology* 4(1), 21–40.

Backus, A. and K. Yağmur. 2017. Differences in Pragmatic Skills between Bilingual Turkish Immigrant Children in the Netherlands and Monolingual Peers. *International Journal of Bilingualism* 23(4), 817–830. 1367006917703455.

Barros García, M. and J. Bachelor. 2018. Pragmatic Instruction May Not Be Necessary among Heritage Speakers of Spanish: A Study of Requests. *Journal of Foreign Language Education and Technology* 3(1), 163–193.

Benmamoun, E., S. Montrul, and M. Polinsky. 2010. Prolegomena to Heritage Linguistics [white paper]. University of Illinois at Urbana-Champaign and Harvard University. Retrieved from www.nhlrc.ucla .edu/pdf/HL-whitepaper.pdf

Bialystok, E. 1993. Symbolic Representation and Attentional Control in Pragmatic Competence. *Interlanguage Pragmatics* 3(1), 43–57.

Biber, D. 1994. An Analytical Framework for Register Studies. In D. Biber and E. Finegan (eds.), *Sociolinguistic Perspectives on Register*. New York: Oxford University Press, 31–56.

Blum-Kulka, S. 1991. Interlanguage Pragmatics: The Case of Requests. In R. Phillipson, E. Kellerman, L. Selinker, M. Sharwood Smith, and M. Swain (eds.), *Foreign/Second Language Pedagogy Research: A Commemorative Volume for Claus Faerch*. Clevedon: Multilingual Matters, 255–272.

Blum-Kulka, S., J. House, and G. Kasper (eds.) 1989. *Cross-Cultural Pragmatics: Requests and Apologies*. New Jersey: Ablex.

Brown, P. and S. Levinson. 1987. *Politeness: Some Universals in Language Usage*. Cambridge: Cambridge University Press.

Cenoz, J. 2003. The Intercultural Style Hypothesis: L1 and L2 Interaction in Requesting Behavior. In V. Cook (ed.), *Effects of the Second Language on the First*. Clevedon: Multilingual Matters, 62–80.

Dubinina, I. 2013. How to ask for a favor: An exploration of speech act pragmatics in heritage Russian. Doctoral dissertation. Retrieved from ProQuest Dissertations & Theses Global (Accession Order No. 3564143).

Dubinina, I. and S. Malamud. 2017. Emergent Communicative Norms in a Contact Language: Indirect Requests in Heritage Russian. *Linguistics* 55(1), 67–116. https://doi.org/10.1515/ling-2016-0039

Elias, M. V. 2013. "Tengo bien harto esperando en la línea": Complaint Strategies by Second-Generation Mexican-American Bilinguals. Master's thesis. Retrieved from ProQuest Dissertations & Theses Global (Accession Order No. 1536477).

Elias, V. 2015. Pragmalinguistic and Sociopragmatic Variation: Refusing among Spanish Heritage Speakers. *IULC Working Papers* 15(1), 1–32.

Fenyvesi, A. (ed.) 2005. *Hungarian Language Contact outside Hungary: Studies on Hungarian as a Minority Language.* Vol. 20. Amsterdam: John Benjamins Publishing.

Finestradt-Martínez, I. and K. Potowski. 2016. Requests and Refusals among Bilingual Mexican Americans. Paper presented at the 8th Workshop on Spanish Sociolinguistics, April 14–16, San Juan, Puerto Rico.

Galante, A. 2018. Linguistic and Cultural Diversity in Language Education through Plurilingualism: Linking the Theory into Practice. In P. Trifonas and T. Aravossitas (eds.), *Handbook of Research and Practice in Heritage Language Education.* Berlin: Springer, 313–330.

García, O. and L. Wei. 2014. *Translanguaging: Language, Bilingualism, and Education.* New York: Palgrave Macmillan.

Goffman, E. 2005. *Interaction Ritual: Essays in Face to Face Behavior.* New Brunswick, NJ: AldineTransaction.

He, A. 2003. Novices and Their Speech Roles in Chinese Heritage Language Classes. In R. Bayley and S. R. Schecter (eds.), *Language Socialization in Bilingual and Multilingual Societies.* Clevedon: Multilingual Matters, 128–145.

He, 2008. Heritage Language Learning and Socialization. In P. Duff and N. Hornberger (eds.), *Encyclopedia of Language and Education: Vol. 8. Language Socialization,* 2nd ed. New York: Springer, 201–216.

He, 2012. Heritage Language Socialization. In A. Duranti, E. Ochs, and B. Schieffelin (eds.), *The Handbook of Language Socialization.* Oxford: Blackwell, 587–609.

Hong, W. 1997. Sociopragmatics in Language Teaching: With Examples of Chinese Requests. *Journal of the Chinese Language Teachers Association* 32(1), 95–107.

Hymes, D. 1974. *Foundations in Sociolinguistics: An Ethnographic Approach.* Philadelphia: University of Pennsylvania Press.

Kasper, G. and S. Blum-Kulka (eds.) 1993. *Interlanguage Pragmatics.* Oxford: Oxford University Press.

Keevallik, L. 2012. Pragmatics of the Estonian Heritage Speakers in Sweden. *Finnisch-Ugrische Mitteilungen* 35, 1–22.

Koike, D. 1989. Pragmatic Competence and Adult L2 Acquisition: Speech Acts in Interlanguage. *Modern Language Journal* 73(3), 279–289. https://doi.org/10.2307/327002

Koo, D. 2002. Realizations of Two Speech Acts of Heritage Learners of Korean: Request and Apology Strategies. Doctoral dissertation. Retrieved from ProQuest Dissertations & Theses Global (Accession Order No. 200300394).

Koo, J. 1995. Politeness Theory: Universality and Specificity. Doctoral dissertation. Retrieved from ProQuest Dissertations & Theses Global (Accession Order No. 304198401).

Kupisch, T. and J. Rothman. 2018. Terminology Matters! Why Difference Is Not Incompleteness and How Early Child Bilinguals Are Heritage Speakers. *International Journal of Bilingualism* 22, 564–582. https://doi.org/10.1177/1367006916654355

Laleko, O. V. 2010. The Syntax-Pragmatics Interface in Language Loss: Covert Restructuring of Aspect in Heritage Russian. Doctoral dissertation. Retrieved from ProQuest Dissertations & Theses Global (Accession Order No. 3408406).

Laleko, O. V. 2011. Restructuring of Verbal Aspect in Heritage Russian: Beyond Lexicalization. *International Journal of Language Studies* 5(3), 13–26.

Lanstyák, I. and G. Szabómihály. 2005. Hungarian in Slovakia. In A. Fenyvesi (ed.), *Hungarian Language Contact outside Hungary: Studies on Hungarian as a Minority Language*. Amsterdam: John Benjamins Publishing, 47–89.

Leech, G. 1983. *Principles of Pragmatics*. London: Longman.

Lohndal, T., J. Rothman, T. Kupisch, and M. Westergaard. 2019. Heritage Language Acquisition: What it Reveals and Why It Is Important for Formal Linguistic Theories. *Language and Linguistics Compass* 13(12). https://doi.org/10.1111/lnc3.12357

Lynch, A. 2003. The Relationship between Second and Heritage Language Acquisition: Notes on Research and Theory Building. *Heritage Language Journal* 1(1), 26–43.

Montrul, S. 2015. *The Acquisition of Heritage Languages*. Cambridge: Cambridge University Press.

Park, E. 2006. Grandparents, Grandchildren, and Heritage Language Use in Korean. In I. Kondo-Brown (ed.), *Heritage Language Development: Focus on East Asian Immigrants*. Amsterdam: John Benjamins Publishing Company, 57–86.

Piccardo, E. 2018. Plurilingualism: Vision, Conceptualization and Practices. In P. Trifonas and T. Aravossitas (eds.), *Handbook of Research and Practice in Heritage Language Education*. Berlin: Springer, 207–226.

Pinto, D. 2012. Pragmatics and Discourse: Doing Things with Words in Spanish as a Heritage Language. In S. Beaudrie and M. Fairclough (eds.), *Spanish as a Heritage Language in the United States*. Washington, DC: Georgetown University Press, 121–138.

Pinto, D. 2018. Heritage Spanish Pragmatics. In K. Potowski (ed.), *The Routledge Handbook of Spanish as a Heritage Language*. Philadelphia: Routledge, 190–202.

Pinto, D. and R. Raschio. 2007. A Comparative Study of Requests in Heritage Speaker Spanish, L1 Spanish, and L1 English. *International Journal of Bilingualism* 11(2), 135–155. https://doi.org/10.1177/13670069070110 020101

Pinto, D. and R. Raschio. 2008. "Oye,¿ qué onda con mi dinero?": An Analysis of Heritage Speaker Complaints. *Sociolinguistic Studies* 2(2), 221–249. https://doi.org/ 10.1558/sols.v2i2.221

Polinsky, M. 2018. *Heritage Languages and Their Speakers*. Vol. 159. Cambridge: Cambridge University Press.

Potowski, K. 2007. *Language and Identity in a Dual Immersion School*. Vol. 63. Clevedon: Multilingual Matters.

Rothman, J. 2007. Heritage Speaker Competence Differences, Language Change, and Input Type: Inflected Infinitives in Heritage Brazilian Portuguese. *International Journal of Bilingualism* 11(4), 359–389. https://doi .org/10.1177/13670069070110040201

Rothman, J. 2009. Understanding the Nature and Outcomes of Early Bilingualism: Romance Languages as Heritage Languages. *International Journal of Bilingualism* 13(2), 155–163. https://doi.org/10.1177/ 1367006909339814

Schieffelin, B. and E. Ochs (eds.) 1986. *Language Socialization across Cultures*. Cambridge: Cambridge University Press.

Sigüenza-Ortiz, C. 1996. Social deixis in a Los Angeles Spanish-English Bilingual Community: Tú and usted Patterns of Address. Doctoral dissertation. Retrieved from ProQuest Dissertations & Theses Global (Accession Order No. 9802759).

Sohn, H. 1999. *The Korean Language*. Cambridge: Cambridge University Press.

Song, J. 2009. Bilingual Creativity and Self-Negotiation: Korean American Children's Language Socialization into Korean Address Terms. In A. Reyes and A. Lo (eds.), *Beyond Yellow English: Toward a Linguistic Anthropology of Asian Pacific America*. Oxford: Oxford University Press, 213–232.

Swann, J., A. Deumert, T. Lillis, and R. Mesthrie (eds.) 2004. *A Dictionary of Sociolinguistics*. Tuscaloosa: The University of Alabama Press.

Taguchi, N. 2015. Pragmatics in Chinese as a Second/Foreign Language. *Studies in Chinese Learning and Teaching* 1(1), 3–17.

Taguchi, N. and C. Roever. 2017. *Second Language Pragmatics*. Oxford: Oxford University Press.

Taguchi, N., H. Zhang, and Q. Li. 2017. Pragmatic Competence of Heritage Learners of Chinese and Its Relationship to Social Contact. *Chinese as a Second Language Research* 6(1), 7–37. https://doi.org/10.1515/caslar-2017-0002

Valdés, G. 2000. The Teaching of Heritage Languages: An Introduction for Slavic-Teaching Professionals. In O. Kagan and B. Rifkin (eds.), *The Learning and Teaching of Slavic Languages and Cultures*. Bloomington, IN: Slavica Publishers, 375–403.

Wang, H. 1995. The Impact of Family Background on the Acquisition of Korean Honorifics. *Korean Language in America* 1, 197–211. www.jstor.org/stable/42922125

Wei, L. 2018. Translanguaging as a Practical Theory of Language. *Applied Linguistics* 39(1), 9–30. https://doi.org/10.1093/applin/amx039

Wolski-Moskoff, I. 2018. Knowledge of Forms of Address in Polish Heritage Speakers. *Heritage Language Journal* 15(1), 116–144.

Youn, S. 2008. *Rater Variation in Paper vs. Web-Based KFL Pragmatic Assessment Using FACETS Analysis.* (Unpublished manuscript, University of Hawai'i, Honolulu). Retrieved from www.hawaii.edu/sls/wp-content/uploads/2014/08/YounSooJung.pdf

Youn, S. and J. Brown. 2013. Item Difficulty and Heritage Language Learner Status in Pragmatic Tests for Korean as a Foreign Language. In S. Ross and G. Kapser (eds.), *Assessing Second Language Pragmatics*. New York: Palgrave MacMillan, 98–128.

Part IV

Heritage Language Education

29

Elementary School Heritage Language Educational Options and Outcomes

Kim Potowski

29.1 K-8 Language Instruction

Children who speak heritage languages in the United States fall into two main categories: those who are still learning English, called "English Learners" (ELs) by their school districts, and those whose English is considered to be strong enough to participate in mainstream English-medium classrooms. These two categories very frequently correspond to the most typical manner of language acquisition experienced by such children, namely late/later onset second language acquisition for the ELs, and bilingual first language acquisition for the non-EL children. As this section hopes to make clear, the EL status of children in the United States is a crucial factor in whether they are likely to receive instruction in their heritage language during their early schooling years.

When a child arrives to a public US elementary school and is deemed to be an EL, the school has a legal responsibility to provide some type of instructional support. This has been the case since 1975, when *Lau v. Nichols* ruled that the lack of supplemental language instruction in public school for students with limited English proficiency violated the Civil Rights Act of 1964.[1] Thus, requiring the child to enroll in all-English medium instruction without any support is illegal. However, *Lau* did not specify what kind of support schools must provide; only that *some* must be provided. The three most common forms of EL services are commonly referred to as *English as a Second Language*, *transitional bilingual*, and *dual language*. Each program type is now briefly described.

---

[1] Parents may request that their children be placed into a mainstream classroom, but by law the school must offer some kind of service.

29.1.1   English as a Second Language

English as a Second Language (ESL) programs provide 100 percent of classroom instruction in English, but a portion of it is tailored to the needs of English learners. It is also typically the only option available when there are fewer than twenty EL children who speak the same language. Thus, if there are nineteen children who speak Gujarati, Polish, or Mandarin, in most schools they will receive ESL services. The majority of school districts around the country with EL students offer only ESL.

29.1.2   Transitional Bilingual Education

When there are twenty or more children who speak the same language, at least six states[2] (Connecticut, Illinois, New Jersey, New York, Texas, and Wisconsin) by law are required to offer the second option, transitional bilingual education (TBE); some school districts opt to offer TBE even if the state does not require it. In TBE programs, a portion of each school day (typically no greater than 25 percent) is taught in the children's home language. However, as the name clearly communicates, the goal is to *transition* students to the mainstream all-English classroom as soon as possible. This typically takes place after 3 years. In some states, an additional 2 years in a TBE program can be requested. Thus, a typical Spanish-speaking EL child who arrives at kindergarten monolingual in Spanish spends kindergarten through third grade in a TBE program and then transitions out "on time" to begin fourth grade in the monolingual mainstream all-English classroom. This means that after June of their third grade year, these children will never encounter another book or text in school written in Spanish until possibly high school, nor will they interact with any academic content in Spanish. We will see ahead that TBE programs are not generally successful at helping children develop and maintain their heritage languages, as they were in fact not designed to do so – meaning that the term "bilingual" in the program title refers to a method and not a goal.

Before moving on to the third program type, we should underscore something about the panorama we have just described. For the majority of heritage speaker children in the United States, a TBE program offered as a result of children's EL status is typically the only way for them to receive any instruction in the heritage language during their early schooling years. Those heritage speaker children who acquired enough English during

---

[2] Policies can change very rapidly, but this was the case as of the publication of www.newamerica.org/education-policy/topics/english-learners/dual-language-learners/legislation/state-legislation/bilingual-mandates/.

Table 29.1 *Percent of U.S. schools offering world language instruction (American Academy of Arts & Sciences 2017)*

Grades	1997	2008	2015	
K-5	31%	25%	K-12	19%
6–8	75%	58%		

"No Child Left Behind"
(2002–2015)

preschool to place out of an EL categorization in Kindergarten will not be in a TBE classroom and thus will not receive any instruction in their HL. While some primary schools do offer "foreign language" instruction, the numbers have declined precipitously over the past 20 years, particularly since the 2002 passing of the now defunct[3] "No Child Left Behind" educational act (see Table 29.1).

We see in the most recent figures from 2015 that only 19 percent of K-12 schools across the United States offer foreign languages. These numbers range greatly from state to state, with 51 percent of students in New Jersey studying foreign language classes but only 9 percent in Arkansas (American Councils for International Education 2017). Not only are the numbers overall relatively low, but the quality of this instruction also varies widely. While some school districts use well-developed curricula with articulated proficiency goals (see Curtain and Dahlberg 2015), other classrooms teach only simple material such as vocabulary for colors, numbers, and days of the week, year after year, with no true proficiency goals. In either case, the instruction is designed for second language learners and not for heritage-speaking children who have already acquired some communicative proficiency in the language. Furthermore, in some school districts that offer K-8 Spanish as a foreign language, the majority of the students are actually heritage Spanish speakers. If the curriculum is adjusted accordingly, these classes can provide meaningful instruction in the HL; Potowski et al. 2008 describe an example from Chicago where a native Spanish language arts approach was incorporated in a curricular spiral, layering

---

[3] It remains unclear what will be the effect on foreign language instruction of its replacement, the Every Student Succeeds Act (ESSA), which went into effect during the 2017–2018 school year.

various literacy and critical thinking skills. It is unclear how many elementary FL classes around the world might have some heritage-speaking children enrolled, but we know of elementary school programs specifically designed for Spanish heritage speakers in Italy (Bonomi and Sanfelici 2018), Germany (Ramos Méndez-Sahlender 2018), and Switzerland (Sánchez Abchi 2018), although not enough is known about how they differ from United States models.

There are also Saturday and community schools in many countries that operate outside of the public and private school systems and offer HL classes on weekends or after school, supplementing the education that students receive in their regular schools (see Chapter 30 this volume). In the United States, many of these are part of the Coalition of Community-Based Heritage Language Schools (www.heritagelanguageschools .org). Some studies suggest that these programs can contribute to individuals' HL proficiency and can put students on the path to the Seal of Biliteracy[4]; others have been shown to be only very moderately successful in this regard (for example, see Chinen and Tucker's 2005 study of Japanese). Some groups have robust community heritage language programs, often but not always attached to religious instruction, including Arabic, Korean, Lithuanian (see Tamošiūnaitė 2013) and Polish. One of the biggest challenges for developing community HL programs in less commonly taught languages is finding qualified teachers, including for Czech and Tamil (Liu, Musica et al. 2011). In different parts of Canada, heritage language programs are available in Cantonese, Cree, Filipino/ Tagalog, German, Greek, Hebrew, Italian, Japanese, Mandarin, Ojibwe, Portuguese, Spanish, and Ukrainian (Guardado and Becker 2013). There are also school-sponsored programs in Inuttitut in the provinces of Nunavut and Nunavik, along with proposed legislation to make such education available in K-12, although there have been implementation challenges (Wright et al. 2000). Several chapters in Trifonas and Aravossitas (2014) describe HL programs in Australia, Canada, China, and Switzerland. However, there is currently no international database for such programs.

Unfortunately, what typically happens is that heritage speakers experience no meaningful opportunities to study in their HL during elementary school. Although this chapter focuses on elementary school, a brief mention of high school is relevant. Again, Spanish in the United States is the most commonly studied context, but other languages and locations are surely reflected to some extent in the description that follows. When

---

[4] The Seal of Biliteracy is an award given by a US school, district, or state to students who have proven written proficiency in two or more languages on high school graduation. It is currently offered in thirty-seven states.

Spanish-speaking students get to high school, they experience one of two things vis-à-vis their heritage language. In one scenario, they are placed into a basic Spanish course designed for and populated by second language students. In these classes the heritage language learner can become bored, sometimes accused of wanting an "easy A," and often told that the way they speak Spanish is "incorrect" because it is informal, belongs to a stigmatized dialect, and/or has English influence. In the second scenario, they are placed into a "Spanish for heritage speakers" (SHL) class (see Chapter 30 in this volume). This is a much better option because these classes are specially designed to take their home-developed communicative competence into account by combining goals and pedagogies from native language arts with those from second language teaching. However, in many cases, the teacher has received no training in how to work with heritage speakers, which usually leads to similar frustrations – students being erroneously or insensitively corrected, having curricular goals that are not a good match for students' skills and interests, etc. (Potowski and Carreira 2004). Unfortunately, the most common option is the first one – heritage speakers of Spanish, Chinese, French, Russian, Arabic, etc., enrolled in basic foreign language classes. Rhodes and Pufahl (2010) found that only 9 percent of US high schools offer SHL,[5] and it is safe to assume that an even smaller percentage of heritage speakers of languages other than Spanish are enrolled in classes in their HL. Similarly, Potowski (in progress) found that there were thirteen counties in the state of Illinois with a population that was 10 percent or more Hispanic, and within these counties, 149 high schools had Hispanic populations that were 10–49 percent Hispanic (and sixty-one additional high schools had populations as high as 49–100 percent Hispanic). Many of these schools offered SHL courses, but of the thirty-three universities in the state that license Spanish teachers, only one offered a methods course[6] where pre-service teachers could study best practices in heritage language teaching. The author is working with the state of Education to create an endorsement[7] in heritage language teaching to encourage high school principals to hire only properly trained teachers to be in charge of heritage language classes. However, given the severe teacher shortages around the country, any added barriers to individuals becoming

---

[5] Leaders at both the American Association of Teachers of Spanish and Portuguese and the American Council of Teachers of Foreign Languages have indicated willingness to launch new surveys to understand nationwide offerings more recently, both for Spanish and other languages (personal communications, November 2019).

[6] There are several high quality online opportunities for professional development in teaching heritage languages, including the National Heritage Language Resource Center's free "Startalk" modules and the University of Wisconsin-Whitewater's Certificate in Heritage Language Education.

[7] An *endorsement* is an official state board of education designation documenting that a pre-determined amount of specialized coursework has been completed.

teachers must be considered with great care. To conclude this topic, it must be noted that high school HL courses in languages other than Spanish, and opportunities for teachers to receive appropriate preparation for the different kinds of teaching that is required for heritage learners, are relatively rare. Mercurio and Scarino (2005) describe how heritage languages were able to gain legitimacy in Australian high schools, first at the state level and then nationally, via "grafting" them onto local curricular structures, but do not measure students' proficiency in their HLs.

29.1.3 Dual Immersion

Finally, the third US elementary school program type for EL children is dual language (also called *dual immersion* and *two-way immersion*). These programs grew out of models in Canada, where "one-way" or full immersion programs were established in the 1960s. In typical one-way immersion programs, all children are native speakers of the country's dominant language, and they are taught the regular school curriculum totally or partially in a foreign language. One-way French immersion began under middle- and upper-class parental pressure for more effective French language education for their children. At that time, Quebec was experiencing ethnolinguistic tensions as Francophones began making demands for linguistic and cultural equality (Genesee 1987: 8). In 1965, parents of an Anglophone Montreal suburb convinced the school district to set up an experimental kindergarten French immersion class. In the United States, Christian (1996: 74) cites the Coral Way Elementary School in Dade County, Florida, as the first two-way bilingual school in the United States. The program was established in 1963 by members of the Cuban community fleeing the Castro regime, who believed their children would soon be returning to Cuban schools. During the 1960s, another fourteen such schools were set up in Dade County. Dual language education programs use a language other than English (LOTE) between 50 and 90 percent of the school day from Kindergarten through eighth grade with the goals of promoting bilingualism, biliteracy, and bicultural appreciation. Most of these programs enroll a balance of children who learned the LOTE at home (many of whom are also ELs) and children who are first learning the LOTE at school. Dual language programs are also designed to address societal power imbalances: Instead of the EL children being the only language learners in the classroom, the home English speakers are expected to learn the LOTE. In this way, the home LOTE-speaking children are positioned as knowledgeable linguistic and cultural models.

The number of schools that have identified themselves with the Center for Applied Linguistics (2007) as having a dual immersion program is 458, including eight different languages, although 93 percent of them operate in

Spanish. However, unofficial estimates place the national number of bilingual dual language schools in the United States at between 1,000 (Maxwell 2012) and more than 2,000 (Watanabe 2011), meaning that there are many programs operating that have not filled out the Center for Applied Linguistics survey. There is literature about programs in Albanian, Arabic, Chinese, French, Haitian Creole, Hebrew, Italian, Japanese, Korean, Navajo, Polish, and Russian (for example, https://fabricejaumont.net/ for the growing list of languages offered in DL programs around New York City), but unfortunately to date no single source documents all of the different languages offered in dual immersion classrooms around the United States. There are also full immersion programs that teach 100 percent of content in a minority language. These exist in some parts of the United States (particularly in Utah and Minnesota) as well as in the Basque Country and in Catalonia (where they run from Kindergarten through university, unlike in the United States, where the majority stop when children are approximately 12 years old) to promote children's bilingualism. There are details about types and distribution of US dual immersion programs in the American Institutes for Research (2015) report.

29.2　Outcomes of Elementary School Programs in the United States

Several nationwide studies have compared student outcomes in the three different elementary school programs for Spanish-speaking ELs just described. Before describing outcomes in heritage language proficiency, it is important to clarify that children's acquisition of the majority language – English, in this case – is not only *not* jeopardized, it is often improved. Figure 29.1 compares the percentage state standardized English reading scores of California graduates of these three program types once they advanced to eleventh grade.

These findings indicate that the more time spent learning in Spanish, the greater the *English* language achievement of Spanish-speaking ELL students. Similar findings emerged from a large-scale study in Houston (Lindholm-Leary 2001), where the author found that in segregated low-income schools, students in dual language programs scored as well as or better in English than similar background students in mainstream programs (they also scored above grade level in assessments conducted in Spanish). Similarly, Steele et al. (2017) found that Portland students randomly assigned to immersion outperformed their peers on state English reading tests by 7 months of learning in Grade 5 and 9 months of learning in Grade 8. In studies involving languages other than Spanish, students at the Nawah'i immersion school in Hawaii, many from poor and working-class families,

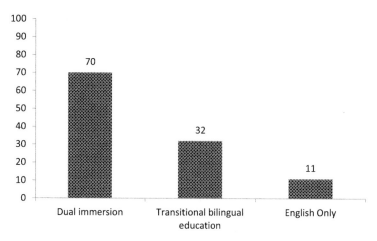

Figure 29.1 Eleventh grade English reading scores of Spanish-speaking ELLs (percentages). *Source*: Thomas and Collier 2009: 55

outscored their non-immersion peers on English standardized tests even though English is not introduced until fifth grade, graduated high school at a rate of 100 percent, and attended college at an 80 percent rate, successes that school leaders attributed to an academically challenging curriculum centered on Hawaiian language and culture (McCarty 2010). It is also worth noting that in the early 1980s, fewer than 50 children spoke Hawaiian but today there are over 4,000 fluent children thanks to Hawaiian-medium schooling.

There are at least three explanations for these seemingly counterintuitive results that greater heritage language study results in stronger English language development. First, there is less chance that EL students will fall behind in their academic subject matter as they gradually develop English proficiency, a gap that usually compounds each year. Children who learn through Russian that "два плюс два - четыре" have learned to add, and do not need to relearn "two plus two is four" once they've acquired the English vocabulary. In addition, scientific studies have demonstrated links between bilingualism and general cognitive benefits, reports of which have become increasingly frequent in mainstream media over the past few years (Barac and Bialystok 2012). This too may contribute to dual language students' improved educational performance. A third explanation is that when children and their languages are positioned as useful resources in the classroom, their self-esteem develops in ways that are conducive to positive school performance (Palmer 2008). EL children in ESL and TBE programs often receive the message that they are deficient and that their heritage language is holding them back from being a successful student in the mainstream classroom. In dual immersion, however, everyone in the school appreciates LOTE proficiency, and for 50 to 90 percent of the school

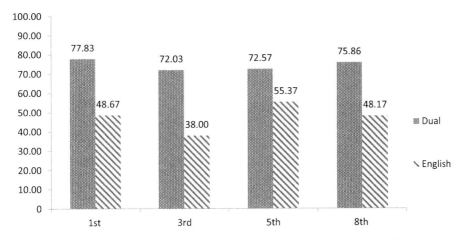

Figure 29.2 Average percent accuracy, Spanish reading exam, dual language vs English program. From Potowski and Marshall (2021)

day the HL children can provide assistance to the other half of students who have just begun to learn the LOTE. When students are positioned as successful, it is more likely that they actually achieve success. An additional attitudinal benefit to DL programs is that it may be the case that language majority children who study through a LOTE alongside native speaking children end up "inoculated" against negative ideologies that lead to linguistic bullying and other xenophobic and racist ideologies that are sadly not uncommon around the world (see http://potowski.org/resources/repres sion for cases of language-focused discrimination, repression, and violence that have taken place in the United States).

Not only does EL students' English benefit in dual immersion; their overall academic achievement as measured by standardized tests has been shown to be higher than in other program types (shown in Figure 29.2 and in Lindholm-Leary 2001, 2013 and in Thomas and Collier 2009). Such findings have been reported in mainstream media, including a study of San Francisco schools conducted by faculty at Stanford University (reported in Myers 2014) and another in Portland (Manning 2015), both finding that dual language resulted in earlier student reclassification as English proficient as well as stronger academic trajectories over time. Thus, DL can contribute to reducing the Latino achievement gap that currently plagues the United States[8] and, if left unchecked, holds potentially negative consequences for the nation's future. One out of every four school-age students in the United States today is Latino, yet the National Center for Educational Statistics reports that Latino fourth and eighth graders score about two

---

[8] This achievement gap is not related only or even mostly to language but rather to poverty and other entrenched problems, but strong levels of bilingualism can play a role in helping these students achieve in school.

grade levels lower than the national average on tests in math and reading. It is unfortunately quite common around the world for immigrant/linguistic minority students to experience lower educational outcomes, so dual language programs would be a solid option to remedy this, although there must be a desire on the part of the mainstream families to learn the minority language – for example, there would need to be sufficient German-speaking families willing to enroll their children in a Turkish-German dual language program, enough French-speaking families in France interested in Arabic, or enough Spanish-speaking families in Mexico who would enroll their children in a school taught half of the day in Zapotec. Another important consideration is that these programs have been proven suitable for students with many kinds of learning challenges, including those with cognitive difficulties, autism, and speech and hearing issues (see Fortune and Menke 2010).

What about development in the heritage language in DL programs? It was mentioned earlier that students who attend a TBE program frequently do not read or write in Spanish again in a school setting once they complete third grade. Various studies have documented the erosion of Spanish as children move from elementary grades to middle school (Merino 1983; Oller and Eilers 2002). A large-scale study comparing the Spanish of over 250 children (Lindholm-Leary 2013) found that those in dual language developed stronger Spanish proficiency as measured by the Language Assessment Scales (De Avila and Duncan 2005) than their peers in English-medium programs and, echoing findings cited earlier, they also scored better on English measures. Bowles & Torres (this volume) reported on a meta-analysis of studies on outcomes of heritage language instruction on heritage language knowledge. They found that at the elementary level, there was a medium weighted mean effect size ($d = .79$) as compared to studies at the university level, where there was a smaller effect size ($d = .42$), suggesting that HL instruction may be more impactful at the elementary level.

To maximize students' Spanish development, we need focused investigations of what their linguistic systems look like and how they change over time so that we can best calibrate specific language arts instruction. Potowski and Marshall (in progress) examined the Spanish of two groups of Latino home-Spanish-speaking students attending the same K-8 school: Thirty-two children enrolled in the mainstream English program (where, if they were classified as ELs, they received ESL services) and 102 children enrolled in the dual language program that taught in Spanish 80 percent of the day in grades K-4, 60 percent in grades 5–6 and 50 percent in grades 7 and 8. Scores on all four Spanish skill tests of the Language Assessment Scales (De Avila and Duncan 2005) were statistically significantly higher for the dual language group, but it was on the literacy tests (reading and

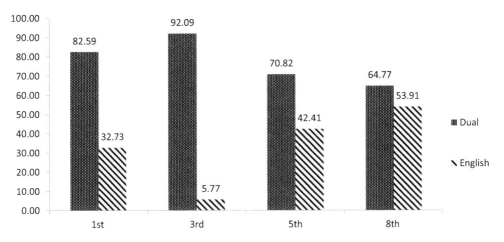

Figure 29.3 Average percent Spanish writing scores, dual language vs English program. From Potowski and Marshall (2021)

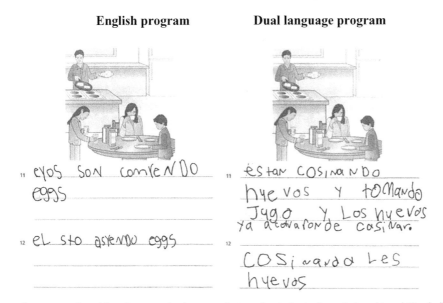

Figure 29.4 Spanish written production, two first-grade students. From Potowski and Marshall (2021)

writing) where the biggest differences were found. This makes sense when we consider that heritage-speaking children, although they listen to and speak the HL each day with family members, typically do not engage in writing and reading it. Figures 29.2 and 29.3 show average percentage Spanish reading comprehension and writing scores for all four grades tested.

Figures 29.4 and 29.5 compare writing samples from two students in first grade and two in fifth grade. Students were asked to describe the drawings in Spanish.

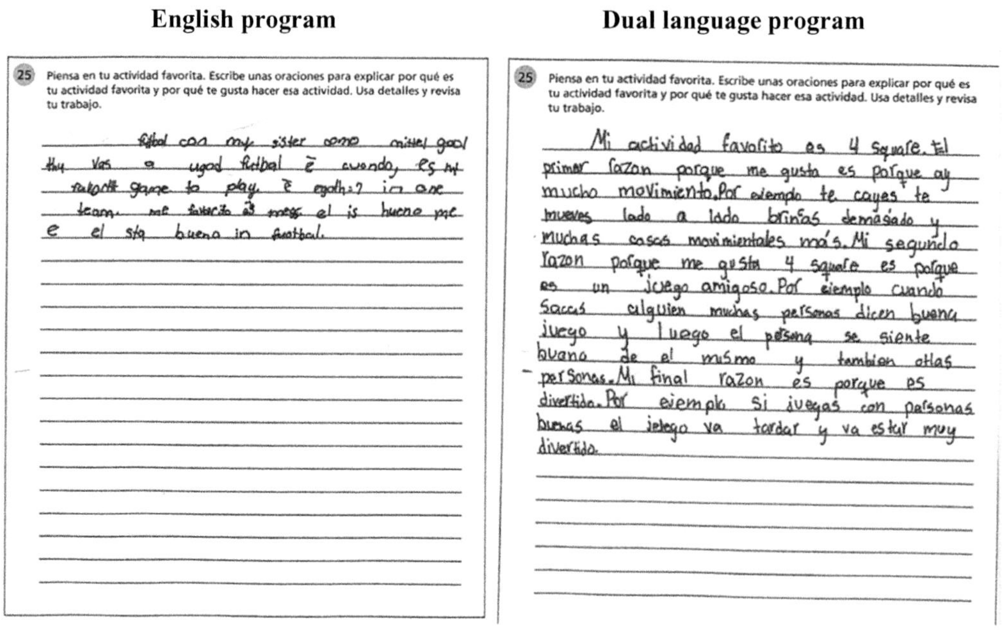

Figure 29.5 Spanish written production, two fifth-grade students. From Potowski and Marshall (2021)

We see in both grade levels compared that the dual language texts are not only longer but they are also lexically richer and more morphosyntactically complex. Thus, although it may be obvious to assume that heritage speakers who study between 50 and 90 percent of the day in their heritage language will develop stronger levels of proficiency in that language, this study provides evidence that this is in fact the case. If these data hold across programs and languages, they suggest that if all heritage-speaking children receive quality instruction through the medium of their heritage language throughout the elementary school years, they will show significantly stronger levels of proficiency as well as literacy development in the heritage language. This would serve to shift the goals of the entire HL field as the students grew up and arrived in high school and university classrooms. Dual language programs at the high school level exist but are unfortunately extraordinarily rare, unlike, for example, in Spain, where they regularly continue beyond elementary school.

In other parts of the world, there are comparable elementary school programs. For example, Nocus et al (2012) found that in French Polynesia, children partially schooled in Tahitian for 300 minutes per week had stronger Tahitian proficiency than a control group schooled entirely in French, without any negative effect on their oral and written French. Similar findings obtained in Papua New Guinea (Malone and Paraide 2011) and in South Africa (Alexander 2004).

Research on dual language educational outcomes is burgeoning but much more is needed, including: (1) More detailed studies of students' HL development over time; (2) Comparisons of HL development in 50–50 vs 90–10 program models; (3) Studies of this nature in other languages in the United States and in all languages around the world in which such programs are offered. There are also several important pitfalls to keep in mind, including what has been called the "gentrification" of dual language programs, whereby middle class white Anglophone students' needs and outcomes take precedence over those of the language minority students (see Jong and Howard 2009; Flores, Tseng, and Tsubtirelu 2020; and Freire et al. 2018).

29.3   Conclusions and Future Directions

Young children around the world who arrive at school fluent or even monolingual in a heritage or indigenous language unfortunately very typically do not develop strong levels of proficiency and literacy in it, and sometimes lose it completely. These are wasted opportunities to develop the world's multilingualism and individuals' biliteracy. Dual language programs are arguably the most successful at not only developing students' proficiency in the dominant school language, which is critical for their future success, but also their abilities in the heritage language. Well-executed curricula in dual language programs may help stem language loss by developing strong proficiency and healthy pride in speaking the HL. Given that 20 percent of all school-aged children in the United States speak a language other than English and that the number of English language learners is expected to increase by an additional 50 percent by 2025, these programs have critical implications for the nation. Heritage language speakers around the globe, instead of waiting until college or even high school, would be best served by elementary school programs designed to develop linguistic proficiency and cultural pride, which can then be articulated into engaging and demanding curricula at higher levels than without this critical early boost.

References

Alexander, N. 2004. The Politics of Language Planning in Post-Apartheid South Africa. *Language Problems & Language Planning* 28(2), 113–130.

American Academy of Arts and Sciences. 2017. *America's Languages: Investing in Language Education for the 21st Century*. Cambridge, MA.

American Councils for International Education. 2017. The National K-12 Foreign Language Enrollment Survey Report. Accessed January 2, 2020 at www.americancouncils.org/sites/default/files/FLE-report-June17.pdf

American Institutes for Research. 2015. Dual Language Education Programs: Current State Policies and Practices. Accessed April 28, 2020 at www.air.org/sites/default/files/downloads/report/Dual-Language-Education-Programs-Current-State-Policies-Feb-2017-rev.pdf

Barac, R. and E. Bialystok. 2012. Bilingual Effects on Cognitive and Linguistic Development: Role of Language, Cultural Background, and Education. *Child Development* 83(2), 413–422. https://doi.org/10.1111/j.1467-8624.2011.01707.x

Bonomi, M. and L. Sanfelici. 2018. Spanish as a Heritage Language in Italy. In K. Potowski (ed.), *The Routledge Handbook of Spanish as a Heritage Language*. London: Routledge, 479–491.

Center for Applied Linguistics. 2007. Directory of Two-Way Bilingual Immersion Programs in the U.S. Accessed June 29, 2013, at www.cal.org/jsp/TWI/SchoolListings.jsp

Chinen, K. and G. R. Tucker. 2005. Heritage Language Development: Understanding the Roles of Ethnic Identity and Saturday School Participation. *Heritage Language Journal* 3(1), 27–59.

Christian, D. 1996. Two-Way Immersion Education: Students Learning through Two Languages. *Modern Language Journal* 80, 66–76.

Curtain, H. and C. Dahlberg. 2015. *Languages and Learners: Making The Match. World Language Instruction in K-8 Classrooms and beyond*. London: Pearson.

De Avila, Edward and Sharon Duncan. 2005. *Language Assessment Scales*. New York: McGraw-Hill.

Flores, N., A. Tseng, and N. Subtirelu (eds.). 2020. *Bilingualism for All?: Raciolinguistic Perspectives on Dual Language Education in the United States*. Multilingual Matters.

Fortune, T. and M. Menke. 2010. *Struggling Learners and Language Immersion Education: Research-Based, Practitioner-Informed Responses to Educators' Top Questions*. Minneapolis, MN: The Center for Advanced Research on Language Acquisition.

Freire, J., V. Valdez, and M. Garrett Delavan. 2018. The (Dis)Inclusion of Latina/o Interests from Utah's Dual Language Education Boom. *Journal of Latinos and Education* 16(4), 276–289.

Genesee, F. 1987. *Learning through Two Languages: Studies of Immersion and Bilingual Education*. Cambridge, MA: Newbury House.

Guardado, M. and A. Becker. 2013. Fostering Heritage Languages and Diasporic Identities: Grassroots Initiatives in Alberta and British Columbia. In K. Arnett and C. Mady (eds.), *Minority Populations in Canadian Second Language Education: New Perspectives on Language and Education*. Bristol: Multilingual Matters, 55–70.

Jong, E. D. and E. Howard. 2009. Integration in Two-Way Immersion Education: Equalising Linguistic Benefits for All Students. *International Journal of Bilingual Education and Bilingualism* 12(1), 81–99.

Lindholm-Leary, K. 2013. Bilingual and Biliteracy Skills in Young Spanish-Speaking Low-SES Children: Impact of Instructional Language and Primary Language Proficiency. *International Journal of Bilingual Education and Bilingualism* 17(2), 144–159.

Lindholm-Leary, K. 2001. *Dual Language Education*. Clevedon: Multilingual Matters.

Liu, N., A. Musica, S. Koscak, P. Vinogradova, and J. Lòpez. 2011. Challenges and Needs of Community-Based Heritage Language Programs and How They Are Addressed. Heritage Briefs Collection. Retrieved from www.cal.org/heritage/pdfs/briefs/challenges-and%20needs-of-community-based-heritage-language-programs.pdf

Malone, S. and P. Paraide. 2011. Mother Tongue-Based Bilingual Education in Papua New Guinea. *International Review of Education* 57(5–6), 705–720.

Manning, R. 2015. Study: Portland Immersion Students Become Better Readers, English Speakers. Retrieved from www.Opb.Org/News/Article/Study-Portland-Immersion-Students-Become-Better-Readers-English-Speakers/

Maxwell, L. 2012, March 28. "Dual" Classes See Growth in Popularity. *Education Week* 31(1), 16–17. Retrieved from https://secure.edweek.org/media/downloads/files/spotlight-deeper-learning.pdf

McCarty, T. 2010. Native American Languages in the USA. In K. Potowski (ed.), *Language Diversity in the USA*. Cambridge: Cambridge University Press, 47–65.

Mercurio, A. and A. Scarino. 2005. Heritage Languages at Upper Secondary Level in South Australia: A Struggle for Legitimacy. *International Journal of Bilingual Education and Bilingualism* 8(2–3), 145–159.

Merino, B. 1983. Language Loss in Bilingual Chicano Children. *Journal of Applied Developmental Psychology* 4, 277–294.

Myers, A. 2014. Students Learning English Benefit More in Two-Language Instructional Programs than English Immersion, Stanford Research Finds. Retrieved from https://news.stanford.edu/news/2014/march/teaching-english-language-032514.html

Nocus, I., P. Guimard, J. Vernaudon, M. Paia, O. Cosnefroy, and A. Florin. 2012. Effectiveness of a Heritage Educational Program for the Acquisition of Oral and Written French and Tahitian in French Polynesia. *Teaching and Teacher Education* 28, 21–31.

Oller, D. and R. Eilers (eds.) 2002. *Language and Literacy in Bilingual Children*. Clevedon: Multilingual Matters.

Palmer, D. 2008. Building and Destroying Students' "Academic Identities": The Power of Discourse in a Two-Way Immersion Classroom. *International Journal of Qualitative Studies in Education* 21(6), 1–24.

Potowski, K., J. Berne, A. Clark, and A. Hammerand. 2008. Spanish for K-8 Heritage Speakers: A Standards-Based Curriculum Project. *Hispania* 91(1), 25–41.

Potowski, K. and M. Carreira. 2004. Towards Teacher Development and National Standards for Spanish as a Heritage Language. *Foreign Language Annals* 37(3), 421–431.

Potowski, K. and M. Marshall. 2021. The Spanish Proficiency of Latino Dual Immersion Students Compared to Peers in an All English Program: A Pseudo-Longitudinal Study across Multiple Domains.

Ramos Méndez-Sahlender, C. 2018. Spanish as a Heritage Language in Germany. In K. Potowski (ed.), *The Routledge Handbook of Spanish as a Heritage Language*. London: Routledge, 492–503.

Rhodes, Nancy and Ingrid Pufahl. 2010. *Foreign Language Teaching in U.S. Schools: Results of a National Survey*. Washington, DC: Center for Applied Linguistics.

Sánchez Abchi, V. 2018. Spanish as a Heritage Language in Switzerland. In K. Potowski (ed.), *The Routledge Handbook of Spanish as a Heritage Language*. London: Routledge, 492–503.

Steele, J., R. Slater, G. Zamarro, T. Miller, J. Li, S. Burkhauser, and M. Bacon. 2017. Effects of Dual-Language Immersion Programs on Student Achievement: Evidence from Lottery Data. *American Educational Research Journal* 54(1 suppl), 282s–302s.

Tamošiūnaitė, A. 2013. Lithuanian Saturday Schools in Chicago: Student Proficiency, Generational Shift, and Community Involvement. *Heritage Language Journal* 10(1), 108–133.

Thomas, W. and V. Collier. 2009. *Educating English Learners for a Transformed World*. Fuente Press, Dual Language Education of New Mexico.

Trifonas, P. and T. Aravossitas. 2014. *Handbook of Research and Practice in Heritage Language Education*. Berlin: Springer.

Watanabe, T. 2011, May 8. Dual-Language Immersion Programs Growing in Popularity. *Los Angeles Times*. Retrieved from www.latimes.com/local/la-xpm-2011-may-08-la-me-bilingual-20110508-story.html

Wright, S., D. Taylor, and J. Macarthur. 2000. Subtractive Bilingualism and the Survival of the Inuit Language: Heritage- versus Second-Language Education. *Journal of Educational Psychology* 92(1), 63–84.

30

Community-Organized Heritage Language Programs

Jin Sook Lee and Huay Chen-Wu

30.1 Introduction

In most countries around the world, the preservation of heritage languages and cultures has been supported by the vitality, resourcefulness, and dedication of individual immigrant and indigenous communities. In immigrant communities, heritage language (HL) education has traditionally occurred outside of mainstream schooling through supplemental programs such as Saturday schools, language camps, and after-school classes. Although its primary goal has been the intergenerational transmission of heritage languages and cultures, community-organized heritage language (CHL) programs have also served as a vehicle to strengthen the cultural identities of ethnic children by fostering a sense of belonging through shared cultural activities and social networking (Lee and Shin 2008; Hancock 2012; Lee and Wright 2014; Nordstrom 2016). However, despite the social and educational importance of these institutions, CHL programs have received little recognition for their added value to the broader educational goals of minority children and for their contributions to the promotion of linguistic and cultural diversity in society. In fact, although they have been in existence for more than 300 years in the United States and over half a century in the United Kingdom, only in the past two decades has there been increased attention to the functions and practices of how such programs serve the needs of the communities in which they exist (Creese et al. 2006; Li 2006; Brinton et al. 2008; Liu 2010; Lytra and Martin 2010; Wiley et al. 2014; Nordstrom 2016).

To date, there are no national records of CHL schools due to their unofficial status in most countries; however, sociolinguist Joshua Fishman's comprehensive survey of HL schools in the United States in the 1980s provides a glimpse into the vastness of these operations. His survey documented over 6,500 HL schools that offered instruction in more than sixty different languages, including Chinese, French, Greek, Hebrew, Italian, Japanese, Korean, Polish, Portuguese, Russian, Spanish, Turkish, Ukrainian, and Yiddish (Fishman 2001). In the United States, the earliest CHL schools date back to the 1880s with roots in German Schools (Ludanyi and Liu 2011), as well as French (Lasserre et al. 2012) and Spanish (Zamora 2013) HL schools. In modern times, the range of languages represented in CHL programs have become even more diverse and the successes of such programs are shaped by the different communities' migration trajectories, histories, as well as current political, social, and economic positions in the dominant society (Shin 2014). In other words, CHL programs are dynamic and are sensitive to the changes in social contexts. Some CHL programs, such as German, French, and Spanish HL schools, continue to exist, but have dwindled in number. For example, French HL schools have been deemed less necessary, despite being one of the most popular foreign languages of study. In one study, native French speakers reported that French maintenance is not a top priority due to the fact that English is being promoted even in the homelands (Lasserre et al. 2012), and for those that are invested in learning French, alternative schools and programs like Le Lycée Français and the FACE French HL program (https://face-foundation .org/language-education/french-heritage-language-program) are available around the world. On the other hand, there are CHL programs that have flourished over time, including Korean, Chinese, and Hindu-Urdu HL schools (Wang 2017). For instance, Chinese CHL schools continue to grow due to the critical nature of foreign policy and the increasing numbers of Chinese American communities (Wong and Lopez 2000).

More recently, there have been expanding efforts to systematically track such programs. For example, the Center for Applied Linguistics has created a directory of the heritage language programs in the United States (www.cal.org/ heritage/profiles/submit.html) and different US states and countries have started registries of HL schools (e.g., California's Department of Education (www.cde.ca.gov/ls/pf/he); The National Resource Centre for Supplemental Education in England (www.supplementaryeducation.org.uk); and the Australian Federation of Ethnic Schools (www.communitylanguagesaustralia .org.au). Yet, because of the lack of formal oversight of such schools, it is difficult to keep an exact record of HL schools as their operational statuses frequently change depending on the shifting needs and resources of the local community.

This chapter presents an overview of the prominent characteristics of CHL programs that distinguish them from programs that exist within the infrastructure of mainstream schooling, such as foreign language courses for HL speakers or maintenance bilingual programs. CHL programs are distinct in that they function outside of the traditional school day and are organized and often operated by community volunteers. In this chapter, we specifically focus on HL programs that exist in diasporic post-immigration contexts, also referred to as Saturday Schools, Weekend Schools, Ethnic Schools, Mother Tongue Schools, Community Schools (i.e., in Canada), Supplemental Schools (i.e., in Australia), and Complementary Schools (i.e., in the United Kingdom). We also limit our discussion to immigrant HL education and leave indigenous HL education for a separate discussion given the critical differences in governmental policies that protect indigenous languages, sociopolitical histories, numbers of living speakers, and perceived instrumental utility of the languages (Fishman 2001; Haynes 2010; Shin 2014). In the following sections, we review the current state of knowledge that surrounds the functions and roles of CHL programs, commonly faced issues within such programs, and types of existing CHL programmatic models. We conclude with a discussion of current work that is being done to support, connect, and promote the interests of CHL programs in order to increase their alignment and visibility so that they may more effectively accomplish the goals of HL education within and across nations.

30.2　Functions and Characteristics of Community-Organized HL Programs

Despite the educational rhetoric that promotes pluralism and linguistic and cultural diversity in mainstream schools, in reality, the linguistic and cultural needs of immigrant children have yet to be adequately addressed in schools (Lee and Oxelson 2006). Scholars have proposed that CHL schools are a response to the lack of support from mainstream educational systems to meet the needs of linguistic minority ethnic children (Zulfiqar 1997; Popkewitz and Brennan 1998; Hall et al. 2002; Li 2006). Such programs help dispel hegemonic ideologies and practices that exist in mainstream society and provide a safe space where the agency of minority communities to affect change in the educational practices of their language, culture, and traditions can be freely expressed. Furthermore, because they operate within local ethnic communities and are not governed by federal funds, they often fly under the radar and are seen as non-threatening entities, giving them the flexibility to organize the curriculum and practices to best meet the needs of their local community (Hall et al. 2002). In other words, the power of CHL programs lies in their autonomy to adapt the goals, curriculum, and pedagogy to the local conditions, available resources, and the strengths and needs of teachers and students in the programs.

Although HL practices and maintenance have remained the responsibility of individual family members, research has shown that family language use alone is not a sufficient condition to promote HL development and counter

HL attrition (Lee and Suarez 2009; Lee and Wright 2014). CHL programs have had a major role in supporting the maintenance and development of both oral and literacy skills in the HL as well as in transferring the cultural knowledge of ethnic communities (Fishman 2001; Kelleher 2010). They have served to resist, or at least slow down, the language shift that leads to loss of the HL experienced by most immigrant communities across generations, yet there is still much about their role in the HL maintenance process that we have yet to understand (Fishman 2001). Moreover, CHL schools are more than a place for language and literacy instruction. The role of CHL programs in strengthening cultural associations and ethnic identity has been widely noted (Lee 2002; Otcu 2010; Hancock 2012; Nordstrom 2016). Along with literacy and language instruction in the HL, curricula usually include the teaching of culture, traditions, and other content such as the history of the homeland. Rosenthal (1987) argues that the ethnic consciousness that results from socialization processes within the family as well as from being a member of a community forms an integral part of one's self-definition and self-esteem. Studies have also found that proficiency in the HL is positively correlated to one's ethnic identity and sense of belonging in one's ethnic group (Kondo-Brown 2006; Phinney et al. 2001). Thus, CHL programs promote a "sense of self-esteem in the many language groups and a fuller understanding of their respective cultural backgrounds" (Curdt-Christiansen 2006: 189).

Depending on the geographic location of CHL programs and the communities they serve, the role of these programs may look slightly different. The scale of CHL programs also varies greatly, from a small class held in someone's living room with a handful of children to a Saturday School in a rented school space with several hundred students. In many communities, religious institutions, such as churches and mosques, are responsible for a fair amount of CHL schooling. Establishing and maintaining a CHL program involves great coordination and involvement among members of the community, cultural and religious centers, and families (Compton 2001; Lee 2014). They are particularly valuable in places with low ethnolinguistic vitality because there are not many places to hear or use the HL outside of the home. In such areas, CHL schools are places for students to nurture their ethnic identity and friendships among co-ethnic peers and for parents to connect with other parents who have similar purposes and goals (Shibata 2000). Furthermore, for those who live in communities sparsely populated by HL speakers, although instruction in the HL via CHL programs may play a critical role, they may not yield the same levels of HL attainment given the lack of opportunities to use the HL outside of CHL school hours. Yet, with technological developments and the availability of the Internet, access to broader communities of HL speakers and HL-based television shows or newspapers can also create motivation and opportunities for further development. Thus, systematic language and literacy instruction that are made available via CHL classes lay an important foundation for HL speakers to continue to develop and maintain their HL (Hashimoto and Lee 2011). On the other hand, participants who attend CHL schools in densely populated communities (e.g., Korean CHL programs in downtown Los Angeles) have the added benefit of being in spaces that create the authentic need for the use of the HL (Lee 2014). HL speakers are able to experience and benefit from the social and cultural capital that their HL affords them within the community, which can add impetus to the motivation to maintain and learn the HL. In addition, certain cultural trends like the rise of K-pop in the Korean community or karaoke in the Khmer community have heightened interest for people from both heritage and non-heritage backgrounds to learn and speak languages. These opportunities for language use can also feed into increasing proficiency in the HL.

While learning of the HL and culture is a critical motivation for attending CHL schools, reasons for attending CHL programs may be more diverse and complex (Walters 2011; Nordstrom 2016). For example, Archer, Francis, and Mau (2010) found that parents in England were motivated to send their children to Chinese CHL schools because they saw it as a way to gain a "potential gateway to Chinese lifestyle and society" (105), facilitate intergenerational communication, and strengthen future careers. Furthermore, Kim (2011) found that Korean immigrant mothers saw CHL schools as a social and emotional support system for both themselves as first-generation immigrant mothers and their Korean American children's development. In addition, Otcu (2010) reported that Turkish CHL schools in the United States, like many other CHL schools, build connections and contentment toward other co-ethnic community members, foster a Turkish American identity in the United States, and support diversity by enabling the members of the school to see their place in relation to other ethnolinguistic groups. Thus, CHLs are sites that promote not only shared beliefs and attitudes regarding the use of the HL in both oral and written forms but also belonging, identity formation, and future professional opportunities (Nordstrom 2016). In addition, they provide a safe place where HL learners are free from minoritization and racism (Archer et al. 2010). They enable a platform for cultural continuity and enrichment as well as the development of language and literacy skills for religious, educational, and social purposes. These aspects become tools for maintenance of cultural identity that positively feed into self-respect and a sense of cultural security, which are key factors that all children need to be successful in any kind of educational setting.

30.3   The Role of CHL Programs in HL Maintenance and Development

The benefits of possessing heritage language and literacy skills with regards to academic achievement, mental health, professional goals, and cultural understanding have been well documented in the literature (Lee and Suarez 2009). For example, studies have shown that HL speakers who are bilingual and biliterate in their HL and the dominant language of society outperform their monolingual counterparts academically; attain better professional opportunities; and have a greater sense of self-esteem, ethnic identity, and appreciation for diversity as well as loyalty to the host country (see Lee and Suarez 2009 for review). Yet, in spite of such benefits, HL maintenance and development continues to be an uphill battle for most families. Knowledge about the considerable advantages of HL maintenance and development is not widespread beyond the academy. Thus, more effort needs to be placed in dissemination of knowledge to the wider public, perhaps through both traditional and social media outlets in order to reach a broader audience.

With even long-term exposure to the HL in informal settings like the home, children of immigrants rarely achieve complete acquisition of their HL (Montrul 2010). Heritage learners often display low literacy skills in the HL and their production skills tend to lag behind their comprehension skills (Carreira and Kagan 2011). Hence, what makes CHL instruction especially challenging is the wide range of language skills and proficiency levels among HL students from limited receptive skills to near native fluency (Kelleher 2010). For example, it is quite common to see heritage speakers who are orally fluent, but illiterate in their HL because they have not had any formal literacy instruction in the HL (Peyton et al. 2001). In addition, it becomes more complicated because HL speakers also come from a wide range of different language varieties (Valdés 2001; Kondo-Brown and Brown 2007). Though many programs opt to teach what is considered the "standard" variety, CHL programs have the flexibility to be able to cater to and instruct in the variety of the HL that is desired and relevant in the local community, unlike many school-based language programs (Peyton et al. 2001).

There is a lack of comprehensive research on the short-term and long-term effects of CHL schooling on HL development and maintenance. According to a survey conducted by the National Heritage Language Resource Center with over 1,700 undergraduate students, the majority of the students that attended CHL schools reported attending them for more than four years (Carreira et al. 2009). However, the longer they were enrolled in the CHL program, the less likely they were to attend regularly, resulting in high absenteeism. Thus, despite the number of years in the program, the actual amount of time of instruction was limited in the experiences of the informants, which likely contributed to the less than ideal outcomes in HL proficiency development. This raises the question of what the minimum threshold should be for instructional contact hours in CHL programs to make a significant difference in HL development. Yet, research has shown that even with brief exposure, those that attended CHL schools tend to have greater HL literacy skills than those who have not (Lao and Lee 2009). Thus, early exposure to literacy in the HL can form the foundation for the development of the HL later in life, when many HL speakers are able to enroll in more formal HL classes at the university level, for example, or continue their HL education in community centers, such as the Korean American Community Center (www.koreanamericancenter.org). Additionally, not only do CHL programs provide more systematic instruction in HL than what generally occurs in the home but they also bring together learning communities that are pursuing similar HL goals. Since learning a language is a social endeavor that requires input, opportunities to practice, and an authentic situation to use the language, CHL programs can offer an optimal setting in which these criteria are met (Norton and Toohey 2011).

CHL programs are attended mainly by children in elementary through middle school grades, but, in general, they are not perceived to be a popular or enjoyable activity among the youth. Aside from reasons ranging from parents and children placing more priority on English development, perceived ineffectiveness of the programs, and physical and financial inability to attend, it is widely known that students stop attending CHL programs when attendance starts to conflict with other mainstream activities that matter for college-going pathways (Lee and Wright 2014; Shin and Lee 2014). As children grow older, their resistance toward attending CHL often increases due to not wanting to be marked as different or seeing CHL programs as being boring or a waste of time (Lee and Shin 2008). Furthermore, the disconnect between the teaching styles and discursive practices of teachers who are not trained in the pedagogical approaches that children in the host country have been assimilated to gives rise to confusion and negative attitudes toward HL learning among students. For example, Curdt-Christiansen (2006) found that at a Chinese Saturday school in Montreal, the traditional way of teaching Chinese with an emphasis on teacher-controlled activities including dictation, reciting, memorizing, and other authoritative discursive practices was seen as too rigid and not engaging, and hence, constrained students' participation in learning. Thus, when the HL teachers' cultural background and discursive practices are in contrast to what students experience in their everyday school activities, the struggle to adjust between these contrasting systems of classroom communication and participation make HL learning and development especially difficult.

Moreover, Otcu (2010) reported that the dominant classroom interaction patterns in Turkish HL classrooms are similar to initiation-response-feedback/follow-up (IRF) sequences (Sinclair and Coulthard 1975), but the literature on language learning discourages IRF interactions because they offer little opportunity to develop complex interactional linguistic competence (Kasper and Rose 2002). Although teachers in CHL schools encourage the use of the HL (Bonacina-Pugh and Gafaranga 2011), in most CHL settings, children prefer to use English or the dominant language of society, especially with each other, or a mixture of the HL and their dominant language (Otcu 2010). There is ample literature that argues for the benefits of translanguaging practices, which has been ascertained to be an effective strategy for language development (Li 2014). Translanguaging is a natural phenomenon in CHL school contexts and an integral part of pupils' identity formation, especially as bilingual beings (García, Zakharia, and Otcu 2012). However, we need more research on the linguistic practices in CHL schools to better understand HL speaker codes and their role in HL development (Li 2006; Lee and Shin 2008).

Given that participation in after-school, summer learning, and other community-based programs has been associated with improved academic achievement and improved linguistic and social development of English language learners (Téllez and Waxman 2010; Hirsch 2011), it is likely that CHL programs may also positively affect HL maintenance and development. However, we have little systematic knowledge of how children's varied understandings and lived experiences in CHL programs impact their linguistic development (Hancock 2012). Before we are able to witness more stories of success in HL learning via CHL schools, instructional practices in CHL programs need to be better aligned with the needs of emerging bilingual students. To do so, we must more carefully examine the linguistic and social welfare of children in CHL programs. Furthermore, CHL programs need to be better positioned in society as a necessary and important learning endeavor rather than seen as an extra workload (Lee 2002; Liu et al. 2010; Lee and Wright 2014). We know that less than four hours of instruction a week is not a sufficient condition for language development to happen. Liu (2010) found in her survey that 63 percent of teachers and 72 percent of parents in Chinese HL programs see limited class time as a major challenge to CHL program effectiveness. Therefore, CHL programmatic efforts must be supported with additional HL use at home, community, and perhaps even in mainstream schooling (see Potowski, this volume, about dual language education).

30.4   Persistent Issues Facing CHL Programs

CHL programs vary greatly with regard to populations served, programmatic structure and organization, staff qualifications, instructional focus, pedagogical methods, instructional materials, alignment with mainstream school programs, and funding sources. Yet, they share many of the same challenges. Previous papers have thoroughly discussed these challenges and presented recommendations and possible solutions to the problems in detail (see Liu et al. 2010; Lee and Wright 2014). Looking forward, here we provide a brief discussion of how the changing demographics of student populations may influence efforts to tackle the persistent challenges that CHL programs continue to face. As the world population experiences greater mobility, increased cultural, geographic, and linguistic crossings are inevitable and the definition of what constitutes an HL learner will continue to evolve. Whether ties to an HL are based on ethnic, familial, circumstantial, or linguistic connections (Van Deusen-Scholl 2003), the profile of a student electing to attend a CHL school has become increasingly diverse (Valdés 2001). CHL programs report not only catering to children of immigrants of different generational statuses but also adoptees, mixed race children, and non-heritage children who are utilizing CHL programs as a means to develop proficiency in the target language. In CHL programs, which also function as a social network for co-ethnic community members, Shin (2010) sheds light on the complex interpersonal relationships toward members that do not fit the traditional mode of an HL learner. She found that they are often stigmatized, which lead them to disconnect with the community of HL speakers. Thus, CHL programs must be sensitive to the different background and needs of the participants, wider range of proficiency levels, and differing levels of home support in the HL. Specific background information of students in the program is critical when deciding on the curriculum, instructional materials, and pedagogical approaches. When the needs of the student population are better addressed, it is likely to contribute to increasing student enrollment and retention, which tend to be unstable for many of the smaller scale CHL programs.

Many CHL programs have already experienced change that reflects the needs and composition of the local community. For example, Southern California's oldest Chinese HL school, Westside Chinese School (https://westsidechineseschool.weebly.com), was founded in 1967 by six Chinese immigrant families. Throughout the years, the school has seen an increase in students who are not of Chinese descent and also has non-Chinese heritage members serving on its school board. To address these changing demographics, the school created additional language tracks for students of mixed-race children and non-heritage speakers, under the assumption that they would have differing needs and levels of support at home. Similarly, Chung (2012) describes a New York-based Korean School that saw its community composition start to shift after the principal began to advertise in English-language periodicals, in addition to Korean-language media. Previously, families with parents who primarily speak Korean were the largest group in the school, but now there are growing numbers of English-dominant parents of Korean heritage and multi-racial families. In her findings, Chung reports that in order to address the needs of English-speaking parents, students' homework is given out in English or bilingually and school meetings are conducted in English so that all parents can be involved. Similarly, Edu-Futuro, a Saturday school in Virginia that was founded in 1999, has seen their program's native English speaker population grow to half of its makeup. As the characteristics of the student population continue to shift with the ebb and flow of changes in the economic, political, and cultural landscapes, CHL curricula and instruction will need to be adjusted to accommodate these changes (Lee and Wright 2014).

Research on HL learners has shown that their linguistic abilities and needs are different enough from those of traditional foreign language students that warrant distinct teaching approaches (see Peyton et al. 2001; Potowski 2003; Kondo-Brown 2006; Kondo-Brown and Brown 2007; Brinton et al. 2008; Montrul 2010). This creates an additional difficulty for CHL programs that already struggle with lack of appropriate teaching resources and teachers for traditional HL learners. While many CHL programs use materials created for native-speaking children, which HL students find both culturally and linguistically unrelatable, CHL teachers may be able to find resources online that are more appropriate for their specific student populations. Technology such as texting apps (e.g., Kakaotalk, HelloTalk) also offer great opportunities to practice language skills in the HL in a non–face-threatening setting (Lee 2006).

But in order to take advantage of online materials and technological advancements for the teaching of HL in CHL programs, teachers need to be properly trained. The recruitment and training of teachers has been one of the greatest challenges throughout the history of CHL programs. Reliance on volunteers from the community to teach and an inability to hire properly trained teachers have been the essence of this persistent issue; however, the situation may begin to improve with growing access to affordable, in-service teacher training opportunities. Liu et al. (2010) describe summer workshops that are offered through local National Foreign Language Resource Centers or universities, as well as opportunities made available through the Overseas Compatriot Affairs Commission of Taiwan that deploys language educators to the United States to conduct teacher training workshops and STARTALK Cross Cultures Teacher Programs, offered by the Strategic Languages Institute, which train teachers in effective classroom assessment designs and tasks.

Needless to say, recruitment and training of HL teachers require financial resources, which CHL programs do not have much access to. Limited funding has been another challenge for CHL programs and the source of many other challenges. Moore and Ingersoll (2010) explain that CHL programs generally receive the majority of their funding from tuition and donations by local constituents. Often, there are little pockets of funding from homeland embassies to promote the HL and culture and from non-profit organizations (e.g., United Way) or governmental agencies to promote linguistic and cultural diversity in the region, but these are scarce and not a stable source of funding. Some foreign governments give aid to heritage organizations and different community-based schools in the form of materials, teachers, pedagogical training, or physical space (García et al. 2012). Canada has one of the best articulated funding policies for HL education, which has attracted the attention of many countries. For example, the federal government supports education in the official minority languages in each province and provides financial support for the development and maintenance of these programs (Duff 2008). But to date, not many other countries have been able to replicate such policies and practices.

With growing visibility of CHL programs and more inclusion of non-HL students in CHL programs, it is likely that there will be greater opportunities to raise public awareness of CHL programs. This may lead to wider support from the community and open additional avenues for collaboration with mainstream educational programs. Thus, it is important for CHL schools to stay updated with their website or social networking site information. Further, information about individual programs on school websites is commonly written only in the HL, hence limiting access to those who do not have literacy skills in that particular HL. Again, with increasing diversity in the backgrounds of students, it should no longer be assumed that parents have proficiency in the HL. CHL programs will need to be mindful about creating multilingual websites that meet the needs of the local population. In the following section, we review the different types of CHL programs and offer glimpses into different model programs.

30.5 Types of CHL Programs

30.5.1 Weekend Schools

Weekend schools, most often referred to as Saturday Schools, exist in a variety of formats: Some are strictly based on language and cultural instruction, while others are taught in religious settings, with religious teachings as the core content. Some of the languages taught in religious settings, like Yiddish, are strongly tied to religion so that one cannot be taught without the other, while others, such as Arabic and Hindi, have both religious and secular uses. There are also languages that often focus on religion but have only secular ties, such as Korean.

The goals of weekend schools range from offering students exposure to HL culture and values to developing high levels of HL proficiency. Many community language programs are taught and run by volunteer native speakers, usually parents, who donate their time, often with minimal or no compensation, as in the case of Lithuanian Saturday Schools in Chicago (Tamošiūnaitė 2013). Additionally, weekend schools may be nonprofit or for-profit, receiving funding through a variety of different sources, for instance, from corresponding foreign governments or local organizations or businesses, but mostly sustained through tuition and community donations.

A vast number of weekend schools are secular. These programs are housed in schools, community centers, or cultural centers on Saturdays or Sundays, usually running from morning to afternoon and up to six hours. For example, Edu-Futuro (https://edu-futuro.org) is a Spanish for Heritage Speakers program in Virginia that partners with the local school district, which provides space for free every Saturday. During this time, students receive language instruction focused on reading, writing, and speaking skills. Often, students are placed in classes by proficiency levels that result in mixed age groups. The negative effect on the morale of the older learners placed in the same class as younger learners has been noted, but due to limited funds, space, and teachers, it is typically not possible to offer separate classes by both age and proficiency level. Proficiency levels are determined mainly through self or parent reports or through informal assessments by teachers since proficiency assessment tools in the diverse HLs are not available or easily accessible. Weekend schools that have a longer school day also teach aspects of culture such as traditional art, cultural music and dance, theatre, and sports like *taekwondo* in order to reinforce students' cultural identity. In addition, some even offer tutoring in SAT/ACT courses, for example, to attract more interest to the school. In some instances, content instruction in religion, history, or geography of the country of the heritage language is also offered. This may vary depending on the student population. Lasserre et al. (2012) found that many of the French CHL schools in the United States are attended by students of Haitian or African descent and so the materials for heritage cultural classes differ accordingly.

Immersion practices are most common in CHL classrooms, not only in language classes but also in cultural classes. The choice of instructional method may be due to the limited bilingual skills of teachers or the strong receptive skills of typical HL learners that make instruction fully in the HL feasible. However, with growing numbers of students that may not have any proficiency in the HL, more multilingual translanguaging strategies will need to be employed in instruction.

Many CHL programs, especially among the more commonly taught HLs, cater to a large range of age groups from pre-K to adults. For example,

Choudhury (2012) describes the Udichi Performing Arts School in New York City that runs for approximately six hours: For the first half of the day, students from 6–18 years of age learn Bengali and attend various music and arts classes, while the second portion of the day is allotted for adults and advanced Bengali learners. The classes are taught in both Bengali and English at the introductory levels, but as the students become more proficient, instruction occurs in only standard Bengali.

On the other hand, some CHL programs, especially among the less commonly taught languages, such as Czech, are geared toward adults (Hrouda 2011). In these contexts, high levels of proficiency in Czech are rarely reached due to limited instructional time and little community support. Other CHL programs that have less community support are those whose HLs are commonly taught as world languages in schools, namely Spanish and French (Zamora 2013). However, there are some Spanish and French CHL schools, as illustrated by En Nuestra Lengua (www-personal.umich.edu/~tsat ter/ENLEnglish/En%20Nuestra%20Lengua%20English/HOME.html), a pre-K-4th grade Saturday morning Spanish heritage program in Michigan that has funding, institutional backing, and high community involvement, enabling the teaching of not only the language but also subject content through the language. In this particular program, parents of enrolled students are highly involved and the Spanish teachers are specifically trained to teach Spanish to heritage students.

Weekend HL schools are also the home for languages that are endangered. The East Turkistan Australian Association has two Saturday Uyghur language schools, in Victoria and South Australia. Not only do the schools teach the language, but they emphasize customs and cultural activities as well. For example, Ana Care (www.facebook.com/anacareandeducation) in Virginia is a Sunday school serving more than fifty students that offers three different courses: Uyghur language, *Usul* (traditional dance), and an Islamic course. These schools play the important roles of uniting people in East Turkistan diasporas and fostering a strong sense of ethnic identity in their students. The existence of these schools is not just significant, but necessary for people from areas where, even in the homeland, their language and culture are at risk of loss.

30.5.2 Religious-Affiliated CHL Programs

Many weekend HL programs are taught in religious institutions, either because of the availability of space for community use or for specific religious purposes. In some communities, religion is directly tied to identity and culture. As García et al. (2012) state, "Yiddish is acquired by Hasidic Jews, Hebrew by Jews, Punjabi by Sikhs, Arabic by Muslims, and Greek by Greek Orthodox, precisely to read holy texts and transmit religious and cultural traditions" (24). Therefore, many parents will send their children to CHL schools in order to continue their religious practices and traditions. The Islamic Arabic Weekend School (https://islamiccenter.sk.ca/islamic-classes/) in Saskatchewan, Canada, offers classes for students and adults on Sunday mornings. In these classes, Arabic and Islam are taught concurrently. For instance, the school's adult class, offered through two levels, is called "Qur'anic Arabic Grammar," in which Arabic grammar is taught in terms of how it is used in the Qur'an. Such programs can be particularly attractive due to the added benefit of receiving both religious and language instruction (Lee and Shin 2008), yet they are often closed to those that do not practice the religion.

Resources and funding are usually stable for religious-based nonprofit programs. For example, Greek language schools are operated and funded by the Greek Orthodox Church (Hantzopoulos 2012). Because the curriculum for the program focuses on literacy skills, translation, and understanding of religious texts, studies have reported that it is less challenging to find instructional materials for languages that are tied specifically to religion. Ghaffar-Kucher and Mahajan (2012) describe that Sikh communities do not need to seek or develop instructional materials and texts for Punjabi because of the available religious texts. Contrarily, while Hindi language programs may teach about Hinduism, because it is not the language of the religion, additional materials are needed.

However, there are also numerous HL communities whose languages are not specifically tied to religion but have CHL programs that are located in religious institutions and are operated on Sundays before or after church or temple services. Depending on the program, some integrate religious teachings in the HL classes as a pathway to spread the gospel, while others strictly teach the HL without any religious inferences. Yet, because of its affiliation to church, for example, where it is common to find an HL-speaking congregation and a separate service in the dominant language of the host country for the youth, HL classes are offered as a way to promote communication intergenerationally among members of the congregation. These programs are usually successful given the preexisting community support and serve multiple social and cultural purposes.

30.5.3 After-School Programs

After-school language programs can occur anywhere from once a week to Monday through Friday for 1–3 hours, generally on school grounds or at community centers, depending on the language and the resources. In locations where mainstream schools have a high population of speakers of a particular HL, CHL programs often rent classrooms after the regular school day is over. For example, a CHL program in Ontario, Canada, has provisions to teach the HL for 2.5 hours per week, where at least twenty-five students participate locally and students are given academic credit for their learning. Other after-school programs couple HL instruction with tutoring in academic subjects from their traditional school curriculum. The shorter classes focus primarily on language, while longer after-school programs include culture and identity-related activities. Makar (2012) describes one after-school program, Finding Our Roots (New York), organized by the Tepeyac Association, that provides support to both students and their families in social, cultural, and academic realms. They offer language (both Spanish and English) instruction to children and adults, as well as a physical education component via soccer and folkloric ballet. Due to the greater range of activities, more frequently than not, after-school language programs are aimed toward language learners from diverse backgrounds, both non-heritage and heritage students. Aierken and Fitzgerald (2017) note that because the limited instructional time in after-school programs often will not lead to high levels of proficiency development, rates of satisfaction and success may increase if the goals of the programs are more limited to the teaching of a specific HL skill, such as learning the alphabet or basic vocabulary words related to a particular topic. Such an approach may serve as smaller developmental steps toward greater proficiency in the HL and culture.

Moreover, after-school CHL programs do not have to be limited to the physical boundaries of a classroom. They may be part of other local community contexts, such as volunteer work and internships in ethnic businesses (Liu 2010); piano, art, or sports lessons in the HL (Shin and Lee 2014); or scout troops with other HL speakers (Guardado 2009). Such programs may not involve actual HL instruction, but the opportunity to use and hear the HL for authentic purposes provides an ideal context for increasing the motivation to learn and practice the HL.

30.5.4 Language Camps

Another type of CHL programs is language camps. There is a wide variety of summer camps for instruction in various languages. Language camps occur primarily during the summer months, although there are some week-long camps that are held during winter vacation or other breaks. Language camps often offer "full-immersion" in the language, with teachers, counselors, and mentors all speaking the language of the camp. Depending on the location/community, these may include day camps, sleep-away camps, and study abroad camps.

Some language camps are open to non-heritage students, but many of the students who attend language camps are usually heritage students. A large portion of these language camps is spent learning the language or being immersed in the language. These language camps generally offer instruction based on proficiency levels, whether through different camp sessions or different classes within the same session. Along with language, there is also an emphasis on culture, which may manifest itself through traditional dance, music (e.g., learning to play the *gayageum*, a traditional Korean zither-like string instrument in Korean language camps), art, writing (e.g., learning calligraphy in Chinese and Japanese), sports (e.g., martial arts), cooking, and celebrating traditional holidays as well as on social co-ethnic networking (e.g., Lithuanian summer camps, www.dainava.org).

Camps may offer scholarships of varying amounts to support the cost of attendance. One organization, Concordia Language Villages in Minnesota (www.concordialanguagevillages.org) offers language camps in the form of day camps, sleep-away camps, and study abroad camps for Romance languages, East Asian languages, Arabic, and Russian, among many others. They also offer four-week long programs for high schoolers, where they can receive academic credit in any of the fourteen languages they offer. There are also week-long programs for adults in some languages, as well as family camps that parents can attend with their children.

In addition, some camps are geared toward adoptive families. Heritage Camps for Adoptive Families in Colorado (www.heritagecamps.org) was originally created as a resource for Korean post-adopted families to encourage the formation of a bicultural identity, but has now spanned to include camps for African/Caribbean, Chinese, Indian/Nepalese, Latin American, Russian/Eastern European/Central Asian, and Southeast Asian/Pacific Islander heritage adoptees. Camp counselors are usually members of the heritage community. While this multi-day long camp does not specifically focus on language learning, there is some exposure to the language through food, music, and other cultural aspects.

Finally, study abroad programs can also serve the purposes of a language camp. American Councils for International Education has a number of study abroad programs across Europe and Asia (www.acstudyabroad.org). These programs are geared for all different types of language learners, college-aged and older, and occur during school semesters or summer. The goal of these programs is immersion in the target language, and they are mostly open to speakers with varying backgrounds and proficiencies. They do, however, have one program that is specifically geared toward HL speakers of Russian. The Russian Heritage Speakers Program is offered in three locations in Russia and one location in Kazakhstan, and through an American university, students can receive college credit on completion of the program. The program is individualized, based on what the students report they need when they apply, and the majority of language teaching happens on a one-to-one basis or in pairs. Students live in dormitories or homestays and engage in cultural activities and excursions.

30.5.5 Expatriate Schools

Less commonly found CHL programs are expatriate schools created for HL-speaking children of expatriates, who plan to go back to the heritage country. These schools offer grade-appropriate curricular instruction that reflects the educational system of the homeland so that students can easily transition into schools in the heritage country on their return. The expectation for students attending such programs is to already possess sufficient levels of oral and literacy skills in the HL so that content can be taught and learned in the HL. The most prominent example of expatriate schools is the Japanese *hokuushoo*. These schools are particularly dedicated to following the Japanese curriculum as dictated by the Japanese government. Kano (2012) states that the Japanese Ministry of Education, or MEXT, officially recognized three Japanese day schools in the United States in 2006, and there were at least eighty-seven weekend schools, which were supplied with at least one teacher by the Japanese government, depending on the number of enrollment. These schools are open to people of all Japanese heritage, including Japanese Americans; however, HL learners often find the curriculum and pace of instruction to be too challenging for them (Chinen et al. 2013). Yet, some parents elect to send their HL learning children to expatriate schools because they find them to be more rigorous in their instruction and more authentic in their treatment of the language and culture. For other languages such as Korean, which also has a large expatriate population in the United States, classes targeted to help children acclimatize into schools on return to the homeland are generally embedded in larger Saturday school settings.

30.5.6 Online Programs and Tools

With advancements in technology, the boundaries of CHL programs are beginning to become blurred. Technology has become part of our daily lives, and devices with Internet connection are usually accessible to both teachers and students, whether they have their own or can access them in community spaces. While current online language learning tools and applications are mainly geared toward foreign language learners rather than HL learners, they can be potential resources for HL education, especially for CHL programs with limited resources. It is important to consider these tools as they can be particularly valuable for HL learners who may be living in areas with low populations of HL speakers or in places with no access to CHL programs. Also, it is likely only a matter of time before hybrid and online CHL programs become commonplace.

In any instructional setting, digital resources and tools can enhance learning as long as they are implemented appropriately. It is critical that CHL teachers receive proper training to enable appropriate and effective use of these online tools for HL education. Kim and Frick (2011) discuss that online tools can encourage collaboration outside school and help support students with homework. Palladino and Guardado (2018) studied the use of digital tools to extend HL learning in two HL schools in Alberta, Canada. They reported that, in both schools, digital tools increased student engagement and fostered students' autonomous learning. Additionally, teachers felt empowered to try new strategies, and the use of resources such as blogs or wikis allowed teachers to give students increased opportunities to engage in writing at all levels, which was especially beneficial for languages that do not use Roman script. Furthermore, when teachers used online tools for their activities, they were able to optimize class time (Palladino and Guardado 2018), which is critical for contexts like CHL programs that operate on a very limited amount of class time per week.

There are also increasing numbers of software/applications and websites that can be used for HL education. While these tools and applications are not necessarily geared toward HL learners, they do provide an accessible option as a starting point. Rosetta Stone, for instance, offers instruction in thirty different languages with different pricing options based on subscription length. A branch of Rosetta Stone, called Rosetta Stone Homeschool, includes about twenty-four languages geared toward a younger audience (www.sonlight.com/RSLT.html). One of the highest grossing language apps, Babbel (www.babbel.com), is another subscription-based program with fourteen different languages. Moreover, Duolingo (www.duolingo.com), a platform that includes a language-learning website and app as well as proficiency assessments in almost forty languages, ranging from Spanish and Chinese to Swahili and Hawaiian, has over 300 million users to date. Basic services on the app and website are free but it also offers premium service for a fee. There are also various online programs such as Yoyo Chinese (www.yoyochinese.com) that utilize Youtube for video-based lessons. Increasingly, there are more videos and channels on Youtube that are geared toward learning languages. These videos, free and short, are usually full of visuals to attract viewers and learners.

Another example of the integration of technology and HL education is Te Kura (www.tekura.school.nz), the largest state-funded distance learning school in New Zealand. Students in New Zealand from ages 5–19 can apply to enroll as full-time students, but there is also an option to enroll in just a single course or part-time. Te Kura offers online courses in Chinese, French, German, Japanese, Māori, Samoan, and Spanish. These courses require either a mobile device, or having a camera and microphone available, as assignment submissions regularly happen through their online learning platform, My Te Kura. Some of these language courses come with beginner and advanced beginner tracks.

The future possibilities of such programs are great, as these online language programs and tools can offer an introduction to the HL or assist in the maintenance of the HL. However, in their current state, they still may not be able to replace the full value of what the physical presence of CHL programs can provide.

30.6 Conclusion

Fishman (1980) states that CHL programs moderate "ethnic uniqueness at the same time that it channels Americanness via the community's own institutions" (243). Although some scholars have questioned whether CHL programs foster ethnic ghettoization (Hall et al. 2002), this may be a concern that can be put to rest given the growing diversification of CHL program student populations. As research has shown, the popularity and robustness of CHL programs can shift based on factors beyond a community's control such as critical political world events or cultural trends. Yet, whether small or large, the existence of some form of CHL program in the community demonstrates the commitment and livelihood of the HL and its speakers.

For the continued survival and prosperity of CHL programs, Lynch (2008) argues for an asset-based approach drawing from available resources in the community to create more innovative partnerships that promote HL education and enhance the experiences of those in the community. For example, CHL programs can integrate instrumental uses of the HL by creating service projects in HL communities where HL learners can work with the elders to document narrative histories of their lives in the homeland, or internships/apprenticeships with mentors who can introduce them to a particular trade or help make connections with local businesses. Such affordances will provide authentic purposes to use the HL, meaningful interactions in the HL, and opportunities to practice the HL in a variety of different settings with different interlocutors – all necessary conditions for HL development. Thus, it is important for CHL programs to conduct an asset inventory at the individual, familial, and community levels within HL communities to identify the range of abilities, experiences, and resources that are available.

Recently, there have been great efforts to consolidate and make accessible resources that communities can share to promote the goals of CHL programs. As previously mentioned, there are national and regional alliances and networks that function to support CHL programs such as the International Languages Educators' Association of Ontario (https://ilea.ca) and the National Coalition of Community-Based Language Schools (https://nhlrc.ucla.edu), a wing of UCLA's National Heritage Language Resource Center that sponsors annual Community-Based Heritage Language Schools conferences (see Section 30.1 for additional HL coalitions). These organizations also support the establishment of CHL schools and provide frameworks to promote programmatic standards in teaching. For example, the National Resource Centre for Supplementary Education in the United Kingdom has also established a nationally recognized teacher accreditation program for CHL program educators. By creating platforms to connect the efforts of CHL programs, local programs are able to benefit via shared resources and increased visibility both locally and nationally. In addition, in the United States, there are numerous HL associations for each language by region, such as the Korean Schools Association of Northern California and one for Southern California, Contemporary Chinese School of Arizona, and The Saturday Schools for European Languages in Washington, DC, as well as national associations such as the American Association of Teachers of Korean, National Council of Associations of Chinese Schools, Chinese School Association, The German Language Conference, the American Association of Teachers of Turkic Language, and the Turkic American Alliance. They offer professional development opportunities for administrators and teachers and organize conferences for HL education in order to advance the knowledge base of HL education. These associations have also weighed in heavily in creating pathways to align the goals of HL education with mainstream educational objectives by developing AP credit-bearing courses in CHL schools and supporting the establishment of SAT II subject tests in various languages. Another resource is the Seal of Biliteracy, a special recognition that is awarded to graduating high school students in forty approved states and Washington D.C that acknowledges achieved proficiency in two or more languages (https://sealofbiliteracy.org). This award is better known within foreign language learning contexts, but the intent of the award is meant to encourage bilingualism in all instances, including HL learners. Although there is still much work to be done to make such resources readily available to all CHL program participants and to increase societal recognition of CHL programs' contributions to our linguistic and cultural prosperity, the establishment of broader coalitions to bring together CHL programs is a critical step in building a more cohesive and collaborative force behind HL development and maintenance efforts across all nations.

References

Aierken, A. and B. Fitzgerald. 2017. Strategies for Launching After-School Language Programs. Retrieved from https://blogs.edweek.org/edweek/global_learning/2017/02/strategies_for_launching_afterschool_language_programs.html

Archer, L. B. Francis, and A. Mau. 2010. The Culture Project: Diasporic Negotiations of Ethnicity, Identity and Culture among Teachers, Pupils and Parents in Chinese Language Schools. *Oxford Review of Education* 36(4), 407–426.

Bonacina-Pugh, F. and J. Gafaranga. 2011. "Medium of Instruction" vs. 'Medium of Classroom Interaction': Language Choice in a French Complementary School Classroom in Scotland. *International Journal of Bilingual Education and Bilingualism* 14(3), 319–334.

Brinton, D. M., O. Kagan, and S. Bauckus (eds.) 2008. *Heritage Language Education: A New Field Emerging*. Henry, IL: Center for Applied Linguistics and Delta Systems.

Carreira, M. and O. Kagan. 2011. The Results of the National Heritage Language Survey: Implications for Teaching, Curriculum Design, and Professional Development. *Foreign Language Annals* 44(1), 40–64.

Carreira, M., L. Jensen, and O. Kagan. 2009. The Heritage Language Learner Survey: Report on the Preliminary Results. UCLA. Retrieved from www .international.ucla.edu/media/files/paper.pdf

Chinen, K., M. O. Douglas, and H. C. Kataoka. 2013. *Japanese Heritage Language Schools in the United States. Heritage Brief*. Washington, DC: Center for Applied Linguistics. Retrieved from www.cal.org/heritage/ pdfs/briefs/japanese-heritage-language-schools-in-the-united-states.pdf

Choudhury, R. 2012. Raising Bilingual and Bicultural Bangladeshi-American Children in New York City: Perspectives from Educators and Parents in a Bengali Community Program. In O. García, Z. Zakharia, and O. Bahar (eds.), *Bilingual Community Education for American Children: Beyond Heritage Languages in a Global City*. Bristol: Multilingual Matters, 60–73.

Chung, J. 2012. Hidden Efforts, Visible Challenges: Promoting Bilingualism in Korean-America. In O. García, Z. Zakharia, and O. Bahar (eds.), *Bilingual Community Education for American Children: Beyond Heritage Languages in a Global City*. Bristol: Multilingual Matters, 87–98.

Compton, C. J. 2001. Heritage Language Communities and Schools: Challenges and Recommendations. In J. K. Peyton, D. A. Ranard, and S. McGinnis (eds.), *Heritage Languages in America: Preserving a National Resource*. McHenry, IL: Center for Applied Linguistics and Delta Systems, 145–166.

Creese, A., A. Bhatt, N. Bhojani, and P. Martin. 2006. Multicultural Heritage and Learner Identities in Complementary Schools. *Language and Education* 20(1), 23–43.

Curdt-Christiansen, X. 2006. Teaching and Learning Chinese: Heritage Language Classroom Discourse in Montreal. *Language, Culture and Curriculum* 19(2), 189–207 https://doi.org/10.1080/07908310608668762

Duff, P. 2008. Heritage Language Education in Canada. In D. Brinton, O. Kagan, and S. Bauckus (eds.), *Heritage Language Education: A New Field Emerging*. New York: Routledge/Taylor & Francis, 71–90.

Fishman, J. 1980. Ethnic Community Mother Tongue Schools in the USA: Dynamics and Distributions. *International Migration Review* 14, 235–247.

Fishman, J. 2001. 300-plus Years of HL Education in the US. In J. Peyton, D. Ranard, and S. McGinnis (eds.), *Heritage Languages in America: Preserving a National Resource*. McHenry, IL: Center for Applied Linguistics and Delta Systems, 81–99.

García, O., Z. Zakharia, and B. Otcu. 2012. *Bilingual Community Education and Multilingualism: Beyond Heritage Languages in a Global City*. Bristol: Multilingual Matters.

Ghaffar-Kucher, A. and A. P. Mahajan. 2012. Salaam! Namaste!: Indian and Pakistani Community-Based Efforts towards Mother Tongue Language Maintenance. In O. García, Z. Zakharia, and O. Bahar (eds.), *Bilingual Community Education for American children: Beyond Heritage Languages in a Global City*. Bristol: Multilingual Matters, 74–86.

Guardado, M. 2009. Speaking Spanish Like a Boy Scout: Language Socialization, Resistance, and Reproduction in a Heritage Language Scout Troop. *The Canadian Modern Language Review* 66, 102–129. https://doi.org/10.3138/cmlr.66.1.101

Hall, K. A., K. Özerk, M. Zulfiqar, and J. E. C. Tan. 2002. "This Is Our School": Provision, Purpose and Pedagogy of Supplementary Schooling in Leeds and Oslo. *British Educational Research Journal* 28(3), 399–418 https://doi.org/10.1080/01411920220137467

Hancock, A. 2012. Unpacking Mundane Practices: Children's Experiences of Learning Literacy at a Chinese Complementary School in Scotland, *Language and Education* 26(1), 1–17 https://doi.org/10.1080/09500782.2011.609280

Hantzopoulos, M. 2012. Going to Greek School: The Politics of Religions, Identity, and Culture in Community-Based Greek Language Schools. In O. García, Z. Zakharia, and O. Bahar (eds.), *Bilingual Community Education for American Children: Beyond Heritage Languages in a Global City*. Bristol: Multilingual Matters, 128–140.

Hashimoto, K. and J. S. Lee. 2011. Heritage Language Literacy Practices: A Case Study of Three Japanese American Families. *Bilingual Research Journal* 34(2), 161–184.

Haynes, E. 2010. *What Is the Difference between Indigenous and Immigrant Heritage Languages in the United States? Heritage Brief*. Washington, DC: Center for Applied Linguistics. Retrieved from www.cal.org/heritage/pdfs/briefs/what-is-the-difference-between-indigenous-and-immigrant-heritage-languages-in-the-united-states.pdf.

Hirsch, B. J. 2011. Learning and Development in After-School Programs. *Phi Delta Kappan* 92(5), 66–69.

Hrouda, S. J. 2011. *Czech Language Programs and Czech as a Heritage Language in the United States. Heritage Brief*. Washington, DC: Center for Applied

Linguistics. Retrieved from www.cal.org/heritage/pdfs/briefs/czech-language-programs-in-the-united-states.pdf

Kano, N. 2012. Japanese Community Schools: New Pedagogy for a Changing Population. In O. García, Z. Zakharia, and O. Bahar (eds.) *Bilingual Community Education for American Children: Beyond Heritage Languages in a Global City*. Bristol: Multilingual Matters, 113–127.

Kasper, G. and K. Rose. 2002. Pragmatic Development in a Second Language. *Language Learning* 51(1), 1–11.

Kelleher, A. 2010. *What Is a Heritage Language Program? Heritage Brief*. Washington, DC: Center for Applied Linguistics. Retrieved from www.cal.org/heritage/pdfs/briefs/What-is-a-Heritage-Language.pdf.

Kim, J. 2011. Korean Immigrant Mothers' Perspectives: The Meanings of a Korean Heritage Language School for Their Children's American Early Schooling Experiences. *Early Childhood Education Journal* 39, 133–141.

Kim, K. and J. T. W. Frick. 2011. Changes in Student Motivation during Online Learning. *Journal of Educational Computing Research* 44(1), 1–23.

Kondo-Brown, K. 2006. *Heritage Language Development: Focus on East Asian Immigrants*. Amsterdam: John Benjamins Publishing Company.

Kondo-Brown, K. and J. D. Brown (eds.) 2007. *Teaching Heritage Students in Chinese, Japanese, and Korean*. Mahwah, NJ: Routledge.

Lasserre, D., S. Lamplugh, and N. Liu. 2012. French Heritage Language Schools in the United States, *Heritage Brief*. Washington, DC: Center for Applied Linguistics. Retrieved from www.cal.org/heritage/pdfs/briefs/french-heritage-language-schools-in-the-united-states.pdf

Lao, R. and J. S. Lee. 2009. Heritage Language Maintenance and Use among 1.5 Generation Khmer College Students. *Journal of Southeast Asian American Education and Advancement* 4, 1–24.

Lee, J. S. 2002. The Korean Language in America: The Role of Cultural Identity and Heritage Language. *Language, Culture, and Curriculum* 15(2), 117–133.

Lee, J. S. 2006. Exploring the Relationship between Electronic Literacy and Heritage Language Maintenance. *Language Learning and Technology* 10(2), 93–113.

Lee, J. S. 2014. Community Support in the Development of Korean as a Heritage Language. In T. Wiley, J. Peyton, D. Christian, S. Moore, and N. Liu (eds.), *Handbook of Heritage, Community, and Native American Languages in the United States: Research, Educational Practice, and Policy*. New York: Routledge, 253–271.

Lee, J. S. and E. Oxelson. 2006. "It's Not My Job": K-12 Teacher Attitudes toward Students' Heritage Language Maintenance. *Bilingual Research Journal* 30(2), 453–477.

Lee, J. S. and S. Shin. 2008. Korean Heritage Language Education in the United States: The Current State, Opportunities and Possibilities. *Heritage Language Journal* 6(1) Retrieved from http://hlj.ucla.edu/ViewPaper.ashx?ID=X5aWPU2Aj8nVf2XLAk2G7w%3d%3d

Lee, J. S. and D. Suarez. 2009. A Synthesis of the Roles of Heritage Languages in the Lives of Immigrant Children. In T. Wiley, J. S. Lee, and R. Rumberger (eds.), *The Education of Linguistic Minority Students in the United States*. Clevedon: Multilingual Matters, 136–171.

Lee, J. S. and W. E. Wright. 2014. The Rediscovery of Heritage and Community Language Education in the United States. *Review of Research in Education* 38(1), 137–165. https://doi.org/10.3102/0091732X13507546

Li, L. 2006. Complementary Schools, Past, Present and Future. *Language and Education* 20(1), 76–83 https:doi.org/10.1080/09500780608668711

Li, L. 2014. Translanguaging Knowledge and Identity in Complementary Classrooms for Multilingual Minority Ethnic Children. *Classroom Discourse* 5(2), 158–175.

Liu, N. 2010. Chinese Heritage Language Schools in the United States. *Heritage Brief*. Washington, DC: Center for Applied Linguistics. Retrieved from www.cal.org/heritage/pdfs/briefs/chinese-heritage-language-schools-in-the-us.pdf

Liu, N., A. Musica, S. Koscak, P. Vinogradova, and J. López. 2010. Challenges and Needs of Community-Based Heritage Language Programs and How They Are Addressed, *Heritage Brief*. Washington, DC: Center for Applied Linguistics. Retrieved from www.cal.org/heritage/pdfs/briefs/challenges-and%20needs-of-community-based-heritage-language-programs.pdf

Ludanyi, R. and N. Liu. 2011. German Heritage Language Schools in the United States, *Heritage Brief*. Washington, DC: Center for Applied Linguistics. Retrieved from: www.cal.org/heritage/pdfs/briefs/german-heritage-language-schools-in-the-united-states.pdf

Lynch, B. K. 2008. Locating and Utilizing Heritage Language Resources in the Community: An Asset-Based Approach to Program Design and Evaluation. In D. Brinton, O. Kagan, and S. Bauckus (eds.), *Heritage language Education: A New Field Emerging*. Henry, IL: Center for Applied Linguistics and Delta Systems, 321–333.

Lytra, V. and P. W. Martin (eds.) 2010. *Sites of Multilingualism: Complementary Schools in Britain Today*. Stoke-on-Trent: Trentham.

Makar, C. 2012. Building Communities through Bilingual Education: The Case of Asociación Tepeyac of New York. In O. García, Z. Zakharia, and O. Bahar (eds.), *Bilingual Community Education for American Children: Beyond Heritage Languages in a Global City*. Bristol: Multilingual Matters, 45–59.

Montrul, S. 2010. Current Issues in Heritage Language Acquisition. *Annual Review of Applied Linguistics* 30, 2–23.

Moore, C. and G. Ingersoll. 2010. Where Do Community-Based Heritage Language Programs Find Funding? *Heritage Brief*. Washington, DC: Center for Applied Linguistics. Retrieved from www.cal.org/heritage/pdfs/briefs/where-do-community-based-heritage-language-programs-find-funding.pdf

Nordstrom, J. 2016. Parents' Reasons for Community Language Schools; Insight from a High-Shift, Non-visible, Middle-Class Community. *Language and Education* 30(6), 519–535.

Norton, B. and K. Toohey. 2011. Identity, Language Learning, and Social Change. *Language Teaching* 44(4), 412–446.

Otcu, B. 2010. Heritage Language Maintenance and Cultural Identity Formation: The Case of a Turkish Saturday School in New York City. *Heritage Language Journal* 7(2), 112–137. Retrieved from www .international.ucla.edu/media/files/otcu-hlj.pdf.

Palladino, V. and M. Guardado. 2018. Extending the Heritage Language Classroom: Experiences of Digital Technology Use in Two Community Schools in Alberta, Canada. *Language, Culture and Curriculum* 31(2), 150–167 https://doi.org/10.1080/07908318.2017.1415923

Peyton, J. K., V. Lewelling, and P. Winke. 2001. *Spanish for Native Speakers: Developing Dual Language Proficiency*. Washington, DC: Center for Applied Linguistics. Retrieved from www.cal.org/resources/digest/spanish_native .html

Peyton, J., D. Ranard, and S. McGinnis (eds.) 2001. *Heritage Languages in America: Preserving a National Resource*. Washington, DC: Center for Applied Linguistics, ERIC, and Delta Systems, Co., Inc.

Phinney, J., I. Romero, M. Nava, and D. Huang. 2001. The Role of Language, Parents, and Peers in Ethnic Identity among Adolescents in Immigrant Families. *Journal of Youth and Adolescence* 30(2), 135–153.

Popkewitz, T. A. and M. Brennan (eds.) 1998. *Foucault's Challenge: Discourse, Knowledge and Power in Education*. New York: Teachers' College Press.

Potowski, K. 2003. Chicago's Heritage Language Teacher Corps: A Model for Improving Spanish Teacher Development. *Hispania* 86(2), 302–311.

Rosenthal, D. 1987. Ethnic Identity Development in Adolescents. In M. Rotheram and J. S. Phinney (eds.), *Children's Ethnic Socialization: Pluralism and Development*. Newbury Park: Sage Publications, 156–180.

Shibata, S. 2000. Opening a Japanese Saturday School in a Small Town in the United States: Community Collaboration to Teach Japanese as a Heritage Language. *Bilingual Research Journal* 24(4), 465–474 https://doi.org/10.1080/ 15235882.2000.10162778

Shin, S. J. 2010. "What about Me? I'm Not Like Chinese but I'm Not Like American": Heritage-Language Learning and Identity of Mixed-Heritage Adults. *Journal of Language, Identity & Education* 9(3), 203–219.

Shin, S. J. 2014. Introduction. In T. Wiley, J. Peyton, D. Christian, S. Moore, and N. Liu (eds.), *Handbook of Heritage, Community, and Native American Languages in the United States: Research, Educational Practice, and Policy*. New York: Routledge, 241–252.

Shin, S. and J. S. Lee. 2014. Expanding Capacity, Opportunity, and Desire to Learn Korean as a Heritage Language. *Heritage Language Journal* 10(3), 64–73.

Sinclair, J. and M. Coulthard. 1975. *Towards an Analysis of Discourse: The Language of Teachers and Pupils*. London: Oxford University Press.

Tamošiūnaitė, A. 2013. Lithuanian Saturday Schools in Chicago: Student Proficiency, Generational Shift, and Community Involvement. *Heritage Language Journal* 10(1).

Téllez, K. and H. C. Waxman. 2010. A Review of Research on Effective Community Programs for English Language Learners. *The School Community Journal* 20(1), 103–119.

Valdés, G. 2001. Heritage Language Students: Profiles and Possibilities. In J. K. Peyton, D. A. Ranard, and Scott McGinnis (eds.), *Heritage Languages in America: Preserving a National Resource*. Washington, DC and McHenry, IL: Center for Applied Linguistics & Delta Systems, 37–77.

Van Deusen-Scholl, N. 2003. Toward a Definition of Heritage Language: Sociopolitical and Pedagogical Considerations. *Journal of Language, Identity, and Education* 2(3), 211–230.

Walters, S. 2011. Provision, Purpose and Pedagogy in a Bengali Supplementary School. *The Language Learning Journal* 39(2), 163–175.

Wang, N. 2017. *Heritage Language Schools in the U.S.: Administration, Sustainability and School Operations*. University of Nebraska. Educational Administration: Dissertations. 282. Retrieved from http:// digitalcommons.unl.edu/cehsedaddiss/282.

Wiley, T. G., J. K. Peyton, D. Christian, S. C. K. Moore, and N. Liu (eds.) (2014). *Handbook of Heritage, Community, and Native American Languages in the United States: Research, Policy, and Educational Practice*. New York: Routledge.

Wong, S. C. and M. G. Lopez. 2000. English Language Learners of Chinese Background. In S. L. McKay and S. C. Wong (eds.) *New Immigrants in the United States*. 263–305. Cambridge: Cambridge University Press.

Zamora, C. 2013. Spanish Heritage Language Schools in the United States, *Heritage Brief*. Washington, DC: Center for Applied Linguistics. Retrieved from www.cal.org/heritage/pdfs/briefs/spanish-heritage-language-schools-in-the-us.pdf.

Zulfiqar, M. 1997. Beyond the National Curriculum: Development of Supplementary Schooling in Britain, *Development Education Journal* 4, 33–34.

31

Curricular and Programmatic Language Development Opportunities for University-Level Heritage Language Learners

Sara Beaudrie

31.1 Introduction

The United States has witnessed a tremendous increase in speakers of minoritized languages. As of 2017, approximately 66.6 million individuals, or one in five, speak a language other than English at home. This population has been steadily increasing for the last three decades, doubling since 1990 and nearly tripling since 1980. Likewise, the student population of color in higher education has grown steadily over the last four decades from 1,690,800 (15.7 percent) in 1976 to 8,254,100 (44.0 percent) in 2017 (National Center for Education Statistics 2018). The ten most spoken non-English languages in the United States are (1) Spanish, (2) Chinese, (3) Tagalog, (4) Vietnamese, (5) Arabic, (6) French, (7) Korean, (8) Russian, (9) German, and (10) Haitian Creole (2017 US Community Survey).

Despite this constant growth in speakers of heritage languages (HL) in the United States, research has consistently shown that these languages are not maintained beyond two or three generations (Veltman 2000; Klee and Lynch 2009; Potowski 2010; Rivera-Mills 2012; among others), which represents significant linguistic and cultural losses at the individual, familial, community, and national levels. In an effort to reverse this loss, practitioners and researchers in HL education strive to provide rich learning experiences for those learners who want to reconnect with their linguistic and cultural heritage. Developing advanced proficiency in linguistic and cultural competencies has been found to increase HL students' sense of personal identity, self-pride, and connectedness to their heritage, their families, and their communities (Li and Duff 2008). Research further suggests that students' HL proficiency contributes to their overall academic success (Cummins 1993; Krashen, Tse, and McQuillan 1998; among others). A recent study found that HL proficiency, and literacy in particular, raises high school graduation rates and access to higher education for Latinx and Asian heritage learners (Jang and Brutt-Griffler 2019). At the national level, heritage speakers have been identified as key actors in efforts to build the multilingual capacity of the United States (Commission on Language Learning, 2017).

In response to the tremendous demand from speakers seeking to study their HL, such courses are becoming more available in public and private colleges and universities in the United States.[1] A recent large-scale survey of HL programs showed that 47 percent of US postsecondary institutions offer language courses specifically designed for HL learners (Carreira 2014, 2017), with their availability depending to a large extent on the size of the HL student population enrolled at the institution (Beaudrie 2011, 2012; Benmamoun and Kagan 2013).

This growth will likely continue for years to come since HL students are highly motivated to enroll in HL courses. In a 2011 survey, Carreira and Kagan queried 1,732 students about their reasons for learning their HL. They found that a majority enrolled in these courses primarily to learn about their cultural and linguistic roots and, secondarily, to connect with communities of speakers in the United States. Reynolds, Howard, and Deák (2009) surveyed 401 L2 and HL learners of nineteen different languages enrolled in beginning-level L2 courses. Results showed a clear difference between L2 and HL learners, with the HL group having higher integrative motivation and more positive attitudes than the L2 group, who expressed instrumental motivation to learn a second language. Similar findings have been obtained in other studies of HL learners' motivation (e.g., Geisherik 2004; Noels 2005; Titus 2014). These studies have also highlighted identity building as a crucial incentive for HL learners to pursue language studies (He 2006).

To serve the growing number of students interested in furthering their HL language abilities, higher education institutions have designed several programmatic options, which vary according to available resources, student population, and institutional support. The average department that offers HL courses has one or two courses (Beaudrie 2012; Carreira 2014,

---

[1] For a historical overview of HL education in the United States, see Carreira and Kagan (2018).

2017), while only 14 percent of departments offer four levels of HL instruction (Carreira 2014, 2017).

This chapter provides an overview of programmatic practices in postsecondary institutions as well as innovative practices emerging from current research in HL education. Traditionally, most postsecondary institutions have offered programs that focus on preparing HL learners to continue their studies toward a minor or major in the language; however, current trends point to an emerging shift toward innovative alternatives and goals for HL instruction. The main contribution of this chapter is to provide practitioners, researchers, and administrators with a review of state-of-the-art curricular and programmatic options for university-level HL learners, including innovations, achievements, current challenges, and future directions. Although the chapter focuses on research and current educational practices primarily in the US context, many insights drawn from this research may be of interest to researchers and practitioners working in international contexts (for an overview of research in international settings, see De Bot and Gorter 2005; Hornberger 2005; Duff 2008; Trifonas and Aravossitas 2014; Fairclough 2015; Kagan et al. 2017; Potowski 2018, section IV; Trifonas and Aravossitas 2018; among others).

31.2 Programmatic Options for Heritage Learners

31.2.1 Heritage Language Programs

HL courses are increasingly available in higher education, particularly for Spanish (see Beaudrie 2012) but also for other languages (Carreira 2017). This is an important development because HL research strongly suggests that HL learners and L2 learners have different language and cultural backgrounds, as well as distinct pedagogical, affective, and motivational needs that support the creation of two separate tracks (Montrul 2010; Benmamoun et al. 2013; Beaudrie et al. 2014; Carreira 2016). The Center for Applied Linguistics (CAL) higher-education HL program database currently profiles fifty-nine programs targeting various heritage languages and distributed all around the United States.

In addition to the availability of HL programs in higher education institutions, researchers have also examined their vibrancy. Carreira (2017) conducted a national survey of 294 programs covering 27 different languages, measuring not only the availability of HL programs but also whether their current state of structural assimilation was sufficient to ensure stability. The author concludes that HL instruction is trending toward institutionalization due to the increasing numbers of programs and the commitment of certain institutions to offer heritage programs, sometimes even with multiple sequences, even though they did not have a critical mass of heritage learners among their enrolled students. In fact, the vast majority of programs (73 percent) offered specialized instruction for HL learners, either in the form of HL courses or through innovative options such as independent studies, study abroad, internships, or tutoring. At the same time, results suggested several obstacles to institutionalization; namely, (1) shortage of course options for HL learners; (2) lack of tenured faculty in charge of those programs; (3) inadequate professional training opportunities; (4) lack of institutional support; (5) lack of pedagogical materials or inadequate materials; (6) low student enrollments; and (7) poor student retention (see also Beaudrie 2011, 2012 for research on HL programs in Spanish; Lee and Shin 2008 for Korean; Luo et al. 2019 for Chinese; Kagan 2014 for Russian). In sum, while much has been accomplished in the past two decades, serious challenges remain to be overcome in the future.

In an effort to help universities overcome some of these obstacles, Beaudrie (2016) advanced guidelines for how to design, implement, and evaluate a successful HL program. Importantly, she calls for a collaborative, integrative, and inclusive approach to HL program design with the inclusion of an evaluation component as key for successful development. Table 31.1 presents the steps for designing or redesigning an HL program (see Beaudrie 2016).

The first step suggests gathering information to be able to argue in favor of the benefits of establishing a new SHL program, including data on the benefits of bilingualism and HL maintenance, comparisons with course offerings at peer institutions, and assessment of students' self-reported needs and motivations. The next step recommends identifying all existing and potential resources and sources of funding in an effort to work collaboratively and efficiently to increase the chances of success. For step 3, a key recommendation is that the teachers in charge of HL courses are selected from among experienced instructors who have received or are willing to receive additional training in heritage language education. For the following step, the course sequence of the program should be followed after considering the language proficiency levels and instructional needs of the

Table 31.1 *Guidelines for establishing a heritage language program.*

Step	Description
STEP 1	Gather information and build an argument for the creation of the HL program
STEP 2	Gather resources for program building
STEP 3	Provide teacher professional development in HL instruction
STEP 4	Decide on program structure and preliminary course content
STEP 5	Identify HL students
STEP 6	Place HL students in appropriate course levels
STEP 7	Promote the program and recruit students
STEP 8	Evaluate the program

target population in combination with the resources available to the program. The next step is to design a quick and accurate procedure for identifying SHL students, distinguishing them from L2 learners. While some institutions are able to meet and identify students on an individual basis, some others have to include an identification tool in their placement exam because there is no personal contact with students. Once students have been identified as HL learners, the next step is to place them in the appropriate course level. A good placement test avoids the time-consuming alternative of placing each student individually in the appropriate course and increases the chances of having maximally homogenous classes, which are pedagogically more effective. Step 7 is program promotion and student recruitment, which, although time consuming, makes a difference in student enrollment levels and the vitality of the program. As with the other steps, a collaborative effort is most effective and more likely to have a big impact. The last step calls for a program evaluation, defined as "the systematic collection of information about the activities, characteristics, and outcomes of programs to make judgments about the program, improve program effectiveness, and/or inform decisions about future programming" (Patton 1997: 23). This step is crucial for ensuring program quality.

Valdés and Parra (2018) continued this line of research by advancing an analytical framework to inform the design, development, and evaluation of a heritage program by taking into account the different interacting elements that should be considered when teaching HL learners. The researchers present these mechanisms as three concentric circles (see Figure 31.1). The innermost circle, "core program elements," contains the fundamental pieces in the process of the curricularization of the heritage language: goals and outcomes; instructional materials; approaches and assessments; instructor competencies; and learner and instructor characteristics. The next circle, "policies, contexts, and traditions," includes contextual forces within the educational climate where heritage programs are immersed, such as educational policies and academic/intellectual areas that inform programs. The outermost circle, "theoretical and ideological mechanisms," includes key influencing forces that intervene in the decision-making process of language teachers, such as ideologies of language, class, race, and identity; conceptualizations of language; and theories of bilingualism and second language acquisition. This framework pushes stakeholders to analyze the relationships between a program's goals and objectives and the students' needs and profiles. It also encourages them to evaluate how these goals and needs are aligned with the program's curriculum, approaches, and materials. Moving beyond the micro level, the authors urge practitioners and researchers to examine the larger ideological system in which a program is embedded, in order to identify its impact on the teaching and learning of heritage learners. This framework aims to move HL education

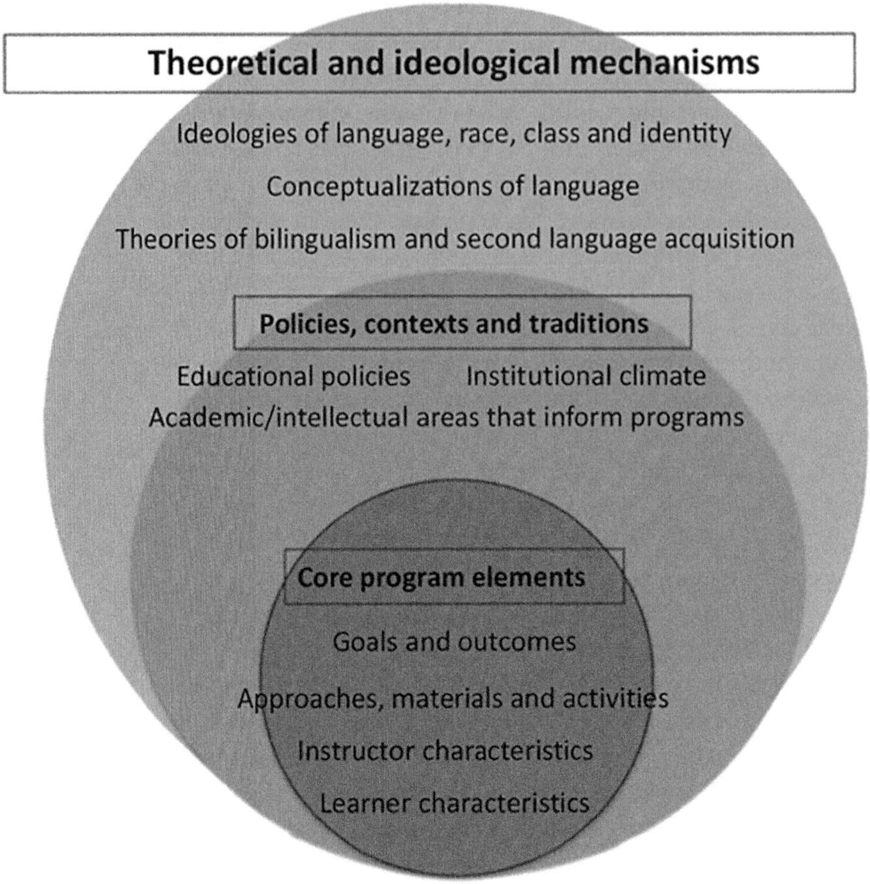

Figure 31.1 Concentric circles informing language curricularization

forward toward a better alignment of pedagogical and curricular practices with student needs through strengthening teacher preparation practices.

While much progress has been made in terms of promoting the need for HL programs within language departments and of presenting sound proposals for curriculum and program design, various challenges still remain.

A challenge identified in current research is the apparent seclusion of heritage programs within language departments (Carreira 2017). Given that most programs offer a limited set of language courses specifically designed for heritage learners, the need to expand HL-appropriate instruction to address higher levels of proficiency is obvious. Teachers and administrators in L2 and content courses are, however, often ill-equipped to address the needs of heritage learners and help them advance their competencies. Therefore, one of the most pressing needs is to integrate HL education throughout the range of curricular offerings in a language department, including upper-division content courses, in order to better address the needs of heritage learners in integrated L2/HL classrooms. Teacher develop-ment opportunities in HL pedagogy should be offered to all pre-service teachers and teaching assistants, as well as to lecturers and professors, so that they can serve HL learners in their non–heritage-specific curricula.

Another challenge discussed earlier is that no clear delineation of the core content of instruction for HL courses has yet been established. On the one hand, research on existing practices shows that the acquisition of academic discourse and/or standard grammar is still the main goal of most HL programs (Valdés et al. 2006; Kondo-Brown 2010; Beaudrie 2011, 2015; Pascual y Cabo 2016). While most HL practitioners respect and value the students' home and local varieties, the main focus of instruction is still on developing "standard" forms and academic discourses. On the other hand, several HL researchers have emphasized that for heritage learners their local language variety, not the "standard" language, has most communi-cative value, and many of them enroll in courses with the main goal of developing that variety (Bernal-Henríquez and Hernández-Chávez 2003; Ducar 2008; Lynch and Potowski 2014; Beaudrie 2015; Fairclough 2016; Toribio and Bullock 2016. Ducar (2008) surveyed 152 students in a large SHL program regarding their perceptions of the teaching and learning of stand-ard and nonstandard varieties of Spanish. The learners did not appear particularly interested in learning formal, academic Spanish, despite the emphasis that Spanish HL educators assigned to expanding learners' know-ledge of this register.

Although the two goals of developing local varieties while acquiring aca-demic registers/varieties are not incompatible, in practice HL practitioners and printed HL materials continue to privilege the latter over the former. For many students, especially for certain languages such as Arabic and Mandarin, their HL, acquired naturally, may actually represent the acquisi-tion of a third language, learned in a classroom setting (Polinsky 2015), and because they learned it largely in conversational contexts at home and in the community, their literacy skills often lag well behind their oral proficiency. Consequently, mastery of formal, academic language may be a daunting task in the limited amount of instructional time currently provided by HL pro-grams. A more innovative programmatic model for heritage learners is one with two tiers: In beginning and intermediate HL courses (first and second academic year), instruction focuses on helping students strengthen and develop their home variety of the language. For fluent heritage speakers (third and fourth academic year) advanced courses have the goal of expanding students' registers/varieties and developing advanced literacy skills. This model is applicable to all languages but it would be particularly beneficial for speakers of dialects such as Egyptian, Iraqi, or Cantonese. HL courses that only present Modern Standard Arabic or Mandarin are not really teaching these students their heritage language (see Albirini, this volume). In addition, for this model to be successful, it is imperative that both sociolinguistic and linguistic inquiry continue to deepen our understanding of local varieties relevant to HL learners, students' linguistic variation at different levels of proficiency, and their mastery of "standard" registers and/or educated varieties. The goal of this type of research should not, however, be to reinforce a "view of fixing heritage grammars from a broken state to an unbroken one via pedagogical intervention" (Rothman et al. 2016: 16). Rather, the pedagogical application of this type of research is to help teachers understand the parameters of variation within HL language use and proficiencies and, for example, recognize language forms that are not present in students' bilingual community and may require further development through instruction (see Beaudrie et al. 2014).

31.2.2 Mixed L2/HL Courses

Although some language programs are able to offer specialized language courses for their HL students, a majority of programs still are not able to do so, whether due to lack of resources, low student enrollments, or absence of trained faculty (Beaudrie 2012; Carreira 2016). As a result, many HL learners take language courses alongside L2 learners, and this has been the main impetus for emerging research on mixed courses over the last decade. This preliminary research has shown that it is possible, at least to some extent, to design tasks that are mutually beneficial for both populations of students.

Bowles (2011) examined oral and written task-based interactions of nine L2-HL pairs and found that L2 and HL learners solved equal proportions of language-related issues, but of different types. While HL learners relied on their L2 partners for metalinguistic issues such as spelling, L2 learners relied on their HL partners for issues of vocabulary and grammar. Subsequent studies confirmed these findings (e.g., Bowles et al. 2014; Henshaw 2015; Valentín-Rivera 2016; Kim et al. 2018; Walls 2018), while also showing that HL and L2 learners have complementary skills that make reciprocal learning possible in carefully manipulated tasks. In fact, Bowles et al. (2014) found that mixed dyads engaged in more target-like talk and were more likely to resolve language issues correctly. However, emerging research suggests that differences between L2 and HL learners' performance may be dependent on language proficiency levels. A recent study (Torres and Cung 2019) compared advanced L2 and heritage learners' peer interaction across modes (face-to-face and written) and pair types and found no differences in terms of linguistic repairs and only significant differences with lexical items in one of the modes (face-to-face).

In an effort to assist teachers with designing learning activities for mixed classes, Carreira (2016) presented a model that moves away from a one-size fits all approach toward a student-centered, individualized approach. This model acknowledges the need to build on the strengths of each group of students while at the same time addressing their individual needs. A core strategy is flexible grouping, where at times L2 and HL students are placed in separate groups, with each group working on a different activity, and at other times mixed L2–HL groups are utilized, depending on students' needs. The gist of Carreira's proposal is to leverage each group's complementary skills to foster reciprocal learning through differentiated instruction. Differentiated instruction assumes that each learner has different needs and, therefore, may need individualized assignments, activities, or assessments (see Carreira 2007; Beaudrie et al. 2014; Carreira and Hitchins Chik 2018).

While emerging research shows that there are potential benefits to mixed classes, various challenges and unanswered questions remain. One of the main challenges in a mixed class is lack of awareness and validation of HL learners' needs. It seems that in many L2 classrooms today, even those that include HL learners, students are still being taught and assessed exclusively according to L2 norms, rendering HL learners invisible (Carreira 2014). This is problematic because research indicates that L2-oriented instruction tends to produce greater gains for L2 learners than for HL learners (Bowles and Torres, this volume; Potowski et al. 2009; Torres 2018).

Another major challenge is in the area of teacher preparation. There is still much to be done to prepare language practitioners to deliver effective differentiated instruction and assessment. As Carreira (2016) explains, in order for L2 and HL students to work effectively together, group work has to be carefully designed so as to take into account students' different levels of proficiency, linguistic gaps, and learning styles. It is imperative to create workshops, conferences, and undergraduate and graduate courses where teachers can be trained to deliver effective instruction for both populations of students. Through action research projects (e.g., Redmond 2013), practitioners can also contribute to our understanding of effective interventions in mixed L2–HL courses.

31.3 Innovative Trends in Heritage Language Education

31.3.1 Critical Language Awareness in Heritage Language Education

Recent research proposals, primarily ones relating to Spanish, have marked the emergence of a "social justice turn" in HL education (Ortega 2017) that explicitly addresses the complex sociopolitical, racial, and ethnolinguistic identities of HL learners as minority language speakers in the United States. These proposals argue that HL curricula and instruction should follow a Critical Language Awareness (CLA) approach that validates and foregrounds learners' own varieties while simultaneously promoting an appreciation of linguistic diversity (Leeman 2005, 2018). Because HL learners typically come to the classroom with low linguistic self-esteem (Martínez 2003; Carreira and Beeman 2014; among others), the CLA approach seeks to increase learners' linguistic self-confidence in their vernacular varieties by making them the central focus for language instruction (Bernal-Henríquez and Hernández-Chávez 2003; Beaudrie 2015). As Beaudrie (2015) states, expanding students' linguistic repertoires to enable them to function in contexts relevant to their lived reality should be a primary goal of SHL instruction. Most importantly, CLA strives to give learners an awareness of the sociopolitical reality behind language use. To that end, the following instructional goals are crucial to a curriculum that takes a social justice approach to HL education (Beaudrie et al. 2019):

1. Students will learn to see language variation as natural and to recognize the intrinsic value of their own variety and all others;
2. Students will develop a consciousness of the political, social, and economic power structures that underlie language use and the arbitrary distribution of so-called prestige and non-prestigious varieties;
3. Students will be able to uncover dominant language ideologies that hide in daily monolingual/bilingual practices;
4. Students will be empowered to exercise agency in making their own decisions about bilingual language use.

Leeman and Serafini (2016) present one of the most complete proposals available for how to incorporate CLA into the HL curriculum. After an in-depth explanation of the sociolinguistic concepts central to implementing a CLA approach, they provide a wealth of concrete classroom activities and assignments to develop students' awareness of multilingualism, language variation, multilingual discourse, code-switching, and language ideologies. Along similar lines, Holguín Mendoza (2017) describes how an SHL program was redesigned to follow a CLA approach. The study measured changes in students' attitudes through a linguistic attitudinal survey containing thirty sentences that incorporated stigmatized words of Mexican Spanish used in spoken US Spanish. The results showed that students as a group increased their sociolinguistic awareness. Similar studies with proposals to help students develop their CLA have been introduced by Leeman, Rabin, and Román-Mendoza (2011); Parra (2013); and Parra et al. (2018).

Despite being a promising innovation, critical approaches to HL instruction so far appear to be limited to Spanish. In addition, Beaudrie's (2015) study of Spanish heritage syllabi revealed that only one of the sixty-three (2 percent) heritage syllabi in the sample presented a critical approach in the course description. More research is needed to find effective strategies to implement this approach and promote its wider use in HL courses.

31.3.2 Community Service-Learning in Heritage Language Education

Another innovation that HL education researchers have advanced is community service-learning (CSL), either as a standalone course or as a curricular component within an HL course. Community service-learning can help learners develop stronger connections with their local community as well as increase their awareness of issues affecting that community. It also promotes learners' awareness of their linguistic competence in local varieties and that this is a valuable resource for the community. Moreover, they can see first-hand the complex relations among language, culture, and social structures of power (Martínez and Schwartz 2010; Leeman et al. 2011; Lowther Pereira 2015; Pascual y Cabo, Prada, and Lowther Pereira, 2017). Studies have also found that CSL approaches benefit students by increasing their pride in their cultural and linguistic expertise (Leeman et al. 2011; see also Moreno and MacGregor-Mendoza 2016; and Guerrero-Rodriguez, Ojeda, and Pascual y Cabo, this volume), which helps address the issue of students' low self-esteem.

The most comprehensive study in this area is Lowther Pereira's book entitled *Community Service-Learning for Spanish Heritage Learners: Making Connections and Building Identities* (2018). She provides step-by-step guidelines for the design and implementation of CLS in language classrooms, together with best practices for HL teachers. She also lists key principles for making CSL experiences successful and tips for developing fruitful community partnerships.

The author also reports on a study conducted to measure CSL's effectiveness both quantitatively and qualitatively. Corroborating previous findings, the results of this study indicated that students strengthened their connections to the local Latinx community and developed greater awareness of social issues affecting them. In addition, students felt their CSL experience influenced their own identity and made a significant difference in their lives. These were found to be the key factors behind students' high level of satisfaction with the course.

Community-service learning, as well as other similar innovations such as community-based instruction (see Carreira and Kagan 2011; Parra 2013; Belpoliti and Fairclough 2016), have a lot of potential in situations where a local community speaks the HL. When this is not the case, creating connections with online communities of speakers may be explored as a good alternative option. Ideally, future research will provide insight into the types of gains obtained through these out-of-class experiences and how they can complement the gains achieved through classroom instruction.

31.3.3 Reconceptualization of HL Programs in Language Departments

As Valdés and Parra (2018) note, HL programs have typically had the status of stepchild in their language departments. A recent innovative proposal seeks to raise their low status. Torres, Pascual y Cabo, and Beusterien (2018) advocate moving heritage programs from the periphery to a central position in the language department by reshaping instruction not only for HL learners but also for L2 learners. They call for the implementation of a "heritage studies" curriculum that has as its main goal validation and promotion of heritage varieties of the language. In addition, it focuses on learning about local HL communities in the United States and fostering stronger connections with them. This program, according to the authors, affords mutual benefits by helping HL learners reconnect with their cultural and linguistic heritage, while teaching L2 learners how to establish informed personal and professional interactions with members of these communities.

A recent study that confirms these benefits was conducted by Pascual y Cabo and Tecedor (forthcoming). The authors redesigned an L2 curriculum to include units on US Latinx communities that filled about 20 percent of class time. Whereas the traditional L2 curriculum explored cultural practices (e.g., foods, festivities, historical landmarks) of countries where Spanish is the official language, the US Hispanic culture curriculum instead explored the cultural practices and histories of Hispanics in the United States. After two semesters of instruction, the authors compared the impact of the US culture curriculum versus the traditional one on students' motivation. They reported that L2 students who participated in the US culture curriculum had significantly higher attitudes and levels of motivation than the students who participated in the traditional curriculum. Thus, instruction that validates and foregrounds US Spanish-speaking communities can benefit L2 students in important ways.

Along the same lines, another promising curricular change to address the current challenges in HL education is through a genre-based pedagogical approach (e.g., Hammond and Derewianka 2001) within a "multiliteracies" framework (New London Group 1996; Kern 2000). This approach moves away from the traditional exclusive focus on academic genres as the main goal of HL instruction and instead enhances learners' resources to make socially situated meanings across different types of text. The main goal of HL instruction becomes to expand learners' communicative repertoires so that they can express meaning in the multiplicity of contexts they will encounter in their everyday lives. As Valdés and Parra (2018: 315) state,

> conceiving the teaching of HLs (in both oral and written modalities) within a more comprehensive notion and broader understanding of "genre" – as "a staged, goal-oriented, and purposeful social activity that people engage in as members of their culture" (Martin 1984: 25) – and literacy in general, appears to open up the possibility for students to analyze and produce different types of texts beyond literary or academic work, including descriptions, narrations, poetry, essays, novels, debates, blogs, art, music, and more. (Martínez 2005; Parra et al. 2017)

Importantly, this approach calls for taking a close look at the types of literacies that students are interested in accessing so as to prioritize these during instruction.

For students to become competent multilingual, biliterate users of their languages, they need first to analyze language use through a critical lens, and then to become comfortable expressing meaning within multiple genres, styles, and registers. As expected, the number of years of education received in the HL makes a difference, since this is reportedly one of the strongest predictors of HL learners' degree of writing proficiency (Gatti 2017). Instructors must always remember, however, that the bilingual writing of HL learners will necessarily differ from the writing of monolinguals on both linguistic and rhetorical levels. Bilingual writing is characterized by the use of detailed descriptions and narrations; inclusion of analogies, testimonies, and examples; and description of personal experiences or general knowledge instead of bibliographic information. Bilinguals' use of linguistic resources also differs in significant ways from monolingual writing, through use of simple rather than complex sentence structures, the use of the indicative rather than the subjunctive, and the simplification of the verb paradigm (Spicer-Escalante 2005, 2007). For different articles that incorporate a multiliteracies model in HL instruction and research studies, see (Martínez 2005; Parra 2016; Samaniego and Warner 2016; Vinogradova 2014; Zapata and Lacorte 2018).

31.3.4 Outcomes of Heritage Language Programs

While comprehensive HL program evaluations or comprehensive research on HL course outcomes have not been conducted at this point, there is emerging research that points to the beneficial learning outcomes of an HL course. Beaudrie (2006) compared the effects of SHL and L2 curricula on the written and oral language development of three groups of learners: two groups of HL learners enrolled in HL and FL courses, and a group of FL learners taking the same FL courses. The results showed that while all groups made significant gains in writing fluency and complexity, only the HL group in the HL course significantly improved their writing accuracy. Both HL groups made greater gains in oral fluency and complexity than the FL group but the HL group in the HL course outperformed both groups in syntactic complexity gains. Importantly, the HL group in the HL course showed the highest level of course satisfaction and the greatest improvement in self-confidence and language attitudes.

Parra, Bravo, and Polinsky (2018) conducted a pre–post design study in which they analyzed quantitative and qualitative changes in the oral narratives of seven advanced-proficiency heritage speakers of Spanish over the course of one semester of macro-based HL instruction and found that there were gains in vocabulary expansion, diversification of verbal tenses, and increased use of subordination. Furthermore, students' confidence levels in their oral language abilities were significantly higher after instruction. Parra, Otero, Flores, and Lavallé (2018) expanded this research study with the same group of participants and found that students also increased their reading fluency and comprehension. After a semester of heritage language instruction, students also improved their self-confidence in their Spanish language use and had a very positive learning experience.

Research studies also suggest that the HL course can have a broader impact, beyond language development. Preliminary research provides evidence that SHL education can make a difference in the students' overall academic success. For example, Pascual y Cabo and Prada (2017) found that the SHL course had a positive impact on student college retention rates. As mentioned previously, Jang and Brutt-Griffler (2019) found that HL proficiency, and literacy in particular, has a positive effect on high school graduation rates and increases access to higher education for Latinx and Asian heritage learners. Moreover, SHL learners often continue to pursue minor and major degrees in Spanish after taking a heritage course (see Holguín Mendoza 2017), which indicates the pivotal role that heritage language programs can have on the success of Spanish language departments more broadly.

31.4 Future Directions

In this chapter I have stressed how the abilities and needs of HL learners differ from those of their L2 peers, as well as how careful curriculum design is needed to meet the needs of HL learners or of both groups in one classroom. This reality highlights the pressing need to develop stronger teacher preparation models for instructors who deliver language or content instruction to heritage learners. Future research needs to focus on identifying practices and programmatic models that successfully prepare educators to work effectively with HL learners. Lacorte (2016) proposed seven key components of an ecological approach to HL teacher development: (1) ideological: addressing language beliefs and attitudes about teaching to foster acceptance of linguistic variation; (2) cultural: understanding students' cultural heritage and their motivations for studying their HL; (3) socio-affective: promoting awareness of students' identity issues, confidence, self-esteem, and social interaction with others; (4) linguistic: recognizing HL proficiencies and the differences between L1, L2, and HL acquisition as well as understanding sociolinguistic issues surrounding minority languages; (5) curricular: developing familiarity with administrative practices such as evaluation of instructional materials, placement and assessment procedures, and creation of community involvement activities; (6) pedagogical: training in different language teaching approaches and a variety of classroom strategies; and (7) providing professional development on issues of interest for instructors working either exclusively with HL learners or with L2 and HL students in mixed courses. While research in this area is still in its infancy, some proposals are beginning to emerge: (1) Arvanitis (2014) presents a culturally responsive pedagogical model for the training of HL teachers; (2) Aravossitas and Oikonomakou (2014) have proposed a curriculum for a professional development course for HL teachers; and (3) Lacorte (2018) proposes increased collaboration between language and education departments to strengthen the preparation of future HL teachers.

Finally, while many advances have been made in linguistic and pedagogical research on HLs, classroom-based research is still in its infancy (for a few exceptions see Lowther Pereira 2010; Helmer 2013, 2014). It is of crucial importance to understand how pedagogical interventions work in actual classrooms as well as to develop a research agenda to understand current achievements, challenges, and further needs of HL learners and teachers. In order to propel the field forward, it is vital to continue to develop three main lines of investigation: (1) what do heritage learners know at different proficiency levels? (2) What specific types of pedagogical interventions are most effective for students at different levels? and (3) How can instructors develop and measure specific learning outcomes for students enrolled in HL classrooms? Research so far has helped us gain a general understanding of heritage learners and general principles for HL instruction. A future research agenda in HL education should include fine-grained empirical and theoretical studies that enable us to understand more precisely the learning paths that students need to follow and how to help them successfully navigate those paths.

31.5   Conclusion

Recent years have witnessed tremendous advances in the field of HL education, in terms of our understanding of these students' linguistic competence, their profiles, their learning needs, and general pedagogical principles that are appropriate for both mixed L2-HL and HL-only courses. Yet, as Bowles (2018) states, we still don't know whether classroom instruction is effective for heritage learners and what type of instruction is most effective for different instructional purposes. Significant gains could be made through more action research studies, collaborative partnerships between practitioners and researchers, and studies that utilize intact classes as the main research site. Classroom research using observational, ethnographic, quasi-experimental, and experimental designs can all provide insights into effect-ive educational practices. Likewise, research on university-level HL curricu-lum, instruction, and programs is almost nonexistent beyond a few state or nationwide surveys on a very limited number of heritage languages. This type of research is essential because it allows us to measure whether the goals of HL education are realized in actual classrooms. It is also crucial to determine whether research advances in pedagogy have entered the class-room setting and what the true impact of these innovations is.

References

Aravossitas, T. and M. Oikonomakou. 2014. Professional Development of Heritage Language Instructors: Profiles, Needs, and Course Evaluation. In P. P. Trifonas and T. Aravossitas (eds.), *Rethinking Heritage Language Education*. Cambridge: Cambridge University Press, 263–284.

Arvanitis, E. 2014. Culturally Responsive Pedagogy: Modelling Teachers' Professional Learning to Advance Plurilingualism. In P. P. Trifonas and T. Aravossitas (eds.), *Rethinking Heritage Language Education*. Cambridge: Cambridge University Press, 245–262.

Beaudrie, S. M. 2006. Spanish Heritage Language Development: A Causal-Comparative Study Exploring the Differential Effects of Heritage versus Foreign Language Curriculum. Doctoral dissertation. Retrieved from ProQuest Dissertation and Theses database (UMI No. 3218230).

Beaudrie, S. M. 2011. Spanish Heritage Language Programs: A Snapshot of Current Programs in the Southwestern United States. *Foreign Language Annals* 44(2), 321–337.

Beaudrie, S. M. 2012. Research on University-Based Spanish Heritage Language Programs in the United States: The Current State of Affairs. In S. Beaudrie and M. Fairclough (eds.), *Spanish as a Heritage Language in the United States: State of the Field*. Washington, DC: Georgetown University Press, 203–221.

Beaudrie, S. M. 2015. Approaches to Language Variation: Goals and Objectives of the Spanish Heritage Language Syllabus. *Heritage Language Journal* 12(1), 1–21.

Beaudrie, S. M. 2016. Building a Heritage Language Program: Guidelines for a Collaborative Approach. In M. Fairclough and S. Beaudrie (eds.), *Innovative Approaches in Heritage Language Teaching: From Research to Practice*. Washington, DC: Georgetown University Press, 80–98.

Beaudrie, S., A. Amezcua, and S. Loza. 2019. Critical Language Awareness for the Heritage Context: Development and Validation of a Measurement Questionnaire. *Language Testing* 36(3), 1–30.

Beaudrie, S., C. Ducar, and K. Potowski. 2014. *Heritage Language Teaching: Research and Practice*. New York: McGraw-Hill.

Belpoliti, F. and M. Fairclough. 2016. Inquiry-Based Projects in the Spanish Heritage Language Classroom: Connecting Culture and Community through Research. *Hispania* 99(2), 258–273.

Benmamoun, E. and O. Kagan. 2013. The Administration of Heritage Language Programs: Challenges and Opportunities. *Heritage Language Journal* 10(2), 143–155.

Benmamoun, E., S. Montrul, and M. Polinsky. 2013. Heritage Languages and Their Speakers: Opportunities and Challenges for Linguistics. *Theoretical Linguistics* 39(3–4), 129–181.

Bernal-Henríquez, Y. and E. Hernández-Chávez. 2003. La enseñanza del español en Nuevo México: ¿Revitalización o erradicación de la variedad chicana? In A. Roca and C. Colombi (eds.), *Mi lengua: Spanish as a Heritage Language in the United States*. Washington, DC: Georgetown University Press, 78–95.

Bowles, M. 2011. Measuring Implicit and Explicit Linguistic Knowledge: What Can Heritage Language Learners Contribute? *Studies in Second Language Acquisition* 33(2), 247–271.

Bowles, M. 2018. Outcomes of Classroom Spanish Heritage Language Instruction: State of the Field and an Agenda for the Future. In K. Potowski (ed.), *The Handbook of Spanish as a Heritage/Minority Language*. New York: Routledge.

Bowles, M. A., R. J. Adams, and P. D. Toth. 2014. A Comparison of L2-L2 and L2-Heritage Learner Interactions in Spanish Language Classrooms. *Modern Language Journal* 98(2), 497–517.

Carreira, M. 2007. Teaching Spanish to Native Speakers in Mixed Ability Language Classrooms. In K. Potowski and R. Cameron (eds.), *Spanish in Contact: Policy, Social and Linguistic Inquiries*. Washington, DC: Georgetown University Press, 61–80.

Carreira, M. 2014. Teaching Heritage Language Learners: A Study of Programme Profiles, Practices, and Needs. In P. Trifonas and T. Aravossitas (eds.), *Rethinking Heritage Language Education*. Cambridge: Cambridge University Press, 20–44.

Carreira, M. 2016. A General Framework and Supporting Strategies for Teaching Mixed Classes. In D. Pascual y Cabo (ed.), *Advances in Spanish as a Heritage Language*. Amsterdam/Philadelphia: John Benjamins, 159–176.

Carreira, M. 2017. The State of Institutionalization of Heritage Languages in Postsecondary Language Departments in the United States. In O. E. Kagan, M. M. Carreira, and C. Hitchins Chik (eds.), *The Routledge Handbook of Heritage Language Education: From Innovation to Program Building*. New York: Routledge, 347–362.

Carreira, M. and T. Beeman. 2014. *Voces: Latino Students on Life in the United States*. Santa Barbara, CA: Praeger Publishers.

Carreira, M. and C. Hitchins Chik. 2018. Differentiated Teaching: A Primer for Heritage and Mixed Classes. In K. Potowski (ed.), *The Handbook of Spanish as a Heritage/Minority Language*. New York: Routledge, 359–374.

Carreira, M. and O. Kagan. 2011. The Results of the National Heritage Language Survey: Implications for Teaching, Curriculum Design, and Professional Development. *Foreign Language Annals* 44, 40–64.

Carreira, M. and O. Kagan. 2018. Heritage Language Education: A Proposal for the Next 50 Years. *Foreign Language Annals* 51, 152–168.

Commission on Language Learning. 2017. *America's Languages: Investing in Language Education for the 21st Century*. Cambridge, MA: American Academy of Arts & Sciences. Available from www.amacad.org/multimedia/ pdfs/publications/researchpapersmonographs/language/Commission-on-Language-Learning_Americas-Languages.pdf

Cummins, J. 1993. The Research Basis for Heritage Language Promotion. In M. Danesi, K. McLeod, and S. Morris (eds.), *Heritage Language and Education: The Canadian Experience*. Oakville, ON: Mosaic Press, 1–21.

De Bot, K. and D. Gorter. 2005. A European Perspective on Heritage Languages, *The Modern Language Journal* 89(4), 612–616.

Ducar, C. M. 2008. Student Voices: The Missing Link in the Spanish Heritage Language Debate. *Foreign Language Annals* 41(3), 415–433.

Duff, P. 2008. Heritage Language Education in Canada. In D. Brinton, O. Kagan, and Bauckus (eds.), *Heritage Language: A New Field Emerging*. New York: Routledge/Taylor and Francis, 71–90.

Fairclough, M. 2015. Spanish as a Heritage Language. In M. Lacorte (ed.), *The Routledge Handbook of Hispanic Applied Linguistics*. New York/London: Routledge, 134–149.

Fairclough, 2016. Incorporating Additional Varieties into the Linguistic Repertoires of Heritage Language Learners: A Multidialectal Approach. In M. Fairclough and S. Beaudrie (eds.), *Innovative Approaches in Heritage Language Teaching: From Research to Practice*. Washington, DC: Georgetown University Press, 143–165.

Gatti, A. 2017. Who Are Heritage Writers? Language Experiences and Writing Proficiency. *Foreign Language Annals* 50(4), 734–753.

Geisherik, A. 2004. The Role of Motivation among Heritage and Non-Heritage Learners of Russian. *Canadian Slavonic Papers* 46(1–2), 9–22.

Hammond, J. and B. Derewianka. 2001. Genre. In R. Carter and D. Nunan (eds.), *The Cambridge Guide to Teaching English to Speakers of Other Languages*. Cambridge: Cambridge University Press, 186–193.

He, A. W. 2006. Toward an Identity Theory of the Development of Chinese as a Heritage Language. *Heritage Language Journal* 4, 1–28.

Helmer, K. A. 2013. A Twice-Told Tale: Voices of Resistance in a Borderlands Spanish Heritage Language Class. *Anthropology and Education Quarterly* 44(3), 269–285.

Helmer, K. A. 2014. 'It's Not Real, It's Just a Story to Just Learn Spanish': Understanding Heritage Language Learner Resistance in a Southwest Charter High School. *Heritage Language Journal* 11(3), 186–206.

Henshaw, F. 2015. Learning Outcomes of L2-Heritage Interactions: The Proof Is in the Posttests. *Heritage Language Journal* 12, 245–270.

Holguín Mendoza, C. 2017. Critical Language Awareness (CLA) for Spanish Heritage Language Programs: Implementing a Complete Curriculum. *International Multilingual Research Journal* 11(5), 1–15.

Hornberger, N. H. 2005. Heritage/Community Language Education: US and Australian Perspectives [Special Issue]. *International Journal of Bilingual Education and Bilingualism* 8(2–3).

Jang, E. and J. Brutt-Griffler. 2019. Language as a Bridge to Higher Education: A Large-Scale Empirical Study of Heritage Language Proficiency on Language Minority Students' Academic Success. *Journal of Multilingual and Multicultural Development* 40(4), 322–337.

Kagan, O. 2014. Russian Heritage Language Learners: From Students' Profiles to Project-Based Curriculum. In T. Wiley, J. Kreeft Peyton, D. Christian, S. C. Moore, and N. Liu (eds.), *Handbook of Heritage, Community, and Native American Languages in the United States: Research, Policy, and Educational Practice*. New York: Routledge, 1–21.

Kagan, O., M. Carreira, and C. Hitchins Chik. 2017. *The Routledge Handbook of Heritage Language Education: From Innovation to Program Building*. New York: Routledge Press.

Kern, R. 2000. *Literacy and Language Teaching*. Oxford: Oxford University Press.

Kim, M., H. Lee, and Y. Kim. 2018. Learning of Korean Honorifics through Collaborative Tasks: Comparing Heritage and Foreign Language Learners. In N. Taguchi andY. Kim (eds.), *Task-Based Approaches to Teaching and Assessing Pragmatics*. Amsterdam: John Benjamins, 28–54.

Klee, C. and A. Lynch. 2009. *El español en contacto con otras lenguas*. Washington, DC: Georgetown University Press.

Kondo-Brown, K. 2010. Curriculum Development for Advancing Heritage Language Competence: Recent Research, Current Practices, and a Future Agenda. *Annual Review of Applied Linguistics* 30, 24–41.

Krashen, S., L. Tse, and J. McQuillan (eds.) 1998. *Heritage Language Development*. Culver City, CA: Language Education Associates.

Lacorte, M. 2016. *Teacher Development in Heritage Language Education. Innovative Strategies for Heritage Language Teaching: A Practical Guide for the Classroom*, 99–119.

Lacorte, M. 2018. Multiliteracies Pedagogy and Heritage Language Teacher Education: A Model for Professional Development. In G. C. Zapata and M. Lacorte (eds.), *Multiliteracies Pedagogy and Language Learning*. London: Palgrave Macmillan, 197–225.

Lee, J. S. and S. J. Shin. 2008. Korean Heritage Language Education in the United States: The Current State, Opportunities, and Possibilities. *Heritage Language Journal* 6(2), 1–20.

Leeman, J. 2005. Engaging Critical Pedagogy: Spanish for Native Speakers. *Foreign Language Annals* 38(1), 35–45.

Leeman, J. 2018. Critical Language Awareness and Spanish as a Heritage Language: Challenging the Linguistic Subordination of US Latinxs. In K. Potowski (ed.), *The Handbook of Spanish as a Heritage/Minority Language*. New York: Routledge, 345–358.

Leeman, J. and E. Serafini. 2016. Sociolinguistics for Heritage Language Educators and Students: A Model of Critical Translingual Competence. In M. Fairclough and S. Beaudrie (eds.), *Innovative Strategies for Heritage Language Teaching: A Practical Guide for the Classroom*. Washington, DC: Georgetown University Press, 56–79.

Leeman, J., L. Rabin, and E. Román-Mendoza. 2011. Identity and Activism in Heritage Language Education. *Modern Language Journal* 95(5), 481–495. https://doi.org/10.1111/j.1540-4781.2001.01237.x

Li, D. and P. Duff. 2008. Issues in Chinese Heritage Language Education and Research at the Postsecondary Level. In A. W. He and Y. Xiao (eds.), *Chinese as a Heritage Language: Fostering Rooted World Citizenry*. Honolulu: National Foreign Language Resource Center, University of Hawaii, 13–36.

Lowther Pereira, K. 2010. Identity and Language Ideology in the Intermediate Spanish Heritage Language Classroom. Unpublished PhD thesis, University of Arizona.

Lowther Pereira, K. 2015. Developing Critical Language Awareness via Service-Learning for Spanish Heritage Speakers. *Heritage Language Journal* 12(2), 159–185.

Lowther Pereira, K. 2018. *Community Service-Learning for Spanish heritage Learners: Making Connections and Building Identities*. Amsterdam/ Philadelphia: John Benjamins.

Luo, H., Y. Li, and M. Li. 2019. Heritage Language Education in the United States: A National Survey of College-Level Chinese Language Programs. *Foreign Language Annals* 52(1), 101–120.

Lynch, A. and K. Potowski. 2014. La valoración del habla bilingüe en los Estados Unidos: Fundamentos sociolingüísticos y pedagógicos en Hablando bien se entiende la gente. *Hispania* 97(1), 32–46.

Martínez, G. A. 2003. Classroom-Based Dialect Awareness in Heritage Language Instruction: A Critical Applied Linguistic Approach. *Heritage Language Journal* 1, 1–14.

Martínez, G. A. 2005. Genres and Genre Chains: Post-Process Perspectives on Heritage Language Writing in a South Texas Setting. *Southwest Journal of Linguistics* 24(1–2), 79–91.

Martínez, G. and A. Schwartz. 2012. Elevating "Low" Language for High Stakes: A Case for Critical, Community-Based Learning in a Medical Spanish for Heritage Learners Program. *Heritage Language Journal* 9(2), 37–49.

Montrul, S. 2010. How Similar Are Adult Second Language Learners and Spanish Heritage Speakers? Spanish Clitics and Word Order. *Applied Psycholinguistics* 31(1), 167–207.

Moreno, G. and P. MacGregor-Mendoza. 2016. Special Issue on Service-Learning and Heritage Language Learners: Impact on Communities, Students, and Classrooms. *Heritage Language Journal* 13.

National Center for Education Statistics (NCES). 2018. Table 306.10. Total fall enrollment in degree-granting postsecondary institutions, by level of enrollment, sex, attendance status, and race/ethnicity or nonresident alien status of student: Selected years, 1976 through 2017. Washington, DC: US Department of Education.

New London Group. 1996. A Pedagogy of Multiliteracies: Designing Social Futures. *Harvard Educational Review* 66(1), 60–92.

Noels, K. A. 2005. Orientations to Learning German: Heritage Language Learning and Motivational Substrates. *Canadian Modern Language Review* 62(2), 285–313.

Ortega, L. 2017. The Study of Heritage Language Speakers from a bilingualism and Social Justice Perspective. 21st Hispanic Linguistics Symposium, Texas Tech University, Lubbock, October 26–28.

Parra, M. L. 2013. Expanding Language and Cultural Competence in Advanced Heritage and Foreign Language Learners through Community Engagement and Work with the Arts. *Heritage Language Journal* 10(2), 252–280.

Parra, M. L. 2016. Understanding Identity among Spanish Heritage Learners: An Interdisciplinary Endeavor. In D. Pascual y Cabo (ed.), *Advances in Spanish as a Heritage Language*. Philadelphia/Amsterdam: John Benjamins, 177–204.

Parra, M. L., M. Bravo, and M. Polinsky. 2018. *De bueno a muy bueno*: How Pedagogical Intervention Boosts Language Proficiency in Advanced Heritage Learners. *Heritage Language Journal* 15(2), 203–241.

Parra, M. L., A. Otero, R. Flores, and M. Lavallé. 2017. Developing a Comprehensive Curriculum for Advanced Heritage Language Learners: Contributions from the Multiliteracies Framework. In Zapata, G. and M. Lacorte (eds.), *Multiliteracies Pedagogy and Language Learning: Teaching Spanish to Heritage Learners*. London: Palgrave Macmillan, 27–66.

Pascual y Cabo, D. 2016. Charting the Past, Present, and Future of Spanish Heritage Language Research. In D. Pascual y Cabo (ed.), *Advances in Spanish as a Heritage Language*. Philadelphia/Amsterdam: John Benjamins, 1–13.

Pascual y Cabo, D. and J. Prada. 2017. Beyond Language: Exploring the Unseen Benefits of Heritage Language Programs. Paper presented at the Third International Conference on Heritage/Community Languages. Los Angeles, California.

Pascual y Cabo, D., J. Prada, and K. Lowther Pereira. 2017. Effects of Community Service-Learning on Heritage Language Learners' Attitudes toward Their Language and Culture. *Foreign Language Annals* 50(1), 71–83.

Patton, Michael. 1997. *Utilization-Focused Evaluation: The New Century Text*. Thousand Oaks, CA: Sage.Polinsky, M. 2015. When L1 Becomes an L3: Do Heritage Speakers Make Better L3 Learners? *Bilingualism: Language and Cognition* 18(2), 163–178.

Potowski, K. 2010. *Language Diversity in the USA*. Cambridge: Cambridge University Press.

Potowski, K. 2018. *Handbook of Spanish as a Heritage/Minority Language*. New York: Routledge.

Potowski, K., J. Jegerski, and K. Morgan-Short. 2009. The Effects of Instruction on Linguistic Development in Spanish Heritage Language Speakers. *Language Learning* 59(3), 537–579.

Redmond, M. L. 2013. *Action Research in the World Language Classroom*. Information Age Publishing.

Reynolds, R., K. Howard, and J. Deák. 2009. Heritage Language Learners in First-Year Foreign Language Courses: A Report of General Data across Learner Subtypes. *Foreign Language Annals* 42(2), 250–269.

Rivera-Mills, S. V. 2012. Spanish Heritage Language Maintenance. In S. M. Beaudrie and M. A. Fairclough (eds.), *Spanish as a Heritage Language in the United States: The State of the Field*. Washington, DC: Georgetown University Press, 21–42.

Rothman, J., I. Tsimpli, and D. Pascual y Cabo. 2016. Formal Linguistic Approaches to Heritage Language Acquisition. In D. Pascual y Cabo (ed.), *Advances in Spanish as a Heritage Language*. Philadelphia/Amsterdam: John Benjamins, 13–26.

Samaniego, M. and C. Warner. 2016. Multiliteracies for the Heritage Language Classroom. In S. Beaudrie and M. Fairclough (eds.), *Innovative Approaches in Heritage Language Pedagogy: From Research to Practice*. Washington, DC: Georgetown University Press, 191–213.

Spicer-Escalante, M. 2005. Writing in Two Languages/Living in Two Worlds: A Rhetorical Analysis of Mexican-American Written Discourse. In M. Farr (ed.), *Latino Language and Literacy in Ethnolinguistic Chicago*. Mahwah, NJ: Lawrence Erlbaum Associates, 217–244.

Spicer-Escalante, M. 2007. Análisis lingüístico de la escritura bilingüe (español-inglés) de los hablantes de español como lengua hereditaria en los Estados Unidos. *Estudios de Lingüística Aplicada* 45, 63–80.

Tecedor, M. and D. Pascual y Cabo. 2020. In Your Own Backyard: Legitimizing Local Communities as a Way to Increase Language Learning Motivation. *Language, Culture and Curriculum*, 33(4), 433–450.

Titus, J. 2014. Russian Heritage Learners' Goals and Motivation. In P. Trifonas and T. Aravossitas (eds.), *Rethinking Heritage Language Education*. Cambridge: Cambridge University Press, 149–164.

Toribio, J. and B. Bullock. 2016. A New Look at Heritage Spanish and Its Speakers. In D. Pascual y Cabo (ed.), *Advances in Spanish as a Heritage Language*. Philadelphia/Amsterdam: John Benjamins, 27–44.

Torres, J. 2018. The Effects of Task Complexity on Heritage and L2 Spanish Development. *Canadian Modern Language Review* 74(1), 128–152.

Torres, J. and B. Cung. 2019. A Comparison of Advanced Heritage Language Learners' Peer Interaction across Modes and Pair Types. *The Modern Language Journal* 103(4), 815–830.

Torres, J., D. Pascual y Cabo, and J. Beusterien. 2018. What's Next: Heritage Language Learners Pave the Path for Spanish Teaching. *Hispania* 100(5), 271–278.

Trifonas, P. and T. Aravossitas. 2014. (eds.) *Rethinking Heritage Language Education*. Cambridge: Cambridge University Press, 149–164.

Trifonas, P. and T. Aravossitas. 2018. (eds.), *Handbook of Research and Practice in Heritage Language Education*. New York: Springer International Publishing.

Valdés, G. and M. L. Parra. 2018. Towards the Development of an Analytical Framework for Examining Goals and Pedagogical Approaches in Teaching Language to Heritage Speakers. In K. Potowski (ed.), *The Handbook of Spanish as a Heritage/Minority Language*. New York: Routledge.

Valdés, G., J. A. Fishman, R. Chávez, and W. Pérez. 2006. *Developing Minority Language Resources: The Case of Spanish in California*. Clevedon: Multilingual Matters.

Valentín-Rivera, L. 2016. Activity Theory in Spanish Mixed Classrooms: Exploring Corrective Feedback as an Artifact. *Foreign Language Annals* 49, 615–634.

Veltman, C. 2000. The American Linguistic Mosaic: Understanding Language Shift in the United States. In S. L. McKay and S. C. Wong (eds.), *New Immigrants in the United States*. Cambridge: Cambridge University Press, 58–93.

Vinogradova, P. 2014. Digital Stores in Heritage Language Education: Empowering Heritage Language Learners through a Pedagogy of Multiliteracies. In T. Wiley, D. Christian, J. K. Peyton, S. Moore, and N. Liu (eds.), *Handbook of Heritage, Community, and Native American Languages in the United States: Research, Educational Practice, and Policy*. London and New York: Routledge and CAL, 314–323.

Walls, L. 2018. The Effect of Dyad Type on Collaboration: Interactions among Heritage and Second Language Learners. *Foreign Language Annals* 51(3), 638–657.

Zapata, G. C. and M. Lacorte (eds.) 2017. *Multiliteracies, Pedagogy and Language Learning: Teaching Spanish to Heritage Speakers*. New York: Palgrave Macmillan.

32

Instructed Heritage Language Acquisition

Melissa A. Bowles and Julio Torres

32.1 Introduction

Instructed heritage language acquisition (IHLA) is a subfield within heritage language (HL) studies that addresses the effects of instruction on HL development. Given the increasing interest in better understanding the pedagogical needs of HL learners (e.g., Beaudrie, Ducar, and Potowski 2014; Torres, Pascual y Cabo, and Beusterien 2017; Carreira and Kagan 2018), studies in the area of IHLA have begun to examine the language development of HL learners who arrive in the instructed setting with some functional knowledge of the HL (Valdés 2001). That is, the studies have *not* focused on those HL learners who have an ancestral connection to the language, but have (almost) no linguistic knowledge of the HL, as these learners most likely behave linguistically like second language (L2) learners. HL learners with functional knowledge in the HL are exposed to their family/community language in a mostly naturalistic environment at an early age. As such, it has been critical to investigate how these HL learners respond to pedagogical interventions as a result of their early bilingual experience, and the effect this experience has on their language development or lack thereof. To date, a number of IHLA studies from different theoretical perspectives such as task-based and processing instruction have been conducted with the aim to address this issue (e.g., Potowski, Jegerski, and Morgan-Short 2009; Torres 2018). However, the field would benefit from an early systematic review through a quantitative meta-analysis of these studies to gauge the overall effects of instruction on HL development. A meta-analysis can also elucidate the theoretical and methodological issues that future empirical studies ought to address to advance our knowledge of the field. Therefore, the goal of this chapter is to report on an exploratory meta-analysis of empirical studies that have examined the effects of instruction on HL learners' language development.

Numerous narrative reviews of IHLA studies have been published in recent years (e.g,. Montrul and Bowles, 2017; Bowles 2018; Sanz and Torres 2018). Although such reviews provide a snapshot of the state of research in the field, a complimentary approach is needed to provide a more complete understanding. One alternative is a vote-counting approach (Hedges and Olkin 1980; Allen 2017), in which all primary research studies addressing a given question are identified and, based on the statistically significant (or nonsignificant) findings, each study is tallied as providing evidence either for or against a given hypothesis. Then, the number of studies with findings supporting or contradicting the hypothesis is tallied, and conclusions are drawn based on the majority finding. Although the procedure for sampling the primary research literature is more comprehensive with the vote-counting approach than in narrative reviews, there are still drawbacks to this method. Most importantly, the vote-counting method relies on probability values, or the statistical significance or non-significance of each individual study's findings, in order to make conclusions. This method is problematic, given that probability values are highly dependent on sample sizes, with larger sample sizes being more likely to yield statistically significant results than smaller sample sizes. In fact, with all other data being equal, two studies observing the same effect may come to opposite conclusions, with one achieving statistically significant differences between groups and the other not finding statistically significant differences, on the basis of sample size alone.

Furthermore, statistical significance conveys only that differences between groups were likely the result of chance at some predetermined level. An alpha level of .05, for instance, indicates simply that the results obtained could have resulted from chance on just 5 out of 100 occasions. The probability value does not convey any information about the magnitude of the difference observed between groups; it merely indicates how likely it is that the results were the product of chance. Thus, a very low probability value could be obtained even with a minuscule difference between groups. Light and Pillemer (1984) sum up these facts, stating, "even if every one of 30 studies in a review reports findings that are statistically significant, a vote count does not tell us whether they are large enough to matter in practice" (75). That is, neither narrative nor vote-counting reviews take into account calculations of effect size, or magnitude of difference between groups.

Quantitative meta-analysis is one method of research synthesis that addresses the aforementioned limitations of both narrative and vote-counting reviews. First, in a meta-analysis, researchers must follow (and report in detail) the principles used to sample the primary literature, and are typically as inclusive as possible in identifying primary studies that have investigated a common research question. Therefore, the sampling procedure is replicable and the synthesis can be built on by other researchers once further studies have been conducted. After primary studies have been identified and coded according to a set of substantive and methodological features, descriptive statistics from each unique sample study are used to gauge the effect size of a given treatment or group. There are several different formulas for the calculation of effect size, but one of the most commonly used in social science research is the standardized mean difference, which is the mean difference between an experimental and a control group, with standard deviations and sample sizes taken into account.

Effect sizes of individual studies can be averaged to determine a mean effect size, summarizing the effectiveness of a given treatment across studies, or they can be compared to provide insight into variables that could have caused differing findings between two studies. Effect sizes have the advantage of not being dependent on sample size, or on probability values. Furthermore, quantitative meta-analyses take into account how frequent and consistent the observed effects are across studies by providing calculations of standard error and confidence intervals.

In instructed Second Language Acquisition (SLA), since Norris and Ortega's (2000) seminal meta-analysis, there has been increased quantitative research synthesis in various subdomains, including grammar (Spada and Tomita 2010; Shintani et al. 2013), vocabulary (Wa-Mbaleka 2006; Chiu 2013), pragmatics (Jeon and Kaya 2006), and pronunciation (Lee, Jang, and Plonsky 2014). To our knowledge, no meta-analyses of research on HL acquisition have been conducted to date. We therefore devote the remainder of this chapter to an exploratory meta-analysis of the effects of IHLA.

In order to understand both the overall effects of HL instruction and to explain potential moderators of those effects, the present study addressed the following research questions:

1. How effective is heritage language instruction overall?
2. What is the relationship between heritage language instruction, learner characteristics (language of instruction, proficiency, age, instructional setting), instruction characteristics (type, target, and duration of instruction), and outcome measures?

32.2   Methods

32.2.1   Identification of Studies
Relevant primary studies were identified using the following techniques, as recommended by Plonsky and Brown (2015), which sometimes resulted in the same study being identified multiple times but was comprehensive.

Since studies investigating the effects of HL instruction are published in a range of venues in education and in linguistics, we searched *Linguistics and Language Behavior Abstracts* (LLBA), the *Education Resources Information Center* (ERIC) database, Google, and Google Scholar using the following subject, abstract, keywords, and combinations thereof: *heritage language instruction*, *heritage language development*, *heritage language acquisition*, and *heritage language learners*. Then we manually searched all issues of *The Heritage Language Journal* as well as draft chapters to appear in an edited volume of empirical studies on the outcomes of HL instruction that was in preparation (Bowles, in press). Finally, to ensure that we had not missed any relevant studies that met our criteria, we conducted ancestry searches by examining the references cited in reviews on HL acquisition and instruction (e.g., Montrul and Bowles 2017) and by contacting the authors of three other chapters in this handbook who were working on related topics (Kim Potowski, Lee Jin Sook, and Sara Beaudrie). We decided to include only studies that were published, accepted, or in press in peer-reviewed journals, conference proceedings, or books. As such, we did not include unpublished theses or dissertations, although we intend to do so in a future study in order to be able to examine potential publication bias. That is, the inclusion of unpublished works would help reduce a bias toward statistically significant results, which can inflate the effects of pedagogical interventions (Plonsky and Brown 2015).

32.2.2 Inclusion and Exclusion Criteria

These search methods resulted in the identification of eighteen unique sample studies (see Appendix 32.A). Then, in order to be included in the meta-analysis, studies had to meet the following inclusion and exclusion criteria. First, they had to have an experimental or quasi-experimental design in which heritage learners were provided with instruction on one or more aspects of their HL. Second, they had to compare one or more instructed groups of heritage learners to an uninstructed (control) group. Studies that did not include a control group of heritage learners (e.g., Pyun and Lee-Smith 2011), those that examined only pre–post-test gains over time in a within-studies design (e.g., Parra et al. 2018), and those that included a control that also received heritage language instruction (e.g., Nocus et al. 2012) were not included. Third, studies had to present quantitative results and include sufficient descriptive statistics to enable the calculation of effect sizes. One study (Potowski, Jegerski, and Morgan-Short 2009) did not meet this criterion, but the authors provided the raw data in response to our request, which we were then able to use to calculate effect sizes. Finally, all studies had to be published, in press, or accepted for publication prior to January 2019. Studies were excluded from the analysis if HL instruction, although a part of the study design, was not an independent variable.

Based on these criteria, a total of eight of the original eighteen unique sample studies were identified for inclusion in the meta-analysis. A summary of the eight studies can be found in Table 32.1. In terms of sample size, the present meta-analysis is similar to meta-analyses on L2 instruction reported in Lee, Jang, and Plonsky (2014), which ranged from 13 to 86 unique sample studies (median: 30). The total N for all included studies was 502, consisting of 341 experimental group participants (median: 32.5) and 161 control group participants (median: 16).

32.2.3 Coding

In order to answer our research questions, each study was coded for both substantive and methodological features, as shown in the coding scheme in Appendix 32.B. As recommended by Plonsky and Oswald (2012), both authors coded the entire sample separately and then discussed and resolved the few cases of disagreement.

32.2.4 Calculation of Effect Sizes

Cohen's *d* effect sizes were calculated based on descriptive statistics (means and standard deviations) or from the results of inferential statistical tests reported in the study, in cases where means and standard deviations were not provided. For small sample sizes, where the degrees of freedom were fifty or less, Cohen's *d* values were corrected following Hedges, Shymansky, and Woodworth (1989).

32.2.5 Combining Effect Sizes

Some meta-analysts believe that each unique study sample should contribute just one effect size to a meta-analysis (Light and Pillemer 1984). Under that logic, in cases where multiple treatments were carried out in a single sample study, then, effect sizes are combined across the range of treatments. In instruction studies this would imply aggregating results across groups that received different instructional treatments. For the present meta-analysis, it was decided that each study could contribute more than one effect size, on the theoretical grounds that an identical sample of participants may perform differently based on a number of factors, including the type of instruction received and the modality and type of assessment used to measure gains. Since several of the studies examined participants' performance on a range of tasks, and with a range of dependent measures, combining them all into one effect size for each study would

Table 32.1 *Summary of studies*

Study	Language	Age (Setting)	Type	Duration	Focus	Outcome measures
Wright et al. (2000)	Inuttitut	Child (Elementary)	Language Arts	3 years	Literacy	Proficiency; Vocabulary; Story comprehension; Literacy
Potowski et al. (2009)	Spanish	Adult (College)	Explicit	4 days	Past subjunctive	Listening; Written production; GJT
Kang (2010)	Korean	Adult (College)	Explicit/Implicit	6 weeks	Past Tense	GJT; Picture description
Cuza et al. (2017)	Spanish	Child (Elementary)	Language Arts		Literacy	Vocabulary; Phonological awareness; Word reading accuracy; Word reading fluency
Torres (2018)	Spanish	Adult (College)	Implicit	1–2 weeks	Present subjunctive	Oral and written production
Bowles & Bello (2019)	Spanish	Adult (College)	Explicit	12 weeks	Writing	CAF; Lexical density, sophistication & diversity
Beaudrie & Holmes	Spanish	Adult (College)	Explicit	2 weeks	Past Tense	Recognition; Written production
Bowles & Fernández	Spanish	Adult (College)	Explicit/Implicit	1 week	Past Subjunctive	AJT; EIT

Note. GJT = grammaticality judgment task; CAF = complexity, accuracy, fluency; AJT = acceptability judgment task; EIT = elicited imitation task have blurred many possible distinctions that could have come to light as a result of the meta-analysis. Therefore, all of the effect sizes calculated for each unique sample study are reported in Figure 32.1, and the relevant effect size estimates for each research question are described in a step-wise fashion. Because each study used multiple assessments and in some cases had several experimental groups, each comparison contributed its own effect size, meaning that our eight unique sample studies provided forty-six effect sizes ($k = 46$).

In order to answer our research questions, it was necessary to combine effect sizes from several studies, which we did by creating a weighted average, weighting each effect size estimate by the reciprocal of its sampling variance (i.e., the reciprocal of its squared standard error). Hedges et al. (1989) refer to this weighting method as "the statistically optimal way to average a group of independent estimates" (46) because it takes into account the sample sizes and sampling errors of each study, rather than treating all studies equally. Due to the heterogeneity that is characteristic of heritage learners, we opted for a random-effects, rather than a fixed-effects, model and used the R packages *meta* and *metafor* for analysis and to create forest plots.

32.2.6 Analysis of the Homogeneity of Effect Sizes

Effect sizes cannot be combined blindly; rather, effect sizes from studies should be combined only when there is good reason to believe that the studies are similar, at least on several dimensions, substantive and/or methodological. Even then, it is essential to quantitatively analyze the studies in terms of both their individual effect sizes and variances. One method of analysis involves a homogeneity test, which determines whether the variability across effect sizes is greater than or less than what would be expected from sampling error alone. The most commonly used homogeneity test in meta-analysis is a Q test. If the Q value is less than the critical value of a χ^2 test with the same number of degrees of freedom, then the group of studies is homogenous. "... [T]his result tells us that the effect sizes do not differ by more than would be expected from sampling error and, hence, are virtual replications in their findings. Even though the studies may differ on a variety of characteristics, methodological and substantive, none of those differences matter in terms of the magnitude of the effects found by the studies." In cases where a group of studies is found to be homogenous, "the mean effect size is clearly a representative and meaningful summary of the distribution of effect size values" (Lipsey and Wilson 2001: 162).

Sometimes, even when studies have been grouped by substantive and methodological variables and are considered to be similar enough to

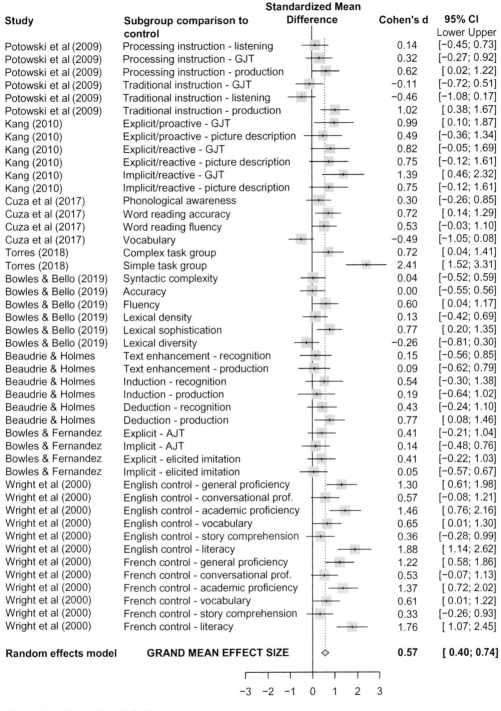

Study	Subgroup comparison to control	Standardized Mean Difference	Cohen's d	95% CI Lower Upper
Potowski et al (2009)	Processing instruction - listening		0.14	[−0.45; 0.73]
Potowski et al (2009)	Processing instruction - GJT		0.32	[−0.27; 0.92]
Potowski et al (2009)	Processing instruction - production		0.62	[0.02; 1.22]
Potowski et al (2009)	Traditional instruction - GJT		−0.11	[−0.72; 0.51]
Potowski et al (2009)	Traditional instruction - listening		−0.46	[−1.08; 0.17]
Potowski et al (2009)	Traditional instruction - production		1.02	[0.38; 1.67]
Kang (2010)	Explicit/proactive - GJT		0.99	[0.10; 1.87]
Kang (2010)	Explicit/proactive - picture description		0.49	[−0.36; 1.34]
Kang (2010)	Explicit/reactive - GJT		0.82	[−0.05; 1.69]
Kang (2010)	Explicit/reactive - picture description		0.75	[−0.12; 1.61]
Kang (2010)	Implicit/reactive - GJT		1.39	[0.46; 2.32]
Kang (2010)	Implicit/reactive - picture description		0.75	[−0.12; 1.61]
Cuza et al (2017)	Phonological awareness		0.30	[−0.26; 0.85]
Cuza et al (2017)	Word reading accuracy		0.72	[0.14; 1.29]
Cuza et al (2017)	Word reading fluency		0.53	[−0.03; 1.10]
Cuza et al (2017)	Vocabulary		−0.49	[−1.05; 0.08]
Torres (2018)	Complex task group		0.72	[0.04; 1.41]
Torres (2018)	Simple task group		2.41	[1.52; 3.31]
Bowles & Bello (2019)	Syntactic complexity		0.04	[−0.52; 0.59]
Bowles & Bello (2019)	Accuracy		0.00	[−0.55; 0.56]
Bowles & Bello (2019)	Fluency		0.60	[0.04; 1.17]
Bowles & Bello (2019)	Lexical density		0.13	[−0.42; 0.69]
Bowles & Bello (2019)	Lexical sophistication		0.77	[0.20; 1.35]
Bowles & Bello (2019)	Lexical diversity		−0.26	[−0.81; 0.30]
Beaudrie & Holmes	Text enhancement - recognition		0.15	[−0.56; 0.85]
Beaudrie & Holmes	Text enhancement - production		0.09	[−0.62; 0.79]
Beaudrie & Holmes	Induction - recognition		0.54	[−0.30; 1.38]
Beaudrie & Holmes	Induction - production		0.19	[−0.64; 1.02]
Beaudrie & Holmes	Deduction - recognition		0.43	[−0.24; 1.10]
Beaudrie & Holmes	Deduction - production		0.77	[0.08; 1.46]
Bowles & Fernandez	Explicit - AJT		0.41	[−0.21; 1.04]
Bowles & Fernandez	Implicit - AJT		0.14	[−0.48; 0.76]
Bowles & Fernandez	Explicit - elicited imitation		0.41	[−0.22; 1.03]
Bowles & Fernandez	Implicit - elicited imitation		0.05	[−0.57; 0.67]
Wright et al (2000)	English control - general proficiency		1.30	[0.61; 1.98]
Wright et al (2000)	English control - conversational prof.		0.57	[−0.08; 1.21]
Wright et al (2000)	English control - academic proficiency		1.46	[0.76; 2.16]
Wright et al (2000)	English control - vocabulary		0.65	[0.01; 1.30]
Wright et al (2000)	English control - story comprehension		0.36	[−0.28; 0.99]
Wright et al (2000)	English control - literacy		1.88	[1.14; 2.62]
Wright et al (2000)	French control - general proficiency		1.22	[0.58; 1.86]
Wright et al (2000)	French control - conversational prof.		0.53	[−0.07; 1.13]
Wright et al (2000)	French control - academic proficiency		1.37	[0.72; 2.02]
Wright et al (2000)	French control - vocabulary		0.61	[0.01; 1.22]
Wright et al (2000)	French control - story comprehension		0.33	[−0.26; 0.93]
Wright et al (2000)	French control - literacy		1.76	[1.07; 2.45]
Random effects model	**GRAND MEAN EFFECT SIZE**		**0.57**	**[0.40; 0.74]**

−3 −2 −1 0 1 2 3

Figure 32.1 Forest plot of all effect sizes

warrant averaging their effect sizes, the Q statistic resulting from the homogeneity test is greater than the critical value of a χ^2 with the relevant number of degrees of freedom. In those cases, the studies are said to be heterogeneous, and the variability observed is larger than that which could be attributed to different samples across the different studies. In such cases, a weighted effect size should not be reported; rather, further analysis is needed to determine if some other difference between studies is likely to have caused the heterogeneity (Lipsey and Wilson 2001: 162). Indeed, such results shed insight into what variables should be controlled for and/or manipulated in future research to move the field forward.

32.3   Results

Before discussing our results, we want to establish that we are interpreting the effect sizes based on the benchmarks set forth by Plonsky and Oswald (2014) for instructed SLA. While we are examining a learner population with a different bilingual profile, the pedagogical interventions adopted in most of these studies are inspired by theoretical and methodological perspectives in instructed SLA. Once the field of IHLA accumulates a larger body of studies, it will be important to take stock of whether Plonsky and Oswald's L2 effect size benchmarks are appropriate for advancing our theoretical knowledge, pedagogical practices, and curricular decisions pertaining to the design of instruction for HL learners. As of now, therefore, it is reasonable to adopt the benchmarks from instructed SLA, which we consider a sister field to IHLA. According to Plonsky and Oswald (2014), d values less than or equal to 0.40 should be considered small, 0.50 to 0.70 medium and 0.80 and above large.

Once the studies were coded for all relevant features, several trends became apparent. Although the studies in this sample date back nearly two decades, the earliest meeting the inclusion criteria being Wright et al. (2000), it is noteworthy that six of the eight (75 percent) have been published since 2010. This trend shows that interest in the effects of HL instruction is growing in tandem with interest in heritage languages more broadly.

Furthermore, it was clear from examining the coding sheet that the overwhelming majority of studies on the effects of HL instruction published to date have been on Spanish (six out of eight studies, or 75 percent of our sample). This is perhaps not surprising given that Spanish is the most widely spoken HL in the United States, where most of these studies were conducted. However, the remaining two studies (25 percent of the sample) were not on other heritage languages that have been widely written about, such as Russian or Chinese. Rather, they dealt with effects of HL instruction on Inuttitut (Wright et al. 2000) and Korean (Kang 2010). We believe it is likely that studies were conducted on these less commonly spoken and taught heritage languages to showcase the value of language revitalization/maintenance efforts in the local communities where those languages are spoken.

Regarding the instructional context, six of the eight studies (75 percent) were conducted at the university level. This replicates findings of instructed SLA research, which is also predominantly conducted with university students (Norris and Ortega 2000, 2001), likely due to convenience sampling. A small number of studies (two out of thirteen or 15.4 percent) were carried out in elementary schools (Wright et al. 2000; Cuza et al. 2017). Most notably, there were no studies meeting our inclusion criteria conducted in middle schools, high schools, or community schools, calling attention to the dire need for further research at both the K-12 level and in community-initiated school programs such as Saturday schools.

Regarding the target of instruction, five of the eight studies (62.5 percent) focused on a particular feature of morphosyntax (e.g., past tense, subjunctive), whereas the remainder focused on aspects of reading, writing, and literacy. Specifically, one study (Bowles and Bello Uriarte 2019) examined gains in linguistic complexity, accuracy, and fluency of writing as a result of heritage instruction in Spanish, and the remaining two focused on vocabulary and literacy gains in elementary school children (Spanish heritage learners in Cuza et al. 2017 and Inuttitut heritage learners in Wright et al. 2000). That is, although there is some emphasis on not just morphosyntax but also on lexical development, at least in these studies, gains in other aspects, such as pragmatic competence, are left completely unaddressed. (Our bibliographic search did identify one study that examined the effects of instruction on HL pragmatic competence (Barros García and Bachelor 2018) but it was excluded from the meta-analysis because it lacked a control group.)

Finally, just five of the eight studies (62.5 percent) contained any kind of delayed post-test to measure the extent to which learning gains as a result of instruction were durable. This echoes findings of early meta-analyses in instructed SLA, where a similar pattern was discovered (Norris and Ortega 2000, 2001). Although longer delays between immediate and delayed post-tests are generally considered better than shorter delays, even results of a delayed post-test conducted just a week or two after instruction would provide some insight into whether effects are transient or longer lasting. Furthermore, it has been attested that learning gains sometimes continue to be made after the instruction has ended and the immediate post-test has taken place (e.g., Morgan-Short, Finger, Grey, and Ullman 2012). Without a delayed post-test, it is impossible to determine to what extent learning gains are maintained across time.

In order to answer our first research question, which asked about the overall effects of HL instruction, we combined the effect sizes of all forty-six experimental-control comparisons reported in the eight unique sample studies meeting our inclusion criteria (see forest plot in Figure 32.1). Heritage speakers are known for their heterogeneity, and our results underscore this fact, since the variance in each study caused the 95 percent confidence intervals around each effect size to be large. Our grand weighted mean effect size is $d = 0.57$, with the 95 percent confidence interval ranging from $d = 0.40$ to 0.74, indicating that overall, HL instruction has a medium-sized, positive impact on learning outcomes. Notably, confidence intervals for effect sizes overlapped zero in twenty-six of the forty-six effect size calculations (56.5 percent), which indicates that there is high variability. It is also important to note that there were some negative effect sizes, likely for a few different reasons. For instance, some treatments showed gains in one type of assessment but not in others. In Potowski et al. (2009), the traditional instruction group performed worse than the uninstructed controls in using the target structure on two measures, listening and a written grammaticality judgment task, but outperformed controls on written production. In Bowles and Bello Uriarte (2019), instructed Spanish heritage learners outperformed uninstructed controls on five out of six measures of linguistic complexity, accuracy, and fluency, but underperformed them on one measure, lexical diversity. The authors attribute this to trade-off effects (e.g., Skehan 2009), a common occurrence whereby gains in one area are accompanied by losses in another. These findings highlight the importance of having multiple measures and would have been obscured if we had chosen to have only one effect size from each study.

With that primary research question answered, we move on to examining the effects of moderator variables, to determine what impact learner characteristics (language of instruction, proficiency, age, instructional setting), instruction characteristics (type, target, and duration of instruction), and outcome measures have on instructed heritage learning.

32.3.1 Language of Instruction

Spanish was the only language represented by more than one study, and the twenty-eight experimental group-control comparisons resulted in a grand mean effect size of $d = 0.33$, with the 95 percent confidence interval ranging between 0.16 and 0.51. For Spanish, then, there was a small effect size for instruction that is slightly smaller than the average across all studies in all languages. Given that there are just two studies in languages other than Spanish (Korean in Kang 2010 and Inuttitut in Wright et al. 2000) it is not possible to determine whether the larger effect sizes observed in them are related to the language per se or to other variables, and this finding should be interpreted with caution.

32.3.2 Age/Setting

As indicated previously, studies that met the inclusion criteria were either conducted in elementary schools or at the college level, so there is a clear divide between studies involving children and those involving adults. The elementary school studies, Cuza et al. (2017) and Wright et al. (2000), contributed sixteen effect sizes to our calculations, yielding a medium weighted mean effect size of $d = 0.79$, with the 95 percent confidence interval ranging from 0.49 to 1.09. By comparison, the university-level studies contributed thirty effect sizes to our calculations, yielding a small-sized weighted mean effect size of $d = 0.42$, with the 95 percent confidence interval ranging from 0.25 to 0.60. This result indicates that HL instruction is more effective with younger, elementary-school aged learners than it is with adult college-aged heritage learners.

32.3.3 Proficiency

We next sought to determine whether HL instruction is more or less effective depending on the starting proficiency level in the language. In this case, differences in the way that proficiency was measured and frequent use of self-assessments or in-house placement tests as the only evaluation of proficiency meant it was not possible to objectively determine the proficiency level of learners in most studies. Therefore, we were unable to do further analysis to determine what impact proficiency may have on efficacy of instruction, and this is an open question that future research will need to address.

32.3.4 Type of Instruction

When we first coded for type of instruction, we used Norris and Ortega's broad categories of *explicit* and *implicit* instruction. However, we found that for the two elementary studies it was difficult to classify the instruction in this binary way, since there were elements of both present. We therefore added a third category, *language arts*, which we believe better captures the way that heritage languages were taught in those studies. There were twenty-two effect sizes containing explicit instruction, and these displayed less heterogeneity, with I^2, a measure of variance not explained by sampling differences, at just 32.8 percent and a Q statistic of $p > 0.05$. These values indicate that the findings across the explicit instruction studies are fairly consistent, and the weighted mean effect was small in size ($d = 0.35$), with the 95 percent confidence interval ranging from 0.18 to 0.52.

In comparison, there were eight effect size calculations involving implicit instruction, but the I^2 statistic indicated that 74 percent of the variance among studies came from something other than sampling error and the Q statistic of $p < 0.05$ indicated that the findings were not consistent. Closer analysis revealed that the simple group in Torres (2018) was an outlier and once it was removed, the I^2 dropped to 32.6 percent and the Q statistic increased above 0.05, showing that the studies could reliably be combined. This resulted in a weighted mean effect size of $d = 0.44$ for implicit instruction, another small effect. However, the 95 percent confidence interval in this case ranges from -0.11 to 0.99, showing that implicit instruction may not have as consistent an effect across participants as explicit instruction does. In other words, it works well for some and less well for others, a pattern that has also been observed in instructed SLA studies (e.g., VanPatten et al. 2013).

Moving on to our third type of instruction, language arts, there were sixteen effect sizes gathered from two studies (Wright et al. 2000; Cuza et al. 2017) with a medium mean effect size of $d = 0.79$, and the lower confidence interval being 0.49 with the upper one being 1.09. This finding suggests that language arts instruction has a larger effect on heritage learners than either explicit or implicit instruction, although it is not possible to tease apart the impact of age on this result, since the only language arts studies were conducted with elementary school-age children.

32.3.5 Focus of Instruction

Regarding focus of instruction, twenty-four effect sizes came from experimental-control comparisons related to specific aspects of morphosyntax (e.g., past tense in Kang 2010 and subjunctive in Torres 2018). For these, the weighted mean effect size was $d = 0.49$, with the 95 percent confidence interval ranging from 0.28 to 0.70. This again represents a small-sized effect of instruction on specific morphosyntactic targets. The remaining twenty-two effect sizes came from studies involving instruction on reading, writing, and/or literacy, and these had a slightly higher weighted mean effect size of $d = 0.63$, with the 95 percent confidence intervals ranging from 0.38 to 0.88. Given that reading and writing tend to be heritage learners' weakest skills, the medium effect size could potentially be attributed to more room for growth in this area, or it could be indicative that reading, writing, and literacy instruction have a bigger impact on heritage learners than does instruction on particular grammatical features.

32.3.6 Duration of Instruction

We initially attempted to code our data for duration of instruction using Norris and Ortega's (2000, 2001) criteria, which are based on number of hours of instruction per week, the longest duration being 7 or more hours. However, duration was not often quantified so precisely in our sample and was frequently reported in number of weeks, months or, in some cases, years (Wright et al. 2000). We therefore modified our coding to reflect this difference and considered studies to be short in duration if they lasted less than 4 weeks, or long if they lasted more than 4 weeks. Short duration comparisons (k = 18) had a mean effect size of d = 0.40, with the 95 percent confidence interval going from 0.16 to 0.64. Long duration comparisons (k = 28) had a larger mean effect size of d = 0.66, with the 95 percent confidence interval ranging from 0.45 to 0.88. That is, longer periods of instruction result in slightly greater learning outcomes.

32.3.7 Outcome Measures

A central question in any language acquisition research is what type of outcome measure to use to assess language knowledge or learning gains. Given the variability that occurs across different types of tests, we examined outcome measures in more detail. First, we grouped together comparisons that involved receptive knowledge measures (tests that do not require participants to produce spoken or written input, k = 20). The average effect size on receptive tests was d = 0.39, with the 95 percent confidence interval ranging from 0.11 to 0.68. Then we grouped together comparisons that involved free production (e.g., spoken or written production based on a prompt, k = 12). This resulted in a mean effect size of d = 0.61, with the 95 percent confidence interval ranging from 0.28 to 0.95. In comparison, performance on constrained production (e.g., elicited imitation and cloze activities, k =19, was even higher, reaching a mean of d = 0.71, with the lower confidence interval at 0.42 and the upper one at 0.99). Therefore, it appears that heritage language gains are largest on constrained production, followed by free production, and then are smallest on tests that measure receptive language use.

32.4 Discussion

In this section, we provide a brief summary of the major results. Due to the interest in meeting the pedagogical needs of HL learners, the aim of the current chapter was to report the results of an exploratory meta-analysis that examined the effects of instruction on HL development. Our first research question asked how effective instruction is on HL learning outcomes. The findings from eight unique pedagogical intervention studies that contributed forty-six effect sizes to our data analysis revealed an overall medium effect size ($d = 0.57$). As such, based on these preliminary studies on instructed HL acquisition, the magnitude of instruction on HL development is moderate. In contrast to Norris and Ortega (2000), who found an overall large effect ($d = 0.96$) for the impact of instruction on L2 outcomes, this finding implies that instruction may have a lesser effect on HL learners. However, more IHLA empirical studies are needed to confirm this trend. Future IHLA studies can compare their experimental groups' magnitude of effect to the range reported here to gain a more reliable picture of the effects of instruction on HL learners. If the effects of instruction are indeed moderate in comparison to L2 learners, it will be critical for researchers to explain how HL learners' early bilingual experience attenuates the impact of instruction. This will also require a theoretical model(s) that can explain and make predictions about HL learners' linguistic development and takes into account the role of instruction.

The IHLA field must also consider whether certain types of instruction are overall more effective than others for HL learning, as the studies mentioned previously employed different pedagogical interventions in their research designs (e.g., processing instruction, feedback, task complexity). For example, Shintani and colleagues' (2013) meta-analysis found that processing instruction was more effective in the development of L2 receptive knowledge compared to non-processing instruction treatments. As such, future studies can contribute to the strands within IHLA studies to gain a more comprehensive picture of the effects of different types of instruction.

The second research question was concerned with the relationship between HL instruction and moderator variables that related to learner and instruction characteristics as well as outcome measures. In what follows, we summarize major observable trends from the results. We found that instruction had the largest effect on elementary school children's HL development through language arts intervention ($d = 0.79$). This finding indicates that children may benefit more from instruction than adult HL learners, especially in school contexts where their HL is supported (e.g., dual immersion schools). One issue, however, is that the outcome measures were not testing particular vulnerable morphosyntactic structures during HL acquisition, but overall proficiency and literacy. In fact, our findings also revealed that instruction was slightly more effective for the development of literacy skills rather than specific morphosyntactic structures. As such, future studies ought to shed more light on whether both HL children and adults benefit more when the instruction is focused on literacy skills.

In examining type of instruction, we also found that language arts instruction was largely more effective ($d = 0.79$) than explicit and implicit pedagogical interventions. However, future studies need to investigate whether HL adults would enjoy the same benefits from a language arts approach as HL bilingual children. While effect sizes were small for the effects of explicit and implicit instruction, the magnitude for implicit instruction was slightly higher, but the wide range of the 95 percent confidence intervals indicated that this was a highly inconsistent finding, whereas the magnitude of the effect for explicit instruction, albeit smaller, was more consistent. These results differ significantly from Norris and Ortega's (2000) findings, as explicit instruction was largely more beneficial (d = 1.13) to L2 outcomes. That is, pedagogical interventions with some sort of metalinguistic information on how the language works do not confer the same degree of benefits to HL learners. Therefore, more research needs to tackle this issue more in depth to understand better whether and to what degree HL learners do or do not make use of the explicit knowledge they gain from explicit instruction.

As far as outcome measures, the findings pointed out that instruction had a bigger impact on participants' performance on constrained production assessments such as an elicited imitation task (d = 0.71), but only small magnitude effects for both free production and receptive tests. The magnitude of effect for constrained production tests falls within the range (0.38 and 0.91) found in Norris and Ortega (2000), who reported that most of their primary studies utilized constrained production measures to examine L2 development. This finding, however, does not align with meta-analyses in which L2 learners demonstrated greater gains in receptive tests (e.g., Shintani et al. 2013).

In sum, the goal of this exploratory quantitative meta-analysis was to provide a comprehensive picture of how instruction impacts HL learning outcomes, based on the published studies to date. However, these results should not be viewed as conclusive, and must be taken with caution. For instance, in this chapter, we did not include unpublished dissertations that investigated HL outcomes. As such, these results may be due to a publication bias. We plan to include unpublished dissertations as part of a future follow-up meta-analysis. Nevertheless, based on these preliminary findings, future primary studies on HL instruction can frame their discussions accordingly. Also, we hope that the findings motivate more focused inquiries with regard to the issues at stake within IHLA.

32.5 Recommendations for Future Research

We would like to conclude the chapter with a few critical recommendations for future research with the aim of improving study designs, reporting practices, and research productivity in the field. These recommendations are not exhaustive, and researchers should pay careful attention to the design of their studies (for helpful guides to research designs, see Mackey and Gass 2012a, 2012b; Phakiti, De Costa, Plonsky, and Starfield 2018, among others). Our recommendations stem from our coding of the entire set of eighteen primary studies initially identified and current directions in the field of instructed SLA.

1. Control group. A few of the studies were eliminated because the study design did not include a control group that was not exposed to the pedagogical intervention(s). The inclusion of a control group is pivotal to understanding the effects of such interventions.

2. Descriptive statistics. We urge researchers to report descriptive statistics, which should include the following at minimum: mean, standard deviations, sample size, power, and effect sizes. Also, ideally, researchers should conduct an *a priori* power analysis to estimate the needed sample size of participants to reach adequate power (www.danielsoper .com/statcalc).

3. Reliability measures. To echo Norris and Ortega (2000), reporting the reliability of assessment instruments is needed to understand "the extent to which measurement error has contributed to overall error of observation and interpretation within the domain" (485).

4. Proficiency. We were unable to examine proficiency as a moderator because the measures were difficult to compare. As such, researchers should include objective standardized tests to complement participants' self-assessments. The "Research and Proficiency Assessment Tools" page available through the National Heritage Language Resource Center website (www.nhlr.ucla.edu) has a few sample standardized tests to measure proficiency.

5. Replication studies. It is difficult to make generalizations based on these studies because of small sample sizes (see #2 for *a priori* power analysis) and because most of the studies were conducted with HL learners of Spanish. One way to address this issue in the field is through replication studies – both direct and conceptual (see Marsden, Morgan-Short, Thompson, and Abugaber 2018 for further discussion in L2 research). Direct replications imply that there are no significant alterations to the original study, and the goal is to provide new data to add to the existing data. To accomplish this goal, researchers are encouraged to make their research materials (e.g., experimental tasks, assessments) available to other researchers to use. HL researchers can contribute to the digital repository available through the National Heritage Language Resource Center under "Research and Proficiency Assessment Tools" on the front page of the website. Further, IRIS (www.iris-database.org), a larger digital repository for second language research instruments, can also serve this purpose, particularly in research that includes both L2 and HL groups. Conceptual replications, on the other hand, allow for significant

alterations to the original study to examine the effects of instruction in a different context (e.g., a different population of HL learners), for example, when appropriate, experimental tasks or treatments can be translated from Spanish to Korean to observe key similarities between HL learners across both languages. Researchers should consult guides that address issues regarding replication studies (e.g., Porte and McManus 2019).

6. Multi-site collaborations. Another alternative to address the small sample size issue is for researchers to collaborate across institutions to gather a larger pool of participants (e.g., Morgan-Short et al. 2018). Multi-site collaborations can work in a few different ways. One is that researchers can collaborate across institutions to examine the same language(s) within a single sociopolitical context, for example, examining the effects of corrective feedback on the development of the Russian case system with HL learners of Russian in the United States. A second possibility is conducting multi-site studies with the same language(s) across different sociopolitical contexts such as examining HL learners of Russian in the United States and in the United Kingdom. Further, a third possibility can be examining different language pairs such as Russian with English in the United States and Russian with Hebrew in Israel.

7. Open Science. A recent call in the field of instructed SLA is for researchers to make their data available for other researchers in the same domain. This would allow for direct replication studies to conduct a more solid analysis by converging new and existing data from the original study. This approach certainly calls for some careful planning and procedures, but it is a new trend in the sciences (see Marsden and Plonsky 2018).

References

Allen, M. 2017. Vote Counting Literature Review Methods. In M. Allen (ed.), *The SAGE Encyclopedia of Communication Research Methods*, Vol. 4. Thousand Oaks, CA: SAGE Publications, Inc. 1868–1870.

Barros García, M. J. and J. W. Bachelor. 2018. Pragmatic Instruction May Not Be Necessary among Heritage Learners of Spanish: A Study on Requests. *Journal of Foreign Language Education and Technology* 3(1), 163–193.

Beaudrie, S. and B. Holmes. In press. The Differential Effects of Three Types of Explicit Computer-Based Grammar Instruction: The Case of Receptive Heritage Learners. In M. A. Bowles (ed.), *Outcomes of University Spanish Heritage Language Instruction in the United States*. Washington, DC: Georgetown University Press.

Beaudrie, S., C. Ducar, and K. Potowski. 2014. *Heritage Language Teaching: Research and Practice*. Columbus, OH: McGraw-Hill.

Bowles, M. 2018. Outcomes of Classroom Spanish Heritage Language Acquisition: State of the Field and an Agenda for the Future. In K. Potowski (ed.), *The Routledge Handbook of Spanish as a Heritage/Minority Language*. New York: Routledge Press, 331–344.

Bowles, M. In press. *Outcomes of University Spanish Heritage Language Instruction in the United States*. Washington, DC: Georgetown University Press

Bowles, M. and A. Bello Uriarte. 2019. What Impact Does Heritage Language Instruction Have on Spanish Heritage Learners' Writing? In M. Sato and S. Loewen (eds.), *Evidence-Based Second Language Pedagogy: A Collection of Instructed Second Language Acquisition Studies*. New York: Routledge.

Fernández, S. and M. Bowles. In press. What Type of Knowledge Do Implicit and Explicit Heritage Language Instruction Result in? In M. A. Bowles (ed.), *Outcomes of University Spanish Heritage Language Instruction in the United States*. Washington, DC: Georgetown University Press.

Bylund, E. and M. Díaz. 2012. The Effects of Heritage Language Instruction on First Language Proficiency: A Psycholinguistic Perspective. *International Journal of Bilingual Education and Bilingualism* 15(5), 593–609.

Carreira, M. and O. Kagan. 2018. Heritage Language Education: A Proposal for the Next 50 Years. *Foreign Language Annals* 51(1), 152–168.

Chinen, K. and G. R. Tucker. 2005. Heritage Language Development: Understanding the Roles of Ethnic Identity and Saturday School Participation. *Heritage Language Journal* 3(1), 27–59.

Chiu, Y. H. 2013. Computer-Assisted Second Language Vocabulary Instruction: A Meta-Analysis. *British Journal of Educational Technology* 44 (2), 52–56.

Cuza, A., L. Miller, A. Pasquarella, and X. Chen. 2017. The Role of Instruction in the Development of Reading and Writing Skills in Spanish as a Heritage Language during Childhood. *Heritage Language Journal* 14(2), 100–123.

Hedges, L. and I. Olkin. 1980. Vote-Counting Methods in Research Synthesis. *Psychological Bulletin* 88(2), 359–369.

Hedges, L., J. Shymansky, and G. Woodworth. 1989. *A Practical Guide to Modern Methods of Meta-analysis*. Washington, DC: National Science Teachers Association.

Jeon, E. H. and T. Kaya. 2006. Effects of L2 Instruction on Interlanguage Pragmatic Development. In J. M. Norris and L. Ortega (eds.), *Synthesizing Research on Language Learning and Teaching*. Amsterdam: John Benjamins, 165–211.

Kang, H. S. 2010. Negative Evidence and Its Explicitness and Positioning in the Learning of Korean as a Heritage Language. *The Modern Language Journal* 94(4), 582–599.

Lee, J., J. Jang, and L. Plonsky. 2014. The Effectiveness of Second Language Pronunciation Instruction: A Meta-analysis. *Applied Linguistics* 36(3), 345–366.

Light, R. and D. Pillemer. 1984. *Summing Up: The Science of Reviewing Research*. Cambridge, MA: Harvard University Press.

Lipsey, M. W. and D. B. Wilson. 2001. *Practical Meta-Analysis*. Thousand Oaks, CA: Sage.

Mackey, A. and S. Gass. 2012a. *Second Language Research: Methodology and Design*. New York: Routledge.

Mackey, A. and S. Gass. 2012b. *Research Methods in Second Language Acquisition: A Practical Guide*. New York: Wiley Blackwell.

Marsden, E. and L. Plonsky. 2018. Data, Open Science, and Methodological Reform in Second Language Acquisition Research. In A. Gudmestad and A. Edmonds (eds.), *Critical Reflections on Data in Second Language Acquisition*. Philadelphia: John Benjamins, 219-228.

Marsden, E., K. Morgan-Short, S. Thompson, and D. Abugaber. 2018. Replication in Second Language Research: Narrative and Systematic Reviews and Recommendations for the Field. *Language Learning* 68, 321–391.

Montrul, S. and M. Bowles. 2010. Is Grammar Instruction Beneficial for Heritage Language Learners? Dative Case Marking in Spanish. *Heritage Language Journal* 7(1), 47–73.

Montrul, S. and M. Bowles. 2017. Instructed Heritage Language Acquisition. In S. Loewen and M. Sato (eds.), *The Routledge Handbook of Instructed Second Language Acquisition*. New York: Routledge Press, 488–502.

Morgan-Short, K., I. Finger, S. Grey, and M. T. Ullman. 2012. Second Language Processing Shows Increased Native-Like Neural Responses after Months of No Exposure. *PLOS One* 7(3), e32974. https://doi.org/10.1371/journal.pone.0032974.

Morgan-Short, K., E. Marsden, J. Heil, B. I. Issa, R. P. Leow, and five authors. 2018. Multisite Replication in Second Language Acquisition Research: Attention to Form during Listening and Reading Comprehension. *Language Learning* 68, 392–437.

Nocus, I., P. Guimard, J. Vernaudon, M. Paia, O. Cosnefroy, and A. Florin. 2012. Effectiveness of a Heritage Educational Program for the Acquisition of Oral and Written French and Tahitian in French Polynesia. *Teaching and Teacher Education* 28, 21–31.

Norris, J. M. and L. Ortega. 2000. Effectiveness of L2 Instruction: A Research Synthesis and Quantitative Meta-Analysis. *Language Learning* 50(3), 417–528.

Norris, J. M. and L. Ortega. 2001. Does Type of Instruction Make a Difference? Substantive Findings from a Meta-Analytic Review. *Language Learning* 51, 157–213.

Parra, M. L., M. Llorente Bravo, and M. Polinsky. 2018. De bueno a muy bueno: How Pedagogical Intervention Boosts Language Proficiency in Advanced Heritage Learners. *Heritage Language Journal* 15(2), 203–241.

Pérez-Núñez, A. 2018. The Acquisition of Spanish Gender Marking in the Writing of Heritage and Second Language Learners: Evidence from the Language Classroom. *Heritage Language Journal* 15(2), 242–267.

Phakiti, A., P. De Costa, L. Plonsky, and S. Starfield. 2018. *The Palgrave Handbook of Applied Linguistics Research Methodology*. London: Palgrave Macmillan.

Plonsky, L. and D. Brown. 2015. Domain Definition and Search Techniques in Meta- analyses of L2 Research (Or Why 18 Meta-analyses of Feedback Have Different Results). *Second Language Research* 31(2), 267–278.

Plonsky, L. and F. L. Oswald. 2012. How to Do a Meta-analysis. In A. Mackey and S. M. Gass (eds.), *Research Methods in Second Language Acquisition: A Practical Guide*. New York: Wiley Blackwell, 275–295.

Plonsky, L. and F. L. Oswald. 2014. How Big Is 'Big'? Interpreting Effect Sizes in L2 Research. *Language Learning* 64, 878–891.

Porte, G. and K. McManus. 2019. *Doing Replication Research in Applied Linguistics*. New York: Routledge.

Potowski, K., J. Jegerski, and K. Morgan-Short. 2009. The Effects of Instruction on Linguistic Development in Spanish Heritage Language Speakers. *Language Learning* 59(3), 537–579.

Pyun, D. O. and A. Lee-Smith. 2011. Reducing Korean Heritage Language Learners' Orthographic Errors: The Contribution of Online and In-Class Dictation and Form- Focused Instruction. *Language, Culture and Curriculum* 24(2), 141–158.

Sanz, C. and J. Torres. 2018. The Prior Language Experience of Heritage Bilinguals. In P. A. Malovrh and A. G. Benati (eds.), *The Handbook of Advanced Proficiency in Second Language Acquisition*. Hoboken, NJ: Wiley Press, 179–198.

Shintani, N., S. Li, and R. Ellis. 2013. Comprehension-Based versus Production-Based Grammar Instruction: A Meta-Analysis of Comparative Studies. *Language Learning* 63(2), 296–329.

Skehan, P. 2009. Modelling Second Language Performance: Integrating Complexity, Accuracy, Fluency, and Lexis. *Applied Linguistics* 30(4), 510–532.

Song, W., W. O'Grady, S. Cho, and M. Lee. 1997. The Learning and Teaching of Korean in Community Schools. *The Korean Language in America* 2, 111–127.

Spada, N. and Y. Tomita. 2010. Interactions between Type of Instruction and Type of Language Feature: A Meta-analysis. *Language Learning* 60(2), 263–308.

Torres, J. 2018. The Effects of Task Complexity on Heritage and L2 Spanish Development. *Canadian Modern Language Review* 74(1), 128–152.

Torres, J., D. Pascual y Cabo, and J. Beusterien. 2017. What's Next? Heritage Language Learners Pave the Path for Spanish Teaching. *Hispania* 100(5), 271–276.

Valdés, G. 2001. Heritage Language Students: Profiles and Possibilities. In J. K. Peyton, D. A. Ranard, and S. McGinnis (eds.), *Heritage Languages in America: Preserving a National Resource*. Washington, DC; McHenry, IL: Center for Applied Linguistics and Delta Systems, 37–80.

VanPatten, B., E. Collopy, J. E. Price, S. Borst, and A. Qualin. 2013. Explicit Information, Grammatical Sensitivity, and the First-Noun Principle: A Cross-Linguistic Study in Processing Instruction. *The Modern Language Journal* 97(2), 506–527.

Wa-Mbaleka, S. 2006. A Meta-analysis Investigating the Effects of Reading on Second Language Vocabulary Learning. Unpublished doctoral dissertation, Northern Arizona University.

Wright, S. C., D. M. Taylor, and J. Macarthur. 2000. Subtractive Bilingualism and the Survival of the Inuit Language: Heritage- versus Second Language Education. *Journal of Educational Psychology* 92(1), 63–84.

Zamora, C. In press. The Secret Is in the Processing: Categorizing How Heritage Learners of Spanish Process. In M. A. Bowles (ed.), *Outcomes of University Spanish Heritage Language Instruction in the United States*. Washington, DC: Georgetown University Press.

Appendix 32.A

Relevant Primary Studies[1]

Barros García and Bachelor (2018)
Beaudrie and Holmes (in press)
Bowles and Bello Uriarte (2019)
Bylund and Díaz (2012)
Chinen and Tucker (2005)
Cuza, Miller, Pasquarella, and Chen (2017)
Fernández and Bowles (in press)
Kang (2010)
Montrul and Bowles (2010)
Nocus, Guimard, Vernaudon, Paia, Cosnefroy, and Florin (2012)
Parra, Llorente Bravo, and Polinksy (2018)
Pérez-Núñez (2018)
Potowski, Jegerski, and Morgan-Short (2009)
Pyun and Lee-Smith (2011)
Song, O'Grady, Cho, and Lee (1997)
Torres (2018)
Wright, Taylor, and Macarthur (2000)
Zamora (in press)

[1] The reader can find the full bibliography for these studies at the end of the Handbook.

Appendix 32.B

Learner Characteristics

I. Participants
- A. *n* size
  1. Total *n*
  2. *n* per cell
- B. How proficiency was defined
  1. Impressionistic judgment
  2. Institutional status (class enrollment)
  3. In-house assessment/placement test
  4. Standardized test (e.g., DELE)
  5. N/A: not assessed/reported
- C. Proficiency level (ACTFL equivalents)
  1. Novice
  2. Intermediate
  3. Advanced
  4. Superior
- D. Language of instruction (heritage language being studied)
- E. Age group
  1. child
  2. adult
- F. Setting
  1. elementary school
  2. middle school
  3. high school
  4. university
  5. community/Saturday school

Research Design

I. Independent variables
    A.   Type of instruction (using definitions from Norris and Ortega 2000, 2001)
        1.   Explicit
        2.   Implicit
        3.   Language arts
    B.   Target of instruction
        1.   Reading/Writing/Literacy
        2.   Specific morphosyntactic structure(s)
        3.   Four skills/broad HL instruction otherwise unspecified
    C.   Duration of instruction
        1.   Short (1–4 weeks)
        2.   Long (More than 4 weeks)
II. Dependent Variables
    A.   Outcome measures (from Norris and Ortega 2000, 2001)
        1.   Receptive
        2.   Productive
            i.   Free constructed
           ii.   Constrained constructed

33

Issues and Practices in Community-Based Experiential Learning for Heritage Speakers in the United States

Paola Guerrero-Rodriguez, Adriana Ojeda,
and Diego Pascual y Cabo

33.1 Introduction

In the context of the United States, early developments within the field of heritage language (HL) education were characterized by the adoption of normative and prescriptive approaches to language teaching that focused on a strict understanding of grammar development (e.g., Fishman 2014; Wiley et al. 2014; Potowski 2018 and references therein). At the time, the emphasis was generally on replacing home language varieties with the more desired (yet arbitrarily chosen) standard versions, and little attention, if any, was paid to relevant cultural, contextual, and affective dimensions (e.g., Train 2003; Leeman 2005; Leeman et al. 2011; Fishman 2014; Wiley et al. 2014; Colombi 2015; Lowther Pereira 2015, 2018; Potowski 2018). Unsurprisingly, the outcomes of such efforts were not always positive, more often than not resulting in a marked deterioration of the relationship between the HL/culture/identity, the individual, and the community (e.g., Fishman 2014; Wiley, et al. 2014; Potowski 2018). This has particularly been the case for Spanish as a HL in the context of the United States (e.g., Valdés 1995, 2001; Villa 2002; Carreira and Beeman 2014), which will be the main focus of this chapter given that most of the literature on community-based experiential service-learning for HL learners consists of studies pertaining to this particular language/community.

Motivated by an increase in holistic awareness of the linguistic, social, cultural, and political challenges that heritage speakers (HSs) generally experience – and fueled by the desire to redress the imbalance observed – our field has continued to develop via the incorporation of transdisciplinary teaching practices, such as sociolinguistically informed curricula, critical language awareness, and critical pedagogies (e.g., Darder 2003; Beaudrie et al. 2014; Fairclough 2014). To be sure, although the nature and the success (or lack thereof) of these approaches has varied over the years, we now have a better idea of not only what to teach but, most importantly, what classroom strategies to use and what educational approaches to embrace (Train 2003; Leeman 2005; Colombi 2015; Lowther Pereira 2015, 2018). For example, we now know that the focus should not be limited to language and its conventions (e.g., Beaudrie et al. 2014). Beyond language, therefore, a key issue in the field of HL education is to ascertain which practices will most effectively address the HSs' socio-affective needs and those of their communities. In this regard, recent scholarship has under-scored the important roles that speakers' and communities' identities, attitudes, and motivations play in said linguistic and personal development (e.g., Beaudrie and Ducar 2005; Ducar 2012; Potowski 2012). To work toward this end, the focus of HL education seems to be shifting toward including areas that support a general development of critical consciousness on social justice, a fortification of a sense of community, the empowerment of oppressed groups, and civic responsibility (e.g., Beaudrie and Fairclough 2012; Fairclough and Beaudrie, 2016; Pascual y Cabo 2016; Potowski 2018). As we see it, the incorporation of these areas within and beyond the HL classroom walls is of great importance to students, as this can further aid in the understanding of their own and others' lived experiences as they relate to (heritage) language use in minoritized contexts. In this regard, one pedagogical model that has recently drawn significant attention, and that has the potential to achieve this overarching goal, is that of community-based service learning (e.g., Leeman et al. 2011; Pascual y Cabo et al. 2017; Lowther Pereira 2018). It is to a description of this model and its multiple applications to HL teaching that we turn next.

33.2 Understanding Community-Based Service Learning (CSL)

CSL can be generally understood as an engaging educational model that combines strategies for reciprocally achieving academic learning objectives and community objectives. It provides students with relevant learning experiences in which they can link theory to practice and apply classroom-developed knowledge to real-life problems beyond the classroom (e.g., Sheffield 2005; Bandy 2016).

In this chapter, we identify three main underpinnings. First, because CSL integrates community service with formal academic instruction, it requires commitment from both the educational institutions and community partners in order to achieve the mutually beneficial exchange of knowledge and resources (e.g., Saltmarsh and Driscoll 2012). Second, the notion of service in CSL should be critically understood by all participants, not be seen as simply a form of volunteering, social/political activism, or free work, but rather as a valuable learning experience that (reciprocally) meets community needs while mutually providing meaningful tasks for students. Third, students' reflections of their CSL experiences play a key role in their process of learning. Through these reflections (whether they are long essays, short journal entries, in-class presentations, or otherwise), students engage in active thinking and examine their own understanding of the issues at hand. Not only does this sort of exploration support the overall learning experience but it also enriches and maximizes it (e.g., Bringle and Hatcher 2003).

If executed appropriately, CSL may yield significant benefits for everyone involved. For example, in addition to improving career development in different areas (i.e., translation and interpretation, social work), CSL students often report experiencing an enhanced sense of engagement and connection with the community, increased civic responsibility, as well as a greater sense of personal efficacy, personal identity, and moral development. (e.g., Eyler and Giles 1999; Astin, Vogelgesang, Ikeda, and Yee 2000; Bandy 2016). Socially, the kind of involvement with the community that CSL encourages usually translates into an increased understanding of intercultural differences, which in turn may also be conducive to reducing stereotypes (e.g., Bandy 2016). Academic institutions also benefit from (and contribute to) a stronger relationship with the community (e.g., Bandy 2016) with all the potential direct and indirect benefits that may ensue reciprocally (i.e., economic, social, cultural, etc.). The community itself also benefits from this relationship in a variety of ways. Not only are students perceived as valuable human resources but their new perspectives, energy, and enthusiasm are sometimes key to achieving the desired community goals (e.g., Bandy 2016). But unbalanced goals between students and community partners may ultimately become CSL's greatest risks. For example, as Mitchell (2008), Stoecker (2016), and many others have pointed out, CSL students driven only by the desire to achieve professional goals may end up not paying enough attention to the needs of the community partner, thus reinforcing undesirable social hierarchies.

To date, CSL has mostly been used in institutions of higher education in social service courses that prepare students for citizenship, social work, health services, marketing, and democracy participation. It was not until the 1990s that CSL started to be implemented in the field of language education. Since then, however, the number of language courses with a CSL designation has increased exponentially. One catalyst for such expansion was the publication of the (2007) report of the MLA *Ad Hoc Committee on Foreign Languages*. Details aside, the MLA report emphasized three main goals: (1) personal and social responsibility, (2) civic knowledge and engagement, and (3) intercultural knowledge. Given its philosophical foundation, CSL was soon identified as an appropriate vehicle to address MLA's goals. Important changes have taken place since then. And while an important body of literature testifies to the effects of service-learning in language education, most CSL studies related to language have focused on its impact in traditional second language learners. General findings highlight its positive impact on students' linguistic skills and increased social consciousness (e.g., Kaplan and Pérez Gamboa 2003; Taylor and Ballengee-Morris 2004; Tapia 2010; Kanost 2014). Little empirical research has examined the implementation of CSL for heritage languages (e.g., Kim and Sohn 2016).

From this brief backstory of CSL, in the next section we delve into some of the specific cases and outcomes of CSL programs applied largely for (heritage) language purposes.

33.3 Community-Based Service Learning and Heritage Languages

Although not originally intended as an HL teaching model per se, CSL's clear focus on social justice, civic responsibility, and community growth makes this a very appealing resource to the HL teaching and learning community. Through well-designed and well-implemented CSL curricula, HSs can gain a fresh perspective on their own lived experiences and those of the communities in which they live. Additionally, when combined with instructional practices that promote critical language awareness and critical pedagogies, HSs can better understand how language works as a tool to manipulate power and social hierarchies in ways that extend far beyond that which traditional classroom settings can offer (e.g., Leeman et al. 2011; Pascual y Cabo et al. 2017; Lowther Pereira 2018). In this way, HSs can invest in their personal (and their communities') development while becoming agents of change (e.g., Leeman 2018).

Although there are multiple findings reported in the CSL literature that could be examined herein, space limitations would not allow us to do justice to all of them. Our focus will therefore be on four main outcomes; namely, combat against stigmatization and linguistic discrimination, identity, sense of belonging, and self-efficacy.

33.3.1 Combat Cultural and Linguistic Discrimination and Promote Language Maintenance

As a whole, the field of HL education is one that challenges status quo linguistic, social, economic, and political hierarchies (e.g., Potowski 2018). It examines and attempts to understand the HS experience from perspectives other than the mainstream. And because HLs are usually subordinated to standard and hegemonic biases, a recurrent experience for most HL learners (regardless of the language examined) is that of linguistic stigmatization and discrimination (e.g., Carreira and Beeman 2014; Potowski 2018). Although this broad topic is generally discussed in the HL class (or at least ought to be), through community-based work, HL learners can achieve a deeper understanding of the role that minoritized languages and cultures may play at the intersections between privilege and oppression, power and opportunities, vulnerability and resilience (Train 2003; Lowther Pereira 2015, 2018; Leeman 2018).

For example, Uehara and Raatior (2016) describe a paid internship CSL program carried out at the University of Hawai'i at Hilo, where (Pacific Islander) heritage and English languages intersect. This particular program offered a different point of view into the complexities of language, culture, and identity for these Pacific Islander students since they have to navigate the American educational system as English Second Language Learners. As part of the CSL experience, students were paired up with different community partners around the nearby islands to work on identity formation, interpersonal communication skills, and overall confidence using their bilingual abilities in different professional contexts. After analyzing data collected via focus groups and individual interviews, Uehara and Raatior (2016) reported significant benefits both to students and to community partners, all emphasizing the role that the students' bi/multilingualism plays in school and self-efficacy. According to Uehara and Raatior (2016), as a result of this experience, a majority of students went from making efforts to avoid speaking in class for fear of ridicule and being perceived as inferior as a result of their accents, to reevaluating their place in American society, reaffirming their identities, and advocating for their communities.

Other alternative means of support that help combat social, cultural, and linguistic discrimination can be found through community-strengthening and empowering initiatives. One particularly illustrative example is the *Oral Narratives of Latin@s in Ohio*, a CSL initiative designed to connect Spanish college-age students with members of the Hispanic community in Ohio to create an oral history project through video recorded interviews (Foulis 2018). In addition to practicing their language skills, through these interviews, students have the opportunity to learn firsthand about the social, linguistic, institutional, and physical barriers often experienced by members of the Latin@ community, an important experience since, as

Foulis (2018) puts it, "our understanding of structural and systematic inequalities is never separate from those who are affected by them" (120–121). The open-access virtual repository currently includes dozens of carefully edited interviews representing a wide range of experiences, which ultimately seek to facilitate and encourage a mutual understanding of other cultures and raise awareness about community activism and involvement (Foulis 2018).

Despite these success stories, effective integration of academic (and non-academic) CSL efforts for minority HL maintenance is challenging and difficult to achieve. For example, in a chapter entitled *The Rediscovery of Heritage and Community Language Education in the United States*, Lee and Wright (2014) note that although some of the HL communities found throughout the United States provide unofficial language instruction for HS children and young adults in non-academic locales such as religious institutions (e.g., mosques, synagogues, temples, churches), public buildings, or in private homes, these classes are generally not recognized as legitimate sources of academic credit, and those enrolled are not able to gain recognition of fluency in the language, even after having attended classes for many years. Due to the unofficial nature of these programs, HSs are sometimes left feeling that the classes are burdensome and a waste of time. Further yet, some HSs have reported feeling like they are some form of punishment because they are often held on weekends (Lee and Wright 2014). The authors argue that many needs – such as the needs for more widespread recognition, teaching materials, resources, and instructors – must be addressed in order for community-based HL programs like these to continue to exist. CSL, through local academic institutions' HL curricula (or even L2 language classes), can be a large part of the missing piece for these programs. Through CSL, students attending local colleges and universities can step in to meet the needs for instruction, materials, and resources. Because CSL would be administered through these local institutions, recognition and awareness would ideally follow the actions of their students.

In their efforts to paint a realistic picture, Lee and Wright (2014) go on to provide a comparison of Korean and Khmer community-based service learning programs in the United Services. While both the Korean and Khmer communities provide HL education programs for their communities, the resources available to them are widely dissimilar. In comparison to the Korean-American community, which is one of the largest Asian communities in the United States, the Khmer-American community has far fewer resources at their disposal – both economic and human. In regards to the Korean-American community, there is support for language programs at the national level as well as support provided by the Korean government itself; additionally, both robust networks for Korean language teachers as well as varied materials and exams exist. On the other hand, no governmental support, widespread language-teaching materials, or standardized exam systems yet exist for the Khmer community to the extent to which they do for the Korean community. Despite this imbalance in resources available to both communities, the efforts to provide community-based service learning programs for the Korean and Khmer-American communities are equally vigorous. Both communities see the preservation of language as an essential piece in the maintenance of their identity; there is a pressing feeling of need to pass on the heritage language – and thus, identity – to future generations. As we see it, this comparison between Korean and Khmer-American communities shows that while there may be differences in the realities and resources available to the communities and their languages in the context of the United States, the underlying motivational factors for preservation and maintenance remain strong.

33.3.2 Sense of Belonging

A commonplace finding in the literature is that HSs often report feeling alienated and devalued not only as legitimate speakers of the HL (e.g., Potowski 2018), but also as members of the academic community more generally (e.g., Strayhorn 2012; Carreira and Beeman 2014; Prada and Pascual y Cabo forthcoming). This points to a need for programs or educational practices that can be put into place to help strengthen a sense of belonging for HSs – a sense of belonging to their heritage communities and their linguistic identities.

In institutions of higher education, for example, in addition to the typical challenges that most adult college students experience, HSs are faced with additional stressors that are unique to them, such as stereotyping and discrimination (e.g., Prada and Pascual y Cabo forthcoming). These feelings may arise and intensify due to inadequate support (e.g., Hurtado and Ponjuan 2005; Pak 2018), which in turn often results in poor personal and academic performance (e.g., Prada and Pascual y Cabo forthcoming). Hence, by providing educational experiences that offer the necessary cultural, social, and academic support, institutions of higher education can contribute to the sense of belonging of HL learners (e.g., Strayhorn 2012), which can further aid in their retention and overall academic success (e.g., Hurtado and Carter 1997; Hausmann et al. 2007; Strayhorn 2008, 2012). This particular idea was the point of departure for Prada and Pascual y Cabo forthcoming, who examined the effects that a sociolinguistically informed Spanish HL program with a strong CSL component has on Spanish HSs' college retention and graduation rates. As part of the CSL component, HL learners were asked to participate in a local after-school Spanish literacy program in which they were paired with Elementary school HSs. Adult and child HSs met twice a week for 10 weeks to work on their Spanish language skills as well as on their identity formation. As part of the study, Prada and Pascual y Cabo compared one- and two-year retention rates of Hispanic students taking at least one Spanish HL class to those of Hispanic students who did not take Spanish HL classes. They predicted that, given the Spanish HL class focus on community building, social justice, identity formation, and cross-cultural sensitivity – which are factors that have been found to affect students' sense of inclusion and belonging – Spanish HL students would reap important personal benefits and academic success. Their findings supported their original prediction, since those students who had taken at least one Spanish HL course displayed higher rates of intentions to persist to degree completion than those who had not. Importantly, in addition to improving HSs' graduation and retention rates, a fostering of HLs' sense of belonging will provide the aforementioned support that these students and future generations of students may feel is lacking.

Recent scholarship has also focused on the extent to which CSL programs lead to a stronger sense of community – and thus a sense of belonging. For example, Pak (2018) observed sixteen Spanish HL learners who were enrolled in a Spanish class for HSs and became involved in a CSL project that spanned the course of a semester. Through a local preparatory program for low income families known as Head Start, students were paired up as tutors with parents who expressed interest in receiving tutoring aid. The tutoring provided by students included preparation for General Educational Development (GED), English conversation skills for specific situations, school-related help for the children, and basic computer skills. Apart from meeting with the parents to complete the tutoring sessions, the university students also completed self-reflective surveys and writing assignments regarding their experiences. After these responses from students were analyzed for naturally emergent themes and patterns throughout, it became evident that the CSL experience proved extremely beneficial for the students. Pak (2018) found that the program allowed students to connect with their sociocultural reality, to feel that they were valued, to develop skills and confidence, and also to strengthen their interest in community engagement. One student, for example, stated the following: "*Gracias a Dios nosotros tuvimos una linda experiencia que al final del proyecto nos sentíamos como familia … Cuando uno es la minoría en un lugar, es bueno ayudarse.*" [Thank God that we had a nice experience; at the end of the project, we felt like a family … When one is a minority in a place, it is good to help each other.] (Pak 2018: 85). Another student mentioned: "*[E]sta experiencia me hizo sentir como si fuera parte de una comunidad, algo que realmente no he sentido antes.*" [This experience has made me feel as if I were a part of community, something that I have not felt before.] (Pak 2018: 85). Through these findings, Pak (2018) argued that CSL can be used to provide opportunities to bring students together and to foster a climate for them to feel connected to a larger community at institutions where there may not otherwise be means of support.

33.3.3 Identity

Apart from providing a sense of belonging, CSL can also be a tool through which HSs regain or fortify their own sense of *identity*. In the context of the United States, recent critical approaches toward HL education have taken strides in finding ways to positively reinforce HSs' identity (e.g., Martínez 2003; Leeman 2005; Trujillo 2009). In this regard, participation in extra- and/or cross-curricular academic experiences that are both culturally and ethno-linguistically sensitive create relevant connections between home and school affirming the HL students' backgrounds and identities, thus making under-represented minority students feel valued and empowered (e.g., Beaudrie, Ducar and Relaño-Pastor 2009; Beaudrie et al. 2014). But the benefits of CSL go beyond identity formation; it provides them with the opportunity to become more critically aware of and in-touch with the political, racial, and power struggles met by members of their own communities. It is through this reinforcement and through these critical experiences that HSs can develop their sense of identity to exert changes in the community (e.g., Leeman 2018). Two ways in which CSL can facilitate social, cultural, and linguistic changes in the community are presented in Leeman, Rabin, and Román-Mendoza (2011) and Pascual y Cabo, Prada, and Lowther Pereira (2017). In their seminal study, Leeman and colleagues (2011) detail the action research done through implementation of community-based experiential service learning for university-level students to teach Spanish as an HL (i.e., language and literacy) to children at a local elementary school. This experience allowed the university-level HL learners an opportunity to directly work with their community while maintaining and developing their own HL. Semi-structured interviews with these students showed that this CSL initiative led to an increase in their awareness of historical and systematic oppression of HSs in the United States. The students not only saw positive effects on their own perceptions and identities but could also foresee there being positive effects on the identities and experiences of other HSs through future iterations of this kind of educational program. Years later, Pascual y Cabo, Prada, and Lowther Pereira (2017) conducted a similar study examining the effects of an after-school Spanish program at a local elementary school. Like Leeman, Rabin, and Román-Mendoza (2011), Pascual y Cabo et al. (2017) designed a CSL curriculum that facilitated direct contact hours between HS children and adults. In addition to documenting many of the findings reported in Leeman et al. (2011), Pascual y Cabo et al. (2017) noted that the

CSL experience provided opportunities for current and future generations that may not have existed previously, allowing HL learners the chance to use their HL under novel and diverse circumstances; to realize their interest in doing further social and educational outreach work; and to revitalize a sense of pride in their identities by positioning themselves as experts in their communities' practices.

Similar findings were reported by Kim and Sohn (2016) for Korean as an HL. In their study, a total of fifty students enrolled in an undergraduate Korean-CSL course offered at UCLA worked with local community partners to serve their varying needs regarding Korean language (i.e., teach, translate/interpret, etc.). At the end of the CSL program, Kim and Sohn (2016) reported increases in HSs' confidence in using their HL, increased feelings of connectedness with their heritage cultures and communities, as well as overall personal growth. Importantly, the students' perspectives shifted over time to focus more on the real-world issues that came up at the CSL sites than their own linguistic and professional development. As a result of this new-found, fostered sense of identity, many of the students continued to serve as volunteers at their respective community partner sites after the academic portion was completed. Combined, the findings reported so far indicate that CSL can provide HL learners with a meaningful, multifaceted, transformative experience that can promote critical language awareness development not only in terms of perceived HL abilities, but, crucially, in terms of language validation and social activism (Leeman et al. 2011; Kim and Sohn 2016; Pascual y Cabo et al. 2017).

33.3.4 Self-Efficacy

In addition to combating against stigmatization, and a gaining of both senses of belonging and identity, students involved in CSL can further strengthen (or gain) a sense of self-efficacy, which, in the words of Bandura, is "a belief in one's capabilities to organize and execute the courses of action required to manage prospective situations" (1995: 2). Self-efficacy is a construct that Sandler (2016) found to be strongly present in her work with HSs in a translation and interpretation program offered to high school students representing different HLs in the Pacific Northwest. These students were considered to have been child language brokers, that is, bilingual children who are asked by their parents to interpret during interactions with English speakers (e.g., at the doctor's office). The parents in such situations often chose to use their children rather than an official interpreter for various reasons, but the effects on the children were not always positive. Although some of the students reported having felt anxiety while engaging as child brokers in the past further expressing that they felt their language skills were weak, Sandler (2016) argues that as long as parental or contextual expectations are not deemed too difficult to attain, situations such as these will eventually help children build a foundation on which their self-efficacy can form. Through a career and technical skill center, these students were able to enroll in translation and interpretation classes that allowed them to practice and refine their HL skills in local communities, resulting in newly formed feelings of fulfillment and confidence. In other words, their feelings of anxiety from past experiences of interpreting for their parents gave way to feelings of self-efficacy after having been involved in communal interpretation and translation through CSL.

Similar findings were reported by Mueller (2005), who described an intergenerational CSL initiative in which German HL learners connected with German-speaking residents at a senior care center in St. Cloud, Minnesota. Students were enrolled in an upper-division German culture course, the purpose of which was to develop an understanding and respect for others and to increase the students' intercultural competency. Throughout the semester, students spent 15 hours with the community partner. Their role was not fixed. Some students organized games and lectures for the residents, others developed a dictionary for the staff, and others simply socialized with the elders. At the end of the semester, based on class discussions and the journals participants kept, students reported sentiments of making a difference in the community, increase in self-confidence, and positive linguistic gains (Mueller 2005).

Beyond language, self-efficacy has also been seen through the lens of culture advisory where students' knowledge of their community practices is valued. For example, the course Culture, Food, and Agriculture, taught under the auspices of the Environmental Studies program from the University of Minnesota-Morris, focused on Native American gardening techniques. Even though there was minimal enrollment of Native American students who acted as advisors to the non-Native American students, this experience allowed them to be positioned as experts, as their heritage background was valued (Chollett 2014). One student commented on the sense of empowerment that they felt through having had the opportunity to be part of this project: "This service-learning project has opened the door to recovering Native American knowledge and health. Not only have the seeds to restore Native traditions been planted in us, but we hope that the seeds are planted in everyone who steps in our garden or learns about our garden through our outreach efforts." (Chollet 2014: 7).

33.4 Conclusion

While traditional methods of instruction based on lectures, readings, and classroom activities can be effective for some students and for some topics, many practitioners seek ways to enhance learning beyond the acquisition of discrete knowledge in a way that is also socially responsible (e.g., Bringle and Hatcher 1999). As discussed previously, one pedagogical model that has the potential to achieve this overarching goal given its intrinsic focus on advocacy, social justice, civic responsibility, and community growth is that of community-based service learning, which aims to draw on learners' previously held knowledge and experiences for the benefit of both learners and the community. Recognizing this potential, and paralleling the observed growing trends in HL education in general, the number of CSL initiatives has increased tremendously (e.g., Leeman et al. 2011; Pascual y Cabo et al. 2017; Lowther Pereira 2018). That said, the number of studies in heritage language research and on CSL is still scarce, particularly if compared to other subdisciplines. In our attempt to introduce the reader to this particular field, specifically as it relates to HL instructional practices, we have provided an overview of its core underpinnings and have presented a discussion of how CSL can positively affect HSs in four specific domains, namely the legitimation of HLs, HS self-efficacy, HS identity, and HS sense of belonging. To be sure, these outcomes are not the only ones, nor are they independent from each other; in fact, they intersect shaping the cultural and linguistic environment for millions of minoritized communities across the United States.

In our efforts to paint a nuanced view of the field, we also presented some of the difficulties associated with carrying out CSL initiatives for HL purposes, which include but are not limited to a lack of available resources (i.e., funding, trained instructors, appropriate materials) and at times perceived credibility from the community (e.g., Lee and Wright 2014). These factors, which are found throughout heritage communities in the United States, highlight the need to support CSL educational programs.

Despite the insights and advances observed herein, there is plenty of room for growth, development, and innovation. A few outstanding topics and questions that future research should address are the following: Most research examining the effects of CSL on HL learners has focused on the socio-affective domain (i.e., attitudes, identity, etc.), but what is there to learn about learners' tangible linguistic gains? In this context, what role does proficiency in the HL play in terms of said linguistic development? Also, to our knowledge, most studies done to date involve young adults in institutions of higher education – we wonder the extent to which the observed benefits could also apply for younger HL learners.

In summary, we would like to point out that although it is not commonplace in the US education system yet, what is clear is that researchers and practitioners involved in HL education are beginning to realize the benefits of community-engaged pedagogical practices and are, thus, relying more and more on this approach for the mutual benefits that can be gained for both HL learners and local communities. Now more than ever before, the conditions are ripe for reshaping current educational strategies, and scholars of many disciplines are paying heed to the opportunities (and challenges) this model presents. Initiatives such as the *Oral Narratives of Latin@s in Ohio* (Foulis 2018), the after-school Spanish HL literacy programs (Leeman et al. 2011; Pascual y Cabo et al. 2017), the translation and interpretation program for child brokers (Sandler 2016), the intergenerational German HL program at a senior care center (Mueller 2005), or the internships for Pacific Islander students (Uehara and Raatior 2016) are all great examples of how to design and implement meaningful CSL initiatives for the benefit of HL learners and the community.

References

Astin, A. W., L. J. Vogelgesang, E. K. Ikeda, and J. A. Yee. 2000. How Service Learning Affects Students. Executive Summary.

Bandura, A. 1995. *Self-Efficacy in Changing Societies*. Cambridge; New York: Cambridge University Press.

Bandy, J. 2016. What Is Service Learning or Community Engagement. Center for Teaching, Vanderbilt University. https://cft.vanderbilt.edu/guides-sub pages/teaching-through-community-engagement.

Beaudrie, S. and C. Ducar. 2005. Beginning Level University Heritage Programmes: Creating a Space for All Heritage Language Learners. *Heritage Language Journal* 3(1), 1–26.

Beaudrie, S., C. Ducar, and K. Potowski. 2014. *Heritage Language Teaching: Research and Practice*. Columbus, OH: McGraw-Hill Education.

Beaudrie, S., C. Ducar, and A. M. Relaño-Pastor. 2009. Curricular Perspectives in the Heritage Language Context: Assessing Culture and Identity. *Language, Culture and Curriculum* 22(2), 157–174.

Beaudrie, S. and M. Fairclough. 2012. Spanish as a Heritage Language in the United States. *Georgetown Studies in Spanish Linguistics*.

Bringle, R. and J. A. Hatcher. 1999. Reflection in Service-Learning: Making Meaning of Experience. *Educational Horizons* 7(4), 179–185.

Bringle, R. G. and J. A. Hatcher. 2003. *Introduction to Service-Learning Toolkit: Reading and Resources for Faculty*. Providence, RI: Campus Compact.

Carreira, M. and T. Beeman. 2014. *Voces: Latino Students on Life in the United States*. Santa Barbara, CA: Praeger.

Chollett, D. L. 2014. The Native American Organic Garden: Using Service Learning as a Site of Resistance. *Culture, Agriculture, Food and Environment* 36(2), 93–104.

Colombi, M. C. 2015. Academic and Cultural Literacy for Heritage Speakers of Spanish: A Case Study of Latin@ Students in California. *Linguistics and Education* 32, 5–15.

Darder, A. 2003. *The Critical Pedagogy Reader.* Hove: Psychology Press.

Ducar, C. 2012. SHL Learners Attitudes and Motivations: Reconciling Opposing Forces. In S. Beaudrie and M. Fairclough (eds.), *Spanish as a Heritage Language in the U.S.: State of the Science.* Washington, DC: Georgetown University Press, 253–282.

Eyler, J. and D. E. Giles Jr. 1999. *Where's the Learning in Service-Learning?* Jossey-Bass Higher and Adult Education Series. San Francisco: Jossey-Bass, Inc..

Fairclough, N. 2014. *Critical Language Awareness.* New York: Routledge.

Fairclough, M. and S. Beaudrie. 2016. *Innovative Strategies for Heritage Language Teaching: A Practical Guide for the Classroom.* Washington, DC: Georgetown University Press.

Fishman, J. 2014. Three Hundred-Plus Years of Heritage Language Education in the United States. In T. G. Wiley, J. K. Peyton, D. Christian, S. C. K. Moore, and N. Liu (eds.), *Handbook of Heritage, Community, and Native American Languages in the United States: Research, Policy, and Educational Practice.* New York: Routledge, 50–58.

Foulis, E. 2018. Participatory Pedagogy: Oral History in the Service-Learning Classroom. *Journal of Higher Education Outreach and Engagement* 22(3), 119–134.

Hausmann, L. R., J. W. Schofield, and R. L. Woods. 2007. Sense of Belonging as a Predictor of Intentions to Persist among African American and White First-Year College Students. *Research in Higher Education* 48(7), 803–839.

Hurtado, S. and D. F. Carter. 1997. Effects of College Transition and Perceptions of the Campus Racial Climate on Latino College Students' Sense of Belonging. *Sociology of Education* 70(4), 324–345.

Hurtado, S. and L. Ponjuan. 2005. Latino Educational Outcomes and the Campus Climate. *Journal of Hispanic Higher Education* 4(3), 235–251.

Kanost, L. 2014. Spanish after Service-Learning: A Comparative Study. *Journal of Service-Learning in Higher Education* 3, 64–80.

Kaplan, B. and T. Pérez-Gamboa. 2003. Stepping Out of the Classroom to Increase Spanish Language Skills and Cultural Awareness. In C. M. Cherry, ed., *Models for Excellence in Second Language Education.* Dimension, 27–35.

Kim, S. and S. Sohn. 2016. Service-Learning, an Integral Part of Heritage Language Education: A Case Study of an Advanced-Level Korean Language Class. *Heritage Language Journal* 13(3), 354–381.

Lee, J. S. and W. E. Wright. 2014. The Rediscovery of Heritage and Community Language Education in the United States. *Review of Research in Education* 38(1), 137–165.

Leeman, J. 2005. Engaging Critical Pedagogy: Spanish for Native Speakers. *Foreign Language Annals* 38(1), 35–45.

Leeman, J. 2018. Critical Language Awareness and Spanish as a Heritage Language: Challenging the Linguistic Subordination of US Latinxs. In K. Potowski (ed.), *Handbook of Spanish as a Minority/Heritage Language*. New York: Routledge, 345–358.

Leeman, J., L. Rabin, and E. Román-Mendoza. 2011. Identity and Activism in Heritage Language Education. *The Modern Language Journal* 95(4), 481–495.

Lowther Pereira, K. 2015. Developing Critical Language Awareness via Service-Learning for Spanish Heritage Speakers. *Heritage Language Journal* 12(2), 159–185.

Lowther Pereira, K. 2018. *Community Service-Learning for Spanish Heritage Learners: Making Connections and Building Identities*. Amsterdam: John Benjamins Publishing Company.

Martínez, G. 2003. Classroom Based Dialect Awareness in Heritage Language Instruction: A Critical Applied Linguistic Approach. *Heritage Language Journal* 1(1). Retrieved from www.international.ucla.edu/CMS/files/martinez_paper.pdf

Mitchell, T. D. 2008. Traditional vs. Critical Service-Learning: Engaging the Literature to Differentiate Two Models. *Michigan Journal of Community Service Learning* 14(2), 50–65.

Mueller, I. 2005. Service Learning, German Culture, and Intercultural Competence. In *The Year of Languages: Challenges, Changes, and Choices: 2005 Report of the Central States Conference on the Teaching of Foreign Languages*. Eau Claire, WI: Crown Prints, 207–218.

Oral Narratives of Latin@s in Ohio. (2018, January 16). Retrieved from https://cfs.osu.edu/archives/collections/ONLO

Pak, C. S. 2018. Linking Service-Learning with Sense of Belonging: A Culturally Relevant Pedagogy for Heritage Students of Spanish. *Journal of Hispanic Higher Education* 17(1), 76–95.

Pascual y Cabo, D. (ed.) 2016. *Advances in Spanish as a Heritage Language*. Amsterdam: John Benjamins Publishing Company.

Pascual y Cabo, D., J. Prada, and K. Lowther Pereira. 2017. Effects of Community Service-Learning on Heritage Language Learners' Attitudes toward Their Language and Culture. *Foreign Language Annals* 50(1), 71–83.

Potowski, K. 2012. Identity and Heritage Language Learners: Moving beyond Essentializations. In S. Beaudrie and M. Fairclough (eds.), *Spanish as a Heritage Language in the US: State of the Science*. Washington, DC: Georgetown University Press.

Potowski, K. (ed.) 2018. *The Routledge Handbook of Spanish as a Heritage Language*. New York: Routledge.

Prada, J. and D. Pascual y Cabo (forthcoming). Can Heritage Language Programs Aid with Student Retention? In M. Bowles (ed.), *Outcomes of University Spanish Heritage Language Instruction in the United States*. Washington, DC: Georgetown University Press.

Saltmarsh, J. and A. Driscoll. 2012. Classification Descriptions: Community Engagement Elective Classification. Retrieved from http://classifications .carnegiefoundation.org/descriptions/community_engagement.php.

Sandler, J. D. 2016. Interpreting Service: Educating Child Language Brokers through Service-Learning. *Heritage Language Journal* 13(3), 434–453.

Sheffield, E. C. 2005. Service in Service-Learning Education: The Need for Philosophical Understanding. *High School Journal* 89(1), 46–53.

Stoecker, R. 2016. *Liberating Service Learning and the Rest of Higher Education Civic Engagement*. Philadelphia: Temple University Press.

Strayhorn, T. L. 2008. Sentido de pertenencia: A Hierarchical Analysis Predicting Sense of Belonging among Latino College Students. *Journal of Hispanic Higher Education* 7(4), 301–320.

Strayhorn, T. L. 2012. *College Students' Sense of Belonging: A Key to Educational Success for all Students*. New York: Routledge.

Tapia, M. N. 2010. Service-Learning Widespread in Latin America. *Phi Beta Kappan* 91(5), 31–32.

Taylor, P. G. and C. Ballengee-Morris. 2004. Service-Learning a Language of "We". *Art Education* 57(5), 6–12.

Train, R. W. 2003. *The (Non) Native Standard Language in Foreign Language Education: A Critical Perspective*.

Trujillo, J. A. 2009. Con todos: Using Learning Communities to Promote Intellectual and Social Engagement in the Spanish Curriculum. In M. Lacorte and J. Leeman (eds.), *Español en Estados Unidos y otros contextos de contacto: Sociolingüística, ideología y pedagogía [Spanish in the United States and other Contact Contexts: Sociolinguistics, Ideology and Pedagogy]*. Madrid: Iberoamericana, 369–395.

Uehara, D. and V. Raatior. 2016. Pacific Islanders in Higher Education: Exploring Heritage Language, Culture and Constructs within a Service Learning Program. *Heritage Language Journal* 13(3), 454–473.

Valdés, G. 1995. The Teaching of Minority Languages as Academic Subjects: Pedagogical and Theoretical Challenges. *The Modern Language Journal* 79(3), 299–328.

Valdés, G. 2001. *Learning and Not Learning English: Latino Students in American Schools*. New York: Teachers College Press.

Villa, D. J. 2002. The Sanitizing of US Spanish in Academia. *Foreign Language Annals* 35(2), 222–230.

Wiley, T. G., J. K. Peyton, D. Christian, S. C. K. Moore, and N. Liu. 2014. *Handbook of Heritage, Community, and Native American Languages in the United States: Research, Policy, and Educational Practice*. New York: Routledge.

34

Developing Spanish Heritage Language Biliteracy

María Cecilia Colombi

34.1   Introduction

Literacy has traditionally been defined from a linguistic perspective. From this point of view, becoming literate is "a mechanical process" involving "the technical acquisition of reading and writing skills" (Al-Kahtany 1996: 548). Nevertheless, from a sociolinguistic perspective all literacy behavior reflects attitudes, values, and practices of particular social, cultural, and/or ethnic groups. In other words, literacy cannot be defined as "a singular knowledge or developmentally-ordered skill set … and unvarying across contexts and situations … Literacy entails much more than the ability to read and write, … literacy practices are enmeshed within and influenced by social, cultural, political, and economic factors, and … literacy learning and use varies by situation and entails complex social interactions" (García et al. 2007:207).

The pedagogical implications of this shift from a traditional literacy curriculum focused on a singular standard (grammar, the literary canon, standard national form of the language) to a sociocultural view of literacy that considers the underlying conception of meaning making (semiosis) as one of negotiating discourse differences are enormous. In the old literacy, learners were passive recipients; in contrast, from a functional approach to literacy, learners are seen as increasingly agents of their own meaning-making process that negotiate discourse differences. A pedagogy of multiliteracies would need to address this fundamental aspect of contemporary teaching and learning. "Literacy teaching is not about skills and competence; it is aimed at creating a kind of person, an active designer of meaning, with a sensibility open to differences, change and innovation. The logic of multiliteracies is one that recognizes that meaning making is an active, transformative process, and a pedagogy based on that recognition is more likely to open up viable life courses for a world of change and diversity" (Cope and Kalantzis 2009:175).

Spanish is the most spoken non-English language in US homes (37 million) followed by Chinese (including Mandarin and Cantonese) (2.8 million); Hindi/Urdu or other Indic languages (2.2 million); French (2.1 million); Tagalog (1.7 million); Vietnamese (1.4 million); German (1.2 million); and Korean (1.1 million) (Pew Hispanic Center 2013). Nevertheless, while the number of heritage speakers of Spanish continues to increase due to the overall growth of the Latinx population, "the share of Latinos who speak the language has declined over the past decade or so: 73% of Latinos spoke Spanish at home in 2015, down from 78% in 2006, according to a Pew Research Center analysis of Census Bureau data" (Pew Hispanic Center 2017a). Due to the decline of home languages, it becomes imperative to design programs that aim at developing advanced literacy in heritage languages. Much of the literature on academic literacy development has concentrated on Spanish as a heritage language in the United States. But Chinese (including Mandarin and Cantonese) has received considerable attention (He and Xiao 2008; He 2015; Mu 2016; Ruan et al. 2016; etc.) as well as Korean and Japanese (Sohn and Shin 2007; Kit-Fong Au and Sae Oh 2009; Kondo-Brown and Brown 2011; Choi 2015; etc.). Moreover, other commonly European languages taught as heritage languages in the United States apart from Spanish are French (Ross and Jaumont 2013), German, Italian, and Portuguese (Rothman and Judy 2014; Wiley et al. 2014).

Heritage speakers (HS) of Spanish in the United States constitute an important student population with unique linguistic and educational needs and challenges, in learning both English and Spanish (Valdés 2001, 2005; Carreira 2007). Valdés' (2001) definition of heritage speakers as a person "who is raised in a home where a non-English language is spoken, who speaks or at least understands the language and, who is to some degree bilingual in that language and in English" (38) is useful to explain the potential variability of speaker competency in the heritage language as well as the diversity of the speakers' linguistic background and experiences. Spanish HS is a good example of a heterogeneous group of learners, both linguistically and culturally. For instance, heritage speakers can range from newly arrived immigrants who are mostly Spanish monolingual speakers to fluent bilinguals of Spanish and English, and others who have not received any instruction in their native tongue. Yet, Polinsky and Kagan (2007) present an even more inclusive definition of HS that considers wider contextual factors such as identity, family, and cultural connections that are not solely limited to language competency. They also define HLs as those who acquired their heritage language to some extent but did not develop it completely before switching to the dominant language. This interpretation focuses on two important elements: the connection speakers feel to the language and the status of the language relative to the dominant language. Therefore, for the purpose of this chapter, a Spanish heritage learner is described as a person who has some knowledge in and a cultural connection to the heritage language that they are studying in a classroom context.

Several studies on bilingualism (Hornberger 2003; García 2009; Grosjean 2010; Montrul 2013; Silva-Corvalán 2014) underline the importance of schooling to develop biliteracy in the heritage language. Heritage speakers' use of Spanish usually revolves around the home or community domains. As a result of having developed their linguistic registers in informal contexts, they have not used Spanish in situations where this particular type of language is utilized to construct knowledge or negotiate membership in an academic or professional community. In light of this fact, they are subsequently less prepared to meet the linguistic and literacy demands of these settings. In order to become legitimate participants then, not only do they need to expand their control over a range of oral and written academic registers but, just as importantly, they *need to negotiate, construct, and index new identities as members of the academic community* [emphasis added] (Achugar and Colombi 2008). A new model of biliteracy learning needs to move from the transmission of language rules ("overt instruction") to one that is centered on learners as agents in their own knowledge processes, capable of contributing their own as well as negotiating differences among communities and situations ("situated practice"), with a critical understanding of the relationships of language and power. In this transformative model of literacy, learners are apprenticed into professional and academic communities as they develop their own agency and identity in those communities.

The heritage language acquisition and development field has expanded in both scope and depth during the last few decades, bringing together new understanding on the nature of how heritage languages are acquired and used in a variety of contexts. Most of these efforts focus on educational institutions where heritage language learners can possibly develop advanced literacy in their home language as well as in English. However, the development of Spanish heritage language biliteracy – particularly at advanced levels – has only recently become a topic of more active research, giving us some insights into how these learners developed advanced biliteracy in educational contexts. Recently, heritage language pedagogy in the United States, and especially the field of teaching Spanish as a heritage language, has placed growing attention on theoretical frameworks that mediate a process of student self-awareness and agency. These pedagogies promote student involvement in multimodal, translingual, and hybrid uses of literacies in and out of school with new technologies with the aim of expanding students' linguistic repertoires and critical language awareness (García et al. 2007; Leeman et al. 2011; Petrov 2013; Lowther Pereira 2015;

Fairclough and Beaudrie 2016; Henshaw 2016; Parra 2016; Parra and Di Fabio 2016; Parra et al. 2018; Zapata and Lacorte 2018). Within these pedagogical frameworks, Systemic Functional Linguistics (SFL), as an explicitly meaning-oriented theory of language and as explicitly education-oriented, has advanced our understanding of the teaching of language literacy in the educational contexts; particularly in K-12 (Christie and Unsworth 2000; Schleppegrell 2004, 2012; Christie & Martin, 2007; Christie and Derewianka 2008; Christie 2012; Brisk 2015; de Oliveira and Silva 2016; Dreyfus et al. 2016; Schleppegrell and Christie 2018) but also in foreign languages (Byrnes and Maxim 2004; Byrnes 2006, 2013; Byrnes et al. 2010; Allen and Maxim 2011; Rhyshina-Pankova 2015) and heritage languages (Colombi 2002, 2006, 2009, 2015; Achugar 2009; Colombi and Magaña 2013; Ignatieva and Colombi 2014; Reznicek-Parrado et al. 2018).

34.2 Biliteracy as a Linguistic and Social Development: Systemic Functional Linguistics

Systemic Functional linguistics, developed by the British linguist Michael Halliday, is a social theory of language that maintains as a fundamental principle the indivisibility of language, meaning, and use (Halliday and Hasan 1976, 1985; Halliday 1978, 1994, 1996a, 1996b, 2009; Halliday and Matthiessen 2004). Halliday and Matthiessen (1999) state that "(t)he construal of human experience [is] … a semantic system; and language plays the central role in storing and exchanging experience but also in constructing it … In linguistic terms, *experience is the reality that we construe for ourselves by means of language* [emphasis added]" (3). From this perspective, then, language is a semiotic meaning-making resource that is always related to social life; language is shaped by social contexts and social contexts are shaped by people using language.

In SFL, the dialectical relationship between language and society is conceptualized as *register* or the variation of language according to situation. Each situational context is realized in linguistic choices that construe our meaning at three levels: experiential or representational, interpersonal, and textual meanings that always operate together. Moreover, the linguistic choices that we make will vary according to the social situation we are in. SFL, as a functional theory of language, proposes that the explicit description of language functions allows for a conscious understanding of the linguistic repertoire that can then be deployed productively in various contexts, according to the different intentions and purposes of the users. But Hasan (1996) reminds us that, the use of language varies depending on variation in social processes; and secondly, not all speakers enjoy the possibility of engaging in all social processes. It follows that pupils will come to the school with different discourse abilities, with different experience of participation in registers – simply because of the differences in their social position. Speaking in the 'voice of one's speech fellowship' will refer not simple to accent and social *dialect* but also to *register repertoire* [emphasis added]–what people use their language for, what social processes they engage in. (396)

The classroom, then, offers heritage speaker learners participation in registers that they may not encounter outside school, but it is important to realize that students will be differently situated to participate in the classroom according to their own life experiences. Therefore, productive language pedagogy or action literacy (Hasan 1996) could help us re-think the teacher–learner experience by focusing on the use of language in different social contexts. Literacy can be understood as a process, "activity" rather than knowledge, a product, something that you acquire one and for all. It is important to understand the development of language as part of human "behaviour potential" that is always related to the "cultural frame" (Hasan 1996). Halliday (1996a, b) tells us that,

> It is more helpful to conceive *literacy as activity rather than knowledge* [emphasis added] ... the concept of literacy from the linguistic point of view [can be summarized in three points:] (1) treating literacy as something that has to do with language; (2) using the conceptual framework of linguistics – the theoretical study of language – as a way of understanding it ... (3) (and understanding) literacy as 'having mastery of written language'. In this sense, if we say that someone is literate it means that they are effectively *using* [emphasis added] the lexicogrammatical patterns that are associated with written text. (339–341)

In other words, this concept of literacy goes beyond knowledge of writing and reading; it implies the ability to make meaning in complex social interactions with linguistic awareness of language practices in relationship to concepts of power and language. This understanding of *register*, *dialect*, code, and genre has enabled researchers to develop descriptions of "advancedness" in second language literacy development that have greatly informed research on literacy development in heritage languages, second languages, and foreign languages (Schleppegrell and Colombi 2002; Byrnes 2006; Achugar and Colombi 2008; etc.).

Productive language pedagogy or action pedagogy, then, seeks to develop students' awareness and competence in language use and meaning, including specific forms of language use, and social context; in other words, it pursues the awareness and growth of students' repertoire of registers. Literate practices are fundamentally social language use practices – and that includes how these practices are socially positioned, and language is the essential resource to learn those practices. As Halliday 1991 describes, we learn language through language and about language. "Learning language" means, of course, learning one's first language, plus any second or foreign languages that are part of the curriculum, including both spoken and written language – emerging literacy, writing skills and so on. Here, language is itself the substance of what is being learnt. "Learning through language" means using language, again both spoken and written, as a tool: as the primary resource for learning other things, subjects – namely, language across the curriculum. "Learning about language" means studying language as the object of study in order to understand how it works: studying the structure of the language, i.e., phonetics, grammar, semantics, and so on. Here language is the object of study, and sometimes in schools this is only considered from the linguistic nature of study but, "there is no reason why it should not become a properly constructed avenue of learning ... So language enters in as substance – we have to learn it to perform; as instrument – we have to learn with it, as a resource; and as object – we have to learn about it, as content. *This is important because nothing else in our educational experience has all these three aspects to it* [emphasis added]" (288) (Figure 34.1).

This pedagogy fosters descriptive and productive instruction of language as a way of raising language development and awareness. Productive language pedagogy follows three stages: recognition, production, and reflection. In heritage language courses, learners have to transform text into system; that is, to construe the instances of language, what they hear and what they read, into a meaning potential. In other words, by learning language and through language, students also learn about language. If we want to express the three aspects of that meaning potential as aspects of language, it can be said that learning language equals to "language skills"; learning through language is extralinguistic, language as a tool to learn other things: "knowledge of content," and learning about language is metalinguistic: "knowledge of language, as content."

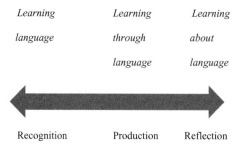

Figure 34.1 Productive language pedagogy

34.3 Productive Language Education: Examples from the Classroom

Spanish heritage learners are often characterized as "having functional proficiency in interpersonal and colloquial registers" (Colombi 2015: 6) but few come to the classroom with explicit Spanish instruction in a formal academic setting (Colombi and Magaña 2013). Thus, for Spanish heritage learners to become active participants in the professional community, they need to learn how to negotiate, construct, and index new identities as members of the academic community (Achugar and Colombi 2008). As such, providing heritage learners with resources to understand how language functions in an academic setting gives them the power to use language for their own purposes (Achugar 2003; Reznicek et al. 2018).

In the field of heritage language pedagogy several questions have been postulated with respect to the variety of Spanish to be used in the classroom from the early 90's (Colombi and Alarcón 1997), such as, what language variety are the students supposed to learn, the Spanish dialect of Spain or Mexico? What is the "standard" to be used in the classroom? Should we use code-switching in the classroom? Socio-functional theories of language have helped us move away from the binary distinction of right and wrong, correct and incorrect, or standard language vs. non-standard language (also, vid. Chapters 26, 28, 29, 31, and 33 this volume). From an SFL perspective, developing knowledge and understanding of the content area and developing control of the linguistic resources that construct and communicate that knowledge and understanding are essentially the same thing (Hasan 1996). The conceptualization of *literacy* as an *activity* serves as a starting point to reformulate the previous questions taking into account the social context. For example, we could ask ourselves the following question: How could our curriculum aim at developing students' multiple literacies in Spanish instead of focusing on the abstract concept of standard language or how to define monolingual speakers of Spanish? The concept of multiple literacies or multiliteracies was first introduced in 1996 by the New London Group and later developed by Kalantzis and Cope (2008), Cope and Kalantzis (2009), and Kalantzis et al. (2016).

Multiple literacy or multiliteracy pedagogy in this context implies the integration of "formal" (or academic) language learning with "informal" (or personal) learning, as well as relating the curriculum closely to learners' personal, social, and cultural backgrounds and aims. Moreover, this pedagogy offers to learners opportunities to interpret and create meaning from form multimodally, that is, through a variety of oral, visual, written, audiovisual, and digital texts. Therefore, advanced literacy from a functional perspective is seen as the capacity to construe experience in language (representational); the capacity to express generalization and abstract ideas

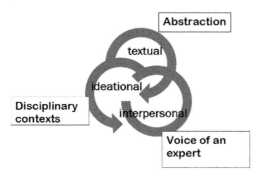

Figure 34.2 Advanced literacy: registerial diagram

in written language (textual); and the ability to enact "expert" roles in disciplinary fields with growing confidence in expressing attitude and evaluation (Schleppegrell and Colombi 2002) (Figure 34.2).

The following sections describe some of the pedagogical practices in a university curriculum for Spanish heritage speakers that stress the relationship between the bilingual continuum and its connection with the social and situational context. These practices emphasize the meaning-making of language in the construal of discourse. They emphasize the explicit instruction of dialect, genre, and register theory as a way of promoting students' language awareness and academic literacy.

34.3.1 Oral–Written Continuum: Genre Pedagogy

Taking into account that, by and large, a great number of heritage students come to the classroom with colloquial repertoires of Spanish but have not been exposed to academic ones, it has proven to be beneficial to examine the difference between oral and written modes of language in context, so as to understand local considerations that motivated specific language choices. In other words, the oral–written continuum refers not only to transmission of a message in a certain medium but includes the context of production as reflected in the three *register* variables of field, mode, and tenor. In Figure 34.3 (Colombi 2009), the pedagogical progression from the more "oral," personal, informal, and congruent texts to the more impersonal and academic ones is presented.

The thematic unit in Figure 34.3 is a snapshot of a unit in a heritage language program curriculum and covers approximately three weeks of instruction. The heritage learners interact with each of those texts in a learning cycle by negotiating the meaning of the text (focus on the field), deconstructing the text (focus on discourse and lexicogrammatical features), and, later on, jointly constructing new texts in relationship to their own experiences and realities (Figure 34.4).

Thematic unit: 'Mexican-American experience in the United States':

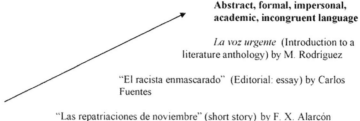

Abstract, formal, impersonal, academic, incongruent language

La voz urgente (Introduction to a literature anthology) by M. Rodríguez

"El racista enmascarado" (Editorial: essay) by Carlos Fuentes

"Las repatriaciones de noviembre" (short story) by F. X. Alarcón

Personal, concrete, informal, congruent language

Fig. 2. Example of a thematic cluster of genres from *Palabra abierta* (Colombi et al., 2007).

Figure 34.3 Thematic unit (Colombi 2009: 45)

Módulo 2 :: Ejercicio 1 - Ubicación dentro el continuo
Ubica dentro del continuo del lenguaje oral-escrito (del cuadro 1) cada uno de los siguientes ejemplos. Considera no solamente si representan la lengua escrita, sino también el nivel de formalidad. Escribe en la línea de la derecha la letra del continuo en el que los ubicarías.

Cuadro 1. Continuo del lenguaje

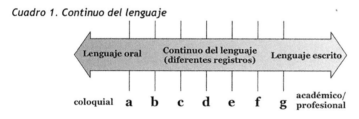

Ejemplo	Ubicación en el continuo
Un discurso presidencial	
Un mensaje para tu compañero de casa	
Un guión de un programa de TV o radio	
Una carta de negocios	
Una entrevista a tu hermana	
Un ensayo para tu clase	

Figure 34.4 Activity #1: Language continuum – recognition. (Adapted from CLAE: http://lenguajeacademico.info)

The three language activities below exemplify the oral (colloquial) – written (formal) language continuum as they move from the simple recognition of the registerial characteristics of each discourse setting (Activity N. 1) to the production and reflection of the lexicogrammatical and discourse features (Activity N. 2 and N. 2.1)

Module 2: Exercise 1 – Oral–written language continuum
In the oral–written language continuum (Figure 34.5) place each of the following examples. Think that they not only represent written language

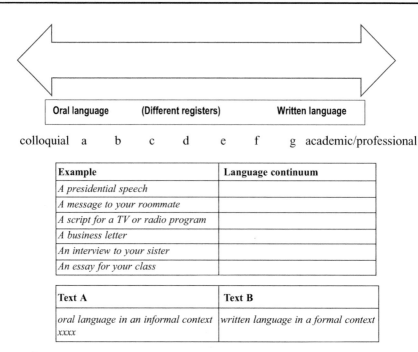

Example	Language continuum
A presidential speech	
A message to your roommate	
A script for a TV or radio program	
A business letter	
An interview to your sister	
An essay for your class	

Text A	Text B
oral language in an informal context *xxxx*	*written language in a formal context*

Figure 34.5 Continuum of language

but also different levels of formality. On the right of the figure, write a letter according to their position in the continuum.

In this activity, learners are asked to situate different speech acts, e.g., a message for your roommate, a business letter, etc. and place them in the language continuum explaining why they place them more toward the colloquial or professional end. The purpose of this activity is to make them aware of the subtle differences in registers, i.e., language use according to the situation. Furthermore, later on, when students are familiarized with the three variables of register: *field* (representational meaning – What is the message about?), *mode* (textual meaning – What is the medium used for the message?) and *tenor* (interpersonal meaning – Who are the participants in that speech act?). This activity represents the first stage in the learning cycle or the recognition stage; the purpose is for students to familiarize themselves with the variation in the use of language according to field, mode, and tenor, i.e., according to the variables in register: A "business" letter is different from a message to your roommate for several reasons, different purpose (field), medium, even if both of them are written (mode), and interactants or participants (tenor).

Notebook of Academic Language ·
Module 1: Activity 1 – Characteristics of academic language
Considering the characteristics of oral and written language studied in the previous lesson (Figure 34.3), **compare and classify** the linguistic

Cuaderno de lenguaje académico

Módulo 1 :: Actividad 1 - Características del lenguaje académico

Tomando en cuenta las características lingüísticas de la lengua oral y de la lengua escrita que se presentaron en el Cuadro 3 de la lectura anterior, **compara** y **clasifica** las características lingüísticas de los textos en la Tabla 1 (abajo). Observa qué característica lingüística resalta cada color del Texto A, y encuentra un equivalente en el Texto B. Completar la Tabla 2 (abajo) con la información que encuentres.

Tabla 1. Ejemplos de texto oral y texto escrito.

Texto A **lengua oral** en un contexto informal	Texto B **lengua escrita** en un contexto formal
Pues este...*Coser y cantar* se trata de una chava que está confundida, y está como buscando por su identidad y platica con su otra parte, o sea que, como que no realiza muy bien que es bilingüe y este... pues tiene broncas internas porque no acepta que es cubana y que también es americana. Ah! y este... también la chava cubana no quiere reconocer, pues que está aquí... y que es... está supuesta a asimilarse, ¿no?, pero la otra si se asimila a la cultura de aquí y solo habla inglés y este...pues nomás es básicamente la lucha de la chava entre su cultura latina y americana.	La obra teatral ejemplifica la dolorosa dicotomía psíquica que puede sufrir un exiliado dentro del ambiente bicultural-bilingüe prevalente en algunas ciudades estadounidenses como Nueva York, Los Ángeles, Miami. Básicamente, la trama se basa en las múltiples discusiones, inconsecuentes en apariencia, que van dibujando la dicotomía psico-lingüística existente en los personajes de la obra ELLA/ SHE. Toda la pieza podría resumirse en el constante enfrentamiento de las «virtudes» hispanas tradicionales versus las «virtudes» anglosajonas adquiridas.

Adaptación del artículo de Mariela A. Gutiérrez, *Dolores Prida: exilio, lengua e identidad.*
http://www.cubaencuentro.com/revista/revista-encuentro/archivo/14-otono-de-1999/dolores-prida-exilio-lengua-e-identidad

Completa la Tabla 2 (abajo). Escribe (o copia) ejemplos de características lingüísticas para cada modalidad: oral y escrita que encuentres en los textos de arriba. Por cada ejemplo puede haber más de una opción. Toma como referencia la información del Cuadro 1 (que se encuentra resumido en la próxima página).

Tabla 2. Comparación y clasificación de las características lingüísticas.

Lengua oral / Texto A	Lengua escrita / Texto B
Léxico de todos los días Ejemplos: una chava, broncas	*Léxico especializado* Ejemplos: los personajes, un exiliado
Gramática no estándar	*Gramática estándar*
Construcciones gramaticales complejas	*Construcciones gramaticales simples*
Baja densidad léxica	*Alta densidad léxica*

Figure 34.6 Activity #2: Language continuum – recognition-production

characteristics of the texts presented in Figure 34.6. Note the words highlighted in Text A, and find an equivalent in Text B. Then, complete the table below the text with the information that you discovered.

Complete Table 34.1. Write (or copy) examples of the linguistic characteristics of each modality: oral and written that you find in the text above.

Table 34.1 *Comparison and classification of linguistic characteristics*

Oral language / Text A	Written language/ Text B
Everyday lexicon	Specialized lexicon
Example: una chava (lass, girl), broncas (rows, fights)	Example: los personajes (characters), un exiliado (an exiled person)
Non standard grammar	Standard grammar
Complex grammatical constructions	Simple grammatical constructions
Low lexical density	High lexical density

Cuaderno de lenguaje académico

Cuadro 1. Características del lenguaje académico

Lengua oral	Lengua escrita
Estructura dinámica El acto comunicativo es espontáneo, no está planeado, es abierto, se va construyendo en el acto mismo.	*Estructura sinóptica* Toma más tiempo escribir que hablar y por eso la lengua escrita se planea y se enfoca en un mensaje claro y organizado.
Léxico de todos los días Las palabras son más informales y menos específicas.	*Léxico especializado* Las palabras deben ser precisas y apropiadas al tema para que el interlocutor entienda claramente el mensaje.
Gramática no estándar En el caso del español de los EE.UU. puede verse interferencia del inglés o construcciones no formales	*Gramática estándar* Las oraciones deben ser entendidas por cualquier persona que hable español
Construcciones gramaticales complejas La lengua oral es dinámica, espontánea y menos consciente lo que ocasiona complejidad gramatical. Las ideas (oraciones generalmente largas y complejas), se unen con la conjunción "y".	*Construcciones gramaticales simples* La legua escrita es más consciente y planeada, por eso requiere estructuras más simples, pero que están construidas con un vocabulario con "más significados".
Baja densidad léxica Se usan más palabras con menos contenido semántico (menos significativas).	*Alta densidad léxica* La idea es comunicar más información a través de palabras que tienen más contenido. Palabras que tiene alta carga semántica como nombres, adjetivos, verbos y adverbios.

Figure 34.7 Activity #2.1: Language continuum – reflection. (Adapted from CLAE: http://lenguajeacademico .info)

For each example, you may find more than one option. As reference you could look at Figure 34.7 (summarized on the next page).

Activity #2 is an example of how learners move from recognition to production and, later on, reflection on language as a "meaning-making

Table 34.2 *Characteristics of academic language*

Oral language	Written language
Dynamic structure The communicative interaction is spontaneous, not planned and open. It is being constructed as it happens.	*Synoptic structure* It takes more time to write than to speak. It is more planned and focused on the message. It is clear and organized.
Everyday lexicon Words are informal and less specific.	*Specialized lexicon* Words are precise and appropriate to the theme discussed so the receiver understands the message clearly.
Nonstandard grammar In the use of Spanish of the United States, there could be some use of English or constructions that are not formal.	*Simple grammatical constructions* Written language is more planned and organized; the structures (sentences) are simple as most of the meaning is in vocabulary with "more meaning."
Low lexical density Words have a lower semantic content (they are less meaningful).	*High lexical density* The idea is to communicate more information with words that have more meaning. Words have a high semantic content like nouns, adjectives, verbs, and adverbs.

resource." In this activity, students interact with a table that presents on the right side a paragraph from a text that they have been reading in class (in this case, a literary analysis of Dolores Prida's play *Coser y Cantar*: "Dolores Prida: exilio, lengua e identidad" by Mariela A. Gutiérrez) and on the left side of the table a more oral version of the same paragraph. Learners are to identify the different lexicogrammatical features of the oral version of the text and compare them with the more written one. Later on, they analyze the linguistic features of the two texts and describe their characteristics explaining why they belong to the colloquial register or academic one. The purpose behind this activity is "*learn language, through language and about language.*"

Notebook of Academic Language

Activity #2.1 is a follow up of Activity #2 when learners discuss from a linguistic point of view why each of the columns is appropriately used in two different registers, a colloquial one and an academic one. Explicit analysis of how the different registers are realized allows them to have a better understanding of how language is used to convey meanings and, later on, to make their own choices in the realizations of their discourse. Thus, the activities presented here serve as an example of the pedagogical cycle (recognition, production, and reflection) with respect to understanding of the oral–written continuum or colloquial–formal registers.

Spanish heritage learners also move in their own production from texts that present more oral–colloquial features to texts that are more academic as they progress in the course and they work with different textual genres such as

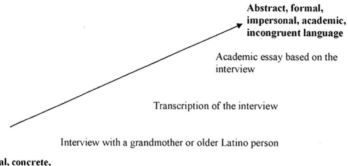

Abstract, formal, impersonal, academic, incongruent language

Academic essay based on the interview

Transcription of the interview

Interview with a grandmother or older Latino person

Personal, concrete, informal, congruent language

Fig. 4. Students' writings on the thematic unit: "Mexican-Americans in the United States".

Figure 34.8 Students' writings (Colombi 2009: 46)

commentaries, responses, reviews, and academic essays. Progression from more personal, concrete, and informal (congruent texts) to more abstract, formal, and impersonal ones (incongruent texts) is exemplified in Figure 34.8.

As part of their course work and looking at the theme of immigration, students have to interview a Latinx person who has immigrated to the United States recently, and then they have to transcribe the interview and talk about it in class. Obviously, the motive behind the interview is for the students to learn firsthand about the experiences of moving from one country to another, changing languages, cultures, and social environments. Later on, students are to write and reflect about the experience in an academic essay; many times in their own essays (Colombi 2009) learners use the knowledge they gathered in the interviews, presenting them in a more academic form, as exemplified in Figure 34.9:

34.3.2   Register–Dialect Continuum: Register Pedagogy

In the context of Spanish as a heritage language in the United States, the concepts of *dialect* and *register* as understood in SFL are particularly relevant to position both Spanish and English in the social context of dominant–non-dominant languages as well as to better understand the variety of Spanishes spoken in the United States in terms of their relationship to the social (and political) power of users of the language. Spanish takes a very special position as a heritage language in the United States; Latinxs constitute the nation's largest ethnic or cultural minority with 58.9 million (18 percent) as of July 1, 2017 (U.S. Census Bureau, 2018). Moreover, Spanish was the first European language to be in contact with the native American languages spoken in the continent when Ponce de León's expedition from Puerto Rico landed in Florida in 1513. Spanish was introduced in the southwest of the

Table 6
Excerpts from student interviews and essays.

1- Interview (oral language) – transcription (Maira)[6]
M- ¿Cómo fue su niñez en el sitio donde nació o se crió?
L- Muy bonita porque tenía a mi papá y mi mamá y mis amigas. Me gustaba ir al campo con mis papas a sembrar semillas de frijoles y maíz.
   Me venia a la casa a bañar, lavar ropa y ayudar a mamá. En la tarde me juntaba con las amigas para jugar baseball...

2- Essay (Maira) thesis statement
... Aunque se supone que una niña de trece años sólo piensa en jugar con las amigas, en realidad, Lucía Mora de niña fue testigo y vivió **el
gran esfuerzo que es trabajar para mantener a la familia.** Esta experiencia es importante porque podemos ver cómo **el valor del trabajo
para una niña quien dejó los juegos de amigas**, la transformó en una mujer a muy temprana edad y aprendió a valerse por sí misma.

3- Essay (Rosalia) Sacrificio para progresar
En los últimos meses el tema de la inmigración ha hecho controversia y las reacciones han sido escuchadas en ambos países divididos por la
frontera: los Estados Unidos y México. La controversia implica a los once millones de inmigrantes que trabajan y viven en los EE. UU. si
tener documentos para hacerlo legalmente. Los inmigrantes ilegales vienen de países localizados en diferentes regiones alrededor del mundo
como centro y sur América pero el mayor número de personas inmigran de México. [En esta composición me enfocaré con **las experiencias
personales de los inmigrantes que han impactado al país estadounidense en la cultura, economía y en los valores sociales.**]

Figure 34.9 Excerpts from students' texts (Colombi 2009: 47)

United States with expeditions that originated from Mexico in the fifteenth
and sixteenth centuries, and, in many places like New Mexico, has stayed
uninterruptedly since then. But the history, vitality, and future of the
Spanish language in the US context is perhaps most obvious in the state
of California. Its very name, *California*,[1] was inspired by Spanish romances
written in the sixteenth century. Indeed, Spanish has been spoken in
California since its very conception. Thus, the Spanish language has influenced California's identity, and its influences are as relevant as ever to us
today. According to Census Data from 2017, 38.9 percent of California's
population is Hispanic/Latinx, comprising the largest cultural/ ethnic
group, and surpassing whites (37.7 percent) (Quick Facts California, U. S.
Census Bureau 2017).

While not all Latinxs/Hispanics in the United States report speaking
Spanish, more than 37 million (out of 58 million) do. The Pew Hispanic
Center found that about half of second-generation self-identified Latinos are
bilingual. But language abilities diminish across generations: Among third-
generation or higher self-identified Latinos fewer than a quarter are bilingual (Pew Hispanic Center 2017b). Whereas Spanish continues to become
more visible across the United States, its integration into the education
system in many states has been disputed, scrutinized, and viewed by many
as a threat to the state's – and the country's – national identity. Movements
such as English Only in the 1980s was behind the passing into law of the
English as an Official Language in several states with strong Latinx populations, such as California, Colorado, Arizona, and Florida. The English Only[2]

---

[1] The name "California" originates from the word "Califa," a mythical paradise island described in Garci Ordóñez de
Montalvo's 1510 romance "Las Sergas de Esplandián."
[2] In fact, thirty-one states have adopted English as their official language, twenty-seven of them since 1980s.

movement is a clear example of the "monolingual ideology" and part of "language pride and language panic" (Hill 2001) that considers bilingualism a serious threat to the national identity. Other movements such as the one illustrated by the approval of Proposition 227 in 1998 in California (similar movements followed in other states like Arizona, Massachusetts, etc.), which was designed to prohibit the implementation of bilingual programs across the state, also exemplify the ideological tensions that surround educational policies in the United States.[3] Therefore, many heritage students enter higher education having had little opportunity to develop academic biliteracy in their family language. These students have only been exposed to their heritage language in familiar or informal social contexts but not in public or academic spaces where English has always been the dominant language. Taking into account the relationship of language and power as a way of constructing discourse as well as in understanding language ideologies, it is evident that the instruction of heritage languages should make explicit the connection between language and culture.

The concepts of *register/dialect* are particularly productive to make clear the connection between academic language as a *register* that is considered prestigious due to the contexts of use and users. Through the pedagogical use of SFL in the classroom, heritage learners can not only be aware of the different uses of language in different contexts but also that they can develop a critical understanding of why certain varieties of language receive higher status than others. Many students have been exposed to teaching practices that value the varieties of Spanish used by "educated speakers of the language" in places such as Spain, Mexico, Colombia, or any other country where Spanish is spoken as the dominant language. Others come to the classroom with only colloquial *registers* of the language through interactions with family members or friends and have never been schooled in Spanish. In other words, heritage speakers of Spanish need to acquire control and agency over their own Spanish first to become confident speakers of the language (Colombi 2015).

The concept of language as an "activity" situated in a social context can be used to raise learners' language consciousness. Halliday's (1978, 2009) conceptualization of *dialect* (as a variety according to the users) and *register* (as a diatypic variety according to use) can be used as a starting point to take a more critical position about language ideologies and attitudes, as well as to reflect on the varieties of Spanish that students bring to the classroom. For example, in Colombi's (2015) study, learners start by writing their own linguistic biography, assessing their own language skills in English and Spanish. A discussion follows to see who has received instruction in

---

[3] Proposition 227 was repealed 20 years later by the approval of Proposition 58 (English Plus) in 2016 in California.

Table 2
Varieties in language.

Dialect ("dialectal variety") – variety "according to the user"	Register ("diatypic variety") – variety "according to the use"

A dialect is:
what you speak (habitually) determined by who you are (socio-region of origen and/or adoption), and expressing diversity of social structure (patterns of social hierarchy)
So in principle dialects are:
  different ways of saying the same thing and tend to differ in:
  phonetics, phonology, lexicogrammar (but not in semantics)
	A register is:
	what you are speaking (at the time) determined by what you are doing (nature or social activity being engaged in) and expressing diversity of social process (social division of labor)
	So in principle registers are:
	  ways of saying different things and tend to differ in:
	  semantics (and hence in lexicogrammar and sometimes phonology as realization of this)

Principal controlling variables:
  social class
  provenance: rural–urban
  generation
  age
  gender
	Principal controlling variables:
	  field (type of social action)
	  tenor (role relationships)
	  mode (symbolic organization)

Typical instances:
  subcultural varieties:
  standard/nonstandard
	Typical instances:
	  occupational varieties:
	  technical/non-technical

Characterized by:
  strongly-held attitudes toward dialects as symbol of social diversity
	Characterized by:
	  major distinctions of spoken/written language in action/language in reflection

Adapted from Halliday (1978, p. 35).

Figure 34.10 *Dialect /register* (Colombi 2015: 10)

(1) Reflection about their own *dialect* of Spanish and use of Spanish and English (autobiography).
(2) Explicit teaching of *dialect/register* concepts from a functional perspective: varying according to the users (geographical region, social class, rural-urban, etc.).
(3) Interaction and analysis of *dialects/registers* in the classroom and in the larger community through their community service.
(4) Discussion of the attitudes and ideologies attributed to the different varieties in different contexts. It is only after the students could really explain **why** certain varieties are *appropriate* in certain contexts and others are not, that they have developed a critical awareness of language; i.e. when they start questioning why certain varieties receive more value than others in society.

Figure 34.11 Activities applying the concepts of *dialect/register* (Colombi 2015: 11)

Spanish and what is considered "proper Spanish," i.e., students start reflecting on their own language. Later on, they analyze the following table on *dialect* and *register* (Figure 34.10).

The difference between a *dialect* or a variety of language will depend on the place where the speaker is born and to the social class/community she belongs to, and *register* as the type of language we use in a social context, that is, the uses of language to achieve different purposes. In this stage of recognition of how language functions in society, learners relate to the idea that "our language is also determined by who we are; that is the basis of *dialect*, and in principle a *dialect* is with us all our lives – it is not subject to choice … Many speakers learn two or more *dialects*, either in succession, dropping the first when they learn the second, or in coordination, switching them according to the context of the situation" (Halliday 1978: 34). The linguistic description of dialect and register can also further their understanding on their linguistic journeys to bilingualism. Figure 34.11 shows how the concepts of *register/dialect* were presented in the classroom using the principles of productive language teaching.

After heritage learners think about the way they speak and how they use language in different contexts (reflection stage), they start working linguistically with the idea that language is socially constructed. Furthermore, whenever possible they are encouraged to use Spanish outside the classroom, i.e., in real situations, such as in community service in schools, clinics, etc., so they can become more aware of the different choices people make in their use of language (production stage). Moreover, it is imperative to bring to the heritage classroom discussions on language attitudes and ideologies to understand and value "all" linguistic repertoires and practices of heritage speakers within the learning context to bring students to reflect on issues of language and power.

34.4 Conclusion

A functional pedagogy of language focuses on how people use language to make meanings with each other as they carry out their social lives. They do this through selections from the sets of choices that are available in language systems. The choices learners can actually make from these systems are, however, constrained by two factors. The first is that meaning is always constructed within the context, and context limits the range of meanings that can be selected. The second factor that limits individuals' linguistic choices is that not everyone within the culture or community has access to all of the possible contexts, and therefore all the possible ways of speaking or writing (Christie and Unsworth 2000). Therefore, academic contexts of instruction are a powerful engine to benefit HL communities themselves as long as we move away from standardized and de-contextualized language pedagogies to social theories of language that will reflect the social, cultural, and political reality of HL students and their communities.

The use of productive teaching pedagogy could be a useful resource to develop a linguistic awareness of language practices in different social contexts. These heritage pedagogical practices start from what is known to the students from their cultural and linguistic context, from the familiar to the professional or academic context, with the aim of extending the linguistic *registerial* repertoire. In addition, heritage speakers learn how to describe use and consciously talk about the value of these linguistic resources in language practices, i.e., they become "apprentices in that professional community," and this is the first step to develop cultural and critical language awareness. They become conscious users of the language (or languages) of schooling, i.e., they can critically assess the value of those choices in society. SFL pedagogy supports meaningful dialogic interaction about language use and power relations.

Diversity, in fact, has become a paradoxical universal. The kind of person who can live well in this world is someone who has acquired the capacity to navigate from one domain of social activity to another, who is resilient in their capacity to articulate and enact their own identities, and who can find ways of entering into dialogue with and learning new and unfamiliar social languages (Cope and Kalantzis 2009). One of the fundamental goals of a pedagogy of multiliteracies is to create the conditions for learning that support the growth of this kind of person: a person comfortable with themselves as well as being flexible enough to collaborate and negotiate with others who are different from themselves in order to forge a common interest. Additionally, the use of functional pedagogical tools is significant, in as much as it describes the use of norms according to the social context and allows students to become independent analysts of language. From this perspective, grammar is never prescriptive but always descriptive and functional, i.e., it becomes a resource to construct meaning as well as a resource to construct their identity as members of the academic community.

In conclusion, a productive pedagogy of heritage biliteracy regards language, in a multimodal world, as a dynamic process of transformation rather than processes of reproduction. That is, language is a "meaning making resource" and not a simple replicator of representational conventions. Language, then is a tool for active citizenship, centered on learners and users as agents in their own knowledge processes, capable of contributing their own as well as negotiating the differences between one community and the next. In the last few decades of research on heritage language pedagogy in the United States, and specially on teaching Spanish as a heritage language, growing attention has been placed on theoretical frameworks that mediate a process of student self-awareness; that is, frameworks that promote student involvement in multimodal, translingual, and multiliteracies as a way to expand students' linguistic repertoires. Recently, the pedagogy of multiliteracies for heritage speakers has been a subject of interest for many researchers (Pascual y Cabo 2016; Zapata and Lacorte 2018). For example, Henshaw (2016) studies the incorporation of technology in the heritage language classroom; other researchers (Leeman et al. 2011; Petrov 2013; Lowther Pereira 2015) analyze the implementation of experiential and critical language learning through service-learning and argue how these pedagogical opportunities serve to promote students' involvement in diverse literacy practices.

References

Achugar, M. 2003. Academic Registers in Spanish in the US: A Study of Oral Texts Produced by Bilingual Speakers in a University Graduate Program. In Roca, A. and M. C. Colombi (eds.), *Mi lengua: Spanish as a Heritage Language in the United States, Research and Practice*. Washington, DC: Georgetown University Press, 213–234.

Achugar, M. 2009. Constructing a Bilingual Professional Identity in a Graduate Classroom. *Journal of Language, Identity & Education* 8(2), 65–87.

Achugar, M. and M. C. Colombi. 2008. Systemic Functional Linguistic Explorations into the Longitudinal Study of Advanced Capacities: The Case of Spanish Heritage Language Learners. In Ortega, L. and H. Byrnes, H. (eds.), *The Longitudinal Study of Advanced L2 Capacities*. New York: Routledge, 36–57.

Al-Kahtany, A. H. 1996. Literacy from a Linguistic and a Sociolinguistic Perspective. *International Review of Education / Internationale Zeitschrift für Erziehungswissenschaft / Revue Internationale de l'Education* 42(6), 547–562.

Allen, H. W. and H. H. Maxim. 2011. *Educating the Future Foreign Language Professoriate for the 21st Century*. Canada: Thompson.

Brisk, M. E. 2015. *Engaging Students in Academic Literacies: Genre-Based Pedagogy for K-5 Classrooms*. New York: Routledge

Byrnes, H. (ed.) 2006. *Advanced Language Learning: The Contribution of Halliday and Vygotsky*. London: Continuum.

Byrnes, H. 2013. Positioning Writing as Meaning-Making in Writing Research: An Introduction. *Journal of Second-Language Writing* 22(2), 95–106.

Byrnes, H. and H. H. Maxim. 2004. *Advanced Foreign Language Learning: A Challenge to College Programs. Issues in Language Program Direction*. Boston, MA: Heinle.

Byrnes, H., H. H. Maxim, and J. M. Norris. 2010. Realizing Advanced L2 Writing Development in Collegiate FL Education: Curricular Design, Pedagogy, and Assessment. *Modern Language Journal*, 94 (monograph issue).

Carreira, M. 2007. Spanish-for-Native-Speaker Matters: Narrowing the Latino Achievement Gap through Spanish Language Instruction. *Heritage Language Journal* 5(1), 147–171.

Christie, F. 2012. Language Education: A Functional Perspective. *Language Learning* 62 (March (Suppl. 1)), 1–247 (monograph issue).

Christie, F. and B. Derewianka. 2008. *School Discourse: Learning to Write across the Years of Schooling*. London: Continuum.

Christie, F. and J. R. Martin (eds.) 2007. *Language, Knowledge and Pedagogy: Functional Linguistic and Sociological Perspectives*. London: Continuum.

Christie, F. and L. Unsworth. 2000. Developing Socially Responsible Language Research. In L. Unsworth (ed.), *Researching Language in Schools and Communities*. London/Washington: Cassell, 1–26.

Choi, J. 2015. A Heritage Language Learner's Literacy Practices in a Korean Language Course in a U.S. University: From a Multiliteracies Perspective. *Journal of Language & Literacy Education* 2(2), 116–133.

CLAE: Corpus del Lenguaje Académico en Español. Retrieved from: www .lenguajeacademico.info

Colombi, M. C. 2002. Academic Language Development in Latino Students' Writing in Spanish. In Schleppegrell, M. J. and M. C. Colombi (eds.), *Developing Advanced Literacy in First and Second Languages*. Mahwah, NJ: Erlbaum, 67–86.

Colombi, M. C. 2006. Grammatical Metaphor: Academic Language Development in Latino Students in Spanish. In Byrnes, H. (ed.), *Advanced Language Learning: The Contribution of Halliday and Vygotsky*. London: Continuum, 147–163.

Colombi, M. C. 2009. A Systemic Functional Approach to Teaching Spanish for Heritage Speakers in the United States. *Linguistics and Education* 20(1), 39–49.

Colombi, M. C. 2015. Academic and Cultural Literacy for Heritage Speakers of Spanish: A Case Study of Latin@ Students in California. *Linguistics and Education* 32, 5–15.

Colombi, M. C. and F. X. Alarcón (eds.) 1997. *La enseñanza del español a hispanohablantes: praxis y teoría*. New York: Houghton Miflin.

Colombi, M. C. and D. Magaña. 2013. Alfabetización avanzada en español en los Estados Unidos en el siglo XXI. In Dumitrescu, D. and G. Piña-Rosales (eds.), *El español en los Estados Unidos: e pluribus unum? Enfoque multidisciplinar*. New York: ANLE, 339–352.

Cope, B. and M. Kalantzis. 2009. "Multiliteracies": New Literacies, New Learning. *Pedagogies: An International Journal* 4, 164–195.

Dreyfus, S., S. Humphrey, A. Mahboob, and J. Martin. 2016. *Genre Pedagogy in Higher Education: The SLATE Project*. Basingstoke: Palgrave Macmillan.

de Oliveira, L. C. and T. Silva (eds.) 2016. *Second Language Writing in Elementary Classrooms: Instructional Issues, Content-Area Writing, and Teacher Education*. New York: Palgrave Macmillan.

Fairclough, M. and S. Beaudrie (eds.) 2016. *Innovative Strategies for Heritage Language Teaching: A Practical Guide for the Classroom*. Washington, DC: Georgetown University Press.

García, O. 2009. *Bilingual Education in the 21st Century: A Global Perspective*. Oxford: Wiley-Blackwell.

García, O., L. Barlett, and J. Kleifgen. 2007. From Biliteracy to Pluriliteracies. In P. Auer and Li Wei (eds.). Handbook of Multilingualism and Multilingual Communication. Berlin/New York: Mouton de Gruyter 10, 207–228.

Grosjean, F. 2010. *Bilingual: Life and Reality*. Cambridge, MA: Harvard University Press.

Ignatieva, N. and M. C. Colombi. 2014. (Coords.). *CLAE: el lenguaje académico en México y los Estados Unidos: un análisis sistémico funcional*. Mexico: Centro de Enseñanza de Lenguas Extranjeras, Universidad Nacional Autónoma de México.

Halliday, M. A. K. 1978. *Language as Social Semiotic: The Social Interpretation of Language and Meaning.* Baltimore: University Park Press.

Halliday, M. A. K. 1991. The Notion of "Context" in Language Education. In Webster, J. (ed.), *Collected Works of M. A. K. Halliday, Language and Education* (Vol. 9). London: Continuum, 269–290.

Halliday, M. A. K. 1994. *An Introduction to Functional Grammar* (2nd ed.) London: Arnold.

Halliday, M. A. K. 1996a. Literacy and Linguistics: A Functional Perspective. In Hasan, R. and G. Williams, G. (eds.), *Literacy in Society.* London/New York: Addison-Wesley Longman, 339–376.

Halliday, M. A. K. 1996b. On Grammar and Grammatics. In Hasan, R., C. Cloran, and D. Butt (eds.), *Functional Descriptions: Theory in Practice.* Amsterdam/Philadelphia: Benjamins, 1–38.

Halliday, M. A. K. 2009. Varieties and Variation in Language: Dialect, Register, Code. In Webster, J. (ed.), *The Essential Halliday* (Vol. 1). London: Continuum, 429–450.

Halliday, M. A. K. and R. Hasan. 1976. *Cohesion in English.* London: Longman.

Halliday, M. A. K. and R. Hasan. 1985. *Language, Context, and Text: Aspects of Language in Social-Semiotic Perspective.* Geelong, Victoria: Deakin University Press.

Halliday, M. A. K. and C. M. I. M. Matthiessen. 1999. *Construing Experience through Meaning: A Language Based Approach to Cognition.* London: Continuum.

Halliday, M. A. K. and C. M. I. M. Matthiessen. 2004. *An Introduction to Functional Grammar* (3rd ed.) London: Arnold.

Hasan, R. 1996. Literacy, Everyday Talk and Society. In Hasan, R. and G. Williams (eds.), *Literacy in Society.* London/New York: Addison-Wesley Longman, 377–424.

He, A. W. 2015. Chinese as a Heritage Language. In Wang, W. S-Y. and C. Sun (eds,), *The Oxford Handbook of Chinese Linguistics.* Oxford: Oxford University Press, 578–589.

He, A. W. and Y. Xiao (eds.) 2008. *Chinese as a Heritage Language: Fostering Rooted World Citizenry.* Honolulu: University of Hawaii Press.

Henshaw, G. G. 2016. Online Courses for Heritage Learners: Best Practices and Lessons Learned. In Pascual y Cabo, D. (ed.), *Advances in Spanish as a Heritage Language.* Amsterdam: John Benjamins, 281–298.

Hill, J. 2001. The Racializing Function of Language Panics. In Dueñas González, R., and M. Ildikó (eds.), *Language Ideologies* (Vol. 2). Mahwah: LEA, 245–267.

Hornberger, N. H. (ed.) 2003. *Continua of Biliteracy: An Ecological Framework for Educational Policy, Research, and Practice in Multilingual Settings. Bilingual Education and Bilingualism, 41.* Clevedon: Multilingual Matters.

Kalantzis, M. and B. Cope. 2008. Language Education and Multiliteracies. In May, S. and N. H. Hornberger (eds.), *Encyclopedia of Language and Education,*

Language Policy and Political Issues in Education (Vol. **1**) (2nd ed.) New York: Springer, 195–211.

Kalantzis, M., B. Cope, E. Chan, and L. Dalley-Trim. 2016. *Literacies*. (2nd ed.) Cambridge: Cambridge University Press.

Kit-Fong Au, T. and J. Sae Oh. 2009. Korean as a Heritage Language. In Li, P., C. Lee, G. Simpson, and Y. Kim (eds.), *The Handbook of East Asian Psycholinguistics*. Cambridge: Cambridge University Press, 268–275.

Kondo-Brown, K. and J. D. Brown (eds.) 2011. *Teaching Chinese, Japanese, and Korean Heritage Language Students*. New York: Routledge.

Leeman, J., L. Rabin, and E. Román-Mendoza. 2011. Identity and Activism in Heritage Language Education. *The Modern Language Journal* **95**(4), 481–495.

Lowther Pereira, K. 2015. Developing Critical Language Awareness via Service-Learning for Spanish Heritage Speakers. *Heritage Language Journal* **12**(2), 159–185.

Montrul, S. 2013. *El bilingüismo en el mundo hispanohablante*. Malden, MA: Wiley-Blackwell.

Mu, G. M. 2016. *Learning Chinese as a Heritage Language: An Australian Perspective*. Bristol: Multilingual Matters.

Parra, M. L. 2016. Critical Approaches to Heritage Language Instruction: How to Forster Students' Critical Consciousness. In Fairclough, M. and S. M. Beaudrie (eds.), *Innovative Strategies for Heritage Language Teaching: A Practical Guide for the Classroom*. Washington, DC: Georgetown University Press, 166–190.

Parra, M. L. and E. G. Di Fabio. 2016. Languages in Partnership with the Visual Arts: Implications for Curriculum Design and Training. In Parkes, L., C. Ryan, and S. Katz-Bourns (eds.), *Issues in Language Program Direction: Integrating the Arts: Creative Thinking About FL Curricula and Language Program Direction*. Boston: Cengage, 11–36.

Parra, M. L., A. Otero, R. Flores, and M. Lavallée. 2018. Designing a Comprehensive Curriculum for Advanced Spanish Heritage Learners: Contributions from the Multiliteracies Framework. In Zapata, G. C. and M. Lacorte (eds.), *Multiliteracies Pedagogy and Language Learning: Teaching Spanish to Heritage Speakers*. Cham, Switzerland: Palgrave McMillan, 27–66.

Pascual y Cabo, D. (ed.) 2016. *Advances in Spanish as a Heritage Language*. Amsterdam: John Benjamins.

Petrov, L. A. 2013. A Pilot Study of Service Learning in a Spanish Heritage Speaker Course: Community Engagement, Identity, and Language in the Chicago Area. *Hispania* **96**(2) 310–332.

Pew Hispanic Center. 2013. Spanish Is the Most Spoken Non-English Language in U.S. Homes, Even among Non-Hispanics. Retrieved from: www.pewresearch.org/fact-tank/2013/08/13/spanish-is-the-most-spoken-non-english-language-in-u-s-homes-even-among-non-hispanics/

Pew Hispanic Center. 2017a. How the U.S. Hispanic Population is Changing. Retrieved from: www.pewresearch.org/fact-tank/2017/09/18/how-the-u-s-hispanic-population-is-changing/

Pew Hispanic Center. 2017b. Use of Spanish Declines among Latinos in Major U.S. Metros. Retrieved from: www.pewresearch.org/fact-tank/2017/10/31/use-of-spanish-declines-among-latinos-in-major-u-s-metros/

Polinsky, M. and O. Kagan. 2007. Heritage Languages: In the "Wild" and in the Classroom. *Language and Linguistics Compass* **1**(5), 368–395.

Reznicek-Parrado, L. M., M. Patiño-Vega, and M. C. Colombi. 2018. Academic Peer Tutors and Academic Biliteracy Development in Students of Spanish as a Heritage Language. *Journal of Spanish Language Teaching* **5**(2), 152–167.

Rothman, J. and T. Judy. 2014. Portuguese Heritage Language in the United States. In Wiley, T. G., J. K. Peyton, D. Christian, S. C. K. Moore, and N. Liu (eds.), *Handbook of Heritage, Community, and Native American Languages in the United States*. New York: Routledge. 132–142.

Rhyshina-Pankova, M. 2015. A Meaning-Based Approach to the Study of Complexity in L2 Writing: The Case of Grammatical Metaphor. *Journal of Second Language Writing* **29**, 51–63.

Ross, J. and F. Jaumont. 2013. French Heritage Language Vitality in the United States. *Heritage Language Journal* **10**(3), 23–33.

Ruan, J., J. Zhang, and C. B. Leung (eds.) 2016. *Chinese Language Education in the United States*. Vol.**14**. New York: Springer.

Schleppegrell, M. 2004. *The Language of Schooling: A Functional Linguistics Perspective*. Mahwah, NJ: Lawrence Erlbaum.

Schleppegrell, M. 2012. Academic Language in Teaching and Learning: Introduction to the Special Issue. *The Elementary School Journal* **112**(3), 409–418.

Schleppegrell, M. and F. Christie. 2018. Linguistic Features of Writing Development: A Functional Perspective. Special issue, *NCTE: The Lifespan Development of Writing*. Urbana, IL: NCTE, 111–150.

Schleppegrell, M. J. and M. C. Colombi (eds.) 2002. *Developing Advanced Literacy in First and Second Languages*. Mahwah, NJ: Erlbaum.

Silva-Corvalán, C. 2014. *Bilingual Language Acquisition: Spanish and English in the First Six Years*. Cambridge: Cambridge University Press.

Sohn, S. O. K. Shin. 2007. True Beginners, False Beginners, and Fake Beginners: Placement Strategies for Korean Heritage Speakers. *Foreign Language Annals* **40**(3), 407–418.

U.S. Census Bureau. 2017 Quick Facts California. Retrieved from www.census.gov/quickfacts/CA

U.S. Census Bureau. 2018. Retrieved on from: www.census.gov/newsroom/facts-for-features/2018/hispanic-heritage-month.html

Valdés, G. 2001. Heritage Languages Students: Profiles and Possibilities. In Peyton, J. K., D. A. Ranard, and S. McGinnis (eds.), *Heritage Languages in*

America: Preserving a National Resource. Washington, DC: Center for Applied Linguistics/Delta Systems, 37–77.

Valdés, G. 2005. Bilingualism, Heritage Language Learners, and SLA Research: Opportunities Lost or Seized? *Modern Language Journal* **89**, 410–426.

Wiley, T. G., J. K. Peyton, D. Christian, S. C. K. Moore, and N. Liu (eds.) 2014. *Handbook of Heritage, Community, and Native American Languages in the United States*. New York: Routledge.

Zapata, G. C. and M. Lacorte (eds.) 2018. *Multiliteracies Pedagogy and Language Learning: Teaching Spanish to Heritage Speakers*. Cham, Switzerland: Palgrave McMillan.

35

Heritage Language Assessment

Kimi Kondo-Brown

35.1   Introduction

Assessment is an indispensable component of sound heritage language (HL) curriculum development and instruction. Effective diagnostic, formative, and summative assessments can provide helpful feedback on HL learners' abilities to perform in the target HL and help them improve them. The results of such assessments can also provide teachers with valuable feedback on their teaching, materials, and assessment procedures. In general, formative assessment is important for learning (Popham 2008), but it is particularly important for instruction of HL learners with different levels of HL proficiency and affective needs (Carreira 2012). Thus, what may make pedagogical HL assessment distinct from other types of pedagogical language assessment is not its critical role in learning and teaching or the processes involved, but rather the fact that pedagogical HL assessment should be conducted in ways that are akin to HL learners' specific language needs as well as the contexts where the assessments are conducted. Also, it should be noted that, in planning and conducting assessment activities in school or classroom settings, including HL assessment, one challenging question that all teachers and administrators inevitably face is how to balance validity and reliability, on one hand, and practicality, on the other hand (Bachman and Palmer 1996; Brown 2005; Green 2014). For example, one-on-one oral testing – which may perhaps require multiple ratings to achieve defensible reliability – may take time and cost much more than paper-and-pencil testing that can be administered to a large group of students all at once. The issue of practicality may be self-evident in conducting assessment, but it is stressed here since it is interrelated with every aspect of HL assessment covered in this chapter.

According to Kondo-Brown's (2010) review of previous research on HL curriculum development, HL learners generally demonstrate higher levels of overall proficiency than second language (L2)[1] learners, but at the same time, HL learners potentially have characteristics that will require attention such as (a) unbalanced development of spoken and written language in the target HL (i.e., fluency in speaking but not in reading/writing); (b) challenges in learning the standard variety, especially among HL learners who have acquired informal varieties at home; (c) lack of metalinguistic knowledge needed for learning the target HL in academic contexts, and so forth. Heritage language learners often study the target HL together with non-HL students in L2 courses or in courses specifically intended for HL learners. In either situation, teachers may assess HL learners by using tools and procedures that draw on the existing approaches and theories in L2 testing and assessment – from discrete-point testing to performance testing and even to alternative assessments such as portfolios (e.g., Bailey 1998; Hughes 2003; Brown 2018). However, as Montrul and Perpiñán (2011) suggested, "L2 and HL learners may perform differently on different tasks and tests, depending on whether they are oral or written, and whether they are designed to tap implicit, intuitive knowledge or explicit, declarative knowledge" (124). Therefore, it is important for teachers to be aware of issues and challenges that are specific to the assessment of HL learners. Indeed, recent literature on HL assessment emphasizes that more attention has to be paid to a number of issues in assessing HL learners (e.g., Llosa 2013; Malone et al. 2014; Son 2017).

It should also be noted here that the HL assessment studies discussed in this chapter were largely conducted in the United States. In the United States, Spanish is by far the most commonly taught language in the formal educational system, followed by such languages as French and German (Fee et al. 2014; Looney and Lusin 2018). However, other languages – which are sometimes labelled as "less commonly taught language (LCTL)" – are also distributed widely in American schools and universities, and they play an important role in HL instruction. A recent national survey indicates that LCTL programs differ considerably in terms of enrollments, types of programs, availability of proficiency tests, and so forth (American Councils for International Education 2017). Thus, while all teachers of HL students may need to cope with differences in proficiency profiles of individual students in the same class, the degree of such differences may vary more in some LCTL classes, especially in mixed-ability ones. In addition, since LCTLs are taught on a much-limited scale, teachers may face assessment issues and

---

[1] In this chapter, the term "second language" is used in a broad sense: "any language learned after one has learnt one's native language" (Richard and Schmidt 2010: 514).

challenges that teachers of commonly taught languages may not have to deal with. For example, proficiency tests that are available for Spanish, French, and German may not be available for many LCTLs.

35.2   Defining Heritage Language Learners for Heritage Language Assessment

The term "heritage language learner" has been defined from different perspectives. From a personal perspective, HL learners can be defined as any individuals who are learning a non-dominant language that has family or ancestral connections and also want to be identified as such. For example, Hornberger and Wang (2008) propose that HL learners in countries like the United States should be broadly defined as "individuals with familial or ancestral ties to a language other than English who exert their agency in determining if they are HLLs [HL learners] of that language" (6). With this definition, neither the individual's home language background nor their proficiency in the target HL is a determining factor. That is, HL learners defined this way may have grown up in a family in which no one has a functional ability to speak the HL.

From a *pedagogical* perspective, a narrower definition of HL learners is not only useful but also necessary to communicate about pedagogical approaches and strategies for HL learners whose linguistic and situational needs are considerably different from the more familiar L2 learners in foreign language classrooms (Kondo-Brown 2002). With this definition, an HL learner in a country like the United States may refer to "a language student who is raised in a home where a non-English language is spoken, who speaks or at least understands the language, and who is to some degree bilingual in that language and English" (Valdés 2001: 38). With this narrower definition of HL learners, the process and outcomes of HL acquisition are regarded as distinctly different from those of L2 acquisition (The UCLA Steering Committee 2000; Valdés 2005). A key determiner in differentiating HL acquisition from L2 acquisition is that "heritage language acquisition begins in the home, as opposed to foreign language acquisition which, at least initially, usually begins in a classroom setting" (The UCLA Steering Committee 2000: 339). It should be noted that although Valdés' definition may be focused on HL learners in countries where English is the dominant language, it can be expanded to HL learners in other countries where English is not the dominant language. For example, Polinsky (2018) defines a "heritage language speaker" in various parts of the world as "a simultaneous or sequential (successive) bilingual whose weaker language corresponds to the minority language of their society and whose stronger language is the dominant language of that society" (9).

In a country like the United States, children of the dominant language group are usually socialized and educated in their first-acquired language (L1) throughout their lives. Such children may become what Valdés and Figueroa (1994) call "elective" bilinguals, who "choose to become bilingual and who seek out either formal classes or contexts in which they can acquire a foreign language" (12). For elective bilinguals, their L1 remains as their stronger language in the process of adding linguistic and cultural competence in an L2 to their linguistic and cultural repertoires (additive bilingualism). Valdés and Figueroa differentiated these elective bilinguals from "circumstantial" bilinguals who become bilinguals because of their circumstantial needs. That is, their L1 is not the society's dominant language, and they need to learn the society's dominant language to meet their communication needs in that language outside their home. For circumstantial bilinguals, their proficiency in their non-dominant L1 may become weaker than that of the dominant language (subtractive bilingualism).

For those who design and conduct HL assessments for pedagogical or research purposes, Valdés and Figueroa's classification of bilingualism – elective vs. circumstantial – is useful because an HL may be understood and assessed as a circumstantial bilingual's non-dominant L1, which "has not been completely acquired because of the switch to another dominant language" (Polinsky 2008: 149). However, as Valdés and Figueroa (1994) noted, they are "not always mutually exclusive" (13). In other words, it does not mean that circumstantial bilinguals do not have agency in their bilingual development. On the contrary, circumstantial bilinguals who have achieved high-level or native-like fluency in both languages, especially literacy skills, have often chosen to invest a substantial amount of time in learning the HL in formal or non-formal school settings (e.g., Kondo-Brown 2006).

35.3   Two Types of Testing for Heritage Language Instruction and Research

Among various pedagogical assessment tools, testing is probably the most widely used assessment procedure for HL learners. In research where HL proficiency is a variable, testing is also a common procedure to measure it. The most common tests used for measuring HL proficiency for research purposes are cloze tests, targeted vocabulary/lexical knowledge tests, and speech production tests (e.g., for measuring the mean length of utterance [MLU]) (see Polinsky 2018: 105–113). Heritage language teachers and researchers basically use two types of testing: criterion-referenced testing (CRT) and norm-referenced testing (NRT). These two types of tests are fundamentally different in terms of their purposes, score distributions, score interpretations, and uses, and therefore, it is very important that they be used as intended. Achievement tests that teachers develop locally and use for pedagogical purposes (e.g., assessing the degree to which students have mastered learning objectives or outcomes of a lesson or course) should be designed, interpreted, and used according to CRT principles (Brown and Hudson 2002). For example, when teachers assign grades and make pass or fail decisions, they should interpret the test scores with reference to the achievement criteria, not by ranking students against each other, i.e., grading on a curve. The use of CRT is particularly important for students (including HL learners) in a "differentiated classroom," in which the teacher plans for diverse student learning needs and goals (Tomlinson and Moon 2013). Also, as Hughes (2003) states, in order to achieve maximum beneficial washback (or backwash) of classroom assessments for students, teachers should use CRT that assesses the very abilities that they want the students to improve. For example, if teachers want to encourage their HL learners to improve academic writing skills, they should use written performance tests for which the students practice academic writing in the target HL, not receptive grammar tests that do not require writing in the language.

Proficiency tests, on the other hand, are designed, analyzed, and interpreted within an NRT framework, and they may be used for pedagogical and research purposes. Proficiency tests are usually based on a given theoretical model of language ability, communicative competence, or whatever proficiency construct the test intends to assess. Such tests are intended to spread the examinees on a continuum of the target language ability or performance being assessed (Brown 2005). Some of the most frequently used NRTs are standardized proficiency tests and locally designed placement tests, which will be discussed later in the chapter. For example, in order to adequately and effectively place HL students of diverse abilities from novice to advanced-level courses, we need to have an NRT that can effectively discriminate abilities at all levels. Also, when researchers conduct an inferential study in which proficiency test scores are collected from a sample of HL learners, one of the assumptions for inferential analyses is that the scores are normally distributed. In addition, in both CRT and NRT, when you develop and use performance tests in which HL learners are asked to demonstrate their ability to perform something (e.g., writing a story), the use of scoring rubrics is recommended because it will allow teachers to generate consistent ratings and provide effective feedback (Arter and McTighe 2001; Stevens and Levi 2005; Brown 2012). Again, rubrics for CRT should be tailored for specific learning objectives or outcomes of a course/lesson. In contrast, rubrics for NRT should be designed to measure a wider range of proficiency (e.g., novice to superior). When the same scoring rubrics are developed and used for students from various backgrounds, it is also important to examine the degree to which rater severity or leniency may be biased toward a specific group of candidates, rating categories, etc. (Kondo-Brown 2002).

Heritage language teachers may use the results of particular achievement or proficiency tests for diagnostic, formative, and summative assessments. *Diagnostic assessment* is conducted to gather information about a student's prior learning (e.g., placement test). In dealing with HL learners, it is particularly important to gather information about their prior learning to find out if they have critically differentiated needs. *Formative assessment* is a process where the teacher gathers evidence of student learning and then uses the information as feedback on their learning, e.g., what they can do or what language needs they have (e.g., quizzes, self-assessments). Finally, *summative assessment* is a process where the teacher gathers and uses cumulative information about student learning at the end of a course or program (e.g., a capstone paper, final presentation). Teachers use the cumulative achievement information not only to assign grades or make pass or fail decisions but also to advise students about their future course of learning. As Bachman (1990) stated, in validating a test, "we are not examining the validity of the test content or of even the test scores themselves, but rather the validity of the way we interpret or use the information gathered through the testing procedure" (283). Thus, in designing tests for HL learners, the test developers and users need to pay careful attention not only to the test content and format but other issues such as score interpretations and their uses.

35.4   Applicability of Second Language Proficiency Tests in Assessing Heritage Language Proficiency

In the United States, one of the most widely used and influential standardized L2 proficiency tests is probably the Oral Proficiency Interview (OPI) developed by the American Council on the Teaching of Foreign Languages (ACTFL). For example, university L2 programs funded by the federal government such as the National Flagship program are required to use the ACTFL and ILR (Interagency Language Roundtable) OPI ratings for assessing the oral proficiency of students (Murphy and Evans-Romaine 2016). Also, in order to comply with the accreditation requirements of the National Council for the Accreditation of Teacher Education (NCATE), many states require world language teacher licensure candidates to achieve a designated ACTFL OPI (or other proficiency) rating. According to the ACTFL website (www.actfl.org/), as of February 2012, the OPI is available for over eighty languages. In the past, the official ACTFL OPI was conducted exclusively in the face-to-face or phone interview formats, but today computer-based

ACTFL OPI (OPIc) tests – which are more affordable and flexible in schedul-ing – are also available for commonly taught languages and some LCTLs.

In the past, the validity issues for the *ACTFL Proficiency Guidelines* as well as the OPI were widely and critically debated (e.g., Bachman and Savignon 1986; Lantolf and Frawley 1985; Fulcher 1996; Salaberry 2000), and future research that generates empirical evidence for validating their criteria and procedures has been called for (Chalhoub-Deville and Fulcher 2003; Malone 2003; Tominaga 2013). For example, Chalhoub-Deville and Fulcher (2003) argued that "ACTFL has a responsibility to its many stakeholders to initiate a comprehensive, focused research program to collect appropriate and meaningful evidence that documents the quality of OPI practices and ratings" (504). In these critical validation studies, the HL background of the candidates has not been a key variable, but a few other studies have examined the usefulness of the *ACTFL Proficiency Guidelines* and OPI in such HLs as Hindi/Urdu, Russian, and Spanish (e.g., Valdés 1989; Kagan and Friedman 2003; Ilieva 2012; Martin et al. 2013; Swender et al. 2014). These studies appear to suggest that there are language-specific issues in using the *Guidelines* or OPI in assessing HL proficiency, and therefore, when these instruments are used for HL learners, it needs to be done cautiously. For example, Valdés (1989) examined the discriminatory power of some of the 14 categories (length of utterance, topic areas, vocabulary, fluency, comprehensibility, etc.) underlying the generic *Guidelines* for assessing pro-ficiency levels for Hispanic HL learners. Valdés concluded that Hispanic HL learners may not quite fit into the stages of language development described in the guidelines and that some performance descriptors may need to be modified to measure Hispanic HL proficiency effectively. More recent literature continues emphasizing the need for future research that will help the ACTFL develop performance descriptors that address differ-ences in linguistics profile between L2 and HL learners (Ilieva and Clark-Gareca 2016).

As Malone, Peyton, and Kim (2014) pointed out, "(re)searchers' lack of consensus regarding the validity of the *ACTFL Proficiency Guidelines* (or, for that matter, any other rubric for delineating language proficiency) compli-cates language assessment in general and HL assessment in particular, representing confusion over a fundamental concept in an already murky subfield" (353). For example, in an earlier study, Lantolf and Frawley (1985) questioned the claim in the *Guidelines* that "all L2 speakers must be meas-ured ultimately in relation to the educated native speaker, who is thus taken as the norm against which all L2 speaker performance is judged" (343). From the HL perspective, Valdés (1989) similarly argued that the *Guidelines*, which were developed based on the norm of an educated native speaker who speaks the standard variety, may disadvantage Hispanic HL learners who speak the non-standard varieties of Spanish. On the other hand, Kagan and Friedman (2003) – who investigated whether the *Guidelines* are appropriate for assessing Russian HL proficiency – did not take issue with using the educated native speaker norm as the reference point. They suggested that the *Guidelines* work for Russian HL learners as well as they do for Russian FL learners. However, at the same time, they found that some HL learners "deviated from the ACTFL descriptors in three areas: pronunciation, fluency (rate of speech), and vocabulary" (Kagan and Friedman 2003: 540). In a related study (Polinsky 2008), child and adult Russian HL speakers' narratives were compared to "fully competent" child and adult speakers of Russian. The analysis of the Russian narrative data indicated that (a) HL speakers use much shorter utterances with fewer embedding and at a much slower rate and (b) adult HL speakers may be characterized by the loss of cases, the restructuring of aspect, and inconsistent use of tense. The results suggest that the use of these variables will be useful for delineating and assessing Russian HL proficiency.

Despite the ongoing challenging issues, given the current public awareness of educational accountability and the national interest in an outcomes-based L2 curriculum (Norris 2006), the *ACTFL Proficiency Guidelines* and OPI will probably remain influential in L2 and HL education. As mentioned previously, in the past, the ACTFL OPIs were available only in face-to-face or phone interview formats, but today computer-based OPIs have become more common for a number of languages, including Spanish. Given this trend, validation studies for the ACTFL OPIc will be needed for both HL and L2 learners. For example, a recent validation study that compared OPIc and OPI ratings suggests that the former may produce higher ratings than the latter (Thomson, Cox, and Knapp 2016). Validation research on HL learners' performances on the ACTFL listening, reading, and writing proficiency tests should also be expanded (e.g., Gatti and O'Neill 2018).

Since these proficiency tests developed by the ACTFL are intended for adults, the ACTFL has recently developed the *Assessment of Performance toward Proficiency in Languages* (AAPPL), a web-based proficiency test intended for younger, non-adult learners. As the development and uses of AAPPL for HL and L2 learners expand in the future, validation research on these instruments will be necessary, too. At the same time, it will also be necessary to examine the uses of some other standards-based online assessment instruments for pre-collegiate or young learners such as the *STAMP* (*Standards-Measurement of Proficiency*), which have been developed based on the ACTFL guidelines. Furthermore, in the United States, validation research will be needed for foreign language Advanced Placement (AP) exams, high-stakes exams that a growing number of high school students from diverse language backgrounds take to earn college credits (Brown and Thompson 2016). AP exams are also used in many states to award the *Seal of Biliteracy* (https://sealofbiliteracy.org/) to high school students. According to

the annual score distributions posted on the College Board website (www
.collegeboard.org), in languages like Spanish, the vast majority of students
taking the exam appear to be HL learners. However, no validation studies
surfaced on foreign language AP exams in which HL background is used as
a variable.

35.5   Placement Tools and Procedures for HL Learners in University Language Programs

According to Brown, Hudson, and Clark's (2004) national L2 placement test
survey, university L2 programs in the United States typically use locally
developed placement tests and self-assessments, but for some languages
such as Spanish, commercial or standardized proficiency tests (e.g.,
WebCAPE) are also widely used. They also reported that receptive tests such
as reading comprehension and grammatical knowledge are much more
commonly used than production tests. Generally speaking, in order to avoid
the misplacement of incoming students – HL learners or not – into courses
of different levels, the use of multiple placement procedures is recommended (e.g., receptive and productive tests), and this is especially true
for HL learners whose linguistic strengths and deficiencies need to be
identified (Fairclough 2012: Ilieva and Clark-Gareca 2016). Also, the additional use of an autobiographic or background questionnaire that includes
self-reported language use and proficiency ratings may be useful for placing
HL learners (see Domingo 2008; Ranjan 2008).

   Although there is no national survey to date that examines the use of
placement tests intended for HL learners, a number of assessment studies
have examined issues concerning the placement of HL learners for
university-level courses, especially Spanish HL placement. A number of
Spanish placement tests have been developed to effectively place HL and
L2 learners into their respective university-level programs. These placement
tests include the computerized placement exam for the Spanish HL program at the University of Arizona (Beaudrie and Ducar 2012); the computerized adaptive placement exam for the Spanish program at the University of
Illinois at Chicago (Potowski et al. 2012); the Spanish placement exam for
Spanish HL sequence at New Mexico State University (MacGregor-Mendoza
2012); the Spanish placement exam for both HL and L2 learners at the
University of New Mexico (Wilson 2012); and the Spanish placement exam,
including a lexical recognition task, for the HL track of the Spanish program at the University of Houston (Fairclough 2011; Fairclough et al. 2010).
Llosa (2013) and Son (2017) provide an excellent review of these Spanish
placement exams developed at US-based individual institutions, and both
emphasize the importance of expanding validation research on HL

placement since it is important and yet very scarce. As Beaudrie (2012) pointed out, "no test should be seen as a final product, but rather as a product in constant need of monitoring, evaluation, and improvement" (vii). In order to further advance research on Spanish placement, future research will need to continue investigating the validity and reliability of existing Spanish placement test items. More work on the linguistic profiles of Spanish HL learners might usefully inform test development as well (see, for example, Montrul and Perpiñán 2011).

Compared to research on Spanish HL placement, research on locally developed placement tests for HL learners in other languages is even scarcer. The target HLs examined in placement testing research seem to be limited to Filipino (Domingo 2008), Hindi (Ranjan 2008), Japanese (Kondo-Brown 2004, 2005), and Korean (Sohn and Shin 2007). For example, Kondo-Brown's (2005) study examined the distributions of test scores of locally made placement tests in multiple-choice formats (listening, grammar, and reading) for university L2 and HL learners. The study compared test score distributions among the four groups divided by their degree of connection to Japanese heritage (i.e., HL learners with a Japanese parent to those who have no connection to Japanese heritage). The study showed that test score distributions for HL learners with a Japanese parent were negatively skewed (i.e., scores were clustered at the upper end of the scale), while score distributions for other groups were similar – more or less evenly and normally distributed over the range of possible scores. These results indicate that, although multiple-choice tests may be more commonly used, some kind of validation study is necessary to examine the degree to which they effectively discriminate well for advanced-level HL learners' proficiency. Also, as discussed earlier, HL linguistic profiling research can inform test developers. For example, Kanno, Hasegawa, Ikeda, Ito, and Long (2008) indicated that, compared to L1 speakers of Japanese, advanced-level Japanese HL learners are weak in academic vocabulary and collocation, especially *kango* (sophisticated lexical compounds written in Chinese characters). Empirical research like this suggests that the use of *kango* in a written test may help discriminate literacy abilities among advanced-level Japanese HL learners.

In a related study, Kondo-Brown (2004) suggested that a simple essay test may serve as an effective placement procedure for discriminating proficiency levels of Japanese HL learners. In the study, students were prompted to write on a topic of their choice (e.g., describe yourself). The scoring rubric was based on a rubric for English L2 writing tests for norm-referenced purposes. Kondo-Brown (2004) showed that scores were more or less evenly distributed over the range of possible scores for both L2 and HL learners. Although a written performance test may not be as practical as a multiple-choice grammar or reading test, the study suggested that it may help discriminate among HL learners whose receptive knowledge and skills are relatively high. Similar results were also reported in the Sohn and Shin's (2007) study of university Korean HL students, that is, the composition test had more discrimination power than the multiple-choice tests. In order to avoid possible misplacement of HL learners, these authors recommended the use of placement tools like a formal academic writing task and a diagnostic oral interview test when performances on the multiple-choice test and the writing test are unbalanced. While practicality is a major concern with any type of performance test, it appears that efforts should be made where possible to develop multiple procedures for assessing HL proficiency for placement purposes.

35.6   Assessment in Pre-collegiate Heritage Language Programs

Pre-collegiate HL learners (including young learners) in countries like the United States may study their HL in (a) various types of bilingual education programs, including dual language programs within the formal education system or (b) in after-school or weekend community-based programs outside the formal education system[2] (Moore 2014). Among various types of bilingual education programs that support HL development, dual language programs may be most desirable because they "provide opportunities for majority and minority language speakers to learn together while capitalizing on multiple sets of realities and backgrounds, with the goal of bilingualism for everyone involved, thus providing a context for HL development" (Moore 2014: 345). Howard, Sugarman, Christian, Lindholm-Leary, and Rogers' (2007) analysis of "effective bilingual and dual language programs" indicates that such programs take assessment and accountability seriously. They reported that effective programs "[use] student achievement data to shape and/or monitor their instructional program," "use assessment measures that are aligned with the school's vision and goals and with appropriate curriculum and related standards," and "require the use of multiple measures in both languages to assess students' progress toward meeting bilingual and biliteracy goals along with the curricular and content-related goals" (Howard et al. 2007: 8). They further argue that more opportunities for professional development in assessment, appropriate infrastructure with a focus on assessment, and adequate budget for assessment are necessary to improve student general academic achievement or other academic outcomes in bilingual programs.

[2] See, for example, a comprehensive online database for dual language and community-based HL programs on the website of the Center for Applied Linguistics (www.cal.org/resource-center/databases-directorie).

From a multilingual assessment perspective, assessing bilingual ability, especially that of young learners in dual programs, is not a simple matter. On the one hand, bilingual education researchers and professionals in general appear to accept and support the view that bilinguals should not be treated as two monolinguals in one (Grosjean 1985; Valdés 2005). From this view, bilinguals are seen as those who have acquired two linguistic systems in particular contexts for specific reasons or purposes and therefore use their linguistic repertoires in highly complex and dynamic ways. The widely discussed concept of "translanguaging" also encourages language educators to view bilinguals' use of two languages holistically (Garcia and Wei 2014). On the other hand, however, the most common practice for teachers of bilingual HL learners is to assess the individual's proficiencies in two languages separately by using the native norm as a reference point for measuring proficiency in each language.

As Shohamy's (2011) multilingual assessment continuum indicates, at one end, multilingual assessment is viewed as assessing two or more languages separately using multiple separate tests, one for each language – the view on which proficiency measurements of bilinguals in dual programs are typically based. On the other end of the continuum, multilingual assessment is viewed as assessing the language repertoire of multilingual individuals as a unified linguistic system. With this view of multilingual assessment, "mixing languages is a legitimate act that does not result in penalties but rather is an effective means of expressing and communicating ideas that cannot be transmitted in one language" (Shohamy 2011: 427). Clearly, this is a highly complex issue, and more future research is needed.

In related work, Guzman-Orth, Lopez, and Tolentino's (2017) reported on "conceptual scoring," which allows bilingual students to use all linguistic recourses in multiple languages in performing tasks. However, the report is largely theoretical, and no empirical evidence is provided. Future research should perhaps expand this line of inquiry. Furthermore, in the United States, a long history of bilingual education politics (see, for example, chapter 9 of Baker and Wright 2017) may have contributed biases to the procedures and interpretations of research that investigates successes and failures of bilingual programs. Therefore, in using research data on bilingual education that discusses the benefits and harm of using and developing HL of language minorities in the mainstream school, care should be taken to interpret the methodology and results by considering the social and political contexts (for more discussion on social and political dimensions of language testing, see McNamara and Roever 2006; Shohamy and Menken 2015).

Community-based HL programs/schools outside the formal system are largely operated and supported by community leaders, parents, and volunteers (see Chapter 30). They differ considerably in terms of curriculum, teaching methods and materials, as well as assessment tools and procedures. There are also serious needs for teacher training to help teachers improve their teaching and assessment of students in their programs/ schools (Caballero 2014). Among the US-based HL programs offered outside the formal education system, one of the largest HL programs is probably *nihongo hoshuu jyugyookoo* (Japanese language supplementary instruction school), or "*hoshuukoo*" in its abbreviated form, which is supported by the Japanese government and local Japanese communities.[3] The *hoshuukoo* has played a critical role in Japanese HL education since students typically attend local "all-English" mainstream schools where instruction in the HL is not available (Sato and Kataoka 2008). There is a growing literature on the *hoshuukoo*, but very little focus on assessment. To date, assessment practices at the *hoshuukoo* are largely unknown and many important questions seem to remain unanswered (e.g., what is assessed at the *hoshuukoo* and how are the results of assessments used). More work is clearly needed on assessment at the *hoshuukoo* to help teachers improve their assessment practices.

As the nation's leading L2 language, it seems that numerous Spanish assessments have been developed for English-Spanish dual language programs (The Center for Applied Linguistics 2007). However, validation studies of these instruments are scarce. Similarly, Hasegawa (2008) – who examined various proficiency measures for Japanese HL learners (e.g., written tests, oral interviews, and self-assessments) – reported that "little information was available for examining the validity" (84).[4] She also noted the issue of balancing practicality and validity. As pointed out earlier, this is an issue that needs to be considered for any type of assessment.

Also, in order to provide adequate assessments for pre-collegiate students, especially young learners, teachers may need to develop and use age-appropriate assessment instruments that consider the learners' cognitive, metalinguistic, and physical abilities to expect positive washback to the learners (Hughes 2003; McKay 2006; Butler 2016). For example, as part of formative assessment, McKay (2006) emphasizes the importance of "on-the-run assessment" (a term adapted from Breen [1997]), or informal, instruction-embedded assessment, for assessing young learners. Her notion of "on-the-run assessment" is also informed by Rea-Dickins' (2001) work on

---

[3] The Japanese Ministry of Education, Culture, Sports, Science and Technology (MEXT) (2016) reported that there were 205 *hoshuukoo* in various parts of the world, of which 88 were located in North America. The *hoshuukoo* offer after-school or weekend immersion programs for young learners of Japanese as a native language or HL (usually from kindergarten to 9th grade). The *hoshuukoo* curriculum may differ from one school to another to some degree, but it should be based on the national academic curriculum guidelines used in public schools in Japan and use board-certified textbooks provided by the Japanese government.

[4] Some of the studies reviewed in Hasegawa's (2008) study were pedagogical case studies that reported the process and outcomes of the assessment tools, and others examined Japanese language proficiency as a research variable, but hardly any study explicitly discussed validity issues, i.e., what intended construct is being measured with the instrument in question.

instruction-embedded classroom assessment. During the on-the-run assessment process, the teacher engages in scaffolding as needed and monitors and provides feedback on the young learners' performance. The theoretical benefits of instruction-embedded assessment are also a basis for dynamic assessment that has "the goal of diagnosing learning potential and promoting development in accordance with this potential" (Lantolf 2009: 360). Given the importance of formative assessment for learning, future empirical research is recommended for validating any approach that integrates instruction and assessment for young HL learners.

35.7   Conclusion

Assessment is an indispensable component of HL instruction and student learning, and yet conducting effective assessment is not easy to do well for most HL teachers, especially for those with administrative and financial restrictions. Nonetheless, in the profession of teaching, assessment is all about providing feedback on student learning and the learners need that. In order to provide support for teachers and inspire them to improve their assessment practices for their HL learners, they need new knowledge (of what needs to be assessed and how) and assessment tools relevant to their situation. To provide such knowledge and tools, research on HL learners and assessment will need to expand and inform teachers of practical implications. Also, given the scarcity of assessment procedures for HL learners for most languages, more professional development opportunities focused on L2 assessment in general and HL assessment in particular will be helpful.

References

American Councils for International Education. 2017. *The National K-16 Foreign Language Enrollment Survey Report.* Retrieved from www .americancouncils.org/sites/default/files/FLE-report.pdf

Arter, J. and J. McTighe. 2001. *Scoring Rubrics in the Classroom.* Thousand Oaks, CA: Corwin Press.

Bachman, L. F. 1990. *Fundamental Considerations in Language Testing.* Oxford: Oxford University Press.

Bachman, L. F. and A. S. Palmer. 1996. *Language Testing in Practice.* Oxford: Oxford University Press.

Bachman, L. F. and S. J. Savignon. 1986. The Evaluation of Communicative Language Proficiency: A Critique of the ACTFL Oral Interview. *The Modern Language Journal* 70(4), 380–390.

Bailey, K. M. 1998. *Learning about Language Assessment: Dilemmas, Decisions, and Directions.* Cambridge, MA: Heinle & Heinle.

Baker, C. and W. E. Wright. 2017. *Foundations of Bilingual Education and Bilingualism* (6th ed.) Bristol: Multilingual Matters.

Beaudrie, S. M. 2012. Introduction: Developments in Spanish Heritage Language Assessment. *Heritage Language Journal* 9(1), i–xi.

Beaudrie, S. and C. Ducar. 2012. Language Placement and beyond: Guidelines for the Design and Implementation of a Computerized Spanish Heritage Language Exam. *Heritage Language Journal* 9(1), 77–99.

Breen, M. P. 1997. The Relationship between Assessment Frameworks and Classroom Pedagogy. In M. P. Breen, C. Barratt-Pugh, B. Derewianka, H. House, C. Hudson, T. Lumley, and M. Rohl (eds.), *Profiling ESL Children: How Teachers Interpret and Use National and State Assessment Frameworks*, Vol. 1. Canberra: Department of Employment, Education, Training and Youth Affairs, 91–128.

Brown, A. V. and G. L. Thompson. 2016. The Evolution of Foreign Language AP Exam Candidates: A 36-year Descriptive Study. *Foreign Language Annals* 49(2), 235–251.

Brown, D. 2018. *Language Assessment: Principles and Classroom Practices* (3rd ed.) White Plains, NY: Pearson Education ESL.

Brown, J. D. 2005. *Testing in Language Program: A Comprehensive Guide to English Language Assessment* (revised ed.) New York: McGraw-Hill.

Brown, J. D. (ed.) 2012. *Developing, Using, and Analyzing Rubrics in Language Assessment with Case Studies in Asian-Pacific Languages*. Honolulu, HI: National Foreign Languages Resource Center Publications.

Brown, J. D. and T. Hudson. 2002. *Criterion-Referenced Language Testing*. Cambridge: Cambridge University Press.

Brown, J. D., T. Hudson, and M. Clark. 2004. *Issues in Placement Survey*. Honolulu: National Foreign Language Resource Center, University of Hawai'i. Retrieved from http://nflrc.hawaii.edu/NetWorks/NW40/SurveyResults.html

Butler, Y. G. 2016. Assessing Young Learners. In D. Tsagari and J. Banerjee (eds.), *Handbook of Second Language Assessment*. Berlin: De Gruyter Mouton, 359–376.

Caballero, A. M. S. 2014. Preparing Teachers to Work with Heritage Language Learners. In T. G. Wiley, J. K. Peyton, D. Christian, S. C. Moore, and N. Liu (eds.), *Handbook of Heritage, Community, and Native American Languages in the United States*. New York: Routledge, 359–369.

Carreira, M. M. 2012. Formative Assessment in HL Teaching: Purposes, Procedures, and Practices. *Heritage Language Journal* 9(1), 100–120.

Chalhoub-Deville, M. snd G. Fulcher. 2003. The Oral Proficiency Interview and the ACTFL Guidelines: A Research Agenda. *Foreign Language Annals* 36(4), 498–506.

Domingo, N. P. 2008.Towards a Heritage-Learner-Sensitive Filipino Placement Test at UCLA. In T. Hudson and M. Clark (eds.), *Case Studies in*

Foreign Language Placement: Practices and Possibilities. Honolulu: University of Hawaii, National Foreign Language Resource Center, 17–28.

Fairclough, M. 2011. Testing the Lexical Recognition Task with Spanish/ English Bilinguals in the United States. *Language Testing* 28(2), 273–297.

Fairclough, M. 2012. A Working Model for Assessing Spanish Heritage Language Learners' Language Proficiency through a Placement Exam. *Heritage Language Journal* 9(1), 121–138.

Fairclough, M., F. Belpoliti, and E. Bermejo. 2010. Developing an Electronic Placement Examination for Heritage Learners of Spanish: Challenges and Payoffs. *Hispania* 93(2), 273–291.

Fee, M., N. C. Rhodes, and T. G. Wiley. 2014. Demographic Realities, Challenges, and Opportunities. In T. Wiley, J. K. Peyton, C. Christian, S. Moore, and N. Liu (eds.), *Handbook of Heritage, Community, and Native American Languages in the United States: Research, Educational Practice, and Policy*. New York: Routledge, 6–18.

Fulcher, G. 1996. Invalidating Validity Claims for the ACTFL Oral Rating Scale. *System* 24(2), 163–172.

Garcia, O. and L. Wei. 2014. *Translanguaging: Language, Bilingualism and Education*. London: Palgrave Macmillan.

Gatti, A. and T. O'Neill. 2018. Writing Proficiency Profiles of Heritage Learners of Chinese, Korean, and Spanish. *Foreign Language Annals* 51(4), 719–737.

Green, A. 2014. *Exploring Language Assessment and Testing: Language in Action*. New York: Routledge.

Grosjean, F. 1985. The Bilingual as a Competent but Specific Speaker-Hearer. *Journal of Multilingual and Multicultural Development* 6(6), 467–477.

Guzman-Orth, D., A. A. Lopez, and F. Tolentino. 2017. *A Framework for the Dual Language Assessment of Young Dual Language Learners in the United States* (Research Report No. RR-17-37). Princeton, NJ: Educational Testing Service. Retrieved from https://doi.org/10.1002/ets2.12165

Hasegawa, T. 2008. Measuring the Japanese Proficiency of Heritage Language Children. In K. Kondo-Brown and J. D. Brown (eds.), *Teaching Chinese, Japanese and Korean Heritage Language Students: Curriculum Needs, Materials, and Assessment*. New York: Lawrence Erlbaum Associates, 77–98.

Hornberger, N. H. and S. C. Wang. 2008. Who Are Our Heritage Language Learners? Identity and Biliteracy in Heritage Language Education in the United States. In D. M. Brinton, O. Kagan, and S. Bauckus (eds.), *Heritage Language Education: A New Field Emerging*. New York: Routledge, 3–35.

Howard, E. R., J. Sugarman, D. Christian, K. J. Lindholm-Leary, and D. Rogers. 2007. *Guiding Principles for Dual Language Education* (2nd ed.) Washington, DC: Center for Applied Linguistics. Retrieved from www.cal .org/ndlf/pdfs/guiding-principles-for-dual-language-education.pdf

Hughes, A. 2003. *Testing for Language Teachers* (2nd ed.) Cambridge: Cambridge University Press.

Ilieva, G. N. 2012. Hindi Heritage Language Learners' Performance during OPIs: Characteristics and Pedagogical Implications. *Heritage Language Journal* 9(2), 18–36.

Ilieva, G. N. and B. Clark-Gareca. 2016. Heritage Language Learner Assessment: Toward Proficiency Standards. In M. Fairclough and S. M. Beaudrie (eds.), *Innovative Strategies for Heritage Language Teaching: A Practical Guide for the Classroom*. Washington, DC: Georgetown University Press, 214–236.

Kagan, O. and D. Friedman. 2003. Using the OPI to Place Heritage Speakers of Russian. *Foreign Language Annals* 36(4), 536–545.

Kanno, K., T. Hasegawa, K. Ikeda, Y. Ito, and M. H. Long. 2008. Prior Language-Learning Experience and Variation in the Linguistic Profiles of Advanced English-Speaking Learners of Japanese. In D. M. Brinton, O. Kagan, and S. Bauckus (eds.), *Heritage Language Education: A New Field Emerging*. New York: Routledge, 215–228.

Kondo-Brown, K. 2002. A FACETS Analysis of Rater Bias in Measuring Japanese Second Language Writing Performance. *Language Testing* 19(1), 1–29.

Kondo-Brown, K. 2004. Do Background Variables Predict Students' Scores on a Japanese Placement Test? Implications for Placing Heritage Language Learners. *Journal of the National Council of Less Commonly Taught Languages* 1, 1–19.

Kondo-Brown, K. 2005. Differences in Language Skills: Heritage Language Learner Subgroups and Foreign Language Learners. *The Modern Language Journal* 89(4), 563–581.

Kondo-Brown, K. (ed.) 2006. *Heritage Language Development: Focus on East Asian Immigrants*. Amsterdam: John Benjamins.

Kondo-Brown, K. 2010. Curriculum Development for Advancing Heritage Language Competence: Recent Research, Innovations, and a Future Agenda. *The Annual Review of Applied Linguistics* 30, 24–41.

Lantolf, J. P. 2009. Dynamic Assessment: The Dialectical Integration of Instruction and Assessment. *Language Teaching* 42(3), 355–368.

Lantolf, J. P. and W. Frawley. 1985. Oral-Proficiency Testing: A Critical Analysis. *The Modern Language Journal* 69, 337–345.

Llosa, L. 2013. Assessing Heritage Language Learners. In A. J. Kunnan (ed.), *The Companion to Language Assessment*. Hoboken, NJ: Wiley & Sons. https://doi.org/10.1002/9781118411360.wbcla121

Looney, D. and N. Lusin. 2018. *Enrollments in Languages other than English in United States Institutions of Higher Education, Summer 2016 and Fall 2016*. Retrieved from www.mla.org/content/download/83540/2197676/2016-Enrollments-Short-Report.pdf

MacGregor-Mendoza, P. 2012. Spanish as a Heritage Language Assessment: Successes, Failures, Lessons Learned. *Heritage Language Journal* 8(1), 1–26.

Malone, M. E. 2003. Research on the Oral Proficiency Interview: Analysis, Synthesis, and Future Directions. *Foreign Language Annals* 36(4), 491–497.

Malone, M., J. K. Peyton, and K. Kim. 2014. Assessment of Heritage Language Learners: Issues and Directions. In T. G. Wiley, J. K. Peyton, D. Christian, S. C. Moore, and N. Liu (Eds.), *Handbook of Heritage, Community, and Rative American Languages in the United States*. New York: Routledge, 349–358.

Martin, C., E. Swender, and M. Rivera-Martinez. 2013. Assessing the Oral Proficiency of Heritage Speakers According to the ACTFL Proficiency Guidelines 2012-Speaking. *Heritage Language Journal* 10(2), 211–225.

McKay, P. 2006. *Assessing Young Language Learners*. Cambridge: Cambridge University Press.

McNamara, T. F. and C. Roever. 2006. *Language Testing: The Social Dimension*. Oxford: Blackwell.

Montrul, S. and S. Perpiñán. 2011. Assessing Differences and Similarities between Instructed Heritage Language Learners and L2 Learners in Their Knowledge of Spanish Tense-Aspect and Mood (TAM) Morphology. *Heritage Language Journal* 8(1), 90–133.

Moore, S. C. 2014. Program Models for Heritage Language Education. In T. G. Wiley, J. K. Peyton, D. Christian, S. C. Moore, and N. Liu (eds.), *Handbook of Heritage, Community, and Native American Languages in the United States*. New York: Routledge, 341–348.

Murphy, D. and K. Evans-Romaine (eds.) 2016. *Exploring the US Language Flagship Program: Professional Competence in a Second Language by Graduation*. Bristol: Multilingual Matters.

Norris, J. M. 2006. The Why (and How) of Assessing Student Learning Outcomes in College Foreign Language Programs. *The Modern Language Journal* 90(4), 576–583.

Polinsky, M. 2008. Heritage Language Narratives. In D. M. Brinton, O. Kagan, and S. Bauckus (eds.), *Heritage Language Education: A New Field Emerging*. New York: Routledge, 149–164.

Polinsky, M. 2018. *Heritage Languages and Their Speakers*. Cambridge: Cambridge University Press.

Popham, W. J. 2008. *Transformative Assessment*. Alexandra, VA: Association for Supervision & Curriculum Development.

Potowski, K., M. A. Parada, and K. Morgan-Short. 2012. Developing an Online Placement Exam for Spanish Heritage Speakers and L2 Students. *Heritage Language Journal* 9(1), 51–76.

Ranjan, R. 2008. The Challenge of Placing Hindi Heritage Students. In T. Hudson and M. Clark (eds.), *Case Studies in Foreign Language Placement: Practices and Possibilities*. Honolulu: University of Hawaii, National Foreign Language Resource Center, 177–186.

Rea-Dickins, P. 2001. Mirror, Mirror on the Wall: Identifying Processes of Classroom Assessment. *Language Testing* 18(4), 429–462.

Richards, J. C. and R. Schmidt. 2010. *Longman Dictionary of language Teaching and Applied Linguistics* (4th ed.) London: Pearson Longman.

Salaberry, R. 2000. Revising the Revised Format of the ACTFL Oral Proficiency Interview. *Language Testing* 17(3), 289–310.

Sato, G. and H. Kataoka (eds.) 2008. *Amerika de sodatsu nihon no kodomotachi [Japanese Children Growing Up in America]*. Tokyo: Akashi.

Shohamy, E. 2011. Assessing Multilingual Competencies: Adopting Construct Valid Assessment Policies. *The Modern Language Journal* 95(3), 418–429.

Shohamy, E. and K. Menken. 2015. Language Assessment: Past to Present Misuses and Future Possibilities. In W. E. Wright, S. Boun, and O. García (eds.), *The Handbook of Bilingual and Multilingual Education*. https://doi.org/10.1002/9781118533406.ch15

Sohn, S-O. and S-K. Shin. 2007. True Beginners, False Beginners, and Fake Beginners: Placement Strategies for Korean Heritage Speakers. *Foreign Language Annals* 40(3), 407–418.

Son, Yung-A. 2017. Toward Useful Assessment and Evaluation of Heritage Language Learning. *Foreign Language Annals* 50(2), 367–386.

Stevens, D. and A. J. Levi. 2005. *Introduction to Rubrics: An Assessment Tool to Save Grading Time, Convey Effective Feedback, and Promote Student Learning*. Sterling, VA: Stylus Publishing.

Swender, E., C. Martin, M. Rivera-Martinez, and O. Kagan. 2014. Exploring Oral Proficiency Profiles of Heritage Speakers of Russian and Spanish. *Foreign Language Annals* 47(3), 423–446.

The Center for Applied Linguistics. 2007. *Spanish-Language Assessments for Dual Language Programs*. Retrieved from www.cal.org/twi/pdfs/assessments.pdf

The Japanese Ministry of Education, Culture, Sports, Science and Technology (MEXT). 2016. *Kaigai de manabu nihon no kodomotachi [Japanese school-age children studying abroad]*. Retrieved from www.mext.go.jp/a_menu/shotou/clarinet/002/001.htm

The UCLA Steering Committee. 2000. Heritage Language Research Priorities Conference Report. *Bilingual Research Journal* 24, 333–346.

Thompson, G. L., T. L. Cox, and N. Knapp. 2016. Comparing the OPI and OPIc: The Effect of Test Method on Oral Proficiency Scores and Student Preference. *Foreign Language Annals* 49(1), 75–92.

Tominaga, W. 2013. The Development of Extended Turns and Storytelling in the Japanese Oral Proficiency Interview. In S. Ross and G. Kasper (eds.), *Assessing Second Language Pragmatics*. Basingstoke: Palgrave Macmillan, 220–257.

Tomlinson, C. A. and T. R. Moon. 2013. *Assessment and Student Success in a Differentiated Classroom*. Alexandria, VA: ASCD.

Valdés, G. 1989. Teaching Spanish to Hispanic Bilinguals: A Look at Oral Proficiency Testing the Proficiency Movement. *Hispania* 72, 392–401.

Valdés, G. 2001. Heritage Language Students: Profiles and Possibilities. In J. K. Peyton, D. A. Ranard, and S. McGinnis (eds.), *Heritage Languages in America: Preserving a National Resource*. McHenry, IL: The Center for Applied Linguistics and Delta Systems, 37–77.

Valdés, G. 2005. Bilingualism, Heritage Language Learners, and SLA Research: Opportunities Lost or Seized? *The Modern Language Journal* 89 (3), 410–426.

Valdés, G. and R. Figueroa. 1994. *Bilingualism and Testing: A Special Case of Bias*. Norwood, NJ: Ablex.

Wilson, D. V. 2012. Developing a Placement Exam for Spanish Heritage Language Learners: Item Analysis and Learner Characteristics. *Heritage Language Journal* 9(1), 27–50.

36

Embracing Opportunity in Heritage Language Revitalization

Maria Schwedhelm, Kate Stemper, and Kendall King

36.1 Introduction

More than two decades ago, Joshua Fishman broadly defined heritage languages (in the US context) as languages of "personal relevance other than English," and identified three categories of heritage languages: Indigenous, colonial, and immigrant (Fishman 1999 in Van Deusen-Scholl 2003: 216). While some heritage languages, notably colonial languages such as French, and many immigrant languages such as Korean, enjoy large numbers of speakers and vibrant communities, longstanding sociohistorical and sociolinguistic oppression has resulted in the extreme endangerment of many Indigenous languages (Van Deusen-Scholl 2003; Hornberger 2006; Hinton et al. 2018). To counter this loss, a growing number of communities have engaged in language revitalization efforts that are tied to broader objectives of ethnic reclamation and cultural resistance, aiming not only to maintain but also to strengthen and reconstruct what has been lost (Hornberger 2006; Shah and Brenzinger 2018). While not all Indigenous languages are endangered, there is a vast amount of overlap between these two categories; here we focus on revitalization efforts of Indigenous, endangered heritage languages, exploring the tensions and opportunities therein.

The learning and teaching of Indigenous, endangered heritage languages happens within a context of revitalization that, similar to that of many other heritage language programs, aims to connect learners to their ancestral or heritage culture. However, in contrast to the cases discussed in the majority of the chapters in the present volume, the language is often not regularly used by the parent generation or perhaps even by the grandparent generation, and is thus moribund, and by definition, endangered. Moreover, in contrast to colonial or immigrant language programming, Indigenous heritage language revitalization efforts are often charged with the monumental task of bringing the language back into daily use within the broader community and raising the status of the language (Hinton 2011). Decades of research point to both the challenges and potential of this work (Hornberger 1987; Fishman 2001; King 2001; Grenoble and Whaley 2006). There is ample evidence that heritage language revitalization is a long-term project that demands changes and engagement across many aspects of community life, work that is ripe with tensions and contradictions. Although each community is distinguished and defined by a particular interplay of internal, historical, and contextual characteristics, as our chapter demonstrates, there are some shared factors, challenges, and questions that most communities must grapple with as they work toward revitalizing their language.

Rather than framing these questions as problems or obstacles, the present chapter considers how communities have responded to challenges to create new opportunities for collaboration and to open new spaces for Indigenous languages. Three recurrent questions in heritage language revitalization include what efforts should be prioritized in language revitalization (Grenoble 2013; Leonard 2017; Austin and Sallabank 2018), who should take responsibility in revitalizing a language (Hornberger 2008; McCarty and Nicholas 2014), and how should revitalization efforts navigate the perceived need to establish linguistic norms and standards while concomitantly supporting linguistic diversity (Hornberger and King 1998; Lane et al. 2017).

Each section of this chapter takes up one of these questions and explores it using a case example of how a particular community has harnessed challenges to develop new approaches to drive language revitalization. First, we consider the question, *how do communities center or prioritize language documentation among other revitalization efforts?* and discuss the creation process of *Ojibwemodaa!*, an interactive language materials project (Hermes et al. 2012). Second, we consider the question of *who should take responsibility in the work of language revitalization and what roles should researchers take in those efforts* and describe the development of an Indigenous language immersion school in an urban Midwestern city. Third, we consider the question of *how linguistic diversity and influence from the dominant language interacts with the demand to establish linguistic norms and standards*, and discuss a project from the Mexican state of Oaxaca designed to promote organic Zapotec literacy development on the Web. The chapter closes with considerations of how the process of negotiating and grappling with these questions in itself creates opportunities and new approaches that accept both ambiguity and pluralism.

36.2 Priorities in Heritage Language Revitalization

A sense of urgency pervades many heritage language revitalization efforts as the number of speakers dwindles, and often, the domains of use are reduced, prompting the question of what efforts should be prioritized. Linguists have traditionally engaged in language description and documentation efforts, often associated with a desire to "save" a language rather than focusing on revitalization through teaching and learning, a priority for most Indigenous communities (Hinton 2001a; Grenoble 2009). This tension, sometimes framed as a dichotomy of linguistic conservation vs. community language revitalization, can stand in the way of fruitful collaborations and creative approaches toward designing Indigenous revitalization. As many scholars have noted, collaborative, cross-disciplinary efforts play an integral part in language revitalization, and there are multiple opportunities for language description and documentation projects to contribute to these efforts (Grenoble 2009; Hermes and Engman 2017; Austin and Sallabank 2018).

In this section, we review some of the varied perspectives on priorities for language revitalization from relevant literature. We then discuss how communities center or prioritize language documentation among other efforts, taking the creation process of *Ojibwemodaa!*, an interactive language learning software, as an example. Finally, we return to the question of *how do communities center or prioritize language documentation among other revitalization efforts*, reframing it in light of the case analyzed here.

36.3 Priorities in Context

Each Indigenous community is different – distinguished and defined by a particular interplay of multiple variables. This means that language revitalization projects must be variably developed to respond appropriately to particular sociopolitical and sociolinguistic contexts, from communities with a relatively large number of Indigenous language speakers and a recent shift to the dominant language in the younger generations (e.g., Mixtec), to communities where nearly all first speakers are elders but there is a new and growing generation of language learners (e.g., Hawaiian), to scenarios where there are no first speakers of the language but language activists have become fluent in the Indigenous language by teaching themselves from documentation sources (e.g., Myaamia). Access to language input, numbers, and age of speakers are only some of the critical variables at play. Other considerations include inter-language dialectal diversity, geographical proximity of speakers, literacy levels, language ideologies, policies, and available funding for educational programs among others, all of which shape the approach toward language revitalization.

What efforts should be prioritized depends not only on the goals of the community, which in turn depend on the situation of the language (Hinton 2001a), but also on local understandings of the meaning of "language."

From a Western academic perspective, "language" is often perceived as an abstract, bounded code that can be accessed through words and grammatical structures, and the success of language revitalization is assessed based on the number of speakers (Leonard 2017:19–21). However, many Indigenous scholars view language as living and inseparable from culture (e.g. Hermes et al. 2012: 392). From this perspective, language revitalization is never *only* about the language, and the goals of language work are driven by and integrated with "non-linguistic" needs (Leonard 2017). In this vein, Leonard (2012) proposed the term "language reclamation" to focus attention on this broader conception of language, defining it as "a larger effort by a community to claim its right to speak a language and to set associated goals in response to community needs and perspectives" (359).

There is increasing awareness among non-Indigenous linguists of the importance of working in collaboration with communities and in response to community needs (Grenoble 2009; McCarty 2018). However, without ideological clarification on different conceptions of language, on the goals of the activities, and on what constitutes success, tensions between non-Indigenous linguists or others engaged in language work and the community (or factions within the community) are likely to arise; instead of strengthening communities, such efforts have the potential to weaken or undermine Indigenous identities and languages (Fishman 1990; Romero-Little 2006; Leonard 2017).

Often, linguists, and those that fund their work (e.g., federal funding agencies such as the U.S. National Science Foundation) have focused their efforts on language description and documentation (Romero-Little 2006; Grenoble 2009), whereas most communities tend to prioritize language revitalization or reclamation centered on the teaching and learning of the Indigenous language (Hinton 2001a; Grenoble 2009). However, as scholars note, and as we will illustrate through the case of *Ojibwemodaa!* software, multiple interrelated approaches including documentation and description can contribute much to language revitalization and reclamation work (e.g., Penfield and Tucker 2011; Grenoble 2013; Hermes and Engman 2017).

Language description aims to record a language as an abstract system, typically in the form of grammars and dictionaries. In turn, language documentation generally emphasizes the creation of audio and video as a "representative and lasting multipurpose record of a natural language" (Himmelmann 1998: 161). Documentation recordings are often transcribed and annotated, and potentially inform description through the creation of grammars, dictionaries, and/or pedagogical materials (Hermes and Engman 2017; Austin and Sallabank 2018). These materials can play an important role in language revitalization, though a common limitation is that they are developed in isolation from other revitalization efforts and/or impose patterns of world language teaching and learning that do not reflect the realities, intellectual traditions, goals, or conceptions of language of the community, and thus often remain unused (Leonard 2017; Austin and Sallabank 2018).

Rather than focusing on the documentation and description of Indigenous languages for conservation, communities tend to focus on revitalization through teaching and learning. Pedagogical models that have been successful in creating new speakers include the master–apprentice program (Hinton 2001b), language and culture classes (Hermes 2012), and bilingual and immersion education (Hinton 2001a). Distinct from pedagogical programs that teach language and culture as curricular content, immersion education aims to integrate Indigenous ways of learning and knowing (and speaking) as media of instruction, a paradigm shift that demands deeper engagement with the local community, and often elders. Starting Indigenous immersion education programs is extremely challenging for multiple reasons, including lack of curriculum, materials, and speaker-teachers (Hinton 2001a; Hermes 2007; Wilson and Kamana 2011; Hermes et al. 2012). In the next section, we describe the production process of *Ojibwemodaa!*, a project that creatively addresses these challenges within the context of the Ojibwe revitalization movement.

36.4   Example Case: The Creation and Development of Ojibwemodaa!

Ojibwemodaa! is an interactive language materials project for language revitalization that involves language documentation and materials creation. What makes this project unique is its approach toward the integration of community and academic efforts through a participatory project that is collaborative, and is "designed from, and centered on, Indigenous epistemologies, philosophies, and languages" (Hermes et al. 2012: 383).

Ojibwe is an Algonquian language spoken in the United States and Canada. It is considered an endangered language, with an estimated few hundred living first speakers in the United States (Treuer et al. 2011). A growing Ojibwe language revitalization movement, however, has given rise to several immersion schools in the southeastern part of the Ojibwe nation, now in the states of Minnesota and Wisconsin, where *Ojibwemodaa!* was created (Hermes et al. 2012). Ojibwe has also seen an increasing number of new speakers, many of whom are teaching or preparing to teach in the immersion schools (Engman 2017). But as in many Indigenous immersion contexts, there are significant shortages in qualified teachers and relevant materials. The school initiatives hold as a main priority the need to develop new speakers and the technology/materials to support that effort (Hermes et al. 2012). This is one of the gaps that *Ojibwemodaa!* aimed to fill.

Technology was taken up as a way to allow language learners to enter into relationships with the language that allowed for meaning making. The focus was as much on the creation process as on the outcome or materials that resulted from that process. Focusing on intergenerational transmission as a goal of heritage language revitalization, the project aimed to use technology to create and re-create discourses from every day interactions, capturing language in context. This was done by involving the community as active participants in the process, where elders and learners made short movies in Ojibwe at a series of summer camps (Hermes et al. 2012). Participants agreed to stay in the Ojibwe language, which "created the feeling of a restored use of the Ojibwe language ... and made for more opportunities for spontaneous joking and speaking" (394).

This process created a type of immersion experience that allowed for constant collaboration, where the ideas for the movies were developed, semi-scripted, and sometimes improvised. There was also a general acknowledgment of the Ojibwe language as living, a grounding that was constantly present "through humor, offering food and tobacco, leaving room for flexibility and spontaneity, or being ready to turn off cameras whenever an elder requests it" (390). This moved the focus from language as content to one of relationality and reciprocity to each other and toward the language. An important aspect of this process was its iterative design, which allowed for constant reevaluation. Tensions arose when documentation goals drove some participants to record long conversations that would be demanding and time-consuming to transcribe and annotate, and be less accessible to learners due to their linguistic complexity. This realization drove the group to opt for shorter videos that could be quickly made available to learners in user-friendly formats. In the end, nineteen short movies were created during the summer camps and later transcribed to create language learning content. Today, *Ojibwemodaa!* has been distributed to hundreds of Ojibwe learners and many conversations from the movies have been adapted into picture books (Rice and Thieberger 2018).

36.5 Priorities Revisited

As the creation of *Ojibwemodaa!* exemplifies, and as most language revitalization scholars and stakeholders agree, language documentation, description, and language revitalization do not need to be mutually exclusive. Indeed, the division between language documentation and language revitalization is somewhat artificial, as most language revitalization projects incorporate different approaches in their overall efforts to bring the Indigenous language back into use. In this vein, Hermes, Bang, and Marin (2012) argue that language revitalization should be understood as both language revitalization and language documentation. To return to the initial question posed, *how to center or prioritize language documentation among other revitalization efforts*, the "answer" needs to be considered in collaboration with communities and in response to community needs. A process of ongoing collaboration, where community members are involved as active participants, allows for the creation of content that is relevant to the context in question and for those who have a stake in the revitalization of their heritage language.

36.6 Roles and Responsibilities in Indigenous Language Revitalization

What has been discursively constructed as a debate in language revitalization is the question of *who should take responsibility in the work of language revitalization* (McCarty and Nicholas 2014). In past literature, this was often framed as a [false] dichotomy between focusing on encouragement of intergenerational transmission of language on the one hand, or focusing on schools as a site of language instruction and language learning on the other (Tollefson 2006). Related to this question is that of the *roles and responsibilities of researchers within language revitalization* due to the intimate and sensitive nature of language revitalization research, especially when home practices are the focus and when conducted by non-Indigenous researchers. In this section, these questions are first reviewed in light of existing perspectives presented in research and literature, and then considered with regard to the development of an Indigenous language immersion school. Lastly, this section reflects on the question of what can be learned by the case example and more broadly on the appropriate roles of researchers.

36.7 Roles and Relationships in Context

With respect to language revitalization and language education in schools, three different questions are typically explored concurrently in literature, even if not always explicitly differentiated. These are (1) *can* schools save Indigenous languages, (2) *how* might schools save Indigenous languages, and (3) do schools have a *responsibility* to save Indigenous languages? Though these are interrelated questions that require nuanced responses, we differentiate them here in order to better frame the focus of this section (responsibility).

The first question, whether or not schools can "save," or revitalize Indigenous languages, has been explored, for example, in Hornberger's (2008) edited volume organized on that theme. There, McCarty (2008) answered this question by arguing that schools cannot *alone* save Indigenous languages, but at the same time, there are few examples of successful language revitalization efforts wherein schools did *not* play a role (161). McCarty explained that although schools cannot be (or perhaps, should not be) the sole catalyst for language revitalization, it is imperative that their role and place in the community be taken up in language revitalization planning. Drawing on concepts from language planning and policy theory, and leading into the second question of *how* schools can save Indigenous languages, McCarty wrote, "[schools] are potential sites of resistance and opportunity … [they] can become strategic platforms for more broad based language planning, from orthographic standardization, to preparing Indigenous teachers, to elevating the status of oppressed and marginalized languages" (161). As such, researchers and language activists alike must be constantly reexamining how and in what ways schools are contributing and *actively* working toward language revitalization, which leads to the question of responsibility.

One well-established viewpoint in research and literature regarding language revitalization is that focus must remain on intergenerational transmission of language, as "it is *the* most vital factor for the maintenance of languages" (Skutnabb-Kangas 2002: 47; Fishman 1990). This goal is reflected in the generally accepted measurement of language "health" and the success of revitalization efforts: The language is being spoken and passed on at home, within families (i.e., Expanded Graded Intergenerational Disruption Scale [EGIDS][1]). However, a singular focus on home and family-based transmission of the language raises the question of the roles and responsibilities of schools. This is further complicated from a historical perspective as "education systems have played a role in the effort to eradicate minority languages, but also in an effort to revive them" (Hinton 2017: 257). These contradictions are evident in Cobarrubias' (1983) taxonomy of state policies toward minority languages, which are also mirrored in the historical practices of schools: (1) Attempting to kill a language; (2) Letting a language die; (3) Unsupported coexistence; (4) Partial support of specific language functions; and (5) Adoption as an official language.

Education policies for Native Americans and colonial schooling in the United States attempted to actively eradicate Indigenous and minority languages and contributed to linguistic genocide and language death (McCarty et al. 2008: 300; Skutnabb-Kangas 2002: 47). It is understandable, then, that Native communities and vested researchers and allies alike would be cautious about relying on schools to support, ground, or aid

---

[1] EGIDS Level 6a: Vigorous, the language is used for face-to-face communication by all generations and the situation is sustainable (www.ethnologue.com/about/language-status).

revitalization efforts. However, because the traumatic forced assimilation experienced in boarding schools (in part) disrupted intergenerational transmission of Native American languages within families and communities, language activists have posed the question *if students are not learning language in school, when and where can they learn it?* (Skutnabb-Kangas 2002: 47; McCarty et al. 2008: 300). Additionally, the absence of Indigenous language learning and use in school often coincides with the absence of other culturally relevant education (Lee 2016). This serves as a strong argument for schools having a responsibility to contribute to language learning, and subsequently for policies and resources to support such efforts.

Hinton argued that although overt, explicit policies to eradicate minority languages are no longer in place (Stage 1 of Cobarrubias's Taxonomy), policies and practices have continued to prevent the use of minority languages and could still be described, per Cobarrubias's taxonomy (stage 2), as "letting a language die" (Hinton 2017: 259). For example, Winstead et al. (2008: 54) described discrepancies regarding the extent to which NCLB (the US federal education policy between 2002 and 2015) provided permissions and support for education of Indigenous languages in federally funded schools. As an example: Section 3125 of the policy stated, "Nothing in this part shall be construed ... to limit the presentation or use of Native American languages." However, Section 3128 of the policy clearly prioritized English, stating that "instruction, staff development, and curricular materials in American Indian/Alaska Native languages are authorized so long as they increase the English proficiency of American Indian/Alaska Native Children." Haynes' (2011) ethnographic account of the "end of Indigenous language classes" at a school in Warm Springs, Oregon demonstrated how the English-centered accountability of NCLB was reflected in the language attitudes of teachers who "considered it more appropriate to teach the tribal languages outside of school time" (149), citing the need to use formal instructional time for tested curricula.

Successful examples of heritage language revitalization, such as the Hawaiian and Maori cases (see Hinton and Hale 2001), are often characterized by large roles for school-based language education. For example, the Hawaiian language revitalization movement was catalyzed by the development of the Hawaiian Punana Leo (preschools) and Kula Kaiapuni Hawai'i (elementary and high schools). These programs created a new generation of Hawaiian speakers and are "by far the most ambitious and advanced language revitalization program in the United States" (Hinton 2016: 474). Originally designed following the "Maori Language Nest" model, these programs are immersion based. Hinton has argued that immersion language education is especially needed in the context of *Indigenous* language learning given the learning goals, the motives for learning, the expectations the community has of the learner, and the effects on the forms and uses of the

Indigenous, endangered language, bearing in mind its often restricted status and functions. These particular needs point to the responsibility of schools to not just provide language instruction, but to take up immersion as "one of the most effective tools for restoring Indigenous language while simultaneously teaching for Native student academic success" (Hermes 2007: 58).

36.8 Example Case: School-Based Language Revitalization Initiatives in Minnesota

We overview one example from recent work with Ojibwe and Dakota (languages Indigenous to land known as the northern midwestern United States and Canada) to illustrate current developments and challenges in school-based language revitalization. Bdote Learning Center is an Ojibwe and Dakota language immersion K-8 school in Minneapolis, Minnesota. Bdote opened as a public charter school in 2014, authorized by Innovative Quality Schools (IQS) – the first single purpose charter school authorizer approved by the Minnesota Department of Education (The Circle 2014). As reported in The Circle (2014), IQS "shared a vision for a school that would not only honor indigenous languages but allow it to deliver academic instruction through the languages."

Bdote serves primarily Native students and families and has welcomed growing enrollments each academic year. Though Bdote opened its doors in 2014, the development of the school began in 2008 when "a group of Indian educators, Native language activists and community members began to discuss a new kind of school for Indian children" (The Circle 2014). The school opened serving K-3 grades, with the intention of adding on a grade each school year; Bdote recently celebrated the completion of its fifth school year and is beginning its sixth with approximately 100 students enrolled across grades K-8. Bdote is a unique language immersion school as it supports immersion language education in *two* languages (Ojibwe and Dakota) across all grades.

In practice, the school is not only a model for what roles schools can take on to support language revitalization but also exemplifies the crucial connections across school, community, and family in language revitalization efforts. Bdote's school vision states, "all students will develop a love of lifelong learning, language and cultural fluency, gain skills and education to determine their own future, and develop a genuine commitment to contribute back to their family, community and nation" (Bdote.org). The centrality of community and family is emphasized and valued among school staff and students, in particular in fostering language development. Staff strive to include family members in students' language development by, for example, sharing take-home vocabulary lists that correspond to what is being focused on in school. Elders, first speakers, dancers, and others are regularly invited to Bdote to help support staff and students with language work and cultural activities.

Recognizing and supporting in practice the inherent linguistic and cultural rights of Native peoples should remain a critical goal of *any* school that serves Native students. However, since the onset of colonial schooling in the late nineteenth century, a "historic continuing assimilationist agenda" within schools has contrasted with "culturally- and community-oriented goals of Native communities" (Lee 2016: 4). From this historical context, Bdote was "created out of a need for language restoration and as a way to engage Native students that were being lost in other schools not reflecting their identities" (Bdote.org). It is notable that this school is striving to create a space for Native languages and practices in a major urban center; many, if not most, American Indian peoples now live (and attend schools) off reservations (Biolsi 2005: 248; McCarty 2013: 7).

Bdote, whose modus operandi is "educating through an Indigenous lens," aims to engage children, their families, and other community members. Bdote's vision explicitly speaks to students developing "a genuine commitment to contribute back to their family, community and nation" (bdote. org); and the school staff have said "their work at the school feels like the most important thing they could be doing for their community" (Shockman 2019). Thus, the ways in which Bdote has taken on the role of supporting language and cultural reclamation also supports the needs to participate in and help build community.

36.9   Roles and Responsibilities Revisited

Schools play a crucial part in Indigenous language revitalization, and language and cultural reclamation within schools is also linked with community development. We argue that while schools *do* have a responsibility to support language revitalization and reclamation, it is *not* a question of schools vs. family and/or community responsibility; they are not mutually exclusive. Rather, we must recognize and further advance the ways schools are supporting communities and families, and how they work together to support students' language development and use. We also note the significance of actions on the part of others either involved in language revitalization (such as researchers) or who have any type of decision-making agency in its regard (such as government representatives or other education policy actors). McCarty, Skutnabb-Kangas, and Magga (2008) wrote, "our efforts in education, research, teaching, and policy making will not save *all* the endangered languages in the world" (308). However, that does not mean a lack of effort is not harmful. While schools such as Bdote put tremendous time and resources toward navigating restrictive policies that may clash with the needs of Native communities and schools, researchers have a responsibility to do work in service of the community. Smith (1999) noted (as have others) that "the term 'research' is inextricably linked to European imperialism and colonialism" (1). Though researchers have provided support to language revitalization efforts through multiple avenues, it is important that those engaging with Indigenous communities in this regard structure research in a way that is first and foremost for the community, supporting the "language community itself [to] take command over all aspects of the use and development of its own language" (McCarty et al. 2008: 306). This is the spirit in which Bdote developed and continues to grow.

36.10   Standardization and Diversity in Heritage Language Education

Endangered heritage languages have long been primarily oral channels. Unlike dominant or official languages such as English or Spanish, most writing systems of heritage Indigenous languages have no standardized norm or are in the relatively early processes of standardization. The development of norms and standards often coincides with educational and status policy and planning (Fishman 1972). "Homogenisation" or "unification" of spoken languages has been seen as facilitating engagement across geographical regions and taken as a precursor to promoting formal education, literacy, and literary development in Indigenous languages; concomitantly, unification efforts can also lead to the erasure of dialectal differences and the domination of one dialect over others (May 2014; Costa et al. 2017; Fitznor 2019). Linguistic heterogenization, in turn, supports "the retention of tradition, ethnolinguistic identity and human heritage" (Albury 2019: 21). Language revitalization efforts thus have to consider how *linguistic diversity interacts with the demands to establish linguistic norms and standards.* Put differently, language activists must ask *how can we approach the apparent demand to establish linguistic norms while concomitantly supporting linguistic diversity?* This section first reviews existing literature that illustrates this dynamic aspect of Indigenous language standardization and second considers perspectives that reframe the question in light of alternative communication practices that challenge standardization regimes (Gal 2018).

36.11   Standardization in Context

Advancing Indigenous literacies is an important part of heritage language revitalization. Literacy facilitates language acquisition through the development and use of materials, dictionaries, books and other teaching and learning resources (Hornberger and King 1998). Literacy has also been described as a human right, a mechanism for participation, and a way to promote language use at national and international levels (Hornberger 1996; Hornberger and King 1998; Cocq and Sullivan 2019). However, community-level debates regarding processes of unification and standardization are common, sometimes impeding revitalization efforts (e.g., Dorian 1994; Hornberger and King 1998; Hinton 2014; Limerick 2017). Drawing from multiple studies from around the world, Nancy Dorian (1994) demonstrated that purist language attitudes can interfere with and even threaten efforts to revive or revitalize a heritage language. She stressed the importance of compromise in the development and promotion of a standard language, noting that language is always changing.

Recognizing the dynamic nature of language remains a challenge. Omnipresent discourses of endangerment (and of revitalization and standardization) draw on assumptions that there is a fixed, "authentic," or "pure" form of the heritage language that needs to be "saved" or "preserved" (Duchêne and Heller 2008; Hermes and Engman 2017). In turn, language varieties that deviate from an idealized norm due to regional, social, or other types of dialectal difference and/or influence from the dominant language tend to be devalued, creating new social hierarchies and discouraging learners who don't see their linguistic heritage and/or language practices reflected in the norm (Hornberger and King 1998; De Korne 2017). Hornberger and King (1998), for example, described the orthographic debate of Quechua in Peru. Similar to Dorian, they found that language planning efforts "for the sake of corpus purity" brought about tensions that can threaten political affiliations, create inter-generational divisions, and ultimately undermine the goal of language revitalization. They suggest suspending judgment, focusing on transformation rather than restoration, and encouraging writing in whatever form.

Furthermore, alphabet histories and trajectories of standardization can also invoke emotions and affect how people perceive competing alphabets (Limerick 2017). Indeed, orthographies are always political, reflecting personal, social, and political issues that can divide communities, becoming a source of disagreement, and turning into "orthography wars" that drain the energy of language activists (Hinton 2014).

Yet language activists are active agents in standardization processes and, as Susan Gal (2018) demonstrated, there are multiple ways that they have subverted and resisted what she calls "the hegemony of modernity's standardization." Gal describes how "standard" languages are constructed as "universal," the language of the "literate" and "educated," whereas on the other side of the axis, Indigenous and other minoritized languages are characterized as "emplaced" and "backward" (233). When minority language standardization processes reproduce this standardization regime, speakers and learners of the language can be subjected to double discrimination vis-a-vis the dominant language as well as the standardized heritage language. Gal illustrated this through the example of Aymara radio in Bolivia policing for "correctness" and purifying against Spanish borrowings (Swinehart 2012). But qualities of "correctedness" are not the only values that might define different linguistic varieties, even when they are normalized (Gal 2018). Language activists can subvert and re-signify these hegemonic discourses by "turning upside down the values of standardizing preservationists" and assigning new qualities or characteristics to different forms of the language (Gal 2018: 237). Taking up the case of Basque, Gal described Urla's (2012) study on "pirate radio," which encouraged the use of rural dialects and code-switching with Spanish in lieu of the standardized variety. Being youth-focused and airing popular international music, the station resisted values of "traditional" or "local/emplaced" associated with rural varieties of Basque.

Scholars and language activists have written about the potential of multimedia and digital media to support Indigenous language acquisition and expand the domains for language use (e.g., Barrett and Cocq 2019; Domeij et al. 2019). However, it also has the potential to resist and re-signify hegemonic discourses of standardization. In the next section, we examine one example from the Mexican state of Oaxaca that resists imposing systematic conventions, focusing instead on creating opportunities for writing on social media and thereby developing literacy while embracing linguistic diversity.

36.12   Example Case: Valley Zapotec Organic Literacy Development on the Web

The potential of digital media to support Indigenous language acquisition relies in part on its promise as an accessible, cost effective, and efficient means to connect across distance (Lillehaugen 2016). Speakers and learners of heritage Indigenous languages can easily create and share reading material in ways that would be challenging through physical publications. The *Voces del Valle* project was conceived as a means to encourage speakers of Valley Zapotec, an Indigenous language from the Southern Mexican state of Oaxaca, to write in their native language through social media (Lillehaugen 2016). Participants committed to writing tweets in Zapotec several times a week, and each participant was assigned a reader with the hope that the interaction would provide motivation for the writers. Participants were speakers of six different varieties of Zapotec, and, of the six varieties, only two had one or more proposals for practical orthographies. Most participants had never written in Zapotec, and facilitators provided an overview of orthographic decision points for Tlacolula Zapotec, but explicitly focused on literacy development and getting participants to write in whatever form was most accessible to them.

The project is rooted in the belief that a standardized orthography is not a prerequisite for a healthy and active writing culture, but rather, that it is possible (and productive) for writing norms to evolve organically (see Brody 2004 in Karan 2014). Participants were not consistent in their orthographic choices, but they were mostly able to understand other participants' posts by reading aloud, even across dialectal differences. Tweets also showed influence from Spanish, subverting common monolingual ideologies that delegitimize multilingual communication practices and may work to discourage multilingual speakers from writing in their heritage language (De Korne 2017).

Past research demonstrates how speakers and learners of Indigenous languages can feel intimidated to write when standardization regimes assign stigmatizing values to language forms and orthographies that deviate from the norm (Karan 2014). Social media, however, potentially provides a more informal and familiar environment where writers can experiment with different forms of the language and orthographies free of the stigmatization that might be present or felt in other domains, such as formal education (Bigelow et al. 2017). Changing the domain of literacy production to social media has the potential of transforming the qualities associated with the participants' diverse communicative practices and flexible orthographic choices. Instead of "local/emplaced" and "backward" they become and thereby re-signify qualities like "global" and "modern" (Gal 2018). Focusing on literacy instead of orthography development or policing might have contributed to the growth of the project, with participants increasing their use of Zapotec writing through other platforms and uptake from Twitter users not involved in *Voces del Valle* (Lillehaugen 2016). Moreover, since the project was implemented, more and more language activists and organizations like Rising Voices (Rising Voices, 2019) are using the Web as a site of activism to increase digital presence and create new spaces for the development of Indigenous literacies.

36.13   Norms and Standards Revisited

This section highlights how linguistic diversity interacts with the demand to establish linguistic norms and standards. Standardization regimes and discourses of authenticity can result in "orthography wars," create new hierarchies and social divisions, and ultimately undermine language revitalization. The field of language revitalization is rooted in the belief that linguistic diversity is not only valuable and desirable to preserve cultures and knowledges, but it is a matter of social justice and human rights

(Skutnabb-Kangas 2000). Yet, there is a perceived demand to establish norms to facilitate language acquisition and expand the presence of the language. While processes for advancing literacy are indeed an important part of heritage language education, these efforts should not be limited to printed materials. As illustrated in the discussion of this case, the use of digital platforms for publishing and sharing in Zapotec has the potential to turn standardization regimes upside down and to create new meanings and opportunities for the continuous development of literacy with and across diversity. This case also helps us reimagine norms and the processes that constitute them. For example: How might conventionalized norms develop organically? And how do we engage in alternative communication practices that support and transform literacy development?

36.14 Concluding Discussion

This chapter has taken up three longstanding points of discussion and research in the field: namely, how do communities center or prioritize language documentation among other revitalization efforts; who should take responsibility in the work of language revitalization and what roles should researchers take in those efforts; and how does linguistic diversity and influence from the dominant language interact with the demand to establish linguistic norms and standards. Our chapter has attempted to illustrate how these points, which are often framed as challenges and obstacles to Indigenous and heritage language revitalization, have been harnessed to develop innovative new approaches to productively drive language revitalization. We close with three broad, takeaways on these issues and considerations going forward.

First, as we hope is evident here, these three questions, and the broader issues on which they rest, are interrelated and interwoven. Central to each of them is the value, importance, and continued struggle for community autonomy, and more broadly, revitalization as a practice and part of decolonization efforts. As illustrated by the examples here, developing Indigenous language teaching and learning materials, documenting a heritage language in everyday interactional domains, and developing a school-community focused on Indigenous heritage language are all efforts that grow community, build community capacity, and strengthen community autonomy. Underlying these three questions is the crucial point that Indigenous heritage language revitalization is about much more than language. Heritage language education and revitalization for Indigenous communities is about survival and reclamation of identity, including the inherent right to exist as autonomous Indigenous peoples.

Second, as suggested previously, the process of negotiating and grappling with these questions in itself creates opportunities and new approaches. While there are no simple or quick answers, the search for what Joshua Fishman (1990) termed "ideological clarification" around these issues is productive, beneficial, and generative. These examples presented here also highlight the fact that this work is necessarily ongoing and continuous. For instance, in the case of Indigenous language immersion schools, balancing the need for state-certified teachers with the need for language speakers is an ongoing challenge and points to areas of further focus, including accessible teacher education and professional development designed for Indigenous language immersion educators, as well as analysis of federal and state education policy regarding teacher certification.

And third, we close by highlighting that there is much more work – academic, hands-on, and community-based – to be done. We need greater bi-directional collaboration across fields, institutions, and communities (McIvor 2018). Indigenous language revitalization work could be sharpened, for instance, by insights from the decades of contributions from heritage language education in other contexts as well as [second] language acquisition more broadly (McIvor 2020). Concomitantly, the study of heritage language learning as a field could also be enriched by greater exposure to Indigenous language learning contexts and the particular teaching and learning methods that have been developed therein, which often differ from those widely studied in the literature (McIvor 2020). This collaboration has the potential to build capacities in many communities, and is essential to maximizing both the knowledge and resources available to maintain and grow revitalization efforts of heritage languages around the world, an ever-more-urgent task.

References

Albury, N. J. 2019. "I've Admired Them for Doing So Well": Where to Now for Indigenous Languages and Literacies? In C. Cocq and K. Sullivan (eds.), *Perspectives on Indigenous Writing and Literacies*. Boston: Brill, 13–28.

Austin, P. K. and J. Sallabank. 2018. Language Documentation and Language Revitalization: Some Methodological Considerations. In L. Hinton, L. Huss, and G. Roche (eds.), *The Routledge Handbook of Language Revitalisation*. London: Routledge, 207–215.

Barrett, J. and C. Cocq. 2019. Indigenous Storytelling and Language Learning: Digital Media as a Vehicle for Cultural Transmission and Language Acquisition. In C. Cocq and K. Sullivan (eds.), *Perspectives on Indigenous Writing and Literacies*. Boston: Brill, 89–112.

Bigelow, M., J. Vanek, K. King, and N. Abdi. 2017. Literacy as Social (Media) Practice: Refugee Youth and Native Language Literacy at School. *International Journal of Intercultural Relations* 60, 183–197.

Biolsi, T. 2005. Imagined Geographies: Sovereignty, Indigenous Space, and American Indian Struggle. *American Ethnologist* 32(2), 239–259. https://doi.org/10.1525/ae.2005.32.2.239

Cobarrubias, J. 1983. Ethical Issues in Status Planning. In J. Cobarubias and J. Fishman (eds.), *Progress in Language Planning: International Perspectives*. New York: Mouton, 4–84.

Cocq, C. and K. Sullivan. 2019. Indigenous Writing and Literacies: Perspectives from Five Continents. In C. Cocq and K. Sullivan (eds.), *Perspectives on Indigenous Writing and Literacies*. Boston: Brill, 1–12.

Costa, J., H. De Korne, and P. Lane. 2017. Standardising Minority Languages: Reinventing Peripheral Languages in the 21st Century. In P. Lane, J. Costa, and H. De Korne (eds.), *Standardizing Minority Languages (Open Access): Competing Ideologies of Authority and Authenticity in the Global Periphery*. New York: Routledge, 1–23.

De Korne, H. 2017. The Multilingual Realities of Language Reclamation: Working with Language Contact, Diversity, and Change in Endangered Language Education. *Language Documentation and Description* 14, 111–135.

Domeij, R., O. Karlsson, S. Moshagen, and T. Trosterud. 2019. Enhancing Information Accessibility and Digital Literacy for Minorities Using Language Technology: The Example of Sámi and other National Minority Languages in Sweden. In C. Cocq and K. Sullivan (eds.), *Perspectives on Indigenous Writing and Literacies*. Boston: Brill, 113–140.

Dorian, N. 1994. Purism vs. Compromise in Language Revitalization and Language Revival. *Language in Society* 23(4), 479–494.

Duchêne, A. and M. Heller (eds.) 2008. *Discourses of Endangerment: Ideology and Interest in the Defence of Languages*. New York: Continuum.

Engman, M. 2017. Revitalizing Language, Reframing Expertise: An Ecological Study of Language in One Teacher-Learner's Ojibwe Classroom. Unpublished doctoral dissertation, University of Minnesota, United States.

Fishman, J. A. 1972. *Language and Nationalism: Two Integrative Essays*. Rowley, MA: Newbury House.

Fishman, J. A. 1990. What Is Reversing Language Shift (RLS) and How Can It Succeed? *Journal of Multilingual & Multicultural Development* 11(1–2), 5–36.

Fishman, J. A. (ed.) 2001. *Can Threatened Languages Be Saved? Reversing Language Shift, Revisited: A 21st Century Perspective* (Vol. 116). Clevedon: Multilingual Matters.

Fitznor, L. 2019. Indigenous Education: Affirming Indigenous Knowledges and Languages from a Turtle Island Indigenous Scholar's Perspective: Pikiskēwinan (Let Us Voice). In C. Cocq and K. Sullivan (eds.), *Perspectives on Indigenous Writing and Literacies*. Boston: Brill, 29–66.

Gal, S. 2018. Visions and Revisions of Minority Languages. In P. Lane, J. Costa, and H. De Korne (eds.), *Standardizing Minority Languages (Open Access): Competing Ideologies of Authority and Authenticity in the Global Periphery*. New York: Routledge, 222–242.

Grenoble, L. 2009. Linguistic Cages and the Limits of Linguists. In J. Reyhner and L. Lockard (eds.), *Indigenous Language Revitalization: Encouragement, Guidance & Lessons Learned*. Flagstaff: Northern Arizona University, 61–69.

Grenoble, L. Unanswered Questions in Language Documentation and Revitalization: New Directions for Research and Action. In Mihas, E., B. Perley, G. Rei-Doval, and K. Wheatley (eds.), *Responses to Language Endangerment. In Honor of Mickey Noonan*. Philadelphia: John Benjamins, 43–57.

Grenoble, L. A. and L. J. Whaley. 2006. *Saving Languages: An Introduction to Language Revitalization*. Cambridge: Cambridge University Press.

Hermes, M. 2007. Moving toward the Language: Reflections on Teaching in an Indigenous-Immersion School. *Journal of American Indian Education* 46 (3), 54–71.

Hermes, M., M. Bang, and A. Marin. 2012. Designing Indigenous Language Revitalization. *Harvard Educational Review* 82(3), 381–402.

Hermes, M. and M. Engman. 2017. Resounding the Clarion Call: Indigenous Language Learners and Documentation. In W. Leonard and H. De Korne (eds.), *Language Documentation and Description*, vol. 14. London: EL Publishing, 59–87

Himmelmann, N. 1998. Documentary and Descriptive Linguistics. *Linguistics* 36, 161–195.

Hinton, L. 2001a. Language Revitalization: An Overview. In L. Hinton and K. Hale (eds.), *The Green Book of Language Revitalization in Practice*. New York: Academic Press, 3–18.

Hinton, L. 2001b. The Master–Apprentice Language Learning Program. In L. Hinton and K. Hale (eds.), *The Green Book of Language Revitalization in Practice*. New York: Academic Press, 217–226.

Hinton, L. 2011. Language Revitalization and Language Pedagogy: New Teaching and Learning Strategies. *Language and Education* 25(4), 307–318.

Hinton, L. 2014. Orthography Wars. In M. Cahill and K. Rice (eds.), *Developing Orthographies for Unwritten Languages*. Dallas, TX: SIL International, 139–168.

Hinton, L. 2016. Hawaiian Language Schools. In S. Lobo, S. Talbot, T. M. Carlston (eds.), *Native American Voices*. London: Taylor & Francis Ltd, 482.

Hinton, L. 2017. Language Endangerment and Revitalization. In T. L. McCarty and S. May (eds.), *Language Policy and Political Issues in Education, Encyclopedia of Language and Education*. New York: Springer International Publishing, 1–16.

Hinton, L. and K. Hale (eds.) 2001. *The Green Book of Language Revitalization in Practice*. New York: Academic Press.

Hinton, L., L. Huss, and G. Roche. 2018. *The Routledge Handbook of Language Revitalization*. New York: Routledge.

Hornberger, N. H. 1987. Bilingual Education Success, but Policy Failure. *Language in Society* 16(2), 205–226.

Hornberger, N. H. 1996. Quechua Literacy and Empowerment in Peru. In N. Hornberger (ed.), *Indigenous Literacies in the Americas: Language Planning from the Bottom Up*. New York: Mouton de Gruyter, 215–236.

Hornberger, N. H. 2006. Voice and Biliteracy in Indigenous Language Revitalization: Contentious Educational Practices in Quechua, Guarani, and Māori Contexts. *Journal of Language, Identity, and Education* 5(4), 277–292.

Hornberger, N. H. (ed.) 2008. *Can Schools Save Indigenous Languages? Policy and Practice on Four Continents*. New York: Palgrave Macmillan.

Hornberger, N. H. and K. A. King. 1998. Authenticity and Unification in Quechua Language Planning. *Language Culture and Curriculum* 11(3), 390–410.

Karan, E. 2014. Standardization: What's the Hurry? In M. Cahill and K. Rice (eds.), *Developing Orthographies for Unwritten Languages*. Dallas, TX: SIL International Publications, 107–138.

King, K. A. 2001. *Language Revitalization Processes and Prospects: Quichua in the Ecuadorian Andes*. Clevedon: Multilingual Matters.

Lane, P., H. De Korne, and J. Costa. 2017. Standardising Minority Languages: Reinventing Peripheral Languages in the 21st Century. In P. Lane, J. Costa, and H. De Korne (eds.), *Standardizing Minority Languages (Open Access)*. New York: Routledge, 1–23.

Lee, T. S. 2016. The Home-School-Community Interface in Language Revitalization in the USA and Canada. In S. M. Coronel-Molina and T. L. McCarty (eds.), *Indigenous Language Revitalization in the Americas*. New York: Routledge, 1–30.

Leonard, W. Y. 2012. Framing Language Reclamation Programmes for Everybody's Empowerment. *Gender and Language* 6(2), 339–367.

Leonard, W. Y. 2017. Producing Language Reclamation by Decolonising 'Language'. In W. Y. Leonard and H. De Korne (eds.), *Language Documentation and Description 14*. London: EL Publishing, 15–36.

Lillehaugen, B. D. 2016. Why Write in a Language That (Almost) No One Can Read? Twitter and the Development of Written Literature. *Language Documentation and Conservation* 10, 356–393.

Limerick, N. 2017. Kichwa or Quichua? Competing Alphabets, Political Histories, and Complicated Reading in Indigenous Languages. *Comparative Education Review* 62(1), 103–124.

May, S. 2014. Justifying Educational Language Rights. *Review of Research in Education* 38(1), 215–241.

McCarty, T. L. 2008. Schools as Strategic Tools for Indigenous Language Revitalization: Lessons from Native America. In N. H. Hornberger (ed.),

Can Schools Save Indigenous Languages? Policy and Practice on Four Continents.
New York: Palgrave Macmillan, 161–179.

McCarty, T. L. 2013. *Language Planning and Policy in Native America: History,
Theory, Praxis.* Clevedon: Multilingual Matters.

McCarty, T. L. 2018. Community-Based Language Planning: Perspectives
from Indigenous Language Revitalization. In L. Hinton, L. Huss, and
G. Roche (eds.), *The Routledge Handbook of Language Revitalization.* New
York: Routledge, 22–35.

McCarty, T. L. and S. E. Nicholas. 2014. Reclaiming Indigenous Languages:
A Reconsideration of the Roles and Responsibilities of Schools. *Review of
Research in Education* 38(1), 106–136.

McCarty, T., T. Skutnabb-Kangas, and O. H. Magga. 2008. Education for
Speakers of Endangered Languages. In B. Spolsky and F. M. Hult (eds.),
The Handbook of Educational Linguistics. Oxford: Blackwell Publishing Ltd,
297–312.

McIvor, O. 2018, November 1. Indigenous Language Revitalization. *Learning
Transforms - UVic Education* [Audio podcast]. Retrieved from: https://t.co/
XCPiMXJkOr

McIvor, O. 2020. Indigenous Language Revitalization and Applied
Linguistics: Parallel Histories, Shared Future?. *Annual Review of Applied
Linguistics 40,* 78–96.

Penfield, S. D. and B. V. Tucker. 2011. From Documenting to Revitalizing an
Endangered Language: Where Do Applied Linguists Fit? *Language and
Education* 25(4), 291–305.

Rice, K. and N. Thieberger. 2018. Tools and Technology for Language
Documentation and Revitalization. In K. Rehg and L. Campbell (eds.) *The
Oxford Handbook of Endangered Languages.* New York: Oxford University
Press, 225–247.

Rising Voices. 2019, January 16. A Year-Long Rotating Twitter Campaign
Will Share the Voices of 50 Indigenous Language Digital Activists.
Retrieved from https://rising.globalvoices.org/blog/2019/01/15/a-year-
long-rotating-twitter-campaign-will-share-the-voices-of-50-indigenous-lan
guage-digital-activists/

Romero-Little, M. E. 2006. Honoring Our Own: Rethinking Indigenous
Languages and Literacy. *Anthropology & Education Quarterly* 37(4), 399–402.

Shah, S. and Brenzinger, M. 2018. The Role of Teaching in Language Revival
and Revitalization Movements. *Annual Review of Applied Linguistics* 38,
201–208.

Shockman, E. 2019. A Minneapolis School is Immersing Students in both
Dakota and Ojibwe. Retrieved from www.mprnews.org/story/2019/04/25/
a-minneapolis-school-is-immersing-students-in-both-dakota-and-ojibwe

Skutnabb-Kangas, T. 2000. *Linguistic Genocide in Education or Worldwide
Diversity and Human Rights?* New York: Routledge.

Skutnabb-Kangas, T. 2002. When Languages Disappear, Are Bilingual Education or Human Rights a Cure? Two Scenarios. In L. Wei, J. M. Dewaele, and A. Housen (eds.), *Opportunities and Challenges of Bilingualism*. New York: Mouton de Gruyter, 45–68.

Smith, L. T. 1999. *Decolonizing Methodologies: Research and Indigenous Peoples*. New York: Zed Books.

Swinehart, K. 2012. Metadiscursive Regime and Register Formation in Aymara Radio. *Language and Communication* 32(2), 102–113.

The Circle. 2014. Bdote Learning Center Opens in South Minneapolis. Retrieved from http://thecirclenews.org/cover-story/bdote-learning-center-opens-in-south-minneapolis/

Tollefson, J. W. 2006. Critical Theory in Language Policy. In T. Ricento (ed.), *An Introduction to Language Policy: Theory and Method*. Malden, MA: Blackwell Publishing Ltd., 24–41.

Treuer, A., N. Jones, and K. Paap. 2011. *Ezhichigeyang: Ojibwe Word List*. Hayward, WI: Waadookodaading Ojibwe Immersion School.

Urla, J. 2012. *Reclaiming Basque: Language, Nation and Cultural Activism*. Reno: University of Nevada Press.

Van Deusen-Scholl, N. 2003. Toward a Definition of Heritage Language: Sociopolitical and Pedagogical Considerations. *Journal of Language, Identity, and Education* 2(3), 211–230.

Wilson, W. H. and K. Kamanā. 2011. Insights from Indigenous language Immersion in Hawai'i. In D. J. Tedick, D. Christian, and T. W. Fortune (eds.), *Immersion Education: Practices, Policies, Possibilities*. Bristol: Multilingual Matters, 36–57.

Winstead, T., A. Lawrence, E. J. Brantmeier, and C. Frey. 2008. Language, Sovereignty, Cultural Contestation, and American Indian Schools: No Child Left behind and a Navajo Test Case. *Journal of American Indian Education* 47(1), 46–64.

37

Heritage Language Planning and Policy

Terrence G. Wiley

37.1   Introduction

This chapter provides a brief overview of many of the issues that emerge when we think about heritage language planning and policy (HLPP). The primary context for this discussion will focus on US planning and policy, with occasional reference to situations elsewhere. Before discussing current directions in HLPP, however, it is useful to reflect on some of the foundational concepts regarding language policy and planning (LPP) and their implications for HLPP.

Traditionally, a distinction has been made between *language planning* and *language policy*, but the two are interrelated. Language policy, or Spolsky's (2004) more inclusive term *language management*, generally refers to formal or explicit plans regarding language use, which are often, but not always, written down in a formal document by a government, official body, or agency (see especially 11–14). As Spolsky (2004) cautions, however, "the existence of an explicit policy does not guarantee that it will be implemented, nor does implementation guarantee success" (11). This definition largely focuses on policy at a macro level, but effective HLP often takes place on a micro level within the community or even the family. Some, such as Schiffman (1996), have also contended that, despite the focus on formal policy, language policies are derived from linguistic culture or cultural practices. It is also important to note that traditionally the focus on language policy has been on "named" languages, and frequently these are official languages of nation states. This traditional emphasis on named languages and their relationship to nation-states and the legacies of colonization has come under scrutiny in recent years by postmodern scholars (see, for example, Pennycook 2006; Makoni and Pennycook 2007; Wee

2011).[1] The postmodernist critique itself, however, has come under scrutiny for its lack of defense language rights and its implications for language minority education (see May 2012, 2014, 2018; Bale 2015; MacSwan 2017; Wiley, in press).

As noted, language planning is intrinsically linked to language policy. Heinz Kloss (1904–1987), was among the first to define language planning as consisting of two interconnected aspects, *corpus planning* and *status planning* (Kloss 1969).[2] Later, Cooper (1989) argued for adding a third component, *acquisition planning*. Corpus planning generally involves purposeful efforts to create, enhance, or change the body or lexicon of a language. It also refers to the coining and acceptance of neologisms, spelling reforms, and standardization as well as the creation and the adoption of new scripts, "in short, to the creation of new forms, the modification of old ones, or the selection from alternative forms in a spoken or written code" (Cooper 1989: 31). Corpus planning likewise may include the standardization of pronunciation, vocabulary, grammar, and spelling. Thus, corpus planning has frequently involved efforts to define, refine, or reform language varieties into named, taught, standardized, "literate" forms.

Corpus planning also encompasses *orthographic planning*, which involves the creation or reform of scripts such as alphabets, syllabaries, and ideographic writing systems. When a decision is made to create orthographies for previously unwritten languages, orthographic planning becomes a major concern. The development of the Cherokee syllabary in 1821 by Sequoyah (1770–1843) is but one noteworthy example, where the choice of a syllabary over an alphabetic system was initially controversial (see Lepore 2002: 63–90). More recently, orthographic planning has had relevance for some HL/CL learners because script reforms have been implemented subsequently in the source countries from which immigrants

---

[1] As noted in Wiley (2014), the construct of "language community" has been scrutinized from a postmodernist perspective. García et al. (2013), for example, contended that the ethnolinguistic communities of New York are transnational, and fluid, thereby leading her and her colleagues to abandon the traditional notion of speech community (see García et al. 2013). They further contend that the shift from Fishman's (1972) definition of speech community, which was based on shared linguistic characteristics and emphasized norms and rules of social use, prioritizes community boundaries as social, not linguistic. García et al. conclude, that "Regardless of whether the notion of 'speech community' uses, social, cultural or linguistic criteria, it results in the view that there are separate social, cultural or linguistic entities, and that these are nested communities within the nation-state" (32). Similarly, postmodern scholars have increasingly challenged the notion of "linguistic inheritance" itself, along with the notion of community language. With Rampton (2006), García et al. conclude: "Language and ethnicity are not simple reflections of 'heritage speech' communities, or of 'practice communities'. They argue that the social action and networks in which individuals are involved in the here-and-now juxtapose multiple linguistic and cultural identities from which we select features at different times to perform our identities" (cited in García et al. 2013: 34); see MacSwan 2017 for a critique).

[2] Kloss' historical work in *The American Bilingual Tradition* continues to have relevance for the study of immigrant heritage languages in the United States because he documented the efforts of groups to maintain and promote their languages and referenced the legal context in which they were able to do so. Nevertheless, Kloss as a scholar is a controversial figure because his early career involved working for the Nazi government in Germany, studying the demographics of German-speaking populations outside of the Reich (see Hutton 1999; Wiley 2002).

previously came. In Chinese heritage communities in the United States, for example, some immigrant parents from Hong Kong and Taiwan learned traditional Chinese characters in school before immigrating, but their children are now more likely to be taught in "simplified" characters, which are now taught in the People's Republic of China. In some communities the choice of script has been controversial (Wiley et al. 2008).

Traditionally, *status planning* has had several areas of focus, including (1) the official recognition of national or common languages; or (2) authoritarian attempts to restrict the use of minority languages (Cooper 1989; Kloss 1998/1977; Leibowitz 2016/1974). Thus, status planning also affects *medium of instruction planning* because it often determines the official designation regarding which language(s) of instruction will be used in schools (Tollefson and Tsui 2014). In broader political contexts, status planning also determines which languages will be used for official and political purposes such as voting, and whether language minority speakers will be accommodated by the provision of bilingual ballots and voting materials. Thus, to the extent that linguistic minority populations include heritage speakers, status planning can have important implications for their linguistic access in economic, political, and educational contexts, particularly in linguistic accommodations when the HL/CL is their dominant language.

Whereas status planning concerns the relationship *between* languages and their standing relative to each other, it can also focus on different varieties of what is purported to be the same language. In this case, status planning becomes a function of corpus planning. Historically, the creation of a standard language often begins with the selection of a written representation of a regional, social, or invented variety, which becomes the basis for grammatical refinement and vocabulary selection. "This initial language choice confers privilege upon those whose speech and writing most closely conform to the newly selected standard," which "inevitably elevates one variety of language over other varieties. Here, again, corpus planning determines status planning, since the process of standardization results in what is usually called the proper or correct variety or sometimes . . . the preferred or power variety" (Wiley 1996: 108).

Thus, although traditional language planning was not overtly seen as being concerned with larger social issues, the ascription of higher status to one language variety over another obviously had implications for the status and social control of groups affected by the policies (Leibowitz 2016/ 1974). The use of the term *dialect*, for example, in popular usage commonly connotes a language that is substandard or of lesser value (Roy 1987). As Weinstein (1983) concluded: "Attaching a positive value to a variety of language transforms it into a form of capital, useful for gaining entry into a community or for claiming economic benefits" (62). Thus, status planning and the labels ascribed to language varieties have status consequences not only for the language varieties to which they are ascribed but also to those who speak them (Wiley 1996). This is equally true for HLs/CLs.

As noted, Cooper (1989) proposed *acquisition planning* as the third, and probably most common, form of language planning. He offered the following definition: "Language policy-making involves decisions concerning the teaching and use of language, and their careful formulation by those empowered to do so, for the guidance of others" (31). Acquisition that takes place through formal education is commonly referred to as *language-in-education planning* (Kaplan and Baldauf 1997). It affects choice of language(s) for medium of instruction policy; it may involve the promotion and spread of a new language, or standardized variety of language; or it might affect the use of languages selected for bilingual or heritage language education. Acquisition planning can also be used to accommodate or even promote minority, community, or heritage languages. In 1977, for example, the first programs under the "heritage" label were offered in Ontario, Canada, where schools were required to offer two and a half hours of instruction per week on request from community groups who could "supply a minimum of 25 students interested in studying a particular language" (Cummins 2005: 591). As Cummins notes, subsequently: [The] "Ontario government replaced [heritage language] with international language, on the grounds that heritage connotes learning about past traditions rather than acquiring language skills that have significance for children's overall educational and personal development" (591).[3]

Acquisition planning has also been associated with mass literacy campaigns such as those in China during the revolutionary period of the early 1950s (Peterson 1997), whereby *pǔtōnghuà*, common speech based on Mandarin, was promoted over other regional varieties. Acquisition planning may also co-occur with corpus planning as in those cases involving the promotion of a new script as, for example, in the promotion of simplified characters in China or *Toyo Kanji* in Japan, or historically *hangul* in Korea. For immigrant communities seeking to stay connected with heritage languages of source countries of their migration, national standard or common languages are sometimes preferred over other varieties spoken in the home (see Bhalla et al., this volume; also Wiley et al. 2008).

Language-in-education planning, as the primary form of language acquisition planning (Paulston and McLaughlin 1994), is carried out or supervised as an extension of governmental policy and is best understood within the

---

[3] Elsewhere in the United Kingdom, Europe, and Australia the term community language is preferred over heritage language (see Horvath and Vaughan 1991 on "community" languages in Europe; also Hornberger 2005 regarding the distinction between heritage and community languages in the United States and Australia).

context of how nation-states attempt to direct socialization within socio-political contexts (Judd 1991). Although schools may play an important role in community-based language planning, they also play a major role in promoting national standard languages and, thereby, help to extend the state's influence over its citizens and residents. Standard languages are explicitly taught through the "pedagogization" of languages in schools (Street and Street 1991). In this regard, Illich (1979) was among the first to note the irony of casting a standardized language as being one's *mother tongue*, since one must go to school to learn the language one supposedly already speaks. Others have elaborated on this as the "invention" of the native speaker (Bonfiglio 2010). Societal multilingualism further compli-cates the notion of mother tongue as applied to defining one's HL (Wiley 2014a). Many people embrace the simplistic notion that writing is merely speech written down or encoded in print. As Haugen (1983) understood, the pedagogization of standardized languages of literacy through schooling facilitates the imposition of the written norms of the formal standard on oral varieties of language, which is facilitated by myriad school-based language policies governing language curricula, syllabi, classroom mater-ials, and activities (Corson 1998).

Language-in-education planning involving attempts to add heritage and community languages (HL/CLs) into the curriculum also relates to status planning, because, as Mercurio and Scarano (2005) have noted, there can be a struggle to accept HL/HCs as "legitimate" objects of study. The addition of HL/CLs has occasionally also created conflicts regarding which languages should have priority in the curriculum. In the United States, for example, the addition of Mandarin into secondary school curricula has sometimes led to the removal of formerly taught European languages.

Historically, much of the momentum for promoting HLs/CLs has fallen outside of formal/governmental language-in-education planning. Rather, the impetus has come through localized efforts in the community or through the family (Spolsky 2012). Thus, it is useful to make a distinction between *macro language planning* and *micro language planning*. In addition, it is important to consider agency in HLPP regarding who attempts to make policy. Traditionally, LPP was characterized as an expert-driven, top down enterprise. It is also important, therefore, to make a distinction between *top down* and *bottom up* planning. The impetus for the latter comes from the community or family. Within the context of US history, top-down language planning also has historically sometimes had a nega-tive impact, particularly on indigenous communities as in the case of the imposition of English-only policies that lead to indigenous language eradi-cation (Adams 1995). Thus, community involvement in HLPP is now seen as essential (see Hornberger 1997; McCarty and Watahomigie 1999; and McCarty 2004).

37.2 Classifying Language Policies and Determining Their Impact

Within LPP broadly, it is sometimes useful to consider motivations for planning and policy formation and to classify them into various policy types. Kloss (1998/1977), for example, noted that policies affecting immigrant languages in the United States could be primarily categorized into various policy orientations ranging from promotion-oriented to restriction-oriented policies. Table 37.1 expands this scheme with reference to policy orientations affecting HLPP.

37.3 Language-as-Resource

During the formative period of language planning scholarship, language planning was largely focused on solving language "problems" either within the contexts of national development or the linguistic integration of language minorities. Later, with the rise of the Civil Rights Movement in the United States, particularly the 1960s, there was an increased focus on minority rights, including language rights. Subsequently, the late Richard Ruíz (1950–2015) argued that orientations toward the role of language in society "are basic to language planning in that they determine the basic questions we ask, the conclusions we draw from the data, and even the data themselves … In short, orientations determine what is thinkable about language in society" (Ruíz 1984: 16). Ruíz observed that much of the focus on language policy to that point had largely focused on language problems and language rights of minorities. Between the two, he concluded that the *language-as-a-problem* orientation was more conspicuous because cultural and social diversity were generally viewed as problems by the dominant society. Thus, language diversity was determined to be a problem too. *Language-as-a-right*, Ruíz's second major orientation, was also a concern, by extension, because, according to Ruíz, "language touches many aspects of social life, any comprehensive statement about language rights cannot confine itself to merely linguistic considerations" (: 22). Leibowitz (2016/ 1974) previously had made a similar point, arguing that whenever language is the focal point as a policy consideration, there is always more at stake for those affected by the policy in other social domains where they are experiencing discrimination in the form of economic, political, or educational access. Thus, language discrimination typically involved other forms of discrimination.

Ruíz (1984), however, concluded that there were many unresolved issues and technical problems associated with the language-as-right orientation, because language planners who operate from orientation are concerned

Table 37.1 *A typology of language planning and policy orientations with a focus on heritage languages*

Policy orientation	Description	Examples
Promotion-oriented	In macro, often "official," contexts, promotion policies utilize state allocated resources through governmental planning typically to further an official/common language or languages in various societal domains, including governmental agencies, schools, or other institutions. In micro contexts, communities or private groups may create internal policies to promote their own languages.	In many countries, the official national language or languages are promoted through the medium of instruction policies, as well as through the printing and distribution of textbooks, laws, and records in the national language(s). In China, for example, through mass literacy campaigns, Mandarin is promoted as *Pǔtōnghuà* or common language. In the United States and United Kingdom, English has been promoted as the common language even without its official recognition. In Wales, Welsh has been also been promoted though governmental policy (Wiley 1996).
Accommodation-oriented	Some policies are designed to accommodate minority or heritage speaker populations. These are also called *expediency-oriented* policies (Kloss 1998/1977). They are sometimes confused with promotion-oriented policies, but they differ in purpose because they are not intended to enhance the broader use of a minority or heritage language. Rather, they are designed to *accommodate* minority speakers, either in the short-term while they are learning the dominant language, or to facilitate access and interaction with governmental agencies. Accommodation policies are sometimes misrepresented as only benefiting minorities; however, they can also benefit the state's ability to communicate with a minority to carry out basic governmental functions.	In 1977 in Ontario, Canada, the province implemented immigrant HL language programs to accommodate smaller immigrant language communities (see Cummins 2005; also Bale and Kawaguchi 2020 for a recent assessment of the program). Common examples of accommodational policies include the widespread use of transitional bilingual education to promote educational access, or the use of translation and interpretation to political participation, or to guarantee legal rights through the provision of interpretation in court proceedings. In the United States, as one of his last official acts, President Clinton signed into law Executive Order 13166 (see www.lep.gov/13166/eo13166.html), which was designed to provide legal and medical access for those of "limited English proficiency." Bilingual tax-forms are an example of an accommodation that helps the state to collect revenue and language minorities to comply with tax laws.
Tolerance-oriented	Tolerance-oriented policies are characterized by the significant absence of governmental interference or involvement in the linguistic life of the language minority or heritage language communities. In a tolerant environment, heritage and minority speakers and communities are left to their own devices to maintain or preserve their languages without any expectation of resources or support from the government.	In US history, most immigrant and indigenous peoples experienced no overt restrictions on the use and maintenance of their community languages until the end of the nineteenth century (Fishman 2014; Kloss 1998/1977). German Americans, for example, had some success, through their own efforts, in maintaining their languages through both public and religious means until the late nineteenth and early twentieth centuries (Toth 1990; see also Fishman 1966).

Table 37.1 (*cont.*)

Policy orientation	Description	Examples
Restriction-oriented	These policies are typically aimed at constraining or eliminating the use of non-official, minoritized, or heritage languages in specific societal contexts such as education, the workplace, media, or other public or official domains.	In US historical educational contexts, restrictive language policies were used extensively during the World War I era. English-only policies were imposed along with other Americanization efforts (Wiley 1998). In 1998, California's Proposition 227 sought to severely limit bilingual education; however, this policy has recently been reversed with the passage of Proposition 58 in 2016 (see Wiley 2019).
Repression-oriented	Repression-oriented policies are a more extreme version of restrictive policies. Restrictive policies become repressive when they are linked to deculturation and have the goal of language eradication or what Skutnabb-Kangas et al. (1995) have termed linguistic genocide, involving the conscious attempt to exterminate minority or heritage languages.	Beginning in colonial British North America, and continuing in the United States under the institution of slavery, those enslaved were not allowed to speak or teach their languages to their children, and they were simultaneously not allowed to become literate in English through compulsory ignorance laws (Weinberg 1995). Deculturation and language eradication policies targeted Native Americans from roughly 1879–1932 (Adams 1995).

with confrontation, activism, and advocacy. Clearly, for contemporary activist scholars this is not problematic. Nevertheless, based on what he saw as limitations of the rights and problems orientations, Ruíz proposed a *language-as-resource orientation* to alleviate conflicts emerging out of the other two orientations. Ruíz also assumed that the language-as-resource orientation might help to enhance the subordinated status of minority language speakers, which he hoped would help to "ease tensions between majority and minority communities" (25–26). Lastly, he believed the resource orientation could "serve as a more consistent way of viewing the role of non-English languages in U.S. society … [because] … it highlights the importance of cooperative language planning" (25–26).

Subsequently, the language-as-resource orientation has been widely embraced and was compatible with efforts to both increase the status of minority languages and enrich or revitalize endangered languages of native peoples and those that were falling into disuse by immigrants who wished to maintain their heritage languages. Meanwhile, Fishman (1991) focused on *planned-language revitalization*, which attempted to provide both practical and theoretical assistance "to communities whose native languages are threatened because their intergenerational continuity is proceeding negatively" (Fishman 1991: 1). Unlike Ruíz, however, he was not as concerned about a conflict between the rights and resource orientations. Thus, he sought to extend promotion-oriented rights to protect the speakers of the world's "endangered" languages, which requires protective rights. His efforts can also be interpreted as using language to promote *ethnic revitalization* (see Tucker 1994). In recent years, the language-as-resource orientation has been more directly criticized because it has been appropriated by some neoliberalists, who seem more interested in promoting language education for global business purposes than in promoting HLs as a community resource (Ricento 2009). This appropriation by neoliberalists, however, seems far from Ruíz's original intent or that of most HL/CL advocates (see Hult and Hornberger 2016 for a retrospective on his work).

37.4 Ideological Policy Shifts Affecting Heritage Language Education in the US Historical Context

As Fishman (2014) has noted, there has been an over 300-year history of heritage language teaching in what has become the United States, spanning from the colonial period through the contemporary national period.

> If we define *heritage languages* as those that (a) are LOTEs (languages other than English) in Michael Clyne's usage (1991, p. 3) and that (b) have a particular family relevance to the learners, then we will find schools devoted to teaching these languages and to developing literacy and promoting further education through these languages among the indigenous, the colonial, and the immigrant groups that have come to this country by choice and good fortune or by force and the winds of cruel history (36).

From an LPP perspective, the primary impetus has come from the more localized efforts of HL communities. Thus, based on the taxonomy of policy types (Table 37.1), most of the efforts to promote HL acquisition planning fall within the *tolerance orientation* and have been carried out at a more micro level of LPP. Within this context, the federal government and various states have largely taken a hands-off approach by neither supporting nor opposing community-based efforts to promote HLs. There have, however, been major exceptions to the climate of tolerance, which Kloss (1998/1977) argued was the prevailing orientation in what he termed "the American bilingual tradition." There were, for example, some nativist sentiments even during the colonial period, as well as prior to the US Civil War with the rise of the anti-immigrant "No Nothing Movement" (Wiley 2013). During the latter nineteenth century, the US government launched the boarding school movement, which incarcerated Native American children in residential schools. The initial objective for the program involved "domestication" through the imposition of English and cultural and linguistic eradication (Adams 1995; McCarty 2004). Immigration also surged during this period. Immigrants, particularly those of German origin, who were the most prolific in promoting German language education, gradually became targeted by nativists, first in several Midwestern states, and then, with the coming of World War I, more widely across the United States. As Fishman (2004) notes,

> German is also a good example of how U.S. foreign policy and other national interests can affect heritage language education (Pavlenko, 2002; Wiley, 1998). World War I led to such severe antiforeigner (and particularly anti-German) propaganda that many ethnic heritage schools were closed, both voluntarily and by state directives. Legislation against foreign language instruction, aimed particularly at the elementary education level, both public and private, was passed. *Meyer* vs. *Nebraska* (1923, 262, US 390) is the U.S. Supreme Court decision that overthrew such legislation, on the grounds that it constituted unjustified state intrusion into the educational preferences of parents and the professional freedom of teachers to practice a legally certified occupation. The Nebraska state government's argument that early exposure to a living foreign language was injurious to the national loyalty and to the intellectual development of children was explicitly rejected by the Supreme Court as contrary to reason and unsupported by evidence. . . . Although the Supreme Court came to the rescue of parents and teachers in connection with the constitutionality of ethnic heritage language education, the atmosphere was already poisoned. We did not fully recover for another quarter century when minority civil rights were more positively located on the national agenda (39).

Thus, the policy orientation in the United States shifted from one of tolerance to *repression* for Native Americans and *restriction* for Germans and other European immigrants (see Table 37.1). These intolerant orientations persisted until the ethnic revival documented by Fishman in *Language Loyalties* (1966), which co-occurred with the Civil Rights Movement of the 1960s and liberalization in US immigration policy. The return of community-based efforts to promote HLs was also contemporaneous with the rise of federally supported bilingual education, even though it was not directly linked to it. Within a decade of the establishment of federal support for bilingual education (BLE), it increasingly became targeted as "affirmative ethnicity" (Epstein 1977) and ethnic revitalization also began to wane. From a policy perspective, those attacking BLE misconstrued it as *promotion-oriented policy*, when in fact it was intended only as an *accommodation*, or *expediency-oriented* policy (see Table 37.1).

The 1980s saw the rise of advocacy for official English and restrictive English-only policies. These were largely successful at the state level, but they failed at the national level. The assault on federally funded bilingual education (BLE) persisted until its demise with the passage of the No Child Left Behind Act of 2002. Moreover, during the 1990s and early 2000s, voters in several states (California, Arizona, and Massachusetts) passed measures to restrict the use of native languages, particularly Spanish, in bilingual education. The demise of federally supported bilingual education and the imposition of restrictive English-only education resulted in denial of opportunities for many language minority students to connect with their family, community, and ancestral languages in school.

To assess this consequence, Fee et al. (2014) analyzed the American Community Survey's demographic data on language and compared it to ACTF school "foreign" language enrollment data to assess how many potential heritage learners in the K-12 population might be reflected among those labeled as foreign language learners. The data were quite revealing. Based on 2007–2008 ACS data, for example, nationally nearly 9 million school-age children lived in homes were Spanish was spoken. Fee et al. then looked at data in selected states. Using California as an example, which had the largest single share of the prospective Spanish-HL population, there were slightly over 2.5 million students in homes where Spanish was spoken. When Fee et al. contrasted the data for Spanish language enrollments in California for 2010, which was the nearest comparable year, they found that only 617,000 students were enrolled in Spanish state-wide. Obviously, that total would have included many students who were not native speakers of Spanish. From this, we can surmise that only a small proportion of the potential HL students from homes where Spanish was spoken had any opportunity to formally study the language. Significantly, bilingual education in California had been restricted between 1998 and 2016. Thus, during that period, both the demise of bilingual education in California and the lack of availability of Spanish classes in many grades and schools greatly diminished the opportunity of language minority students to learn through Spanish, their "heritage" language, or even to have contact with it as a "foreign" language (see Fee et al. 2014). There were similar findings for other states (see also Wiley et al. 2016).

With the 2016 passage of Proposition 58 in California, the schools in the state are now free to promote dual language education – assuming they have the resources. This, and similar trends in other states, have now signaled a policy shift with more positive implications for HL learners and the promotion of HLs (Wiley 2019). To some degree, however, bilingual educators and foreign language educators have tended to pursue separate policy agendas for promoting language education. Bilingual educators have tended to focus on "mother tongue" education for language minorities. This population, however, could also be labeled "heritage" learners. Meanwhile, foreign language educators have often taught heritage learners, but, until recently, they have been taught their home/community languages as "foreign" languages.

Gradually through the efforts of the late Olga Kagan (1947–2018) and her colleagues, including the editors of this volume, there has been a growing recognition that there need to be curricular adjustments for HL learners given that they often have considerable knowledge and facility in their HLs despite having had little – or interrupted – formal education in them. From the standpoint of acquisition policy, there have been some attempts to articulate bilingual education within foreign language education, or in two-way/dual immersion programs; however, these efforts have often been carried out at a more local or micro policy level, with some progressive schools or universities offering innovative instruction. Despite some positive endeavors (including those noted in this volume), there remains a need for a more comprehensive national policy that links various elements of language education together from elementary through university-level instruction.

37.5   Efforts to Envision a Comprehensive National Policy

Ironically, the late 1990s marked a positive turning point for HL policy even as federally supported bilingual education was in decline after more than two decades of being attacked by those advocating English-only instruction for language minority students and those who saw it as "affirmative ethnicity" (Epstein 1977). Some scholars began focusing on the relationship between HL language loss and language acquisition (see, for example, Polinsky 1995). Around the same time, a growing number of language educators also began advocating for a more specific focus on HL learners. In 1998, Krashen, Tse, and McQuillan published *Heritage Language Development*. In 1999, the first National Conference on Heritage Languages was held in Long Beach, California. It was co-sponsored by California State University, Long Beach, in collaboration with the Center for Applied Linguistics in Washington, DC, and the National Foreign Language Center (NFLC). A working group was formed following the conference to identify research priorities for the emerging field (Wiley et al. 2014: ix).[4] A report of the committee's work was published in the *Bilingual Research Journal* (see UCLA 2000/2001). A second conference followed in 2002, which was sponsored by the Center for Applied Linguistics and the NFLC. An increasing body of work specifically focused on heritage language learning quickly followed. The Center for Applied Linguistics, for example, published *Heritage Languages in America: Preserving a National Resource* (Peyton et al. 2001). With the establishment of the National Heritage Language Resource Center at UCLA, initially led by the late Russell Campbell (1927–2003), the center was able to assume national leadership in

[4] Among the participants were James Alatis, Russell Campbell, Donna Christian, Lily Wong Fillmore, Joshua Fishman, Joy Peyton, Ana Roca, Guadalupe Valdés, and me, among others. The following year, under the leadership of Russell Campbell, a smaller group of us were joined by Reynaldo Macías and Joseph LoBianco. We began formulating a research and policy agenda for the field, meeting regularly at UCLA. As noted, a report by the committee was subsequently published (see UCLA, 2000/2001).

promoting HL research with relevance for acquisition policy. Much of the initial focus was on HL learners who were enrolled in "foreign" language instruction; however, there was increasing interest in community-based efforts (see McCarty and Watahomigie 1999; Spolsky 2001; Valdés 2001; Kagan 2005; Wiley 2005a, 2005b, 2007a, 2007b; Polinsky and Kagan 2007; Peyton et al. 2008).

Moreover, with increasing evidence regarding the pace of language shift, and thereby first language loss (Rumbaut 2009), there were signs of increasing support for HL education as well as dual language instruction. Research on immigrant HL and language minority parents demonstrated strong support for bilingual and community language education in languages such as Spanish, Chinese, Korean, and indigenous languages, when parents have the opportunity to choose them (e.g., Krashen 1996; McCarty 2004; Wiley 2005a; Wiley et al. 2008; Rumbaut 2009). There was also increasing evidence at the community level for the promotion of heritage and community languages by newer immigrant populations such as Koreans, Chinese, and Indians (You 2009; Liu 2010; Pu 2012; see also Bhalla, Liu, and Wiley this volume). During the early 2000s, McGinnis (2005) had even concluded that for the teaching of Chinese, community-based efforts often seemed more advanced than K-12 and university efforts to teach the language. Thus, he recommended closer articulation and planning among all stakeholders.

Thus, increasingly, it became clear that what was missing was a national comprehensive policy framework that could link those interested in the promotion of foreign languages at the K-12 and higher education levels with heritage and community-based education efforts. In other words, there was a need for a macro policy framework that could link community- and more micro-based promotion efforts together. Ironically, at the federal level, it was the Department of Defense (DOD) rather than Education that led many of the efforts to promote the importance of HL education, although the DOD was focused mostly on critical and strategic language promotion through such programs as STARTALK and the Flagship program (Bale 2008). A further continuing challenge is promoting heritage and community language educational policies in the United States in the wake of the demise of federally sponsored Title VII bilingual education (Wiley and Wright 2004; González 2007; Wiley 2013).

Spolsky (2001, October 2002) was among the first to offer a general framework for a comprehensive national language policy that would include HL policy. Spolsky's five basic principles on which such a national policy could be based may be summarized as including:

> ... the development of policies designed to ensure (1) no linguistic discrimination; (2) the provision of adequate programs for the teaching of English to all; (3) the development of respect for both plurilingual capacity and ... diverse individual languages; (4) the development of approaches that

enhance the status and enrich the knowledge of heritage language and community languages: (5) the development of a multi-branched language-capacity program that strengthens and integrates a variety of language programs that: assures the heritage programs connect with advanced training programs; builds on heritage, immersion and overseas-experience approaches to constantly replenish a cadre of efficient plurilingual citizens capable of professional work using their plurilingual skills; and provides rich and satisfying language programs that lead to a plurilingual population with knowledge of and respect for other languages and cultures (Wiley 2014b: 50).

Spolsky's first two principles are closely connected, since freedom from discrimination necessitates the need for policies of linguistic accommodation where translation and interpretation are needed to provide linguistic access to ensure basic services or to protect human and civil rights. His second principle, which emphasizes the necessity for instruction in English, is needed to ensure that language minorities are not linguistically isolated so that they may have social, economic, and political access and participation. Importantly, Spolsky (October 2002) noted that the demise of federal Title VII bilingual education programs weakened the range of educational opportunities for language minorities to develop their heritage and community languages (Wiley 2014b).

The sunsetting of the federal bilingual education also diminished opportunities for learners to develop respect for both plurilingual capacity and diverse individual languages (Spolsky's third principle). Similarly, as the No Child Left Behind Act of 2002 became law, there was a subsequent reduction of emphasis on foreign language instruction which further reduced the capacity to promote multilingualism. Thus, Spolsky correctly understood that a new comprehensive national policy initiative was needed to link heritage language education with bilingual education, foreign language education, and effort to preserve and promote native languages (Spolsky, October 2002; Wiley 2014b).

Spolsky's fourth principle, for improving the standing of heritage language and community languages, traditionally falls under language status promotion. In this regard, Ruíz (1995) had noted that promotion may either be internal (endoglossic) to language communities or (exoglossic); that is, aimed at promoting languages more widely. He further notes that in the United States, Native American language promotion efforts have tended to be mostly endoglossic, or focused on status promotion within the community. Thus, efforts to promote language status should be sensitive to a community's aspirations regarding whether the goal for the promotion is more on language development within the community, and/or more broadly in larger society (Spolsky, October, 2002; Wiley 2014b). Spolsky's last principle, which focused on the building of a multi-branched language-capacity network, requires the development of a comprehensive language policy that would link HL/community-based promotion efforts to K-12 language programs, as well as university programs. Thus, there would be a comprehensive K-university level program (Spolsky, October 2002; Wiley 2014b).

In the United States, despite the importance of federal policy, there continues to be a need for official recognition of heritage-community language learners at the state level, since states have primary responsibility for public education. As noted, this involves what Mercurio and Scarano (2005) call a "struggle for legitimacy." First, this involves moving community languages into the curriculum that have not previously been taught, which is traditionally related to promoting their status in the curriculum. Moreover, once "less commonly taught" languages are in the curriculum, there is a need for HL curriculum and instruction to be differentiated from foreign language teaching. Moreover, as Action and Dalphinis (2000) have noted, non-standardized heritage and community languages have not been traditionally used as mediums of instruction. Thus, including them is a major challenge for some communities that may not have, or want, a written standard (see Bale and Kawaguchi's 2020 discussion regarding this issue in Ontario's HL program). As Spolsky (2001) cautioned, this requires critical dialog and input from the communities involved. Thus, to create a successful national or state macro-policy there is a need for an inclusive micro-policy involving input and leadership from the community. In summary, Spolsky (2001) endorsed:

> [T]he need for the community to (1) recognize the importance of plurilingual competence in its members; (2) support programs that assure that everyone can develop full control of English for access to educational, economic, social and cultural development; (3) support efforts to assure that everyone can develop a high level of proficiency in the community language for the maintenance of tradition and culture by raising children bilingually by (a) providing opportunities for developing oral and literacy skills in both languages, (b) ensuring the use of the community language in public domains as well as private, (c) assisting in the maintenance and cultivation of the community language, provides ways of passing traditional language and culture between the generations, (d) providing community schools, (e) persuading the public schools to respect and support community language maintenance, (f) and encouraging and respect efforts by other language groups to do the same (Wiley 2014: 51).

Spolsky's (2001; October 2002) recommendations provided a useful guide for an inclusive national language policy. So, what progress has been made? In recent years, despite the persistence of anti-immigrant and English-only lobbying at both the federal and state levels, there has been increasing public support for increasing language development and multilingualism;

some states, such as Utah, and more recently California, have embraced policies designed to promote multilingualism more broadly (Wiley 2019). More recently, other positive developments have been the endorsement of inclusive language development policies by high profile commissions. The American Academy of Arts and Sciences, for example, with rare bipartisan congressional endorsement, formed the Commission on Language Learning. The commission was brought together by an interdisciplinary team of experts, for the purpose of promoting "a national strategy to improve access to as many languages as possible for people of every region, ethnicity, and socioeconomic background … and that instruction should begin as early in life as possible. Its primary goal, therefore, is for every school in the nation to offer meaningful instruction in world languages as part of their standard curricula" (Commission on Language Learning 2017: viii).

From an ideological perspective, however, the commission first framed its arguments for the promotion of languages largely in neoliberal discursive terms. The commission noted with concern that the monolingual majority in the United States trails most European nations as well as China in developing linguistic knowledge and skills in second languages among its citizens. Importantly – given the legacy of associating bilingualism with deficits (Hakuta 1986) – the commission next embraced the social, economic, and cognitive benefits of bilingualism, and endorsed "heritage" language instruction, particularly for Native Americans in accordance with the Native American Languages Act in "English-based schools with appropriate curricula and materials" (x). The commission also stressed that language is a resource for the United States in an increasing globalized world. More constructively, the commission endorsed improving linguistic access "for people of every region, ethnicity, and socioeconomic background" (viii). The commission depicted languages of the home primarily as "heritage languages," and (1) endorsed support for the intergenerational transition of HLs. Reflecting similar notions to those previously developed by Spolsky (2001; October 2002), the commission supported (2) encouraging HL speakers to pursue further academic instruction in their languages and more "learning opportunities for HL speakers in classroom or school settings"; (3) expanding "efforts to create college and university curricula designed specifically" for them as well as "course credit for proficiency" in an HL; (4) providing "targeted support and programming for Native American languages as defined in the Native American Languages Act"; (5) increasing "support for Native American languages being used as primary languages of education, and for the development of curricula and education materials for such programs"; and (6) providing "opportunities for Native Americans and others to study Native American languages in English-based schools with appropriate curricula and materials" (Commission on Language Learning 2017: x).

37.6 Conclusion

Recommendations such as Spolsky's and those of the commission can be taken as positive for envisioning a comprehensive macro language framework that includes HLs. The greater challenge is more of a political one involving how to generate sufficient broad-based support to implement articulated K-university programs in language education that are supported by the provision of sufficient resources. In doing so, however, there is also a need to come to terms with the legacies of the restrictive ideologies of the Americanization and English-only movements of the prior century, as well as those that continue to be promoted, often in association with anti-immigrant or racist agendas. Thus, to move an effective national HLLP policy forward, there is also a need to be informed by the history of language policies toward immigrant and minority groups (Fishman 2014; Wiley, in press). That history needs to interrogate why there was a lapse of federal support for bilingual education, as well as why there were prior attempts to eradicate Native American languages during the Boarding school era, or to restrict German and other foreign languages during World War I, as well as to not accommodate instruction for non–English-speaking Chinese children without the intervention of the Supreme Court in *Lau* v. *Nichols*, 414 U.S. 563 (1974). Further, as noted, the history of language policy and planning has all too often been imposed from the top-down. Thus, there is an ongoing need to reorient policymaking from the bottom-up to ensure that language planning and policy formation for the promotion of, and efforts to revitalize and restore, heritage, community, and indigenous languages are done in partnership with those who are the objects of HLPP promotion efforts.

References

Action, T. and M. Dalphinis. 2000. *Language, Blacks, and Gypsies: Languages without a Written Tradition and Their Role in Education.* Salem, MA: Witing & Birch.

Adams, D. W. 1995. *Education for Extinction: American Indians and the Boarding School Experience, 1875–1928.* Lawrence: University of Kansas Press.

Bale, J. 2008. When Arabic is the "Target" Language: National Security, Title VI, and Arabic Language Programs, 1958–1991. Dissertation. Tempe: Arizona State University.

Bale, J. 2015. Language Policy and Global Political Economy. In T. Ricento (ed.), *Language Policy and Political Economy: English in Global Context.* Oxford: Oxford University Press. 72–95.

Bale, J. and M. Kawaguchi. 2020. Heritage-Language Education Policies, Anti-Racist Activism, and Discontinuity in 1970s and 1980s Toronto. *Critical Inquiry in Language Studies* 17(1), 5–25.

Bhalla, S., N. Liu, and T. G. Wiley (2021). Asian Heritage Languages in the United States: Chinese and Hindi Language Communities. In S. Montrul and M. Polinsky (eds.), *The Cambridge Handbook of Heritage Languages and Linguistics*. Cambridge: Cambridge University Press, 206–229.

Bonfiglio, T. P. 2010. *Mother Tongues and Nations: The Invention of the Native Speaker*. New York: De Gruyter Mouton.

Clyne, M. 1991. *Community Language*. Cambridge: Cambridge University Press.

Commission on Language Learning. 2017. *America's Languages: Investing in Language Education for the 21st Century*. Cambridge, MA: American Academy of Arts and Sciences.

Cooper, R. L. 1989. *Language Planning and Social Change*. Cambridge: Cambridge University Press.

Corson, D. 1998. *Language Polices in Schools. A Resource for Teachers and Administrators*. Mahwah, NJ: Lawrence Erlbaum Associates.

Cummins, J. 2005. A Proposal for Action: Strategies for Recognizing Heritage Language Competence as a Learning Resource within the Mainstream Classroom. *The Modern Language Journal* 89(4), 586–592.

Epstein, N. 1977. *Language, Ethnicity, and the Schools*. Washington, DC: Institute for Educational Leadership.

Executive Order 13166. Retrieved May 7, 2020 from www.lep.gov/13166/eo13166.html.

Fee, M., N. C. Rhodes, and T. G. Wiley. 2014. Demographic Realities, Challenges, and Opportunities. In T. G. Wiley, J. K. Peyton, D. Christian, S. K. Moore, and N. Liu. (eds.), *Handbook on Heritage, Community, and Native American Language Education in the United States: Research, Policy and Practice*. London: Routledge, 6–18.

Fishman, J. A. (ed.) 1966. *Language Loyalty in the United States*. The Hague: Mouton.

Fishman, J. A. 1972. *Readings in the Sociology of Language*. The Hague: Mouton.

Fishman, J. A. 1991. *Reversing Language Shift*. Clevedon: Multilingual Matters.

Fishman, J. A. 2014. Three Hundred-plus Years of Heritage Language Education in the United States. In T. G. Wiley, J. K. Peyton, D. Christian, S. K. Moore, and N. Liu. (eds.), *Handbook on Heritage, Community, and Native American Language Education in the United States: Research, Policy and Practice*. London: Routledge, 36–53.

García, O., Z. Zakharia, and B. Otcu. 2013. *Heritage Bilingual Community Education*. Bristol: Multilingual Matters.

González, J. M. 2007. It's Time to Get another Horse. *International Multilingual Research Journal* 1(1), 39–44.

Hakuta, K. 1986. *Mirror of Language: The Debate on Bilingualism*. New York: Basic Books.

Haugen, E. 1983. The Implementation of Corpus Planning: Theory and Practice. In J. Cobarrubias and J. A. Fishman (eds.), *Progress in Language Planning*. 269–289. The Hague: Mouton.

Hornberger, N. 1997. Language Planning from the Bottom Up. In N. Hornberger (ed.), *Indigenous Literacies in the Americas: Language Planning from the Bottom Up*. Berlin and New York: Mouton de Gruyter, 357–366.

Hornberger, N. (ed.) 2005. Heritage/Community Language Education: US and Australian Perspectives. *International Journal of Bilingual Education and Bilingualism* 8(2–3).

Horvath, B. M. and P. Vaughan. 1991. *Community Languages: A Handbook*. Clevedon: Multilingual Matters.

Hult, F. M. and N. H. Hornberger. 2016. Orientations in Language Planning Revisited: Problem, Right and Resource as an Analytical Heuristic. *Bilingual Review/Revista Bilingüe* 33(3).

Hutton, Christopher. 1999. *Linguistics and the Third Reich: Mother-Tongue Fascism, Race, and the Science of Language*. London: Routledge.

Illich, I. 1979. Vernacular Values and Education. *Teacher's College Record* 81(1), 31–75.

Judd, E. 1991. Language-in-Education Policy and Planning. In W. Grabe and R. Kaplan (eds.), *Introduction to Applied Linguistics*. Reading, MA: Addison-Wesley, 169–188.

Kagan, O. E. 2005. In Support of a Proficiency-Based Definition of Heritage Language Learners: The Case of Russian. *International Journal of Bilingual Education and Bilingualism* 8(2–3), 213–229.

Kaplan, R. B. and R. B. Baldauf Jr. 1997. *Language Planning: From Practice to Theory*. Clevedon: Multilingual Matters.

Kloss, H. 1969. Research Possibilities on Group Bilingualism: A Report. Quebec: International Center for Research on Bilingualism.

Kloss, H. 1998. *The American Bilingual Tradition, Revised Edition*. Washington, DC and McHenry, IL: Center for Applied Linguistics & Delta Systems. Revised reprint of Kloss, H. (1977). *The American Bilingual Tradition*. Rowley, MA: Newbury House Publishers.

Krashen, S. D. 1996. *Under Attack: The Case against Bilingual Education*. Culver City, CA: Language Education Associates.

Krashen, S. D., J. McClellan, and L. Tse. 1998. *Heritage Language Development*. Los Angeles: Language Education Associates.

Leibowitz, A. H. 2016. Language as a Means of Social Control. In T. Ricento (ed.), *Language Policy and Planning*, Vol. 1. London: Routledge, 221–257. Reprint. Leibowitz, A. H. (1974, August). Language as a Means of Social Control. Eric Document No. ED O93 168, Eric Clearing House, Washington, DC; 1974.

Lepore, J. 2002. *A is for American: Letters and other Characters in the Newly United States*. New York: Alfred A. Knopf.

Liu, N. 2010. The Role of Confucius Institutes in Chinese Language-Community Language Schools: Stakeholders' Views. Dissertation. Tempe: Arizona State University.

MacSwan, J. 2017. A Multilingual Perspective on Translanguaging. *American Educational Research Journal* 54(1), 167–201.

Makoni, S. and A. Pennycook. 2007. *Disinventing and Reconstructing Language*. Bristol: Multilingual Matters.

May, S. 2012. Contesting Hegemonic and Monolithic Constructions of Language Rights 'Discourse'. *Journal of Multicultural Discourses* 7(1), 21–27.

May, S. 2014. Overcoming Disciplinary Boundaries: Connecting Language, Education and (Anti)Racism. In R. Race and V. Lander (eds.), *Advancing Race and Ethnicity in Education*. London: Palgrave Macmillan, 128–144.

May, S. 2018. Unanswered Questions: Addressing the Inequalities of Majoritarian Language Policies. In L. Lim, C. Stroud, and L. Wee (eds.), *The Multilingual Citizen: Towards a Politics of Language for Agency and Change*. Bristol: Multilingual Matters, 65–74.

McCarty, T. L. 2004. Dangerous Difference: A Critical-Historical Analysis of Language Education Policies in the United States. In J. W. Tollefson and A. B. M. Tsui (eds.), *Medium of Instruction Policies: Which Agenda? Whose Agenda?* Mahwah, NJ: Lawrence Erlbaum, 71–93.

McCarty, T. L. and L. J. Watahomigie. 1999. Indigenous Community-Based Language Education in the USA. In S. May (ed.), *Indigenous Community-Based Education*. Clevedon: Multilingual Matters, 79–94.

McGinnis, S. 2005. More than a Silver Bullet: The Role of Chinese as a Heritage Language in the United States. *The Modern Language Journal* 89 (4), 592–594.

Mercurio, A. and A. Scarino. 2005. Heritages Languages at the Upper Secondary Level in South Australia: A Struggle for Legitimacy. [Special Issue] Heritage/Community Language Education: U.S. and Australian Perspectives. *In International Journal of Bilingualism and Bilingual Education* 8(2–3), 145–159.

Meyer vs. *Nebraska* (1923, 262, US 390).

Paulston, C. B. and S. McLaughlin. 1994. Language-in-Education Policy and Planning. In W. Grabe (ed.), *Annual Review of Applied Linguistics, 14*. Cambridge: Cambridge University Press, 53–81.

Pavlenko, A. 2002. We Have Room for but One Language Here: Language and National Identity in the US at the Turn of the 20th Century. *Multilingua – Journal of Cross-Cultural and Interlanguage Communication* 21(2–3), 163–196.

Pennycook, A. 2006. Postmodernism in Language Policy. In T. Ricento (ed.), *An Introduction to Language Policy: Theory and Practice*. London: Blackwell, 60–76.

Peterson, G. 1997. *The Power of Words: Literacy and Revolution in South China, 1945–1949*. Vancouver: University of British Columbia Press.

Peyton, J. K., D. A. Ranard, and S. McGinnis (eds.) 2001. *Heritage Languages in America: Preserving a National Resource*. Washington, DC and McHenry, IL.: Center for Applied Linguistics & Delta Systems.

Peyton, J. K., M. Carreira, S. Wang, and T. G. Wiley. 2008. Heritage Language Education in the United States: A Need to Reconceptualize and Restructure. In K. A. King, N. Schilling-Estes, L. W. Fogle, J. J. Lou, and B. Soukup (eds.), *Sustaining Linguistic Diversity: Endangered and Minority Languages and Language Varieties*. Washington, DC: Georgetown University Press.

Polinsky, M. 1995. American Russian: Language Loss Meets Language Acquisition. In *Formal Approaches to Slavic Linguistics*. Cornell Meeting. Ann Arbor: Michigan Slavic Publications.

Polinsky, M. and O. Kagan. 2007. Heritage Languages: In the "Wild" and in the Classroom. *Language and Linguistics Compass* 1(5), 368–395.

Pu, C. 2008. Chinese American Children's Bilingual and Biliteracy Development in Heritage Language and Public Schools. Doctoral Dissertation. San Antonio: University of Texas.

Pu, C. 2012. Community-Based Heritage Language Schools: A Chinese Example. *Kappa Delta Pi Record* 48(1), 29–34, https://doi.org/10.1080/00228958.2012.654717

Rampton, B. 2006. *Language in Late Modernity: Interaction in an Urban School*. Cambridge: Cambridge University Press.

Ricento, T. 2009. Problems with the 'Language-as-Resource' Discourse in the Promotion of Heritage Languages in the US. In R. Salaberry (ed.), *Language Allegiances and Bilingualism in the US*. Clevedon: Multilingual Matters, 110–131.

Roy, J. D. 1987. The Linguistic and Sociolinguistic Position of Black English and the Issue of Bidialectism in Education. In P. Homel, M. Palij, and D. Aaronson (eds.), *Childhood Bilingualism: Aspects of Linguistic, Cognitive, and Social Development*. Hillsdale, NJ: Lawrence Erlbaum Associates, 231–242.

Ruíz, R. 1984. Orientations in Language Planning. *NABE Journal* 8(2), 15–34.

Ruíz, R. 1995. Language Planning Considerations in Indigenous Communities. *Bilingual Research Journal* 19(1), 71–81.

Rumbaut, R. 2009, A Linguistic Graveyard? The Evolution of Language Competencies, Preferences, and Use among Young Adult Children of Immigrants. In T. G. Wiley, J. S. Lee, and R. Rumberger (eds.), *The Education of Language Minority Immigrants in the United States*. Bristol: Multilingual Matters, 35–71.

Schiffman, H. F. 1996. *Linguistic Culture and Language Policy*. London: Routledge.

Skutnabb-Kangas, T., R. Phillipson, and M. Rennet (eds.) 1995. *Linguistic Human Rights: Overcoming Linguistic Discrimination*. Berlin: Mouton de Gruyter.

Spolsky, B. 2001. Heritage Languages and National Security: An Ecological View. In Steven J. Baker (ed.), *Language Policy: Lessons from Global Models*. Monterey, CA: Monterey Institute of International Studies, 103–114.

Spolsky, B. October 2002. National Policy Statement on Heritage Language Development: Toward an Agenda for Action. Conference Paper. Heritage Languages in America: Building on Our National Resources. Tysons Corner, VA.

Spolsky, B. 2004. *Language Policy*. Cambridge: Cambridge University Press.

Spolsky, B. 2012. Family Language Policy – The Critical Domain. *Journal of Multilingual and Multicultural Development* 33(1), 1–9.

Street, J. C. and B. V. Street. 1991. The Schooling of Literacy. In B. Barton and R. Ivanic (eds.), *Writing in the Community*. London: Sage, 143–166.

Tollefson, J. W. and A. B. M. Tsui. 2014. Language Diversity and Language Policy in Education. *Review of Research in Education* 38(1), 189–214.

Toth, C. R. 1990. *German-English Bilingual Schools in America: The Cincinnati Tradition in Historical Context*. New York: Peter Lang.

Tucker, G. R. 1994. Concluding Thoughts: Language Planning Issues for the Coming Decade. In W. Grabe (ed.), *Annual Review of Applied Linguistics, 14*. New York: Cambridge University Press, 277–286.

University of California, Los Angeles (UCLA). 2000/2001. Heritage Language Research Priorities Conference Report. (Los Angeles, CA: Author.) *Bilingual Research Journal* 24(4), 333.

Valdés, G. 2001. Heritage Language Students: Profiles and Possibilities. In J. K. Peyton, D. A. Ranard, and S. McGinnis (eds.), *Heritage Languages in America: Preserving a National Resource*. Washington, DC and McHenry, IL: Center for Applied Linguistics and Delta Systems, 37–80.

Wee, L. 2011. *Language without Rights*. Oxford: Oxford University Press.

Weinberg, M. 1995. *A Chance to Learn: A History of Race and Education in the United States*. Long Beach, CA: California State University Press.

Weinstein, B. 1983. *The Civic Tongue: Political Consequences of Language Choices*. New York: Longman.

Wiley, T. G. 1996. Language Planning and Language Policy. In S. McKay and N. Hornberger (eds.), *Sociolinguistics and Language Teaching*. Cambridge: Cambridge University Press, 103–147.

Wiley, T. G. 1998. The Imposition of World War I English-only Policies and the Fate of German in North America. In T. Ricento and B. Burnaby (eds.), *Language and Politics in the United States and Canada*. Philadelphia: Lawrence Erlbaum, 211–241.

Wiley, T. G. 2002. Heinz Kloss Revisited: National Socialist Ideologue or Champion of Language-Minority Rights? *International Journal of the Sociology of Language* 154(154), 83–97.

Wiley, T. G. 2004. Language Planning, Language Policy, and the English-only Movement. In E. Finegan and J. R. Rickford (eds.), *Language in the U.S.A.: Theme for the Twenty-first Century*. Cambridge: Cambridge University Press, 319–338.

Wiley, T. G. 2005a. Discontinuities in Heritage and Community Language Education: Challenges for Educational Language Policies. [Special Issue]

Heritage/Community Language Education: U.S. and Australian Perspectives. *The International Journal of Bilingual Education and Bilingualism* 8(2–3), 222–229.

Wiley, T. G. 2005b. The Reemergence of Heritage and Community Language Policy in the U.S. National Spotlight. *The Modern Language Journal* 89(4), 595–601.

Wiley, T. G. 2007a. Beyond the Foreign Language Crisis: Toward Alternatives to Xenophobia and National Security as Bases for U.S. Language Policies. *Modern Language Journal* 91(2), 252–255.

Wiley, T. G. 2007b. The Foreign Language "Crisis" in the U.S.: Are Heritage and Community Languages the Remedy? *Critical Inquiry in Language Studies* 4(2–3), 179–205.

Wiley, T. G. 2013. A Brief History and Assessment of Language Rights in the United States. In J. W. Tollefson (ed.), *Language Policies in Education: Critical Issues*, Second Edition. London: Routledge, Taylor & Francis, 61–90.

Wiley, T. G. 2014a. Policy Considerations for Promoting Heritage, Community, and Native American Languages. In T. G. Wiley, J. K. Peyton, D. Christian, S. K. Moore, and N. Liu (eds.), *Handbook on Heritage, Community, and Native American Language Education in the United States: Research, Policy and Practice*. London: Routledge, 45–53.

Wiley, T. G. 2014b. The Problem of Defining Heritage and Community Languages and Their Speakers: On the Utility and Limitations of Definitional Constructs. In T. G. Wiley, J. K. Peyton, D. Christian, S. K. Moore, and N. Liu (eds.), *Handbook on Heritage, Community, and Native American Language Education in the United States: Research, Policy and Practice*. London: Routledge, 19–26.

Wiley, T. G. 2019. The Rise, Fall, and Rebirth of Bilingual Education in U.S. Educational Policy: The Case of California. In T. Ricento (ed.), *Language Politics and Policies: Perspectives from Canada and the United States*. Cambridge: Cambridge University Press, 135–152.

Wiley, T. G. (in press). The Grand Erasure: Whatever Happened to "Bilingual Education" and Language Minority Rights? In J. MacSwan (ed.), *Language(s): Multilingualism and Its Consequences*. Bristol: Multilingual Matters.

Wiley, T. G. and W. Wright. 2004. Against the Undertow: Language-Minority Education and Politics in the Age of Accountability. *Educational Policy* 18(1), 142–168.

Wiley, T. G., J. K. Peyton, and D. Christian. 2014. Preface. In T. G. Wiley, J. K. Peyton, D. Christian, S. K. Moore, and N. Liu (eds.), *Handbook on Heritage, Community, and Native American Language Education in the United States: Research, Policy and Practice*. London: Routledge, ix–xiii.

Wiley, T. G., B. Arias, J. Renn, and S. Bhalla. 2016. Language and the Fulfilment of the Potential of All Americans. Commissioned Report for the American Academy of Arts and Sciences, Commission on Language

Learning. Washington, DC: Center for Applied Linguistics. Retrieved May 10, 2020 from www.cal.org/resource-center/publications/aaas-language-fulfillment

Wiley, T. G., G. De Klerk, M-Y. Li, N. Liu, Y. Teng, and P. Yang. 2008. Language Attitudes toward Chinese "Dialects" among Chinese Immigrants and International Students. In A. He and Y. Xiao (eds.), *Chinese as a Heritage Language in the United States*. National Foreign Language Resource Center. University of Hawaii at Manoa. Honolulu: University of Hawaii Press.

You, B-K. 2009. Stakeholder Views of Korean and Chinese Heritage and Community language (HL-CL) Schools and Education in Phoenix: A comparative study. Dissertation. Tempe: Arizona State University.

Index